How well do **you** want to do in this course?

A better grade starts here.

Register today for your S.O.S. Edition's online grade-boosting tools.

(Your registration code is included at the back of this textbook.)

LONGMAN

Introducing the **S.O.S. Edition** for *The American People, Sixth Edition...*

Get ready to Study... Organize... and Succeed!

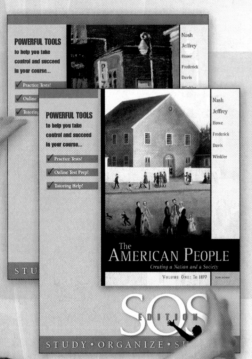

We give you the tools to take control and succeed in your course!

✓ Practice Tests
✓ Online Test Prep
✓ Tutor Center – Live Tutor Support

Want help mastering the course?

Looking to change that B to an A?

Our S.O.S Edition for *The American People, Sixth Edition,* offers a study and review system that helps you master the principles of American history, save time studying, and perform better on exams.

With the purchase of this textbook, you get a powerful combination of tools that includes Practice Tests with Answers, live tutoring assistance from our Tutor Center, and access to our online testing and review system. With the S.O.S. Edition tools, you can test with confidence and complete your course with greater comprehension and higher grades!

Read on to find out how...

How will you **benefit** from using the S.O.S. Edition tools?

✓ **Reinforces** textbook concepts.

✓ Provides **feedback** on your learning progress.

✓ Helps you **maximize** your study time.

✓ Adds **variety** to your study routine.

✓ **Supports** you with live tutors who can answer your questions and help you master the text.

✓ Gives you more **control** over your grade!

" Taking the pre- and post-tests enhances their test-taking skills, and ultimately helps them earn better grades on their chapter exams. "

— *Professor Teresa R. Stalvey,*
North Florida Community College*

A better grade is right here at your fingertips!

WWW.SOSEDITION.COM

What's the best way to **review** concepts and **practice** for exams?

It's built right into your textbook!

Printed Practice Tests with Answers

Practice makes perfect when you have the right tools. What better way to review textbook concepts than with tools built into the back of your textbook. Master the text material by utilizing the Practice Tests at the end of your S.O.S. Edition. You'll find multiple-choice, short answer, true/false questions, and vocabulary words for every chapter, organized by the major text sections to help you quickly connect the concepts. Answers are included for all questions to help you measure your performance. What's more, all Practice Tests are perforated so you can remove them and take them with you!

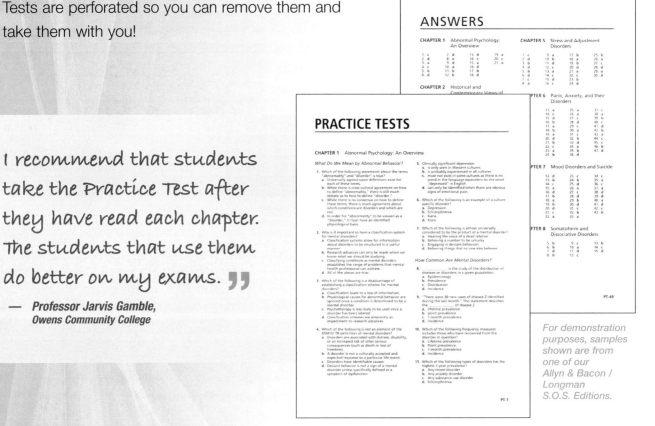

> " I recommend that students take the Practice Test after they have read each chapter. The students that use them do better on my exams. "
>
> — **Professor Jarvis Gamble, Owens Community College**

For demonstration purposes, samples shown are from one of our Allyn & Bacon / Longman S.O.S. Editions.

you go out and buy a magnet to help you with a repetitive-stress injury caused by typing too many term papers!

WHAT DO WE MEAN BY ABNORMAL BEHAVIOR?

This is an easy question to ask but a surprisingly difficult one to answer. Is talking to yourself abnormal? What about feeling depressed for weeks and weeks after a break-up? Or drinking a bottle of vodka with friends on the weekend? Drawing the line between what is abnormal and what is just human behavior can be difficult sometimes. No two of us are alike, and although some of us can exhibit behaviors that are considered quirky, indulgent, or experimental, others with similar behavior may be considered mentally ill, afflicted, or addicted.

It may come as a surprise to you that there is still no universal agreement about what we mean by *abnormality* or *disorder*. This is not to say we do not have definitions.

The S.O.S. Edition Practice Tests (right) include questions for every major section of the textbook (above), providing you with a thorough review of the material.

PRACTICE TESTS

CHAPTER 1   Abnormal Psychology: An Overview

What Do We Mean by Abnormal Behavior?

1. Which of the following statements about the terms "abnormality" and "disorder" is true?
   a. Universally agreed upon definitions exist for each of these terms.
   b. While there is cross-cultural agreement on how to define "abnormality," there is still much debate as to how to define "disorder."
   c. While there is no consensus on how to define these terms, there is much agreement about which conditions are disorders and which are not.
   d. In order for "abnormality" to be viewed as a "disorder," it must have an identified physiological basis.

2. Why is it important to have a classification system for mental disorders?
   a. Classification systems allow for information about disorders to be structured in a useful manner.
   b. Research advances can only be made when we know what we should be studying.
   c. Classifying conditions as mental disorders establishes the range of problems that mental health professional can address.
   d. All of the above are true.

3. Which of the following is a disadvantage of establishing a classification scheme for mental disorders?
   a. Classification leads to a loss of information.
   b. Physiological causes for abnormal behavior are ignored once a condition is determined to be a mental disorder.
   c. Psychotherapy is less likely to be used once a disorder has been labeled.
   d. Classification schemes are inherently an impediment to research advances.

4. Which of the following is *not* an element of the DSM-IV-TR definition of mental disorders?
   a. Disorders are associated with distress, disability, or an increased risk of other serious consequences (such as death or loss of freedom).
   b. A disorder is not a culturally accepted and expected response to a particular life event.
   c. Disorders have identifiable causes.
   d. Deviant behavior is not a sign of a mental disorder unless specifically defined as a symptom of dysfunction.

5. Clinically significant depression
   a. is only seen in Western cultures.
   b. is probably experienced in all cultures.
   c. must not exist in some cultures as there is no word in the language equivalent to the word "depressed" in English.
   d. can only be identified when there are obvious signs of emotional pain.

6. Which of the following is an example of a culture-specific disorder?
   a. Depression
   b. Schizophrenia
   c. Kana
   d. Koro

7. Which of the following is almost universally considered to be the product of a mental disorder?
   a. Hearing the voice of a dead relative
   b. Believing a number to be unlucky
   c. Engaging in deviant behaviors
   d. Believing things that no one else believes

How Common Are Mental Disorders?

8. _____ is the study of the distribution of diseases or disorders in a given population.
   a. Epidemiology
   b. Prevalence
   c. Distribution
   d. Incidence

9. "There are 30 new cases of disease Z identified during the last month." This statement describes the _____ of disease Z.
   a. lifetime prevalence
   b. point prevalence
   c. 1-month prevalence
   d. incidence

10. Which of the following frequency measures includes those who have recovered from the disorder in question?
   a. Lifetime prevalence.
   b. Point prevalence.
   c. 1-month prevalence
   d. Incidence

11. Which of the following types of disorders has the highest 1-year prevalence?
   a. Any mood disorder
   b. Any anxiety disorder
   c. Any substance-use disorder
   d. Schizophrenia

A better grade is right here at your fingertips!

WWW.SOSEDITION.COM

Jump-start your grade with our online test prep system!

Who doesn't want better grades?

Designed specifically to help enhance your performance, this S.O.S. Edition's online test preparation system gauges your prior knowledge of content and creates a Study Plan to help you pinpoint exactly where additional study and review is needed. You can follow the plan as a guide to focus your efforts and improve upon areas of weakness by utilizing the printed Practice Tests in the back of the textbook. Additional testing features in this program help you assess your progress with the textbook material to reach your ultimate goal of success in the course.

> **❝** I like the fact that I can take a pre-test before I study the course material to test how much I know, and then I can take the post-test to see my improvement. **❞**
> — *Natalie Ricks, student**

Knowing what to study is key to your success.

Pre-Test

Why waste time studying what you already know? Pre-Tests help you measure your level of understanding of the material in each chapter. After logging in to the S.O.S.

Edition online program, you'll find the Table of Contents for your textbook, with links to Pre-Tests and Post-Tests that cover all of the chapters in the book. Choose the Pre-Tests and Post-Tests that cover a chapter of interest. Completing the Pre-Test will help you assess your existing knowledge of the subject matter. When you complete all of the questions and submit the test, you will receive a proficiency rating and a study plan based on the results. These results will help you focus your study efforts where they're needed most.

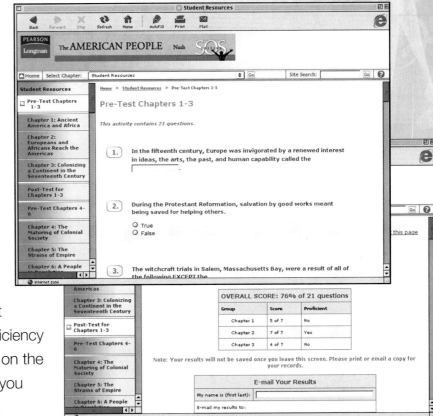

Post-Test

Measure your progress with Post-Tests that include questions covering each chapter.
Organized exactly like the Pre-Tests, the Post-Tests show you how much you've improved, or
where you need
continued help.
Continue to take the
Post-Tests as often
as you like, revisiting
your progress in the
Study Plan, which
is updated every
time a test is taken.

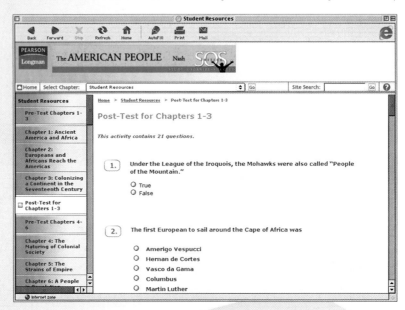

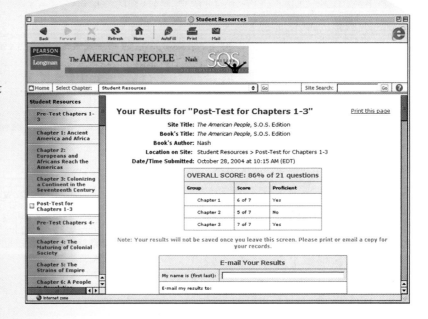

Individualized Study Plan

Maximize your study time by reviewing and following your very own Study Plan created from the results of your Pre- and Post-Tests. The Study Plan quickly identifies your areas of weakness and strength in a clear outline, directing you back to specific areas in your textbook (section heads) for further study. Be sure to either email or print your study results. This way you can immediately pinpoint where additional time is needed, so you can feel confident about where you're saving time! Use this customized guide to re-study material as necessary for mastery of the material and success on your tests and in your course.

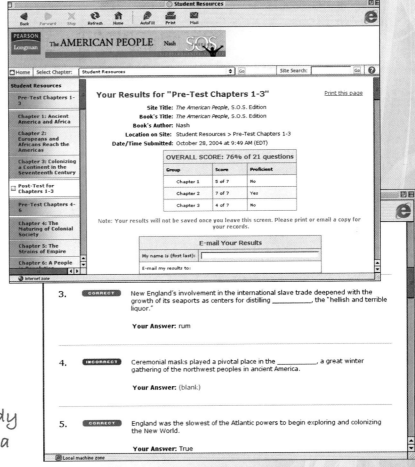

" The Individualized Study Plans help me study at a faster pace by focusing on my underscored areas. "

— *Kim Skains, student**

A better grade is right here at your fingertips!

WWW.SOSEDITION.COM

Need additional assistance studying or completing assignments?

One-on-One Tutoring!

The Tutor Center
www.ablongman.com/tutorcenter

Our Tutor Center from Addison-Wesley Higher Education provides one-on-one tutoring to registered students. Our tutors are qualified college instructors who assist students with both questions and concepts from the textbook as well as any publisher-authored technology used in the course. The center is open during peak student studying hours from **Sunday to Thursday, 5PM to midnight EST,** when professors are usually unavailable. Students are offered multiple channels for tutor contact — toll-free phone, email, fax, and interactive web — affording various learning opportunities, both auditory and visual, to get through even the most difficult concepts. **Be sure to visit our website for more details!**

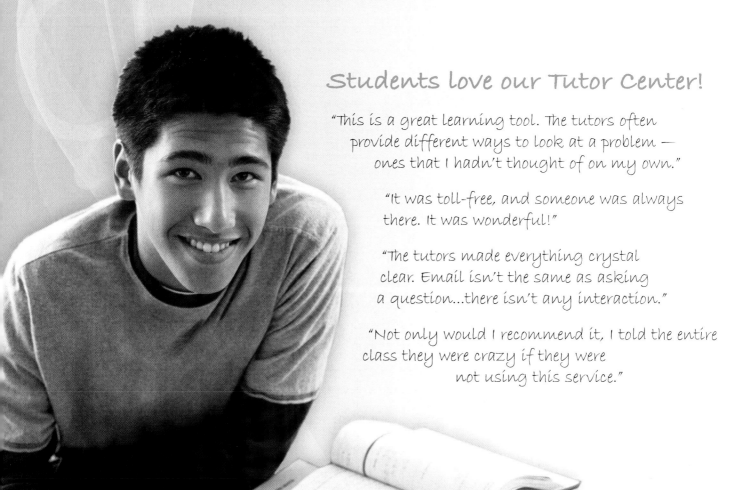

Students love our Tutor Center!

"This is a great learning tool. The tutors often provide different ways to look at a problem — ones that I hadn't thought of on my own."

"It was toll-free, and someone was always there. It was wonderful!"

"The tutors made everything crystal clear. Email isn't the same as asking a question...there isn't any interaction."

"Not only would I recommend it, I told the entire class they were crazy if they were not using this service."

A support service that's available when your instructor isn't! Our qualified tutors are on hand to assist you during key studying hours – from Sunday to Thursday, 5PM to midnight EST, during the school term.

Addison-Wesley • Allyn & Bacon • Benjamin Cummings • Longman

The
Tutor
Center

"What I benefited from the most was the Tutor Center. I am a working mother, and to have the opportunity to come home late at night and still be able to have someone to help me is a true blessing."

— *Jennifer Kelly, student*

A better grade is right here at your fingertips!

WWW.SOSEDITION.COM

Getting started on the path to success is **quick** and **easy!**

✓ **Take advantage of the Practice Tests**

At any point in your studies, you can use these tests to quiz yourself, prepare for exams, or simply gain understanding of the most important concepts in each chapter of this textbook.

✓ **Access your online resources**

The Student Starter Kit packaged with this textbook gives you a **FREE 6-month subscription** to the S.O.S. Edition's program and Tutor Center resources. You'll find your access code under the tear-off tab in the back of your book. **Follow these quick and easy steps...**

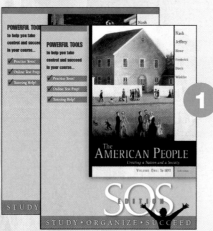

1 **GET YOUR CODE.**

Open your S.O.S. Edition to the inside back cover to find your code.

2 **LOG ON TO www.sosedition.com** and **CHOOSE YOUR TEXTBOOK.**

3 CLICK "REGISTER" AND ENTER YOUR ACCESS CODE.

4 THAT'S IT!

You'll find the table of contents for your book with links to Pre-Test, Post-Test, and Study Plan to get started.

A better grade is right here at your fingertips!

S.O.S. EDITION

THE AMERICAN PEOPLE

Creating a Nation and a Society

VOLUME ONE: TO 1877

General Editors **GARY B. NASH**
University of California, Los Angeles

JULIE ROY JEFFREY
Goucher College

JOHN R. HOWE
University of Minnesota

PETER J. FREDERICK
Wabash College

ALLEN F. DAVIS
Temple University

ALLAN M. WINKLER
Miami University of Ohio

PEARSON
Longman

New York   San Francisco   Boston
London   Toronto   Sydney   Tokyo   Singapore   Madrid
Mexico City   Munich   Paris   Cape Town   Hong Kong   Montreal

Publisher:	Priscilla McGeehon
Executive Marketing Manager:	Sue Westmoreland
Supplement Editor:	Kristi Olson
Media Editor:	Patrick McCarthy
Cover Designer:	Rubin Pfeffer (S.O.S. Edition)
Manufacturing Buyer:	Roy Pickering
Printer and Binder:	Quebecor-World-Dubuque
Cover Printer:	The Lehigh Press, Inc.

Please visit our website at http://www.ablongman.com

Volume One ISBN 0-321-31727-0

1 2 3 4 5 6 7 8 9 10—QWD—07 06 05 04

THE AMERICAN PEOPLE

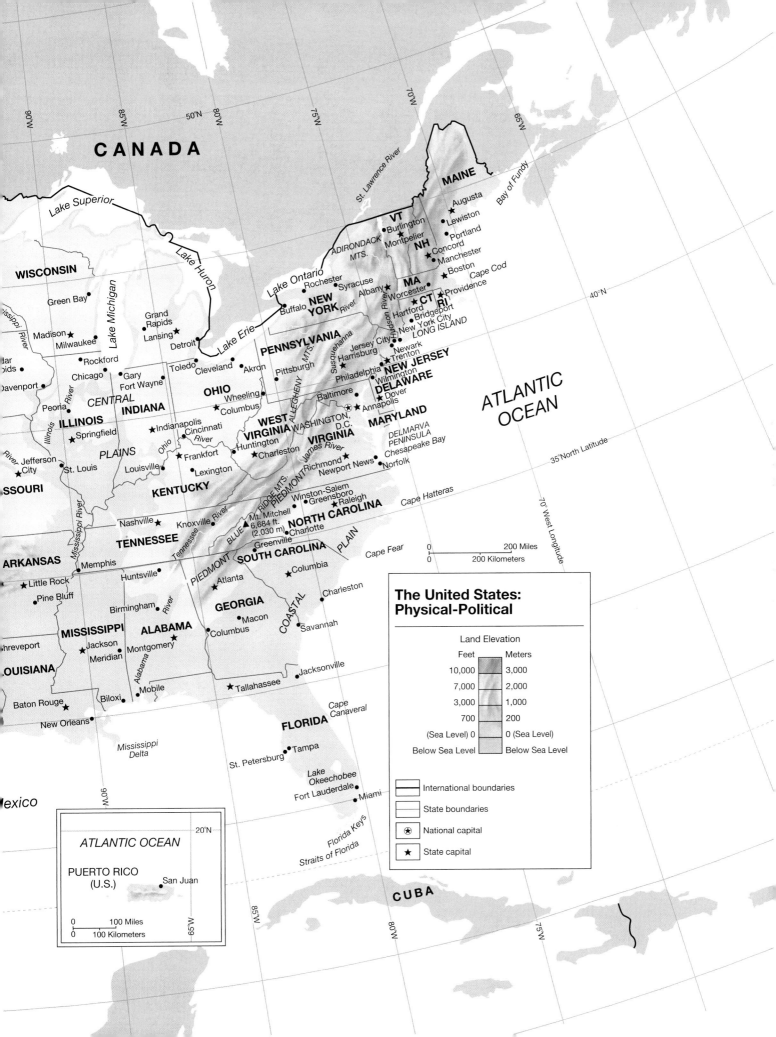

THE AMERICAN PEOPLE

Creating a Nation and a Society

Sixth Edition
VOLUME ONE: TO 1877

General Editors

GARY B. NASH
University of California, Los Angeles

JULIE ROY JEFFREY
Goucher College

JOHN R. HOWE
University of Minnesota

PETER J. FREDERICK
Wabash College

ALLEN F. DAVIS
Temple University

ALLAN M. WINKLER
Miami University of Ohio

PEARSON
Longman

New York   San Francisco   Boston
London   Toronto   Sydney   Tokyo   Singapore   Madrid
Mexico City   Munich   Paris   Cape Town   Hong Kong   Montreal

Vice President and Publisher:	Priscilla McGeehon
Acquisitions Editor:	Ashley Dodge
Development Manager:	Lisa Pinto
Senior Development Editor:	Dawn Groundwater
Executive Marketing Manager:	Sue Westmoreland
Supplement Editor:	Kristi Olson
Media Editor:	Patrick McCarthy
Production Manager:	Douglas Bell
Project Coordination, Text Design, and Electronic Page Makeup:	Elm Street Publishing Services, Inc.
Cover Designer/Manager:	John Callahan
Cover Illustration:	Joseph Beekman Smith's painting of "Wesley Chapel on John Street," old John Street United Methodist Church
Cartographer:	Maps.com
Photo Research:	Photosearch, Inc.
Recovering the Past Spinning Wheel Image:	George Pickow/Getty Images
Manufacturing Buyer:	Alfred C. Dorsey
Printer and Binder:	Quebecor-World-Versailles
Cover Printer:	The Lehigh Press, Inc.

For permission to use copyrighted material, grateful acknowledgment is made to the following copyright holders:

p. 395   "The Tar Baby Tricks Brer Rabbit" from Faulkner, William J. ed., *Days When the Animals Talked: Black American Folktales and How They Came To Be.* © AFRICA WORLD PRESS, 1993.

p. 457   Journal of Mary Stuart Bailey (1852) from Sandra L. Myers ed., *Ho for California: Women's Overland Diaries* from the Huntington Library, CA, 1980. Reprinted with the permission of the Henry E. Huntington Library.

p. 457   Journal of Robert Robe [1851] from *Washington Historic Quarterly,* January 1928. Reprinted with permission.

Library of Congress Cataloging-in-Publication Data

The American people: creating a nation and a society / general editors, Gary B. Nash . . .
[et al.].—6th ed.
     p. cm.
     Includes biblitographical references and index.
     ISBN 0-321-12525-8 (Volume One)
     1. United States—History.   I. Nash, Gary B.

E178.1.A49355 2004
973—dc21   2002040662

Please visit our website at http://www.ablongman.com

Single Volume Edition ISBN 0-321-12524-X
Volume One ISBN 0-321-12525-8
Volume Two ISBN 0-321-12526-6

1 2 3 4 5 6 7 8 9 10—WCV—06 05 04 03

◆ Brief Contents

✦ Detailed Contents

✦ Specialized Contents

Recovering the Past

Analyzing History

Maps

International Maps, Charts, and Tables

Figures

TABLES

The Yoruba people of West Africa have an old saying, "However far the stream flows, it never forgets its source." Why, we wonder, do such ancient societies as the Yoruba find history so important, whereas today's American students question its relevance? This book aims to end such skepticism about the usefulness of history.

As we begin the twenty-first century in an ethnically and racially diverse society caught up in an interdependent global society, history is of central importance in preparing us to exercise our rights and responsibilities as free people. History cannot make good citizens, but without history we cannot understand the choices before us and think wisely about them. Lacking a collective memory of the past, we would be unaware of the human condition and the long struggles of men and women everywhere to deal with the problems of their day and to create a better society. Unfurnished with historical knowledge, we deprive ourselves of knowing about the huge range of approaches people have taken to political, economic, and social life; to solving problems; and to conquering the obstacles in their way. Unaware of how events beyond our national boundaries have affected our own history, we are less able to deal with the challenges of contemporary globalism.

History has a deeper, even more fundamental importance: the cultivation of the private person whose self-knowledge and self-respect provide the foundation for a life of dignity and fulfillment. Historical memory is the key to self-identity, to seeing one's place in the long stream of time, in the story of humankind.

When we study our own history, that of the American people, we see a rich and extraordinarily complex human story that stretches back to the last ice age when nomadic hunters arrived in the Americas from Siberia. This country, whose written history began thousands of years later with a convergence of Native Americans, Europeans, and Africans, has always been a nation of diverse peoples—a magnificent mosaic of cultures, religions, and skin shades. This book explores how American society assumed its present shape and developed its present forms of government; how as a nation we have conducted our foreign affairs and managed our economy; how as individuals and in groups we have lived, worked, loved, married, raised families, voted, argued, protested, and struggled to fulfill our dreams and the noble ideals of the American experiment.

Several ways of making the past understandable distinguish this book from most textbooks written in the last 20 years. While this book covers public events like presidential elections, diplomatic treaties, and economic legislation, we have attempted to integrate this broad national narrative with the private human stories that pervade them. Within a chronological framework, we have woven together our history as a nation, as a people, and as a society. When, for example, national political events are discussed, we analyze their impact on social and economic life at the state and local levels. Wars are described not only as they unfolded on the battlefield and in the salons of diplomats but also on the home front, where they are history's greatest motor of social change. The interaction of ordinary Americans with extraordinary events runs as a theme throughout this book.

Above all, we have tried to show the "humanness" of our history as it is revealed in people's everyday lives. We have often used the words of ordinary Americans to capture the authentic human voices of those who participated in and responded to epic events such as war, slavery, industrialization, and reform movements.

GOALS AND THEMES OF THE BOOK

Our primary goal is to provide students with a rich, balanced, and thought-provoking treatment of the American past. By this, we mean a history that treats the lives and experiences of Americans of all national origins and cultural backgrounds, at all levels of society, and in all regions of the country. It also means a history that seeks connections between the many factors—political, economic, technological, social, religious, intellectual, and biological—that have molded and remolded American society over four centuries. And, finally, it means a history that encourages students to think about how we have all inherited a complex past filled with both notable achievements and thorny problems. The only history befitting a democratic nation is one that inspires students to initiate a frank and searching dialogue with their past.

Historians continually revise their understanding of what happened in the past. Historians reinterpret history both because they find new evidence on old topics and also because new sensibilities inspire them to ask questions about the past that did not interest earlier historians. It is this continual questioning of the past that has led to historical research and writing on many topics previously ignored or scanted.

Through this book, we also hope to promote class discussions, which can be organized around seven questions that we see as basic to the American historical experience:

1. How has this nation been peopled, from the first inhabitants to the many groups that arrived in slavery or servitude during the colonial period down to the voluntary immigrants of today? How have these waves of newcomers contributed to the American cultural mosaic? To what extent have different immigrant groups preserved elements of their ethnic, racial, and religious heritages? How have the tensions between cultural assimilation and cultural preservation been played out, in the past and today?

2. To what extent have Americans developed a stable, democratic political system flexible enough to address the wholesale changes occurring in the last two centuries, and to what degree has this political system been consistent with the principles of our nation's founding?

3. How have economic and technological changes affected daily life, work, family organization, leisure, sexual behavior, the division of wealth, and community relations in the United States?

4. How did the European settlement of the Americas alter the landscape? How have environmental factors shaped American society, and how have Americans changed in their attitudes and policies concerning the natural environment?

5. What role has American religion played in the development of the nation? How has religion served to promote or retard social reform in our history? Whatever their varied sources, how have the recurring reform movements in our history dealt with economic, political, and social problems in attempting to square the ideals of American life with the reality?

6. In what ways have global events and trends had an impact on the shape and character of American life? How has the United States affected the rest of the world? To what extent has the United States served as a model for other peoples, as an interventionist savior of other nations around the globe, and as an interfering expansionist in the affairs of other nations?

7. How have American beliefs and values changed over more than four hundred years of history, and how have they varied between different groups—women and men; Americans of many colors and cultures; people of different regions, religions, sexual orientations, ages, and classes?

In writing a history that revolves around these themes, we have tried to convey two dynamics that operate in all societies. First, we observe people continuously adjusting to new developments, such as industrialization and urbanization, over which they seemingly have little control; yet we realize that people are not paralyzed by history but are the fundamental creators of it. They retain the ability, individually and collectively, to shape the world in which they live and thus in considerable degree to control their own lives.

Second, we emphasize the connections that always exist among social, political, economic, and cultural events. Just as our individual lives are never neatly parceled into separate spheres of activity, the life of a society is made up of a complicated and often messy mixture of forces, events, and accidental occurrences. In this text, political and economic, technological and cultural factors are intertwined like strands in a rope.

STRUCTURE OF THE BOOK

The chapters of this book are grouped into three parts that relate to major periods in American history from 1492 to 1877. The title of each part suggests a major theme that helps to characterize the period.

Every chapter begins with an outline that provides an overview of the chapter's organization. Next, a personal story, called *American Stories,* recalls the experience of an ordinary or lesser-known American. Chapter 3, for example, is introduced with an account of the life of Anthony Johnson who came to Virginia as a slave but who managed to gain his freedom along with his wife, Mary. This brief anecdote introduces the overarching themes and major concepts of the chapter, in this case the tri-racial character of American society, the gradual tightening of racial slavery, and the instability of late seventeenth century colonial life. In addition, *American Stories* launches the chapter by engaging the student with a human account, suggesting that history was shaped by ordinary as well as extraordinary people. Following the personal story and easily identifiable by its visual separation from the anecdote and the body of the chapter, a *brief chapter overview* links the story to the text. Students should read these crucial transition paragraphs carefully for three reasons: first, to identify the three or four major themes of the chapter; second, to understand the organizational structure of the chapter, and third, to see how the chapter's themes are related to the organizing questions of this book.

We aim to facilitate the learning process for students in other ways as well. Every chapter ends with pedagogical features to reinforce and expand the narrative. A *Timeline* reviews the major events and developments covered in the chapter. A *Conclusion* briefly summarizes the main concepts and developments elaborated in the chapter and serves as a bridge to the following chapter. A list of *Recommended Readings* provides supplementary sources for further study or research; an annotated selection of novels and films, called *Fiction and Film,* is also included. Finally, a special annotated section of suggested Web sites, *Discovering U.S. History Online,* offers students information on electronic sources relating to chapter themes. Each map, figure, and table has been chosen to relate clearly to the narrative.

SPECIAL FEATURES

Five distinctive features help contribute to student learning of history.

- **Recovering the Past.** A distinctive feature of this book is the two-page *Recovering the Past* presented in each chapter. These RTPs, as the authors affectionately call them, introduce students to the fascinating variety of evidence—ranging from household inventories, folk tales, and diaries to census returns and photography—that historians have learned to employ in reconstructing the past. Each RTP gives basic information about the source and its use by historians and then raises questions, called *Reflecting on the Past,* for students to consider as they study the example reproduced for their inspection.
- New to this edition, an **international context for American history.** Believing that in today's global society it is particularly important for students to think across national boundaries and to understand the ways in which our history intersects with the world, we have provided an international framework. Rather than developing a separate discussion of global events, we have woven an international narrative into our analysis of the American past. Chapter 13, for example, discusses the international context for American expansionism. Chapter 10 examines the international character of reform. We have shown the ways in which the United States has

been influenced by events in other parts of the world and the connection between the history of other nations and our own. We have also drawn attention to those aspects of our history that appear to set the nation apart. New tables, charts, and maps provide an additional dimension for this international context. These are identified by a global icon (☉) and are accompanied by *Reflecting on the Past* questions.

- **Analyzing History.** This feature brings together, in visually engaging ways, a variety of socioeconomic data that illustrates the ways in which complex changes are closely intertwined at particular moments in American history. One chart, for example, shows the migration of black and white peoples into Trans-Appalachia in the late eighteenth and early nineteenth centuries. Our goal is not only to show connections but also to encourage visual literacy by helping students read and interpret statistics and graphs. We have written captions for this feature to assist students in analyzing these materials and have posed *Reflecting on the Past* questions to encourage them to think about the implications of the data presented.
- **Discovering U.S. History Online.** Suggested Web sites, carefully evaluated for this edition, allow students to explore particular areas that relate to each chapter. These sites can also provide the basis for written evaluations, essays, and other learning activities.
- **Illustration Program.** Color illustrations— paintings, cartoons, photographs, maps, and figures—amplify important themes while presenting visual evidence for student reflection and analysis. Captions on all photographs, maps, and figures are designed to help students understand and interpret the information presented. Many map captions pose questions for students to think about. Summary tables, which we refer to as "talking boxes," recap points discussed in the narrative, pulling the material together in a format designed for ease of student study. An example of a "talking box" is "Significant Factors Promoting Economic Growth, 1820–1860" in Chapter 10.

THE SIXTH EDITION

The sixth edition of *The American People* has benefited from both the helpful comments of scholars and the experience of teachers and students who used previous editions of the book. While some of the modifications are small, this edition incorporates substantial changes.

Major Changes

- A new chapter (Chapter 1) on the pre-contact period called "Ancient America and Africa" begins the book. This chapter covers indigenous people in the Americas before 1492 and ancient Africa on the eve of European contact.
- Several chapters have been reorganized and revised. Chapters 1–5 have been reorganized to reflect new material on ancient Africa, the Americas, and the early Caribbean.
- This edition also has an important new focus. Because we believe it is not enough to understand only the history of our own nation in today's world, we have reconceptualized the way in which we present the story of our past. We have woven important international materials and themes into the narrative and added many new maps and tables to illuminate the connection between the United States and the world. Chapter 11, for example, includes a new section on the expansion of the cotton South in a global economy and slavery in Latin America to provide a comparative perspective for the southern experience.
- We have strengthened our coverage of the role of Asian Americans and religion. Chapter 13, for example, includes new coverage of the Chinese who came to the West in the middle of the nineteenth century. Chapter 15 includes new material on the role of religion during the Civil War.
- This edition also features several smaller changes, with several new anecdotes. An expanded map program as well as carefully selected new visual materials provide students with additional ways of understanding chapter discussions. Revised bibliographies with annotated sections on film and fiction and a carefully selected list of helpful Web sites provide avenues for further explorations outside of the classroom.

Other Chapter Changes

- *Chapter 1* contains revised coverage on Africa and the Americas on the eve of 1492; a new vignette on women in Europe, Africa, and the Americas; and several new maps.
- *Chapter 2* features an expanded section on the Spanish conquest of the Americas, with a new subsection on Caribbean colonization experiments; new material on African bondage and early slave trade; a new RTP on illustrated travel accounts; and a new vignette of the cultural, social, and linguistic broadening of the sixteenth-century Atlantic world.

- *Chapter 3* has been reconfigured to treat European settlements in North America and the Caribbean to 1692. The discussion of slavery has been woven into each regional picture rather than dealt with as a whole.
- *Chapter 4* includes expanded coverage of French and Spanish settlements and has incorporated slavery into each sectional description of maturing European colonies in North America.
- *Chapter 5* provides expanded coverage of the War of Jenkins' Ear and King George's War to emphasize the Caribbean zone of conflict; a greater emphasis on the Seven Year's War as world war; and includes several new maps.
- *Chapter 6* now includes material, formerly in Chapter 5, describing the final slide into independence. Significant new material on the smallpox epidemic of 1775–1782 that ravaged large areas of Spanish Mexico and North America has been added. The chapter now discusses the consequences of the Revolutionary War and American independence from England and its empire. The chapter also includes a new RTP on military muster roles.
- *Chapter 7* features a clearer organization of the section "Toward the New National Government" as well as new material on the Anti-Federalists.
- *Chapter 8* now ends with the conclusion of Jefferson's two administrations rather than with the election of 1800. This new breaking point makes clearer the story of the initial creation of the new national government through the Federalist years as well as the very different path the Jeffersonians pursued. The decade of the 1790s has been more explicitly set in the context of the larger age of democratic revolutions that showed up most dramatically in France, but also in other areas of Europe as well, and in the Caribbean with the Haitian revolution. The chapter emphasizes the ways in which the United States was involved, ideologically, diplomatically, politically, and demographically in the Atlantic world. Finally the chapter considers the challenges posed by events in revolutionary France to the gendered structure of American politics and includes some new material on freedom of the press during Jefferson's administrations.
- *Chapter 9* is somewhat differently configured because material has been shifted into Chapter 8. The discussion of urban life has been broadened, and the treatment of free African-American communities now includes coverage of the very different free African-American experience in New Orleans. The analysis of the War of 1812 and the

United States' involvement in the Americas is now joined by a new section titled "The End of Neo-Colonialism." The discussion of politics clarifies the accelerating development of political parties and white male democracy and includes new material on women. A new RTP on census returns is also included.

- *Chapter 10* has been reworked to put America's first industrial revolution into an international context.
- *Chapter 11* features two new major sections on the expansion of the cotton South in a global economy and slavery in Latin America to provide a comparative perspective for the southern experience. The chapter includes an expanded discussion of yeoman and non-slaveholding farmers, religion, maroons, and African-American Seminoles, and a new section on paternalism and honor in the plantation class.
- *Chapter 12* has new international content that provides a comparative framework for understanding American reform, religion, and politics. The chapter has increased coverage of religion and better connects both revivalism and religion to the chapter's themes. Additional voices for African Americans show points of view beyond Frederick Douglass'.
- *Chapter 13* has a new anecdote featuring a missionary to the western Indians and highlights the international context that helped to shape

the westward movement. It includes new material on the Chinese who came to the West in the middle of the nineteenth century.

- *Chapter 14* features an expanded discussion of the United States' place in the larger world.
- *Chapter 15* relates the Civil War to European wars of nationalism and offers a new discussion reflecting recent scholarship on southern nationalism. As a result, the chapter's explanation of why the South lost the war has been modified. The chapter provides an explanation of Lee's aggressive tactics and makes clearer the links between the home front and the military front. Material on religion's role in the war has been added.
- *Chapter 16* has been largely rewritten to reflect scholarship and language usage. There is a new section on white farmers during Reconstruction and greater emphasis on religion.

Our aim has been to write a balanced and vivid history of the development of the American nation and its society. We have also tried to provide the support materials necessary to make teaching and learning enjoyable and rewarding. The reader will be the judge of our success. We welcome your comments.

Gary B. Nash
Julie Roy Jeffrey

✦ SUPPLEMENTS

FOR QUALIFIED ADOPTERS: INSTRUCTOR SUPPLEMENTS

Instructor's Manual, written by Neal Brooks and Ingrid Sabio, Essex Community College. This guide was written based on ideas generated in "active learning" workshops and is tied closely to the text. In addition to suggestions on how to generate lively class discussion and involve students in active learning, this supplement also offers a file of exam questions and lists of resources, including films, slides, photo collections, records, and audiocassettes. ISBN: 0-321-18636-2.

Test Bank. This test bank, prepared by Jeanne Whitney, Salisbury State University, contains more than 3,500 objective, conceptual, and essay questions. All questions are keyed to specific pages in the text. ISBN: 0-321-18639-7.

TestGen EQ Computerized Testing System. This flexible, easy-to-master computerized test bank on a dual-platform CD includes all of the items in the printed test bank and allows instructors to select specific questions, edit existing questions, and add their own items to create exams. Tests can be printed in several different fonts and formats and can include figures, such as graphs and tables. ISBN: 0-321-18640-0.

History Digital Media Archive CD-ROM. The Digital Media Archive CD-ROM contains electronic images and interactive and static maps, along with media elements such as video. These media assets are fully customizable and ready for classroom presentation or easy downloading into your PowerPoint™ presentations or any other presentation software. ISBN: 0-321-14976-9.

Companion Website, www.ablongman.com/nash. Instructors can take advantage of the Companion Website that supports this text. The instructor section of the Website includes the instructor's manual, teaching links, downloadable maps and images from the text in PowerPoint™.

PowerPoint™ Presentations. These presentations contain an average of 15 PowerPoint™ slides for each chapter. These slides may include key points and terms for a lecture on the chapter, as well as four-color slides of some important maps, graphs, and charts within a particular chapter. The presentations are available for download at www.ablongman.com/nash.

CourseCompass®, www.ablongman.com/coursecompass. Combines the strength of the content from *The American People,* Sixth Edition, with state-of-the-art eLearning tools. CourseCompass™ is an easy-to-use online course management system that allows professors to tailor content and functionality to meet individual course needs. Every CourseCompass™ course includes a range of pre-loaded content—all designed to help students master core course objectives. Organized by era, CourseCompass™ allows you to access maps, map exercises, and primary sources as well as test questions from the print test bank and the full text of several of our best-selling supplements. *The American People* CourseCompass™ site is available at no additional charge for students whose professor has requested that a student Access Kit be bundled with the text.

BlackBoard and WebCT. Longman's extensive American history content is available in these two major course management platforms: BlackBoard and WebCT. All quickly and easily customizable for use with *The American People,* Sixth Edition, the content includes multiple primary sources, maps, and map exercises. Book specific testing is simply uploaded.

The History Place Premium Website, www.ushistoryplace.com. Available at no additional cost when requested as a bundle component by the professor, the site offers extraordinary breadth and depth, featuring unmatched interactive maps, timelines, and activities; hundreds of source documents, images, and audio clips; a powerful TestFlight student self-assessment tool; and much more.

A Guide to Teaching American History Through Film. Written by Randy Roberts, Purdue University, this guide provides instructors with a creative and practical tool for stimulating classroom discussion. The sections include "American Films: A Historian's Perspective," a list of films, practical suggestions, and bibliography. The film listing is presented in narrative form, developing connections between each film and the topics being discussed. ISBN: 0-673-99798-7.

Comprehensive American History Transparency Set. This collection includes more than 200 four-color American history map transparencies on subjects ranging from the first Native Americans to the end of the Cold War, covering wars, social trends, elections, immigration, and demographics. ISBN: 0-673-97211-9.

Discovering American History Through Maps and Views Transparency Set. Created by Gerald Danzer, the recipient of the AHA's James Harvey Robinson Prize for his work in the development of map transparencies, this set of 140 four-color acetates is a unique instructional tool. The collection includes cartographic and pictorial maps, views and photos, urban plans, building diagrams, and works of art. ISBN: 0-673-53766-8.

Text-specific Transparency Set. A set of four-color transparency acetates showing maps from the text. ISBN: 0-321-18641-9.

Video Lecture Launchers. Prepared by Mark Newman, University of Illinois at Chicago, these video lecture launchers (each two to five minutes in duration) cover key issues in American history from 1877 to the present. The launchers are accompanied by an *Instructor's Manual.* ISBN: 0-321-01869-9.

"This Is America" *Immigration Video.* Produced by the American Museum of Immigration, this video tells the story of American immigrants, relating their personal stories and accomplishments. By showing how the richness of our culture is due to the contributions of millions of immigrant

Americans, the videos make the point that America's strength lies in the ethnically and culturally diverse backgrounds of its citizens. ISBN: 0-321-01865-6.

FOR STUDENTS

Multimedia Edition CD-ROM for The American People, **Sixth Edition.** This unique CD-ROM takes students beyond the printed page, offering them a complete multimedia learning experience. It contains the full annotatable textbook on CD-ROM, with contextually placed media—audio, video, interactive maps, photos, figures, Web links, and practice tests—that link students to additional content directly related to key concepts in the text. The CD also contains the Study Guide, Map Workbooks, a primary source reader, and more than a dozen supplementary books most often assigned in American history courses. Free when packaged with the text. ISBN: 0-321-18788-1.

Study Guide. This two-volume study guide, created by Neal Brooks and Ingrid Sabio, Essex Community College, includes chapter outlines, significant themes and highlights, a glossary, learning enrichment ideas, sample test questions, exercises for identification and interpretation, and geography exercises based on maps in the text. Volume One: ISBN: 0-321-18637-0; Volume Two: ISBN: 0-321-18638-9.

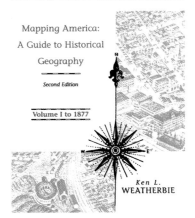

Longman American History Atlas. A four-color reference tool and visual guide to American history that includes almost 100 maps and covers the full scope of history. Atlas overhead transparencies available to adopters. *$3.00 when bundled.* ISBN: 0-321-00486-8.

Mapping America: A Guide to Historical Geography, **Second Edition.** A two-volume workbook by Ken L. Weatherbie, Del Mar College, that presents the basic geography of the United States and helps students place the history of the United States into spatial perspective. *Free when bundled.* Volume One: ISBN: 0-321-00487-6; Volume Two: ISBN: 0-321-00488-4.

Mapping American History. A workbook created by Gerald A. Danzer for use in conjunction with *Discovering American History Through Maps and Views* and designed to teach students to interpret and analyze cartographic materials as historical documents. *Free when bundled.* ISBN: 0-673-53768-4.

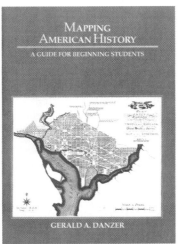

Companion Website for The American People, **Sixth Edition,** www. ablongman.com/nash. The online course companion provides a wealth of resources for students using *The American People,* Sixth Edition. Students can access chapter summaries, interactive practice test questions, and Web links for every chapter. The Website is a comprehensive online study guide for students.

iSearch Guide for History (with Research Navigator™). This guidebook includes exercises and tips on how to use the Internet for the study of history. It also includes an access code for Research Navigator™—the easiest way

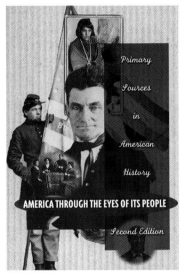

for students to start a research assignment or research paper. Research Navigator™ is composed of three exclusive databases of credible and reliable source material including EBSCO's ContentSelect™ Academic Journal Database, New York Times Search by Subject Archive, and "Best of the Web" Link Library. This comprehensive site also includes a detailed help section. ISBN: 0-321-14282-9.

America Through the Eyes of Its People. A comprehensive anthology that makes primary sources widely available in an inexpensive format, balancing social and political history and providing up-to-date narrative material. *Free when bundled.* ISBN: 0-673-97738-2.

Sources of the African American Past. Edited by Roy Finkenbine, University of Detroit at Mercy, this collection of primary sources covers key themes in the African-American experience from the West African background to the present. Balanced between political and social history, it offers a vivid snapshot of the lives of African Americans in different historical periods and includes documents representing women and different regions of the United States. Available at a minimum cost when bundled with the text. ISBN: 0-673-99202-0.

Women and the National Experience, **Second Edition.** Edited by Ellen Skinner, Pace University, this primary source reader contains both classic and unusual documents describing the history of women in the United States. The documents provide dramatic evidence that outspoken women attained a public voice and participated in the development of national events and policies long before they could vote. Chronologically organized and balanced between social and political history, this reader offers a striking picture of the lives of women across American history. Available at a minimum cost when bundled with the text. ISBN: 0-321-00555-4.

Reading the American West. Edited by Mitchel Roth, Sam Houston State University, this primary source reader uses letters, diary excerpts, speeches, interviews, and newspaper articles to let students experience how historians research and how history is written. Every document is accompanied by a contextual headnote and study questions. The book is divided into chapters with extensive introductions. Available at a minimum cost when bundled with the text. ISBN: 0-321-04409-6.

A Short Guide to Writing About History, **Fourth Edition.** Richard Marius, Harvard University, Melvin E. Page Eastern Tennessee University. This engaging and practical text helps students get beyond merely compiling dates and facts; it teaches them how to incorporate their own ideas into their papers and to tell a story about history that interests them and their peers. Covering both brief essays and the documented resource paper, the text explores the writing and researching processes, different modes of historical writing including argument, and concludes with guidelines for improving style. ISBN: 0-321-09300-3.

Retracing the Past, **Fifth Edition.** This two-volume set of readers is edited by Ronald Schultz, University of Wyoming, and Gary B. Nash. These secondary source readings cover economic, political, and social history with special emphasis on women, racial and ethnic groups, and working-class people. Volume One: ISBN: 0-321-10137-5; Volume Two: ISBN: 0-321-10138-3.

American History in a Box. This unique primary source reader offers students the opportunity to experience written documents, visual materials, material culture artifacts, and maps in order to learn firsthand what history is and what historians actually do. It was written and put together by Julie Roy Jeffrey and Peter Frederick, two of the authors of *The American People,* Sixth Edition. Volume One (to 1877): ISBN: 0-321-30005-2; Volume Two (since 1865): ISBN: 0-321-03006-0.

The History Place Premium Website, www.ushistoryplace.com. Available at no additional cost when requested as a bundle component by the professor, the site is a continually updated American history Website of extraordinary breadth and depth, which features unmatched interactive maps, timelines, and activities; hundreds of source documents, images, and audio clips; and much more.

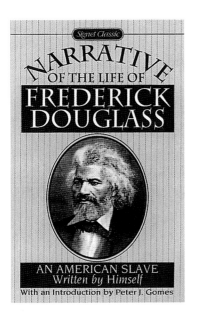

The Library of American Biography Series. Each of the interpretative biographies in this series focuses on a figure whose actions and ideas significantly influenced the course of American history and national life. Brief and inexpensive, they are ideal for any American history survey course. Available to students at a discount.

Penguin Books

The partnership between Penguin-Putnam USA and Longman Publishers offers students a discount on many titles when you bundle them with any Longman survey. Among these include

- Frederick Douglass, *Narrative of the Life of Frederick Douglass*
- L. Jesse Lemisch (Editor), *Benjamin Franklin: The Autobiography & Other Writings*
- Upton Sinclair, *The Jungle*
- Harriet Beecher Stowe, *Uncle Tom's Cabin*

◆ ACKNOWLEDGMENTS

The authors wish to thank the following reviewers who gave generously of their time and expertise and whose thoughtful and constructive work have contributed greatly to this edition:

Cara Anzilotti, *Loyola Marymount University*

Virginia H. Bellows, *Tulsa Community College*

Marjorie Berman, *Red Rocks Community College*

S. Charles Bolton, *University of Arkansas at Little Rock*

James Brett Adams, *University of Oklahoma*

Roger Bromert, *Southwest Oklahoma State University*

Neal Brooks, *Community College of Baltimore County—Essex*

Thomas P. Carroll, *John A. Logan College*

Kathleen Carter, *Highpoint University*

Mark Clark, *Oregon Institute of Technology*

Stephanie Cole, *University of Texas—Arlington*

William Furdell, *University of Great Falls*

Kathleen Gorman, *Minnesota State University—Mankato*

Amy Greenberg, *Pennsylvania State University*

Maurice Greenwald, *University of Pittsburgh*

David J. Grettler, *Northern State University*

David Gutzke, *Southwest Missouri State University*

James Hedtke, *Cabrini College*

Craig Hendricks, *Long Beach City College*

Carol Sue Humphrey, *Oklahoma Baptist University*

Edmund Irlbacher, *Orange County Community College*

Shawn Johansen, *Frostburg State University*

Jeremy Johnston, *Northwest College*

Anne Klejment, *University of St. Thomas*

Lawrence Lowther, *Central Washington University*

Robert F. Marcom, *San Antonio College*

Joanne Maypole, *Front Range Community College*

Sylvia W. McGrath, *Stephen F. Austin State University*

Thomas M. McLuen, *Spokane Falls Community College*

John McWilliams, *Pennsylvania State University*

Earl F. Mulderink III, *Southern Utah State University*

Tom Murphy, *Temple College*

Cassandra L. Newby-Alexander, *Norfolk State University*

Sean O'Neill, *Grand Valley State University*

Anne Paulet, *Humboldt State University*

Dolores Davison Peterson, *Foothill College*

Gene B. Preuss, *Texas Tech University*

David Richards, *State University College of New York at Oneonta*

Steven Riess, *Northeastern Illinois University*

Arthur T. Robinson, *Santa Rosa Junior College*

Dale J. Schmitt, *East Tennessee State University*

John A. Trickel, *Richland College*

Steve Tripp, *Grand Valley State University*

Michael P. White, *Temple College*

Over the years, as previous editions of this text were being developed, many of our colleagues read and criticized the various drafts of the manuscript. For their thoughtful evaluations and constructive suggestions, the authors wish to express their gratitude to the following reviewers:

Richard H. Abbott, *Eastern Michigan University*

John Alexander, *University of Cincinnati*

Kenneth G. Alfers, *Mountain View College*

Terry Alford, *North Virginia Community College*

Gregg Andrews, *Southwest Texas State University*

Robert Asher, *University of Connecticut, Storrs*

Harry Baker, *University of Arkansas at Little Rock*

Michael Batinski, *Southern Illinois University*

Gary Bell, *Sam Houston State University*

Virginia Bellows, *Tulsa Community College*

Spencer Bennett, *Siena Heights College*

Jackie R. Booker, *Western Connecticut State University*

James Bradford, *Texas A&M University*

Neal Brooks, *Essex Community College*

Jeffrey P. Brown, *New Mexico State University*

Dickson D. Bruce, Jr., *University of California, Irvine*

David Brundage, *University of California, Santa Cruz*

Colin Calloway, *Dartmouth University*

D'Ann Campbell, *Indiana University*

Jane Censer, *George Mason University*

Vincent A. Clark, *Johnson County Community College*

Neil Clough, *North Seattle Community College*

Matthew Ware Coulter, *Collin County Community College*

David Culbert, *Louisiana State University*

Mark T. Dalhouse, *Northeast Missouri State University*

Bruce Dierenfield, *Canisius College*

John Dittmer, *DePauw University*

Gordon Dodds, *Portland State University*

Richard Donley, *Eastern Washington University*

Dennis B. Downey, *Millersville University*

Robert Downtain, *Tarrant County Community College*

Robert Farrar, *Spokane Falls Community College*

Bernard Friedman, *Indiana University–Purdue University at Indianapolis*

Bruce Glasrud, *California State University, Hayward*

Brian Gordon, *St. Louis Community College*

Richard Griswold del Castillo, *San Diego State University*

Carol Gruber, *William Paterson College*

Colonel Williams L. Harris, *The Citadel Military College*

Robert Haws, *University of Mississippi*

Jerrold Hirsch, *Northeast Missouri State University*

Frederick Hoxie, *University of Illinois*

John S. Hughes, *University of Texas*

Link Hullar, *Kingwood College*

Donald M. Jacobs, *Northeastern University*

Delores Janiewski, *University of Idaho*

David Johnson, *Portland State University*

Richard Kern, *University of Findlay*

Robert J. Kolesar, *John Carroll University*

Monte Lewis, *Cisco Junior College*

William Link, *University of North Carolina, Greensboro*

Patricia M. Lisella, *Iona College*

Paul K. Longmore, *San Francisco State University*

Rita Loos, *Framingham State College*

Ronald Lora, *University of Toledo*

George M. Lubick, *Northern Arizona University*

Suzanne Marshall, *Jacksonville State University*

John C. Massman, *St. Cloud State University*

Vern Mattson, *University of Nevada at Las Vegas*

Art McCoole, *Cuyamaca College*

John McCormick, *Delaware County Community College*

Sylvia McGrath, *Stephen F. Austin University*

James E. McMillan, *Denison University*

Otis L. Miller, *Belleville Area College*

Walter Miszczenko, *Boise State University*

Norma Mitchell, *Troy State University*

Gerald F. Moran, *University of Michigan, Dearborn*

William G. Morris, *Midland College*

Marian Morton, *John Carroll University*

Roger Nichols, *University of Arizona*

Paul Palmer, *Texas A&I University*

Al Parker, *Riverside City College*

Judith Parsons, *Sul Ross State University*

Carla Pestana, *Ohio State University*

Neva Peters, *Tarrant County Community College*

James Prickett, *Santa Monica College*

Noel Pugash, *University of New Mexico*

Juan Gomez-Quiñones, *University of California, Los Angeles*

George Rable, *Anderson College*

Joseph P. Reidy, *Howard University*

Leonard Riforgiato, *Pennsylvania State University*

Randy Roberts, *Purdue University*

Mary Robertson, *Armstrong State University*

David Robson, *John Carroll University*

Jud Sage, *Northern Virginia Community College*

Phil Schaeffer, *Olympic College*

Sylvia Sebesta, *San Antonio College*

Herbert Shapiro, *University of Cincinnati*

David R. Shibley, *Santa Monica College*

Ellen Shockro, *Pasadena City College*

Nancy Shoemaker, *University of Connecticut*

Bradley Skelcher, *Delaware State University*

Kathryn Kish Sklar, *State University of New York at Binghampton*

James Smith, *Virginia State University*

John Snetsinger, *California Polytechnic State University, San Luis Obispo*

Jo Snider, *Southwest Texas State University*

Stephen Strausberg, *University of Arkansas*

Katherine Scott Sturdevant, *Pikes Peak Community College*

Nan M. Sumner-Mack, *Hawaii Community College*

Cynthia Taylor, *Santa Rosa Junior College*

Tom Tefft, *Citrus College*

John A. Trickel, *Richland College*

Donna Van Raaphorst, *Cuyahoga Community College*

Morris Vogel, *Temple University*

Michael Wade, *Appalachian State University*

Jackie Walker, *James Madison University*

Paul B. Weinstein, *University of Akron—Wayne College*

Joan Welker, *Prince George's Community College*

Kenneth H. Williams, *Alcorn State University*

Mitch Yamasaki, *Chaminade University*

Charles Zappia, *San Diego Mesa College*

GARY B. NASH received his Ph.D. from Princeton University. He is currently Director of the National Center for History in the Schools at the University of California, Los Angeles, where he teaches colonial and revolutionary American history. Among the books Nash has authored are *Quakers and Politics: Pennsylvania, 1681–1726* (1968); *Red, White, and Black: The Peoples of Early America* (1974, 1982, 1992, 2000); *The Urban Crucible: Social Change, Political Consciousness, and the Origins of the American Revolution* (1979); *Forging Freedom: The Formation of Philadelphia's Black Community, 1720–1840* (1988); and *First City: Philadelphia and the Forging of Historical Memory* (2002). A former president of the Organization of American Historians, his scholarship is especially concerned with the role of common people in the making of history. He wrote Part I and served as a general editor of this book.

JULIE ROY JEFFREY earned her Ph.D. in history from Rice University. Since then she has taught at Goucher College. Honored as an outstanding teacher, Jeffrey has been involved in faculty development activities and curriculum evaluation. She was Fulbright Chair in American Studies at the University of Southern Denmark, 1999–2000. Jeffrey's major publications include *Education for Children of the Poor* (1978); *Frontier Women: The Trans-Mississippi West, 1840–1880* (1979, 1997); *Converting the West: A Biography of Narcissa Whitman* (1991); and *The Great Silent Army of Abolitionism: Ordinary Women in the Antislavery Movement* (1998). She collaborated with Peter Frederick on *American History in a Box,* two volumes (2002). She is the author of many articles on the lives and perceptions of nineteenth-century women. Her research continues to focus on abolitionism as well as on history and film. She wrote Parts III and IV in collaboration with Peter Frederick and acted as a general editor of this book.

JOHN R. HOWE received his Ph.D. from Yale University. At the University of Minnesota, he has taught the U.S. history survey and courses on the American revolutionary era and the early republic. His major publications include *The Changing Political Thought of John Adams, The Role of Ideology in the American Revolution,* and *From the Revolution Through the Age of Jackson.* In 2003, The University of Massachusetts Press will publish his most recent book on conceptions of language in the political writing of the American revolutionary era. His present research deals with the social politics of verbal discourse in late eighteenth and early nineteenth century Boston. He has received a Woodrow Wilson Graduate Fellowship, a John Simon Guggenheim Fellowship, and a Research Fellowship from the Charles Warren Center for Studies in American History.

PETER J. FREDERICK received his Ph.D. in history from the University of California, Berkeley. Innovative student-centered teaching in American and African-American history has been the focus of his career at California State University, Hayward, and since 1970 at Wabash College (1992–1994 at Carleton College). Recognized nationally as a distinguished teacher and for his many articles and workshops on teaching and learning, Frederick was awarded the Eugene Asher Award for Excellence in Teaching by the AHA in 2000. He has also written several articles on life-writing and a book, *Knights of the Golden Rule: The Intellectual as Christian Social Reformer in the 1890s.* With Julie Jeffrey, he recently published *American History in a Box.* He coordinated and edited all the "Recovering the Past" sections and coauthored Parts III and IV.

ALLEN F. DAVIS earned his Ph.D. from the University of Wisconsin. A former president of the American Studies Association, he is a professor of history at Temple University and editor of *Conflict and Consensus in American History* (9th edition, 1997). He is the author of *Spearheads for Reform: The Social Settlements and the Progressive Movement* (1967); *American Heroine: The Life and Legend of Jane Addams* (1973); and *Postcards from Vermont: A Social History* (2002). He is coauthor of *Still Philadelphia* (1983); *Philadelphia Stories* (1987); and *One Hundred Years at Hull-House* (1990). Davis wrote Part V of this book.

ALLAN M. WINKLER received his Ph.D. from Yale University. He has taught at Yale and the University of Oregon, and he is now Distinguished Professor of History at Miami University of Ohio.

An award-winning teacher, he has also published extensively about the recent past. His books include *The Politics of Propaganda: The Office of War Information, 1942–1945* (1978); *Home Front U.S.A.: America During World War II* (1986, 2000); *Life Under a Cloud: American Anxiety About the Atom* (1993, 1999); and *The Cold War: A History in Documents* (2000). His research centers on the connections between public policy and popular mood in modern American history. Winkler wrote Part VI of this book.

FEATURES OF THIS BOOK

We have included a number of tools to help you in your study of American history.

- Each chapter begins with a personal story called *American Stories*, recalling the experience of an ordinary or lesser-known American. A *brief chapter overview* links this opening story to the major themes of the chapter.
- An *outline* provides an overview of the chapter topics and organization.
- *Summary* tables ("talking boxes") recap points discussed in the chapter for easy reference.
- Each international map or table is identified by a global icon ⊕ and contains *Reflecting on the Past* questions for you to consider.
- *Recovering the Past* essays in each chapter examine different kinds of historical evidence ranging from household inventories, folktales, and diaries to advertising, and popular music. *Reflecting on the Past* questions raise points for you to consider.
- *Analyzing History* graphics help you in reading and interpreting graphs and statistics. Each ends with *Reflecting on the Past* questions.
- A carefully selected program of *illustrations*—paintings, cartoons, photographs, maps, and figures—amplify important themes while presenting visual evidence for your reflection and analysis.
- A *timeline* reviews the major events and developments covered in the chapter.
- A *Conclusion* briefly summarizes the main concepts and developments discussed in the chapter.
- *Recommended Readings* are included at the end of every chapter, offering you research suggestions for scholarly resources, as well as a brief list of fiction and film (feature films and documentaries) related to chapter topics and themes.
- At the end of each chapter there is also an annotated list of suggested Web sites called *Discovering U.S. History Online* that relate to chapter topics and themes. Though these Web addresses were checked for accuracy before publication of this text, the changing nature of Web sites suggests that at least a few might be outdated links by the time you investigate them. These and additional Web suggestions will be updated regularly on the text's Web site at http://www.ablongman.com/nash.

In addition to the specific Web sites recommended for the chapters, you may also want to visit some of the following *major history Web sites* that have content that relates to all periods of American history.

Smithsonian Institution—National Museum of American History

americanhistory.si.edu/

Library of Congress Web Site

www.loc.gov/

Library of Congress American Memory Project

memory.loc.gov/ammem/amhome.html

National Archives and Records Administration Home Page

www.nara.gov

"The Digital Classroom"

www.nara.gov/education/teaching/teaching.html

"The Exhibit Hall"

www.nara.gov/exhall/

Documents for the Study of American History (AMDOCS)

www.ukans.edu/carrie/docs/amdocs_index.html

United States Census Bureau

www.census.gov/

The African-American Mosaic—A Library of Congress Resource Guide

lcweb.loc.gov/exhibits/african/intro.html

National Women's History Project

www.nwhp.org

National Gallery of Art

www.nga.gov/home.htm

Historical Maps: The Perry Castaneda Library Map Collection

www.lib.utexas.edu/Libs/PCL/Map_collection/historical/history_main.html

University of California—Berkeley Library Digital Map Collection

www.lib.berkeley.edu/EART/digital/tour.html

THE AMERICAN PEOPLE

1

Ancient America and Africa

Portuguese troops storm Tangiers in Morocco in 1471 as part of the ongoing struggle between Christianity and Islam in the mid-fifteenth century Mediterranean world. *(The Art Archive/Pastrana Church, Spain/Dagli Orti)*

✦ *American Stories*

FOUR WOMEN'S LIVES HIGHLIGHT THE CONVERGENCE OF THREE CONTINENTS

In what historians call the "early modern period" of world history—roughly the fifteenth to seventeenth century when peoples from different regions of the earth came into close contact with each other—four women played key roles in the convergence and clash of societies from Europe, Africa, and the Americas. Their lives highlight some of this chapter's major themes, which developed in an era when the people of three continents began to encounter each other and the shape of the modern world began to take form.

Born in 1451, Isabella of Castile was a banner-bearer for *reconquista*—the centuries-long Christian crusade to expel the Muslim rulers who had controlled Spain for centuries. Pious and charitable, the queen of Castile married Ferdinand, the king of Aragon, in 1469. The union of their kingdoms forged a stronger Christian Spain now prepared to realize a new religious and military vision. Eleven years later, after ending hostilities with Portugal, Isabella and Ferdinand began consolidating their power. By expelling Muslims and Jews, the royal couple pressed to enforce Catholic religious conformity. Their religious zeal also led them to sponsor four voyages of Christopher Columbus as a means of extending Spanish power across the Atlantic. The first was commissioned in 1492, only a few months after what the spanish considered a "just and holy war" against infidels culminated in the surrender of Moorish Granada, the last stronghold of Islam in Christian Europe. Sympathizing with Isabella's fervent piety and desire to convert the people of distant lands to Christianity, Columbus, after 1493 signed his letters "Christopher Columbus, Christ Bearer."

On the other side of the Atlantic resided an Aztec woman of influence, also called Isabella by the Spanish, who soon symbolized the mixing of her people with the Spanish. Her real name was Tecuichpotzin, which meant "little royal maiden" in Nahuatl, the Aztec language. The first-born child of the Aztec ruler Moctezuma II and Teotlalco, his wife, she entered the world in 1509— before the Aztecs had seen a single Spaniard. But when she was eleven, Tecuichpotzin witnessed the arrival of the conquistadors under Cortés. When her father was near death, he asked the conqueror to take custody of his daughter, hoping for an accommodation between the conquering Spanish and the conquered Aztecs. But Tecuichpotzin was reclaimed by her people and soon was married to her father's brother, who became the Aztec ruler in 1520. After he died of smallpox within two months, the last Aztec emperor claimed the young girl as his wife.

But then in 1521, the Spanish siege of Tenochtitlán, the Aztec island capital in Lake Texcoco, overturned the mighty Indian empire and soon brought Tecuichpotzin into the life of the victorious Spanish. In 1526, she learned that her husband had been tortured and hanged for plotting an insurrection against Cortés. Still only nineteen, she soon succumbed to the overtures of Cortés, agreeing to join his household and live among his Indian mistresses. Pregnant with Cortés's child, she was married off to a Spanish officer. Another marriage followed, and in all she bore seven children, all descendants of Moctezuma II. All became large landowners and figures of importance. Tecuichpotzin was in this way a pioneer of *mestizaje*—the mixing of races—and thus one of the leading Aztec women who launched the creation of a new society in Mexico.

Elizabeth I, daughter of Henry VIII who had established the Church of England and rejected the authority of the Catholic pope in Rome, became the key figure in encouraging English expansion overseas. Through her long rule of nearly a half-century, she inspired Protestant England to challenge Catholic Spain and France. Even Pope Sixtus V acknowledged that she was "a great woman, and were she only Catholic she would be without her match." He also remarked, "She is only a woman, yet she makes herself feared by Spain, by France, by the Emperor, by all." Commissioning buccaneers such as John Hawkins and Francis Drake, and sponsoring promoters of colonization such as Walter Raleigh and the Richard Hakluyts (both uncle and nephew), Elizabeth assured the planting of English colonies in North America. They would grow mightily after her death in 1603 and eventually challenge the

Dutch, French, and Spanish, who also saw the Americas as a source of great wealth and power.

Elizabeth I's vitality, ambition, and wit suited her perfectly to lead England forward, even though her nation, when she assumed the throne in 1558, was weak in comparison to France, Spain, and even Portugal. Investing her own money in voyages of exploration and settlement, she encouraged others from the middle and upper classes to do the same. In backing a 20-year conflict with the Spanish—a religious conflict and also a struggle for maritime power—she opened a gateway to the Americas for the English.

On the west coast of Africa was another powerful woman. Born around 1595 and named because she entered the world with the umbilical cord wrapped around her neck (which was believed to foretell a haughty character), Queen Njinga led fierce resistance to the Portuguese slave trade and the Portuguese attempts to control Angola. She knew the Portuguese had been trading for slaves in Angola and had even converted King Affonso I to Catholicism in the 1530s. She also knew that by the time Queen Elizabeth came to power in 1558 in England, the Portuguese had trapped her people into incessant wars in order to supply slaves to their Portuguese trading partners. Only when she assumed the throne of Ndongo (present-day Angola) in 1624 did Queen Njinga's people begin to resist

Portuguese rule. Leading her troops in a series of wars, she gave a fierce battle cry that legend says was heard for miles, making her a heroic figure in Angolan history.

In opening this book, Chapter 1 sets the scene for the intermingling of Europeans, Africans, and Native Americans in the New World, what Europeans called North and South America, by examining the backgrounds of the peoples of three continents and glimpsing the changes occurring with each of their many societies as the time for an historic convergence neared. Too often in historical writing, Europeans reaching the Americas are portrayed as the carriers of a superior culture that inevitably vanquished people living in a primitive if not "savage" state. This renders Native Americans and Africans passive and static people—so much dough to be kneaded by advanced Europeans. But recent historical scholarship tells us that Africans and Native Americans were critically important participants in the making of American history—part of a complex, intercultural birthing of a "new world." By examining the state of the societies of West Africa, North and South America, and Western Europe in the late fifteenth century, we will be better prepared to see how the complex, multicultural shaping of American history took place.

THE PEOPLES OF AMERICA BEFORE COLUMBUS

Thousands of years before the European exploratory voyages in the 1490s, the history of humankind in North America began. Thus, American history can begin with some basic questions: Who were the first inhabitants of the Americas? Where did they come from? What were they like? How had the societies they formed changed over the millennia that preceded European arrival? Can their history be reconstructed from the mists of prehistoric time?

Migration to the Americas

Almost all the evidence suggesting answers to these questions comes from ancient sites of early life in North America. Archaeologists have unearthed skeletal remains, pots, tools, ornaments, and other objects to reach tentative dates for the arrival of humans in America to about 35,000 B.C.E.—about

the same time that humans began to settle Japan and Scandinavia.

Nearly every Native American society has its own creation story about its origins in the Americas. For example, many Indian societies believe they were the first people in North America, people who emerged out of the earth or from underneath the waters of a large lake. However, paleo-anthropologists, scientists who study ancient peoples, generally agree that the first inhabitants of the Americas were sojourners from Asia. Nomadic bands from Siberia, hunting big game animals such as bison, caribou, and reindeer, began to migrate across a land bridge connecting northeastern Asia with Alaska. Geologists believe that this land bridge, perhaps 600 miles wide, existed most recently between 25,000 and 14,000 years ago, when massive glaciers locked up much of the earth's moisture and left part of the Bering Sea floor exposed. Ice-free passage through Canada was possible only briefly at the beginning and end of this period, however. At other times, melting glaciers flooded the land bridge and blocked foot traffic to Alaska. Scholars are divided on the exact timing, but the main migration apparently occurred between 11,000 and 14,000 years ago, although possibly much earlier. Some new archaeological finds suggest multiple migrations, both by sea and land, from several regions of Asia and even from Europe.

Hunters, Farmers, and Environmental Factors

Once on the North American continent, these early wanderers began trekking southward and then eastward, following vegetation and game. Even to reach what is now the Pacific Northwest took many centuries. In time, they reached the tip of South America—some 15,000 miles from the Asian homeland to Tierra del Fuego, the southernmost limit of South America. Moving eastward, they traversed some 6,000 miles from Siberia to the eastern edge of North America. American history has traditionally emphasized the "westward movement" of people, but for thousands of years before Columbus's arrival, the frontier moved southward and eastward. Thus did people from the "Old World" discover the "New World" thousands of years before Columbus.

Archaeologists have excavated ancient sites of early life in the Americas, unearthing tools, ornaments, and skeletal remains that can be scientifically dated. In this way, they have tentatively reconstructed the dispersion of these first Americans over an immense land mass. Although much remains unknown, archaeological evidence suggests that as centuries passed and population increased, the earliest inhabitants evolved into separate cultures, adjusting to various environments in distinct ways. Europeans who rediscovered the New World thousands of years later would lump together the myriad societies they found. But by the late 1400s, the "Indians" of the Americas were enormously diverse in the size and complexity of their societies, the languages they spoke, and their forms of social organization.

Archaeologists and anthropologists have charted several phases of so-called Native American history. The Beringian period of initial migration ended about 14,000 years ago. During the Paleo-Indian era, 14,000 to 10,000 years ago, big-game hunters flaked hard stones into spear points and chose "kill sites" where they slew herds of Pleistocene mammals. This more reliable food source allowed population growth, and nomadism began to give way to settled habitations or local migration within limited territories.

Then during the Archaic era, from about 10,000 to 2,500 years ago, great geological changes brought further adaptations to the land. As the massive Ice Age glaciers slowly retreated, a warming trend turned vast grassland areas from Utah to the highlands of Central America into desert. The Pleistocene mammals were weakened by more arid conditions, but human populations ably adapted. They learned to exploit new sources of food, especially plants. In time, a second technological breakthrough took place, what historians call the agricultural revolution.

Learning how to plant, cultivate, and harvest allowed humans certain control over once-ungovernable natural forces. Anthropologists believe that this process began independently in widely separated parts of the world—Africa, Asia, Europe, and the Americas—about 9,000 to 7,000 years ago. Though agriculture developed very slowly, it eventually brought dramatic changes in human societies everywhere.

Historians have sometimes imagined that these early people lived in a primordial paradise in harmony with their surroundings. But recent archaeological evidence points to examples of environmental devastation that severely damaged the biodiversity of the Americas. The first wave of intruders found a wilderness teeming with so-called megafauna: saber-toothed tigers, woolly mammoths, gigantic ground sloths, huge bison, and monstrous bears. But by about 10,000 years ago, these animals were almost extinct. Both overhunting and a massive shift of climate that deprived the huge beasts of their grazing environment were to blame.

The depletion of the megafauna left the hemisphere with a much restricted catalogue of animals. Left behind were large animals such as elk, buffalo, bear, and moose. But the extinction of the huge beasts forced people to prey on new sources of food such as turkeys, ducks, and guinea pigs. Their reduced food supply may have gradually reduced their population.

Over many centuries in the Americas, salinization and deforestation put the environment under additional stress. For example, in what is today central Arizona, the Hohokam civilization collapsed hundreds of years ago, much like that in ancient Mesopotamia, when the irrigation system became too salty to support agriculture. At New Mexico's Chaco Canyon, the fast-growing Anasazi denuded a magnificently forested region in their search for firewood and building materials. This, in turn, led to the erosion of rich soil that impoverished the region for the Anasazi.

Migration Routes from Asia to the Americas

The red arrows indicate the general flow of migrating societies over thousands of years before Europeans reached the Americas. Based on fragile archaeological evidence, these migratory patterns are necessarily tentative, and new discoveries support the theory of early Stone Age arrivals by boat. **Reflecting on the Past** Can you reconcile Native American creation myths with archaeological evidence of the first humans reaching the Americas by crossing the Bering Straits land bridge? If so, how?

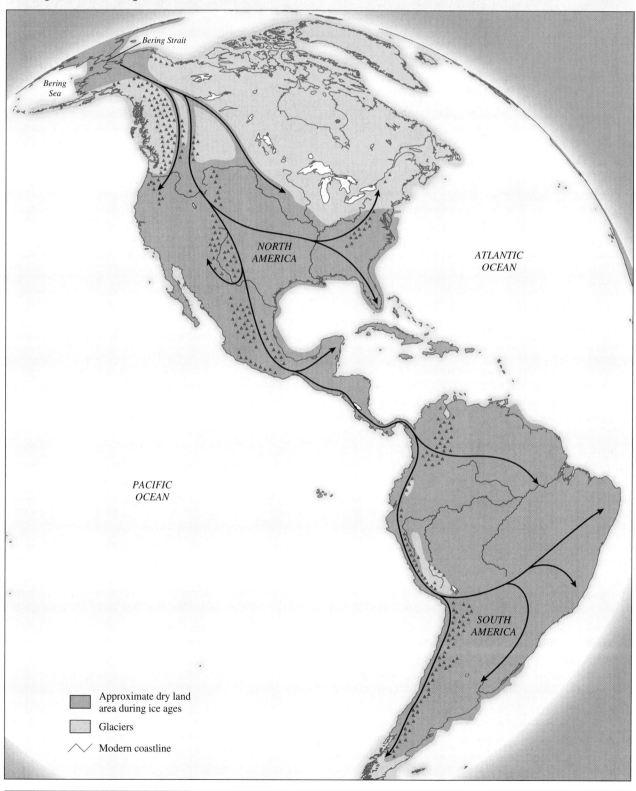

agriculture triggered other major changes. As more ample food fueled population growth, large groups split off to form separate societies. Greater social and political complexity developed because not everyone was needed as before to secure the society's food supply. Men cleared the land and hunted game, while women planted, cultivated, and harvested crops. Many societies empowered religious figures, who organized the common followers, directed their work, and exacted tribute as well as worship from them. In return, the community trusted them to ward off hostile forces.

Everywhere in the Americas, regional trading networks formed. Along trade routes carrying commodities such as salt for food preservation, obsidian rock for projectile points, and copper for jewelry

The skeleton shown here of a saber-tooth cat was recovered from a tar pit in downtown Los Angeles, where excavation of the pits began in 1908. Roving animals, including dinosaurs, giant sloths, and wolves, were trapped in the sticky asphalt bog and preserved for as long as 40,000 years. *(Ed Ikuta/Courtesy of the George C. Page Museum)*

When Native Americans learned to domesticate plant life, they began the long process of transforming their relationship to the physical world. Like all living organisms, human beings depend on plants to survive. For both humans and animals, plants are the source of life-sustaining fuel. The ultimate source of this energy is the sun. But in tapping solar energy, humans and animals had to rely on plants because they are the only organisms capable of producing significant amounts of organic material through the photosynthetic process. Plant life was—and still is—the strategic element in the chain of life.

Dating the advent of agriculture in the Americas is difficult, but archaeologists estimate it at about 5000 B.C.E. Agriculture had already been developed in Southwestern Asia and in Africa and spread to Europe at about the time people in the Tehuacán Valley of central Mexico first planted maize and squash. Over the millennia, humans progressed from doorside planting of a few wild seeds to systematic clearing and planting of fields. As the production of domesticated plant food ended dependence on gathering wild plants and pursuing game, settled village life began to replace nomadic existence. Increases in food supply brought about by

At the bottom of this pictograph, the Aztecs displayed the conquest of two villages—Colhuacan pueblo and Tenayucan pueblo—on the western side of Lake Texcoco. These were the first two victories that marked the beginning of the consolidation of Aztec power in central Mexico less than a century before Columbus's voyages. Note the importance of corn in the upper part of the pictograph and the prickly pear cactus, the meaning of Tenochtitlán, and the eagle, symbol of their war god, in the center. *(Bodleian Library, University of Oxford [MS Arch. Seld.A.1. fol. 2r])*

also traveled technology, religious ideas, and agricultural practices. By the end of the Archaic period, about 500 B.C.E., hundreds of independent kin-based groups, like people in other parts of the world, had learned to exploit the resources of their particular area and to trade with other groups in their region. For centuries thereafter, native societies grew in size, developed more sophisticated agricultural techniques, and in some areas adopted a sedentary life.

Mesoamerican Empires

Of all the large-scale societies developing in the Americas during Europe's medieval period, the most impressive were in Mesoamerica—the middle region bridging the great land masses of South and North America. The Valley of Mexico, now dominated by Mexico City, became the center of the largest societies that emerged in the centuries before the Spanish arrived early in the sixteenth century. Successor to the earlier Olmec and Toltec civilizations, the Aztec people, according to their legends, were forced by more advanced people to serve as soldiers in their captors' armies, and in this way the Aztecs became skilled warriors. After years of wandering, the militant Aztec people around the early 1300s reached the town-dotted agricultural

Valley of Mexico. There they encountered the descendants of the ancient Toltec civilization, which had collapsed in the twelfth century. In less than two centuries, the Aztecs built a mighty empire, rivaling any known over the centuries in Europe, Asia, or Africa, by using their warrior skills to subjugate smaller tribes. By the time of Columbus's first voyage in 1492, the Aztecs controlled most of central Mexico with a huge population, estimated at 10 to 20 million people. Extracting tribute from conquered peoples—beans, maize, and other foodstuffs; cotton fabrics; bird feathers for war costumes; animal furs; and labor on state projects such as canals, temples, and irrigation—the Aztecs built a great capital in Tenochtitlán ("Place of the Prickly Pear Cactus")—a canal-ribbed city island in the great lake of Texcoco. Connected to the mainland by three broad causeways and supplied with drinkable water by an impressive aqueduct, Tenochtitlán boasted a population of perhaps 150,000, comparable to the medieval city-state of Venice and certainly one of the world's greatest cities on the eve of the Columbian voyages.

Aztec society was as stratified as any in Europe, and the supreme ruler's authority was as extensive as that of any European or African king. Every Aztec was born into one of four classes: the nobility, including the emperor's household, priests, and mili-

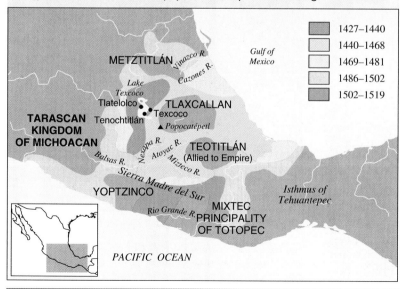

Expansion of the Aztec Empire, 1427–1519

In the century before Europeans breached the Atlantic to find the Americas, the Aztecs' rise to power brought 10 to 20 million people under their sway—more than the entire population of Spain and Portugal at this time.

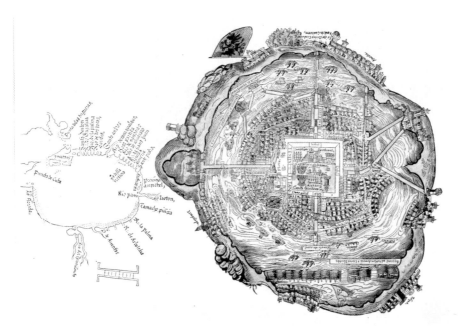

The plan of Tenochtitlán, later Mexico City, is from the Latin edition of Cortés's "Second Letter," on his conquest of the Aztec. Cortés's account was widely published in Europe, where Germans, French, and English were astounded to hear of such an extraordinary Aztec metropolis with floating gardens, causeways, and monumental architecture. *(The Granger Collection, New York)*

tary officers; free commoners with rights to land and organized in precincts with temples and schools; serfs, who were like those in Europe bound to the soil and toiling on the lands of nobles; and slaves, who had rights akin to slaves in ancient Rome or Greece.

When they arrived in 1519, Spaniards could hardly believe the grandeur they saw in the immense Aztec capital that covered about ten square miles and boasted some forty towers, one of them, according to the first Spaniards entering the city, higher than the cathedral of Seville, the largest in Spain. "When we saw so many cities and villages built in the water and other great towns on dry land and that straight and level causeway going towards Mexico," wrote one Spaniard in the army of Cortés, "we were amazed and said that it was like the enchantments they tell of in the legend of Amadis. . . . Some of our soldiers even asked whether the things that we saw were not a dream." Indeed, they had found their way to the most advanced civilization in the Americas, where through skilled hydraulic engineering, the Aztecs cultivated chinampas, or "floating gardens," around their capital city where a wide variety of flowers and vegetables grew. Unprepared for encountering such a civilization built by what they considered savage people, the Spaniards could not believe their eyes when they saw monumental architecture, bustling city markets, elaborate stone sculpture, beautiful jewelry set with precious stones, an army of skilled artisans, and a priesthood that presided over multiple religious ceremonies, where human sacrifices were made to the gods at the Temple of the Sun to ensure rich harvests (and according to some scholars, to frighten their enemies).

Regional North American Cultures

While the regions north of Mesoamerica were never populated by societies of the size and complexity of the Aztecs, some of them, particularly in what is now the American Southwest, felt the influence radiating northward from the Valley of Mexico. But throughout the vast expanses of North America in the last epoch of pre-Columbian development, the so-called post-Archaic phase, many distinct societies evolved through a complex process of growth and environmental adaptation. In the southwestern region of North America, for example, Hohokam and Anasazi societies (the ancestors of the present-day Hopi and Zuñi) had developed a sedentary village life thousands of years before the Spanish arrived in the 1540s. By about 700 to 900 C.E., descendants of these people abandoned the ancient pit houses dug in cliffs and began to construct rectangular rooms arranged in apartment-like structures.

By about 1200 C.E., "Pueblo" people, as the Spanish later called them, were developing planned villages composed of large, terraced, multistoried buildings, each with many rooms and often constructed on defensive sites that would afford the Anasazi protection from their northern enemies. The largest of them, containing about 800 rooms, was at Pueblo Bonito in Chaco Canyon. By the time

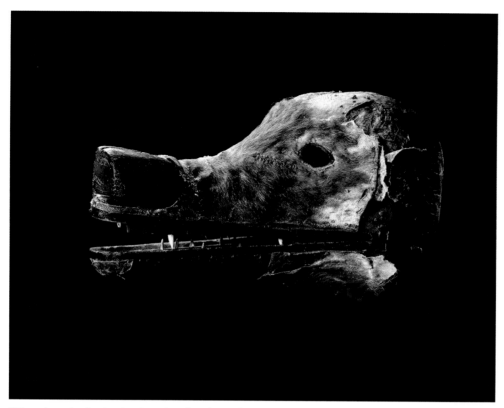

This mask, made of red cedar, sinew, bearskin, glass, and paint, was created about 1840 by an unknown artist of the Kwakwaka'wakw people of British Columbia. Grizzly bear masks were displayed in villages and used in ritual dances, partly to control the behavior of children, who were warned by their parents that the grizzly bear would get them if they misbehaved. *(Courtesy of the Royal British Columbia Museum, Victoria, British Columbia [CPN 9187])*

the Spanish arrived in the 1540s, the indigenous Pueblo people were using irrigation canals, dams, and hillside terracing to water their arid maize fields. In their agricultural techniques, their skill in ceramics, their use of woven textiles for clothing, and their village life, Pueblo society resembled that of peasant communities in many parts of Europe and Asia. Don Juan de Oñate reported home in 1599 after reaching the Pueblo villages on the Rio Grande that the Indians "live very much the same as we do, in houses with two and three terraces. . . ."

Far to the north, on the Pacific coast of the Northwest, native people formed societies around cedar and salmon. Tlingit, Kwakiutl, Salish, and Haida people lived in villages of several hundred, drawing their sustenance from salmon and other spawning fish. Plank houses displayed elaborately carved red cedar pillars and were guarded by gigantic totem poles depicting animals with supernatural power such as the bear, bald eagle, killer whale, sea otter, wolf, and frog. Reaching this region much later than most other parts of the hemisphere, early European explorers were amazed at the architectural and artistic skills of the Northwest indigenous people. "What must astonish most," wrote one

French explorer in the late eighteenth century, "is to see painting everywhere, everywhere sculpture, among a nation of hunters."

Carving and painting soft wood from deep cedar forest surrounding their villages, Northwest native people defined their place in the cosmos with ceremonial face masks. The masks often represented animals, birds, and fish—reminders of magical ancestral spirits that inhabited what they understood as the four interconnected zones of the cosmos: the Sky World, the Undersea World, the Mortal World, and the Spirit World.

Ceremonial masks played a pivotal place in the Potlatch, a great winter gathering where through song, dance, and ritual Northwest peoples gave meaning to their existence and reaffirmed their goal of achieving harmony and balance in their world. In the Potlatch ceremonial dances, native leaders honored their family lineage and signified their chiefly authority in the tribe. By giving away many of their possessions, chiefs satisfied tribe members and in this way maintained their legitimacy. Such largesse mystified and often disturbed Europeans, who prized the individual accumulation of wealth. Attempts by American and Canadian authorities to suppress Potlatch ceremonies in the late nineteenth century never succeeded.

Far to the east, Native American societies evolved over thousands of years. From the Great Plains of the mid-continent to the Atlantic tidewater region, a variety of tribes came to be loosely associated in four main language groups: Algonquian, Iroquoian, Muskhogean, and Siouan. Their existence in eastern North America has been traced as far back as about 9000 B.C.E. Like other tribal societies, they had been transformed by the agricultural revolution. Gradually, they adopted semi-fixed settlements where they combined agriculture, food gathering, game hunting, and fishing. In time, these societies developed trading networks linking together societies occupying a vast region.

Among the most impressive of these societies were the mound-building societies of the Mississippi and Ohio valleys. When European settlers first crossed the Appalachian Mountains a century and a half after arriving on the continent, they were astounded to find hundreds of ceremonial mounds and gigantic sculptured earthworks in geometric designs or in the shapes of huge humans, birds, or writhing serpents. Believing all "Indians" to be forest primitives, they reasoned that these were the remains of an ancient civilization that had found its way to North America—perhaps Phoenicians, survivors of the sunken island of Atlantis, or the Lost Tribes of Israel spoken of in European mythology.

Archaeologists now conclude that the Mound Builders were the ancestors of the Creeks, Choctaws, and Natchez. Their societies, evolving slowly over the centuries, had developed considerable complexity

Pre-Columbian Societies of the Americas

Once described as nomadic hunter–gatherers, indigenous peoples in the Americas were agriculturalists and urban dwellers in many areas and populated the land as densely as did people in many other parts of the world.

The ruins of Pueblo Bonita in Chaco Canyon, New Mexico, mark the center of Anasazi culture in the twelfth century C.E. This San Juan River basin town may have contained one thousand people living in apartment-like structures larger than any built in North America until the late nineteenth century. (© David Muench)

Archaeological Artifacts

The recovery of the past before there were extensive written records is the domain of archaeology. Virtually our entire knowledge of Indian societies in North America before the arrival of European colonizers is drawn from the work of archaeologists who have excavated the ancient living sites of the first Americans. Many Native Americans today strongly oppose this rummaging in the ancient ancestral places; they particularly oppose the unearthing of burial sites. But the modern search for knowledge about the past goes on.

Archaeological data have allowed us to overcome the stereotypical view of Native Americans as a primitive people whose culture was static for thousands of years before Europeans arrived in North America. This earlier view allowed historians to argue that the tremendous loss of Native American population and land accompanying the initial settlement and westward migration of white Americans was more or less inevitable. When two cultures, one dynamic and forward-looking and the other static and backward, confronted each other, historians have frequently maintained, the more advanced or "civilized" culture almost always prevailed.

Much of the elaborate early history of people in the Americas is unrecoverable. But many fragments of this long human history are being recaptured through archaeological research. Particularly important are studies that reveal how Indian societies were changing during the few centuries immediately preceding the European arrival in the New World. These studies give us a much better chance to interpret the seventeenth-century interaction of Native Americans and Europeans because they provide an understanding of Indian values, social and political organization, material culture, and religion as they existed when the two cultures first met.

One such investigation has been carried out over the last century at the confluence of the Mississippi and Missouri Rivers near modern-day East St. Louis, Illinois. Archaeologists have found the center of a vast Mississippi culture that began about 600 C.E., reached its peak about 300 years before Columbus's voyages, and then declined through a combination of drought, dwindling food supplies, and internal tensions. Cahokia is the name given to the urban

center of a civilization that at its height dominated an area as large as New York State. At the center of Cahokia stood one of the largest earth constructions built by ancient man anywhere on the planet. Its base covering 16 acres, this gigantic earthen temple, containing 22 million cubic feet of hand-moved earth, rises in four terraces to a height of 100 feet, as tall as a ten-story modern office building. The central plaza, like those of the Aztecs and Mayans, was oriented exactly on a north–south axis in order to chart the movement of celestial bodies. The drawing shown opposite indicates some of the scores of smaller geometric burial mounds near this major

Pottery effigy vessels in the shape of human heads. (*National Museum of the American Indian, New York*)

A reconstructed view of Cahokia, the largest town in North America before European arrival, painted by William R. Iseminger. The millions of cubic feet of earth used to construct the ceremonial and burial mounds must have required the labor of tens of thousands of workers over a long period of time. *(Cahokia Mounds State Historic Site)*

temple. Notice the outlying farms, a sure sign of the settled (as opposed to nomadic) existence of the people who flourished ten centuries ago in this region. How does this depiction of ancient Cahokia change your image of Native American life before the arrival of Europeans?

By recovering artifacts from Cahokia burial mounds, archaeologists have pieced together a picture, still tentative, of a highly elaborate civilization along the Mississippi bottomlands. Cahokian manufacturers mass-produced salt, knives, and stone hoe blades for both local consumption and export. Cahokian artisans made sophisticated pottery, ornamental jewelry, metalwork, and tools. They used copper and furs from the Lake Superior region, black obsidian stone from the Rocky Mountains, and seashells from the Gulf of Mexico, demonstrating that the people at Cahokia were involved in long-distance trade. In fact, Cahokia was a crucial crossroads of trade and water travel in the heartland of North America.

The objects shown opposite, unearthed from graves by archaeologists, are an example of the culture of the Mississippi Mound Builders. The round-faced pottery bottles in the form of heads, each about 6 inches tall and wide, show a sense of humor in early Mississippi culture. Holes in the ears of the bottles once held thongs so that the objects could be hung or carried. Other objects, such as a figure of a kneeling woman found in Tennessee, had holes under the arms for a similar purpose.

The fact that some graves uncovered at Cahokia contain large caches of finely tooled objects and that other burial mounds contain many skeletons unaccompanied by any artifacts leads archaeologists to conclude that this was a more stratified society than those encountered by the first settlers along the Atlantic seaboard. Anthropologists believe that some of the Mississippi culture spread eastward before Cahokia declined, but much mystery still remains concerning the fate and cultural diffusion of these early Americans.

Reflecting on the Past What other conclusions about Cahokian culture can you draw from figures such as these? Are there archaeological sites in your area that contain evidence of Native American civilization?

North American Mound-building Cultures

Plows, shovels, and bulldozers have obliterated many of the earthworks created at hundreds of mound-building sites in the eastern half of North America.

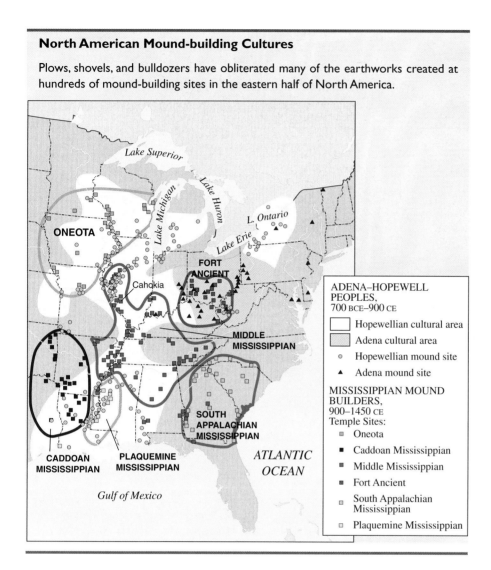

by the advent of Christianity in Europe. In southern Ohio alone about ten thousand mounds, used as burial sites, have been pinpointed, and archaeologists have excavated another one thousand earth-walled enclosures, including one enormous fortification with a circumference of about three and one-half miles, enclosing one hundred acres, or the equivalent of fifty modern city blocks. From the mounded tombs, archaeologists have recovered a great variety of items that have been traced to widely separated parts of the continent: large ceremonial blades chipped from obsidian rock formations in what is now Yellowstone National Park; embossed breastplates, ornaments, and weapons fashioned from copper nuggets from the Great Lakes region; decorative objects cut from sheets of mica from the southern Appalachians; conch shells from the Atlantic seaboard; and ornaments made from shark and alligator teeth and shells from the Gulf of Mexico. All of this material shows that the

Mound Builders participated in a vast trading network linking together hundreds of Indian villages across the continent.

The mound-building societies of the Ohio valley declined many centuries before Europeans reached the continent, perhaps attacked by other tribes or damaged by severe climatic changes that undermined agriculture. By about 600 C.E., another mound-building agricultural society arose in the Mississippi valley. Its center, the city of Cahokia with at least 20,000 (and possibly as many as 40,000) inhabitants, stood near present-day St. Louis. Great ceremonial plazas, flanked by a temple that rose in four terraces to a height of 100 feet, marked this first metropolis in America. This was the urban center of a far-flung Mississippi culture that encompassed hundreds of villages from Wisconsin to Louisiana and from Oklahoma to Tennessee.

Before the mound-building cultures of the continental heartlands declined, perhaps through cli-

Native American Trade Networks in 1400

By recovering objects such as shell necklaces, stone tools, and decorative copper from ancient sites of Indian habitation, and by determining their place of origin, anthropologists have developed this approximate map of Native American trading networks in the century before the arrival of Europeans.

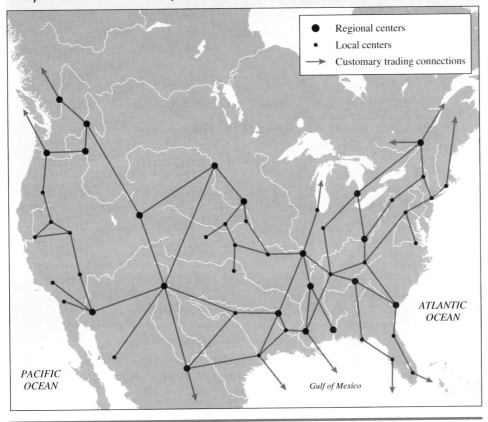

matic changes, their influence was already transforming the woodlands societies along the Atlantic coastal plain. The numerous small tribes that settled from Nova Scotia to Florida never equaled the larger societies of the midcontinent in earthwork sculpture, architectural design, or development of large-scale agriculture. But they were far from the "savages" that the first European explorers described. When Europeans arrived, they encountered scores of local tribes of the Eastern woodlands. Each maintained cultural elements peculiar to its people, although they shared in common many things such as agricultural techniques, the sexual division of labor, pottery design, social organization, and toolmaking. But the most important common denominator among them was that each had mastered the local habitat in a way that sustained life and ensured the perpetuation of their people.

In the far north were Abenakis, Penobscots, Passamaquoddys, and others, who lived by the sea and supplemented their diet with maple sugar and a few foodstuffs. Farther south, in what was to become New England, were Massachusetts, Wampanoags, Pequots, Narragansetts, Niantics, Mahicans, and others—small tribes occupying fairly local areas and joined together only by occasional trade. South of them, in the mid-Atlantic area, were Lenape, Susquehannock, Nanticoke, Pamunkey, Shawnee, Tuscarora, Catawba, and other peoples, who added limited agriculture to their skill in using natural plants for food, medicine, dyes, and flavoring and had developed food procurement strategies that exploited all the resources around them—cleared land, forests, streams, shore, and ocean. Most of these eastern woodlands tribes lived in waterside villages. Locating their fields of maize near fishing grounds, they often migrated seasonally

One of the hundreds of symbolic mounds built by people of the Hopewell culture, this mound, in the shape of a serpent, is near present-day Cincinnati. Nearly a quarter-mile long and about 20 feet across, the coiled earthen serpent is devouring a frog or an egg. In 1887, Frederick Putnam, a Harvard archaeologist, saved the mound from destruction. *(National Museum of the American Indian, New York)*

between inland and coastal village sites or situated themselves astride two ecological zones. In the Northeast, their birchbark canoes, light enough to be carried by a single man, helped them trade and communicate over immense territories.

One of the most heavily populated regions of the North American continent was the Southeast, where rich and complex cultures, some of them joined in loose confederacies, were located. Belonging to several language groups, these peoples traced their ancestry back at least 8,000 years. Some of the most elaborate pottery-making in the eastern half of the continent occurred in the Southeast, beginning about 2000 B.C.E. Hopewell burial mound techniques also influenced these cultures, and a few hundred years before Spanish explorer Hernando de Soto marched through the area in the 1540s, grandiose ceremonial centers, whose construction involved earthmoving on a vast scale, had become a distinct feature of this region. Called "Mississippian" societies by archaeologists, the tribes of the Southeast learned how to do elaborate pottery and basket weaving and conduct long-distance trade. Favored by a global warming trend that increased the annual average temperature by a few degrees for about four hundred years after 900, agriculture flourished in this region. This led in some cases, as with the Natchez, to the development of highly stratified societies where chiefs and commoners were sharply divided and where priests led ritual ceremonies, meant to ensure successful crops and community well-being, that were based on the seasons and the solar cycle. These people were the ancestors of the powerful Creeks and Yamasees in the

Georgia and Alabama regions, the Apalachees in Florida and along the Gulf of Mexico, the Choctaws, Chickasaws, and Natchez of the lower Mississippi Valley, the Cherokees of the southern Appalachian mountains, and several dozen smaller tribes scattered along the Atlantic coast. But after the "Little Ice Age," which occurred for several centuries after about 1300, the ancestors had abandoned their mounded urban centers and devolved into less populous, less stratified, and less centralized societies.

The Iroquois

Far to the north of the declining southeastern mound-building societies, Iroquoian-speaking people were following a contrary path for several centuries before the arrival of Europeans. The most important of those that were beginning a process of growth and consolidation were the Iroquois. Their territory stretched from the Adirondack Mountains to the Great Lakes and from what is now northern New York to Pennsylvania. Five tribes comprised what Europeans later called the League of the Iroquois: the Mohawk ("People of the Flint"), Oneidas ("People of the Stone"), Onondagas ("People of the Mountain"), Cayugas ("People at the Landing"), and Senecas ("Great Hill People"). The Iroquois confederation was a vast extension of the kinship group that characterized the northeastern woodlands pattern of family settlement and embraced perhaps 10,000 people at the time Europeans began to build settlements in the northeastern region of the continent in the sixteenth century. Living across major Indian trade routes in the Northeast, they were positioned between what would become French and English zones of settlement, which would ensure that the Iroquois would be deeply caught up with the onrush of Europeans.

Not long before Europeans began coming ashore in eastern North America, the loosely organized and strife-ridden Iroquois strengthened themselves by creating a more cohesive political confederacy. By learning to suppress intra-Iroquois blood feuds, villages gained stability, population increased, and the Iroquois developed political mechanisms for solving internal problems and presenting a more unified front in parlaying with their Algonquian neighbors for the use of hunting territories to the north or in admitting dependent tribes to settle on their territory. This facilitated the development of a coordinated Iroquois policy for dealing with the European newcomers.

Work in the palisaded villages of Iroquoia, some bustling with more than a thousand people, was performed communally and land was owned not by individuals but by all in common. An individual family might till their own patch of land, but it was understood that this usage in no way implied private ownership. Likewise, hunting was a communal enterprise. Though individual hunters differed in their ability to stalk and kill deer, the collective bounty of the hunting party was brought back to the village and divided among all. Similarly, several families occupied a longhouse, but the house itself, like all else in the community, was common property. "No hospitals [poorhouses] are needed among them," wrote a French Jesuit in 1657, "because there are neither mendicants nor paupers as long as there are any rich people among them. Their kindness, humanity, and courtesy not only makes them liberal with what they have, but causes them to possess hardly anything except in common. A whole village

must be without corn, before any individual can be obliged to endure privation." One historian has called this "upside down capitalism," where the goal was not to pile up material possessions but to reach the happy situation where they could give what they had to others.

Out of extended kinship groups, the Iroquois organized village settlements. Like many Africans, the Iroquois had matrilineal families where family membership was determined through the female rather than male line. A typical Iroquois family comprised an old woman, her daughters with their husbands and children, and her unmarried granddaughters and grandsons. Sons and grandsons remained with their kinship group until they married; then they joined the family of their wife or the family of their mother's brother. If this puzzled Europeans, whose men controlled women strictly, so did the Iroquois woman's prerogative of divorce; if she desired it, she merely set her husband's possessions outside the longhouse door.

Iroquois society also invested the community's women with a share of political power in ways the Europeans found strange. Political authority in the villages derived from the matrons or senior women of the *ohwachiras*—a group of related families. These women named the men representing the clans at village and tribal councils and appointed the 49 sachems or chiefs who met periodically when the confederated Five Nations met. These civil chiefs were generally middle-aged or elderly men who had gained fame earlier as warriors but now gained their prestige at the council fires. The political power of the women also extended to the ruling councils, where they caucused behind the circle of chiefs and made sure that the tribal council did not move too far from the will of the women

When the Frenchman Jacques le Moyne arrived in what is now South Carolina in 1565, he painted Indian women cultivating the soil and planting corn. Le Moyne's painting did not survive, but it was rendered as shown here by the Flemish engraver Theodor de Bry, who purchased it from Le Moyne's widow in 1588. DeBry took some liberties; for example, he put European-style hoes with metal blades into the hands of the women, whereas they tilled with large fish bones fitted to sticks. Iroquois women would have tilled the soil in much the same way.

A typical Iroquois village in the sixteenth century might have contained 30 or more longhouses of this kind. Averaging about 100 feet in length, they had interior compartments for individual families. *(Courtesy of The Newberry Library, Chicago)*

who appointed them. The male chiefs were secure in their positions only so long as they could achieve a consensus with the women who had placed them in office.

Power divided between men and women was seen further in the tribal economy and in military affairs. While men did most of the hunting and fishing, the women were the community's primary agriculturists. In tending the crops, they became vital to sustaining the community. When men were away on weeks-long hunting expeditions, women were left entirely in charge of village daily life. If "the forest belonged to the men," one historian explains, "the village was the woman's domain." In military affairs women played a significant role, for they supplied the moccasins and food for warring expeditions. A decision to withhold these supplies was tantamount to vetoing a military foray. Clan matrons often initiated war by calling on the Iroquois warriors to bring them enemy captives to replace fallen clan members.

In raising children, Iroquois parents were more permissive than Europeans. They did not believe in harsh physical punishment, encouraged the young to imitate adult behavior, and were tolerant of fumbling early attempts. The mother nursed and protected the infant while hardening it by baths in cold water. Weaning ordinarily began at age three or four. Childhood interest in the anatomy and in sexual experimentation was accepted as normal. All this con-

trasted with European child-rearing techniques, which stressed accustoming the child to authority from an early age through frequent use of physical punishment, condemning early sexual curiosity, and emphasizing obedience and respect for authority.

The approach to authority in Iroquois society, like most other Indian societies in North America, lacked most of the complicated machinery developed by Europeans to direct individual lives. No laws and ordinances, sheriffs and constables, judges and juries, or courts or jails—the apparatus of authority in Europe—existed in pre-contact North America. Yet the Iroquois set boundaries of acceptable behavior firmly. They prized the autonomous individual yet maintained a strict code of right and wrong. But they governed behavior by imparting a sense of tradition and attachment to the group through communally performed rituals. Europeans dealt with crime through investigation, arrest, prosecution, and sentencing. But in Indian society, those who stole food, to take one example, were "shamed" and ostracized until the culprits atoned for their actions and proved ready for re-entry into village communal life.

Pre-contact Population

For many decades, anthropologists and historians estimated that the population of the Americas, and especially North America, was small, only about 10 percent of Europe's population at the time of

Indian Population of the Americas in World Context, 1500

Because they are from a time when censuses were rare in most parts of the world, all population figures are estimates. Some demographers believe that 100 million people inhabited the Americas in 1500. New research and lively debate will no doubt alter these figures. **Reflecting on the Past** What is the population today of the areas listed below, and how do you account for differing distribution of the world's population?

China	100–150 million
India	75–150 million
Southwest Asia	20–30 million
Japan and rest of Asia	30–50 million
Europe (including Russia)	70–90 million
Africa	50–70 million
Americas	50–70 million

Columbus's voyages initiated in 1492. Only recently have scholars conceded that most estimates made in the past were grossly understated because of the conventional view that Indian societies peopled by nomadic hunters and gatherers could not be very large.

But with massive archaeological research in recent decades, and with a firmer understanding of how sophisticated many Native American societies were five hundred years ago in agricultural techniques capable of sustaining large societies, the population estimates have soared. Today's scholars believe that the pre-contact population north of the Rio Grande River, on the eve of European exploration of the Americas, contained at least 4 million people, of whom perhaps half lived east of the Mississippi River and some 700,000 settled along the eastern coastal plain and in the piedmont region accessible to the early European settlers. Though estimates vary widely, the firmest counts

Indian Population Density in North America, c. 1500

Historical demographers have devised estimates of Native American population density in North America before the arrival of Europeans. Estimates are based on the "carrying capacity" of different ecological regions: rainfall, access to fish and animals, soil fertility, and length of growing season are all factors in the capacity of the land to support human life.

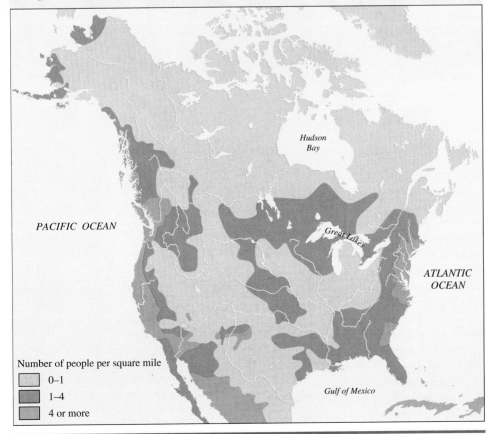

Number of people per square mile
- 0–1
- 1–4
- 4 or more

about 50 to 70 million people living in the entire hemisphere when Europeans first arrived. This contrasted with some 70 to 90 million in Europe (including Russia) around 1500, about 50 to 70 million in Africa, and 225 to 350 million in Asia. The colonizers were not coming to a "virgin wilderness," as they often described it, but to a land inhabited for thousands of years by people whose village existence in some ways resembled that of the arriving Europeans and whose population matched that of the Europeans to the west of Russia.

In some important ways, however, Indian culture differed sharply from that of Europeans. Horses and oxen, for example, did not exist in the New World. Without large draft animals, Indians had no incentive to develop wheeled vehicles or, for that matter, the potter's wheel. Many inventions—such as the technology for smelting iron, which had diffused widely in the Old World—had not crossed the ocean barrier to reach the New World. The opposite was also true: valuable New World crops, such as corn and potatoes developed by Indian agriculturists, were unknown in the Old World before Columbus.

Contrasting Worldviews

The gulf separating people in Europe and North America was shaped not only by their material cultures but also by the way they viewed their relationship to the environment and defined social relations in their communities. Having evolved in complete isolation from each other, European and Indian cultures exhibited a wide difference in values. Colonizing Europeans called themselves "civilized" and typically described the people they met in the Americas as "savage," "heathen," or "barbarian." Lurking behind the physical confrontation that took place when Europeans and Native Americans met were latent conflicts over humans' relationship to the environment, the meaning of property, and personal identity.

Europeans and Native Americans conceptualized their relationship to nature in starkly different ways. Regarding the earth as filled with resources for man to use and exploit for human benefit, Europeans took seriously God's proclamation to Adam and Eve in the book of Genesis: "Subdue the earth and have dominion over every living thing that moves on the earth." While Christians believed that God ruled the cosmos and alone commanded supernatural forces such as earthquakes, hurricanes, drought, and flood, Europeans gradually gained confidence that they could comprehend the natural world—and therefore eventually control it. Separating the secular and sacred parts of life, they placed their own re-

lationship to the natural environment mostly in the secular sphere. Native Americans, however, did not distinguish between the secular and sacred. For them, every aspect of the natural world was sacred, inhabited by a variety of "beings," each pulsating with spiritual power and all linked together to form a sacred whole. Consequently, if one offended the land by stripping it of its cover, the spiritual power in the land—called "manitou" by some eastern woodlands tribes—would strike back. If one overfished or destroyed game beyond one's needs, the spirit forces in fish or animals would take revenge, because humans had broken the mutual trust and reciprocity that governed relations between all beings—human or nonhuman. To neglect reciprocal obligations in Nature's domain was to court sickness, hunger, injury, or death. Illustrating this point, Mohawks told the story to Europeans in the seventeenth century that in traversing Lake George, in what is today upstate New York, they always rested their canoes to make an offering of burnt tobacco at a rock they believed contained the spiritual power to control the often-violent winds.

This figure of a pelican was extracted in the 1890s from deep muck on Key Marco, Florida. It is dated through carbon 14 tests to about 1000 C.E. Anthropologists believe that the figure was part of a shrine. *(University of Pennsylvania Museum [Neg. #40708])*

Because they regarded land as a resource to be exploited for man's gain, Europeans had little difficulty in seeing land as a privately held commodity. This belief was fundamental. Fences contained animals but also symbolized exclusively held property. Inheritance became the way to transmit land from one generation to another within the same family. Courts settled property disputes and mediated the dispersal of property through sale or will. Property was the basis not only of sustenance but also of independence, wealth, status, political rights, and identity. The social structure directly mirrored patterns of land ownership, with a land-wealthy elite at the apex of the social pyramid and a propertyless mass at the bottom.

Native Americans also had concepts of property and boundaries. But they believed that land had sacred qualities and should be held in common. As one German missionary explained the Indian view in the eighteenth century, the Creator "made the Earth and all that it contains for the common good of mankind. Whatever liveth on the land, whatsoever groweth out of the earth, and all that is in the rivers and waters . . . was given jointly to all and everyone is entitled to his share."

Communal ownership sharply limited social stratification and increased a sense of sharing in most Indian communities, much to the amazement of Europeans accustomed to wide disparities of wealth. Observing the Iroquois of the eastern woodlands in 1657, a French Jesuit noted that they had no almshouses because "their kindness, humanity and courtesy not only makes them liberal with what they have, but causes them to possess hardly anything except in common. A whole village must be without corn, before any individual can be obliged to endure privation." Not all Europeans were acquisitive, competitive individuals. The majority were peasant farmers living from the soil, living in kin-centered villages with little contact with the outside world, and exchanging goods and labor through barter. But in Europe's cities, a wealth-conscious, ambitious individual who valued and sought wider choices and greater opportunities to enhance personal status was coming to the fore. In contrast, Native American traditions stressed the group rather than the individual and valor rather than wealth.

There were exceptions. The empires of the Aztec in Central America and the Inca in South America were highly developed, populous, and stratified. So, in North America, were a few tribes such as the Natchez. But on the eastern and western coasts of the continent and in the Southwest—the regions of contact in the sixteenth and seventeenth centuries—the European newcomers encountered a people whose cultural values differed strikingly from theirs.

European colonizers in North America also found disturbing the matrilineal organization of many tribal societies. Contrary to European practice, family membership among most tribes was determined through the female line and divorce was the woman's prerogative (she merely set her husband's possessions outside their dwelling door). Clans were composed of several matrilineal kin groups related by a blood connection on the mother's side. To Europeans, this was a peculiar and dangerous reversal of their male-dominated hierarchy.

In Native American societies, women also held subordinate positions, but not nearly to the extent found among European women. While European women were excluded almost entirely from political affairs, senior women in many Native American villages designated the men who sat in a circle to deliberate and make decisions and stood behind them to lobby and instruct. Village chiefs were male, but the elder women of their clans, as was the case with the Iroquois, often chose them. If the men moved too far from the will of the women who appointed them, these chiefs were removed or "dehorned." "Our ancestors," the Oneida chief Good Peter explained, "considered it a great transgression to reject the counsel of their women, particularly the female governesses. Our ancestors considered them mistresses of the soil. . . . The women, they are the life of the nation."

The role of women in the tribal economy reinforced the sharing of power between male and female. Men hunted, fished, and cleared land, but women controlled the cultivation, harvest, and distribution of crops, supplying probably three-quarters of their family's nutritional needs. When the men were away hunting, the women directed village life. Europeans, imbued with the idea of male superiority and female subordination, perceived such sexual equality as another mark of savagery.

In economic relations, Europeans and Indians differed in ways that sometimes led to misunderstanding and conflict. Over vast stretches of the continent, Indians had built trading networks for centuries before Europeans arrived, making it easy for them to trade with arriving Europeans and incorporate new metal and glass trade items into their culture. But trade for Indian peoples was also a way of preserving interdependence and equilibrium between individuals and communities. This principle of reciprocity displayed itself in elaborate ceremonies of gift giving and pipe smoking that preceded the exchange of goods. Europeans saw trade largely as economic exchange, with the benefit of

Carved from marble seven to eight hundred years ago, these shrine figures, male and female, were found in a tomb in northwestern Georgia. The Indian carvings, known to us only as part of a South Appalachian Mississippi culture, are thought to be representations of ancestor gods. *(Lynn Johnson/Aurora & Quanta Productions)*

building good will between two parties sharply limited in comparison with Indians.

In the religious beliefs of Native Americans, the English saw a final damning defect. Europeans built their religious life around the belief in a single divinity, written scriptures, a trained and highly literate clergy, and churches with structured ceremonies. Native American societies, sharing no literary tradition, had less structured religious beliefs. Believing that human life could be affected, positively or negatively, by the mysterious power pervading everything in nature—in rocks, water, the sun, the moon, and animals—Indian people sought to conciliate these spirits and maintain proper relationships with them, even the spirits of the fish, beaver, and deer they hunted. Pueblo people, for example, living in arid lands where rainfall dictated their well-being, expressed their thanks for rain by performing frequent ritual dances.

For Europeans, the Indians' polytheism or belief in several gods, was pagan and devilish. Europeans

understood that Indians had religious leaders called shamans, who used medicinal plants and magical chants to heal the sick and facilitated the people's quests to communicate with the spiritual world. But Europeans regarded the shamans as especially dangerous because they occupied powerful roles among a spiritually misled people. Their fear and hatred of infidels intensified by the Protestant Reformation, Europeans saw a holy necessity to convert—or destroy—these enemies of their God.

AFRICA ON THE EVE OF CONTACT

Half a century before Columbus reached the Americas, a Portuguese sea captain, Antam Gonçalves, made the first European landing on the west coast of sub-Saharan Africa. If he had been able to travel the length and breadth of the immense continent, he would have encountered a rich variety of African states, peoples, and cultures that had developed over many millennia. What Europeans considered African backwardness and cultural impoverishment was a myth perpetuated after the slave trade had begun transporting millions of Africans to the New World. During the period of early contact with Europeans, Africa, like pre-Columbian America, was recognized as a diverse continent with a long history of cultural evolution.

The Spread of Islam

"The seat of Mansa Sulayman [the sultan, or ruler] was a sprawling, unwalled town set in a 'verdant and hilly' country," wrote Arab geographer Abu Abdallah Ibn Battuta in 1351 after visiting the capital of the Mali Kingdom at about the same time that the Aztecs rose to eminence in Mesoamerica. "The sultan had several enclosed palaces there . . . and covered [them] with colored patterns so that it turned out to be the most elegant of buildings." The 47-year-old Ibn Battuta, born into a family of Muslim legal scholars in Tangier, Morocco, on the southern shore of the Mediterranean Sea, was struck with Mali's splendor. "Surrounding the palaces and mosques were the residences of the citizenry, mud-walled houses roofed with domes of timber and reed." Keenly interested in their laws, Ibn Battuta wrote that "Amongst their good qualities is the small amount of injustice amongst them, for of all people they are the furthest from it. Their sultan does not forgive anyone in any matter to do with injustice. . . .

In this beautiful tapestry hanging in the Collegiate Church of Pastrana in Spain, we can see Dom Afonso V, the Portuguese king, leading his troops in 1471 in an attack on Tangiers, a Muslim stronghold in North Africa. The Portuguese campaigns of conquest in North Africa from the 1450s to the 1470s were a response to the fall of Constantinople to the Ottomans in 1453, a terrible blow to the Catholic world in its prolonged struggle with Islam. *(Bettmann/Corbis)*

There is also the prevalence of peace in their country, the traveler is not afraid in it nor is he who lives there in fear of the thief or of the robber." With Ibn Battuta traveled the Muslim faith, or commitment to Islam (meaning "submission to Allah").

This account of the greatest traveler of premodern times opens a window to the two themes of this section: the spread of Islam and the rise of great empires in West and Central Africa—a region then called the Sudan (the word comes from *al-Sudan*, the Arabic term for "black people"). Ibn Battuta had traveled for more than 20 years through much of the eastern hemisphere before reaching Mali, visiting territories equivalent to some 44 present-day countries and traversing 73,000 miles.

Spreading rapidly in Arabia after Muhammad, the founder of Islam, began preaching in 610 C.E., Islam rose to global eminence after several centuries. By the tenth century, Egypt was predominantly Muslim, and Islam was spreading southward from Mediterranean North Africa across the Sahara Desert into northern Sudan, where it took hold especially in the trading centers. In time, Islam encompassed much of the Eastern Hemisphere and became the main intermediary for exchanging goods, ideas, and technologies across a huge part of the world. When Portuguese traders initiated the slave traffic in West Africa in the 1400s, they found that many of the Africans they forced onto slave ships were devout Muslims.

The Kingdoms of Central and West Africa

The vast region of West Africa, to which Islam was spreading by the tenth century, embraced widely varied ecological zones—partly a vast desert, partly grasslands, and partly tropical forests. As in Europe and the Americas at that time, most people tilled the soil, leading to sophisticated agricultural techniques and livestock management by the time of first contact with Europeans. Part of their skill in farming derived from the development of iron production, which began among the Nok in present-day Nigeria about 450 B.C.E., long before it reached Europe. Over many centuries, more efficient iron implements for cultivating and harvesting increased agricultural productivity, in turn spurring population growth. With large populations came greater specialization of tasks and thus greater efficiency and additional technical improvements. The pattern was similar to the agricultural revolution that occurred in the Americas, Europe, the Far East, the Middle East, and elsewhere.

Cultural and political development in West Africa proceeded at varying rates, largely dependent on ecological conditions. Regions blessed by good soil,

Spread of Islam in Africa, c. 1500

This map shows the extensive reach of Islam in Africa by 1500. On most of the North African Mediterranean coast and in the powerful Mali and Songhai kingdoms, the Muslim faith predominated. **Reflecting on the Past** Do you think enslaved Africans who had converted to Islam practiced their faith after arriving in the American colonies? How would they do so on slave plantations?

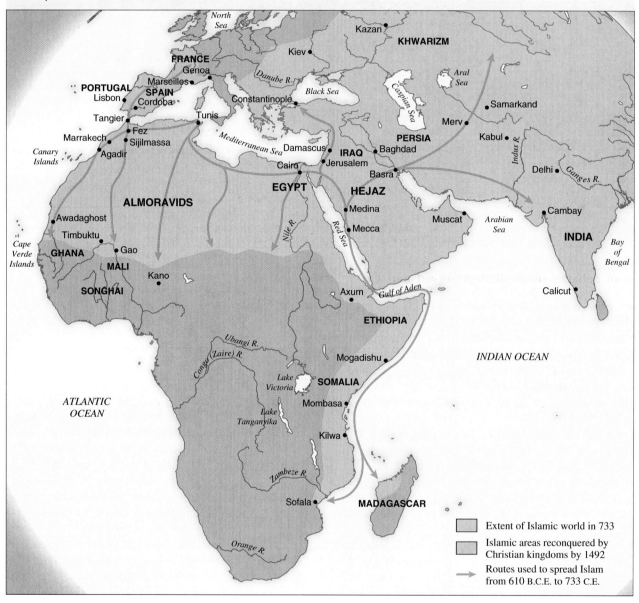

adequate rainfall, and abundance of minerals, as in coastal West Africa, began engaging in interregional trade. This, in turn, brought population growth and cultural development. But where deserts were inhospitable or forests impenetrable, social systems remained small and changed at a crawl. For example, the Sahara Desert, once a land of flowing rivers and lush green pastures and forests, had been depopulated by climate changes that brought higher temperatures and lower rainfall. As desertification occurred between about 4000 B.C.E. and 2500 B.C.E., Sahara people moved southward in search of more fertile land, first to oases situated along a strip of grasslands, or savanna, on the desert's southern border, then farther south to the fertile rain forests of the Niger River basin where they built some of Africa's greatest empires.

The Ghana Empire The first of these empires was Ghana. Developing between the fifth and eleventh centuries, when the Roman Empire collapsed and medieval Europe stagnated, it embraced an immense territory between the Sahara and the Gulf of Guinea and stretched from the Atlantic Ocean to the Niger River. Though Ghana was mostly a land of small villages, it became a major empire noted for its extensive urban settlement, skillfully designed buildings, elaborate sculpture and metalwork, long-distance commerce, and a complex political and military structure. Ideally positioned for trade, Ghana became a wealthy empire built primarily on trade rather than military conquest, partly because of the trading contacts with Muslim Arabs, who had crossed the Sahara Desert in camel caravans to control the region by the eleventh century. From the south came kola nuts, palm oil, copper, and gold. From the north came imported items like ceramics, glass, oil lamps, and—absolutely essential—the salt from Saharan mines that preserved and flavored food. By the late 900s, Ghana controlled more than 100,000 square miles of land and hundreds of thousands of people. Gold was so plentiful that to support its value the kings maintained a royal monopoly over ingots, or bars, allowing the traders only gold dust. Even so, a pound of gold was traded for a pound of salt.

A thriving caravan trade with Arab peoples across the Sahara to Morocco and Algeria brought extensive Muslim influence by the eleventh century, when the king of Ghana boasted an army of 200,000 and maintained trading contacts as far east as Cairo and Baghdad. Gold—important in Europe, the Middle East, and North Africa for use as coin and jewelry—fueled trade. With the exhaustion of gold mines in Europe and Asia, Ghanaian gold made Kumbi-Saleh, Ghana's capital, the busiest and wealthiest marketplace in West Africa. By Europe's Middle Ages, two-thirds of the gold circulating in the Christian Mediterranean region was coming from Ghana.

As trade in Ghana grew more profitable, Arab merchants came to live in the empire, and especially in the capital city of Kumbi-Saleh. With the trading of goods came the exchange of ideas. Arabs brought the first system of writing and numbers to West Africa, and the Ghanaian kings adopted Arab script and appointed Arabs to government positions. As these Arabs gained influence in Ghana, they spread the Islamic faith. Most of Ghana's rulers held tightly to their traditional religion and rejected the Muslim

principle of patriarchy where royal succession would follow the father's lineage. But many Ghanaians, especially in the cities, converted to Islam. By 1050, Kumbi-Saleh boasted 12 Muslim mosques.

The Mali Empire An invasion of North African Muslim warriors beginning in the eleventh century introduced a period of religious strife that eventually destroyed the kingdom of Ghana. Rising to replace it was the Islamic kingdom of Mali, dominated by Malinke, or Mandingo people. Through effective agricultural production and control of the gold trade, Mali flourished. The cultivation of rice and harvesting of inland deltas for fish helped support the thriving trade for salt, gold, and copper. Under Mansa Musa, a devout Muslim who assumed the throne in 1307, Mali came to control territory three times as great as the kingdom of Ghana. Famed for his 3,500-mile pilgrimage across the Sahara and through Cairo all the way to Mecca in 1324, with an entourage of some 50,000, Mansa Musa drew the attention of Mediterranean merchants. Dispensing lavish gifts of gold as he proceeded east, he made Mali gold legendary. Mansa Musa's image on maps of the world

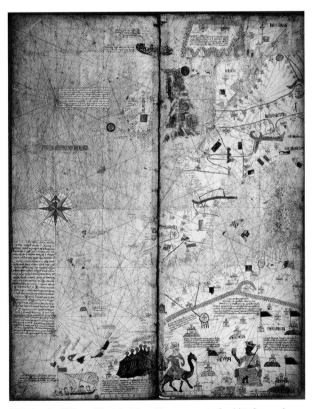

This detail of Mansa Musa holding a large nugget of gold is from a huge six-panel map created in 1375 in Catalan, now part of Spain. The panel was labeled "Mansa Musa: Lord of the Negroes of Guinea." The writing to the right of Mansa Musa includes these words: "So abundant is the gold which is found in his country that he is the richest and most noble king in all the land." (*Bibliothèque Nationale de France, Paris*)

The Empires of Ghana, Mali, and Songhai

These ancient empires, each in their turn, controlled vast areas of West Africa. Ghana, which built its wealth on trade, was at its height from about 900 to 1100 C.E. Mali's devout Muslim leader, Mansa Musa, commissioned large mosques and turned Timbuktu into a center of Islamic learning. Songhai began its rise to power after the death of Mansa Musa.   **Reflecting on the Past** Why would some Europeans send their sons to Timbuktu to study? What evidence can you find that Muslim ideas contributed to European scientific and cultural knowledge?

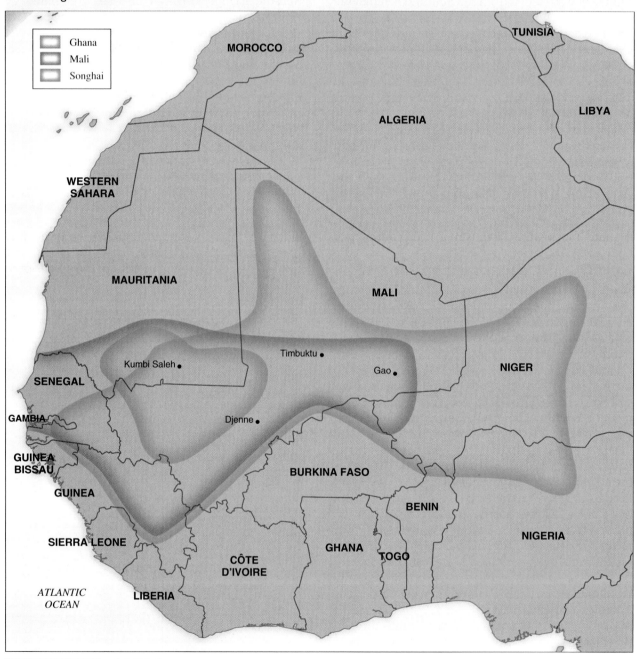

for centuries thereafter testified to his importance in advertising the treasures of western Africa.

Coming home, Mansa Musa brought Muslim scholars and artisans with him who were instrumental in establishing Timbuktu, at the center of the Mali Empire, as a city of great importance. Noted for its extensive wealth, its Islamic university developed a distinguished faculty, who instructed North Africans and southern Europeans who came to study. Traveling there in the 1330s, Ibn Battuta wrote admiringly of "the discipline of its officials and provincial governors, the excellent condition of public finance, and . . . the respect accorded to the decisions of justice and to the authority of the sovereign."

The Songhai Empire After Mansa Musa died in 1332, power in West Africa began to shift to the Songhai, centered on the middle Niger River. A mixture of farmers, traders, fishermen, and warriors, the Songhai declared independence from Mali in 1435 and began a slow ascendancy. Just as Mali had grown out of a state in the empire of Ghana, the new Songhai Empire grew out of a region that had once been part of Mali. By the time Portuguese traders in the late 1400s were establishing firm commercial links with the Kongo, far to the south, the Songhai Empire was at its peak under the rule of Sonni Ali (1464–1492) and Muhammad Ture (1493–1528).

Yet Songhai, too, collapsed, as some tribes that were resentful of Muslim kings began to break away. But the most dangerous threat came from Morocco, in North Africa, whose rulers coveted Songhai's sources of salt and gold—the two critical commodities in the African trade. Equipped with guns procured in the Middle East, Morocco's ruler conquered Timbuktu and Gao in 1591. The North Africans remained in loose control of western Sudan for more than a century, as the last great trading empire of West Africa faded. At a time when England, France, Spain, and other centralized kingdoms in Europe were emerging—and sending ships to forge trading connections on Africa's west coast, the great empires of West Africa slowly devolved into smaller states. Looking back over the long centuries of the tragic Atlantic slave trade, it seems that by a melancholy quirk of history, local west African conflicts made it easier for European slave traders to convince tribal leaders to send out warrior parties to capture tradeable slaves.

The Kongo Kingdom Farther south along the Atlantic coast and in Central Africa lay the vast kingdom of Kongo, first encountered by Europeans in 1482, just a decade before Columbus sailed across the Atlantic, when the Portuguese ship captain Diego Cao anchored in the mouth of the mighty Kongo River. Kongo's royal capital, Mbanza, was built on a fertile plateau surrounded by rain forests 100 miles east of the coast and 50 miles south of the Kongo River. A trade center for a kingdom of several million people, Mbanza also became a center of trade relations with the Portuguese, who by the 1490s were sending Catholic missionaries to the court of King Mani-Kongo. Thus was Mani-Kongo's son baptized Affonso I, and it was under Affonso's rule, in the early 1500s, that a flourishing trade in slaves with the Portuguese began.

Like Kongo, the kingdom of Benin developed long before seaborne Europeans reached western Africa. Benin, which became so important in the English slave trade, was formed in about 1000 C.E. west of the Niger Delta. When Europeans reached Benin City hundreds of years later, they found a walled city with broad streets and hundreds of buildings. It was through Benin City that thousands of slaves procured in the interior passed on their way for exchange with the Portuguese, and later the English, at coastal Calabar, where one of the main slave forts stood. One of Benin's most important chroniclers, Olaudah Equiano, endured just such a trip. He was born in a village in "a charming fruitful vale," far into the interior of the kingdom of

Before Europeans reached West Africa, Niger River craftsmen were producing terra cotta figures such as this horseman. With outstretched arms, the rider holds the reins. His helmet, heavy necklace, shoulder quiver, and dagger fastened to his arm all signify his warrior nobility. *(Equestrian Figure, Inland Niger Delta region, Mali, Possibly 13–15th century, Terracotta, H. 70.5 [27 ¾ in.], Museum purchase, 86–12–2, Photograph by Frank Khoury, National Museum of African Art, Smithsonian Institution)*

In the Benin kingdom of West Africa, people celebrated the leopard as "king of the bush." Copper alloy leopards of this kind were usually placed at the king's side when he sat in state to symbolize the king's ominous power combined with prudent reserve. *(© 1978 Dirk Bakker)*

Benin, which he regarded as "the most considerable" of "a variety of kingdoms" in the "part of Africa known by the name of Guinea." Equiano's story has a timelessness that allows it to stand for the experiences over several centuries of millions of Africans who were born in western Africa, the ancestral homelands of most of today's African Americans.

African Slavery

The idea that slavery was a legitimate social condition in past societies offends modern values, and it is difficult for many Americans to understand why Africans would sell fellow Africans to European traders. But there were no people who identified themselves as Africans four centuries ago; rather, they thought of themselves as Ibos or Mandingos, or Kongolese, or residents of Mali or Songhai. Moreover, slavery was not new for Africans or any other people in the fourteenth century. It had flourished in ancient Rome and Greece, in large parts of eastern Europe, in southwestern Asia, and in the Mediterranean world in general. In times of pillage and conquest, invading people everywhere sold prisoners into slavery. Conquerors could not tolerate holding massive numbers of the enemy in their midst and therefore often sold them to distant lands as slaves, where their threat would be neutralized. This seemed more merciful than mass execution—and more profitable.

Slavery had existed in Africa for centuries, but it had nothing to do with skin color. Like other peoples, Africans accepted slavery without question as a condition of servitude and slaveholding as a mark of wealth. To own slaves was to be wealthy; to trade slaves was a way of increasing one's wealth. Olaudah Equiano described how his tribe traded slaves to "mahogany-coloured men from the south west" of his village: "Sometimes we sold slaves to them but they were only prisoners of war, or such among us as had been convicted of kidnaping, or adultery, and some other crimes which we esteemed heinous." In this way, African societies for centuries conducted an overland slave trade that carried captured people from West Africa across the vast Sahara Desert to Christian Roman Europe and the Islamic Middle East.

From the tenth to fifteenth century, about five thousand West Africans were sold eastward as sugar workers in Egypt, as domestic servants and craftsmen throughout the Arabic world, and as soldiers in North Africa. Islam had facilitated this process by establishing secure trade routes connecting West Africa with the Mediterranean world and the lands east of it. By the time Songhai rose to prominence in West Africa, the kingdom became a major supplier of enslaved captives across the Sahara to North Africa. This trade gave Songhai's elite access to European trade goods—Venetian beads, fine cloth, and horses, the latter especially important to Songhai warriors who were waging war against neighboring peoples. Though this slave traffic was on the rise, it was still an occasional rather than a highly organized trade, and it was carried out to provide Mediterranean trading partners with soldiers, household servants, and artisans rather than gangs of field workers.

In this way, the peoples of West Africa held to a conception of slavery very different from that which would develop in the European colonies of the Americas. "Those prisoners which were not sold or redeemed," remembered Equiano, "we kept as slaves; but how different was their condition from that of slaves in the West-Indies! With us, they do no more work than other members of the community, even their master. Their food, clothing, and lodging were nearly the same as theirs, except they were not permitted to eat with the free-born." Slaves in Africa had restricted rights and blocked opportunities for upward movement. Yet they were entitled to certain rights, including education, marriage, and parenthood. Most important in the African practice

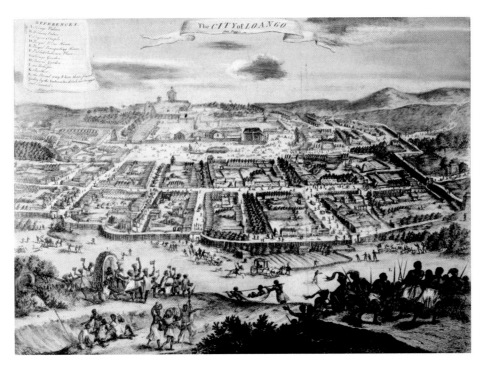

The city of Loango, at the mouth of the Congo River on the west coast of Africa, was larger at the time of this drawing in the mid-eighteenth century than all but a few seaports in the British colonies in North America. *(The Granger Collection, New York)*

of slavery was that the enslaved served as soldiers, administrators, sometimes as royal advisors, and even occasionally as royal consorts. Also key was the possibility of freedom that would be blocked in North America: the status of slave was not necessarily lifelong but was revocable; and slavery did not automatically pass on to the female slave's children.

The African Ethos

Many of Africa's peoples—Ashanti, Mandingo, Coromantee, Yoruba, Fon, Hausa, Ibo, Whydah, Ga, and others—eventually became African Americans. Indeed, they would become at least two-thirds of all the immigrants who crossed the ocean to the Western Hemisphere in the three centuries after Europeans began colonizing there. They came from a rich diversity of cultures, but most of them shared certain ways of life that differentiated them from Europeans.

As in Europe, the family was the basic unit of social organization. By maintaining intimate connections between man and woman, parent and child, sister and brother, enslaved Africans developed an important defense against the cruelties of slavery. Unlike Europeans, however, where patriarchy put the father and husband at the center of family life, Africans organized themselves in a variety of kinship systems. In many African societies, like many Native American ones, the family was matrilineal, in which property rights and political inheritance descended through the mother rather than the father. When a chief died, the son of his sister inherited his position. After marrying, a man joined his bride's people. This matrilineal tradition carried over into slavery, as African women continued to have an influence not typical in European family organization. In Africa, each person was linked to others in the village, his or her identity defined by family relationships. Individualism, which would become so prized in English society transplanted to North America, was an alien, distasteful, and nearly meaningless concept to Africans.

Widespread across Africa was a belief in a Supreme Creator of the cosmos and in a pantheon of lesser deities associated with natural forces such as rain, animals, and the fertility of the earth. Because these deities could intervene in human affairs, they were elaborately honored. West Africans, like most North American Indians, held that spirits dwelt in the trees, rocks, and rivers around them, and hence they exercised care in the treatment of these natural objects.

Africans also worshiped ancestors, who they believed mediated between the Creator and the living. Because the dead played such an important role for the living, relatives held elaborate funeral rites to ensure the proper entrance of a deceased relative into the spiritual world. The more ancient an ancestor, the greater was this person's power to affect the

The tall, netted headdress, with hanging strands of beads, signifies the royal status of Idia, the Queen Mother of the Edo people (later Ibo) in the Benin kingdom in the mid-1500s. In this cast copper alloy and iron sculpture, the Queen Mother wears a collar of coral beads. Note the scarifications across the forehead. (© 1980 Dirk Bakker)

living; thus the "ancient ones" were devoutly worshiped. Deep family loyalty and regard for family lineage flowed naturally from ancestor worship.

Finally, West Africans believed in spirit possession, where the gods spoke to men and women through priests and other religious figures. "Though we had no places of public worship," Equiano remembered, "we had priests and magicians, or wise men . . . held in great reverence by the people. They calculated time, foretold events, . . . and when they died, they were succeeded by their sons." This was the complex religious heritage that Africans brought with them to the Americas, and no amount of desolation or physical abuse could wipe out these deeply rooted beliefs. In fact, people enduring the kind of daily stress inherent in the master–slave relationship typically drew on their deepest emotive sources for sustenance and thus kept alive their religious beliefs and ritual patterns.

While differing from the religious beliefs of their European slave owners, Africans shared some com-

mon ground. Both cultural groups recognized a physical world where everyone lived and an "other world" inhabited by the souls of the dead. Both believed that the "other world" could not be seen but could be known through revelations that spiritually gifted persons could interpret. These roughly shared foundations of religious feeling made it possible for a hybrid African Christianity to develop. In fact, in the Kingdom of Kongo and several small kingdoms close to the Niger Delta, extensive contact with the Portuguese had allowed Christianity to graft itself on African religious beliefs by the time English colonies were planted in North America in the seventeenth century. African religious customs, funeral rites, sacred images, and charms for protection against evil spirits lost some of their power during enslavement, though how fast this happened is murky and clearly varied from place to place. But even to the present day, African religious beliefs and practices still hold at least partial sway among some African Americans.

Social organization in much of West Africa by the time Europeans arrived was as elaborate as in fifteenth-century Europe. At the top of society stood the king, supported by nobles and priests, usually elderly men. Beneath them were the great mass of people, mostly cultivators of the soil in innumerable villages. "Agriculture is our chief employment," recalled Equiano, "and everyone, even the children and women, are engaged in it. Thus we are habituated to labour from our earliest years" and "everyone contributes something to the common stock." In urban centers, craftsmen, traders, teachers, and artists lived beneath the ruling families. At the bottom of society toiled the slaves. As in ancient Greece and Rome, they were "outsiders"—war captives, criminals, or sometimes people who sold themselves into servitude to satisfy a debt. The rights of slaves were restricted, and their opportunities for advancement were narrow. Nevertheless, as members of the community, they were entitled to protection under the law and allowed the privileges of education, marriage, and parenthood. Their servile condition was not permanent, nor was it automatically inherited by their children, as would be the fate of Africans enslaved in the Americas.

EUROPE ON THE EVE OF INVADING THE AMERICAS

In the ninth century, about the time that the Mound Builders of the Mississippi valley were constructing their urban center at Cahokia and the kingdom of Ghana was rising in West Africa, western Europe was an economic and cultural backwater. The center of political power and economic vitality in the Old World had shifted eastward to Christian Byzantium, which controlled Asia Minor, the Balkans, and parts of Italy. The other dynamic culture of this age, Islam, had spread through the Middle East, spilled across North Africa, and penetrated Spain and West Africa south of the Sahara.

Within a few centuries, an epic revitalization of western Europe occurred, creating the conditions that enabled its leading maritime nations vastly to extend their oceanic frontiers. By the late fifteenth century, a 400-year epoch of militant overseas European expansion was underway. Not until the second half of the twentieth century was this process of Europeanization reversed; then colonized people began to regain their autonomy and cultural identity through wars of national liberation—a process now nearing completion.

The Rebirth of Europe

The rebirth of western Europe, which began around 1000 C.E., owed much to a revival of long-distance trading from Italian ports on the Mediterranean and to the rediscovery of ancient knowledge that these contacts permitted. The once mighty cities of the Roman Empire had stagnated for centuries, but now Venice, Genoa, and other Italian ports began trading with peoples facing the Adriatic, the Baltic, and the North seas. These new contacts brought wealth and power to the Italian commercial cities, which gradually evolved into merchant-dominated city–states that freed themselves from the rule of feudal lords in control of the surrounding countryside. By the late 1400s, sailing ships were crossing all the sea basins of the Eastern Hemisphere—the China Sea, the Indian Ocean, the Persian Gulf, the Red and Black seas, and the Mediterranean, thus creating a zone of intercultural communication never before achieved.

While merchants led the emerging city–states, western Europe's feudal system gradually weakened. For centuries, warrior aristocrats, not kings, had exercised the normal powers of the state: the power to tax, wage war, and administer the law. In the thirteenth and fourteenth centuries, however, kings began to reassert their political authority and to undertake efforts to unify their realms. One of their primary goals was to curb the power of the great feudal lords who dominated entire regions and to force lesser nobles into dependence on and obedience to the crown.

Concurrently in the fourteenth century, the mass of peasant people suffered greatly. Famine struck many parts of Europe after 1300 because the production of food did not keep up with population increases. Malnutrition reduced the resistance of millions when the Black Death (bubonic plague) struck with fury. It first devastated China, wiping out nearly one-third of the population, and then moved eastward following trade routes to India and the Middle East, hitting hardest in the cities. Then in 1348 it reached western Europe and North Africa. Over the next quarter century, some 30 million Europeans died, a blow from which Europe did not recover demographically for centuries. This unprecedented human misery produced economic disruption, violent worker strikes, and peasant uprisings. Yet the Black Death promoted the unification of old realms into early modern states. The nobilities with which monarchs had to contend were reduced in size, for the plague defied class distinction. Ironically, feudal lords treated their peasants better for a time because their labor, tremendously reduced by the plague, became more valuable.

Early developments in England led to a distinctive political system. In 1215, the English aristocracy curbed the powers of the king when they forced him to accept the Magna Carta. On the basis of this charter, a parliament composed of elective and hereditary members eventually gained the right to meet regularly to pass money bills. Parliament was thus in a position to act as a check on the Crown, an arrangement unknown on the European continent. During the sixteenth century, the Crown and Parliament worked together toward a more unified state, with the English kings wielding less political power than their European counterparts.

Economic changes of great significance also occurred in England during the sixteenth century. To practice more profitable agriculture, great landowners began to "enclose" (consolidate) their estates, throwing peasant farmers off their plots and turning many of them into wage laborers. The formation of this working class was the crucial first step toward industrial development.

Continental Europe lagged behind England in two respects. First, it was far less affected by the move to "enclose" agricultural land. Part of the explanation lies in the values of continental aristocrats, who regarded the maximization of profit as unworthy of gentlemen. French nobles could lose their titles for commercial activities. Second, continental rulers were less successful in engaging the interests of their nobilities, and these nobles never shared governance with their king, as did English aristocrats through their participation in Parliament. In France, a noble faction assassinated Henry III in 1589, and the nobles remained disruptive for nearly another century. In Spain, the final conquest of the Muslims and expulsion of the Jews, both in

The Black Death of the mid-fourteenth century killed nearly 40,000 people in the region of Prague. Five centuries later, a Czech woodcarver fashioned the bones of thousands of Black Death victims into a chapel where visitors are astounded to see a bone altar, bone chalices, the bone chandelier that is pictured here, and gigantic bone bells. Every bone in the human body is used in the chandelier. (© Lubomir Stiburek)

1492, strengthened the monarchy's hold, but regional cultures and leaders remained strong. The continental monarchs would thus warmly embrace doctrines of royal absolutism—the unqualified authority of the king or queen—developed in the sixteenth century.

The New Monarchies and the Expansionist Impulse

In the second half of the fifteenth century, ambitious monarchs coming to power in France, England, and Spain sought social and political stability in their kingdoms. Louis XI in France, Henry VII in England, Isabella of Castile, and Ferdinand of Aragon all created armies and bureaucratic state machinery strong enough to quell internal conflict, such as the English War of the Roses (1459–1487), and to raise taxes sufficient to support their regimes. In these countries, and in Portugal as well, eco-

nomic revival and the reversal of more than a century of population decline and civil disorder nourished the impulse to expand. This impulse was also fed by Renaissance culture. Ushering in a new, more secular age, the Renaissance (Rebirth) encouraged innovation (in science as well as in art and music), freedom of thought, richness of expression, and an emphasis on human abilities. Beginning in Italy and spreading northward through Europe, the Renaissance peaked dramatically in the late fifteenth century when the age of overseas exploration began.

The exploratory urge had two initial objectives: first, to circumvent overland Muslim traders by finding an eastward oceanic route to Asia; second, to tap the African gold trade at its source. Since the tenth century, Muslim middlemen in North Africa had brought the precious metal to Europe from West Africa. Now the possibility arose of bypassing these non-Christian traffickers. Likewise, Christian Europeans dreamed of eliminating Muslim traders

Venice's throbbing life along the Grand Canal is apparent in this painting of a procession making its way across the Rialto Bridge toward a balcony. Warehouses and handsome mansions flank the canal. *(Scala/Art Resource, NY)*

from the commerce with Asia. Since 1291, when Marco Polo returned to Venice with tales of Eastern treasures such as spices, silks, perfumes, medicines, and jewels, Europeans had bartered with the Orient. But the difficulties of the long eastward overland route through the Muslim world kept alive the hopes of Christian Europeans that an alternative water route existed. Eventually, Europe's mariners found they could voyage to Cathay (China) by both eastward and westward water routes.

Portugal seemed the least likely of the rising nation–states to lead the expansion of Europe outside its continental boundaries, yet it forged into the lead at the end of the fifteenth century. A poor country of only 1 million inhabitants, Portugal had gradually overcome Moorish control in the twelfth and thirteenth centuries and, in 1385, had wrenched itself free of domination by neighboring Castile. Led by Prince Henry the Navigator, for whom trade was secondary to the conquest of the Muslim world, Portugal breached the unknown. In the 1420s, Henry began dispatching Portuguese mariners to probe the unknown Atlantic "sea of darkness." His intrepid sailors were aided by important improvements in navigational instruments, mapmaking, and ship design, all promoted by the prince, all necessary to venture more widely into the

In Columbus's era, the astrolabe was the most important astronomical computer, where the celestial sphere was projected onto the equator's plane. Once the moveable arm was set, the entire sky was visible. Europeans adopted it in the twelfth century from the Islamic world, where it had been used for centuries. *(Courtesy of Adler Planetarium & Astronomy Museum, Chicago, Illinois [W-264])*

Atlantic Ocean vastness. Symbolizing the increasingly interconnected world, the compass, invented by the Chinese, was copied by Middle Eastern Arabs then by the Portuguese.

Portuguese captains operated at sea on three ancient Ptolemaic principles: that the earth was round, that distances on its surface could be measured by degrees, and that navigators could "fix" their position at sea on a map by measuring the position of the stars. The invention in the 1450s of the quadrant, which allowed a precise measurement of star altitude necessary for determining latitude, represented a leap forward from the chart-and-compass method of navigation. Equally important was the design of a lateen-rigged caravel, adapted from a Moorish ship design. Its triangular sails permitted ships to sail into the wind, allowing them to travel southward along the African coast—a feat the square-rigged European vessels could never perform—and return northward against prevailing winds.

By the 1430s, the ability of Prince Henry's captains to break through the limits of the world known to Europeans had carried them to Madeira, the Canary Islands, and the more distant Azores, lying off the coasts of Portugal and northwestern Africa. These were soon developed as the first European-controlled agricultural plantations, located on the continent's periphery and designed to produce cash crops such as sugar that could be marketed in Europe. Thus, the Madeiras, Canaries, and Azores became a kind of laboratory for much larger European colony building much farther from the colonizers' homelands.

From islands off the West African coast, the Portuguese sea captains pushed farther south. By the time of Prince Henry's death in 1460, Portuguese mariners had navigated their way down the west coast of Africa. While carrying their Christian faith to new lands, they began a profitable trade in ivory, slaves, and especially gold. Now, they were poised to capitalize on the connection between Europe and Africa, though not yet knowing that a stupendous land mass, to become known as America, lay far across the Atlantic Ocean.

Timeline

35,000 B.C.E.	First humans cross Bering Land Bridge to reach the Americas
12,000 B.C.E.	Beringian epoch ends
6000 B.C.E.	Paleo-Indian phase ends
500 B.C.E.	Archaic era ends
500 B.C.E.–1000 C.E.	Post-Archaic era in North America
600 C.E.–1100	Rise of mound-building center at Cahokia
632–750	Islamic conquest of North Africa spreads Muslim faith
800–1026	Kingdom of Ghana controls West Africa's trade
1000	Norse seafarers establish settlements in Newfoundland Kingdom of Benin develops
1000–1500	Kingdoms of Ghana, Mali, Songhai in Africa
1200s	Pueblo societies develop village life in southwest of North America
1235	Defeating the Ghanaian king, Mali becomes a West African power
1291	Marco Polo's return from East Asia to Venice quickens European trade with Eastern Hemisphere
1300s	Rise of Aztec society in Valley of Mexico
1300–1450	Italian Renaissance
1324	Mansa Musa's pilgrimage to Mecca expands Muslim influence in West Africa
1420s	Portuguese sailors explore west coast of Africa
1435	Kingdom of Songhai declares independence from kingdom of Mali
1450–1600	Northern European Renaissance
1460s–1590s	Kingdom of Songhai controls West Africa's trading societies
1469	Marriage of Castile's Isabela and Aragon's Ferdinand creates Spain
1500s	Quickening of western European trade and production of consumer goods

✦ Conclusion

THE APPROACH OF A NEW GLOBAL AGE

All the forces that have made the world of the past five hundred years "modern" began to come into play by the late fifteenth century. As the stories about four important women of this era demonstrate, deep transformations were underway in West Africa, in southern and western Europe, and in the Americas. West African empires had reached new heights, some had been deeply influenced by the Islamic faith, and many had become experienced in trans-regional trade. Muslim scholars, merchants, and long-distance travelers were becoming the principal mediators in the interregional exchange of goods, ideas, and technical innovations. Meanwhile, the Renaissance initiated in Italy, which worked its way northward, brought new energy and ambition to a weakened, disease-ridden, and tired Europe. Advances in maritime technology also allowed Europeans to make contact with the peoples of West Africa and develop the first slave-based plantation societies in tropical islands off the West African coast. In the Americas, large empires in Mexico and—as we will see in Chapter 2, Peru—were growing more populous and consolidating their power while in North America the opposite was occurring—a decay of powerful mound-building societies and a long-range move toward decentralized tribal societies. The scene was set for the great leap of Europeans across the Atlantic where the convergence between the peoples of Africa, the Americas, and Europe would occur.

✦ Recommended Reading

The Peoples of America Before Columbus

Kathleen J. Bragdon, *Native People of Southern New England, 1500–1650* (1996); Thomas E. Emerson, *Cahokia and the Archaeology of Power* (1997); Brian M. Fagan, *The Great Journey: The Peopling of Ancient America* (1987) and *Ancient North America: The Archaeology of a Continent* (1991); Stuart Fiedel, *The Prehistory of the Americas* (1987); R. Douglas Hurt, *Indian Agriculture in America: Prehistory to the Present* (1987); Alvin M. Josephy, Jr., *America in 1492: The World of the Indian Peoples Before the Arrival of Columbus* (1992); Philip Kopper, *The Smithsonian Book of North American Indians: Before the Coming of Europeans* (1986); Kenneth Macgowan and Joseph A. Hester, Jr., *Early Man in the New World* (1983); Daniel K. Richter and James H. Merrell, *Beyond the Covenant Chain: The Iroquois and Their Neighbors in Indian North America, 1600–1800* (1987); Lynne Sebastian, *The Chaco Anasazi: Sociopolitical Evolution in the Prehistoric Southwest* (1994); Lynda N. Shaffer, *Native Americans Before 1492: The Moundbuilding Centers of the Eastern Woodlands* (1992); Dean Snow, *The Archaeology of North America: American Indians and Their Origins* (1976); Biloine W. Young and Melvin L. Fowler, *Cahokia: The Great Native American Metropolis* (2000).

Africa on the Eve of Contact

Edward W. Bovill, *The Golden Trade of the Moors*, rev. ed. (1995); George E. Brooks, *Landlords and Strangers: Ecology, Society, and Trade in Western Africa, 1000–1630* (1993); Graham Connah, *African Civilizations: Precolonial Cities and States in Tropical Africa: An Archaeological Perspective* (1987); Ann Hilton, *The Kingdom of Kongo* (1985); Nehemia Levtzion and Randall Pouwels, eds., *A History of Islam in Africa* (2000); Paul E. Lovejoy, *Transformations in Slavery: A History of Slavery in Africa* (1983); John S. Mbiti, *An Introduction to African Religion* (1975); Roland Oliver and Anthony Atmore, *The African Middle Ages, 1400–1800* (1981); Ronald Segal, *Islam's Black Slaves: The Other Black Diaspora* (2001); John Thornton, *Africa and Africans in the Making of the Atlantic World, 1400–1600*, 2nd ed. (1998).

Europe on the Eve of Invading the Americas

Robert Bartlett, *The Making of Europe: Conquest, Colonization and Cultural Change* (1993); Jerry Bentley, *Old World Encounters: Cross Cultural Contacts and Exchanges in Pre-Modern Times* (1993); F. Braudel, *The Mediterranean and the Mediterranean World in the Age of Phillip II*, 2 vols. (1978); Carlo M. Cipolla, *Guns, Sails, and Empires: Technological Innovations and the Early Phases of European Expansion, 1400–1700* (1966) and *Before the Industrial Revolution: European Society and Economy, 1000–1700* (1976); Ralph Davis, *The Rise of the Atlantic Economies* (1973); W. H. McNeill, *The Rise of the West* (1963); J. H. Plumb, *The Italian Renaissance* (1986).

Fiction and Film

Peter Forbath's *Lord of the Kongo* (1996) tells the dramatic story of a young Portuguese sailor counted among those interacting with the Kongo people of West Africa in the early 1500s. Chinua Achebe's *Things Fall Apart* (1958) is already a classic—an unsentimental depiction of tribal life in Nigeria before and after the arrival of Europeans. Barbara Tuckman's *A Distant Mirror* (1978) is the most engaging novel ever written about the European Middle Ages—and particularly about the calamitous 14th century when England and France waged the Hundred Years War (1337–1429). In *The Man on a Donkey* (1952), H. F. M. Prescott brings alive the tumultuous English era of Henry VIII.

Search of the First Americans (1992), part of the Nova series produced by the Public Broadcasting System (PBS), provides a fascinating introduction to the peopling of the Americas before the Columbian voyages. *Secrets of the Lost Red Paint People*, also in this series, shows how archaeologists have reconstructed—always tentatively—the ancient world of the Americas. Films for the Humanities and Sciences in Princeton, New Jersey, has produced a five-part series of short films to recreate the history and culture of some of the great West African societies, particularly those from which today's African Americans in North American and the West Indies have derived. In *The Agony and the Ecstasy* (1965), derived from Irving Stone's biography of Michaelangelo, Charlton Heston and Rex Harrison bring alive the Italian

Renaissance. *Luther,* John Osborne's play that captivated London theatergoers, appeared on film, with Stacy Keach playing Luther, in 1974. *The Return of Martin Guerre* (1982), called by some the best historical movie ever made, depicts French peasant life in the era when Europeans were awakening to overseas exploration and settlement.

◆ Discovering U.S. History Online

Ancient Mesoamerican Civilizations
www.angelfire.ca/humanorigins
This page supplies information regarding Meso-american civilizations with well-organized essays, links, and photos.

Cahokia Mounds
www.medicine.wustl.edu/~mckinney/cahokia/cahokia.html
This online presentation of the historical Cahokia Mounds offers background information, an interactive map of the site, a satellite map, and other photos.

Pre-Contact Cultural Areas
www.kstrom.net/isk/maps/houses/housingmap.html
www.kstrom.net/isk/maps/cultmap.html
These clickable maps give regional cultural information about pre-contact native peoples of North America.

Vikings in the New World
www.emuseum.mnsu.edu/prehistory/vikings/vikhome.html
This site explores the history of some of the earliest European visitors to the Americas.

Civilizations in Africa
www.wsu.edu:8080/~dee/CIVAFRCA/CIVAFRCA.HTM
This site offers a region-by-region, broad overview of the pre-conquest civilizations in Africa.

The Slave Kingdoms
www.pbs.org/wonders
Part of the PBS online exhibition "Wonders of the African World," this section describes the West African cultures during the slave trade as well as both African and European participation in the slave trade.

The Ancient West African City of Benin
www.nmafa.si.edu/exhibits/beninsp.htm
A brief description and exhibit example from each of the three sections of this Smithsonian Institute exhibit give a view through art of the extent of cultural development at the time of European contact and subsequent slave trade.

Life in Elizabethan England
www.renaissance.dm.net/compendium/home.html
A compendium of information about everyday life, politics, and religion in England prior to "the westward fever."

Life in Sixteenth Century France
www.lepg.org/index.html
This detailed site offers "a guide to the history, culture, and daily life of 16th century France."

Renaissance
www.learner.org/exhibits/renaissance
An exploration of the European Renaissance, this interactive site seeks to discover and describe "the forces that drove this rebirth in Europe, and in Italy in particular."

2 Europeans and Africans Reach the Americas

Slave Deck of the Albanoz, watercolor done by a young naval officer in a Spanish slave ship captured by the *HMS Albanoz*. *(National Maritime Museum, Greenwich, England)*

◆ *American Stories*

OLD WORLD SOJOURNERS MINGLE WITH NEW WORLD INHABITANTS

Just 15 years after conquistadors led by Hernán Cortés toppled the Aztec Empire in Mexico, Spanish horsemen, searching for Indians to capture as slaves, happened upon some 600 Indians in northwestern Mexico. Traveling with the natives were an African and three Spaniards, all dressed in native garb. The horsemen were "thunderstruck to see me so strangely dressed and in the company of Indians," noted Alvar Núñez Cabeza de Vaca, one of the three Spaniards accompanying the Indians. "They went on staring at me for a long space of time, so astonished that they could neither speak to me nor manage to ask me anything."

De Vaca, his two Spanish companions, and the African had been lost for eight years and were presumed dead. They had been part of the 1528 expedition that had tried to plant a permanent Spanish settlement in what the

Spanish called La Florida. Establishing themselves near the swamplands of Tampa Bay, the Spanish adventurers encountered starvation, disease, a leadership crisis, and hostile Indians. Captured by Apalachee Indians who enslaved them, de Vaca and his companions soon adopted Indian ways, adapted to a new environment, and used their cleverness to convince the Indians that they possessed magical healing power. The African, already a slave of one of the captured Spaniards and known as Estevan (sometimes called Estanvanico or Esteban), became an accomplished linguist, healer, guide, and negotiator. When they fled their captors, the four fugitives plunged into the wilderness and headed west. Paddling crude boats across the Gulf of Mexico, they shipwrecked on the Texas coast and took refuge among merciful Indians.

Such forays into a rugged and uncharted territory cast the Spanish and African adventurers into unaccustomed roles and sorely tested their ability to survive among the indigenous people who generally opposed their intrusion into their homelands. De Vaca, a conquistador experienced in enslaving Indians, had become an Indian slave himself before the flight to Texas. Estevan's status as the slave of a Spanish conquistador all but dissolved in the process of becoming an Indian slave and then a refugee from Indian enslavement. In his journal, de Vaca described Estevan as "a black," "a Moor," and "an Arabian." But these were only words describing his skin color (dark), his religion (Islam), and his geographical homeland (Morocco). What mattered in this strange and often hostile land was not Estevan's blackness or even his slave status. What counted, in this time before the idea of racial categories, were his linguistic abilities, his fortitude, and his cleverness as a go-between. Estevan, an Atlantic creole—a man who originated on one land bordering the Atlantic—became a new man in the process of the cultural, linguistic, and social braiding that was occurring throughout the sixteenth-century Atlantic world.

For five years, Estevan, his master Andrés Dorantes, de Vaca, and another Spaniard traveled west for about 2,500 miles. Often following friendly Indian guides, the four travelers came to be regarded as holy men, possessing the power to heal. Reaching present-day New Mexico, they found Indians who, according to de Vaca, described them as "four great doctors, one of them black, the other three white, who gave blessings [and] healed the sick." On one occasion, the natives gave Estevan a sacred gourd rattle. Then, in 1536, the foursome stumbled upon the Spanish expedition in northern Mexico. Three years later, after joining a new Spanish expedition, Estevan blazed a trail for Francisco Vasquez de Coronado's *entrada* of 1540. In what would later be called Arizona, Estevan was selected to forge ahead into Zuñi country with Indian guides, in search of the fabled seven gold-filled cities of Cibola. His gift for acquiring native languages and his long experience with peoples of the vast territory north of New Spain made him the logical choice. But on this trip, Estevan met his death at the hands of Zuñi warriors, perhaps angry at his consorting with Zuñi women.

The voyages of Christopher Columbus from 1492 to 1504 brought together people like Estevan and de Vaca from three previously unconnected continents. Together, they made a new world, their lives intersecting, their cultural attributes interacting. In this chapter, we follow the epoch-making voyages of Columbus, the arrival of Spanish conquistadors, their remarkable conquest of vast territories in Mesoamerica and the southern regions of North America, and the momentous effect of plants, animals, and germs as they traveled westward and eastward across the Atlantic. We will also see how the phenomenal exploits of Hernán Cortés and Francisco Pizarro, and the discovery of immense quantities of silver, attracted the attention of other Europeans, first the French, then the Dutch and English. Latecomers in the race to exploit the treasures of the Americas while providing a place for the downtrodden and opportunity-blocked settlers of Europe, the English, as we will see, finally appeared on the scene in the Americas a century after the Columbian voyages.

BREACHING THE ATLANTIC

When Ferdinand and Isabella married in 1469 to unite the independent states of Aragon and Castile, they launched this new Spanish nation into its golden age, beginning with the four voyages of Christopher Columbus to the Americas between 1492 and 1504. Meanwhile, the Portuguese extended their influence along the west coast of Africa and all the way to the Far East. In a short period of time, these epic maritime exploits began to shrink the globe, as contact between peoples in different parts of the world increased markedly. Then came the great leap across the Atlantic Ocean, triggering global changes of unimaginable significance. Western Europeans were becoming the most dynamic force in the world and were on the verge of exerting a greater global influence than the people of any single region had ever exerted.

The Columbian Voyages

Leading the way for Spain was an Italian sailor, Christopher Columbus. The son of a poor Genoese weaver, Columbus had married into a prominent family of Lisbon merchants, thus making important contacts at court. Celebrated for hundreds of years as the intrepid explorer who initiated permanent contact between Europe and the Americas, Columbus is attacked by some today as the ruthless exploiter of Indian peoples and lands. But Columbus is best understood in the context of his own times—an age of great brutality and violence and also an age in which Catholic Spain was engaged in the final stages of expelling the Moorish people who had controlled southern Spain for centuries. Columbus's urge to explore was nourished by ideas and questions about the geographic limits of his world, and he was inspired by notions of contributing to the reconquest of Moorish Spain. The Latin inscription on the tomb of his monarchs, Isabella and Ferdinand, captures the missionary mood of the era: "Overthrowers of the Mahometan sect and repressors of heretical stubbornness."

Like many sailors, Columbus had listened to sea tales about lands to the west. He may have heard Icelandic sagas about the voyages of Leif Eriksson and several thousand Norse immigrants who reached Newfoundland five centuries before during an era of global warming that allowed them to cross unexplored expanses of water. Other ideas circulated that the Atlantic Ocean stretched to India and eastern Asia. Could one reach the Indies by sailing west rather than by sailing east around Africa, as the Portuguese were attempting? Columbus hungered to know.

For nearly ten years, Columbus tried unsuccessfully to secure financial backing and royal sanction in Portugal for exploratory voyages. Many mocked his modest estimates of the distance westward from Europe to Japan, which he reckoned at 3,500 miles rather than contemporary estimates of 10,000 to 12,000 miles—far beyond the limit of small European ships, which could not carry enough food and water to keep sailors alive over such distances. Finally, in 1492, Spain's Queen Isabella commissioned him. With three tiny ships and a crew of about 90 men, Columbus sailed west. Strong winds, lasting ten days, blew the ships far into the Atlantic. There they were becalmed. In the fifth week at sea—longer than any European sailors had been out of the sight of land—mutinous rumblings swept through the crews. But Columbus pressed on. On the seventieth day, long after Columbus had calculated he would reach Japan, a lookout sighted land about 3,000 miles from Seville. On October 12, 1492, the sailors clambered ashore on a tiny island in the Bahamas (just east of Florida), which Columbus named San Salvador (Holy Savior). Grateful sailors "rendered thanks to Our Lord, kneeling on the ground, embracing it with tears of joy."

Believing he had reached Asia, Columbus was rewarded for his colossal miscalculations of the earth's circumference with a landfall in the island-

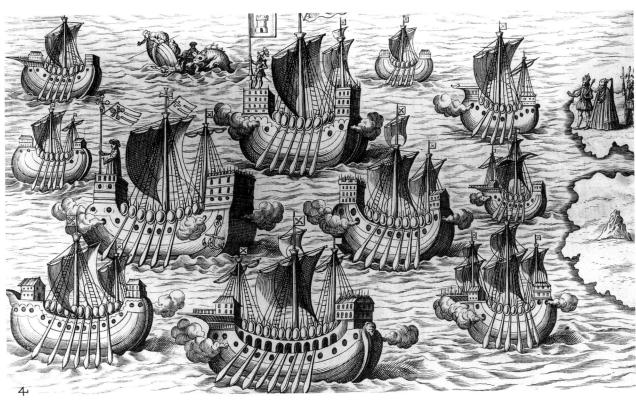

In this fanciful depiction of Columbus's second voyage across the Atlantic, a large fleet is propelled by oars as well as wind. Waving goodbye are Queen Isabella and King Ferdinand (upper right). A sea monster (upper left) may threaten the expedition. *(Courtesy, American Antiquarian Society)*

speckled Caribbean. Here he explored for ten weeks. After landing on a heavily populated island that he named Hispaniola (shared today by Haiti and the Dominican Republic) and on Cuba (which he thought was the Asian mainland), he set sail for Spain with cinnamon, coconuts, a bit of gold, and several kidnaped natives. Homeward bound, he penned a report of what he believed were his Asian discoveries: hospitable people, fertile soils, magnificent harbors, and gold-filled rivers.

Quickly printed and distributed throughout Europe, Columbus's report brought him financing between 1494 and 1504 for three much larger expeditions to explore the newfound lands. The second voyage, carrying over 1,200 Spaniards in 17 ships, initiated the first extended contact between Europeans and Native Americans. In an ominous display of what was to come, Columbus's men captured some 1,600 Tainos on Hispaniola and carried 550 of them back to Spain as slaves in 1495. Only 350 survived the stormy voyage to Spain. Here began the Atlantic slave trade that would alter the history of the world, though it began in the reverse direction of what would soon become its dominant flow. Although his discoveries seemed less significant than the Portuguese exploits in the South Atlantic, Columbus led Spain to the threshold of a mighty empire. He reaped few rewards, however, dying unnoticed and penniless in 1506. To the end, he believed that he had found the water route to Asia.

While Spain began to project its power westward across the Atlantic, the Portuguese extended their influence in different directions—southward toward West Africa and then eastward to East Asia. In 1497, Vasco da Gama became the first European to sail around the Cape of Africa, where he picked up a Hindu pilot in East Africa who guided him all the way across the Indian Ocean in 1498. This allowed the Portuguese to colonize the Indian Ocean and to reach modern Indonesia and south China by 1513. By forcing trade concessions in the islands and coastal states of the East Indies, the Portuguese unlocked the fabulous Asian treasure houses that, since Marco Polo's time, had whetted European appetites. By 1500, they had captured control of the African gold trade monopolized for centuries by North African Muslims. The gleaming metal now traveled directly to Lisbon by sea rather than by camel caravan across the Sahara to North African Muslim ports such as Tunis and Algiers.

Columbus's Four Voyages

The different courses taken by Columbus on his four Atlantic crossings were prompted by his desire to explore the island-rich Caribbean Sea. He departed on his second voyage only months after reaching Seville with news about the first epic voyage.

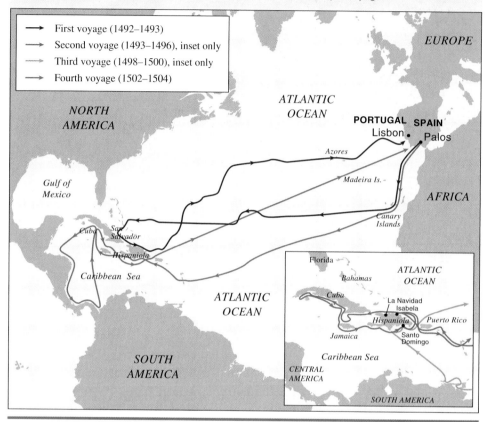

⟶ First voyage (1492–1493)
⟶ Second voyage (1493–1496), inset only
⟶ Third voyage (1498–1500), inset only
⟶ Fourth voyage (1502–1504)

Religious Conflict During the Era of Reconnaissance

The expansion of Spain and Portugal into areas of the world where they had little previous influence profoundly affected patterns of economic activity in Europe. Its commercial center now shifted away from the ports of the Mediterranean to the Atlantic ports facing the New World. But this fast-growing commercial power also had a deeply religious aspect because it occurred in the midst of—and magnified—an era of religious conflict and reformation.

Shortly after Columbus's Atlantic voyages, the people of western Europe were torn by religious schisms that magnified national rivalries. At the heart of Europe's religious strife was a continental movement to cleanse the Christian church of corrupt practices and return it to the purer ways of early Christianity. Criticism of the worldliness of the Catholic church mounted during the Renais-

sance. Then a German monk, Martin Luther, became the first to break successfully with Rome, initiating the Protestant Reformation that changed both theology and practice. As Protestant sects multiplied, Catholics began to reform their Church, and the two groups began a long battle for the souls of Europeans.

Luther was preparing for a legal career in 1505 when a bolt of lightning nearly struck him during a violent thunderstorm. Trembling with fear, he vowed to become a monk. But in the religious order of Saint Augustine, he lost faith in the power of the age-old rituals and sacraments of the Church—the Mass, confession, pilgrimages to holy places, even crusades against Muslim infidels. Salvation did not come through these practices but through an inward faith, or "grace," that God conferred on those He chose. Good works, Luther believed, did not earn grace but were the external evidence of grace won through faith. Luther's position implied a rev-

Portuguese Voyages of Exploration

The four voyages by Portuguese sea captains between 1482 and 1500 show how those who sailed southward and eastward opened up distant parts of the world to Europeans in the same era when Columbus was sailing westward to the Americas. **Reflecting on the Past** Did Columbus share his Atlantic Ocean experiences with the Portuguese sea captains who reached the Indian Ocean? If so, how? What did Columbus learn from the Indian Ocean voyagers that helped him in his Atlantic Ocean voyages?

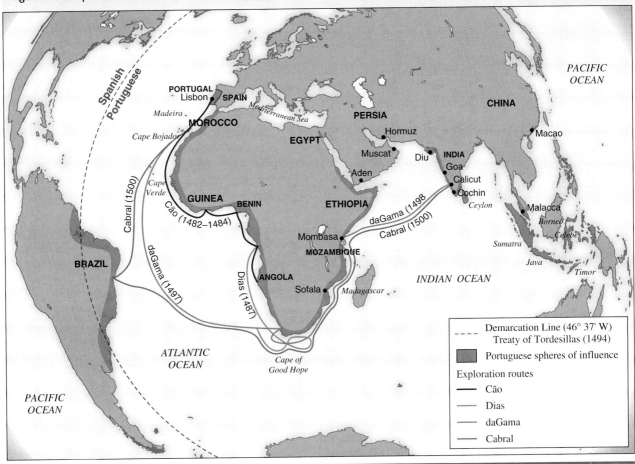

olutionary rejection of the Church's elaborate hierarchy of officials, who presided over the rituals intended to guide individuals along the path toward salvation.

Luther's doctrine of private "justification by faith" did not immediately threaten the Church. But in 1517, he openly attacked the sale of "indulgences" for sins by which the pope raised money for the building of St. Peter's in Rome. By purchasing indulgences, individuals had been told, they could reduce their time (or that of a deceased relative) in purgatory. Luther drew up 95 arguments against this practice and called on Christians to practice true repentance. The spread of printing, invented less than 70 years before, allowed the rapid circulation of his ideas. The printed word and the ability to read it were to become revolutionary weapons throughout the world.

Luther's cry for reform soon inspired Germans of all classes. He denounced five of the seven sacraments of the Church, retaining only baptism and communion. He attacked the upper clergy for luxurious living and urged priests, who were nominally celibate but were often involved in irregular sexual relations, to marry respectably. He railed against the "detestable tyranny of the clergy over the laity" and called for a priesthood of all believers. He urged people to seek faith individually by reading the

In this painting by Hans Holbein the Younger, John Calvin (1509–1564) is portrayed as a man of letters, books, and solemn religiosity. "What I have taught and written," wrote Calvin, "did not grow in my brain, but that I hold it from God." *(The Granger Collection, New York)*

Bible, which he translated into German and made widely available for the first time in printed form. Most dangerously, he called on the German princes to assume control over religion in their states, directly challenging the authority of Rome and further undermining the functions of its clergy.

The basic issue dividing Catholics and Protestants thus centered on the source of religious authority. To Catholics, religious authority resided in the organized Church, headed by the pope. To Protestants, the Bible was the sole authority, and access to God's word or God's grace did not require the mediation of the Church.

Building on Luther's redefinition of Christianity, John Calvin, a Frenchman, brought new intensity and meaning to the Protestant Reformation. In 1536, at age 26, he published a ringing appeal to every Christian to form a direct, personal relationship with God. By Calvin's doctrine, God had saved a few souls at random before Creation and damned the rest. Human beings could not alter this predestination, but those who were good Christians must

struggle to understand and accept God's saving grace if He chose to import it. Without mediation of ritual or priest but by "straight-walking," one was to behave as one of God's elect, the "saints." This radical theology, even more insistent on individual godliness than Luther's, spread among all classes throughout Europe.

Calvin proposed reformed Christian communities structured around the elect few. To remake the corrupt world and follow God's will, communities of "saints" must control the state, rather than the other way around. Elected bodies of ministers and dedicated laymen, called presbyteries, were to govern the Church, directing the affairs of society down to the last detail so that all, whether saved or damned, would work for God's ends.

Calvinism, as a fine-tuned system of self-discipline and social control, was first put into practice in the 1550s in the city-state of Geneva, near the French border of Switzerland. Here the brilliant and austere leader established what he intended to be a model Christian community. A council of 12 elders drove nonbelievers from the city, rigidly disciplined daily life, and stripped the churches of every appeal to the senses—images, music, incense, and colorful clerical gowns. Religious reformers from all over Europe flocked to the new holy community, and Geneva soon became the continental center of the reformist Christian movement and a haven for refugee Protestant leaders. The city was, wrote John Knox of Scotland in 1556, "the most perfect school of Christ that ever was in the earth since the days of the apostles."

Calvin's radical program converted large numbers of people to Protestantism throughout Europe. Like Lutheranism, it recruited most successfully among the privileged classes of merchants, landowners, lawyers, and the nobility and among the rising middle class of master artisans and shopkeepers.

Sixteenth-century monarchs initially regarded attacks on the Catholic church with horror. But many local princes adopted some version of the reformed faith. The most important monarch to break with Catholicism was Henry VIII of England. When Pope Clement VII refused him permission to divorce and remarry, Henry declared himself head of the Church of England, or Anglican church. Although it retained many Catholic features, the Church of England moved further in a Protestant direction under Henry's son Edward. But when Mary, Henry's older Catholic daughter, came to the throne, she vowed to reinstate her mother's religion by suppressing Protestants. Her policy created Protestant martyrs, and many were relieved when she died in

1558, bringing Henry's younger Protestant daughter, Elizabeth, to the throne. During her long rule, the flinty Elizabeth steered Anglicanism along a middle course between the radicalism of Geneva and the Catholicism of Rome.

The countries most affected by the Reformation—England, Holland, and France—were slow in trying to colonize the New World, so Protestantism did not gain an early foothold in the Americas. Catholicism in Spain and Portugal remained almost immune from the Protestant Reformation. Thus, even while under attack, Catholicism swept across the Atlantic virtually unchallenged in the colonies of Spain and Portugal during the century after Columbus's voyages.

THE SPANISH CONQUEST OF AMERICA

From 1492 to 1518, Spanish and Portuguese explorers opened up vast parts of Asia and the Americas to European knowledge. Yet during this age of exploration, only modest attempts at settlement were made, mostly by the Spanish on the Caribbean islands of Cuba, Puerto Rico, and Hispaniola. The three decades after 1518, however, became an age of conquest. In some of the bloodiest chapters in recorded history, the Spanish nearly exterminated the native peoples of the Caribbean islands, toppled and plundered the great inland empires of the Aztec and Inca in Mexico and Peru, gained control of territories ten times as large as their Spanish homeland, discovered fabulous silver mines, and built an oceanic trade of enormous importance to all of Europe. This short era of conquest had immense consequences for global history.

Portugal, meanwhile, restricted by one of the most significant lines ever drawn on a map, concentrated mostly on building an eastward oceanic trade to southeastern Asia. In 1493, to settle a dispute, the pope had demarcated Spanish and Portuguese spheres of exploration in the Atlantic. Drawing a north–south line 100 leagues (about 300 miles) west of the Azores, the pope confined Portugal to the eastern side. One year later, in the Treaty of Tordesillas, Portugal obtained Spanish agreement to move the line 270 leagues farther west. Nobody knew at the time that a large part of South America, as yet undiscovered by Europeans, bulged east of the new demarcation line and therefore fell within the Portuguese sphere. In time, Portugal would develop this region, Brazil, into one of the most profitable areas of the Americas.

Treaty of Tordesillas

The Treaty of Tordesillas, promulgated by Pope Alexander VI, drew a line dividing all claims to land in the Americas between Portugal and Spain. Until the arrival of the Spanish and Portuguese in the Americas, never before had such small numbers of people established their dominance over such a large and populous area.

Caribbean Experiments

Columbus's second Atlantic expedition in 1493 established the first Spanish colony in the New World on the island of Hispaniola (or Santo Domingo), and this proved to be the testing ground for all future Spanish colonization. Taíno—the first New World indigenous people to encounter Europeans—had never seen a people like the Spanish and touched the soldiers pouring ashore "to ascertain if they were flesh and bones like themselves." Columbus thought the Taíno as strange as the natives found him and his sailors. Their hair, Columbus wrote in his journal, was "straight and coarse like horsehair" and their heads very broad, "more so than any other race that I have ever seen."

Columbus arrived with 17 ships and about 1,200 men. Coming ashore with the Spaniards were seeds and cuttings for propagating European crops; chickens, cattle, sheep, goats, and pigs; and, hidden in sacks of seed, weeds. All of these transfers across

Greater Antilles in 1520

In the West Indies explored by Columbus, most of the inhabitants, as shown on this map, were Taínos. Columbus's knowledge that Marco Polo had found 7,448 islands dotting the China Sea convinced him that the Taínos were "the people of the Great Khan [of China]."

the Atlantic would prove to be the agents of ecological change, as we will see. But for now, Columbus was seeking gold, which he had heard from Marco Polo's account of East Asia was plentiful. When he found no gold, Columbus visited Cuba and then returned to Spain with six Taíno captives.

Seeing that the island was teeming with Taíno Indians—their number has been estimated as high as 3 million—the Spanish used military force, including huge mastiffs and horses, to subdue them and turn them into a captive labor force to work on ranches. Similar conquests brought the people of Puerto Rico under Spanish control in 1508 and the people of Cuba in 1511. But Spanish diseases soon touched off a biological holocaust that killed most of the Indians within a single generation—a preview of what would soon occur elsewhere in the Americas. Some Taíno women married Spanish men and produced the first mestizo society in the Americas. But by 1550, the Taíno no longer existed as a distinct people.

Spanish immigration to the Caribbean islands was underway by 1510, closely followed by the importation of enslaved Africans who were put to work on the first sugar plantations created in the Americas. Over the course of the sixteenth century, about a quarter-million Spaniards—most of them young, single men—immigrated to the Americas. But the islands dotting the Caribbean sea became a backwater, reaching their potential as cash-crop economies much later. For now, they served as laboratories for larger experiments in Mexico and South America, launching pads from which to mount invasions of the Mesoamerican mainland, and places to build fortified ports such as San Juan, Puerto Rico, and Havana, Cuba.

The Conquistadors' Onslaught at Tenochtitlán

Within a single generation of Columbus's death in 1506, Spanish conquistadors explored, claimed, and conquered most of South America (except Brazil), Central America, and the southern parts of North America from Florida to California. Led by audacious explorers and military leaders, and usually accompanied by enslaved Africans, they established Spanish authority and Catholicism over an area that dwarfed their homeland in size and population. They were motivated by religion, pride of nation,

The crouching male figure shown here was fashioned from wood by a Taíno carver on Hispaniola (now the Dominican Republic). The stern visage may have been intended to warn Taínos not to drink the poisonous cassava juice extracted from the tuber that provided them with their main flour for bread. *(Nelson A. Rockefeller Collection/Boltin Picture Library)*

Following two years of sparring with the Aztecs and their subject people, Cortés assaulted Tenochtitlán and, after a four-month siege, dramatically brought the Aztec Empire to its knees.

The Spanish use of horses and firearms provided an important advantage; so did a murderous smallpox epidemic in 1520 that felled thousands of Aztec. Support from local peoples oppressed by Moctezuma's tyranny was also important in overthrowing the Aztec ruler. Cortés was exceedingly lucky in being given a Nahuatl woman named Malinche who the Spanish would rename Doña Marina. Fluent in both Mayan and Nahuatl, the Aztec language, Malinche became Cortés's interpreter, giving him an advantage over the native Indians he encountered. Native peoples regarded Malinche as a traitor, and so her name passed down in the Mexican vocabulary as *malinchista*—a person betraying his people. In two years, the conquistadors from the other side of the Atlantic had destroyed the empire that had brought Mesoamerica to the peak of thousands of years of development.

In the next few decades, foraying from the Valley of Mexico, the Spanish extended their dominion over the Mayan people of the Yucatán, Honduras, and Guatemala. Disease was always their companion, mowing down the native peoples even before the Spanish arrived.

In the second conquest, the intrepid Francisco Pizarro, marching from Panama through the jungles of Ecuador and into the towering Andes mountains of Peru with a mere 168 men, most of them not even soldiers, toppled the Inca Empire. Like the Aztec, the populous Inca lived in a highly organized social system. But also like the Aztec, they were riddled by smallpox and weakened by violent internal divisions. This ensured Pizarro's success in capturing their capital at Cuzco in 1533. From there, Spanish soldiers marched farther afield, plundering other gold- and silver-rich Inca cities. Further expeditions into Chile, New Granada (Colombia), Argentina, and Bolivia in the 1530s and 1540s brought under Spanish control an empire larger than any in the Western world since the fall of Rome.

By 1550, Spain had overwhelmed the major centers of native population throughout the Caribbean, Mexico, Central America, and the west coast of South America. Spanish ships carried gold, silver, dyewoods, and sugar east across the Atlantic and transported African slaves, colonizers, and finished goods west. In a brief half century, Spain had exploited the advances in geographic knowledge and marine technology of its Portuguese rivals and

and dreams of personal enrichment. "We came here," explained one Spanish foot soldier in the legion of Hernán Cortés, "to serve God and the king, and also to get rich."

In two bold and bloody strokes, the Spanish overwhelmed the ancient civilizations of the Aztec and Inca. In 1519, hearing of a great empire in Mexico's interior, Cortés set out from Cuba, unauthorized by its governor, with 11 ships, 550 Spanish soldiers, several hundred Cuban Indians, some enslaved Africans, and well-fed mounts and pack horses that had thrived on Hispaniola. Reaching the coast of Mexico at Veracruz, he marched over rugged mountains to attack Tenochtitlán (modern-day Mexico City), the capital of Moctezuma II's Aztec empire. Seizing towns subject to the Aztec rule, Cortés enlisted Indian support against their hated overlords.

In this painting for a Spanish book on the conquest of the Aztecs, Cortés meets Moctezuma. Standing behind Cortés is his mistress and interpreter, Malinche, or Doña Marina as the Spanish renamed her. From *Lienzo de Tlaxcala, Antigüedades Mexicanas 1892 (American Museum of Natural History Library [AMNH#314372])*

Anthropologists who discovered the Royal Tombs of the Moche people found many small sculptures of what they called the "Decapitator." *(Photograph by Susan Einstein, Courtesy of UCLA Fowler Museum of Cultural History)*

brought into harsh but profitable contact with each other the people of three continents. The triracial character of the Americas was already firmly established by 1600.

For nearly a century after Columbus's voyages, Spain enjoyed almost unchallenged dominion over the fabulous hemisphere newly revealed to Europeans. Greedy buccaneers of various nations snapped at the heels of homeward-bound Spanish treasure fleets with cargoes of silver, but this was only a nuisance. France made gestures of contesting Spanish or Portuguese control by planting small settlements in Brazil and Florida in the mid-sixteenth century, but they were quickly wiped out. England remained island-bound until the 1580s. Until the seventeenth century, only Portugal, which staked

The Inca Empire in 1500

The Inca Empire in 1500 was gigantic, extending along the west coast of South America for some 2,600 miles and containing an estimated 14 million people. Only the Ottoman and Chinese empires in the Old World controlled more land than the Inca.

Inca Empire
• Inca town
— Inca road

out important claims in Brazil in the 1520s, challenged Spanish domination of the Americas.

The Great Dying

Spanish conquest of major areas of the Americas set in motion one of the most dramatic and disastrous population declines in recorded history. Spanish contacts with the natives of the Caribbean basin, central Mexico, and Peru in the early sixteenth century triggered a biological epidemic. The population of the Americas on the eve of European arrival had grown to an estimated 50 to 70 million or more. In some areas, such as central Mexico, the highlands of Peru, and certain Caribbean islands, population density exceeded that of most of Europe. But though they were less populous than the peoples of the Americas, the European colonizers had one extraordinary biological advantage: for centuries Old World peoples had been exposed to nearly every lethal microbe that infects humans on an epidemic scale in the temperate zone. Over the centuries, Europeans had built up immunities to these diseases. Such biological defenses did not eliminate smallpox, measles, diphtheria, and other afflictions, but they limited their deadly power. Geographic isolation, however, had kept these diseases from the peoples of the Americas. The closing of the Bering Land Bridge, thousands of years before, had provided a "cold filter" through which no raging diseases could pass. So, too, one seeming liability actually advantaged the indigenous people: their lack of large domesticated animals, which were the major disease carriers. Arriving Europeans therefore unknowingly encountered a huge component of the human race that was utterly defenseless against the "domesticated" infections the Europeans and their animals carried inside their bodies.

The results were catastrophic. In 1518, the smallpox virus erupted on Hispaniola. The Spanish priest Bartolomé de las Casas recorded that "of that immensity of people that was on this island and which we have seen with our own eyes" only about one thousand were spared among a population of between 1 and 3 million that had existed when Columbus arrived in 1493. Now the Spanish had an invaluable ally—the deadly smallpox virus—to carry with them in their invasion of Mexico in 1519. Of some 15 million inhabitants in central Mexico before Cortés's arrival, nearly half perished within 15 years. In the Valley of Mexico, where the Aztec capital of Tenochtitlán stood, the estimated population was 1.5 to 3 million before the conquistadors arrived. Eighty years later, in 1600, only 70,000 native people could be counted.

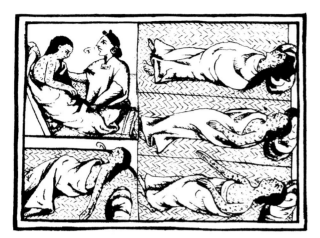

Aztec victims of smallpox, contracted during Cortés's invasion of Tenochtitlán in the 1520s. The woodcut is from the sixteenth-century work *Historia de las Casas de Nueva Espana* by Fray Bernardo de Sahagun. According to the account of the disease, "The sores were so terrible that the victims could not lie face down, . . . nor move from one side to the other. And when they tried to move even a little, they cried out in agony." *(Biblioteca Medicea Laurenziana)*

Demographic disaster also struck the populous Inca peoples of the Peruvian Andes, speeding ahead of Pizarro's conquistadors. Smallpox "spread over the people as great destruction," an old Indian told a Spanish priest in the 1520s. "There was great havoc. Very many died of it. They could not stir, they could not change position, nor lie on one side, nor face down, nor on their backs. And if they stirred, much did they cry out. . . . And very many starved; there was death from hunger, [for] none could take care of [the sick]." Such terrifying sickness led many natives to believe that their gods had failed them, and this belief left them ready to acknowledge the greater power of the Spaniards' God. Microbic onslaughts came in waves—one from 1545 to 1548, another from 1576 to 1581. By 1600, the Aztec population had been reduced to a tenth—perhaps even a twentieth—80 years after the Spanish conquest.

In most areas where Europeans intruded in the hemisphere for the next three centuries, the catastrophe repeated itself. Whether Protestant or Catholic, whether French, English, Spanish, or Dutch, whether male or female, every newcomer from the Old World participated accidentally in the spread of disease that typically eliminated, within a few generations, at least two-thirds of the native population. Millions of Native Americans who had never seen a European died of European diseases, which swept like wildfire through densely populated regions.

The first historian to appreciate the role played by disease in the Spanish conquest, writing more

than a half-century ago, accurately described the role of the pathogens unleashed in the New World: these "forerunners of civilization, the companions of Christianity, the friends of the invader" were "more terrible than the conquistadors on horseback, more deadly than sword and gunpowder, they made the conquest . . . a walkover compared with what it would have been without their aid."

The enslavement and brutal treatment of the native people intensified the lethal effects of European diseases. After their spectacular conquests of the Inca and Aztec, the Spanish enslaved thousands of native people and assigned them work regimens that severely weakened their resistance to disease. Some priests like Bartolomé de las Casas waged lifelong campaigns to reduce the exploitation of the Indians, but they had only limited power to control the actions of their colonizing compatriots.

The Columbian Exchange

Much more than lethal microbes crossed the Atlantic with the Spaniards as they conquered the Caribbean islands and then large parts of Central and South America. With them came animal and plant life that altered ecosystems and transformed the landscape. Westward-bound Spanish ships brought wheat, rye, barley, oats, and other European grains; fruits such as cherries, peaches, pears, lemons, oranges, melons, and grapes; vegetables such as radish, salad greens, and onions. All of these, unknown in the New World, perpetuated European cuisine and were gradually incorporated into Indian diets. But much more important were the herd animals of the Europeans: cattle, goats, horses, burros, pigs, and sheep. The burro pulling a wheeled cart could move ten times as much corn or cordwood as a human beast of burden. The horse could carry a messenger twice the speed of the fleetest runner. Still more transformative were livestock. Cattle, sheep, goats, and pigs flourished, grazing in the vast grasslands of the Americas and safe from the large carnivores that attacked them in the Old World but did not exist in the Americas. Cattle reproduced so rapidly that feral livestock swarmed across the countryside, often increasing tenfold in three or four years. They flourished so well that in time they ate themselves out of their favorable environment, stripping away plant life, which soon led to topsoil erosion and eventually to desertification.

Pigs were even harder on the environment. Reproducing at staggering rates, they tore into the manioc tubers and sweet potatoes in the Greater Antilles where Columbus first introduced eight of

ANALYZING HISTORY

THE COLUMBIAN EXCHANGE

In the last several millennia of world history, the Columbian Exchange, as historian Alfred Crosby has termed it, stands as the most significant geographical rearrangement of organisms with profound environmental and human consequences.

Reflecting on the Past Can you determine why inhabitants of the Americas had few domesticated animals before the arrival of Europeans? Why were infectious diseases rare in the pre-Columbian Americas? What is the relationship between the lack of domesticated animals and the general absence of infectious diseases?

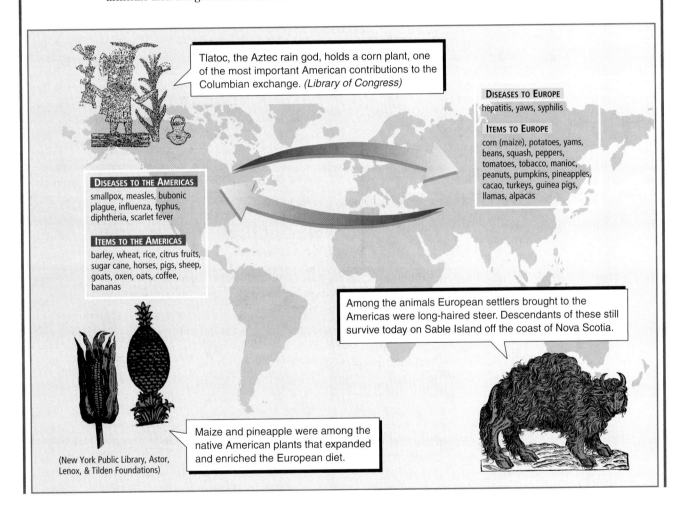

Tlatoc, the Aztec rain god, holds a corn plant, one of the most important American contributions to the Columbian exchange. *(Library of Congress)*

DISEASES TO EUROPE
hepatitis, yaws, syphilis

ITEMS TO EUROPE
corn (maize), potatoes, yams, beans, squash, peppers, tomatoes, tobacco, manioc, peanuts, pumpkins, pineapples, cacao, turkeys, guinea pigs, llamas, alpacas

DISEASES TO THE AMERICAS
smallpox, measles, bubonic plague, influenza, typhus, diphtheria, scarlet fever

ITEMS TO THE AMERICAS
barley, wheat, rice, citrus fruits, sugar cane, horses, pigs, sheep, goats, oxen, oats, coffee, bananas

Among the animals European settlers brought to the Americas were long-haired steer. Descendants of these still survive today on Sable Island off the coast of Nova Scotia.

Maize and pineapple were among the native American plants that expanded and enriched the European diet.

(New York Public Library, Astor, Lenox, & Tilden Foundations)

them in 1493. They devoured guavas and pineapples, ravaged lizards and baby birds, and in short stripped the land clean. Similar swine explosions occurred on the mainland of Mexico and Central America, where along with cattle they devastated the grasslands. Meat, leather, and milk were never lacking for the Spanish intruders; all were there for the taking because, as the main historian of the "Columbian Exchange" explains, Old World hoofed animals took to the savannas and meadows of the Americas "like Adam and Eve returning to Eden."

Spaniards brought the flora and fauna that they prized most to the Americas, but also traveling with them were unwelcome passengers. Among the most destructive were weeds, the seeds of which could never be strained out of sacks of fruit and vegetable seed. Once they took root, weeds proved hard to control in an age lacking the chemicals used today. Therefore, invasive weeds, including clover that crowded out native flora, entered the Americas. So did rats, pesky stowaways impossible to keep off ships bound across the Atlantic. Reproducing as fast

In this pictograph of an ancient Aztec myth, maize plays a central role; the first female spreads kernels of maize, or corn, while her husband tries to divine the future. *(Bibliothèque de l'Assemblée Nationale, Paris [Plate No. 20, Codex Borbonicus])*

as pigs, they decimated native small animals, spread diseases, and added a new dimension to the human struggle for life. Rabbits, shipmates of the rats, also multiplied prodigiously in the Americas.

The "Columbian Exchange" had its eastbound dimension but mainly this advantaged Europeans and Africans—and eventually Asians—whereas the westbound traffic had brought, above all, death-dealing microbic infections. Syphilis and yaws, apparently not known in Europe until about 1500, were afflictions of the Americas that created misery in the Old World as they traveled eastward, although they were never remotely on the scale of the scathing smallpox epidemics. On the other hand, table foods from the Americas such as pumpkins, pineapples, squash, peanuts, and beans enriched the European diet. So did guinea pigs and turkeys. Tomatoes, known as "love apples" for their supposed stimulus to sexual potency, became a staple of European cuisine. Llamas and alpacas produced wool for warmth.

But far more important was the spread in Europe of Indian maize and potatoes. The spread was gradual because it took generations to understand the fundamental advantage the potato had over Old World grains. From its first introduction in northern Spain in the late 1500s, the potato slowly spread northward and eastward through Europe. From the North Sea to the Ural Mountains, farmers on the northern European plain learned slowly that by substituting potatoes for rye—the only grain that would thrive in the short and often rainy summers—they could quadruple their yield in calories per acre. Columbus had been dead for more than a century before potato and corn production took hold in Europe. But when this happened, as it did in Ireland in the mid-1660s, the transition to New World potato allowed for population growth and strengthened the sinew of Europe's diet.

The same phenomenon occurred with the introduction of New World Indian maize (to be renamed corn). First, in mountain valleys where summer rains permitted corn cultivation, such as in Spain, Greece, and the Balkans, corn became the staple grain. Maize also reached Africa and China as early as the 1550s; the New World sweet potato also made its entry into China.

Silver, Sugar, and Their Consequences

The small amount of gold that Columbus brought home from the Caribbean islands raised hopes that this metal, which along with silver formed the standard of wealth in Europe, might be found in the transatlantic paradise. Some gold was gleaned from the Greater Antilles and later from Colombia, Brazil, and Peru. But though men pursued it fanatically to the far corners of the hemisphere, more than three centuries would pass before they discovered gold in windfall quantities in North America. All of the

Spanish efforts between 1500 and 1650 produced only about 180 tons of gold.

Silver was another matter. It proved most abundant—so plenteous, in fact, that when bonanza strikes were made in Bolivia in 1545 and then in northern Mexico in the next decade, much of Spain's New World enterprise focused on its extraction. For most of the sixteenth century, the Spanish Empire in America was a vast mining community. Sixteen thousand tons of silver were scooped from Spain's colonies in the Americas between 1500 and 1650.

Native people, along with some African slaves, provided the first labor supply for the mines. The Spaniards permitted the highly organized Indian societies to maintain control of their own communities but exacted from them huge labor drafts for mining. By imposing themselves at the top of a highly stratified social order that had previously been organized around tributary labor, the Spanish enriched themselves beyond the dreams of even the most visionary explorers. At Potosí, in Bolivia, 58,000 workers labored at elevations of up to 13,000 feet to extract the precious metal from a fabulous sugarloaf "mountain of silver." The town's population reached 120,000 by 1570, making it much larger than any in Spain at the time. Thousands of other workers toiled in the mines of Zacatecas, Taxco, and Guanajuato. By 1660, they had scooped up so many

million pounds of silver from the Americas that the gleaming metal tripled the entire European supply.

The massive flow of bullion from the Americas to Europe triggered profound changes. It financed further conquests and settlement in Spain's American empire, spurred long-distance trading in luxury items such as silks and spices from East Asia, and supported agricultural development in the New World of sugar, coffee, cacao, and indigo. The bland diet of Europeans gradually changed as items such as sugar and spices, previously luxury articles for the wealthy, became accessible to ordinary people.

The enormous increase of silver in circulation in Europe after the mid-sixteenth century also caused a "price revolution." As the supply of silver increased faster than the volume of goods and services that Europeans could produce, the value of the metal declined. Put differently, prices rose. Between 1550 and 1600, they doubled in many parts of Europe and then rose another 50 percent in the next half century. Land-owning farmers got more for their produce, and merchants thrived on the increased circulation of goods. But artisans, laborers, and landless agricultural workers (the vast majority of the population) suffered because their wages did not keep pace with rising prices. As one of the first English immigrants to America lamented, skilled artisans "live in such a low condition as is little better than beggary."

In this cutaway depiction of the Potosí mountain range in Mexico, enslaved Indian workers dig silver and carry it up a rope ladder made of ox hides. Deep inside the mountain, the miners hold candles. The illustration appeared in 1601 in a translation of the Jesuit missionary José de Acosta's *Historia natural y moral de las Indias. (Map Division, New York Public Library, Astor, Lenox and Tilden Foundations)*

This 1823 lithograph by William Clark romanticizes gang labor in the sugar fields of the British West Indies by decorously clothing men and women in trousers, jackets, and skirts. In reality, enslaved Africans worked semi-naked under the punishing sun. However, this depiction accurately reflects the use of female labor in the harvesting of sugar cane. *(By Permission of the British Library)*

Overall, the price revolution brought a major redistribution of wealth and increased the number of people in western Europe living at the margins of society. It thus built up the pressure to emigrate to the Americas, Europe's new frontier. At the same time, rising prices stimulated commercial development. Expansion overseas fed expansion at home and intensified changes toward capitalist modes of production already underway in the sixteenth century.

While the Spaniards organized their overseas empire around the extraction of silver from the highlands of Mexico, Bolivia, and Peru, the Portuguese staked their future on sugar production in the lowlands of Brazil. Spanish colonial agriculture supplied the huge mining centers, but the Portuguese, adapting techniques of cultivation worked out earlier on their Atlantic islands off the coast of Africa, produced sugar for export markets.

Whereas the Spanish mining operations rested primarily on the backs of the native labor force, the lowland Portuguese sugar planters scattered the indigenous people and replaced them with platoons of African slaves. By 1570, this regimented workforce was producing nearly 6 million pounds of sugar annually; by the 1630s, output had risen to 32 million pounds per year. High in calories but low in protein, the sweet "drug food" revolutionized the tastes of millions of Europeans and stimulated the

oceanic transport of millions of African slaves across the Atlantic.

From Brazil, sugar production jumped to the island-speckled Caribbean. Here, in the early seventeenth century, England, Holland, and France challenged Spain and Portugal for the riches of the New World. Once they secured footholds in the West Indies, Spain's enemies stood at the gates of the Hispanic New World empire. This ushered in a long period of conflict "beyond the line"—where European treaties had no force. Through contraband trading with Spanish settlements, piratical attacks on Spanish treasure fleets, and outright seizure of Spanish-controlled islands, the Dutch, French, and English in the seventeenth century gradually sapped the strength of the first European empire outside of Europe.

Spain's Northern Frontier

The crown jewels of Spain's New World empire were silver-rich Mexico and Peru, with the islands and coastal fringes of the Caribbean representing lesser, yet valuable, gemstones. Distinctly third in importance were the northern borderlands of New Spain—the present-day Sun Belt of the United States. Yet the early Spanish influence in Florida, the Gulf region, Texas, New Mexico, Arizona, and California indelibly marked the history of the United States. Spanish control of the southern fringes of North America began in the early 1500s and did not end for three centuries, when Mexico wrested independence from Spain in 1821. Far outlasting Spanish rule were the plants and animals they introduced to North America, ranging from sheep, cattle, and horses to various grasses and weeds that crowded out native plants.

Horses were of special importance. They had arrived with Columbus in 1493 but did not thrive in the tropical climate of the Greater Antilles. But once the Spanish reached the three great temperate grasslands of the Americas—the Argentine pampas, the Venezuelan llanos, and the North American Great Plains stretching all the way from southern Canada to northern Mexico—horses flourished. Flourishing with them were cattle, which were the foundation of the Spanish economy on their northern frontier. Horses and cattle were both tough on the grasslands, destroying ground cover and clearing the way for an invasion of European weeds and less nutritious grasses.

Spanish explorers began charting the southeastern region of North America in the early sixteenth century, beginning with Juan Ponce de León's expeditions to Florida in 1515 and 1521 and Lucas Vasquez d'Ayllón's short-lived settlement at Winyah Bay in South Carolina in 1526. For the next half century, Spaniards planted small settlements along the coast as far north as the Chesapeake Bay, where their temporary encampment included enslaved Africans. The Spanish traded some with the natives, but the North American coast, especially Florida,

was chiefly important to the Franciscan friars, who attempted to gather the local tribes into mission villages and convert them to Catholicism.

The Spanish made several attempts to bring the entire Gulf of Mexico region under their control. From 1536 to 1542, Hernán de Soto, a veteran of Pizarro's conquest of the Inca a few years before, led a military expedition of about 600 men deep into the homelands of the Creeks and Choctaws. Yearning to find another Tenochtitlán or Cuzco, he explored westward from Tampa Bay across the Mississippi River to present-day Arkansas and east Texas. But he found only agricultural-based tribes, influenced by Mayan and Aztec people, who lived in sizeable villages and built ceremonial pyramids.

De Soto's expedition at first found receptive natives, but they could not provide what the Spanish most wanted—gold. Pillaging thickly settled Indian villages for furs and freshwater pearls, seizing food supplies, and enslaving Indians to serve as human pack animals, de Soto's men cut a brutal swath as far north as North Carolina and as far west as Arkansas. Death preceded them and intensified in their wake. For example, reaching the chiefdom of Cofitachequi (in present-day Georgia), they found vacated villages and funereal houses packed with skeletons. New outbreaks of disease further ravaged the native people as the Spanish explorers moved on. De Soto never conquered the peoples that his train of soldiers encountered; instead, the environment and tenacious Indian resistance conquered him. After seeing their leader die a miserable death, de Soto's men and enslaved Africans limped back to Mexico

James Walker's *Vaqueros in a Horse Corral* speaks beautifully of the Spanish origins of the cowboy in the American West. *(Gilcrease Museum of American Art, Tulsa, OK)*

The Spanish *Entradas* in North America

The *entradas* of the Spanish conquistadors were all motivated by gold fever as well as the mission to claim vast territories across the lower tier of North America for the Spanish. Most of the early explorers became governors of Spanish colonies in South America.

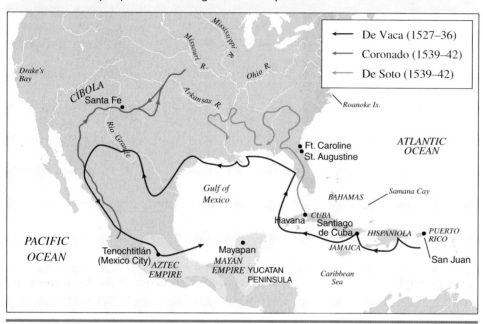

with what was left of their forces. Little could the English know that their Spanish enemies were paving the way for them in North America's southeastern sector by spreading lethal microbes that devastated Indian societies and broke up the great chiefdoms of the lower South.

In 1559, Spaniards again marched northward from Mexico in an attempt to establish their authority in the lower Gulf region. Everywhere they went, they enslaved Indians to carry provisions. In 1565, they sought to secure Florida. Building a fort at St. Augustine, they evicted their French rivals at Fort Caroline, 40 miles to the north. St. Augustine became the center of Spain's northeastern frontier, and Florida remained a Spanish possession for more than two centuries.

The Southwest became a more important region of early Spanish activity in North America. Francisco Vásquez de Coronado explored the region from 1540 to 1542, leading an expedition of several hundred Spanish soldiers, a number of Africans, and a baggage train of some 1,300 friendly Indians, servants, and slaves. Coronado never found the Seven Cities of Cíbola, reported by earlier Spanish explorers to be fabulously decorated in turquoise and gold. But he opened much of Arizona, New Mexico, and Colorado to eventual Spanish control, hap-

pened upon the Grand Canyon, and probed as far north as the Great Plains. His interior explorations, together with the nearly simultaneous expedition of de Soto in the Southeast, established Spanish claims to the southern latitudes of North America and gave them contacts, often bloody, with the populous corn-growing Indian societies of the region.

The Southwest, like Florida and the Gulf region, had no golden cities. In New Mexico, however, Franciscan friars tried to harvest souls. A half-century after Coronado's exploratory intrusions, Don Juan de Oñate led 129 soldiers, about 500 Spanish settlers, and 10 Franciscan friars up the Rio Grande in 1598 to find some 60,000 Pueblo gathered in scores of settled towns where they had practiced agriculture for centuries. Santa Fe, established in 1610, became the administrative center of northern New Spain. For the next 70 years, the Franciscans tried to graft Catholicism onto Pueblo culture by building churches on the edges of ancient native villages. As long as the priests were content to overlay Indian culture with a veneer of Catholicism, they encountered little resistance because the Pueblo found advantage in Spanish military protection from their Apache enemies and valued access to mission livestock and grain during years of drought. So, outwardly, they professed the Christian faith. But secretly the Pueblo still practiced their traditional religion in the underground Pueblo ceremonial chambers called kivas. Meanwhile, Spanish settlers—never more than one thousand in 1680—carved out cattle ranches and built small towns.

ENGLAND LOOKS WEST

By the time England awoke to the promise of the New World, Spain and Portugal were firmly entrenched there. But by the late sixteenth century, the conditions necessary to propel England overseas had ripened. During the early seventeenth century, the English, as well as the Dutch and French, began overtaking their southern European rivals. For the English, the first challenge came in the Caribbean, where between 1604 and 1640 the English planted several small colonies producing tobacco and later sugar. Few guessed that some secondary and relatively unproductive settlements then being planted on the North American mainland would in time be among England's most prized possessions.

England Challenges Spain

England was the slowest of the Atlantic powers to begin exploring and colonizing the New World. Although far more numerous than the Portuguese, the English in the fifteenth century had little experience with long-distance trade and few contacts with cultures beyond their island aside from the French, against whom they had waged the Hundred Years' War (1337–1453). Only the voyages of John Cabot (the Genoa-born Giovanni Caboto) gave England any claim in the New World sweepstakes. But England never followed up on Cabot's voyages to Newfoundland and Nova Scotia—the first northern crossing of the Atlantic since the Vikings—a few years after Columbus's first voyage.

At first, England's interest in the far side of the Atlantic centered primarily on fish. This high-protein food, basic to the European diet, was the gold of the North Atlantic. Early North Atlantic explorers found the waters off Newfoundland and Nova Scotia teeming with fish—not only the ordinary cod but also the delectable salmon. But the fishermen of Portugal, Spain, and France, more than those of England, began making annual spring trips to the offshore fisheries in the 1520s. Not until the end of the century would the French and English drive Spanish and Portuguese fishermen from the Newfoundland Banks.

Exploratory voyages along the eastern coast of North America hardly interested the English. It was for the French that Cartier and Verrazano sailed between 1524 and 1535. Looking for straits westward to India, through the northern land mass that was still thought to be a large island, they made contact with many Indian tribes and charted the coastline from the St. Lawrence River to the Carolinas. They established the northern latitudes as a suitable place for settlement but found nothing of immediate value to take home. The time had not yet arrived when Europeans would leave their homelands to resettle in North America rather than go there merely to extract its riches or plunder the Spanish colonies.

Changes in the late sixteenth century, however, propelled the English overseas. The rising production of woollen cloth, a mainstay of the English economy, had sent merchants scurrying for new markets after 1550. Their success in establishing trading companies in Russia, Scandinavia, the Middle East, and India vastly widened England's commercial orbit and raised hopes for developing still other spheres. Meanwhile, population growth and rising prices depressed the economic conditions of ordinary people and made them look across the ocean for new opportunities.

The cautious policy of Queen Elizabeth I, who ruled from 1558 to 1603, did not at first promote overseas colonies, favoring Protestantism as a vehicle of national independence rather than a missionary project. Ambitious and talented, she had to contend with Philip II, king of Spain and her fervently Catholic brother-in-law, whose long reign nearly coincided with hers. Regarding Elizabeth as a Protestant heretic, Philip plotted incessantly against her. The pope added to Catholic–Protestant tensions in England by excommunicating Elizabeth in 1571 and absolving her subjects from paying her allegiance—in effect, inciting them to overthrow her.

The smoldering conflict between Catholic Spain and Protestant England broke into open flames in 1587. Two decades before, Philip II had sent 20,000 Spanish soldiers into his Netherlands provinces to suppress Protestantism. Then, in 1572, he had helped arrange the massacre of thousands of French Protestants. By the 1580s, Elizabeth was providing covert aid to the Protestant Dutch revolt against Catholic rule. Philip vowed to crush the rebellion and decided as well to launch an attack on England to wipe out this growing center of Protestant power.

Elizabeth fed the flames of the international Catholic–Protestant conflict in 1585 by sending

European Exploration of North America

The English and French dominated European explorations of North America in the late fifteenth and sixteenth centuries. Verrazano, an Italian sea captain, sailed in the service of the French king.

6,000 English troops to aid the Dutch Protestants. A year later, the colorful sea dog Francis Drake, who had been raiding Spanish shipping on the coasts of Mexico and Peru, bombarded Spanish St. Augustine in Florida for two days, looted the city, and touched off an epidemic that the Florida Indians attributed to the "English God that made them die so fast." Two years later, infuriated by Drake's piracy and support

of Protestant rebels in the Netherlands, Philip dispatched a Spanish armada of 130 ships carrying 30,000 men and 2,400 artillery pieces. Sails blazing with crusaders' crosses, the fleet set forth to conquer Elizabeth's England. For two weeks in the summer of 1588, a sea battle raged off the English coast. A motley collection of smaller English ships, with Drake in the lead, defeated the Armada, sinking

Under the leadership of Elizabeth I, here displayed in royal finery and resting her hand on the globe, England challenged and ultimately overturned Spain's domination of worldwide sea trade. Behind the placid face was a determined and sometimes ruthless ruler. *(By kind permission of the Marquess of Tavistock and Trustees of the Bedford Estate)*

many of the lumbering Spanish galleons and then retiring as the legendary "Protestant wind" blew the crippled Armada into the North Sea.

The Spanish defeat prevented a crushing Catholic victory in Europe and brought a temporary stalemate in the religious wars. It also solidified Protestantism in England and brewed a fierce nationalistic spirit there. Shakespeare's love of "this other Eden, this demi-paradise" spread among the people; and with Spanish naval power checked, both the English and the Dutch found the seas more open to their rising maritime and commercial interests.

The Westward Fever

In the last decades of the sixteenth century, the idea of overseas expansion began to capture the imagination of important elements of English society. Urging them on were two Richard Hakluyts, uncle and nephew. In the 1580s and 1590s, they devoted themselves to advertising the advantages of colonizing on the far side of the Atlantic. For nobles at court, colonies offered new baronies, fiefdoms, and estates. For merchants, the New World promised exotic produce to sell at home and a new outlet for English cloth and other goods. For militant Protestant clergy, there awaited a continent filled with heathen people to be saved from devilish savagery and Spanish Catholicism. For the commoner, opportunity beckoned in the form of bounteous land that was almost for the taking. The Hakluyts' pamphlets publicized the idea that the time was ripe for England to break the Iberian monopoly on the riches of the New World.

However, England's first effort at colonizing occurred in Ireland, and this delayed English efforts to plant colonies on the other side of the Atlantic. In the 1560s and 1570s, the English extended control over Ireland through brutal military conquest. The emerald island became a turbulent frontier for thousands of career-hungry younger sons of gentry families as well as landless commoners. Many of the leaders first involved in New World colonizing served in Ireland, and many of their ideas about the legitimacy of colonial conquest and about how to deal with a "savage" and "barbaric" people stemmed from their Irish experience.

The first English attempts at overseas settlement were small, feeble, and ill-fated. Whereas the Spanish encountered unheard-of wealth and scored astounding victories over ancient and populous civilizations, the English at first met only failure in relatively thinly settled lands. Their efforts on the eastern coast of North America were centered in the temperate zone because the French had already established themselves in the fish- and fur-rich northern region and the Spanish had established a grip on the near-tropical zone conducive to producing cash crops in what is now the American Southeast.

Working with leftovers, England began—unsuccessfully—to mount small settlements, first in 1583 in Newfoundland. Hard on the heels of this, a reconnaissance expedition organized by Walter Raleigh, one of Queen Elizabeth's favorite courtiers, scouted the Carolina coast and hastened homeward carrying two natives and a string of tales about rich soil,

Illustrated Travel Accounts

English travel accounts of New World settlements had a threefold purpose: first, to convince investors that purchasing stock issued by colonizing companies would reward them richly; second, to attract colonists through promotional descriptions of an exotic new world; and third, to serve as a Protestant weapon against colonizing Catholic countries, especially Spain. These pamphlets have furnished historians with rich ethnographic evidence of Indian lifeways in the Americas, a source of information on English attitudes toward Native Americans, and insights into how new technologies in book publishing fed the Protestant-Catholic conflict.

In 1588, Thomas Harriot (1560–1623), a minister, mathematician, and scientist trained at Oxford, published the first popular pamphlet describing and promoting English colonization. It came off the press as the English were repelling the Spanish Armada trying to destroy the English navy. In *A Briefe and True Report of the New Found Land of Virginia, directed to the Investors, Farmers and Wellwishers of the project of Colonizing and Planting there*, Harriot described what he had seen in eastern North America as a member of the second expedition to the Roanoke colony in 1585. Harriot enthusiastically described the pleasant climate and fertile land that would make farming easy, while boasting the commodities that English colonists could easily procure in Virginia—furs, pearls, iron, timber, precious metals, and more. Also on this voyage was a talented water colorist, John White, whose many paintings depicted Native Americans living in villages, practicing agriculture, and engaging in dances, religious activities, and child-rearing—a people who seemed to be ones with whom the English could settle peacefully (see figure opposite).

Harriot's *Briefe and True Report* became a model for English colonial promotional pamphlets. In 1589, he teamed up with Théodore de Bry, a Protestant engraver who in 1570 had fled Liège, his Belgian hometown, to escape the Spanish Inquisition, and taken refuge in Strasbourg, a Protestant stronghold and a center of engraving and the book trade. Once in London, de Bry created new copperplate engravings of White's watercolor paintings for a second edition of the *Briefe and True Report*. Taking artistic liberties, de Bry made the Indians seem more civilized to the English (see figures at top of next page). In 1590, Harriot's re-issued, illustrated *Briefe Report* at-tracted great attention, appearing as the first volume of a series of European travel accounts gathered by de Bry and advertised as *The Grand Voyages to America*. When John Smith published his *Generall Historie of Virginia, New England, and the Summer Isles* in 1624, the first lengthy eyewitness account of early English settlement in North America, it used many of de Bry's engravings, copied from John White's water colors.

De Bry's engravings introduced large numbers of Europeans to images of Indian life in the Americas and to impressions of the first encounters of Europeans with the indigenous people. A few Europeans had seen crude woodcuts of native life in the Americas in earlier sixteenth-century travel

English viewers of this water color of an Indian town on the bank of Pamlico River (in present-day Beaufort County, North Carolina) might see that though they called them "savages," the Eastern Woodlands natives tilled their maize fields (shown on the right), enjoyed dancing (lower right), and buried their chiefs (see tomb in lower left) in ways familiar to Europeans. At the upper right is a small, elevated watch man's hut. (© *British Museum*)

John White's picture of a man and woman squatting on a mat at a meal of soaked maize. Harriot noted that "they are very sober in their eating and drinking, and consequently very long lived because they do not oppress nature." In De Bry's reinterpretation of this image, the man and woman's posture, with legs extended, is much like that of Europeans at a picnic. Both figures have much lighter skin than in White's water color. The woman's face has been prettified by European standards, while the man has acquired musculature familiar to Europeans through Leonardo da Vinci paintings. De Bry has added fish, nuts, and a gourd to the scene. *(left: British Museum [1906-5-9-1(20)/PS207965]; right: Corbis)*

accounts. But not until de Bry's copperplate engravings, which offered clear, precise details, did book illustration advance to the point where a panoramic view of the European colonization of the Americas become available to the many. The great Catholic-Protestant conflict in sixteenth- and seventeenth-century Europe, being played out in the Americas, could thus be presented to a wide audience through the de Bry-illustrated travel accounts.

Théodore de Bry's illustrations were based on Las Casas's accounts of actual incidents, but his imagination ran free in creating chilling images. In this engraving, a huge conquistador holds a child by the legs and prepares to dash its brains out against a rock. Another Spaniard ignites a fire to burn thirteen Indians hanging from a crude gallows, while other conquistadors (in the background) hunt down fleeing Indians. *(From the Collections of the James Ford Bell Library, University of Minnesota, Minneapolis, Minnesota)*

Just before he died in 1598, de Bry published a Latin version of Bartolomé de Las Casas's *Short Account of the Destruction of the Indies*, first published in 1541 by the Spanish Dominican friar who had lived for nearly forty years in New Spain. Las Casas gave his life to converting the Indians to Catholicism and was intent on stopping the cruel Spanish treatment of them. His book was filled with details on horrific Spanish torture and killing of Indian women and children as well as adult males. Protestants had earlier republished Las Casas's exposé in French, English, and other languages, eager to offer proof of Catholic Spain's depravity in the Americas. But de Bry's illustrations for the 1598 edition published in Frankfurt showed Spanish ruthlessness with such graphic horror as to terrify the reader.

After their father's death, Jean-Théodore and Jean-Israël de Bry published another 22 illustrated volumes of voyages to the Americas, including eight volumes with illustrations emphasizing how the Spanish Catholics brutalized the native people. Published in English, German, French, and Latin editions, the illustrated books promoted the idea of English superiority while providing Europeans with graphic material on the exotic peoples on the other side of the Atlantic.

Reflecting on the Past Look at these four illustrations and imagine that you saw them in England as you prepared to cross the Atlantic among a group of colonists. Having never lived outside the small village where you had been born, how do the Indians appear to you? How will you prepare yourself for encounters with them? How will you be able to avert the violence of the Spanish colonists?

61

John White, whose watercolors on Roanoke Island provided fascinating ethnographic detail of Native Americans, also painted this mythical Pict male with blue skin to accompany his Roanoke drawings. The Picts were an ancient people—the ancestors of seventeenth-century Britons. White pictured them as tattooed, savage, bloodthirsty people. Here a male holds the head of a slain enemy. If Britons could evolve from such savages, suggested White, then the natives of North America could be patiently schooled in English ways. (© *British Museum [1906-5-9-1(24)/PS211689]*)

friendly Indians, and mineral wealth. A second voyage in 1585 and a third in 1587, composed of 91 men, 17 women, and 9 children, planted a small colony on Roanoke Island. But this first English foothold in a hemisphere dominated by Spanish and Portuguese colonizers failed. The voyages to Roanoke were too small and poorly financed to establish successful settlements. They served only as tokens of England's rising challenge to Spain in North America and as a source of valuable information for colonists later settling the area.

The Roanoke colony also failed resoundingly as the first sustained contact between English and Native American peoples. Although one member of the first expedition reported that "we found the people most gentle, loving, and faithful, void of all guile and treason," relations with the local tribes quickly soured and then turned violent. Charges

flew back and forth, the English believing that the local Indians had stolen a silver cup and the Indians angered by English raids on their winter supply of corn. Aware of their numerical disadvantage and afraid of a coordinated attack against them, the English turned their muskets on a local leader to intimidate the natives with their superior technology. In 1591, when a relief expedition reached Roanoke, none of the settlers could be found. Most likely these "lost colonists" succumbed to Indian attacks. It was an ominous beginning for England's overseas ambitions.

Discouraged Englishmen took another generation to try again. Small groups of men sent out to establish a tiny colony in Guiana, off the South American coast, failed in 1604 and 1609, and another group that set down in Maine in 1607 lasted only one year. Although they would flourish in time, even the colonies founded in Virginia in 1607 and Bermuda in 1612 floundered badly for several decades.

English merchants, sometimes supported by gentry investors, undertook these first tentative efforts. They risked their capital hoping that small-scale ventures in North America might produce the profits of their other overseas commercial ventures. They had their queen's blessing though little royal backing in subsidies, ships, and naval protection. The Spanish and Portuguese colonizing efforts were national enterprises that were sanctioned, capitalized, and coordinated by the crown. The English colonies were private ventures, organized and financed by small partnerships of merchants who pooled their slender resources.

English colonization could not succeed until these first merchant adventurers solicited the wealth and support of the prospering middle class. This support grew steadily in the first half of the seventeenth century, but even then, investors were drawn far more to the quick profits promised in West Indian tobacco production than to the uncertainties of mixed farming, lumbering, and fishing on the North American mainland. In the 1620s and 1630s, most of the English capital invested overseas went into establishing tobacco colonies in tiny Caribbean islands, including St. Christopher (1624), Barbados (1627), Nevis (1628), Montserrat (1632), and Antigua (1632).

Apart from the considerable financing required, the vital element in launching a colony was a suitable body of colonists. About 80,000 streamed out of England between 1600 and 1640, as economic, political, and religious developments pushed them from their homeland at the same time that dreams of opportunity and adventure pulled them westward. In the next 20 years, another 80,000 departed.

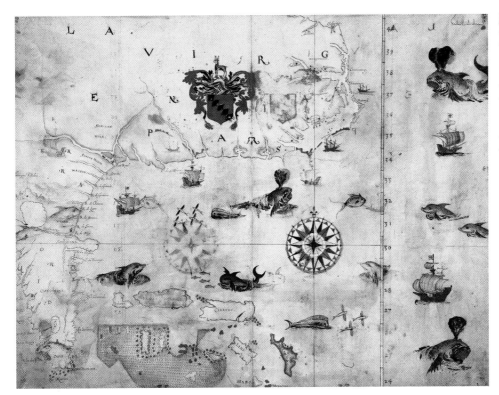

John White's chart of the east coast of North America, from the Chesapeake Bay to the tip of Florida, drew upon knowledge of French and Spanish attempts at colonization. Small red dots indicate places where White believed Europeans had made landfalls. Dolphins, flying fish, and spouting whales decorate the map, along with the coat of arms of Walter Raleigh. (© *British Museum [1906-5-9-1(2)/PS225251]*)

Economic difficulties in England prompted many to try their luck in the New World. The changing agricultural system, combined with population growth and the unrelenting increase in prices caused by the influx of New World silver, produced a surplus of unskilled labor, squeezed many small producers, and spread poverty and crime. By the late 1500s, wrote Richard Hakluyt, the roads were swarming with "valiant youths rusting and hurtful for lack of employment," and the prisons were "daily pestered and stuffed full of them."

A generation later, beginning in 1618, the renewed European religious wars between Protestants and Catholics devastated the continental market for English woollen cloth, bringing unemployment and desperate conditions to the textile regions. Probably half of England's households lived on the edge of poverty. "This land grows weary of her inhabitants," wrote John Winthrop of East Anglia, "so as a man, which is the most precious of all creatures, is near more vile among us than a horse or a sheep."

Religious persecution and political considerations intensified the pressure to emigrate from England in the early seventeenth century. How these forces operated in specific situations will be considered in the next chapter. The largest number of emigrants went to the West Indies. The North American mainland colonies attracted perhaps half

as many, and the Irish plantations in Ulster and Munster still fewer. For the first time in their history, large numbers of English people were abandoning their island homeland to carry their destinies to new frontiers.

Anticipating North America

The early English settlers in North America were far from uninformed about the indigenous people of the New World. Beginning with Columbus's first description of the New World, published in several European cities in 1493 and 1494, reports and promotional accounts circulated among the participants in early voyages of discovery, trade, and settlement. This literature became the basis for anticipating the world that had been discovered beyond the setting sun.

Colonists who read or listened to these accounts got a dual image of the native people. On the one hand, the Indians were depicted as a gentle people who eagerly received Europeans. Columbus had written of the "great amity toward us" that he encountered in San Salvador in 1492 and had described the Arawaks there as "a loving people" who "were greatly pleased and became so entirely our friends that it was a wonder to see." Verrazano, the first European to touch the eastern edge of North America, wrote optimistically about the native people in 1524. The natives, graceful of limb and tawny-colored, he related, "came toward us joyfully uttering loud cries of wonderment, and showing us the safest place to beach the boat."

This positive image of the Native Americans reflected both the friendly reception that Europeans often actually received and the European vision of the New World as an earthly paradise where wartorn, impoverished, and persecuted people could build a new life. The strong desire to trade with the native people also encouraged a favorable view because only a friendly Indian could become a suitable partner in commercial exchange.

A counterimage of a savage, hostile Indian, however, also entered the minds of settlers coming to North America. Like the positive image, it originated in the early travel literature. As early as 1502, Sebastian Cabot had paraded in England three Eskimos he had kidnapped on an Arctic voyage. They were described as flesh-eating savages and "brute beasts" who "spake such speech that no man could understand them." Many other accounts portrayed the New World natives as crafty, brutal, loathsome halfmen, who lived, as Amerigo Vespucci put it, without "law, religion, rulers, immortality of the soul, and private property."

The English had another reason for believing that all would not be friendship and amiable trading when they came ashore. For years they had read accounts of the Spanish experience in the Caribbean, Mexico, and Peru—and the story was not pretty. Many books described in gory detail the wholesale violence that occurred when Spaniard met Mayan, Aztec, or Inca. Accounts of Spanish cruelty, even genocide, were useful to Protestant pamphleteers, who labeled the Catholic Spaniards "hell-hounds and wolves." Immigrants embarking for North America wondered whether similar violent confrontations awaited them.

Another factor nourishing negative images of the Indian stemmed from the Indians' possession of the land necessary for settlement. For Englishmen, rooted in a tradition of the private ownership of property, this presented moral and legal, as well as practical, problems. As early as the 1580s, George Peckham, an early promoter of colonization, had admitted that the English doubted their right to take the land of others. In 1609, Anglican minister Robert Gray wondered, "By what right can we enter into the land of these savages, take their rightful inheritance from them, and plant ourselves in their places, being unwronged or unprovoked by them?"

The problem could be partially solved by arguing that English settlers did not intend to take the Indians' land but wanted only to share it with them. In return, they would offer the natives the advan-

John White, governor of the second expedition to Virginia in 1587, rendered the first pictorial records of native life in the Americas. This watercolor of a tattooed noblewoman of Pomeiock shows her right arm resting in a chain of pearls or copper beads. Her young daughter holds a prized English doll in an Elizabethan dress. (© British Museum)

tages of a more advanced culture and, most important, the Christian religion. This argument would be repeated for generations. As the governing council in Virginia put it in 1610, the settlers "by way of merchandizing and trade, do buy of [the Indians] the pearls of earth, and sell to them the pearls of heaven."

A more ominous argument arose to justify English rights to native soil. By denying the humanity of the Indians, the English, like other Europeans, claimed that the native possessors of the land disqualified themselves from rightful ownership of it. "Although the Lord hath given the earth to children of men," one Englishman reasoned, "the greater part of it [is] possessed and wrongfully usurped by wild beasts and unreasonable creatures, or by brutish savages, which by reason of their godless ignorance and blasphemous idolatry, are worse than those beasts which are of the most wild and savage nature."

Defining the Native Americans as "savage" and "brutish" did not give the English arriving in the New World the power to dispossess the Indians of their soil, but it armed them with a moral justification for doing so when their numbers became sufficient. Few settlers arriving in North America doubted that their technological superiority would allow them to overwhelm the indigenous people. For their part, many natives probably perceived the arriving Europeans as impractical, irreligious, aggressive, and strangely intent on accumulating material wealth.

AFRICAN BONDAGE

For almost four centuries after Columbus's voyages to the New World, European colonizers transported Africans out of their homelands in the largest forced migration in history. Estimates vary widely, but the number of Africans arriving in the New World was probably not less than 9.6 million. Millions more perished while being marched from the African interior to coastal trading forts or during the passage across the Atlantic (which claimed about 1.4 million lives). Nearly as many were traded across the Sahara to Red Sea and Indian Ocean slave markets during the centuries from 650 to 1900.

African peoples, fed into the merciless slave trade, were crucially important in building the first transoceanic European colonial empires. Once the slave trade began, locales for producing desired commodities such as sugar, coffee, rice, and tobacco moved from the Old World to the Americas. This gradually shifted Europe's orientation from the Mediterranean Sea to the Atlantic Ocean. Africa became an essential part of the immense Atlantic-basin system of trade and communication by providing Europeans with the human labor needed to unlock the profits buried in productive American soils. Without African labor, the overseas colonies of European nations would never have flourished as they did.

While the economic importance of enslaved Africans can hardly be overstated, it is equally important to understand the cultural interchange that occurred when some 9.6 million Africans arrived in the Western hemisphere. Of all the newcomers who peopled the New World between 1519, when the first black slaves arrived in the Americas directly from Africa, and the early nineteenth century, the Africans were by far the most numerous, probably outnumbering Europeans two or three to one. As a result, African slavery became the context in which European life would evolve in many parts of the Americas. At the same time, the slave trade etched lines of communication for the movement of crops, agricultural techniques, diseases, and medical knowledge among Africa, Europe, and the Americas.

European slave traders carried most Africans to the West Indies, Brazil, and Spanish America. Fewer than one out of every 20 reached North America, which remained a fringe area for slave traders until the early eighteenth century. Yet those who came to the American colonies, about 10,000 in the seventeenth century and 350,000 in the eighteenth century, profoundly affected the destiny of North American society. In a prolonged period of labor scarcity, their labor and skills were indispensable to colonial economic development, while their African customs mixed continuously with that of their European masters. Moreover, the racial relations that grew out of slavery so deeply marked society that the problem of race has continued to be one of this nation's most difficult problems.

The Slave Trade

The African slave trade did not begin as a part of the colonization of the Americas but as an attempt to fill a labor shortage in the Mediterranean world. As early as the eighth century, Arab and Moorish traders had driven slaves across Saharan caravan trails for delivery to Mediterranean ports. Seven centuries later, Portuguese merchants became the first European slave traders. For Africans, the Portuguese were nothing more than a new trading partner who could provide guns, horses, copper and brass, and especially textiles.

When Portuguese ship captains reached the west coast of Africa by water, they tapped into a slave-trading network that had operated in central and west Africa for many generations. Slaveholding was deeply rooted in African societies, regarded as a natural part of human organization, and was important in enhancing one's status and augmenting one's ability to produce wealth. However, slaves were employed in a wide variety of occupations, often serving as soldiers, administrators, and even occasionally as royal advisors.

Many Africans were relegated to slavery by judicial decree for crimes they had committed, but far more were captives in the wars between the numerous states of central and west Africa. Songhai—the largest state in Africa in the 1500s—waged several wars of territorial conquest, capturing slaves as it expanded its empire. The economy of the kingdom of Dahomey depended heavily for several centuries on commerce in slaves. One former slave, Francisco Feliz de Sousa, came to own a fleet of slave ships. But the early trade in human flesh was mainly in the

The Islamic Slave Trade

Though much less noticed than the Atlantic slave trade, the Islamic slave traffic across the Sahara Desert, Red Sea, and Indian Ocean was equally important numerically. The Islamic slave trade continued long after the Atlantic slave trade came to a halt in the late nineteenth century. **Reflecting on the Past** Why has the Islamic slave trade received less attention than the Atlantic slave trade? Why did the Islamic slave trade continue after abolitionists succeeded in ending the Atlantic slave trade?

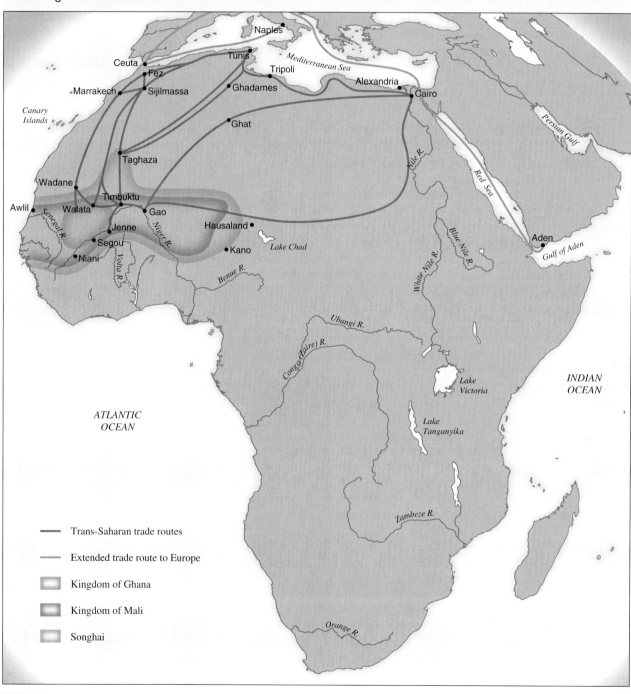

West African Slaving Forts

Europeans fought lustily for control of slaving forts on the West African coast, and many forts changed hands several times during the long period of the Atlantic slave trade. **Reflecting on the Past** How did West Africans participating in the slave trade adjust to the languages of different European slave traders? Or did the European slave trades learn a variety of African languages in order to trade at the coastal forts?

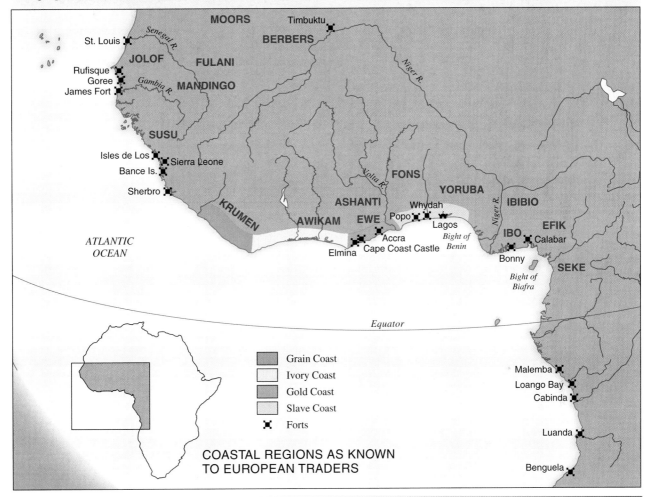

hands of the Spanish and Portuguese, who carried some 100,000 enslaved Africans to the Iberian peninsula before Columbus's first voyage across the Atlantic.

More than anything else, sugar transformed the African slave trade. For centuries, sugar cane had been grown in the Mediterranean countries to sweeten the diet of the wealthy. As sugar's popularity grew, the center of production shifted to Portugal's Atlantic islands of Madeira and São Tomé, off the west coast of Africa. Here in the 1460s, a European nation for the first time established an overseas colony organized around slave labor. From Madeira,

the cultivation of sugar spread to Portuguese Brazil and Spanish Santo Domingo. By the seventeenth century, with Europeans developing a taste for sugar almost as insatiable as their craving for tobacco, they vied fiercely for the tiny islands dotting the Caribbean and for control of the trading forts on the West African coast. African kingdoms, eager for European trade goods, fought each other to supply the "black gold" demanded by white ship captains.

Many European nations competed for trading rights on the West African coast. In the seventeenth century, when slave traders brought about 1 million Africans to the New World, the Dutch replaced the

Portuguese as the major supplier. The English, meanwhile, hardly counted in the slave trade. Not until the 1690s, when they began their century-long rise to maritime greatness, did the English challenge the Dutch. But by the 1690s, the English were the foremost European slave traders. Paradoxically, the first nations to forswear chattel slavery—Holland, France, and England—became leaders in raising their New World plantations on the foundation of African slave labor.

In the eighteenth century, European traders carried at least 6 million Africans to the Americas. By this time African slave labor figured so importantly in the colonial world that one Englishman called slavery the "strength and the sinews of this western world."

Once established on a large scale, the Atlantic slave trade dramatically altered slave recruitment in Africa. When criminals and "outsiders" were insufficient in number to satisfy the growing European demand, African kings highly desirous of European goods and others imported from Asia waged war against neighboring tribes. European guns abetted the process. By 1730, Europeans were providing some 180,000 weapons a year, spreading kidnaping and organized violence while strengthening the most militarily effective kingdoms. Again and again, coastal and interior kings invaded the hinterlands of western and central Sudan to procure slaves. Perhaps three-quarters of the slaves transported to

English North America came from the part of western Africa that lies between the Senegal and Niger rivers and the Gulf of Biafra.

In this forcible recruitment of slaves, young males—most of them 10 to 24 years old—were preferred over women. This demonstrated the preference of New World plantation owners for male field laborers, and it also reflected the decision of vanquished African villagers to yield up more men than women to raiding parties because women were the chief agriculturists in their society and, in matrilineal and matrilocal kinship systems, were too valuable to be sacrificed.

The Middle Passage

Even the most vivid accounts of the slave trade cannot convey the pain and demoralization that accompanied the initial capture and subsequent march to slave-trading forts on the West African coast or the dreaded "middle passage" across the Atlantic. Olaudah Equiano, an eighteenth-century Ibo from what is now Nigeria, described how raiders from another tribe kidnapped him and his younger sister when he was only 11 years old. He passed from one trader to another while being marched to the coast. Many slaves attempted suicide or died from exhaustion or hunger on these forced marches. But Equiano survived. Reaching the coast, he encountered the next humiliation, con-

This rare depiction of enslaved Africans being ferried out to European slave ships was first published in Jean Barbot's *A description of the coasts of north and south-Guinea* (1688). At the right is the slave fort of Manfroe while three other slaving stations appear to the left of it. *(New York Public Library, Rare Book Collection, Astor, Lenox and Tilden Foundations)*

The pain of a slave coffle, in which enslaved Africans were tied together with forked branches and bark rope, shows in this eighteenth-century print. About one-eighth of the slaves marched toward coastal holding pens were children. *(Mansell Collection/TimePix)*

finement in barracoons, or fortified enclosures on the beach, where a surgeon from an English slave ship inspected him. Equiano was terrified by the light skins, language, and long hair of the English and was convinced that he "had got into a world of bad spirits and that they were going to kill me."

More cruelties followed. European traders often branded the African slaves they purchased with a hot iron to indicate which company had procured them. The next trauma came with the ferrying of slaves in large canoes to the ships anchored in the harbor. An English captain recounted the desperation of Africans who were about to lose touch with their ancestral homeland and embark on a vast unknown ocean. "The Negroes are so loath to leave their own country," he wrote, "that they have often leaped out of the canoes, boat and ship, into the sea, and kept under the water till they were drowned."

Conditions aboard the slave ships were miserable, even though the traders' goal was to deliver alive as many slaves as possible to the other side of the Atlantic. Equiano recounted the scene below decks, where manacled slaves were crowded together like corpses in coffins. "With the loathsomeness of the stench, and crying together, I became so sick and low that I was not able to eat, nor had I the least desire to taste anything." The refusal to take food was so common that ship captains devised special techniques to cope with slaves who were determined to starve themselves to death rather than reach the New World in chains. Slavers flogged their captives brutally and applied hot coals to their lips. If this did not suffice, they force-fed the slaves with a mouth wrench. Yet for all the attempts to terrify the Africans into passive commodities, the slaves rebelled on about one of ten slave ships crossing the Atlantic.

The Atlantic passage, which usually took four to eight weeks, was so physically depleting and psychologically wrenching that one of every seven captives died en route. Many others arrived in the Americas deranged or near death. In all, the relocation of any African may have averaged about six months from the time of capture to the time of arrival at the plantation of a colonial buyer. During this protracted personal crisis, the slave was completely cut off from the moorings of a previous life—language, family and friends, tribal religion, familiar geography, and status in a local community. Still

Timeline

1440s	Portuguese begin kidnaping Africans and trading with them for slaves on Africa's western coast
1460s	Using African labor, sugar plantations in Portuguese Madeira become major exporters
1492	Christopher Columbus lands on Caribbean islands Spanish expel Moors (Muslims) and Jews
1493–1504	Columbus makes three additional voyages to the Americas
1493	Spain plants first colony in Americas on Hispaniola
1494	Treaty of Tordesillas
1497–1585	French and English explore northern part of the Americas
1498	Vasco da Gama reaches India after sailing around Africa
Early 1500s	First Africans reach the Americas with Spanish
1508–1511	Spanish conquistadors subjugate native people on Puerto Rico and Cuba
1513	Portuguese explorers reach China
1517	Luther attacks Catholicism and begins Protestant Reformation
1520	First disease contracted from Spanish devastates Aztec people
1521	Cortés conquers the Aztec
1528	Spain plants first settlement on Florida coast
1528–1536	Cabeza de Vaca *entrada* across southern region of North America
1530s	Calvin calls for religious reform
1533	Pizarro conquers the Inca
1534	Church of England established
1540–1542	Coronado explores the Southwest
1558	Elizabeth I crowned queen of England
1585	English plant settlement on Roanoke Island
1588	English defeat the Spanish Armada
1590	Roanoke settlement fails
1603	James I succeeds Elizabeth I

awaiting these victims of the European demand for cheap labor was adaptation to a new physical environment, a new language, a new work routine, and a life of unending bondage for themselves and their children.

Slavery in Early Spanish Colonies

Before a single enslaved African touched soil in the English colonies, thousands of slaves were already present in North America. They came first with fifteenth-century Spanish explorers such as Ponce de Leon, Vasquez de Ayllon, de Soto, and Coronado. The Morocco-born Estevan was indispensable to

Coronado's expedition in North America's Southwest, serving as guide, healer, linguist, and diplomat to Indian tribes. The importance of Africans on these arduous expeditions gave slavery a distinct character in the early Spanish colonies. Laboring in fields, in fort and church construction, and on supply trains, they were also valuable as soldiers, guides, and linguistic go-betweens with Indian people. In this way, slavery had little of the caste-like character it developed in the English colonies. Also contributing to the greater flexibility of Spanish slavery was the frequent crossing of blood among Spaniards, Indians, and Africans.

✦ *Conclusion*

CONVERGING WORLDS

The Iberian voyages of the late fifteenth and early sixteenth centuries, linking Europe and Africa with the Americas, brought together people such as the Spanish conquistador Alvar Núñez Cabeza de Vaca, the Moroccan captive Estevan, and chiefs of Creek villages in the southeastern sector of North America. Here were the beginnings of a communications network that ultimately joined every region of the globe and linked the destinies of widely disparate peoples living on many parts of the immense Atlantic basin.

Other nations would follow Spain, but it was the Spanish who first erected colonial regimes that drew upon homeland traditions of law, religion, government, and culture. The Spanish also initiated maritime and commercial enterprises profoundly affecting patterns of production, with the Americas destined to become the great producer of foodstuffs to be exported to Europe. Part of this fledgling global economy was the trade in human beings—Africans carried to Spain and Portugal, then to the Atlantic islands off the west coast of Africa, and finally to the Americas in one of the most tragic chapters of human history. Accompanying this, and paving the way for European settlement, was the greatest weapon possessed by Europeans—the germs carried in their bodies that decimated the indigenous people of the Americas in the greatest biological holocaust in the annals of history.

The English immigrants who began arriving on the eastern edge of North America in the early seventeenth century came late to a New World that other Europeans had been colonizing for more than a century. The first English arrivals, the immigrants to Virginia, were but a small advance wave of the large, varied, and determined fragment of English society that would flock to the western Atlantic frontier during the next few generations. Like Spanish, Portuguese, and French colonizers before them, they would establish new societies in the newfound lands in contact with the people of two other cultures—one made up of ancient inhabitants of the lands they were settling and the other composed of those brought across the Atlantic against their will. We turn now to the richly diverse founding experience of the English latecomers in the seventeenth century and their contests with French, Dutch, and Spanish contenders for control of North America.

◆ Recommended Reading

Breaching the Atlantic
A. G. Dickens, *The English Reformation* (1964); J. H. Elliot, *The Old World and the New, 1492–1650* (1970); Hubert Jedin and John Dolan, eds., *Reformation and Counter Reformation* (1980); H. A. F. Kamen, *The Iron Century: Social Change in Europe, 1550–1660* (1971); William D. Phillips, Jr., and Carla Rahn Phillips, *The Worlds of Christopher Columbus* (1992); Kirkpatrick Sale, *The Conquest of Paradise: Christopher Columbus and the Columbian Legacy* (1990); Eric Wolf, *Europe and the People without History* (1982).

The Spanish Conquest of America
Inga Clendinnen, *The Aztecs* (1991); David N. Cooke, *Born to Die: Disease and New World Conquest* (1998); Alfred Crosby, Jr., *The Columbian Exchange: Biological and Cultural Consequences of 1492* (1972) and *Ecological Imperialism: The Biological Expansion of Europe, 900–1900* (1986); Charles Gibson, *The Aztecs Under Spanish Rule* (1964); Paul E. Hoffman, *A New Andalucia and a Way to the Orient: The American Southeast During the Sixteenth Century* (1990); Charles Hudson, *Knights of Spain, Warriors of the Sun: Hernando de Soto and the South's Ancient Chiefdoms* (1997); Oakah L. Jones, Jr., *Los Paisanos: Spanish Settlers on the Northern Frontier of New Spain* (1979); James Lockhart and Stuart B. Schwartz, *Early Latin America* (1983); R. C. Padden, *The Hummingbird and the Hawk: Conquest and Sovereignty in the Valley of Mexico, 1503–1541* (1962); M. Leon Portilla, *The Broken Spears: The Aztec Account of the Conquest of Mexico* (1962); Ann F. Ramenofsky, *Vextors of Death: The Archaeology of European Contact* (1987); Edward Spicer, *Cycles of Conquest: The Impact of Spain, Mexico, and the United States on the Indians of the Southwest, 1533–1960* (1962); David E. Stannard, *American Holocaust: Columbus and the Conquest of the New World* (1992); Hugh Thomas, *Conquest: Montezuma, Cortés, and the Fall of Old Mexico* (1993).

England Looks West
Kenneth R. Andrews, *Trade, Plunder, and Settlement: Maritime Enterprise and the Genesis of the British Empire, 1480–1630* (1985); Nicholas P. Canny, *The Elizabethan Conquest of Ireland* (1976); De Lamar Jensen, *Reformation Europe, Age of Reform and Revolution* (1981); Karen Kupperman, *Facing Off in Early America* (2000) and *Roanoke: The Abandoned Colony* (1984); Peter Laslett, *The World We Have Lost* (1971); David B. Quinn, *England and the Discovery of America, 1481–1620* (1974) and *Set Fair for Roanoke: Voyages and Colonies, 1584–1606* (1985); A. L. Rowse, *The Expansion of Elizabethan England* (1955); Keith Wrightson, *English Society, 1580–1680* (1982).

African Bondage
Robin Blackburn, *The Making of New World Slavery, 1492–1800* (1997); Philip Curtin, *The Atlantic Slave Trade: A Census* (1969) and *The Rise and Fall of the Plantation Complex* (1990); David B. Davis, *The Problem of Slavery in Western Culture* (1966); Carl N. Degler, *Neither Black nor White: Slavery and Race Relations in Brazil and the United States* (1971); Richard S. Dunn, *Sugar and Slaves: The Rise of the Planter Class in the English West Indies, 1624–1713* (1972); David Eltis, *The Rise of African Slavery in the Americas* (2000); H. Hoetink, *Slavery and Race Relations in the Americas* (1973); Patrick Manning, *Slavery and African Life: Occidental, Oriental, and African Slave Trades* (1990); James A. Rawley, *The Transatlantic Slave Trade* (1981); Walter Rodney, *West Africa and the Atlantic Slave Trade* (1969); Frank Tannenbaum, *Slave and Citizen* (1956); Hugh Thomas, *The Slave Trade* (1997); John Thornton, *Africa and Africans in the Making of the Atlantic World, 1440–1680*, 2nd ed. (1998).

Fiction and Film
In the feature film *Conquest of Paradise* (1992), Gerard Depardieu plays Christopher Columbus, but Boston's WGBH seven-part *Columbus and the Age of Discovery* (1991) is much more comprehensive and authentic. In the miniseries *Roanoke*, PBS explores the friction between Indians and colonizers in the first attempt of the English to plant a North American settlement. Louise Erdrich's poem titled "Captivity," which can be found in

her *Jacklight* collection (1984), is a valuable Indian-centered reading of one of the most popular Indian captivity accounts ever published—Mary Rowlandson's *A Narrative of the Captivity, Sufferings and Removes of Mrs. Mary Rowlandson*, first published in 1682. Boston's WGBH has produced a superb four-part video series on

Africans in America (1998). The first two parts cover slavery and slave culture in the seventeenth and eighteenth centuries. Much shorter is the BBC production *A Son of Africa: The Slave Narrative of Olaudah Equiano*, a half-hour video of the only eighteenth-century slave who wrote an autobiography.

✦ Discovering U.S. History Online

1492: An Ongoing Voyage
www.lcweb.loc.gov/exhibits/1492/intro.html
An exhibit of the Library of Congress, Washington D.C., this site provides brief essays and images about early civilizations and contact in the Americas.

The European Voyages of Exploration
www.ucalgary.ca/applied_history/tutor/eurvoya
This site has images and texts for nearly every facet of European exploration.

Jamestown
www.iath.virginia.edu/vcdh/jamestown/images/
white_debry_html/introduction.html
This site presents Theodor de Bry's engravings of America alongside John White's original drawings, giving "the opportunity to use this material as a pedagogical resource on English views of native people."

Spain, The United States, & The American Frontier
www.international.loc.gov/intldl/eshtml/
A joint effort of American and Spanish national libraries, this bilingual site presents primary materials and several exhibits about the pre-conquest to contact period between the two countries.

The Columbus Doors
www.xroads.virginia.edu/~CAP/COLUMBUS/
colhome.html
Via the topics covered by the panels on the Capitol Columbus doors, historians discuss the Columbus myth and how is has changed over time.

Florida History Timeline
www.palmm.fcla.edu/fh/outline/outline.html
This Web site gives an overview of pre- and post-colonial Florida.

Sir Francis Drake
www.mcn.org/2/oseeler/drake.htm
This comprehensive site covers much of Drake's life and voyages.

John Cabot
www.heritage.nf.ca/exploration/cabot.html
Giovanni Caboto, or John Cabot, sailed for England to the New World in the late fifteenth century. This site describes his voyages as well as England's goals.

Africans in America
www.pbs.org/wgbh/aia/part1/1narr2.html
This site offers a brief background and a few illustrations of the English foray into slavery and colonization in the Americas.

African American Odyssey: Slavery— The Peculiar Institution
lcweb2.loc.gov/ammem/aaohtml/exhibit/aopart1.html
A web exhibit that includes paintings, original documents, engravings, and broadsides, along with background information on each.

Slave Movement During the Eighteenth and Nineteenth Centuries
dpls.dacc.wisc.edu/slavedata/index.html
This site provides downloadable primary source data from the slave trade.

Afro-Louisiana History and Genealogy
www.ibiblio.org/laslave/
The author has compiled a thorough database of "African slave names, genders, ages, occupations, illnesses, family relationships, ethnicity, places of origin, prices paid by slave owners, and slaves' testimony and emancipations" from slave inventories recorded by the French and Spanish proprietors in Louisiana.

3

Colonizing a Continent in the Seventeenth Century

Cecil Calvert grasping a map of Maryland held by his grandfather, the second Lord Baltimore; detail of a painting by Gerard Soest, court painter to Charles II. *(Enoch Pratt Free Library, Baltimore)*

◆ *American Stories*

AN AFRICAN ON THE VIRGINIA FRONTIER

Anthony Johnson, an African, arrived in Virginia in 1621 with only the name Antonio. Caught as a young man in the Portuguese slave-trading net, he had passed from one trader to another in the New World until he reached Virginia. There he was purchased by Richard Bennett and sent to work at Warrasquoke, Bennett's tobacco plantation situated on the James River. In the next year, Antonio was brought face-to-face with the world of triracial contact and conflict that would shape the remainder of his life. On March 22, 1622, the Powhatan tribes of tidewater Virginia fell on the white colonizers in

74

a determined attempt to drive them from the land. Of the 57 people on the Bennett plantation, only Antonio and four others survived.

Antonio—his name anglicized to Anthony—labored on the Bennett plantation for some 20 years, slave in fact if not in law, for legally defined bondage had not yet fully taken hold in the Virginia colony. During this time, he married Mary, another African trapped in the labyrinth of servitude, and fathered four children. In the 1640s, Anthony and Mary Johnson gained their freedom after half a lifetime of servitude. Probably at this point they chose a surname, Johnson, to signify their new status. Already past middle age, the Johnsons began carving out a niche for themselves on Virginia's eastern shore. By 1650, they owned 250 acres, a small herd of cattle, and two black servants. In a world in which racial boundaries were not yet firmly marked, the Johnsons had entered the scramble of small planters for economic security.

By schooling themselves in the workings of the English legal process, carefully cultivating white patronage, and working industriously on the land, the Johnsons gained their freedom, acquired property, established a family, warded off contentious neighbors, and hammered out a decent existence. But by the late 1650s, as the lines of racial slavery tightened, the customs of the country began closing in on Virginia's free blacks.

In 1664, convinced that ill winds were blowing away the chances for their children and grandchildren in Virginia, the Johnsons began selling their land to white neighbors. The following spring, most of the clan moved north to Maryland, where they rented land and again took up farming and cattle raising. Five years later, Anthony Johnson died, leaving his wife and four children. The growing racial prejudice of Virginia followed Johnson beyond the grave. A jury of white men in Virginia declared that because Johnson "was a Negroe and by consequence an alien," the 50 acres he had deeded to his son Richard before moving to Maryland should be awarded to a local white planter.

Johnson's children and grandchildren, born in America, could not duplicate the modest success of the African-born patriarch. By the late seventeenth century, people of color faced much greater difficulties in extricating themselves from slavery. When they did, they found themselves forced to the margins of society. Anthony's sons never rose higher than the level of tenant farmer or small freeholder. John Johnson moved farther north into Delaware in the 1680s, following a period of great conflict with Native Americans in the Chesapeake region. Members of his family married local Indians and became part of a triracial community that has survived to the present day. Richard Johnson stayed behind in Virginia. When he died in 1689, just after a series of colonial insurrections connected with the overthrow of James II in England, he had little to leave his four sons. They became tenant farmers and hired servants, laboring on plantations owned by whites. By now, slave ships were pouring Africans into Virginia and Maryland to replace white indentured servants, the backbone of the labor force for four generations. To be black had at first been a handicap. Now it became a fatal disability, an indelible mark of degradation and bondage.

Anthony and Mary Johnson's story is one of thousands detailing the experiences of seventeenth-century immigrants who arrived in North America. Their story is not about those European immigrants who sought both spiritual and economic renewal in the New World. But their lives became intertwined with those who were trying to escape European war, despotism, material want, and religious corruption. Like free immigrants and indentured servants from Europe, the Johnsons had to cope with new environments, new social situations, and new mixings of people who before had lived on different continents. Mastering the North American environment involved several processes that would echo down the corridors of American history. Prominent among them were the molding of an African labor force and the gradual subjection of Native American tribes who contested white expansion. Both developments occurred in the lifetimes of Anthony and Mary Johnson and their children. Both involved a level of violence that made this frontier of European expansion not a zone of pioneer equality and freedom but one of growing inequality and servitude.

This chapter reconstructs the manner of settlement and the character of immigrant life in six areas of early coloniza-tion: the Chesapeake Bay, southern New England, the French and Dutch area from the St. Lawrence River to the Hudson River, the Carolinas, Pennsylvania, and the Spanish toeholds on the southern fringe of the continent. A comparison of these various colonies will show how the colo-nizers' backgrounds, ideologies, modes of settlement, and uses of labor—free, slave, and indentured—produced dis-tinctly different societies in North America in the seven-teenth century. The chapter also shows how these regional societies changed over the course of the seventeenth cen-tury and how they experienced internal strain, a series of Indian wars, and reactions to England's attempts to reorga-nize its overseas colonies

THE CHESAPEAKE TOBACCO COAST

In 1607, a generation after the first Roanoke expedi-tion, a group of merchants established England's first permanent colony in North America at James-town, Virginia. Thus began the first permanent English colony in North America. But for the first generation, its permanence was anything but as-sured; even into the second and third generation of settlement along the waters that flowed into the huge Chesapeake Bay, the English colonizers were plagued with internal discord and violent clashes with the native peoples.

Jamestown, Sot Weed, and Indentured Servants

Under a charter from James I, the Virginia Company of London operated as a joint-stock company, an early form of a modern corporation that sold shares of stock and used the pooled capital to outfit and supply overseas expeditions. Although the king's charter to the company began with a concern for bringing Christian religion to native people who "as yet live in darkness and miserable ignorance of the true knowledge of God," most of the settlers proba-bly agreed with Captain John Smith, who emerged as their strongest leader. "We did admire," he wrote, "how it was possible such wise men could so tor-ment themselves with such absurdities, making reli-gion their colour, when all their aim was profit."

Profits in the early years proved elusive, however. Expecting to find gold, a rewarding trade with Indians for beaver and deer skins, and a water route

The Great English Migration, 1630–1660

This map shows that more than half of all the early English immigrants to the Americas went to the West Indies. Even a larger proportion of the Africans brought to the English colonies found themselves sold in England's Caribbean Islands.

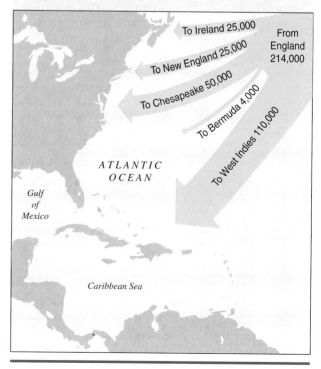

To Ireland 25,000
From England 214,000
To New England 25,000
To Chesapeake 50,000
To Bermuda 4,000
To West Indies 110,000

ATLANTIC OCEAN

Gulf of Mexico

Caribbean Sea

No one knows exactly what the Jamestown settlement looked like in its early years; this twentieth-century mural by Stanley King is a conjectured rendering based on archaeological evidence. New archaeological findings at the site of the Jamestown fort are adding to our knowledge of the first English Virginians. *(National Park Service, Colonial National Historical Park)*

to China, the original investors and settlers got a rude shock. Dysentery, malaria, drought, and malnutrition carried off most of the first colonists. More than 900 settlers, mostly men, arrived in the colony between 1607 and 1609; only 60 survived.

Seeking occupational diversity, the Virginia Company sent French silk artisans, Italian glassmakers, and Polish potash burners to Jamestown. But one-third of the first immigrants were gold-seeking adventurers with unroughened hands, a proportion of gentlemen six times as great as in the English population. Many others were unskilled servants, some with criminal backgrounds, who (according to John Smith) "never did knowe what a days work was." Both types adapted poorly to wilderness conditions, and Smith got few of the carpenters, fishermen, blacksmiths, and farmers he wanted.

The Jamestown colony was also hampered by the common assumption that Englishmen could exploit the Indians as Cortés and Pizarro had done. But the English found that the some 24,000 local Powhatan Indians were not densely settled and so could not be easily subjugated. Unlike Spain, England had sent neither an army of conquistadors nor an army of priests to subdue the natives. Instead, relations with the small groups that the able Powhatan had united into a confederacy turned bitter almost from the beginning. Powhatan brought supplies of maize to the sick and starving Jamestown colony during the first autumn. However, John Smith, whose military

Early Chesapeake Settlement

Only the major Indian villages in the early 1600s are indicated on this map. Note that the town sites are all oriented to the rivers—the source of both food and transportation.

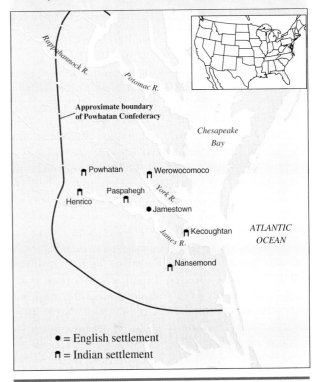

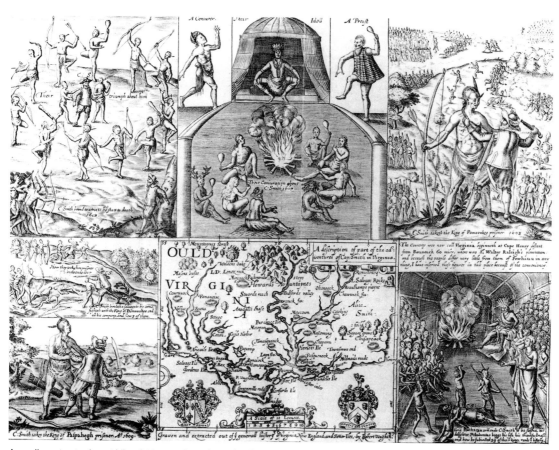

A small caption in the middle of this set of panels reads, "A description of part of the adventures of Cap: Smith in Virginia." The images were rendered by Robert Vaughan, an English engraver, and were published in *The Generall Historie of Virginia, 1624, by Captain John Smith.* In the lower right panel, an oversized Pocohantas (at the right) begs for the life of Smith, whose head is on a block, ready for dismemberment by an Indian executioner.

experience in eastern Europe had schooled him in dealing with people he regarded as "barbarians," raided Indian food supplies and tried to cow the local tribes. In the midst of one of the most severe droughts in centuries, which reduced the maize supply, Powhatan withdrew from trade with the English and sniped at their flanks. Many settlers died in the "starving times" of the first years.

Still, the Virginia Company of London poured in more money and settlers, many enticed with promises of free land after seven years' labor for the company. In 1618, the company even offered 50 acres of land outright to anyone journeying to Virginia. To people on the margins of English society, the promise of free land seemed irresistible. More than 9,000 crossed the Atlantic between 1610 and 1622. Yet only 2,000 remained alive at the end of that period. "Instead of a plantation," wrote one English critic, "Virginia will shortly get the name of a slaughter house."

Beside the offer of free land, a crucial factor in the migration was the discovery that tobacco grew splendidly in Chesapeake soil. Francis Drake's boat-load of the "jovial weed" (so named for its intoxicating effect), procured in the West Indies in 1586, popularized it among the upper class and launched an addiction that continues to this day.

Even James I's denunciation of smoking as "loathsome to the eye, hateful to the nose, harmful to the brain, and dangerous to the lungs" failed to halt the smoking craze. The "sot weed" became Virginia's salvation. Planters shipped the first crop in 1617, and tobacco cultivation spread rapidly. Tobacco yielded enough profit for settlers to plant it even in the streets and marketplace of Jamestown. By 1624, Virginia exported 200,000 pounds of the "stinking weed"; by 1638, though the price had plummeted, the crop exceeded 3 million pounds. Tobacco became to Virginia in the 1620s what sugar was to the West Indies and silver to Mexico and Peru. In London, men joked that Virginia was built on smoke.

Because tobacco required intensive care, Virginia's planters had to find a reliable supply of cheap labor. They found it by recruiting mostly English and Irish laborers along with a scattering

By the end of the 1600s, most young European males were addicted to tobacco. Like the young Dutchmen shown in this painting, they practiced various tricks such as the "ring," "whiffle," "gulp," and "retention" as part of the smoking cult. *(Adriaen Brouwer, "The Smokers," The Metropolitan Museum of Art, Bequest of Michael Friedsam, 1931, The Friedsam Collection [32.100.21] © 1989 The Metropolitan Museum of Art)*

from Sweden, Portugal, Spain, Germany, and even Turkey and Poland. They came as indentured servants, willingly selling a portion of their working lives in exchange for free passage to America. About four of every five seventeenth-century immigrants to Virginia—and later, Maryland—were indentured. Nearly three-quarters of them were male, mostly between 15 and 24 years old. Many came from the armies of the unemployed. Others were orphans, political prisoners, or convicts who escaped the gallows by going abroad. Some were younger sons unlikely to inherit a father's farm or shop, or young men fleeing an unfortunate marriage. Others were drawn simply by the prospect of adventure. But overwhelmingly, indentured servants came from the lower rungs of the social ladder at home.

Life for indentured servants often turned into a nightmare. Only about one in twenty realized the dream of freedom and land. If malarial fever or dysentery did not quickly kill them, they often succumbed to brutal work routines. Even by the middle of the seventeenth century, about half died during the first few years of "seasoning." Masters bought and sold their servants as property, gambled for them, and worked them to death, for there was little motive for keeping them alive beyond their term of labor. "My Master Adkins," wrote one servant in 1623, "hath sold me for £150 like a damned slave." When servants neared the end of their contract, masters found ways to add time and were backed by courts that they controlled.

Contrary to English custom, masters often put women servants to work at the hoe. Sexual abuse was common, and servant women paid dearly for illegitimate pregnancies. The courts fined them heavily and ordered them to serve an extra year or two to repay the time lost during pregnancy and childbirth. They also deprived mothers of their illegitimate children, indenturing them out at an early age. For many servant women, marriage was the best release from this hard life. Many accepted the purchase of their indenture by any man who suggested marriage.

Expansion and Indian War

As Virginia's population increased, spurred by the growth of tobacco production, violence mounted between white colonizers and the Powhatan tribes. In 1614, the sporadic hostility of the early years ended temporarily with the arranged marriage of Powhatan's daughter, the fabled Pocahontas, to planter John Rolfe. However, the profitable cultivation of tobacco created an intense demand for land. As more and more settlers pushed inland, the local tribes pondered their future.

In 1617, when Powhatan retired, leadership of the Chesapeake tribes fell to Opechancanough. This proud and talented leader began preparing an all-out attack on his English enemies. The English murder of Nemattanew, a Powhatan war captain and religious prophet, triggered a fierce Indian assault in 1622 that dealt Virginia a staggering blow. More than one-quarter of the white population fell, and the casualties in cattle, crops, and buildings were equally severe.

The devastating attack bankrupted the Virginia Company. The king annulled its charter in 1624 and established a royal government, which allowed the elected legislative body established in 1619, the House of Burgesses, to continue lawmaking in concert with the royal governor and his council.

The Indian assault of 1622 fortified the determination of the surviving planters to pursue a ruthless new Indian policy. John Smith, writing from England two years later, noted the grim satisfaction that had followed the Indian attack. Many, he reported, believed that "now we have just cause to destroy them

Ætatis suæ 21. Aͦ. 1616.

Matoaks als Rebecka daughter to the mighty Prince
Powhatan Emperour of Attanoughkomouck als Virginia
converted and baptized in the Christian faith, and
Wife to the worthell Mr Tho: Rolff.

Painted at the time she was presented to the court of King James I,
Pocahontas appears in a red velvet jacket over a dark dress with gold
buttons. She holds a fan of three ostrich feathers. We can only imagine how her elaborate shoulder collar of white lace must have felt for
a 22-year-old woman accustomed to loose-fitting, comfortable
clothes. *(National Portrait Gallery, Smithsonian Institution/Art Resource, NY)*

by all means possible." Bolstered by instructions
from London to "root out [the Indians] from being
any longer a people," the Virginians conducted annual military expeditions against the native villages
west and north of the settled areas. The "flood of
blood," as the English poet John Donne called it in
1622, had cost the colony dearly, but it justified a
policy of "perpetual enmity," even though the
Indians had attacked in 1622 because of "our own
perfidious dealing with them."

Population growth after 1630 and settlers' perpetual need for fresh acreage because tobacco
quickly exhausted the soil intensified the pressure
on Indian land. The tough, ambitious planters soon
encroached on Indian territories, provoking war in
1644. The Chesapeake tribes, Virginians came to believe, were merely obstacles to be removed from the
path of English settlement.

Proprietary Maryland

By the time Virginia had achieved commercial success in the 1630s, another colony on the Chesapeake
took root. The founder's main aim was not profit but

rather a refuge for Catholics and a New World version of England's manor-dotted countryside.

George Calvert, an English nobleman, designed
and promoted the new colony. Closely connected to
England's royal family, he had received a huge grant
of land in Newfoundland in 1628, just three years after James I had made him Lord Baltimore. In 1632,
Charles I, James's son, prepared to grant him a more
hospitable domain of 10 million acres. To honor the
king's Catholic wife, Henrietta Maria, Calvert named
it Terra Maria—or Maryland.

Catholics were an oppressed minority in
England, and Calvert planned his colony as a haven
for them. But knowing that he needed more than a
small band of Catholic settlers, the proprietor invited others, too. Catholics, never a majority in his
colony, were quickly overwhelmed by Protestants
who jumped at the offer of free land with only a
modest yearly fee to the Calverts.

Lord Baltimore died in 1632, leaving his 26-year-
old son, Cecilius, to carry out his plans. The charter
guaranteed the proprietor control over all branches

Population of the Chesapeake Colonies, 1610–1750

As indicated in this chart, it was not until the 1690s,
when Chesapeake planters began turning to Africa for
their labor, that the black population in the Chesapeake colonies began to rise rapidly.

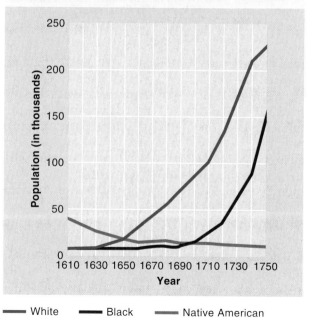

White   Black   Native American

Source: U.S. Bureau of the Census.

of government, but young Calvert learned that his colonists would not be satisfied with fewer liberties than they enjoyed at home or could find in other colonies. Hence, the Lords Baltimore were obliged to give up their charter-given right to initiate all colonial laws, subject only to the advice and consent of the people.

Arriving in 1634, immigrants ignored Calvert's plans for 6,000-acre manors for his relatives and 3,000-acre manors for lesser aristocrats, each to be worked by serflike tenants. The settlers took up their free land, imported as many indentured servants as they could afford, maintained generally peaceful relations with local Indian tribes, grew tobacco on scattered riverfront plantations like their Virginia neighbors, and governed themselves locally as much as possible. Although Maryland grew slowly at first—in 1650, it had a population of only 600—it developed rapidly in the second half of the seventeenth century. By 1700, its population of 33,000 was half that of Virginia.

Daily Life on the Chesapeake

Though immigrants to the Chesapeake Bay region dreamed of bettering the life they had known in England, most found life dismal. Only a minority could marry and rear a family, because marriage had to be deferred until the indenture was completed. And there were three times more men than women. Once made, marriages were fragile. Either husband or wife was likely to succumb to disease within about seven years. The vulnerability of pregnant women to malaria frequently terminated marriages, and death claimed half the children before they reached adulthood. Few children had both parents alive while growing up. Grandparents were almost unknown.

In a society so numerically dominated by men, widows were prized, and they remarried quickly. Such conditions produced complex families, full of stepchildren and stepparents, half-sisters and half-brothers. In the common case of marriage between a widow and a widower, each with children from a previous marriage, the web of family life became particularly complex, and the tensions attending child rearing unusually thick.

The household of Robert Beverley of Middlesex County illustrates the tangled family relationships in this death-filled society. When Beverley married Mary Keeble in 1666, she was a 29-year-old widow who had borne seven children during her first marriage. At least four of them were still alive to join the household of their mother's new husband. They gained five half-brothers and half-sisters during their mother's 12-year marriage to Beverley. When Mary Keeble Beverley died at age 41, her husband quickly remarried a recent widow, Katherine Hone. Beverley's second wife brought her son into the household and in the next nine years produced four more children with Beverley before his death in 1687. Thus, between 1666 and 1687, Beverley had married two widows who bore him nine children and had been stepfather to the eight children his two wives had produced with previous husbands. Not one of these 17 children, from an interlocking set of four marriages, reached adulthood with both a living mother and father.

We think of the churches of the colonial South as handsome, steepled, red brick buildings, but this unpainted clapboard church is typical of the rudimentary buildings erected by early colonists in the Chesapeake region. *(Harold Wickliffe Rose Papers, Yale University Library, New Haven, CT)*

RECOVERING THE PAST

Houses

Homesteading is central to our national experience. For 300 years after the founding of the first colonies, most Americans were involved in taming and settling the land. On every frontier, families faced the tasks of clearing the fields, beginning farming operations, and building shelter for themselves and their live-stock. The kinds of structures they built depended on available materials, their resources and aspirations, and their notions of a "fair" dwelling. The plan of a house and the materials used in its construction re-veal much about the needs, resources, priorities, and values of the people who built it.

By examining archaeological remains of early or-dinary structures and by studying houses that are still standing, historians are reaching new under-standings of the social life of pioneering societies. Since the 1960s, archaeologists and architectural historians have been studying seventeenth-century housing in the Chesapeake Bay and New England regions. They have discovered a familiar sequence of house types—from temporary shanties and lean-tos to rough cabins and simple frame houses to larger and more substantial dwellings of brick and finished timber. This hovel-to-house-to-home pat-tern existed on every frontier, as sodbusters, gold miners, planters, and cattle raisers secured their hold on the land and then struggled to move from subsistence to success.

What is unusual in the findings of the Chesapeake researchers is the discovery that the second phase in the sequence—the use of temporary, rough-built structures—lasted for more than a century. Whereas many New Englanders had rebuilt and extended their temporary clapboard houses into timber-framed, substantial dwellings by the 1680s, Chesa-peake settlers continued to construct small, rickety buildings that had to be repaired continually or abandoned altogether every 10 to 15 years.

The William Boardman house shown below, built around 1687, is an example of the "orderly, fair, and

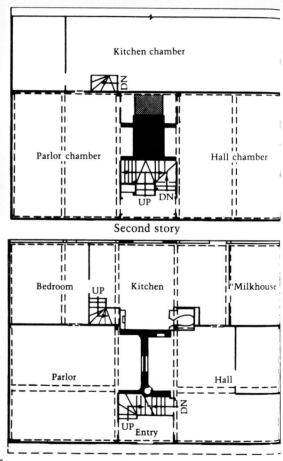

William Boardman house, Saugus, Massachusetts, c. 1687; a floor plan of the house is shown above. *(The Society for the Preservation of New England Antiquities)*

82

well-built" houses of late-seventeenth-century Massachusetts. Its plan shows a typical arrangement of space: the hall, used for cooking, eating, working, and socializing; the parlor; a sleeping room for the parents; and a lean-to for kitchen chores and activities such as dairying. The great central chimney warmed the main downstairs room. Upstairs were two rooms used for both storage and sleeping. As you examine the exterior of the building, note the materials that have been used and the arrangement and treatment of windows, doors, and chimney. What impression of the Boardman family might visitors have as they approached the house? What kind of privacy and comfort did the house provide for family members?

The house shown above is a typical reconstructed tobacco planter's house. It has some of the same features as the Boardman house, for both are products of an English building tradition. But there are some major differences between the two. In the Chesapeake house, the chimney is not built of brick but of mud and wood, and there is no window glass, only small shutters. The exterior is rough, unfinished planking. The placement of doors and windows and the overall dimensions indicate that this house has only one room downstairs and a loft above. The builders of this house clearly enjoyed less privacy and comfort than the Boardmans.

Historians have puzzled over this contrast between the architecture of the two regions. Part of the explanation may lie in the different climatic conditions and different immigration patterns of New England and the Chesapeake. In the southern region, disease killed thousands of settlers in the early decades. The imbalance of men and women produced a stunted and unstable family life, hardly conducive to an emphasis on constructing fine homes. In New England, good health prevailed almost from the beginning, and the family was at the heart of society. It made more sense, in this environment, to make a substantial investment in larger and more permanent houses. Some historians argue, moreover, that the Puritan work ethic impelled New Englanders to build solid homes—a compulsion unknown in the culturally backward, "lazy" South.

Archaeological evidence combined with data recovered from land, tax, and court records, however, suggests another reason for the impermanence of housing in the Chesapeake region. Living in a labor-intensive tobacco world, it is argued, planters large and small economized on everything possible in order to buy as many indentured servants and slaves as they could. Better to live in a shanty and have ten slaves than to have a handsome dwelling and nobody to cultivate the fields. As late as 1775, the author of *American Husbandry* calculated that in setting up a tobacco plantation, five times as much ought to be spent on purchasing 20 black fieldhands as on the "house, offices, and tobacco-house."

Only after the Chesapeake region had emerged from its prolonged era of mortality and gender imbalance and a mixed economy of tobacco, grain, and cattle had replaced the tobacco monoculture did the rebuilding of the region begin. Excavated house sites indicate that this occurred in the period after 1720. New research reveals that the phases of home building and the social and economic history of a society were closely interwoven.

Reflecting on the Past   What do houses today reveal about the resources, economic livelihood, priorities, and values of contemporary Americans? Do class and regional differences in house design continue?

Plagued by horrendous mortality, the Chesapeake remained, for most of the seventeenth century, a land of immigrants rather than a land of settled families. Churches and schools took root very slowly. The large number of indentured servants further destabilized community life. Strangers in a household, they served their time and moved on, or died, replaced by other strangers, purchased fresh from England.

The region's architecture reflected the difficult conditions. Life was too uncertain, the tobacco economy too volatile, and the desire to invest every available shilling in field labor too great for men to build grandly. At first they lived in primitive huts and shanties, hardly more than windbreaks. Even by the early eighteenth century, most Chesapeake families lived in a crude house without interior partitions. Eating, dressing, working, and loving all took place with hardly a semblance of privacy. For nearly two centuries, most ordinary Virginians and Marylanders were "pigg'd lovingly together," as one planter put it. Even prosperous planters did not begin constructing fully framed, substantial homesteads until a century after the colony was founded.

The crudity of life also showed in the household possessions of the Chesapeake colonists. Struggling farmers and tenants were likely to own only a straw mattress, a simple storage chest, and the tools for food preparation and eating—a mortar and pestle to grind corn, knives for butchering, a pot or two for cooking stews and porridges, wooden trenchers and spoons for eating. Most ordinary settlers owned no chairs, dressers, plates, or silverware. Among middling planters, the standard of living was raised only by possession of a flock mattress, coarse earthenware for milk and butter, a few pewter plates and porringers, a frying pan or two, and a few rough tables and chairs. To be near the top of Chesapeake society meant having three or four rooms, sleeping more comfortably, sitting on chairs rather than squatting on the floor, and owning such ordinary decencies as chamber pots, candlesticks, bed linen, a chest of drawers, and a desk. Only a few boasted such luxuries as clocks, books, punch bowls, wine glasses, and imported furniture. Four generations elapsed in the Chesapeake settlements before the frontier quality of life slowly gave way to more refined living.

Bacon's Rebellion Engulfs Virginia

The rough and crooked road that the Chesapeake colonies had followed in the seventeenth century reached an explosive point in 1675–1676 when both a war between the red and white populations and

civil war among the colonizers occurred. Before this ended, hundreds of whites and Indians lay dead in Virginia and Maryland, Virginia's capital of Jamestown lay smoldering, and English troops were crossing the Atlantic to suppress what the king labeled an outright rejection of his authority. This tangled conflict was called Bacon's Rebellion after the headstrong Cambridge-educated planter Nathaniel Bacon, who arrived in Virginia at age 28.

Bacon and many other ambitious young planters detested the Indian policy of Virginia's royal governor, Sir William Berkeley. In 1646, after the second Indian uprising against the Virginians, the Powhatan tribes had been granted exclusive rights to territory beyond the limits of white settlement. Stable Indian relations suited the established planters, some of whom traded profitably with the Indians, but became obnoxious to new settlers. Nor did harmonious conditions please the white ex-indentured servants who hoped for cheap frontier land.

Land hunger and dissatisfaction with declining tobacco prices, rising taxes, and lack of opportunity erupted into violence in the summer of 1675. A group of frontiersmen used an incident with a local tribe as an excuse to attack the Susquehannocks, whose rich land they coveted. Governor Berkeley denounced the attack, but few supported his position. As he explained, he faced "a people where six parts of seven at least are poor, indebted, discontented, and armed." Although badly outnumbered, the Susquehannocks prepared for war. Rumors swept the colony that the Susquehannocks were offering large sums to gain western Indian allies or that New England tribes would support them.

Thirsting for revenge, the Susquehannocks attacked during the winter of 1675–1676 and killed 36 Virginians. That spring, the hot-blooded Nathaniel Bacon became the frontiersmen's leader. Joined by hundreds of runaway servants and some slaves, he attacked friendly and hostile Indians alike. Governor Berkeley refused to sanction these attacks and declared Bacon a rebel, sending 300 militiamen to drag him to Jamestown for trial. Bacon headed into the wilderness for "a more agreeable destiny" and recruited more followers, including many substantial planters. Frontier skirmishes with Indians had turned into civil war.

During the summer of 1676, Bacon's and Berkeley's troops maneuvered, while Bacon's men continued their forays against local Indian tribes. Then Bacon boldly captured and razed Jamestown, obliging Berkeley to flee across Chesapeake Bay.

Virginians at all levels had chafed under Berkeley's rule. High taxes, an increase in the governor's powers

Bacon's Rebellion

In Bacon's Rebellion, Governor Berkeley fled to the Eastern Shore because it was the only part of Virginia strongly loyal to him. Berkeley raised a militia there by promising them tax exemption for 21 years.

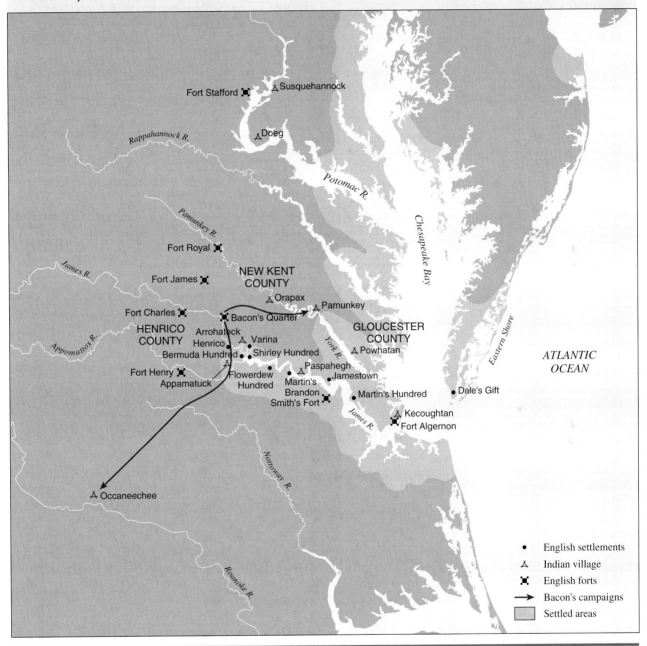

at the expense of local officials, and the monopoly that Berkeley and his friends held on the Indian trade were especially unpopular. This opposition surfaced in the summer of 1676 as Berkeley's and Bacon's troops pursued each other through the wilderness. Berkeley tried to rally public support by holding new assembly elections and extending the vote to all freemen, whether they owned property or not. But the new assembly turned on the governor, passing laws to make government more responsive to the common people and to end rapacious officeholding. It also legalized enslaving Native Americans.

Time was on the governor's side, however. Having crushed the Indians, Bacon's followers began drifting home to tend their crops. Meanwhile, 1,100 royal troops were dispatched from England. By the time they arrived in January 1677, Nathaniel Bacon lay dead of swamp fever and most of his followers had melted away. Berkeley hanged 23 rebel leaders without benefit of trial.

As royal investigators who arrived in 1677 reported, Bacon's followers "seem[ed] to wish and aim at an utter extirpation of the Indians." Even a royal governor could not restrain such men, with their hopes of land ownership and independence.

Hatred of Indians, bred into white society during the war, became a permanent feature of Virginia life. A generation later, in 1711, the legislature spurned the governor's plea for quieting the Indian frontier with educational missions and regulated trade, instead voting military appropriations of £20,000 "for extirpating all Indians without distinction of Friends or Enemys." The remnants of the once populous Powhatan Confederacy lost their last struggle for the world they had known. Now they moved farther west or submitted to a life on the margins of white society as tenant farmers, day laborers, or domestic servants.

After Bacon's Rebellion, an emerging planter aristocracy annulled most of the reform laws of 1676. But the war relieved much of the social tension among white Virginians. Newly available Indian land created fresh opportunities for small planters and former servants. Equally important, Virginians with capital to invest were turning from the impoverished rural villages of England and Ireland to the villages of West Africa to supply their labor needs. This halted the influx of poor white servants who, once free, had formed a discontented mass at the bottom of Chesapeake society. A racial consensus, uniting whites of different ranks in the common pursuit of a prosperous, slave-based economy, began to take shape.

Bacon's Rebellion caused rumblings outside Virginia. Many of his followers fled to North Carolina, joining disgruntled farmers there, who were distressed by recent Indian uprisings, export duties on tobacco, and quitrents controlled by a mercenary elite. Led by George Durant and John Culpeper, they drove the governor from office and briefly seized power.

In Maryland, Protestant settlers chafed under high taxes, quitrents, and officeholders regarded as venal, Catholic, or both. Declining tobacco prices and a fear of Indian attacks increased their touchiness. A month after Bacon razed Jamestown, insurgent small planters tried to seize the Maryland government. Two leaders were hanged for the attempt. In 1681, Josias Fendall and John Coode, "two rank Baconists" according to Lord Baltimore, led another abortive uprising. After their attempt to kidnap the Catholic proprietor failed, the authorities executed Fendall and banished Coode from the colony.

In all three southern colonies, the volatility of late-seventeenth-century life owed much to the region's peculiar social development. Where family formation was retarded by imbalanced gender ratios and fearsome mortality, and where geographic mobility was high, little social cohesion or attachment to community could grow. Missing in the southern colonies were the stabilizing power of mature local institutions, a vision of a larger purpose, and the presence of experienced and responsive political leaders.

The Southern Transition to Slave Labor

English colonists on the mainland of North America at first regarded Native Americans as the obvious source of labor. But European diseases ravaged native societies, and Indians, more at home in the environment than the white colonizers, were difficult to subjugate. Indentured white labor proved the best way to meet the demand for labor during most of the seventeenth century.

However, beginning in 1619, a few Africans entered the Chesapeake colonies to labor in the tobacco fields alongside white servants. But as late as 1671, when some 30,000 slaves toiled in English Barbados, fewer than 3,000 served in Virginia. They were still outnumbered there at least three to one by white indentured servants.

Only in the last quarter of the seventeenth century did the southern labor force begin to change into one in which black slaves performed most of the field labor. Three reasons explain this shift. First, the rising commercial power of England, at the expense of the Spanish and Dutch, swelled English participation in the African slave trade. This allowed southern planters, beginning in the 1680s, to purchase slaves more readily and cheaply than before. Second, the supply of white servants from England began drying up. Third, Bacon's Rebellion, involving rebellious former servants seeking land, led white planters to seek a more pliable labor force. Consequently, by the 1730s, the number of white indentured servants had dwindled to insignificance. Black hands, not white, tilled and harvested Chesapeake tobacco and Carolina rice. Nothing had greater priority in starting a plantation than procuring slave labor.

In enslaving Africans, English colonists in North America merely copied their European rivals in the New World and emulated their countrymen on

ANALYZING HISTORY

THE ATLANTIC SLAVE TRADE

The enslavement of Africans and their forced migration to many parts of the world has no precedent in human history.

Reflecting on the Past To what degree did climate and other environmental factors determine the development of slave-based societies in the Americas? What differences marked the Atlantic slave trade from the slave trade across the Sahara and through the Red Sea and Indian Ocean?

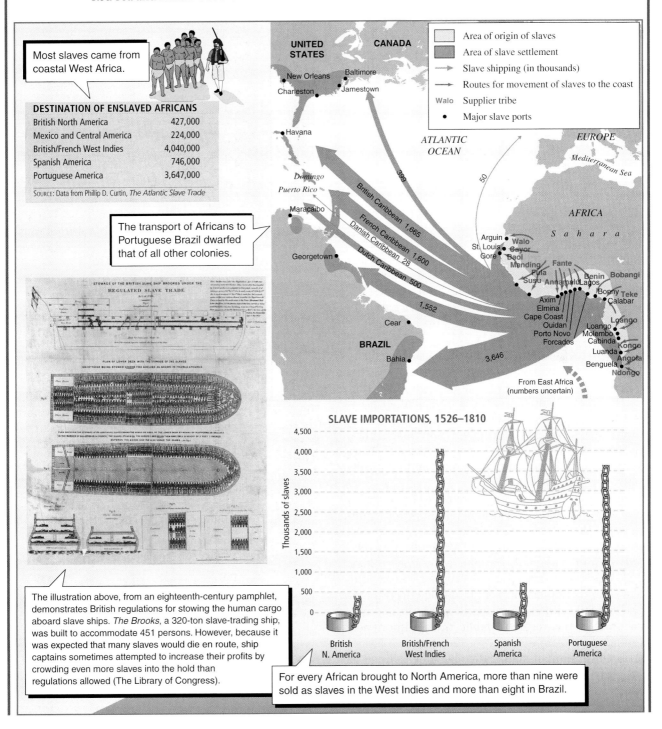

Most slaves came from coastal West Africa.

DESTINATION OF ENSLAVED AFRICANS

British North America	427,000
Mexico and Central America	224,000
British/French West Indies	4,040,000
Spanish America	746,000
Portuguese America	3,647,000

SOURCE: Data from Phillip D. Curtin, *The Atlantic Slave Trade*

The transport of Africans to Portuguese Brazil dwarfed that of all other colonies.

The illustration above, from an eighteenth-century pamphlet, demonstrates British regulations for stowing the human cargo aboard slave ships. *The Brooks*, a 320-ton slave-trading ship, was built to accommodate 451 persons. However, because it was expected that many slaves would die en route, ship captains sometimes attempted to increase their profits by crowding even more slaves into the hold than regulations allowed (The Library of Congress).

SLAVE IMPORTATIONS, 1526–1810

For every African brought to North America, more than nine were sold as slaves in the West Indies and more than eight in Brazil.

Barbados, Jamaica, and the Leeward Islands. There, from the 1630s on, Englishmen had used brutal repression to mold Africans into a sugar- and tobacco-producing slave labor force. Human bondage would later become the subject of intense moral debate, but in the seventeenth century, all but a few whites accepted it without question.

The System of Bondage

The first Africans brought to the American colonies were probably sold as bound servants, who served their term and then, like Anthony and Mary Johnson, gained their freedom. Once free, they could buy land, hire out their labor, and move as they pleased. Their children, like those of white indentured servants, were born free. But gradually, Chesapeake planters began to draw tighter lines around the activities of black servants. By the 1640s, Virginia forbade blacks, free or bound, to carry firearms. In the 1660s, marriages between white women and black servants were banned as "shameful matches" and the "disgrace of our Nation." By the end of the century, when incoming Africans increased from a trickle to a torrent, even the few free blacks found themselves pushed to the margins of society. Slavery, which had existed for centuries in many societies as the lowest social status, was now becoming a caste reserved for those with black skin. Step by step, white society turned the black servant from a low-status human being into a chattel, or commodity.

In this dehumanization of Africans, which the English largely copied from their colonial rivals, the key step was instituting hereditary lifetime service. Once servitude ended only by death, all other privileges quickly vanished. When a mother's slave condition legally passed on to her newborn black infant (which was not the case in slavery in Africa), slavery became self-perpetuating, passing automatically from one generation to the next.

Slavery became not only a system of forced labor but also a pattern of human relationships legitimated by law. By the early eighteenth century, most provincial legislatures limited black rights. Borrowed largely from England's Caribbean colonies, "Black codes" forced Africans into an ever narrower world. Slaves could not testify in court, engage in commercial activity, hold property, participate in the political process, congregate in public, travel without permission, or legally marry or be parents. Nearly stripped of human status, they became defined as property, and, as such the masters' treatment of them was rarely tempered by legal restraints.

This portrait, painted about 1780 after Equiano had purchased his freedom, shows him as a successful Londoner with hair and clothes in the style of a fashionable Englishman. In 1792, Equiano married an English woman and had two daughters with her. He died five years later. *(Robert Albert Memorial Museum, Exeter, Devon England/The Bridgeman Art Library)*

Eliminating slave rights did not eliminate slave resistance. With every African in chains a potential rebel, the rapid increase in the slave population brought anxious demands for strict control and justifications for brutality. "The planters," wrote one Englishman in Jamaica, "do not want to be told that their Negroes are human creatures. If they believe them to be of human kind, they cannot regard them as no better than dogs or horses." Thus occurred one of the great paradoxes of modern history. Many Old World immigrants imagined the Americas as a liberating and regenerating arena. Yet the opportunity to exploit its resources led to a historic process by which masses of Africans were wrenched from their homelands and forced into a system of slavery that could be maintained only by increasing intimidation and brutality.

MASSACHUSETTS AND ITS OFFSPRING

While some English settlers in the reign of James I (1603–1625) scrambled for wealth on the Chesapeake, others in England looked to the wilds of North America as a place to build a tabernacle to

God. The society they fashioned aimed at unity of purpose and utter dedication to reforming the corrupt world. American Puritanism would powerfully affect the nation's history, especially by nurturing a belief in America's special mission in the world. But the "New England way" also represented an attempt to banish diversity on a continent where the arrival of streams of immigrants from around the globe was destined to become the primary phenomenon.

Puritanism in England

England had been officially Protestant since 1558. Many English in the late sixteenth century, however, thought the Church of England was still riddled with Catholic vestiges. Some demanded the end of every taint of "the Bishop of Rome and all his detestable enormities." Because they wished to purify the Church of England, they were dubbed Puritans.

People attracted to the Puritan movement were not only religious reformers but also men and women who hoped to find in religion an antidote to the changes sweeping over English society. The growth of turbulent cities, the increase of wandering poor, rising prices, and accelerating commercial activity made them fear for the future and long for restraining gentry-dominated medieval institutions such as the church, guilds, and local government.

The concept of the individual operating as freely as possible, maximizing both opportunities and personal potential, is at the core of our modern system of beliefs and behavior. But many in Elizabethan England dreaded the crumbling of traditional restraints. They wanted to preserve the ideal of community—the belief that people were bound together by reciprocal rights, obligations, and responsibilities. Symptoms of the "degeneracy of the times" included the defiling of the Sabbath by Maypole dancing, card playing, fiddling, bowling, and all the rest of the roistering and erotic behavior reflected in Shakespeare's dramatic portrayals of "Merrie England." Puritans vowed to reverse the march of disorder by imposing a new discipline.

One part of their plan was a social ethic stressing work as a primary way of serving God. This emphasis on work made the religious quest of every member of society equally worthy. The labor of a mason was just as valuable in God's sight as that of a merchant, and so was his soul. The "work ethic" would banish idleness and impart discipline throughout the community. Second, Puritans organized themselves into religious congregations where each member hoped for personal salvation but also supported all others in their quest. Third, Puritans assumed responsibility for coercing and controlling "unconverted" people around them.

In 1603, when King James VI of Scotland succeeded his cousin, the childless Elizabeth (becoming James I of England), he claimed to be responsible only to God. This led to his collision with the rising power of the Puritans. They occupied the pulpits in hundreds of churches, gained control of several colleges at Oxford and Cambridge, and obtained many seats in Parliament where they challenged the king's power. James responded by harassing them, removing dozens of Puritan ministers from their pulpits, and threatening many others. "I will harry them out of the land," he vowed, "or else do worse."

When Charles I succeeded to the throne in 1625, the situation worsened for Puritans. Determined to strengthen the monarchy and stifle dissent, the king summoned a new Parliament in 1628 and one year later adjourned this venerable body (which was the Puritans' main instrument of reform) when it would not accede to royal demands. The king then appointed William Laud, the bishop of London, to high office and turned him loose on the Puritans, whom Laud called "wasps" and the "most dangerous enemies of the state."

By 1629, as the king began ruling without Parliament, many Puritans were turning their eyes to northern Ireland, Holland, the Caribbean, and, especially, North America. They were convinced that God intended them to carry their religious and social reforms beyond the reach of persecuting authorities. A declining economy added to their discouragement about England, for the depression in the cloth trades was most severe in Puritan strongholds. Many Puritans decided that they should transport a fragment of English society to some distant shore and complete the Protestant Reformation.

Puritan Predecessors in New England

Puritans were not the first European colonizers to reach northeastern North America. A short-lived attempt at settlement in Maine had been made in 1607. Seven years later, the aging Chesapeake war dog John Smith, hired to hunt whales off the North American coast, coined the term "New England" after visiting the area. No permanent settlement took root, however, until the Pilgrims—actually outnumbered by non-Pilgrims—arrived in Plymouth in 1620. Unlike the Puritans who followed, these humble Protestant farmers did not expect to convert a sinful world. Rather, they wanted to be left alone to

The reconstruction of the settlement at Plymouth resists romanticizing the past as is the case with so many other historical reconstructions. Here we see re-enactors working with tools of the early seventeenth century amid a row of houses leading down to the waterfront. *(Plimoth Plantation)*

realize their radical vision of a pure and primitive life. Instead of reforming the Church of England, they left it and hence were called Separatists. They had first fled from England to Amsterdam in 1608, then to Leyden when they found the commercial capital of Holland too corrupt, and, finally, in 1620, to North America.

Arriving at Cape Cod in November 1620, the Pilgrims were weakened by a stormy nine-week voyage and were ill-prepared for the harsh winter ahead. Misled by John Smith's glowing report of a warm, fertile country, they discovered instead a severe climate and a rockbound coast. By the following spring, half the *Mayflower* passengers were dead, including 13 of the 18 married women.

The survivors, led by the staunch William Bradford, settled at Plymouth. Squabbles soon erupted with local Indians, whom Bradford considered "savage and brutish men, which range up and down, little otherwise than the wild beasts." In 1622,

they found themselves nearly overwhelmed by the arrival of 60 non-Pilgrims, sent out by the London Company, which had helped the Pilgrims finance their colony. For two generations, the Pilgrims tilled the soil, fished, and tried to keep intact their religious vision. But with the much larger Puritan migration that began in 1630, the Pilgrim villages nestled around Cape Cod Bay became a backwater of the thriving, populous Massachusetts Bay Colony, which absorbed them in 1691.

Errand into the Wilderness

In 11 ships, about 1,000 Puritans set out from England in 1630 for the Promised Land—the vanguard of a movement that by 1642 brought about 18,000 colonizers to New England. Led by John Winthrop, a talented, Cambridge-educated member of the English gentry, they operated under a charter from the king to the Puritan-controlled Massachusetts Bay Company. The Puritans set about building their utopia convinced they were carrying out a divine task. "God hath sifted a nation," wrote one Puritan, "that he might send choice grain into this wilderness."

Their intention was to establish communities of pure Christians who collectively swore a covenant with God. Puritan leaders agreed to punish harshly civil and religious transgressors. Dreaming of homogeneous communities where the good of the group outweighed individual interests, Winthrop counseled that "We must delight in each other, make others' conditions our own, rejoice together, mourn together, labor and suffer together."

Puritans willingly gave up freedoms that other English settlers sought. An ideology of rebellion in England, Puritanism in North America became an ideology of control—and of a powerful mission that is still part of a distinctive American perspective. As Winthrop reminded the first settlers, "we shall be as a city upon a hill [and] the eyes of all people are upon us."

As in Plymouth and Virginia, the first winter tested the strongest souls. More than 200 of the first 700 settlers perished, and 100 others, disillusioned and sickened by the forbidding climate, soon returned to England. But Puritans kept coming, settling along the rivers that emptied into Massachusetts Bay. A few years later, they pushed south into what became Connecticut and Rhode Island, as well as northward along the rocky coast.

Motivated by their militant work ethic and sense of mission, and led by men experienced in local government, law, and exhortation, the Puritans thrived. The early leaders of Virginia were soldiers of fortune or roughneck adventurers with predatory instincts, men who had no families or had left them at home; ordinary Chesapeake settlers were mostly young men with little stake in English society who sold their labor to cross the Atlantic. But the early leaders in Massachusetts were university-trained ministers, experienced members of the lesser gentry, and men with a compulsion to fulfill God's prophecy for New England. Most ordinary settlers came as free men and women in families. Artisans and farmers from the middle ranks of English society, they established tight-knit communities in which, from the outset, the brutal exploitation of labor rampant in the Chesapeake had no place.

Relying mostly on free labor, the Puritans built an economy based on agriculture, fishing, timbering, and trading for beaver furs with local Indians. Even before leaving England, the directors of the Massachusetts Bay Company transformed their

Reverend William Ames, pictured here, was one of the Puritans' most respected theologians. His portrait was painted in the Netherlands, where he was a professor at the University of Franeker. When his widow arrived in Massachusetts in 1637 with her children, she had the portrait with her. Ames has one hand over his heart, the other grasps a paper—perhaps a sermon—and gloves. *(Courtesy of the Harvard University Portrait Collection, Gift of Ephraim Hyde to Harvard College [#H043])*

commercial charter into a rudimentary government. In North America, they laid the foundations of self-government. Free male church members annually elected a governor and deputies from each town, who formed one house of a colonial legislature, the General Court. The other house was composed of the governor's assistants, later to be called councillors. Consent of both houses was required to pass laws.

The Puritans also established the first printing press in the English colonies and founded Harvard College, which opened its doors in 1636 to train clergymen. The Puritan leaders also launched a brave attempt in 1642 to create a tax-supported school system, open to all wanting an education.

In spite of these accomplishments, the Puritan colony suffered many of the tensions besetting people bent on human perfection. Nor did Puritans prove any better at reaching an accommodation with the Native Americans than their less pious countrymen on the Chesapeake. Surrounded by seemingly boundless land, Puritans found it difficult to stifle acquisitive instincts and to keep families confined in compact communities. "An over-eager desire after the world," wrote an early leader, "has so seized on the spirits of many as if the Lord had no farther work for his people to do, but every bird to feather his own nest." Those remaining at the nerve center in Boston agitated for broader political rights and even briefly ousted Winthrop as governor in 1635, when the colony's clergy backed the stiff-necked Thomas Dudley. After a few years, Governor Winthrop wondered if the Puritans had not gone "from the snare to the pit."

Winthrop's troubles multiplied in 1633 when Salem's Puritan minister, Roger Williams, began to voice disturbing opinions. The contentious and visionary young man argued that the Massachusetts Puritans were not truly pure because they would not completely separate from the polluted Church of England (which most Puritans still hoped to reform). Williams also denounced mandatory worship, which he said "stinks in God's nostrils," and argued that government officials should not interfere with religious matters but confine themselves to civil affairs. "Coerced religion," he warned, "on good days produces hypocrites, on bad days rivers of blood." Today honored as the earliest spokesman for the separation of church and state, Williams in 1633 seemed to strike at the heart of the Bible commonwealth, whose leaders regarded civil and religious affairs as inseparable. Williams also charged the Puritans with illegally intruding on Indian land.

For two years, Puritan leaders could not quiet the determined young Williams. Convinced that he would split the colony into competing religious groups and undermine authority, the magistrates vowed to deport him to England. Warned by Winthrop, Williams fled southward through winter snow with a small band of followers to found Providence in what would become Rhode Island.

Even as they were driving Williams out, the Puritan authorities confronted another threat: a magnetic woman of extraordinary talent and intellect. Arriving in 1634 with her husband and seven children, Anne Hutchinson was a devout Puritan who quickly gained respect among Boston's women as a midwife, healer, and spiritual counselor. She soon began to discuss religion, suggesting that the "holy spirit" was absent in the preaching of some ministers. Before long Hutchinson was leading a movement labeled *antinomianism*, which stressed the mystical nature of God's free gift of grace while discounting the efforts the individual could make to gain salvation.

No likeness of Anne Hutchinson was ever painted, so her face in this sculpture standing outside the Massachusetts Statehouse in downtown Boston is entirely the work of the artist. The monument was erected in 1922. The sculptor, Cyrus E. Dallin, is famous for his "Appeal to the Great Spirit," an Indian figure showing desperation but defiance, much like Anne Hutchinson. *(Kevin Fleming/Corbis)*

By 1636, Boston was dividing into two camps—those who followed the male clergy and those drawn to the theological views of a gifted though untrained woman without official standing. Her followers included most of the community's malcontents—merchants and artisans who chafed under the price controls the magistrates imposed in 1635 to stop inflation, young people resisting the rigid rule of their elders, and women disgruntled by male authority. Hutchinson doubly offended the male leaders of the colony because she boldly stepped outside the subordinate position expected of women. "The weaker sex" set her up as a "priest" and "thronged" after her, wrote one male leader. Another described a "clamour" in Boston that "New England men . . . usurp over their wives and keep them in servile subjection."

Determined to remove this thorn from their sides, the clergy and magistrates put Hutchinson on trial in 1637. After long interrogations, they convicted her of sedition and contempt in a civil trial and banished her from the colony "as a woman not fit for our society." Six months later, the Boston church excommunicated her for preaching 82 erroneous theological opinions. She had "highly transgressed and offended and troubled the church," pronounced the presiding clergyman, and "therefore in the name of our Lord Jesus Christ, I do cast you out and deliver you up to Satan and account you from this time forth to be a heathen and a leper." In the last month of her eighth pregnancy, Hutchinson, with a band of supporters, followed Roger Williams's route to Rhode Island.

Ideas proved harder to banish. The magistrates could never enforce uniformity of belief nor curb the appetite for land. Growth, geographic expansion, and commerce with the outside world all eroded the ideal of integrated, self-contained communities vibrant with piety. Leaders never wearied of reminding Puritan settlers that the "care of the public must oversway all private respects." But they faced the nearly impossible task of containing land-hungry immigrants in an expansive region. By 1636, groups of Puritans had swarmed not only to Rhode Island but also to Hartford and New Haven, where Thomas Hooker and John Davenport led new Puritan settlements in what became Connecticut.

New Englanders and Indians

The charter of the Massachusetts Bay Company spoke of converting "the natives to the knowledge and obedience of the only true God and Saviour of mankind and the Christian faith." But the instructions that Governor John Winthrop carried from

Early New England

Maine and New Hampshire became the frontier to which New England settlers migrated when their towns and farmlands became too crowded.

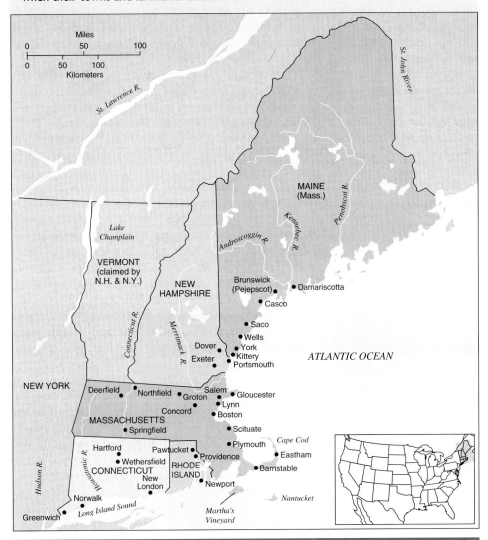

England reveal other Puritan thoughts about the native inhabitants. According to Winthrop's orders, all men were to receive training in the use of firearms, a reversal of the sixteenth-century English policy of disarming the citizenry in order to quell public disorders. New England magistrates prohibited Indians from entering Puritan towns and threatened to deport any colonist selling arms to an Indian or instructing one in their use.

Only sporadic conflict with local tribes occurred at first because disease had left much of New England vacant. In 1616, visiting English fishermen had triggered a ferocious outbreak of respiratory viruses and smallpox that wiped out three-quarters of some 125,000 Indians. Five years later, an

Englishman exploring the area described walking through a forest where human skeletons covered the ground.

The Puritans believed that God had intervened on their side, especially when smallpox returned in 1633, killing thousands more natives and allowing new settlers to find land. Many surviving Indians welcomed the Puritans because they now had surplus land and through trade hoped to gain English protection against tribal enemies to the north.

The settler pressure for new land, however, soon reached into areas untouched by disease. Land hunger mingled with the Puritan sense of mission made an explosive mix. To a people brimming with messianic zeal, the heathen Indians represented a mocking challenge to the building of a religious commonwealth that would "shine as a beacon" back to decadent England. Puritans believed that God would blame them for not civilizing and Christianizing the natives and would punish them with his wrath.

Making the "savages" of New England strictly accountable to the ordinances that governed white behavior was part of this quest for fulfilling their mission. They succeeded with the smaller, disease-ravaged tribes of eastern Massachusetts. But their attempts to control the stronger Pequots led to the bloody war in 1637. The Puritan victory assured English domination over all the tribes of southern New England except the powerful Wampanoags and Narragansetts of Rhode Island and removed the last obstacle to expansion into the Connecticut River valley. Missionary work, led by John Eliot, began among the remnant tribes in the 1640s. After a decade of effort, about 1,000 Indians had been settled in four "praying villages," learning to live according to the white man's ways.

The Web of Village Life

Unlike the dispersed Chesapeake tobacco planters, the Puritans established small, tightly settled villages that were vital centers of life. Most were "open field" agricultural communities where farmers trudged out from the village each morning to cultivate narrow strips radiating out from the town. They grazed their cattle on common meadow and cut firewood on common woodland. In other towns, Puritans employed the "closed field" system of self-contained farms that they had known at home. Both systems re-created common English patterns of agriculture.

In both systems, families lived close together in towns built around a common, with a meetinghouse and tavern. These small, communal villages kept families in close touch so that each could be alert not only to its own transgressions, but also to those of its neighbors. "In a multitude of counsellors is safety," Puritan ministers were fond of advising, and the little villages of 50 to 100 families perfectly served the need for moral surveillance, or "holy watching." To achieve godliness and communal unity, Puritans also prohibited single men and women from living by themselves, beyond patriarchal authority and group observation. Left to themselves, men and women would stray from the path, for, as Thomas Hooker put it, "every natural man and woman is born full of sin, as full as a toad of poison." Virginia planters counted the absence of restraint as a blessing. New Englanders feared it as the Devil.

At the center of every Puritan village stood the meetinghouse. These plain wooden structures, sometimes called "Lord's barns," gathered in every soul in the village, twice a week. No man stood higher in the community than the minister. He was the spiritual leader in these small, family-based, community-oriented settlements, which viewed life as a Christian pilgrimage.

The unique Puritan mixture of strict authority and incipient democracy, of hierarchy and equality, can be seen in the way the Massachusetts town distributed land and devised local government. Each town was founded by a grant of the General Court. Only groups of Puritans who had signed a compact signifying their unity of purpose received settlement grants. "We shall by all means," read the town of Dedham's covenant, "labor to keep off from us such as are contrary minded, and receive only such unto us as may be probably of one heart with us."

After receiving a grant, townsmen met to parcel out land. They awarded individual grants according to the size of a man's household, his wealth, and his usefulness to the church and town. Such a system perpetuated existing differences in wealth and status. Yet some towns wrote language into their covenants that to the modern ear has an almost socialistic ring. "From each according to his ability to each as need shall require," read one. But it was not socialism that the Puritans had in mind; rather, they believed that the community's welfare transcended individual ambitions or accomplishments and that unity demanded limits on the accumulation of wealth. Every family should have enough land to sustain it, and prospering men were expected to use their wealth for the community's benefit. Repairing the meetinghouse, building a school, aiding a widowed neighbor—such were the proper uses of wealth.

Having felt the sting of centralized power in church and state, Puritans emphasized local exercise of authority. Until 1684, only male church members could vote, and as the proportion of males who were church members declined, so did the proportion of men who could vote. These voters elected selectmen, who allocated land, passed local taxes, and settled disputes. Once a year, all townsmen gathered for the town meeting, which Thomas Jefferson later called the "wisest invention ever devised by the wit of man for the perfect exercise of self-government." At the town meeting, the citizens selected town officers for the next year and decided matters large and small.

The appointment of many citizens to minor offices—surveyors of hemp, informers about deer, purchasers of grain, town criers, measurers of salt, fence viewers, and many others—bred the tradition of local government. All officeholders were annually subject to electoral approval, and about one of every ten adult males in many towns was selected each year for some office, large or small. In New England, nobody could acquire a reputation for sobriety and industry without finding himself elected to a local post.

The predominance of families also lent cohesiveness to Puritan village life. Strengthening this family orientation was the remarkably healthy environment of the Puritans' "New Israel." Whereas the germs carried by English colonizers devastated neighboring Indian societies, the effect on the newcomers of entering a new environment was the opposite. The low density of settlement prevented infectious diseases from spreading, and the isolation of the New England villages from the avenues of Atlantic commerce, along which diseases as well as cargo flowed, minimized biological hazards.

The result was a spectacular natural increase in the population and a life span unknown in Europe. At a time when the population of western Europe was barely growing—deaths almost equaled births—the population of New England, discounting new immigrants, doubled every 27 years. The difference was not a higher birthrate. New England women typically bore about seven children during the course of a marriage, but this barely exceeded the European norm. The crucial factor was that chances for survival after birth were far greater than in England because of the healthier climate and better diet. In most of Europe, only half the babies born lived long enough to produce children themselves. Life expectancy for the population at large was less than 40 years. In New England, nearly 90 percent of the infants born in the seventeenth century survived to marriageable age, and life expectancy exceeded 60 years—longer than for the American population as a whole at any time until the early twentieth century. About 25,000 people immigrated to New England in the seventeenth century, but by 1700, they had produced a population of 100,000. By contrast, some 75,000 immigrants to the Chesapeake colonies had yielded a population of only about 70,000 by the end of the century.

Women played a vital role in this family-centered society. In addition to being a wife, mother, and housekeeper, the puritan woman also kept the vegetable garden; salted and smoked meats; preserved vegetables and dairy products; and spun yarn, wove cloth, and made clothes.

The presence of women and a stable family life shaped New England's regional architecture. As communities formed, the Puritans converted early

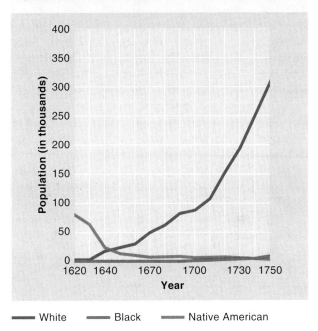

Population of the New England Colonies, 1620–1750

The fact that white population growth was far more rapid in New England than in the Chesapeake region reflected higher birthrates, a healthier environment, and a reliance on free labor.

Source: U.S. Bureau of the Census.

economic gains into more substantial housing rather than investing in bound labor as Chesapeake colonists did, which retarded family formation and rendered the economy unstable. In New England, well-constructed one-room houses with sleeping lofts quickly replaced the early "wigwams, huts, and hovels." Families then added parlors and lean-to kitchens as soon as they could. Within a half century, New England immigrants accomplished a general rebuilding of their living structures, whereas the Chesapeake lagged far behind.

A final binding element in Puritan communities was the stress on literacy and education, eventually to become a hallmark of American society. Placing religion at the center of their lives, Puritans emphasized the ability to read catechisms, psalmbooks, and especially the Bible. In literacy, Puritans saw guarantees that they would not succumb to the savagery they perceived all around them in the new land. Through education, they could preserve their central values.

Though eager to be left alone, Puritans could not escape events in England. In 1642, King Charles I pushed England into revolution by violating the country's customary constitution and continuing earlier attacks against Puritans. By 1649, the ensuing civil war climaxed with the trial and beheading of the king. Thereafter, during the so-called Commonwealth period (1649–1660), Puritans in England could complete the reform of religion and society at home. Meanwhile, migration to New England abruptly ceased.

The 20,000 English immigrants who had come to New England by 1649 were scattered from Maine to Long Island. Governor Winthrop of Massachusetts and Roger Williams of Rhode Island deplored this dispersion and condemned the "depraved appetite" for new and better land. Yet, in a terrain so rock-strewn that its pastures were said to produce Yankee sheep with sharpened noses, it was natural that farmers should seek better plow land.

Funeral testimonies, like this one, were cheaply printed as broadsides and were passed out to mourners. When Lydia Minot died in 1667, giving birth to her sixth child, she was memorialized with anagrams and acrostics—popular literary exercises in the seventeenth century. Note the hourglass, coffin, and shovel, which are all symbols of death, at the middle of the broadside. *(Courtesy of the Massachussets Historical Society)*

In 1643, to combat the problems of dispersion, Puritan leaders established the Confederation of New England, intended to coordinate government among the various Puritan settlements (Rhode Island was pointedly excluded) and to provide more effective defense against the French, the Dutch, and the Indians. This first American attempt at federalism functioned fitfully for a generation and then dissolved.

Although the Puritans fashioned stable communities, developed the economy, and constructed effective government, their leaders, as early as the 1640s, complained that the founding vision of Massachusetts Bay was faltering. Material concerns seemed to transcend religious commitment; the individual prevailed over the community. In 1638, the General Court declared a day of humiliation and prayer to atone for the colony's "excess idleness and contempt of authority." A generation later, the synod of 1679—a convention of Puritan Churches—cried out that the "church, the commonwealth and the family are being destroyed by self-assertion." If social diversity increased and the religious zeal of the founding generation waned, that was only to be expected. One second-generation Bay colonist put the matter bluntly. His minister had noticed his absence in church and found him later that day at the docks, unloading a boatload of cod. "Why were you not in church this morning?" asked the clergyman. Back came the reply: "My father came here for religion, but I came for fish."

King Philip's War in New England

For religious leaders concerned about declining piety, continued difficulties with Indian tribes of southern New England signaled new signs of God's displeasure. The Wampanoags and Narragansetts, whose fertile land lay within the boundaries of Plymouth and Rhode Island, tried to keep their distance from the Puritans. But the New Englanders coveted Indian territories. As they quarreled among themselves over provincial boundaries, they gradually reduced the Indians' land base.

By the 1670s, when New England's population had grown to about 50,000, younger Indians brooded over their situation. Their leader, Metacomet (called King Philip by the English), was the son of Massasoit, the Wampanoag chief who had allied with the first Plymouth settlers in 1620. Metacomet had watched his older brother preside over the deteriorating position of his people after their father's death in 1661. Becoming chief in his turn, Metacomet faced one humiliating challenge after another, climaxing in 1671, when Plymouth forced him to surrender a large

Three of Arthur and Joanna Mason's five children were captured in this 1670 painting. The nine-year-old boy on the left holds a silver-headed walking stick, signifying his status as male heir. His six-year-old sister in the middle holds a yellow fan and red and yellow ribbons. The four-year-old sister to the right holds a rose, which Puritans used as a symbol of innocence associated with childhood. *(Fine Arts Museum of San Francisco, Gift of Mr. and Mrs. John Rockefeller 3rd, 1979 .7.3)*

stock of guns and accept his people's subjection to English law. Metacomet began organizing a resistance movement. Insurrection was triggered in 1675 by the execution of three Wampanoags for murdering John Sassamon, a Christianized Indian educated at Harvard who had allegedly warned Plymouth of an impending Indian attack.

But a deeper cause of the war was the rising anger of the young Wampanoag males. As would happen repeatedly in the next two centuries, younger Native Americans refused to imitate their fathers, who had permitted the colonizers' encroachments and abridgment of their sovereignty. Rather than submit further, they attempted a pan-Indian offensive against an ever-stronger intruder. For the young tribesmen, revitalization of their ancient culture through war became as important a goal as defeating the enemy.

In the summer of 1675, the Wampanoags unleashed daring hit-and-run attacks on villages in the Plymouth colony. By autumn, many New England tribes, including the powerful Narragansetts, had joined Metacomet. Towns all along the frontier reeled under Indian attacks. By November, Indian warriors had devastated the entire upper Connecticut River valley, and by March 1676, they were less than 20 miles from Boston and

Providence. As assumptions about English military superiority faded, New England officials passed America's first draft laws. Widespread draft evasion, with eligible men between ages 16 and 60 "skulking from one town to another," and friction among the New England colonies hampered a counteroffensive.

Metacomet's offensive faltered in the spring of 1676, sapped by food shortages and disease. The powerful Mohawks' refusal to join the New England tribes was an additional blow. Then Metacomet fell in a battle near the Wampanoag village where the war had begun. The head of this "hell-hound, fiend, serpent, caitiff and dog," as one colonial leader branded him, was displayed in Plymouth for 25 years.

At war's end, several thousand colonists and perhaps twice as many Indians lay dead. Of some 90 Puritan towns, 52 had been attacked and 13 completely destroyed. Some 1,200 homes lay in ruins and 8,000 cattle were dead. The estimated cost of the war exceeded the value of all personal property in New England. Not for 40 years would the frontier advance beyond the line it had reached in 1675. Indian towns were devastated even more completely, including several inhabited by "praying Indians" who had converted to Christianity and allied with the whites. An entire generation of young men had been nearly annihilated. Many of the survivors, including Metacomet's wife and son, were sold into slavery in the West Indies.

Slavery in New England

The Wampanoag captives sold as slaves in the West Indies continued New England's involvement in the dirty business of slavery. Coerced labor never became the foundation of New England's workforce, for labor-intensive crops such as sugar and rice would not grow in colder climates. Slavey took root mainly in the cities, where slaves worked as artisans and domestic servants.

But northern colonial economies became enmeshed in the Atlantic commercial network, which depended on slavery and the slave trade. New England's merchants eagerly pursued profits in the slave trade as early as the 1640s. By 1676, New England slavers were packing their holds with slaves from Madagascar, off the coast of East Africa, and transporting them 6,000 miles to the western side of the Atlantic. By 1750, half the merchant fleet of Newport, Rhode Island, reaped profits from carrying human cargo. In New York and Philadelphia, building and outfitting slave vessels proved profitable.

New England's involvement in the international slave trade deepened with the growth of its seaports as centers for distilling rum—the "hot, hellish and terrible liquor." Made from West Indian sugar, rum became one of the principal commodities traded for slaves on the African coast. As the number of slaves in the Caribbean multiplied—from about 50,000 in 1650 to 500,000 in 1750—New England's large fish-

King Philip's War, 1675–1676

The home base of Metacomet, or King Philip, was within the Plymouth Colony, but he carried the war to the westernmost Massachusetts towns.

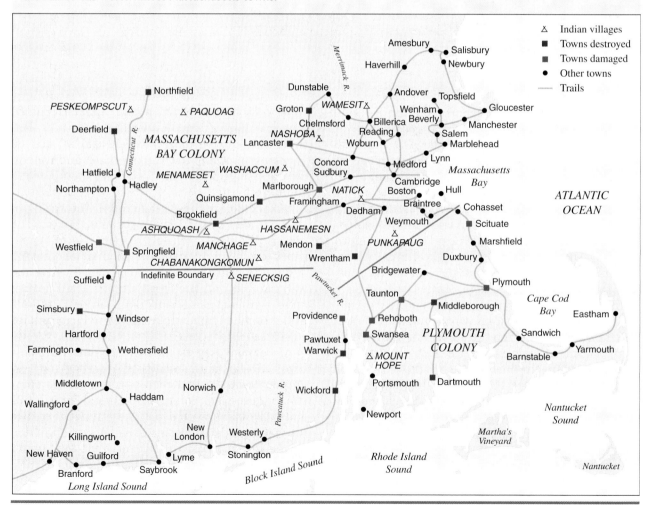

ing fleet found important markets for their cod. Wheat from the middle colonies and barrel staves and hoops from North Carolina also serviced the slave-based West Indies economy. In short, every North American colony participated in the slave business.

FROM THE ST. LAWRENCE TO THE HUDSON

The New Englanders were not the only European settlers in the northern region, for both France and Holland created colonies there. While English settlers founded Jamestown, the French were settling Canada, where they had failed in the 1540s.

France's America

Henry IV, the first strong French king in half a century, sent Samuel de Champlain to explore deep into the territory even before the English had obtained a foothold on the Chesapeake. Champlain established a small settlement in Port Royal, Acadia (later Nova Scotia), in 1604 and another at Quebec in 1608. French trading with Indians for furs had already begun in Newfoundland, and Champlain's settlers hoped to keep making these easy profits. But the holders of the fur monopoly in France did not encourage immigration to the colony, fearing that settlement would reduce the forests from which the furs were harvested. New France therefore remained so lightly populated that English marauders easily seized and held Quebec from 1629 to 1632.

In 1609–1610, Champlain allied with the Algonquian Indians of the St. Lawrence region in attacking their Iroquois enemies to the south, earning their enmity. This drove the Iroquois to trade furs for European goods with the Dutch on the Hudson River; when the Iroquois exhausted the furs of their own territory, they turned north and west, determined to seize the forest-rich resources from the Hurons, French allies in the Great Lakes region.

When the Iroquois descended on them in the 1640s, the Hurons were already decimated by a decade of epidemics that spread among them as Jesuit priests entered their villages. In the "beaver wars" of the 1640s and 1650s, the Iroquois used Dutch guns to attack Huron parties carrying beaver pelts to the French. By mid-century, Iroquois attacks had scattered the Hurons, all but ending the French fur trade and reducing the Jesuit influence to a few villages of Christianized Hurons.

The bitterness bred in these years colored future colonial warfare, driving the Iroquois to ally with the English against the French. But for the time being, in the mid-seventeenth century, the English remained unhindered by the beleaguered French colonists, who numbered only about 400.

England Challenges the Dutch

By 1650, the Chesapeake and New England regions each contained about 50,000 settlers. Between them lay the mid-Atlantic area controlled by the Dutch, who planted a small colony named New Netherland at the mouth of the Hudson River in 1624 and in the next four decades extended their control to the Connecticut and Delaware river valleys. South of the Chesapeake lay a vast territory where only the Spanish, from their mission frontier in Florida, challenged the power of Native American tribes.

Although for generations they had been the Protestant bulwarks in a mostly Catholic Europe, England and Holland became bitter commercial rivals in the mid-seventeenth century. By the time the Puritans arrived in New England, the Dutch had become the mightiest carriers of seaborne commerce in western Europe. By one contemporary estimate, Holland owned 16,000 of Europe's 20,000 merchant ships. The Dutch had also muscled in on Spanish and Portuguese transatlantic commerce, trading illegally with Iberian colonists who gladly violated their government's commercial policies to obtain cloth and slaves more cheaply. By 1650, the Dutch had temporarily overwhelmed the Portuguese in Brazil, and soon their vast trading empire reached the East Indies, Ceylon, India, and Formosa (now Taiwan). The best shipbuilders, mariners, and businessmen in western Europe, they validated the dictum of Sir Walter Raleigh that "whosoever commands the sea commands the trade; whosoever commands the trade of the world commands the riches of the world, and consequently the world itself."

In North America, the Dutch West India Company's New Netherland colony was small, profitable, and multicultural. Agents fanned out from Fort Orange (Albany) and New Amsterdam (New York City) into the Hudson, Connecticut, and Delaware river valleys. There they established a lucrative fur trade with local tribes by hooking into the sophisticated trading network of the Iroquois Confederacy, which stretched to the Great Lakes. The Iroquois welcomed the Dutch presence, who were few in number, did not have voracious appetites for land, and willingly exchanged desirable goods for the pelts of animals plentiful in the vast Iroquois territory. At Albany, the center of the Dutch–Iroquois trade, relations remained peaceful

The fort at the tip of Manhattan, flying an English flag, shows prominently in this 1664 map of Dutch New Amsterdam just after it had been bloodlessly conquered by a small English fleet. The park-filled city and the Governor's garden fronting on the Hudson River were separated by a wall from the farmlands of "upper" Manhattan. *(By Permission of the British Library)*

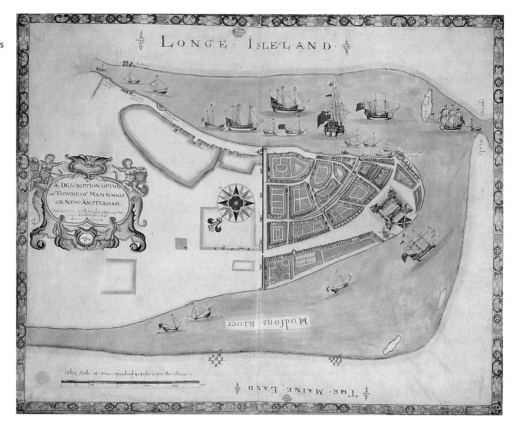

and profitable for several generations because both peoples served each other's needs.

Although the Dutch never settled more than 10,000 people in their mid-Atlantic colonies, their commercial and naval powers were impressive. The Virginians learned this in 1667 when brazen Dutch raiders captured 20 tobacco ships on the James River and confiscated virtually the entire tobacco crop for that year.

By 1650, England was ready to challenge Dutch maritime supremacy. War broke out three times between 1652 and 1675, as the two Protestant nations competed to control the emerging worldwide capitalist economy. In the second and third wars, New Netherland became an easy target for the English. They captured it in 1664 and then, after it fell to the Dutch in 1673, recaptured it almost immediately. By 1675, the Dutch had been permanently dislodged from the North American mainland. But they remained mighty commercial competitors of the English around the world.

New Netherland—where from the beginning Dutch, French Huguenots, Walloons from present-day Belgium, Swedes, Portuguese, Finns, English, refugee Portuguese Jews from Brazil, and Africans had commingled in a babel of languages and religions—now became New York, so named because

From her expensive dress, pearls, and exquisite headdress, one would never know that Catharina Ten Eyck van Zandt (1692–1772) was the daughter and granddaughter of Dutch shoemakers and married to a craftsman who made wooden pulleys for New York's ship captains. Van Zandt married at age 18 and bore 15 children. *(© Collection of the New-York Historical Society [26353])*

Charles II gave it (along with the former Dutch colonies on the Delaware River) to his brother the duke of York, later King James II. Under English rule, the Dutch colonists remained ethnically distinct for several generations, clinging to their language, their Dutch Reformed Calvinist churches, and their architecture. In time, however, English immigrants overwhelmed the Dutch, and gradual intermarriage among the Dutch, the French Huguenots (Protestants), and the English—the three main groups—diluted ethnic loyalties. But New York retained its polyglot, religiously tolerant character, and its people never allowed religious concerns or utopian plans to interfere with the pragmatic conduct of business.

PROPRIETARY CAROLINA: A RESTORATION REWARD

In 1663, three years after he was restored to his father's throne, England's Charles II granted a vast territory named Carolina to a group of supporters during his years of exile. Its boundaries extended from Virginia southward to central Florida and westward to the Pacific. Within this potential empire, eight London-based proprietors, including several involved in Barbados sugar plantations, gained governmental powers and semifeudal rights to the land. The system of governance planned for Carolina had both feudal and modern features. To lure settlers, the proprietors promised religious freedom and offered land free for the asking. But onto this generous land offer they grafted a scheme for a semimedieval government in which they, their deputies, and a few noblemen would monopolize political power. Reacting to a generation of revolutionary turbulence in England, they designed Carolina as a model of social and political stability in which a hereditary aristocracy would check boisterous small landholders.

Carolina realities bore faint resemblance to these hopes. The rugged sugar and tobacco planters who streamed in from Barbados and Virginia, where depressed economic conditions made a new beginning seem attractive, claimed their 150 acres of free land, as well as additional acreage for each family member or servant they brought. But they ignored proprietary regulations about settling in compact rectangular patterns and reserving two-fifths of every county for an appointed nobility. In government, they also did as they pleased. Meeting in assembly for the first time in 1670, they refused to accept the proprietors' Fundamental Constitutions of 1667 and ignored orders from the proprietors' governor. Most of the settlers already knew how to run a slave society from having lived in Barbados, and from that experience they shaped local government.

The Indian Debacle

Carolina was the most elaborately planned colony in English history but the least successful in achieving harmony. The London proprietors had intended otherwise. Mindful of the violence that had plagued other settlements, they projected a well-regulated Indian trade, run exclusively by their appointed agents. But the aggressive settlers from the West Indies and the Chesapeake flouted all this. Those from Barbados, accustomed to exploiting African slave labor, saw that if the major tribes of the Southeast—the Cherokee, Creek, and Choctaw—could be drawn into trade, the planters might reap vast wealth, which the Spanish in Florida had failed to tap.

It was not the beaver that beckoned in the Carolina Indian trade, as in the North, but the deerskin, much desired in Europe for making warm, durable clothing. While the Carolina colonists found the natives eager to barter for European trade goods, the business soon turned into a trade in Indian slaves. To the consternation of the London proprietors, capturing Indians for sale in New England and the West Indies became the cornerstone of commerce in Carolina in the early years, plunging the colony into a series of wars. Planters and merchants selected a tribe, armed it, and rewarded it handsomely for bringing in enemy captives. But even strong tribes found that after they had used English guns to enslave their weaker neighbors, they themselves were scheduled for elimination. The colonists claimed that "thinning the barbarous Indian natives" was needed to make room for white settlement, and the "thinning" was so thorough that by the early eighteenth century the two main tribes of the coastal plain, the Westos and the Savannahs, were nearly extinct.

Early Carolina Society

Carolina's fertile land and warm climate convinced many that it was a "Country so delicious, pleasant, and fruitful that were it cultivated doubtless it would prove a second Paradize." In came Barbadians, Swiss, Scots, Irish, French Huguenots, English, and migrants from northern colonies. But far from creating paradise, this ethnically and religiously diverse people clashed abrasively in an atmosphere of fierce competition, ecological exploitation, brutal race relations, and stunted social institutions. Decimating the coastal Indians made it easier to expand the initial settlements around

Restoration Colonies: New York, the Jerseys, Pennsylvania, and the Carolinas

After founding the Restoration colonies from the 1660s to the 1680s, England's colonists claimed the entire seaboard between Spanish Florida and French Canada.

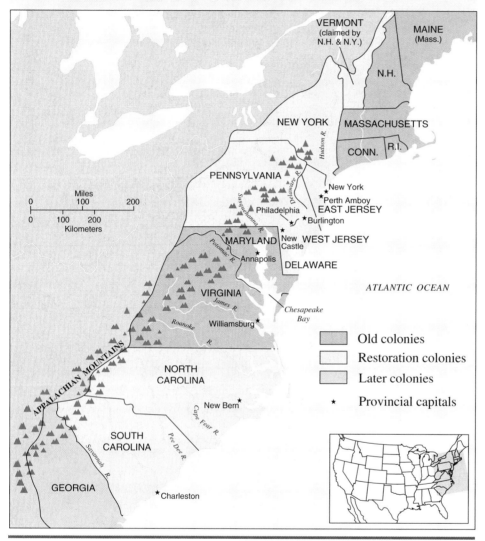

Charleston. Along the twisting rivers that flowed to the coast, planters staked out claims and experimented with a variety of exotic crops, including sugar, indigo, tropical fruits, tobacco, and rice. After much experimentation, planters found a profitable staple crop that would flourish in this forbidding environment: rice.

Rice cultivation required backbreaking labor to drain swamps, build dams and levees, and hoe, weed, cut, thresh, and husk the crop. Many early settlers had owned African slaves in Barbados, so their early reliance on slave labor came naturally. On widely dispersed plantations, black labor came

to predominate. In 1680, four-fifths of South Carolina's population was white. But by 1720, when the colony had grown to 18,000, black slaves outnumbered whites two to one.

As in Virginia and Maryland, the low-lying areas of coastal Carolina were so disease-ridden that population grew slowly in the early years. "In the spring a paradise, in the summer a hell, and in the autumn a hospital," remarked one traveler. Malaria and yellow fever, especially dangerous to pregnant women, were the main killers that retarded population growth, and the scarcity of women further limited natural increase. Like the West Indies, the rice-

This painting of Mulberry Plantation in South Carolina shows the mansion house, built in 1708, and rows of slave huts constructed in an African style. Most enslaved Africans lived in far more primitive structures in the eighteenth century. *(Gibbes Museum/Carolina Art Association)*

growing region of Carolina was at first more a place to accumulate a fortune than to rear a family.

In healthier northern Carolina, a different kind of society emerged amid pine barrens along a sandy coast. Settled largely by small tobacco farmers from Virginia seeking free land, the Albemarle region developed a mixed economy of livestock grazing, tobacco and food production, and the extraction of naval stores—lumber, turpentine, resin, pitch, and tar.

In 1701, North and South Carolina became separate colonies, but their distinctiveness had already emerged. Slavery took root only slowly in North Carolina, which was still 85 percent white in 1720. A land of struggling white settlers (called "Lubberland" by one prosperous Virginia planter), its healthier climate and settlement by families rather than by single men with servants and slaves gave it a greater potential for sustained growth. But in North as well as South Carolina, several factors inhibited the growth of a strong corporate identity: the pattern of settlement, ethnic and religious diversity, and a lack of shared assumptions about social and religious goals.

THE QUAKERS' PEACEABLE KINGDOM

Of all the utopian dreams imposed on the North American landscape in the seventeenth century, the most remarkable was the Quakers'. During the English civil war, the Society of Friends, as the Quakers called themselves, had sprung up as one of the many radical sects searching for a juster society

and a purer religion. Their visionary ideas and defiance of civil authority cost them dearly in fines, brutal punishment, and imprisonment. After Charles II and Parliament stifled radical dissent in the 1660s, they, too, sent many converts across the Atlantic. More than any other colony, the society they founded in Pennsylvania foreshadowed the religious and ethnic pluralism of the future United States.

The Early Friends

Like Puritans, the Quakers regarded the Church of England as corrupt and renounced its formalities and rituals, which smacked of Catholicism. But Quakers went much further, rejecting all Church officials and institutions and holding that every believer could find grace through the "inward light," a redemptive spark in every human soul. Rejecting original sin and eternal predestination, Quakers offered a radical alternative to Calvinism.

Quakers were persecuted in England after their movement, led by George Fox and Margaret Fell, gathered momentum in the 1650s. Other Protestants regarded them as dangerous fanatics, for the Quakers' doctrine of the "light within" took precedence even over Scripture and elevated all lay people to the position of the clergy.

Garbing themselves in plain black cloth and practicing civil disobedience, the Quakers also threatened social hierarchy and order. They refused to observe the customary marks of deference, such as doffing one's hat to a superior, believing that God made no social distinctions. They used the familiar "thee" and "thou" instead of the formal and deferential "you," they resisted taxes supporting the

The likenesses of William Penn and Hannah Callowhill Penn, his second wife, were done by Francis Place, an amateur artist. After Penn died in 1718, his widow became an absentee director of the family affairs in Pennsylvania until she died in 1726. *(Top: The Historical Society of Pennsylvania [1957.8]; Bottom: The Historical Society of Pennsylvania [1957.7])*

Church of England, and they refused to sign witnesses' oaths on the Bible, regarding this as profane. Most shocking, they renounced the use of force in human affairs and therefore refused to perform militia service.

Quakers also affronted traditional views when they insisted on the spiritual equality of the sexes and the right of women to participate in church matters on an equal, if usually separate, footing with men. Quaker leaders urged women to preach and to establish separate women's meetings. Among Quakers who fanned out from England to preach the doctrine of the inward light, 26 of the first 59 to cross the Atlantic were women. All but four of them were unmarried or without their husbands and therefore living, traveling, and ministering outside male authority.

Intensely committed to converting the world, Quakers ranged westward to North America and the Caribbean in the 1650s and 1660s. Nearly everywhere, they faced jeers, prison, mutilation, deportation, and death. Puritan Massachusetts warned them "to keep away from us and such as will come to be gone as fast as they can, the sooner the better." Hungering to serve in what they called "the Lamb's War" (the crusade of the meek), the Quakers vowed to test the Puritans' resolve and kept coming. To enforce religious conformity, the Bay Colony magistrates, in 1659, hanged two Quaker men on the Boston Common and threatened to do the same to Mary Dyer, an old woman who had followed Anne Hutchinson a quarter century before. Led from the colony, she returned the next year, undaunted, to meet her death at the end of a rope.

Early Quaker Designs

By the 1670s, the English Quakers were looking for a place in the New World to carry out their millennial dreams and escape severe repression. They found a leader in William Penn. His decision to identify with this radical and persecuted sect was surprising, for he was the son of Sir William Penn, the admiral who had captured Jamaica from Spain in 1654. But in 1666, the 23-year-old Penn was converted to Quakerism and thereafter devoted himself to the Friends' cause.

In 1674, Penn joined other Friends in establishing a North American colony, West Jersey. They had bought the land from one of the proprietors of New Jersey, itself a new English colony recently carved out of the former New Netherland. For West Jersey, Penn helped fashion a constitution—extraordinarily liberal for its time—that allowed virtually all free males to vote for legislators and local officials. Settlers were guaranteed freedom of religion and trial by jury. As Penn and the other trustees of the colony explained, "We lay a foundation for [later] ages to understand their liberty as men and Christians, that they may not be brought in bondage, but by their own consent; for we put the power in the people."

The last phrase, summing up the document, would have shocked anyone of property and power in England or North America at the time. Most regarded "the people" as ignorant, dangerous, and certain to bring society to a state of anarchy if allowed to rule themselves. Nowhere in the English world had ordinary citizens, especially those who did not own land, enjoyed such extensive privileges. Nowhere had a popularly elected legislature received such broad authority.

Despite these idealistic plans, West Jersey sputtered at first. Only 1,500 immigrants arrived in the first five years, and for several decades the colony was caught up in tangled claims to the land and government. The center of Quaker hopes lay across the Delaware River, where in 1681, Charles II granted William Penn a territory almost as large as England, paying off a large royal debt to Penn's father. Charles II also benefitted by getting the pesky Quakers out of England. Thus Penn and the Quakers came into possession of the last unassigned segment of the eastern coast of North America, which was one of the most fertile.

Pacifism in a Militant World: Quakers and Indians

On the day Penn received his royal charter for Pennsylvania, he wrote a friend, "My God that has given it to me will, I believe, bless and make it the seed of a nation." The nation that Penn envisioned was unique among colonizing schemes. Penn intended to make his colony an asylum for the persecuted and a refuge from arbitrary state power. Puritans had strived for social homogeneity and religious uniformity, excluding all not of like mind. In the Chesapeake and Carolina colonies, aggressive, unidealistic men had sought to exploit their lands and bondspeople. But Penn dreamed of inviting to his forested colony people of all religions and national backgrounds, offering them peaceful coexistence. His state would neither claim authority over citizens' consciences nor demand military service of them.

The Quakers who began streaming into Pennsylvania in 1682 quickly absorbed earlier Dutch, Finnish, and Swedish settlers. They participated in the government by electing representatives who initiated laws. They were primarily farmers, and like colonists elsewhere, they avidly acquired land, which Penn sold at reasonable rates. But unlike other colonizers, the Quakers practiced pacifism, holding the ethic of love and nonresistance embodied in the Sermon on the Mount as literally binding on them.

Even before arriving, Penn laid the foundation for peaceful relations with the Delaware tribe inhabiting his colony. "The king of the Country where I live, hath given me a great Province," he wrote to the Delaware chiefs, "but I desire to enjoy it with your Love and Consent, that we may always live together as Neighbors and friends." In this single statement Penn dissociated himself from the entire history of European colonization in the New World and from the widely held negative view of Indians. Recognizing the Indians as the rightful owners of the land included in his grant, Penn pledged not to sell one acre until he had first purchased it from local chiefs. He also promised to regulate strictly the Indian trade and to ban alcohol sales.

The Quaker accomplishment is sometimes disparaged with the claim that there was little competition for land in eastern Pennsylvania between the natives and the newcomers. However, a comparison between Pennsylvania and South Carolina, both established after the restoration of Charles II to the English throne in 1660, shows the power of pacifism. A quarter century after initial settlement, Pennsylvania had a population of about 20,000 whites. Penn's peaceful policy had so impressed Native American tribes that Indian refugees began migrating into Pennsylvania from all sides. During the same 25 years, South Carolina had grown to only about 4,000 whites, while becoming a cauldron of violence. Carolinians spread arms through the region to facilitate slave dealing, shipped some 10,000 members of local tribes off to New England and the West Indies as slaves, and laid waste to the Spanish mission frontier in Florida.

As long as the Quaker philosophy of pacifism and friendly relations with the local Indians held sway, interracial relations in the Delaware River valley contrasted sharply with those in other parts of North America. But ironically, the Quaker policy of toleration, liberal government, and exemption from military service attracted thousands of immigrants to the colony (especially in the eighteenth century) whose land hunger and disdain for Indians undermined Quaker trust and friendship. Germans and Scots-Irish flooded in, swelling the population to 31,000 by 1720. Neither shared Quaker idealism

Edward Hicks painted *Penn's Treaty with the Indians* in the nineteenth century. It is a romanticized version of the Treaty of Shackamaxon by which the Lenape chiefs ceded the site of Philadelphia to Penn. The treaty was actually made in 1682, but Hicks was correct in implying that the Lenape held Penn in high regard for his fair treatment of them. *(Hicks, Edward,* Penn's Treaty with the Indians, *Gift of Edgar William and Bernice Chrysler Garbisch,* © 2000 *Board of Trustees, National Gallery of Art, Washington,* c. 1840/1844, canvas, .617 × .765 [24¹⁄₄ × 30¹⁄₈])

PENNS TREATY with the INDIANS, made 1681 without an Oath, and never broken. The foundation of Religious and Civil LIBERTY, in the U.S. of AMERICA.

about racial harmony. Driven from their homelands by hunger and war, they pressed inland and, sometimes encouraged by the land agents of Penn's heirs, encroached on the lands of the local tribes. This created conflict with the natives who had sought sanctuary in Pennsylvania. By the mid-eighteenth century, a confrontation of displaced people, some red and some white, was occurring in Pennsylvania.

Building the Peaceable Kingdom

Although Pennsylvania came closer to matching its founder's goals than any other European colony, Penn's dreams never completely materialized. Nor could he convince people to settle in compact villages, which he believed necessary for his "holy experiment." Instead, they created open country networks without any particular centers or boundaries. Yet a sense of common endeavor persisted.

Quaker farmers prized family life and emigrated almost entirely in kinship groups. This helped them maintain their distinctive identity. So did other practices such as allowing marriage only within their society, carefully providing land for their offspring, and guarding against too great a population increase (which would cause too rapid a division of farms) by limiting the size of their families.

Settled by religiously dedicated farming families, Pennsylvania boomed. Its countryside became a rich grainland. By 1700, the port capital of Philadelphia overtook New York City in population, and a half century later, it was the largest city in the colonies, bustling with artisans, mariners, merchants, and professionals.

The Limits of Perfectionism

Despite commercial success and peace with Native Americans, not all was harmonious in early Pennsylvania. Politics were often turbulent, in part because of Pennsylvania's weak leadership. Penn was a much-loved proprietor, but he did not tarry long in his colony, returning to England in 1684 and revisiting his colony briefly in 1700. This left a leadership vacuum.

A more important cause of disunity resided in the Quaker attitude toward authority. In England, balking at authority was almost a daily part of Quaker life. But in Pennsylvania, the absence of persecution eliminated a crucial binding element from Quaker society. The factionalism that developed among them demonstrated that people never unify so well as when under attack. Rather than looking inward and banding together, they looked outward to an environment filled with opportunity. Their squabbling filled Penn with dismay. Why, he asked, were his settlers so "governmentish, so brutish, so susceptible to scurvy quarrels that break out to the disgrace of the Province?"

Meanwhile, Quaker industriousness and frugality helped produce great material success. After a generation, social radicalism and religious evangelicalism began to fade. As in other colonies, settlers discovered the door to prosperity wide open, and in they surged.

Where Pennsylvania differed from New England and the South was in its relations with Native Americans, at least for the first few generations. It also departed from the Puritan colonies in its immigration policy. Pennsylvania, it is said, was the first community since the Roman Empire to allow people of different national origins and religious persuasions to live together under the same government on terms of near equality. English, Highland Scots, French, Germans, Irish, Welsh, Swedes, Finns, and Swiss all settled in Pennsylvania. This ethnic mosaic was further complicated by a medley of religious groups, including Mennonites, Lutherans, Dutch Reformed, Quakers, Baptists, Anglicans, Presbyterians, Catholics, Jews, and a sprinkling of mystics. Their relations may not always have been friendly, but few attempts were made to discriminate against dissenting groups. Pennsylvanians thereby laid the foundations for the pluralism that was to become the hallmark of American society.

NEW SPAIN'S NORTHERN FRONTIER

Spain's outposts in Florida and New Mexico, preceding all English settlements on the eastern seaboard, fell into disarray between 1680 and the early eighteenth century just as the English colonies were sinking deep roots. Trying to secure a vast northern frontier with only small numbers of settlers, the Spanish relied on forced Indian labor. This reliance proved to be their undoing in Florida and New Mexico.

Popé's Revolt

During the 1670s, when the Franciscans developed a new zeal to root out traditional Indian religious ceremonies, the Pueblo people turned on the Spanish intruders. In years of harsh rule, the Spanish had extracted tribute labor from the Pueblo, who at the same time suffered the ravaging effects of European diseases. Both of these punishing long-term effects contributed to Pueblo alienation. But pushing the Pueblo to the edge was an assault on their religion. Launching a campaign to restrict native religious ceremonies in the 1670s, the Spanish friars began to seize the Pueblo kivas (underground ceremonial religious chambers), to forbid native dances, and to destroy priestly Indian masks and prayer sticks.

In August 1680, led by Popé, a much-persecuted medicine man from San Juan pueblo, about two dozen Pueblo villages scattered over several hundred miles rose up in fury. They burned Spanish ranches and government buildings, systematically destroyed Spanish churches, lay waste to Spanish fields, and killed half of the friars. As the Spanish governor in Santa Fe watched the church go up in flames, he reported his shock at the "scoffing and ridicule which the wretched and miserable Indian rebels made of the sacred things, intoning . . . prayers of the church with jeers."

Spanish settlers, soldiers, and friars streamed back to El Paso, abandoning their northern frontier in the Southwest for more than a decade. Only in 1694 did a new Spanish governor, the intrepid Diego de Vargas, regain Santa Fe and gradually subdue most of the Pueblo. Learning from Popé's rebellion, the Spanish declared a kind of cultural truce, easing their demands for Pueblo labor tribute and tolerating certain Pueblo rituals in return for nominal acceptance of Christianity. Periodic tension and animosity continued, but the Pueblo had to come to terms with the Spanish because of their need for defense against their old enemies—the Navajo, Ute, and Apache.

Decline of Florida's Missions

The Franciscan missions, established in Florida along the Atlantic coast and inland to the west in the Florida panhandle, had firmed up New Spain's grip of the southeast corner of North America. By 1675, 40 Franciscan priests had converted some 20,000 Guales, Timucuas, and others. Yet few Spanish settlers could be persuaded to settle in Florida. As the governor of Cuba put it frankly in 1673, "It is hard to get anyone to go to St. Augustine because of the horror with which Florida is painted. Only hoodlums and the mischievous go there from Cuba."

Much devastated by disease, the Florida Indians and their Franciscan spiritual shepherds were as severely pummeled as those in New Mexico in the late seventeenth century. Rapidly settling in South Carolina, the English were eager to use Indian allies to attack the Spanish Indian villages and sell the

Spanish Missions in New Mexico and Florida in the Late Seventeenth Century

The extensive Spanish missionary activity in Florida and New Mexico had no English parallel.

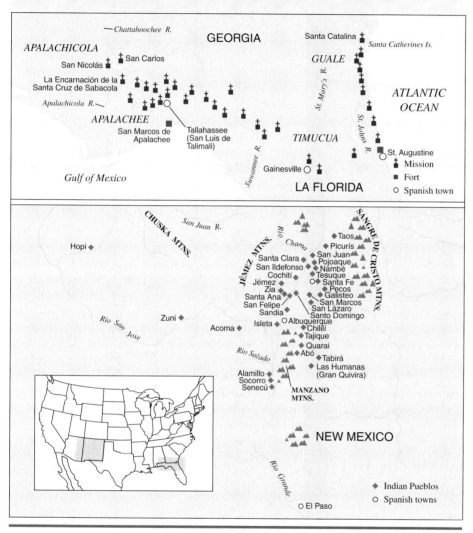

captives into slavery. The resentment of missionized Indians, wearying under demands on their labor, further weakened the tenuous Spanish hold on them. The attacks of Carolinians in the early 1680s destroyed a number of Spanish missions. When England and Spain went to war in 1701—called Queen Anne's War in the colonies—the Carolinians attacked Florida. Burning mission villages to the ground, they slaughtered the Spanish friars and captured some 4,000 women and children to be sold as slaves. The Spanish mission frontier was thoroughly devastated, and only St. Augustine remained as a Spanish stronghold. Unlike New Mexico, there was no Spanish reconquest. From this time onward,

English and French traders, offering more attractive trade goods, would have the main influence over Florida Indians.

AN ERA OF INSTABILITY

A dozen years after the King Philip's War in New England and Bacon's Rebellion in Virginia, a series of insurrections and a searing witchcraft incident convulsed colonial society. The rebellions were triggered by the Revolution of 1688, known thereafter to English Protestants as the Glorious Revolution because it ended forever the notion that kings ruled by "divine right" and marked the last serious Catholic challenge to Protestant supremacy. But these colonial disruptions also signified a struggle for social and political dominance in the expanding colonies. So did the Salem witchcraft trials in Massachusetts.

Organizing the Empire

From the beginning of colonization, the English assumed that overseas settlements existed to promote the national interest at home. Mercantilist theory held that colonies served as outlets for English manufactured goods, provided foodstuffs and raw materials, stimulated trade (and hence promoted a larger merchant navy), and filled royal coffers by exporting commodities such as sugar and tobacco on which duties were paid. In return, colonists benefited from English military protection and guaranteed markets.

Beginning with a small step in 1621, when the king's council forbade tobacco growers to export their crop to anywhere but England, the Crown slowly began to regulate its colonies in order to mold them into a unified empire. However, not until 1651, when the colonists traded freely with the commercially aggressive Dutch, did Parliament consider regulating colonial affairs. It passed a navigation act requiring that English or colonial ships, manned by English or colonial sailors, carry all goods entering England, Ireland, and the colonies, no matter where those goods originated. These first steps toward a regulated empire were also the first steps to place England's power behind national economic development.

In 1660, after the monarchy was restored, Parliament passed a more comprehensive navigation act that listed colonial products (tobacco, sugar, indigo, dyewoods, and cotton) that could be shipped only to England or other English colonies. Like its predecessor, the act took dead aim at Holland's domination of Atlantic commerce, while increasing England's revenues by imposing duties on the enumerated articles. Later navigation acts closed loopholes in the 1660 law and added other enumerated articles. This regulation bore lightly on the colonists, for the laws lacked enforcement mechanisms.

After 1675, international competition and war led England to impose greater imperial control. That year marked the establishment of the Lords of Trade, a committee of the king's privy council empowered to make and enforce decisions regulating the colonies. Their chief goal was to create more uniform governments in North America and the West Indies that would do the Crown's will. Although movement toward imperial centralization often sputtered, the trend was unmistakable, especially to colonists who felt the sting of royal customs agents sent to enforce the navigation acts. England was becoming the shipper of the world, and its state-regulated policy of economic nationalism was essential to commercial greatness.

The Glorious Revolution in North America

When Charles II died in 1685, his brother, the duke of York, became King James II. This set in motion a chain of events that nearly led to civil war. Like Charles, James II professed the Catholic faith. But unlike Charles II, who had disclosed this only on his deathbed, the new king announced his faith immediately on assuming the throne. Consternation ensued. Protestant England recoiled when James issued the Declaration of Indulgence, which granted liberty of worship to all. Although religious toleration is cherished today, it was unacceptable to most English Protestants 300 years ago. Belief that the declaration was primarily a concession to Catholics hardened when the king began creating Catholic peerages to fill the House of Lords, appointed Catholics to high government posts, and demanded that Oxford and Cambridge open their doors to Catholic students. In 1687, the king dismissed a resistant Parliament. When his wife, supposedly too old for childbearing, bore a son in 1688, a Catholic succession loomed.

Convinced that James aimed at absolute power, Protestant leaders in 1688 invited a Dutch prince, William of Orange, to seize the throne with his wife, Mary, who was James's Protestant daughter. James abdicated rather than fight. It was a bloodless victory for Protestantism, for parliamentary power and the limitation of kingly prerogatives, and for the merchants and gentry of England.

The response of New Englanders to these events stemmed from their previous experience with royal authority and their fear of "papists." In 1676, New England became a prime target for efforts to reorganize the empire and crack down on smuggling, which had prevailed there for two generations. Charles II annulled the Massachusetts charter in 1684, and two years later James II appointed Sir Edmund Andros, a crusty professional soldier and former governor of New York, to rule over the newly created Dominion of New England. Soon the Dominion gathered under one government all the English colonies from Maine to New Jersey. Puritans now had to swallow the bitter fact that they were subjects of London bureaucrats who cared more about shaping a disciplined empire than about New England's special religious vision.

At first, New Englanders accepted Andros, though coolly. But he soon earned their hatred by

The center of government and official news in colonial New England was Boston's town house, built in 1657. Note the stocks and shipping post at lower left. *(From* Boston's First Town-House, 1657–1711, *1930, by Charles A. Lawrence/The Bostonian Society)*

invading freedoms they cherished. He imposed taxes without legislative consent, ended trial by jury, abolished the General Court of Massachusetts (which had met annually since 1630), muzzled Boston's town meetings, and challenged land titles. He also mocked the Puritans by converting a Boston Puritan meetinghouse into an Anglican chapel, held services there on Christmas Day—a gesture that to Puritans stank of popery—and overturned their practice of suppressing religious dissent.

When news reached Boston in April 1689 that William of Orange had landed in England, Bostonians streamed into the streets to the beat of drums. They imprisoned Andros, a suspected papist, and overwhelmed the fort in Boston harbor, which held most of the governor's small contingent of red-coated royal troops. Andros escaped, disguised in women's clothing, but was quickly recaptured. Boston's ministers, along with merchants and former magistrates, led the rebellion, but city folk of the lower orders supplied the foot soldiers. For three years, an interim government ruled Massachusetts while the Bay colonists awaited a new charter and a new royal governor.

Although Bostonians had dramatically rejected royal authority and the "bloody Devotees of Rome" as well as arbitrary power, no internal revolution occurred. However, growing social stratification and the emergence of a political elite caused some citizens to argue that men of modest means but common sense might better be trusted with power. "Anarchy" was the word chosen by Samuel Willard, minister of

Boston's Third Church, to tar the popular spirit he saw unloosed in Boston in the aftermath of Andros's ouster. But such egalitarian rumblings came to little.

In New York, the Glorious Revolution was similarly bloodless at first but far more disruptive. Royal government melted away on news of James's abdication. Displacing the governor's "popishly affected dogs and rogues," German-born militia captain Jacob Leisler established an interim government and ruled with an elected Committee of Safety for 13 months until a governor appointed by King William arrived.

Leisler's government enjoyed popularity among small landowners and urban laboring people. Most of the upper echelon, however, detested him as an upstart—a common foot soldier of the Dutch West India Company who arrived in 1660 and had leapfrogged into the merchant class by marrying a wealthy widow. After the English seized the Dutch colony in 1664, he was often at odds with English leaders. "Up jump into the saddle hott brain'd Capt. Leisler," sneered one aristocrat after Leisler's takeover. Such antipathy was returned in kind by lower- and middle-class Dutch inhabitants. Many Dutch merchants had readily adjusted to the English conquest of New Netherland in 1664, and many incoming English merchants had married into Dutch families. But beneath the upper class, where economic success softened ethnic friction, Anglo-Dutch hostility was common. Ordinary Dutch families felt that the English were crowding them out of the society they had built.

The Glorious Revolution ignited this smoldering social conflict. Leisler shared Dutch hostility toward New York's English elite, and his sympathy for the common people, mostly Dutch, earned him the hatred of the city's oligarchy. Leisler freed imprisoned debtors, planned a town-meeting system of government for New York City, and replaced merchants with artisans in important offices. By the autumn of 1689, Leislerian mobs were attacking the property of some of New York's wealthiest merchants. Two merchants, refusing to recognize Leisler's authority, were jailed.

Leisler's opponents were horrified at the power of the "rabble." They believed that ordinary people had no right to rebel against authority or to exercise political power. When a new English governor arrived in 1691, the anti-Leislerians embraced him and charged Leisler and seven of his assistants with treason for assuming the government without royal instructions.

In the ensuing trial, Leisler and Jacob Milbourne, his son-in-law and chief lieutenant, were convicted of treason by an all-English jury and hanged. Leisler's popularity among the artisans of the city was evident when his wealthy opponents could find no carpenter in the city who would make a ladder for the scaffold. After his execution, peace gradually returned to New York, but for years provincial and city politics reflected the deep rift between Leislerians and anti-Leislerians.

The Glorious Revolution also focused dissatisfactions in several southern colonies. Because Maryland was ruled by a Catholic proprietor, the Protestant majority seized power in July 1689 on word of the Glorious Revolution and used it for their own purposes. They vowed to cleanse Maryland of popery and to reform a corrupt customs service, cut taxes and fees, and extend the rights of the representative assembly. The militant Protestant John Coode, formerly a fiery Anglican minister who had been involved in a brief rebellion in 1681, assumed the reins of government and held them until the arrival of Maryland's first royal governor in 1692.

In neighboring Virginia, the wounds of Bacon's Rebellion were still healing when word of the Glorious Revolution arrived. The fact that Virginia lived under a Catholic governor, Lord Howard of Effingham, and a number of Catholic officials, fostered rumors of a Catholic plot. News of the revolution in England led a group of planters, suffering a prolonged drop in tobacco prices, to try an overthrow of the governor, but the governor's council defended itself, partly by removing Catholics from positions of authority.

The Glorious Revolution brought lasting political changes to several colonies. The Dominion of New England collapsed. Connecticut and Rhode Island regained the right to elect their own governors, but Massachusetts (now including Plymouth) and New Hampshire became royal colonies with governors appointed by the king. In Massachusetts, a new royal charter in 1691 eliminated Church membership as a voting requirement. The Maryland proprietorship was abolished (to be restored in 1715 when the Calverts became Protestant), and Catholics were barred from office. Everywhere Protestant Englishmen celebrated their liberties.

The Social Basis of Politics

The colonial insurrections associated with the Glorious Revolution revealed social and political tensions that accompanied the transplanting of English society to the North American wilderness. Still hardly beyond the frontier stage, the immature societies along the coast were fluid, unruly, and competitive, lacking the stable political systems and acknowledged leadership class thought necessary for social order.

The emerging colonial elite tried to foster stability by upholding a stratified Old-World-style society where children were subordinate to parents, women to men, servants to masters, and the poor to the rich. Hence, leaders everywhere tried to maintain social gradations and subordination. Puritans did not file into church on Sundays and occupy the pews randomly; seats were "doomed," or assigned according to customary yardsticks of respectability—age, parentage, social position, wealth, and occupation. Even in fluid Virginia, lower-class people were hauled before courts for horse racing because this was a sport legally reserved for men of social distinction.

But this social ideal proved difficult to maintain. Regardless of previous rank, settlers rubbed elbows so frequently and faced such raw conditions together that those without pedigrees often saw little reason to defer to men of superior rank. "In Virginia," explained John Smith, "a plain soldier that can use a pickaxe and spade is better than five knights." Colonists everywhere gave respect not to those who claimed it by birth but to those who earned it by deed.

Adding to the difficulty of reproducing a traditional social order was the social fluidity in frontier society. A native elite gradually formed, but it had no basis, as in Europe, in legally defined and hereditary social rank. Planters and merchants, accumulating large estates, aped the English gentry by cultivating

On both sides of the Atlantic, most people took witches seriously. The book *Full and Plain Evidence Concerning Witches and Apparitions*, published in London in 1681, showed devil-inspired witches flying over a house, entering an attic window, and hovering in one of the rooms. *(By permission of the Houghton Library, Harvard University)*

the arts, building fine houses, and acquiring symbols of respectability such as libraries, coaches, and racehorses. Yet their place was rarely secure. New competitors nipped constantly at their heels.

Amid such social flux, the elite never commanded general allegiance to the ideal of a fixed social structure. Ambitious men on the rise such as Nathaniel Bacon and Jacob Leisler, and thwarted men below them who followed their lead, rose up against the constituted authorities, which they almost certainly would not have dared to do so in their homelands. When they gained power during the Glorious Revolution, in every case only briefly, the leaders of these uprisings linked themselves with a tradition of English struggle against tyranny and oligarchical power. They vowed to make government more responsive to the ordinary people, who composed most of their societies.

Witchcraft in Salem

The ordinary people in the colonies, for whom Bacon and Leisler tried to speak, could sometimes be misled, as the tragic events of the Salem witch hunts demonstrated. In Massachusetts, the deposing of Governor Andros left the colony in political limbo for three years, and this allowed what might have been a brief outbreak of witchcraft in the little community of Salem to escalate into a bitter and bloody battle. The provincial government, caught in transition, reacted only belatedly.

On a winter's day in 1692, 9-year-old Betty Parris and her 11-year-old cousin Abigail Williams began to play at magic in the kitchen of a small house in Salem, Massachusetts. They enlisted the aid of Tituba, the slave of Betty's father, Samuel Parris, the minister of the small community. Tituba told voodoo tales from her Caribbean past and baked "witch cakes." The girls soon became seized with fits and began making wild gestures and speeches. Soon other young girls in the village were behaving strangely. Village elders extracted confessions that they were being tormented by Tituba and two other women, both social outcasts.

What began as the innocent play of young girls turned into a ghastly rending of a farm community capped by the execution of 20 villagers accused of witchcraft. In the seventeenth century, people still took literally the biblical injunction "Thou shalt not suffer a witch to live." For centuries throughout western Europe, people had believed that witches followed Satan's bidding and did evil to anyone he designated. Communities had accused and sentenced women to death for witchcraft far more often than men. In Massachusetts, more than 100 people, mostly older women, had been accused of witchcraft before 1692, and more than a dozen had been hanged.

In Salem, the initial accusations against three older women quickly multiplied. Within weeks, dozens had been charged with witchcraft, including several prominent members of the community. But formal prosecution of the accused witches could not proceed because neither the new royal charter of 1691 nor the royal governor to rule the colony had yet arrived. For three months, while charges spread, local authorities could only jail the accused without trial. When Governor William Phips arrived from England in May 1692, he ordered a special court to try the accused. By then, events had careened out of control.

All through the summer, the court listened to testimony. By September it had condemned about two dozen villagers. The authorities hanged 19 of them on barren "Witches Hill" outside the town and crushed 80-year-old Giles Corey to death under heavy stones. The trials rolled on into 1693, but by then, colonial leaders, including many of the clergy,

recognized that a feverish fear of one's neighbors, rather than witchcraft itself, had possessed the little village of Salem.

Many factors contributed to the hysteria. Among them were generational differences between older Puritan colonists and the sometimes less religiously motivated younger generation, old family animosities, population growth and pressures on the available farmland, and tensions between agricultural Salem Village and the nearby commercial center called Salem Town. An outbreak of food poisoning may also have caused hallucinogenic behavior, and a new Indian war on the Massachusetts–Maine frontier caused near-hysteria. Probably nobody will ever fully understand the exact mingling of causes, but the fact that most of the individuals charged with witchcraft were women underscores the relatively weak position of women in Puritan society. The relentless spread of witchcraft accusations suggests the anxiety of this tumultuous era. War, economic disruption, the political takeover of the colony by Andros and then his overthrow, and erosion of the early generation's utopian vision all became a deadly mix.

Timeline

1607	Jamestown settled
1616–1621	Native American population in New England decimated by European diseases
1617	First tobacco crop shipped from Virginia
1619	First Africans arrive in Jamestown
1620	Pilgrims land at Plymouth
1622	Powhatan tribes attack Virginia settlements
1624	Dutch colonize mouth of Hudson River
1630	Puritan immigration to Massachusetts Bay
1632	Maryland grant to Lord Baltimore (George Calvert)
1633–1634	Native Americans in New England again struck by European diseases
1635	Roger Williams banished and flees to Rhode Island
1636	Anne Hutchinson exiled to Rhode Island
1637	New England wages war against the Pequot people
1640s	New England merchants enter slave trade Virginia forbids blacks to carry firearms
1642–1649	English civil war ends great migration to New England
1643	Confederation of New England
1650–1670	Judicial and legislative decisions in Chesapeake colonies solidify racial lines
1651	Parliament passes first navigation act
1659–1661	Puritans hang two Quaker men and one Quaker woman on Boston Common
1660	Restoration of King Charles II in England
1662	Half-Way Covenant in New England
1663	Carolina charter granted to eight proprietors
1664	English capture New Netherland and rename it New York Royal grant of the Jersey lands to proprietors
1673–1685	French expand into Mississippi valley
1675–1677	King Philip's War in New England
1676	Bacon's Rebellion in Virginia
1680	Popé's revolt in New Mexico
1681	William Penn receives Pennsylvania grant
1684	Massachusetts charter recalled
1688	Glorious Revolution in England, followed by accession of William and Mary
1689	Overthrow of Governor Andros in New England Leisler's Rebellion in New York
1690s	Transition from white indentured servitude to black slave labor begins in Chesapeake region
1692	Witchcraft hysteria in Salem

✦ *Conclusion*

THE ACHIEVEMENT OF NEW SOCIETIES

Nearly 200,000 immigrants who had left their European homelands reached North America in the seventeenth century. Coming from a variety of social backgrounds and spurred by different motives, they represented the rootstock of distinctive societies that would mature in the North American colonies of England, France, Holland, and Spain. For three generations, North America served as a social laboratory for religious and social visionaries, political theorists, fortune seekers, social outcasts, and, most of all, ordinary men and women seeking a better life than they had known in their European homelands.

By the end of the seventeenth century, 12 English colonies on the eastern edge of North America (and several others in the West Indies) had secured footholds in the hemisphere and erected the basic scaffolding of colonial life. So had Spanish and French colonies lying north, south, and west of the English. The coastal Indian tribes were reeling from disease and a series of wars that secured the English colonists' land base along 1,000 miles of coastal plain. Though never controlling the powerful Indian tribes of the interior, the colonists had established a profitable trade with them. English settlers had overcome a scarcity of labor by copying the other European colonists in the hemisphere, who had linked the west coast of Africa to the New World through the ghastly trade in human flesh. Finally, the English colonists had engaged in insurrections against what they viewed as arbitrary and tainted governments imposed by England.

The embryo of British America carried into the eighteenth century contained peculiarly mixed features. Disease, stunted family life, and the harsh work regimen imposed by the planters who commanded the labor of the vast majority ended the dreams of most who came to the Southern colonies. Yet population inched upward, and the bone and sinew of a workable economy formed. In the northern colonies, to which the fewest immigrants came, life was more secure. Organized around family and community, favored by a healthier climate, and motivated by religion and social vision, the Puritan and Quaker societies thrived. Still physically isolated from Europe, the colonists developed a large measure of self-reliance. Slowly, they began to identify themselves as the permanent inhabitants of a new land rather than as transplanted English, Dutch, or Scots-Irish. Viewing land and labor as the indispensable elements of a fruitful economy, they learned to exploit without apologies the land of one dark-skinned people and the labor of another. Yet even as they attained a precarious mastery in a triracial society, they were being culturally affected by the very people to whose land and labor they laid claim. Although utopian visions of life in North America still preoccupied some, most colonists had awakened to the reality that life in the New World was a mixture of unpredictable opportunity and sudden turbulence, unprecedented freedom and debilitating wars, racial intermingling and racial separation. It was a New World in much more than a geographic sense, for the people of three cultures who now inhabited it had remade it. And, while doing so, people like Anthony and Mary Johnson (whom we met at the beginning of the chapter) were remaking themselves.

✦ Recommended Reading

The Chesapeake Tobacco Coast
Ira Berlin, *Many Thousands Gone: The First Two Centuries of Slavery in North America* (1998); T. H. Breen and Stephen Innes, *"Myne Owne Ground": Race and Freedom on Virginia's Eastern Shore, 1640–1676* (1980); Kathleen M. Brown, *Good Wives, Nasty Wenches, and Anxious Patriarchs: Gender, Race, and Power in Colonial Virginia* (1996); Frederic W. Gleach, *Powhatan's World and Colonial Virginia: A Conflict of Cultures* (1997); Michael A. Gomez, *Exchanging Our Country Marks: The Transformation of African Identities in the Colonial and Antebellum South* (1998); Allan Kulikoff, *Tobacco and Slaves: The Development of Southern Cultures in the Chesapeake, 1680–1800* (1986); Karen Kupperman,

Settling with the Indians: The Meeting of English and Indian Cultures in America, 1580–1640 (1980); Edmund S. Morgan, *American Slavery, American Freedom: The Ordeal of Colonial Virginia* (1975); David B. Quinn, ed., *Early Maryland in a Wider World* (1982); Darrett B. Rutman and Anita H. Rutman, *A Place in Time: Middlesex County, Virginia, 1650–1750* (1984); Alden Vaughan, *American Genesis: Captain John Smith and the Founding of Virginia* (1975); Lorena Walsh, *From Calabar to Carter's Grove: The History of a Virginia Slave Community* (1997); Wilcomb Washburn, *The Governor and the Rebel* (1957); J. Leitch Wright, *The Only Land They Knew: The Tragic Story of the American Indians in the Old South* (1981).

Massachusetts and Its Offspring
Virginia D. Anderson, *New England's Generation: The Great Migration and the Formation of Society and Culture in the Seventeenth Century* (1991); Richard Archer, *Fissures in the Rock: New England in the Seventeenth Century* (2001); James Axtell, *The European and the Indian* (1981); Bernard Bailyn, *The New England Merchants in the Seventeenth Century* (1955); Kathleen J. Bragdon, *Native People of Southern New England, 1500–1650* (1996); Colin G. Calloway, *New Worlds for All: Indians, Europeans, and the Remaking of Early America* (1997); David Cressy, *Coming Over: Migration and Communication Between England and New England in the Seventeenth Century* (1987); John Demos, *A Little Commonwealth: Family Life in Plymouth Colony* (1970); James Drake, *King Philip's War: Civil War in New England, 1675–1676* (1999); David D. Hall, *Worlds of Wonder, Days of Judgment: Popular Religious Belief in Early New England* (1989); Christopher Hill, *Society and Puritanism in Pre-Revolutionary England*, 2nd ed. (1967); Stephen Innes, *Creating the Commonwealth: The Economic Culture of Puritan New England* (1995) and *Labor in a New Land* (1983); Jill Lepore, *The Name of the War: King Philip's War and the Origins of American Identity* (1998); Kenneth Lockridge, *A New England Town* (1970); Gloria L. Main, *Peoples of a Spacious Land: Families and Cultures in Colonial New England* (2001); Calvin Martin, *Keepers of the Game: Indian–Animal Relationships and the Fur Trade* (1978); Robert Middlekauff, *The Mathers* (1971); Perry Miller, *Errand into the Wilderness* (1956); Edmund S. Morgan, *The Puritan Dilemma: The Story of John Winthrop* (1958); Gary B. Nash, *Red, White, and Black*, 4th ed. (2000); Darrett B. Rutman, *Winthrop's Boston* (1965); Neal Salisbury, *Manitou and Providence: Europeans, Indians, and the Making of New England, 1500–1643* (1982); Roger Thompson, *Sex in Middlesex: Popular Mores in a Massachusetts County, 1649–1699* (1986).

From the St. Lawrence to the Hudson
James Axtell, *The Invasion Within: The Contest of Cultures in Colonial North America* (1985); Denys Delâge, *Bitter Feast: Amerindians and Europeans in Northeastern North America, 1600–64*, Trans. Jane Brierley (1993); Joyce Goodfriend, *Before the Melting Pot: Society and Culture in Colonial New York City, 1664–1730* (1992); Francis Jennings, *The Ambiguous Iroquois Empire* (1984); Daniel K. Richter, *The Ordeal of the Longhouse: The Peoples of the Iroquois League in the Era of European Colonization* (1992); Daniel K. Richter and James H. Merrell, eds., *Beyond the Covenant Chain: The Iroquois and Their Neighbors in Indian North America, 1600–1800* (1987); Robert C. Ritchie, *The Duke's Province: A Study of Politics and Society in Colonial New York, 1660–1691* (1977); Ian K. Steele, *Warpaths: Invasions of North America* (1994); Bruce G. Trigger, *Children of the Aataentsic: A History of the Huron People, 1600–1664* (1976); Richard White, *The Middle Ground: Indians, Empires, and Republics in the Great Lakes Region, 1650–1815* (1991).

Proprietary Carolina: A Restoration Reward
Verner Crane, *The Southern Frontier, 1670–1732* (1929); Alan Gallay, *The Indian Slave Trade: The Rise of the English Empire in the American South, 1670–1717* (2002); Patricia Galloway, *Choctaw Genesis, 1500–1700* (1995); Daniel C. Littlefield, *Rice and Slaves: Ethnicity and the Slave Trade in Colonial South Carolina* (1981); M. Eugene Sirmans, *Colonial South Carolina* (1966); Richard Waterhouse, *A New World Gentry: The Making of a Merchant and Planter Class in South Carolina, 1670–1770* (1989); Robert M. Weir, *Colonial South Carolina* (1983).

The Quakers' Peaceable Kingdom
J. William Frost, *The Quaker Family in Colonial America* (1972); Barry J. Levy, *Quakers and the American Family* (1988); Gary B. Nash, *Quakers and Politics: Pennsylvania, 1681–1726* (1968); Sharon V. Salinger, *"To Serve Well and Faithfully": Labor and Indentured Servitude in Pennsylvania* (1987); Sally Schwartz, *A Mixed Multitude: The Struggle for Toleration in Colonial Pennsylvania* (1987); Frederick B. Tolles, *Meeting House and Counting House: The Quaker Merchants of Colonial Philadelphia* (1948).

New Spain's Northern Frontier
Ramon A. Gutiérrez, *When Jesus Came, the Corn Mothers Went Away: Marriage, Sexuality, and Power in New Mexico, 1500–1846* (1992); A. H. Johns, *Storms Brewed in Other Men's Worlds: The Confrontation of Indians, Spanish, and French in the Old Southwest* (1975); Andrew L. Knout, *The Pueblo Revolt of 1680* (1995); Jane Landers, *Black Society in Spanish Florida* (1999); D. W. Meinig, *The Shaping of America: Atlantic America, 1492–1800* (1986); Jerald T. Milanich, *Florida Indians and the Invasion of Europe* (1995); Marvin T. Smith, *Archaeology of Aboriginal Culture Change in the Interior Southeast: Depopulation During the Early Historical Period* (1987); David J. Weber, *The Spanish Frontier in North America* (1992).

An Era of Instability
Paul Boyer and Steven Nissenbaum, *Salem Possessed: The Social Origins of Witchcraft* (1974); John P. Demos, *Entertaining Satan: Witchcraft and the Culture of Early New England* (1982); Carol F. Karlsen, *The Devil in the Shape of a Woman* (1987); David Lovejoy, *The Glorious Revolution in America* (1972); Mary Beth Norton, *In the Devil's Snare: The Salem Witchcraft Crisis of 1692* (2000); Elizabeth Reis, *Damned Women: Sinners and Witches in Puritan New England* (1997); Richard Weisman, *Witchcraft, Magic, and Religion in 17th-Century Massachusetts* (1984).

Fiction and Film
Nathaniel Hawthorne's *The Scarlet Letter* (1850) is an American classic on Puritan love, infidelity, and morality; Hollywood's version, by the same title, features Demi Moore and Gary Oldman (1995). John Barth's *The Sotweed Factor* (1960) is a rollicking and ribald novel about indentured servitude, tobacco planting, love, and brutishness in seventeenth-century Maryland. *Black Robes* (1991), a gripping film made in Canada, evokes

all the cruelty of the contact between early French Jesuit missionaries and the Iroquois people. The film is based on Brian Manning's novel of the same name. Werner Herzog's *Aguirre: The Wrath of God* (1972) is a surreal film about the early Spanish conquest of much of the Americas in the sixteenth century. A much milder film on early Indian–European contact is *Squanto: A Warrior's Tale* (1994), featuring Adam Beach. *Three Sovereigns for Sarah* (1985), a PBS miniseries starring Vanessa Redgrave, stunningly dramatizes the Salem witchcraft trials. Arthur Miller's play *The Crucible* (1953) is on the same topic and is as engaging today as it was three decades ago when it played on stages around the country. Wayne Carlin, *The Wished For Country* (2002) is a compelling historical novel about the indentured servants, Africans, and Native Americans who met each other in early Maryland and how, from their intermingling, the triracial Wesort people emerged.

◆ Discovering U.S. History Online

Jamestown

www.nps.gov

Using the search facility on the main page, search for Jamestown. Essays on the historical significance of Jamestown, some of the personalities, manufacturing and industries, timelines, and bibliographies make up this informative site.

Jamestown Rediscovery

www.apva.org

This site has excellent material on the archaeological excavation of Jamestown.

Plymouth Colony, 1620–1691

www.etext.virginia.edu/users/deetz

This collection of searchable texts, mostly primary sources, provides information about the late seventeenth-century Plymouth Colony.

The Pilgrim Story

www.pilgrimhall.org/museum.htm

Well-illustrated with images from the museum, this online exhibit gives an overview of the pilgrims' origins and their settlement in the New World.

Colonization—New England

www.foundingfathers.info/us-history/New-England/
www.foundingfathers.info/us-history/NewEngland/

A history of colonization of New England, including the "Massachusetts Bay Colony," "King Philip's War," and "Puritan Laws and Character" is presented via a reprint of a turn-of-the-century textbook with links to definitions and illustrations.

Divining America: Religion and the National Culture

www.nhc.rtp.nc.us:8080/tserve/eighteen/ekeyinfo/
puritan.htm

An illustrated essay on Puritan ideas and how they intersected with American history.

Long Island

www.lihistory.com/3/chap3cov.htm

This is one chapter of a well-organized site on the history of Long Island, New York, originally published as a series of articles in a local newspaper.

The People of Colonial Albany

www.nysm.nysed.gov/albany/index.html

This site gives detailed information about the settlers of Albany using essays, biographical information, portraits, maps, architecture, and more. Some information is presented about the pre-European native settlers of the area.

Investigations in the Richard B. Russell Dam and Lake Area

www.cr.nps.gov/seac/brochure3/front.htm

This brochure, adapted for the Web, presents prehistorical and historical cultural findings from this Georgia/South Carolina archaeological site.

History of North Carolina and South Carolina

www.usahistory.info/southern/North-Carolina.html
www.usahistory.info/southern/South-Carolina.html

Histories of the Carolinas are presented via a reprint of a turn-of-the-century textbook with links to illustrations and other documents.

William Penn

www.xroads.virginia.edu/~CAP/PENN/pnhome.html

William Penn was an extraordinary colonial figure, and this site is a good introduction to the man and some of his achievements.

Cultural Readings: Colonization and Print in the Americas

www.library.upenn.edu/special/gallery/kislak/index/
cultural.html

This site presents primary sources—including books, manuscripts, illustrations, and maps—from the colonial period.

The Golden Crescent: Crossroads of Florida and Georgia

www.cr.nps.gov/goldcres/

This site presents the cultural history and pre-history of the European, African, and native inhabitants of the region.

New Spain: The Frontiers of Faith

www.humanities-interactive.org/newspain/

An illustrated exhibit of documents from the Thomas Gilcrease Institute pertaining to the Spanish colonies in the New World.

Salem Witchcraft Trials, 1692

www.law.umkc.edu/faculty/projects/ftrials/salem/salem.htm

Images and primary documents comprise this account of the events in Salem.

Salem Witch Trials: Documentary Archive and Transcription Project

etext.lib.virginia.edu/salem/witchcraft/

Richly illustrated with documents and map images, this site presents both primary and secondary source material on the Salem witch trials.

4 The Maturing of Colonial Society

Joseph Beekman Smith, *Wesley Chapel on John Street, New York City—1768* (detail), completed 1817–1844 (based on earlier sketches). *(Old John Street United Methodist Church, New York)*

◆ *American Stories*

A STRUGGLING VIRGINIAN FINDS HIS PLACE

As a youth, Devereaux Jarratt knew only the isolated life of the small southern planter. Born in 1733 on the Virginia frontier, he was the third son of an immigrant yeoman farmer. In New Kent County, where Jarratt grew up, class status showed in a man's dress, his leisure habits, his house, even in his religion. A farmer's "whole dress and apparel," Jarratt recalled later, "consisted in a pair of coarse breeches, one or two shirts, a pair of shoes and stockings, an old felt hat, and a bear skin coat." In a maturing colonial society that was six generations old by the mid-eighteenth century, such simple folk stepped aside and tipped their hats when prosperous neighbors went by. "A periwig, in those days," recollected Jarratt, "was a distinguishing badge of gentle folk, and when I saw a man riding the road, near our house, with a wig on, it would so alarm my fears . . . that, I dare say, I would run off, as for my life."

As the colonies grew rapidly after 1700, economic development brought handsome gains for some, opened modest opportunities for many, but produced disappointment and privation for others. Jarratt remembered that his parents "neither sought nor expected any title, honors, or great things, either for themselves or their children. They wished us all brought up in some honest calling that we might earn our bread, by the sweat of our brow, as they did." But Jarratt was among those who advanced. His huge appetite for learning was apparent to his parents when as a small child he proved able to repeat entire chapters of the Bible before he had learned to read. That earned him some schooling. But at age 8, when his parents died, he had to take his place behind the plow alongside his brothers. Then, at 19, Jarratt was "called from the ax to the quill" by a neighboring planter's timely offer of a job tutoring his children.

Tutoring put Jarratt in touch with the world of wealth and status. Gradually, he advanced to positions in the households of wealthy Virginia planters. His modest success also introduced him to the world of evangelical religion. In the eighteenth century, an explosion of religious fervor dramatically reversed the growing secularism of the settlers. Jarratt first encountered evangelicalism in the published sermons of George Whitefield, an English clergyman.

But it was later, at the plantation of John Cannon, "a man of great possessions in lands and slaves," that Jarratt personally experienced conversion under the influence of Cannon's wife. He later became a clergyman in the Anglican church, which was dominated in the South by wealthy and dignified planters. He never lost his religious zeal and desire to carry religion to the common people. In this commitment to spiritual renewal, he participated in the first mass religious movement to occur in colonial society.

From the time of Jarrett's immigrant parents' arrival to the height of his career, a virtual population explosion occurred in the English colonies. In 1680, some 150,000 settlers clung to North America's eastern edge. By 1750, they had swelled sevenfold to top 1 million. Such growth staggered English policymakers, who uneasily watched the population gap between England and its American colonies closing rapidly. A high marriage rate, large families, lower mortality than in Europe, and heavy immigration accounted for much of the population boom.

Population growth and economic development gradually transformed eighteenth-century British America. Three variations of colonial society emerged: the farming society of the North, the plantation society of the South, and the urban society of the seaboard commercial towns. Although they shared some important characteristics, each was distinct. Even within regions, diversity increased in the eighteenth century as incoming streams of immigrants, mostly from Germany, Ireland, and France, and especially from Africa, added new pieces to the emerging American mosaic.

Until the late seventeenth century, the Spanish, French, and English settlements in North America were largely isolated from each other. But when a long period of war erupted in Europe between these colonizing nations, North America and the Caribbean now became important theaters of international conflict—a development that would reach a climax in the second half of the eighteenth century.

Despite their diversity and lack of cohesion, the colonies along the Atlantic seaboard were affected similarly by population growth and economic development. Everywhere except on the frontier, class differences and an involvement with slavery grew. A commercial orientation spread from north to south, especially in the towns, as local economies matured and forged links with the Atlantic basin network of trade. To these realities, Native Americans and the swelling number of enslaved Africans had to adjust—or, in some cases, resist. The exercise of political power of elected legislative assemblies and local bodies produced seasoned leaders, a tradition of local autonomy, and a widespread belief in a political ideology stressing the liberties that freeborn Englishmen should enjoy. All English-

settled regions experienced a deep-running religious awakening that was itself connected to secular changes. All these themes will be explored as we follow the way scattered frontier settlements developed into mature provincial societies.

THE NORTH: A LAND OF FAMILY FARMS

Although New England strove to maintain its homogeneity by making non-English immigrants unwelcome, the mid-Atlantic colonies swarmed with waves of immigrants from the Rhineland and Ireland, showing how connected were the destinies of people on opposite sides of the Atlantic. About 90,000 Germans flocked in during the eighteenth century, many fleeing "God's three arrows"—famine, war, and pestilence. They settled where promoters promised cheap and fertile land, low taxes, and freedom from military duty—mostly between New York and South Carolina, with Pennsylvania absorbing most. Coming mostly in families, they turned much of the mid-Atlantic hinterland into a German-speaking region. Place names still mark their zone of settlement: Mannheim, New Berlin, and Herkimer, New York; Bethlehem, Ephrata, Nazareth, and Hanover, Pennsylvania; Hagerstown and Frederick, Maryland; Mecklenberg and New Hanover, North Carolina.

Even more Protestant Scots–Irish arrived. Mostly poor farmers, they streamed into the same backcountry areas where Germans were settling, especially in New York and Pennsylvania, and many went farther, into the mountain valleys of the Carolinas and Georgia. No major Indian wars occurred between 1715 and 1754, but the frontier bristled with tension as the new settlers pushed westward.

Northern Agricultural Society

In the mid-eighteenth-century northern colonies, especially New England, tightknit farming families that were organized in communities of several thousand people dotted the landscape. New Englanders staked their future on a mixed economy. They cleared forests for timber used in barrels, ships, houses, and barns. They plumbed the offshore waters for fish that fed both local populations and the ballooning slave population of the West Indies. And they cultivated and grazed as much of

Pious German farmers often had moral stories displayed on the stove plates they purchased in Pennsylvania, Virginia, and North Carolina. This one, forged in 1741 with a German inscription, translates as "Cain killed his brother, Abel." *(Furnace, Durham, Stoveplate. Philadelphia Museum of Art: Purchased with Museum Funds, 1899 [1899.1142])*

the thin-soiled, rocky hills and bottomlands as they could recover from the forest.

The farmers of the middle colonies—Pennsylvania, Delaware, New Jersey, and New York—drove their wooden plows through much richer soils than New Englanders. They enjoyed the additional advantage of settling an area cleared by Native Americans who had relied more on agriculture than New England tribes. Thus favored, mid-Atlantic farm families produced modest surpluses of corn, wheat, beef, and pork. By the mid-eighteenth century, New York and Philadelphia ships were carrying these foodstuffs not only to the West Indies, always a primary market, but also to areas that could no longer feed themselves—England, Spain, Portugal, and even New England. In this way, they strengthened ties within the Atlantic basin.

German Settlement Areas, 1775   **Scots-Irish Settlement Areas, 1775**

Most German and Scots-Irish immigrants in the 1700s were farmers, and they quickly moved into the interior, where land was cheapest and most available.

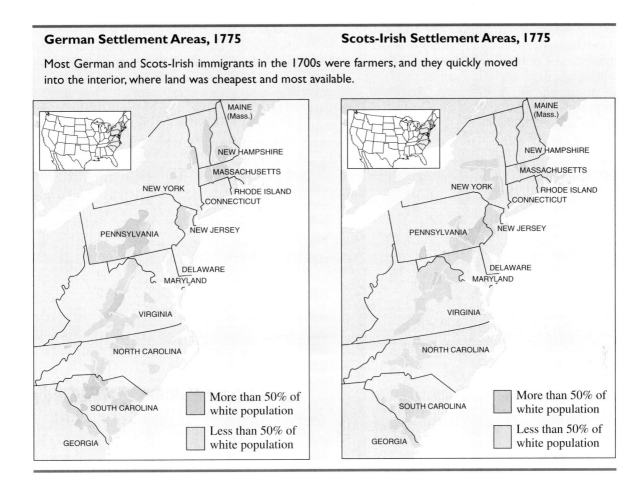

In the North, the broad ownership of land distinguished farming society from every other agricultural region of the Western world. Although differences in circumstances and ability led gradually toward greater social stratification, in most communities, few were truly rich or abjectly poor. Except for indentured servants, most men lived to purchase or inherit a farm of at least 50 acres. With their family's labor, they earned a decent existence and provided a small inheritance for each of their children. Settlers valued land highly, for freehold tenure ordinarily guaranteed both economic independence and political rights.

Amid widespread property ownership, a rising population pressed against a limited land supply by the eighteenth century, especially in New England. Family farms could not be divided and subdivided indefinitely, for it took at least 50 acres (of which only a quarter could usually be cropped) to support a family. In Concord, Massachusetts, for example, the founders had worked farms averaging about 250 acres. A century later, in the 1730s, the average farm had shrunk by two-thirds, as farm owners struggled to provide an inheritance for the three or four sons that the average marriage produced.

Decreasing soil fertility compounded the problem of dwindling farm size. When land had been plentiful, farmers planted crops in the same field for three years and then let it lie fallow seven years or more until it regained its strength. But on the smaller farms of the eighteenth century, farmers reduced fallowing to only a year or two. Such intense use of the soil reduced crop yields, forcing farmers to plow marginal land or shift to livestock production. Thus, Jared Eliot, New England's first agricultural essayist, referred to "our old land which we have worn out."

The diminishing size and productivity of family farms drove many New Englanders to the frontier or out of the area. "Many of our old towns are too full of inhabitants for husbandry, many of them living on small shares of land," bemoaned one Yankee. In Concord, one of every four adult males migrated from town every decade from the 1740s on, and in many towns out-migration was even greater. Some drifted to New York and Pennsylvania, and others sought opportunities as artisans in the coastal towns or took to the sea. More went to western Massachusetts, New Hampshire, Maine, and Nova Scotia.

Wherever they took up farming, northern cultivators engaged in agricultural work routines that were far less intense than in the South. The growing season was shorter, and cereal crops required incessant labor only during spring planting and autumn harvesting. This seasonal rhythm led many northern cultivators to fill out their calendars with work as clockmakers, shoemakers, carpenters, and weavers.

Unfree Labor

In the northern colonies, where shorter growing seasons than in the South curbed the cultivation of staple crops, the demand for labor was not so intense as in the West Indies and southern colonies. Yet slaves and indentured servants made up much of the incoming human tide after 1713. The westward traffic in servants became a regular part of the commerce linking Europe and North America.

Shipboard conditions for servants worsened in the eighteenth century and were hardly better than on slave ships. Official attempts to reduce the "tight packing" of indentured immigrants were of little help. Crammed between decks in stifling air, they suffered from smallpox and fevers, rotten food, impure water, cold, and lice. "Children between the ages of one and seven seldom survive the sea voyage," lamented one German immigrant, "and par-

ents must often watch their offspring suffer miserably, die, and be thrown into the ocean." As one Virginia observer remarked of an incoming troop of servants in 1758, "I never see such parcels of poor wretches, some almost naked and what had clothes was as black as chimney sweepers and almost starved." The shipboard mortality rate of about 15 percent in the colonial era made this the most unhealthy of all times to seek American shores.

Most indentured servants, especially males, found the labor system harsh. Merchants sold them, one shocked Britisher reported in 1773, "as they do their horses, and advertise them as they do their beef and oatmeal." Fleeing brutal masters was common, as testified by the notices of runaway servants that filled colonial newspapers.

Every servant's goal was to secure a foothold on the ladder of opportunity. "The hope of buying land in America," a New Yorker noted, "is what chiefly induces people into America." However, many died before finishing their time; others won freedom only to toil for years as poor day laborers and tenant farmers. The relatively few seventeenth-century indentured servants who had survived the fearful Chesapeake death often rose in society. Eighteenth-century servants had better chances to complete the labor contract but much less opportunity after-

Like enslaved Africans, white indentured servants often fled the harsh conditions under which they labored. Advertisements for the recovery of runaway servants (left) filled the colonial newspapers. No explanation is given for the sale of the servant girl's time (right). Was her performance unsatisfactory? Did her master unexpectedly need cash? *(Historical Society of Pennsylvania, Philadelphia)*

Slaves Imported to North America, 1701–1775

Overwhelmingly, Africans transported to the American colonies arrived from the 1730s to the 1770s. Rapid natural increase, as well as importation, swelled the African population to about 500,000 by the outbreak of the American Revolution.

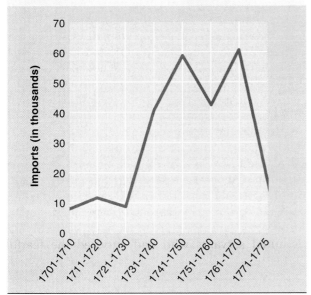

Source: R. C. Simmons, *The American Colonies: From Settlement to Independence*, 1976

wards to enter the propertied ranks. The chief beneficiaries of the system of bound white labor were the masters.

The number of enslaved Africans in the northern colonies grew in the eighteenth century but not nearly as fast as the indentured servant population. Slaves made up less than 10 percent of the population in all northern colonies and in most only 3 to 4 percent. Along with occasional Indian slaves, they typically worked as artisans, farmhands, or personal servants. Whereas about two-thirds of all southern slaves worked on plantations with at least ten of their fellows by the 1720s, in the North the typical slave labored alone or with only a few others. Living in the same house as the master, slaves adapted to European ways much faster than in the South, where the slave quarters perpetuated African folkways. Slavery was also less repressive in the North.

Northern slavery grew fastest in the ports. Artisans invested profitably in slaves; ship captains purchased them for maritime labor; and an emerging urban elite of merchants, lawyers, and landlords displayed its wealth with slave coachmen and per-

sonal servants. By the beginning of the eighteenth century, more than 40 percent of New York City's households owned slaves. Even in Quaker Philadelphia, slaveholding increased sharply in the eighteenth century. Struggling white artisans resented slave workers for undercutting their wages, and the white citizenry feared black arsonists and rebels. Yet these reservations were outweighed by high labor demand and by the advantage of purchasing lifelong servants for just two years' worth of a free white laborer's wages.

Changing Values

Boston's weather on April 29, 1695, began warm and sunny, noted the devout merchant Samuel Sewall in his diary. But by afternoon, lightning and hailstones "as big as pistol and musket bullets" pummeled the town. Sewall dined that evening with Cotton Mather, New England's prominent Puritan clergyman. Mather wondered why "more ministers' houses than others proportionately had been smitten with lightning." The words were hardly out of his mouth before hailstones began to shatter the windows. Sewall and Mather fell to their knees in prayer "after this awful Providence." These two third-generation Massachusetts Puritans understood that God was angry with them as leaders of a people whose piety was giving way to worldliness. Massachusetts was becoming "sermon-proof," explained one dejected minister.

In other parts of the North, the expansive environment and the Protestant emphasis on self-discipline and hard work were also breeding qualities that would become hallmarks of American culture: ambitiousness, individualism, and materialism. In Europe, most tillers of the soil expected little from life. Lacking access to new land, impoverished peasant farmers viewed life simply as a perpetual struggle against famine and disease. But in America, one colonist remarked, "Every man expects one day or another to be upon a footing with his wealthiest neighbor."

Commitment to religion, family, and community did not disappear, but fewer people saw daily existence just as a preparation for the afterlife. They began to regard land not simply as a source of livelihood but as a commodity to be bought and sold for profit.

A slender almanac, written by the twelfth child of a poor Boston candlemaker, captured the new outlook with wit and charm. Born in 1706, Benjamin Franklin climbed the ladder of success spectacularly. Running away from a harsh apprenticeship to an older brother when he was 16, he abandoned a declining Boston for a rising Philadelphia. By 23, he had learned the printer's trade and was publishing the *Pennsylvania Gazette*. Three years later, he began *Poor Richard's Almanack,* which, next to the Bible, was the most widely read book in the colonies. Franklin filled it with quips, adages, and homespun philosophy: "The sleeping fox gathers no poultry." "Lost time is never found again." "It costs more to maintain one vice than to raise two children." "Sloth makes all things difficult but industry all easy." Ever cocky, Franklin caught the spirit of the rising secularism of the eighteenth century. He embodied the growing utilitarian doctrine that good is whatever is useful and the notion that the community is best served through individual self-improvement and accomplishment.

Women and the Family in the Northern Colonies

In 1662, Elnathan Chauncy, a Massachusetts schoolboy, copied into his writing book that the soul "consists of two portions, inferior and superior; the superior is masculine and eternal; the feminine inferior and mortal." This lesson had been taught for generations on both sides of the Atlantic. It was part of a larger conception of God's design that assigned degrees of status and stations in life to all individuals. In that world, women were subordinate, taught from infancy to be modest, patient, and compliant. Regarded by men as weak of mind and large of heart, they existed for and through men, subject first to their fathers and then to their husbands.

European women usually accepted these narrowly circumscribed roles. Few complained, at least openly, that their work was generally limited to housewifery and midwifery. They silently accepted exclusion from the early public schools and laws that transferred to their husbands any property or income they brought into a marriage. Nor could women speak in their churches or participate in governing them (except in Quaker meetinghouses), and they had no legal voice in politics. Few women chose a husband for love because parental guidance prevailed in a society in which producing legal heirs was the means of transmitting property. Once wed, women expected to remain so until death, for they could rarely obtain a divorce.

On the colonial frontier, women's lives changed in modest ways. One European woman in ten women did not marry. But in the colonies, where men outnumbered women for the first century, a spinster was almost unheard of, and widows remarried with astounding speed. "A young widow with 4 or 5 children, who among the middling or inferior ranks of people in Europe would have little chance for a second husband," observed one Englishman, "is in America frequently courted as a sort of fortune." *Woman* and *wife* thus became nearly synonymous.

A second difference concerned property rights. Single women and widows in the colonies, as in England, could make contracts, hold and convey property, represent themselves in court, and conduct business. Under English common law, a woman forfeited these rights, as well as all property, when she married. In the colonies, however, legislatures and courts gave wives more control over property brought into marriage or left at their husbands' death. They also enjoyed broader rights to act for and with their husbands in business transactions. In addition, young colonial women slowly gained the right of consenting to a marriage partner—a right that came by default to the thousands of female indentured servants who completed their labor contracts and had no parents within 3,000 miles to dictate to them.

Although colonial society did not encourage or reward female individuality, women worked alongside their husbands in competent and complementary ways. Women had limited career choices and rights but broad responsibilities. The work spaces and daily routines of husband and wife overlapped and intersected far more than today. Farm women as well as men worked at planting, harvesting, and milking cows. Women also made candles and soap,

Part of becoming the "ideal" woman was learning patience and exactitude. Young Rebecca Jones, a Philadelphia teenager, spent hundreds of hours working birds, animals, and sprigs of flowers into her compartmented sampler, which also recorded the exact time of her birth. *(Courtesy of the Atwater Kent Museum of Philadelphia)*

Childbirth was an oft-repeated event in the lives of most colonial wives. In this portrait of the Cheney family, the older woman is a nanny or mother-in-law; the younger woman holding a baby is Mr. Cheney's second wife. (The Cheney Family, *Gift of Edgar and Bernice Chrysler,* © 2000 Board of Trustees, National Gallery of Art, Washington, c. 1795, canvas, .490 × .650 [19¼ × 25⅝])

butter and cheese, and smoked meat; they made cloth and sometimes marketed farm products. A merchant's wife kept shop, handled accounts when her husband voyaged abroad, and helped supervise the servants and apprentices. "Deputy husbands" and "yoke mates" were revealing terms used by New Englanders to describe eighteenth-century wives.

Despite conventional talk of inferiority, women within their families and neighborhoods neverthe-less shaped the world around them. Older women modeled the behavior of young women, aided the needy, and subtly affected menfolk, who held for-mal authority. Women outnumbered men in church life and worked within their families to promote re-ligion in outlying areas, to seat and unseat minis-ters, and to influence morals. Periodically, they ap-peared as visionaries and mystics.

Women held vital responsibilities as midwives. Until the late eighteenth century, the "obstetrick art" was almost entirely in their hands. Midwives coun-seled pregnant women, delivered babies, supervised postpartum recovery, and participated in infant baptism and burial ceremonies. Mrs. Phillips, an immigrant to Boston in 1719, was a familiar figure as she hurried through the streets to attend the lying-in of about 70 women each year. In her 42-year ca-reer, she delivered more than 3,000 infants. Because colonial women were pregnant or nursing infants for about half the years between the ages 20 and 40 and because childbirth was dangerous, the circle of female friends and relatives attending childbirth created strong networks of mutual assistance.

In her role as wife and mother, the eighteenth-century northern woman differed somewhat from her English counterpart. Whereas English women married in their mid-twenties, American women typically took husbands a few years earlier because of more favorable life prospects. This head start in-creased their childbearing years. Hence, the average colonial family included five children (two others typically died in infancy), whereas the English fam-ily contained fewer than three. Gradually, marriage age crept up and the number of children per family inched down.

Northern child-rearing patterns differed consid-erably. In the seventeenth century, stern fathers dominated Puritan family life, and few were reluc-tant to punish unruly children. "Better whip'd than damn'd," advised Cotton Mather, reinforcing many parents' belief that breaking the young child's will created a pious and submissive personality. Quaker mothers, however, tended to use love rather than guilt to mold their children. Attitudes toward choos-ing a marriage partner also separated early Puritans and Quakers. Puritan parents usually arranged their children's marriages but allowed them the right to veto. Young Quaker men and women made their own matches, subject to parental veto. These differ-ences aside, all children played roles, from an early age, in contributing to the family economy.

The father-dominated family of New England gradually declined in the eighteenth century. In its place rose the mother-centered family, in which af-fectionate parents encouraged self-expression and independence in their children. This "modern" approach, on the rise in Europe as well, brought the colonists closer to the methods of parenthood found among the coastal Native Americans, who initially had been disparaged for their lax approach to rearing their young.

Ecological Transformation

Wherever Europeans settled in the Americas, they brought with them animals, plant life, diseases, and ways of viewing the natural resources—all with enormous consequences. The introduction of grazing animals profoundly altered New Spain's landscape. Breeding prolifically in an environment generally free of animal predators, the cattle, horses, pigs, sheep, and goats devoured the tall grasses and most palatable plant species. Within a half century, huge areas had little or no ground cover. Then, new unwelcome plant species took hold—stinging nettles, dandelions, and nightshade.

In England's North American colonies, the rapid increase of settlers after 1715 had different environmental effects. First, the demand for wood—for building and heating houses, for producing the charcoal necessary for ironmaking, for shipbuilding and barrelmaking—swiftly depleted coastal forests. Just for heating and cooking, the typical northern farmhouse required an acre of trees each year. An iron furnace needed 20,000 acres of forest to produce a thousand tons of iron. A 40-acre field required 8,000 fence rails. Rapid and often wasteful harvesting of the forests had many effects. As the colonists chopped down the forest canopy that had previously moderated the weather, the summers became hotter and winters became colder. Snow melted sooner and watersheds emptied faster, in turn, causing soil erosion and drought.

A second ecological transformation occurred when animals brought by Europeans began to replace animals already in North America. European colonists were a livestock people, skilled in mixed farming and herding of domesticated cattle, horses, pigs, sheep, and goats. Multiplying rapidly in a favorable environment, pigs and cattle "swarm like vermin upon the earth," reported one Virginia account as early as 1700. Native grasses and shrubs disappeared so quickly that the European livestock began to die for lack of grazing land.

Meanwhile, native fur-bearing animals—beaver, deer, bear, wolf, raccoon, and marten—rapidly became extinct in the areas of settlement. Prized for their skins or hated as predators of domesticated animals, these species were hunted relentlessly. One broken link in the ecological chain affected others. For example, the dams and ponds of the beaver,

which had been breeding grounds for many species of wild ducks, soon were drained and converted to meadows for cattle.

Animals prized for dinner-table fare also quickly reached extinction along the East Coast. Wild turkeys were a rarity in Massachusetts by the 1670s. Deer disappeared by the early 1700s in settled areas. "Hunting with us exists chiefly in the tales of other times," wrote Yale's president in the late eighteenth century.

All these environmental changes were linked not only to the numbers of Europeans arriving in North America but also to their ways of thinking about nature. Transplanted Europeans saw only the possibility of raising valuable crops as if the ecosystem was composed of unconnected elements, each ripe for exploitation. Land, lumber, fish, and fur-bearing animals could be converted into sources of cash that would buy imported commodities that improved one's material condition. The New England writer Edward Johnson described the process as early as 1653: Who would have imagined, he mused, "that this wilderness should turn a mart for merchants in so short a space, Holland, France, Spain, and Portugal coming hither for trade?" Supplying these Europeans were the farmers, woodcutters, and fishermen who consigned to the marketplace portions of the ecosystem that Native Americans regarded as essential for sustaining life.

Coming from homelands where land was scarce, the settlers viewed their ability to reap nature's abundance in North America as proof of their success. From their perspective, they were correct because, in fact, colonial agriculture was abundantly successful in terms of what the settlers obliged the land to yield up. Yet the "rage for commerce" and for an improved life produced wasteful practices on farms and in forests and fisheries. "The grain fields, the meadows, the forests, the cattle, etc.," wrote a Swedish visitor in the 1750s, "are treated with equal carelessness." Accustomed to the natural abundance once the native peoples had been driven from the land, and seeing no limits to the land that was available, the colonists embarked on ecologically destructive practices that over a period of many generations profoundly altered the natural world of North America.

THE PLANTATION SOUTH

Between 1690 and 1760, the southern white tidewater settlements changed from a frontier society with high immigration, a surplus of males, and an unstable social organization to a settled society composed mostly of native-born families. But while a mature southern culture took form from the ocean to the piedmont after 1715, Scots-Irish and German immi-

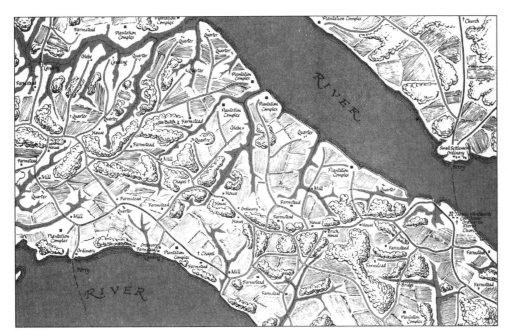

The distribution of cultivated fields, dwellings, and commercial buildings in the tidewater landscape created "communities" without towns (rendered from historical and archaeological evidence). *(From* The Transformation of Virginia, 1740–1790 *by Rhys Isaac. © 1982 by the University of North Carolina Press. Published for the Institute of Early American History and Culture. Used by permission of the publisher.)*

grants flooded into the backcountry of Virginia, the Carolinas, and the new colony of Georgia, which was founded in 1732 as a debtors' haven and a buffer between Spanish Florida and the Carolinas. New England nearly tripled in population, but the southern colonies quadrupled; in the South, the fast-growing slave population accounted for much more of the growth than in the North. Virginia, with a population of nearly 340,000 by 1760, remained by far the largest colony in North America.

The Tobacco Coast

Tobacco production in Virginia and Maryland expanded rapidly in the seventeenth century, with exports reaching 25 million pounds annually during the 1680s. But then two decades of war in Europe made Atlantic basin commercial traffic more dangerous, driving up transportation costs and dampening the demand for tobacco. Stagnation in the tobacco market lasted from the mid-1680s until about 1715.

Yet in this period the Upper South underwent a profound social transformation. First, African slaves replaced European indentured servants so rapidly that by 1730 the unfree labor force was overwhelmingly black. Second, planters responded to the depressed tobacco market by diversifying their crops. They shifted some tobacco fields to grain, hemp, and flax; increased their herds of cattle and swine; and became more self-sufficient by developing local industries to produce iron, leather, and textiles. By the 1720s, when a profitable tobacco trade with France created a new period of prosperity, the economy was much more diverse and resilient. Third, the population structure changed rapidly. African

slaves grew from about 7 percent to more than 40 percent of the region's population between 1690 and 1750, and the drastic imbalance between white men and women disappeared. Families rather than single men now predominated. The earlier frontier society of white immigrants, mostly living short, unrewarding lives as indentured servants, grew into an eighteenth-century plantation society of native-born freeholder families.

Notwithstanding the influx of Africans, slave owning was far from universal. As late as 1750, a majority of families owned no slaves at all. Not more than one-tenth of slaveholders held more than 20 slaves. Nonetheless, the common goal was the large plantation where slaves made the earth yield up profits to support an aristocratic life for their masters.

The Chesapeake planters who acquired the best land and accumulated enough capital to invest heavily in slaves created a gentry lifestyle that set them apart from ordinary farmers such as Devereaux Jarratt's father. By the eighteenth century, the development of the northern colonies had produced prosperous farmers worth several thousand pounds. But such wealth paled alongside the estates of men such as Charles Carroll of Maryland and Robert "King" Carter and William Byrd of Virginia, who counted their slaves by the hundreds, their acres by the thousands, and their fortunes by the tens of thousands of pounds.

Ritual display of wealth marked southern gentry life. Racing thoroughbred horses and gambling on them recklessly, sometimes for purses of £100 (at a time when a laboring man earned £40 per year), became common sport for young gentlemen, who had often been educated in England. Planters began to construct stately brick Georgian mansions, filled with imported furniture, attended by liveried black slaves, and graced by formal gardens and orchards.

Some observers saw the cultivated aristocratic lifestyle as a veneer. "If a [man] has Money, Negroes, and Land enough," scoffed a Scottish newcomer, "he is a complete Gentleman. These hide all his defects, usher him into the best of company, and draw upon him the smiles of the fair Sex." Affected or not, the emerging Chesapeake planter elite controlled the county courts, officered the local militia, ruled the parish vestries of the Anglican Church, made law in their legislative assemblies, and passed to their sons the mantle of political and social leadership.

For all their airs, these southern squires were essentially agrarian businessmen. They spent their days haggling over credit, land, slaves, and tenant leases; scheduling planting and harvesting; conferring with overseers; and disciplining slaves. Tobacco cultivation (unlike that of wheat and corn) claimed the planter's attention year-round as the crop moved through the many stages of planting, transplanting, topping, cutting, curing, and packing. A planter's reputation rested on the quality of his crop. To personalize their tobacco, planters stamped their hogsheads of leaf with their initials or emblem. "Question a planter on the subject," explained one observer, "and he will tell you that he cultivates such or such a kind [of tobacco], as for example, Colonel Carter's sort, John Cole's sort or [that of] some other leading crop master."

Planters' wives also shouldered many responsibilities. They superintended cloth production and the processing and preparation of food while ruling over households crowded with children, slaves, and visitors. An aristocratic veneer gave the luster of gentility to plantations from Maryland to North Carolina, but in fact these were large working farms, often so isolated from one another that the planter and his wife lived a "solitary and unsociable existence," as one phrased it. With only infrequent contact with the outside world, they learned to be independent as they managed their own little communities of servants, slaves, and family members.

The Rice Coast

The plantation economy of the Lower South in the eighteenth century rested on rice and indigo. Rice exports surpassed 1.5 million pounds per year by 1710 and reached 80 million pounds by the eve of the Revolution. Indigo, a smelly blue dye obtained from plants for use in textiles, became a staple crop in the 1740s after Eliza Lucas Pinckney, a wealthy South Carolina planter's wife, experimented successfully with its cultivation. Within a generation, indigo production had spread into Georgia. It soon ranked among the leading colonial exports, widely used in England where textile production was centered.

The expansion of rice production, exported to the West Indies and Europe, transformed the swampy coastal lowlands around Charleston, where planters imported thousands of slaves after 1720. By 1740, slaves composed nearly 90 percent of the region's inhabitants. White population declined as wealthy planters entrusted their estates to resident overseers. They wintered in cosmopolitan Charleston and summered in Newport, Rhode Island, their refuge from seasonal malaria along the rice coast. At mid-century, a shocked New England visitor described it as a society "divided into opulent and lordly planters, poor and spiritless peasants, and vile slaves."

Three Africans are pictured here rolling hogsheads of tobacco and hammering home the top of one of them. In colonial Virginia, it became almost impossible to think about tobacco without calling slaves to mind. *(Duke University Library)*

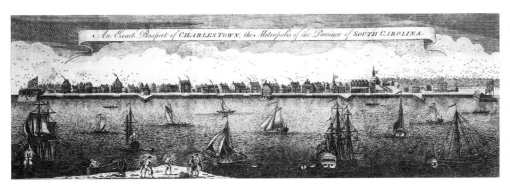

This engraved view of Charleston's waterfront a few decades before the American Revolution shows that it was little more than a waterside village, yet it was the southern colonies' busiest seaport. The two tallest buildings (designated D and E) were churches. *(Courtesy, American Antiquarian Society)*

Throughout the plantation South, the courthouse became a central male gathering place. All classes came to settle debts, dispute over land, sue and be sued. When court was over, a multitude lingered on, drinking, gossiping, and staging horse races, cockfights, wrestling matches, footraces, and fiddling contests—all considered tests of male prowess.

The church, almost always Anglican in the South before 1750, also became a center of community gathering. A visiting northerner described the animated socializing before worship: men "giving and receiving letters of business, reading advertisements, consulting about the price of tobacco and grain, and settling either the lineage, age, or qualities of favourite horses." Then, people filed into church, with lesser planters entering first and standing attentively until the wealthy gentry, "in a body" took their pews at the front. After church, socializing continued, with young people strolling together and older ones extending invitations to Sunday dinner. New England's pious Sabbath was little in evidence.

The Backcountry

While the southern gentry matured along the tobacco and rice coasts, settlers poured into the upland backcountry. As late as 1730, only hunters and Indian fur traders had known this vast expanse of hilly red clay and fertile limestone soils from Pennsylvania to Georgia. Over the next four decades, it attracted some 250,000 inhabitants, nearly half the southern white population.

Thousands of land-hungry German and Scots-Irish settlers spilled into the interior valleys along the eastern side of the Appalachians. They squatted on land, lived tensely with neighboring Indians in a region where boundaries were shadowy, and built a subsistence society of small farms. This "mixed medley from all countries and the off scouring of America," as one colonist described them, remained isolated from the coastal region for several generations, which helped these pioneers cling fiercely to folkways they had brought across the Atlantic.

Crude backcountry life appalled many visitors from the more refined seaboard. In 1733, William Byrd described a large Virginia frontier plantation as a "poor, dirty hovel, with hardly anything in it but children that wallowed about like so many pigs." Charles Woodmason, a stiff-necked Anglican minister who tramped between settlements in the Carolina upcountry, was shocked. "Through the licentiousness of the people many hundreds live in concubinage—swopping their wives as cattle and living in a state of nature more irregularly and unchastely than the Indians."

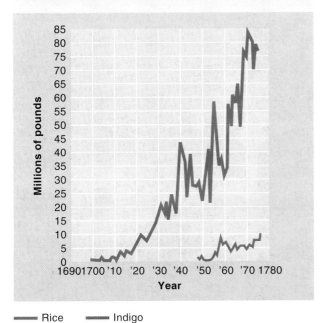

Rice and Indigo Exports from South Carolina and Georgia, 1698–1775

Just as Virginia had been built on tobacco, South Carolina and Georgia were built on rice. Much of it was sent to the West Indies to feed the huge population of enslaved Africans there.

━━━ Rice   ━━━ Indigo

Source: U.S. Bureau of the Census

These comments reflected the poverty of frontier life and the lack of schools, churches, and towns. Most families plunged into the backcountry with only a few crude household possessions, tools, perhaps a pair of oxen, a few chickens and swine, and the clothes on their backs. They lived in rough-hewn log cabins and planted their corn, beans, and wheat between the tree stumps. Women toiled alongside men. For a generation, everyone endured a poor diet, endless work, and meager rewards.

By the 1760s, the southern backcountry had begun to emerge from the frontier stage. Small marketing towns such as Camden, South Carolina; Salisbury, North Carolina; Winchester, Virginia; and Fredericktown, Maryland, became centers of craft activity, church life, and local government. Farms began producing surpluses for shipment east. Density of settlement increased, creating a social life known for harvest festivals, log-rolling contests, horse races, wedding celebrations, dances, and prodigious drinking bouts. Class distinctions remained narrow compared with the older seaboard settlements, as many backcountry settlements acquired the look of permanence.

Family Life in the South

As the South emerged from the early era of withering mortality and stunted families, male and female roles gradually became more physically and functionally separated. In most areas, the white gender ratio reached parity by the 1720s, depriving women

of their leverage in the marriage market. The growth of slavery also changed white women's work role, with the wealthy planter's wife becoming a domestic manager in "the great house." In a description of his daughters' daily routine, William Byrd II pointed to the emerging female identity: "They are every day up to their elbows in housewifery, which will qualify them effectually for useful wives and if they live long enough for notable women."

The balanced gender ratio and the growth of slavery also brought changes for southern males. The planters' sons had always been trained in horsemanship, the use of a gun, and the rhythms of agricultural life. Learning how to manage and discipline slaves was as important as lessons with tutors such as Devereaux Jarratt. Bred to command, southern planters' sons developed a self-confidence and authority that propelled many of them into leadership roles during the American Revolution.

On the small farms of the tidewater region and throughout the back settlements, women's roles closely resembled those of northern women. Women labored in the fields alongside their menfolk. "She is a very civil woman," noted an observer of a southern frontierswoman, "and shows nothing of ruggedness or immodesty in her carriage; yet she will carry a gun in the woods and kill deer and turkeys, shoot down wild cattle, catch and tie hogs, knock down beeves with an ax, and perform the most manful exercises as well as most men in those parts."

Marriage and family life were more informal in the backcountry. With vast areas unattended by

Indigo production, mostly the work of enslaved Africans in South Carolina, was dirty, smelly, and debilitating. This eighteenth-century engraving shows each step, from the plant at lower right to tending vats of boiling water. An overseer (top right) supervises the slaves. *(The Folger Shakespeare Library)*

ministers and with courthouses out of reach, most couples married or "took up" with each other until an itinerant clergyman on horseback appeared to bless the marriages and baptize the children. Respectable clergymen saw the frontier settlers living in lascivious abandon. But the upcountry hunters and farmers were really only the first of many generations of pioneers who made do as best they could on the forest's edge, where the institutions of settled society had not yet arrived.

Enslaved Africans in the Southern Colonies

From the late seventeenth century, the slave population grew rapidly—from about 15,000 in 1690 grew to 80,000 in 1730 and 325,000 in 1760. By then, when they composed one-fifth of the colonial population, Africans were growing in number far more from natural increase than from importation. The generation after 1730 witnessed the largest influx of African slaves in the colonial period, averaging about 5,000 a year. In the entire period from 1700 to 1775, more than 350,000 African slaves entered the American colonies.

Most of these miserable captives were auctioned off to southern planters, but some landed in the northern cities, especially New York and Philadelphia. Merchants sold them there to artisans, farmers, and upper-class householders seeking domestic servants.

The basic struggle for Africans toiling on plantations 5,000 miles from their homes was to create strategies for living as satisfactorily as possible despite horrifying treatment. The master hoped to convert the slave into a mindless drudge who obeyed every command and worked efficiently for his profit. But attempts to cow slaves rarely succeeded completely. Masters could set the external boundaries of existence for their slaves, controlling physical location, work roles, diet, and shelter. But the authority of the master class impinged far less on how slaves established friendships, fell in love, formed kin groups, reared children, worshiped their gods, buried their dead, and organized their leisure time.

In these aspects of daily life, slaves in the Americas drew on their African heritage to shape their existence to some degree, thus laying the foundations for an African-American culture. At first, this culture had many variations because slaves came from many areas in Africa and lived under different conditions in the colonies. But common elements emerged, led by developments in the South, where about 90 percent of American slaves labored in colonial times.

Arriving in North America, Africans entered a relatively healthy environment compared with other slave-labor areas in the Western Hemisphere. In the southern colonies, where the ghastly mortality of the early decades had subsided by the time Africans were arriving in large numbers, the slave's chance for survival was much better than in the West Indies or Brazil. This, as well as a more even gender ratio, led to a natural increase in the North American slave population unparalleled elsewhere.

Visiting French Louisiana in 1735, Alexander de Batz painted members of the Illinois tribe who traded at New Orleans. Note the hatted African, who apparently has been adopted by the Illinois. *(Peabody Museum, Harvard University, Photography by Hillel Burger)*

Although slave codes severely restricted the lives of slaves, the possibility for family life increased as the southern colonies matured. Larger plantations employed dozens and even hundreds of slaves, with many of the men laboring in skilled crafts, and the growth of roads and market towns permitted them greater opportunities to forge relationships beyond their own plantation. By the 1740s, a growing proportion of Chesapeake slaves were American-born, had established families, and lived in plantation outbuildings where from sundown to sunup they could fashion personal lives.

In South Carolina, African slaves drew on agricultural skills practiced in Africa and made rice the keystone of the coastal economy by the early eighteenth century. Their numbers increased rapidly, from about 4,000 in 1708 to 90,000 by 1760. Working mostly on large plantations in swampy lowlands, they endured the most life-sapping conditions on the continent. But they outnumbered whites three to one by 1760 and hence could maintain more of their African culture than slaves in the Chesapeake region. Many spoke Gullah, a "pidgin" mixing several African languages. They often gave African names to their children—names like Cudjoe, Cuffe, Quashey, and Phibbi—and kept alive African religious customs.

Resistance and Rebellion

Slaves not only adapted to bondage but also resisted and rebelled in ways that constantly reminded their masters that slavery's price was eternal vigilance. Slaveowners interpreted rebelliousness as evidence of the "barbarous, wild savage natures" of Africans, as a South Carolina law of 1712 phrased it. Some planters, like Virginia's Landon Carter, believed that "slaves are devils and to make them free is to set devils free." But from the African point of view, the struggle against enslavement was essential to maintaining meaning and dignity in a life of degrading toil. Resisters' goals varied: to rejoin family members, to flee, to convince masters to improve their condition, or to avenge sadistic overseers.

"Saltwater" Africans, fresh from their homelands, often fought slavery fiercely. "They often die before they can be conquered," said one white. Commonly, initial resistance took the form of fleeing—to renegade frontier settlements, to interior Indian tribes (which sometimes offered refuge), or to Spanish Florida. Rebellions, such as those in New York City in 1712 and at Stono, South Carolina, in 1739, mostly involved newly arrived slaves. There was no North American parallel, however, for the massive slave uprisings of the West Indies and Brazil, where Africans vastly outnumbered their masters and therefore had a special incentive for rebelling.

The relatively small rebellions that did occur (or were feared) led to atrocious repression. Near Charleston in 1739, officials tortured and hanged 50 black rebels. Their decapitated heads, impaled on posts, warned other potential insurrectionists. In New York City a year later, officials responded to a rumored insurrection by hanging 18 slaves and 4 white allies and burning 13 other slaves at the stake.

Open rebelliousness often gave way to more subtle forms of resistance as slaves learned English, adjusted to work routines, and began forming families. Dragging out jobs, pretending illness or ignorance, and breaking tools were ways of avoiding physical exhaustion and indirect forms of opposing slavery itself. More direct resistance included truancy, arson directed against the master's barns and houses, crop destruction, pilfering to supplement their food supply, and direct assaults on masters, overseers, and drivers. Overall, slave masters did extract labor and obedience from their slaves; if they had not, the slave system would have collapsed. But they did so only with difficulty. To push slaves too hard could be costly. One South Carolina planter drove his slaves late into the night cleaning and barreling a rice crop in 1732. When he awoke in the morning, he found his barn, with the entire harvest in it, reduced to ashes.

Black Religion and Family

The balance of power was always massively stacked against the slaves. Only the most desperate challenged the system directly. But most slaves struggled to find meaning and worth in their existence, no matter how brutal and discouraging the slave system that manacled them. In this quest, religion and family played a central role—one destined to continue far into the postslavery period.

Africans brought to the New World a complex religious heritage that no desolation or physical abuse could crush. People enduring the daily travail that accompanied slavery typically turned for relief to their deepest emotional sources. Coming from cultures where the division between sacred and secular activities was less clear than in Europe, slaves made religion central to their existence. But until the mid-eighteenth century, most slaves died strangers to Christianity. Then they began to blend African religious practices with the religion of the master class, using this hybrid religion both to light the spark of resistance and to find comfort from oppression.

The religious revival that began in the 1720s in the northern colonies and spread southward thereafter made important contributions to African-American religion. Evangelicalism stressed personal

> Philadelphia, Auguſt 24, 1762.
>
> RUN away from the Subſcriber Yeſterday, a Mulattoe Man Slave, named Joe, alias Joſeph Boudron, a middle-ſized Man, a briſk lively Fellow, about 23 Years of Age, was born at Guadaloupe, has lived ſome Time in New-York, and Charles-Town, in South-Carolina, ſpeaks good Engliſh, French, Spaniſh, and Portugueſe: Had on when he went away, an old whitiſh coloured Broadcloth Coat, faced with Pluſh, and Metal Buttons, a Calicoe Jacket, black knit Breeches, blue Worſted Stockings, new Shoes, with large Braſs Buckles, Check Shirt, an old laced Hat, and has other Things not known; he is a good Cook, and much uſed to the Seas, where it is thought he intends, or for New-York. Any Perſon that takes up ſaid Runaway, and brings him to me, or ſecures him in any Goal in this Province, ſhall have Two Piſtoles Reward, and if in any other Province, Four Piſtoles, and reaſonable Charges, paid by me
>
> THOMAS BARTHOLOMEW, junior.
>
> N. B. All Maſters of Veſſels and others are deſired not to carry him off, or harbour him, on any Account.

Colonial newspapers, from Boston to Charleston, were filled with ads for runaway slaves. This ad, from the *Pennsylvania Gazette* (August 26, 1762), indicates that Joe (who has renamed himself Joseph Boudron) is an accomplished linguist who speaks English, French, Spanish, and Portuguese. *(The Historical Society of Pennsylvania [Pennsylvania Gazette, 8/26/1762])*

rebirth, used music and body motion, and produced an intense emotional experience. The dancing, shouting, rhythmic clapping, and singing that came to characterize slaves' religious expression represented a creative mingling of West African and Christian religions.

Besides religion, the slaves' greatest refuge from their dreadful fate lay in their families. In West Africa, all social relations were centered in kinship, which included dead ancestors. Torn from their native societies, slaves placed great importance on rebuilding extended kin groups.

Most English colonies prohibited slave marriages. But in practice, slaves and masters struck a bargain. Slaves desperately wanted families, and masters found that slaves with families would work harder and be less inclined to escape or rebel (for few slaves wanted to leave loved ones at the mercy of an angry master).

Slaves fashioned a family life only with difficulty, however. The general practice of importing three male slaves for every two females stunted family formation. Female slaves, much in demand, married in their late teens, but males usually had to wait until their mid- to late twenties. But as natural increase swelled the slave population in the eighteenth century, the gender ratio became more even.

Slave marriages were rarely secure because they could be abruptly severed by the sale of either husband or wife. This happened repeatedly, especially when a deceased planter's estate was divided among his heirs or his slaves were sold to his credi-

tors to satisfy debts. Children usually stayed with their mothers until about age eight; then they were frequently torn from their families through sale, often to small planters needing only a hand or two. Few slaves escaped separation from family members at some time during their lives.

White male exploitation of black women represented another assault on family life. How many black women were coerced or lured with favors into sexual relations with white masters and overseers cannot be known, but the sizable mulatto (mixed-race) population at the end of the eighteenth century indicates that the number was large. Interracial liaisons, frequently forced, were widespread, especially in the Lower South. In 1732, the *South-Carolina Gazette* called racial mixing an "epidemical disease." It was a malady that had traumatic effects on slave attempts to build stable relationships.

In some interracial relationships, the coercion was subtle. In some cases, black women sought the liaison to gain advantages for themselves or their children. These unions nonetheless threatened both the slave community and the white plantation ideal. They bridged the supposedly unbridgeable gap between slave and free society and produced children who did not fit into the separate racial categories that the colonists wished to maintain.

Despite such obstacles, slaves fashioned intimate ties as husband and wife, parent and child. If monogamous relationships did not last as long as in white society, much of the explanation lies in slave life: the shorter life span of African Americans, the shattering of marriage through sale of one or both partners, and the call of freedom that impelled some slaves to run away.

Whereas slave men struggled to preserve their family role, many black women assumed a position in the family that differed from that of white women. Plantation mistresses usually worked hard in helping manage estates, but nonetheless the ideal grew that they should remain in the house guarding white virtue and setting standards for white culture. In contrast, the black woman remained indispensable to both the work of the plantation and the functioning of the slave quarters. She toiled in the fields and slave cabins alike. Paradoxically, black women's constant labor made them more equal to men than was the case of women in white society.

Above all, slavery was a set of power relationships designed to extract the maximum labor from its victims. Hence, it regularly involved cruelties that filled family life with tribulation. But slaves in North America were unusually successful in establishing families because they lived in a healthier environment; toiled in less physically exhausting circumstances than slaves on sugar and coffee plantations; and were better clothed, fed, and treated than Africans in the West Indies, Brazil, and other parts of the hemisphere. In these more tropical areas, plantation owners imported large numbers of male slaves, literally worked them to death, and then purchased replacements from Africa. Family life in the American colonies brimmed with uncertainty and sorrow, but slaves nonetheless made it the greatest monument to their will to endure captivity and eventually gain their freedom.

CONTENDING FOR A CONTINENT

From earliest beginnings, the colonists of the English colonies occupied only a narrow strip of coastal plain in eastern North America. Even by 1750, when they numbered about 1.2 million, only a small fraction of them, along with their African slaves, lived farther than 100 miles from the Atlantic Ocean. But between them and the Pacific Ocean lay rich soils in the river valleys of the Ohio and Mississippi and beyond that a vast domain that they had hardly even imagined. Growing rapidly, the English colonists were beginning to elbow up against the French and Spanish settlements. In the interior of North America, France posed the greatest threat to English colonists, but on their southern flank the Spanish presented another challenge. On the other side of the continent, the Spanish were

moving northward up the California coast until they reached the limits of Russian settlement in northern California.

France's Inland Empire

In 1661, France's Louis XIV, determined to make his country the most powerful in Europe, looked to North America and the Caribbean with keen interest. New France's timber would build the royal navy, its fish would feed the growing mass of slaves in the French West Indies, and its fur trade, if greatly expanded, would fill the royal coffers. From French Caribbean islands came precious sugar.

Under able governors such as Count Frontenac, New France grew in population, economic strength, and ambition in the late seventeenth century. In 1673, Louis Joliet and Father Jacques Marquette, a Jesuit priest, explored an immense territory watered by the Mississippi and Missouri rivers. A decade later, military engineers and priests began building forts and missions in the Great Lakes region and the Mississippi valley. In the 1682, René Robert de La Salle canoed down the Mississippi all the way to the Gulf of Mexico and planted a settlement in Texas at Matagorda Bay. The French solidified their claim to the North American heartland and the lower Mississippi valley when the Canadian leader Pierre le Moyne d'Iberville established a small settlement at Biloxi in 1699 and then a settlement three years later at Mobile.

In the first half of the eighteenth century, the French developed a system of forts, trading posts, and agricultural villages throughout the heart of the continent, threatening to pin the English to the seaboard. French success in this vast region hinged partly on shrewd dealing with the Indian tribes, which retained sovereignty over the land but gradually succumbed to French diseases, French arms, and French-promoted intertribal wars.

Because France's interior empire was organized primarily as a military, trading, and missionizing operation, male French settlers arrived with few French women. Thus, for a long time, French men were in a state of need when they encountered Indians—not only for trading partners, allies, and religious converts but also for wives. These needs produced a mingling of French and Indian peoples—what the French called *metissage*—in the North American interior. Such interracial marriages, called "the custom of the country," were welcomed by the Indians as well as the French. Marital alliances cemented trade and military relations. French traders entered Indian kinship circles, making trade flow smoothly, while Indians gained protection against their enemies and access to provi-

French North America, 1608–1763

Though thinly settled by colonists, the vast region west of the Proclamation Line claimed by France was held by a combination of forts and trading posts.

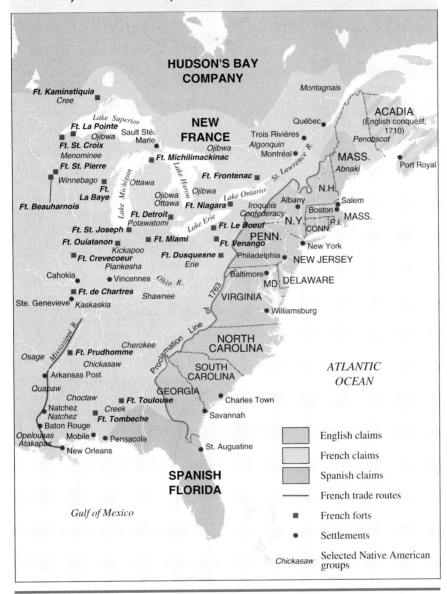

sions and weapons at French trading posts. Though the French sometimes fought fiercely with Indian peoples, the North American heartland was a cultural melting pot, as well as a marketplace.

Thinly dotted with small farming communities, the French presence in the continent's vast heartland created a shield against the expansive British to the east. As the French population grew to about 70,000 by 1750, they demonstrated how European settlers and Indian peoples could coexist. Almost all French settlements in North America's interior were mixed-race, or *meti*, communities—a sharp contrast to the English colonies.

In 1718, French pioneers of the interior and those along the Gulf of Mexico were inundated when France settled New Orleans at great cost by transporting almost 7,000 whites and 5,000 African slaves to the mouth of the Mississippi River. Disease rapidly whittled down these numbers, and an uprising of the powerful Natchez in 1729 discouraged further French immigration. Most of the survivors settled around the little town of New Orleans and on long, narrow plantations stretching back from the Mississippi River. In its economy and society, New Orleans resembled early Charleston, South Carolina. But French New Orleans was run and financed by

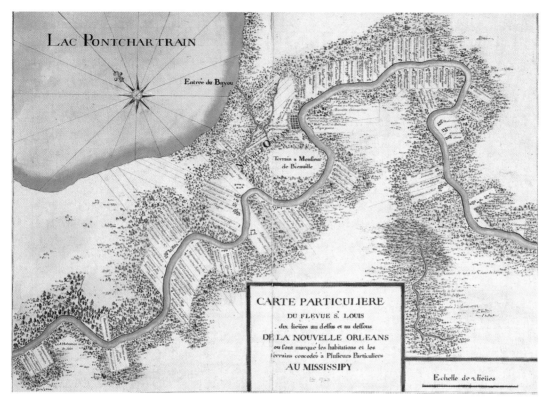

This map of New Orleans Parish in 1723, when the colony was still struggling, shows every plantation fronting on the Mississippi River. *(Courtesy of The Newberry Library, Chicago)*

royal government and knew nothing of representative political institutions. Its people had no elections, no assembly, no newspapers, and no taxes.

French slaves were critically important to the development of Louisiana. Arriving with skills as rice growers, indigo processors, metal workers, river navigators, herbalists, and cattle keepers, Africans became the backbone of the economy. Like male slaves in the Spanish colonies, they mingled extensively with Indian women, producing mixed-race children known locally as *grifs*. African women also made interracial liaisons with French immigrants, often soldiers in search of partners. Always precariously in charge of limited numbers of French settlers—by 1765, blacks outnumbered whites—French governors in Louisiana used enslaved Africans extensively as militiamen and sometimes granted them freedom for military service. Moreover, paternalistic French law gave slaves some protection in courts. All in all, the chance of gaining freedom in fluid French Louisiana exceeded that of any other colony in North America's Southeast, and the absorption of free blacks into white society, particularly if they were of mixed-race descent, was shockingly common from the English point of view. When the Spanish took over the colony in 1769, they guaranteed slaves the right to buy freedom with money earned in their free time. Soon a free black class emerged, headed by substantial people like Simon Calfat, who ran various enterprises, helped other slaves pay for their freedom, and headed a company of free black militia. When Americans acquired the colony in 1803, they suppressed freedom purchase and discouraged manumission.

A Generation of War

The growth of French strength and ambitions brought British America and New France into deadly conflict beginning in the late seventeenth century. Religious hostility overlaid commercial rivalry. Protestant New Englanders regarded Catholic New France as a satanic challenge to their divinely sanctioned mission. When the European wars began in 1689, precipitated by Louis XIV's territorial aggression in western and central Europe, conflict between England and France quickly extended into every overseas theater where the two powers had colonies. In North America, the battle zone included New York, New England, and eastern Canada.

In two wars, from 1689 to 1697 and 1701 to 1713, the English and French, while fighting in Europe, also sought to oust each other from the Americas. The zone of greatest importance was the Caribbean, where slaves produced huge sugar fortunes. But both home governments valued the North American settlements greatly as a source of the timber and fish that sustained the sugar-producing West Indian colonies.

The English struck three times at the centers of French power—at Port Royal, which commanded the access to the St. Lawrence River, and at Quebec, the capital of New France. In 1690, during King William's War (1689–1697), their small flotilla captured Port Royal, the hub of Acadia (which was returned to France at the end of the war). The English assault on Quebec, however, failed disastrously. In Queen Anne's War (1701–1713), New England attacked Port Royal three times before finally capturing it in 1710. A year later, when England sent a flotilla of 60 ships and 5,000 men to conquer Canada, the land and sea operations foundered before reaching their destinations.

With European-style warfare miserably unsuccessful in America, both England and France attempted to subcontract military tasks to their Indian allies. This policy occasionally succeeded, especially with the French, who gladly sent their own troops into the fray alongside Indian partners. The French and their Indian allies wiped out the frontier outpost of Schenectady, New York, in 1690; razed Wells, Maine, and Deerfield, Massachusetts, in 1703; and battered other towns along the New England frontier during both wars.

Retaliating, the English-supplied Iroquois stung several French settlements and left New France "bewildered and benumbed" after a massacre near Montreal in 1689. Assessing their own interests, and too powerful to be bullied by either France or England, the Iroquois sat out the second war in the early eighteenth century. Convinced that neutrality served their purposes better than acting as mercenaries for the English, they held to the principle that "we are a free people uniting ourselves to whatever sachem [chief] we wish."

Though England had rebuffed France after a generation of war, New England suffered grievous economic and human losses. In time, Nova Scotia would provide a new frontier for Puritan farmers. But the two wars between 1689 and 1713 struck hard at New England's economy. Massachusetts bore the heaviest burden. Probably one-fifth of all able-bodied males in the colony participated in the Canadian campaigns, and of these, about one-quarter never lived to tell of the terrors of New England's first major experience with international warfare. At the end of the first war, in 1697, one leader bemoaned that Massachusetts was left "quite exhausted and ready to sink under the calamities and fatigue of a tedious consuming war." The war debt was £50,000 sterling in Massachusetts alone, a greater per capita burden than the national debt today. At the end of the second conflict, in 1713, war widows were so numerous that the Bay Colony faced its first serious poverty problem. In addition, wartime taxes and price inflation had eaten deeply into the pocketbooks of most working families.

The colonies south of New England remained on the sidelines during most of the two wars. But war at sea between European rivals affected even those who sat out the land war. In Queen Anne's War, New York lost one of its best grain markets when Spain, allied with France, outlawed American foodstuffs in its Caribbean colonies. The French navy plucked off nearly one-quarter of the port's fleet and disrupted Philadelphia grain merchants' access to the Caribbean.

The burdens and rewards fell unevenly on the participants, as usually happens in wartime. Some lowborn men could rise spectacularly. William Phips, the twenty-sixth child in his family, had been a poor sheep farmer and ship's carpenter in Maine who seemed destined to go nowhere. Then he won a fortune by recovering a sunken Spanish treasure ship in the West Indies in 1687. For that feat, he was given command of the expedition against Port Royal in 1690. Victory there catapulted him to the governorship of Massachusetts in 1691; thereafter his status was secure.

Other men, already rich, got richer. Andrew Belcher of Boston, who had grown wealthy on provisioning contracts during King Philip's War, supplied warships and outfitted the New England expeditions to Canada. He became a local titan, riding in London-built coaches, erecting a handsome mansion, and purchasing slaves to symbolize his rise to the pinnacle of New England society.

Most men, especially those who did the fighting, gained little, and many lost all. The least securely placed New Englanders—indentured servants, apprentices, recently arrived immigrants, unskilled laborers, fishermen, and ordinary farmers—supplied most of the voluntary or involuntary recruits, and they died in numbers that seem staggering today. Antipopery, dreams of glory, and promises of plunder in French Canada lured most of them into uniform. Having achieved no place on the paths leading upward, they grasped at straws and usually failed again.

In 1713, the Peace of Utrecht, which ended Queen Anne's War, capped the century-long rise of England and the decline of Spain in the rivalry for the sources of wealth outside Europe. England, the big winner, received Newfoundland and Acadia (re-

Queen Anne's War: Major Battles and Territorial Changes

Like every other Anglo-French conflict in the seventeenth and eighteenth century, Queen Anne's War was fought in the Caribbean as well as in North America. The sugar- and coffee-rich islands of the West Indies, teeming with enslaved Africans, made them prizes in the competition for empire.

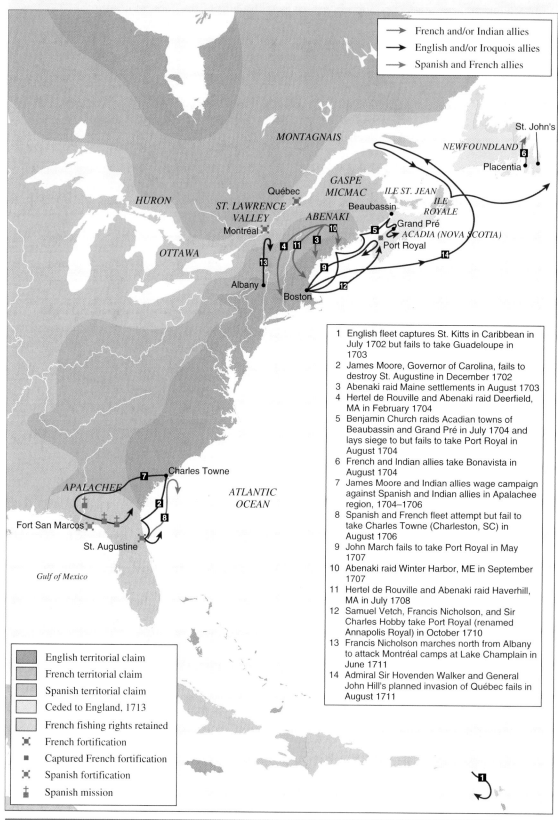

1. English fleet captures St. Kitts in Caribbean in July 1702 but fails to take Guadeloupe in 1703
2. James Moore, Governor of Carolina, fails to destroy St. Augustine in December 1702
3. Abenaki raid Maine settlements in August 1703
4. Hertel de Rouville and Abenaki raid Deerfield, MA in February 1704
5. Benjamin Church raids Acadian towns of Beaubassin and Grand Pré in July 1704 and lays siege to but fails to take Port Royal in August 1704
6. French and Indian allies take Bonavista in August 1704
7. James Moore and Indian allies wage campaign against Spanish and Indian allies in Apalachee region, 1704–1706
8. Spanish and French fleet attempt but fail to take Charles Towne (Charleston, SC) in August 1706
9. John March fails to take Port Royal in May 1707
10. Abenaki raid Winter Harbor, ME in September 1707
11. Hertel de Rouville and Abenaki raid Haverhill, MA in July 1708
12. Samuel Vetch, Francis Nicholson, and Sir Charles Hobby take Port Royal (renamed Annapolis Royal) in October 1710
13. Francis Nicholson marches north from Albany to attack Montréal camps at Lake Champlain in June 1711
14. Admiral Sir Hovenden Walker and General John Hill's planned invasion of Québec fails in August 1711

named Nova Scotia), and France recognized English sovereignty over the fur-rich Hudson Bay territory. France retained Cape Breton Island, controlling the entrance to the St. Lawrence River. In the Caribbean, France yielded St. Kitts and Nevis to England. Spain lost its provinces in Italy and the last of its holdings in the Netherlands to the Austrian Habsburgs. Spain also surrendered Gibraltar and Minorca to England and awarded the English the lucrative privilege of supplying the Spanish empire in the Americas with African slaves.

Spain's Frail North American Grip

Spain's grip on its colonies in North America had always been tenuous. On the East Coast, the growth of South Carolina's slave-based plantation society in the late seventeenth century stemmed partly from the English use of Indian allies to attack Spanish Indian missions and outposts and sell the captives into slavery. From this time forward, English and French traders, with more attractive trade goods to offer, held sway over Florida Indians.

After the Peace of Utrecht in 1713, Spain maintained a fragile hold on the southern tier of the continent. But the Spanish settlements stagnated in the first half of the eighteenth century. Spain's priority was not to expand in North America but to preserve its holdings by keeping others away from what were admittedly marginal, money-losing settlements. That in itself proved difficult, for this defensive mentality had to compete with the commercially minded English and French, whose colonial population, especially the former's, was growing rapidly. Small, impoverished Spanish frontier outposts and Indian missions in Florida, Texas, and New Mexico could do little to halt the expansion of British and French America.

Hispanics, mestizos, and detribalized Indians began to increase modestly in Texas, New Mexico, and California in the first half of the eighteenth century, but by 1745 in Florida they had only one-tenth the population of the English in South Carolina. New Mexico's Hispanic population of about 10,000 at mid-century could defend the vast region only because no European challenger appeared.

As in New France, racial intermixture and social fluidity were more extensive in New Spain than in the English colonies because Spanish male colonizers greatly outnumbered Spanish women. By precisely how much is uncertain because the Spanish never defined racial groups as distinctly as the English. The word *Spaniard* on a census might mean a white immigrant from Mexico or a part-Indian person who "lived like a Spaniard." Social

The mixing of races in Spain's New World colonies is vividly displayed in paintings of interracial families, widely produced in Mexico in the eighteenth century. In each painting shown here, the mother and father of different racial ancestries produces a child with a different racial term. In panel 5, for example, the mulatto mother and Spanish father produce a "Morisco" child. Paintings such as these spread the view that interracial mixing was the natural path of human affairs when people of different racial backgrounds converged.

mobility was considerable because the Crown was willing to raise even a common person to the status of *hidalgo* (minor nobleman) as an inducement to settle in New Spain's remote northern frontier. Most of the immigrants became small ranchers, producing livestock, corn, and wheat for export to southward Spanish provinces.

Native Americans had mixed success in resisting Spanish domination. In New Mexico, an early nineteenth-century Spanish investigator saw the key to Pueblo cultural autonomy as the underground kivas, which were "like impenetrable temples, where they gather to discuss mysteriously their misfortunes or good fortunes, their happiness or grief. The doors of these *estufas* are always closed to us." The tribes of California, however, were less successful in maintaining cultural cohesion. In the 1770s, the Spanish rapidly completed their western land and

Spanish Missions in California

As colonists in the British colonies on the eastern seaboard careened toward revolution, Spanish Franciscan priests were building a string of missions on the other side of the continent, hoping to convert Indians to Catholicism while capturing their labor.

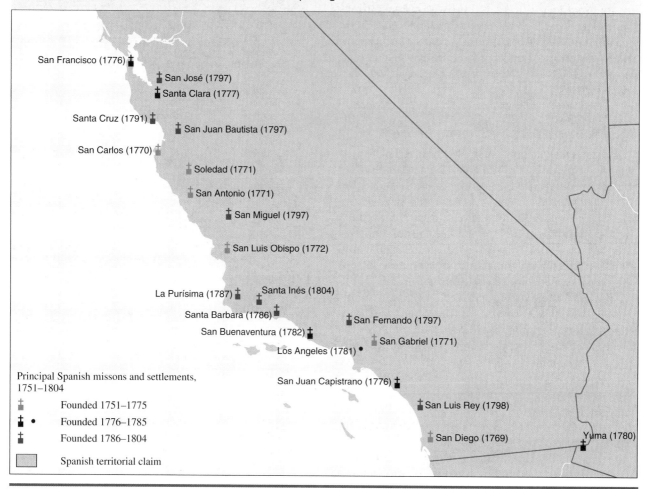

San Francisco (1776)
San José (1797)
Santa Clara (1777)
Santa Cruz (1791)
San Juan Bautista (1797)
San Carlos (1770)
Soledad (1771)
San Antonio (1771)
San Miguel (1797)
San Luis Obispo (1772)
La Purísima (1787)
Santa Inés (1804)
Santa Barbara (1786)
San Fernando (1797)
San Buenaventura (1782)
San Gabriel (1771)
Los Angeles (1781)
San Juan Capistrano (1776)
San Luis Rey (1798)
San Diego (1769)
Yuma (1780)

Principal Spanish missons and settlements, 1751–1804

Founded 1751–1775
Founded 1776–1785
Founded 1786–1804
Spanish territorial claim

sea routes from San Diego to Yerba Buena (San Francisco) to block Russian settlement south of their base in northern California. California's Spanish pioneers were Franciscan missionaries, accompanied by royal soldiers. The priests would choose a good location and then attract a few Indians to be baptized and resettled around the missions, which they helped build. Visiting relatives would then be induced to stay. These Indians lived under an increasingly harsh regimen until they were reduced to a condition of virtual slavery. The California mission, with its extensive and profitable herds and grain crops, theoretically belonged to the Indian converts, but they did not enjoy the profits. Priests even hired them out to immigrant Spaniards. Ironically, the spiritual motives of the priests pro-

duced the same reduction and degradation of tribal Americans as elsewhere.

Cultural and Ecological Changes Among Interior Tribes

During the first half of the eighteenth century, the inland tribes proved their capacity to adapt to the contending European colonizers in their region while maintaining political independence. Yet extensive contact with the French, Spanish, and English slowly brought ominous changes to Native American societies. European trade goods, especially iron implements, textiles, firearms and ammunition, and alcohol, altered Indian ways of life. Subsistence hunting, limited to satisfying tribal food requirements, turned into commercial hunting, restricted only by the quantity of trade goods desired. Indian males, gradually wiping out deer and beaver east of the Mississippi River, spent more time trapping and hunting away from the villages. Women were also drawn into the new economy, skinning animals and fashioning pelts into robes. Among some tribes, all this became so time-consuming that they had to procure food from other tribes.

The fur trade altered much in traditional Native American life. Spiritual beliefs that the destinies of humans and animals were closely linked eroded when trappers and hunters declared all-out war on the beaver and other fur-bearing animals in order to exchange pelts for attractive trade goods. Competition for furs sharpened intertribal tensions, often to the point of war. The introduction of European weaponry, which Indians quickly mastered, intensified these conflicts.

Tribal political organization in the interior also changed in the eighteenth century. Earlier, most tribes had been loose confederations of villages and clans. Creek, Cherokee, and Iroquois gave primary loyalty to the village, not to the tribe or confederacy. But trade, diplomatic contact, and war with Europeans required coordinated policies, so villagers gradually adopted more centralized leadership. For example, the basic unit of Cherokee political authority was the nearly autonomous village. But tension with Creek neighbors and intermittent hostilities with the English pressed home the need for coordinated decision making. By 1750, the Cherokee had formed an umbrella political organization that gathered together the fragmented authority of the villages and formed a more centralized tribal "priest state." When this proved inadequate, warriors began to assume the dominant role in tribal councils, replacing the civil chiefs.

While incorporating trade goods into their material culture and adapting their economies and political structures to new situations, the interior tribes held fast to tradition in many ways. They saw little reason to replace what they valued in their own culture. What they saw of the colonists' law and justice, religion, education, family organization, and child rearing usually convinced Native Americans that their own ways were superior.

The Indians' refusal to accept the superiority of white culture frustrated English missionaries, eager to win Native Americans from "savage" ways. A Carolinian admitted that "they are really better to us than we are to them. We look upon them with scorn and disdain, and think them little better than beasts in human shape, though if well examined, we shall find that, for all our religion and education, we pos-

sess more moral deformities and evils than these savages do."

Overall, interior tribes suffered from contact with the British colonizers. Decade by decade, the fur trade spread epidemic diseases, intensified warfare, depleted game animals, and drew Native Americans into a market economy where their trading partners gradually became trading masters.

THE URBAN WORLD OF COMMERCE AND IDEAS

Only about 5 percent of the eighteenth-century colonists lived in towns as large as 2,500, and no city boasted a population above 16,000 in 1750 or 30,000 in 1775. Yet urban societies were at the leading edge of the transition to "modern" life. In the seaboard centers, the barter economy first gave way to a commercial economy, a social order based on assigned status turned into one based on achievement, rank-conscious and deferential politics changed to participatory and contentious politics, and small-scale craftsmanship was gradually replaced by factory

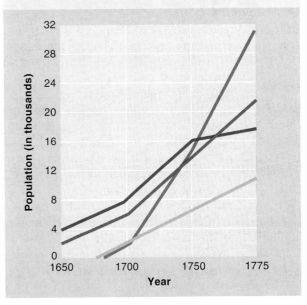

Urban Population Growth, 1650–1775

By 1755, Boston had lost its lead as British North America's largest city. Plagued by costly wars and economic difficulties, its population leveled off, whereas that of other cities grew.

━━ Boston   ━━ New York   ━━ Philadelphia   ━━ Charleston

Source: Gary B. Nash, *The Urban Crucible*, 1979

production. Into the cities flowed European ideas, which radiated outward to the hinterland.

Sinews of Trade

In the half century after 1690, Boston, New York, Philadelphia, and Charleston blossomed into thriving commercial centers. Their growth accompanied the development of the agricultural interior, to which the seaports were closely linked. As the colonial population rose and spread out, minor seaports such as Salem, Newport, Providence, Annapolis, Norfolk, and Savannah gathered 5,000 or more inhabitants.

Cities were trade centers. Through them flowed colonial export staples (tobacco, rice, furs, wheat, timber products, and fish) and the imported goods that colonists needed: manufactured and luxury goods from England (glass, paper, iron implements, and cloth); wine, spices, coffee, tea, and sugar from other parts of the world; and the human cargo to fill the labor gap. In these seaports, the pivotal figure was the merchant. Frequently engaged in both retail and wholesale trade, the merchant was also money-lender (for no banks yet existed), shipbuilder, insurance agent, land developer, and often coordinator of artisan production.

By the eighteenth century, the American economy was integrated into an Atlantic trading system that connected settlers to Great Britain, western Europe, Africa, the West Indies, and Newfoundland. The rulers of Great Britain, like those of other major trading nations of western Europe, pursued mercantilist trade policies. Mercantilism's core idea was that a country must gain wealth by increasing exports, taxing imports, regulating production and trade, and exploiting colonies. These policies governed British treatment of their North American and Caribbean colonies.

The colonists could never produce enough exportable raw materials to pay for the imported goods they craved, so they had to earn credits in England by supplying the West Indies and other areas with foodstuffs and timber products. They also accumulated credit by providing shipping and distribution services. Sailing from Boston, Salem, Newport, and Providence, New Englanders became the most ambitious participants in the carrying trade. A much higher proportion of New England's population made its living in maritime enterprise than in any other colonial region.

The Artisan's World

Although merchants stood first in wealth and prestige in the colonial towns, artisans were far more numerous. About two-thirds of urban adult males (slaves excluded) labored at handicrafts. By the

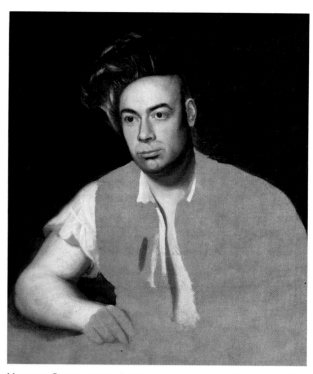

Not many Boston artisans became prosperous enough to have their portrait painted. But a few did, including Paul Revere and Nathaniel Hurd, the engraver shown here. Hurd came from a long line of artisans: his great-grandfather was a tailor, his grandfather a joiner, and his father a silversmith. Hurd's open collar and rolled-up sleeves show him in his working outfit. This unfinished portrait was probably a study for a more elegant portrait that showed Hurd in an embroidered silk blouse. *(Memorial Art Gallery of the University of Rochester, Marion Stratton Gould Fund)*

mid-eighteenth century, the colonial cities contained scores of specialized "leather apron men" besides the proverbial butcher, baker, and candlestick maker. Handicraft specialization increased as the cities matured, but every artisan worked with hand tools, usually in small shops.

Work patterns for artisans were irregular, dictated by weather, length of daylight, erratic delivery of raw materials, and shifting consumer demand. When ice blocked northern harbors, mariners and dockworkers endured slack time. If prolonged rain delayed the slaughter of cows in the country or made impassable the rutted roads into the city, the tanner and the shoemaker laid their tools aside. The hatter depended on the supply of beaver skins, which could stop abruptly if disease struck an Indian tribe or war disrupted the fur trade. Every urban artisan knew "broken days," slack spells, and dull seasons. Ordinary laborers dreaded winter, for it was a season when cities had "little occasion for the labor of the poor," and firewood could cost several months' wages.

Urban artisans took fierce pride in their crafts. While deferring to those above them, they saw themselves as the backbone of the community, contributing essential products and services. "Our professions rendered us useful and necessary members of our community," the Philadelphia shoemakers asserted, "Proud of that rank, we aspired to no higher." This self-esteem and desire for community recognition sometimes jostled with the upper-class view of artisans as "mere mechanicks," part of the "vulgar herd."

Striving for respectability, artisans placed a premium on achieving economic independence. Every craftsman began as an apprentice, spending five or more teenage years in a master's shop, then, after fulfilling his contract, becoming a "journeyman," selling his labor to a master and frequently living in his house where he ate at his table and sometimes married his daughter. He hoped to complete within a few years the three-step climb from servitude to self-employment. After setting up his own shop, he could control his work hours and acquire the respect that came from economic independence. But in trades requiring greater organization and capital, such as distilling and shipbuilding, the rise from journeyman to master often proved impossible.

In good times, urban artisans did well. They expected to earn a "decent competency" and eventually to purchase a small house. But success was far from automatic, even for those following Poor Richard's advice about hard work and frugal living. An advantageous marriage, luck in avoiding illness, and an ample inheritance were often critical. In Philadelphia, about half the artisans in the first half of the eighteenth century died leaving enough personal property to have ensured a comfortable standard of living. Another quarter left more, often including slaves and indentured servants. New England's artisans did not fare so well because their economy was weaker.

Urban Social Structure

Population growth, economic development, and war altered the urban social structure between 1690 and 1765. Stately townhouses displayed fortunes built through trade, shipbuilding, war contracting, and—probably most profitable of all—urban land development. "It is almost a proverb," a Philadelphian observed in the 1760s, "that every great fortune made here within these 50 years has been by land." A merchant's estate of £2,000 sterling was impressive in the early eighteenth century. Two generations later, North America's first millionaires were accumulating estates of £10,000 to £20,000 sterling.

The rise of Thomas Hancock, on whose fortune his less commercially astute nephew, John Hancock, would later construct a shining political career, provides a glimpse of how war could catapult an enterprising trader to affluence. An opportune marriage to the daughter of a prosperous merchant provided bookseller Hancock with a toehold in commerce and enough capital to invest in several vessels. By 1735, he had made enough money, much of it from smuggling tea, to build a mansion on Beacon Hill. When war broke out with Spain in 1739, Hancock obtained lucrative supply contracts for military expeditions to the Caribbean and Nova Scotia. He also invested heavily in privateers, who engaged in private warfare against enemy shipping and auctioned the enemy vessels they overpowered. When peace returned in 1748, Hancock was riding through Boston in a London-built four-horse chariot emblazoned with a heraldic shield.

Alongside urban wealth grew urban poverty. From the beginning, every city had its disabled, orphaned, and widowed who required aid. But after 1720, poverty marred the lives of many more city dwellers. Many were war widows with numerous children and no means of support. Others were rural migrants or recent immigrants who found fewer chances for

Wealth Distribution in Colonial America

Percentage of wealth held by the richest 10% and the poorest 30% of the population in two cities and one rural area.

Year	Richest 10%	Poorest 30%
Boston		
1684–1699	41.2	3.3
1700–1715	54.5	2.8
1716–1725	61.7	2.0
1726–1735	65.6	1.9
1736–1745	58.6	1.8
1746–1755	55.2	1.8
1756–1765	67.5	1.4
1766–1775	61.1	2.0
Philadelphia		
1684–1699	36.4	4.5
1700–1715	41.3	4.9
1716–1725	46.8	3.9
1726–1735	53.6	3.7
1736–1745	51.3	2.6
1746–1755	70.1	1.5
1756–1765	60.3	1.1
1766–1775	69.9	1.0
Chester County, Pennsylvania		
1693	23.8	17.4
1715	25.9	13.1
1730	28.6	9.8
1748	28.7	13.1
1760	29.9	6.3
1782	33.6	4.7

Source: Gary B. Nash, *The Urban Crucible*, 1979.

Household Inventories

Historians use probate records to examine social changes in American society. They include wills, the legal disposition of estates, and household inventories taken by court-appointed appraisers that detail the personal possessions left at death. Inventories have been especially valuable in tracing the transformation of colonial communities.

Like tax lists, inventories can be used to show changes in a community's distribution of wealth. But they are far more detailed than tax lists, providing a snapshot of how people lived at the end of their life. Inventories list and value almost everything a person owned—household possessions, equipment, books, clothes and jewelry, cash on hand, livestock and horses, crops and stored provisions. Hence, through inventories, we can measure the quality of life at different social levels. We can also witness how people made choices about investing their savings—in capital goods of their trade such as land, ships, and equipment; in personal goods such as household furnishings and luxury items; or in real property such as land and houses.

Studied systematically (and corrected for biases, which infect this source as well as others), inventories show that by the early 1700s, ordinary householders were improving their standard of living. Finished furniture such as cupboards, beds, tables, and chairs turn up more frequently in inventories. Pewter dinnerware replaces wooden bowls and spoons, bed linen makes an appearance, and books and pictures are sometimes noted.

Among an emerging elite before the Revolution, much more fashionable articles of consumption appear. The partial inventory of Robert Oliver, a wealthy merchant and officeholder living in a Boston suburb, is reproduced here. You can get some idea of the dignified impression Oliver wished to make by looking at his furniture and dishes and by noticing that he owned a mahogany tea table, damask linen, and a bed with curtains. The inventory further suggests the spaciousness of Oliver's house and show's how he furnished each room.

It is helpful when studying inventories to categorize the goods in the following way: those that are needed to survive (basic cooking utensils, for example); those that make life easier or more comfortable (enough plates and beds for each member of the family, for example); and those that make life luxurious (slaves, silver plates, paintings, mahogany furniture, damask curtains, spices, wine, and so forth). Oliver had many luxury goods as well as items that contributed to his use of leisure time and his personal enjoyment. Which items in his inventory do you think were needed only to survive comfortably? Which were luxuries? What other conclusions can you draw about the lifestyle of rich colonial merchants like Oliver?

Beyond revealing a growing social differentiation in colonial society, the inventories help the historian understand the reaction during the Great Awakening to what many ordinary colonists regarded as sinful pride and arrogance displayed by the elite. By the 1760s, this distrust of affluence among simple folk had led to outright hostility toward men who surrounded themselves with the trappings of aristocratic life. Even the ambitious young John Adams, a striving lawyer, was shocked at what he saw at the house of a wealthy merchant in Boston. "Went over the House to view the furniture, which alone cost a thousand Pound sterling," he exclaimed. "A seat it is for a noble Man, a Prince. The Turkey Carpets, the painted Hangings, the Marble Tables, the rich Beds with crimson Damask Curtains . . . are the most magnificent of any Thing I have ever seen."

Such a description takes on its full meaning only when contrasted with what inventories tell us about life at the bottom of society. The hundreds of inventories for Bostonians dying in the decade before the American Revolution show that fully half of them died with less than £40 personal wealth and one-quarter with £20 or less. The inventories and wills of Jonathan and Daniel Chandler of Andover, Massachusetts, show the material circumstances of less favored Americans who suffered from the economic distress afflicting New England since the 1730s. Note that Daniel Chandler was a shoemaker.

Reflecting on the Past   How do the possessions of these brothers compare with Oliver's partial inventory? An examination of these contrasting inventories helps explain the class tension that figured in the revolutionary experience.

Household Inventory of Robert Oliver, Wealthy Merchant

Dorchester Jan.ʸ 11.ᵗʰ 1763.

Inventory of what Estates Real & Personall, belonging to Coll.º Robert Oliver [Esquire] late of Dorchester Deceased, that has been Exhibited to us the Subscribers, for Apprizement. Viz.ᵗ

In the Setting Parlour Viz.ᵗ	
	£4.—.—
a looking Glass	0.6.0
a Small Ditto	@ 6/ 3.12.—
12 Metzitens pictures Glaz'd	4.—.—
8 Cartoons D.º Ditto	—.4.—
11 small Pictures	—.10.—
4 Maps	—.10.—
1 Prospect Glass	—.4.—
2 Escutchons Glaz'd	—.6.—
1 pair small hand Irons	—.8.—
1 Shovel & Tongs	—.1.—
1 Tobacco Tongs	—.2.—
1 pair Bellowes	—.2.—
1 Tea Chest	—.1.—
2 Small Waters	1.—.—
1 Mehogony Tea Table	—.2.—
8 China Cups & Saucers	—.—.1
1 Earthen Cream Pott	—.—.4
1 Ditto. Sugar Dish	1.—.—
1 Black Walnut Table	0.6.—
1 Black Ditto Smaller	0.1.—
1 Round painted Table	@ 6/ 2.2.—
7 Leather Bottom Chairs	1.3.—
1 Arm.d Chair Common	1.12.—
1 Black Walnut Desk	
1 pair Candlesticks snuffers & Stand Base Mettle	—.1.—
4	
6 Wine Glasses 1 Water Glass	1.—.—
a parcell of Books	0.4.—
a Case with Small Bottles	22.1.5

In the Entry & Stair Case Viz.ᵗ	
	£0.10.—
17 pictures	0.10.0

In the Kitchen Chamber Viz.ᵗ	
a Bedstead & Curtains Compleat	£4.—.—
a Bed Bolster & 2 pillows	5.—.—
a Under Bed & 1 Chair	0.1.—
2 Rugs & 1 Blankett	@ 6/ 0.18.—
	09.19.0

In the Dining Room Viz.ᵗ	
	£0.3.—
1 pair of andirons	0.7.—
7 Bass Bottoms Chairs	0.3.—
1 Large Wooden Table	0.1.—
1 Small Ditto. Oak	0.6.—
1 Small looking Glass	0.6.—
1 Old Desk	0.2.—
1 Case with 2 Bottles	0.12.—
1 Warming pan	2.0.0

In the Marble Chamber Viz.ᵗ		
		£8.—.—
1 Bedstead & Curtains Compleat		8.—.—
1 feather Bed, Bolster & 2 pillows		2.8.—
1 Chest of Drawers		1.—.—
1 Buroe Table	@ 6/	1.16.—
6 Chairs Leather'd Bottoms		—.6.—
1 Small dressing Glass		1.—.—
1 Small Carpett		—.18.—
1 White Cotton Counterpin		1.12.—
1 pair Blanketts		1.4.—
1 pair holland Sheets	@ 12ˢ/p.ʳ	1.16.—
3 pair Dowlases D.º New	@ 4/	0.14.—
3 pair & 1 Ditto Coarser	@ 3/	0.9.—
3 pair Cotton & Linnen D.º	@ 2/	0.8.—
4 pair Servants Ditto	@ 1/	0.4.—
4 Coarse Table Cloth	@ 1/	0.4.—
10 Ditto Kitchen Towels	@ 12/	3.—.—
5 Diaper Table Cloths	@ 18/	5.8.—
6 Damask Table Cloths	@ 3	0.12.—
4 N: England Diaper D.º	@ 2/	0.8.—
4 pair Linnen pillow Cases	@ 1/	0.5.—
5 Coarser Ditto	@ 6ᵈ	0.3.—
6 Diaper Towels	@ 2/	0.14.—
7 Damask Ditto	@ 24/doz.ⁿ	3.6.—
2 doz.ⁿ & 9 Damask Napkins		0.1.—
1 Gauze Tea Table Cover		£43.13.0

Household Inventory of Jonathan Chandler

(d. 1745)

Cash	£18p
Gun	1p
Psalmbook	8p
	£19p
Debts	£5p
Total	£14p

Household Inventory of Daniel Chandler

(d. 1752), Shoemaker

Bible	
Shoe knife	
Hammer	Total £12
Last (shoe shaper)	
Various notes	

employment than existed earlier. Boston was hit especially hard. Its economy stagnated in the 1740s, and taxpayers groaned under the burden of paying for heavy war expenditures. Cities devised new ways of helping the needy, such as building large almshouses where the poor could be housed and fed more economically. But many of the indigent preferred "to starve in their homes" rather than endure the discipline and indignities of the poorhouse. Boston's poor women also resisted laboring in the linen factory that was built in 1750 to enable them to contribute to their own support through spinning and weaving. Despite the warnings of Boston's ministers that "if any would not work, neither should they eat," they refused to leave their children at home to labor in America's first textile factory.

The increasing gap between the wealthy and the poor was recorded in the urban eighteenth-century tax lists. The top 5 percent of taxpayers increased their share of the cities' taxable assets from about 30 to 50 percent between 1690 and 1770. The bottom half of the taxable inhabitants saw their share of the wealth shrink from about 10 to 4 percent. Except in

Boston, the urban middle classes continued to gain ground. But the growth of princely fortunes amid increasing poverty made some urban dwellers reflect that Old World ills were reappearing in the New.

The Entrepreneurial Ethos

As the cities grew, new values took hold. In the traditional view of society, economic life was supposed to operate according to what was fair, not what was profitable. Regulated prices and wages, quality controls, supervised public markets, and other such measures seemed natural because a community was defined as a single body of interrelated parts, where individual rights and responsibilities formed a seamless web.

In their commercialized cities, most urban dwellers grew to regard the subordinating of private interests to the commonweal as unrealistic. Prosperity required the encouragement of acquisitive appetites rather than self-denial, for ambition would spur economic activity as more people sought more goods. The new view held that, if people were allowed to pursue their material desires

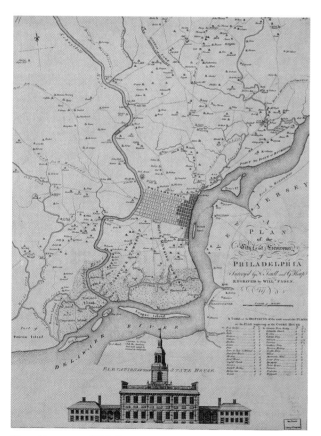

The grid pattern of Philadelphia's straight streets contrasts sharply with Boston's crooked and irregular roads and alleys. Topography had everything to do with this. Surrounded by water, which created an irregular shoreline, and dominated by three high hills, leveled in the nineteenth century, Boston's streets were laid out in the manner of goat paths. *(Library of Congress Geography & Maps Division)*

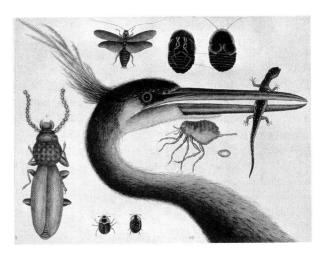

In two trips to the Americas between 1712 and 1726, the Englishman Mark Catesby captured the flora and fauna of the British colonies, both on the North American mainland and in the West Indies. His work, published in 1747 as *Natural History of Carolina, Florida, and the Bahama Islands*, became the first illustrated natural history of the British colonies. Portrayed here is the American bison, unknown in Europe, and chiggers, heron, and eft (the latter held in the heron's beak). *(Colonial Williamsburg Foundation)*

competitively, they would collectively form a natural, impersonal market of producers and consumers that would advantage everyone.

Hence, as the colonial port towns took their places in the Atlantic world of commerce, merchants became accustomed to making decisions according to the emerging commercial ethic that rejected traditional restraints on entrepreneurial activity. If wheat fetched 8 shillings a bushel in the West Indies but only 5 in Boston, a grain merchant felt justified in sending all he could purchase from local farmers to the more distant buyer. Indifferent to individuals and local communities, the new transatlantic market responded only to the invisible laws of supply and demand.

Tension between the new economic freedom and the older concern for the public good erupted only with food shortages or galloping inflation. Because the American colonies experienced none of the famines that ravaged Europe in this period, such crises were rare, usually occurring during war, when demand for provisions rose sharply. Such a moment struck in Boston during Queen Anne's War. Merchant Andrew Belcher contracted to ship wheat to the Caribbean, where higher prices would yield greater profit than in Boston. Ordinary neighbors, threatened with a bread shortage and angered that a townsman would put profit ahead of community needs, attacked one of Belcher's grain-laden ships

and tried to seize the grain. The grand jury, composed of substantial members of the community, hinted its approval of the violent action against Belcher by refusing to indict the rioters.

The two conceptions of community and economic life continued to rub against each other for decades. Urban merchants, shopkeepers, land speculators, and ambitious artisans cleaved more and more to the new economic formulas, while many clergymen continued to preach the traditional message: "Let no man seek his own, but every man another's wealth." By the mid-eighteenth century, the pursuit of a profits was winning out over the old community-oriented social compact.

The American Enlightenment

Ideas not only about economic life but also the nature of the universe and the improvement of the human condition filtered across the Atlantic. In the eighteenth century, an American version of the European intellectual movement called the Enlightenment came into focus.

In what is called the Age of Reason, European thinkers rejected the pessimistic Calvinist concept of innate human depravity, replacing it with the optimistic notion that a benevolent God had blessed humankind with the supreme gift of reason. Thinkers like John Locke, in his influential *Essay Concerning Human Understanding* (1689), argued that God had not predetermined the content of the human mind but had instead given it the capacity to acquire knowledge. All Enlightenment thinkers prized this acquisition of knowledge, for it allowed humankind to improve its condition. As the great mathematician Isaac Newton demonstrated, systematic investigation could unlock the secrets of the physical universe. Moreover, scientific knowledge could be applied to improve society.

The scientific and intellectual advances of the seventeenth and eighteenth centuries encouraged a belief in "natural law" and fostered debate about the "natural" human rights. In Europe, French philosophers Voltaire and Denis Diderot explored the issue of equality. From 1750 to 1772, Diderot published his *Encyclopedia*, which treated such topics as equality, liberty, reason, and rights. These ideas spread in Europe and the Americas, eventually finding expression in movements for reform, democracy, and liberation—all of deep interest to those beginning to oppose slavery and the slave trade as abominations.

Eighteenth-century Americans began to make significant contributions to the advancement of science. Naturalists such as John Bartram of Philadelphia gathered and described American plants from all over eastern North America as part of the transatlantic attempt to classify all plant life into one universal system. Professor John Winthrop III of Harvard made an unusually accurate measurement of the earth's distance from the sun. Foremost of all was Benjamin Franklin, whose spectacular (and dangerous) experiments with electricity, the properties of which were just becoming known, earned him an international reputation.

Franklin's true genius as a figure of the Enlightenment came in his practical application of scientific knowledge. Among his inventions were the lightning rod, which nearly ended the age-old danger of fires when lightning struck wooden buildings; bifocal spectacles; and a stove that heated rooms more cost-effectively than the open fireplace. Franklin made his adopted city of Philadelphia a center of the American Enlightenment. He led the founding of America's first circulating library in 1731, an artisans' debating club for "mutual improvement" through discussion of the latest ideas from Europe, and an intercolonial scientific association that in 1769 became the American Philosophical Society.

Most colonists were not educated enough to participate actively in the American Enlightenment, and only a handful read French Enlightenment authors like Voltaire. But the efforts of men such as Franklin exposed thousands, especially in the cities, to new currents of thought. This kindled hopes that Americans, blessed by an abundant en-

Benjamin Lay was regarded as eccentric and a troublemaker, even by his fellow Quakers. Known primarily as a fervent opponent of slavery and the slave trade as early as the 1730s, he was also in the vanguard of many reform movements such as temperance and vegetarianism. The portrait shows Lay's dwarf-like stature. *(National Portrait Gallery, Smithsonian Institution/Art Resource, NY)*

vironment, might achieve the Enlightenment ideal of a perfect society.

Even as the traffic in slaves peaked, religious and humanitarian opposition to slavery arose. A few individuals, mostly Quaker, had objected to slavery on moral grounds since the late seventeenth century. But the idea grew in the 1750s that slavery contradicted the Christian concept of brotherhood and the Enlightenment notion of the natural equality of all humans. Abolitionist sentiment was also fed by the growing belief that a slave master's authority "depraved the mind," as the Quaker John Woolman argued. An introspective tailor from New Jersey, in the 1750s Woolman dedicated his life to a crusade against slavery. He traveled thousands of miles on foot to convince every Quaker slaveholder of his or her wrongdoing. Only a few hundred masters freed their slaves in the mid-eighteenth century, but men such as Woolman had planted the seeds of abolitionism.

THE GREAT AWAKENING

Many of the social, economic, and political changes occurring in eighteenth-century colonial society converged in the Great Awakening, the first of many religious revivals that would sweep America during the next two centuries. The timing and character of the Awakening varied from region to region. But everywhere, this quest for spiritual renewal challenged old sources of authority and produced patterns of thought and behavior that helped fuel a revolutionary movement in the next generation.

Fading Faith

Early eighteenth-century British America remained an overwhelmingly Protestant culture. Puritanism—that is, the Congregational church—dominated all of New England except Rhode Island. Anglicanism held sway in much of New York and throughout the South except the backcountry. In the mid-Atlantic and in the back settlements, German Mennonites, Dunkers, Moravians, and Lutherans; Scots-Irish Presbyterians; and English Baptists and Quakers all mingled. Yet only about one-third of the colonists belonged to one of these groups; those who went to no church at all remained the majority. In many areas, ministers and churches were simply unavailable. In the most populous colony, Virginia, only 60 parsons in 1761 served a population of 350,000—one for every 5,800 people.

Most colonial churches were voluntary ("congregated") groups, formed for reasons of conscience, not because of government compulsion. Catholics, Jews, and nonbelievers could not vote or hold office. But the persecution of Quakers and Catholics had largely passed, and by 1720 some dissenting groups had gained the right to use long-obligatory church taxes to support their own congregations.

The clergy often administered their congregations with difficulty. Anglicans and several German sects maintained close ties to mother churches across the Atlantic, whereas other denominations attempted to centralize authority. However, most efforts to tighten organization and discipline failed. For example, Anglican ministers had to be ordained in England and regularly report to the bishop of London. But in his Chesapeake parish, an Anglican priest faced wealthy planters who controlled the vestry (the local church's governing body), set his salary, and would drive him out if he challenged them too forcefully. In Connecticut, the Saybrook Platform of 1708 created a network, or "consociation," of Congregational churches, but individual churches still preserved much of their autonomy.

Though governing their churches frustrated many clergymen, religious apathy was a more pressing problem. As early as the 1660s, New England's Congregational clergy had adopted the Half-Way Covenant in order to combat religious indifference. It allowed children of church members, if they adhered to the "forms of godliness," to join the church even if they could not demonstrate that they had undergone a conversion experience. They could not, however, vote in church affairs or take communion.

Such compromises and innovations could not halt the creeping religious apathy that many ministers observed. An educated clergy, its energies often drained by doctrinal disputes, appealed too much to the mind and not enough to the heart. As one Connecticut leader remembered it, "the spirit of God appeared to be awfully withdrawn."

The Awakeners' Message

The Great Awakening was not a unified movement but rather a series of revivals that swept different regions between 1720 and 1760 with varying degrees of intensity. The first stirrings came in the 1720s in New Jersey, where a Dutch Reformed minister, Theodore Frelinghuysen, excited his congregation through emotional preaching about the need to be "saved" rather than offering the usual theological abstractions. A neighboring Presbyterian, Gilbert Tennent, soon took up the Dutchman's techniques, with similar success.

From New Jersey, the Awakening spread to Pennsylvania in the 1730s, especially among Presbyterians, and then broke out in the Connecticut River valley. There its greatest leader was Jonathan Edwards in Northampton, Massachusetts. Later a philosophical giant in the colonies, as a young man Edwards gained renown by frightening his parishioners with the fate of "sinners in the hands of an angry God." "How manifold have been the abominations of your life!" Edwards preached. "Are there not some here that have debased themselves below the dignity of human nature, by allowing in sensual filthiness, as swine in the mire . . . ?" Edwards paraded one sin after another before his trembling congregants and drew such graphic pictures of the hell awaiting the unrepentant that his Northampton neighbors were soon preparing frantically for the conversion by which they would be "born again." His *Faithful Narrative of the Surprizing Work of God* (1736), which described his town's awakening, was the first published revival narrative. This literary form would be used many times in the future to fan the flames of evangelical religion.

In 1739, these regional brushfires of evangelicalism were drawn together by a 24-year-old Anglican priest from England, George Whitefield. Inspired by John Wesley, the founder of English Methodism, Whitefield used his magnificent speaking voice in dynamic open-air preaching before huge gatherings. Whitefield barnstormed seven times along the American seaboard, beginning in 1739. In Boston, he preached to 19,000 in three days and at a farewell sermon left 25,000 writhing in fear of damnation. In

Jonathan Edwards (1703–1758) was the first major philosopher in the American colonies. A leader of the Great Awakening in Massachusetts, he was ousted by his congregation for reprimanding the children of church members for reading *The Midwife Rightly Instructed,* an obstetric guide that was as close as curious children could come to learning about sex. *(Corbis)*

Samson Occom, a Mohegan born in Connecticut, was attracted to Christianity, like so many others who were "outsiders," by the emotional and populistic appeal of the Great Awakening preachers. On a trip to England, Occom raised £12,000 for an evangelical school for Indians, later to become Dartmouth College. *(Courtesy of the Boston Public library, Print Department)*

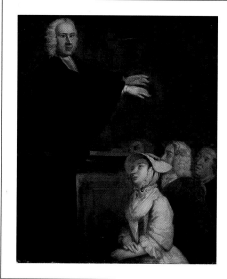

George Whitefield, who first toured the American colonies in 1739 and 1740, sent thousands of souls "flying to Christ" with his emotional sermons. More Americans heard Whitefield on his many seaboard itineracies than any other figure in the eighteenth century. *(National Portrait Gallery, London)*

his wake came American preachers whom he had inspired, mostly young men like Devereaux Jarratt.

The appeal of the Awakeners lay both in the medium and the message. They preached that the established, college-trained clergy was too intellectual and tradition-bound. Congregations were dead, Whitefield declared, "because dead men preach to them." "The sapless discourses of such dead drones," cried another Awakener, were worthless. The fires of Protestant belief could be reignited only if individuals assumed responsibility for their own conversion.

An important form of individual participation was "lay exhorting," which horrified most established clergymen. "Exhorting" meant that anyone—young or old, female or male, black or white—spontaneously recounted a conversion experience and preached "the Lord's truth." This shattered the trained clergy's monopoly and gave new importance to the oral culture of common people, whose impromptu outpourings contrasted sharply with the controlled literary culture of the gentry. Through lay exhorting, all manner of people, including women, children, servants, and slaves, defied assigned roles.

How religion, social change, and politics became interwoven in the Great Awakening can be seen by examining two regions swept by revivalism. Both Boston, the heartland of Puritanism, and interior Virginia, a land of struggling small planters and slave-rich aristocrats, experienced the Great Awakening, but in different ways and at different times.

Revivalism in the Urban North

In Boston, Whitefield-inspired revivalism blazed up amid political controversy about paper money and land banks. Since 1739, the citizens had argued about remedies for the severe depreciation of the province's paper currency, which had been issued to finance military expeditions against French Canada. When the English government ordered Massachusetts to retire all paper money by 1741, one group proposed a land bank to issue private bills of credit backed by land. Another group proposed a silver bank to distribute bills of credit backed by silver. Controversy over the land and silver banks pitted large merchants, who preferred the fiscally conservative silver bank, against local traders, artisans, and the laboring poor, who preferred the land bank.

Whitefield's arrival in Boston coincided with the currency furor. At first, Boston's elite applauded Whitefield's ability to call the masses to worship. It seemed that the master evangelist might restore social harmony by redirecting people from earthly matters such as the currency dispute toward concerns for their souls. But when he left Boston in 1740, others followed him who were more critical of the "unconverted" clergy and the self-indulgent accumulation of wealth. One was 25-year-old James Davenport, who appeared anything but respectable to the elite.

Finding every meetinghouse closed to him, even those whose clergy had embraced the Awakening, Davenport preached daily on the Boston Common, aroused religious ecstasy among thousands, and stirred up feeling against the city's leading figures. Respectable people decided that revivalism had got out of hand when ordinary people began verbally attacking opponents of the land bank in the streets as "carnal wretches, hypocrites, fighters against God, children of the devil, cursed Pharisees." A revival that had begun as a return to religion among backsliding Christians had overlapped with political affairs. Hence, it threatened polite culture, which stressed order and discipline from ordinary people.

Southern Revivalism

The Great Awakening was ebbing in New England and the middle colonies by 1744, although aftershocks continued for years. But in Virginia, where the initial religious earthquake was barely felt, tremors of enthusiasm rippled through society from the mid-1740s onward. As in Boston, the Awakeners challenged and disturbed the gentry-led social order.

Whitefield stirred some religious fervor during his early trips through Virginia. Traveling "New Light" preachers, led by the brilliant orator Samuel Davies, were soon gathering large crowds both in the backcountry and in the traditionally Anglican parishes of the older settled areas. By 1747, worried Anglican clergyman convinced the governor to issue a proclamation restraining "strolling preachers." As in other colonies, Virginia's leaders despised traveling evangelists, who, like lay exhorters, conjured up a world without properly constituted authority. When the Hanover County court gave the fiery James Davenport a license to preach in 1750, the governor ordered the suppression of all circuit riders.

New Light Presbyterianism, challenging the gentry-dominated Anglican church's spiritual monopoly, spread in the 1750s. Then, in the 1760s, came the Baptists. Renouncing finery and ostentatious display, and addressing each other as "brother" and "sister," the Baptists reached out to thousands of unchurched people. Like northern revivalists, they focused on the conversion experience. Many of their preachers were uneducated farmers and artisans who called themselves "Christ's poor" and insisted that heaven was populated more by the humble poor than by the purse-proud rich. Among the poorest of all, Virginia's 140,000 slaves in 1760, the evangelical message began to take hold.

The insurgent Baptist movement in rural Virginia became both a quest for a personal, emotionally satisfying religion among ordinary folk and a rejection of gentry values. Established Anglican pulpits denounced the Awakeners as furiously as had respectable New England divines. In both regions, social changes had weakened the cultural authority of the upper class and, in the context of religious revival, produced a vision of a society drawn along more equal lines.

Legacy of the Awakening

By the time George Whitefield returned to North America for his third tour in 1745, the revival had burned out in the North. Its effects, however, were long-lasting. Notably, it promoted religious pluralism and nourished the idea that all denominations were equally legitimate. Whitefield had anticipated this tendency when he sermonized: "Father Abraham, whom have you in heaven? Any Episcopalians? And the answer came back, No! Any Presbyterians? No! Any Independents or Methodists? No, no, no! Whom have you there? And the final answer came down from heaven, We don't know the names here. All who are here are Christians."

By legitimizing the dissenting Protestant groups that had sprung up in seventeenth-century England, the Great Awakening gave them all a basis for living together in relative harmony. From this framework of denominationalism came a second change—the separation of church and state. Once a variety of churches gained legitimacy, it was hard to justify one denomination claiming special privileges. In the seventeenth century, Roger Williams had tried to sever church and state because he believed that ties with civil bodies would corrupt the Church. But during the Awakening, groups such as the Baptists and Presbyterians in Virginia constituted their own religious bodies and broke the Anglican monopoly as *the* Church in the colony. This undermining of the church–state tie would be completed during the Revolutionary era.

A third effect of the revival was to legitimate community diversity. Almost from their beginnings, Rhode Island, the Carolinas, and the middle colonies had recognized this. But uniformity had been prized elsewhere, especially in Massachusetts and Connecticut. There, the Awakening split Congregational churches into New Lights and Old Lights. Mid-Atlantic Presbyterian churches faced similar schisms. In hundreds of rural communities by the 1750s, two or three churches existed where only one had stood before. People learned that the fabric of community could be woven from threads of many hues.

New eighteenth-century colonial colleges reflected the religious pluralism. Before 1740, there existed only Puritan Harvard (1636) and Yale (1701) and Anglican William and Mary (1693). But between 1746 and 1769, six new colleges were added: Dartmouth, Brown, Princeton, and what are now Columbia, Rutgers, and the University of Pennsylvania.

None was controlled by an established church, all had governing bodies composed of men of different faiths, and all admitted students regardless of religion. Eager for students and funds, they made nonsectarian appeals and combined the traditional Latin and Greek curricula with natural sciences and natural philosophy.

Last, the Awakening nurtured a subtle change in values that crossed over into politics and daily life. Especially for ordinary people, the revival experience created a new feeling of self-worth. People assumed new responsibilities in religious affairs and became skeptical of dogma and authority. Many, especially the fast-growing Baptists, decried the growing materialism and deplored the new acceptance of self-interested behavior. He who was "governed by regard to his own private interest," Gilbert Tennent preached, was "an enemy to the public," for in true Christian communities, "mutual love is the band and cement." By learning to oppose authority and create new churches, thousands of colonists unknowingly rehearsed for revolution.

Founded in 1701, Yale College was one of only three institutions of higher learning in the colonies before the Great Awakening. Students customarily entered Yale at 16 and some even earlier. *(Yale University Art Gallery [1940.317])*

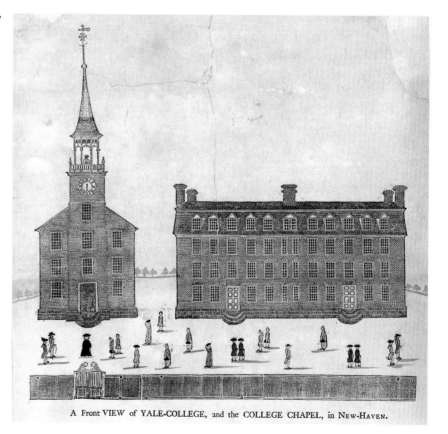

A Front VIEW of YALE-COLLEGE, and the COLLEGE CHAPEL, in NEW-HAVEN.

POLITICAL LIFE

"Were it not for government, the world would soon run into all manner of disorders and confusions," wrote a Massachusetts clergyman early in the eighteenth century. "Men's lives and estates and liberties would soon be prey to the covetous and the cruel," and every man would be "as a wolf" to his neighbors. Few colonists or Europeans would have disagreed. Government existed to protect life, liberty, and property.

But how should political power be divided—in England, between the English government and the American colonies, and within each colony? Colonists naturally drew heavily on inherited political ideas and institutions—almost entirely English ones, for it was English charters that sanctioned settlement, English governors who ruled, and English common law that governed the courts. But meeting unexpected circumstances in a new environment, colonists modified familiar political forms.

Structuring Colonial Governments

All societies consider it essential to determine the final source of political authority. In England, the notion of the God-given, supreme monarchical authority was crumbling even before the planting of the colonies. In its place arose the belief that stable government depended on blending and balancing the three pure forms of government: monarchy, aristocracy, and democracy. Unalloyed, each would degenerate into oppression. Monarchy, the rule of one, would become despotism. Aristocracy, the rule of the few, would turn into corrupt oligarchy. Democracy, the rule of the many, would descend into anarchy or mob rule. Most colonists believed that the Revolution of 1688 in England had vindicated and strengthened a carefully balanced political system.

In the colonies, political balance was achieved somewhat differently. The governor, as the king's agent (or, in proprietary colonies, the agent of the proprietor to whom the king delegated authority), represented monarchy. Bicameral legislatures arose in most of the colonies in the seventeenth century, and in most provinces they had upper houses of wealthy men appointed by the governor; as a pale equivalent of Britain's House of Lords, it formed a nascent aristocracy. The assembly, elected by white male freeholders, replicated the House of Commons and was the democratic element. Every statute required the governor's assent (except in Rhode Island and Connecticut), and all colonial laws required final approval from the king's privy council. This royal check operated imperfectly, however. A law took months to reach England and months more before word of its final approval or rejection. In the meantime, the laws took force in the colony.

Colonial Foundations of the American Political System

1606 Virginia companies of London and Plymouth granted patents to settle lands in North America.

1619 First elected colonial legislature meets in Virginia.

1634 Under a charter granted in 1632, Maryland's proprietor is given all the authority "as any bishop of Durham" ever held—more than the king possessed in England.

1635 The council in Virginia deports Governor John Harvey for exceeding his power, thus asserting the rights of local magistrates to contest authority of royally appointed governors.

1643 The colonies of Massachusetts, Plymouth, Connecticut, and New Haven draw up articles of confederation and form the first intercolonial union, the United Colonies of New England.

1647 Under a charter granted in 1644, elected freemen from the Providence Plantations draft a constitution establishing freedom of conscience, separating church and state, and authorizing referenda by the towns on laws passed by the assembly.

1677 The Laws, Concessions, and Agreements for West New Jersey provide for a legislature elected annually by virtually all free males, secret voting, liberty of conscience, election of justices of the peace and local officeholders, and trial by jury in public so that "justice may not be done in a corner."

1689 James II deposed in England in the Glorious Revolution and royal governors, accused of abusing their authority, ousted in Massachusetts, New York, and Maryland.

1701 First colonial unicameral legislature meets in Pennsylvania under the Frame of Government of 1701.

1735 John Peter Zenger, a New York printer, acquitted of seditious libel for printing attacks on the royal governor and his faction, thus widening the freedom of the press.

1754 First congress of all the colonies meets at Albany (with seven colonies sending delegates) and agrees on a Plan of Union (which is rejected by the colonies and the English government).

1765 The Stamp Act Congress, the first intercolonial convention called outside England's authority, meets in New York.

Behind the formal structure of politics stood rules governing who could participate as voters and officeholders. In England, land ownership conferred political rights (women and non-Christians were uniformly excluded). Only men with property producing an annual rental income of 40 shillings could vote or hold office. The colonists closely followed this principle, except in Massachusetts, where until 1691 Church membership was the basic requirement. As in England, the poor and propertyless were excluded, for they lacked the "stake in society" that supposedly produced responsible voters.

In England, the 40-shilling freehold requirement kept the electorate small; but in the colonies, where land was cheap, it conferred the vote on 50 to 75 percent of the adult free males. However, as the proportion of landless colonists increased in the eighteenth century, the franchise contracted.

Though voting rights were broadly based, most men assumed that the wealthy and socially prominent should hold the main political positions. Balancing this elitism, however, was the notion that the entire electorate should periodically judge the performance of those entrusted with political power and reject those who were found wanting. Following the precedent of England's Glorious Revolution, in British America the people were assumed to have the right to badger their leaders, to protest openly, and, in extreme cases of abuse of power, assume control and put things right. Crowd action, frequently effective, gradually achieved a kind of legitimacy.

The Crowd in Action

What gave special power to the common people when they assembled to protest oppressive authority and the trampling of traditional English liberties was the general absence of effective police power. In the countryside, where most colonists lived, only the county sheriff insulated civil leaders from angry farmers. In the towns, the sheriff had only the night watch to keep order. As late as 1757, New York's night watch was described as a "parcell of idle, drinking vigilant snorers, who never quelled any nocturnal tumult in their lives." In theory, the militia stood ready to suppress public disturbances, but crowds usually included many militiamen.

Boston's Impressment Riot of 1747 vividly illustrates the people's readiness to defend their inherited privileges and the weakness of law enforcement. It began when Commodore Charles Knowles brought his Royal Navy ships to Boston for provisioning—and to replenish the ranks of mariners thinned by desertion. When Knowles sent press

gangs to fill the crew vacancies from Boston's waterfront population, they scooped up artisans, laborers, servants, and slaves, as well as merchant seamen from ships riding at anchor in the harbor.

But before the press gangs could hustle away their victims, a crowd of angry Bostonians seized several British officers, surrounded the governor's house, and demanded the release of their townsmen. When the sheriff and his deputies tried to intervene, the mob mauled them. The militia refused to respond. An enraged Knowles threatened to bombard the town, but negotiations amid further tumult averted a showdown. Finally, Knowles released the impressed Bostonians. After the riot, a young politician named Samuel Adams defended Boston's defiance of royal authority. The people, he argued, had a "natural right" to band together against press gangs that deprived them of their liberty. He labeled local magnates who supported the governor in this incident "tools to arbitrary power."

The Growing Power of the Assemblies

While the Impressment Riot of 1747 was dramatic, a more gradual and restrained change was underway—the growing ambition and power of the legislative assemblies—that was far more important. For most of the seventeenth century, royal and proprietary governors had exercised greater power in relation to the elected legislatures than did England's king in relation to Parliament. Governors could dissolve the lower houses and delay their sitting, control the election of their speakers, and in most colonies initiate legislation with their appointed councils. They had authority to appoint and dismiss judges at all levels of the judiciary and to create chancery courts, which sat without juries. Governors also controlled the expenditure of public monies and had authority to grant land to individuals and groups, which they sometimes used to confer vast estates on their favorites.

Since the seventeenth century, Virginia, Massachusetts, and New York had been royal colonies, with crown-appointed governors. In the eighteenth century, royal government came to New Jersey (1702), South Carolina (1719), and North Carolina (1729), replacing proprietary regimes.

Many royal governors were competent military officers or bureaucrats, but some were corrupt recipients of patronage posts. Some never even came over, preferring to pocket the salary and pay part of it to another man who went to serve as lieutenant governor. One committed suicide a week after arriving. But most governors were not crazy, corrupt, or absent; they were merely mediocre. They also

When frontier farmers marched on Philadelphia in 1763 to demand more protection on the frontier, a miniature civil war almost broke out. Philadelphians had little use for the "Paxton Boys," who had murdered 20
harmless Christian Indians in retaliation for frontier raids. *(The Library Company of Philadelphia)*

lacked the extensive patronage power that enabled ministers of government in England to manipulate elections and buy off opponents.

Eighteenth-century legislatures challenged the swollen powers of the colonial governors. Bit by bit, they won new rights: to initiate legislation, to elect their own speakers, to settle contested elections, to discipline members, and to nominate provincial treasurers who disbursed public funds. Most important, they won the "power of the purse"—the authority to initiate money bills, specifying how much money should be raised by taxes and how it should be spent. Thus, the elected assemblies gradually transformed themselves into governing bodies reflecting the interests of the electorate. Governors complained bitterly about the "levelling spirit" and "mutinous and disorderly behavior" of the assemblies, but they could not stop their rise.

Local Politics

Binding elected officeholders to their constituents became an important feature of the colonial political system. In England, the House of Commons was filled with representatives from "rotten boroughs" (ancient places left virtually uninhabited by population shifts) and with men whose vote was controlled by the government because they had accepted

offices, contracts, or gifts. Nevertheless, its members claimed to represent the entire nation rather than narrow local interests. American assemblies, by contrast, contained mostly representatives sent by voters who instructed them on particular issues and held them accountable.

Royal governors and colonial grandees who sat as councillors often deplored this localist, popular orientation. Sniffed one aristocratic New Yorker, the assemblies were crowded with "plain, illiterate husbandmen [small farmers], whose views seldom extended farther than the regulation of highways, the destruction of wolves, wildcats, and foxes, and the advancement of the other little interests of the particular counties which they were chosen to represent." In actuality, most lower-house members were merchants, lawyers, and substantial planters and farmers, who by the mid-eighteenth century constituted the political elite in most colonies. But they took pride in upholding their constituents' interests, for they saw themselves as bulwarks against oppression and arbitrary rule, which history taught them were most frequently imposed by monarchs and their appointed agents.

Local government was usually more important to the colonists than provincial government. In the North, local political authority generally rested in the towns (which included surrounding rural areas).

The New England town meeting decided a wide range of matters, arguing until it could express itself as a single unit. "By general agreement" and "by the free and united consent of the whole" were phrases denoting a collective assent rather than a democratic competition among differing interests and points of view.

In the South, the county was the primary unit of government, and by the mid-eighteenth century, a landed squirearchy of third- and fourth-generation families had achieved political dominance. They ruled the county courts and the legislature, and substantial farmers served in minor offices such as road surveyor and deputy sheriff. At court sessions, usually four times a year, deeds were read aloud and then recorded, juries impaneled and justice dispensed, elections held, licenses issued, and proclamations read aloud. On election days, gentlemen treated their neighbors (on whom they depended for votes) to "bumbo," "kill devil," and other alcoholic treats.

The Spread of Whig Ideology

Whether in local or provincial affairs, a political ideology called Whig, or "republican," had spread widely by the mid-eighteenth century. This body of thought, inherited from England, rested on the belief that concentrated power was historically the enemy of liberty and that too much power lodged in any person or group usually produced corruption and tyranny. The best defenses against concentrated power were balanced government, elected legislatures adept at checking executive authority, prohibition of standing armies (almost always controlled by tyrannical monarchs to oppress the people), and vigilance by the people in watching their leaders for telltale signs of corruption.

Much of this Whig ideology reached the people through the newspapers that began appearing in the seaboard towns in the early eighteenth century. By 1763, some 23 papers circulated in the colonies. Many papers reprinted pieces from English Whig writers railing against corruption and creeping despotism. Though limited to a few pages and published only once or twice a week, the papers passed from hand to hand and were read aloud in taverns and coffeehouses, so that their contents probably reached most urban households and a substantial minority of rural farms.

The new power of the press and its importance in guarding the people's liberties against would-be tyrants (such as haughty royal governors) were dramatically illustrated in the Zenger case in New York. Young John Peter Zenger, a printer's apprentice, had

John Peter Zenger symbolized freedom of the press, but it wasn't until the nineteenth century that his image was ever created. This engraving showing the burning of Zenger's newspaper, and the stocks awaiting him, is a modern re-creation of the scene. *(Bettmann/Corbis)*

been hired in 1733 by the anti-government faction of Lewis Morris to start a newspaper that would publicize the tyrannical actions of Governor William Cosby. In Zenger's *New-York Weekly Journal*, the Morris faction fired salvos at Cosby's interference with the courts and his alleged corruption.

Arrested for seditious libel, Zenger was defended brilliantly by Andrew Hamilton, a Philadelphia lawyer hired by the Morris faction to convince the jury that Zenger had been simply trying to inform the people of attacks on their liberties. Although the jury acquitted Zenger, the libel laws remained very restrictive. But the acquittal did reinforce the notion that the government was the people's servant, and it brought home the point that public criticism could keep people with political authority responsible to the people they ruled. Such ideas about liberty and corruption, raised in the context of local politics, would shortly achieve a much broader significance.

Timeline

1682	La Salle canoes down Mississippi River and claims Louisiana for France
1689–1697	King William's War
1700	Spanish establish first mission in Arizona
1702–1713	Queen Anne's War
1704	*Boston News-Letter*, first regular colonial newspaper, published
1712	First northern slave revolt erupts in New York City
1713	Peace of Utrecht
1714	Beginning of Scots-Irish and German immigration
1715–1730	Volume of slave trade doubles
1718	French settle New Orleans
1720s	Natural increase of African population begins
1732	Benjamin Franklin publishes first *Poor Richard's Almanack*
1734–1736	Great Awakening begins in Northampton, Massachusetts
1735	Zenger acquitted of seditious libel in New York
1739	Slave revolt in Stono, South Carolina
1739–1740	Whitefield's first American tour spreads Great Awakening
1740s	Slaves compose 90 percent of population on Carolina rice coast. Indigo becomes staple crop in Lower South
1747	Impressment riot in Boston
1750s	Quakers initiate campaign to halt slave trade and end slavery
1760	Africans compose 20 percent of colonial population
1760s–1770s	Spanish establish California mission system
1769	American Philosophical Society founded at Philadelphia

✦ *Conclusion*

AMERICA IN 1750

The English colonies in North America, robust and expanding, matured rapidly between 1690 and 1750. Transatlantic commerce linked them closely to Europe, Africa, and other parts of the Americas. Churches, schools, and towns—the visible marks of the receding frontier—appeared everywhere. A balanced gender ratio and stable family life had been achieved throughout the colonies. Men such as Devereaux Jarratt, the son of an immigrant yeoman farmer, were able to move up in society despite frequent obstacles. Seasoned political leaders and familiar political institutions functioned from Maine to Georgia.

Yet the sinew, bone, and muscle of American society had not yet fully knit together. The polyglot population, one-fifth of it bound in chattel slavery and its Native American component still unassimilated and uneasily situated on the frontier, was a kaleidoscopic mixture of ethnic and religious groups. While developing rapidly, its economy showed weaknesses, particularly in New England, where land resources had been strained. The social structure reflected the colonizers' emergence from a frontier stage, but the consolidation of wealth by a landed and mercantile elite was matched by pockets of poverty appearing in the cities and some rural areas. Full of strength, yet marked by awkward incongruities, colonial America in 1750 approached an era of strife and momentous decisions. Much of that strife involved the growing power of France's inland empire in North America and the way that wars in Europe were become globe-encircling conflicts.

✦ Recommended Reading

The North: A Land of Family Farms
Bernard Bailyn, *Voyagers to the West: A Passage in the Peopling of America on the Eve of the American Revolution* (1986); John L. Brooke, *The Heart of the Commonwealth: Society and Political Culture in Worcester County, Massachusetts, 1713–1861* (1989); Richard Bushman, *From Puritan to Yankee* (1967); Jon Butler, *The Huguenots in Colonial America* (1983); David W. Conroy, *In Public Houses: Drink and the Revolution of Authority in Colonial Massachusetts* (1995); Thomas J. Davis, *A Rumor of Revolt: The "Great Negro Plot" in Colonial New York* (1985); Cornelia Hughes Dayton, *Women Before the Bar: Gender, Law, and Society in Connecticut, 1639–1789* (1995); R. J. Dickson, *Ulster Immigration to Colonial America, 1718–1775* (1966); Aaron S. Fogleman, *Hopeful Journeys: German Immigration, Settlement, and Political Culture, 1717–1775* (1996); Patrick Griffin, *The People with No*

Name: Ireland's Ulster Scots, America's Scots Irish, and the Creation of a British Atlantic World, 1689–1764 (2001); Graham Russell Hodges, *Root and Branch: African Americans in New York and East Jersey, 1613–1863* (1999); Christopher M. Jedrey, *The World of John Cleaveland: Family and Community in Eighteenth-Century New England* (1979); Sung Bok Kim, *Landlord and Tenant in the Colony of New York: Manorial Society, 1664–1775* (1976); Ned Landsman, *Scotland and Its First American Colony* (1985); James Lemon, *The Best Poor Man's Country: A Geographical Study of Early Southeastern Pennsylvania* (1972); Carolyn Merchant, *Ecological Revolutions: Nature, Gender, and Science in New England* (1989); William Piersen, *Black Yankees: The Development of an African-American Subculture in Eighteenth-Century New England* (1988); Laurel T. Ulrich, *Good Wives: Image and Reality in the Lives of Women in Northern New England, 1650–1750* (1982) and *The Age of Homespun: Objects and Stories in the Creation of an American Myth* (2001); Daniel Vickers, *Farmers and Fishermen: Two Centuries of Work in Essex County, Massachusetts, 1630–1850* (1994); Marianne S. Woceck, *The Beginnings of Mass Migration to North America* (1999).

The Plantation South

Alex Bontemps, *The Punished Self: Surviving Slavery in the Colonial South* (2001); T. H. Breen, *Tobacco Culture: The Mentality of the Great Tidewater Planters on the Eve of the Revolution* (1985); Joyce E. Chaplin, *An Anxious Pursuit: Agricultural Innovation and Modernity in the Lower South, 1730–1815* (1993); Paul G. E. Clemens, *The Atlantic Economy and Colonial Maryland's Eastern Shore: From Tobacco to Grain* (1980); Carville Earle, *The Evolution of a Tidewater Settlement System* (1975); Rhys Isaac, *The Transformation of Virginia, 1740–1790* (1982); Winthrop D. Jordan, *White Over Black* (1968); Cynthia A. Kierner, *Beyond the Household: Woman's Place in the Early South, 1700–1835* (1998); Allan Kulikoff, *Tobacco and Slaves: The Development of Southern Culture in the Chesapeake, 1680–1800* (1986); Philip D. Morgan, *Slave Counterpoint: Black Culture in the Eighteenth-Century Chesapeake and Low-Country* (1998); Gerald Mullin, *Flight and Rebellion: Slave Resistance in Eighteenth-Century Virginia* (1972); Michael Mullin, *Africa in America: Slave Acculturation and Resistance in the American South* (1992); Anthony Penna, *Nature's Bounty: Historical and Modern Environmental Perspectives* (1999); Timothy Silver, *A New Face on the Countryside: Indians, Colonists, and Slaves in South Atlantic Forests, 1500–1800* (1990); Daniel Blake Smith, *Inside the Great House: Planter Family Life in Eighteenth-Century Chesapeake Society* (1980); Mechal Sobel, *The World They Made Together: Black and White Relations in Eighteenth-Century Virginia* (1987); Gregory Stiverson, *Poverty in the Land of Plenty: Tenancy in Eighteenth-Century Maryland* (1980); Marvin L. Michael Kay and Lorin Lee Cary, *Slavery in North Carolina, 1748–1775* (1995); Betty Wood, *Slavery in Colonial Georgia,*

1730–1775 (1984); Peter H. Wood, *Black Majority: Negroes in South Carolina from 1670 Through the Stono Rebellion* (1974).

Contending for a Continent

Kathryn E. Holland Braund, *Deerskins and Duffels: The Creek Indian Trade with Anglo-America, 1685–1815* (1993); Gwendolyn Midlo Hall, *Africans in Colonial Louisiana* (1992); Thomas Ingersoll, *Mammon and Manon in Early New Orleans: The First Slave Society in the Deep South, 1717–1819* (1999); Robert H. Jackson and Edward Castillo, *Indians, Franciscans, and Spanish Colonization* (1995); Michael N. McConnell, *A Country Between Us: The Upper Ohio Valley and Its Peoples, 1724–1774* (1992); Claudio Saunt, *A New Order of Things: Property, Power, and the Transformation of the Creek Indians, 1733–1816* (1999); Marc Simmons, *Coronado's Land: Essays on Daily Life in Colonial New Mexico* (1991); Daniel Usner, Jr., *Indians, Settlers, and Slaves in a Frontier Exchange Economy: The Lower Mississippi Valley Before 1783* (1992) and *American Indians in the Lower Mississippi Valley* (1998); Richard White, *The Middle Ground: Indians, Empires, and Republics in the Great Lakes Region, 1650–1815* (1991).

The Urban World of Commerce and Ideas

Russell R. Menard, *The Economy of British America, 1607–1789* (1985); Gary B. Nash, *The Urban Crucible: Social Change, Political Consciousness, and the Origins of the American Revolution* (1979); Edwin J. Perkins, *The Economy of Colonial America*, 2nd ed. (1988); Sharon V. Salinger, *Taverns and Drinking in Early America* (2002); Billy G. Smith, *The "Lower Sort": Philadelphia's Laboring People, 1750–1800* (1990); G. B. Warden, *Boston, 1687–1776* (1970); Esmond Wright, *Franklin of Philadelphia* (1986); Karin Wulf, *Not All Wives: Women of Colonial Philadelphia* (2000).

The Great Awakening

Patricia Bonomi, *Under the Cope of Heaven: Religion, Society, and Politics in Colonial America* (1986); Alan Heimert, *Religion and the American Mind: From the Great Awakening to the Revolution* (1966); Susan Juster, *Disorderly Women: Sexual Politics and Evangelicalism in Revolutionary New England* (1994); Frank J. Lambert, *"Pedlar in Divinity": George Whitefield and the Trans-atlantic Revivals* (1994); Henry May, *The American Enlightenment* (1976); Gerald R. McDermott, *Jonathan Edwards Confronts the Gods* (2000); Perry Miller, *From Colony to Province* (1953); Nina Reid-Maroney, *Philadelphia's Enlightenment, 1740–1800: Kingdom of Christ, Empire of Reason* (2001); Thomas P. Slaughter, *The Natures of John and William Bartram* (1996); Harry S. Stout, *The Divine Dramatist: George Whitefield and the Rise of Modern Evangelicalism* (1991); Patricia Tracy, *Jonathan Edwards, Pastor* (1979).

Political Life

Bernard Bailyn, *The Origins of American Politics* (1968); Patricia Bonomi, *A Factious People: Politics and Society in Colonial New York* (1977); William Pencak, *War, Politics, and Revolution in Provincial Massachusetts* (1981); Charles Sydnor, *American Revolutionaries in the Making: Political Practices in Washington's Virginia* (1965); Alan Tully, *Forming American Politics: Ideas, Interests, and Institutions in Colonial New York and Pennsylvania* (1994); Robert Zemsky, *Merchants, Farmers, and River Gods: An Essay on Eighteenth-Century American Politics* (1971).

Fiction and Film

Kenneth Roberts, king of historical novelists on eighteenth-century America, movingly describes the Seven Years' War in *Northwest Passage* (1937); Spencer Tracy starred in the Hollywood version with the same title. James Fenimore Cooper's *The Last of the Mohicans* (1836) is another American classic, but much more to the taste of today's students is Hollywood's movie by the same title (1992), starring Daniel Day-Lewis and Madeleine Stowe.

✦ Discovering U.S. History Online

History Buff's Reference Library

www.historybuff.com/library/refseventeen.html

Brief journalistic essays on newspaper coverage of sixteenth- to eighteenth-century American history.

Bethlehem, Pennsylvania

www.bdhp.moravian.edu/

A cooperative effort of area libraries, this site examines the history of the Moravian community of Bethlehem, Pennsylvania.

Martha Ballard's Diary

www.dohistory.org

Focusing on the life of Martha Ballard, a late eighteenth-century New England woman, this site employs selections from her diary, excerpts from a book and film about her life, and other primary documents that enable students to conduct their own historical investigation.

Georgia: Early Colonial Period

www.members.aol.com/jeworth/gboindex.htm

This site aims to supply information that will shed light on the "almost-forgotten era of Georgia history when American Indians, Spanish missionaries, and English traders briefly shared the land."

Colonial Williamsburg

www.history.org/Almanack/almanack.cfm

Sections of this view of colonial Williamsburg include "Meet the People," "See the Places," and "Colonial Life."

Excerpts from Slave Narratives

www.vi.uh.edu/pages/mintz/primary.htm

This site offers online access to slave narratives dating from the seventeenth century.

Two Centuries of Louisiana History

www.lsm.crt.state.la.us/cabildo/cabildo.htm

This state-run site focuses on the diverse ethnic heritage of Louisiana's people. The early sections cover pre-contact and colonial Louisiana.

Military Artifacts of Spanish Florida, 1650–1821

www.artifacts.org/default.htm

Along with an extensive display of military artifacts, this "Internet Museum" also provides background information on the age of Spanish exploration and settlement as well as details about her rival, Bourbon France.

Colonial Currency

etext.lib.virginia.edu/users/brock

This site includes useful primary and secondary documents on early American currency.

Newspaper Articles from the Sixteenth to Eighteenth Century

www.discovery.com/guides/history/historybuff/library/refseventeen.html

Brief journalistic essays on newspaper coverage of sixteenth- to eighteenth-century American history.

North American Women's Letters and Diaries

www.lib.uchicago.edu/efts/asp/NAWLD

At this site, students can find rich firsthand accounts of colonial life from women's perspectives.

White Oak Fur Post

www.whiteoak.org

This site documents an eighteenth-century fur trading post among the Indians in the region that would become Minnesota.

Religion in Eighteenth-Century America

www.lcweb.loc.gov/exhibits/religion/rel02.html

Providing an overview of eighteenth-century religion in the American colonies, this site draws on primary source material such as paintings of clergymen, title pages of published sermons, and other artifacts.

Benjamin Franklin

www.english.udel.edu/lemay/franklin

This richly illustrated site relates the story of Franklin's life and political involvement in seven parts.

5

The Strains of Empire

A View of the Town of Concord (April 1775), attributed to Ralph Earle. *(Courtesy Concord Museum, Concord, MA)*

✦ *American Stories*

A SHOEMAKER LEADS A BOSTON MOB

In 1758, when he was 21 years old, Ebenezer MacIntosh of Boston laid down his shoemaker's awl and enlisted in the Massachusetts expedition against the French on Lake Champlain—one battle in the war that was raging between England and France in North America, the Caribbean, and Europe. The son of a poor Boston shoemaker who had fought against the French in a previous war, MacIntosh had known poverty all his life. Service against the French offered the hope of plunder or at least an enlistment bounty worth half a year's wages. One among thousands of colonists who fought against the "Gallic menace" in the Seven Years' War, MacIntosh contributed his mite to the climactic struggle that drove the French from North America.

But a greater role lay ahead for the poor Boston shoemaker. Two years after the Peace of Paris in 1763, England imposed a stamp tax on the American colonists. In the massive protests that followed, MacIntosh emerged as the street leader of the Boston crowd. In two nights of the most violent attacks on private property ever witnessed in North America, a Boston crowd nearly destroyed the houses of two of the colony's most important officials. On August 14, they tore through the house of Andrew Oliver, a wealthy merchant and the appointed distributor of stamps for Massachusetts. Twelve days later, MacIntosh led the crowd in attacking the mansion of Thomas Hutchinson, a wealthy merchant who served as lieutenant governor and chief justice of Massachusetts. "The mob was so general," wrote the governor, "and so supported that all civil power ceased in an instant."

For the next several months, the power of the poor Boston shoemaker grew. Called "General" MacIntosh and "Captain-General of the Liberty Tree" by his townspeople, he soon sported a militia uniform of gold and blue and a hat laced with gold. Two thousand townsmen followed his commands on November 5, when they marched in orderly ranks through the crooked streets of Boston to demonstrate their solidarity in resisting the hated stamps.

Five weeks later, a crowd publicly humiliated stamp distributor Oliver. Demanding that he announce his resignation before the assembled citizenry, they marched him across town in a driving December rain. With MacIntosh at his elbow, he finally reached the "Liberty Tree," which had become a symbol of resistance to England's new colonial policies. There the aristocratic Oliver ate humble pie. He concluded his resignation remarks with bitter words, hissing sardonically that he would "always think myself very happy when it shall be in my power to serve the people."

"To serve the people" was an ancient idea embedded in English political culture, but it assumed new meaning in the American colonies during the epic third quarter of the eighteenth century. Few colonists in 1750 held even a faint desire to break the connection with England, and fewer still might have predicted the form of government that 13 independent states in an independent nation might fashion. Yet in a whirlwind of events, 2 million colonists moved haltingly toward a showdown with mighty England. Little-known men like Ebenezer MacIntosh as well as his well-known and historically celebrated townsmen Samuel Adams, John Hancock, and John Adams were part of the struggle. Collectively, ordinary people such as MacIntosh influenced—and in fact sometimes even dictated—the revolutionary movement in the colonies. Though we read and speak mostly of a small group of "founding fathers," the wellsprings of the American Revolution can be fully discovered only among a variety of people from different social groups, occupations, regions, and religions.

This chapter addresses the tensions in late colonial society, the imperial crisis that followed the Seven Years' War (in the colonies, often called the French and Indian War), and the tumultuous decade that led to the "shot heard round the world" fired at Concord Bridge in April 1775. It portrays the origins of a dual American Revolution. Ebenezer MacIntosh, in leading the Boston mob against Crown officers and colonial collaborators who tried to implement a new colonial policy after 1763, helped set in motion a revolutionary movement to restore ancient liberties thought by the Americans to be under deliberate attack in England. This movement eventually escalated into the war for American independence.

But MacIntosh's Boston followers were also venting years of resentment at the accumulation of wealth and power by Boston's aristocratic elite. Behind every swing of the ax, every shattered crystal goblet, and splintered mahogany chair lay the fury of a Bostonian who had seen the city's conservative elite try to dismantle the town meeting, suffered economic hardship, and lost faith that opportunity and just relations still prevailed in his town. This sentiment, which called for the reform of a colonial society that had become corrupt, self-indulgent, and dominated by an elite, fed an idealistic commitment to reshape American society even while severing the colonial bond. As distinguished from the war for independence, this was the American Revolution.

THE CLIMACTIC SEVEN YEARS' WAR

After a brief period of peace following King George's War (1744–1748), France and England fought the fourth, largest, and by far most significant of the wars for empire that had begun in the late seventeenth century. Known variously as the Seven Years' War, the French and Indian War, and (to modern historians) the Great War for Empire, this global conflict in part represented a showdown for control of North America's interior between the Allegheny Mountains and the Mississippi River. In North America, the Anglo-American forces ultimately prevailed, and their victory dramatically affected the lives of all the diverse people living in the huge region east of the Mississippi—English, German, and Scots-Irish settlers in the English colonies; French and Spanish colonizers in Canada, Florida, and interior North America; African slaves in a variety of settlements; and, perhaps most of all, the powerful Native American tribes of the interior.

War and the Management of Empire

England began constructing a more coherent administration of its far-flung colonies after the Glorious Revolution of 1688. In 1696, a professional Board of Trade replaced the old Lords of Trade; the Treasury strengthened the customs service; and Parliament created overseas vice-admiralty courts, which functioned without juries to prosecute smugglers who evaded the trade regulations set forth in the Navigation Acts. Parliament began playing a more active role after the reign of Queen Anne (1702–1714) and continued to do so when the weak, German-speaking King George I came to the throne. Royal governors received greater powers, got more detailed instructions, and came under more insistent demands from the Board of Trade to enforce British policies. England was quietly installing the machinery of imperial management tended by a corps of colonial bureaucrats.

The best test of an effectively organized state is its ability to wage war. Four times between 1689 and 1763, England matched its strength against France, its archrival in Europe, North America, and the Caribbean. These wars of empire had tremendous consequences for the home governments, their colonial subjects in the Americas, and the North American Indian tribes drawn into the bloody conflicts.

We have already seen (in Chapter 4) how the Peace of Utrecht, which ended Queen Anne's War (1702–1713), brought victor's spoils of great importance to England. The generation of peace that followed was really only a time-out, which both England and France used in the years until 1739 to strengthen their war-making capacity. Britain's productive and efficiently governed New World colonies made important contributions. Though known as a period of "salutary neglect," this was actually an era when king and Parliament increased their control over colonial affairs.

Concerned mainly with economic regulation, Parliament added new articles such as fur, copper, hemp, tar, and turpentine to the list of items produced in the colonies that had to be shipped to England before being exported to another country. Parliament also curtailed colonial production of articles important to England's economy: woollen cloth (1699), beaver hats (1732), and finished iron products (1750). Most important, Parliament passed the Molasses Act in 1733. Attempting to stop the trade between New England and the French West Indies, where Yankee traders exchanged fish, beef, and pork for molasses to convert into rum, Parliament imposed a prohibitive duty of six pence per gallon on French slave-produced molasses. This turned many of New England's largest merchants and distillers into smugglers, for a generation schooling them, their ship captains, crews, and allied waterfront artisans in defying royal authority.

The generation of peace ended abruptly in 1739 when England declared war on Spain. The immediate cause was the ear of an English sea captain, Robert Jenkins. Spanish authorities had deprived him of that appendage eight years before for smuggling in their colonies. Encouraged by his government, Jenkins publicly displayed his pickled ear in 1738 to whip up war fever against Spain. The real cause, however, was England's determination to continue its drive toward commercial domination of the Atlantic basin. The British Navy captured Porto Bello in Spanish Panama in 1739, but four expeditions against Spanish strongholds in 1740–1742 were disasters. Admiral Edward Vernon recruited some 3,500 American colonists for these attacks, enticing them with dreams of capturing mountains of Spanish silver and gold. But the Spanish withstood attacks against St. Augustine in Florida; Havana, Cuba, Cartagena, and Colombia; and Panama. Most of the American colonists died of yellow fever, dysentery, and outright starvation, and those who limped home, including George Washington's father, Lawrence Washington, who renamed his Virginia plantation after Admiral Vernon, had little booty to show for their efforts.

From 1744 to 1748, the Anglo-Spanish war merged into a much larger Anglo-French conflict, called King George's War in North America and the War of Austrian Succession in Europe. Its scale far exceeded that of previous conflicts. As military priorities became paramount, the need increased for discipline within the empire. In addition, unprecedented military expenditures led Britain to ask its West Indian and American colonies to share in the costs of defending—and extending—the empire and to tailor their behavior to home country needs. But for American colonists, except for war contractors such as Boston's Thomas Hancock, the war was costly. All New Englanders swelled with pride in June 1745 after Massachusetts volunteers, coordinating their attacks with British naval forces, captured the massive French fortress of Louisbourg, on Cape Breton Island, guarding the approach to the St. Lawrence River, after a six-week siege. But the losses were staggering. "One half of our militia [died] like rotten sheep," reported one Boston leader, who believed that one-fifth of all Massachusetts adult males had perished, leaving thousands of widows and orphaned children. New Englanders were bitter when, at war's end in 1748, the British government handed the prized Fort Louisbourg back to France in exchange for French withdrawal from conquests in

parts of British-controlled India and an agreement to spare the British army trapped in Europe.

Outbreak of Hostilities

The return of peace in 1748 did not relieve the tension between English and French colonists in North America. Reaching back to the early seventeenth century and fueled by religious hatred, it was intensified by the spectacular population growth of the English colonies: from 250,000 in 1700 to 1.25 million in 1750, and to 1.75 million in the next decade. Three-quarters of the increase came in the colonies south of New York, propelling thousands of land-hungry settlers toward the western trading empire of the French and their Indian allies.

Promoting this westward rush were fur traders and land speculators. The fur traders were penetrating a French-influenced region, where they offered native trappers and hunters better prices and, sometimes, higher-quality goods than the French. In the 1740s and 1750s, speculators (including many future revolutionary leaders) formed land companies to capitalize on the seaboard population explosion. The farther west the settlement line moved, the closer it came to the western trading empire of the French and their Indian allies.

Colonial penetration of the Ohio valley in the 1740s established the first English outposts in the continental heartland. This challenged the French where their interest was vital. While the English controlled most of the eastern coastal plain of North America, the French had nearly encircled them to the west by building a chain of trading posts and forts along the St. Lawrence River, through the Great Lakes, and southward into the Ohio and Mississippi valleys all the way to New Orleans.

Confronted by English intrusions, the French resisted. They attempted to block further English expansion west of the Alleghenies by constructing new forts in the Ohio valley and by prying some tribes loose from their new English connections. As a French emissary warned a western tribe in the 1750s, the English "are much less anxious to take away your peltries than to become masters of your lands, and your blindness is so great that you do not perceive that the very hand that caresses you will scourge you like negroes and slaves, so soon as it will have got possession of your lands."

By 1753, the French were driving the English traders out of the Ohio River valley and establishing a line of forts between Lake Erie and the forks of the Ohio River, near present-day Pittsburgh. There, near Fort Duquesne on May 28, 1754, the French smartly

The War of Jenkins' Ear in the Southern Colonies and the Caribbean

The War of Jenkins' Ear was especially unsettling in the colonies because slave revolts broke out in New York and South Carolina during the course of the war. In each case, the Spanish enemy was suspected of having played a role in the revolts.

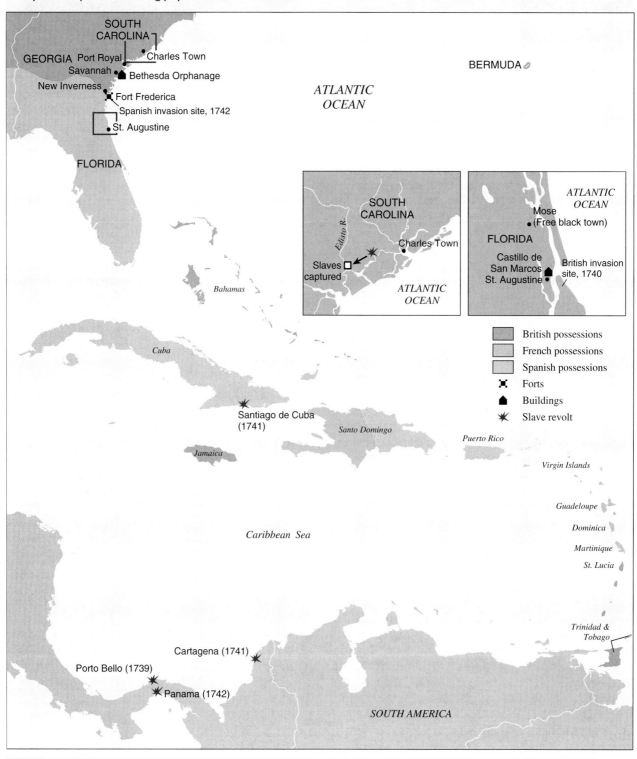

In this dramatic painting, colonial assault groups prepare to go ashore on Cape Breton Island to capture the nearby Louisbourg Fort. The colonial forces were commanded by William Pepperell, a merchant, shipbuilder, and land speculator who—for capturing the French fortress—was the first American to be knighted by the English. *(Anne S. K. Brown Military Collection)*

rebuffed an ambitious 21-year-old Virginia militia colonel named George Washington, dispatched by his colony's government to expel them from the region and drive them from the very site where the Ohio Company, a syndicate of wealthy Virginia speculators, had built an Indian trading post. The skirmish produced only a few casualties, but it quickly escalated into a global war that rearranged the balance of power not only in North America but in Europe and the entire Atlantic world.

Men in the capitals of Europe, not in the colonies, made the decision to force a showdown in the interior of North America. England's powerful merchants, supported by American clients, had been emboldened by English success in overwhelming the mighty French fortress at Louisbourg. Now, they argued, the time was ripe to destroy the French overseas trade. Convinced, the English ministry ordered several thousand troops to North America in 1754; in France, 3,000 regulars embarked to meet the English challenge.

With war looming, the colonial governments attempted to coordinate efforts. Representatives of seven colonies met at Albany, New York, in June 1754 to plan a colonial union and rewin the allegiance of the Iroquois, whose grievances had grown sharply after a group of land speculators, the Kayaderossera partners, had tried to grab nearly a million acres of Mohawk land. Both failed. The 150 Iroquois chiefs left with 30 wagonloads of gifts but made no firm commitment to fight the French. Benjamin Franklin designed a plan for an intercolonial government to manage Indian affairs, provide for defense, and have

The Americans and British relied heavily on the Iroquois in attempting to vanquish the French in the Seven Years' War. "Old Hendrick," the Mohawk chief pictured here, is shown in elaborate European apparel given him by King George II in 1740 to help seal a diplomatic alliance. Chief Hendrick died at the Battle of Lake George in 1755, fighting alongside the British against the French. *(Courtesy of the John Carter Brown Library at Brown University)*

the power to pass laws and levy taxes. But even the clever woodcut displayed in the *Pennsylvania Gazette* that pictured a chopped-up snake with the insignia "Join or Die" failed to overcome the long-standing jealousies that had thwarted previous attempts at intercolony cooperation. "Everyone cries a union is necessary," sighed Franklin, "but when they come to the manner and form of the union, their weak noodles are perfectly distracted."

With his newly arrived British regiments and hundreds of American recruits, General Edward Braddock slogged across Virginia in the summer of 1755, each day cutting a few miles of road through forests and across mountains. A headstrong professional soldier who regarded his European battlefield experience as sufficient for war in the American wilderness, Braddock had contempt for the woods-wise French regiments and their stealthy Indian allies.

As Braddock neared Fort Duquesne, the entire French force and the British suddenly surprised one another in the forest. The French had 218 soldiers and Canadian militiamen and 637 Indian allies, while Braddock commanded 1,400 British regulars supported by 450 Virginians commanded by Washington. But only a few Indian scouts were with them. Pouring murderous fire into Braddock's tidy lines, the French and their Indian allies won. Braddock perished, and two-thirds of the British and Americans were killed or wounded. Washington, his uniform pierced by four bullets, had two horses shot from beneath him. Although they had 1,000 men in reserve down the road, the Anglo-American force beat a hasty retreat.

The Seven Years' War, 1754–1756

In the 1755 campaigns of the Seven Years' War, the British suffered losses except in Nova Scotia, where they captured Fort Beauséjour, which led to the deportation of the French-speaking Catholic Acadians.

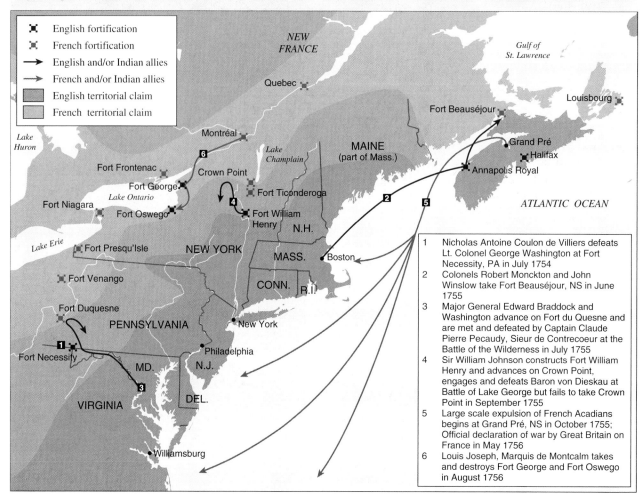

1 Nicholas Antoine Coulon de Villiers defeats Lt. Colonel George Washington at Fort Necessity, PA in July 1754
2 Colonels Robert Monckton and John Winslow take Fort Beauséjour, NS in June 1755
3 Major General Edward Braddock and Washington advance on Fort du Quesne and are met and defeated by Captain Claude Pierre Pecaudy, Sieur de Contrecoeur at the Battle of the Wilderness in July 1755
4 Sir William Johnson constructs Fort William Henry and advances on Crown Point, engages and defeats Baron von Dieskau at Battle of Lake George but fails to take Crown Point in September 1755
5 Large scale expulsion of French Acadians begins at Grand Pré, NS in October 1755; Official declaration of war by Great Britain on France in May 1756
6 Louis Joseph, Marquis de Montcalm takes and destroys Fort George and Fort Oswego in August 1756

Braddock's ignominious retreat brought almost every tribe north of the Ohio River to the French side. Throughout the summer, French-supplied Indian raiders torched the Virginia and Pennsylvania backcountry. "The roads are full of starved, naked, indigent multitudes," observed one officer. One French triumph followed another during the next two years. Never was disunity within the English colonies so glaring. With its Indian allies, French Canada, only 70,000 inhabitants strong, had badly battered 1.5 million colonists supported by the British army.

Farther north, the Anglo-American forces had more success. A month before Braddock's debacle, British regulars with Massachusetts volunteers overpowered Fort Beauséjour, the French fort on the neck of land that connected Nova Scotia, held by the English since the Peace of Utrecht, and the French Canadian mainland. This quickly led to the expulsion of the French Acadians, who had been promised the right to practice Catholicism and keep their land while promising neutrality in any war between the English and French. When they refused to swear oaths of unqualified allegiance to the English king, which would revoke their religious freedom and oblige them to fight against fellow Frenchmen on the Canadian mainland, the British rounded up about six thousand Acadians, herded them aboard ships, and dispersed them among the English colonies. Their confiscated land was given to New Englanders looking for a new agricultural frontier. Another seven to ten thousand Acadians escaped to the Canadian mainland, and in time, about three thousand of those deported to the English colonies made their way to French Louisiana. The English justified this ethnic cleansing—the first time a civilian population was relocated by force—as a wartime security measure.

The French won most of the battles in 1756, including a victory at Fort William Henry on Lake George, where the Indian allies of the French proved essential. At this point, Britain declared war on France, and the French and Indian War in North America turned into a world war where France, Austria, and Russia pitted themselves against England and Prussia. The turning point in the war came after the energetic William Pitt became England's secretary of state in 1757. "I believe that I can save this nation and that no one else can," he boasted, abandoning Europe as the main theater of action against the French and throwing his nation's military might into the American campaign. The forces he dispatched to North America in 1757 and 1758 dwarfed all preceding commitments: about 23,000 British troops and a huge fleet with 14,000

mariners. But even forces of this magnitude, when asked to engage the enemy in the forests of North America, were not necessarily sufficient to the task without Indian support, or at least neutrality. "A doubt remains not," proclaimed one English official in the colonies, "that the prosperity of our colonies on the continent will stand or fall with our interest and favour among them."

Tribal Strategies

Anglo-American leaders knew that the support of the Iroquois and their tributary tribes was crucial and could be secured in only two ways: through purchase or by a demonstration of power that would convince the tribes that the English would prevail with or without their assistance. The Iroquois knew that their interest lay in playing off one European power against the other. "To preserve the balance between us and the French," wrote a New York politician, "is the great ruling principle of modern Indian politics."

The first English stratagem for securing Iroquois support failed in 1754 when colonial negotiators heaped gifts on the Iroquois chiefs at the Albany

The Iroquois warrior depicted here shows the blending of Indian and European weaponry. His snowshoes and the war club held in his right hand are native in origin. His English musket, slung over his shoulder, and the steel axe fastened at his belt are European trade items.
(© Collection of the New-York Historical Society)

The Seven Years' War, 1757–1760

The British-American victory over France and its Indian allies in the Seven Years' War did not bring peace on the western frontier. After the war, Pontiac led the warriors of several tribes in attacks on settlers and British forts.

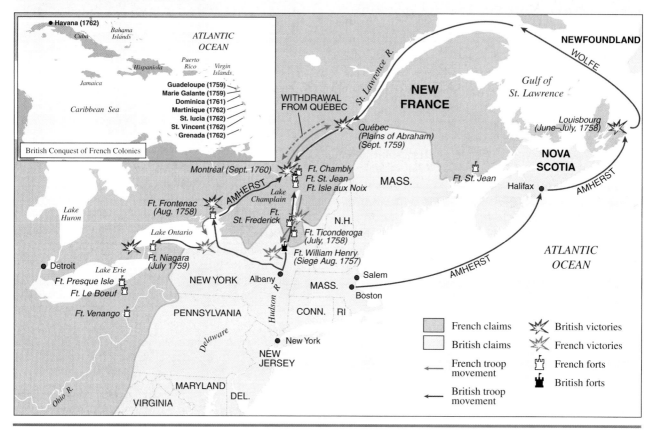

Congress but received in return only tantalizing half-promises of support against the French. The second alternative fizzled because the English proved militarily inferior to the French in the first three years of the war. Hence, the westernmost of the Iroquois Six Nations, the Seneca, fought on the side of the French in the campaigns of 1757 and 1758, while the Delaware, a tributary tribe, harassed the Pennsylvania frontier.

In 1758, the huge English military buildup began to produce victories. The largest army ever assembled in North America to that point, some 15,000 British and American soldiers, including the Bostonian Ebenezer MacIntosh, suffered terrible casualties and withdrew from the field after attempting to storm Fort Ticonderoga on Lake Champlain in June 1758. Then the tide turned. Troops under Sir Jeffrey Amherst captured Louisbourg, on Cape Breton Island, and Fort Duquesne fell to another army of 6,000 led by General John Forbes. The resolute Pitt had mobilized the fighting power of the English nation and put more men in

the field than existed in all of New France. The colonists, in turn, had put aside intramural squabbling long enough to overwhelm the badly outnumbered French.

The victories of 1758 finally moved the Iroquois away from neutrality. Added incentive to join the Anglo-American side came when the English navy bottled up French shipping in the St. Lawrence River, cutting the Iroquois off from French trade goods. By early 1759, foreseeing a French defeat in North America, the Iroquois pledged 800 warriors for an attack on Fort Niagara, the strategic French trading depot on Lake Ontario.

But dramatic Anglo-American victories did not always guarantee Indian support. Backcountry skirmishes with the Cherokee from Virginia to South Carolina turned into a costly war from 1759 to 1761. In 1760, the Cherokee mauled a British army of 1,300 under Amherst. The following summer, a much larger Anglo-American force invaded Cherokee country, burning towns and food supplies. English control of the sea interrupted the Indians' supply of

French arms. Beset by food shortages, lack of ammunition, and a smallpox epidemic, the Cherokee finally sued for peace.

Other Anglo-American victories in 1759, the "year of miracles," decided the outcome of the bloodiest war yet known in the New World. The capture of Fort Niagara, the critical link in the system of forts that joined the French inland empire with the Atlantic, was followed by the conquest of sugar-rich Martinique in the West Indies. The culminating stroke came with a dramatic victory at Québec. Led by 32-year-old General James Wolfe, 5,000 troops scaled a rocky cliff and overcame the French on the Plains of Abraham. The capture of Montreal late in 1760 completed the shattering of French power in North America. The theater of operations shifted to the Caribbean, where fighting continued, as in Europe, for three more years. But in the American colonies, the old English dream of destroying the Gallic menace had finally come true.

Consequences of the Seven Years' War

The Treaty of Paris, ending the Seven Years' War in 1763, brought astounding changes to European and Indian peoples in North America. The Spanish, who had tried to check the French southern influence directed from Louisiana, now acquired New Orleans and all of the vast Louisiana territory west of the Mississippi. Although this could provide a buffer against English aspirations in the continent's heartland, Spain's king surrendered Spanish Florida to the British—a pragmatic decision because England agreed to compensate Spain with Havana, which the British had captured during the war.

The Treaty of Paris dealt a harsh blow to the interior Indian tribes. Unlike the coastal Native Americans, whose population and independence had ebbed rapidly through contact with the colonizers, the inland tribes had maintained their strength and sometimes even grown more unified through relations with settlers. Although they came to depend on European trade goods, Native Americans had turned this commercial connection to their advantage so long as more than one source of trade goods existed.

The Indian play-off system came to a crashing halt when the French ceded Canada and all territory east of the Mississippi, except for New Orleans, to England in the Treaty of Paris. For the interior tribes, only one source of trade goods remained. Two centuries of European rivalry for control of eastern North America ended abruptly. Iroquois, Cherokee, Creek, Ojibway, Shawnee, and scores of other interior tribes were now forced to adjust to this reality.

After making peace, the British government launched a new policy designed to separate Native

The storming of French Québec in 1759 was the decisive blow in England's campaign to end the French domination of Canada and the lands west of the Appalachians. The heroic exploits of General James Wolfe made him a hero throughout England and the colonies. (A View of the Taking of Quebec, September 13, 1759, *National Army Museum, London*)

Americans and colonizers by creating a racial boundary roughly following the crestline of the Appalachian Mountains from Maine to Georgia. The Proclamation of 1763 reserved all land west of the line for Indian nations. White settlers who were already there were told to withdraw.

Though well-intended, this attempt to legislate interracial accord failed completely. Even before the proclamation was issued, the Ottawa chief Pontiac, concerned that the elimination of the French threatened the old treaty and gift-giving system, had gathered together many of the northern tribes that had aided the French assaults on the English forts during the Seven Years' War. Although Pontiac's pan-Indian movement to drive the British out of the Ohio valley collapsed in 1764, it served notice that the interior tribes would fight for their lands.

London could not enforce the Proclamation of 1763. Staggering under an immense wartime debt,

England decided to maintain only small army garrisons in America to regulate the interior. Nor could royal governors stop land speculators and settlers from privately purchasing land from trans-Appalachian tribes or simply encroaching on their land. Under such circumstances, the western frontier seethed after 1763.

Although the epic Anglo-American victory redrew the map of North America, the war also had important social and economic effects on colonial society. It convinced the colonists of their growing strength, yet left them debt-ridden and weakened in manpower. The wartime economy spurred economic development and poured British capital into the colonies, yet rendered them more vulnerable to cyclic fluctuations in the British economy.

Military contracts, for example, brought prosperity to most colonies during the war years. Huge orders for ships, arms, uniforms, and provisions en-

North America After 1763

At the Treaty of Paris in 1763, France surrendered huge claims west of the Mississippi River to Spain and east of the river to England. England also acquired Florida from Spain.

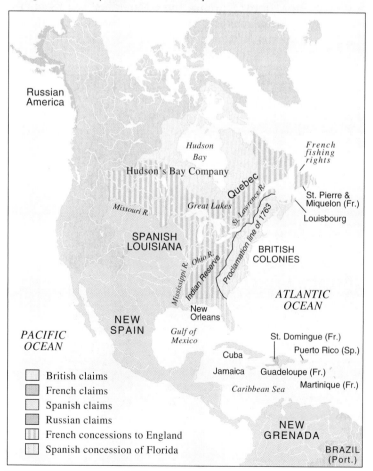

riched northern merchants and provided good prices for farmers as well. Urban artisans enjoyed full employment and high wages, as tailors' needles flashed to meet clothing contracts, shoemakers stitched for an unprecedented demand for shoes, and bakers found armies clamoring for bread. Privateers—privately outfitted ships licensed by colonial governments to attack enemy shipping— enriched the fortunate few. On a single voyage in 1758, John MacPherson snared 18 French ships. The prize money was lavish enough to allow this son of a Scottish immigrant to pour £14,000 into creating a country estate outside Philadelphia, to which he retired in splendor.

The war, however, required heavy taxes and took a huge human toll. Privateering carried many fortune seekers to a watery grave, and the wilderness campaigns from 1755 to 1760 claimed thousands of lives. Garrison life brought wracking fevers (which claimed more victims than enemy weapons), and battlefield medical treatment was too primitive to save many of the wounded. Boston's Thomas Hancock predicted at the beginning of the war that "this province is spirited to [send] every third man to do the work of the Lord." But the Lord's work was expensive. Thomas Pownall, assuming the governorship of Massachusetts in August 1757, found not the "rich, flourishing, powerful, enterprizing" colony he expected but a province "ruined and undone."

The human cost of the war was high, especially in New England, which bore the brunt of the fighting. Probably half of all New England men of military age served in the war and perhaps three-quarters of those between the ages of 17 and 24. The magnitude of human loss in Boston was probably greater than in any war fought by Bostonians up until this time or in the future. The wartime muster lists show that nearly every working-class Bostonian tasted military service at some point during the long war. When peace came, Boston had a deficit of almost 700 men in a town of about 2,000 families. The high rate of war widowhood feminized poverty and required expanded poor relief to maintain husbandless women and fatherless children.

Peace ended the casualties but also brought depression. When the bulk of the British forces left North America in 1760, the economy slumped badly, especially in the coastal towns. "The tippling soldiery that used to help us out at a dead lift," mused a New York merchant, "are gone to drink [rum]in a warmer region [the Caribbean], the place of its production."

Although even some wealthy merchants went bankrupt, the greatest hardships after 1760 fell on laboring people. Those with the smallest wages had the thinnest savings to cushion them against hard times. How quickly their security could evaporate showed in Philadelphia, where early in the contractionary cycle many poor people, unable to pay their property taxes, were "disposing of their huts and lots to others more wealthy than themselves." Established craftsmen and shopkeepers were caught between rising prices and reduced demand for their goods and services. A New York artisan expressed a common lament in 1762. Thankfully, he still had employment, he wrote in the *New-York Gazette*. But despite every effort at unceasing labor and frugal living, he had fallen into poverty and found it "beyond my ability to support my family ... [which] can scarcely appear with decency or have necessaries to subsist." His situation, he added, "is really the case with many of the inhabitants of this city."

The Seven Years' War paved the way for a far larger conflict in the next generation. The legislative assemblies, for example, which had been flexing their muscles at the expense of the governors in earlier decades, accelerated their bid for political power. During wartime, knowing that their governors must obtain military appropriations, they extracted concessions as the price for raising revenues. The war also trained a new group of military and political leaders. In carrying out military operations on a scale unknown in the colonies and in shouldering heavier political responsibilities, men such as George Washington, Samuel Adams, Benjamin Franklin, Patrick Henry, and Christopher Gadsden acquired the experience that would serve them well in the future.

In spite of severe costs, the Seven Years' War left many colonists buoyant. New Englanders rejoiced at the final victory over the "Papist enemy of the North." Frontiersmen, fur traders, and land speculators also celebrated the French withdrawal, for the West now appeared open for exploitation. This "Garden of the World," trumpeted a Boston almanac publisher, was larger than France, Germany, and Poland combined, "and all well provided with rivers, a very fine wholesome air, a rich soil, ... and all things necessary for the conveniency and delight of life." A new frontier now seemed to await those whom opportunity had passed by on the crowded seaboard.

The colonists also felt a new sense of identity after the war. Surveying a world free of French and Spanish threats, they began reassessing subordination to England and the advantages of standing alone. As a French diplomat predicted at the war's end, the colonists would soon discover "that they stand no longer in need of your protection. You will call on them to contribute towards supporting the

The reputation of the young George III has vacillated over many decades, even in feature films produced in the 1990s. Known primarily for losing the American colonies, he was competent and intelligent in many matters. In this portrait by David Ramsey, the young king is regally clad in ermine and brocade. *(Colonial Williamsburg Foundation)*

burden which they have helped to bring on you; they will answer you by shaking off all dependence."

The British, however, viewed the matter differently at the end of the Seven Years' War. From their perspective, the colonists were unreliable, had fought poorly, and were "an obstinate and ungovernable people, utterly unacquainted with the nature of subordination," as one British officer put it. Many royal army officers who had fought alongside the Americans had little but contempt for the "martial virtue" of the colonists. "He could take a thousand grenadiers to America," boasted one officer, "and geld all the males, partly by force and partly by a little coaxing."

THE CRISIS WITH ENGLAND

At the end of the Seven Years' War, George Grenville became the chief minister of England's 25-year-old king, George III. He inherited a national debt that had billowed from £75 million to £145 million and a nation of wearied taxpayers. To reduce the debt, Grenville proposed new taxes in England and others in America, asking the colonists to bear their share of running the empire. Grenville's particular concern was financing the 10,000 British regulars left in North America after 1763 to police French-speaking Canada and the Indians—and to remind unruly Americans that they were still subjects. Grenville's revenue program opened a rift between England and its colonies that in a dozen years would become a revolution.

Sugar, Currency, and Stamps

In 1764, Grenville pushed through Parliament several bills that in combination pressed hard on colonial economies. First came the Revenue Act (or Sugar Act) of 1764. While reducing the tax on imported French molasses from six to three pence per gallon, it added various colonial products to the list of commodities that could be sent only to England. It also required American shippers to post bonds guaranteeing observance of the trade regulations before loading their cargoes. Finally, it strengthened the vice-admiralty courts to prosecute violators of the trade acts.

Many colonial legislatures grumbled about the Sugar Act because a strictly enforced duty of three pence per gallon on molasses pinched more than the loosely enforced six-pence duty. But only New York objected that any tax by Parliament to raise revenue (rather than to control trade) violated the rights of overseas English subjects who were unrepresented in Parliament.

Next came the Currency Act. In 1751, Parliament had forbidden the New England colonies to issue paper money as legal tender, and now it extended that prohibition to all the colonies. In a colonial economy chronically short of hard cash, this constricted trade.

The move to tighten up the machinery of empire confused the colonists because many of the new regulations came from Parliament. Before, Parliament had let the king, his ministers, and the Board of Trade run overseas affairs. In a world where history taught that power and liberty were perpetually at war, generations of colonists had viewed Parliament as a bastion of English liberty, the bulwark against despotic political rule. Now Parliament began to seem like a violator of colonial rights.

In protesting new parliamentary regulations, colonial leaders were uncertain about where Parliament's authority began and ended. The colonists had always implicitly accepted parliamentary power overseas because it was easier to evade distasteful trade regulations than to contest this power. But the exact limits of that authority were vague.

After Parliament passed the Sugar Act in 1764, Grenville announced his intention to extend to America the stamp duties—already imposed in England—on every newspaper, pamphlet, almanac, legal document, liquor license, college diploma, pack of playing cards, and pair of dice. He gave the colonies a year to suggest alternative ways of raising revenue. The colonies objected, but none provided another plan. Knowing that colonial property taxes were slight compared with those in England, Grenville dismissed the petitions that poured in from the colonies and drove the bill through Parliament. The Stamp Act became effective in November 1765.

Colonial reaction to the Stamp Act ranged from disgruntled submission to mass defiance. The breadth of the reaction shocked the British government—and many Americans as well. Lieutenant Governor Hutchinson of Massachusetts believed that "there is not a family between Canada and Pensacola that has not heard the name of the Stamp Act and but very few . . . but what have some formidable apprehensions of it." In many cases, resistance involved not only discontent over England's tightening of the screws on the American colonies but also internal resentments born out of local events. Especially in the cities, the defiance of authority and destruction of property by people from the middle and lower ranks redefined the dynamics of politics, setting the stage for a 10-year internal struggle for control among the various social elements alarmed by the new English policies.

Stamp Act Riots

In late 1764, Virginia's House of Burgesses had strenuously objected to the proposed stamp tax, citing the economic hardship it would cause and arguing that it was their "inherent" right to be taxed only by their own consent. It became the first legislature to react to the news of the Stamp Act. Virginians were already worried by a severe decline in tobacco prices and heavy war-related taxes, which mired most planters in debt. Led by 29-year-old Patrick Henry, a fiery lawyer newly elected from a frontier county, the House of Burgesses in May 1765 debated seven strongly worded resolutions. Old-guard burgesses regarded some of them as treasonable. The legislature finally adopted the four more moderate resolves, including one proclaiming that it was their "inherent" right to be taxed only by their own consent.

From the time of his election to the Virginia House of Burgesses at the age of 29, Patrick Henry was an outspoken proponent of American rights. In this portrait, he pleads a case at a county courthouse crowded with local planters. *(Virginia Historical Society, Richmond, VA)*

Many burgesses had left for home before Henry introduced his resolutions, so less than a quarter of Virginia's legislators voted for the four moderate resolves. But within a month, newspapers of other colonies published all seven resolutions, which included a defiant assertion that Virginians did not have to pay externally imposed taxes and branded as an "enemy to this, his Majesty's colony" anyone who denied Virginia's exclusive right to tax itself. Henry and the aggressive young burgesses had hurled words of defiance at Parliament for other colonies to reflect on and match.

Governor Francis Bernard of Massachusetts called the Virginia resolves an "alarm bell for the disaffected." Events in Boston in August 1765 amply confirmed his view. On August 14, Bostonians hung an rag-dressed effigy of stamp distributor Andrew from an elm tree in the south end of town. When the sheriff tried to remove it at the order of Lieutenant Governor Thomas Hutchinson, who was Oliver's brother-in-law, a hostile crowd intervened. In the evening, workingmen began gathering for a mock funeral. Led by Ebenezer MacIntosh, they cut down Oliver's effigy and boisterously carried it through the streets. Then they leveled Oliver's new brick office on the wharves, rumored to be the distribution point for the hated stamps.

As night fell, the crowd reduced Oliver's luxurious mansion to a shambles. The stamp distributor promptly asked to be relieved of his commission. Twelve days later, MacIntosh led the crowd again in an all-night bout of destruction of the handsomely appointed homes of two British officials and Hutchinson, a haughty man, who was as unpopular with the common people as his great-great-grandmother, Anne Hutchinson, had been popular. Military men "who have seen towns sacked by the enemy," one observer reported, "declare they never before saw an instance of such fury."

In attacking the property of men associated with the stamp tax, the Boston crowd demonstrated not only its opposition to parliamentary policy but also its resentment of a local elite. For decades, ordinary Bostonians had aligned politically with the Boston "caucus," which led the colony's "popular party" against conservative aristocrats such as Hutchinson and Oliver. They had also read in the *Boston Gazette* that the new parliamentary legislation had been proposed by "mean mercenary hirelings among yourselves, who for a little filthy lucre would at any time betray every right, liberty, and privilege of their fellow subjects."

But the "rage-intoxicated rabble" had suddenly broken away from the leaders of the popular party and gone farther than they had intended. Hutchinson

was one of their main targets. Characterized by young lawyer John Adams as "very ambitious and avaricious," Hutchinson was, in the popular view, chief among the "mean mercenary hirelings" of the British. In the aftermath of the destruction of his house—what Governor Bernard called "a war of plunder, of taking away the distinction between rich and poor"—the more cautious political leaders knew that they would have to struggle to regain control of the protest movement.

Protest took a more dignified form at the Stamp Act Congress, called by Massachusetts and attended by representatives of nine colonies, who met in New York in October 1765. English authorities branded this first self-initiated intercolonial convention a "dangerous tendency." The delegates formulated 12 restrained resolutions that accepted Parliament's right to legislate for the colonies but denied its right to tax them directly.

Violent protests against the Stamp Act also wracked New York and Newport, Rhode Island. Leading the resistance were groups calling themselves the Sons of Liberty, composed mostly of artisans, shopkeepers, and ordinary citizens. By late 1765, effigy-burning crowds all over America were convincing stamp distributors to resign. Colonists defied English authority even more directly by forcing most customs officers and court officials to open the ports and courts for business after November 1 without using the hated stamps required after that date. This often took months of pressure and sometimes mob action, but the Sons of Liberty, often led by new faces in local politics, got their way by going outside the law.

In March 1766, Parliament debated the furious American reaction to the Stamp Act. Lobbied by many merchant friends of the Americans, Parliament voted to repeal it. Some members warned that to retreat before colonial defiance of the law would ultimately be fatal. But the legislators bowed to expediency, though they also passed the Declaratory Act, which asserted Parliament's power to enact laws for the colonies in "all cases whatsoever."

The crisis had passed, yet nothing was solved. Americans had begun to recognize a grasping government trampling its subjects' rights. The Stamp Act, one New England clergyman foresaw, "diffused a disgust through the colonies and laid the basis of an alienation which will never be healed." Stamp Act resisters had politicized their communities as never before. The established leaders, generally cautious in their protests, were often displaced by those lower down on the social ladder. Men such as New York ship captains Alexander McDougall and Isaac Sears mobilized common citizens and raised

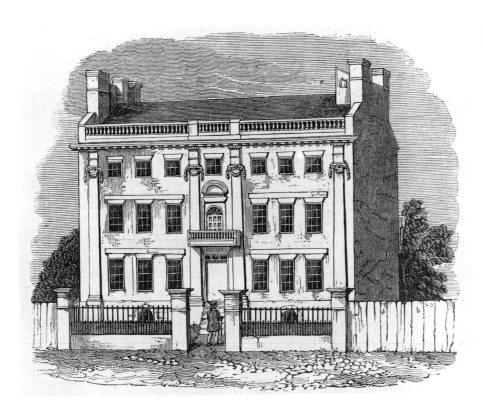

Thomas Hutchinson inherited the family house in Boston's North End. Every window shown here was smashed on August 26, 1765. Some in the furious crowd also reached the roof by midnight and worked until daylight in cutting down a large cupola. By dawn, according to one account, the mansion was "a mear Shell." *(Courtesy of the Society for the Preservation of New England Antiquities [#10600-A])*

political consciousness, employing mass demonstrations and street violence to humble stamp distributors and force open the courts and seaports. Scribbled John Adams in his diary: "The people have become more attentive to their liberties, ... and more determined to defend them. ... Our presses have groaned, our pulpits have thundered, our legislatures have resolved, our towns have voted; the crown officers have everywhere trembled, and all their little tools and creatures been afraid to speak and ashamed to be seen."

Gathering Storm Clouds

Ministerial instability in England hampered the quest for a coherent, workable American policy. Attempting to be a strong king, George III chose ministers who commanded little respect in Parliament. This led to strife between Parliament and the king's chief ministers; that in turn led to a shuffling of chief ministers and a chaotic political situation just when the king was trying to overhaul the empire's administration.

To manage the colonies more effectively, the Pitt-Grafton ministry appointed by the king in 1767 obtained new laws to reorganize the customs service, establish a secretary of state for American affairs, and install in the port cities three new vice-admiralty courts, which did not use juries to try accused smugglers. Still hard-pressed for revenue—for at home the government faced severe unemployment, tax protests, and riots over the high price of grain—the ministry pushed through Parliament the relatively small Townshend duties on paper, lead, painters' colors, and tea. A final law suspended New York's assembly until that body ceased defying the Quartering Act of 1765, which required public funds for support of British troops garrisoned in the colony since the end of the Seven Years' War. New York knuckled under in order to save its legislature.

Massachusetts led the colonial protests against the Townshend Acts. Its House of Representatives sent a circular letter to each colony objecting to the new Townshend duties, small though they were. Written by Samuel Adams, the letter attacked as unconstitutional the plan to underwrite salaries for royal officials in America from customs duties. Under instructions from England, Governor Bernard dissolved the legislature after it refused to rescind the circular letter. "The Americans have made a discovery," declared Edmund Burke before Parliament, "that we mean to oppress them; we have made a discovery that they intend to raise a rebellion. We do not know how to advance; they do not know how to retreat."

Showing more restraint than they had in resisting the Stamp Act, most colonists only grumbled and petitioned. But Bostonians protested stridently. In

City Plan of Boston, 1772

Boston's many churches became important political meeting places in the tumultuous decade leading to the outbreak of war in 1775. Old South Meeting House, holding as many as 5,000 people, became the gathering place of "body of the people." Faneuil Hall was the usual site of town meetings, but when crowds exceeded its capacity of 1,200, meetings were adjourned and reconvened at Old South Meeting House.

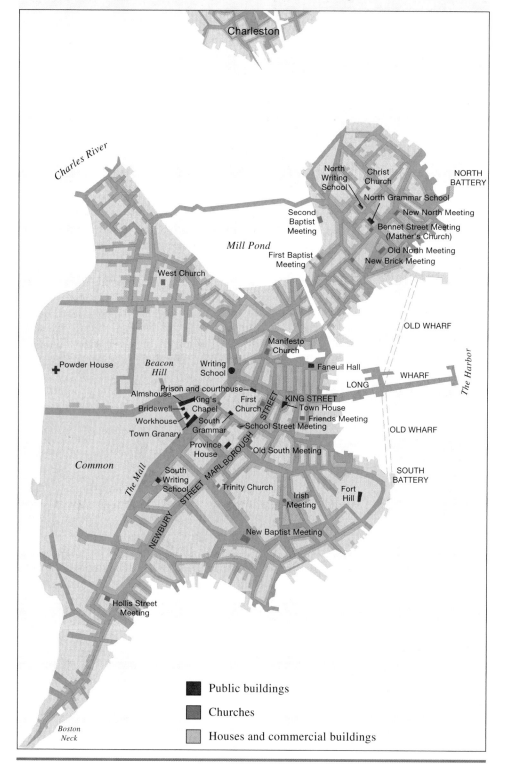

Charleston

Charles River

North Writing School

Christ Church

NORTH BATTERY

North Grammar School

Second Baptist Meeting

New North Meeting

Mill Pond

Bennet Street Meeting (Mather's Church)

First Baptist Meeting

Old North Meeting

New Brick Meeting

West Church

OLD WHARF

Manifesto Church

The Harbor

Powder House

Beacon Hill

Writing School

Faneuil Hall

WHARF

Prison and courthouse

LONG

Almshouse

King's Chapel

First Church

KING STREET

Bridewell

Town House

Workhouse

South Grammar

Friends Meeting

OLD WHARF

Town Granary

School Street Meeting

Province House

Old South Meeting

Common

The Mall

South Writing School

SOUTH BATTERY

Trinity Church

Irish Meeting

Fort Hill

New Baptist Meeting

Hollis Street Meeting

■ Public buildings

■ Churches

Houses and commercial buildings

Boston Neck

the summer of 1768, after customs officials seized a sloop owned by John Hancock for a violation of the trade regulations, an angry crowd mobbed them. They fled to a British warship in Boston harbor and remained there for months. Newspapers warned of new measures designed to "suck the life blood" from the people and predicted that troops would be sent to "dragoon us into passive obedience." To many, the belief grew that the English were plotting "designs for destroying our constitutional liberties."

Troops indeed came. The attack on the customs officials convinced the English that the Bostonians were insubordinate and selfish. The ministry dispatched two regiments from England and two more from Nova Scotia, meant to bring the Bostonians to a proper state of subordination and make them an example. Cries went up against maintaining standing armies in peacetime, but radical Bostonians who proposed force to prevent the troops from landing got little support from delegates called to a special provincial convention. On October 1, 1768, red-coated troops marched into Boston without resistance.

Thereafter, the colonists' main tactic of protest against the Townshend Acts became economic boycott. First in Boston and then in New York and Philadelphia, merchants and consumers adopted nonimportation and nonconsumption agreements, pledging neither to import nor to use British goods.

These measures promised to bring the politically influential English merchants to their aid, for half of British shipping was engaged in commerce with the colonies, and one-quarter of all English exports were consumed there. When the southern colonies also adopted nonimportation agreements in 1768, a new step toward intercolonial union had been taken.

Many colonial merchants, however, especially those with official connections, saw nonimportation agreements as lacking legal force and refused to be bound by them. They had to be persuaded otherwise by street brigades, usually composed of artisans for whom nonimportation was a boon to home manufacturing. Crowd action welled up again in the seaports, as patriot bands attacked the homes and warehouses of offending merchants and "rescued" incoming contraband goods seized by customs officials.

England's attempts to discipline its American colonies and oblige them to share the costs of governing an empire lay in shambles by the end of the 1760s. Using troops to restore order undermined the respect for the mother country on which colonial acceptance of its authority ultimately depended. American newspapers denounced new extensions of British authority. Colonial governors quarreled with their legislatures. Customs officials met with determined opposition and were widely accused of arbitrary actions and excessive zeal in

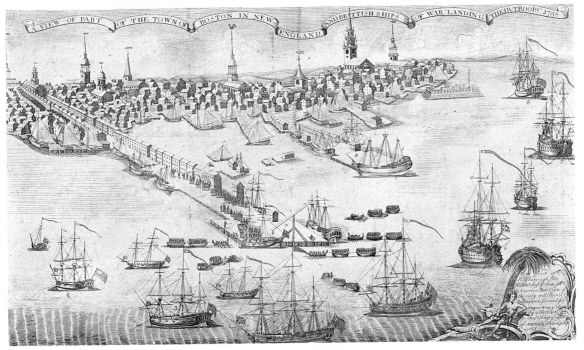

Rather than quelling the disorder as King George III hoped, the occupation of Boston by British troops in 1768 increased tensions. In this engraving by Paul Revere, the red-coated troops are debarking at the Long Wharf. *(Courtesy the Henry Francis du Pont Winterthur Museum)*

Paul Revere was not only a noted silver-smith and political activist but also a man who put art to work in the cause of revolutionary politics. This engraving became known throughout the colonies and convinced many people to involve themselves in what had been mainly New England's cause. The smiling British redcoats are reviled in verse: "While faithless P[resto]n and his savage Bonds, / With murd'rous Rancour stretch their bloody Hands, / Like fierce Barbarians grinning o'er their Prey, / Approve the Carnage and enjoy the Day." *(American Antiquarian Society)*

enforcing the Navigation Acts. The Townshend duties had failed miserably, yielding less than £21,000 by 1770 while costing British business £700,000 through the colonial nonimportation movement.

On March 5, 1770, Parliament repealed all the Townshend duties except the one on tea (which the new minister of state, Lord North, explained was retained "as a mark of the supremacy of Parliament and an efficient declaration of their right to govern the colonies"). On that same evening in Boston, British troops fired on an unruly crowd of heckling citizens. For months, Bostonians had been baiting the "lobsterbacks," as they dubbed the red-coated British soldiers. They hated them for competing with townspeople for menial jobs when off duty, as well as for their military presence. On this evening, a taunting crowd had first hurled insults and snow-balls and then surged toward a sentry. After a squad of redcoats joined the sentry, someone cried, "Fire!" When the smoke cleared, five bloody bodies, including that of Ebenezer MacIntosh's brother-in-law, stained the snow-covered street. Bowing to furious popular reaction, Thomas Hutchinson, recently appointed governor, ordered the British troops out of town and arrested the commanding officer and the soldiers involved. They were later acquitted, with two young patriot lawyers, John Adams and Josiah Quincy, Jr., providing a brilliant defense.

In spite of the potential of the "Boston massacre" for galvanizing the colonies into further resistance, opposition to English policies, including boycotts, subsided in 1770. Popular leaders such as Samuel Adams in Boston and Alexander McDougall in New York, who had made names for themselves as the standard-bearers of American liberty, had few issues left, especially when the depression that had helped sow discontent ended. Yet the fires of revolution had not been extinguished but merely dampened.

The Growing Rift

From 1770 to 1772, relative quiet descended over the colonies. Then in June 1772, England created a new furor by announcing that it, rather than the provincial legislature, would henceforth pay the salaries of the royal governor and superior court judges in Massachusetts. Even though the measure saved the colony money, it looked like a scheme, undermining a right set forth in the colony's charter to impose a despotic government. Judges paid from London presumably would obey London.

Boston's town meeting protested loudly and created a Committee of Correspondence "to state the rights of the colonists . . . and to communicate and publish the same to the several towns and to the world." Crown supporters called the committee "the foulest, subtlest, and most venomous serpent ever issued from the egg of sedition." By the end of 1772,

Steps on the Road to Revolution

1763   Treaty of Paris ends Seven Years' War between England and France; France cedes Canada to England.
        Proclamation of 1763 forbids white settlement west of Appalachian Mountains.

1764   Sugar Act sets higher duties on imported sugar and lower duties on molasses and enlarges the power of vice-admiralty courts.
        Currency Act prohibits issuance of paper money by colonies.

1765   Stamp Act requires revenue-raising stamps purchased from British-appointed stamp distributors on printed documents.
        Stamp Act Congress meets in New York.
        Quartering Act requires colonies to furnish British troops with housing and certain provisions.
        Sons of Liberty formed in New York City and thereafter in many towns.

1766   Declaratory Act asserts Parliament's sovereignty over the colonies after repealing Stamp Act.
        Rent riots by New York tenant farmers.

1767   Townshend Revenue Acts impose duties on tea, glass, paper, paints, and other items.
        South Carolina Regulators organize in backcountry.

1768   British troops sent to Boston.

1770   British troops kill four and wound eight American civilians in Boston Massacre.

1771   Battle of Alamance pits frontier North Carolina Regulators against eastern militia led by royal governor.

1772   British schooner *Gaspee* burned in Rhode Island.
        Committee of Correspondence formed in Boston and thereafter in other cities.

1773   Tea Act reduces duty on tea but gives East India Company right to sell directly to Americans.
        Boston Tea Party dumps £10,000 of East India Company tea into Boston harbor.

1774   Coercive Acts close port of Boston, restrict provincial and town governments in Massachusetts, and send additional troops to Boston.
        Québec Act attaches trans-Appalachian interior north of Ohio River to government of Quebec.
        First Continental Congress meets and forms Continental Association to boycott British imports.

1775   Battles of Lexington and Concord cause 95 American and 273 British casualties; Americans take Fort Ticonderoga.
        Second Continental Congress meets and assumes many powers of an independent government.
        Dunmore's Proclamation in Virginia promises freedom to slaves and indentured servants fleeing to British ranks.
        Prohibitory Act embargoes American goods.
        George III proclaims Americans in open rebellion.

1776   Thomas Paine publishes *Common Sense.*
        British troops evacuate Boston.
        Declaration of Independence.

---

another 80 towns in Massachusetts had created committees. In the next year, all but three colonies established Committees of Correspondence in their legislatures.

Samuel Adams was by now the leader of the Boston radicals, for the influence of laboring men like Ebenezer MacIntosh had been quietly reduced. Adams was an experienced caucus politicker and a skilled political journalist, and (despite his Harvard degree) he had deep roots among the laboring people. He organized the working ranks through the taverns, clubs, and volunteer fire companies and secured the support of wealthy merchants such as John Hancock, whose ample purse financed patriotic celebrations and feasts that kept politics on everyone's mind and helped build interclass bridges. In England, Adams became known as one of the most dangerous firebrands in America.

In 1772, Rhode Islanders gave Adams a new issue. The British commander of the royal ship *Gaspee* was roundly hated for hounding the fishermen and small traders of Narragansett Bay. When his ship ran aground while pursuing a suspected smuggler, Rhode Islanders took their revenge, burning the stranded vessel to the waterline. A Rhode Island court then convicted the *Gaspee*'s captain of illegally seizing what he was convinced was smuggled sugar and rum. London reacted with cries of high treason. An investigating committee found the lips of Rhode Islanders sealed. The event was tailor-made for Samuel Adams, who used it to "awaken the American colonies, which have been too long dozing upon the brink of ruin."

The final plunge into revolution began when Parliament passed the Tea Act in early 1773, allowing the practically bankrupt East India Company to ship its tea directly to North America. By eliminating English middlemen and English import taxes, this provided Americans with the opportunity to buy their tea cheaply from the company's agents in

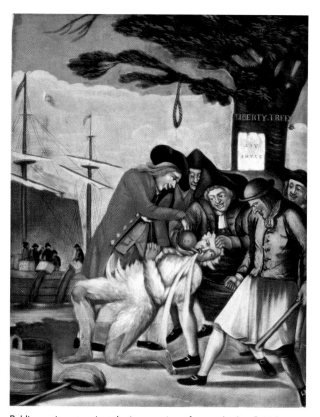

Public sentiment against the importation of tea and other British goods often found expression in a coat of tar and feathers applied to the bare skin of the offending importer. Note the symbols in *The Bostonians Paying the Excise-Man*: the Liberty Tree with a hangman's noose and the overturned copy of the Stamp Act. In the background, Bostonians dump chests of tea into the harbor. *(Library of Congress)*

the colonies. Even with the small tax to be paid in the colonies, Indian tea would now undersell smuggled Dutch tea. The Americans would get inexpensive tea, the Crown a modest revenue, and the East India Company a new lease on life. The company soon had 600,000 pounds of tea in 2,000 chests ready for shipment to America.

Parliament greatly miscalculated the American response. For several years, merchants in Philadelphia and New York had been flagrantly smuggling Dutch tea. As a consequence, imports of English tea in the two seaports plummeted from 500,000 pounds in 1768 to a mere 650 pounds in 1772. The merchants bitterly denounced the new act for giving the East India Company a monopoly on the American tea market. Other monopolies would follow, they predicted, and middlemen of all kinds would be eliminated. The colonists also objected that the government was shrewdly trying to gain acceptance of Parliament's taxing power. As Americans drank the taxed tea, they would also be swallowing the English right to tax them.

Showing that their principles were not entirely in their pocketbooks, Americans staged mass meet-

ings that soon forced the resignation of the East India Company's agents, and citizens vowed to stop the obnoxious tea at the water's edge.

Governor Hutchinson of Massachusetts brought the tea crisis to a climax, convinced that to yield again to popular pressure would forever cripple English sovereignty in America. The popular party led by Samuel Adams had been urging the citizens to demonstrate that they were not yet prepared for the "yoke of slavery" by sending the tea back to England. When Hutchinson refused, 5,000 Bostonians packed Old South Church on December 16, 1773, noisily passing resolutions urging the governor to grant the tea ships clearance papers to return to England with their cargoes. But Hutchinson was not swayed. "This meeting," despaired Samuel Adams, "can do no more to save the country."

At nightfall, a band of Bostonians who were dressed as Indians, boarded the tea ships, broke open the chests of tea, and flung £10,000 worth of the East India Company's property into Boston harbor. George Hewes, a 31-year-old shoemaker, recalled how he had garbed himself as a Mohawk, blackened "face and hands with coal dust in the

This portrait of George Robert Twelve Hewes was painted in 1835 when the last survivor of the Boston Tea Party was called "The Centenarian," though he was 93 years old. A biography of the poor shoemaker, written by Benjamin Bussey Thatcher, came off the press in the same year. *(Courtesy of The Bostonian Society)*

shop of a blacksmith," and joined men of all ranks in marching stealthily to the wharves to do their work. In time, this would be remembered as The Boston Tea Party.

Now the die was cast. Lord North, the king's chief minister, called the Bostonians "fanatics" and argued that the dispute was no longer about taxes but about whether England had any authority over the colonies. George III put it succinctly: "We must master them or totally leave them to themselves and treat them as aliens."

Thoroughly aroused, Parliament passed the Coercive Acts, stern laws that Bostonians promptly labeled the "Intolerable Acts." The acts closed the port of Boston to all shipping until the colony paid for the destroyed tea and barred local courts from trying British soldiers and officials for acts committed while suppressing civil disturbances. To hamstring the colony's truculent political assemblies, Parliament amended the Massachusetts charter to transform the council from an upper legislative chamber, elected by the lower house, to a body appointed by the governor. This stripped the council of its veto power over the governor's decisions.

The act also struck at local government by authorizing the governor to prohibit all town meetings except for one annual meeting to elect local officers of government. Finally, General Thomas Gage, commander in chief of British forces in America, replaced Thomas Hutchinson as governor. "This is the day, then," declared Edmund Burke in the House of Commons, "that you wish to go to war with all America, in order to conciliate that country to this."

Lord North's plan to strangle Massachusetts into submission and hope for acquiescence elsewhere in the colonies proved popular in England. Earlier, the colonies had gained supporters in Parliament for their resistance to what many regarded as attacks on their fundamental privileges. Now this support evaporated. After a decade of debating constitutional rights and mobilizing sentiment against what many believed was a systematic plot to enslave free-born citizens, the Americans found their maneuvering room severely narrowed.

When the Intolerable Acts arrived in May 1774, Boston's town meeting urged all the colonies to ban trade with England. This met with faint support. But a second call, for a meeting in Philadelphia of delegates from all colonies, received a better response. The Continental Congress, as it was called, now began to transform a 10-year debate conducted by separate colonies into a unified American cause.

In September 1774, 55 delegates from all the colonies except Georgia converged on Carpenters' Hall in Philadelphia. The discussions centered not

Royal Governor Thomas Hutchinson called Sam Adams "[the greatest] incendiary in the King's dominion" whereas his cousin, John Adams, called him "a plain, simple, decent citizen of middling stature, dress, and manners." Boston's premier painter, John Singleton Copley, painted Adams in just this way—in a simple wool suit with no embroidery and a partially unbuttoned waistcoat, suggesting the patriot leader's disdain for proper appearances. *(Samuel Adams, about 1772; John Singleton Copley, American [1738–1815], Oil on canvas; 49 ½ × 39 ½ in. [125.7 × 100.3 cm], Deposited by the city of Boston, 30.76c. Courtesy of the Museum of Fine Arts, Boston. Reproduced with permission. © 1999 The Museum of Fine Arts, Boston. All Rights Reserved.)*

on how to prepare for a war that many sensed was inevitable but on how to resolve sectional differences that most delegates feared were irreconcilable. Overcoming prejudices and hostilities was as important as the formal debates. New Englanders were eyed with suspicion especially for their reputed intolerance and self-interest. "We have numberless prejudices to remove here," wrote John Adams from Philadelphia. "We have been obliged to keep ourselves out of sight, and to feel pulses, and to sound the depths; to insinuate our sentiments, designs, and desires by means of other persons, sometimes of one province, and sometimes of another."

The Continental Congress was by no means a unified body. Some delegates, led by cousins Samuel and John Adams from Massachusetts and Richard Henry Lee and Patrick Henry of Virginia, argued for outright resistance to Parliament's Coercive Acts. Moderate delegates from the middle colonies,

The Québec Act of 1774

Most colonists hated the Québec Act, which attached the trans-Appalachian interior north of the Ohio River to the British government in Québec, because they believed this act passed by Parliament, like others during the prewar years, was aimed at the heart of colonial liberty. It not only sealed off the western lands from colonial speculators but guaranteed the right of French Catholics to practice their religion freely—an offense, especially, to New England Puritans.

West Indies. To keep reluctant southern colonies in the fold, some exceptions were made for the export of southern staple commodities.

By the time the Congress adjourned in late October, leaders from different colonies had transformed Boston's cause into a national movement. "Government is dissolved [and] we are in a state of nature," Patrick Henry argued dramatically. "The distinctions between Virginians, Pennsylvanians, New Yorkers, and New Englanders are no more. I am not a Virginian, but an American." Many other delegates were a long way from that, but still the Congress agreed to reconvene in May 1775.

By the time the Second Continental Congress met, the fabric of government became badly torn in most colonies. Revolutionary committees, conventions, and congresses, entirely unauthorized by law, were replacing legal governing bodies. Assuming authority in defiance of royal governors, who suspended truculent legislatures in many colonies, they often operated on instructions from mass meetings where the legal franchise was ignored. These extralegal bodies created and armed militia units, bullied merchants and shopkeepers refusing to obey popularly authorized boycotts, levied taxes, operated the courts, and obstructed English customs officials. By the end of 1774, all but three colonies defied their own charters by appointing provincial assemblies without royal authority. In the next year, this independently created power became evident when trade with England practically ceased.

THE IDEOLOGY OF REVOLUTIONARY REPUBLICANISM

In the tumultuous years between 1763 and 1774, the colonists had been expressing many reactions to the crisis with Britain. Mostly these took the form of newspaper articles and pamphlets written by educated lawyers, clergymen, merchants, and planters. But the middling and lower ranks of society had also expressed themselves in printed broadsides, appeals in the newspapers, and even ideologically laden popular rituals such as tarring and feathering and burning in effigy. Gradually, the colonists pieced together a political ideology, borrowed partly from English political thought, partly from the theories of the Enlightenment, and partly from their own experiences. Historians call this new ideology "revolutionary republicanism." But because the colonists varied widely in interests and experiences, no single coherent ideology united them all.

led by Joseph Galloway of Pennsylvania and James Duane of New York, urged restraint and further attempts at reconciliation. After weeks of debate, the delegates agreed to a restrained Declaration of Rights and Resolves. It attempted to define American grievances and justify the colonists' defiance of English policies and laws by appealing to the "immutable laws of nature, the principles of the English constitution, and the several [colonial] charters and compacts" under which they lived. More concrete was the Congress's agreement on a plan of resistance. If England did not rescind the Intolerable Acts by December 1, 1774, a ban would take effect on all imports and exports between the colonies and Great Britain, Ireland, and the British

Liberty always had to struggle against power, as American colonists saw it. In this cartoon, England (power) forces Liberty (America in the form of a woman) to drink the "Bitter Draught" of tea. Uncompliant, America spits the tea into England's face while another corrupt Englishman peeks under her petticoat. *(Massachusetts Historical Society)*

A Plot Against Liberty

Many American colonists agreed with earlier English Whig writers who charged that corrupt and power-hungry men were slowly extinguishing the lamp of liberty in England. The so-called country party represented by these Whig pamphleteers proclaimed itself the guardian of the true principles of the English constitution and opposed the "court" party—the king and his appointees.

From this perspective, every ministerial policy and parliamentary act in the decade after the Stamp Act appeared as a subversion of English liberties. Most Americans regarded resistance to such blows against liberty as wholly justified.

The belief that England was carrying out "a deep-laid and desperate plan of imperial despotism . . . for the extinction of all civil liberty," as the Boston town meeting expressed it in 1770, spread rapidly in the next few years. By 1774, John Adams was writing of the "conspiracy against the public liberty [that] was first regularly formed and begun to be executed in 1763 and 1764." From London, America's favorite writer, Benjamin Franklin, described the "extreme corruption prevalent among all orders of men in this old rotten state." Another pamphleteer reached the conclusion that England was no longer "in a condition at present to suckle us, being pregnant with vermin that corrupt her milk and convert her blood and juices into poison."

Among many Americans, especially merchants, the attack on constitutional rights blended closely with the threats to their economic interests contained in the tough new trade policies. Merchants saw a coordinated attack on their "lives, liberties, and property," as they frequently phrased it. If a man was not secure in his property, he could not be secure in his citizenship, for it was property that gave a man the independence to shape his identity.

Revitalizing American Society

The continuing crisis over the imperial relationship by itself inspired many colonists to resist impending tyranny. But for others, the revolutionary mentality was also fed by a belief that an opportunity was at hand to revitalize American society. They believed that the colonies had been undergoing a silent transformation and that the growing commercial connections with the decadent and corrupt mother country had injected poison into the American bloodstream. They worried about the luxury and vice they saw around them and came to believe that resistance to England would return American society to a state of civic virtue, spartan living, and godly purpose.

The colonial protest movement got much of its high-toned moralism from its fervent supporters, the colonial clergy. This was especially true in New England, where so secular a man as John Adams groaned at the "universal spirit of debauchery, dissipation, luxury, effeminacy and gaming." As in most revolutionary movements, talk of moral regeneration, of a society-wide rebirth through battle against a corrupt enemy, ennobled the cause, inspiring people in areas that had been stirred a generation before by the Great Awakening.

THE TURMOIL OF A REBELLIOUS PEOPLE

The long struggle with England over colonial rights between 1763 and 1774 did not occur in a unified society. Social and economic change, which accelerated in the late colonial period, brought deep unrest and calls for reform from many quarters. By the end of the Seven Years' War, faith in the internal social systems of the colonies had waned among many colonists, just as allegiance to the mother country and to the British mercantile system had worn thin.

Many of the colonists who struggled for security in the aftermath of the Seven Years' War hoped that migration to frontier land would improve their fortunes. A flood of new immigrants from Ireland and Germany after the Treaty of Paris in 1763 added to the pressure to reach the trans-Appalachian river valleys. However, the western option involved much violence with Indian tribes. Therefore, most colonists chose to work out their destinies at home or in other communities along the coastal plain to which they migrated in search of opportunity.

As agitation against English policy intensified, previously passive people took a more active interest in politics. In this charged atmosphere, the constitutional struggle with England spread quickly into uncharted territory. Groups emerged—slaves, urban laboring people, backcountry farmers, evangelicals, women—who enunciated goals of their own that were sometimes only loosely connected to the struggle with England. The stridency and potential power of these groups frightened many in the upper class. Losing control of the protests they had initially led, many would abandon the resistance movement against England.

Urban People

Although the cities contained only about 5 percent of the colonial population, they were the core of revolutionary agitation. As centers of communications, government, and commerce, they led the way in protesting English policy, and they soon contained the most politicized citizens in America. Local politics could be rapidly transformed as the struggle against England meshed with calls for internal reform.

Philadelphia offers a good example of popular empowerment. Before the Seven Years' War, craftsmen had usually acquiesced to local leadership by merchant and lawyer politicos. But economic difficulties in the 1760s and 1770s led them to band to-

In January 1774, after British customs officer John Malcolm bullied a small boy and then beat George Robert Twelve Hewes (who had intervened), a Boston crowd tarred and feathered Malcolm. As shown here, Bostonians force Malcolm into a cart, which was dragged through town to the hoots of the crowd. *(Corbis)*

TO THE
Delaware Pilots.

WE took the Pleasure, some Days since, of kindly admonishing you *to do your Duty*; if perchance you should meet with the *(Tea,)* SHIP POLLY, CAPTAIN AYRES; a THREE DECKER which is hourly expected,

We have now to add, that Matters ripen fast here; and that *much is expected from those Lads who meet with the Tea Ship.*----There is some Talk of A HANDSOME REWARD FOR THE PILOT WHO GIVES THE FIRST GOOD ACCOUNT OF HER.----How that may be, we cannot *for certain* determine: But ALL agree, that TAR and FEATHERS will be his Portion, who pilots her into this Harbour. And we will answer for ourselves, that, whoever is committed to us, as an Offender against the Rights of *America*, will experience the utmost Exertion of our Abilities; as

THE COMMITTEE FOR TARRING AND FEATHERING.

Not only Bostonians took action against the Tea Act. This Philadelphia broadside from "The Committee for Tarring and Feathering," issued several weeks before the Boston Tea Party, exhorts pilots on the Delaware River to watch for an arriving tea ship. *(Rare Book Collection, New York Public Library, Astor, Lenox and Tilden Foundations)*

gether within their craft and community. Artisans played a central role in forging and—equally important—enforcing a nonimportation agreement in 1768. They called public meetings, published newspaper appeals, organized secondary boycotts against foot-dragging merchants, and tarred and feathered their opponents. Cautious merchants complained that mere artisans had "no right to give their sentiments respecting an importation" and called the craftsmen a "rabble." But artisans, casting off their customary deference, forged ahead.

By 1772, artisans were filling elected municipal positions and insisting on their right to participate equally with their social superiors in nominating assemblymen and other important officeholders. They also began lobbying for reform laws. The craftsmen called for elected representatives to be more accountable to their constituents. Genteel Philadelphians muttered, "It is time the tradesmen were checked—they ought not to intermeddle in state affairs—they will become too powerful."

By 1774, the Philadelphia working-class's meddling in state affairs reached a bold new stage—a de facto assumption of governmental powers by committees created by the people at large. Craftsmen had first assumed such extralegal authority in policing the nonimportation agreement in 1769. Now, responding to the Intolerable Acts, they proposed a radical slate of candidates for a committee to enforce a new economic boycott. Their ticket drubbed one nominated by conservative merchants.

The political support of the new radical leaders centered in the 31 companies of the Philadelphia militia, composed mostly of laboring men, and in the extralegal committees now controlling the city's economic life. Their leadership helped overcome the conservatism of the regularly elected Pennsylvania legislature, which was resisting the movement of the Continental Congress toward independence. In addition, the new radical leaders demanded internal reforms: curbing the accumulation of wealth by "our great merchants" who were "making immense fortunes at the expense of the people"; abolishing the property requirement for voting; allowing militiamen to elect their officers; and imposing stiff fines, to be used for the support of the families of poor militiamen, on men who refused militia service.

Philadelphia's radicals never controlled the city. They always jostled for position with prosperous artisans and shopkeepers of more moderate views and with cautious lawyers and merchants. But mobilization among artisans, laborers, and mariners, in other cities as well as Philadelphia, became part of the chain of events that led toward independence. Whereas most of the patriot elite fought only to change English colonial policy, the people of the cities also struggled for internal reforms and raised notions of how an independent American society might be reorganized.

Patriot Women

Colonial women also played a vital role in the movement toward revolution, and they drew upon revolutionary arguments to define their own goals. They signed nonimportation agreements, harassed noncomplying merchants, and helped organize "fast days," on which communities prayed for deliverance from English oppression. But the women's most important role was to facilitate the boycott of English goods. The success of the nonconsumption pacts depended on substituting homespun cloth for English textiles on which colonists of all classes had always relied. From Georgia to Maine, women and

Poetry

Poetry is one of the most ancient and universal of the arts. Making its effect by the rhythmic sound and imagery of its language, poetry often expresses romantic love, grief, and responses to nature. But other kinds of poetry interest historians: reflections of human experience, often expressed with deep emotion; and political verses, often written to serve propagandistic goals. For generations, American historians have drawn on poetry to recapture feelings, ideas, and group experiences. For example, American Indian creation myths have often taken poetic form; the poems of Anne Bradstreet and Michael Wigglesworth in seventeenth-century Massachusetts tell us much about Puritan mentality and attitudes on topics running from marriage to death; the poetry of the American Transcendentalists tells us about nineteenth-century notions of heroism and who was admired; and Langston Hughes, Arno Bontemps, and other poets of the Harlem Renaissance have expressed through poetry the bittersweet nature of the African-American experience. All this material is grist for the historian's mill.

The revolutionary generation created poetry of great interest to historians. The newspapers of several port cities published weekly "Poet's Corner" satires, drinking songs, and versed commentary on the issues of the day. Verse was widely used to provoke public discussion; in 1767 poets prompted the boycott of British goods to obtain Parliament's reversal of the hated Townshend duties.

A year later, Philadelphia's John Dickinson composed a "Liberty Song" that became the first set of verses learned in all the colonies. Boston's Sons of Liberty began using this "Liberty Song" in annual ceremonies celebrating their resistance to the Stamp Act. Soon the verses were printed in newspapers throughout the colonies and were used widely in public gatherings. Set to music and easily learned, the verses cultivated anti-British feeling and a sense of the need for intercolonial cooperation:

> COME join Hand in Hand, brave AMERICANS all,
> And rouse your bold Hearts at fair LIBERTY'S Call;
> No tyrannous Acts shall suppress your just Claim,
> Or stain with Dishonor AMEÏRICA's Name.

Of all the poets of the revolutionary era, none has fascinated today's historians more than Phillis Wheatley, a young slave in Boston who wrote her first poem at age 14 in 1767. Within six years, she be-

came North America's first published black poet. Boston's "Ethiopian poetess" had been brought from Africa to Boston at age seven and purchased by a prospering tailor named John Wheatley. Soon her master and his wife discovered that she was a prodigy. After learning English so well in 16 months that she could read the most difficult passages of the Bible, she soon showed an uncanny gift for writing. Much of her writing was inspired by deep religious feelings, but she soon was caught up in the dramatic events in Boston that were bringing revolution closer and closer. In her poem entitled "To the King's Most Excellent Majesty," she saluted King George III for repealing the Stamp Act; in "On the Death of Mr. Snider [Seider], Murder'd by Richardson," she lambasted the British customs officer who murdered a teenage member of a crowd protesting the British soldiers who occupied Boston in 1768.

Wheatley was anything but radical. She had so thoroughly imbibed Christianity from her master and mistress that she wrote in one of her first poems that "Twas mercy brought me from my *Pagan* land." Many times she used poetry to implore slaves to "fly to Christ." But by 1772, she was inserting a muffled plea for an end of slavery in her odes to American rights and American resistance to British policies.

That Wheatley's poems were published in London in 1773 is remarkable. Women were not supposed to write publicly in the eighteenth century, and certainly not black women. Nonetheless, her master, supported by Boston friends and proud of his slave prodigy, shipped a sheaf of poems to a bookseller in England, who obtained the support of the Countess of Huntingdon for publishing them. They appeared under the title *Poems on Various Subjects, Religious and Moral*. Even more remarkable was that Wheatley, only 20 years old, took a ship to London to see her book come off the press. Her master and mistress financed the trip, hoping that sea air would clear her clogged lungs. There she was introduced to important reformers and public dignitaries, received a copy of Milton's *Paradise Lost* from the lord mayor of London, and met with Benjamin Franklin. She returned to Boston in 1774.

Reflecting on the Past   Read the two poems that follow: Wheatley's "On the Death of Mr. Snider [Seider], Murder'd by Richardson," composed in 1770, and her poem addressed to the King's minister in charge of colonial affairs, penned two years later. As modern readers, you may find the poetry stilted, but Wheatley's style was modeled on poetic conven-

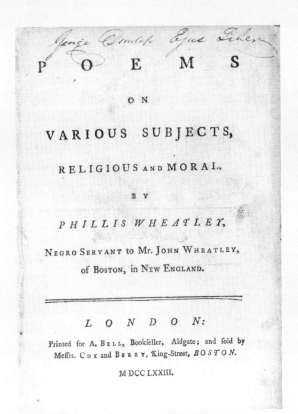

(Left) Wheatley worshiped at Old South Meeting House, which held some 5,000 people. In the 1770s, people frequently gathered there for political rallies and deliberations. This partly explains Wheatley's growing interest in the political battles raging in Boston. (Right) Wheatley's patroness in England specifically requested a drawing of Phillis for the frontispiece of this volume of poetry. Scipio Moorhead, slave of Boston's Presbyterian minister, did the drawing. Wheatley's mistress, Susannah Wheatley, called it a fine likeness. *(From the copy in the Rare Book Collection, The University of North Carolina at Chapel Hill)*

tions of the eighteenth century. What change can you discern in Wheatley's political consciousness between 1770 and 1772? Do you consider her poem on Seider's murder by a British customs officer propagandistic? How does she relate the plight of enslaved Africans to the American colonists' struggle? More generally, how effective do you think poetry is in arousing sentiment and mobilizing political energy? Can you think of verse serving as lyrics in popular protest music today?

On the Death of Mr. Snider, Murder'd by Richardson (1770)

In heaven's eternal court it was decreed
How the first martyr for the cause should bleed
To clear the country of the hated brood
We whet his courage for the common good.
Long hid before, a vile infernal here
Prevents Achilles in his mid career
Wherev'r this fury darts his Poisonous breath
All are endanger'd to the shafts of death

To the Right Honourable William, Earl of Dartmouth, His Majesty's Principal Secretary of State for North America (1772)

HAIL, happy day, when, smiling like the morn,
Fair Freedom *rose New-England to adorn:*
The northern clime beneath her genial ray,
Dartmouth, congratulates thy blissful sway:
Elate with hope her race no longer mourns,
Each soul expands, each grateful bosom burns,
While in thine hand with pleasure we behold
The silken reigns, and Freedom's *charms unfold.*
No more, America, *in mournful strain*
Of wrongs, and grievance unredress'd complain,
No longer shalt thou dread the iron chain,
Which wanton Tyranny with lawless hand
Had made, and with it meant t' enslave the land.
Should you, my lord, while you peruse my song,
Wonder from whence my love of Freedom *sprung,*
Whence flow these wishes for the common good,
By feeling hearts alone best understood,
I, young in life, by seeming cruel fate
Was snatch'd from Afric's *fancy'd happy seat:*
What pangs excruciating must molest,
What sorrows labour in my parent's breast?
Steel'd was that soul and by no misery mov'd
That from a father seiz'd his babe belov'd:
Such, such my case. And can I then but pray
Others may never feel tyrannic sway?

As marketgoers and consumers, urban women played a crucial role in applying economic pressure on England during the prerevolutionary decade. This British cartoon, published in 1775, derisively depicts a group of North Carolina women signing an anti-tea agreement. A slave woman looks on while a bewigged Whig focuses on something other than tea. *(Library of Congress)*

children began spinning yarn and weaving cloth. "Was not every fireside, indeed a theatre of politics?" John Adams remembered after the war. Towns often vied patriotically in the manufacture of cotton, linen, and woollen cloth, with the women staging open-air spinning contests to publicize their commitment. In 1769, the women of tiny Middletown, Massachusetts, set the standard by weaving 20,522 yards of cloth, about 160 yards each.

After the Tea Act in 1773, the interjection of politics into the household economy increased as patriotic women boycotted their favorite drink. Newspapers carried recipes for tea substitutes and recommendations for herbal teas. In Wilmington, North Carolina, women paraded solemnly through the town and then made a ritual display of their patriotism by burning their imported tea.

Women's perception of their role was also changed by colonial protests and petitions against England's arbitrary uses of power. The more male leaders talked about England's intentions to "enslave" the Americans and England's callous treatment of its colonial "subjects," the more American

women began to rethink their own domestic situations. The language of protest against England reminded many American women that they too were badly treated "subjects" of their husbands, who often dealt with them cruelly and exercised power over them arbitrarily.

Most American women, still bound by the social conventions of the day, were not ready to occupy such new territory. But the protests against England had stirred up new thoughts about what seemed "arbitrary" or "despotic" in their own society. Hence, many agendas for change appeared and with them a new feeling that what had been endured in the past was no longer acceptable.

Protesting Farmers

In most of the agricultural areas of the colonies, where the majority of settlers made their livelihoods, passions over English policies awakened only slowly. After about 1740, farmers had benefited from a sharp rise in the demand for foodstuffs in England, southern Europe, and the West Indies. Rising prices and brisk markets brought a higher standard of living to thousands of rural colonists, especially south of New England. Living far from harping English customs officers, impressment gangs, and occupying armies, the colonists of the interior had to be drawn gradually into the resistance movement by their urban cousins. Even in Concord, Massachusetts, only a dozen miles from the center of colonial agitation, townspeople found little to protest in English policies until England closed the port of Boston in 1774. They concerned themselves

A road sign in North Carolina is one of the few reminders that a bloody battle was fought at Alamance between small farmers and a militia commanded by the colony's governor in 1771. *(© 2002 Steven H. J. Rankin)*

with local issues—roads, schools, the location of churches—but rarely with the frightful offenses to American liberty that Bostonians perceived.

Yet some parts of rural America seethed with social tension in the prewar era. The dynamics of conflict, shaped by the social development of particular regions, eventually became part of the momentum for revolution. In three western counties of North Carolina and in the Hudson River valley of New York, for example, widespread civil disorder marked the prerevolutionary decades. The militant rhetoric and tactics small farmers used to combat exploitation formed rivulets that fed the mainstream of revolutionary consciousness.

For years, the small farmers of western North Carolina had suffered exploitation by corrupt county court officials appointed by the governor and a legislature dominated by eastern planter interests. Sheriffs and justices, allied with land speculators and lawyers, seized property when farmers could not pay their taxes and sold it, often at a fraction of its worth, to their cronies. The legislature rejected western petitions for lower taxes, paper currency, and lower court fees. In the mid-1760s, frustrated at getting no satisfaction from legal forms of protest, the farmers formed associations—the so-called Regulators—that forcibly closed the courts, attacked the property of their enemies, and whipped and publicly humiliated judges and lawyers. When their leaders were arrested, the Regulators stormed the jails and released them.

In 1768 and again in 1771, Governor William Tryon led troops against the Regulators. Bloodshed was averted on the first occasion, but on the second, at the Battle of Alamance, two armies of more than 1,000 fired on each other. Nine men died on each side before the Regulators fled the field. Seven leaders were executed in the ensuing trials. Though the Regulators lost the battle, their protests became part of the larger revolutionary struggle. They railed against the self-interested behavior of a wealthy elite and asserted the necessity for people of humble rank to throw off deference and assume political responsibilities.

Rural insurgency in New York flared up in the 1750s, subsided, and then erupted again in 1766. The conditions under which land was held precipitated the violence. The Hudson River valley had long been controlled by a few wealthy families with enormous landholdings, which they leased to small tenant farmers. The Van Rensselaer manor, for example, totaled a million acres, the Phillipses' manor nearly half as much. Hundreds of tenants with their families paid substantial annual rents for the right to farm on these lands, which had been acquired as

virtually free gifts from royal governors. When tenants resisted rent increases or purchased land from Indians who swore that manor lords had extended the boundaries of their manors by fraud, the landlords began evicting them.

As the wealthiest men of the region, the landlords had the power of government, including control of the courts, on their side. Organizing themselves and going outside the law became the tenants' main strategy, as with the Carolina Regulators. By 1766, while New York City was absorbed in the Stamp Act

Timeline

1696	Parliament establishes Board of Trade
1701	Iroquois set policy of neutrality
1702–1713	Queen Anne's War
1713	Peace of Utrecht
1733	Molasses Act
1739–1742	War of Jenkins' Ear
1744–1748	King George's War
1754	Albany conference
1755	Braddock defeated by French and Indian allies Acadians expelled from Nova Scotia
1756–1763	Seven Years' War
1759	Wolfe defeats the French at Québec
1759–1761	Cherokee War against the English
1760s	Economic slump
1763	Treaty of Paris ends Seven Years' War Proclamation line limits westward expansion
1764	Sugar and Currency acts Pontiac's Rebellion in Ohio valley
1765	Colonists resist Stamp Act Virginia House of Burgesses issues Stamp Act resolutions
1766	Declaratory Act Tenant rent war in New York Slave insurrections in South Carolina
1767	Townshend duties imposed
1768	British troops occupy Boston
1770	"Boston Massacre" Townshend duties repealed (except on tea)
1771	North Carolina Regulators defeated
1772	*Gaspee* incident in Rhode Island
1773	Tea Act provokes Boston Tea Party
1774	"Intolerable Acts" First Continental Congress meets in Philadelphia

furor, tenants led by William Prendergast began resisting sheriffs who tried to evict them from lands they claimed. The militant tenants threatened landlords with death and broke open jails to rescue friends. British troops from New York were used to break the tenant rebellion. Prendergast was tried

and sentenced to be hanged, beheaded, and quartered. Although he was pardoned, the bitterness of the Hudson River tenants endured through the Revolution. Most of them, unlike the Carolina Regulators, fought for the British because their landlords were patriots.

✦ *Conclusion*

ON THE BRINK OF REVOLUTION

The colonial Americans who lived in the third quarter of the eighteenth century participated in an era of political tension and conflict that changed the lives of nearly everyone. The Seven Years' War removed French and Spanish challengers and nurtured the colonists' sense of separate identity. Yet it left them with difficult economic adjustments, heavy debts, and growing social divisions. The colonists heralded the Treaty of Paris in 1763 as the dawning of a new era, but it led to a reorganization of England's triumphant yet debt-torn empire that had profound repercussions in America.

In the prerevolutionary decade, as England and the colonies moved from crisis to crisis, a dual disillusionment penetrated ever deeper into the colonial consciousness. Pervasive doubt arose concerning both the colonies' role, as assigned by England, in the economic life of the empire and the sensitivity of the government in London to the colonists'

needs. At the same time, the colonists began to perceive British policies—instituted by Parliament, the king, and his advisors—as a systematic attack on the fundamental liberties and natural rights of British citizens in North America.

The fluidity and diversity of colonial society and the differing experiences of Americans during and after the Seven Years' War evoked varying responses to the disruption that accompanied the English reorganization of the empire. In the course of resisting English policy, many previously inactive colonists, such as the humble shoemaker Ebenezer MacIntosh, entered public life to challenge gentry control of political affairs. Often occupying the most radical ground in the opposition to England, they simultaneously challenged the growing concentration of economic and political power in their own communities. What lay ahead was not only war with England but protracted arguments about how the American people, if they prevailed in their war for independence, should refashion their society.

✦ Recommended Reading

The Climactic Seven Years' War
Fred Anderson, *A People's Army: Massachusetts Soldiers and Society in the Seven Years' War* (1984) and *Crucible of War: The Seven Years' War and the Fate of Empire in British North America, 1754–1766* (2000); Gregory Dowd, *A Spirited Resistance: The North American Indian Struggle for Unity, 1745–1815* (1992); Richard Harding, *Amphibious Warfare in the Eighteenth Century: The British Expeditions to the West Indies* (1991); Tom Hatley, *The Dividing Paths: Cherokees and South Carolinians through the Era of Revolution* (1993); Francis Jennings, *Empire of Fortune: Crowns, Colonies, and Tribes in the Seven Years' War in America* (1988); John Oliphant, *Peace and War on the Anglo-Cherokee Frontier, 1756–63* (2001); Howard H. Peckham, *Pontiac and the Indian Uprising* (1947); Ian K. Steele, *Betrayals: Fort William Henry and the "Massacre"* (1990).

The Crisis with England
John Brewer, *Party Ideology and Popular Politics at the Accession of George III* (1976); Ian R. Christie, *Crisis of Empire: Great Britain and the American Colonies,*

1754–1783 (1966); Michael Kammen, *Empire and Interest* (1970); John Shy, *Toward Lexington: The Role of the British Army in the Coming of the American Revolution* (1965); Peter D. G. Thomas, *Tea Party to Independence: The Third Phase of the American Revolution* (1991); Alfred F. Young, *The Shoemaker and the Tea Party: Memory and the American Revolution* (1999).

The Ideology of Revolutionary Republicanism
Bernard Bailyn, *The Ideological Origins of the American Revolution* (1967); Ruth Bloch, *Visionary Republic: Millennial Themes in American Thought, 1750–1800* (1985); Richard Bushman, *King and People in Provincial Massachusetts* (1985); Jay Fliegelman, *Prodigals and Pilgrims: The American Revolution Against Patriarchal Authority, 1750–1800* (1982); Nathan O. Hatch, *The Sacred Cause of Liberty: Republican Thought and the Millennium in Revolutionary New England* (1977); Pauline Maier, *From Resistance to Revolution: Colonial Radicals and the Development of American Opposition to Britain, 1765–1776* (1972); Edmund S. Morgan, *Inventing the People: The Rise of Popular Sovereignty in*

England and America (1988); Gary B. Nash, *The Urban Crucible: Social Change, Political Consciousness, and the Origins of the American Revolution* (1979).

The Turmoil of a Rebellious People

Jon Butler, *Becoming America: The Revolution before 1776* (2000); Edward Countryman, *A People in Revolution* (1981); David Hackett Fischer, *Paul Revere's Ride* (1994); Eric Foner, *Tom Paine and Revolutionary America* (1976); Robert Gross, *The Minutemen and Their World* (1976); Ruth Herndon, *Unwelcome Americans: Living on the Margin in Early New England* (2001); Dirk Hoerder, *Crowd Action in Revolutionary Massachusetts, 1765–1780* (1977); Linda K. Kerber, *Women of the Republic: Intellect and Ideology in Revolutionary America* (1980); Henry Mayer, *A Son of Thunder: Patrick Henry and the American Republic* (1991); Mary Beth Norton, *Liberty's Daughters: The Revolutionary Experience of American Women, 1750–1800* (1980); Steven Rosswurm, *Arms, Country, and Class: The Philadelphia Militia and the "Lower Sort" During the American Revolution* (1987); Alfred E. Young, ed., *The American Revolution: Essays in the History of American Radicalism* (1976).

Fiction and Film

Americans have written novels about the American Revolution almost from the day the firing stopped. James Fenimore Cooper's *The Spy: A Tale of the Neutral Ground* (1822) is the best of the early ones. Historian Paul Leicester Ford's *Janice Meredith: A Story of the American Revolution* (1899) remains absorbing a century after its publication. In the modern period, Kenneth Roberts's four novels on the Revolution have entertained American readers for two generations: *Arundel* (1933); *Oliver Wiswell* (1940); *Rabble in Arms* (1953); and *The Battle of Cowpens: The Great Morale-Builder* (1958). *Oliver Wiswell* is especially notable for its recreation of a Loyalist's view of the Revolution. *Mary Silliman's War* (Heritage Film and Citadel Film, 1993) shows the Revolution through the eyes of a Connecticut family where husband and wife must reconcile their differing views on the Patriots and Loyalists. The English film on George III, *The Madness of King George* (1994), brings alive the era of the American Revolution and turns the king into the deeply psychotic ruler that some at the time believed he was. *Liberty* (Middlemarch Films, 1997) is a docudrama produced for television that has many high moments but neglects the internal struggles within the Patriot ranks for reforming American society.

◆ Discovering U.S. History Online

Exploring the West from Monticello: An Exhibition of Maps and Navigational Instruments
www.lib.virginia.edu/exhibits/lewis_clark/home.html
Maps and charts reveal knowledge and conceptions about the known and the unknown. This site includes a number of eighteenth-century maps.

Maps of the French and Indian War
www.masshist.org/maps/MapsHome/Home.htm
In addition to contemporary maps, this site explains the political significance of the maps and gives a background of the wars.

1755: The French and Indian War
www.web.syr.edu/~laroux/
This amateur site presents information about French soldiers who came to New France between 1755 and 1760 to fight in the French and Indian War as well as a list of key places.

Religion and the American Revolution
www.lcweb.loc.gov/exhibits/religion/rel02.html
Providing an overview of eighteenth-century religion in the American colonies, this site draws on primary source material such as paintings of clergyman, title pages of published sermons, and other artifacts.

A Century of Lawmaking
www.memory.loc.gov/ammem/amlaw/lwjc.html
A searchable version of "the daily proceedings of the Congress as kept by the office of its secretary, Charles Thomson."

Phillis Wheatley (1753–1784)
www.csustan.edu/english/reuben/pal/chap2/wheatley.html
This online essay on Phillis Wheatley includes samples of her poetry and a bibliography.

Thomas Paine
www.thomaspaine.org
This official site contains a large archive of Paine's work, including *Common Sense*, and information about the association.

The Freedom Trail
www.freedomtrail.org/index.html
This site presents the story of colonial protest via Boston historical sites.

The Trial of John Peter Zenger
www.jurist.law.pitt.edu/trials20.htm
A thorough essay on the trial, with links to primary documents.

Georgia's Rare Map Collection
www.scarlett.libs.uga.edu/darchive/hargrett/maps/revamer.html
This site contains maps of colonial and revolutionary America.

6

A People in Revolution

William Mercer, *Battle of Princeton*, c. 1786–1790. Because infantry weapons were inaccurate at long distances, lines formed in close proximity, where weapons were more deadly and combat was intensely personal. Here, General Washington directs the American force. *(Historical Society of Pennsylvania)*

✦ *American Stories*

STRUGGLING FOR INDEPENDENCE

Among the Americans wounded and captured at the Battle of Bunker Hill in the spring of 1775 was Lieutenant William Scott of Peterborough, New Hampshire. Asked by his captors how he had come to be a rebel, "Long Bill" Scott replied:

> The case was this Sir! I lived in a Country Town; I was a Shoemaker, & got [my] living by my labor. When this rebellion came on, I saw some of my neighbors get into commission, who were no better than myself. . . . I was asked to enlist, as a private soldier. My ambition was too great for so low a rank. I offered to enlist upon having a lieutenant's commission, which was granted. I imagined my self now in a way of promotion. If I was killed in battle, there would be an end of me, but if my Captain

was killed, I should rise in rank, & should still have a chance to rise higher. These Sir! were the only motives of my entering into the service. For as to the dispute between Great Britain & the colonies, I know nothing of it; neither am I capable of judging whether it is right or wrong.

Scott may have been trying to gain the sympathy of his captors, but people fought in America's Revolutionary War for a variety of reasons—fear and ambition as well as principle among them. We have no way of knowing whether Long Bill Scott's motives were typical. Certainly many Americans knew more than he about the colonies' struggle with England, but many did not.

In the spring of 1775, the Revolutionary War had just begun. So had Long Bill's adventures. When the British evacuated Boston a year later, Scott was transported to Halifax, Nova Scotia. After several months' captivity, he managed to escape and make his way home to fight once more. He was recaptured in November 1776 near New York City, when its garrison fell to a surprise British assault. Again Scott escaped, this time by swimming the Hudson River at night with his sword tied around his neck and his watch pinned to his hat.

During the winter of 1777, he returned to New Hampshire to recruit his own militia company. It included two of his eldest sons. In the fall, his unit helped defeat Burgoyne's army near Saratoga, New York, and later took part in the fighting around Newport, Rhode Island. When his light infantry company was ordered to Virginia in early 1778, Scott's health broke, and he was permitted to resign from the army. After only a few months' recuperation, however, he was at it again. During the last year of the war, he served as a volunteer on a navy frigate.

For seven years, the war held Scott in its harsh grasp. Scott's oldest son died of camp fever after six years of service. In 1777, Long Bill sold his New Hampshire farm to meet family expenses. He lost a second farm in Massachusetts shortly afterward. After his wife died, he turned their youngest children over to relatives and set off to beg a pension or job from the government.

Long Bill's saga was still not complete. In 1792, he rescued eight people when their boat capsized in New York harbor. Three years later, General Benjamin Lincoln took Scott with him to the Ohio country, where they surveyed land that was opening for white settlement. At last he had a respectable job and even a small government pension as compensation for his nine wounds. But trouble would still not let him go. While surveying on the Black River near Sandusky, Scott and his colleagues contracted "lake fever." Though ill, he guided part of the group back to Fort Stanwix in New York, then returned for the others. It was his last heroic act. A few days after his second trip, on September 16, 1796, he died.

American independence and the Revolutionary War that accompanied it were not as hard on everyone as they were on Long Bill Scott, yet together they transformed the lives of countless Americans. The war lasted seven years, longer than any other of America's wars until Vietnam nearly two centuries later. And unlike the nation's twentieth-century conflicts, it was fought on American soil, among the American people. It called men by the thousands from shops and fields, disrupted families, destroyed communities, spread disease, and made a shambles of the economy.

America's struggle for independence echoed far beyond the boundaries of the original 13 states. The war against England was quickly internationalized as France, Spain, and other nations, driven by their own imperial ambitions and the realities of European power politics, joined in the struggle against England. The Treaty of Paris (1783) and other diplomatic accords following the Revolutionary War not only secured American independence but also redrew the contours of imperial ambition in North America and recast relations between England and the nations of western Europe.

More than that, America's fight for independence ushered in an extended Age of Revolution that, over the following half century, would see a king toppled and aristocratic privilege overthrown in France, republican reforms erupt throughout Europe, and independence movements undercut European imperialism in Haiti and Latin America.

Amid their struggle for independence, the American people mounted a political revolution of profound importance. Politics and government were transformed in keeping with republican principles and the rapidly changing circumstances of public life. How could individual liberty be reconciled with the need for public order? Who should be considered republican citizens? Women as well as men? Free black as well as white Americans? These were among the puzzling questions with which the American people wrestled at the nation's beginning.

As political activity quickened under the pressure of war and revolution, people clashed repeatedly over the best way to write new constitutions and organize new governments in the states. How much power should the new governments have? How democratic could they safely be? And what should the national government be like? Seldom has the nation's political agenda been fuller or more troubled than during these critical years.

The American Revolution dominated the lives of all who lived through it. But it had different consequences for men than for women, for black slaves than for their white masters, for Native Americans than for frontier settlers, for overseas merchants than for urban workers, for northern businessmen than for southern planters. Our understanding of the experience out of which the American nation emerged must begin with the Revolutionary War, for liberty came at a high cost.

BURSTING THE COLONIAL BONDS

By the spring of 1775, tension between the colonies and England was at the breaking point. In each of the colonies extra-legal committees and assemblies organized continuing resistance to the Intolerable Acts, while in England, Parliament and the king's ministers prepared to crush the colonial challenge to British authority. The outbreak of fighting at Lexington and Concord decisively transformed the imperial crisis. No longer was it limited to a struggle over competing theories of Parliamentary authority and colonial rights, for now the firing had commenced and men on both sides lay dying. Within little more than a year of that fateful event, England's empire was severed.

The Final Rupture

The final spark to the revolutionary powder keg was struck in April 1775. General Gage had assumed the governorship of Massachusetts 11 months earlier and occupied Boston with 4,000 troops—one for every adult male in the town. In early April, the government in London ordered Gage to arrest "the principal actors and abettors" of insurrection in Massachusetts. Under cover of night, he sent 700 redcoats out of Boston to seize colonial arms in nearby Concord. But Americans learned of the plan, and when the troops reached Lexington at dawn, 70 armed "Minutemen"—townsmen available on a minute's notice—were waiting. In the ensuing skirmish, 18 Massachusetts farmers fell, 8 of them mortally wounded.

Marching six miles west to Concord, the British encountered another firefight. Withdrawing, the redcoats made their way back to Boston, harassed by militiamen firing from farmhouses and from behind stone walls. Before the bloody day ended, 273 British and 95 Americans lay dead or wounded. News of the bloodshed swept through the colonies. Within weeks, thousands of men besieged the British troops in Boston. According to one colonist, everywhere "you see the inhabitants training, making firelocks, casting mortars, shells, and shot."

As fighting erupted around Boston, the Second Continental Congress assembled in May 1775 in Philadelphia. Many delegates knew one another from the earlier Congress. But fresh faces appeared, including Boston's wealthy merchant, John Hancock; a young planter-lawyer from Virginia, Thomas Jefferson; and the much-applauded Benjamin Franklin, who had arrived from London only four days before the Congress convened.

Meeting in the statehouse where the king's arms hung over the entrance and the inscription on the tower bell read "Proclaim liberty throughout the land unto all the inhabitants thereof," the Second Congress set to work. Though its powers were unclear and its legitimacy uncertain, the desperate situation required that it act. After a spirited debate, Congress authorized a continental army of 20,000 and, partly to cement Virginia to the cause, chose George Washington as commander in chief. Over succeeding weeks, it issued a "Declaration of Causes of Taking-up Arms," sent the king an "Olive Branch Petition" humbly begging him to remove the obstacles to reconciliation, made moves to secure the neutrality of the interior Indian tribes, issued paper money, erected a postal system, and approved plans for a military hospital.

While debate continued over whether the colonies ought to declare themselves independent, military action grew more intense. The fiery Ethan Allen and his Green Mountain Boys from eastern New York captured Fort Ticonderoga, controlling the Champlain valley, in May 1775. On New Year's Day in 1776, the British shelled Norfolk, Virginia. Still, many members of the Congress dreaded a final rupture and hoped for reconciliation. Such hopes finally crumbled at the end of 1775 when news arrived that the king, rejecting the Olive Branch Petition and proclaiming the colonies in "open and avowed rebellion," had dispatched 20,000 additional British troops to quell the insurrection. Those fatal words made Congress's actions treasonable and turned all who obeyed the Congress into traitors.

Thomas Paine's *Common Sense*

As the crisis deepened, a pamphlet appeared that would speed the move toward independence. Published in Philadelphia on January 9, 1776, Thomas Paine's *Common Sense* soon appeared in bookstalls all over the colonies. In scathing language, Paine denied the very legitimacy of monarchy. "Of more worth is one honest man to society," he scoffed, "than all the crowned ruffians that ever lived." It was Paine's unsparing rejection of monarchy that made his pamphlet seem so radical. From that it was a logical step to call openly for Americans to act in defense of their liberties. "O ye that love mankind," he declared. "Ye that dare oppose not only the tyranny, but also the tyrant, stand forth!" Paine's ringing challenge had the desired effect. "The public sentiment which a few weeks before shuddered at the tremendous obstacles, with which independence was envisioned," declared Edmund Randolph of Virginia in amazement, now "overleaped every barrier."

The pamphlet's astounding popularity—it went through 25 editions in 1776 and sold more copies than any printed piece in colonial history—stemmed not only from its argument but also from its style. Shunning the elaborate, legalistic language of most pamphlets written by lawyers and clergymen, Paine wrote for the common people who read little more than the Bible. Using biblical imagery and plain language, he appealed to their Calvinist heritage and millenial yearnings: "We have it in our power to begin the world over again," he exulted. "The birthday of a new world" was at hand. It was language that could be understood on the docks, in the taverns, on the streets, and in the farmyards.

Many Whig leaders found his pungent rhetoric and egalitarian call for ending hereditary privilege and concentrated power too strong. They denounced the disheveled immigrant as a "crack-brained zealot for democracy" and a dangerous man who appealed to "every silly clown and illiterate mechanic." But thousands who read or listened to *Common Sense* were radicalized by it and came to believe not only that independence could be wrestled from England, but also that a new social and political order could be created in North America.

Declaring Independence

By the time Paine's hard-hitting pamphlet appeared, members of Congress were talking less gingerly about independence. When England embargoed all trade to the colonies and ordered the seizure of American ships, the Congress declared American ports open to all countries. "Nothing is left now," Joseph Hewes of North Carolina admitted, "but to fight it out." It was almost anticlimactic when Richard Henry Lee introduced a congressional resolution on June 7 calling for independence. After two days of debate, the Congress ordered a committee chaired by Jefferson to begin drafting such a document.

Though it would become revered as the new nation's birth certificate, the Declaration of Independence was not a highly original statement. It drew heavily on the Congress's earlier justifications of American resistance, and its theory of government had already been set forth in scores of pamphlets over the previous decade. The ringing phrases that "all men are created equal, that they are endowed by their Creator with certain unalienable Rights, that among these are Life, Liberty, and the pursuit of Happiness" were familiar in the writing of many American pamphleteers.

Jefferson's committee presented the declaration to Congress on June 28. The proposals were read and ordered to "lie on the table" until the following

Monday, July 1. "This morning is assigned for the greatest debate of all," noted John Adams when the Congress reconvened. "May Heaven prosper the new-born republic, and make it more glorious than any former republics have been." On July 2, 12 delegations voted "yes," with New York abstaining, thus allowing the Congress to say that the vote for independence was unanimous. Two more days were spent polishing the document. The major change was the elimination of a long argument blaming the king for slavery in America. On July 4, Congress sent the document to the printer.

Four days later, Philadelphians thronged to the state house to hear the Declaration of Independence read aloud. They "huzzahed" the reading, tore the king's arms from above the state house door, and later that night, amid cheers, toasts, and clanging church bells, hurled this symbol of more than a century and a half of colonial dependency on England into a roaring fire. Across the land, people raised toasts to the great event: "Liberty to those who have the spirit to preserve it," and "May Liberty expand sacred wings, and, in glorious effort, diffuse her influence o'er and o'er the globe." Independence had been declared; the war, however, was yet to be won.

THE WAR FOR AMERICAN INDEPENDENCE

The war began in Massachusetts in 1775, but within a year its focus shifted to the middle states. After 1779, the South became the primary theater. Why did this geographic pattern develop, what was its significance, and why did the Americans win?

The War in the North

For a brief time following Lexington and Concord, British officials thought of launching forays out from Boston into the surrounding countryside. They soon reconsidered, however, for the growing size of the continental army and the absence of significant Loyalist strength in the New England region urged caution. Even more important, Boston became untenable after the Americans placed artillery on the strategic Dorchester Heights. On March 7, 1776, the British commander General William Howe decided to evacuate the city.

Fearing retaliation against Loyalists and wishing not to destroy lingering hopes of reconciliation, Howe spared the city from the torch. The departing troops, however, left it in a shambles. British officers had taken over the elegant homes of John Hancock and others, dragoons had used the Old South

Meeting House as a riding school after tearing out the pews, and the Old North Church had been demolished for firewood. All around lay trampled gardens, uprooted trees, and filth. "Almost everything here, appears Gloomy and Melancholy," lamented one returning resident.

For a half dozen years after Boston's evacuation, British ships prowled the New England coast, confiscating supplies and attacking coastal towns. Yet away from the coast, there was little fighting. Most New Englanders had reason to be thankful for their good fortune.

The British established their new military headquarters in New York City. Their decision was strategically sound, for New York offered important advantages: a central location, a spacious harbor, control of the Hudson River, a major water route into the interior, and access to the abundant grain and livestock of the Middle Atlantic states. In addition, Loyalist sentiment ran deep among the inhabitants of the city and its environs.

In the summer of 1776, Washington moved his troops south from Boston, determined to challenge the British for control of New York City. It proved a terrible mistake. Outmaneuvered and badly outnumbered, he suffered defeat, first at the Battle of Long Island and then in Manhattan itself. By late October, the city was firmly in British hands. It would remain so until the war's end.

Meanwhile, King George III instructed his two chief commanders in North America, the brothers General William and Admiral Richard Howe, to make a final effort at reconciliation with the colonists. In early September, they met with three delegates from the Congress on Staten Island, in New York harbor. But when the Howes demanded revocation of the Declaration of Independence before negotiations could begin, all hope of reconciliation vanished.

For the next two years, the war swept back and forth across New Jersey and Pennsylvania. Reinforced by German mercenaries hired in Europe, the British moved virtually at will. Neither the state militias nor the continental army—weakened by losses, low morale, and inadequate supplies—offered serious opposition. At Trenton in December 1776 and at Princeton the following month, Washington surprised the British and scored victories that prevented the Americans' collapse. Survival, however, remained the rebels' primary goal.

American efforts during the first year of the war to invade Canada and bring that British colony into the rebellion also fared badly. In November 1775, American forces under General Richard Montgomery had taken Montreal. But the subsequent assault against Quebec ended with almost

Military Operations in the North, 1776–1780

During the early years of the war, fighting was most intense in upper New York and the mid-Atlantic states. Note the importance of water routes to military strategies.

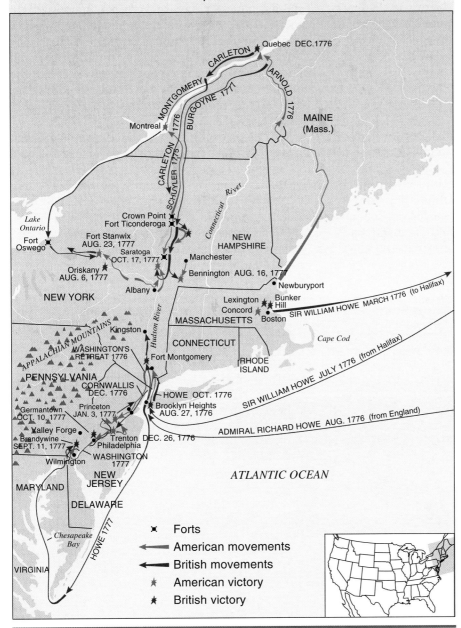

100 Americans killed or wounded and more than 300 taken prisoner. The American cause could not survive many such losses.

Washington had learned the painful lesson at New York that his troops were no match for the British in frontal combat. He realized, moreover, that if the continental army was defeated, American independence would certainly be lost. Thus, he decided on a strategy of harassing the British, making

the war as costly for them as possible, and protecting the civilian population as best he could while avoiding major battles. He would follow that strategy for the rest of the war.

As a consequence, the war's middle years turned into a deadly chase that neither side proved able to win. In September 1777, the British took Philadelphia, sending the Congress fleeing into the countryside, but then hesitated to press their advantage.

On numerous occasions British commanders failed to act decisively, either reluctant to move through the hostile countryside or uncertain of their instructions. Offsetting British domination of the Middle Atlantic region was the American victory in October at Saratoga, New York, where General Burgoyne surrendered with 5,700 British soldiers. That victory prompted France to join the struggle against England.

Congress and the Articles of Confederation

As war erupted, the Continental Congress turned to the task of creating a more permanent and effective national government. It was a daunting assignment, for prior to independence the colonies had quarreled repeatedly over colonial boundaries, control of the Indian trade, and commercial advantage within the empire. The crisis with England had forced them together, and the Congress embodied that tenuous union.

As long as hopes of reconciliation with England lingered, the Congress's uncertain authority posed no serious problems. But as independence and the prospects of an extended war loomed, pressure to establish a more durable government increased. On June 20, 1776, shortly before independence was declared, Congress appointed a committee, chaired by John Dickinson of Pennsylvania, to draw up a plan of perpetual union. So urgent was the crisis that the committee responded in a month's time, and debate on the proposed Articles of Confederation quickly began.

The delegates promptly clashed over whether to form a strong, consolidated government or a loosely joined confederation of sovereign states. As the debate went on, those differences sharpened. Dickinson's draft, outlining a government of considerable power, generated strong opposition. American experience with a "tyrannous" king and Parliament had revealed the dangers of a central government unmindful of the people's liberties.

Western Land Claims Ceded by the States, 1782–1802

Based on their colonial charters, seven of the original states claimed land west of the Appalachian Mountains. Eventually those states ceded their western claims to the Congress, making ratification of the Articles of Confederation and the creation of new western states possible.

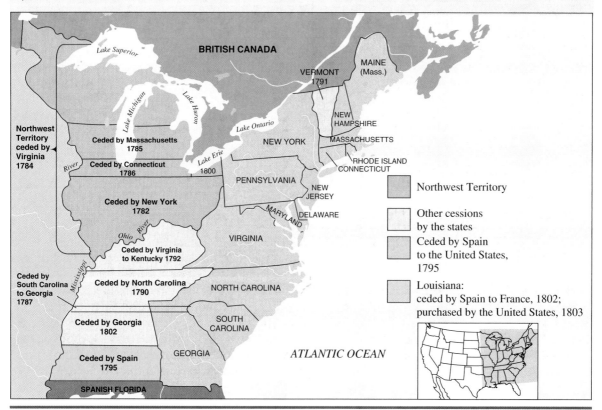

As finally approved, the Articles of Confederation represented a compromise. Article 9 gave the Congress sole authority to regulate foreign affairs, declare war, mediate boundary disputes between the states, manage the post office, and administer relations with Indians living outside state boundaries. The Articles also stipulated that the inhabitants of each state were to enjoy the "privileges and immunities" of the citizens of every other state. Embedded in that clause was the basis for national, as distinguished from state, citizenship.

At the same time, the Articles sharply limited what the Congress could do and reserved broad governing powers to the states. For example, the Congress could neither raise troops nor levy taxes but could only ask the states for such support. Article 2 stipulated that each state was to "retain its sovereignty, freedom and independence," as well as "every power . . . which is not by this confederation expressly delegated to the United States in Congress assembled." Nor could the Congress's limited powers be easily expanded, because the Articles could be amended only by the unanimous agreement of all 13 states.

Though the Congress sent the Articles to the states for approval in November 1777, they were not ratified until March 1781. Ratification required approval by all the states, and that was hard to obtain. The biggest impediment was a bitter dispute over control of the lands west of the Appalachian Mountains. Some states had western claims tracing back to their colonial charters, but other states, such as Maryland and New Jersey, did not. In December 1778, the Maryland assembly announced that it would not ratify until all the western lands had been ceded to the Congress. For several years, ratification hung in the balance while politicians and land speculators jockeyed for advantage. Finally, in 1780, New York and Virginia agreed to transfer their western lands to the Congress. Those decisions paved the way for Maryland's ratification in early 1781. Approval of the Articles was now assured.

Meanwhile, Congress managed the war effort as best it could, using the unratified Articles as a guide. Events quickly proved its inadequacy, because Congress could do little more than pass resolutions and implore the states for support. If they refused, as they frequently did, the Congress could only protest and urge cooperation. Its ability to function was further limited by the stipulation that each state's delegation cast but one vote. Disagreements within state delegations sometimes prevented them from voting at all. That could paralyze the Congress, because most important decisions required a nine-state majority.

As the war dragged on, Washington repeatedly criticized the Congress for its failure to support the army. Acknowledging its own ineffectiveness, the Congress in 1778 temporarily granted Washington extraordinary powers, asking him to manage the war on his own. In the end, the Congress survived because enough of its members realized that disaster would follow its collapse.

The War Moves South

As the war in the North bogged down in a costly stalemate, British officials adopted an alternative strategy: invasion and pacification of the South. Royal officials in the South encouraged the idea with reports that thousands of Loyalists would rally to the British standard. The southern coastline with its numerous rivers, moreover, offered maximum advantage to British naval strength. Then there were the slaves, that vast but imponderable presence in southern society. If they could be lured to the British side, the balance might tip in Britain's favor. In any case, the threat of slave rebellion would weaken white southerners' will to resist. Persuaded by these arguments, the British shifted the primary theater of military operations to the South during the war's final years.

Georgia—small, isolated, and largely defenseless—was the initial target. In December 1778, Savannah, the state's major port, fell before a seaborne attack of 3,500 men. For nearly two years, the Revolution in the state virtually ceased. Encouraged by their success, the British turned to the Carolinas, with equally impressive results. On May 12, 1780, Charleston surrendered after a month's siege. At a cost of only 225 casualties, the British captured the entire 5,400-man American garrison. It was the costliest American defeat of the war.

After securing Charleston, the British quickly extended their control north and south along the coast. At Camden, South Carolina, the British killed nearly 1,000 Americans and captured 1,000 more, temporarily destroying the southern continental army. With scarcely a pause, the British pushed on into North Carolina. There, however, British officers quickly learned the difficulty of extending their lines into the interior: distances were too large, problems of supply too great, the reliability of Loyalist troops too uncertain, and popular support for the revolutionary cause too strong.

In October 1780, Washington sent Nathanael Greene south to lead the continental forces. It was a fortunate choice, for Greene knew the region and the kind of war that had to be fought. Determined, like Washington, to avoid large-scale encounters,

Military Operations in the South, 1778–1781

The war in the South was fought both along the coast and in the interior.

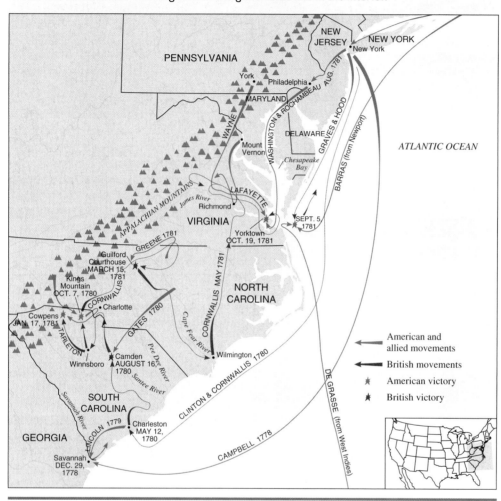

Greene divided his army into small, mobile bands. Employing what today would be called guerrilla tactics, he harassed the British and their Loyalist allies at every opportunity, striking by surprise and then disappearing into the interior. Nowhere was the war more fiercely contested than through the Georgia and Carolina backcountry. Neither British nor American authorities could restrain the violence. Bands of private marauders, roving the land and seizing advantage from the war's confusion, compounded the chaos.

In time, the tide began to turn. At Cowpens, South Carolina, in January 1781, American troops under General Daniel Morgan won a decisive victory, suffering fewer than 75 casualties to 329 British deaths, and taking 600 men prisoner. In March, at Guilford Court House in North Carolina, Cornwallis won, but at a cost that forced his retreat to Wilmington, near the sea.

In April 1781, convinced that British authority could not be restored in the Carolinas while the rebels continued to use Virginia as a supply and staging area, Cornwallis moved north. With a force of 7,500, he raided deep into Virginia, sending Governor Jefferson and the Virginia legislature fleeing from Charlottesville into the mountains. But again Cornwallis found the costs of victory high, and again he turned back to the coast for protection and resupply. On August 1, he reached Yorktown.

Cornwallis's position was secure as long as the British fleet controlled Chesapeake Bay, but that advantage did not last long. In 1778, the French government, still smarting from its defeat by England in the Seven Years' War and buoyed by the American victory at Saratoga in 1777, had signed an alliance with the Congress, promising to send its naval forces into the war. Initially, the French concentrated their fleet in the West Indies, hoping to seize

At Yorktown, Cornwallis asserted he was ill and sent a subordinate, Brigadier General Charles O'Hara, to yield the symbolic sword of surrender. *(Library of Congress)*

some of the British sugar islands. But on August 30, 1781, after repeated American urging, the French admiral Comte de Grasse arrived off Yorktown. Reinforced by a second French squadron from the North, de Grasse established naval superiority in Chesapeake Bay. At the same time, Washington's continentals, supplemented by French troops, marched south from Pennsylvania.

As Washington had foreseen, French entry turned the tide of war. Cut off from the sea and pinned down on a peninsula between the York and James Rivers by 17,000 French and American troops, Cornwallis's fate was sealed. On October 19, 1781, near the Virginia hamlet of Yorktown, he surrendered. While a military band played "The World Turned Upside Down" and hundreds of civilians looked on, nearly 7,000 British troops laid down their arms.

Learning the news in London a month later, Lord North, the king's chief minister, exclaimed, "Oh, God! It is all over." On February 27, 1782, the House of Commons cut off further support of the war. North resigned the following month. In Philadelphia, citizens poured into the streets to celebrate while the

Congress assembled for a solemn ceremony of thanksgiving. Though the preliminary articles of peace were not signed until November 1782, everyone knew after Yorktown that the Americans had won their independence.

Native Americans in the Revolution

The Revolutionary War drew in countless Native Americans as well as colonists and Englishmen. It could hardly have been otherwise, for the lives of all three peoples had been intertwined since the first English settlements more than a century earlier.

Though small tribes still struggled to maintain their identities along the eastern seaboard and though Indians still roamed the streets of America's port cities, the coastal tribes were mostly gone by the time of the Revolution, their villages displaced by white settlement, their numbers thinned by warfare and disease. Powerful tribes, however, still controlled the interior between the Appalachians and the Mississippi River. The Iroquois Six Nations, a confederation numbering 15,000 people, controlled a huge area stretching westward from Albany, New York, and dominated the "western tribes" of the Ohio valley—the Shawnee, Delaware, Wyandotte, and Miami. In the Southeast, five tribes—the Choctaw, Chickasaw, Seminole, Creek, and Cherokee, 60,000 people in all—dominated the interior.

Far outnumbering the few white settlers that had pushed across the Appalachians, the interior tribes were more than a match, militarily and diplomatically, for the Anglo-Americans. As the imperial crisis between England and its colonies deepened, Native and European Americans eyed each other warily across this vast "middle ground."

When the Revolutionary War began, British and American officials urged neutrality on the Indians. The British, expecting the conflict to be short, wished to disrupt the interior as little as possible, while the Americans worried about Indian attacks from the west when confronting British power along the coast. The Native Americans, however, were too important militarily for either side to ignore. By the spring of 1776, both were actively seeking Indian alliances. Recognizing their stake in the white man's conflict, Native Americans up and down the interior debated their options.

Alarmed by encroaching white settlement and eager to take advantage of the colonists' troubles with England, a band of Cherokee, led by the warrior Dragging Canoe, launched a series of raids in July 1776 in what is today eastern Tennessee. In retaliation, Virginia and Carolina militias laid waste a group of Cherokee towns. Thomas Jefferson expressed satisfaction at the outcome. "I hope that the Cherokees

Indian Battles and the War in the West, 1775–1783

Though most battles were fought along the coastal plain, the British and their Indian allies opened a second front far to the west.

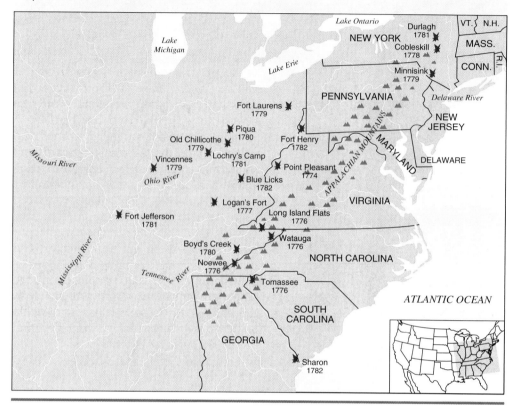

will now be driven beyond the Mississippi," he wrote. "Our contest with Britain is too serious . . . to permit any possibility of [danger] . . . from the Indians." The Cherokee never again mounted a sustained military effort against the rebels. Seeing what had befallen their neighbors, the Creek stayed aloof. Their time for resistance would come in the early nineteenth century, when white settlers began to push onto their lands.

In the Ohio country, the struggle lasted longer. For several decades before the Revolution, explorers such as Daniel Boone had contested with the Shawnee and others for control of the region bordering the Ohio River. The Revolutionary War intensified these conflicts. In February 1778, George Rogers Clark led a ragtag band of Kentuckians through icy rivers and across 180 miles of forbidding terrain to attack a British outpost at Vincennes, in present-day Indiana. Though heavily outnumbered, Clark fooled the British and their Indian allies into believing that his force was much larger, and the British surrendered without a shot. Though skirmishes between Indians and marauding American

forces continued for several years, Clark's victory tipped the balance in the war's western theater.

The Devastation of the Iroquois

To the northeast, an even more deadly scenario unfolded. At a council in Albany, New York, in August 1775, representatives of the Iroquois Six Nations listened while American commissioners urged them to remain at home and keep the hatchet buried deep. "The determination of the Six Nations," replied Little Abraham, a Mohawk leader, "[is] not to take any part; but as it is a family affair, to sit still and see you fight it out." Iroquois neutrality, however, did not last long.

After U.S. troops raided deep into Mohawk territory west of Albany, the British argued with words, rum, and trade goods that the Iroquois should join them against the rebels. Most did so in the summer of 1777, at the urging of Joseph Brant, a Mohawk warrior who had visited England several years earlier and proclaimed England's value as an ally against American expansion.

It was a fateful decision for Indians and whites alike. Over the next several years, the Iroquois and their British allies devastated large areas in central New York and Pennsylvania, destroying property and terrorizing the inhabitants. An officer of the Pennsylvania militia reported somberly, "Our country is on the eve of breaking up. There is nothing to be seen but disolation, fire & smoak."

The Americans' revenge came swiftly. During the summer of 1779, General John Sullivan led a series of punishing raids into the Iroquois country, burning villages; killing men, women, and children; and destroying fields of corn. His motto was blunt: "Civilization or death to all American savages." By war's end, the Iroquois had lost as many as one-third of their people as well as countless towns. Their domination of the northeastern interior was permanently shattered.

Not all the Eastern Woodland tribes sided with England in the Revolutionary War. The Oneida and the Tuscarora, members of the Iroquois confederation, fought with the Americans, their decision driven by intertribal politics and effective diplomacy by emissaries of the Continental Congress. In New England, the Stockbridge, a small tribe surrounded by a sea of white settlement, contributed warriors and scouts, while farther to the south the Catawba, similarly dependent on the Americans for trade and diplomacy, also signed on. The Indians who fought for American independence, however, reaped little reward. Though General Sullivan spared the Oneida and Tuscarora villages, the British and their Iroquois allies destroyed them in turn. And although a number of Indian warriors were compensated by grateful state governments once the war was over, tribes allied with the victorious American cause enjoyed no protection from the accelerating spread of white settlement.

Most Indians had sound reason for opposing American independence, because England provided them with trade goods, arms, and markets for their furs. England, moreover, had promised protection against colonial expansion, as the Proclamation Line of 1763 had demonstrated. At the peace talks that ended the Revolutionary War, however, the British ignored their Indian allies. They received neither compensation for their losses nor guarantees of their land, for the boundary of the United States was set far to the west, at the Mississippi River.

Though the Indians' struggle against white expansion would continue, their own anticolonial war of liberation had failed. The American Revolution, declared a gathering of Indian chiefs to the Spanish

Mohawk chief Joseph Brant (Thayendanegea) played a major role in the Iroquois's decision to enter the war on the side of Britain. *(The National Gallery of Canada, Ottawa)*

governor at Saint Louis in 1784, had been "the greatest blow that could have been dealt us."

Negotiating Peace

In September 1781, formal peace negotiations began in Paris between the British commissioner, Richard Oswald, and the American emissaries, Benjamin Franklin, John Adams, and John Jay. The negotiations were complicated by the involvement in the war of several European countries seeking to weaken Great Britain. The Americans' main ally, France, had entered the war in February 1778. Eight months later, Spain declared war on England, though it declined to recognize American independence. Between 1780 and 1782, Russia, the Netherlands, and six other European countries joined in a League of Armed Neutrality aimed at protecting their maritime trade against British efforts to control it. America's Revolutionary War had quickly become internationalized. It could hardly have been otherwise, given England's centrality to the European balance of power and the long-standing competition among European powers for colonial dominance in North America.

England's American Empire Divides

The majority of England's New World colonies did not rebel in 1776. **Reflecting on the Past** What difference did it make that Canada and England's Caribbean colonies did not join the 13 North American colonies in throwing off English authority?

BRITISH CANADA

MAINE
(Mass.)

N.H.

NEW YORK

MASS.

PENN.

R.I.

N.J.

CONN.

MD.

DEL.

VIRGINIA

NORTH CAROLINA

SOUTH CAROLINA

GEORGIA

Gulf of Mexico

ATLANTIC OCEAN

BAHAMAS

ANTIGUA

NEVIS

MONTSERRAT

JAMAICA

DOMINICA

ST. LUCIA

BARBADOS

Caribbean Sea

ST. VINCENT

TOBAGO

New World Possessions of Britain

Rebelled

Did not rebel

Dependent on French economic and military support, the Congress instructed the American commissioners to follow the advice of the French foreign minister Vergennes. But as the American commissioners soon learned, he was prepared to let the exhausting war continue in order to weaken England and tighten America's dependence on France. Even more alarming, Vergennes suggested that the new nation's boundary should be set no farther west than the crest of the Appalachian Mountains, and he hinted that the British might retain areas they controlled at the war's end. That would have left New York City and other coastal enclaves in British hands.

In the end, the American commissioners ignored their instructions and, without a word to Vergennes, arranged a provisional peace agreement with the British emissaries. It was fortunate that they did so, for the British were prepared to be generous. In the Treaty of Paris signed in September 1783, England recognized American independence and agreed to set the western boundary of the United States at the Mississippi River. Britain promised as well that U.S. fishermen would have the right to fish the waters off Newfoundland and that British forces would evacuate American territory "with all convenient speed" once hostilities had ended. In return, the Congress would recommend that the states restore the civil rights and property of the Loyalists. Both sides agreed that prewar debts owed the citizens of one country by the citizens of the other would remain valid. Each of these issues would trouble Anglo-American relations in the years ahead, but for the moment it seemed a splendid outcome to a long and difficult struggle.

The Ingredients of Victory

In spite of English fears and congressional hopes, only half of Britain's New World colonies (13 out of 26) joined the rebellion against British authority. Congressional efforts to enlist Canadian support foundered because the colony, given its strategic location at the western end of the North Atlantic sea routes, had become a center of British military force. The colony's French Catholic majority, moreover, harbored vivid memories of bitter conflicts during the Seven Years' War with England's Protestant colonists to the south.

Hoping to weaken England and gain access to crucial trade goods, Congress made overtures as well to white planters on Jamaica, Barbados, and other British sugar islands in the Caribbean. But a variety of circumstances argued for their continuing loyalty to England. Given the planters' close social and cultural ties with London, many were only temporary "sojourners" on the islands rather than permanent residents. In addition, the islands' sugar economies were heavily dependent on British markets and sources of capital, as well as on British military force for protection against Spanish and Dutch raiders and the slave majorities in their midst. Congressional non-importation and non-exportation policies, moreover, threatened to cut off supplies of North American foodstuffs critical to maintaining slave populations, while reports that slavery was being questioned in some of the rebelling colonies struck fear into planters' hearts.

Canada's loyalty meant that it could continue to serve as a convenient staging area for British supply, as well as a threatened point of invasion from the north. And although Britain was forced to defend its Caribbean colonies against French and Dutch attack, the absence of rebellion there meant that British military resources could be concentrated in North America.

Even without the support of Canada and the Caribbean islands, the 13 weak and disunited North American states were able to defeat Great Britain, the most powerful nation in the Atlantic world. How was that so? Certainly Dutch loans and French military resources, were crucially important. At the height of the war, France fielded a force of more than 10,000 men in North America.

More decisive, though, was the American people's determination not to submit. Often the Americans were disorganized and uncooperative. Repeatedly, the war effort seemed about to collapse as continental troops drifted away, state militias refused to march, and supplies failed to materialize. Neither Congress nor the states proved capable of providing consistent direction to the struggle. Yet as the war progressed, the people's estrangement from England deepened and their commitment to the "glorious cause" grew stronger. To subdue the colonies, England would have had to occupy the entire eastern third of the continent, and that it could not do.

Even though state militias frequently refused to go beyond their own borders and after the first months of the war engaged in relatively few battles, they provided a vast reservoir of manpower capable of intimidating Loyalists, gathering intelligence, and harassing British forces that would otherwise have been free to engage the continental army. And though Washington frequently disparaged the militia's fighting qualities, he gradually learned to utilize them in the war effort.

The American victory owed much as well to Washington's administrative and organizational talents. Against massive odds, often by the sheer force of his will, he held the continental army together

John Jay, John Adams, and Benjamin Franklin (the three figures on the left in the unfinished painting by Benjamin West) meet with the British commissioners in Paris to negotiate preliminary conditions of peace in 1783. *(Benjamin West,* Commissioners of the Preliminary Peace Negotiations with Great Britain, *c. 1783/Courtesy, The Henry Francis du Pont Winterthur Museum)*

and created a military force capable of winning selected encounters and surviving over time. Had he failed, the Americans could not possibly have won.

In the end, however, it is as accurate to say that Britain lost the war as that the United States won it. With vast economic and military resources, Britain enjoyed clear military superiority over the Americans. Its troops were more numerous, better armed and supplied, and more professional. Until the closing months of the contest, Britain enjoyed naval superiority as well, enabling its forces to move up and down the coast virtually at will.

Britain, however, could not capitalize on its advantages. It had difficulty extending its command structures and supply routes across several thousand miles of ocean. Because information flowed erratically across the water, strategic decisions made in London were often based on faulty or outdated intelligence. Given the difficulties of supply, British troops often had to live off the land, thus reducing their mobility and increasing the resentment of Americans whose crops and animals they commandeered.

Faced with these circumstances, British leaders were often overly cautious. Burgoyne's attempt in 1777 to isolate New England by invading from Canada failed because Sir William Howe decided to attack Philadelphia rather than move northward up the Hudson River to join him. Similarly, neither Howe nor Cornwallis pressed his advantage in the central states during the middle years of the war, when more aggressive action might have crushed the continentals.

Just as important, British commanders generally failed to adapt European battlefield tactics to the realities of the American war. They were willing to fight only during specified times of the year and used formal battlefield maneuvers, even though the wooded American terrain was better suited to the use of smaller units and irregular tactics.

Washington and Greene were more flexible, often employing a patient strategy of raiding, harassment, and strategic retreat. Behind this strategy lay a willingness, grounded partly in necessity, to allow England control of territory along the coast. But it was based as well on the conviction that popular support for the revolutionary cause would grow and that the costs of subduing the colonial rebellion would become greater than the British government could bear. As a much later American war in Vietnam would also reveal, a guerrilla force can win if it does not lose, while a regular army loses if it does not consistently win.

The American strategy proved sound. As the war dragged on and its costs escalated, Britain's will began to waver. After France and Spain entered the conflict, Britain had to worry about Europe, the

Caribbean, and the Mediterranean as well as North America, while unrest in Ireland and food riots in London tied down additional English troops. As the cost in money and lives increased and prospects of victory dimmed, opposition to the war mounted. It was spearheaded by long-time critics of imperial policy such as Edmund Burke and given popular voice by the followers of John Wilkes and other English radicals who saw in America's rebellion the promise of political reform at home. With the defeat at Yorktown, support for the war collapsed. Britain's effort to hold onto its 13 North American colonies had failed.

The war of American independence, Britain's longest colonial conflict of the modern era, left its mark on England in ways beyond the loss of her North American colonies. Contested not only in North America but in India, the Mediterranean, West Africa, and the Caribbean as well, the war required the mobilization of military forces (nearly 400,000 fighting men by 1782) and the levying of taxes on a scale that decisively strengthened the central government—as major wars always do. The mingling of officers and recruits from every class and area of the realm, moreover, helped fashion a stronger sense of British identity.

At the same time, the government's American policy generated intense criticism concerning the justice and necessity of the conflict among a radical coalition of London tradesmen, professionals, and reformist politicians. And although such criticism was often harshly suppressed once the fighting began, charges of ministerial despotism and parliamentary corruption fed into calls for parliamentary reform. Meaningful political reform would not begin for another half century, but the arguments of late-eighteenth-century radicals helped lay the essential groundwork.

Though Britain's empire was severely shaken by the events of 1776–1783, it survived and would expand to truly global dimensions in the following century. Still, the loss of the immensely valuable North American colonies weakened the empire in the short run and brought the adoption of harsher, more centralized forms of imperial control.

THE EXPERIENCE OF WAR

In terms of loss of life and destruction of property, the Revolutionary War pales by comparison with America's more recent wars. Yet modern comparisons are misleading, for the War of American Independence proved terrifying to the people caught up in it.

Recruiting an Army

Estimates vary, but on the American side as many as 250,000 men may at one time or another have borne arms. That amounted to one out of every two or three adult white males. Though a majority of recruits were native born, many who fought for American freedom came from the thousands of

This watercolor painting offers a humorous, even mocking, depiction of the variety of uniforms worn by American troops. (*Anne S. K. Brown Military Collection, Brown University*)

As this painting suggests, military recruiting was a community affair in the eighteenth century. What do you suppose the man with upraised arms is doing? What role might the women be playing in the recruitment process? *(William T. Ranney & Charles F. Blauvelt, Recruiting for the Continental Army, c. 1857–59, oil on canvas, 533 ¾ × 82 ¼ in, Munson-Williams-Proctor Institute, Museum of Art, Utica, New York, Gift of T. Proctor Eldred)*

British and European immigrants who streamed into North America during the middle decades of the eighteenth century. Of the 27 men enrolled in Captain John Wendell's New York company, for example, more than half had been born abroad, the majority in Ireland but others in Germany and the Netherlands. And while the motives of these men were as various as those of native born soldiers, many had come to America seeking to better their lives and eagerly embraced the Revolution's democratic promise. They were the vanguard of a transatlantic political network that, over the late eighteenth and early nineteenth centuries, would link the American republic to English reformers and French radicals during the age of democratic revolutions.

As the war began, most state militias were not effective fighting forces. This was especially true in the South, where Nathanael Greene complained that the men "came from home with all the tender feelings of domestic life" and were not "sufficiently fortified . . . to stand the shocking scenes of war, to march over dead men, [or] to hear without concern the groans of the wounded." The militia did serve as a convenient recruiting system, for men were already enrolled, and arrangements were in place for calling them into the field on short notice. This was of special importance before the continental army took shape. Given its grounding in local community life, the militia also legitimated the war among the people and secured their commitment to the revolutionary cause. And what better way to separate Patriots from Loyalists than by mustering the local company and seeing who turned out?

During the early years of the war, when enthusiasm ran high, men of all ranks—from the rich and middle classes as well as the poor—volunteered to fight the British. But as the war went on, casualties increased, enlistment terms grew longer, military discipline became more harsh, and the army filled with conscripts. Eventually, the war was transformed, as wars so often are, into a poor man's fight as wealthier men hired substitutes, communities filled their quotas with strangers lured by enlistment bonuses, and state laws subjected "vagrants" and men with "no family . . . or visible means of support" to impressment. Convicts, out-of-work laborers, free and unfree blacks, even British deserters filled the continental army with an array of "Tag, Rag, and Bobtail" soldiers.

For the poor and the jobless, whose ranks the war rapidly swelled, military bonuses and the promise of board and keep proved attractive. But often the bonuses failed to materialize, and pay was long overdue. Moreover, life in the camps was harsh, and soldiers frequently heard from home of their families' distress. As the war dragged on and desertion rates rose as high as 25 percent, Washington imposed harsher discipline in an effort to hold his troops in line.

Occasionally, frustration spilled over into open revolt. In 1779, Sergeant Samuel Glover and a group of soldiers from the North Carolina line, who had been unpaid for 15 months, refused to obey the commands of their superior officer "until they had justice done them." Glover was executed for insubordination. His widow later apologized to the North

Carolina assembly for her husband's conduct but asked sorrowfully, "What must the feeling of the man be who . . . with poverty staring him full in the face, was denied his pay?"

Throughout the war, soldiers suffered from shortages of supplies. At Valley Forge during the terrible winter of 1777–1778, men went without shoes or coats. In the midst of that winter's gloom, Washington wrote, "There are now in this army 4,000 men wanting blankets, near 2,000 of which have never had one, altho' some of them have been 12 months in service." Declared one despairing soul, "I am sick, discontented, and out of humour. Poor food, hard lodging, cold weather, fatigue, nasty cloathes, nasty cookery, vomit half my time, smoaked out of my senses. The Devil's in't, I can't Endure it. Why are we sent here to starve and freeze?"

The states possessed food and clothing enough, but state assemblies were often reluctant to strip their own people of wagons, blankets, and shoes for use elsewhere. Moreover, mismanagement often stood in the way. Neither the state governments nor the Congress could effectively administer a war of such magnitude. Wagon transport was slow and costly, and the British fleet made coastal travel perilous. Though many individuals served honorably as supply officers, others exploited the army's distress. Washington commented bitterly on the "speculators, various tribes of money makers, and stock-jobbers" whose "avarice and thirst for gain" threatened the country's ruin.

Swarms of camp followers further complicated army life. Wives and prostitutes, personal servants and slaves, con men and sutlers swarmed around the continental army camps. While often providing essential services, they slowed the army's movement and threatened its discipline.

The Casualties of Combat

The death that soldiers dispensed to each other on the battlefield was intensely personal. Because the effective range of muskets was little more than 100 yards, soldiers came virtually face-to-face with the men they killed. According to eighteenth-century practice, armies formed on the battlefield in ranks and fired in unison. After massed volleys, the lines often closed for hand-to-hand combat with knives and bayonets. Such encounters were indelibly etched in the memory of individuals who survived them. Partisan warfare in the South, with its emphasis on ambush and cyclic patterns of revenge, personalized combat even more.

British officers expressed shock at the "implacable ardor" with which the Americans fought. The Americans' ferocity is attributable in part to the fact that this was a civil war. Not only did Englishmen fight Americans, but American Loyalists and Patriots fought each other as well. As many as 50,000 colonists fought for the king in some of the war's most bitter encounters. They figured importantly in Burgoyne's invasion from Canada and in the attacks on Savannah and Charleston. Loyalist militia units joined Indian allies in destructive sweeps through central New York, Pennsylvania, and the backcountry of the Carolinas. "The rage of civil discord," lamented one individual, "hath advanced among us with an astonishing rapidity. The son is armed against the father, the brother against the brother, family against family."

The passion with which American Patriots fought derived as well from their belief that the very future of human liberty depended on their success. In such a historic crusade, nothing was to be spared that might bring victory.

Medical treatment, whether for wounds or the diseases that raged through military camps, frequently did more harm than good. Casualties poured into hospitals, overcrowding them beyond capacity. Dr. Jonathan Potts, the attending physician at Fort George in New York, reported that "we have at present upwards of one thousand sick crowded into sheds & labouring under the various and cruel disorders of dysentaries, bilious putrid fevers and the effects of a confluent smallpox. . . ." The entire medical staff consisted of "four seniors and four mates" in addition to Potts himself.

Surgeons, operating without anesthetics and with the crudest of instruments, threatened life as often as they preserved it. Few understood the causes or proper treatment of infection. Doctoring consisted mostly of bleeding, blistering, and vomiting (which was "deemed of excellent use, by opening and squeezing all the glands of the body, & then shaking from the nervous system, the contaminating poison"). One doctor reported that "we lost no less than from 10 to 20 of camp diseases, for one by weapons of the enemy."

No one kept accurate records of how many soldiers died, but the most conservative estimate runs to over 25,000, a higher percentage of the total population than for any other American conflict except the Civil War. For Revolutionary War soldiers, death was an imminent reality.

Civilians and the War

While the experience of war varied from place to place depending on people's proximity to battle, vulnerability to economic disruption, and racial and

Military Muster Rolls

In almost all of America's wars, patriotism has run high and bombastic rhetoric has inspired citizens to arms. The American Revolutionary War was no exception. But people fought for other than patriotic reasons, as the account of "Long Bill" Scott makes clear. It is always difficult to assess human motivations in something as complex as war. If we knew which Americans bore arms, however, it would help us understand why people fought and perhaps even understand what the war meant to them.

As we see in this chapter, the social composition of the revolutionary army changed markedly as the war went along. At the beginning, men from all walks of life and every class fought in defense of American liberty. Within a short time, however, that began to change. As the war lengthened and its costs increased, men who could afford to do so hired substitutes or arranged to go home, whereas men of less wealth and influence increasingly carried the burden of fighting. Many of them did so out of choice, for the army promised adventure, an escape from the tedium of daily life, a way to make a living, and even, as for "Long Bill" Scott, the chance to rise in the world. And so thousands of poorer men hired out to defend American liberty. Such a decision, of course, was more attractive to them because other opportunities were limited.

Enlistment lists of the continental army and the state militias offer one important source for studying the social history of the Revolutionary War. Although eighteenth-century records are imperfect by modern standards, recruiting officers did keep track of the men they signed up so that bounties and wages could be paid accurately. These lists usually give the recruit's name, age, occupation, place of birth, residence, and length of service.

Such lists exist for some of America's earliest wars. The muster rolls for New York City and Philadelphia during the Seven Years' War, for example, show that these two cities contributed 300 and 180 men per year, respectively, to the war effort. Most of the enlistees in that earlier war were immigrants—about 90 percent of New York's recruits and about 75 percent of Philadelphia's. Their occupations—mariner, laborer, shoemaker, weaver, tailor—indicate that they came primarily from the lowest ranks of the working class. Many were former indentured servants and many others were servants running away from their masters to answer the recruiting sergeant's drum. In these Middle Atlantic port towns, successful, American-born artisans left the bloody work of bearing arms against the French to those beneath them on the social ladder. Enlistment lists for Boston, however, reveal that soldiers from that city were drawn from higher social classes.

A comparison of the Revolutionary War muster rolls from different towns and regions provides a view of the social composition of the revolutionary army and how it changed over time. It also offers clues to social conditions in different regions during the war and how they might have affected military recruitment.

The lists shown here of Captain Wendell's and Captain White's companies from New York and Virginia give "social facts" on 81 men. What kind of group portrait can you draw from the data? Some occupations, such as tanner, cord-wainer, and chandler, may be unfamiliar, but they are defined in standard dictionaries. How many of the recruits come from middling occupations (bookkeeper, tobacconist, shopkeeper, and the like)? How many are skilled artisans? How many are unskilled laborers? What proportions are foreign and native-born? Analyze the ages of the recruits. What does that tell you about the kind of fighting force that was assembled? How do the New York and Virginia companies differ in terms of these social categories and occupations? How would you explain these differences?

To extract the full meaning of the soldiers' profile, you would have to learn more about the economic and social conditions prevailing in the communities from which these men are drawn. But already you have glimpsed how social historians are trying to go beyond the history of military strategy, tactics, and battles to understand the "internal" social history of the Revolutionary War.

Reflecting on the Past How would social historians describe and analyze more recent American wars? What would a social profile of soldiers who fought in Vietnam or Afghanistan, including their age, region, race, class, extent of education, and other differences, suggest to a social historian of these wars?

New York Line—1st Regiment

Captain John H. Wendell's Company, 1776–1777

Men's Names	Age	Occupation	Place of Birth	Place of Abode
Abraham Defreest	22	Yeoman	N. York	Claverack
Benjamin Goodales	20	do [ditto]	Nobletown	do
Hendrick Carman	24	do	Rynbeck	East Camp
Nathaniel Reed	32	Carpenter	Norwalk	Westchester
Jacob Crolrin	29	do	Germany	Bever Dam
James White	25	Weaver	Ireland	Rynbveck
Joseph Battina	39	Coppersmith	Ireland	Florida
John Wyatt	38	Carpenter	Maryland	
Jacob Reyning	25	Yeoman	Amsterdam	Albany
Patrick Kannely	36	Barber	Ireland	N. York
John Russell	29	Penman	Ireland	N. York
Patrick McCue	19	Tanner	Ireland	Scholary
James J. Atkson	21	Weaver	do	Stillwater
William Burke	23	Chandler	Ireland	N. York
Wm Miller	42	Yeoman	Scotland	Claverack
Ephraim H. Blancherd	18	Yeoman	Ireland	White Creek
Francis Acklin	40	Cordwainer	Ireland	Claverack
William Orr	29	Cordwainer	Ireland	Albany
Thomas Welch	31	Labourer	N. York	Norman's Kill
Peter Gasper	24	Labourer	N. Jersey	Greenbush
Martins Rees	19	Labourer	Fishkill	Flatts
Henck Able	24	do	Albany	Flatts
Daniel Spinnie	21	do	Portsmouth	
Patrick Kelly	23	Labourer	Ireland	Claverack
Richd James Barker	12	do	America	Rynbeck
John Patrick Cronkite	11			Claverack
William Dougherty	17		Donyal, Ireland	Sch^ty

Virginia Line—6th Regiment

Captain Tarpley White's Company, December 13th, 1780

Name	Age	Trade	Where Born — State or Country	Where Born — Town or County	Place of Residence — State or Country	Place of Residence — Town or County
Win Bails, Serjt	25	Baker	England	Burningham	Virg.	Leesburg
Arthur Harrup"	24	Carpenter	Virg.	Southampton	"	Brunswick
Charles Caffatey"	19	Planter	"	Caroline	"	Caroline
Elisha Osborn"	24	Planter	New Jersey	Trenton	"	Loudon
Benj Allday	19	"	Virg.	Henrico	"	Pawhatan
Wm Edwards Senr	25	"	"	Northumberland	"	Northumberland
James Hutcherson	17	Hatter	Jersey	Middlesex	"	P.Williams
Robert Low	31	Planter	"	Powhatan	"	Powhatan
Cannon Row	18	Planter	Virg.	Hanover	Virg.	Louisa
Wardon Pulley	18	"	"	Southampton	"	Hallifax
Richd Bond	29	Stone Mason	England	Cornwell	"	Orange
Tho Homont	17	Planter	Virg.	Loudon	"	Loudon
Tho Pope	19	Planter	"	Southampton	"	Southampton
Tho Morris	22	Planter	"	Orange	"	Orange
Littlebury Overby	24	Hatter	"	Dinwiddie	"	Brunswick
James [Pierce]	27	Planter	"	Nansemond	"	Nansemond
Joel Counsil	19	Planter	"	Southampton	"	Southampton
Elisha Walden	18	Planter	"	P.William	"	P.William
Wm Bush	19	S Carpenter	Virg.	Gloucester	Virg.	Glocester
Daniel Horton	22	Carpenter	"	Nansemond	"	Nansemond
John Soons	25	Weaver	England	Norfolk	"	Loudon
Mara Lumkin	18	Planter	Virg.	Amelia	"	Amelia
Wm Wetherford	27	Planter	"	Goochland	"	Lunenburg
John Bird	16	Planter	"	Southampton	"	Southampton
Tho Parsmore	22	Planter	England	London	"	Fairfax
Josiah Banks	27	Planter	Virg.	Gloucester	"	Gloucester
Richd Roach	28	Planter	England	London	"	Culpeper
Joseph Holburt	33	Tailor	"	Middlesex	"	Federickb^g
Henry Willowby	19	Planter	Virg.	Spotsylvania	"	Spotsylvania
Thos Pearson	22	Planter		Pennsylvany	"	Loudon
Jno Scarborough	19	Planter	Virg.	Brunswick	"	"
Chas Thacker	21	Planter	"		"	"
Nehemiah Grining	20	Planter	Virg.	Albemarle	Virg.	Albemarle
Ewing David	19	Planter	"	King W^m	"	Brunswick
Isaiah Ballance	17	Shoemaker	"	Norfolk	"	Norfolk
Wm Alexander	20	Planter	Virg.	Northumbl^d	Virg.	Northumbl^d
Wm Harden	26	Planter	"	Albemarle	"	Albemarle
John Ward	20	Sailor	England	Bristol	"	Northumbl^d
Daniel Cox	19	Planter	Virg.	Sussex	"	Sussex
George Kirk	21	Planter	"	Brunswick	"	Brunswick
John Nash	19	Planter	"	Northumbl^d	"	Northumbl^d
Wm Edward, Jr.	19	Planter	"	Northumbl^d	"	Albemarle
John Fry	20	Turner	"	Albemarle	"	"
Jno Grinning	25	Hatter	"	Albemarle	"	
Daniel Howell	30	Planter	"	Loudon	"	Loudon
Milden Green	25	Planter	"	Sussex	"	Sussex
Matthias Cane	32	Planter	"	Norfolk	"	Norfolk
Wm Mayo	21	Joiner	"	Dinwiddie	"	Dinwiddie
Jas Morgan	25	Shoemaker	England	Shropshire	"	Stafford
Mathew Catson	19	Planter	Pennsylvania	York	"	Berkly
Wm B[rown]	22	Planter		"		
Richd Loyd	42	Planter	Virg.	Surry	Virg.	Surry
Abram Foress	33	Planter	"	Gloster	Virg.	Gloster
Wm White	19	Planter	"	"	"	Gloster

ethnic makeup, it touched the lives of virtually every American. Noncombatants experienced the realities of war most intensely in densely settled areas along the coast. The British concentrated their military efforts there, taking advantage of their naval power and striking at the political and economic centers of American life. At one time or another, British troops occupied every major port city: Boston for a year at the war's start, New York from 1777 to 1783, Philadelphia over the winter and spring of 1777–1778, Charleston in 1780–1781, and Savannah two years earlier.

The disruptions of urban life were profound. In September 1776, a fire consumed 500 houses, nearly a quarter of the dwellings in New York City. About half the town's inhabitants fled when the British occupation began and were replaced by an equal number of Loyalists who streamed in from the surrounding countryside. Ten thousand British and German troops added to the crowding. Makeshift shelters of sailcloth and timber, patched together by the growing number of the poor, stretched along Broadway. An American officer somberly reported what he found as his troops entered New York at the war's end: "Close on the eve of an approaching winter, with an heterogeneous set of inhabitants, composed of almost ruined exiles, disbanded soldiery, mixed foreigners, disaffected Tories, and the refuse of the British army, we took possession of a ruined city."

In Philadelphia, the occupation was shorter and the disruptions were less severe, but the shock of invasion was no less real. Elizabeth Drinker, living alone after local Patriots had exiled her Quaker husband, found herself the unwilling landlady of a British officer and his friends. Though the officer's presence may have protected her from the plundering that went on all around, she was constantly anxious, confiding to her journal that "I often feel afraid to go to Bed." During the occupation, British soldiers frequently tore down fences for their campfires and confiscated food to supplement their own tedious fare. Even Loyalists complained of the "dreadful consequences" of British occupation.

Along the entire coastal plain, British landing parties descended without warning, seizing supplies and terrorizing inhabitants. In 1780 and 1781, the British mounted punishing attacks along the Connecticut coast. Over 200 buildings in Fairfield were burned, and much of nearby Norwalk was destroyed. The southern coast, with its broad, navigable rivers, was even more vulnerable. In December 1780, Benedict Arnold, the American traitor who was by then fighting for the British, ravaged

In September 1776, as American troops fought unsuccessfully for control of New York, nearly a quarter of the city was destroyed by a fire apparently set by a defiant Patriot woman. Not until the war ended did cleanup of the ruins and reconstruction of the city begin. *(Library of Congress)*

Virginia's James River valley, uprooting tobacco, confiscating slaves, and creating panic among whites. Similar devastation befell the coastal regions of Georgia and the Carolinas.

Such punishing attacks sent civilians fleeing into the interior. During the first years of the war, the port cities lost nearly half their population, while inland communities struggled to cope with the thousands of refugees who streamed into them. So many Bostonians crowded into Concord, Massachusetts, by July 1775 that they decided to hold a town meeting there. By March 1776, Concord's population had expanded by 25 percent, creating problems of housing, social order, and public health.

Not all refugee traffic moved inland, away from the coast. Settlers from the interior fled eastward for safety as Loyalist rangers and their Indian allies fought Patriot militias in a violent, often chaotic struggle. By 1783, the white population along the Mohawk River west of Albany, New York, had declined from 10,000 to 3,500. According to one observer, after nearly five years of warfare in Tryon County, 12,000 farms had been abandoned, 700 buildings burned, thousands of bushels of grain destroyed, nearly 400 women widowed, and perhaps 2,000 children orphaned. Similar disasters unfolded up and down the backcountry from Maine to Georgia.

As they moved across the countryside, the armies lived off the land, taking what they needed. In an effort to protect the surrounding population during the desperate winter of 1777–1778, Washington prohibited his troops from roaming more than a half mile from camp. In New Jersey, Britain's German mercenaries raised additional fears, particularly among women. A committee of the Congress, taking affidavits from women in April 1777, reported that it had "authentic information of many instances of the most indecent treatment, and actual ravishment of married and single women." Such was the nature of that "most irreparable injury," however, that the persons suffering it, "though perfectly innocent, look upon it as a kind of reproach to have the facts related and their names known." Whether the report had any effect is unknown.

Wherever the armies went, they generated a swirl of refugees, who spread vivid tales of the war's devastation. This refugee traffic, together with the constant movement of soldiers between army and civilian life, brought the war home to countless people who did not experience it first hand. Moreover, disease followed the armies like an avenging angel, ravaging soldiers and civilians alike.

Smallpox proved the most deadly pathogen. During the 1770s and 1780s, a smallpox epidemic,

global in its fullest dimensions, surged across Mexico and North America. Driven by the movement of people and exchange of trade goods, the disease wreaked its devastating effects from the Atlantic coast to the Pacific, and from the Southwest across the Rockies and Great Plains to Hudson's Bay in Canada.

The human toll is impossible to measure exactly, but before it was spent the virus appears to have killed more than 130,000 people and maimed countless more—Indians and Englishmen, African- and European-Americans among them. By comparison, just over 25,000 continental soldiers died during the same years. Because a crash program of inoculation launched by Washington in 1777 (the first large-scale immunization program in American history) protected the continental army, and because many English troops (in addition to the large number of foreign-born continental soldiers) carried immunity from earlier exposure to the disease at home, the plague did not significantly affect the war's outcome. Still, it took a terrible toll virtually everywhere—throughout New England and the mid-Atlantic states where it was spread by returning soldiers; on Britain's disease-infested prison ships; among thousands of black Loyalists in the Chesapeake region; across wide areas of the South where partisan warfare spread the disease in epidemic fashion; in the backcountry where the virus raced through Indian populations, reducing their capacity to resist the rebels; and beyond the Mississippi, where agricultural tribes such as the Mandans, Hidatsas, and Arikaras were virtually wiped out, leaving them prey to Sioux marauders from the east. The pox, declared one observer gloomily, "spread its destructive and desolating power, as the fire consumes the dry grass of the field."

The Loyalists

Among the Americans suffering losses were those who remained loyal to the Crown. Though many Loyalist émigrés established successful lives in England, the Maritime Provinces of Canada, and the British West Indies, others found the uprooting an ordeal from which they never recovered. On September 8, 1783, Thomas Danforth, formerly a prosperous lawyer from Cambridge, Massachusetts, appeared in London before the official commission appointed to receive Loyalist claims. In explaining the consequences of his loyalty, Danforth declared that after devoting his whole life to "preparing himself for future usefulness," he was now "near his fortieth year, banished under pain of death, to a distant country, where he has not the most remote family connection . . . cut off from his profession, from every hope of importance in life." Without assistance he would sink to "a station much inferior to that of a menial servant," his financial affairs in disarray, his future uncertain. Many of the several thousand Loyalists who appeared before the king's commission gained partial reimbursement for their losses, though it proved meager compensation for the loss of house and property, expulsion from their communities, and relocation in a distant land. The vast majority of Loyalists never had the opportunity to make their case before the commission, and thus secured nothing.

Although we do not know how many colonists remained loyal to England, tens of thousands evacuated with British troops from New York, Charleston, and Savannah at the end of the war. At least as many slipped away to England, Canada, or the West Indies while fighting was still underway. Additional thousands who wished the Revolution had never occurred stayed on in the new nation, struggling to rebuild their lives. The incidence of loyalism dif-

Loyalists, or "Tories," as the Patriots called them, often suffered the indignities of tarring, feathering, and public humiliation for their loyalty to England. *(Corbis-Bettmann)*

fered from region to region. Loyalists were fewest in New England and most numerous around New York City, where British authority was most stable.

Many Patriots were determined to exact revenge against those who had rejected the revolutionary cause. In each state, revolutionary assemblies enacted laws depriving Loyalists of the vote, confiscating their property, and banishing them from their homes. In 1778, the Georgia assembly declared 117 persons guilty of treason, expelled them from the state on pain of death, and declared their possessions forfeit. Two years earlier, the Connecticut assembly had passed a remarkably punitive law threatening anyone who criticized either the assembly or the Continental Congress with immediate fine and imprisonment. Probably not more than a few dozen Loyalists actually died at the hands of the revolutionary regimes, but thousands found their livelihoods destroyed, their families ostracized, and themselves subject to physical attack.

Punishing Loyalists—or people accused of loyalism, a distinction that was often unclear in the confusion of the times—was politically popular. Most Patriots argued that such "traitors" had put themselves outside the protection of American law. Others, however, argued that republics were intended to be "governments of law and not of men" and worried that no one's rights would be safe when the rights of any were disregarded. No other wartime issue raised so starkly the nettlesome question of balancing individual liberty against the requirements of public security. That issue would return to trouble the nation in the years ahead.

Why did so many Americans remain loyal, often at the cost of personal danger and loss? Customs officers, members of the governors' councils, and Anglican clergy often remained with the king who had appointed them. Loyalism was common as well among groups specially dependent on British authority—for example, settlers on the Carolina frontier who believed themselves mistreated by the planter elite along the coast, and ethnic Germans in the middle states who feared domination by the Anglo-American majority. Other Loyalists made their choice because they believed it futile to oppose English power and doubted that independence could be won.

Still others based their loyalism on principle, as Samuel Seabury made clear. "Every person owes obedience to the laws of the government," he insisted, "and is obliged in honour and duty to support them. Because if one has a right to disregard the laws of the society to which he belongs, all have the same right; and then government is at an end." William Eddis worried about the kind of society independence would bring when revolutionary crowds showed no respect for the rights of Loyalist dissenters such as he. "If I differ in opinion from the multitude," he asked, "must I therefore be deprived of my character, and the confidence of my fellow-citizens; when in every station of life I discharge my duty with fidelity and honour?" Loyalists such as Eddis and Seabury claimed to be upholding reason and the rule of law against revolutionary disorder. Their loss to American society weakened the forces of conservatism in America and facilitated revolutionary change.

African Americans and the War

The revolution caught up thousands of American blacks in its toils. In the northern states, both free and enslaved blacks were enlisted in support of the revolutionary cause. In the South, nearly 400,000 slaves constituted a vast and uncertain force, viewed by the British as a resource to be exploited and by southern whites as a source of vulnerability and danger. Sizing up the opportunities provided by the war's confusion, southern blacks struck out for their own freedom by seeking liberty behind English lines, journeying to the north, or fleeing to mixed-race settlements in the interior. Before the war was over, it generated the largest slave rebellion in American history prior to the Civil War.

Hearing their masters' talk about liberty, growing numbers of black Americans questioned their own oppression. In the North, slaves petitioned state legislatures for their freedom, while in the South, pockets of insurrection appeared. In 1765, more than 100 South Carolina slaves, most of them young men in their 20s and 30s, fled their plantations. The next year, slaves paraded through the streets of Charleston chanting, "Liberty, liberty!"

In November 1775, Lord Dunmore, Virginia's royal governor, issued a proclamation offering freedom to all slaves and servants, "able and willing to bear arms," who would leave their masters and join the British forces at Norfolk. Within weeks, 500 to 600 slaves responded.

Among them was Thomas Peters. Kidnapped from the Yoruba tribe in what is now Nigeria and brought to Louisiana by a French slave trader in 1760, Peters resisted enslavement so fiercely that his master sold him into the English colonies. By 1770, Peters was toiling on the plantation of William Campbell, an immigrant Scots planter, on the Cape Fear River, near Wilmington, North Carolina.

Peters's plans for his own declaration of independence may have ripened as a result of the rhetoric of liberty he heard around his master's house, for

James Armistead Lafayette, a Virginia slave, served as a spy against the British for the French general Lafayette. In recognition of his service, the Virginia General Assembly granted him his freedom in 1786. (Valentine Museum, Richmond, VA)

William Campbell was a leading member of Wilmington's Sons of Liberty and talked enthusiastically about inalienable rights. By mid-1775, the Cape Fear region, like many areas of the coastal South, buzzed with rumors of slave uprisings. After the British commander of Fort Johnston encouraged Negroes to "elope from their masters," the state assembly banned the importation of new slaves, dispatched patrols to disarm all blacks, and imposed martial law. When 20 British ships entered the Cape Fear River in March 1776 and disembarked royal troops, Peters seized the moment to redefine himself as a man, instead of William Campbell's property, and escaped. Before long, he would fight with the British-officered Black Pioneers.

How many African Americans sought liberty behind British lines is unknown, but as many as 20 percent may have done so. Unlike their white masters, blacks saw in England the promise of freedom, not tyranny. As the war dragged on, English commanders pressed blacks into service. A regiment of black soldiers, formed from Virginia slaves who responded to Dunmore's proclamation, marched into battle, their chests covered by sashes emblazoned with the slogan "Liberty to Slaves."

Some of the blacks who joined England achieved their freedom. At the war's end, several thousand were evacuated with the British to Nova Scotia. Their reception by the white inhabitants, however, was generally hostile. By 1800, most had left Canada to settle in the free black colony of Sierra Leone in West Africa. Thomas Peters was a leader among them.

Many of the slaves who fled behind British lines, however, never won their freedom. Under the terms of the peace treaty, hundreds were returned to their American owners. Several thousand others, their value as field hands too great to be ignored, were transported to harsher slavery on West Indian sugar plantations. England was not intent on abolishing slavery.

Other blacks took advantage of the war's confusion to flee. Some went north, following rumors that slavery had been abolished there. Others sought refuge among Indians in the southern interior. The Seminoles of Georgia and Florida generally welcomed black runaways and through intermarriage absorbed them into tribal society. Blacks met a more uncertain reception from the Cherokee and Creek. While some were taken in, others were returned to their white owners for bounties, and still others were held in slavelike conditions by new Indian masters.

Fewer blacks fought on the American side than on England's, in part because neither the Congress nor the states were eager to see them armed. Faced with the increasing need for troops, however, the Congress and each of the states except Georgia and South Carolina eventually relented and pressed blacks into service. Of those who served the Patriot cause, many received the freedom they were promised. The patriotism of countless others, however, went unrewarded.

THE FERMENT OF REVOLUTIONARY POLITICS

The Revolution altered people's lives in countless ways that reached beyond the sights and sounds of battle. No areas of American life were more powerfully changed than politics and government. Who would have a voice in revolutionary politics, and who would be excluded? How vigorously would notions of political equality be pursued, or how tenaciously would people cling to the more traditional belief that citizens should defer to their political leaders? And how would the new state governments balance the need for order and the security of property against demands for democratic openness and accountability? These were some of the explosive questions that had to be addressed. Seldom has American politics been more heated; seldom has it struggled with more daunting problems than at the nation's founding.

Mobilizing the People

Under the pressure of revolutionary events, politics absorbed people's energies as never before. The politicization of American society was evident in the flood of printed material that streamed from American presses. Newspapers multiplied and pamphlets by the thousands fanned political debate. Declared one contemporary in amazement, it was

a spectacle . . . without a parallel on earth. . . . Even a large portion of that class of the community which is destined to daily labor have free and constant access to public prints, receive regular information of every occurrence, [and] attend to the course of political affairs. Never were political writings so cheap, so universally diffused, so easy of access.

Pulpits rocked with political exhortations as well. Religion and politics had never been sharply separated in colonial America, but the Revolution drew them more tightly together. Some believed that God had designated revolutionary America as the place of Christ's Second Coming and that independence foretold that glorious day. Others of a less millennial persuasion thought of America as a "New Israel"—a covenanted people specially chosen by God to preserve liberty in a threatening world. Giving the metaphor a classical twist, Samuel Adams called on Bostonians to join in creating a "Christian Sparta."

In countless sermons, Congregational, Presbyterian, and Baptist clergy exhorted the American people to repent the sins that had brought English tyranny upon them and urged them to rededicate themselves to God's purposes by fighting for American freedom. It was language that people who were nurtured in Puritan piety and the Great Awakening instinctively understood.

The belief that God sanctioned their revolution strengthened Americans' resolve. It also encouraged them to identify their own interests with divine intent and thus offered convenient justification for whatever they believed necessary to do. This was not the last time Americans would make that dangerous equation.

By contrast, Loyalist clergy, such as Maryland's Jonathan Boucher, urged their parishioners to support the king as head of the Anglican church. During the months preceding independence, as the local Committee of Safety interrupted worship to harass him, Boucher carried a loaded pistol into the pulpit while he preached submission to royal authority.

Belief in the momentous importance of what they were doing increased the intensity of revolutionary politics. As independence was declared, people throughout the land raised toasts to the great event: "Liberty to those who have the spirit to preserve it," and "May Liberty expand sacred wings, and, in glorious effort, diffuse her influence o'er and o'er the globe." Inspired by the searing experience of

Ordinary men and women took to the streets in political rallies, such as this mock parade of 1780 in Philadelphia, in which Benedict Arnold, an American general who deserted to the British, was burned in effigy. Such rallies were filled with powerful symbols. *(American Antiquarian Society)*

rebellion, war, and nation building, Americans believed they held the future of human liberty in their hands. Small wonder that they took their politics so seriously.

The expanding array of extralegal crowds and committees that erupted during the 1770s and 1780s provided the most dramatic evidence of the people's new political commitment. Prior to independence, crowds had taken to the streets to protest measures like the Stamp Act. After 1776, direct political action increased as people gathered to administer roughhewn justice to Loyalists and, as one individual protested, even direct "what we shall eat, drink, wear, speak, and think."

Patriots of more radical temperament defended these activities as legitimate expressions of the popular will. More conservative republicans, however, worried that such behavior threatened political stability. Direct action by the people had been necessary in the struggle against England, but why such restlessness after the yoke of English tyranny had been thrown off? Even Thomas Paine expressed concern. "It is time to have done with tarring and feathering," he wrote in 1777. "I never did and never would encourage what may properly be called a mob, when any legal mode of redress can be had."

The expansion of popular politics resulted from an explosive combination of circumstances: the momentous events of revolution and war; the efforts of Patriot leaders to mobilize popular support for the struggle against England; and the determination of artisans, workingmen, farmers, and other

In celebration of American independence, Patriots and their slaves toppled the statue of King George III that stood at Bowling Green in New York City. *(Library of Congress)*

common folk to apply the principles of liberty to the conditions of their own lives.

A Republican Ideology

Throughout history, as people have moved from colonial subordination to independence, they have struggled to define their identities as free and separate nations. It was no different with the American Revolutionary generation. What did it mean to be no longer English, but American? "Our style and manner of thinking," observed Thomas Paine in amazement, "have undergone a revolution. . . . We see with other eyes, we hear with other ears, and think with other thoughts than those we formerly used." The ideology of revolutionary republicanism, pieced together from English political ideas, Enlightenment theories, and religious beliefs, constituted that revolution in thought (see Chapter 5). Many of its central tenets were broadly shared among the American people, but its larger meanings were sharply contested throughout the Revolutionary era.

In addition to the rejection of monarchy that Thomas Paine had so eloquently expressed in *Common Sense*, the American people also rejected the system of hierarchical authority on which monarchy was based, a system that promised the Crown's protection in return for obedience by the people. Under a republican system, by contrast, public authority was created by the people contracting together for their mutual good. In that fundamental change lay much of the American Revolution's radical promise.

Basic to republican belief as well was the notion that governmental power, when removed from the people's close oversight and control, threatened to expand at the expense of liberty. Recent experience with England had burned that lesson into people's consciousness. Although too much liberty could degenerate into political chaos, history seemed to demonstrate that trouble most often arose from too much government, not too little. "It is much easier to restrain the people from running into licentiousness," went a typical refrain, "than power from swelling into tyranny and oppression."

Given the need to limit governmental power, how could political order be maintained? The revolutionary generation offered an extraordinary answer to that question. Order was not to be imposed from above through traditional agencies of central control such as monarchies, standing armies, and state churches. In a republic, political discipline had to emerge from the self-regulated behavior of citizens, especially from their willingness to put the public good ahead of their private interests. In a republic, explained one pamphleteer, "each individ-

ual gives up all private interest that is not consistent with the general good." This radical principle of "public virtue" was an essential ingredient of republican belief.

By contrast, political "faction," or organized self-interest, was regarded as the "mortal disease" to which popular governments throughout history had succumbed. Given the absence in republics of a strong central government capable of imposing political order, factional conflict could easily spin out of control. This fear added to the intensity of political conflict in revolutionary America by encouraging people to attribute the worst motives to their opponents.

The idea of placing responsibility for political order with the people and counting on them to act selflessly for the good of the whole alarmed countless Americans, for what if the people proved unworthy? If the attempt was made, warned one individual darkly, "the bands of society would be dissolved, the harmony of the world confused, and the order of nature subverted." A strong incentive to loyalism lurked in such concerns.

Few Patriots were so naive as to believe that the American people were altogether virtuous. During the first years of independence, when revolutionary enthusiasm ran high, however, many believed that public virtue was sufficiently widespread to support republican government, while others argued that the American people would learn public virtue by its practice. The revolutionary struggle would serve as a "furnace of affliction," refining the American character as it strengthened people's capacity for virtuous behavior. It was an extraordinarily hopeful but risk-filled undertaking.

The principle of political equality was another controversial touchstone of republicanism. It was broadly assumed that republican governments must be grounded in popular consent, that elections should be frequent, and that citizens must be vigilant in defense of their liberties. But agreement often ended there.

Some Americans took the principle of political equality literally, arguing that every citizen should have an equal voice and that public office should be open to all. This position was most forcefully articulated by tenants and small farmers in the interior, as well as by workers and artisans in the coastal cities, who had long struggled to claim a political voice. More cautious citizens emphasized that individual liberty must be balanced by political order, arguing that stable republics required leadership by men of ability and experience, an "aristocracy of talent" that could give the people direction. Merchants, planters, and large commercial farmers who were used to providing such leadership saw no need for radical changes in the existing distribution of political power.

Forming New Governments

These differences of ideology and self-interest burst through the surface of American politics during the debates over new state constitutions. Fashioning new governments would not be easy, for the American people had no experience with government making on such a scale and had to undertake it in the midst of a disruptive war. In addition, there were sharp divisions over the kinds of governments they wished to create. One person thought it the "most difficult and dangerous business" that was to be done. Events proved those words prophetic.

Rather than create new systems of government, Connecticut and Rhode Island continued under their colonial charters, simply deleting all reference to the British Crown. The other 11 states, however, set their charters aside and wrote new constitutions. Within two years following 1776, all but Massachusetts had completed the task. By 1780, it had done so as well.

Given their recent experience with England and the prompting of republican theory, constitution makers began with two overriding concerns: to limit the powers of government and to make public officials closely accountable. The only certain way of accomplishing these goals was by establishing a fundamental law, in the form of a written constitution, that could serve as a standard for controlling governmental behavior.

In most states, the provincial congresses, extralegal successors to the defunct colonial assemblies, wrote the first constitutions. But this made people increasingly uneasy. If governmental bodies wrote the documents, they could change them as well, and what would then protect liberty against the abuse of governmental power? Some way had to be found of grounding the fundamental law not in the actions of government, but directly in the people's sovereign will.

Massachusetts first perfected the new procedures. In 1779, its citizens elected a special convention for the sole purpose of preparing a new constitution, which was then sent to the people for ratification.

Through trial and argumentation, the revolutionary generation gradually worked out a clear understanding of what a constitution was and how it should be created. In the process, it established some of the most basic doctrines of American constitutionalism: that sovereignty resides in the people; that written constitutions, produced by specially elected conventions and ratified by the people, embody their sovereign will; and that governments must function within clear constitutional limits. No principles have been more important to the preservation of American liberty.

The governments described by these new constitutions were considerably more democratic than the colonial regimes had been. Most state officials were now elected, many of them annually rather than every two or three years as before. The assemblies, moreover, were now larger and more representative

Massachusetts was the first state to elect a special convention to draw up a new constitution and then return that constitution to the people for approval. The new government—along with Boston's officials, courts, and the Merchants' Exchange—met in the old colonial statehouse. *(I. N. Phelps Stokes Collection, Miriam and Ira D. Wallach Division of Art, Prints and Photographs, The New York Public Library, Astor, Lenox and Tilden Foundations)*

than they had been prior to 1776, and many of the powers formerly exercised by colonial governors— control over the budget, veto power over legislation, and the right to appoint various state officials—were either abolished or reallocated to the assemblies.

Different Paths to the Republican Goal

At the same time, constitution making generated heated controversy, especially over how democratic the new governments should be. In Pennsylvania, a coalition of western farmers, Philadelphia artisans, and radical leaders such as Thomas Paine, Timothy Matlack, and Thomas Young pushed through the most democratic state constitution of all. Drafted less than three months after independence, during the most intense period of political reform, it rejected the familiar English model of two legislative houses and an independent executive. Republican governments, the radicals insisted, should be simple and easily understood. The constitution thus provided for a single, all-powerful legislative house—its members annually elected and its debates open to the public. There was to be no governor; legislative committees would handle executive duties. A truly radical assumption underlay this unitary design: that only the "common interest of society" and not "separate and jarring private interests" should be represented in public affairs. Property-

holding requirements for public office were abolished, and the franchise was opened to every taxpaying, white male over 21. A bill of rights guaranteed every citizen religious freedom, trial by jury, and freedom of speech.

The most radical proposal of all called for the redistribution of property. "An enormous proportion of property vested in a few individuals," declared the proposed constitution, "is dangerous to the rights, and destructive of the common happiness of mankind." Alarmed conservatives just managed to have the offending language removed.

Debate over the constitution polarized the state. Men of wealth condemned the document's supporters as "coffee-house demagogues" seeking to introduce a "tyranny of the people." The constitution's proponents—tradesmen, farmers, and other small producers—shot back that their critics were "the rich and great men" who had no "common interest with the body of the people."

In 1776, the radicals had their way, and the document was approved. The Pennsylvania constitution, together with its counterparts in Vermont and Georgia, represented the most radical thrust of revolutionary republicanism. Its guiding principle, declared Thomas Young, was that "the people at large [are] the true proprietors of governmental power." As later events would reveal, the struggle for political

---

Occupational Composition of Several State Assemblies in the 1780s

Membership in the revolutionary assemblies reflected differences in the economies and societies of the various states. Those differences often generated political conflict throughout the Revolutionary era. What are the major differences between northern and southern state assemblies, and how do you explain them?

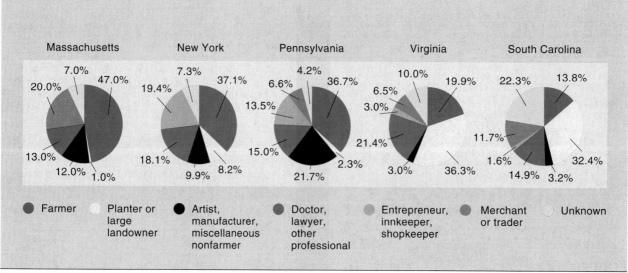

Source: Jackson T. Main, *Political Parties Before the Constitution*, 1973.

control in Pennsylvania was not over, for in 1790 a more conservative constitution would be approved. For the moment, however, the lines of political power in Pennsylvania had been decisively redrawn.

In Massachusetts, constitution making followed a more cautious course. There the disruptions of war were less severe and the continuity of political leadership was greater. The constitution's main architect, John Adams, readily admitted that the new government must be firmly grounded in the people, yet he warned against "reckless experimentation" and regarded the Pennsylvania constitution as far too democratic. He thought a balance between two legislative houses and an independent executive was essential to preserving liberty.

Believing that society was inescapably divided between "democratic" and "aristocratic" forces, Adams sought to isolate each in separate legislative houses where they could guard against each other. Following Adams's advice, the Massachusetts convention provided for a popular, annually elected assembly and a senate apportioned on the basis of wealth. The constitution also provided for an independent governor empowered to veto legislation, make appointments, command the militia, and oversee state expenditures. To qualify for election to the state House of Representatives, Senate, or governorship, candidates had to possess specific amounts of personal property.

When the convention sent the document to the town meetings for approval on March 2, 1780, farmers and Boston artisans attacked it as "aristocratic." The citizens of Dorchester warned that the property requirement for the franchise would exclude "half the people of this commonwealth" from voting, while the inhabitants of Petersham feared that "rich and powerful men" would control the proposed government. Despite such objections, the convention reconvened in June, declared the constitution approved, and the document went into effect four months later.

Women and the Limits of Republican Citizenship

While men of the revolutionary generation battled over sharing political power, they were virtually unanimous in the belief that women should be excluded from public affairs. Though women participated in revolutionary crowds and other political activities, they continued to be denied the franchise. Except on scattered occasions, women had neither voted nor held public office during the colonial period. Nor, with rare exceptions, did they do so in revolutionary America.

In New Jersey, the constitution of 1776 opened the franchise to "all free inhabitants" meeting property and residency requirements. During the 1780s, numerous women took advantage of that opening and cast their votes, leading one disgruntled male to protest, "It is evident that women, generally, are neither by nature, nor habit, nor education . . . fitted to perform this duty with credit to themselves, or advantage to the public." Reflecting that widely held, male belief, the New Jersey Assembly in 1807 again disenfranchised women. The author of that law, John Condict, had narrowly escaped defeat several years earlier when women voted in conspicuous numbers for his opponent. In no other state did women even temporarily secure the vote. Not until the twentieth century would women secure the franchise, the most fundamental attribute of citizenship.

Prior to independence, most women had accepted the principle that political involvement fell outside the feminine sphere. The Revolution altered that attitude, for women felt the urgency of the revolutionary crisis as intensely as men. "How shall I impose a silence upon myself," wondered Anne Emlen in 1777, "when the subject is so very interesting, so much engrossing conversation & what every

Though women were discouraged from public writing, Mercy Otis Warren, related by both birth and marriage to leading Massachusetts Patriots, published pamphlets and plays dealing with revolutionary politics. *(Courtesy, Museum of Fine Arts, Boston. Reproduced with permission ©1999 The Museum of Fine Arts, Boston. All Rights Reserved.)*

member of the community is more or less concerned in?" With increasing frequency, women wrote and spoke to each other about public events, especially as they affected their own lives. Declared Eliza Wilkerson of South Carolina during the British invasion of 1780, "None were greater politicians than the several knots of ladies, who met together. All trifling discourses of fashions, and such low chat were thrown by, and we commenced perfect statesmen."

As the war progressed, increasing numbers of women spoke out publicly. A few, such as Mercy Otis Warren and Esther DeBerdt Reed of Philadelphia, published essays explaining women's urgent desire to contribute to the Patriot cause. In her 1780 broadside "The Sentiments of an American Woman," Reed declared that women wanted to serve like "those heroines of antiquity, who have rendered their sex illustrious," and called on women to renounce "vain ornament" as they had earlier renounced English tea. The money not spent on clothing and hair styles would be the "offering of the Ladies" to Washington's army. In Philadelphia, women responded by collecting $300,000 in continental currency from over 1,600 individuals. Refusing Washington's proposal that the money be mixed with general funds in the national treasury, they insisted on using it to purchase materials for shirts so that each soldier might know he had received a contribution directly from the women.

Even women's traditional roles assumed new political meaning. With English imports cut off and the army badly in need of clothing, spinning and weaving took on patriotic significance. Coming together as Daughters of Liberty, women made shirts and other items of clothing. Charity Clarke, a New York teenager, acknowledged that she "felt Nationaly" as she knitted stockings for the soldiers. Though "heroines may not distinguish themselves at the head of an army," she informed an English cousin, a "fighting army of amazons . . . armed with spinning wheels" would emerge in America.

The most traditional female role, the care and nurture of children, took on special political resonance during the Revolutionary era. How could the republic be sustained once independence had been won? Only by a rising generation of republican citizens schooled in the principles of public virtue and ready to assume the task. How would they be prepared? During their formative years by their "Republican Mothers," the women of the Revolution.

Most women did not press for full political equality, since the idea flew in the face of long-standing social convention, and its advocacy exposed a woman to public ridicule. Women, however, did speak out in defense of their rights. Male lawmakers, Abigail Adams reminded her husband John, should think about the rights of women as well as men. Choosing words that had been used over and over in the protests against England, she wrote: "Do not put such unlimited power into the hands of the husbands. . . to use us with cruelty and indignity. Remember, all men would be tyrants if they could." Borrowing directly from the republican ideology used to protest Parliament's attempts to tax the colonies, she warned that American women "will not hold ourselves bound by any laws in which we

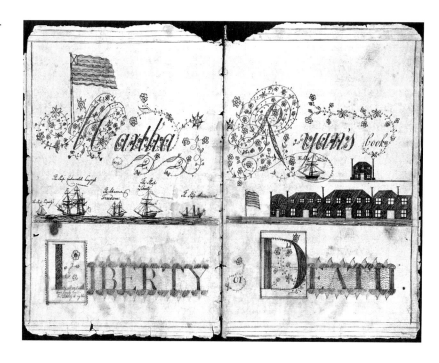

Martha Ryan, a young North Carolina girl, decorated the cover of her copybook with political themes. *(From the Ryan Cipher Book, #1940, Southern Historical Collection, The Library of the University of North Carolina at Chapel Hill)*

have no voice, or representation" and even promised that women would "foment a rebellion" if men did not heed their rightful claims. Though John consulted Abigail on many things, his response to this spirited challenge is unknown.

While women developed new ties to the public realm during the revolutionary years, the assumption that politics was an exclusively male domain did not easily die. Indeed, republican ideology, so effectively invoked in support of American liberty against the English king and Parliament, actually sharpened political distinctions between women and men. The independent judgment required of republican citizens assumed a level of economic self-sufficiency that was denied married women by the long-established principle of *coverture* (a legal doctrine that transferred women's property to their husbands, in effect designating them political as well as economic dependents).

Republican virtue, moreover, was understood to encompass such "manly" qualities as rationality, self-discipline, and public sacrifice, qualities believed inconsistent with "feminine" attributes of emotion and self-indulgence. Finally, the desperate struggle against England strengthened patriarchal values by celebrating military heroism and government making.

In time, new challenges to male political hegemony would emerge. When they did, women would find guidance in the universal principles enshrined in the Declaration of Independence that the women of the Revolution had helped to defend.

Timeline	
1775	Lexington and Concord
	Second Continental Congress
	Lord Dunmore's proclamation to slaves and
	servants in Virginia
	Iroquois Six Nations pledge neutrality
1776	Thomas Paine's *Common Sense*
	British evacuate Boston and seize New York City
	Declaration of Independence
	Eight states draft constitutions
	Cherokee raids and American retaliation
1777	British occupy Philadelphia
	Most Iroquois join the British
	Americans win victory at Saratoga
	Washington's army winters at Valley Forge
1778	War shifts to the South
	Savannah falls to the British
	French treaty of alliance and commerce
1779	Massachusetts state constitutional convention
	Sullivan destroys Iroquois villages in New York
1780	Massachusetts constitution ratified
	Charleston surrenders to the British
	Pennsylvania begins gradual abolition of slavery
1780s	Virginia and Maryland debate abolition of slavery
	Destruction of Iroquois Confederacy
1781	Cornwallis surrenders at Yorktown
	Articles of Confederation ratified by states
1783	Peace treaty with England signed in Paris
	Massachusetts Supreme Court abolishes slavery
	King's Commission on American Loyalists
	begins work

✦ *Conclusion*

THE CRUCIBLE OF REVOLUTION

When Congress declared independence and launched its struggle for national liberation in July 1776, it steered the American people into uncharted and turbulent seas and changed the destinies of countless people like Long Bill Scott. The break with England and accompanying war redrew the contours of American life and changed the destinies of the American people. Though the war ended in victory, liberty had its costs, as lives were lost, property was destroyed, and local economies were deranged. The conflict altered relationships between Indians and whites, for it left the Iroquois and Cherokee severely weakened and opened the floodgates of western expansion. Though women participated in revolutionary activities and achieved enhanced status as "Republican Mothers," they were still denied the vote.

By 1783, a new nation had come into being where none had existed before, a nation based not on age-encrusted principles of monarchy and aristocratic privilege but on the doctrines of republican liberty. That was the greatest change of all. However, the political transformations that were set in motion generated angry disputes whose outcome could be but dimly foreseen. How might individual liberty be reconciled with the need for public order? Who should be accorded full republican citizenship, and to whom should it be denied? How should constitutions be written and republican governments be organized? Thomas Paine put the matter succinctly: "The answer to the question, can America be happy under a government of her own, is short and simple—as happy as she pleases; she hath a blank sheet to write upon." The years immediately ahead would determine whether America's republican experiment, launched with such hopefulness in 1776, would succeed.

Success would depend as well on the new nation's position in a hostile Atlantic world. Though American independence had been acknowledged, the long-established web of connections tying the United States to England and Europe remained strong. Wartime alliances had revealed that North America remained an object of imperial ambition and European power politics, while the cutoff of Atlantic trade had made clear how dependent the nation still was on overseas commerce. The new American republic, moreover, served as a model and, on occasion, an asylum for political radicals intent on reforming the corrupt systems of England and France. At the same time, many Americans regarded their republic as a beacon for the struggles of oppressed people elsewhere. In these ways as well, the meaning of American independence remained to be worked out in the years ahead.

✦ Recommended Reading

Bursting the Colonial Bonds
Bernard Bailyn, *Faces of Revolution* (1991); Stephen Conway, *The British Isles and the War of American Independence* (2000); Eric Foner, *Tom Paine and Revolutionary America* (1976); Eliga Gould, *The Persistence of Empire: British Political Culture in the Age of the American Revolution* (2000); Robert Gross, *The Minutemen and Their World* (1976); Woody Holton, *Forced Founders: Indians, Debtors, Slaves, and the Making of the American Revolution in Virginia* (1999); Andrew Jackson O'Shaughnessy, *An Empire Divided: The American Revolution and the British Caribbean* (2000).

The War for American Independence
Colin Calloway, *The American Revolution in Indian Country* (1995); Jonathan Dull, *A Diplomatic History of the American Revolution* (1985); John Ferling, ed., *The World Turned Upside Down: The American Victory in the War of Independence* (1988); Tom Hatley, *The Dividing Paths: Cherokees and South Carolinians Through the Revolutionary Era* (1993); Ronald Hoffman and Peter Albert, eds., *Arms and Independence: The Military Character of the American Revolution* (1984) and *Peace and the Peacemakers: The Treaty of 1783* (1986); Isabel Kelsey, *Joseph Brant, 1743–1807: Man of Two Worlds* (1984); Holly Mayer, *Belonging to the Army: Camp Followers and Community During the American Revolution* (1996); Anthony Wallace, *The Death and Rebirth of the Seneca* (1969).

The Experience of War
Bernard Bailyn, *The Ordeal of Thomas Hutchinson* (1974); Robert Calhoon, *The Loyalists in Revolutionary America, 1760–1781* (1973); Lawrence Cress, *Citizens in Arms: The Army and the Militia in American Society to the War of 1812* (1982); Elizabeth Fenn, *Pox Americana: The Great Smallpox Epidemic of 1775–82* (2001); Sylvia Frey, *The British Soldier in America: A Social History of Military Life in the Revolutionary Period* (1981) and *Water from the Rock: Black Resistance in a Revolutionary Age* (1991); Sidney Kaplan, *The Black Presence in the Era of the American Revolution, 1770–1800* (1973); Gary B. Nash, *Race and Revolution* (1990); Charles Neimeyer, *America Goes to War: A Social History of the Continental Army* (1996); Mary Beth Norton, *The British Americans: The Loyalist Exiles in England, 1774–1789* (1972).

The Ferment of Revolutionary Politics
John Buchanan, *The Road to Guilford Courthouse: The American Revolution in the Carolinas* (1997); Joy Day Buel and Richard Buel, Jr., *The Way of Duty: A Woman and Her Family in Revolutionary America* (1995); Edith Gelles, *Portia: The World of Abigail Adams* (1992); Ronald Hoffman and Peter Albert, eds., *Women in the Age of the American Revolution* (1989); Linda Kerber, *Women of the Republic* (1980); Cynthia Kerner, *Southern Women in Revolution, 1776–1800* (1998); Mark Kruman, *Between Authority and Liberty: State Constitution Making in Revolutionary America* (1997); Edmund Morgan, *Inventing the People: The Rise of Popular Sovereignty in England and America* (1988); Mary Beth Norton, *Liberty's Daughters* (1980); Jeffrey Richards, *Mercy Otis Warren* (1995); Norman Risjord, *Representative Americans: The Revolutionary Generation* (1980); John Selby, *The Revolution in Virginia, 1775–1783* (1988); Alan Taylor, *Liberty Men and Great Proprietors: The Revolutionary Settlement on the Maine Frontier, 1760–1820* (1990); Peter Thompson, *Rum, Punch, and Revolution: Taverngoing and Public Life in Eighteenth Century Philadelphia* (1999); Gordon Wood, *The Creation of the American Republic, 1776–1787* (1969); Al Young, ed., *Beyond the American Revolution: Explorations in the History of American Radicalism* (1993).

Fiction and Film
The Broken Chain, a made-for-television historical drama produced and aired in 1994, tells the story of the Mohawk war chief Joseph Brant, who fought with England during the Revolutionary War and then led many of his people to Canada following the peace of 1783. *The Way of Duty*, a PBS documentary-drama based on a book by the historians Richard and Joy Buel, traces the challenging experiences of a Connecticut woman and her family during the American Revolution. James Fenimore Cooper's dramatic novel *The Pilot* (1824) offers an imaginative account of naval warfare and seafaring life during the Revolution. In the more recently published novel *Oliver Wiswell* (1940), Kenneth Roberts depicts the Revolution as seen through the eyes of an American Loyalist.

✦ Discovering U.S. History Online

Articles of Confederation
www.yale.edu/lawweb/avalon/artconf.htm

The full text of the articles is presented, along with other relevant documents such as Benjamin Franklin's draft, John Dickinson's draft, and discussion of the Articles of Confederation in Jefferson's autobiography.

The American Revolution and Its Era: Maps and Charts of North America and the West Indies, 1750–1789
www.memory.loc.gov/ammem/gmdhtml/armhtml/armhome.html

This site gives geographical context to the American Revolution.

American Revolution
www.nps.gov/revwar/

This site includes a timeline of the war, links to all Revolutionary War national parks, as well as special exhibits.

North America Map Archive
www.uoregon.edu/~atlas/america/maps.html

This map collection includes an interactive map that shows America's configuration after the 1783 Treaty of Paris, including states and claimed territories.

Revolutionary Battles
www.wpi.edu/Academics/Depts/MilSci/BTSI

With an aim to instruct in military strategy, this site gives detailed information about four key revolutionary battles and their causes.

Oneida Indian Nation, 1777
www.one-web.org/1777.html

This site presents a several-part essay that explains the role the Oneida tribe played in the American Revolution. The discussion features quotes from Oneida oral history as well as contemporary publications.

Indians and the American Revolution
www.americanrevolution.org/ind1.html

This site presents the annotated text of a presentation by a former director of American Studies at the Smithsonian Institution in which he outlined the involvement of various Native American tribes in the American Revolution.

Spy Letters of the American Revolution
www.si.umich.edu/spies/

The story of the American Revolution is told through letters of its spies. This site gives context to the letters with a timeline, overall stories, maps of routes, and descriptions of their methods.

Archiving Early America
www.earlyamerica.com

Via this site, students can access writings, maps, and images of leading men and women reproduced from newspapers and magazines of the Revolutionary era.

Black Loyalists
www.collections.ic.gc.ca/blackloyalists

Using primary sources from the collections, this site explores the history of the African-American Loyalists who earned their freedom by serving with the British and then fled to Canada to settle.

Intelligence in the War of Independence
www.cia.gov/cia/publications/warindep

This collection of primary documents explains how intelligence was organized, how it operated, and the techniques used during the War for Independence.

Was the American Revolution Inevitable?
www.bbc.co.uk/history/society_economy/empire/american_revolution_01.shtml

This essay explores the war from the British perspective.

The Army Medical Department, 1755–1818
www.armymedicine.army.mil/history/booksdocs/rev/gillett1/default.htm

An online complete, illustrated text of a volume describing the army's medical practices from the time of the Revolutionary War and the first quarter century of the nation.

The American Revolution: National Discussions of Our Revolutionary Origins
www.revolution.h-net.msu.edu

This site accompanies the PBS series "Liberty!" with essays and resource links to a rich array of sites containing information on the American Revolution. Included are the Bill of Rights, slave documents, and maps of the era.

Biographies of America's Founding Fathers
www.colonialhall.com

The biographical sketches of America's founding fathers presented are taken from the 1829 book *Lives of the Signers of the Declaration of Independence* by the Rev. Charles A. Goodrich.

Women in the American Revolution
www.rims.k12.ca.us/women_american_revolution/

Brief biographies of 25 women who played a role in the Revolutionary War. This site also includes a comprehensive bibliography of online sources.

The Charters of Freedom
www.archives.gov/exhibit_hall/charters_of_freedom/charters_of_freedom.html

This government site includes images and full text as well as background of three early documents: the Declaration of Independence, the Constitution, and the Bill of Rights.

7 Consolidating the Revolution

Ratification of the U.S. Constitution by the states in 1788 brought an end to the revolutionary years and ushered in a dramatically new era in the nation's history. *(John Feingersh/Stock, Boston)*

✦ *American Stories*

EXTENDING THE REVOLUTION

Timothy Bloodworth of New Hanover County, North Carolina, knew what the American Revolution was all about, for he had experienced it firsthand. A man of humble origins, Bloodworth had known poverty as a child. Lacking any formal education, he had worked hard during the middle decades of the eighteenth century as an innkeeper and ferry pilot, self-styled preacher and physician, blacksmith and farmer. By the mid-1770s, he owned nine slaves and 4,200 acres of land, considerably more than most of his neighbors.

His unpretentious manner and commitment to political equality earned Bloodworth the confidence of his community. In 1758, at the age of 22, he was elected to the North Carolina colonial assembly. Over the next three decades, he was deeply involved in the political life of his home state.

When the colonies' troubles with England drew toward a crisis, Bloodworth spoke ardently of American rights and mobilized support for independence. In 1775, he helped form the Wilmington Committee of Safety. Filled with revolutionary fervor, he urged forward the process of republican political reform and, as commissioner of confiscated property for the district of Wilmington, pressed the attack on local Loyalists.

In 1784, shortly after the war ended, the North Carolina assembly named Bloodworth one of the state's delegates to the Confederation Congress. There he learned for the first time about the problems of governing a new nation. As the Congress struggled through the middle years of the 1780s with the intractable problems of foreign trade, war debt, and control of the trans-Appalachian interior, Bloodworth shared the growing conviction that the Articles of Confederation were too weak. He supported the Congress's call for a special convention to meet in Philadelphia in May 1787 for the purpose of taking action necessary "to render the constitution of the federal government adequate to the exigencies of the Union."

Like thousands of other Americans, Bloodworth eagerly awaited the convention's work. And like countless Americans, he was stunned by the result, for the proposed constitution described a government that seemed to him certain not to preserve republican liberty but to endanger it.

Once again sniffing political tyranny on the breeze, Bloodworth resigned his congressional seat and in August 1787 hurried back to North Carolina to help organize opposition to the proposed constitution. Over the next several years, he worked tirelessly for its defeat.

Alarmed by the prospect of such a powerful central government, Bloodworth protested that "we cannot consent to the adoption of a Constitution whose revenues lead to aristocratic tyranny, or monarchical despotism, and open a door wide as fancy can point, for the introduction of dissipation, bribery and corruption to the exclusion of public virtue." Had Americans so quickly forgotten the dangers of consolidated power? Were they already prepared to turn away from their brief experiment in republicanism?

Alarmed by a variety of provisions in the document, Bloodworth demanded the addition of a federal bill of rights to protect individual liberties. Echoing the language of revolutionary republicanism, he warned the North Carolina ratifying convention that "without the most express restrictions, Congress may trample on your rights. Every possible precaution should be taken when we grant powers," he continued, for "Rulers are always disposed to abuse them."

Bloodworth also feared the sweeping authority Congress would have to make "all laws which shall be necessary and proper" for carrying into execution "all other powers vested . . . in the government of the United States." That language, he insisted, "would result in the abolition of the state governments. Its sovereignty absolutely annihilates them."

In North Carolina, the arguments of Bloodworth and his Anti-Federalist colleagues carried the day. By a vote of 184 to 84, the ratifying convention declared that a bill of rights "asserting and securing from encroachment the great Principles of civil and religious Liberty, and the unalienable rights of the People" must be approved before North Carolina would concur. The convention was true to its word. Not until November 1789, well after the new government had gotten underway and Congress had forwarded a national bill of rights to the states for approval, did North Carolina, with Timothy Bloodworth's cautious endorsement, finally enter the new union.

Just as Timothy Bloodworth knew the difficulties of achieving American independence, so he learned the problems of preserving American liberty once independence had been won. As a member of the Confederation Congress, Bloodworth confronted the continuing vestiges of colonialism: the patronizing attitudes of England and France, their continuing imperial ambitions in North America, and the republic's ongoing economic dependence on Europe. He also observed the Congress's inability to pay off the war debt, pry open foreign ports to American commerce, or persuade the states to join in a common tariff policy against England. As a southerner, Bloodworth was equally alarmed by the willingness of a congressional majority to forego free navigation of the Mississippi River, deemed essential for development of the southern backcountry, in exchange for northern commercial advantages in Europe. Finally, he worried about political turmoil in the states as issues of taxation, debt, and paper money, continuing to fester during the 1780s, led discontented citizens to challenge public authority openly.

By 1786, Bloodworth, like countless other Americans, was caught up in an escalating debate between the Federalists, who believed that the Articles of Confederation were fatally deficient and must be replaced by a stronger national government, and the Anti-Federalists, who were deeply troubled by the dangers consolidated power posed to individual liberties.

That debate over the future of America's republican experiment came to a head in the momentous Philadelphia convention of 1787, which produced not reform but dramatic change in the national government. With ratification of the new Constitution, the Revolutionary era came to an end, and the American people opened a portentous new chapter in their history.

STRUGGLING WITH THE PEACETIME AGENDA

As the war ended, daunting problems of demobilization and adjustment to the novel conditions of independence troubled the new nation. Whether the Confederation Congress could effectively deal with the problems of the postwar era remained unclear.

Demobilizing the Army

Demobilizing the army presented the Confederation government with immediate challenges, for when the fighting stopped, many of the troops refused to go home until the Congress redressed their grievances. Trouble first arose in early 1783 when officers at the continental army camp in Newburgh, New York, sent a delegation to complain about arrears in pay and other benefits that the Congress had promised them during the dark days of the war. When Congress called on the army to disband, an anonymous address circulated among the officers, attacking the "coldness and severity" of the Congress and hinting darkly at more direct action if grievances were not addressed.

Several Congressmen encouraged the officers' muttering, hoping the crisis would lend urgency to their own calls for a stronger central government. Most, however, found the challenge to Congress's authority alarming. Washington moved quickly to calm the situation. Promising that the Congress

The Resignation of General Washington, 1783. By resigning his commission in 1783 and returning to private life, Washington affirmed the supremacy of civilians over military authority. Note the women in the balcony observing the ceremony. Though distanced from the floor of Congress, they pay close attention to the proceedings. *(U.S. Capital Historical Society)*

Old Northwest Survey Patterns

The Land Ordinance passed by Congress in 1785 provided for townships divided into lots of 640 acres. Its purpose was to promote the rapid and orderly settlement of the Old Northwest.

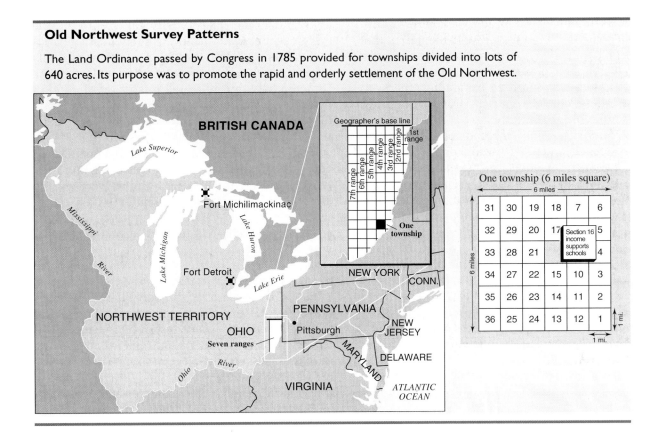

would treat the officers justly, he counseled patience and urged his comrades not to tarnish the victory they had so recently won. His efforts succeeded, for the officers reaffirmed their confidence in the Congress and agreed to disband.

Officers were not the only ones to take action. In June, several hundred disgruntled continental soldiers and Pennsylvania militiamen gathered in front of Philadelphia's Independence Hall, where both Congress and Pennsylvania's Executive Council were meeting. When the state authorities would not guarantee the Congress's safety, it fled to Princeton, New Jersey. Once there, tension eased when Congress issued the soldiers three months' pay and furloughed them until they could be formally discharged. By early November, the crisis was over, but congressional authority had been seriously damaged.

Over the next several years, the Congress shuffled between Princeton and Annapolis, Trenton and New York City, its transience visible evidence of its steadily eroding authority. A hot-air balloon, scoffed the *Boston Evening Herald,* would "exactly accommodate the itinerant genius of Congress," because it could "float along from one end of the continent to the other . . . and when occasion requires . . . suddenly pop down into any of the states they please." Never had the Congress been so openly mocked.

Opening the West

The Confederation Congress was not without significant accomplishments during the postwar years. Most notable were the two great land ordinances of 1785 and 1787. The first provided for the systematic survey and sale of the region west of Pennsylvania and north of the Ohio River. The area was to be laid out in townships six miles square, which were in turn to be subdivided into lots of 640 acres each. Thus began the rectangular grid pattern of land survey and settlement that to this day characterizes the Midwest and distinguishes it so markedly from the irregular settlement patterns of the older, colonial areas to the east.

Two years later, Congress passed the Northwest Ordinance. It provided for the political organization of the same interior region, first under congressionally appointed officials, then under popularly elected territorial assemblies, and ultimately as new states to be incorporated into the Union "on an equal footing with the original states in all respects whatsoever." These laws represented a dramatic change from the days of England's colonial administration. Rather than seeking to restrain white settlement as Parliament had attempted to do in the Proclamation Line of 1763, the central government in America's "Empire of Liberty" sought ways to promote settlement's expansion via land laws and Indian policies. In addition, settlements in the American West would not remain colonies subordinate to an imperial power, but would be fully incorporated as new states into the expanding American nation. These changes carried profound importance for the country's future.

Both ordinances enjoyed broad political support, for they opened land to settlers and profits to speculators. Income from land sales, moreover, promised to help reduce the national debt. While permitting slave owners already living north of the Ohio River to retain their chattels, the Ordinance of 1787 prohibited the importation of new slaves into the region. This made the area more attractive to white farmers who worried about competing with slave labor and living among blacks. Southern delegates in the Congress accepted the restriction because they could look forward to slavery's expansion south of the Ohio River. During the 1780s, the country's interior seemed large enough to accommodate everyone's needs.

Despite these accomplishments, however, Congress could neither get British troops out of the western posts south of the Great Lakes nor guarantee free navigation of the Mississippi. Nor was it able to clear the tribes of the Ohio region out of white settlers' way. These failings fueled doubts that the Confederation government was capable of promoting westward expansion.

During the immediate postwar years, the Congress operated as if the Native Americans of the interior were "conquered" peoples—allies of England who had lost the war and come under U.S. control. Such claims were grounded as well in notions of Indian inferiority. Even the most sympathetic whites believed that Native Americans must forego their Indian ways, become "civilized," and adopt Christianity before they could coexist with white society. Most whites doubted that such "improvements" were possible, and argued that the Indians must simply be driven out of white settlers' way. George Washington gave blunt expression to the prevailing view. "The gradual extension of our settlements," he explained, "will as certainly cause the savage as the wolf to retire; both being beasts of prey though they differ in shape."

For a few years, the conquest strategy seemed to work. During the mid-1780s, the Congress imposed several important land treaties on the interior tribes, among them the Iroquois. Their numbers sharply reduced and their once proud confederation shattered, many Iroquois had fled into Canada. Pressured by Congress and the New York government, those who remained deeded away much of

their land. At the Treaty of Fort Stanwix in 1784, the first treaty between the newly independent government and an Indian tribe, the Six Nations officially made peace, ceded most of their lands to the United States, and retreated to small reservations. By the 1790s, little remained of the once imposing Iroquois domain but a few islands in a spreading sea of white settlement. On these "slums in the wilderness," the Iroquois struggled against disease and poverty, their traditional lifeways gone, their self-confidence broken. The Iroquois were not the only tribe to lose their land. In January 1785, representatives of the Wyandotte, Chippewa, Delaware, and Ottawa tribes relinquished claim to most of present-day Ohio.

Often exacted under the threat of force, the treaties generated widespread resentment among Indians. Two years after the Fort Stanwix negotiations, the Iroquois repudiated the treaty, asserting that they were still sovereigns of their own soil and "equally free as . . . any nation under the sun." The Revolution left behind a legacy of bitterness: among Indians because they had suffered defeat and betrayal by their English allies, among white Americans because the Indians had sided with England and thus threatened the Revolution's success. Such bit-

The figure of Columbia, symbolic of the new republic, was often represented as an Indian maiden, embodying the innocence and freedom of America. *(Library of Congress)*

"Utmost Good Faith" Clause from the Northwest Ordinance (1787)

The following articles shall be considered as articles of compact between the original States and the people and States in the said territory and forever remain unalterable, unless by common consent, to wit:

> The utmost good faith shall always be observed towards the Indians; their land and property shall never be taken from them without their consent; and, in their property, rights, and liberty, they shall never be invaded or disturbed, unless in just and lawful wars authorized by Congress, but laws founded in justice and humanity, shall from time to time be made for preventing wrongs being done to them, and for preserving peace and friendship with them.

---

terness would trouble Indian–white relations for years to come.

By the mid-1780s, tribal groups above and below the Ohio River were resisting white expansion into the interior. While the Creek resumed hostilities in Georgia, north of the river the Shawnee, Delaware, and Miami asserted that the Ohio River was the proper boundary between them and the United States, and prepared for the defense of their homeland. When white settlers continued to press into the region, Native Americans launched a series of devastating raids, bringing white settlement to a virtual halt. By the end of 1786, the entire region from the Great Lakes to the Gulf of Mexico was embroiled in warfare. With the continental army disbanded, there was little that the Congress could do.

Congress's inability to open the interior to white settlement alarmed countless Americans: speculators facing the loss of their investments; farmers wanting to leave the crowded lands of the East; revolutionary soldiers eager to start afresh on the rich soil of Kentucky and Ohio that they had been promised as payment for military service; and leaders such as Thomas Jefferson who believed that America's "empire of liberty" depended on an expanding nation of yeoman farmers.

The Congress also failed to resolve problems with European nations that continued to claim areas of the trans-Appalachian west. In June 1784, Spain—still in possession of Florida, the Gulf Coast, and vast areas west of the Mississippi—closed the mouth of the Mississippi River to American shipping. The act outraged western settlers dependent on getting their produce to market by floating it downstream to New Orleans where ocean-going vessels picked it up. Land speculators were alarmed as well, for closure of the Mississippi would discour-

age development of the southern backcountry and reduce their profits. Rumors spread that Spanish agents were urging American frontiersmen to break away from the new nation and seek affiliation with Spain. Sensing the danger, Washington commented uneasily that settlers throughout the West were "on a pivot." "The touch of a feather," he warned, "would turn them away."

When Spain refused to reopen the Mississippi, the Congress's secretary for foreign affairs, John Jay, offered to relinquish American claims to free transit of the river in return for a commercial treaty opening Spanish ports to American shipping. Though the bargain pleased merchants in the northeastern states, southern delegates in Congress were outraged at Jay's betrayal of their interests and opposed it. Stalemated, the Congress could take no action at all.

Wrestling with the National Debt

Further evidence of the Confederation's weakness was the Congress's inability to deal effectively with the nation's war debt, estimated at $35 million. Much of the debt was held by French and Dutch bankers. Unable to make regular payments against the loan's principal, the Congress had to borrow additional money just to pay the accumulating interest. Things were no better at home. In response to the incessant demands of its creditors, the government could only delay and try to borrow more.

In 1781, the Congress appointed Robert Morris, a wealthy Philadelphia merchant, as superintendent of finance and gave him broad authority to deal with the nation's troubled affairs. Morris urged the states to stop issuing paper money and persuaded the Congress to demand that the states pay their requisitions in specie (gold and silver coin). In addition, he persuaded Congress to charter the Bank of North America and took steps to make federal bonds more attractive to investors.

Though Morris made considerable progress, the government's finances remained shaky. Lacking authority to tax, Congress continued to depend on the states' willingness to meet their financial obligations. This arrangement, however, proved unworkable. Desperate, the Congress, in October 1781, requested $8 million from the states. Two and a half years later, less than $1.5 million had come in. In January 1784, Morris resigned, partly in despair over the government's financial situation and partly to recoup his personal fortunes.

By 1786, federal revenue totaled $370,000 a year, not enough, one official lamented, to provide for "the bare maintenance of the federal government."

North America After the Treaty of Paris, 1783

Though victorious in its struggle for independence, the United States was surrounded by British and Spanish possessions, while Russia and France continued to harbor imperial ambitions in the Americas as well. **Reflecting on the Past** What problems and opportunities did European claims on areas of North America pose for the United States?

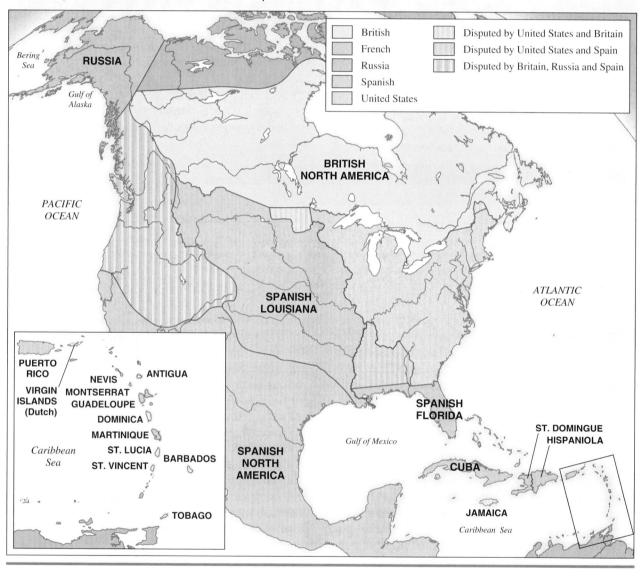

Declared a congressional committee, Americans "must decide whether they will support their rank as a nation, by maintaining the public faith at home and abroad. . . ."

Not all Americans were alarmed. Some pointed out approvingly that several state governments, having brought their own financial affairs under control, were beginning to assume responsibility for portions of the national debt. Others, however, saw this as additional evidence of the Congress's weak-

ening condition and wondered how long a government unable to maintain its credit could endure.

Surviving in a Hostile Atlantic World

The Congress's difficulties dealing with its creditors and failure to counter Spain's closure of the Mississippi pointed to a broader problem in American foreign relations. Even after the United States had formally won independence, Britain, France, and

Spain continued to harbor imperial ambitions in North America. Before the century was over, France would regain most of the continent west of the Mississippi River. Meanwhile, Great Britain's Union Jack still flew over Canada and British troops still occupied strategic outposts on American Soil, while Spain continued to conjure up grim memories of past New World conquests.

The Revolutionary War had dramatically transformed America's relations with the outside world. England, once the nurturing "mother country," had become the enemy, while France, long the mortal foe of England and the colonies alike, was at best an uncertain friend. As an imperial power and an absolute monarchy, it feared colonial rebellions and regarded republicanism as deeply subversive. Moreover, French efforts to manipulate the peace process for its own advantage had taught the Americans a hard lesson in the dangers of power politics.

The reason for America's diplomatic troubles was clear: the country was new, weak, and republican in an Atlantic world dominated by strong, monarchical governments and divided into exclusive, warring empires.

Nothing revealed the difficulties of national survival more starkly than the Congress's futile efforts to rebuild America's overseas commerce. When the Revolutionary War ended, familiar and highly desired English goods once again flooded American markets. Few American goods, however, flowed the other way. John Adams learned why. In 1785, he arrived in London as the first American minister to England. The Congress had ordered him to negotiate a commercial treaty. After endless rebuffs, he reported in frustration that England had no intention of reopening the empire's ports to American shipping. British officials testily reminded him that Americans had desired independence and must now live with its consequences.

Progress was slow as American merchants searched for new commercial arrangements during the 1780s. While England remained intractable, France and Spain withdrew wartime trading privileges and returned to a policy of maritime restrictions against American commerce. Congressional efforts to secure authorization from the states to regulate foreign trade were unavailing because each state wanted to channel its trade for its own advantage. As a result, overseas trade continued to languish and economic hardship deepened.

By the late 1780s, the per capita value of American exports had fallen a startling 30 percent from the 1760s. No wonder that merchants and artisans, carpenters and shopkeepers, sailors and dock workers—all dependent on shipbuilding and overseas commerce—suffered. In an Atlantic world divided into exclusive, imperial trading spheres, the United States lacked the political unity and the economic muscle to protect its essential interests.

SOURCES OF POLITICAL CONFLICT

Revolutionary politics took different forms in each state, depending on the impact of the war, the extent of Loyalism, patterns of social conflict, and the disruptions of economic life. Everywhere, though, citizens struggled with a bewildering, often intractable array of issues.

Separating Church and State

Among the most explosive issues was deciding the proper relationship between church and state. Prior to 1776, only Rhode Island, New Jersey, Pennsylvania, and Delaware had allowed full religious liberty. The other colonies all had established churches endorsed by the government and supported by public taxes. There, civil authorities grudgingly tolerated "dissenters" such as the Methodists and Baptists, whose numbers were growing among ordinary folk and who noisily pressed their case for full religious liberty.

With independence, pressure built for severing all ties between church and state. Such arguments were strengthened by the belief that throughout history, alliances between governmental and church authorities had brought religious oppression, and that voluntary choice was the only safe basis for religious association. The issue, however, remained hotly contested.

In Massachusetts, Congregationalists fought to preserve their long-established privileges. To separate church and state, they argued, was to risk infidelity and social disorder. Isaac Backus, the most outspoken of New England's Baptists, protested that "many, who are filling the nation with the cry of *liberty* and against *oppressors* are at the same time themselves violating that dearest of all rights, *liberty of conscience.*"

Massachusetts's 1780 constitution guaranteed everyone the right to worship God "in the manner and season most agreeable to the dictates of his own conscience." While protecting the right of conscience and permitting religious pluralism, however, the constitution empowered the legislature to require towns to ensure the public worship of God; provide tax support for "public protestant teachers

This nineteenth-century print says it gives "A Correct View of the Old Methodist Church in John Street, New York. The first erected in America. Founded A.D. 1768." Methodists and Baptists were among the "dissenting" groups pressing for full religious freedom during the Revolutionary era. *(The Metropolitan Museum of Art, Bequest of Edward W. C. Arnold, 1954. The Edward W. C. Arnold Collection of New York Prints, Maps and Pictures. [54.90.168])*

of piety, religion, and morality"; and "enjoin attendance" on religious instruction for residents who could conscientiously participate. A common religion and shared morality, avowed John Adams, were essential supports to liberty and republican government. Religious freedom, he believed, consisted of "the right of each individual to discharge divine duties—which duties the Constitution helped to define." Still unsatisfied, Isaac Backus continued to protest that religious toleration fell far short of true religious freedom. In Massachusetts, laws linking church and state were not repealed until 1833.

In Virginia, the Baptists pressed their cause against the Protestant Episcopal Church, successor to the Church of England. The adoption in 1786 of Thomas Jefferson's Bill for Establishing Religious Freedom, rejecting all connections between church and state and removing all religious tests for public office, decisively settled the issue. Three years later, that statute served as a model for the First Amendment to the new federal Constitution.

But even most supporters of religious freedom were not prepared to extend it universally. The wartime alliance with Catholic France together with congressional efforts to entice Catholic settlers in Quebec to join the resistance against England had weakened long-established prejudices. Still anti-Catholic biases remained strong, especially in New England. The people of Northbridge, Massachusetts, wanted to exclude "Roman Catholics, pagons, or Mahomitents" from public office. Disestablishment

did not always end religious discrimination, but it helped to implant the principle of religious freedom firmly in American law.

Slavery under Attack

The place of slavery in a republican society also vexed the revolutionary generation. How, asked many, could slavery be reconciled with the inalienable right to life, liberty, and the pursuit of happiness?

During the several decades preceding 1776, the trade in human chattels had flourished. While the 1760s had witnessed the largest importation of slaves in colonial history, the Revolutionary War halted the slave trade almost completely. Though southern planters talked of replacing their lost chattels once the war ended, a combination of revolutionary principles, a reduced need for field hands in the depressed Chesapeake tobacco economy, the continuing natural increase among the existing slave population, and anxiety over black rebelliousness argued for the slave trade's permanent extinction. By 1790, every state except South Carolina and Georgia had outlawed slave importations.

Ending the slave trade had powerful implications, for it reduced the infusion of new Africans into the black population. As a result, an ever higher proportion of blacks was American born, thus speeding the cultural transformation by which Africans became African Americans.

Slavery itself came under attack during the Revolutionary era, with immense consequences for

Resettlement of Black Loyalists after the Revolution

Thousands of American blacks departed the new nation with British troops at the end of the Revolutionary War. As the map indicates, their destinations and futures differed dramatically. **Reflecting on the Past** What difference did resettlement outside the United States make in the lives of black Loyalists?

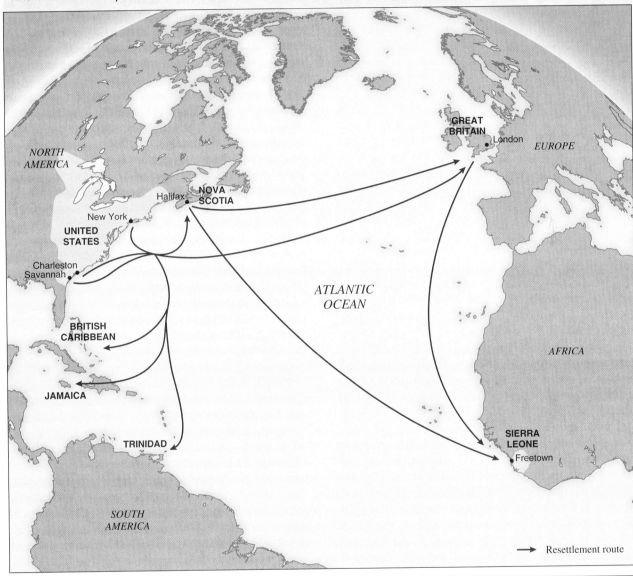

blacks and for the nation's future. As the crisis with England heated up, catchwords such as *liberty* and *tyranny,* mobilized by colonists against British policies, reminded citizens that one-fifth of the colonial population was in chains. Samuel Hopkins, a New England clergyman, accosted his compatriots for "making a vain parade of being advocates for the liberties of mankind, while . . . continuing this lawless, cruel, inhuman, and abominable practice of enslaving your fellow creatures." Following independence, antislavery attacks intensified.

In Georgia and South Carolina, where blacks outnumbered whites more than two to one and where slave labor remained essential to the prosperous rice economy, slavery escaped significant challenge. Committed to the doctrine of racial superiority and fearing the black majority, whites shuddered at the prospect of black freedom and wound the local slave codes even tighter.

In Virginia and Maryland, by contrast, whites argued openly whether slavery was compatible with republicanism, and in these states significant change did occur. The weakened demand for slave labor in the depressed tobacco economy facilitated the debate. Though neither state abolished slavery, both passed laws making it easier for owners to manumit (that is, to free) their slaves without continuing to be responsible for their behavior. Moreover, increasing numbers of blacks bought their own or their families' freedom, or simply ran away. By 1800, more than one of every ten blacks in the Chesapeake region was free, a dramatic increase from 30 years before. Even so, their freedom was limited, since many found themselves obligated to work for others as indentured servants.

The majority of free blacks lived and worked in Baltimore, Richmond, and other towns, where they formed communities that served as centers of an expanding African-American society, as well as havens for slaves escaping from the countryside. In the Chesapeake region, the conditions of life for black Americans slowly changed for the better.

The most dramatic breakthrough occurred in the North. There, slavery was either abolished or put on the road to gradual extinction. Such actions were possible in the North because blacks were a numerical minority—in most areas, they constituted no more than four percent of the population—and slavery had neither the economic nor social importance that it did in the South. In 1780, the Pennsylvania assembly passed a law stipulating that all newborn blacks were to be free when they reached age 21. It was a cautious but decisive step. Other northern states adopted similar policies of gradual emancipation.

Northern blacks joined in the attacks on slavery. Following independence, they eagerly petitioned state assemblies for their freedom. "Every Principle from which America has acted in the course of their unhappy difficulties with Great Britain," declared one group of Philadelphia blacks, "pleads stronger than a thousand arguments in favor of our petition."

In scattered instances, free blacks participated actively in revolutionary politics. When the first draft of the Massachusetts constitution, explicitly excluding blacks and mulattoes from the franchise, was made public, William Gordon, a white clergyman, voiced his protest. "Would it not be ridiculous . . . and unjust to exclude freemen from voting . . . though otherwise qualified, because their skins are black?" he questioned. "Why not . . . for being long-nosed, short-faced, or . . . lower than five feet nine?" In the end, Massachusetts's constitution made no mention of race, and there, as well as in Pennsylvania and New York, African Americans occasionally cast their ballots.

If civic participation by blacks was scattered and temporary in the North, it was almost totally absent in the South. With the brief exception of North Carolina, free African Americans could neither vote nor enjoy such basic rights of citizenship as protection of their persons and property under the law. In the South, blacks (the vast majority of them slaves) remained almost entirely without political voice, except in the petitions against slavery and mistreatment that they pressed upon the state regimes. Even as freemen, blacks continued to encounter pervasive discrimination.

Still, remarkable progress had been made. Prior to the Revolution, slavery had been an accepted fact of northern life. After the Revolution, it no longer was. That change made a vast difference in the lives of countless black Americans. The abolition of slavery in the North, moreover, widened the sectional divergence between the North and South, with enormous consequences for the years ahead. In addition, there now existed a coherent, publicly proclaimed antislavery argument, closely linked in Americans' minds with the nation's founding. The first antislavery organizations had been created as well. Although another half century would pass before antislavery became a significant force in American politics, the groundwork for slavery's final abolition had been laid.

Politics and the Economy

The devastating economic effects of independence and the Revolutionary War plagued the American economy throughout the 1770s and 1780s. The cutoff of long-established patterns of overseas trade with England sent American commerce into a 20 year tailspin. While English men-of-war prowled the coast, American ships rocked idly at empty wharves, New England's once booming shipyards grew quiet, and communities whose livelihood depended on the sea sank into depression. Virginia tobacco planters, their British markets gone and their plantations open to seaborne attack, struggled to survive. Farmers in the middle and New England states often prospered when hungry armies were nearby, but their profits plummeted when the armies moved on.

Not everyone suffered equally. With British goods excluded from American markets and the wearing of homespun clothes deemed patriotic, American artisans often prospered. (The slogan "Buy American" has a long tradition.) People with the right political connections, moreover, could make handsome profits from government contracts. Henry Knox, some-

Exports and Imports, 1768–1783

Nonimportation affected colonial commerce during the late 1760s and early 1770s, but exports as well as imports plummeted with the Coercive Acts and the outbreak of war.

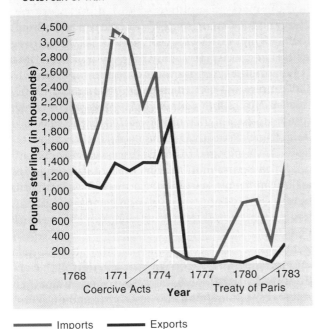

Source: U.S. Bureau of the Census.

The issue of taxation, seared into Americans' consciousness by their troubles with England, generated similarly heated controversy. As the costs of the war mounted, so did taxes. Between 1774 and 1778, Massachusetts levied more than £400,000 in taxes, a stunning increase over colonial days. One anguished soul complained that taxes took nearly one-third of the inhabitants' incomes. Massachusetts was not unique.

As taxes skyrocketed, farmers, artisans, and others of modest means argued that taxes should be payable in depreciated paper money or government securities. Lacking the hard money that states required in payment, they faced foreclosure of their property. Officials responded that allowing payment in depreciated paper would deprive governments of critically needed revenue.

Controversy swirled as well around efforts to control soaring prices. The upward spiral of prices was staggering. In Massachusetts, a bushel of corn that sold for less than a dollar in 1777 went for nearly $80 two years later, and in Maryland the price of wheat increased several thousandfold.

Every state experimented with price controls at one time or another. Seldom were such efforts effective; always they generated controversy. In Boston a

time merchant and commander of the continental artillery, observed that he was "exceedingly anxious to effect something in these fluctuating times, which may make ... [me] easy for life." In the eighteenth century, as now, the boundary between private interest and public duty was often unclear.

But even as some prospered, countless others saw their affairs fall into disarray. Intractable issues such as price and wage inflation, skyrocketing taxation, and mushrooming debt set people sharply against each other. Heated debates arose over whether the states' war debts should be paid off at face value or at some reduced rate. Arguing for full value were the states' creditors—merchants and other persons of wealth who had loaned the states money and had bought up large amounts of government securities at deep discounts. These people spoke earnestly of upholding the public honor and giving fair return to those who had risked their own resources in the revolutionary cause. Opposed were common folk angered by the speculators' profits. No one, they argued, should reap personal advantage from public distress.

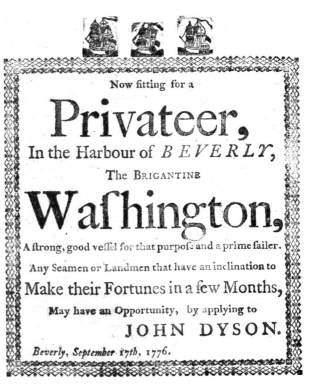

As this Massachusetts broadside suggests, the lure of adventure and hope for quick profits enticed countless young men into dangerous but exciting service aboard American privateers. (*American Antiquarian Society*)

Wholesale Price Index, 1770–1789

Prices skyrocketed as Congress and the state governments printed huge amounts of paper money to cover the costs of the war and as the British blockage reduced the supply of goods. The resulting inflation was the worst in U.S. history.

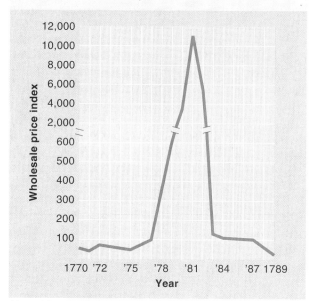

Note: 1850–1859 = 100

Source: U.S. Bureau of the Census.

crowd of women angered by the escalating cost of food tossed a merchant suspected of monopolizing commodities into a cart and dragged him through the city's streets, while "a large concourse of men stood amazed."

In general, the poor and those not yet integrated into the market economy supported price controls. They believed that goods should carry a "just price" that was fair to buyer and seller alike. In keeping with that principle, a crowd in New Windsor, New York, seized a shipment of tea bound for Albany in 1777 and sold it for what they deemed a fair offering.

Merchants, shopkeepers, and others accustomed to a commercial economy, however, believed that supply and demand should govern economic transactions. "It is contrary to the nature of commerce," observed Benjamin Franklin, "for government to interfere in the prices of commodities." Attempts to regulate prices only created a disincentive to labor, which was "the principal part of the wealth of every country."

Disputes over paper money also divided the American people. Faced with the uncontrollable escalation of wartime expenses, Congress and the states did what colonial governments had done before and American governments have done ever since: they printed money. In the first year of the war alone, they issued more than $400 million in various kinds of paper, and that was just the beginning. Only the citizens' willingness to accept such paper supported its value. That willingness rapidly

Lacking sufficient gold and silver to cover the escalating costs of war, Congress printed massive amounts of paper money, which, in spite of the printed pledge, rapidly depreciated in value. (*Smithsonian Institution*)

disappeared as the flood of paper increased. Congressional bills of credit that in 1776 were pegged against gold at the ratio of 1.5 to 1 had slipped five years later to 147 to 1. State currencies depreciated just as alarmingly. In 1780, New York exchanged its old currency for new at the rate of 128 to 1.

Immense quantities of counterfeit currency produced by unscrupulous Americans out to make a profit, as well as by British agents intent on disrupting the American war effort, added to the confusion. So worthless did American currency become that a crowd paraded the streets of Philadelphia in 1781 with paper money stuck in their hats as cockades and leading a dog plastered with congressional dollars.

The disastrous monetary depreciation had ominous social consequences. James Lovell reported nervously that "sailors with clubs" were parading the streets of Boston "instead of working for paper." With property values in disarray, it seemed at times as if the very foundations of society were coming unhinged. "The war," wrote Thomas Paine,

> has thrown property into channels where before it never was.... Monies in large sums ... enable ... [profiteers] to roll the snow ball of monopoly and forestalling ... [and] while these people are heaping up wealth ... the remaining part are jogging on in their old way, with few or no advantages.

The poor suffered most severely, for they were most vulnerable to losses in the purchasing power of wages and military pay. But they were not alone. Farmers and merchants, planters and artisans also faced growing debt and uncertainty.

Rarely has the American economy been in such disarray as at the nation's founding. There were no ready solutions to the problems of debt, taxation, price control, and paper money, for such issues often exceeded the capacity of politics for compromise and resolution. Divisive and intractable, they continued to heighten political tensions during the postwar years.

POLITICAL TUMULT IN THE STATES

The many issues embroiling American politics—church and state, slavery and the slave trade, taxation, debt relief, paper money, and arguments over political equality—came together with explosive force in the mid-1780s. The political crisis that resulted spurred demands for a new and more powerful national government.

The Limits of Republican Experimentation

In a pattern that would frequently recur in American history, the postwar era witnessed growing social and political conservatism. Exhausted by the war's ordeal, many Americans focused their energies on the immediate problems troubling their personal lives. With the patriotic crusade against England successfully concluded, the initial surge of republican reform subsided. As a consequence, political leadership fell increasingly to men convinced that republican experimentation had gone too far, that individual liberty threatened to overbalance political order, and that the "better sort" of men, not democratic newcomers, should occupy public office.

The most dramatic change occurred in Pennsylvania, where the democratic constitution of 1776 was replaced in 1790 by a far more conservative document. The new constitution provided for a strong governor who could veto legislation and control the militia, and a conservative senate designed to balance the more democratic assembly. Gaining control even of the assembly by the mid-1780s, the conservatives proceeded to dismantle much of the radicals' program, stopped issuing paper money, and rechartered the Bank of North America. Pennsylvania's experiment in radical republicanism was over.

Shays's Rebellion

The conservative resurgence generated surprisingly little controversy in Pennsylvania. Elsewhere, however, popular opposition to hard money and high-tax policies resulted in vigorous protest. Nowhere was the situation more volatile than in Massachusetts. The controversy that erupted there in 1786 echoed strongly of equal rights and popular consent, staples of the rhetoric of 1776.

Given the war's disruption of economic affairs, increasing numbers of Massachusetts citizens found by the mid-1780s that they had to borrow money simply to pay their taxes and support their families. Those who were better off borrowed so they could speculate in western land and government securities. Because there were no commercial banks in the state, people borrowed from each other in a complicated, highly unstable pyramid of credit that reached from wealthy merchants along the coast to shopkeepers and farmers in the interior.

Trouble began when English goods glutted the American market, forcing down prices. In 1785, a number of English banks, heavily overcommitted in the American trade, called in their American loans. When American merchants tried in turn to collect

This woodcut from *Bickerstaff's Genuine Boston Almanack* of 1787 depicts a county convention framing a petition for redress of grievances to the Massachusetts government. *(Library of Congress)*

debts due them by local storekeepers, a credit crisis surged through the state's economy.

Hardest hit were small farmers and laboring people in the countryside and small towns. Caught in a tightening financial bind, they turned to the state government for "stay laws" suspending the collection of private debts and thus easing the threat of foreclosure against their farms and shops. They also demanded new issues of paper money with which to pay both debts and taxes. The largest creditors, most of whom lived in commercial towns along the coast, fought such relief proposals because they wanted to collect what was owed them in hard money. They also feared that new paper money would quickly depreciate, further confounding economic affairs.

By 1786, Massachusetts farmers, desperate in the face of mounting debt and a lingering agricultural depression, were petitioning the Massachusetts assembly for relief in words that echoed the colonial protests of the 1760s. Their appeals, however, fell on deaf ears, for commercial and creditor interests now controlled the government. Turning aside appeals for tax relief, the government passed a law calling for full repayment of the state debt and levied a new round of taxes that would make payment possible. No matter that, as one angry citizen charged, "there was not . . . the money in possession or at command among the people" to pay what was due. Between 1784 and 1786, 29 towns defaulted on their tax obligations.

As frustrated Americans had done before and would do again when the law proved unresponsive to their needs, Massachusetts farmers took matters into their own hands. A Hampshire County convention of delegates from 50 towns condemned the state senate, court fees, and tax system. It advised against violence, but crowds soon began to form.

The county courts drew much of the farmers' wrath, because they issued the writs of foreclosure that private creditors and state officials demanded. On August 31, 1786, armed men prevented the county court from sitting at Northampton, and on September 5, angry citizens closed down the court at Worcester. When farmers threatened similar actions elsewhere, an alarmed Governor James Bowdoin dispatched 600 militiamen to protect the state Supreme Court, then on circuit at Springfield.

About 500 insurgents had gathered nearby under the leadership of Daniel Shays, a popular Revolutionary War captain recently fallen on hard times. A "brave and good soldier," Shays had returned home in 1780, tired and frustrated, to await payment for his military service. Like thousands of others, he had a long wait. Meanwhile, his farming went badly, debts accumulated, and, as he later recalled, "the spector of debtor's jail . . . hovered close by." Most of the men who gathered around Shays were also debtors and veterans.

The Continental Congress, worried about a possible raid on the federal arsenal at Springfield and urged by the Massachusetts delegates to take action, authorized 1,300 troops, ostensibly for service against the Indians but actually to be ready for use against Shays and his supporters. For a few weeks, Massachusetts teetered on the brink of civil conflict.

The insurrection collapsed in eastern Massachusetts in late November, but to the west it was

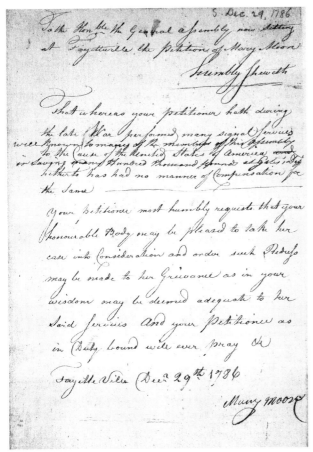

Following the war, hundreds of women petitioned state legislatures to recover property and seek redress for other war related grievances. In this petition, Mary Moore seeks compensation from the North Carolina Assembly. *(Courtesy of the North Carolina Division of Archives and History)*

far from over. When several insurgent groups refused Governor Bowdoin's order to disperse, he called out a force of 4,400 men, financed and led by worried eastern merchants. On January 26, 1787, Shays led 1,200 men toward the federal arsenal at Springfield. When they arrived, its frightened defenders opened fire, killing four of the attackers and sending the Shaysites into retreat.

Over the next several weeks, the militia chased the remnants of Shays's followers across the state and sent Shays himself fleeing into Vermont for safety. By the end of February, the rebellion was over. In March, the legislature pardoned all but Shays and three other leaders; in another year, they too were forgiven.

Similar challenges to public authority, fired by personal troubles and frustration over unresponsive governments, erupted in six other states. In Charles County, Maryland, a "tumultuary assemblage of the people" rushed into the courthouse in June 1786 and closed it down. Like the Massachusetts rebels,

they demanded paper money and the suspension of debt proceedings. The governor condemned the "riotous and tumultuous" proceedings and warned against further "violence and outrages." In South Carolina in May 1785, an incensed Hezekiah Mayham, being served by the sheriff with a writ of foreclosure, forced him to eat it on the spot. Warned Judge Aedanus Burke, not even "5,000 troops, the best in America" could enforce obedience to the court under such conditions.

Across the states, politics was in turmoil. While many felt betrayed by the Revolution's promise of equal rights and were angered by the "arrogant unresponsiveness" of government, others were alarmed by the "democratic excesses" that the Revolution appeared to have unleashed. What the immediate future might hold seemed exceedingly uncertain.

TOWARD A NEW NATIONAL GOVERNMENT

By 1786, belief was spreading among members of Congress and other political leaders that the nation was in crisis and that the republican experiment was in danger of foundering. Explanations for the crisis and prescriptions for its resolution varied, but attention focused on the inadequacies of the Articles of Confederation. Within two years, following a raucous and deeply divisive political struggle, a new constitution had replaced the Articles, altering forever the course of American history.

The Rise of Federalism

The supporters of a stronger national government called themselves Federalists (leading their opponents to adopt the name Anti-Federalists). Led by men such as Washington, Hamilton, Madison, and Jay, whose experiences in the continental army and Congress had strengthened their national vision, the Federalists believed that the nation's survival was at stake. Such men had never been comfortable with the more democratic impulses of the Revolution. While committed to moderate republicanism, they believed that democratic change had carried too far, property rights needed greater protection, and an "aristocracy of talent" should lead the country.

The Revolution, lamented John Jay, "laid open a wide field for the operation of ambition," especially for "men raised from low degrees to high stations and rendered giddy by elevation." It was time, he insisted, to find better ways of protecting "the worthy against the licentious."

Federalist leaders feared the loss of their own social and political power, but they were concerned as well about the collapse of the orderly world they believed essential to the preservation of republican liberty. In 1776, American liberty had required protection against overweening British power. Now, however, danger arose from excessive liberty that threatened to degenerate into license. "We have probably had too good an opinion of human nature," concluded Washington somberly. "Experience has taught us, that men will not adopt and carry into execution measures the best calculated for their own good, without the intervention of a coercive power." What America now needed was a "strong government, ably administered."

The Federalists regarded outbursts like Shays's uprising in Massachusetts not as evidence of genuine social distress but as threats to social and political order. Although they were reassured by the speed with which the Shaysites had been dispatched, the episode persuaded them of the need for a stronger national government managed by the "better sort."

Congress's inability to handle the national debt, establish public credit, and restore overseas trade also troubled the Federalists. Sensitive to America's economic and military weakness, smarting from French and English arrogance, and aware of continuing Anglo-European designs on North America, the Federalists called for a new national government capable of extending American trade, spurring economic recovery, and protecting national interests.

Beyond that, the Federalists shared a vision of an expanding commercial republic, its people spreading across the rich lands of the interior, its merchant ships connecting America with the markets of Europe and beyond. That vision, so rich in national promise, seemed clearly at risk.

The Grand Convention

The first step toward governmental reform came in September 1786, when delegates from five states who were gathered in Annapolis, Maryland, to discuss interstate commerce, issued a call for a convention to revise the Articles of Confederation. In February, the Confederation Congress cautiously endorsed the idea. Before long, it became clear that far more than a revision of the Articles was afoot.

During May 1787, delegates representing every state except Rhode Island began assembling in Philadelphia. The city bustled with excitement as they gathered, for the roster read like an honor roll of the Revolution. From Virginia came the distinguished lawyer George Mason, chief author of Virginia's trailblazing bill of rights, and the already legendary George Washington. Proponents of the convention had held their breath while Washington

considered whether to attend. His presence vastly increased the prospects of success. James Madison was there as well. No one, with perhaps the single exception of Alexander Hamilton, was more committed to nationalist reform. Certainly, no one had worked harder to prepare for the convention than he. Poring over treatises on republican government and natural law that his friend Thomas Jefferson sent from France, Madison brought to Philadelphia a clear design for a new national government. That design, presented to the convention as the Virginia Plan, would serve as the basis for the new constitution. Nor did anyone rival the diminutive Madison's contributions to the convention's work. Tirelessly, he took the convention floor to argue the nationalist cause or buttonhole wavering delegates to strengthen their resolve. Somehow, he also found the energy to keep extensive notes of the debates in his personal shorthand. Those notes constitute our essential record of the convention's proceedings.

Two distinguished Virginians were conspicuously absent. Thomas Jefferson was in Paris as minister to France, and the old patriot Patrick Henry, an ardent champion of state supremacy, feared what the convention would do and wanted no part of it.

James Madison of Virginia, only 36 years old when the Philadelphia convention met, worked tirelessly between 1786 and 1788 to replace the Articles of Confederation with a new and more effective national constitution. *(Mead Art Museum, Amherst Collection, Bequest of Herbert L. Pratt, 1895, [1945.82])*

From Pennsylvania came the venerable Benjamin Franklin, too old to contribute significantly to the debates but still able to call quarreling members to account and reinspire them in their work. His colleagues from Pennsylvania included the erudite Scots lawyer James Wilson, whose nationalist sympathies had been inflamed when a democratic mob, resentful of privileged lawyers and merchants, attacked his elegant Philadelphia townhouse in 1779. Robert Morris, probably the richest man in America, was there as well. Massachusetts was ably represented by Elbridge Gerry and Rufus King, while South Carolina sent John Rutledge and Charles Pinckney. Roger Sherman led Connecticut's contingent.

The New York assembly sent a deeply divided delegation. Governor George Clinton, long a personal enemy of Alexander Hamilton and determined to protect New York's autonomy as well as his own political power, saw to it that several Anti-Federalist skeptics made the trip to Philadelphia. They were no match for Hamilton, however.

Born in the Leeward Islands, the "bastard brat of a Scots-peddlar" and a strong-willed woman with a troubled marriage, Hamilton used his immense intelligence and ingratiating charm to rise rapidly in the world. Sent to New York by wealthy sponsors, he quickly established himself as a favorite of the city's mercantile community. While still in his early twenties, he became Washington's wartime aide-de-camp. That relationship served Hamilton well for the next 20 years. Returning from the war, he married the wealthy Elizabeth Schuyler, thereby securing his personal fortune and strengthening his political connections. Together with Madison, Hamilton had promoted the abortive Annapolis convention. At Philadelphia, he was determined to drive his nationalist vision ahead.

Meeting in Independence Hall, where the Declaration of Independence had been proclaimed little more than a decade earlier, the convention elected Washington as its presiding officer, adopted rules of procedure, and, after spirited debate, voted to close the doors and conduct its business in secret.

Drafting the Constitution

Debate focused first on the Virginia Plan, introduced on May 29 by Edmund Randolph. It outlined a potentially powerful national government and effectively set the convention's agenda. According to its provisions, there would be a bicameral Congress, with the lower house elected by the people and the upper house, or Senate, chosen by the lower house from nominees proposed by the state legislatures. The plan also called for a president who would be named by the Congress, a national judiciary, and a Council of Revision, whose task was to review the constitutionality of federal laws.

The smaller states quickly objected to the Virginia Plan's call for proportional rather than equal representation of the states. On June 15,

This painting by Thomas Rossiter, done in the early nineteenth century, provides an imaginative portrayal of the Philadelphia convention, with George Washington presiding and a rising sun, symbolic of the new nation, shining behind him. *(Independence National Historical Park Collection)*

William Paterson introduced a counterproposal, the New Jersey Plan. It urged retention of the Articles of Confederation as the basic structure of government while conferring on Congress the long-sought powers to tax and regulate foreign and interstate commerce. After three days of heated debate, by a vote of seven states to three, the delegates adopted the Virginia Plan as the basis for further discussions. It was now clear that the convention would set aside the Articles for a much stronger national government. The only question was how powerful the new government would be.

At times over the next four months, it seemed that the Grand Convention would collapse under the weight of its own disagreements and the oppressive summer heat. How were the conflicting interests of large and small states to be reconciled? How should the balance of power between national and state governments be struck? How could an executive be created that was strong enough to govern but not so strong as to endanger republican liberty? And what, if anything, would the convention say about slavery and the slave trade, issues on which northerners and southerners, antislavery and proslavery advocates so passionately disagreed?

At one extreme was an audaciously conservative proposal, made by Hamilton, for a Congress and president elected for life and a national government so powerful that the states would become little more than administrative agencies. Finding his plan under attack and his influence rapidly eroding, Hamilton withdrew from the convention in late June. He would return a month later but make few additional contributions to the convention's work.

At the other extreme stood the ardent Anti-Federalist Luther Martin of Maryland. Rude and unkempt, Martin opposed anything that threatened state sovereignty or smacked of aristocracy. Increasingly isolated by the convention's nationalist inclinations, Martin also returned home, in his case to spread the alarm.

By early July, with tempers frayed and frustration growing over the apparent deadlock, the delegates agreed to recess, ostensibly for Independence Day but actually to let Franklin, Roger Sherman of Connecticut, and several others make a final effort at compromise. All agreed that only a bold stroke could prevent a collapse.

That stroke came on July 12, as part of what has become known as the Great Compromise. The reassembled delegates settled one major point of controversy by agreeing that representation in the lower house should be based on the total of each state's white population plus three-fifths of its

blacks. Though African Americans were not accorded citizenship and could not vote, the southern delegates argued that they should be fully counted for this purpose. Delegates from the northern states, where relatively few blacks lived, did not want them counted at all, but the bargain was struck. As part of this compromise, the convention agreed that direct taxes would also be apportioned on the basis of population and that blacks would be counted similarly in that calculation. On July 16, the convention accepted the principle that the states should have equal votes in the Senate. Thus the interests of both large states and small were effectively accommodated.

The convention then submitted its work to a committee of detail for drafting in proper constitutional form. That group reported on August 6, and for the next month the delegates hammered out the language of the document's seven articles. On several occasions, differences seemed so great that it was uncertain whether the convention could proceed. In each instance, however, agreement was reached, and the discussion continued.

Determined to give the new government the stability that state governments lacked, the delegates created an electoral process designed to bring persons of wide experience and solid reputation into national office. An Electoral College of wise and experienced leaders, selected at the direction of state legislatures, would meet to choose the president. The process functioned exactly that way during the first several presidential elections.

Selection of the Senate would be similarly indirect, for its members were to be named by the state legislatures. (Not until 1913, with ratification of the Seventeenth Amendment, would the American people elect their senators directly.) Even the House of Representatives, the only popularly elected branch of the new government, was to be filled with people of standing and wealth, for the Federalists were confident that only well-established politicians would be able to attract the necessary votes.

The delegates' final set of compromises touched the fate of black Americans. At the insistence of southerners, the convention agreed that the slave trade would not formally end for another 20 years. As drafted, the Constitution did not contain the words *slavery* or *slave trade*, but spoke more vaguely about not prohibiting the "migration or importation of such persons as any of the states now existing shall think proper to admit." The meaning, however, was entirely clear.

Despite Gouverneur Morris's impassioned charge that slavery was a "nefarious institution" that would

Gradually, as Indian-white conflict intensified and as white Americans turned to the ancient republics of Greece and Rome for inspiration, Columbia came to be represented as a white woman clothed in the flowing robes of classical attire. In this painting by Samuel Jacobs, Columbia offers the promise of education to a group of black Americans. *(The Library Company of Philadelphia)*

bring "the curse of Heaven on the states where it prevails," the delegates firmly rejected a proposal to abolish slavery, thereby tacitly acknowledging its legitimacy. More than that, they guaranteed slavery's protection, by writing in Section 2 of Article 4 that "No person held to service or labour in one state, . . . [and] escaping into another, shall, in consequence of any law . . . therein, be discharged from such service, but shall be delivered up on claim of the party to whom such service or labour may be due." Through such convoluted language, the delegates provided federal sanction for the capture and return of runaway slaves. This fugitive slave clause would return to haunt northern consciences in the years ahead. At the time, however, it seemed a small price to pay for sectional harmony and a new government. Northern accommodation to the demands of the southern delegates was eased, moreover, by knowledge that southerners in the Confederation Congress, still meeting in New York City, had agreed to prohibit new slaves from entering the Northwest Territory.

Although the Constitution's unique federal system of government called for shared responsibilities between the nation and the states, it decisively strengthened the national government. Congress would now have the authority to levy and collect taxes, regulate commerce with foreign nations and

between the states, devise uniform rules for naturalization, administer national patents and copyrights, and control the federal district in which it would eventually be located. Conspicuously missing was any statement reserving to the states all powers not explicitly conferred on the central government. Such language had proved crippling in the Articles of Confederation. On the contrary, the Constitution contained a number of clauses bestowing vaguely defined grants of power on the new government. Section 8 of Article 1, for example, granted Congress the authority to "provide for the . . . general welfare of the United States" as well as to "make all laws . . . necessary and proper for carrying into execution . . . all . . . powers vested by this Constitution in the government of the United States." Later generations would call these phrases "elastic clauses" and would use them to expand the federal government's activities.

In addition, Section 10 of Article 1 contained a litany of powers now denied the states, among them issuing paper money, passing laws impairing the obligation of contracts, and entering into agreements with foreign powers other than by the consent of Congress. A final measure of the Federalists' determination to ensure the new government's supremacy over the states, was the assertion in Article 6 that the Constitution and all laws and treaties passed under it were to be regarded as the "supreme Law of the Land."

When the convention had finished its business, 3 of the 42 remaining delegates refused to sign the document. The other 39, however, affixed their names and forwarded it to the Confederation Congress along with the request that it be sent on to the states for approval. On September 17, the Grand Convention adjourned.

Federalists versus Anti-Federalists

Ratification presented the Federalists with a more difficult problem than they had faced at Philadelphia, for the debate now shifted to the states where sentiment was sharply divided and the political situation was more difficult to control. Recognizing the unlikelihood of gaining quick agreement by all 13 states, the Federalists stipulated that the Constitution should go into effect when any nine agreed to it. Other states could then enter the Union as they were ready. Ratification was to be decided by specially elected conventions rather than by the state assemblies. Approval by such conventions would give the new Constitution greater legitimacy by grounding it in the consent of the people.

In the Confederation Congress, opponents of the new Constitution charged that the Philadelphia Convention had grossly exceeded its authority. But after a few days' debate, the Congress dutifully forwarded the document to the states for consideration. Word of the dramatic changes being proposed spread rapidly. In each state, Federalists and Anti-Federalists, the latter now actively opposing the Constitution, prepared to debate the new articles of government.

Although levels of Federalist and Anti-Federalist strength differed from state to state, opposition to the Constitution was widespread and vocal. Some critics warned that a stronger central government would threaten state interests. Others, like Timothy Bloodworth, charged the Federalists with betraying revolutionary republicanism. Like all "energetic" governments, they warned, the one being proposed would be corrupted by its own power. Far from the watchful eyes of the citizenry, its officials would behave as power wielders always had, and American liberty, so recently preserved at such high cost, would again come under attack.

The Anti-Federalists were aghast at the Federalists' vision of an expanding "republican empire." "The idea of . . . [a] republic, on an average of 1,000 miles in length, and 800 in breadth, and containing 6 millions of white inhabitants all reduced to the

same standards of morals, . . . habits . . . [and] laws," exclaimed one incredulous critic, "is itself an absurdity, and contrary to the whole experience of mankind." Such an extended republic would quickly fall prey to factional conflict and internal disorder. The Anti-Federalists continued to believe that republican liberty could be preserved only in small, homogeneous societies, where the seeds of faction were few and public virtue guided citizens' behavior.

Nor did the Anti-Federalists believe that the proposed separation of executive, legislative, and judicial branches or the intended balance between state and national governments would prevent power's abuse. Government, they insisted, must be kept simple, for complexity only confused the people and cloaked selfish ambition.

Though joined by a common belief in the dangers of central government, Anti-Federalists were also motivated by conflicting agendas. Some opposed the new national government not because it was anti-democratic, but because it threatened their own, long-established and state-based political power. In the South, many Anti-Federalists held slaves, and their appeals to local authority did not always mean support for political equality, even among whites. Other opponents of the proposed constitution, genuinely democratic in belief, were suspicious of all political elites and regarded the states as democratic bulwarks against consolidated power. Allied as well in opposition were countless cottagers, tenant farmers, and less affluent mechanics, fiercely egalitarian in attitude, whose concerns seldom reached beyond the circumstances of their daily lives.

Federalist spokesmen moved quickly to counter the Anti-Federalists' attack, for many of those criticisms carried the sanction of the revolutionary past. Their most important effort was a series of essays penned by James Madison, Alexander Hamilton, and John Jay and published in New York under the pseudonym Publius. The *Federalist* essays, as they were called, were written to promote ratification in New York but were quickly reprinted elsewhere.

Madison, Hamilton, and Jay moved systematically through the Constitution, explaining its virtues and responding to the Anti-Federalists' attacks. In the process, they described a political vision fundamentally different from that of their Anti-Federalist opponents.

No difference was more dramatic than the Federalists' treatment of governmental power. Power, the Federalists now argued, was not the enemy of liberty but its guarantor. Where government was not sufficiently "energetic" and "efficient" (these were favorite Federalist words), demagogues

The eagle, an important symbol of the new nation, appeared on water pitchers, whiskey bottles, flags, newspaper mastheads, and fabrics of all kinds. The flag also became an important icon. While its red and white stripes represented the 13 original states, its blue field of stars was modified as new states entered the Union. (quilt: *Magnette, Edith, Quilt, Index of American Design,* © *2000 Board of Trustees, National Gallery of Art, Washington, c. 1941, watercolor and graphite on paperboard, .759 × .506 [29 ⅞ × 19 ¹⁵/₁₆]*; pine chest: *from the Collections of Henry Ford Museum & Greenfield Village [57.28.61]*)

and disorganizers would find opportunity to do their nefarious work. It is far better, Hamilton wrote in *Federalist No. 26,* "to hazard the abuse of . . . confidence than to embarrass the government and endanger the public safety by impolitic restrictions of . . . authority."

The authors of the *Federalist* also countered the Anti-Federalists' warning that a single, extended republic encompassing the country's economic and social diversity would lead inevitably to factional conflict and destroy republican liberty. Turning the Anti-Federalists' classic, republican argument on its head, they explained that political divisions were the inevitable accompaniment of human liberty. Wrote Madison in *Federalist No. 10:* "Liberty is to faction what air is to fire, an aliment without which it instantly expires." To suppress faction would bring the destruction of liberty itself.

Earlier emphasis on public virtue as the guarantor of political order, the Federalists explained, had been naive, for few people would consistently put the public good ahead of their own interests. Politics had to heed this harsh fact of human nature and provide for peaceful compromise among conflicting groups. That could be best accomplished by expanding the nation so that it included innumerable factions. Out of the clash and accommodation of multiple social and economic interests would emerge compromise and the best possible approximation of the public good.

The Federalists' argument established the basic rationale for modern democratic politics, but it left the Anti-Federalists sputtering in frustration. Where in the Federalists' scheme was there a place for that familiar abstraction, the public good? What would become of public virtue in a system built on the notion of competing, private interests? In such a free market of competition, the Anti-Federalists warned, the wealthy and powerful would thrive, while ordinary folk would suffer.

As the ratification debate revealed, the two camps held sharply contrasting visions of the new republic. The Anti-Federalists remained much closer to the original republicanism of 1776, with its suspicion of power and wealth, its emphasis on the primacy of local government, and its fears of national development. They envisioned a decentralized republic filled with citizens who were self-reliant, guided by public virtue, and whose destiny was determined primarily by the states rather than the nation. Anxious about the future, they longed to preserve the political world of an idealized past.

RECOVERING THE PAST

Patriotic Paintings

The questions that historians ask are limited only by their own imagination and the evidence left behind for them to study. In addition to written documents such as household inventories and militia rolls, and material artifacts like tombstones and the archaeological residue of burial mounds, historians also examine paintings and other forms of visual evidence for information about the past.

While revealing the development of artistic styles and techniques, paintings also provide important windows into past eras for social and cultural historians by revealing how people looked and did their work, as well as what the landscape and built environment were like. Paintings offer insights additionally into the values and attitudes of past times, for they are often intended to enlighten and instruct, as well as please the viewer's eye.

So it was with Charles Willson Peale, who, as a member of the Pennsylvania militia, carried paint kits and canvas along with his musket as he followed George Washington during the Revolutionary War. Before it was over, he had completed four portraits of the general.

And so it was, even more spectacularly, with the artist John Trumbull, who recorded on canvas some of the most dramatic events of the nation's founding. Slighted for promotion during the Rhode Island campaign early in the war, Trumbull resigned his commission to become a painter. After a frustrating start, he sailed for London, where he studied with the artist Benjamin West, another transplanted American. Imprisoned briefly at the urging of angry American Loyalists, Trumbull was deported to the United States. Returning to England at the war's end, he was urged by West and Thomas Jefferson to paint an ambitious series of "national history" canvases. Over the next four decades, in addition to numerous portraits, religious subjects, and landscapes, Trumbull fashioned the most famous sequence of patriotic paintings ever undertaken by an American artist.

Included were four canvases, depicting crucial military and civil turning points in the struggle for American independence, commissioned by Congress in the early nineteenth century and now hanging in the capitol rotunda in Washington, D.C.—The

Surrender of General Burgoyne at Saratoga, The Surrender of Lord Cornwallis at Yorktown, The Declaration of Independence, and *The Resignation of General Washington* as commander of the continental army. In addition to those monumental works, Trumbull fashioned a number of heroic battle scenes, including *The Death of General Warren at the Battle of Bunker Hill,* shown opposite.

Though Trumbull knew Warren and others who fought at Bunker Hill, had witnessed the battle from a distance, and was familiar with the techniques of military combat from his own months in the army, he was not primarily concerned with literal accuracy as he composed his painting. Guided by the canons of classical aesthetics popular at the time, he was more interested in the power of artistic "invention" to impart "ideal" truths through the use of brush and pigment.

Examine the painting carefully. How has the artist arranged the figures in relationship to each other? What facial expressions and postures has he given to the people depicted? In what ways do the banners, clouds, and uses of light and color contribute to the painting's overall effect? What messages about the Revolutionary War did Trumbull want viewers to carry away from the canvas?

In all his historical canvases, Trumbull was intent on promoting national pride and constructing public memory. How does this painting serve those purposes? Why was the creation of a shared public memory so important during the early years of the new republic? Might Trumbull have had future generations of Americans as well as his own contemporaries in mind as he did his work?

Art and politics have been intimately related throughout our history, for painting and theater, music and other forms of performance art have been employed to challenge as well as celebrate political leaders and their policies.

Reflecting on the Past   Think for a moment about the connections between art and politics in our own time. Why have controversies recently swirled around the National Endowments for the Arts and the Humanities? Should the government provide financial assistance for the arts? If so, should such assistance be accompanied by restrictions on the political messages such art might convey? Is art ever nonpolitical?

John Trumbull, *The Death of General Warren at the Battle of Bunker Hill.* (Francis G. Mayer/Corbis)

The Federalists, on the other hand, persuaded that America's situation had changed dramatically since 1776, embraced the idea of nationhood and looked forward with anticipation to the development of a rising "republican empire," fueled by commercial development and led by men of wealth and talent. Both Federalists and Anti-Federalists claimed to be heirs of the Revolution, yet they differed fundamentally in what they understood that heritage to be.

The Struggle over Ratification

No one knows what most Americans thought of the proposed Constitution, for no national plebiscite on it was ever taken. Probably no more than several hundred thousand people participated in the elections for the state ratifying conventions, and many of the delegates carried no binding instructions from their constituents on how they should vote. A majority of the people probably opposed the document, either out of indifference or alarm. Fortunately for the Federalists, they did not have to persuade most Americans but needed only to secure majorities in nine of the state ratifying conventions, a much less formidable task.

They set about it with determination. As soon as the Philadelphia Convention adjourned, its members hurried home to organize the ratification movement in their states. In Delaware and Georgia, New Jersey and Connecticut, where the Federalists were confident of their strength, they pressed quickly for a vote. Where the outcome was uncertain, as in New York, Massachusetts, and Virginia, they delayed, hoping that word of ratification elsewhere would work to their benefit.

It took less than a year to secure approval by the necessary nine states. Delaware, Pennsylvania, and New Jersey ratified first, in December 1787. Approval came a month later in Georgia and Connecticut. Massachusetts ratified in February 1788, but only after considerable political maneuvering. In an effort to woo Anti-Federalist delegates and persuade the uncommitted, Federalist leaders there agreed to forward a set of amendments outlining a federal bill of rights along with notice of ratification. The strategy worked, for it brought Samuel Adams and John Hancock into line, and with them the crucial convention votes that they controlled.

Maryland and South Carolina were the seventh and eighth states to approve. That left New Hampshire and Virginia vying for the honor of being ninth and putting the Constitution over the top. There was staunch opposition in both states. The New Hampshire convention met on February 13. Sensing that they lacked the necessary votes, the

Ratification of the Constitution

Votes of State Ratifying Conventions

State	Date	For	Against
Delaware	December 1787	30	0
Pennsylvania	December 1787	46	23
New Jersey	December 1787	38	0
Georgia	January 1788	26	0
Connecticut	January 1788	128	40
Massachusetts	February 1788	187	168
Maryland	April 1788	63	11
South Carolina	May 1788	149	73
New Hampshire	June 1788	57	47
Virginia	June 1788	89	79
New York	July 1788	30	27
North Carolina	November 1789	194	77
Rhode Island	May 1790	34	32

Federalists adjourned the convention until mid-June and worked feverishly to build support. When the convention reconvened, it took but three days to secure a Federalist majority. New Hampshire ratified on June 21.

Two massive gaps in the new Union remained—Virginia and New York. Clearly, the nation could not endure without them. In Virginia, Madison gathered support by promising that the new Congress would immediately consider a federal bill of rights. Other Federalists spread the rumor that Patrick Henry, among the most influential Anti-Federalist leaders, had changed sides, a charge that Henry angrily denied. His oratory, however, proved no match for the careful politicking of Madison and others. On June 25, the Virginia convention voted to ratify by the narrow margin of 10 votes.

The New York convention gathered on June 17 at Poughkeepsie, with the Anti-Federalist followers of Governor Clinton firmly in command. Hamilton worked for delay, hoping that news of the results in New Hampshire and Virginia would turn the tide. For several weeks, approval hung in the balance while the two sides maneuvered for support. On July 27, approval squeaked through, 30 to 27. That left two states still uncommitted. North Carolina (with Timothy Bloodworth's skeptical approval) finally ratified in November 1789. Rhode Island did not enter the Union until May 1790, more than a year after the new government had gotten underway.

The Social Geography of Ratification

A glance at patterns of Federalist and Anti-Federalist strength in the state ratifying conventions reveals their different sources of political support.

Federalist strength was concentrated in areas along the coast and navigable rivers, and was strongest in cities and towns. Merchants and businessmen supported the Constitution most ardently. Enthusiasm also ran high among urban laborers, artisans, and shopkeepers—surprisingly so, given the Anti-Federalists' criticism of wealth and power and their emphasis on democratic equality. City artisans and workers, after all, had been in the vanguard of democratic reform during the Revolution. But in the troubled circumstances of the late 1780s, they worried primarily about their livelihoods and believed that a stronger government could better promote overseas trade and protect American artisans from foreign competition.

On July 4, 1788, a grand procession celebrating the Constitution's ratification wound through the streets of Philadelphia. Seventeen thousand strong, it graphically demonstrated the breadth of support for the Constitution. At the head of the line marched lawyers, merchants, and others of the city's elite. Close behind came representatives of virtually every trade in the city, from ship's carpenters to shoemakers, each trade with its own floats, flags, and mottoed

Federalist and Anti-Federalist Areas, 1787–1788

Distinct geographic patterns of Federalist and Anti-Federalist strength developed during the ratification debate. This map shows areas whose delegates to the state ratifying conventions voted for and against the Constitution.

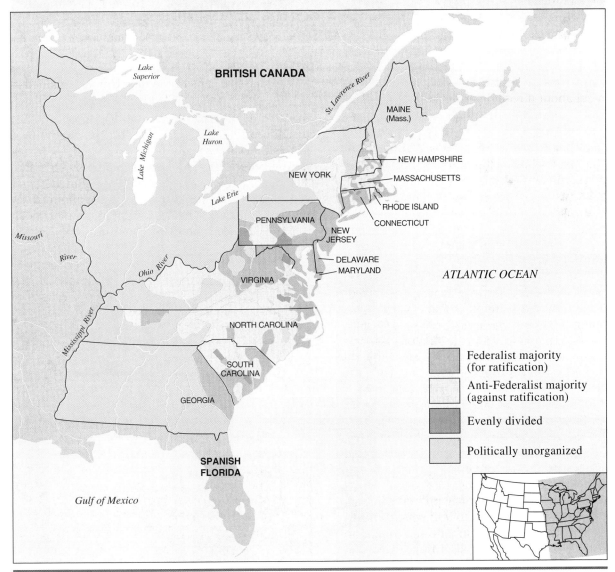

The federal ship *Hamilton* formed the centerpiece of a grand procession in New York City celebrating the successful ratification of the new Constitution.

banners. "May commerce flourish and industry be rewarded," declared the mariners and shipbuilders. "May the federal government revive our trade," exclaimed the bakers. "Home-brewed is best," insisted the maltsters. For the moment, declared the democratic-minded physician Benjamin Rush in amazement, "rank. . . forgot all its claims." Within a few years, political disputes would divide merchants and artisans once again. For the moment, however, people of all ranks joined in celebrating the new Constitution.

Elsewhere differences of class and geography defined political alignments more sharply. The Constitution found support among commercial farmers and southern planters eager for profit and anxious about overseas markets. But in the interior, Federalist enthusiasm waned and Anti-Federalist sentiment increased. The centers of Anti-Federalism lay away from the coast, in central New England, upstate New York, the Virginia Piedmont and southside, and western Carolina. Among ordinary farmers living outside the market economy, local loyalties and the republicanism of 1776 still held sway, for they found Federalist visions of an expanding "American empire" alarming.

Why did the Federalists finally prevail? After all, their opponents had only to tap into people's deep-seated fears of central government and appeal to their local loyalties. The Federalists, by contrast, had to explain how republicanism had suddenly be-

come compatible with a strong national government and an expanding empire. Moreover, they faced the complicated task of coordinating ratification in the various states.

The Federalists' task was simplified by the widespread perception that the Articles of Confederation were inadequate and that America's experiment in republican independence was doomed unless deci-

Timeline	
1784	Treaty of Fort Stanwix with the Iroquois Spain closes the Mississippi River to American navigation
1785	Treaty of Hopewell with the Cherokee Land Ordinance for the Northwest Territory Jay–Gardoqui negotiations

1786	Virginia adopts "Bill for Establishing
	    Religious Freedom"
	Annapolis Convention calls for revision of the
	    Articles of Confederation

1786–1787	Shays's Rebellion
1787	Northwest Ordinance Constitutional Convention *Federalist Papers* published by Hamilton, Jay, and Madison
1788	Constitution ratified

sive action was taken. More than anything, however, the Federalists succeeded because of their determination and political skill. Most of the Revolution's major leaders were Federalists. Time and again these worthies spoke out for the Constitution, and time and again their support proved decisive. Their experience in the continental army and as members of the Continental and Confederation Congresses fired their vision of what the nation might become. They brought their vision to the ratification process and asked others to share it. Altogether, it was an impressive political performance. With their success, the Federalists turned the American republic in a new and fateful direction.

✦ *Conclusion*

COMPLETING THE REVOLUTION

Only five years had passed between England's acknowledgment of American independence in 1783 and ratification of the new national Constitution, yet to many Americans it seemed far longer than that. At war's end, the difficulties of sustaining American liberty were already evident. The experience of the 1780s added to these difficulties as the American people struggled to survive in a hostile Atlantic environment and cope with troublesome issues of church and state, slavery and the slave trade, and an economy shattered by the cut off of overseas trade and rampant inflation. Throughout the resulting political turmoil, Americans continued to argue over how democratic their experiment in republicanism could safely be, and even whether it could survive.

At the same time, the American people retained an immense reservoir of optimism about the future. Had they not defeated mighty England? Was not their Revolution destined to change the course of history and provide a model for all mankind? Did not America's wonderfully rich interior contain the promise of limitless economic and social opportunity? Though Timothy Bloodworth and others continued to worry, countless Americans, still filled with the enthusiasm of their new beginning, answered with a resounding "Yes." Much would depend, of course, on their new Constitution and the government soon to be created under it. As the ratification debate subsided and the Confederation Congress prepared to adjourn, the American people looked eagerly and anxiously ahead.

✦ Recommended Reading

Struggling with the Peacetime Agenda
Richard Buel, *In Irons: Britain's Naval Supremacy and the American Revolutionary Economy* (1998); Eric Hinderaker, *Elusive Empires: Constructing Colonialism in the Ohio Valley, 1673–1800* (1997); Ronald Hoffman et.al., eds., *The Economy of Early America: The Revolutionary Period, 1763–1790* (1985); Cathy Matson and Peter Onuf, *A Union of Interests: Political and Economic Thought in Revolutionary America* (1990); Peter Onuf, *Statehood and Union: A History of the Northwest Ordinance* (1987); Jack Rakove, *The Beginnings of National Politics: An Interpretive History of the Continental Congress* (1979).

Sources of Political Conflict
Dee Andrews, *The Methodists and Revolutionary America, 1760–1800* (2000); Ira Berlin and Ronald Hoffman, eds., *Slavery and Freedom in the Age of the American Revolution* (1983); Thomas Curry, *First Freedoms: Church and State in America to the Passage of the First Amendment* (1986); David B. Davis, *The Problem of Slavery in the Age of the Democratic Revolution* (1975); Ronald Hoffman and Peter Albert, eds., *Religion in a New Age* (1994); James Hutson, ed., *Religion and the New Republic: Faith in the Founding of America* (2000); Susan Juster, *Disorderly Women: Sexual Politics and Evangelicalism in Revolutionary New England* (1994); William McLaughlin, *Soul Liberty: The Baptists' Struggle in New England, 1630–1833* (1991); Gary Nash and Jean Soderlund, *Freedom by Degrees: Emancipation in Pennsylvania and Its Aftermath* (1991); T. Stephen Whitman, *The Price of Freedom: Slavery and Manumission in Baltimore and Early National Maryland* (1997).

Political Tumult in the States
Robert Gross, ed., *In Debt to Shays: The Bicentennial of an Agrarian Rebellion* (1993); Ronald Hoffman et al., *An Uncivil War: The Southern Backcountry During the American Revolution* (1985); Ronald Hoffman and Peter Albert, eds., *Sovereign States in an Age of Uncertainty* (1978); Jackson T. Main, *Political Parties Before the Constitution* (1973); Robert Olwell, *Masters, Slaves, and Subjects: The Culture of Power in the South Carolina Low Country, 1740–1790* (1998); David Szatmary, *Shays's Rebellion: The Making of an Agrarian Rebellion* (1988); Albert Tillson, Jr., *Gentry and Commonfolk: Political Culture on a Virginia Frontier, 1740–1789* (1991); Gordon Wood, *The Radicalism of the American Revolution* (1992).

Toward a New National Government
Lance Banning, *The Sacred Fire of Liberty: James Madison and the Founding of the Federal Republic*

(1995); Richard Beeman et al., *Beyond Confederation: Origins of the Constitution and American National Identity* (1987); Stephen Boyd, *The Politics of Opposition: Antifederalists and the Acceptance of the Constitution* (1979); Patrick Conley and John Kaminsky, eds., *The Constitution and the States* (1988); Saul Cornell, *The Other Founders: Anti-Federalism and the Dissenting Tradition in America, 1788–1828* (1999); Frederick Marks III, *Independence on Trial: Foreign Affairs and the Making of the Constitution* (1973); Richard Morris, *Witnesses at the Creation: Hamilton, Madison, Jay, and the Constitution* (1985); Jack Rakove, *Original Meanings: Politics and Ideas in the Making of the Constitution* (1996); Gary Wills, *Explaining America: The "Federalist"* (1981); Gordon Wood, *The Creation of the American Republic, 1776–1787* (1969).

Fiction and Film

The visually lush commercial film *Jefferson in Paris* (1995) combines a depiction of Jefferson's years as U.S. minister to France (1785–1789) with commentaries on themes of liberty and slavery involving events leading to the French Revolution and Jefferson's controversial liaison with his slave girl Sally Hemmings. The documentary film *Unearthing the Slave Trade* (1994) uses the recent discovery and excavation of an old black burying ground near Wall Street in New York City, where deceased slaves were interred from about 1712 to 1790, to depict the life of urban slaves in eighteenth-century America. Herman Melville's novel *Israel Potter* (1855) tells the story of a fictitious Revolutionary War sailor who encounters Benjamin Franklin, Ethan Allen, and John Paul Jones during his adventures and ends up in England as a gardener to King George III. In *Those Who Love: A Biographical Novel of Abigail and John Adams* (1965), Irving Stone traces the life story of this remarkable couple, largely through Abigail's eyes, as they move from early courtship through the end of John's presidency in 1800.

✦ Discovering U.S. History Online

1777–1815: The Revolutionary War to the War of 1812

www.tax.org/Museum/1777-1815.htm

This essay explores by timeline the way the new nation dealt with finances, debt, and taxes.

Indian Affairs: Laws and Treaties

www.digital.library.okstate.edu/kappler

This site offers a digitized and searchable version of U.S. treaties, laws, and executive orders pertaining to Native American tribes. Volume two contains treaties from 1770–1890.

Colonial Currency

www.etext.lib.virginia.edu/users/brock/

This site includes informative primary and secondary sources on early American currency.

Evolution of Territories and States from the Old "Northwest Territory"

www.jlindquist.com/mapsupp1.html

This site includes a link to the full text of the Northwest Ordinance of 1787, tables and maps showing the geographical evolution of the territory, photos of the area, and an image of the map showing Jefferson's concept for the states to be carved out of the territory.

Religion and the American Revolution

www.lcweb.loc.gov/exhibits/religion/rel03.html

Providing an overview of eighteenth-century religion in the American colonies, this site draws on primary source material such as paintings of clergymen, title pages of published sermons, and other artifacts.

A Struggle from the Start

www.hartford-hwp.com/HBHP/exhibit/index.html

A local history, this site presents a virtual exhibit of the history of Hartford's African-American community from 1638 to the present, including the post-revolutionary period.

Shays' Rebellion

www.sjchs-history.org/shays.html

A brief, illustrated explanation of the rebellion and its participants.

Within These Walls

www.americanhistory.si.edu/house/default.asp

Part of the museum's "Hands on History," this virtual exhibit tells the story of five families who lived in one house over 200 years, including the Choate family (1757–1772).

You Be the Historian

www.americanhistory.si.edu/hohr/springer

Part of the Smithsonian's online museum, this exhibit enables students to examine artifacts from the home of New Castle, Delaware, residents Thomas and Elizabeth Springer and interpret the lives of a late eighteenth-century American family.

The Quock Walker Case

www.pbs.org/wgbh/aia/part2/2h38.html

This site presents the background of the case as well as the full text of the document.

The Founders' Constitution

www.press-pubs.uchicago.edu/founders/

An online anthology of the five-volume print edition, this site presents the full text (searchable) of the Constitution and of such "fundamental documents" as the Northwest Ordinance. Many primary source letters revealing the formation of the ideas that would become the constitution are also available on the site.

A Procedural Guide to the Electoral College

www.archives.gov/federal_register/electoral_college/electoral_college.html

This site explains how the Electoral College works as well as how it was established.

The Federalist

www.law.emory.edu/FEDERAL/federalist
www.law.emory.edu/FEDERAL/usconst.html

This searchable site, which presents a collection of the most important *Federalist Papers* as well as the complete text of the Constitution, is especially useful for its information about the Bill of Rights and other constitutional amendments.

Documents from the Continental Congress and the Constitutional Convention, 1774–1789

www.memory.loc.gov/ammem/bdsds/bdsdhome.html

This site allows access to the Continental Congress Broadside Collection (253 titles) and the Constitutional Convention Broadside Collection (21 titles), containing documents relating to the work of Congress and the drafting and ratification of the Constitution. Items include extracts of the journals of Congress, resolutions, proclamations, committee reports, treaties, and early printed versions of the U.S. Constitution and the Declaration of Independence.

Independence Hall National Historical Park

www.nps.gov/inde/visit.html

This National Park Service site contains images and historical accounts of Independence Hall and other Philadelphia buildings closely associated with the founding of the United States.

Creating a Nation

In December 1790, the national government moved from New York to Philadelphia, where it stayed until moving to the new capital in the District of Columbia in 1799. While in Philadelphia, the House and Senate met in Congress Hall, adjacent to the Philadelphia State House depicted here. In this image, a variety of people, including several Indians, mingle in the State House yard. *(William Birch,* The State House, *Philadelphia, 1800, Historical Society of Pennsylvania)*

◆ *American Stories*

QUESTIONING AUTHORITIES

In October 1789, David Brown arrived in Dedham, Massachusetts. Born about 50 years earlier in Bethlehem, Connecticut, Brown served in the revolutionary army. After the war, he shipped out on an American merchantman to see the world. His travels, as he reported, took him to "nineteen different . . . Kingdoms in Europe, and nearly all the United States." For two years before settling in Dedham, he visited scores of Massachusetts towns, supporting himself as a day laborer while discussing the troubled state of public affairs with local townspeople.

Initially, the people of Dedham took little notice of Brown, but he soon made his presence felt. Though he had little formal schooling, he was a man of powerful opinions and considerable natural ability. His reading and personal experience had persuaded him that government was a conspiracy of the rich to exploit farmers, artisans, and other common folk, and he was quick to make his opinions known.

The object of his wrath was the central government recently established under the new national constitution. Though he could cite no evidence, he accused government leaders of engrossing the nation's western lands for themselves. "Five hundred [people] out of the union of five millions receive all the benefit of public property and live upon the ruins of the rest of the community," he fumed in one of his numerous pamphlets. Such a government, he warned, would soon lose the confidence of the people.

In the highly charged political climate of the 1790s, Brown's exaggerated attacks on the new government brought a sharp response. In 1798, John Davis, the federal district attorney in Boston, issued a warrant for Brown's arrest on charges of sedition, while government-supported newspapers attacked him as a "rallying point of insurrection and disorder." Fearing arrest, Brown fled to Salem, where he was caught and charged with intent to defame the government and aid the country's enemies. Lacking $400 bail, he was clapped in prison.

In June 1799, Brown came before the U.S. Circuit Court, Justice Samuel Chase presiding. Chase's behavior was anything but judicious. Convinced that critics of the administration were enemies of the republic, Chase was determined to make Brown an example. Confused and hoping for leniency, Brown pleaded guilty to the charges against him.

Ignoring Brown's plea, Chase directed the federal prosecutor to "examine the witness . . . so that the degree of his guilt might be duly ascertained." Before passing sentence, Chase demanded that Brown provide the names of his accomplices and a list of subscribers to his writings. When Brown refused, protesting that he would "lose all my friends," Chase sentenced him to a fine of $480 and 18 months in jail, no matter that Brown could not pay the fine and faced the prospect of indefinite imprisonment.

In rendering judgment, Chase castigated Brown for his "disorganizing doctrines and . . . falsehoods, and the very alarming and dangerous excesses to which he attempted to incite the uninformed part of the community." Not all citizens, Chase thought, should be allowed to comment so brashly on public affairs. For nearly two years, Brown languished in prison. Not until the Federalist party was defeated in the election of 1800 and the Jeffersonian Republicans had taken office was he freed.

David Brown discovered how easy it was for critics of the government to get into trouble during the 1790s, one of the most tumultuous decades in American political history. Though independence had been won, the struggle over political power and control of the revolutionary heritage continued. As Benjamin Rush, Philadelphia physician and revolutionary patriot, explained: "The American War is over, but this is far from being the case with the American Revolution. On the contrary, nothing but the first act of the great drama is closed. It remains [for us] . . . to establish and perfect our new forms of government."

Those efforts proceeded differently in the states than at the center of the new government in Philadelphia. In the states, government remained close to the people and politics had primarily to do with events that impinged on daily life. There the fires of controversy, fanned to a white heat during the 1770s and 1780s, continued to burn.

By contrast, the new national government dealt with issues that transcended local concern. It was distant from popular politics, just as the Founders had intended. Only the House of Representatives was directly elected, and it as well as the Senate was filled with heroes of the Revolution, gentlemen concerned with maintaining reputation among their peers, as well as with issues of state. The dignitaries that filled the Congress would soon divide over foreign and domestic policies into competing Federalist and

Jeffersonian-Republican coalitions. But they were united initially in the belief that the nation's well-being depended on the leadership of gentlemen such as themselves, men of wisdom and experience prepared to govern according to their own best judgment.

At first, the politics of congressional dignitaries and the more rapidly evolving, democratic politics among the people proceeded along parallel but separate trajectories. Before long, however, the decade's events began to force them together into the nation's first political parties. When that happened, a new era of American politics took shape.

Controversy first erupted over domestic policies designed to stabilize the new government's finances and promote the country's economic development. Those policies revealed deep-seated conflicts between economic interests and raised difficult questions of how the new constitution should be interpreted. What was the proper balance of power between state and national governments? How should governing authority be allocated between the executive branch and Congress? And what was to be the role of the new federal courts?

Within a few years, the French Revolution and the successful revolt by black Haitians against French colonial power in the Caribbean—the two most dramatic events in a larger web of democratic insurgencies against established authority that reached from Ireland and Europe to the Americas—further inflamed congressional politics and roused the people at large. By the last years of the 1790s, political divisions, intensified by the prospect of war with France and Federalist measures such as the Alien and Sedition Acts, brought the nation to the brink of political upheaval. That prospect was narrowly avoided by the Federalists' defeat and Thomas Jefferson's election as president in 1800.

Having captured both the presidency and control of Congress, the Jeffersonian Republicans set about the task of purging the government of Federalist influence. At home, they successfully refashioned domestic policies, promoted the country's westward expansion, and set the government on a new constitutional path emphasizing state rather than central authority. Abroad, they struggled, less successfully, to protect American commerce on the high seas, oppose the continuing impressment of American sailors, and avoid embroilment in European war.

Adding to the political crisis of the early republic were widespread anxiety over the nation's still unproven "experiment" in creating an extended republican empire, conflicts over the desirability of political democracy, dangers to the nation's security posed by a hostile Atlantic environment, and the absence of fully developed parties capable of forging political compromise.

As political controversy grew during these troubled years, it caught up countless people like David Brown in its toils. By the time Thomas Jefferson had left office in 1809, it was apparent how fragile, and yet how resilient, America's new government had proven to be.

LAUNCHING THE NATIONAL REPUBLIC

Once the Constitution had been ratified, its Anti-Federalist critics seemed ready to give the new experiment a chance. They were determined, however, to watch closely for the first signs of danger. It was not many months before they sounded the alarm.

Beginning the New Government

On April 16, 1789, George Washington, unanimously elected president by the Electoral College, started north from Virginia toward New York City for his inauguration. His feelings were mixed as he set forth. "I bade adieu to Mount Vernon, to private life, and to domestic felicity," he confided to his diary, "and with a mind oppressed with more anxious and painful sensations than I have words to express, set out for New York . . . with the best disposition to render service to my country in obedience to its call, but with less hope of answering its expectations." He had good reason for such foreboding.

The president-elect was the object of constant adulation as he journeyed north. In villages and towns, guns boomed their salutes, children danced in the streets, church bells pealed, and dignitaries toasted his arrival. On April 23, accompanied by a flotilla of boats, Washington was rowed on an elegant, flower-festooned barge from the New Jersey shore to New York City, where throngs of citizens and newly elected members of Congress greeted the

This imaginative scene of President-elect Washington's reception in Trenton, New Jersey, during his trip from Virginia to New York City for his first inauguration depicts the popular adulation that surrounded him, as well as the sharply different political roles of men and women. *(Library of Congress)*

weary traveler. Over the streets of the city stretched gaily decorated arches, while young women in white robes strewed flowers in his path. That evening, bonfires illuminated the city.

Inaugural day was April 30. Shortly after noon, on a small balcony overlooking a crowded Wall Street, Washington took the oath of office. "It is done," exulted New York's chancellor, Robert Livingston. "Long live George Washington, President of the United States!" With the crowd roaring its approval and 13 guns booming in the harbor, the president bowed his way off the balcony and into Federal Hall. Late into the night, celebrations filled the air.

Though hopefulness attended the new government's beginning, the first weeks were tense, because everyone knew how important it was that the government be set on a proper republican course. "Things which appear of little importance in themselves and at the beginning," the president warned, "may have great and durable consequences."

When Washington addressed the first Congress, republican purists complained that the ceremony smacked too much of the English monarch's speech from the throne at the opening of Parliament. Congress then had to decide how to reply, and whether it should address Washington with a title. Vice President Adams proposed "His Most Benign Highness," while others offered the even gaudier suggestion "His Highness, the President of the United States, and Protector of the Rights of the Same." Howls of outrage arose from those who

thought titles had no place in a republic. Good sense finally prevailing, Congress settled on the now familiar "Mr. President." Every decision seemed filled with significance, for people believed they were setting the new government's direction for years to come. That belief gave politics a special intensity.

The Bill of Rights

Among the Congress's first tasks was consideration of the constitutional amendments that several states had made a condition of their ratification. Although Madison, Hamilton, and other Federalists had argued that a national bill of rights was unnecessary, they were ready to keep their promise that such amendments would be considered. That would reassure the fearful, head off calls for a second constitutional convention, and build support for the new regime. "We have in this way something to gain," Madison shrewdly observed, "and if we proceed with caution, nothing to lose."

From the variety of proposals offered by the states, Madison culled a set of specific propositions for Congress to consider. After extensive debate, Congress reached agreement in September 1789 on twelve amendments and sent them to the states for approval. By December 1791, ten had been ratified. Those ten became the national Bill of Rights. Among other things, they guaranteed freedom of speech, press, and religion; pledged the right of trial by jury and due process of law; forbade "unreasonable searches and seizures"; and protected individuals

FEDERAL HALL.
The Seat of Congress

President Washington took the oath of office on the balcony of Federal Hall in New York City, where the new national government first met. The shield of the United States and 13 stars emblazoned its cornice, while arrows (symbolizing war) and olive branches (symbolizing peace) appeared above the windows. *(Museum of the City of New York)*

against self-incrimination in criminal cases. The Bill of Rights was the most important achievement of these early years, for it has protected citizens' democratic rights ever since.

The People Divide

During its first months in office, Washington's administration enjoyed almost universal support. The honeymoon, however, did not last long, for criticism of the administration's policies soon began. By the mid-1790s, opposition groups had formed a coalition known as the Jeffersonian Republicans, while the administration's supporters rallied under the name of Federalists.

Disagreement began in January 1790, when Secretary of the Treasury Alexander Hamilton submitted to Congress the first of several major policy statements on the country's economic future. Seldom in the nation's history has a single official so dominated public affairs as did Hamilton during these early years. A man of extraordinary intelligence and ambition, Hamilton preferred to act be-

hind the scenes, shaping events beyond the public eye. His instincts for locating and seizing the levers of political power were unerring.

An ardent proponent of America's economic development, Hamilton, perhaps more than any of the nation's founders, foresaw the country's future strength and was determined to promote its growth by encouraging domestic manufacturing and overseas trade. The United States, he was fond of saying, was a "Hercules in the cradle." He believed that competitive self-interest, whether of nations or individuals, was the surest guide to behavior. He most admired ambitious entrepreneurs eager to tie their fortunes to America's rising empire, and he believed that a close alliance between them and government officials was essential to achieving American greatness.

At the same time, Hamilton's politics were profoundly conservative. He continued to be deeply impressed by the stability of the British monarchy and confident governing style of the British upper class, while distrusting the people's wisdom and fearing their purposes. "The people," he asserted, "are turbulent and changing; they seldom judge or determine right." That stark belief guided his entire public career.

Believing that the Constitution as written was not "high-toned" enough, Hamilton was eager to give it proper direction. His opportunity came when Washington named him secretary of the treasury. Recognizing the potential importance of his office, he was determined to use it to build the kind of nation he envisioned.

In his first "Report on the Public Credit," Hamilton recommended funding the remaining Revolutionary War debt by enabling the government's creditors to exchange their badly depreciated securities at face value for new, interest-bearing government bonds. The foreign-held debt Hamilton set at $11.7 million; the domestic debt, including back interest, he fixed at $40.4 million. Second, he proposed that the federal government assume responsibility for the $21.5 million in remaining state war debts. These actions, he hoped, would stabilize the government's finances, establish its credit, build confidence in the new nation at home and abroad, and tie business and commercial interests firmly to the new administration.

Consideration of Hamilton's economic program quickly became embroiled in Congress's first extended debate over slavery. It was stimulated by petitions from mid-Atlantic Quakers and the Pennsylvania Abolition Society lamenting the "licentious wickedness of the African trade for slaves" and deploring the "inhuman tyranny and blood guiltiness

Alexander Hamilton used the office of secretary of the treasury and his personal relationship with President Washington to shape national policy during the early 1790s. *(The White House, © White House Historical Association)*

inseparable from it." Going beyond moral condemnations, the petitions called on Congress to end the slave trade abroad and ameliorate the conditions of slavery at home.

In the House of Representatives, Southern delegates warned that arguments implying that Congress possessed authority over domestic slavery threatened to "blow the trumpet of civil war," and defended the slave trade as rescuing blacks from African savagery. Northern delegates, even many who professed antislavery sentiments, held back, alarmed that the debate threatened to erode southern support for Hamilton's financial program and thus deny its benefits to the northern states. To put the troublesome issue to rest, they agreed to language stating that "Congress has no authority to interfere in the emancipation of slaves, or in the treatment of them." Lamented the Philadelphia Quaker John Pemberton, the funding system is so much the darling of northerners that they are eager "to obtain the favor" of southern delegates.

When debate on Hamilton's Report picked up again, the proposal to fund the foreign debt aroused little controversy. His plans for handling the government's domestic obligations, however, generated immediate opposition. In the House of Representatives, James Madison, Hamilton's recent ally in the ratification process, protested the unfairness of funding depreciated securities at face value because it would reward speculators, some anticipating Hamilton's proposals, who had acquired them at a fraction of their initial worth. Madison and his southern colleagues knew as well that northern businessmen held most of the securities and that funding would bring little benefit to the South.

Hamilton was not impressed. The speculators, he observed, "paid what the commodity was worth in the market, and took the risks." They should therefore "reap the benefit." If his plan served the interests of the wealthy, that was exactly as he intended, for it would further strengthen ties between wealth and national power. After considerable grumbling, Congress endorsed the funding plan.

Federal assumption of the remaining state debts, another important part of Hamilton's program, aroused greater criticism. States with the largest unpaid obligations, such as Massachusetts, thought assumption a splendid idea. But others, such as Virginia and Pennsylvania, which had already retired much of their debt, were adamantly opposed. Critics also warned that assumption would strengthen the central government at the expense of the states, since wealthy individuals would now look to it rather than the states for a return on their investments. Moreover, with its increased need for revenue to pay off the accumulated debt, the federal government would have additional reason to exercise its newly acquired power of taxation. That was exactly what Hamilton intended.

Once again, Congress endorsed Hamilton's bill, in good measure because Madison and Jefferson supported it as part of an agreement to move the seat of government from New York to Philadelphia and eventually to a special federal district on the Potomac River. Southerners hoped that moving the government away from northern commercial centers would enable them to control its development and keep it more closely aligned with their own agrarian interests.

Opposition to the funding and assumption scheme, however, did not die. In December 1790, the Virginia assembly passed a series of resolutions, framed by that old Anti-Federalist Patrick Henry, warning that southern agriculture was being subordinated to the interests of northern commerce, and that the national government's powers were expanding dangerously. Hearing of the Virginia resolutions, Hamilton confided privately that "This is the first symptom of a spirit which must either be killed, or will kill the Constitution." The contest for control of the new government was now vigorously joined.

As the controversy grew, Hamilton introduced the second phase of his financial program, a national bank capable of handling the government's

The revolutionary generation found inspiration in the republican eras of ancient Greece and Rome. This bust of Thomas Jefferson, cast in the classical style, was completed in 1789 by the French sculptor Jean-Antoine Houdon. *(Collection of the New-York Historical Society)*

financial affairs and pooling private investment capital for economic development. He had the Bank of England and its ties to the royal government clearly in mind, though he was careful not to say so publicly.

Congressional opposition to the bank came almost entirely from the South. Nowhere, the bank's southern critics protested, did the constitution authorize the creation of a national bank. More practically, it seemed obvious that the bank would serve the needs of northern merchants and manufacturers far better than those of southern agrarians. Northern and middle state delegates, however, combined to secure passage of the bank bill.

When Washington asked his cabinet for advice on the bank's constitutionality, Hamilton urged approval. Following the constitutional doctrine of "implied powers"—the principle that the government had the authority to make any laws "necessary and proper" for exercising the powers specifically granted it by the Constitution—he argued that Congress could charter such a bank under its power to collect taxes and regulate trade. Secretary of State Jefferson, however, urged a veto. He saw in Hamilton's argument a blueprint for the indefinite expansion of federal authority and insisted that the government possessed only those powers specifically itemized in the Constitution. Because the Constitution said nothing about chartering banks, the bill was uncon-

stitutional and should be rejected. To Jefferson's distress, Washington followed Hamilton's advice and signed the bank bill into law.

In December 1790, in his second "Report on the Public Credit," Hamilton proposed a series of excise taxes, including one on the manufacture of distilled liquor. This so-called Whiskey Tax was intended to signal the government's intention to use its taxing authority to increase federal revenue. The power to tax and spend, Hamilton knew, was the power to govern. The Whiskey Tax became law in March 1791.

Finally, in his "Report on Manufactures" issued in December 1791, Hamilton called for tariffs (i.e., taxes) on imported European goods as a way of protecting American industries; bounties to encourage the expansion of commercial agriculture; and a network of federally sponsored internal improvements such as roads and lighthouses. These were intended to stimulate commerce and bind the nation more tightly together. Neither northern merchants nor southern agrarians, however, wanted tariffs that might reduce overseas trade and raise the cost of living, so Congress never endorsed this report.

All the while, criticism of Hamilton's program continued to mount. In October 1791, opposition leaders in Congress established a newspaper, the *National Gazette,* that vigorously attacked the administration's policies. Hamilton responded with a series of anonymous articles in the administration's paper, *The Gazette of the United States,* accusing Jefferson (inaccurately) of having opposed the Constitution and charging him (also inaccurately) of fomenting opposition to the government. Alarmed at the division within his administration, Washington pleaded for restraint.

Congressional criticism of Hamilton's policies reached a climax in January 1793, when Representative William Branch Giles of Virginia introduced resolutions calling for an inquiry into the condition of the Treasury, accusing Hamilton of using the office for his own benefit, and censuring his conduct. Though Hamilton vigorously defended himself and none of the resolutions passed, the month-long debate revealed how acrimonious politics had become at the nation's capital.

Political conflict was now spreading beyond the circle of governing officials in Philadelphia. In northern towns and cities, artisans and other working people generally supported Hamilton's efforts to improve credit and stimulate economic development. With their own economic circumstances improving, they seemed undisturbed by constitutional issues or the benefits that Hamilton's policies brought to a privileged few. Before many years were out, many such folk would move into the political opposition, but for the moment their support of the administration was secure.

The Whiskey Rebellion

The farmers of western Pennsylvania voiced their opposition to government policies in dramatic fashion. Their anger focused on the Whiskey Tax. Ever since the trouble with England 30 years earlier, Americans had been sensitive to taxation and suspicious of its connections with governmental power. Farmers had special reason to dislike this particular tax. Their livelihood depended on transporting surplus grain over the Appalachians to eastern markets. Shipping it in bulk was prohibitively expensive, so they distilled the grain and moved it more efficiently as whiskey. The Whiskey Tax threatened to make this unprofitable. The farmers also protested that people charged with tax evasion had to stand trial in federal court hundreds of miles away in Philadelphia.

Westerners' frustration went even deeper than that, for they sensed control of their local affairs slipping away as the backcountry was caught up in a market economy and system of politics dominated by the more populous, commercialized areas to the east. In places like South Carolina, the integration of coastal and interior regions went more smoothly because of similar agricultural interests and shared racial antipathy to the state's black majority. In the more economically diverse and racially homogenous states to the north, however, conflicts between coastal and backcountry regions sharpened.

Hamilton cared little what the farmers thought about the Whiskey Tax or local self-reliance. The government needed revenue, and the farmers would have to bear the cost. George Clymer, federal supervisor of revenue for Pennsylvania, was similarly unsympathetic. Referring to the "moral and personal weakness" of "lesser folk," Clymer publicly castigated the "sordid shopkeepers" who retailed Pennsylvania whiskey and the "depraved" farmers who produced it. Angered by Federalist arrogance as much as the tax, farmers quickly made their resentment known.

Trouble was brewing by the summer of 1792 as angry citizens gathered in mass meetings across western Pennsylvania. In August, a convention at Pittsburgh denounced the Whiskey Tax and vowed to prevent its collection. Like opponents of the Stamp Act in 1765, they concluded that liberties would be lost if resistance did not soon begin. Alarmed, Washington issued a proclamation warning against such "unlawful" gatherings and insisting that the tax would be enforced. As collections began, the farmers took matters into their own hands.

In July 1794, when federal marshal David Lennox, in company with John Neville, a local excise inspector, attempted to serve papers on several recalcitrant farmers near Pittsburgh, an angry crowd of 500 armed men surrounded Neville's home and demanded his resignation. Learning that Neville had fled, they ordered the dozen soldiers trapped in the house to lay down their arms and come out. Fearing for their safety, the soldiers refused, and for several hours the two sides exchanged gunfire. After several men had been wounded, the soldiers finally surrendered, whereupon Neville's house was put to the torch. Similar episodes involving angry crowds, the erection of liberty poles reminiscent of the Revolution, and the hoisting of banners bearing slogans such as "Liberty and No Excise. O Whiskey!" erupted across the state. At Parkinson's Ferry, a convention of over 200 delegates debated armed resistance and talked ominously about seceding from the United States.

Fearing that the protests might spread through the entire backcountry from Maine to Georgia, and worried by rumors that Spanish emissaries and western adventurers were plotting secession among settlers in Kentucky and the western Carolinas, Washington called out federal troops to restore order. For more than a year, Hamilton had been urging the use of force against the protesters. To him the insurrection was not evidence of an unjust policy needing change but a test of the administration's ability to govern. Suppressing the rebellion, Hamilton explained, "will . . . add to the solidity of everything in this country." He eagerly volunteered to accompany the troops west.

In late August, a force of nearly 13,000 men, larger than the average strength of the continental army during the Revolutionary War, marched into western Pennsylvania. At its center was Colonel William McPherson's "Pennsylvania Blues," an upper-class, strongly Federalist cavalry regiment. At its head rode the president and secretary of the treasury. Persuaded by aides of the danger to his safety, Washington returned to Philadelphia, but Hamilton pressed ahead. When later criticized for accompanying the army to Pittsburgh, he replied that he had "long since . . . learned to hold public opinion of no value." The battle for which Hamilton hoped never materialized, however, for as the federal army approached, the "Whiskey Rebels" dispersed. Of 20 prisoners taken, two were convicted of treason and sentenced to death. In a calmer mood, Washington later pardoned them both.

President Washington and Treasury Secretary Hamilton led a federal army of nearly 13,000 troops into western Pennsylvania in 1794. Rebellious farmers, protesting the government's excise tax on whiskey, dispersed as the army approached. *(The Metropolitan Museum of Art, Gift of Edgar William and Bernice Chrysler Garbisch, 1963 [63.201.2] Photograph © 1983 The Metropolitan Museum of Art)*

As people quickly realized, the "Whiskey Rebellion" had never threatened the government's safety. "An insurrection was ... proclaimed," Jefferson scoffed, "but could never be found." Even such an ardent Federalist as Fisher Ames was uneasy at the sight of federal troops marching against American citizens. "Elective rulers," he warned, "can scarcely ever employ the physical force of a democracy without turning the moral force, or the power of public opinion, against the government." The American people would have additional reason to ponder Ames's warning in the years immediately ahead.

Though the whiskey rebels were quickly dispersed, the affray gave clear indication that the gentry-based politics of Congress and the locally based politics of the people were becoming more closely joined.

THE REPUBLIC IN A THREATENING WORLD

Because the nation was so new and the outside world so threatening, foreign policy generated extraordinary excitement during the 1790s. This was especially so after the tumultuous events of the French and Haitian Revolutions burst onto the international scene. The revolution in France and the European war that accompanied it threatened to draw America in, while across Europe, Ireland, and the Caribbean, political insurgents, invoking the Declaration of Independence and America's colonial rebellion as inspiration for their own cause, extended what historians call the age of democratic revolution. As the American people argued over the meaning of these events for their young, still vulnerable republic, they revealed again how sharply they were divided.

The Promise and Peril of the French Revolution

France's revolution began in 1789 as an effort to reform an arbitrary but weakened monarchy. Pent-up demands for social justice, however, quickly outran attempts at moderate reform, and by 1793, when the recently proclaimed republican regime beheaded Louis XVI, France had plunged into a genuinely radical revolution. As revolutionary leaders extended their attack on the French aristocracy and Catholic church, conservatives across Europe rallied in opposition, their fears fueled by the accounts of French aristocrats fleeing the chaos. By the end of 1793, Europe was locked in a deadly struggle between France and a counterrevolutionary coalition led by Prussia and Great Britain.

For more than a decade, the French Revolution dominated European affairs. Before it was finished, it would transform the course of Western history. The revolution also cut like a plowshare through the surface of American politics, threatening the nation's security and dividing the American people against each other.

The outbreak of European war posed thorny diplomatic problems for Washington's administration. Under international law, neutral countries could continue to trade with belligerent nations as long as such trade did not include goods directly related to the war effort. American merchants eagerly took advantage of that opportunity because it promised handsome profits. Within a few years, shipbuilding surged and American commerce was booming. By 1800, American ships were carrying an astonishing 92 percent of all commerce between America and Europe. American merchants were also reaching beyond those familiar routes. As early as 1784, the New York merchant ship *Empress of China* had made the first American voyage to the Orient; others soon followed.

For the first time since the Revolutionary War, prosperity returned to the nation's coastal cities. Though the benefits of America's expanding commerce were most evident among urban merchants and sailors, artisans and tavern keepers, renewed prosperity radiated as well into the surrounding countryside, where cargoes of agricultural and forest goods, as well as the provisions required by ships' crews, were produced.

America's expanding commerce, however, quickly encountered problems, for while both England and France sought access to American goods, each was determined to prevent those goods from reaching the other, if necessary by stopping American ships and confiscating their cargoes. Neither belligerent was willing to bind itself by the formalities of international law when locked in such a deadly struggle.

America's relations with England were additionally complicated by the Royal Navy's practice of impressing American sailors into service aboard its warships to meet the growing demand for seamen. Washington faced the difficult problem of upholding the country's neutral rights and protecting its citizens without getting drawn into the European conflict.

The French treaty of 1778 compounded the government's dilemma, for it appeared to require that the United States aid France much as France had assisted the American states a decade and a half earlier. Americans sympathetic to the French cause argued that the commitment still held. Others, fearing the consequences of American involvement and the political infection that closer ties with revolutionary France might bring, insisted that the treaty had lapsed when the French king was overthrown.

The American people's intense reaction to the European drama further complicated the situation. At first, the French Revolution seemed an extension of America's own struggle against England, and was thus to be celebrated as an event linking France and the United States in a universal contest for liberty. Even France's swing toward social revolution did not immediately dampen American enthusiasm.

By the mid-1790s, however, after France's revolutionary regime launched its attack on organized Christianity, many people pulled back in alarm. What connection could there possibly be between the principles of 1776 and the chaos so evident in France? Insisted a staunchly Federalist newspaper,

This scene of bustling commercial activity in New York City in 1797 reveals the benefits that expanded neutral trade brought to the nation's major seaports. *(The New-York Historical Society)*

RECOVERING THE PAST

Foreign Travel Journals

Historians utilize many different kinds of sources in their quest to recover the American past. Among the most revealing are travel accounts penned by foreign visitors eager to learn about the United States and record their impressions of it. From the days of earliest explorations to our own time, travelers have been fascinated by the people, customs, institutions, and physical setting of North America. Out of this continuing interaction between America and its foreign visitors has emerged a rich and fascinating travel literature that reveals much not only about America but about the travelers who have visited it as well.

During the second quarter of the nineteenth century, a stream of perceptive European visitors—Alexis de Tocqueville, Harriet Martineau, and Francis Grund among them—toured the United States, eager to record their impressions of what Jacksonian America was like. Fifty years earlier, the American Revolution fanned similar interest in the minds of Europeans fascinated by the newly independent nation and anxious to discern its implications for them. Among the most opinionated and engaging of these earlier commentators was the Frenchman Moreau de Saint Méry.

Born on the French island of Martinque in January 1750, de Saint Méry established a successful legal practice before moving to France, where relatives introduced him to polite, Parisian society. In the late 1780s, he became an ardent champion of political reform during the early days of the French Revolution. As the revolution entered its radical phase, however, he was forced to flee to the United States for safety. Arriving at Norfolk, Virginia, with his wife and two children, de Saint Méry settled in Philadelphia, where he remained from October 1794 to August 1798. While there, he mingled with civic and cultural leaders, opened a bookstore that served as a rendezvous for French émigrés who also had fled the revolution's turmoil, and published a French-language paper that reported the latest news from home. In the late summer of 1798, de Saint Méry returned safely to France.

As with all such travel accounts, de Saint Méry's commentary must be read with a critical eye, for travelers disagreed over what they thought important and worth reporting, and interpreted what they saw in very different ways. In nearly 400 pages of commentary, de Saint Méry touched on numerous aspects of American life, but none in more frank and compelling fashion than relations between the sexes. The selections that follow (somewhat re-arranged for greater continuity) provide tantalizing insights into the behavior and sexual mores of American men and women in the early years of the republic.

What did de Saint Méry find most interesting about gender relations in Philadelphia? How did religion, class, and ethnicity shape men's and women's behavior? What forms of behavior did he approve and disapprove?

The explicit commentary of de Saint Méry is unique among the numerous accounts left by foreign travelers in the early republic, most of whom showed far more interest in America's racial makeup, political practices, and physical environment. Thus, de Saint Méry's observations may be idiosyncratic and should be approached with caution.

What other kinds of sources might enable us to evaluate the accuracy of such travel accounts? In what ways is a traveler's own nationality, gender, religion, or class likely to shape his or her impressions of the United States? Similarly, how important is it to know travelers' motives for coming, how long they stayed, which parts of the country they visited, and with whom they associated while here?

Reflecting on the Past Does the gendered world of late eighteenth-century Philadelphia, as described by de Saint Méry, seem strange or familiar, attractive or distasteful to your own sensibilities? If you were to visit another country today, how accurate do you think you could be in assessing the social behavior and cultural values of its people? To what extent would your values, perhaps like those of Moreau de Saint Méry, color your impressions? Might it be more difficult to understand some foreign cultures than others? Why?

Moreau de Saint Méry's American Journal

American men, generally speaking, are tall and thin . . . [and] seem to have no strength. . . . They are brave, but they lack drive. Indifferent toward almost everything, they sometimes behave in a manner that suggests real energy; then follow it with a "Oh-to-hell-with-it" attitude which shows that they seldom feel genuine enthusiasm.

Their dinner consists of . . . English roast surrounded by potatoes . . . baked or fried eggs, boiled or fried fish, salad which may be thinly sliced cabbage . . . [and] sweets to which they are excessively partial. . . . The entire meal is washed down with cider, weak or strong beer . . . [and] wine . . . which they keep drinking right through dessert, toward the end of which any ladies who are at the dinner leave the table and withdraw by themselves, leaving the men free to drink as much as they please. . . . Toasts are drunk, cigars are lighted, diners run to the corners of the room hunting night tables and vases which will enable them to hold a greater amount of liquor. . . . Finally the dinner table is deserted because of boredom, fatigue or drunkenness. . . .

American women are pretty, and those of Philadelphia are prettiest of all. . . . Girls ordinarily mature in Philadelphia at the age of fourteen, and reach that period without unusual symptoms. . . . But they soon grow pale. . . . After eighteen years old they lose their charms. . . . Their hair is scanty, their teeth bad. . . . In short, while charming and adorable at fifteen, they are faded at twenty-three, old at thirty-five, decrepit at forty or forty-five. . . .

American women carefully wash their faces and hands, but not their mouths, seldom their feet and even more seldom their bodies. . . . They are greatly addicted to finery and have a strong desire to display themselves—a desire . . . inflamed by their love of adornment. They cannot, however, imitate that elegance of style possessed by Frenchwomen. . . .

One is struck by the tall and pretty young girls one sees in the streets, going and coming from school. They wear their hair long, and skirts with closed seams. But when nubility has arrived they put up their hair with a comb, and the back of the skirt has a placket. At this time, they . . . become their own mistresses, and can go walking alone and have suitors. . . .

They invariably make their own choice of a suitor, and the parents raise no objection because that's the custom of the country. The suitor comes into the house when he wishes; goes on walks with his loved one whenever he desires. On Sunday he often takes her out in a cabriolet, and brings her back in the evening without anyone wanting to know where they went. . . . Although in general one is conscious of widespread modesty in Philadelphia, . . . the disregard . . . of some parents for the manner in which their daughters form relationships to which they . . . have not given their approval is an encouragement to indiscretions. . . .

A young woman trusts in her suitor's delicacy and charges him with maintaining for her a respect which she is not always able to command. Each day both of them are entrusted to no one but each other. . . . Her servant . . . leaves the house as soon as night as arrived. . . . Her father, her mother, her entire family have gone to bed. The suitor and his mistress remain alone; and sometimes, when the servant returns, she finds them asleep and the candle out, such is the frigidity of love in this country. . . .

When one considers the unlimited liberty which young ladies enjoy, one is astonished by their universal eagerness to be married. . . . When a young woman marries, she enters a wholly different existence. She is no longer a . . . butterfly who denies herself nothing and whose only laws are her whims and her suitor's wish. She now lives only for her husband, and to devote herself without surcease to the care of her household and her home. . . . The more her husband is capable of multiplying . . . the pleasures of matrimony . . . the more her health may suffer, most of all when she has a child; for sometimes while nursing it, or as soon as it is weaned, she has already conceived another. . . .

In spite of conjugal customs which would seem to indicate a state of happiness, they do not produce the happiness which would be expected to result. . . . This is evidenced by the multiplicity of second marriages. . . . The men in particular remarry oftenest. . . . Divorce is obtained with scandalous ease. From this alone one can judge the extent of loose habits. . . .

Bastards are extremely common in Philadelphia. There are two principal reasons for this. In the first place, the city is full of religious sects, but none of them give their clergymen any authority to enforce obedience. Consequently there is no way of inspiring shame in women who become mothers for no reason except the pleasure they get out of it. In the second place, once an illegitimate child is twelve months old, a mother can disembarrass herself of him by farming him out for twenty-one years. This makes it possible for her to commit the same sin for a second time. It never occurs to her that her child can never know her, and that the whole business is shameful. . . .

There are streetwalkers . . . in Philadelphia. These are very young and very pretty girls, elegantly dressed, who promenade two by two, arm in arm and walking very rapidly, at an hour which indicates that they aren't just out for a stroll. . . . Anyone who accosts them is taken to their home . . . [where] they fulfill every desire for two dollars, half of which is supposed to pay for the use of the room. Quaker youths are frequent visitors in the houses of ill fame, which have multiplied in Philadelphia and are frequented at all hours. There is even a well-known gentleman who leaves his horse tied to the post outside one of these houses, so that everyone knows when he is there and exactly how long he stays. . . .

Source: *Moreau de St. Méry's American Journey, 1793–1798*, trans. and ed., Kenneth Roberts and Anna M. Roberts. (New York: Doubleday & Co., 1947), pp. 265, 281–283, 312–313.

"In America no barbarities were perpetrated—no men's heads were stuck upon poles—no mangled ladies' bodies were carried thro' the streets in triumph.... Whatever blood was shed, flowed gallantly in the field." The writer betrayed a selective memory of America's often violent revolution and conveniently ignored the brutality meted out in France by supporters of monarchy. Even so, the differences were indeed profound.

For the Federalists, revolutionary France symbolized social anarchy and threatened the European order on which they believed the nation's commercial and diplomatic security depended. With increasing vehemence, they castigated the revolution, championed England as the defender of European civilization, and sought ways of linking England and the United States more closely together.

In this 1792 print from *The Lady's Magazine* of Philadelphia, a kneeling woman presents Columbia with a copy of Mary Wollstonecraft's "A Vindication of the Rights of Woman," one of the most outspokenly feminist writings of the time. Note the cap, symbol of the French Revolution, on Columbia's staff. *(The Library Company of Philadelphia [Per 5.7.51708.0])*

Many citizens, however, continued to support France. While decrying the revolution's excesses, they noted how difficult it was to uproot deeply embedded forces of reaction. Though Jefferson regretted the shedding of innocent blood, he believed that political liberty would ultimately emerge from the turmoil. John Bradford, editor of the *Kentucky Gazette*, thought similarly. "Instead of reviling the French republicans as monsters," he wrote, "the friends of royalty in this country should rather admire their patience in so long deferring the fate of their perjured monarch." In Bradford's judgment, England was not a bastion of civilized order, but of political privilege and oppression.

The turmoil in France challenged American assumptions about the gendered basis of politics as well. In France, women were conspicuously evident in revolutionary crowds and joined in arguments over issues of political equality. During the Terror, Jacobin radicals effectively purged women from public politics, but not before word of radical feminist activity reached North American shores, where it echoed loudly in the political consciousness of American women.

As Federalists and Jeffersonian Republicans mounted public rallies to denounce or praise revolutionary France, women took active part. In August 1794, Philadelphia citizens gathered to celebrate the progress of French liberty. Mimicking the public festivals popular in revolutionary France, a crowd of women and men paraded down Market Street to the French minister's residence. There, women dressed in gowns emblazoned with the French tri-color, gathered around an "alter of liberty" to recite patriotic odes before finally dispersing.

Many women participated as spectators, performers, and playwrights in patriotic, theatrical displays, while women such as Anne Willing Bingham, wife of a Federalist senator and daughter of a socially prominent Philadelphia family, opened dinner parties and social salons to political talk, a practice that would become a regular part of civic life at the nation's capital. In all of these ways, middle- and upper-class women explored the boundaries of American citizenship, fashioned new political identities, and claimed a wider presence in the public sphere.

Democratic Revolutions in Europe and the Atlantic World

The revolution in France was but the most dramatic among an array of democratic insurgencies throughout Europe and the Atlantic world that, during the 1790s, challenged aristocratic power, pro-

The Outbreak of Democratic Insurgencies

During the 1790s, numerous democratic insurgencies erupted in Europe and the Caribbean. **Reflecting on the Past** In what ways were these insurgencies shaped by the American and French Revolutions?

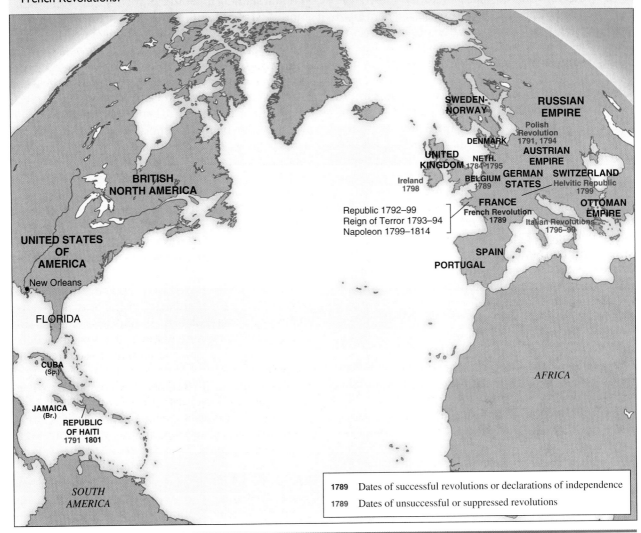

moted democratic values, and in the process generated disquiet among the American people.

Supported by invading armies from revolutionary France and guided by the doctrine of natural rights traced to both the American and French revolutions, rebellions against long-entrenched privilege erupted from the Netherlands to the Italian peninsula. Though some of these movements were repressed, others resulted in the creation of new states, such as the Batavian and Cisalpine Republics.

Democratic insurgencies erupted as well in Latin America and the Caribbean. By far the most important occurred on the island of San Domingue, soon

to be known as Haiti. There, beginning in 1791, a multiracial coalition, inspired by events in revolutionary France, rose in rebellion against French colonial rule. Conflict quickly developed between white landowners seeking to preserve their privileges while throwing off the colonial yoke, poor whites demanding access to land, mixed-race mulattoes chafing under years of discrimination, and black slaves angered by brutal repression. For more than a decade, these black and white Haitians conducted a furious and bloody struggle against a combined French and British army of 30,000. (Though France's mortal enemy in Europe, England feared the prospect of rebellion among the 300,000 slaves on its nearby possession, Jamaica, and was eager to help out.) The conflict devastated the island's sugar economy and caused more than 100,000 casualties among whites and blacks alike.

In 1798, the island's black majority, led by the charismatic Toussiant L'Ouverture, seized control of the rebellion, making the abolition of slavery its primary goal. Six years later, the victorious Haitian rebels established Haiti as the first black nation-state in the Americas.

Haitian revolutionaries found inspiration in the American as well as French Revolution—just as later slave revolts throughout the Americas would look to the Haitian rebellion. But while Haitian rebels celebrated the Declaration of Independence as a manifesto of universal freedom, whites in North America followed events on that troubled island with a mixture of enthusiasm and dread. On the one hand, the Haitian revolt affirmed the universal relevance of the U.S. struggle for liberty and struck another blow against European colonialism in the New World. During the height of the Haitian insurgency, American warships ferried black troops from one part of the island to another in preparation for battle.

U.S. citizens, however, contemplated with dread the effect on North American slaves of a successful black rebellion so close by. The Haitian achievement, moreover, cast doubt on racial assumptions that blacks were incapable of comprehending liberty's true meaning. White southerners were especially anxious. The governor of North Carolina issued a proclamation warning white Haitians and their slaves, fleeing the island's chaos, to stay away. When Haitian officials appealed in "the name of humanity" for "fraternal aid," the Congress demurred. And in late 1798, proposals for a commercial treaty with the island aroused deep-seated fears. If Haiti should become an independent state, warned Pennsylvania Senator Albert Gallatin, it might become "a dangerous neighbor" offering asylum to runaway slaves. When the new black republic was proclaimed in 1804, the U.S. government withheld recognition. Not until after the American Civil War were diplomatic relations established.

Though each of the democratic insurgencies that erupted during the 1790s was inspired by its own history of social injustice, they shared a common dedication to human liberty. And though they were scattered widely across Europe and the Atlantic basin, news about them circulated in the United States via newspapers, networks of personal correspondence, and an expanding human traffic of soldiers, rebels, emigres, and political idealists who crisscrossed the Atlantic during these tumultuous years. Several hundred black and mulatto Haitians had been mobilized by France to fight in the American Revolutionary War, and they carried home reports of that victorious struggle. Similarly, French soldiers and officers such as LaFayette transported American notions of liberty to France, where they helped fuel the cause of political reform.

During the mid-1790s, Joel Barlow and other Americans, motivated by curiosity and democratic principle, journeyed to France, eager to witness the further unfolding of universal liberty. The American expatriate Thomas Paine, seeking asylum in France after being hounded out of England for his radical views, churned out new political tracts, was granted honorary French citizenship, and served briefly in the revolutionary Convention before running afoul of the Terror. At the same time, shifting political fortunes sent a stream of French emigres to North America (among them Moreau de Saint Méry, the subject of this chapter's "Recovering the Past" feature), bringing with them vivid tales of political tumult.

As the 1790s progressed, growing numbers of English and Irish radicals fleeing the deepening political conservatism in Britain took passage for North America. When they arrived, many joined the Jeffersonian opposition as newspaper editors and activists, adding to the party's democratic commitment and anti-British stance. As they settled in, they contributed to a transatlantic web of radical dissent.

That web was strengthened as well by a multiracial underclass of sailors, runaway slaves, and white commonfolk from the far corners of the Atlantic world—restive men, and occasionally women, who circulated in and out of North American ports. Their rough appearance, vivid tales of injustice, and ready challenges to local authorities added to the country's political clamor.

The Democratic-Republican Societies

Political clubs served as weapons of democratic reform throughout the Atlantic world during the 1790s, providing safe havens where dissidents could gather to read political tracts, discuss political issues, and plot political change. The Jacobin clubs in France were the best known, but similar clubs sprouted up elsewhere, including the United States.

As early as 1792, ordinary citizens began to form "constitutional societies" dedicated to "watching over the rights of the people" and giving the alarm in case of governmental encroachments on American liberty. During the early 1790s, several dozen societies, modeled after the Sons of Liberty and Committees of Correspondence that had mobilized

The Haitian Revolution

Not only did the Haitian Revolution resonate with issues of racial ideology, it also proved a focal point of European imperial competition in the Americas and of French political battles at home. For white Americans, the Haitian Revolution conjured up frightening visions of black rebellion and cast doubt on the universal relevance of America's own revolution. **Reflecting on the Past** In what ways was the United States sympathetic or unsympathetic to the Haitian Revolution?

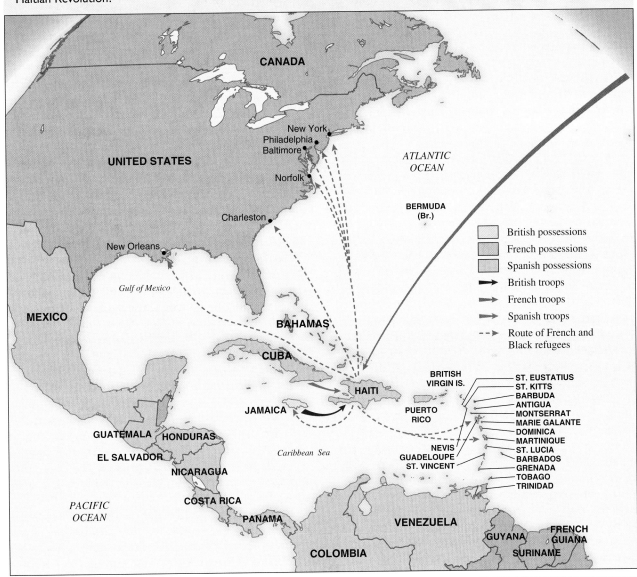

patriots against England 20 years earlier, formed in opposition to Hamilton's financial program. The French Revolution stoked the fires of democratic enthusiasm and stimulated the societies' growth.

That growth was spurred by the arrival in April 1793 of Citizen Edmund Genêt, the French republic's minister to the United States. When Genêt landed at Charleston, South Carolina, he sparked a firestorm of democratic enthusiasm. His instructions were to court popular support and negotiate a commercial treaty with the United States. Shortly after his arrival, however, he began commissioning American privateers to prey on British shipping in the Caribbean and enlisting American seamen for expeditions against Spanish Florida. Both were clear violations of American neutrality.

As he traveled north toward Philadelphia, Genêt met enthusiastic receptions. His popularity, however, soon led him astray. In open defiance of diplomatic protocol, he urged Congress to reject Washington's recently issued neutrality proclamation and side with revolutionary France. That was the final straw. On August 2, the president demanded Genêt's recall, charging that his conduct threatened "war abroad and anarchy at home." Washington's decision drew cries of protest.

If Genêt failed as a diplomat, he succeeded in fanning popular enthusiasm. With his open encouragement, the largest of the new popular associations, the Democratic Society of Pennsylvania, called for the formation of similar societies elsewhere and challenged them to join in supporting France and promoting the "spirit of freedom and equality" at home.

Although a full network of popular societies never materialized, about 40 organizations scattered from Maine to Georgia sprang up. Working people—artisans and laborers in the cities, small farmers and tenants in the countryside—provided the bulk of membership. Federalist critics derided them as "the lowest orders of . . . draymen . . . broken hucksters, and trans-Atlantic traitors." That final canard was in reference to the growing tide of Irish immigrants, fleeing hard times and political repression at home, who combined demands for Irish independence from England with a commitment to political equality and a relish for rough-and-tumble politics.

The societies' leaders were most often doctors, lawyers, and tradesmen, men of acknowledged respectability. But leaders and followers alike were united by a common determination to preserve the "principles of '76" against the "royalizing" tendencies of Washington's administration. Committed to an awakened citizenry, the societies organized public celebrations, issued addresses filled with democratic principles, and fired off petitions sharply critical of administration policies to the president and Congress. They labeled Washington's proclamation of neutrality a "pusillanimous truckling to Britain, despotically conceived and unconstitutionally promulgated." Several of the societies openly urged the United States to enter the war on France's behalf.

West of the Appalachians, local democratic societies agitated against England's continuing occupation of frontier posts south of the Great Lakes, and berated Spain for closing the Mississippi River at New Orleans to American shipping. Everywhere they protested the Excise Tax, opposed the administration's overtures to England, and demanded that public officials attend to the people's wishes.

They campaigned as well for a press free from control by Federalist "aristocrats." Declared William Manning, a Massachusetts farmer who had marched to the "Concord fight" in 1775 and who continued to praise the principles for which he had earlier fought: a laboring man may as well "hunt for pins in a haymow" as try to collect accurate knowledge from the "promiscuous piles of contradictions" appearing in the Federalist press.

President Washington and his supporters were incensed by the societies' support of Genêt and their criticism of the government. Such "nurseries of sedition," thundered Fisher Ames, threatened to revolutionize America as the Jacobins had revolutionized France. In January 1794, a Virginia Federalist berated Kentucky's Democratic Society as "that horrible sink of treason, that hateful synagogue of anarchy, that odious conclave of tumult, that frightful cathedral of discord, that poisonous garden of conspiracy, that hellish school of rebellion and opposition to all regular and well-balanced authority!" So inflamed had public discourse become.

As controversy escalated, another circumstance added to the anxiety gripping politicians at the Philadelphia capital. Through the summer of 1793, an unrelenting heat wave descended on southeastern Pennsylvania, searing trees and gardens, threatening supplies of potable water, and raising a stench in the refuse-filled streets. Even more alarming, from early August to mid-October a deadly epidemic of yellow fever gripped the city, sending wealthier citizens fleeing to the countryside for safety and taking a terrible toll on those forced to stay behind. The poor and elderly were most vulnerable and fared worst. Blacks also died in large numbers when the Free African Society, responding to appeals from the mayor, volunteered nurses to tend the sick and labor to bury the dead. The belief that blacks were naturally immune to the fever's ravages proved tragically false.

Before early frosts finally destroyed the swarms of mosquitoes that carried the deadly pestilence through the city's crowded streets, well over 4,000 black and white Philadelphians, more than 10 percent of the city's population, had died. Yellow fever was not new to Philadelphia and would return before the decade was out, but never again did it reap such a deadly harvest.

Jay's Controversial Treaty

The uproar over Jay's Treaty with England further heightened political tensions at mid-decade. Alarmed by deteriorating relations with England, Washington sent Chief Justice John Jay to London in

Cartoons became powerful weapons in the superheated political press of the 1790s. This Jeffersonian cartoon lampoons William Cobbett, one of the Federalists' most acid-penned pamphleteers who wrote under the pseudonym Peter Porcupine. While Columbia swoons over the political division, the English Lion urges Cobbett to "sow the seeds of discord" and the Devil mutters "More scandal. Let us destroy this Idol Liberty." *(The Historical Society of Pennsylvania [HSP], "Caricature against William Cobbett, editor of the Porcupine Gazette," 1796, [Accession #Bb612Se31])*

the spring of 1794 with instructions to negotiate a range of troublesome issues carried over from the Revolutionary War. The treaty that the chief justice brought home in early 1795 contained British promises to withdraw from the western posts and permit American ships selective access to British West Indian ports. However, it totally ignored a host of other lingering problems. When its terms were made public, they triggered an explosion of protest.

The administration's pleas that the agreement headed off an open breach with England and was the best that could be obtained failed to pacify its critics. In New York City, Hamilton was stoned while defending the treaty at a mass meeting. The "rabble," sniffed one Federalist, attempted "to knock out Hamilton's brains to reduce him to an equality with themselves." Southern planters were angry because the agreement brought no compensation for their lost slaves. Westerners complained that the British gave no indication of evacuating the military posts, while merchants and sailors railed against Jay's failure to pry fully open the West Indies trade or stop impressment. After a long and acrimonious debate, the Senate ratified the treaty by the narrowest margin.

The administration made better progress on the still volatile issue of free transit of the Mississippi River at New Orleans. In the Treaty of San Lorenzo, negotiated by Thomas Pinckney in 1795, Spain for the first time recognized the United States' boundaries under the peace treaty of 1783 (the Mississippi River to the west and the 31st parallel to the south) and thus gave up all claim to U.S. territory. Spain also granted Americans free navigation of the Mississippi and the right to unload goods for transshipment at New Orleans, but only for three years. What would happen after that was uncertain.

Still in possession of vast western areas of the continent, Spain strengthened its hold over "New California," stretching from San Diego to San

Francisco Bay. Unable to conquer the southwestern Indians by force, Spanish officials turned to trade and missionary activity as ways of extending colonial hegemony in the region. Spanish merchants also competed with American, Russian, and British traders along the northwest coast for control of the lucrative "China trade" in furs.

By mid-decade, American political harmony had disappeared in Congress and among the people at large, as divisions deepened on virtually every important issue of foreign and domestic policy. Estranged from the administration, Jefferson resigned as secretary of state in July 1793. He soon joined politicians such as Madison and Albert Gallatin of Pennsylvania in open opposition to Washington's policies.

THE POLITICAL CRISIS DEEPENS

By 1796, bitter controversy surrounded the national government. That controversy intensified during the last half of the 1790s until the very stability of the country seemed threatened.

The Election of 1796

The presidential election of 1796 reflected the political storms buffeting the nation. In September, in what came to be called his Farewell Address to the nation, Washington deplored the deepening political divisions, warned against political alliances with foreign nations, and announced that he would not accept a third term as president (thus setting a precedent that would last until 1940). He had long been contemplating retirement, for he was now 64 and was exhausted by the controversy swirling around him.

With Washington out of the picture, the contest quickly narrowed to John Adams versus Jefferson. Both had played distinguished roles during the Revolution, when they had shared in the electrifying task of drafting the Declaration of Independence. They had joined forces again during the 1780s, when Adams served as first U.S. minister to Great Britain and Jefferson as minister to France. They came together a third time in the early 1790s, Adams as vice president and Jefferson as secretary of state.

Though they had earned each other's respect, they differed in many ways. Short, rotund, and fastidious, Adams contrasted sharply in appearance with the tall and frequently disheveled Jefferson. At once intensely ambitious and deeply insecure about the judgments of his contemporaries and of history, Adams struggled constantly to burnish his public reputation. Jefferson, by contrast, charted his course more quietly, frequently withdrawing to

John Adams, Washington's vice president, won a narrow victory over Jefferson for the presidency in 1796. His administration foundered on conflicts over foreign policy abroad and the suppression of political dissent at home. *(Adams National Historic Site/U.S. Department of the Interior, National Park Service)*

private life. Jefferson's mind was more expansive and his interests more wide reaching. Politician and political theorist, he was also an avid naturalist, architect, and philosopher. Adams's interests were more tightly focused on legal and constitutional matters.

By the mid-1790s, the two statesmen differed fundamentally in their visions of the nation's future. Though he feared Hamilton's ambition and distrusted his infatuation with England, Adams was a committed Federalist. He believed in a vigorous national government, was appalled by the French Revolution, and feared "excessive democracy." Jefferson, while firmly supporting the Constitution, was alarmed by Hamilton's financial program, viewed France's revolution as a logical if chaotic extension of America's struggle for freedom, and hoped to expand American democracy at home. By 1796, he had become the leader of an increasingly vocal political opposition, the Jeffersonian Republicans.

The election of 1796 bound Jefferson and Adams together once again, this time in a deeply strained and ill-fated alliance. With Washington gone, Adams became the Federalists' candidate for president. Though Jefferson did not openly oppose him, his followers campaigned vigorously on Jefferson's behalf. In the election, Adams received 71 electoral votes and became president. Jefferson came in second with 68 and, as the Constitution then specified, assumed the vice presidency. The narrowness of Adams's majority—his enemies gleefully reminded him that he was only a "President of three votes"—foreshadowed the troubles that lay ahead.

Adams later recalled his inaugural day. "A solemn scene it was indeed, and it was made more affecting by the presence of the General [Washington], whose countenance was as serene and unclouded as the day. He seemed to enjoy a triumph over me. Methought I heard him say, 'Ay! I am fairly out and you fairly in! See which of us will be the happiest'." The answer was not long in coming.

The War Crisis with France

Adams had no sooner taken office than he confronted a deepening crisis with France generated by French naval vessels interfering with American merchant ships in the Caribbean. That crisis would push the nation to the brink of civil conflict.

Hoping to ease relations between the two countries, he sent three commissioners to Paris to negotiate an accord. When they arrived, agents (identified only as "X," "Y," and "Z") of the French foreign minister, Talleyrand, made it clear that the success of the American mission depended on a substantial loan to the French government and a $240,000 "gratuity" (more accurately, a bribe) for themselves. The two staunchly Federalist commissioners, John Marshall and Charles Pinckney, indignantly sailed home. The third commissioner, Elbridge Gerry, alarmed by Talleyrand's intimation that if all three Americans left, France would declare war, stayed on.

When Adams reported to Congress on the so-called XYZ Affair, American opinion was outraged. The Federalists quickly exploited the French blunder. Secretary of State Pickering urged an immediate declaration of war, while Federalist congressmen thundered against the insult to American honor and promised "millions for defense, but not one cent for tribute." Adams now found himself an unexpected hero. When he attended the theater in Philadelphia, audiences cheered themselves hoarse with shouts of "Adams and Liberty!" Caught up in the anti-French furor and emboldened by the petitions of support that flooded in from around the country, the president lashed out at "enemies" at home and abroad. The nation, he warned ominously, had never been in greater danger. Emotions were further inflamed by the so-called Quasi War, a series of encounters between American and French naval ships on the high seas.

For the moment, the Republicans were in disarray. Publicly, they deplored the French government's behavior and pledged to uphold the nation's honor. But among themselves, they voiced alarm over the Federalists' intentions. They had good reason for concern, because the Federalists soon mounted a crash program to repel foreign invaders and root out "traitors" at home.

The Alien and Sedition Acts

In May 1798, Congress called for the rapid development of a naval force capable of defending the American coast against French attack. In July, it moved closer to an open breach with France by repealing the treaty of 1778 and calling for the formation of a 10,000-man army. The army's stated mission was to repel a French invasion, but this seemed an unlikely danger given France's desperate struggle in Europe. The Jeffersonian Republicans, remembering the speed with which the Federalists had deployed troops against the Whiskey Rebels only a few years earlier, feared the army would be used against them.

As criticism of the army bill mounted, Adams had second thoughts. He was still enough of an old revolutionary to worry about the dangers of a standing army. "This damned army," he burst out, "will be the ruin of the country." The navy, he believed, should be America's first line of defense. He was further angered when members of his party sought to put Hamilton in command of the troops. To the dismay of hard-line Federalists, Adams issued only a few of the officers' commissions that Congress had authorized. Without officers, the troops could not be mobilized.

Fearful of foreign subversion and aware that French as well as Irish immigrants were active in the political opposition, the Federalist-dominated Congress acted to curb the flow of aliens into the country. In June 1798, the Naturalization Act raised from 5 to 14 years the residence requirement for citizenship, while the Alien Act authorized the president to expel aliens whom he judged "dangerous to the peace and safety of the United States." Imprisonment and permanent exclusion from citizenship awaited those who were warned to leave but refused to go. The following month, the Alien Enemies Act empowered the president in time of war to arrest, imprison, or banish the subjects of any hostile nation without specifying charges against them or providing opportunity for appeal. The Federalist Congressman Harrison Gray Otis explained that there was no need "to invite hordes of

Wild Irishmen, or the turbulent and disorderly of all parts of the world, to come here with a view to distract our tranquility."

The implications of these acts for basic political liberties were ominous enough, but the Federalists were not yet finished. In mid-July, Congress passed the Sedition Act, aimed directly at the Jeffersonian opposition. The bill made it punishable by fine and imprisonment for anyone to conspire in opposition to "any measure or measures of the government" or to aid "any insurrection, riot, unlawful assembly, or combination." Fines and imprisonment also awaited those who dared to "write, print, utter, or publish . . . any false, scandalous and malicious writing" bringing the government, Congress, or the president into disrepute.

The Federalist moves stunned the Jeffersonian Republicans, for they threatened to smother all political opposition. The Federalists left no room for doubts on the matter. With an open declaration of war, predicted Congressman James Lloyd of Delaware, "traitors and sedition mongers who are now protected and tolerated, would . . . be easily restrained or punished." The Federalists now equated their own political domination with the nation's survival.

Under the terms of the Alien Act, Secretary of State Pickering launched investigations intended to force all foreigners to register with the government. The act's chilling effects were immediately apparent. Toward the end of July, Pickering noted approvingly that large numbers of aliens, especially people of French ancestry, were leaving the country. As prosecutions under the Sedition Act went forward, 25 people, among them David Brown of Dedham, were arrested. Fifteen were indicted, and ten were ultimately convicted, the majority of them newspaper printers and editors.

Representative Matthew Lyon, a cantankerous, acid-tongued congressman from Vermont, learned the consequences of political indiscretion, even for members of Congress. Born in Ireland, Lyon had come to America as a young indentured servant, bringing with him undying enmity toward England and disrespect for privilege of every sort. A veteran of the war for American independence, he took his revolutionary principles seriously.

During a heated debate over the Sedition Act, Lyon spat in the face of Federalist Congressman Roger Griswold of Connecticut, thus earning the derisive sobriquet of the "Spitting Lion." Two weeks later, Griswold exacted revenge by caning Lyon on the House floor. Later that year, Lyon was hauled into court, fined $1,000, and sentenced to four months in prison. His crime? Reference in a personal letter to President Adams's "unbounded thirst for ridiculous pomp, foolish adulation, and selfish avarice."

Local Reverberations

David Brown was not the only ordinary citizen to experience the enmity of Federalist authorities, for the political conflict penetrated deep into American communities. On July 27, 1798, President and Mrs. Adams passed through Newark, New Jersey, on their

A fight erupted in the House of Representatives in 1798 when Matthew Lyon, a Jeffersonian from Vermont, spat on the Federalist Roger Griswold. As the two congressmen battle, other representatives and a dog look on. *(Print Collection, Miriam and Ira D. Wallach Division of Art, Prints and Photographs, The New York Public Library, Astor, Lenox and Tilden Foundations)*

way from Philadelphia to their home in Quincy, Massachusetts. As the nation's first couple moved along Broad Street around 11 o'clock that morning, they were greeted by firing cannon, ringing church bells, and cheering citizens.

Not all Newark's residents shared in the moment's enthusiasm. Luther Baldwin happened to be coming toward John Burnett's dram shop when one of the tavern's customers, noting that the cannon continued to fire after the president had passed by, commented acidly, "There goes the President and they are firing at his a––." A "little merry with drink," Baldwin replied that "he did not care if they fired thro' his a––." Whereupon, the Federalist tavern keeper cried out that Baldwin had spoken sedition and must be punished. Within a year he was hauled before a federal Circuit Court, where he was convicted of speaking "seditious words tending to defame the President and Government of the United States," fined, and committed to jail until both fine and court fees were paid.

Jeffersonian Republicans made a field day of Baldwin's trial. The New York *Argus* wondered in mock astonishment whether the "most enthusiastic Federalists and Tories" supposed that anyone "would feel . . . justification in firing at such a disgusting target as the a–– of J. A.?" There was danger as well as humor, however, in the Federalists' overreaction. When so much is made of such a "ridiculous expression" as Baldwin's, the *Argus* warned, the "malignancy of the federal faction" was plainly revealed.

Though some Jeffersonian leaders found it difficult to set aside long-established notions of leadership by a "natural aristocracy of talent," the Jeffersonian coalition benefitted from the continuing spread of democratic sentiment. That was illustrated by an episode that occurred in New York City in 1795.

In November of that year, two Irish-American ferrymen, Thomas Burke and Timothy Crady, refused to obey the order of Gabriel Furman, a New York merchant and Federalist alderman, to take him across the East River from Brooklyn to Manhattan ahead of schedule. Angered by the "rascals" impudence, Furman threatened to have them arrested. Undaunted, Crady shot back that he and Burke "were as good as any buggers," and promised to use his boathook on anyone who interfered.

When the ferry landed on the Manhattan shore, Furman had the two arrested, brandishing his cane at them as they were taken off to jail where they were charged with vagrancy and denied bail. Eventually they were hauled before Mayor Varick and three other Federalist aldermen, sitting as a Court of General Sessions. The judges quickly decided to make examples of the two insolent Irishmen. "You rascals," Varick allegedly said, "we'll learn you to insult men in office." The two ferrymen were not allowed to speak on their own behalf, nor were friendly witnesses permitted to testify. The magistrates found the two guilty of insulting an alderman and threatening a constable, sentenced them to two months at hard labor, and ordered that 25 lashes be laid on Crady's back for good measure.

Within a month, the two ferrymen bolted from jail and disappeared into the woods of Pennsylvania, never to be heard from again. The episode, however, was not yet over, for a young Jeffersonian lawyer named William Keteltas publicly castigated the "tyranny and partiality of the court," arguing that Burke and Crady had been punished to "gratify the pride, the ambition and insolence of men in office." The authorities had supposedly acted to protect the mayor's reputation, but what about the reputation of the ferrymen? After Keteltas was upbraided for his insolence, 2,000 citizens carried him through the streets chanting "The Spirit of '76" and waving a banner sardonically inscribed "What, you rascal, insult your superiors?" Given the Jeffersonian Republicans' opposition to Federalist arrogance and challenge to the Alien and Sedition Acts, such social tensions worked steadily to their political advantage.

The Virginia and Kentucky Resolutions

With little prospect of reversing the actions of the Federalist-dominated Congress, Jeffersonian Republicans turned to the states for redress. Building on the firestorm of protest that greeted the Alien and Sedition Acts, the Virginia and Kentucky assemblies mounted direct challenges to the Federalist laws. The Kentucky Resolutions, drafted by Jefferson and passed on November 16, 1798, declared that the national government had violated the Bill of Rights. Faced with the arbitrary exercise of federal power, the resolutions continued, each state "has an equal right to judge [of infractions] by itself" and decide on the proper "mode and measure of redress." Nullification (declaring a federal law invalid within a state's borders) was the "rightful remedy" for unconstitutional laws. The Virginia Resolutions, written by Madison and passed the following month, asserted that when the central government threatened the people's liberties, the states "have the right and are in duty bound to interpose for arresting the progress of the evil." It would not be the last time in U.S. history that state leaders would claim authority to set aside a federal law.

The Kentucky and Virginia resolutions received little support elsewhere, and the Alien and Sedition

Divisive Issues of the 1790s

Issues	Federalist Party	Jeffersonian Republican Party
Domestic Policy		
Paying the national debt	Favors—Fund remaining debt at face value.	Favors—But wants discrimination between original holders and speculators.
Assumption of remaining state debts	Favors—As way of strengthening central government.	Opposes—As unfair to Southern States and source of power for central government.
Bank of the United States	Favors—To stabilize national economy, promote economic growth, and enhance power of central government.	Opposes—As exceeding central government's constitutional authority, and adding to consolidation of central authority.
Whiskey Tax	Favors—To provide revenue for central government.	Opposes—Warns of dangers in taxing power of central government.
Whiskey Rebellion	Favors—Suppression of rebellion as challenge to central government.	Opposes—Use of federal force to suppress protest.
Alien and Sedition Acts	Favors—As necessary to protect national security.	Opposes—As infringement of constitutional rights and threat to political opposition.
Federal army	Favors—As necessary to defend against possible French invasion.	Opposes—As dangerous enhancement of federal authority and threat to political opposition.
Foreign Policy		
French Revolution	Initially endorses political reform in France, but alarmed by radicalism following 1793. Fears French influence in U.S. Cheers England as bastion of political order.	Endorses political reform in France. Continues cautious support following 1793. Suspicious of British motives.
Jay's Treaty	Supports as best agreement possible, and as promoting trade with England.	Opposes—Criticizes treaty's silence concerning impressment, return of confiscated slaves, etc.
XYZ Affair	Expresses outrage over affront to American dignity.	Also expresses outrage, though worries over domestic political fallout.
Declaration of war with France	Favors, following XYZ Affair—Badly divided when Adams opts for peace.	Opposes—As unnecessary and threatening dangerous domestic repercussions.

Acts were not enforced in the South. Still, the resolutions indicated the depth of popular opposition to the Federalist program.

As the Federalists pressed ahead, some of their opponents prepared for open conflict. The Virginia assembly called for the formation of a state arsenal at Harpers Ferry, reorganization of the militia, and a special tax to pay for these preparations. In Philadelphia, Federalist patrols walked the streets to protect government officials from angry crowds. As a precaution, President Adams smuggled arms into his residence. As 1799 began, the country seemed on the brink of upheaval.

Within a year, however, the political cycle turned again, this time decisively against the Federalists. From Europe, the president's son, John Quincy Adams, sent assurances that Talleyrand was prepared to negotiate an honorable accord. Alarmed at the political furor consuming the nation and fearful that war with France "would convulse the attachments of the country," Adams eagerly seized the opening. "The end of war is peace," he explained, "and peace was offered me." He had also concluded that his only chance of reelection lay in fashioning a peace coalition from elements of both parties.

Adams's cabinet was enraged when they learned of the new mission, for the Federalist war program depended for its legitimacy on continuation of the French crisis. After Secretary of State Pickering ignored the president's orders to dispatch the new commissioners, Adams dismissed him and personally instructed the commissioners to depart. By year's end, the envoys secured an agreement releasing the United States from the 1778 alliance and restoring peaceful relations between the two nations.

The "Revolution of 1800"

As the election of 1800 approached, the Federalists were in disarray, having squandered the political advantage handed them by the XYZ Affair in 1798. With peace a reality, they stood before the nation charged with exercising federal power unconstitutionally, suppressing political dissent, and intending to use a federal army against American citizens. Followers of Hamilton were furious at Adams's "betrayal." When the president announced his intention of standing for reelection, they plotted his defeat.

Emotions were running high as the election approached. In Philadelphia, gangs of young Federalists, showing their sympathy with England by wear-

ing black cockades in their caps, clashed with other groups sporting the tricolored cockade of France. "A fray ensued," one observer reported, "the light horse were called in, and the city was so filled with confusion . . . that it was dangerous going out."

The arch-Federalist Fisher Ames berated the Jeffersonian Republicans as "fire-eating salamanders" and "poison-sucking toads," while they returned the abuse in kind. In the heat of the moment, no compromise seemed possible. This election,

Jefferson declared, will "fix the national character" by determining whether "republicanism or aristocracy" will prevail. In Virginia, rumors of a slave insurrection briefly interrupted the political feuding, but the scare passed and Federalists and Jeffersonian Republicans were soon at each others' throats once again.

Election day was tense throughout the country, but passed without serious incident. As the results were tallied, it became clear that the Jeffersonian

The Presidential Election of 1800

Though the federal government was little more than a decade old, the electoral vote in 1800 revealed the sectional divisions that already troubled national politics.

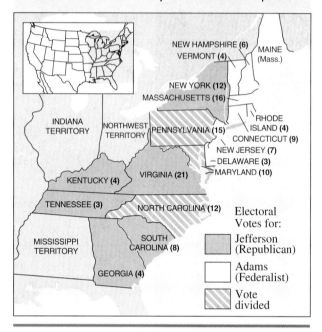

Electoral Votes for:

- Jefferson (Republican)
- Adams (Federalist)
- Vote divided

Republicans had handed the Federalists a decisive defeat. The two Jeffersonian candidates for president, Jefferson and Aaron Burr of New York, each had 73 electoral votes, compared to Adams's 65.

Because of the tie vote, the election was thrown into the House of Representatives, as provided in the Constitution, where a deadlock quickly developed. After a bitter struggle in which the Federalists backed Burr, believing him less dangerous than Jefferson, the House finally elected Jefferson, 10 states to 4, on the thirty-sixth ballot. (Seeking to prevent a recurrence of such a crisis, the next Congress passed and the states then ratified the Twelfth Amendment, providing for separate Electoral College ballots for president and vice president.) The magnitude of the Federalists' defeat was even more evident in congressional elections, where they lost their majority in both House and Senate.

The election's outcome revealed the strong sectional divisions now evident in the country's politics. The Federalists dominated New England because of regional loyalty to Adams, the area's commercial ties with England, and fears, fed by local ministers and politicians, that their opponents intended to import social revolution from France. From Maryland south, political control by the Jeffersonians was almost as complete. In the middle states, where issues of foreign and domestic policy

cut across society in more complicated ways, the election was more closely contested. These sectional differences would continue to shape American politics in the years ahead.

The political alignment evident in the election of 1800 resembled but did not duplicate the Federalist/Anti-Federalist division of 1788. Federalist support was strongest among merchants, manufacturers, and commercial farmers situated within easy reach of the coast—groups that had supported the Constitution in 1788. In New York City and Philadelphia, Federalists were most numerous in wards where houses were largest and addresses most fashionable.

The Jeffersonian coalition included most of the old Anti-Federalists, including farmers in both North and South, but was much broader as well. The Jeffersonians marshaled support among urban workers and artisans, many of whom had once been staunch Federalists, and included leaders such as Madison and Jefferson who had helped create the Constitution and set the new government on its feet. Unlike the Anti-Federalists, the Jeffersonians were ardent supporters of the Constitution, but insisted that it be implemented in ways consistent with political liberty and a strong dependence on the states.

Motivated by electoral self-interest, political principle, and the determination of ordinary men to claim their rights as republican citizens, the Jeffersonian Republicans mounted elaborate parades, organized sophisticated get-out-the-vote campaigns in New York City and other urban centers, and utilized the popular press to mobilize the people. And when Jeffersonian leaders hesitated to enlist the people, they were pushed ahead by the growing tide of popular politics.

In the election of 1800, control of the federal government passed for the first time from one political party to another, not easily but peacefully and legally. The "Revolution of 1800," Jefferson claimed, was "as real a revolution in the principles of our government as that of 1776 was in its form." The coming years would show whether he was correct.

RESTORING AMERICAN LIBERTY

The Jeffersonians took office in 1801 with several objectives in mind: calming the political storms that had threatened the country's unity, consolidating their recent electoral victory, rescuing the government from Federalist mismanagement, and setting it on a proper republican course.

The Jeffersonians Take Control

In November 1800 the government had moved from Philadelphia to the new capital in the District

Unlike highly commercial, cosmopolitan centers such as New York and Philadelphia that had served as earlier capitals, Washington seemed lost in the woods of southern Maryland and northern Virginia. *(Library of Congress)*

of Columbia. When the politicians arrived, they were stunned by its primitiveness and isolation. Missing were the comfortable accommodations, sophisticated surroundings, and convenient access to the broader Atlantic world offered by New York and Philadelphia, earlier seats of the national government. To the amazement of arriving politicians, the new capital was little more than a swampy village of 5,000 inhabitants on the banks of the Potomac River.

Boasting that Washington would in time become the "Rome of the New World," Congress had commissioned a Frenchman, Pierre L'Enfant, to develop a plan for the capital city's development. Aided by a black mathematician and surveyor, Benjamin Banneker, L'Enfant produced a magnificent design, replete with plazas and broad boulevards radiating outward from a government center anchored by the Capitol and presidential mansion. Little of that grand design, however, had materialized by 1800. The Capitol wing containing the House chamber was finished, but the Senate chamber and president's house were still under construction.

To rid the government of Federalist pomp, Jefferson planned a simple inauguration. Shortly before noon on March 4, he walked to the Capitol from his nearby boardinghouse. Dressed as a plain citizen, the president-elect read his short inaugural address, Chief Justice John Marshall (a fellow Virginian but staunch Federalist, recently appointed to the Supreme Court by John Adams) administered

the oath of office, and a militia company fired a 16-gun salute.

Despite the modesty of the occasion, it was filled with significance. Mrs. Samuel Harrison Smith, Washington resident and political observer, described the moment's drama. "I have this morning witnessed one of the most interesting scenes a free people can ever witness," she wrote to a friend. "The changes of administration, which in every . . . age have most generally been epochs of confusion, villainy, and bloodshed, in this our happy country take place without any species of distraction or disorder." Countless Americans shared her sense of pride and relief.

In his inaugural speech, Jefferson enumerated the "essential principles" that would guide his administration: "equal and exact justice to all," support of the states as "the surest bulwarks against anti-republican tendencies," "absolute acquiescence" in the decisions of the majority, supremacy of civil over military authority, reduction of government spending, "honest payment" of the public debt, freedom of the press, and "freedom of the person under the protection of the habeas corpus." Though Jefferson never mentioned the Federalists, his litany of principles reverberated with the dark experience of the 1790s.

The president spoke also of political reconciliation. "Every difference of opinion," he declared, "is not a difference of principle. . . . We are all republicans—we are all federalists." Not all his followers

Only the wing housing the House of Representatives had been completed when Congress first met in the new capital in 1800. *(Library of Congress)*

welcomed that final flourish, for many were eager to scatter the Federalists to the political winds. Jefferson eventually agreed that a "general sweep" of Federalist officeholders was necessary, and by 1808 virtually all government offices were in Republican hands.

Politics and the Federal Courts

Having lost Congress and the presidency, the Federalists turned to the federal judiciary for protection against the expected Jeffersonian onslaught. In the last months of the Adams administration, the Federalist-controlled Congress had passed a new Judiciary Act increasing the number of circuit courts, complete with judges, marshals, and clerks. Before leaving office, Adams filled many of those offices with staunch Federalists. Our opponents, observed Jefferson bitterly, "defeated at the polls, have retired into the Judiciary, and from that barricade . . . hope to batter down all the bulwarks of Republicanism." Something had to be done. In January 1802, the new Congress repealed the Federalist Judiciary Act by a strict party vote.

As Federalists sputtered in anger, exultant Jeffersonians prepared to purge several highly partisan Federalist judges from the bench. In March 1803, the House of Representatives impeached federal District Judge John Pickering. The grounds were not the "high crimes and misdemeanors" required by the Constitution, but the Federalist diatribes with which Pickering regularly assaulted defendants and juries. Impeachment, declared Representative William Branch Giles of Virginia, is nothing more than a declaration by Congress that an individual holds "dangerous opinions," which if allowed to go into effect "will work the destruction of the Union." Although Giles's speech echoed the language of repression used by Federalists only a few years earlier, the Jeffersonian-controlled Senate convicted Pickering by a straight party vote.

Emboldened by their success, the Jeffersonian Republicans next impeached Supreme Court Justice Samuel Chase, charging him with "intemperate and inflammatory political harangues," delivered "with intent to excite the fears and resentment of the . . . people . . . against the Government of the United States." When the trial revealed that Chase had committed no impeachable offense, he was acquitted and returned triumphantly to the bench.

Chase was a sorry hero, but constitutional principles are often established in the defense of less than heroic people. Had Chase's impeachment succeeded, Chief Justice Marshall would almost certainly have been next, and that would have precipitated a serious constitutional crisis. Sensing the danger, the Jeffersonians pulled back, content to allow time and attrition to cleanse the courts of Federalist control. The vital principle of judicial independence had been narrowly preserved.

Dismantling the Federalist War Program

The Jeffersonians had regarded the Federalists' war program as a threat to liberty, and quickly dismantled it. Jefferson ended prosecution of newspaper

Federal Revenues and Expenditures, 1790–1810 (in thousands of dollars)

Year	Revenues		Expenditures	
1790	Customs	4,399	Military	634
	Other	19	Interest on public debt	2,349
		4,418	Other	1,426
				4,409
1800	Customs	9,081	Military	6,010
	Internal revenue	809	Interest on public debt	3,375
	Other	793	Other	1,466
		10,683		10,851
1810	Customs	8,583	Military	3,948
	Internal revenue	7	Interest on public debt	2,845
	Sale of public lands	697	Other	1,447
	Other	793		8,240
		10,080		

Note: In constant dollars, the estimated revenue of the federal government in 2001 was $2,136 trillion and its estimated expenditures were $1,856 trillion.

Source: U.S. Bureau of the Census and Statistical Abstract of the U.S.: 2001.

editors under the Sedition Act, freed its victims, and in 1802 let it lapse. While several Federalist editors felt the government's displeasure after 1800, Jefferson never duplicated the Federalists' attempts to stifle political dissent. As a consequence, the doctrine of freedom of the press, listed in the first amendment to the Constitution among the bedrock principles of American liberty, was solidly affirmed.

For Jeffersonians such as James Madison, as for civil libertarians ever since, freedom of the press meant opportunity, even for the most radical critics, to comment on public issues without fear of official reprisal. Jefferson agreed. "Error of opinion may be tolerated," he explained in his first inaugural address, "where reason is left free to combat it." Affirming freedom of the press was especially important at a time of political crisis and when the press was becoming an essential vehicle of democratic politics. The American people would often struggle to reaffirm that freedom in the years ahead.

Jefferson also undercut the Alien Acts by dismantling the hated inspection system. In 1802, Congress restored the requirement of 5 rather than 14 years of residence before a foreigner could become a citizen. The Federalists' provisional army was also quickly disbanded; no longer would federal troops intimidate American citizens.

Finally, Jefferson was determined to reduce the size of the federal government. Tiny by modern standards, the government had fewer than 3,000 civilian employees, only 300 of them, including the cabinet and Congress, in Washington. (That amounted to one federal official for every 1,914 citizens, compared with one for approximately every 68 citizens today.) The "principal care of our persons and property," he declared, should be left to the states because they were more closely attuned to the needs of the people and could be held more closely accountable. The federal government, he thought, should do little more than oversee foreign policy, deliver the mail, deal with Indians on federal land, and administer the public domain.

The Jeffersonian Republicans may not have "revolutionized" the government as they claimed, but they reduced its size and limited its powers.

BUILDING AN AGRARIAN NATION

The Jeffersonian Republicans did more than reverse Federalist initiatives and reshape the government, for they were determined to implement their own vision of an expanding, agrarian nation. That vision was mixed and inconsistent, because the Jeffersonian party was made up (as major American parties have always been) of often conflicting groups: southern patricians determined to maintain a gentry-led, slavery-based agrarian order; lower- and middle-class southern whites committed to black servitude but ardent proponents of political equality among whites; northern artisans who brought to the Jeffersonian party an aversion to slavery (though rarely a commitment to racial equality) together with a fierce dedication to honest toil and their own economic interests; western farmers devoted to self-sufficiency on the land; and northern intellectuals committed to political democracy. In time, this diversity would splinter the Jeffersonian coalition. For the moment, however, these groups found unity not only in their common Federalist enemies, but also in a set of broadly shared principles that guided the government through Jefferson's two administrations (1801–1809).

The Jeffersonian Vision

Political liberty, the Jeffersonians believed, could survive only under conditions of broad economic and social equality. Their strategy centered on the independent, yeoman farmer—self-reliant, industrious, and concerned for the public good. Such qualities were deemed essential to democratic citizenship.

The Jeffersonian vision was clouded, however, because industriousness generated wealth, wealth bred social inequality, and inequality threatened to destroy the very foundation of a democratic society. The solution to that dilemma lay in rapid territorial expansion that would provide land for the nation's yeoman citizens, draw restless people out of crowded eastern cities, preserve the social equality that democratic liberty required, and delay, perhaps even prevent, the cycle of political growth, maturity, and decay that had been the fate of all past nations.

Calls for expanding white settlement were strengthened by the somber writings of an English clergyman and political economist named Thomas Malthus. In 1798, Malthus published an essay that jolted Europeans and Americans alike. Observing the increasingly crowded conditions of his native England, Malthus argued that "the power of population" was "greater than the power in the earth to produce subsistence for man." Hopes for a steadily improving quality of life, he warned, were a delusion, for the future would be filled with increasing misery as population outran the supply of food.

Jefferson took Malthus's warnings seriously but believed that the Englishman failed to understand that the United States' vast reservoir of land would enable its people to escape Europe's fate. In Europe, Jefferson explained, "the quantity of food is fixed . . . [while] supernumerary births add only to mortality. Here the immense extent of uncultivated and fertile lands enables every one who will labor to marry young and to raise a family of any size. Our food, then, may increase geometrically with our laborers, and our births, however multiplied, become effective." Territorial expansion was thus indispensable to the Jeffersonian vision of the nation's future.

In addition, occupation of the West would secure the nation's borders against continuing threats from England, France, and Spain. Finally, the Jeffersonians calculated that the new western states, committed to democratic forms of politics, would strengthen their own political control and ensure the Federalists' demise.

Time would reveal that American exceptionalism—the idea that the United States could avoid Europe's woes by continental expansion—was more limited than Jefferson imagined. Yet from the perspective of the early nineteenth century, the Jeffersonians offered a compelling vision of the nation's future.

The Windfall Louisiana Purchase

The goal of securing agrarian democracy by territorial expansion explains Jefferson's most dramatic accomplishment, buying the Louisiana Territory in 1803. The purchase nearly doubled the nation's size.

In 1800, Spain ceded the vast trans-Mississippi region called Louisiana to France. Jefferson was profoundly disturbed by such clear evidence that European nations still coveted North American territory. His fears were well grounded, for in October 1802 the Spanish commander at New Orleans, which Spain had retained, once again closed the Mississippi River to American commerce. Spain's action raised consternation both in Washington and in the West.

In January 1803, the president sent his young associate James Monroe to Paris with instructions to purchase New Orleans and West Florida (which contained Mobile, the only good harbor on the Gulf Coast). When Monroe arrived, he was surprised to find the ruler of France, Napoleon Bonaparte, prepared to sell all of Louisiana (although not West Florida). Faced with the successful black rebellion against French rule in Haiti and a renewed threat of war with England, Napoleon feared American designs on Louisiana and knew he could not keep American settlers out. In April, the deal was struck. For $15 million, the United States obtained nearly 830,000 square miles of new territory.

Federalists reacted with alarm to news of the acquisition, fearing correctly that the states to be carved from Louisiana would be staunchly Jeffersonian. They worried as well that a rapidly expanding frontier would "decivilize" the entire nation.

Territorial expansion did not end with Louisiana. In 1810, American adventurers fomented a revolt in Spanish West Florida and proclaimed an independent republic. Two years later, over vigorous

Exploring the Trans-Mississippi West, 1804–1807

With the nation nearly doubled in size following the Louisiana Purchase, President Jefferson sent out exploring expeditions to map the region and establish an American presence there.

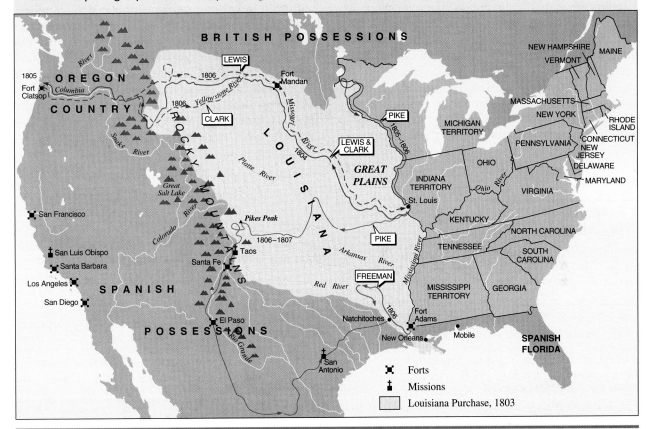

Spanish objections, Congress annexed the region. In the Adams-Onis (or Transcontinental) Treaty of 1819, Spain ceded East Florida as well. As part of that agreement, the United States also extended its territorial claims to include the Pacific Northwest.

Opening the Trans-Mississippi West

If the country's expanding domain was to serve the needs of the agrarian nation, it would have to be explored and prepared for white settlement. In the summer of 1803, Jefferson dispatched an expedition led by his secretary, Meriwether Lewis, and a young army officer named William Clark to explore the Northwest, make contact with the Native Americans, open the fur trade, and bring back scientific information about the area. For nearly two and a half years, the intrepid explorers, assisted by the Shoshoni woman Sacajawea, made their way across thousands of miles of hostile and unmapped terrain—up the Missouri River, through the Rockies via the Bitterroot Valley and Lolo Pass, down the Columbia to the Pacific coast, and back again, finally reemerging at St. Louis in September 1806. Lewis and Clark's journey, which some have called the greatest wilderness trip ever recorded, fanned people's interest in the Trans-Mississippi West and demonstrated the feasibility of an overland route to the Pacific.

In 1805 and 1806, Lieutenant Zebulon Pike explored the sources of the Mississippi River in northern Minnesota, then undertook an equally bold venture into the Rocky Mountains, where he surveyed the peak that still bears his name. In the following decade, the government established a string of military posts from Fort Snelling, at the confluence of the Minnesota and Mississippi Rivers, to Fort Smith on the Arkansas. They were intended to secure the nation's frontier, promote the fur trade, and support white settlement.

The Jeffersonians' blueprint for an agrarian democracy also guided changes in federal land policy. While Federalists had viewed public land as a commodity to be sold as a way of generating government revenue, Jeffersonians were principally concerned to speed its settlement. Accordingly, the Land Act of 1801 reduced the minimum required purchase from 640 to 320 acres, established a credit system, and offered discounts for cash sales. Over the next year and a half, settlers, speculators, and land companies bought nearly four times as much federal land as during the entire 1790s. Although these new policies fostered widespread speculation and contributed to the Panic of 1819, they speeded the movement of public land into private hands.

A FOREIGN POLICY FOR THE NEW NATION

While Jefferson was preoccupied with refashioning the government during his first term of office, his second term was dominated by foreign policy. As Washington and John Adams had discovered, and as James Madison would later learn, dealing with a volatile and dangerous Atlantic world proved no easy task.

Jeffersonian Principles

During the early years of the nineteenth century, the Jeffersonians struggled to fashion a foreign policy appropriate for the expanding agrarian nation. Several goals guided their efforts: protecting American interests on the high seas, clearing the Great Lakes region of foreign troops, breaking free of the country's historic dependence on Europe, and avoiding war.

Jeffersonian foreign policy was based on the principle of "no entangling alliances" with Europe that Washington had articulated in his Farewell Address of 1796. England was still the principal enemy, but France, now that the revolution had ended in Napoleon Bonapart's dictatorial rule, was suspect as well.

Second, the Jeffersonians emphasized the importance of overseas commerce for the nation's well-being. Foreign trade would provide markets for the country's agricultural produce and bring manufactured goods in return. Federalists had nurtured domestic manufacturing by offering tariff protection against European goods, but the Jeffersonians hoped to keep large-scale manufacturing in Europe. They feared the concentrations of wealth and dependent working classes that domestic manufacturing would bring.

Peace was the Jeffersonians' third goal. War they regarded as objectionable not only because people were killed and property destroyed, but also because war endangered liberty by inflaming politics, stifling free speech, swelling public debt, and expanding governmental power. The Jeffersonians understood the dangers lurking throughout the Atlantic world and knew that protecting the nation's interests might require force. Between 1801 and 1805, Jefferson dispatched naval vessels to the Mediterranean to defend U.S. commerce against the Barbary States (Algiers, Morocco, Tripoli, and Tunis). War, however, was to be a policy of last resort.

Struggling for Neutral Rights

After a brief interlude of peace, European war resumed in 1803. Once again Britain and France seized American shipping. Britain's overwhelming naval superiority made its attacks especially serious, while its continuing refusal to negotiate on issues of impressment, occupation of the Great Lakes fur-trading posts, and reopening the West Indian trade heightened Anglo-American tension.

In response to British seizures of U.S. shipping, Congress passed the Non-Importation Act in 1806,

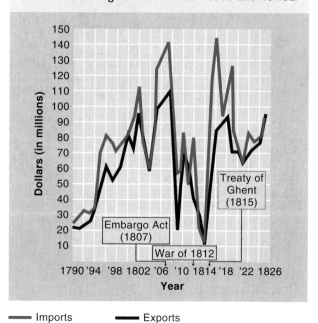

American Foreign Trade, 1790–1825

American overseas trade fluctuated dramatically as tensions with England and France ebbed and flowed.

Dollars (in millions)

Embargo Act (1807)

War of 1812

Treaty of Ghent (1815)

— Imports   — Exports

Source: U.S. Bureau of the Census.

The tranquility of Crowninshield Wharf in Salem, Massachusetts, reveals ships idled and docks emptied by Jefferson's embargo. *(Courtesy the Peabody Essex Museum, Salem, Massachusetts)*

banning British imports that could be produced domestically or acquired elsewhere. A month later, Britain blockaded the European coast. In retaliation, Napoleon forbade all commerce with the British Isles.

Tension between Britain and the United States reached the breaking point in June 1807, when the British warship *Leopard* stopped the frigate *Chesapeake* off the Virginia coast and demanded that four crew members be handed over as British deserters. When the American commander refused, protesting that the sailors were U.S. citizens, the *Leopard* opened fire, killing 3 men and wounding 18. After the *Chesapeake* limped back into port with the story, cries of outrage rang across the land.

Knowing that the United States was not prepared to confront Britain militarily, Jefferson proposed that U.S. ships withdraw from the Atlantic. In December 1807, Congress passed the Embargo Act, forbidding

Timeline

1789	George Washington inaugurated as first president Outbreak of the French Revolution
1790	Slave trade outlawed in all states except Georgia and South Carolina Hamilton's "Reports on the Public Credit"
1791	Bill of Rights ratified Whiskey Tax and national bank established Hamilton's "Report on Manufactures"
1792	Washington reelected
1793	Outbreak of war in Europe Washington's Neutrality Proclamation Jefferson resigns from cabinet Controversy over Citizen Genêt's visit
1794	Whiskey Rebellion in Pennsylvania
1795	Controversy over Jay's Treaty with England
1796	Washington's Farewell Address John Adams elected president
1797	XYZ Affair in France
1798	Naturalization Act Alien and Sedition Acts Virginia and Kentucky Resolutions

1798–1800	Undeclared naval war with France
1799	Trials of David Brown and Luther Baldwin
1800	Capital moves to Washington
1801	Jefferson elected president Judiciary Act New Land Act
1802	Judiciary Act repealed
1803	Louisiana Purchase Napoleonic wars resume
1803–1806	Lewis and Clark expedition
1804	Jefferson reelected
1805–1807	Pike explores the West
1806	Non-Importation Act
1807	Embargo Act Chesapeake–Leopard Affair Congress prohibits slave trade

American vessels from sailing for foreign ports. Urging the embargo was one of Jefferson's most ill-fated decisions.

The embargo had relatively little effect on Britain, since British shipping profited from the withdrawal of commercial competition and British merchants found new sources of agricultural produce in Latin America. The embargo's impact at home, however, was far-reaching. U.S. exports plummeted 80 percent in a year, while imports dropped by more than half. New England was hardest hit. In ports such as Salem, Boston, and Providence, ships rocked idly at the wharves and thousands of workers were unemployed as depression settled in.

Everywhere, coastal communities, heavily dependent on overseas trade, openly violated the embargo. Attempts to police it failed, while English goods were smuggled across the Canadian border. When federal officials declared martial law and sent in troops in an effort to control the situation near Lake Champlain in upstate New York, local citizens fired on U.S. revenue boats and recaptured confiscated goods.

Throughout the Federalist Northeast, bitterness threatened to escalate into open rebellion. Connecticut's Federalist governor, in language reminiscent of the Virginia and Kentucky Resolutions, declared that if Congress exceeded its authority, the states were duty-bound "to interpose their protecting shield between the rights and liberties of the people and the assumed power of the general government." Faced with the embargo's ineffectiveness abroad and disastrous political consequences at home, Congress repealed the measure in 1809.

As Jefferson's presidency ended, officials found themselves in a quandary. How could American rights on the high seas be protected and the country's honor upheld without being drawn into a European war, and without further inflaming American politics? The nation would continue to struggle with that dilemma in the years immediately ahead.

✦ *Conclusion*

A PERIOD OF TRIAL AND TRANSITION

The decade of the 1790s was a time of continuing political crisis. Scarcely had the new government begun to be formed under the Constitution than divisions appeared, first among political leaders in the Congress but increasingly among the people at large. Hamilton's domestic policies generated the initial conflict, but it was the French Revolution, European war, Jay's Treaty, and the Federalist war program that galvanized political energies and set Federalists and Jeffersonian Republicans so adamantly against each other, involving countless citizens like David Brown in the confusion. The Haitian rebellion together with other democratic insurgencies in Ireland, Europe, and the Americas further inflamed the country's politics.

In control of the federal government following the election of 1800, the Jeffersonians labored to set it on a more democratic course. At home, they fashioned domestic policies designed to redirect authority to the states and promote the country's agrarian expansion. Abroad they attempted, with more ambiguous results and at considerable political cost, to protect American rights in a hostile Atlantic world while avoiding European entanglements.

As Thomas Jefferson left the presidency in 1809 and his Virginia colleague, James Madison took office, politics at the seat of national government and the more democratic politics brewing in the states had drawn more closely together, as politicians perfected the techniques of democratic politics, including a highly partisan press and better organized political parties. That political transition, emerging in the midst of deep-seated controversy, would continue in the years immediately ahead.

✦ Recommended Reading

Launching the National Republic
Kenneth Bowling and Donald Kemon, eds., *Neither Separate nor Equal: Congress in the 1790s* (2000); David Currie, *The Constitution in Congress: The Federal Period, 1789–1801* (1997); Stanley Elkins and Eric McKitrick, *The Age of Federalism* (1993); Joseph Ellis, *Founding Brothers: The Revolutionary Generation* (2000); Ronald Hoffman and Peter Albert, eds., *Launching the "Extended Republic": The Federalist Era* (1996); Leonard Levy, *Origins of the Bill of Rights* (1999); Stephen

Schechter and Richard Bernstein, eds., *Contexts of the Bill of Rights* (1990); Thomas Slaughter, *The Whiskey Rebellion* (1986).

The Republic in a Threatening World
Stuart Andrews, *The Rediscovery of America: Transatlantic Crosscurrents in an Age of Revolution* (1998); Albert Bowman, *The Struggle for Neutrality: Franco-American Diplomacy During the Federalist Era* (1974); Susan Branson, *These Fiery Frenchified Dames: Women and Political Culture in Early National Philadelphia* (2001); Michael Durey, *Transatlantic Radicals and the Early American Republic* (1997); J. Worth Estes and Billy G. Smith, eds., *A Melancholy Scene of Devastation: The Public Response to the 1793 Yellow Fever Epidemic* (1997); Daniel Lang, *Foreign Policy in the Early Republic* (1985); Peter Linebaugh and Marcus Rediker, *The Many-Headed Hydra: Sailors, Slaves, Commoners, and the Hidden History of the Revolutionary Atlantic* (2000); Thomas Ott, *The Haitian Revolution, 1789–1804* (1973); R. R. Palmer, *The Age of the Democratic Revolution*, 2 vols. (1959–64); David Wilson, *United Irishmen, United States: Immigrant Radicals in the Early Republic* (1998).

The Political Crisis Deepens
Joyce Appleby, *Capitalism and the New Social Order: The Republican Vision of the 1790s* (1984); Aliene Austin, *Matthew Lyon: "New Man" of the Democratic Revolution, 1749–1800* (1981); Doron Ben-Atar and Barbara Oberg, eds., *Federalists Reconsidered* (1998); John Hoadley, *Origins of American Political Parties, 1789–1803* (1986); Leonard Levy, *Freedom of the Press from Zenger to Jefferson* (1966); David McCulloch, *John Adams* (2000); Simon Newman, *Parades and the Politics of the Street* (1997); Jeffrey Pasley, *"The Tyranny of Printers": Newspaper Politics in the Early American Republic* (2001); James Roger Sharp, *American Politics in the Early Republic* (1998); Charles Steffen, *The Mechanics of Baltimore: Workers and Politics in the Age of Revolution, 1763–1812* (1984); Bernard Weisberger, *America Afire: Jefferson, Adams, and the Revolutionary Election of 1800* (2000).

Restoring American Liberty
Noble Cunningham, *The Process of Government Under Jefferson* (1978); Joseph Ellis, *American Sphinx: The Character of Thomas Jefferson* (1997); Annette Gordon-Reed, *Thomas Jefferson and Sally Hemmings: An American Controversy* (1997); Merrill Peterson, *Thomas Jefferson and the New Nation* (1970); James Simon, *What Kind of Nation: Thomas Jefferson, John Marshall, and the Epic Struggle to Create a United States* (1999).

Building an Agrarian Nation
Lance Banning, *The Jeffersonian Persuasion: The Evolution of a Party Ideology* (1978); Donald Jackson, *Thomas Jefferson and the Stony Mountains: Exploring the American West from Monticello* (1981); Drew McCoy, *The Elusive Republic* (1980); James Ronda, *Lewis and Clark Among the Indians* (1984).

A Foreign Policy for the New Nation
Robert Allison, *The Crescent Observed: The United States and the Muslim World, 1776–1805* (1995); Lester Langley, *The Americas in the Age of Revolution, 1750–1850* (1996); Reginald Horsman, *The Diplomacy of the New Republic, 1776–1815* (1985); James Lewis, Jr., *The American Union and the Problem of Neighborhood: The United States and the Collapse of the Spanish Empire, 1783–1829* (1998); Ernest May, *The Making of the Monroe Doctrine* (1975); J.C.A. Stagg, *Mr. Madison's War* (1983).

Fiction and Film
Adapted from Laurel Thatcher Ulrich's prize-winning book, the docudrama *A Midwife's Tale* (1997) depicts the daily life of nurse-midwife Martha Ballard, who delivered a thousand babies and served her New England community during the closing years of the eighteenth century. The initial installment of C-SPAN's *American Presidents: Life Portraits* series (1999) effectively portrays the challenges and accomplishments of the nation's first president, George Washington. In the novel *Fever* (1996), John Weidman offers a vivid account of the yellow fever plague that killed thousands of people and threatened social chaos in Philadelphia in 1793. The essayist and novelist Gore Vidal explores the tangled politics and personalities of the early republic via a largely sympathetic portrayal of Aaron Burr (who killed Alexander Hamilton in a duel in 1804) in *Burr: A Novel* (1973).

✦ Discovering U.S. History Online

Birth of the Nation: The First Federal Congress 1789–1791
www.gwu.edu/~ffcp/
This online exhibit "provides an overview of the work of and issues faced by this seminal Congress."

The Bradford House—Whiskey Rebellion—Whiskey Insurrection
www.bradfordhouse.org

David Bradford was a prominent figure in the "Whiskey Insurrection." His home has been restored as a museum; its online site includes a description of the rebellion, its causes, Bradford's role, and the end results.

George Washington's Mount Vernon Estate and Gardens
www.mountvernon.org
Pictures and documents from Mount Vernon, the home of the first president, George Washington.

The Papers of George Washington
http://gwpapers.virginia.edu
This richly illustrated site is the online site of George Washington's papers and includes the text of many of the documents, maps, images, and articles about Washington and his time.

The French Revolution
www.woodberry.org/acad/hist/FRWEB
This well-organized site provides an illustrated introduction to the French Revolution, its events, and people.

John Adams
www.whitehouse.gov/WH/glimpse/presidents/html/ja2.html
This site contains biographical information about the second president and links to his inaugural address, his more quotable phrases, and information about his wife, Abigail.

The Haitian Revolution of 1791–1803
www.webster.edu/~corbetre/haiti/history/revolution/revolution1.htm
This site presents a four-part historical essay on the Haitian Revolution and its significance.

Benjamin Rush, Yellow Fever, and the Birth of Modern Medicine
www.geocities.com/bobarnebeck/fever1793.html
An "online book with companion essays and primary documents," this site offers details on issues of disease and public health in Philadelphia during the 1790s.

Learning About the Senate: Series of Historical Minutes, 1790–1850
www.senate.gov/pagelayout/history/b_three_sections_with_teasers/essays.htm
This government site details some of the key issues facing the Senate including Jay's Treaty, complaints from early constituents, and confirming Supreme Court justices.

The Alien and Sedition Acts
www.yale.edu/lawweb/avalon/alsedact.htm
The full text of these acts is available on this site.

Nullification Issues
www.jmu.edu/madison/nullification
This illustrated site presents the Virginia and Kentucky Resolutions, how James Madison responded to them, a letter from Andrew Jackson, and the Senate debate.

Building the Capitol for a New Nation
www.loc.gov/exhibits/us.capitol/s0.html
Compiled from holdings in the Library of Congress, this site contains detailed information on the design and early construction of the Capitol building in Washington, D.C.

Thomas Jefferson
www.ipl.org/div/potus/tjefferson.html
This site contains basic factual data about Jefferson's election and presidency, speeches, and online biographies.

The Louisiana Purchase Exhibit
www.sec.state.la.us/purchase/purchase-index.htm
A colorful, illustrated presentation of the details of the Louisiana Purchase, the negotiations, documents, and a series of historical maps.

Thomas Jefferson Digital Archive
www.etext.virginia.edu/jefferson/
This site is the virtual home for numerous resources about Jefferson and his times.

Monticello: The Home of Thomas Jefferson
www.monticello.org
This site explores Jefferson's ideas through an examination of Monticello, Jefferson's unique home.

Lewis and Clark: The Journey of the Corp of Discovery
www.pbs.org/lewisandclark
This is a companion site to Ken Burns's film, containing a timeline of the expedition, a collection of related links, a bibliography, and over 800 minutes of unedited, full-length Real Player interviews with seven experts featured in the film.

British-American Diplomacy, 1782–1863
www.yale.edu/lawweb/avalon/diplomacy/britain/brtreaty.htm
An online archive of important treaties and conventions between England and the United States.

Napoleonic War Series
www.wtj.com/wars/napoleonic
Exploration of this site gives context to America's relations with Europe during the early part of the nineteenth century.

Birth of the Navy, Prelude to the War of 1812
www.mariner.org/usnavy/08/08a.htm
This illustrated chapter of the online book includes "Impressment of American Soldiers," "The *Chesapeake* Affair of 1807," "American Reaction to the *Chesapeake* Affair," and "Entanglement in World Affairs," as well as the text of original documents.

War of 1812
www.city-net.com/~markd/roots/history/us_war_of_1812.htm
A brief essay covering the foreign conflicts in the period leading up to the War of 1812.

9

Society and Politics in the Early Republic

Detail from Thomas Coke Ruckle, *Fairview Inn or Three Mile House on Old Frederick Road* (near Baltimore), 1829. At country inns, people on the move bought supplies, exchanged goods, and secured information about the routes that lay ahead. *(Maryland Historical Society, Baltimore, Maryland)*

✦ *American Stories*

CREATING NEW LIVES

In May 1809, Mary and James Harrod gathered their five children, loaded a few belongings (tools, seeds for the summer planting, and several prized pieces of furniture) on a wagon, closed the door on their four-room cabin, fell in line with a dozen other families, and headed west from Spotsylvania County, Virginia, toward a new life in Kentucky. They left behind 15 years of wearying effort trying to wring a modest living from 10 acres of marginal upland, and a family cemetery that held two of their other children and Mary's parents.

Beyond the Appalachian Mountains, 450 difficult miles ahead, lay additional hard work and uncertainty. Though central Kentucky, where the Harrods would settle, contained few Indian villages, powerful tribes from north and south of the Ohio River hunted there and fought over its control. They also fought the growing tide of white settlers. The first years would be especially hard for James and Mary as they "opened up" the land, planted the first crops, and erected a cabin. They would be lonesome as well, for the Harrods would be unlikely to see even the chimney smoke of their nearest neighbors.

Yet James and Mary were hopeful as they trudged west. The land agent who had sold them their claim had promised rich, fertile soil that in time would support a good life. And they had been excited at the prospect of joining the swelling stream of migrants seeking new lives in the trans-Appalachian West. They looked forward as well to escaping Virginia's slave society with its arrogant planters and oppressed slaves—no place for poor whites to live. Once in Kentucky, they settled on their own plot of land, joined with others in fashioning a new community, and took responsibility for their own lives.

In April 1795, Ben Thompson started north from Queen Anne's County, Maryland, for New York City. Ben knew little beyond farming, but he was ambitious, and when he arrived in New York he listened carefully to the ship's captains who talked about life at sea while they recruited men for their crews. Ben was lucky, for he arrived just as American overseas commerce, stimulated by renewed war in Europe, was entering a decade of unprecedented prosperity. Sailors were in demand, pay was good, and few questions were asked. For five years, Ben sailed the seas. Having enough of travel, he returned to New York and hired out as an apprentice to a ship's carpenter.

About the same time, Phyllis Sherman left her home in Norwalk, Connecticut. She also headed for New York, where she took a job as a maid in the household of one of the city's wealthy merchants. As fate would have it, Phyllis and Ben met, fell in love, and in the spring of 1802 were married.

There is little of note in this except that Ben and Phyllis were former slaves and were married in the African Methodist Episcopal Zion Church. Ben had cast off his slave name, Cato, as a sign of liberation, while Phyllis kept the name her master had given her. Ben was doubly fortunate, for he had purchased his freedom just as cotton production began to expand through the Old Southwest, creating a growing demand for field slaves shipped in from the Chesapeake. In another decade, he would have faced greater difficulty securing his independence. Phyllis had been freed as a child when slavery ended in Connecticut. As she grew up, she tired of living as a servant with her former owner's family and longed for the companionship of other blacks. She had heard that there were people of color in New York City, and she was correct. In 1800, it contained 6,300 African Americans, more than half of them free.

Though life in New York was better than either Ben or Phyllis had known before, it was hardly easy. They shared only marginally in the city's commercial prosperity. In 1804, they watched helplessly as yellow fever carried off their daughter and many of their friends. And while they found support in newly established African-American churches and the expanding black community, they had to be constantly on guard because slave ships still moved in and out of the port and slave catchers pursued southern runaways in the city's streets.

During the early decades of the nineteenth century, the American republic consisted of several distinctive regions, loosely joined by transportation and communication. In the Northeast, farmers struggled to wrest a living from long-cultivated land. To the South, cotton was beginning to emerge as the dominant staple crop. As it did, the region's sagging economy, together with its system of slave labor, began a fateful expansion. West of the Appalachian Mountains, a new region of white settlement took shape generating conflict with the area's Indian inhabitants and dramatically altering the nation's social, economic, and political life. These years witnessed as well the accelerated growth of American cities.

In the early republic, thousands of people like Mary and James Harrod, Ben Thompson, and Phyllis Sherman seized opportunities to improve their lives. In doing so, they strengthened American values of social equality, individual opportunity, political democracy, and personal autonomy. Those values would help to transform the nation.

This transformation—some have called it the "opening" of American society—was driven as well by an expanding market economy with its relentless discipline of supply and demand, pursuit of individual profit, and impersonal, contractual relationships. As the market expanded, it weakened long-standing commitments to a "just price" and other values of an earlier "moral economy."

In addition, the wave of religious revivalism known as the Second Great Awakening that swept through American society beginning about 1800 strengthened belief in individualism and equality. The Gospel message carried by swarms of untutored, itinerant Methodist and Baptist preachers, stressed universal salvation, the equality of all believers before God, and the individual's responsibility for her or his own soul.

Not all Americans benefited equally from the changes of these early nineteenth-century years. Doctrines of equality,

opportunity, and individual autonomy resonated far more powerfully in the lives of white men than of white women. In the South, African Americans found their lives harshly constrained by a revitalized system of slavery, while in the North, free blacks faced an increasingly racialized society. West of the Appalachians, Native Americans confronted a swelling tide of white settlement sweeping across their homeland.

Discrepancies between the nation's values and the conditions of many Americans' lives, together with moral energies released by the Great Awakening, fueled a flurry of reform movements aimed at alleviating poverty and distress and improving women's lives.

Patterns of change in the early republic appeared as well in the political arena, where democratic forces—energized during the revolutionary struggle against England and strengthened during the tumultuous administrations of Washington, Adams, and Jefferson—were promoted by a new generation of political leaders eager to claim their place in shaping the nation's future.

The years of the early republic brought as well a diplomatic revolution of major importance. Following the War of 1812, the American people broke free of their centuries-old dependence on Europe and turned their energies toward exploiting the vast North American continent. At the same time, the United States asserted a bold, new role among the emerging nations of Latin America, as those nations also threw off the yoke of European colonialism.

A NATION OF REGIONS

In the early republic, the vast majority of Americans drew their living from the land. In 1800, fully 83 percent of the labor force was engaged in agriculture; that figure had hardly changed 25 years later. Yet in the nation's regions, people occupied the land in very different ways.

The Northeast

In the Northeast, a region stretching from eastern Pennsylvania and New Jersey to New England, family farms dominated the landscape. On New England's rock-strewn land, farmers often abandoned field crops for the greater profits to be made from dairying and livestock. On the richer agricul-

tural lands of New York and Pennsylvania, farmers cultivated the land intensively, planting crops year after year rather than following the customary practice of allowing worn-out fields to lie fallow and recover their fertility. In 1776, the mid-Atlantic landscape had an unkempt appearance, with wide areas still covered by timber and fallow lands lapsing into brush. Fifty years later, the countryside looked increasingly orderly, its carefully cultivated fields marked by hedges and stone walls.

Farmers along the Hudson River valley and in southeastern Pennsylvania produced an agricultural surplus, the produce left over after they had met their families' needs, and exchanged it in nearby towns for commodities such as tea, sugar, window glass, and tools. Yet the goal, reported a European

Agricultural Productivity in 1800 and 2001

	Wheat		Cotton	
	Worker-Hours per Acre	Yield per Acre	Worker-Hours per Acre	Yield per Acre
1800	56.0	15 bushels	185	147 pounds
2001	2.4	40 bushels	4.6	698 pounds

Source: U.S. Bureau of the Census.

visitor, "was for every farmer to produce anything he required within his own family; and he was esteemed the best farmer, to use a phrase of the day, 'who did everything within himself.' "

Across much of the rural Northeast, cash often played a small part in economic exchanges. People, noted an observant Frenchman, "supply their needs in the countryside by direct reciprocal exchanges. The tailor and the bootmaker go and do the work of their calling at the home of the farmer . . . who . . . provides the raw material for it and pays for the work in goods. . . . They write down what they give and receive on both sides, and at the end of the year they settle a large variety of exchanges with a very small quantity of coin."

Most farms were not large. By 1800, the average farm in longer-settled areas of New England and the mid-Atlantic states was no more than 100 to 150 acres, down substantially from half a century before. That was primarily a result of the continuing division of farm property from fathers to sons. Even in southeastern Pennsylvania, long known as "the best poor man's country" and the most productive agricultural region in the entire Northeast, economic opportunity was declining. Continuous

cropping had robbed the soil of fertility, forcing farmers to bring more marginal land under cultivation, thus bringing a steady decline in productivity.

By 1800, nearly 20 percent of male taxpayers in southeastern Pennsylvania were single, clear evidence that young men were delaying marriage until they could establish themselves financially. In some localities, as many as 30 percent of married taxpayers were landless.

Most farmers owned only a few animals and knew little about scientific breeding. They typically allowed their animals to graze in common fields or forage in the open countryside. Even in winter, most farmers neither sheltered their animals nor provided them with fodder.

Whereas the majority of northeasterners made their living from the land, growing numbers of rural folk also worked for wages as artisans or day laborers in nearby towns, or toiled in the small-scale manufactories—grain and saw mills, potash works, and iron forges—that dotted the rural landscape. Farm women contributed to the family economy by helping with the livestock, preserving food, and making clothes for sale or exchange with neighbors. As the practice grew of men working for wages outside the family setting, women's unwaged domestic labor began to be regarded as less valuable.

Frustrated by the backwardness of American agriculture, leading citizens like John Adams joined in creating associations, such as the Massachusetts Society for Promoting Agriculture, that compiled agricultural libraries and issued publications promoting "scientific" techniques. Elkanah Watson, a prosperous businessman turned gentleman farmer, promoted the raising of fine-fleeced merino sheep

Though this Pennsylvania scene features cattle rather than merino sheep, it reveals the interests of farmers and more elegantly attired gentlemen in the commercial benefits of "scientific" livestock breeding. Note what appear to be plowing contests in the background. *(John A. Woodside*, A Country Fair in Pennsylvania, *1824, from the Collection of Harry T. Peters, Jr. Museum of The City of New York)*

Rural Industry in the North

Prior to the expansion of urban industrialization beginning in the 1830s, American manufacturing was small in scale and was often scattered across the countryside.

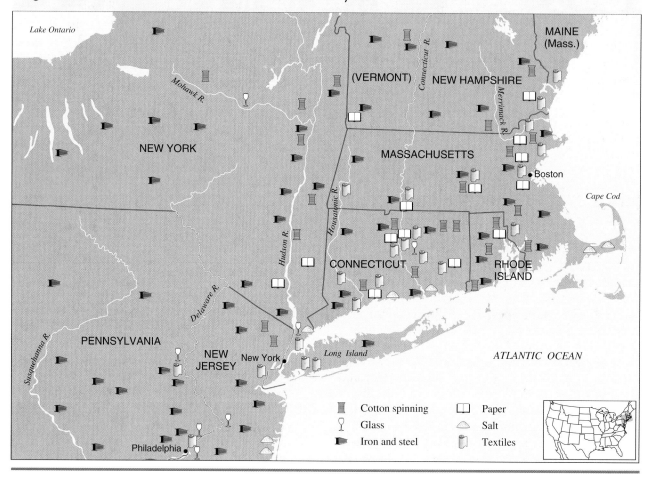

Cotton spinning		Paper	
Glass		Salt	
Iron and steel		Textiles	

that agricultural reformers promised would bring newfound prosperity.

Watson was instrumental as well in creating the nation's first agricultural fairs in western Massachusetts. Part visionary and part huckster, Watson intended the fairs' displays of equipment, animals, and produce not only to educate farmers but to "excite a lively spirit of competition" and thus energize them as well. His efforts succeeded beyond his fondest hopes, for within a few years rural folk by the thousands were converging on the annual Berkshire gatherings. In a short while, these precursors to the county fairs that have remained a staple of rural and small town American life had spread from Maine to Virginia and as far west as Illinois.

By 1830, the demands of the Northeast's expanding population for new agricultural land and a wide variety of wood products had transformed the region's once heavily forested landscape. Numerous iron furnaces, scattered across the countryside, con-

sumed firewood voraciously. The Union Furnace in New Jersey exhausted a forest of nearly 20,000 acres in less than 15 years and had to be abandoned. That sorry tale was duplicated by other ironworks in New York and Massachusetts. The production of pot ash and turpentine, planking for wooden houses and fencing further depleted forest ranges.

But more than anything else, it was the demand for heating fuel during the long winter months that made the woodcutter's axe ring. Rural households burned from 20 to 30 cords of firewood annually in the highly inefficient open fireplaces that warmed their homes. As the region's coastal cities grew and nearby wood lots were exhausted, fuel had to be fetched from far inland. By 1800, Bostonians were dependent on wood shipped in from Maine and New Hampshire. As fuel prices rose, wealthier urbanites purchased more efficient Franklin stoves or switched from wood to coal, while the poor shivered. Much of the coastal region had been denuded of trees by the

As settlers moved west, they cleared the land of trees for agriculture and produced lumber for houses and fences, as this sketch of a sawmill in upstate New York suggests. *(Library of Congress)*

early nineteenth century, though in some areas deserted farmlands lapsed into new growth forest, contributing a bit of ecological renewal.

The South

Life was very different in the South, a region stretching from Maryland to Georgia along the coast, and west to the newly forming states of Alabama and Mississippi. In 1800, much of southern agriculture was in disarray. Low prices, worn-out land, and the loss of slaves during the Revolutionary War had left the Chesapeake's tobacco economy in shambles. One English traveler reported that throughout much of the Shenandoah Valley, crops were "so intermixed with extensive tracts of waste land, worn out by the culture of tobacco . . . that on the whole the country had the appearance of barrenness."

In hopes of boosting their sagging fortunes, southern planters experimented with wheat and other grains. Regional recovery began in earnest, however, when they turned to a new staple crop—cotton. In 1790, the South had produced no more than 3,135 bales of cotton; by 1820, output had mushroomed to 334,378 bales. In 1805, cotton accounted for 30 percent of the nation's agricultural exports; by 1820, it exceeded half. Across both the old coastal South and the newly developing states of Alabama, Mississippi, and Tennessee, cotton was becoming king.

A fortuitous combination of circumstances fueled the transformation: the growing demand for raw cotton by textile mills in England and the American Northeast; wonderfully productive virgin soil; a long, steamy growing season; an ample supply of slave labor; and southern planters' long experience in producing and marketing staple crops.

Planters were most successful in cultivating the long-staple variety. Its silky fibers were highly valued and could easily be separated from the cotton's seeds. The delicate long-staple plant, however, grew only where soil and climate were right—on the sea islands off the coast of Georgia and South Carolina. The hardier, short-staple variety could be successfully cultivated across large areas of the South. But its fibers clung tenaciously to the plant's sticky, green seeds. A slave could clean no more than a pound of short-staple cotton a day.

A solution began to appear in 1793 when Eli Whitney, a Yankee school teacher living in the South, set his mind to the problem of short-staple cotton and its seeds. Within a few days, he had designed a functioning model of what he called a "cotton gin." It was disarmingly simple, nothing more than a box containing a roller equipped with wire teeth, designed to pull the fibers through a comblike barrier, thus stripping them from the seeds. A hand crank activated the mechanism. The implications of Whitney's invention were immediately apparent, for

Slave labor, provided by women as well as men, followed the spread of cotton cultivation into new lands of the southern interior. This Benjamin Latrobe sketch is of *An Overseer Doing His Duty.* *(Maryland Historical Society, Baltimore, Maryland)*

Though others had tinkered with mechanical devices for stripping cotton fibers from their seeds, Eli Whitney was the first to develop a successful gin. *(Library of Congress)*

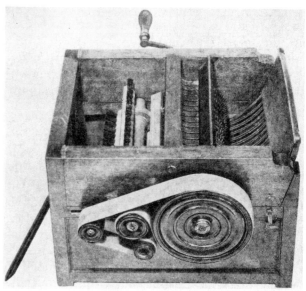

This model of the original cotton gin was deposited in the Smithsonian Museum by Whitney's son in 1884. *(National Museum of American History, Smithsonian Institution)*

with this crude device a laborer could clean up to 50 pounds of short-staple cotton a day.

As we shall see in later chapters, the swing to cotton marked a momentous turning point in the South's—and the nation's—history. Not only did it raise the value of southern land and open economic opportunity for countless southern whites, but it also increased the demand for black field hands and breathed new life into slavery. Some of the escalating demand for slave labor was met from overseas. In 1803, Georgia and South Carolina imported 20,000 new slaves, as southern planters and northern suppliers rushed to meet the need before the slave trade ended in 1807. Much of the demand for agricultural labor, however, was met by the internal slave trade that moved African Americans from the worn-out lands of the Chesapeake to the lush cotton fields of the southern interior.

Trans-Appalachia

West of the Appalachian Mountains, a third region of settlement was forming as the nineteenth century began. In the eighteenth century, British colonists had called the regions west of white settlement the "backcountry," the land that lay behind them as they faced east, toward the Atlantic and Europe. As attention shifted toward settlement of the trans-Appalachian West, however, people spoke increasingly of an ever-expanding "frontier."

In the early republic, most Americans did not move far during their lifetimes. As late as 1820, persistence rates, that is, people's tendency to stay in the same community over a decade's time, had changed little from the eighteenth century. As a result, generational continuity and extended kin networks still characterized life in older, eastern communities.

Even so, growing numbers of Americans were now moving across the land. Not all travelled from older settled areas westward to the interior. In New England, for example, increasing numbers of young men and women fled the region's rock-strewn farms for opportunities in Boston and various mill towns sprouting up along the region's swift-flowing rivers. The Philadelphia hinterland witnessed a similar movement of rural people to the city.

The most dramatic change, however, was the accelerating spread of settlement into the interior. Trans-Appalachia, a broad and shifting "middle ground" of settlement and encounter, extended from the mountains to the Mississippi River and from the Great Lakes to the Gulf of Mexico. In 1790, scarcely 100,000 white settlers had lived there. By 1810, augmented by people like Mary and James Harrod, their number had swollen to nearly one million. A decade later, there were over a million more. They came by wagon through the Cumberland Gap and other tortuous routes into Kentucky and Tennessee, or clambered aboard flatboats at Pittsburgh in the spring, when the water was high, to float down the Ohio River to destinations at Wheeling, Cincinnati, and Louisville. The human tide appeared to grow with each passing year. The woods are full of new settlers driven by "Genesee fever," wrote an amazed observer near Batavia in western New York in 1805. "Axes are resounding, and the trees literally falling around us as we passed." America, exclaimed the British traveler Morris Birkbeck, "is breaking up and going west!"

Settlers were drawn by the promotions of speculators seeking their fortunes in the sale of western land. Wealthy individuals like George Washington and groups of investors like the Ohio Company, their fortunes made in Atlantic commerce, monopolized large areas of the interior. They counted on the swelling tide of white settlement to increase land values and ensure their profit. By 1800, absentee landlords had engrossed as much as 75 percent of areas in present day West Virginia, Tennessee, and the western Carolinas. Between 1790 and 1820, land companies hawked vast areas of New York, Ohio, and Kentucky to prospective settlers like the Harrods. The most extravagant ventures often failed, but countless others returned handsome profits to their investors.

North of the Ohio River, settlement followed the grid pattern prescribed in the Land Ordinance of 1785. There, free-labor agriculture took hold and towns such as Columbus and Cincinnati emerged to provide services and cultural amenities for the surrounding population. South of the Ohio, white settlers with their black slaves distributed themselves more randomly across the land, much as their ancestors had done back east. In Kentucky and Tennessee, free-labor agriculture was soon challenged by the spread of slavery-based cotton.

As people poured into the region, they established churches and schools. Transylvania University, founded in Lexington, Kentucky, was the first college west of the Appalachians.

Historians think of the trans-Appalachian frontier not as a distinct line separating areas of white and Indian settlement, but as a shifting "borderland" where diverse groups of European, Native, and African Americans encountered each other. As people of differing ethnicity, race, class, and regional origin mingled, they brought competing social, economic, and cultural values. Those differences often generated tension. But as settlers created new communities, they fashioned new ways of life and strengthened the belief that America was a land of opportunity always under construction.

Given its newness and diversity, Trans-Appalachia retained a reputation for its rough and colorful ways. While life could be depressingly lonesome for families lost in the hollows of the Cumberland Mountains of eastern Tennessee, in towns such as Louisville along the Ohio River boatmen and gamblers, con men and speculators gave civic life a raucous quality. Everywhere the transiency of the population and large numbers of young, unattached males kept society unsettled.

The drama of human migration together with the grandeur of the natural surroundings stoked people's imaginations. No characters were more famous in popular folklore than western adventurers like

ANALYZING HISTORY

THE MOVEMENT OF WHITE AND BLACK POPULATION INTO TRANS-APPALACHIA, 1790–1830

Once regarded as the backcountry, Trans-Appalachia had grown to nearly two million people by the early nineteenth century. In the area north of the Ohio River, free-labor agriculture took hold. South of the Ohio, slave labor quickly became dominant.

Reflecting on the Past Compare the population size and rate of growth in the Old Southwest and Old Northwest. How did they differ, and why? The sale of federal lands dropped precipitously in the decade following 1819. Can you explain why? Between 1790 and 1820, seven new states were carved out of Trans-Appalachia. What were the consequences of that for the nation?

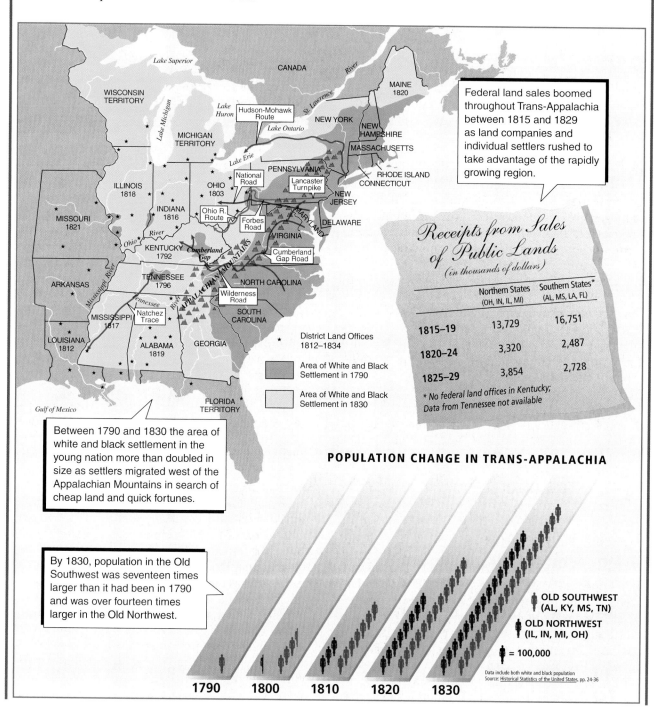

Federal land sales boomed throughout Trans-Appalachia between 1815 and 1829 as land companies and individual settlers rushed to take advantage of the rapidly growing region.

Receipts from Sales of Public Lands
(in thousands of dollars)

	Northern States (OH, IN, IL, MI)	Southern States* (AL, MS, LA, FL)
1815–19	13,729	16,751
1820–24	3,320	2,487
1825–29	3,854	2,728

* No federal land offices in Kentucky; Data from Tennessee not available

Between 1790 and 1830 the area of white and black settlement in the young nation more than doubled in size as settlers migrated west of the Appalachian Mountains in search of cheap land and quick fortunes.

By 1830, population in the Old Southwest was seventeen times larger than it had been in 1790 and was over fourteen times larger in the Old Northwest.

POPULATION CHANGE IN TRANS-APPALACHIA

OLD SOUTHWEST (AL, KY, MS, TN)
OLD NORTHWEST (IL, IN, MI, OH)
= 100,000

Data include both white and black population
Source: Historical Statistics of the United States, pp. 24-36

1790 1800 1810 1820 1830

Daniel Boone. None was more colorful than the mythical riverman Mike Fink, "half man, half alligator," who could "whip his weight in grizzly bears." And nothing revealed the West's rawness more graphically than the eye-gouging, ear-biting, no-holds-barred, "rough and tumble" brawls that regularly erupted.

As settlers arrived, they began the long process of transforming the region's heavily forested land. In the mountainous areas of western Pennsylvania, entire hillsides were denuded of trees that anxious travelers dragged behind their wagons as makeshift brakes during the jolting ride downhill. Believing, erroneously, that open areas were infertile, Ohio farmers staked their claims where the trees grew thickest and set about the arduous task of clearing the land. They followed the time-honored practice of cutting a girdle of bark off the trees, then setting them on fire or leaving them to die in place while planting crops around the decaying hulks. By this method, a family could clear from three to five acres a year for cultivation. "The scene is truly savage," observed an English traveler used to the orderly landscape of his own country. "Immense trees stripped of their foliage, and half consumed by fire extend their sprawling limbs . . . now bleached by the weather."

The relentless demand for wood generated by the growing white population—for log cabins and barns, fences and fuel, potash and turpentine—added to the assault on the region's forests. As expanding areas of Trans-Appalachia came under the farmer's plow, forests and wildlife gave way.

The Nation's Cities

Though most Americans lived on the land or in small towns, increasing numbers dwelt in the nation's expanding cities. From 1790 to 1830, the nation's population increased by nearly 230 percent, but urban places of more than 2,500 residents grew almost twice as fast.

Patterns of urban development differed from region to region. The most dramatic growth occurred in the port cities of the Northeast, stimulated by the region's booming economy. By 1830, the Northeast contained four cities of more than 50,000. New York alone held over 100,000 people. Away from the coast, inland cities such as Lowell and Springfield, Massachusetts, and Albany and Troy, New York, proliferated as service centers for their surrounding areas.

In Trans-Appalachia, fledgling cities such as Pittsburgh, Lexington, Cincinnati, and Chicago dotted the region's rivers and lakes, their growth promoted by ambitious entrepreneurs eager to speculate in land and control the transportation routes of the interior. Still small villages in 1790, these interior cities held 30 percent of the nation's urban population by 1830.

Francis Guy, *Winter Scene in Brooklyn*, c. 1817–1820. Many neighborhoods of early nineteenth-century cities retained a small-town atmosphere, as this Brooklyn scene reveals. *(The Brooklyn Museum, 97.13, Gift of the Brooklyn Institute of Arts and Sciences)*

y
RECOVERING THE PAST

Census Returns

Across the nation's history, the American population has changed dramatically, not only in size and geographic distribution but also in birth and death rates, marriage age, and family size. In the early nineteenth century, for example, the average life expectancy of white Americans was about 45 years, and men tended to outlive women. In our own time, the average life expectancy has reached 74, and women on average live longer than men. Populations have differed as well across regions, urban and rural settings, and among racial, ethnic, and class groups.

Changes in the demographic profile of the American population have powerful effects on the nation's economic, social, and political development. The changing size and makeup of the labor force shape economic activity, while changing proportions of older and younger Americans affect consumer habits and put different demands on health care and educational systems—as the aging of Baby Boomers in our own time is again making clear. When mortality rates were high, as was often the case in early American history, parents had more children in an effort to stabilize their families. As mortality declined during the nineteenth century, so too did birthrates and family size.

Demographic information can tell us a great deal about the life experiences of ordinary Americans. Indeed, demographic data is often the major source of information about otherwise anonymous individuals. For all these reasons, historians spend considerable time analyzing populations and the ways they change.

Two kinds of demographic data have proved most important. One consists of birth, death, and marriage records, often found in church or town registers. These records chronicle the basic demographic events in people's lives. If they are complete and continuous enough, they allow historians to trace the life course of individuals and to reconstruct patterns of family and community life.

Here we offer an example of the second kind of demographic data, a census. The material is from the Federal Census of 1820. Article 1, Section 2 of the Constitution called for an enumeration (or counting) of the nation's population every 10 years, "in such manner" as Congress required. The information was to be used in determining the periodic reapportionment of the House of Representatives and allocation of direct taxes to the states. The first decennial census was taken in 1790.

Compared with modern census inquiries, the first federal censuses collected limited information. The 1790s census, for example, gathered data under six headings: "Name of head of family," "Free white males, 16 years and upwards," "Free white males, under 16," "Free white females," "All other free persons," and "Slaves." As the nation grew, the demand for additional information increased. In 1820, Congress for the first time called for the collection of economic data. In the decades following, categories of social and economic data were gradually expanded.

This "Recovering the Past" feature contains data from three cities—New York City; Charleston, South Carolina; and Cincinnati, Ohio—located in different sections of the country. What do they tell you about the racial, gender, and age profiles of these cities? How do they differ? Do you find significant age and gender differences between white and black populations? Between free blacks and slaves? How do you explain the differences that you find? In making your calculations, be sure to take into account both absolute numbers and proportions of the total populations.

Why were there no slaves in Cincinnati, while there were still slaves in New York? What kinds of people might have been included under the heading "Foreigners not naturalized?" The economic data included in the 1820 census was very general. What conclusions are you able to draw concerning economic activities in the three cities? Can you explain the differences?

Reflecting on the Past How would the federal census of 2000 differ from the census displayed here? Why do disputes often arise over the kinds of information to be gathered?

Data from the Federal Census of 1820

	New York City	Charleston	Cincinnati
Free white males, 25 and under	36,122	3,780	3,419
Free white males, 26 and over	21,331	2,119	1,672
Free white males, total	57,453 (44)	5,899 (23)	5,091 (51)
Free white females, 25 and under	37,438	3,297	3,137
Free white females, 26 and over	20,070	2,033	1,152
Free white females, total	57,508 (44)	5,330 (21)	4,289 (43)
Total white population	114,961 (88)	11,229 (44)	9,380 (93)
Free colored males, 25 and under	2,201	394	120
Free colored males, 26 and over	1,993	229	99
Free colored males, total	4,194 (3)	623 (2)	219 (2)
Free colored females, 25 and under	3,342	467	132
Free colored females, 26 and over	2,832	385	82
Free colored females, total	6,174 (5)	852 (3)	214 (2)
Male slaves, 25 and under	144	3,656	0
Male slaves, 26 and over	33	2,039	0
Male slaves, total	177 (1)	5,695 (22)	0 (0)
Female slaves, 25 and under	233	4,347	0
Female slaves, 26 and over	108	2,610	0
Female slaves, total	341 (1)	6,957 (27)	0 (0)
Total black population	10,886 (8)	14,127 (55)	433 (0)
Foreigners not naturalized	5,390 (4)	425 (2)	241 (2)
Total city population	131,237	25,781	10,054
Persons engaged in agriculture	386	164	29
Persons engaged in commerce	3,142	1,138	63
Persons engaged in manufacturing	9,523	887	211

Notes: New York City did not then include Kings, Queens, or Suffolk Counties. Figures in parentheses represent percentages of each city's total population.

In the South, urban development centered in long-established port cities such as Charleston, Savannah, and New Orleans. As during the colonial period, they served as commercial entrepots, exporting agricultural products and importing manufactured goods. Baltimore's population grew by nearly 500 percent between 1790 and 1830, its location at the head of Chesapeake Bay giving it easy access to the mid-Atlantic interior.

Though increasing rapidly in population, America's cities were small in area. In these "walking cities," residents got about mostly on foot and could easily stroll from one side of town to the other. Still, urban growth brought increasing congestion. Asa Greene, a New York physician, observed ruefully that to cross Broadway "you must button your coat tightly about you . . . settle your hat firmly on your head, look up street and down street . . . to see what carts and carriages are upon you, and then run for your life."

Philadelphia led the way in street paving, but in most cities dust and mud brought constant complaints. One alarmed citizen, finding a man embedded up to his neck in a mud hole following a violent downpour, offered to help pull him out. "No need to worry," replied the man, "I have a horse underneath me." So, at least, went a popular fable.

More than mud clogged urban streets in the early nineteenth century, for residents dumped their garbage there, privies leached into open drains, and wandering cows, goats, and sheep roamed freely, leaving their droppings behind. Packs of stray dogs added to the confusion.

Under such conditions, diseases like typhoid and dysentery, spread by contaminated well water, took a continuous toll. Not until 1832 with construction of the Croton Aqueduct, did New York City establish a safe and adequate water supply. Ignorance about the causes and etiology of disease put urban populations continuously at risk.

Urban families had long maintained small garden plots and a milk cow. As populations grew and land values increased, however, gardens and cows gradually disappeared, further weakening diet and health.

The rigors of poor diet, frequent disease, and inadequate medical care often brought life to an early end. Scarcely half of urban dwellers could expect to reach the age of 45. Unlike today, women on average died sooner than men, their bodies weakened by frequent childbirth. While birthrates had begun the long decline that would carry through the nineteenth and twentieth centuries, white women could still expect to bear from four to eight children. Immigrant and black women averaged even more.

Though buildings and streets were virtually devoid of the commercial signage that would emblazon American cities by the middle of the nineteenth century, urban economies hummed with activity. True industrialization would not hit northeastern cities until the second half of the nineteenth century, but by the 1820s, Philadelphia was becoming a center of textile manufacturing, while places like New York City and Newark, New Jersey, were producing shoes, iron goods, and other products. As these enterprises expanded, artisans' shops began to give way to factory-based wage labor.

As urban economies grew, the gap between richer and poorer inhabitants widened. Prosperous merchants, reaping the rewards of overseas trade and investing their profits in budding manufacturing enterprises, rested securely at the top. Their households were graced by fine table linens, imported china, store-bought furniture, and tailor-made clothes—the artifacts of an expanding consumer economy. Below them came an aspiring middle class of artisans, shopkeepers, and professional men whose families shared modestly in the general prosperity. At the bottom of urban society spread an underclass of common laborers, dock workers, and the unemployed, their lives a continuous struggle for survival.

Although rich and poor had lived close together in eighteenth century cities, rising land values now forced the lower classes into crowded alleys and tenements, while more prosperous urban dwellers clustered in fashionable neighborhoods.

The wars of the American and French Revolutions, sharply reduced European immigration between the 1770s and 1820s. Even so, America's urban populations were racially and ethnically diverse. In places such as New York and Philadelphia, Irish, German, British, and African Americans, together with travelers from around the world, jostled for space on the cities' sidewalks. In southern cities such as Charleston and Richmond, half the population was black. All along the Atlantic and Gulf coasts, sailors, often speaking unfamiliar tongues, filled harbor-front taverns with colorful stories of far-off lands, adding raucous behavior and, at times, an edge of danger to urban life.

To the west, cities like New Orleans and St. Louis reflected their multinational origins. Established as a French colony in 1718, New Orleans came under Spanish rule following 1763. When it became part of the United States in 1803, urban life was dominated by French and Spanish creole families. For several decades, U.S. citizens remained a minority among the city's white population. Of the city's 27,000 people, nearly 13,000 were black.

In this panorama by Boqueto de Woiserie, the American eagle flies over the French colonial city of New Orleans following the Louisiana Purchase of 1803. *(Chicago Historical Society)*

Upriver from New Orleans, the smaller town of St. Louis had a similarly colorful flavor. At different times part of French and Spanish North America, the town retained the multinational character of its origins. Enslaved blacks constituted nearly one-third of the town's 1,000 souls, while a mixture of French, Spanish, and American men and women made up the rest.

INDIAN–WHITE RELATIONS IN THE EARLY REPUBLIC

Indian–white relations took a dramatic turn in the early years of the nineteenth century. In 1790, vast areas of Trans-Appalachia were still controlled by Native American tribes. North of the Ohio River, the Shawnee, Delaware, and Miami formed a western confederacy capable of mustering several thousand warriors. South of the river lived five major tribal groups: the Cherokee, Creek, Choctaw, Chickasaw, and Seminole. Together, they totaled nearly 60,000 people. By 1830, however, the balance of power throughout Trans-Appalachia had shifted decisively as white settlers, many of them bringing their black slaves with them south of the Ohio River, streamed into the region.

As the tide of white settlement grew, tribal groups devised various strategies of resistance and survival. Among the Cherokee, many sought peaceful accommodation. Others, like the Shawnee and the Creek, rose in armed resistance. Neither strategy was altogether successful, for by 1830 the Indians faced a future of continued acculturation, military defeat, or forced migration to lands west of the Mississippi River.

Less dramatic but no less important, the social and cultural separation of Indians and white Americans sharpened during these years. As late as the 1780s, Indians still walked the streets of New York and Philadelphia, while countless Indians and white Americans interacted regularly as friends or enemies, traders or marriage partners. By 1830, such contacts were much less common and racial separation increased as Native Americans were confined on reservations or forced to move farther west.

The Goals of Indian Policy

During the years from 1790 to 1830, the federal government established policies that would govern Indian–white relations through much of the nineteenth century. Intended in part to promote the assimilation of Native Americans into white society, they actually speeded the transfer of Indian land to white settlers and set the stage for a later, more dramatic program of Indian removal.

With the government's initial "conquest" theory rendered obsolete by the Indians' refusal to regard themselves as a conquered people (see Chapter 7), U.S. officials shifted course by recognizing Indian rights to the land they inhabited. Henry Knox,

Washington's first secretary of war, laid out the government's new position in 1789. The Indians, he explained, "being the prior occupants of the soil, possess the right of the soil." It should not be taken from them "unless by their free consent, or by the right of conquest in case of just war." In the Indian Intercourse Act of 1790, Congress declared that public treaties, ratified by the Congress, would henceforth be the only legal means of obtaining Indian land. Through treaty negotiations, vast areas of tribal land throughout Trans-Appalachia passed into the possession of white settlers, tribal leaders agreeing to cessions in return for trade goods, yearly annuity payments, and assurances that treaty boundaries would be respected.

The treaty process, however, did not satisfy the demand for western land, as white settlers pushed illegally into tribal areas and state governments contracted their own treaty agreements without congressional approval. Again and again, tribal leaders resisted the terms that state and federal negotiators pressed upon them, and appealed to Washington to uphold boundary agreements. (In the late twentieth century, tribal groups would cite violations of the Indian Intercourse Act in federal court suits seeking the recovery of ancestral land.)

Federal policy was also intended to regulate the fur trade, in which both Native Americans and white traders eagerly participated. The Indians, in return for their abundant furs, secured the blankets, guns, and rum that they valued highly, while white traders acquired desirable furs in exchange for inexpensive trade goods.

Though the fur trade brought handsome profits to companies such as John Jacob Astor's American Fur Company (1808), it often worked to the Indians' disadvantage. Rum devastated Indian communities, while trade goods frequently transmitted diseases such as measles and smallpox. Indians often became dependent on the trade because it provided

Indian Land Cessions, 1750–1830

As white settlers streamed across the nation's interior, state and federal governments wrung land cessions from the Indians. By 1830, only the southeastern tribes still controlled significant areas of their ancestral land east of the Mississippi River. Labels in red indicate the major Native American tribes.

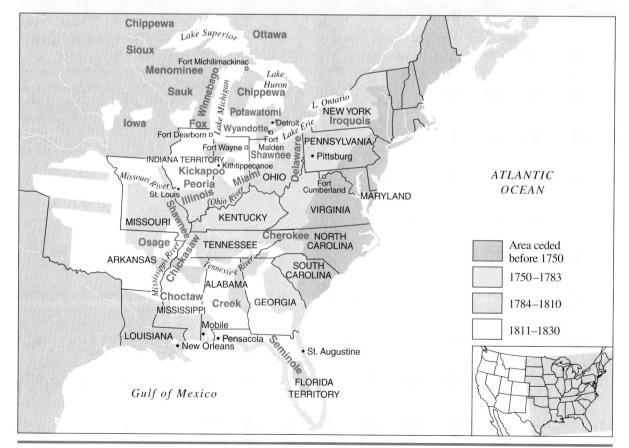

the only reliable supplies of coveted goods such as iron kettles and firearms. As the demand for furs and pelts increased, Native Americans frequently overtrapped their hunting grounds, forcing them to compete with other tribes for new sources of furs farther west.

In an effort to reduce trading fraud and the resulting conflict, Congress created government trading posts, or "factories," where Indians could come for fairer treatment. Often, however, Indians found themselves deeply in debt to government traders.

A third objective of federal Indian policy was to "civilize" Native Americans, then assimilate them into white society. Education and Christianization were the major instruments of assimilationist policy. After the revolution, Moravians, Quakers, and Baptists sent scores of missionaries to live among the Indians, preach the Gospel, and teach the benefits of white civilization. John Stewart, a freeborn, part-Indian mulatto, was one such missionary. From 1815 to his death in 1821, he preached to the Wyandotte near Sandusky, Ohio. Among the most selfless were Quaker missionaries who labored with the Iroquois in New York, attempting to inspire conversion and improve the conditions of Iroquois life. In spite of the missionaries' best efforts, however, most Native Americans remained aloof, because the chasm between Christianity and their own religions was wide (see Chapter 2), and the missionaries' denigration of Indian culture was clearly apparent.

Education was the other weapon of assimilation. In 1793, Congress appropriated $20,000 to promote literacy, agriculture, and vocational instruction among Indians. Federal officials encouraged missionaries to establish schools in which Indian children could learn Christianity, the three R's, and vocational skills. But the vast majority of Indian children never attended because they and their parents distrusted the alien environment of the schools.

Although the assimilationists cared deeply about the physical and spiritual fate of Native-American people, they showed little sympathy for Indian culture, for they demanded that Native Americans give up their language, religion, dress, and extended family arrangements and adopt the ways of white society. Assimilation or removal were the stark alternatives posed by even the most benevolent whites.

Strategies of Survival: The Iroquois and Revitalization

Faced with the steady loss of land and tribal autonomy, Native Americans devised various strategies of resistance and survival. In June 1799, a middle-aged

warrior named Handsome Lake began to preach a message of hope and redemption among the Seneca tribe of the once powerful Iroquois nation. Like so many of his people, Handsome Lake had been beaten down by the experience of the preceding 30 years. As a young man, he had joined England in the fight against American independence. Wounded on several occasions, his spirit broken by the American victory, he had watched helplessly as the Seneca's land was taken and his people were confined on New York reservations. Handsome Lake's own life had crumbled as well. On several occasions, alcohol and depression had brought him close to death.

As he lay on his bunk, scarcely breathing, Handsome Lake experienced a vision. From that vision he fashioned a message of renewal for the Seneca people. The Great Spirit, he explained, had given him two "gospels" to share with them. The first was a religious gospel. In it, Handsome Lake preached the imminence of the world's destruction; the dangers of spiritual sins such as witchcraft, abortion, and drunkenness; and the promise of salvation through the rituals of *Gaiwiio*, a new form of worship combining elements of Christianity with the ceremonies of the Seneca's traditional religious calendar.

Handsome Lake also preached a social gospel, offering guidance for the reconstruction of Seneca life. Here again he called for a mingling of old and new ways. Drawing ideas from federal officials and nearby Quaker missionaries, Handsome Lake urged the importance of temperance, peace, land retention, acculturation, and domestic morality.

Though his authoritarian manner alienated some supporters, his message offered renewed pride as Indians and inspired a social and cultural revitalization among a people hungering for guidance. His gospels originated in a vision transmitted by the Great Spirit. In Seneca culture, no source of truth was more powerful. He also commanded the attention of his people because he had shared with them the humiliation of defeat and the poverty of reservation life. Finally, his gospels had effect because they were supported by other tribal leaders, among them his half sister Gayantgogwus, who spoke for tribal women before the Great Council, and Cornplanter, the community's political leader and Handsome Lake's half brother.

Strategies of Survival: The Cherokee and Accommodation

Far to the south, the Cherokee followed a different path of accommodation. As the nineteenth century began, the Cherokee still controlled millions of acres in Tennessee, Georgia, and the western Carolinas. Their land base, however, was shrinking.

Southern state governments, responding to white demands for Indian land, acted to undercut tribal autonomy. In 1801, Tennessee unilaterally brought Cherokee lands under state authority. As violence escalated along the borders between white and Indian settlements, state officials demanded that Native Americans accused of horse stealing and other crimes stand trial in state courts. The Cherokee, who had their own system of justice and distrusted the state courts with their all-white juries and exclusion of Indian testimony, rejected Tennessee's demands.

Soon a group of full-blood leaders called for armed resistance. Better to stand and fight, they argued, than follow the false path of accommodation. Others, including mixed-bloods like John Ross, insisted that accommodation offered the best hope for survival. After a bitter struggle, the accommodationists won out and began bringing the tribe's scattered villages under a common government, the better to protect their freedom and prevent the further loss of land. In 1808, the Cherokee National Council adopted a written legal code combining elements of American and Indian law, and in 1827, it devised a written constitution patterned after those of nearby states. The council also issued a bold declaration that the Cherokee were an independent nation with full sovereignty over their lands. In 1829, the Cherokee government made it an offense punishable by death for any member of the tribe to transfer land to white ownership without the consent of tribal authorities.

Meanwhile, the process of social and cultural accommodation, encouraged by Cherokee leaders such as Ross and promoted by white missionaries and government agents, went forward. As the Cherokee turned from their traditional hunting, gathering, and farming economy to settled agriculture, many moved from village settlements onto individual farmsteads. Others established sawmills, country stores, and blacksmith shops. In contrast to traditional practices of communal ownership, the concept of private property took hold.

The majority of Cherokee people kept their crude log cabins and continued to live a hand-to-mouth existence. But some, especially mixed-bloods like Joseph Vann who learned English and understood how to deal with white authorities, accumulated hundreds of acres of fertile land and scores of black slaves.

Since the mid-eighteenth century, the Cherokee had held a few runaway blacks in slavelike conditions. During the early nineteenth century, Cherokee slavery expanded and became more harsh. By 1820, there were nearly 1,300 black slaves in the Cherokee nation. A tribal law of 1824 forbade intermarriage with blacks. The accelerating spread of cotton cultivation increased the demand for slave labor among the Cherokee, as it did among southern whites. Within the tribe, slave ownership became a mark of social standing.

By 1820, the strategy of peaceful accommodation had brought clear rewards. Tribal government was stronger, and the sense of Cherokee identity was reasonably secure. But success would prove the Cherokee people's undoing. As their self-confidence grew, so did the hostility of neighboring whites impatient to acquire their land. That hostility would soon erupt in a final campaign to drive the Cherokee from their land forever (see Chapter 12).

Patterns of Armed Resistance: The Shawnee and the Creek

Not all tribes proved so accommodating to white expansion. Faced with growing threats to their political and cultural survival, the Shawnee and Creek nations rose in armed resistance. Conflict was smoldering as the nineteenth century began; it burst into flame during the War of 1812.

In the late 1780s, chieftains such as Little Turtle of the Miami and Blue Jacket of the Shawnee had led a series of devastating raids across Indiana, Ohio, and western Pennsylvania, panicking white settlers and challenging U.S. control of the Old Northwest. After two efforts to quell the uprising failed, President Washington determined to smash the Indians' resistance once and for all. In 1794, a federal army led by the old Revolutionary War general Anthony Wayne defeated 2,000 Indian warriors in the Battle of Fallen Timbers. Shortly after, in the Treaty of Greenville, the assembled chiefs ceded the southern two-thirds of Ohio. That cession opened the heart of the Old Northwest to white control. Subsequent treaties further reduced the Indians' land base, driving the tribes more tightly in upon each other.

By 1809, two Shawnee leaders, the brothers Tecumseh and Tenskwatawa, the latter known to whites as "the Prophet," were traveling among the region's tribes warning of their common danger and forging an alliance against the invading whites. They established headquarters at an ancient Indian town named Kithtippecanoe in northern Indiana. Soon it became a gathering point for Native Americans from across the region responding to the messages of cultural pride, land retention, and pan-Indian resistance proclaimed by the Shawnee brothers.

Between 1809 and 1811, Tecumseh carried his message south to the Creek and the Cherokee. His

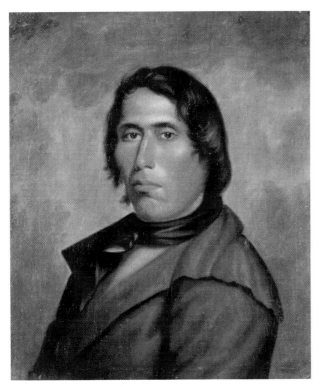

Though Tecumseh's vision of a Pan-Indian alliance reaching from the Great Lakes to the Gulf of Mexico never materialized, he led Indian tribes of the Northwest in militant opposition to white territorial expansion. *(Woodfin Camp & Associates)*

speeches rang with bitterness. "The white race is a wicked race," he told his listeners. "Since the days when the white race first came in contact with the red men, there has been a continual series of aggressions. The hunting grounds are fast disappearing, and they are driving the red men farther and farther to the west." The only hope was "a war of extermination against the paleface." Though the southern tribes refused to join, by 1811 over 1,000 fighting men had gathered at Kithtippecanoe.

Alarmed, the governor of the Indiana Territory, William Henry Harrison, surrounded the Indian stronghold with a force of 1,000 soldiers. After a successful all-day battle, he burned Kithtippecanoe to the ground.

The Indians, however, were not yet defeated. Over the next several months, Tecumseh's followers, taking advantage of the recent outbreak of the War of 1812 with England and aided by British troops from Canada, mounted devastating raids across Indiana and southern Michigan. With the British, they crushed American armies at Detroit and Fort Nelson and followed up with forays against Fort Wayne. The tide finally turned at the Battle of the Thames near Detroit, where Harrison inflicted a grievous defeat on a combined British and Indian force. Among those slain was Tecumseh.

The American victory at the Thames signaled the collapse of Tecumseh's confederacy and an end to Indian resistance in the Old Northwest. Beginning in 1815, American settlers surged once more across Ohio and Indiana, then into Illinois and Michigan. The balance of power in the Old Northwest had decisively shifted.

To the south, the Creek challenged white intruders with similar militancy. By 1800, white settlers were pushing onto Creek lands in northwestern Georgia and central Alabama. Although some Creek urged accommodation, others, called Red Sticks, who had listened eagerly to Tecumseh's message, prepared to fight. The embers of this smoldering conflict were fanned into flame by an aggressive Tennessee militia commander named Andrew Jackson. In 1808, citing Creek atrocities against "defenseless women and children," Jackson urged President Jefferson to endorse a campaign against the "ruthless foe."

He got his chance in the summer of 1813, when the Red Sticks carried out a series of devastating frontier raids, capping their campaign with an assault on Fort Mims on the Alabama River where they killed as many as 500 men, women and children. News of the tragedy elicited bitter cries for revenge. "When the tomahawk and the scalping knife are drawn in the cabins of our peaceful and unsuspecting citizens," declared the Tennessee legislature, "it is time, high time to prepare . . . for defense."

At the head of 5,000 Tennessee and Kentucky militia, augmented by warriors from other tribes eager to punish their traditional Creek enemies, Jackson launched his long-awaited attack. As he moved south, the fighting grew more ferocious. Davey Crockett, one of Jackson's soldiers, later reported that the militia volunteers shot the Red Sticks down "like dogs." The Indians gave like measure in return.

The climactic battle of the Creek War came in March 1814 at Horseshoe Bend, on the Tallapoosa River in central Alabama. There, in the fortified town of Tohopeka, 1,000 Red Stick warriors made their stand against 1,400 state troops, 600 Cherokee, and opponents of the Red Sticks from within the Creek tribe. While American cannon fire raked the Red Stick defenses, allied warriors crossed the river to cut off retreat. In the battle that followed, over 800 Native Americans died, more than in any other Indian–white battle in American history.

Jackson followed up his victory with a scorched-earth sweep through the remaining Red Stick towns. With no hope left, Red Eagle, one of the few remaining Red Stick leaders, walked alone into Jackson's camp. "General Jackson," he said, "I am not afraid of you. I fear no man, for I am a Creek warrior. I have nothing to request in behalf of myself; you can kill me if you desire. But I come to beg you to send for the women and children of the war party, who are now starving in the woods. . . . I am now done fighting."

Jackson allowed Red Eagle and his followers to return home, but in August 1814 exacted his final revenge by constructing Fort Jackson on the Hickory Ground, the most sacred spot of the Creek nation. During the following months, he seized 22 million acres, nearly two-thirds of the Creek domain. Before his Indian-fighting days were over, Jackson would acquire for the United States, through treaty or conquest, nearly three-fourths of Alabama and Florida, one-third of Tennessee, and one-fifth of Georgia and Mississippi.

Indian–white conflict in the South did not end with the Creek defeat at Horseshoe Bend. For nearly a decade, the Second Seminole War, costly in both lives and money, would continue to ravage much of Florida. As Tecumseh's death had signaled the end of Indian resistance in the North, however, so Jackson's defeat of the Creek broke the back of Indian defenses in much of the South. With the possibility of armed resistance gone, Native Americans gave way before the swelling tide of white settlement.

PERFECTING A DEMOCRATIC SOCIETY

Throughout our nation's history, the American people have launched a variety of reform movements aimed at achieving social justice and bringing the conditions of daily life into conformity with democratic ideals. The first of those reform eras occurred in the early nineteenth century.

The Revolutionary Heritage

Reform was inspired by democratic ideals fostered during the Revolution and still fresh in countless Americans' minds. Preeminent among them was the principle of social equality. In part, this meant equality of opportunity—the notion that people should have a chance to rise as far as ability and ambition would carry them. Such an idea appealed to social democrats, for it spoke of setting privilege aside and giving everyone an equal chance. Social conservatives could also embrace it, for it could be used to justify the inequalities that individual effort often produced. The doctrine of social equality had a powerful moral dimension as well, because it implied an equality of worth among individuals, no matter what their social standing might be. Though Americans generally accepted differences of wealth and social position, they were less willing to tolerate social pretension or the assumption that such differences made some people better than others.

The Revolution also fostered a belief in the "youthfulness" of America, compared to the "old" and "decadent" nations of Europe. This sense of America's uniqueness, combined with the seemingly limitless land of the interior, offered the promise of creating a nation unlike any that had existed before, one in which ordinary citizens could create new lives for themselves and their families.

The Evangelical Impulse

A surge of evangelical Christianity also inspired the reform impulse. Throughout our history, religion has been a major force in American public life. This was true in the early republic when a wave of Protestant enthusiasm known as the Second Great Awakening swept across the American nation. From its beginnings in the 1790s through much of the nineteenth century, in settings ranging from the Cane Ridge district of backwoods Kentucky to the cities of the Northeast, Americans by the tens of thousands sought personal salvation and social belonging in the shared experience of religious revivalism.

Displayed most spectacularly at Methodist and Baptist camp meetings, the revivals reached across boundaries of class and race. Rough-hewn itinerant preachers, black as well as white, many of them theologically untrained but all of them afire with religious conviction, spread the Gospel message.

In 1809, Benjamin Latrobe, principal architect of the new Capitol building in Washington, D.C., and a shrewd observer of the American scene, visited a Methodist camp meeting on the Leesburg Road in northern Virginia. As his group approached the meeting ground, Latrobe reported, "we could distinguish among the trees, half concealed by the underwood, houses, chaises, light wagons, hacks, & a crowd of men and women, in the midst of whom we presently arrived."

Positioning himself at the head of the clearing, Latrobe watched in fascination as a blacksmith named Mr. Bunn "spoke with immense rapidity & exertion . . . of the judgement to come." As Bunn exhorted the assembled throng, "a general groaning & shrieking was . . . heard from all Quarters" while the preacher "threw out both his arms sideways at full length, & shook himself violently." Every time Bunn pronounced "the stroke of grace," Latrobe continued, he brought his hands together with an astonishing clap. "The stroke again," Bunn shouted, "and another stroke, and another . . . and now it works, it works. . . . There it is, now she has it, glory! glory! glory!"

Perhaps no one represented the Awakening's religious fervor and egalitarian values more vividly

This depiction of a Second Great Awakening camp meeting reveals the highly emotional nature of such gatherings, the semi-permanent nature of such encampments, the conspicuous place of women in the revivals, and the mingling of social classes that took place. *(Collection of the New-York Historical Society)*

than Lorenzo Dow. Self-declared "holy man" claiming visionary powers and unabashed salesman of his own religious writings, Dow travelled the length and breadth of the land bringing a potent combination of Gospel message and Jeffersonian politics to frontier hamlets and eastern cities alike. During 1804 alone, he preached to as many as 800 gatherings. The following year his travels carried him over 10,000 miles. His boundless energy, communicative gifts, and common touch may well have made him the most widely known American of his time.

Though the salvation of souls was the central purpose of revival camp meetings, observers such as Latrobe perceived that it ministered to other human needs as well. "The illumination of the woods, the novelty of a camp especially to the women and children, the dancing and singing, & the pleasure of a crowd, so tempting to the most fashionable," he noted, imparted a powerful sense of social belonging in a society undergoing rapid change.

Offering a simple message that ordinary folks could readily grasp, itinerant preachers such as Dow emphasized the equality of all believers before God, held out the promise of universal salvation, and declared each individual responsible for his or her own soul. In the process, they strengthened values of equality and individualism. The power of their message was registered in the explosive growth of Methodist and Baptist churches. By mid-century, they would surpass Presbyterians and Congregationalists as the nation's largest denominations.

The Awakening also called on believers to demonstrate their faith by going into the world to lift up the downtrodden. That religious impulse would provide much of the energy for antebellum reforms such as temperance and abolition (see Chapter 12). Its influence was evident as well in earlier efforts at perfecting American society.

Alleviating Poverty and Distress

In the early republic, as at other times in the nation's history, social ideals jarred awkwardly against reality. One source of tension was the contrast between the affirmations of democratic equality and deepening social divisions.

As the nineteenth century began, women continued to hold far less property than men. For black slaves, ownership of anything more than the most simple possessions was unattainable. Though the condition of free blacks such as Ben Thompson and Phyllis Sherman was better, they, too, held little of the country's wealth.

Among white males, property was most broadly shared in rural areas of the North, where free labor and family-farm agriculture predominated, and least so in the South, where planters' control of slave labor and the best land permitted them to monopolize the region's resources. The most even distribution of wealth existed on the edges of white settlement in Trans-Appalachia, but it was essentially an equality of want. There, larger numbers of settlers, well over 50 percent in some areas of southern Appalachia,

The Hot Corn Seller

Among the urban poor, women as well as men peddled food and other commodities in an effort to make ends meet. *(Niccolino Calyo, The Hot Corn Seller, c. 1840. Museum of the City of New York)*

lived as tenants, unable to gain ownership of their land from absentee landlords. Poor transportation deprived them of access to outside markets.

Though America, unlike Europe, contained no permanent and destitute underclass (at least among white citizens), poverty was real and increasing. In the South, it was most evident among poor whites living on the sandy pine barrens of the backcountry. In the North, port cities held growing numbers of the poor. Boston artisans and shopkeepers, who together had owned 20 percent of the city's wealth in 1700, held scarcely half as much a century later.

Recurring economic recessions hit the urban poor with particular force, while winter added to hard times as shipping slowed and jobs disappeared. During the winter of 1805, New York's Mayor DeWitt Clinton worried about the potentially disruptive behavior of 10,000 impoverished New Yorkers. During the winter of 1814–1815, relief agencies assisted nearly one-fifth of the city's population. In rural New England and southeastern Pennsylvania, propertyless men and women, the "strolling poor," roamed the countryside searching for work.

Three other groups were conspicuous among the nation's poor. One consisted of old Revolutionary War veterans like Long Bill Scott, who had found poverty as well as adventure in the war. State and federal governments were peppered with petitions from grizzled veterans and their widows, describing their misery and seeking relief. Women and children suffered disproportionately from poverty. Between 1816 and 1821, they outnumbered men in New York City almshouses.

For every American who actually suffered poverty's effects, several others lived just beyond its reach. The thinness of their margin of safety became clear during the depression of 1819–1822. Triggered by a financial panic caused by the unsound practices of hundreds of newly chartered state banks, a deep depression settled over the land, sending unemployment soaring. In Ohio, the governor reported that "the greater part of our mercantile citizens are in a state of bankruptcy," while "the citizens of every class are . . . delinquent in discharging even the most trifling of debts." In the South, farms and plantations were abandoned as cotton and tobacco exports fell. By the early 1820s, the depression was lifting, but it left behind broken fortunes and shattered dreams.

Alleviating poverty was one goal of the early reformers. In New York City, private and public authorities established over 100 relief agencies to aid orphans and widows, prostitutes and poverty-stricken seamen. Across the nation, a "charitable revolution" increased benevolent institutions from 50 in 1790 to nearly 2,000 by 1820. Most of these ventures drew a distinction between the "worthy poor," respectable folk who were victims of circumstance and merited help, and the "idle poor," who were deemed to lack character and deserved their fate. No matter that a New York commission in 1823 found only 46 able-bodied adults among the 851 inmates of the city's poorhouses.

Poverty was not the only target of reform. Municipal authorities and private charities also established orphanages, asylums for the insane, and hospitals for the sick. Many such efforts were short-lived, but they attested to the continuing strength of revolutionary and religious ideals, and they provided a foundation for the more ambitious reforms that would come later in the century.

Women's Lives

Women's lives did not change dramatically during these early nineteenth-century years. But developments occurred that set the stage for later, more significant breakthroughs.

Divorce was one area where women achieved greater equality. When a neighbor asked John Backus, a silversmith in Great Barrington, Massachusetts, why he kicked and struck his wife, John replied that it was partly because his father had treated his mother in the same way. We do not know whether John's mother tolerated such abuse, but his wife did not. She complained of cruelty and secured a divorce. More and more women followed her example.

Securing a divorce was not easy, for most states allowed it only on grounds of adultery, and South Carolina did not permit it at all. Moreover, *coverture* laws required married women to transfer their property to their husbands, making divorce a risky economic proposition. And though new laws enabling women to file for divorce in court rather than secure legislative approval made the process easier, women faced the uncomfortable task of persuading all-male courts of their husbands' infidelities.

Even so, legal remedies for unacceptable marriages were becoming more available to women. In Massachusetts during the decade after 1783, 50 percent more women than men filed for divorce, with an almost equal rate of success. Part of the explanation can be found in the war's disruptions, which led some men to desert their families, thus encouraging their wives to take action. The trans-Appalachian West lured men away as well. It seems just as certain, however, that women took to heart prevailing values of individualism and equality, leading them to expect more of marriage. Changes in patterns of divorce involved new ways of thinking about sexuality and women's autonomy.

Changes also occurred in women's education. Given their prospective role as "Republican Mothers," young women would have to prepare for their responsibilities as keepers of public morality and nurturers of republican citizens. Judith Sargeant Murray demanded that and more of women's education. In a series of essays, Murray criticized parents who "pointed their daughters" exclusively toward marriage and dependence. "They should be enabled to procure for themselves the necessaries of life; independence should be placed within their grasp," she wrote. "A woman should reverence herself."

Between 1790 and 1830, a number of female academies were established. Most, such as Susanna Rowson's Young Ladies Academy in Philadelphia, were in the Northeast. Timothy Dwight, the future president of Yale, opened his academy at Greenfield Hill in Connecticut to girls and taught them the same subjects he taught boys. Benjamin Rush prescribed bookkeeping, reading, geography, history, and singing ("because it soothes cares and is good for the lungs") as proper elements of girl's education. In addition to the "three R's," the curriculum of several New England academies included "purposive exercise," such as horseback riding, walking, and gymnastics, all intended to promote physical and personal improvement.

Female academies in the early republic provided young middle- and upper-class women with the knowledge and skills necessary for their roles as Republican Mothers. *(Jacob Marling,* The Crowning of Flora, *1816/The Chrysler Museum of Art, Norfolk, VA, Gift of Edgar William and Bernice Chrysler Garbisch 80.118.20)*

Enlightened educators like Murray and Dwight, however, were the exception. Most proposals for female education assumed that girls should be taught separately and that the curriculum should be less demanding than for boys. Warning that intellectual activity would "unsex" women, the Boston minister John Gardner declared that "Women of masculine minds have generally masculine manners, and a robustness of person ill calculated to inspire the tender passions." Even ardent supporters of female learning like Murray conceded that education was primarily important so that women might function more effectively within the domestic sphere. Still, by 1830, literacy for white females was at an all-time high.

Women were affected in various ways by changes in American religious life. Prior to the Revolution, women had been excluded from positions of leadership in Congregational and Anglican churches. For women to exercise religious authority when church and state were closely allied was to challenge male political dominance. When the First Amendment to the U.S. Constitution shattered the traditional connection between church and state, however, women's religious activism could be more readily accepted without seeming to threaten the gendered basis of the political order.

Though women had long outnumbered men in church membership, the Second Great Awakening drew them into the churches in even greater numbers. Lacking public tax support as church and state drew apart, ministers relied on female volunteers to raise funds and promote missionary as well as charitable projects. In that way, churches offered women limited entrance into public life.

As time went on, however, women found their place among evangelical Methodists and Baptists increasingly limited. Whereas women had previously served as religious exhorters and participated in church governance, they found themselves marginalized as evangelical churches, seeking "respectability" and broader social acceptance, adopted the strictly gendered policies of the older Congregational and Presbyterian denominations. In matters of church discipline, women were more frequently charged with "disorderliness" and condemned for "disobedience" than their male brethren, thus calling into question a once robust tradition of piety in which men and women shared spiritual truth and ministered equally to each other's souls.

Race, Slavery, and the Limits of Reform

As we saw in Chapter 7, the Revolution initiated the end of slavery in the northern states and challenged it in the Upper South. Even as slavery withered in the North, however, southern slavery continued to expand while private manumissions declined. Although the nation's population of free blacks grew from 60,000 to 185,000 between 1790 and 1810, the slave population increased from 720,000 to 1,200,000.

In the South, the spread of cotton cultivation sent the value of slave labor soaring, while revolutionary idealism faded with the passage of time. Equally important were two slave rebellions that generated alarm among southern whites. Panic-stricken refugees fleeing the successful revolt of black Haitians on the Caribbean island of Saint Domingue (see Chapter 8) spread terror through the South by fueling rumors that Haitian incendiaries would soon be landing. In response, southern whites tightened their "Black Codes," cut the importation of new slaves from the Caribbean, and sought out malcontents among their own chattels.

A second shock occurred closer to home in the summer of 1800, when a rebellion just outside Richmond, Virginia, was nipped in the bud. A 24-year-old slave named Gabriel devised a plan to arm 1,000 slaves for an assault on the city. Gabriel and his accomplices were American-born blacks who spoke English and worked at skilled jobs that provided a good bit of personal freedom. They fashioned their own ideology of liberation by appropriating the revolutionary tradition of Virginia's whites and applying it to the conditions of their own lives.

A drenching downpour delayed the attack, providing time for several house servants (subsequently granted freedom by the Virginia Assembly) to sound the alarm. No whites died in the abortive rebellion, but scores of slaves and free blacks were arrested, and 25 suspects, including Gabriel, were hanged at the order of Governor James Monroe. The carnage both alarmed and saddened Thomas Jefferson. "There is strong sentiment that there has been hanging enough," he confided to Monroe. "The other states and the world at large will forever condemn us if we . . . go one step beyond absolute necessity." In the midst of panic, however, the line between necessity and revenge was hard to find.

In the early nineteenth century, antislavery appeals all but disappeared from the South. Even religious groups that had once denounced slavery now grew quiet. "A majority of the (white) people of the southern states," declared Congressman Peter Early of Georgia in 1806, deprecate slavery as a "political evil" but do not consider it a crime or believe it "immoral to hold human flesh in bondage." Confederate spokesmen would be saying much the same thing at the time of the Civil War.

Slavery continued to have a conspicuous presence in the nation's capital. When Maryland ceded

Blacks and Slavery, 1790–1820

Though regions had differed in the importance of slavery and the number of blacks in their population as the Revolutionary War ended, those differences increased significantly over the next 30 years.

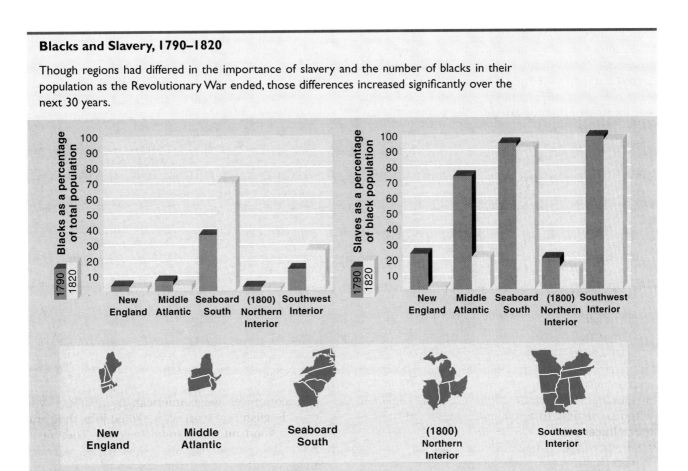

Source: U.S. Bureau of the Census.

land for the new District of Columbia, Congress retained the state's legal code sanctioning slavery. Slave servants attended to the needs of southern Congressmen, while slave markets, driven by the expanding cotton economy, thrived in the shadow of the Capitol building.

In the Northeast, antislavery sentiment was also weakening. There, the gradual abolition of slavery soothed many consciences. And with racial domination no longer enforced by law, whites invoked the doctrine of black inferiority to justify racial exclusiveness and ensure their own continued control. At the same time, the conviction that immutable racial differences separated whites from blacks generated conciliatory attitudes toward slave owners in the South. In the eighteenth century, ideas of racial exclusiveness had competed with Enlightenment beliefs in the common humanity of all mankind. Now, rigid ideas of racial difference were increasingly dominant.

The hardening of racial attitudes was evident in the growing sentiment for colonizing free blacks in western Africa (areas that would become Liberia and Sierra Leone). The American Colonization Society typified these attitudes. Founded in 1816 with the encouragement of leaders such as Henry Clay, James Madison, and John Marshall, the Society enjoyed widespread support among northern white men and women. While detesting slavery and proclaiming their own benevolent intentions, northern members were uneasy over the growing number of free blacks in their midst and wondered whether the two races could peacefully coexist. White churches, wishing to combine Christian conversion with colonization, offered financial support and religious sanction for the Society's work. Southern slave owners saw in colonization a convenient way of reducing the South's free black population and ridding themselves of troublesome bondsmen. The Colonization Society never sent many American blacks abroad, but it helped to allay white anxieties.

A few black leaders, such as Paul Cuffe, saw advantage in the idea of colonization, believing it offered the best promise of true freedom in the face of rising white hostility. The mass of free blacks, however, vigorously opposed it. They condemned the ideology of black racial inferiority on which colonization was based and chose instead to demand their rights as Americans. In joining together to oppose colonization, American blacks demonstrated a new public militance, and gained experience in political organizing that would prove valuable for the abolitionist crusade that lay ahead.

Not all northern whites succumbed to the new racism, for the states of Massachusetts, Rhode Island, and Pennsylvania would soon become hotbeds of a resurgent, multiracial abolition movement. Blacks, moreover, enjoyed greater liberty in the cities of the Northeast than elsewhere in the nation. Nonetheless, during the early years of the republic, the revolutionary promise of equality rang increasingly hollow for most African Americans.

Racism reared its ugly head in the West as well. Though the Northwest Ordinance prohibited owners from bringing new slaves into the old Northwest Territory, slavery was hotly contested in states such as Illinois. In 1823, a proslavery mob torched the state capital and threatened Governor Edward Coles for his efforts to end *de facto* slavery in the state. And proposals for a new state constitution included calls, ultimately unsuccessful, for legalizing slavery within the state's borders.

In Cincinnati, white citizens watched anxiously as the city's black population grew. By 1829, one out of every ten residents was black, almost twice as many as ten years before. In July of that year, city leaders announced that they would begin enforcing the state's black laws by requiring black residents to carry certificates certifying their free status. Those who refused would have to leave the city.

While whites debated the new policy, black leaders petitioned the Ohio legislature for repeal of the "obnoxious black laws." Soon an anti-black coalition of city leaders, unskilled workers fearing competition for jobs, and members of the Cincinnati Colonization Society began to form. In late August, several hundred whites invaded the town's black neighborhoods, where they encountered armed defenders. In the ensuing confrontation, one raider was killed and two others injured. Though the mayor declared that the blacks had fired in self-defense and white opinion supported the mayor's judgment, over half the city's blacks fled. Many sought sanctuary in Canada.

With northern antislavery sentiment weakening and southern slavery on the increase, the federal government acted to strengthen the South's peculiar institution. American diplomats continued to press England for the return of chattels confiscated during the Revolutionary War and War of 1812. And while the constitution outlawed the importation of slaves in 1808, governmental efforts to suppress the continuing trade were sporadic.

Forming Free Black Communities

During the half-century following independence, vibrant black communities appeared in port cities along the Atlantic coast. As the lives of Ben Thompson and Phyllis Sherman revealed, emancipation in the North and the increase of freedmen and women in the Upper South enabled growing numbers of African Americans to seek the companionship of people of color in places such as New York, Philadelphia, and Baltimore. On the eve of independence, 4,000 slaves and a few hundred free blacks had called the port cities home; by 1830, 40,000 African Americans did so.

The men sought employment as laborers or sailors, the women as domestics. In rural areas, free blacks such as Phyllis Sherman had lived in isolation. In the port cities, black communities provided a measure of security and better chances of finding a marriage partner, establishing a family, and participating in community organizations.

Family formation was eased because many of the migrants were women, thus correcting a long-standing imbalance in the black urban population. Initially, former slaves formed extended households that included relatives, friends, and boarders. As circumstances allowed, single-family units were formed. By 1820, most blacks in the northern cities lived in autonomous households.

As their numbers grew, African Americans created organizations independent of white control and capable of serving the needs of black communities. Schools educated children excluded from white academies, while mutual-aid societies offered help to the down-and-out, and fraternal associations, such as the first African American Masonic Lodge established in Boston in 1797, provided fellowship and mutual support. It was black churches, however, that emerged as cornerstones of black community life, a position they would occupy throughout the nation's history.

Following the Revolution, growing numbers of free blacks joined integrated Methodist and Baptist congregations in cities such as Philadelphia and New York. They were drawn by those church's strongly biblical theology, enthusiastic worship, and antislavery stand. By 1790, 20 percent of Methodist church members were black. As the numbers of black communicants grew, however, they found themselves segregated in galleries, excluded from leadership roles, and even denied communion. Although many black Christians were reluctant to

In his watercolor of a black Methodist church meeting, Paul Svinin, a traveler from Russia, reveals his amazement at the physical emotion displayed by the worshippers. "African" churches and other organizations were rare before 1800 but grew steadily in the ensuing decades. (*The Metropolitan Museum of Art, Rogers Fund, 1942 [42.95.19]*)

withdraw from biracial congregations, others sought opportunity to control their religious lives by breaking away.

In 1794, a small group of black Methodists led by Richard Allen, a slave-born, itinerant preacher, organized the Bethel African American Methodist Church in Philadelphia. Originally established within American Methodism, Allen's congregation moved toward separatism by requiring that only "Africans and descendants of the African race" be admitted to membership. In 1815, it rejected all oversight by the white Methodist leadership, and a year later it joined a similar congregation in Baltimore to form the African Methodist Episcopal Church—the first independent black denomination in the United States. Though not as numerous as black Methodists, black Baptists also formed separate churches in places such as Boston (1805), Philadelphia (1810), New Orleans (1826), and St. Louis (1827).

Located in the heart of black communities, these churches not only nurtured African-American forms of worship, but also provided education for black children and burial sites for families excluded from white cemeteries. Equally important, they offered secure places where the basic rituals of family and community life—marriages, births, funerals, and anniversaries—could be celebrated and where community norms could be enforced. By 1830, a rich cultural and institutional life had taken root in the black neighborhoods of American cities.

White hostility, however, remained a reality of black urban life, especially during hard times when free blacks competed with white laborers for scarce jobs and affordable housing. Overt violence against free blacks was infrequent during the early decades of the century, but even so, blacks found themselves increasingly segregated in residence, employment, and social life. Faced with that harsh reality, black leaders such as Richard Allen, Prince Hall, and Absolom Jones spoke earnestly about the meaning of black "freedom" in a white republic and struggled to create a sense of civic identity for Americans of African descent.

Black urban life was far different in the South than in the nation's northeastern cities. While blacks constituted a large percentage of southern urban populations, the vast majority were slaves. Of Charleston's 14,127 blacks (slightly over 50 percent of the city's population), 90 percent were slaves. That circumstance, combined with the South's rigid "Black Codes," frustrated black community building. Opportunities to come together for their own betterment were even fewer among the vast majority of southern blacks living on plantations.

In New Orleans, on the other hand, lenient policies concerning black freedom, property rights, and racial mixing during the years of Spanish colonial control had produced the largest free black (*libre*) and mixed race (*mulatto*) populations in North America. While racial hierarchies were clearly evident within the three-tiered social order of whites, free blacks, and slaves, a growing and increasingly self-confident population of *libres*, its ranks augmented by manumitted slaves and black refugees fleeing the chaos of revolutionary Haiti, prospered. In 1805, *libres* constituted one-third of the city's black population; by 1820, they numbered 46 percent.

Several developments threatened the privileges of the city's free black residents. Among them were the thousands of new slaves imported to provide labor for the burgeoning sugar economy (what one historian has called the "re-Africanization" of Louisiana), white alarm over black rebellion in nearby Haiti, and the introduction of a more rigid racial ideology by the growing number of white American settlers. Still, New Orleans *libres* continued to own urban property, carriages, small businesses, even slaves, and constituted a uniquely prosperous and independent free black community.

THE END OF NEO-COLONIALISM

Following the election of 1808, James Madison, second in the "Virginia dynasty" of presidents, assumed office. As American ships once more ventured into the Atlantic following the embargo's collapse, and as the British Navy renewed its depredations, war fever continued to mount. Within a few years, conflict with England erupted in the War of 1812. The war brought an end to a period of neo-colonialism when the United States, though formally independent, was still vulnerable to the actions of England and other European imperial powers. During the administrations of James Monroe (1817–1825), the Jeffersonian Republicans fashioned a momentous new role for the United States within the Americas as well.

The War of 1812

The election of 1810 brought to Congress a new group of western and southern leaders, firmly Jeffersonian in party loyalty but impatient with the administration's bumbling foreign policy and demanding tougher measures. These War Hawks included such future political giants as Henry Clay of Kentucky and John C. Calhoun of South Carolina.

For too long, the War Hawks cried, the United States had tolerated Britain's presence on American soil, encouragement of Indian raids, and attacks on American commerce. They talked freely of expanding the nation's boundaries north into Canada and south into what was still Spanish Florida. Most of all, these young nationalists resented British arrogance and America's continuing humiliation. No government, they warned, could last unless it pro-

tected the nation's interests and upheld the nation's honor. Nor could the Jeffersonian party survive unless it proved able to govern.

Responding to the growing pressure, President Madison finally asked Congress for a declaration of war on June 1, 1812. Opposition came entirely from the New England and Middle Atlantic states—ironically, the regions most adversely affected by Britain's European blockade—whereas the loudest shouts for war emanated from the South and West. Rarely had sectional alignments been more sharply drawn.

Rarely, either, had American foreign policy proven less effective. Madison decided to abandon economic for military coercion just as the British government, under domestic pressure to seek accommodation, suspended its European blockade. Three days later, unaware of Britain's action (it took three weeks for news to cross the Atlantic), the Congress declared war.

The war proved a strange affair. Britain beat back several American forays into Canada and launched a series of attacks along the Gulf Coast. As it had done during the Revolutionary War, the British navy blockaded American coastal waters, while landing parties launched punishing attacks along the eastern seaboard. On August 14, 1814, a British force occupied Washington, torched the Capitol and president's mansion (soon to be called the White House after being repaired and whitewashed), and sent the president, Congress, and panic-stricken American troops fleeing into Virginia. Britain, however, did not press its advantage, for it was preoccupied with Napoleon's armies in Europe and wanted to end the American quarrel.

On the American side, emotions ran high between the war's Federalist critics and Jeffersonian Republican supporters. In the summer of 1812, a crowd of 1,000 men and women in Baltimore, inspired by partisan politics, working-class animosity toward Federalist "aristocrats," and eagerness for war related jobs, demolished the printing office of a Federalist newspaper that criticized the war. When copies of the paper again appeared on the city's streets, a crowd gathered once again. After Federalist defenders opened fire from inside the office, the crowd rolled up a cannon and sent a round of grapeshot into the building. Several people lay dead on both sides before the militia finally carted the Federalists off to the safety of jail.

The encounter was not yet over, for the following night, a third crowd assembled in front of the city jail, seized ten prisoners, including James Lingan, an old Revolutionary War general, and left their badly beaten bodies, stripped of their fine clothing, sprawling in the street.

The War of 1812

The War of 1812 scarcely touched the lives of most Americans, but areas around the Great Lakes, Lake Champlain, Chesapeake Bay, and the Gulf Coast witnessed significant fighting.

Fortunately, the Baltimore riots were not duplicated elsewhere, but emotions continued to run high throughout the country. In Federalist New England, opposition to the war veered toward outright disloyalty. In December 1814, delegates from the five New England states met at Hartford, Connecticut, to debate proposals for secession. Cooler heads prevailed, but before adjourning, the Hartford Convention asserted the right of a state to "interpose" its authority against "unconstitutional" acts of the government. Now it was New England's turn to play with the nullification fire. As the war dragged on, Federalist support soared in the Northeast, while elsewhere bitterness grew over New England's disloyalty.

Before the war ended, American forces won several impressive victories, among them Commander Oliver Hazard Perry's defeat of the British fleet on

Lake Erie in 1813. That victory proved a turning point of the war in the Old Northwest, for it secured American dominance on the Great Lakes, ended the threat of a British invasion from Canada, and weakened the British–Indian alliance that had menaced American interests in the region. The most dramatic American triumph was Andrew Jackson's smashing victory in 1815 over an attacking British force at New Orleans. But it had little to do with the war's outcome, for it occurred after preliminary terms of peace had already been signed.

Increasingly concerned about affairs in Europe, the British government offered to begin peace negotiations. Madison eagerly accepted, and on Christmas Eve in 1814, at Ghent, Belgium, the two sides reached agreement. Britain agreed to evacuate the western posts, but the treaty ignored other outstanding issues, including impressment, neutral rights, and American access to Canadian fisheries. It simply declared the fighting over, called for the return of prisoners and captured territory, and provided for joint commissions to deal with lingering disputes.

Still, the war left its mark on the American nation. Four thousand African Americans, constituting nearly 20 percent of American seamen, fought in the war, demonstrating their patriotism and challenging white racial stereotypes. At least as many free and enslaved blacks took the opportunity, as had occurred during the American Revolution, to serve the British as spies, messengers, and guides. A hundred or so newly liberated slaves accompanied the troops that burned the Capitol and White House in the summer of 1814.

The British attack on Fort McHenry in Baltimore harbor inspired a young officer, Francis Scott Key, to compose a poem, titled "The Star Spangled Banner," that was then set to a familiar English tune. (In 1931, Congress designated it the official national anthem.) In addition, the war made Andrew Jackson a hero and established him as a political figure of national significance. Most important, the conflict was quickly designated a "Second War of American Independence" that finally secured the country against outside interference. That belief fed a surge of postwar nationalism.

Following 1815, the nation turned its principal energies to the task of internal development—occupying the continent, building the economy, and reforming American society. At the same time, European countries, preoccupied with their own problems of national unification and economic development, entered what would prove to be almost a century free of general war. In the past, European wars had drawn America in; they would do so again in the twentieth century. For the remainder of the nineteenth century, however, that fateful link was broken. Finally, the focus of European colonialism was shifting to Africa and Asia, and that diverted European attention from the Americas as well.

The United States and the Americas

While disengaging from Europe, the president and Congress fashioned new policies for Latin America that would guide the nation's hemispheric relations for years to come. Many cheered when Spain and Portugal's Latin American colonies, holding up the American Revolution as a model of liberation, began their struggle for independence in 1808. But U.S. leaders were skeptical that the racially mixed populations of Latin America, with their history of brutal colonialism, could govern themselves effectively. They were also reluctant to recognize the new governments of Colombia, Mexico, Chile, and Argentina for fear of disrupting delicate efforts then underway to secure Florida from Spain. In addition, there was concern that the newly independent countries might attempt to form a South American confederacy. "In a single mass," Jefferson mused, "they would be a very formidable neighbor."

Still, North Americans were happy to see European colonialism weakened and held out hope that newly independent nations, no longer suffering under imperial restrictions, would offer the prospect of increased trade. Eventually, President Monroe sent Congress a message proposing formal recognition of the Latin American republics. Congress quickly agreed.

Trouble arose, however, in November 1822, when the major European powers talked of helping Spain regain its American empire. Such prospects alarmed Great Britain as well as the United States, and in August 1823, the British foreign secretary broached the idea of Anglo-American cooperation to thwart Spain's intentions.

Secretary of State John Quincy Adams opposed the idea. John Adams's son had joined the Jeffersonian camp several years earlier as part of the continuing exodus from the Federalist Party. Filled with the new spirit of nationalism so evident following the War of 1812 and suspicious of British intentions, Adams urged that the United States not "come in as a cockboat in the wake of the British man-of-war." He called instead for independent action based on two principles: a sharp separation between the Old World and the New, and U.S. dominance in the Western Hemisphere.

Monroe agreed that the United States should issue its own policy statement. In his annual message of December 1823, he outlined a new Latin American policy. Though known as the Monroe Doctrine, Adams had devised it.

The doctrine asserted four basic principles: (1) the American continents were closed to new European colonization, (2) the political systems of the Americas were separate from those of Europe, (3) the United States would consider as dangerous to its peace and safety any attempts to extend Europe's political influence into the Western Hemisphere, and (4) the United States would neither interfere with existing colonies in the New World nor meddle in Europe's affairs. Though promulgated with Latin America primarily in mind, the Doctrine was also aimed at Russian ambitions on the northern Pacific coast.

Monroe's bold declaration had little immediate effect, for the United States possessed neither the economic nor military power to enforce it. By the end of the nineteenth century, when the nation's might had increased, however, it would become clear what a fateful moment in the history of the Americas Monroe's declaration had been.

KNITTING THE NATION TOGETHER

At the Philadelphia convention in 1788, Federalists and Anti-Federalists had argued whether such a diverse and sprawling republic could survive. After the vast area of Louisiana was added and white settlement surged into Trans-Appalachia, those concerns increased. Given the country's primitive modes of travel, restricted forms of communication, and limited central government, the problem of holding the country together continued to bedevil the American people. Although the nation would not be securely unified until after the Civil War, progress was clearly evident in the early republic.

Conquering Distance

It has been estimated that within half an hour of President Kennedy's assassination in Dallas, Texas, in 1963, 68 percent of the American people had learned the news. By contrast, when George Washington died in December 1799 in Alexandria, Virginia, it took five days for word to reach Philadelphia (scarcely 140 miles away), 11 days to get as far as Boston, and over three weeks to penetrate west to Lexington, Kentucky.

More dramatic breakthroughs in conquering distance would come with the transportation revolution beginning in the second quarter of the century (see Chapter 10). But by the 1820s, improvements in transportation and communication had already begun to knit the nation more effectively together.

In the absence of modern technologies such as telephones, television and the Internet, human travel and circulation of the printed word were the only ways of communicating across space. In 1800, it took two days to go by coach from New York to Philadelphia and more than a week to Pittsburgh. Over the following decades, northeastern states engaged in a flurry of turnpike construction. One of the earliest pikes opened between Philadelphia and Lancaster, Pennsylvania, in 1794. When it proved profitable, dozens of others quickly followed. By 1811, the New York legislature had chartered 137 turnpike companies and the New England states 200 more.

Most turnpikes consisted of little more than dirt roadways cut through the woods with tree stumps, sawed off just low enough to clear wagon axles, left in place. Turnpikes, moreover, were few and their tolls high. People most often made their way on horseback along crude trails that wound across the countryside, following paths of least topographic resistance.

In summer, travel along these byways raised clouds of dust; in spring, they dissolved into mud. The usual rate of travel, whether on foot or horseback, was little more than 3 or 4 miles an hour. At that pace, a trip of 25 miles filled a day. Even such a modest goal was impossible to achieve if there were mountains to cross or rivers to ford. Still, travel times in the Northeast had been halved by 1830.

In the first federal road building project, Congress in 1806 authorized construction of a National Road from Cumberland, Maryland, to the West. By 1818, it had reached Wheeling on the Ohio River and had reduced travel time between its terminals from eight days to three.

Given the difficulties of overland routes, Americans traveled via coastal and inland waterways whenever possible. During the early years of the century, the first steamboats appeared along the Atlantic coast and began to ply the waters of the Ohio and Mississippi rivers. In 1807, Robert Fulton launched his 160-ton sidewheeler *Clermont*, demonstrating the feasibility of steam travel. Four years later, the *New Orleans* made the first successful run over the falls of the Ohio River at Cincinnati, then continued down the Mississippi to New Orleans. Within a few decades, steamboats would revolutionize transportation on the nation's interior river system. For the moment, however, westerners

The turnpike system reduced travel time through the countryside. Here an express coach makes its way through the forest. (*Album of Western Sketches: Highways and Byeways of the Forest, a Scene on "the Road"; 1836 By: George Tattersall. English, 1817–1849 [active U.S. 1836]; Pen and brown ink with brush and brown wash, heightened with white gouache, over graphite pencil, on gray paper; Sheet: 21.0 × 29.8 cm [8 ¼ × 11 ¾ in.]; Museum of Fine Arts, Boston; Gift of Maxim Karolik; [56.400.11] © 2003 The Museum of Fine Arts, Boston)*

still depended on flatboats to float their cargoes downstream and keelboats for the laborious task of poling upriver.

Between 1790 and 1830, significant breakthroughs occurred in print communication as well. When Washington assumed the presidency, only 92 newspapers were under publication. Most were weeklies, and virtually all were printed in cities along the Atlantic coast. The majority had no more than 600 subscribers. By 1830, the number of newspapers had increased to over 1,000, about one-third of them dailies. The first paper printed west of the mountains, the *Pittsburgh Gazette*, appeared in 1786. By 1800, 21 western papers were being published, some in places as far inland as St. Louis.

By 1820, the ratio of newspapers to population was higher in the United States than in Great Britain. The English traveler Frances Trollope commented in amazement on Americans' "universal reading" of papers, while another visitor claimed that "there is scarcely a hamlet that has not its newspaper." The widespread practice of reading newspapers aloud in taverns, shops, and homes further extended their reach.

The swelling demand for newspapers was spurred by rising literacy rates (most notably among women and lower-class men), the demand for information generated by the nation's expanding market economy, democratic belief in the importance of an informed citizenry, and the growing importance of papers as an instrument of party politics.

As the circulation of papers brought information about distant people and events into formerly isolated communities, it expanded people's horizons and strengthened Americans' sense of shared experience. Only a newspaper, noted one observer, "can drop the same thought into a thousand minds at the same moment."

During the early nineteenth century, the American postal system expanded similarly. When Washington was inaugurated, there were only 75 post offices in the entire country. As late as 1792, there were none in the entire trans-Appalachian West. By 1820, nearly 8,500 post offices were scattered throughout the nation. During these same decades, the number of letters carried by the postal system increased ninefold. It cost 25 cents to send a letter 30 miles or more—a prohibitive sum for most folks when daily wages averaged only a dollar. Still, the cost of mailing a letter had declined by half.

Strengthening American Nationalism

Improvements in travel and communication, together with the sense of national pride fostered by the War of 1812, strengthened American nationalism in the years of the early republic. So, too, did the galvanizing experience of the Second Great Awakening. It reinforced belief in America as God's chosen nation and tied Americans together in networks of shared religious identity, woven by the hundreds of itinerant Protestant ministers who car-

In the early republic, celebrations of Independence Day mingled military processions with patriotic displays and neighborhood conviviality. *(The Historical Society of Pennsylvania (HSP),* "Fourth of July Celebration," *India ink and watercolors on paper by Lewis Krimmel, Accession #Bc882K897)*

ried the Gospel message into communities in every part of the country. The flood of printed tracts circulated by religious organizations reinforced the sense of religious unity.

Rituals of patriotic celebration on occasions such as Washington's birthday and the Fourth of July also helped unify the country. Although Federalists and Jeffersonian Republicans, northerners and southerners, black and white Americans filled these occasions with their own, often conflicting meanings, all were eager to claim a voice in shaping the nation's heritage. Reports of these local celebrations, carried across the land via newspapers and correspondence, knitted communities together in a national conversation of patriotism.

National unity was further strengthened by several key decisions of the Supreme Court. In a series of trailblazing cases, the Court, led by Chief Justice John Marshall, laid down some of the most basic doctrines of American constitutional law. In *Marbury* v. *Madison* (1803), the Court established the principle of judicial review, that is the assertion that the Court had the authority to judge the constitutionality of congressional laws and executive actions. In the case of *Martin* v. *Hunter's Lessee* (1816), the

Court claimed appellate jurisdiction over the decisions of state courts.

Three years later, in another landmark decision, *McCulloch* v. *Maryland*, the Court denied claims by the Maryland legislature that Congress had exceeded its authority in chartering the Second Bank of the U.S. (1816) and ruled that the state could not tax operations of the bank's Baltimore branch. In a unanimous decision, Marshall issued a ringing endorsement of the doctrine of loose, as opposed to strict, construction of the Constitution. "Let the end (of a Congressional law) be legitimate," he declared, "let it be within the scope of the constitution, and all means which are appropriate . . . to that end, which are not prohibited, but consist with the letter and spirit of the constitution, are constitutional." The Bank's charter would thus stand.

No state, he further argued, possessed the right to tax a nationally chartered bank, because "the power to tax involves the power to destroy." The principle of national supremacy lay at the very center of Marshall's finding. The doctrines elaborated in these path breaking decisions would continue to shape the nation's history in the years ahead.

John Marshall, appointed chief justice of the United States by President Adams in 1801, served in that position for 34 years. Under his leadership, the Supreme Court established some of the most basic principles of American constitutional law. *(Boston Atheneum)*

The Specter of Sectionalism

Despite the surge of national spirit following the War of 1812, Federalist talk of disunion had revealed just how fragile national unity was. That was starkly evident in the Missouri crisis of 1819–1820.

Since 1789, politicians had labored to keep the explosive issue of slavery tucked safely beneath the surface of political life, for they understood how quickly it could jeopardize the nation. Their fears were borne out in 1819 when Missouri's application for admission to the Union raised anew the question of slavery's expansion. The Northwest Ordinance of 1787 had prohibited slavery north of the Ohio River while allowing its expansion to the south. But Congress had said nothing about slavery's place in the vast Louisiana territory west of the Mississippi.

Though there were several thousand slaves in the Missouri Territory, Senator Rufus King of New York demanded that Missouri prohibit slavery before entering the Union. His proposal triggered a fierce debate over Congress's authority to regulate slavery in the trans-Mississippi West. Southerners were adamant that the vast area must remain open to their slave property and were determined to preserve the equal balance of slave and free states in the Senate. Already by 1819, the more rapidly growing population of the free states had given them a 105-to-81 advantage in the House of Representatives. Equality in the Senate offered the only sure protection for southern interests. Northerners, however, vowed to keep the territories west of the

The House of Representatives, depicted in this 1821 painting by Samuel F. B. Morse, later inventor of the telegraph, rang with debate over the Missouri Compromise and other explosive issues. *(Samuel F. B. Morse, The Old House of Representatives, 1882, 86 ¹⁄₂ × 130 ³⁄₄ in, oil on canvas. In the Collection of the Corcoran Gallery of Art, Washington, D.C., Museum Purchase, Gallery Fund 11.14)*

Missouri Compromise of 1820

In the early nineteenth century, politicians struggled to contain the explosive issue of slavery's expansion. In 1820, they did so by balancing Missouri's admission as a slave state with Maine's as a free state and drawing the Missouri Compromise line separating free territories from slave territories.

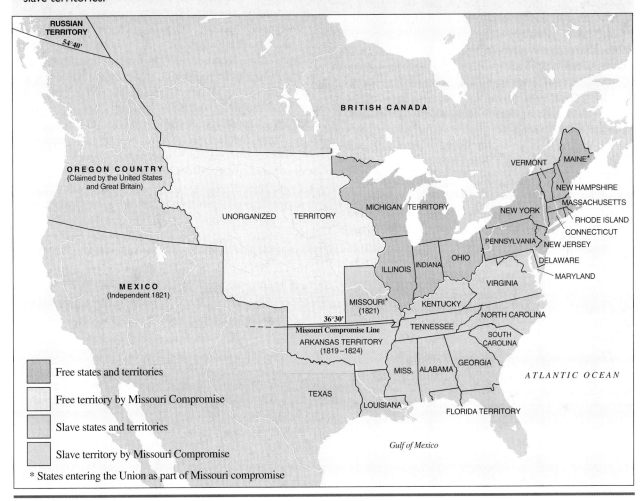

RUSSIAN TERRITORY
54°40'

BRITISH CANADA

OREGON COUNTRY
(Claimed by the United States and Great Britain)

UNORGANIZED TERRITORY

MICHIGAN TERRITORY

VERMONT MAINE*
NEW HAMPSHIRE
MASSACHUSETTS
NEW YORK
RHODE ISLAND
CONNECTICUT
PENNSYLVANIA NEW JERSEY
OHIO
DELAWARE
MARYLAND

MEXICO
(Independent 1821)

ILLINOIS INDIANA

VIRGINIA

MISSOURI*
(1821)

KENTUCKY

36°30'

NORTH CAROLINA

Missouri Compromise Line
ARKANSAS TERRITORY
(1819–1824)

TENNESSEE

SOUTH CAROLINA

GEORGIA

MISS. ALABAMA

ATLANTIC OCEAN

TEXAS

LOUISIANA

FLORIDA TERRITORY

Gulf of Mexico

Free states and territories

Free territory by Missouri Compromise

Slave states and territories

Slave territory by Missouri Compromise

* States entering the Union as part of Missouri compromise

Mississippi open to free labor, which meant closing them to slavery.

For nearly three months, Congress debated the issue. During much of the time, free blacks, listening intently to northern antislavery speeches, filled the House gallery. "This momentous question," worried the aged Jefferson, "like a fire-bell in the night, [has] awakened and filled me with terror." Northerners were similarly alarmed. The Missouri question, declared the editor of the New York *Daily Advertiser,* "involves not only the future character of our nation, but the future weight and influence of the free states. If now lost—it is lost forever."

In the end, compromise prevailed. Missouri gained admission as a slave state, while Maine (formerly part of Massachusetts) came in as a counterbalancing free state. A line was drawn west from

Missouri at latitude 36° 30′ to the Rocky Mountains. Lands north of that line would be open to slavery; areas to the south of it would not.

Controversy erupted again when antislavery forces in Congress protested a clause in the Missouri constitution excluding free blacks and mulattoes from the state. They argued that the denial of citizenship and civil rights to free blacks in Missouri would set a precedent for similar denials by other states. The Missouri legislature assured Congress that the offending clause would not be used to abridge the rights of any U.S. citizens, thus assuaging congressional critics and ensuring Missouri's admission to the union. In spite of such assurances, however, free blacks continued to be excluded from the state.

For the moment, the issue of slavery's expansion had been put to rest. It would not be long, however, before the problem would set North and South even more violently against each other.

POLITICS IN TRANSITION

While Indian relations, social reform, foreign policy, and sectional tensions dominated the nation's agenda in the early republic, American politics continued to evolve. Gradually the Federalist–Jeffersonian party system collapsed, a victim of Federalist folly and an increasingly unmanageable Jeffersonian majority. As that happened, new political alignments got underway. By the late 1820s, America was poised on the threshold of a new political era.

The Demise of the Federalists

For a while following the election of 1800, Federalists had maintained a drumfire of attack on the Jeffersonians, including the charge published by a Federalist editor in 1803 that Jefferson had sired several children by his slave girl Sally Hemmings. But the Federalists were discredited by accusations of disloyalty during the War of 1812 and were tainted by their lingering aristocratic image. While some Federalists endorsed broad suffrage as essential to social stability and governmental legitimacy, many did not. "The tendency of universal suffrage," declared one New York Federalist, "is to jeopardize the rights of property and the principles of liberty. . . . There is a tendency in the majority to tyrannize over the minority and trample down their rights . . . [and] in the indolent . . . to cast the burthens of society upon the industrious and the virtuous." Whatever they might think about the suffrage, Federalists continued to believe that political leadership should be restricted to "the wise and the good." Saddled with this outlook, the Federalist Party gradually collapsed.

Repelled by the increasingly democratic temper of public politics, many Federalists retired to the solace of private life. Others turned their energies to cultural commentary, where in literary journals such as *The North American Review* they continued to promote Federalist values: distrust of individualism, emphasis on communal responsibility and the common good, a clearly established social hierarchy, and political leadership by the wise and good. Those values, though increasingly at odds with American democratic politics, would continue to find advocates throughout the nineteenth century.

Division Among the Jeffersonians

During the early decades of the nineteenth century, the Jeffersonian Republicans monopolized the pres-

idency and dominated Congress. But their political success, spurred by the Federalists' decline, fresh recruits in the East, and the admission of new states in the West, proved their undoing. No single party could contain the nation's swelling diversity of economic and social interests, its growing sectional divisions, and the ambitions of a new generation of political leaders.

In response to pressures from constituents in the West and Northeast, Madison's administration launched a Federalist-like program of national development. In March 1816, he signed a bill creating a second Bank of the United States (the first Bank's charter had expired in 1811), intended to stimulate economic expansion and regulate the loose currency-issuing practices of countless state-chartered banks. At Madison's urging, Congress also passed America's first protective tariff, a set of duties on imported woollen and cotton goods, iron, hats, and sugar intended to protect American industries that had sprung up during the embargo. He also launched a federally subsidized network of roads and canals. By the early 1820s, Henry Clay and others, now calling themselves National Republicans, were proposing an even more ambitious program of tariffs and internal improvements, under the name the American System.

The administration's program of nationally directed economic development drew sharp criticism from so-called Old Republicans, southern politicians who regarded themselves as guardians of the Jeffersonian conscience. Speaking in opposition to the bank bill, Congressman John Randolph of Virginia warned that "the question is whether . . . the state governments are to be swept away; or whether we . . . still . . . regard their integrity and preservation as part of our policy." Over the following decade, the Old Republicans continued to sound the alarm, even as their numbers dwindled.

Collapse of the Federalist–Jeffersonian Party System

The final collapse of the Federalist–Jeffersonian system of politics was triggered by the presidential election of 1824. For the first time since 1800, when the "Virginia dynasty" of Jefferson, Madison, and Monroe began, there was competition for the presidency from every major wing of the Jeffersonian party. Of the five candidates, John Quincy Adams of Massachusetts and Henry Clay of Kentucky advocated federal programs of economic development. William Crawford of Georgia and Andrew Jackson of Tennessee clung to traditional Jeffersonian principles of limited government, agrarianism, and states' rights. In between stood John Calhoun of South Carolina, just beginning his fateful passage from nationalism to Southern nullification.

When none of the presidential candidates received an electoral majority, the election, as in 1800, moved into the House of Representatives. There, an alliance of Adams and Clay supporters gave the New Englander the election, even though he trailed Jackson in electoral votes, 84 to 99. The Jacksonians' charges of a "corrupt bargain" gained credence when Adams appointed Clay secretary of state.

Adams's ill-fated administration revealed the disarray in American politics. His stirring calls for federal road and canal building, standardization of weights and measures, a national university, and government support for science and the arts quickly fell victim to sectional conflicts, political factionalism, and his own scorn for the increasingly democratic politics of the time. Against the urging of his political advisers, Adams declined an invitation to attend the Maryland Agricultural Society's annual cattle show. Presidents, he thought, should stand above such efforts to court popular favor. That attitude, relic of a bygone era, was political suicide in the increasingly democratic politics of the 1820s. Within a year of his inauguration, Adams's administration had foundered. For the rest of his term, politicians jockeyed for position in the political realignment that was underway.

Women at the Republican Court

At the center of national politics in Washington, the female relatives and friends of government officials fashioned new political roles for women. Much as aristocratic women had long exerted influence at English and European courts, so elite American women such as Margaret Bayard Smith forged an American style of parlor politics. Initiated at Philadelphia in the 1790s when a national governing community was first taking shape, parlor politics became an integral part of the Washington scene after 1800.

As political actors in their own right, women visited the Supreme Court and attended sessions of Congress, frequently circulating on the House and Senate floors and even sitting in members' seats. "The House of Representatives," observed Bayard Smith, "is a lounging place for both sexes, where acquaintance is as easily made as at public amusements." Women also filled the House galleries as electoral votes were counted in the 1808 presidential election, and followed the debates over war in 1812.

They also utilized networks of friendship, dinner parties, and social gatherings to reinforce political alliances, lobby political appointments, and promote legislation. In the process, they contributed to the new government's effectiveness while contesting the lines separating public (male) and private (female) spheres.

Though many women participated in the capital's parlor politics, no one pursued it more aggressively than Louisa Catherine Adams, who launched what she called "my campaign" for her husband John Quincy Adams's candidacy in the disputed presidential election of 1824. During his term in office, she continued to work the Washington scene.

If privileged women found it possible to fashion political influence at the republican court in Washington, however, other women continued to find themselves politically isolated during these years. That was in part because of a conservative backlash against the radically feminist politics evident earlier during the French Revolution. For anxious American males, the political rights of American women at home could be easily tarred with the brush of French "anarchy" abroad.

Finally, as male-dominated political parties grew in importance and as voting became the defining act of political participation, American political democracy became more rigidly gendered.

A New Style of Politics

While women, blacks, and Native Americans continued to be excluded from the franchise, white men now flocked to the polls in unprecedented numbers. In state elections, voter turnout at times reached as high as 80 percent of the qualifying electorate, far higher than previously.

A combination of circumstances explains the dramatic increase, among them the growing strength of democratic beliefs and decisions by state governments to abolish long-established property-owning requirements for the franchise. It was in the states, moreover, that government acted most directly on people's lives—building roads and canals, regulating banks and stray cattle, enforcing temperance, and regulating poor relief—thus activating individuals' self-interest and drawing them into the political arena. And it was in the states that a new generation of political leaders such as Martin Van Buren and Henry Clay, men uninhibited by their elders' fear of political "faction" and skilled in party organization and the use of a partisan press, first perfected the techniques of mass, democratic politics. By the 1820s, successful politicians of every persuasion vied for voters' support through registration drives, party conventions, and popular campaigning.

Election days were often raucous affairs in the increasingly
democratic, male-dominated
politics of the early republic,
as this Philadelphia scene
amply testifies. *(The Historical
Society of Pennsylvania [HSP],
India ink and watercolors on
paper of "Election Day at the
State House, 1816" by John
Lewis Krimmel, Accession
#Bc47K897)*

The election of Andrew Jackson to the presidency in 1828 represented the culmination of these democratic changes, for it brought the techniques of mass politics, developed initially in the states, to presidential electioneering. When the presidential election became a genuine popular referendum, American politics was changed forever.

✦ *Conclusion*

THE PASSING OF AN ERA

Vast in area by the standards of European nations, the United States consisted of diverse, often conflicting, and as yet only loosely joined regions. Within those regions ordinary citizens like Mary and James Harrod, Ben Thompson, and Phyllis Sherman struggled to fashion new lives. Their efforts gave human expression to the nation's values of social equality, individual opportunity, and personal autonomy.

Those values, strengthened by the country's revolutionary heritage and the Great Awakening, inspired reforms intended to improve the conditions of American life. Though the lives of many white women improved, gendered restrictions continued to limit women's opportunities. The reinvigoration of chattel slavery in the South imperiled the lives of countless black slaves, while deepening racism in the North impeded the efforts of free blacks to create new communities. To the west, Native Americans, pursuing strategies of accommodation and resistance, gradually gave way in the face of expanding white settlement.

During these same years, American leaders fashioned important new relationships with the outside world. Following the War of 1812, the United States finally ended its neo-colonial dependence on England and Europe, while in the Monroe Doctrine it defined a portentous new relationship with the emerging nations of Latin America.

As the country grew, American nationalism was strengthened by improvements in travel and print communication, the widely shared experience of the Great Awakening, and a series of path-breaking decisions handed down by the Supreme Court. At the same time, sectional tensions continued to simmer, breaking ominously through the surface of political life in the Missouri Crisis.

These years brought decisive changes to American political life as well. Though privileged, white women had influence in the nation's capital, most women found themselves politically marginalized as sophisticated political parties enlisted men by the tens of thousands in electoral politics.

By the 1820s, the American people had turned from an era of founding, when the nation was new and the outcome of the republican experiment un-

Timeline

1790	Indian Intercourse Act
1790s	Second Great Awakening begins
1793	Invention of the cotton gin
1794	Battle of Fallen Timbers
1795	Treaty of Greenville
1800	Gabriel's Rebellion
1803	*Marbury v. Madison*
1806	National Road begun
1807	Fulton's steamboat *Clermont* launched
1808	James Madison elected president
1811	Battle of Kithtippecanoe
1812	Madison reelected War declared against Great Britain
1813	Battle of the Thames
1813–1814	Creek War

1814	Treaty of Ghent Battle of Horseshoe Bend
1814–1815	Hartford Convention
1815	Battle of New Orleans
1816	James Monroe elected president Second Bank of the United States chartered American Colonization Society founded African Methodist Episcopal Church established
1819	Adams–Onis Treaty with Spain *McCulloch v. Maryland*
1819–1822	Bank panic and depression
1819–1820	Missouri Compromise
1822	Diplomatic recognition of Latin American republics
1823	Monroe Doctrine proclaimed
1824	John Quincy Adams elected president
1827	Cherokee adopt written constitution

certain, to a new era of national development. That transition was dramatized on July 4, 1826, the fiftieth anniversary of American independence, when two of the remaining revolutionary patriarchs, John Adams and Thomas Jefferson, died within a few hours of each other. "The sterling virtues of the Revolution are silently passing away," mused George McDuffie of South Carolina during that jubilee year, "and the period is not distant when there will be no living monument to remind us of those glorious days of trial." As the anniversary celebrations ended and the revolutionary founders faded into memory, the American people had reason to ponder what the future would bring.

◆ Recommended Reading

A Nation of Regions

Michael Allen, *Western Rivermen, 1763–1861* (1990); Stephen Aron, *How the West Was Lost: The Transformation of Kentucky from Daniel Boone to Henry Clay* (1996); Jeremy Atack and Fred Bateman, *To Their Own Soil: Agriculture in the Antebellum North* (1987); Joan Cashin, *A Family Venture: Men and Women on the Southern Frontier* (1991); Andrew R. L. Cayton and Fredrika Teute, eds., *Contact Points: American Frontiers from the Mohawk Valley to the Mississippi, 1750–1830* (1998); William David, *A Way Through the Wilderness: The Natchez Trace and the Civilizing of the Southern Frontier* (1995); Robert Doherty, *Society and Power: Five New England Towns, 1800–1860* (1977); Daniel Dupre, *Transforming the Cotton Frontier: Madison County, Alabama, 1800–1840* (1997); John Mack Farragher, *Daniel Boone: The Life and Legend of an American Pioneer* (1992); Stephen Hahn and Jonathan Prude, *The Countryside in the Age of Capitalist Transformation* (1985); James Lemon, *The Best Poor Man's Country* (1972); Robert Mitchell, ed., *Appalachian Frontiers: Settlement, Society, and Development in the Preindustrial Era* (1991); John Otto, *The Southern Frontiers, 1607–1860*

(1989); Howard Rock et al., *American Artisans: Crafting Social Identity* (1995); Richard Wade, *The Urban Frontier: The Rise of Western Cities, 1790–1830* (1959).

Indian–White Relations in the Early Republic

Gregory Dowd, *Spirited Resistance: The North American Indian Struggle for Unity, 1745–1815* (1992); R. David Edmunds, *Tecumseh and the Quest for Indian Leadership* (1984); Fred Hoxie et. al., eds., *Native Americans and the Early Republic* (1999); William McLaughlin, *Cherokee Renascence in the New Republic* (1986); Theda Perdue, *Cherokee Women: Gender and Culture Change, 1700–1835* (1998); Francis Paul Prucha, *American Indian Policy in the Formative Years* (1970); Anthony F. C. Wallace, *Jefferson and the Indians* (1999); Richard White, *The Middle Ground: Indians, Empires, and Republics in the Great Lakes Region, 1650–1815* (1991).

Perfecting a Democratic Society

Norma Basch, *Framing American Divorce: From the Revolutionary Generation to the Victorians* (1999); Jeanne Boydston, *Home and Work: Housework, Wages, and the Ideology of Labor in the Early Republic* (1991); Lee Chambers-Schiller, *Liberty, A Better Husband* (1984); Paul

Conkin, *Cane Ridge: American Pentecost* (1990); Nancy Cott, *The Bonds of Womanhood: "Women's Sphere" in New England, 1780–1835* (1977); Robert Cray, Jr., *Paupers and Poor Relief in New York City and Its Rural Environs, 1700–1830* (1988); Cathy Davidson, *Revolution and the Word: The Rise of the Novel in America* (1986); Sylvia Frey and Betty Wood, *Come Shouting to Zion: African-American Protestantism in the American South and British Caribbean to 1830* (1998); Kimberly Hanger, *Bounded Lives, Bounded Places: Free Black Society in New Orleans, 1769–1803* (1997); Nathan Hatch, *The Democratization of American Christianity* (1989); Joan Jensen, *Loosening the Bonds: Mid-Atlantic Farm Women, 1750–1850* (1986); Susan Juster, *Disorderly Women: Sexual Politics and Evangelicalism in Revolutionary New England* (1994); Cynthia Kierner, *Beyond the Household: Women's Place in the Early South, 1700–1835* (1998); Joanne Pope Melish, *Disowning Slavery: Gradual Emancipation and "Race" in New England, 1780–1860* (1998); Michael Meranze, *Laboratories of Virtue: Punishment, Revolution, and Authority in Philadelphia, 1760–1835* (1996); Gary B. Nash, *Forging Freedom: The Formation of Philadelphia's Black Community, 1720–1840* (1988); James Sidbury, *Plowshares into Swords: Race, Rebellion, and Identity in Gabriel's Virginia, 1730–1810* (1997); Laurel Thatcher Ulrich, *A Midwife's Tale: The Life of Martha Ballard . . . 1785–1812* (1990); T. Stephen Whitman, *The Price of Freedom: Slavery and Manumission in Baltimore and Early National Maryland* (1997); John Wigger, *Taking Heaven by Storm: Methodism and the Rise of Popular Christianity in America* (1998); Julie Winch, *A Gentleman of Color: The Life of James Forten* (2002); Conrad Wright, *The Transformation of Charity in Post-Revolutionary New England* (1992).

The End of Neo-Colonialism
Robert Allison, *The Crescent Obscured: The United States and the Muslim World, 1776–1815* (1995); Reginald Horsman, *The Diplomacy of the New Republic, 1776–1815* (1985); Lester Langley, *The Americas in the Age of Revolution, 1750–1850* (1996); James Lewis, Jr., *The American Union and the Problem of Neighborhood: The United States and the Collapse of the Spanish Empire, 1783–1829* (1998); Ernest May, *The Making of the Monroe Doctrine* (1975); J. C. A. Stagg, *Mr. Madison's War* (1983).

Knitting the Nation Together
Andrew Burstein, *America's Jubilee: How in 1826 a Generation Remembered Fifty Years of Independence* (2001); Herbert Johnson, *The Chief Justiceship of John Marshall, 1801–1835* (1997); Richard John, *Spreading the News: The American Postal System from Franklin to Morse* (1995); Thomas Leonard, *The Power of the Press: The Birth of American Political Reporting* (1986); Len Travers, *Celebrating the Fourth: Independence Day and the Rites of Nationalism in the Early Republic* (1997); David Waldstreicher, *In the Midst of Perpetual Fetes: The Making of American Nationalism, 1776–1820* (1997).

Politics in Transition
Catherine Allgor, *Parlor Politics* (2000); Andrew Cayton, *The Frontier Republic: Ideology and Politics in the Ohio Country, 1780–1825* (1986); Marshall Foletta, *Coming to Terms with Democracy: Federalist Intellectuals and the Shaping of American Culture* (2001); Joanne Freeman, *Affairs of Honor: National Politics in the New Republic* (2001); David Konig, ed., *Devising Liberty: Preserving and Creating Freedom in the New American Republic* (1995); Drew McCoy, *The Last of the Fathers: James Madison and the Republican Legacy* (1989); Paul Nagel, *John Quincy Adams: A Public Life, A Private Life* (1997); Donald Ratcliffe, *Party Spirit in a Frontier Republic: Democratic Politics in Ohio, 1793–1821* (1998); Ronald Schultz, *The Republic of Labor: Philadelphia Artisans and the Politics of Class, 1720–1830* (1993); Alan Taylor, *William Cooper's Town: Power and Persuasion on the Frontier in the Early American Republic* (1995); Steven Watts, *The Republic Reborn: War and the Making of Liberal America, 1790–1820* (1987).

Fiction and Film
In the classic American novel *Rip Van Winkle* (1829), Washington Irving explores the transiency of historical memory via the story of an eighteenth-century New Yorker who mysteriously falls asleep during the American Revolution and awakes decades later to find his community radically changed and himself the object of intense curiosity. *Scandalmonger* (2000), a novel by the *New York Times* columnist William Safire, describes personal intrigue within high political circles in the early republic. *Tecumseh: The Last Warrior* (1995), a made-for-television historical drama, offers an imaginative rendering of the Shawnee leader who sought to unite tribes north and south of the Ohio River against invading white settlers in the early nineteenth century. *Lewis and Clark: The Journey of the Corps of Discovery* (1997), a PBS documentary by Ken Burns, tells the story of this pathbreaking expedition and reveals the dramatic landscape through which it passed.

✦ Discovering U.S. History Online

Turns of the Centuries Exhibit
www.americancenturies.mass.edu/turns/index.jsp
Web site visitors can examine museum artifacts from three "turn-of-the-century" eras: 1680–1720, 1780–1820, and 1880–1920. The exhibits for each era demonstrate "Family Life," "Native American Indians," "African Americans," "Newcomers," and "The Land."

Birch's Views of Philadelphia in 1800

www.ushistory.org/birch

This site presents a facsimile of 29 engravings of Philadelphia at the beginning of the nineteenth century.

Nineteenth-Century Views of Manhattan

www.nypl.org/research/chss/spe/art/print/exhibits/movingup/opening.htm

An annotated exhibition of nineteenth-century prints that demonstrate the urban growth in early nineteenth-century Manhattan.

Charlottesville: A Brief Urban History

www.iath.virginia.edu/schwartz/cville/cville.history.html

This illustrated history focuses on development of Charlottesville in the nineteenth-century.

The Seminole Tribe of Florida

www.seminoletribe.com/history/index.shtml

This site is dedicated to the rich history and culture of the Seminole, including the campaigns Andrew Jackson led against the tribe before and during his presidency.

The Iroquois of the Northeast

www.carnegiemuseums.org/cmnh/exhibits/north-south-east-west/iroquois/index.html

A virtual exhibit of the Iroquois and their way of life.

Native Americans in North Georgia

www.ngeorgia.com/history/findex.html

This site presents a several-part history of Georgia's Native Americans, especially the Creeks and Cherokees.

Divining America: Religion and the National Culture, the 19th Century

www.nhc.rtp.nc.us:8080/tserve/nineteen.htm

Using essays and contemporary photos and primary sources, this site includes several essays including "Evangelicalism, Revivalism, and Second Great Awakening" and "Evangelicalism as a Social Movement."

Colonization

www.loc.gov/exhibits/african/afam002.html

Explores the roots of the colonization movement, including the American Colonization Society.

A History of African Americans of Delaware and Maryland's Eastern Shore

www.udel.edu/BlackHistory

A collection of several essays on blacks in these colonies, especially the growth of antebellum free black communities.

Eastern State Penitentiary

www.easternstate.com/history

A timeline and detailed history of this prison, which opened "in 1829 as a part of a controversial movement to change the behavior of inmates through 'confinement in solitude with labor.'"

Judith Sargent Murray Society

www.hurdsmith.com/judith/

Presents her biography, an illustrated tour of her world, and several of her published essays.

Casebook: The War of 1812

warof1812.casebook.org/index.html

A detailed presentation of the War of 1812, this site presents the people, battles, press coverage contemporary to the war, primary source documents, and a timeline.

James Madison

www.jmu.edu/madison

This site explores many aspects of James Madison's career and the historical events and ideas he influenced.

Nationalism

www.fordham.edu/halsall/mod/modsbook17.html

This site has collected essays (public domain texts) on the surging global nationalism of the early nineteenth century, giving context to America's own rising patriotism during those years.

The Marshall Cases for the American Revolution

www.odur.let.rug.nl/~usa/D/1801-1825/marshallcases/marxx.htm

This site presents thorough descriptions and text excerpts from court records of John Marshall's six best-known cases as well as a brief biography.

The Missouri Compromise

www.darien.k12.ct.us/jburt/approject/civilwar/1820/per3/index.htm

Created for a class project, this site offers a topical presentation of the Missouri Compromise.

The History of the First Locomotives in America

www.history.rochester.edu/steam/brown/

This site presents a complete reprint of the volume on early nineteenth-century railroad development.

Thomas Jefferson

www.loc.gov/exhibits/jefferson

This extensive, illustrated exhibit presents Jefferson's life and ideas, including the progression of his ideas of federalism and his legacy.

Martin Van Buren—His Early Years

www.mindspring.com/~braniff/mvb-earl.htm

Part of a larger site on Martin Van Buren, this page gives a year-by-year description of his early years.

History of the Fourth of July

www.pbs.org/capitolfourth/history.html

This site presents a colorful illustrated history of Fourth of July celebrations.

10 Economic Transformations in the Northeast and the Old Northwest

This picture of an 1845 fair suggests the cornucopia of goods made available in the early stages of industrialization. *(B. J. Harrison,* Fair of the American Institute at Niblo's Garden, *1845/Museum of the City of New York)*

✦ *American Stories*

DISCOVERING SUCCESS IN THE MIDST OF FINANCIAL RUIN

For her first 18 years, Susan Warner was little touched by the far-reaching economic and social changes that were transforming the character of the country and her own city of New York. Whereas some New Yorkers toiled to make a living by taking in piecework and others responded to unsettling new means of producing goods by joining trade unions to agitate for wages that would enable them to "live as comfortable as others," Susan was surrounded by luxuries and privilege. Much of the year was spent in the family's town-house in St. Mark's Place, not far from the home of the enormously rich real estate investor and fur trader John Jacob Astor. There Susan acquired the social graces and skills appropriate for a girl of her position and background. She had dancing and singing lessons, studied Italian and French, and learned the etiquette involved in receiving visitors and making calls. When hot weather made life in New York unpleasant, the Warners escaped to the cooler airs of Canaan, where they had a summer house. Like any girl of her social class, Susan realized that her carefree existence could not last forever. With her marriage, which she confidently expected some time in the future, would come significant new responsibilities as a wife and mother but not the end of the comfortable life to which she was accustomed.

It was not marriage and motherhood that disrupted the pattern of Susan's life but financial disaster. Sheltered as she had been from the unsettling economic and social changes of the early nineteenth century, Susan discovered that she, too, was at the mercy of forces beyond her control. Her father, heretofore so successful a provider and parent, lost most of his fortune during the financial Panic of 1837. Like others experiencing a sharp economic reversal, the Warners had to make radical adjustments. The fashionable home in St. Mark's Place and the pleasures of New York were exchanged for a more modest existence on an island in the Hudson River. Susan turned "housekeeper" and learned how to do tasks once relegated to others: sewing and making butter, pudding sauces, and johnny cake.

The change of residence and Susan's attempt to master domestic skills did not halt the family's financial decline. Prized possessions, including the piano and engravings, all symbols of the life the Warners had once taken for granted, eventually went up for auction. "When at last the men and the confusion were gone," Susan's younger sister, Anna, recalled, "then we woke up to life."

Waking up to life meant facing the necessity of making money. But what could Susan do to reverse sliding family fortunes? True, some women labored as factory operatives, domestics, seamstresses, or schoolteachers, but it was doubtful Susan could even imagine herself in any of these occupations. Her Aunt Fanny, however, had a suggestion that was more congenial to the genteel young woman. Knowing that the steam-powered printing press had revolutionized the publishing world and created a mass readership, much of it female, Aunt Fanny told her niece, "Sue, I believe if you would try, you could write a story." "Whether she added 'that . . . would sell,' I am not sure," recalled Anna later, "but of course that was what she meant."

Taking Aunt Fanny's advice to heart, Susan started to write a novel that would sell. She constructed her story around the trials of a young orphan girl, Ellen Montgomery. As Ellen suffered one reverse after another, she learned the lessons that allowed her to survive and eventually triumph over adversity: piety, self-denial, discipline, and the power of a mother's love. Entitled *The Wide, Wide World*, the novel was accepted for publication only after the mother of the publisher, George Putnam, read it and told her son, "If you never publish another book, you must make *The Wide, Wide World* available for your fellow men." A modest 750 copies were printed. Much to the surprise of the cautious Putnam, if not to his mother, 13 editions were published within two years. *The Wide, Wide World* became the first American novel to sell more than one million copies. It was one of the bestsellers of the century.

Long before she realized the book's success, Susan, who was now much aware of the need to make money, was working on a new story. Drawing on her own experience of economic and social reversal, Susan described the spiritual and intellectual life of a young girl thrust into poverty after an early life of luxury in New York. Entitled *Queechy,* this novel was also a great success.

Though her fame as a writer made Susan Warner unusual, her books' popularity suggested how well they spoke to the concerns and interests of a broad readership. The background of social and financial uncertainty, with its sudden changes of fortune, so prominent in several of the novels, captured the reality and fears of a fluid society in the process of transformation. While one French writer was amazed that "in America a three-volume novel is devoted to the history of the moral progress of a girl of thirteen," pious heroines like Ellen Montgomery, who struggled to master their passions and urges toward independence, were shining exemplars of the new norms for middle-class women. Their successful efforts to mold themselves heartened readers who believed that the future of the nation depended on virtuous mothers and who struggled to live up to new ideals. Susan's novels validated their efforts and spoke to the importance of the domestic sphere. "I feel strongly impelled to pour out to you my most heartful thanks," wrote one woman. None of the other leading writers of the day had been able to minister "to the highest and noblest feelings of my nature *so much as yourself.*"

Susan Warner's life and her novels serve as an introduction to the far-reaching changes that this chapter explores. Between 1820 and 1860, as Susan Warner discovered, economic transformations in the Northeast and the Old Northwest reshaped economic, social, cultural, and political life. Though most Americans still lived in rural settings, economic growth and the new industrial mode of production affected them through the creation of new goods, opportunities, and markets. In cities and factory towns, the new economic order ushered in new forms of work, new class arrangements, and new forms of social strife.

After discussing the factors that fueled antebellum growth, the chapter turns to the industrial world, where so many of the new patterns of work and life appeared. An investigation of urbanization reveals shifting class arrangements and values as well as rising social and racial tensions. Finally, an examination of rural communities in the East and on the frontier in the Old Northwest highlights the transformation of these two sections of the country. Between 1840 and 1860, industrialization and economic growth increasingly knit them together.

ECONOMIC GROWTH

Between 1820 and 1860, the American economy entered a new and more complex stage of development as it moved away from its reliance on agriculture as the major source of growth toward an industrial and technological future. In this period of general national expansion, real per capita output grew an average of 2 percent annually between 1820 and 1840 and slightly less between 1840 and 1860. This doubling of per capita income over a 40-year period suggests that many Americans were enjoying a rising standard of living.

As the Warners discovered so dramatically, economic expansion was unpredictable. Periods of boom (1822–1834, mid-1840s–1850s) alternated with periods of bust (1816–1821, 1837–1843). As never before, Americans faced dramatic and recurrent shifts in the availability of jobs and goods and in prices and wages. Particularly at risk were working-class Americans, a third of whom lost their jobs during years of depression. Moreover, because regional economies were increasingly linked, problems in one area tended to affect conditions in others.

The Trans-Atlantic Context for Growth

American economic growth was linked to and influenced by events elsewhere in the world, particularly in Great Britain. Britain was the home of the Industrial Revolution, the event that some historians believe to be among the most important of human history in terms of its impact on material life. For the first time, production of goods proceeded at a faster pace than the growth of population.

The industrial revolution that began in Britain in the eighteenth century was a complex process involving many technological innovations that spurred new developments and efficiencies. Among the most important developments was the discovery in the 1780s of a way to eliminate carbon and other substances from pig iron. This opened the way for cheap, durable iron machines that led to the increased production of goods. Another milestone, the improvement of the steam engine, originally used to pump water out of coal mines, eventually led to railroads and steamboats, thus revolutionizing transportation. Steam-powered machinery also transformed the production of cloth, moving it from cottages to factories. The British textile industry was the giant of the early Industrial Revolution. The use of machinery allowed the production of more and cheaper textiles. The industry became a prime market for American cotton as well as cotton from India and Brazil. British demand for raw cotton helped to cement the South's attachment to slavery.

By 1850, Great Britain was the most powerful country in the world, and its citizens were the richest. In following decades, its factories and mines were churning out most of the world's coal and over half of its iron and textiles. Not surprisingly, Americans would look to England and English know-how as they embarked on their own course of industrialization. While American industrial development did not mimic the British, there were many similarities between the two countries' experiences.

Other global trends affected the United States. In the late eighteenth century, Europe experienced an unprecedented burst of population growth. Behind the spurt lay the disappearance of deadly epidemics like the plague, continuing agricultural improvements that led to large harvests, and the cultivation of New World foods like white potatoes and corn. These crops yielded more per acre than traditional European crops and thus may have been the most important factor in the sudden surge of population.

With about 188 million people in 1800, Europe became a source of immigration to the United States and helped fill its needs for labor.

Factors Fueling Economic Development

The United States enjoyed abundant natural resources that facilitated economic changes and, thanks to European immigration, the expanding population necessary for economic expansion. The size of American families was shrinking—in 1800, the average white woman bore seven children; by 1860, the number had declined to five. Thus immigration from Europe provided the new workers, new households, and new consumers so essential to economic development as well as the capital and technological ideas that helped to shape American growth.

Improved transportation played a key role in bringing about economic and geographic expansion. Early in the century, high freight rates discouraged production for distant markets and the exploitation of resources, while primitive transportation hindered western settlement. Canal-building projects in the 1820s and 1830s dramatically transformed this situation. The 363-mile-long Erie Canal, the last link in a chain of waterways binding New York City to the Great Lakes and the Northwest, was the most

Significant Factors Promoting Economic Growth, 1820–1860

Factor	Important Features	Contribution to Growth
Abundant natural resources	Acquisition of new territories (Louisiana Purchase, Florida, trans-Mississippi West); exploitation and discovery of eastern resources	Provided raw materials and energy vital to economic transformation
Substantial population growth	Increase from 9 million in 1820 to over 30 million in 1860—due to natural increase of population and, especially after 1840, to rising immigration; importance of immigration from Ireland, Germany	Provided workers and consumers necessary for economic growth; immigration increased diversity of workforce with complex results, among them supply of capital and technological know-how
Transportation revolution	Improvement of roads; extensive canal building, 1817–1837; increasing importance of railroad construction thereafter; by 1860, 30,000 miles of tracks; steamboats facilitate travel on water	Facilitated movement of peoples, goods, and information; drew people into national economy market; stimulated agricultural expansion, regional crop specialization; decreased costs of shipping goods; strengthened ties between Northeast and Midwest
Capital investment	Investments by European investors and U.S. interests; importance of mercantile capital and banks, insurance companies in funneling capital to economic enterprises	Provided capital to support variety of new economic enterprises, improvements in transportation
Government support	Local, state, and national legislation; loans favoring enterprise; judicial decisions	Provided capital, privileges, and supportive climate for economic enterprises
Industrialization	New methods of producing goods, with and without involvement of machinery	Produced more numerous, cheaper goods for mass market; transformed classes and nature of work; affected distribution of wealth and individual opportunity

impressive of these new canals. The volume of goods and people it carried at low cost as well as the economic advantages it conferred on those within its reach (suggested by both the figure on inland freight rates and the table on economic growth) prompted the construction of over 3,000 miles of canals by 1840, primarily in eastern and midwestern states.

Even at the height of the canal boom, politicians, promoters, and others, impressed with Britain's success with steam-powered railways, also supported the construction of railroads. Unlike canals that might freeze during the winter, railroads could operate year-round and could be built almost anywhere. These advantages encouraged Baltimore merchants, envious of New York's water link to the Northwest, to begin the Baltimore & Ohio Railroad in 1828.

Despite the interest in and advantages of railroads, there were technical problems: the first trains jumped their tracks and spewed sparks, setting nearby fields ablaze. But such difficulties were quickly overcome. By 1840, there were 3,000 miles of track, more than in all the countries of Europe. Another 5,000 miles were laid during the 1840s, and by the end of the 1850s, total mileage soared to 30,000. Like the canals, the new railroads strengthened the links between the Old Northwest and the East.

Improved transportation so profoundly influenced American life that some historians use the term *transportation revolution* to refer to its impact. Canals and railroads bound the country together in a new way. They provided farmers, merchants, and manufacturers with cheap and reliable access to distant markets and goods and encouraged Americans to settle the frontier and cultivate virgin lands. The economic opportunities they opened fostered technological innovations that could increase production. Eventually, the strong economic and social ties the waterways and then the railways fostered between the Northwest and the East led people living in the two regions to share political outlooks.

Railroads exerted enormous influence, especially in terms of the pattern of western settlement. As the railroads followed—or led—settlers westward, their routes could determine whether a city, town, or even homestead survived. The railroad transformed Chicago from a small settlement into a bustling commercial and transportation center. In 1850, the city contained not one mile of track, but within five years, 2,200 miles of track serving 150,000 square miles terminated in Chicago.

The dramatic rise in railroad construction in the two decades before the Civil War contributed to

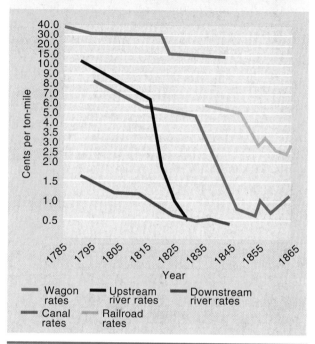

Inland Freight Rates

As this chart makes dramatically clear, the transportation revolution had a tremendous impact on the cost of shipping goods and materials to markets and factories.

faster economic growth after 1839. Goods, people, commercial information, and mail flowed ever more predictably, rapidly, and cheaply. In 1790, an order from Boston took two weeks to reach Philadelphia; in 1836, it took only 36 hours.

Improved transportation stimulated agricultural expansion and regional specialization. Farmers began to plant larger crops for the market, concentrating on those most suited to their soil and climate. By the late 1830s, the Old Northwest had become the country's granary, and New England farmers turned to dairy or produce farming. In 1860, American farmers were producing four to five times as much wheat, corn, cattle, and hogs as they had in 1810. Their achievements meant plentiful, cheap food for American workers and more income for farmers to spend on the new consumer goods.

Capital and Government Support

Internal improvements, the exploitation of natural resources, and the cultivation of new lands all demanded capital. Between 1790 and 1861, over $500 million in foreign capital, most of it from Great Britain, was invested in state bonds, transportation, and land. Foreign investors financed as much as

The Transportation Revolution

This map shows the impact of the transportation revolution. Note the components of that revolution: roads, canals, and then railroad lines. What were the important regional connections opened up by transportation improvements? How would you compare northern and southern development? What were the commercial results of the new transportation networks?

one-third of all canal construction and bought about one-quarter of all railroad bonds.

American mercantile capital fueled growth as well. As Chapter 8 suggested, the merchant class prospered in the half century after the Revolution. Now merchants invested in schemes ranging from canals

to textile factories. Many ventured into the production of goods and became manufacturers themselves. Other prosperous Americans also eagerly sought opportunities to put their capital to work.

Local and state government played their part by enthusiastically supporting economic growth. States

This view of the junction of the Erie and Champlain Canals around 1830 suggests the ambitious construction efforts that lay behind the improvement of transportation. The Erie Canal stretched for 363 miles and was the last link in a chain of waterways connecting New York to the Great Lakes and the Northwest. Irish immigrants who flooded into the country during the antebellum period provided the muscle power for building the Erie Canal and worked on many other transportation projects. One of the laborers' songs captures the pride and magnitude of "such a great undertaking. . . . To dig through the vallies so level, through rocks for to cut a canal." *(© Collection of the New-York Historical Society)*

often helped new ventures raise capital by passing laws of incorporation, by awarding entrepreneurs special privileges such as tax breaks or monopolistic control, by underwriting bonds for improvement projects, which increased their investment appeal, and by providing loans for internal improvements. New York, Pennsylvania, Ohio, Indiana, Illinois, and Virginia publicly financed almost 75 percent of the canal systems in their states between 1815 and 1860.

The national government also encouraged economic expansion by cooperating with states on some internal improvements, such as the National Road linking Maryland and Illinois. Federal tariff policy shielded American products, and the Second Bank of the United States provided the financial stability investors required. So widespread was the enthusiasm for growth that the line separating the public sector from the private often became unclear.

The law also helped promote aggressive economic growth. Judicial decisions created a new understanding of property rights. The case of *Palmer* v. *Mulligan,* decided by the New York State Supreme Court in 1805, laid down the principle that property ownership included the right to develop property for business purposes. Land was increasingly defined as a productive asset for exploitation, not merely subsistence, as earlier judicial rulings had suggested.

Investors and business operators alike wanted to increase predictability in the conduct of business. Contracts lay at the heart of commercial relationships, but contract law hardly existed in 1800. A period of rapid development ensued. A series of important Supreme Court decisions between 1819 and 1824 established the basic principle that contracts were binding. In *Dartmouth College* v. *Woodward,* the Court held that a state charter could not be modified unless both parties agreed, and it declared in *Sturges* v. *Crowninshield* that a New York law allowing debtors to repudiate their debts was unconstitutional.

A New Mentality

As the discussion of the links between law and economic growth suggests, economic expansion depends on intangible factors as well as more obvious ones such as improved transportation. When a farmer decided to specialize in apples for the New York market rather than to concentrate on raising food for his family, he was thinking in a new way, much like those who invested in banks that would, in turn, finance a variety of economic enterprises. The entrepreneurial outlook, or as one newspaper editor put it, the *"universal desire to get forward,"* was shared by millions of Americans. By encouraging investment, new business and agricultural ventures, and land speculation, entrepreneurialism played a vital role in antebellum economic development.

Europeans often recognized another intangible factor when they described Americans as energetic and open to change. As one Frenchman explained in 1834, "All here is circulation, motion, and boiling agitation. Experiment follows experiment; enterprise succeeds to enterprise." An American observer agreed: "Every man seems born with some steam engine within him, driving him into an incessant and restless activity of body and mind . . . every head and every hand busy, with a thousand projects, . . . working from morning till night with the most intense industry."

Others described an American mechanical "genius." The American was "a mechanic by nature," one Frenchman insisted. "In Massachusetts and Connecticut, there is not a labourer who had not invented a machine or tool." This observer exaggerated the uniqueness of American inventiveness. Many American innovations drew on British precedents and were introduced by immigrants well acquainted with the British originals. Nor was every ordinary laborer an inventor. Many of the changes that improved efficiency came from machinists as they made adjustments to British equipment or tinkered with malfunctioning mill machines to get them back in working order. But every invention and improvement attracted scores of imitators. In 1854, the government patent office issued 56 patents for harvesting implements and 39 for seed planters; the next year, it issued 40 for sewing machines.

Mechanically minded Americans prided themselves on developing efficient and productive tools and machines. The McCormick harvester was the product of two generations of the McCormick family who dreamed of replacing scythes and sickles with a horsedrawn reaping machine and worked for years to realize that dream. Like the McCormicks, John Jervis experimented for years to modify the heavy, rigid English railroad engine into a lighter, more flexible engine suited to American conditions. The Colt revolver, Goodyear vulcanized rubber products, and the sewing machine were developed, refined, and developed further. Such improvements cut labor costs and increased efficiency. By 1840, the average American cotton textile mill was about 10 percent more efficient and 3 percent more profitable than its British counterpart.

Although the shortage of labor in the United States stimulated technological innovations that replaced humans with machines, the rapid spread of education after 1800 also contributed to innovation and increased productivity. By 1840, most whites

were literate. In that year, public schools nationwide were educating 38.4 percent of white children between the ages of 5 and 19. The belief that education spurred economic growth helped foster enthusiasm for public education, particularly in the Northeast. The development of the Massachusetts common school illustrates the connections many saw between education and progress.

Although several states had decided to use tax monies for education by 1800, Massachusetts moved first toward mass education by mandating in 1827 that taxes pay the whole cost of the state's public schools. Several years later, the state set up a permanent elementary education fund and in 1836 forbade factory managers to hire children who had not spent three of the previous twelve months in school. Despite the legislation, the Massachusetts school system limped along. School buildings were often run-down, even unheated. Because school curricula were virtually nonexistent, students often lounged idly at their desks.

Under the leadership of Horace Mann, the reform of state education for white children began in earnest in 1837. Mann intended to regularize the

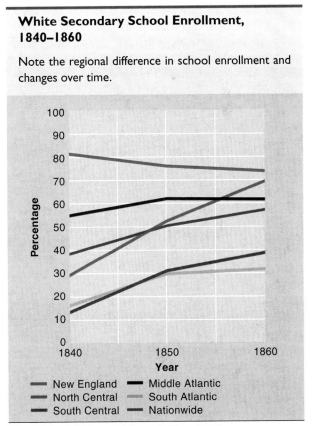

White Secondary School Enrollment, 1840–1860

Note the regional difference in school enrollment and changes over time.

Source: Albert W. Niemi, *U.S. Economic History* (1975).

operation of schools and attract more students to them. He and others pressed for graded schools, uniform curricula, teacher training, and a school year of at least six months. Believing that the power of local districts over their schools prevented improvement, he sought to reduce local control. Mann's success inspired reformers elsewhere in the country. For the first time in American history, primary education became the rule for over half of white children between the ages of 5 and 19 outside the South. The expansion of education created a whole new career of schoolteaching that attracted mostly young women.

Mann believed that education promoted inventiveness. It "had a market value." Businessmen often agreed. Prominent industrialists in the 1840s were convinced that education produced workers who could handle complex machinery without undue supervision and were superior employees—reliable, punctual, industrious, and sober. Manufacturers valued education not merely because of its intellectual content but also because it encouraged habits essential to a disciplined and productive workforce.

Ambivalence Toward Change

While supporting education as a means to economic growth, many Americans, like their European counterparts, also firmly believed in its social value. They expected the public schools to mold student character and promote "virtuous habits" and "rational self-governing" behavior. Many school activities sought to instill good habits. Students learned facts by rote because memory work and recitation taught them discipline and concentration. Nineteenth-century schoolbooks reinforced classroom goals. "It is a great sin to be idle," children read in one 1830 text, and another encouragingly pointed out, "He who rises early and is industrious and temperate will acquire health and riches."

The concern with education and character indicates that Americans both welcomed economic progress and feared its results. The improvements in transportation that encouraged trade and emigration, for example, created anxieties that civilization might disintegrate as people moved far from their place of birth and familiar institutions. Others worried that rapid change undermined the American family. Schools, which taught students to be deferential, obedient, and punctual, could counter the worst by-products of change. The schools served as much as a defense against change as they did its agent.

Other signs of cultural uneasiness appeared. In the eighteenth century, Benjamin Franklin emphasized the importance of hard work in his celebrated *Poor Richard's Almanack.* In the 1830s, popularizers restated Franklin's message. As the publishing revolution lowered costs and speeded the production of printed material, authors poured out tracts, stories, and manuals on how to get ahead. Claiming that hard work and good character led to success, they touted the virtues of diligence, punctuality, temperance, and thrift. These habits probably did assist economic growth. Slothful workers are seldom productive. Industry and perseverance often pay off. But the success of early nineteenth-century economic ventures frequently depended on the ability to take risks and to think daringly. The emphasis these publicists gave to the safe but stolid virtues and behavior suggests their fear of social disintegration. Their books and tracts aimed to counter unsettling effects of change and ensure the dominance of middle-class values.

The Advance of Industrialization

As had been true for Great Britain in the eighteenth century, the advance of industrialization in the United States fueled economic growth in the decades before the Civil War. As was also the case in Britain, economic changes spilled over to transform many other aspects of life. The types of work people did, the places where they labored, the relationships they had with their bosses were all affected by new modes of production. The American class system was modified as a new working class dependent on wages emerged and as a new middle class took shape.

Factory production moved away from the decentralized system of artisan or family-based manufacturing using hand tools and reorganized work by breaking down the manufacture of an article into

This daguerreotype shows a blacksmith, surrounded by his tools, hammering a horseshoe on an anvil. Some workers, like blacksmiths, continued to work in traditional ways, almost untouched by the advent of industrialization. Others found their work life dramatically changed as machines replaced some of the tasks once done by hand. *(The Library of Congress, LC-USZC4-4075)*

discrete steps. Initially, early manufacturers often relied on what came to be called the "putting-out" system. Their strategy was to gain control of the raw materials from which goods were fashioned—leather in the case of shoes; cotton, flax, and wool for textiles—and the arrangements for marketing the finished products. Some steps in the manufacturing process they farmed out to workers in shops and homes, paying them on a piecework basis, for the pieces they were able to "put out." Manufacturers consolidated other steps in their own central shops.

The putting-out system not only reorganized production but also entangled rural families in the market economy and affected their relationships with one another. Early pieceworkers might labor as a family unit, leaving men to exercise their power as fathers and husbands. But by the 1830s, men were moving into the workplace, while wives and daughters continued to take in piecework. Usually, the women worked only intermittently. They took in shoes or made palm-leaf hats to pay off a family debt or to earn some cash for a desirable new good like cotton cloth or an iron cook stove. While most outworkers were not highly paid, they enjoyed earning their own cash and store credit. Piecework provided them with a new kind of independence even as they continued to stay at home.

The putting-out system persisted even as some manufacturers moved to consolidate all the steps of production under one roof. Hand labor gradually gave way to power-driven machinery such as wooden "spinning jennies." Often manufacturers sought the help of British immigrants who had the practical experience and technical know-how that few Americans possessed. As factory workers replaced artisans and home manufacturers, the volume of goods rose, and prices dropped dramatically. The price of a yard of cotton cloth fell from 18 to 2 cents over the 45 years preceding the Civil War.

The transportation improvements that provided the opportunity to reach large markets encouraged the reorganization of the production process and the use of machinery. The simple tastes and rural character of the American people suggested the wisdom of manufacturing inexpensive everyday goods like cloth and shoes rather than luxuries for the rich.

Between 1820 and 1860, textile manufacturing became the country's leading industry. Textile mills sprang up across the New England and Middle Atlantic states, regions with swift-flowing streams to power the mills, capitalists eager to finance the ventures, children and women to tend the machines, and numerous cities and towns with ready markets for cheap textiles. Early mills were small affairs, containing only the machines for carding and spinning.

The thread was then put out to home workers to be woven into cloth. The early mechanization of cloth production did not replace home manufacture but supplemented it.

Experiments were underway that would further transform the industry. Closeted in the attic of a Boston house in 1813, Francis Cabot Lowell, a merchant, and Paul Moody, a mechanic, worked to devise a power loom capable of weaving cloth. Lowell's study of mechanical looms during his earlier tour of English and Scottish cotton factories guided their work. Eventually, they succeeded, and the loom they devised was soon installed in a mill at Waltham, Massachusetts, capitalized at $300,000 by Lowell and his Boston Associates.

The most important innovation of the Waltham operation was Lowell's decision to bring all the steps of cotton cloth production together under one roof. The Waltham mill thus differed from mills in Rhode Island and Great Britain, where spinning and weaving were separate operations. Through this centralizing of the entire manufacturing process and workforce in one factory, cloth for the mass market could be produced more cheaply and more profitably. The work of maintaining the equipment in good order encouraged machinists to improve upon existing machines. Constant innovation thus helped mills to make cloth ever more cheaply and quickly. In 1823, the Boston Associates expanded their operations to East Chelmsford on the Merrimack River, a town they renamed Lowell.

Most New England mills followed the Lowell system. But in the Middle Atlantic states, the textile industry was more varied. Philadelphia became a center for fine textiles, and Rhode Island factories produced less expensive materials. Maryland manufacturers, like those in Philadelphia, focused on quality goods. The cumulative impact of the rise of the textile industry was to supplant the home production of cloth, even though some women would continue to spin and weave for their families for some years to come, and hand-loom weavers would survive for another generation. In the process, Americans were transformed from a people clad in earth-colored homespun into a nation decked out in more colorful clothing.

Textile mills were an important component of the increasingly industrial character of the Northeast. The majority of the South's cotton went to England, but an increasing share flowed to northeastern mills. Other manufacturing concerns, such as shoemaking, also contributed to the Northeast's economy. By 1860, fully 71 percent of all manufacturing workers lived in this region of the country. Still other important manufacturing operations reached west

The Growth of Cotton Textile Manufacturing, 1810–1840

The concentration of textile manufacturing in New England suggests the changing economic and social trends in that region.

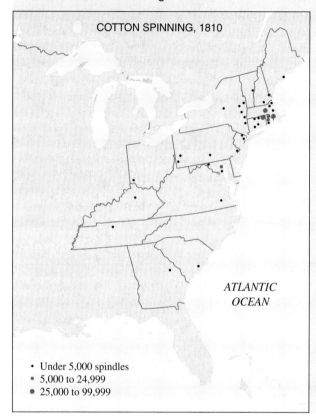

COTTON SPINNING, 1810

- Under 5,000 spindles
- 5,000 to 24,999
- 25,000 to 99,999

ATLANTIC OCEAN

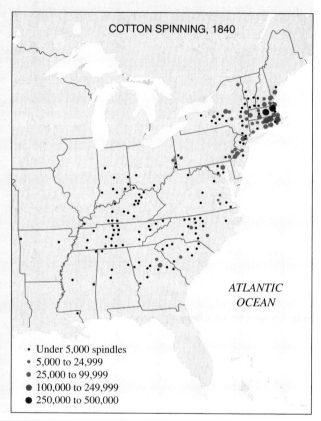

COTTON SPINNING, 1840

- Under 5,000 spindles
- 5,000 to 24,999
- 25,000 to 99,999
- 100,000 to 249,999
- 250,000 to 500,000

ATLANTIC OCEAN

and south from New England. The processing of wheat, timber, and hides using power-driven machinery was common in most communities of 200 families or more. Although one-third of them were clustered in Philadelphia, paper mills were widespread. The ironworking and metalworking industry stretched from Albany, New York, south to Maryland, and west to Cincinnati.

Environmental Consequences

Although canals, railroads, steamboats, and the growth of industry undergirded economic growth, their impact on the environment was far-reaching and often harmful. Steamboats and early railroads, for example, depended on wood for fuel. So, too, did home heating stoves. Armed with new steel axes, lumbermen and farmers kept up with the increased demand for wood, and the eastern forest and the wildlife that lived there rapidly disappeared. Better transportation, which encouraged western settlement, also promoted forest clearance as individual settlers cleared land for crops and cut wood for housing. Sawmills and milldams interfered with

spawning habits of fish, clogged their gills with sawdust, and even changed the flow of rivers. The process of ecological change, spurred by the desire for wood, recurred as lumber companies and entrepreneurs moved from the East to exploit the forests of the Great Lakes and the Gulf states.

As late as 1840, wood was the main source for the country's energy needs. But the high price of wood and the discovery of anthracite coal in Pennsylvania signaled the beginning of a shift to coal as the major source of power. While the East gradually regained some of its forest cover, the heavy use of coal resulted in air pollution. Steam engines and heating stoves poured out dirty fumes into the air. In New York City, one could see the evidence of pollution everywhere—in the gray cloud hanging over the city; in the smoke rising from its machine shops, refineries, and private houses; and in the acrid smells and black soot that were a part of daily life. Pittsburgh, considered by some the dirtiest city in the United States, was surrounded by "a dense black smoke" and rained down "flakes of soot" on houses and people alike.

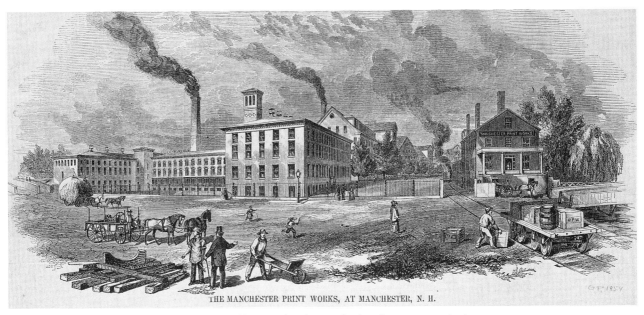

Gleason's Pictorial, one of the many modestly priced publications that the introduction of steam-powered printing presses put within reach of the reading public, pictures the Manchester Print Works in New Hampshire in 1854. Although the smokestacks spewing forth black clouds of smoke hint at the pollution that accompanied the Industrial Revolution, nineteenth-century viewers most likely were impressed by the dignified mill building and the seemingly spacious surroundings. Men appear in the foreground, but over half the workers in this calico factory were female. *(Library of Congress)*

Textile mills located along rivers and streams might present a prettier picture than the shops and refineries of New York because they used water as the source of power. But mills also adversely affected the environment. Dams and canals supporting industrial activities contributed to soil erosion. "Industrial operations," declared the Vermont fish commissioner in 1857, are "destructive to fish that live or spawn in fresh water. . . . The thousand deleterious mineral substances, discharged into rivers from metallurgical, chemical, and manufacturing establishments, poison them by shoals."

Some Americans were aware of the environmental consequences of rapid growth and change. Author James Fenimore Cooper had one of his characters in his novel *The Pioneers* condemn those who destroyed nature "without remorse and without shame." The popularity in the 1820s of a song with the lines "Woodman, / Spare that Tree / Touch not a single bough" suggested sympathy for that point of view. Yet most Americans accepted the changing environment as an inevitable part of progress.

EARLY MANUFACTURING

Industrialization created a more efficient means of producing more goods at much lower cost than had been possible in the homes and small shops of an

earlier day. Philadelphian Samuel Breck's diary reveals some of the new profusion and range of goods. "Went to town principally to see the Exhibition of American Manufactures at the Masonic Hall," he noted in 1833. "More than 700 articles have been sent. . . . porcelains, beautiful Canton cotton . . . soft and capacious blankets, silver plate, cabinet ware, marble mantels, splendid pianos and centre tables, chymical drugs, hardware, saddlery, and the most beautiful black broadcloth I ever saw."

Two examples illustrate how industrialization transformed American life in both simple and complex ways. Before the nineteenth century, local printing shops depended on manual labor to produce books, newspapers, and journals. The cost of reading material was high enough to make a library a sign of wealth. Many literate families of moderate means had little in their homes to read other than a family Bible and an almanac.

Between 1830 and 1850, however, adoption and improvement of British inventions revolutionized the printing and publishing industries. Like other changes in production, the transformation of publishing involved not only technological but also managerial and marketing innovations. A $2.5 million market in 1830, the book business quintupled by 1850.

As books and magazines dropped in cost and grew in number, far more people could afford them.

Without this new mass market of readers, Susan Warner's literary success would hardly have been possible. But the implications of the changes in publishing went beyond bestsellers. The presence of inexpensive reading material inspired and nourished literacy. Easy access to reading material also encouraged a new sort of independence. No longer needing to rely solely on the words of the "better sort" for information, people could form their own views on the basis of what they read. At the same time, however, readers everywhere were exposed repeatedly to the mainstream norms, values, and ideas expressed in magazines and books. Even on the frontier, pioneer women could study inexpensive ladies' magazines and books of domestic advice or be inspired by the pious example of Ellen Montgomery in *The Wide, Wide World*. Their husbands could follow the latest political news, market prices, or theories about scientific farming while the children learned their letters and the moral lesson in McGuffey readers. The proliferation of printed matter had an enormous impact on people's stock of information, values, tastes, and use of leisure time.

Just as printed materials wrought great changes in American life, the making of inexpensive timepieces affected its pace and rhythms. Before the 1830s, when few Americans could afford a clock, it was difficult to make exact plans or to establish rigid schedules. But the production of timepieces soared in the 1830s, and by mid-century, peddlers had carried inexpensive, mass-produced wooden clocks everywhere. Even on the frontier, "in cabins where there was not a chair to sit on," according to one observer, "there was sure to be a Connecticut clock." Free of nature's irregular divisions of the day, Americans could decide how to use their time and coordinate their activities. Clocks encouraged a more disciplined use of time and undergirded the economic changes taking place. Timepieces, for example, were essential for the successful operation of steamboats and railroads, which ran on schedules.

Clocks also imposed a new rhythm in many workplaces. For some Americans, the clock represented a form of oppression rather than liberation. An early mill song put it directly: "The factory bell begins to ring / And we must all obey, / And to our old employment go / Or else be turned away."

A NEW ENGLAND TEXTILE TOWN

The process of industrialization and its impact on work and the workforce are ably illustrated by Lowell, the "model" Massachusetts textile town, and Cincinnati, a bustling midwestern industrial center.

Though there were similarities between the process of industrialization in these two communities, significant differences also existed. The example of Lowell points out the importance of women in the early manufacturing workforce, whereas Cincinnati shows the uneven pace of industrialization.

Lowell was a town, planned and built expressly for industrial purposes in the 1820s. Planners gave most attention to the shops, mills, and workers' housing, but the bustling town had a charm that prompted visitors to see it as a model factory community. In 1836, Lowell, with 17,000 inhabitants, aspired to become the "Manchester of America." It was the country's most important textile center.

Lowell's planners realized the difficulty of persuading men to leave farming for millwork but saw that they might recruit unmarried women relatively cheaply for a stint. Unlike mill owners farther south, they decided not to depend on child labor. By hiring women who would work only until marriage, they hoped to avoid the depraved and depressed workforce so evident in Great Britain. They hoped that New England factory communities, because of their special arrangements, would become models for the world.

By 1830, women composed nearly 70 percent of the Lowell textile workforce, with men and children filling the remaining positions. The women who came to Lowell for jobs were the first women to work outside their homes in large numbers. Some had already labored for wages by taking in piecework. Now they became some of the first Americans to experience the full impact of the factory system.

Working and Living in a Mill Town

At the age of 15, Mary Paul wrote to her father asking him "to consent to let me go to Lowell if you can." This young Vermont woman was typical of those flocking to Lowell and other New England textile towns. As the planners had anticipated, the bulk of the workforce was made up of young unmarried women, most between the ages of 15 and 29.

These women, from New England's middling rural families, came to the mills for a variety of reasons, but desperate poverty was not one of them. The decline of home manufacture deprived many women, especially daughters in farming families, of their traditional productive role. Some rural young women took in piecework to replace or supplement regular chores. Millwork offered them more money than piecework, as well as the possibility of independence. As Sally Rice from Vermont explained, "I am almost nineteen years old. I must of course have something of my own before many more years have

This depiction of Lowell workers, engraved in the 1850s by the American Banknote company, shows neatly dressed young women carefully tending to their machines. Their concentration on their task suggests that they had to pay close attention to their repetitive work. The engraving gives little idea of the tedium, noise, and other difficulties of millwork that the young women often mentioned in their letters. *(Print Collection, Miriam and Ira D. Wallach Division of Art, Prints and Photographs. The New York Public Library, Astor, Lenox and Tilden Foundations)*

passed over my head." Early millwork paid women relatively well. Domestic servants' weekly wages hovered around 75 cents, and seamstresses' 90 cents, whereas in the mid-1830s, women could make between $2.40 and $3.20 a week in the mill. The lure of the "privileges" of the new environment also drew young women to Lowell.

Few considered their decision to come to Lowell a permanent commitment. Most young women were like Mary Paul and Sally Rice. They came to work for a few years, felt free to go home or to school for a few months, and then returned to millwork. Once married—and the majority of women did marry—they left the millwork force forever.

New manufacturing work was regimented and exhausting. The day began at dawn or even earlier and ended about 7 in the evening. The standard schedule was 12 hours a day, 6 days a week, with only a half-hour for breakfast and lunch. The clock tower atop the attractive four- to six-story brick mills symbolized the new control of work.

Within the factory, the organization of space facilitated production. In the basement was the waterwheel, which was the source of power (unlike Britain, where the steam engine was used). Above, successive floors were completely open, each containing the machines necessary for the different steps of cloth making: carding, spinning, weaving, and dressing. Elevators moved materials from one floor to another. On a typical floor, rows of machines stretched the length of the low room, tended by operatives who might watch over several machines at the same time. From his elevated desk at the end of the room, the overseer watched the workers. The male supervisor and two or three children roamed the aisles to survey the work and to help out. The rooms were noisy, poorly lit, and badly ventilated. Overseers, believing that humidity would prevent threads from breaking, often nailed the windows shut.

Although machines, not operatives, did the basic work of production, workers had to ensure that their machines worked properly. The lowest-paid women workers who watched over the spinning frames and drawing frames pieced together broken yarn once the machines had automatically halted. The better-paid weavers made skillful interventions in the production process, repairing warp yarns and rapidly replacing shuttle bobbins when they ran out of yarn so that production would slow down for only a moment. "I can see myself now," recalled Harriet Robbins, "racing down the alley, between the spinning frames, carrying in front of me a bobbin-box bigger than I was . . . so as not to keep the spinning-frames stopped long."

Involving an adaptation to a new work situation, millwork also entailed a new living situation for women operatives. The companies provided substantial quarters for their overseers and housing for male workers and their families. Hoping to attract respectable females to Lowell and to avoid English-style industrial slums, the mill owners constructed company boardinghouses for women workers. Headed by female housekeepers, the boardinghouse maintained strict rules, including a 10 o'clock curfew to ensure a well-rested workforce. Little personal privacy was possible. Normally, four or six women shared a small room, which contained little more than the double beds in which they slept together.

Amid such intimate working and living conditions, young women formed close ties with one another and developed a strong sense of community. Strong group norms dictated acceptable behavior, clothing, and speech and shared leisure activities at lectures, night classes, sewing and literary circles, and church. At work, experienced operatives initiated newcomers into the mysteries of tending machines, stood in for each other, and shared work assignments.

Female Responses to Work

Although millwork offered better wages than other occupations open to women, all female workers had limited job mobility. The small number staying in the mills for more than a few years did receive increases in pay and promotions to more responsible positions. A top female wage earner took home 40 percent more than a newcomer. But she never could earn as much as male employees, who at the top of the job ladder earned 200 percent more than men at the bottom. Because only men could hold supervisory positions, economic and job discrimination characterized the early American industrial system.

Job discrimination generally went unquestioned, for most female operatives accepted gender differences as part of life. But the sense of sisterhood, so much a part of the Lowell work experience, supported open protest, most of it focused against a system that workers feared was turning them into a class of dependent wage earners. Lowell women's critique of the new industrial order drew on both the sense of female community and the revolutionary tradition and exposed the social gap between owners and operatives.

Trouble broke out when hard times hit Lowell in February 1834. Falling prices, poor sales, and rising inventories prompted managers to announce a 15 percent wage cut. This was their way of protecting profits—at the expense of their employees. The millworkers sprang into action. Petitions circulated, threatening a strike. Meetings followed. At one lunchtime gathering, when the company agent fired an apparent ringleader, "she declared that every girl in the room should leave with her," then "made a signal, and . . . they all marched out & few returned the ensuing morning." The strikers roamed the streets, appealing to other workers, and they visited other mills. In all, about a sixth of the town's workforce turned out.

Though this work stoppage was brief, involved only a minority of workers, and failed to prevent the wage reduction, it demonstrated some women's concern about the impact of industrialization on the labor force. Strikers, taunted as unfeminine for their "amazonian display," refused to agree that workers were inferior to bosses. Pointing out that they were daughters of free men, strikers (as the words of their song suggest) sought to link their

protest to their fathers' and grandfathers' efforts to throw off the bonds of British oppression during the Revolution.

Let oppression shrug her shoulders,
And a haughty tyrant frown,
And little upstart Ignorance,
In mockery look down.
Yet I value not the feeble threats
Of Tories in disguise,
While the flag of Independence
O'er our noble nation flies.

The women viewed threatened wage reductions as an unjust attack on their economic independence and also on their claim to equal status with their employers. Revolutionary rhetoric that once held only political meaning took on economic overtones as Lowell women confronted industrial work.

During the 1830s, wage cuts, long hours, increased workloads, and production speedups, mandated by owners' desires to protect profits, constantly reminded Lowell women and other textile workers of the possibility of "wage slavery." In Dover, New Hampshire, 800 women turned out and formed a union in 1834 to protest wage cuts. In the 1840s, women in several New England states agitated for the 10-hour day, and petitions from Lowell prompted the Massachusetts legislature to hold the first government hearing on industrial working conditions.

The Changing Character of the Workforce

Most protest efforts met with limited success. The short tenure of most women millworkers prevented permanent labor organizations. Protests mounted in hard times often failed because mill owners could easily replace striking workers. Increasingly, owners found that they could do without the Yankee women altogether. The waves of immigration in the 1840s and 1850s created a new pool of labor. The newcomers were desperate for jobs and would accept lower wages than New England farm girls. Gradually, the Irish began to replace Yankee women in the mills. Representing only 8 percent of the Lowell workforce in 1845, the Irish composed nearly half the workers by 1860.

As the example of Lowell suggests, the reality of massive immigration had a far-reaching effect on American life in the antebellum period. Immigration, of course, had been a constant part of the country's experience from the early seventeenth century. But it occurred on an unprecedented scale after 1845, as the nearby figure makes clear. What had been a trickle in the 1820s—some 128,502 for-

Immigration: Volume and Sources, 1840–1860

This chart captures the growing ethnic diversity of the country in the years before the Civil War. What is only implied is the element of religious diversity that immigration also introduced. Most of the Irish immigrants and half of the Germans were Roman Catholics. The presence of immigrants who differed so dramatically from Protestant Americans in background and culture contributed to the tensions of the period.

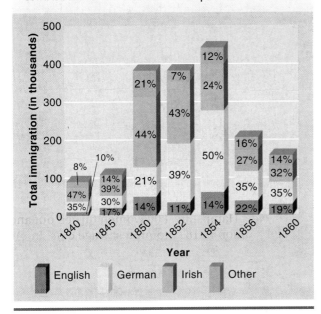

eigners came to U.S. shores during that decade—became a torrent in the 1850s, with more than 2.8 million migrants to the United States. Although families and single women emigrated, the majority of the newcomers were young European men of working age.

This vast movement of people, which began in the 1840s and continued throughout the nineteenth century, resulted from Europe's population explosion and the new farming and industrial practices that undermined or ended traditional means of livelihood. Poverty and the lack of opportunity heightened the appeal of leaving home. As one Scottish woman wrote to an American friend in 1847, "we can not mak it better [here]. All that we can duo is if you can give us any encouragement [is] to ama[grate?] to your Country."

Famine uprooted the largest group of immigrants: the Irish. In 1845, a terrible blight attacked and destroyed the potato crop, the staple of the Irish diet. Years of devastating hunger followed. One million Irish starved to death between 1841 and 1851; another million and a half emigrated. Although not all came to the United States, those

who did arrived almost penniless in eastern port cities without the skills needed for good jobs. With only their raw labor to sell, employers, as one observer noted, "will engage Paddy as they would a dray horse." Yet, limited as their opportunities were, immigrants saved money to send home to help their families or to pay for their passage to the United States.

German immigrants, the second largest group of newcomers during this period (1,361,506 arrived between 1840 and 1859), were not facing such drastic conditions. But as Henry Brokmeyer observed, "Hunger brought me . . . here [and] hunger is the cause of European immigration to this country." Some Germans, however, arrived with sufficient resources to go west and buy land. (The significance of this German midwestern presence is suggested by the fact that as late as 1940, German was one of the most common "street" languages in Minnesota.) Others like Brokmeyer had the training to join the urban working class as shoemakers or as cabinetmakers or tailors.

The arrival of so many non-British newcomers made American society more diverse than it had ever been. The consequences of this diversity were complex, as discussions in this and subsequent chapters will make clear. Because over half of the Irish and German immigrants were Roman Catholics, a religion long feared and disliked by Protestants, religious differences acerbated economic and ethnic tensions.

The impact of the Irish presence in Lowell was far-reaching. As the ethnic makeup of the workforce changed in the city, so did its gender composition. More men came to work in the mills. By 1860, some 30 percent of the Lowell workers were male. All these changes made the Yankee women expendable and increased the costs of going "against the mill."

It was easy for New England women to blame the Irish for declining pay and deteriorating conditions. Gender no longer unified women workers, not only because there were more men in the mills but also because Irish women and New England women had little in common. The Irish mill girl who started working as early as age 13 to earn money for her family's survival had a different perspective on work than the older Yankee woman who was earning money for herself. Segregated living conditions further divided the workforce and undermined the likelihood of united worker actions in the 1850s.

Lowell itself changed as the Irish crowded into the city and New England women gradually left the mills. With owners no longer feeling the need to continue paternalistic practices, boardinghouses disappeared. A permanent workforce, once a nightmare to

Changing Occupational Distribution, 1820–1860

The decline of agriculture and the increased involvement in industrial pursuits are represented in this table.

	1820	1840	1860
Agriculture	78.8%	63.1%	52.9%
Mining	0.4	0.6	1.6
Construction	—	5.1	4.7
Manufacturing	2.7	8.8	13.8
Trade	—	6.2	8.0
Transport	1.6	1.8	2.0
Service	4.1	5.0	6.4
Other	12.4	9.4	10.6

Source: U.S. Bureau of the Census.

owners, had become a reality by 1860, and Lowell's reputation as a model factory town faded away.

Factories on the Frontier

Cincinnati, a small Ohio River settlement of 2,540 in 1810, grew to be the country's third-largest industrial center by 1840. With a population of 40,382, it contained a variety of industries at different stages of development. Cincinnati manufacturers who turned out machines, machine parts, hardware, and furniture were quick to mechanize for increased volume and profits. Other trades like carriage making and cigar making moved far more slowly toward mechanization. Alongside these concerns, artisans like coopers, blacksmiths, and riverboat builders still labored in small shops, using traditional hand tools. The new and the old ways coexisted in Cincinnati, as they did in most manufacturing communities.

No uniform work experience prevailed in Cincinnati. The size of the shop, the nature of work, the skills required, and the rewards all varied widely. In 1850, most Cincinnati workers toiled in small or medium-sized shops, but almost 20 percent labored in factories with over 100 employees. Some craftsmen continued to use a wide array of skills as they produced goods in time-honored ways. Others used their skills in new factories, but they tended to focus on more specialized and limited tasks. In furniture factories, for example, machines did the rough work of cutting, boring, and planing, while some artisans worked exclusively as varnishers, others as carpenters, and still others as finishers. No single worker made a chair from start to finish. But all used some of their skills and earned steady wages. Though in the long run, machines threatened to replace them, these skilled factory workers often had reason in the short run to praise the factory's opportunities.

Less fortunate was the new class of unskilled factory laborers who performed limited tasks either with or without the assistance of machinery. In the meatpacking industry, for example, workers sat at long tables. Some cleaned the ears of the hogs, others scraped the bristles, others had the unenviable task of gutting the dead animals. Whereas owners in the industry profited from efficient new operations, workers received low wages and had little job security. Because they had no skills to sell, they were easily replaced and casually dismissed during business slowdowns.

The experience of Cincinnati's working women differed from that of their male counterparts. Cincinnati's large black community was so economically marginal that a majority of black women labored as washerwomen, cooks, or maids. Many white women were "outworkers" for the city's growing ready-to-wear clothing industry. Manufacturers purchased the cloth, cut it into basic patterns, and then contracted the work out to women to be finished in small workshops or at home. Like many other urban women, Cincinnati women sought this employment because husbands or fathers could not earn enough to support the family and because outwork often allowed them to labor at home. Middle-class domestic ideology prescribed that home was the proper sphere for women. Many working men supported this view because they feared female labor would undercut their wages and destroy order in the family. Outwork, then, allowed poor married women to supplement their family income while honoring social norms.

Paid by the piece, female outworkers were among the most exploited of Cincinnati's workers. Long days spent sewing in darkened rooms not only often failed to bring an adequate financial reward but also led to health problems, including ruined eyes and curved spines. The successful marketing of sewing machines in the 1850s contributed to worsening working conditions and lower pay. The sewing machine made stitching easier, so the pool of potential workers increased and the volume of work that bosses expected grew. As tasks were further subdivided, work also became more monotonous. As one Cincinnati citizen observed, "As many as 17 hands" were employed on a single pair of pants.

Cincinnati employers claimed that the new industrial order offered great opportunities to most of the city's male citizens. Manufacturing work encouraged the "manly virtues" so necessary to the "republican citizen." Not all Cincinnati workers agreed. Like workers in Lowell and other manufacturing communities, Cincinnati's laborers rose up against their bosses in the decades before the Civil War.

In 1848, an unknown photographer took this picture of Cincinnati. The prominence of steamboats in the picture suggests the role that location and improvements in transportation played in the city's growth. Although the countryside is visible in the background, the rows of substantial commercial and industrial buildings make Cincinnati's status as a bustling urban center clear. *(Public Library of Cincinnati and Hamilton County, Ohio)*

The workingman's plight, as Cincinnati labor leaders analyzed it, stemmed from his loss of independence. Even though a manufacturing job provided a decent livelihood for some people, the new industrial order was changing the nature of the laboring class itself. A new kind of worker had emerged. Rather than selling the products of his skills, he had only his raw labor to sell. His "wage slavery," or dependence on wages, promised to be lifelong. The reorganization of work signaled the end of the progression from apprentice to journeyman to master and undermined traditional skills. Few workers could expect to rise to the position of independent craftsman. Most would labor only for others, just as slaves labored for their masters. Nor would wages bring to most that other form of independence: the ownership of shop and home. The expression "wage slavery" contained a deep truth about the changed conditions of many American workingmen.

Workers also resented the masters' attempts to control their lives. In the new factories, owners insisted on a steady pace of work and uninterrupted production. Artisans who were used to working in spurts, stopping for a few moments of conversation or a drink, disliked the new routines. Those who took a dram or two at work found themselves discharged. Even outside the workplace, manufacturers attacked Cincinnati's working-class culture. Crusades to abol-

ish volunteer fire companies and to close down saloons, both attacked as nonproductive activities, suggested how little equality the Cincinnati worker enjoyed in an industrializing society.

The fact that workers' wages in Cincinnati, as in other cities, rose more slowly than food and housing costs compounded discontent over changing working conditions. The working class sensed it was losing ground at the very time the city's rich were growing visibly richer. In 1817, the top tenth of the city's taxpayers owned over half the wealth, whereas the bottom half possessed only 10 percent. In 1860, the share of the top tenth had increased to two-thirds, while the bottom half's share had shrunk to 2.4 percent. Cincinnati workers may not have known these exact percentages, but they could see growing social and economic inequality in the luxurious mansions that the city's rich were building and in the spreading blight of slums.

In the decades before the Civil War, Cincinnati workers formed unions, turned out for fair wages, and rallied in favor of the 10-hour day. Like the Lowell mill girls, they cloaked their protest with the mantle of the Revolution. Striking workers staged parades with fifes and drums and appropriated patriotic symbols to bolster their demands for justice and independence. Although they did not see their bosses as a separate or hostile class, labor activists insisted that masters were denying workers a fair share of profits. This unjust distribution doomed them to economic dependency. Because the republic depended on a free and independent citizenry, the male workers warned that their bosses' policies threatened to undermine the republic itself.

Only in the early 1850s did Cincinnati workers begin to suspect that their employers formed a distinct class of parasitic "nonproducers." Although most strikes still revolved around familiar issues of better hours and wages, signs appeared of the more hostile labor relations that would emerge after the Civil War.

As elsewhere, skilled workers were in the forefront of Cincinnati's labor protest and union activities. But their victories proved temporary. Depression and bad times always harmed labor organizations and canceled out employers' concessions. Furthermore, Cincinnati workers did not readily unite to protest new conditions. The uneven pace of industrialization meant that these workers, unlike the Lowell mill women, had no common working experience. Moreover, growing cultural, religious, and ethnic diversity compounded differences in the workplace. By 1850, almost half the people in the city were foreign-born, most of them German, whereas only 22 percent had been in 1825.

As the heterogeneity of the American people increased, ethnic and religious tensions simmered. Immigrants, near the bottom of the occupational ladder, faced limited job choices and suspicion of their faith, habits, and culture. Protestant workers frequently felt that they had more in common with their Protestant bosses than with Catholic Irish or German fellow workers. These tensions exploded in Cincinnati in the spring of 1855. Americans attacked barricades erected in German neighborhoods, crying out death threats. Their wrath visited the Irish as well. Ethnic, cultural, and social differences often drove workers apart and concealed their common grievances. In many cases, disunity served economic progress by undermining workers' efforts for higher pay, shorter hours, and better working conditions, thus enabling businesses to maximize productivity and profits while minimizing the cost of labor.

URBAN LIFE

Americans experienced the impact of economic growth most dramatically in the cities. In the four decades before the Civil War, the rate of urbanization in the United States was faster than ever before or since. In 1820, about 9 percent of the American people lived in cities (defined as areas containing a population of 2,500 or more). Forty years later, al-most 20 percent of them did. Older cities like Philadelphia and New York mushroomed, while new cities like Cincinnati, Columbus, and Chicago sprang up. Although urban growth was not confined to the East, it was most dramatic there. By 1860, more than one-third of the people living in the Northeast were urban residents, compared with only 14 percent of westerners and 7 percent of southerners. Although the majority of northerners still lived on farms or in small farm towns, the region was clearly urbanizing.

The Process of Urbanization

Three distinct types of cities—commercial centers, mill towns, and transportation hubs—emerged during these years of rapid economic growth, while the increase of population in many overgrown seaports and inland centers turned them into real metropoli. Although the lack of water power limited industrial development, commercial seaports like Boston, Philadelphia, and Baltimore expanded steadily and developed diversified manufacturing

The balloon frame, the most important technological improvement in building in the years before the Civil War, allowed the rapid construction of housing in new and old sections of the country. First introduced in 1839 in Chicago, the balloon frame was made of small, light, mill-cut pieces of lumber joined by factory-produced nails. Unlike the older forms of building construction that had used heavy timbers joined by handmade pegs and mortise-and-tenon joints, balloon frames were easy to put together and demanded only a few workers. Since this construction is still used today, you have probably seen examples of the balloon frame. (*Engraving by W. W. Wilson, From Edward Shaw,* The Modern Architect, *1855, Constructing a Balloon Frame House, The Metropolitan Museum of Art, Harris Brisbane Dick Fund, 1934. [34.46.9])*

Urban Growth in 1820 and 1850

In 1820, there were few very large cities in the United States, and most of them were located along the Atlantic coast. This map shows urban growth by 1850. What are the important features of the map and what forces lie behind them? *(Data Source: Statistical Abstract of The United States)*

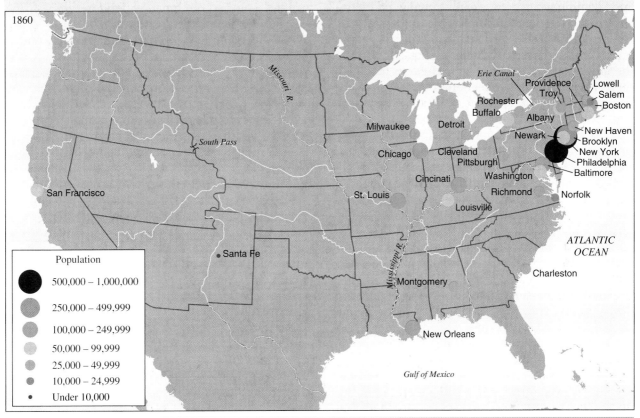

to supplement the older functions of importing, exporting, and providing services and credit. New York replaced Philadelphia as the country's largest and most important city. The completion of the Erie Canal allowed New York merchants to gain control of much of the trade with the West. By 1840, they had also seized the largest share of the country's import and export trade.

Access to water power fueled the development of a second kind of city, exemplified by Lowell, Massachusetts; Trenton, New Jersey; and Wilmington, Delaware. Situated inland along the waterfalls and rapids that provided the power to run their mills, these cities burgeoned, as American industry, especially the production of textiles, expanded in the decades before the Civil War.

Between 1820 and 1840, one-quarter of the increase in urban population occurred west of the Appalachian Mountains, where a third type of city arose. Louisville, Cleveland, and St. Louis were typical of cities that had served as transportation service and distribution centers from the earliest days of frontier settlement. Chicago acted as "grand depot, exchange, counting-house, and metropolis" for its hinterlands. Like most of these western cities, Chicago was a commercial rather than an industrial center. In the 1850s, selling lumber to prairie farmers who needed it for fences and housing was one of Chicago's most significant commercial activities.

As the number of urban dwellers grew, their needs helped generate economic growth. City dwellers rarely had gardens or animals, so they had to purchase their food. This encouraged farmers to turn to commercial farming. Cities also provided a growing market for other products, including shoes, clothing, furniture, and carriages. The iron industry sold more than a half million cast-iron stoves yearly, mainly to city dwellers, and city governments purchased cast-iron pipes for sewers and the water supply and city merchants erected cast-iron buildings.

Until 1840, the people eagerly crowding into cities came mostly from the American countryside.

Then ships began to spill their human cargoes into seaboard cities, and a growing number of immigrants began their lives anew in the United States. Immigrants who could afford to leave the crowded port cities for the interior, many of them Germans and Scandinavians, did so. But many had little choice but to remain in eastern cities and search for work there. By 1860, fully 20 percent of the people living in the Northeast were immigrants; in some of the largest cities, they and their children made up more than half the population. The Irish, fleeing famine and poverty at home, were the largest foreign group in the Northeast.

A look at Philadelphia reveals the character, rhythms, rewards, and tensions of urban life during the antebellum period. The city was one of the giants of the age. An inland port, a bustling mercantile city, a center of shops producing textiles, metals, and a host of other products, Philadelphia stood second only to New York. Though William Penn's "green country town" boasted an attractive appearance and an orderly plan, speculators, interested only in profit, relied on the grid pattern as the cheapest and most efficient way to divide land for development. They built monotonous miles of new streets, new houses, and new alleys with "not a single acre left for public use, either for pleasure or health," as merchant Samuel Breck observed.

A few cities, like New York and Boston, did lay aside areas where residents could escape from the noises, sights, and smells of urban life. Frederick Law Olmsted and Calvert Vaux designed New York's picturesque Central Park, adorning it with grass, trees, and tranquil lakes. Olmsted envisioned the park as a place where all classes of New Yorkers could come together to enjoy themselves in a "quiet and orderly" manner. As with so much else of urban life, however, it was mainly the middle and upper classes who had the time to spend in the park and the money to pay for transportation to it.

As the example of Central Park suggests, not all citizens enjoyed the benefits of urban life. Overwhelmed by rapid growth, city governments provided few of the services we consider essential today and usually only to those who paid for them. Poor families devoted many hours to securing necessities that affluent citizens had at their fingertips. Water is a case in point. By 1801, Philadelphia had constructed a system of waterworks that drew water from the Schuylkill River and then pumped it through wooden pipes to street hydrants. Only by paying a special fee could Philadelphians have water brought into their homes, so most of the city's residents went without. In the 1820s, the city expanded the water system by constructing the Fairmount waterworks, but the more abundant supply of water again benefited those who could afford to pipe it into their homes.

In 1849, Isaac Parrish's report on the sanitary conditions in Philadelphia lamented some of the consequences. "There is . . . a general absence of bathing apparatus, and even of hydrants," he wrote, "in the houses of the poorer classes, and especially in confined courts and alleys of the populous districts of the city." An earlier inspection, carried out by Mathew Carey in 1837, had pointed to an even more

Although this panoramic view of Philadelphia in about 1855 shows individual buildings and empty lots, it is the grid street pattern that stands out as the main feature of the city. By imposing the grid pattern on varied landscapes, Americans created similar types of urban spaces all over the country. This picture does not hint at the underside of Philadelphia life; its purpose seems to be to highlight the importance of the nation's second-largest city. *(The Historical Society of Pennsylvania)*

Wealth Distribution in Three Eastern Cities in the 1840s

Americans and foreign visitors often commented on the rough equality they believed characterized American life. Wealth distribution figures, although incomplete, suggest a different picture of American society.

Level of Wealth	Percentage of Population	Approximate Noncorporate Wealth Owned	Percentage Noncorporate Wealth
Brooklyn in 1841			
$50,000 or more	1	$10,087,000	42
$15,000 to $50,000	2	$14,000,000	17
$4,500 to $15,000	9	$15,730,000	24
$1,000 to $4,500	15	$12,804,000	12
$100 to $1,000	7	$11,000,000	4
Under $100	66	—	—
New York City in 1845			
$50,000 or more	1	$85,804,000	40
$20,000 to $50,000	3	$55,000,000	26
Boston in 1848			
$90,000 or more	1	$47,778,500	37
$35,000 to $90,000	3	$34,781,800	27
$4,000 to $35,000	15	$40,636,400	32
Under $4,000	81	$16,000,000	4

Source: Edward Pessen, *Riches, Class, and Power Before the Civil War* (1973).

basic problem: 253 persons crowded into 30 tenements without even one privy. The ability to pay for services determined not only comfort but health.

Class Structure in the Cities

The drastic differences in the quality of urban life reflected social fluidity and the growing economic inequality that characterized Philadelphia and other American cities. In sharp contrast to the colonial period, the first half of the nineteenth century witnessed a dramatic rise in the concentration of wealth in the United States. The pattern was most extreme in cities.

Because Americans believed that capitalists deserved most of their profits, the well-to-do profited handsomely from this period of growth, whereas workers lost ground. The merchants, brokers, lawyers, bankers, and manufacturers of Philadelphia's upper class gained control of more and more of the city's wealth. By the late 1840s, the wealthiest 4 percent of the population held about two-thirds of the wealth. The economic pattern was similar in other American cities, as the nearby table on wealth distribution indicates. The houses of the city's elite were spacious and filled with new conveniences. Samuel Breck's house in 1839 was elegant and luxurious, with "parlours 14 feet high, . . . furnaces, water closet and shower and common bath up stairs, marble mantels and fireplaces in dressing rooms." Costing $22,500, Breck's "splendid house" represented wages that would take an ordinary

Philadelphia textile factory operative 75 years of work to earn.

The widening gap between the upper class and the working class did not translate into mass suffering, because more wealth was being generated. But the growing inequality hardened class lines, nourished social tensions, and contributed to the labor protests of the antebellum period.

Between 1820 and 1860, a new working and middle class were in the process of formation in Philadelphia and elsewhere. As preindustrial ways of producing goods yielded to factory production and as the pace of economic activity quickened, some former artisans and skilled workers took advantage of newly created opportunities. Perhaps 10 to 15 percent of Philadelphians in each decade before the Civil War were able to improve their occupations and places of residence. They became businessmen, factory owners, mill supervisors, clerks, bookkeepers, engineers, or shopkeepers. Increasingly, membership in this middle class meant having a nonmanual occupation and a special place of work suited to activities that demanded brainpower rather than brawn. But as new opportunities opened up for some, downward occupational mobility increased. Former artisans or journeymen joined a new class of permanent manual workers, dependent on wages for their livelihood. Fed by waves of immigrants, the lower class was growing at an accelerating rate. Moreover, within the working class itself, the percentage of unskilled wage earners living in poverty or on its brink increased from 17 to 24 percent between 1820 and 1860. At the same time, the proportion of craftsmen, once the heart of the laboring class, shrank from 56 to 47 percent.

The Urban Working Class

As with so much else in urban life, housing patterns reflected social and economic divisions. The poorest rented quarters in crowded, shacks, shanties, and two-room houses. Because renters moved often, from one cramped lodging to another, it was difficult for them to create close-knit neighborhoods that might offer fellowship and assistance to offset the harsh conditions of daily life.

Substantial houses fronting the main streets concealed the worst urban housing, which was in back alleys or even in backyards. Many visitors did not even realize slums lay behind the rows of brick housing, nor did they know of the uncollected garbage, privy runoffs, and fetid decay in the dark, unpaved alleys. In his diary, Philadelphia shopkeeper Joseph Sill left a description of living conditions at the bottom. "In the afternoon," he wrote, "Mrs. S & I went to the lowest part of the City to see some poor persons who had call'd upon us for Charity. We found one woman, with two children, & expecting soon to be confined, living in a cellar, part of which was unfloored, & exhibited much wretchedness; but it was tolerably clean. Her husband is a Weaver, & had his loom in the Cellar, but has only occasional work."

What the Sills witnessed during their visit to the weaver's family was not just poverty but the transformation of working-class family life. Men could no longer be sure of supporting their wives and children, even when they were employed. Children as young as 10 might be working for wages or helping with piecework. Women might be taking in work at home. Making ends meet colored family relations. Men felt they had lost much of their authority and power. Sons, earning their own money, did not necessarily respect their fathers. Husbands found themselves having to help with housework when wives were too busy. Observed one immigrant, "the idea of either husband or wife acknowledging one or the other to be 'Boss' [was] quite out of the question." With wives responsible for buying food at urban markets, husbands sometimes felt their wives were careless with their hard-earned money. When one woman failed to explain clearly what she had done with the grocery money, her angry husband "said if she did not give him a full account . . . he would kill her or something like that." The squabble ended in murder. This family was an extreme case, but family violence was not uncommon in working-class quarters.

Middle-Class Life and Ideals

Like the Sills, other members of the new middle class profited from the dramatic increase in wealth in antebellum America. They lived in pleasantly furnished houses, enjoying more peace, more privacy, and more comfort than the less affluent. Franklin stoves gave warmth in winter, and iron cookstoves made cooking easier. Conveniences like Astral lamps made it possible to read after dark. Bathing stands and bowls ensured higher standards of cleanliness. Rugs muffled sounds and kept in the heat.

Material circumstances were one badge of middle-class status, but there were others as well. The acceptance of certain norms and values also identified a person as a member of the new middle class. Genteel behavior and the careful observance of elaborate rules of etiquette (for example, a gentleman was expected to back out of a parlor after making a call upon a lady), the appropriate clothes and conversation, an elegantly furnished parlor for the entertainment of visitors—all served to establish the standing of a middle-class family.

New expectations about the roles of men and women, prompted partly by economic change, also shaped middle-class life. In the seventeenth and eighteenth centuries, the labor of men and women, adults and children, all contributed to the family's economic welfare. But improved transportation, new products, and the rise of factory production and large businesses changed the family economy. Falling prices for processed and manufactured goods like soap, candles, clothing, and even bread made it unnecessary for women, except on the frontier, to continue making these items at home.

As men increasingly involved themselves in a money economy, whether through commerce or market farming, women's and children's contributions to the family welfare became relatively less significant. Although middle-class women and children still worked in their homes as their husbands left to "bring home the bacon," they often neither produced vital goods nor earned money. Even the rhythm of their lives, oriented to housework rather than the demands of the clock, separated them from the bustling commercial world where their husbands now labored. By 1820, the notion that the sexes occupied separate spheres emerged. Men's sphere was the public world, whereas women's was the domestic.

Men were charged with the task of financial support, a responsibility that (as Susan Warner's family experience suggested) was a heavy one in a changing economy. Women's duties included working at home—not as producer but as housekeeper. As the popular book *Whisper to a Bride* counseled readers, "For his sake . . . acquaint thyself with the knowledge that appertaineth unto a wife and housekeeper. If thou art deficient in this knowledge, rest not, till thou hast acquired it. It cometh readily to an attentive mind, and groweth with experience."

The role of housekeeper had both pleasure and frustration built into it. Susan Warner's celebration of domestic life in her novels suggested the satisfactions derived from a cozy household. Yet it was sometimes impossible to achieve the new standards of cleanliness, order, and beauty. Catharine Beecher's "Words of Comfort for a Discouraged Housekeeper" listed just a few of the problems—an inconvenient house, sick children, poor domestics—that undermined efforts to create a perfect, harmonious home.

Although women were expected to become "systematic, neat and thorough" housekeepers, whatever the personal costs might be, they were also given more elevated responsibilities as moral and cultural guardians of their own families and, by extension, of society as a whole. Believing that women were innately pious, virtuous, unselfish, and modest (all characteristics that men lacked), publicists built on the argument developed during the Revolutionary era. By training future citizens and workers to be obedient, moral, patriotic, and hardworking, mothers ensured the welfare of the republic. Just as important, they preserved important values in a time of rapid change. Because men had none of women's virtues and were daily caught up in the fast-paced world of business, wives were responsible for helping husbands cope with temptations and tensions. In the words of one preacher, a wife was the "guardian angel" who "watches over" her husband's interests, "warns him against dangers, comforts him under trial; and by . . . pious, assiduous, and attractive deportment, constantly endeavors to render him more virtuous, more useful, more honourable, and more happy."

This view, characterizing women as morally superior to and different from men, had important consequences for female life. Although the concept of domesticity seemed to confine women to their homes, it actually prompted women to take on activities in the outside world. If women were the guardians of morality, why should they not carry out their tasks in the public sphere? "Woman," said

Sarah Hale, editor of the popular magazine *Godey's Lady's Book*, was "God's appointed agent of *morality.*" Such reasoning lay behind the tremendous growth of voluntary female associations in the early decades of the nineteenth century. Initially, most involved religious and charitable activities. Women supported orphanages, paid for and distributed religious tracts and Bibles, established Sunday schools, and ministered to the poor. The associations provided women with congenial companions and suitable tasks for their "moral character." In the 1830s, as we shall see in Chapter 12, women added specific moral concerns like the abolition of slavery to their missionary and benevolent efforts. As these women took on more active and controversial tasks, they often clashed with men and with social conventions about "woman's place."

The notion of separate spheres established norms for middle-class men and women but were far more flexible than they appeared. Men played a much greater part in the household and in child rearing than gender proscriptions would suggest. Many women were active in the public world. Obviously, men were not always aggressive and rational nor were all women pious, disinterested, selfless, virtuous, cheerful, and loving. But these ideas influenced how men and women thought of themselves. It helped promote "male" and "female" behavior by encouraging particular choices, and it

This daguerreotype shows two children posed on an upholstered bench. Each child holds a book. While we do not know the identity of these children or even if they were related, the image reveals new middle-class norms. The fact that the children are holding books suggests the importance now attached to primary education. Note the groomed hair styles and clothing. Neat appearance and cleanliness were also important middle-class values. The fact that the children are the subject of this picture hints at the importance attached to children in the middle-class family. *(The Library of Congress, LC-USZ6-1988 DLC)*

RECOVERING THE PAST

Family Paintings

Although paintings are often admired and studied for artistic reasons alone, their value as historical documents should not be overlooked. In an age before the camera, paintings, sketches, and even pictures done in needlework captured Americans at different moments of life and memorialized their significant rituals. Paintings of American families in their homes, for example, reveal both an idealized conception of family life and the details of its reality. In addition, the paintings provide us with a sense of what the houses of the middle and upper classes (who could afford to commission art) were like.

Artists trained in the European tradition of realism painted family scenes and portraits, but so did many painters who lacked formal academic training, the so-called primitive artists. Their art was abstract in the sense that the artists tended to emphasize what they knew or felt rather than what they actually saw.

Some primitive artists were women who had received some drawing instruction at school. They often worked primarily for their own pleasure. Other artists were craftsmen, perhaps house or sign painters, who painted pictures in their leisure time. Some traveling house decorators made a living by making paintings and wall decorations. Many primitive paintings are unsigned, and even when we know the painter's identity, we rarely know more than a name and perhaps a date. Primitive artists flourished in the first three-quarters of the nineteenth century, eventually supplanted by the camera and inexpensive prints.

We see below a painting of the Sargent family done by an unknown artist around 1800. Though not an exact representation of reality, it does convey what the artist and the buyer considered important. Like any piece of historical evidence, this painting must be approached critically and carefully. Our questions focus on four areas: (1) the individual family members and their treatment, (2) the objects associated with each, (3) the implied or apparent rela-

Anonymous, *The Sargent Family,* 1800. *(National Gallery of Art)*

H. Knight, *The Family at Home,* 1836. *(Private collection)*

tionship between family members, and (4) the domestic environment. The painting gives us an idealized version of what both the painter and the subjects felt ought to be as well as what actually was. First, study the family itself. Describe what you see. How many family members are there, and what is each one doing? What seems to be the relationship between husband and wife? Why do you think Mr. Sargent is painted with his hat on? Who seems to dominate the painting, and how is this dominance conveyed (positioning, attitude or facial expression, eye contact, clothing)? What can you conclude about different "spheres" and roles for men and women?

Why do you think the artist painted two empty chairs and included a ball and a dog in this scene of family life? What do these choices suggest about attitudes toward children and their upbringing? What seems to be the role of the children in the family? What does the painting suggest about how this family wished to be viewed? How do your conclusions relate to information discussed in this chapter?

Take a look at the room in which the Sargents are gathered. Make an inventory of the objects and furnishings in it. The room seems quite barren in comparison with present-day interiors. Why? Why do you think the chairs are placed near the window and door? What kind of scene does the window frame?

The *Family at Home,* painted by H. Knight in 1836, is a more detailed painting showing a larger family gathering almost 40 years later. Similar questions can be asked about this painting, particularly in relationship to the different treatment of boys and girls and the positioning and objects associated with each gender. There are many clues about the different socialization of male and female children. The family's living room can be contrasted with the Sargent family's room to reveal some of the changes brought about by industrialization.

Reflecting on the Past   How do these nineteenth-century homes and gender roles differ from those in colonial New England and the Chesapeake?

helped many men and women make psychological sense of their lives.

New norms, effectively spread by the publishing industry, also influenced rural and urban working women. The insistence on marriage and service to family discouraged married women from entering the workforce. Many took in piecework so that they could remain at home. Those who had to work often bore a burden of guilt. Though the new feminine ideal may have suited urban middle-class women, it created difficult tensions in the lives of working-class women.

As family roles were reformulated, a new view of childhood emerged. Working-class children still worked or scavenged for goods to sell or use at home, but middle-class children were no longer expected to contribute economically to the family. Middle-class parents now came to see childhood as a special stage of life, a period of preparation for adulthood. In a child's early years, mothers were to impart important values, including the necessity of behaving in accordance with gender prescriptions. Harsh punishments lost favor. As Catharine Beecher explained, "Affection can govern the human with a sway more powerful than the authority of reason or [even] the voices of conscience." Schooling also prepared a child for the future, and urban middle-class parents supported the public school movement.

Children's fiction, which poured off the printing presses, also socialized children. Stories pictured modest youngsters happily making the correct choices of playmates and activities, obeying their parents, and being dutiful, religious, loving, and industrious. Occasionally, as in *The Child at Home* (1833), the reader could discover the horrible consequences of wrongdoing. The young girl who refused to bring her sick mother a glass of water saw her promptly die. Heavy-handed moralizing made sure that children got the proper message.

The growing publishing industry helped spread new ideas about family roles and appropriate family behavior. Novels, magazines, etiquette and child-rearing manuals, and schoolbooks all carried the message from northern and midwestern centers of publishing to the South, to the West, and to the frontier. Probably few Americans lived up to the new standards established for the model parent or child, but the standards increasingly influenced them.

New notions of family life supported the widespread use of contraception for the first time in American history. Because children required so much loving attention and needed careful preparation for adulthood, many parents desired smaller families. The declining birthrate was evident first in the Northeast, particularly in cities and among the middle class. Contraceptive methods included abortion, which was legal in many states until 1860. This medical procedure terminated perhaps as many as one-third of all pregnancies. Other birth control methods included coitus interruptus and abstinence. The success of these methods for family limitation suggests that many men and women adopted the new definitions of the female as naturally affectionate but passionless and sexually restrained.

Mounting Urban Tensions

The social and economic changes transforming U.S. cities in the half century before the Civil War produced urban violence on a scale never before witnessed in the United States, not even during the Revolution. Festering ethnic, racial and religious tensions often triggered mob actions that lasted for days. Baltimore, Philadelphia, Boston, and New York experienced at least 35 major riots between 1830 and 1860, while those cities whose populations reached 20,000 by 1850 also witnessed scenes of urban disorder.

American cities were slow to establish a modern police force (London had organized one in 1829). Most still had the traditional constable-and-watch system. The night watch lit city streetlights and patrolled the streets to preserve order and arrest suspicious characters. During the day, constables investigated health hazards, carried out court orders, and apprehended criminals against whom complaints had been lodged. Neither group tried to prevent crimes or discover offenses. Neither wore uniforms. Certainly, neither was able to "prevent a tumult."

An unsavory Philadelphia riot in August 1834 reveals the range of antagonisms contributing to urban disorder. The riot started on a hot summer evening. Several hundred white Philadelphians wrecked a building on South Street that contained a merry-go-round patronized by both blacks and whites. A general melee followed. As the *Philadelphia Gazette* reported, "At one time it is supposed that four or five hundred persons were engaged in the conflict, with clubs, brickbats, paving stones, and the materials of the shed in which the flying horses were kept." Spurred by the taste of blood, the white mob moved into the crowded, racially mixed neighborhood, where they continued their orgy of destruction, looting, and intimidation of black residents. Similar mayhem followed on the next two nights. Intermittent rioting broke out the succeeding night as well, but the presence of 300 special constables, a troop of mounted militia, and a company of infantry prevented the violence from reaching the pitch of the previous nights.

This cartoon was one of a series entitled "Life in Philadelphia." Philadelphia had a large, free African-American community that often became the target for racial animosity. The negative attitude of the cartoonist is apparent here. Notice the exaggerated racial features of the two figures and the over-elaborate clothing of the dandified man passing his card to the woman coming up from the basement. The verbal message reinforced the visual one. The man asks, "Is Miss Dinah at home?" The woman replies, "Yes sir but she bery potickly engaged in washing de dishes." He replies, "Ah! I'm sorry I cant have the honour to pay my devours to her. Give her my card." *(The Print & Picture Collection, The Free Library of Philadelphia)*

An investigation following the riots revealed at least $4,000 of damage to two black churches and more than 36 private homes. At least one black had been killed, and numerous others were injured. As one shocked eyewitness reported, "The mob exhibited more than fiendish brutality, beating and mutilating some of the old, confiding and unoffending blacks with a savageness surpassing anything we could have believed men capable of."

Many rioters bragged that they were "hunting the nigs." Riots, however, are complicated events, and this racial explanation does not reveal the range of causes underlying the rampage of violence and destruction. The rioters were young and generally of low social standing. Many were Irish. Some had criminal records. A number of those arrested, however, were from a "class of mechanics of whom better things are expected": weavers, house painters, a cabinetmaker, a carpenter, a blacksmith, and a plasterer. While no professional people or businessmen seem to have been involved, onlookers egged the mob on. As one paper reported, these

spectators "countenanced" the operations of the mob "and in one or two instances coincided with their conduct by clapping." The rioters revealed that in the event of an "attack by the city police, they confidently counted" on the assistance of these bystanders.

The mob's composition hints at some of the reasons for participation. Many of the rioters were at the bottom of the occupational and economic ladder and competed with blacks for jobs. This was particularly true of the newly arrived Irish immigrants, who were attempting to replace blacks in low-status jobs. Subsequent violence against blacks suggested that economic rivalry was an important component of the riot. "Colored persons, when engaged in their usual vocations," the *Niles Register* observed, "were repeatedly assailed and maltreated. . . . Parties of white men have insisted that no blacks shall be employed in certain departments of labor."

If blacks threatened the dream of advancement of some whites, this was not quite the complaint of the skilled workers. These men were more likely to have experienced the negative impact of a changing economic system that was undermining the small-scale mode of production. The dream of a better life seemed increasingly illusory as their declining wages drew them closer to unskilled workers than to the middle class. Like other rioters, they were living in one of the poorest and most crowded parts of the city. Their immediate scapegoats were blacks, but for them, the real but intangible villain was the economic system itself. Trade union organizing and a general strike a year later would highlight the grievances of this group.

Urban expansion also contributed to the racial violence. Most of the rioters lived either in the riot area or nearby. All had experienced the overcrowded and inadequate living conditions caused by the city's rapid growth. The racial tensions generated by squalid surroundings and social proximity go far to explain the outbreak of violence. The same area would later become the scene of race riots and election trouble and became infamous for harboring criminals and juvenile gangs. The absence of middle- and upper-class participants did not mean that these groups were untroubled during times of growth and change, but their material circumstances cushioned them from some of the more unsettling forces.

The city's police proved unable to control the mob, thus prolonging the violence. Philadelphia, like other eastern cities, was in the midst of creating its police force. In 1833, a small force had been added to the constable-and-watch system. Its task was to deter crime by walking the city streets. But the police were too few to cope with the angry mob.

Finally, the character of the free black community itself was a factor in producing those gruesome August events. Not only was the community large and visible, but it also had created its own institutions and its own elite. Whites resented "dressy blacks and dandy coloured beaux and belles" returning from "their proper churches." The mob vented its rage against black affluence by targeting the solid brick houses of middle-class blacks and robbing them of silver and watches. Black wealth threatened the notion of the proper social order held by many white Philadelphians and seemed unspeakable when whites could not afford life's basic necessities or lacked jobs.

Ten years later another riot in Philadelphia illustrated the depth of religious and ethnic animosity in that city. Sparked by Catholic objections to the city's policy of using the St. James version of the Bible in the public schools, the controversy escalated from a disagreement over the use of the Protestant Bible to

the accusation that Irish Catholics intended to "trample our free Protestant institutions in the dust." A mass rally organized by the nativists in an Irish immigrant neighborhood got out of hand and ended in violence. In the nights and days that followed, six people were killed and much immigrant property destroyed. Two Catholic churches were burned to the ground. As had been the case in 1834, the mob contained working class men and boys. Also supporting the nativist cause, however, were middle-class men like lawyers and doctors. Both groups resented the presence of Irish immigrants and feared that these outsiders threatened American culture, religion, and politics.

When the rioters torched St. Augustine's Catholic Church the second night of the disturbances, the city's mayor attempted to reason with the crowd. Rather than listen to the mayor, someone in the crown threw a stone at him, knocking him down. And cheers went up as the church steeple toppled. Without an armed police force, city officials like the mayor were powerless to stop mob actions. Each chaotic event made the London model more attractive, and eventually residents and city officials in Philadelphia (and in other large cities) supported an expanded, quasi-military, preventive, and uniformed police force. By 1855, most sizable eastern cities had established such forces.

The Black Underclass

Between 1800 and 1860, the number of free blacks in the United States grew dramatically, from 108,435 in 1800 to 488,070 in 1860. Most of these lived in northeastern cities, although Baltimore had the largest free African-American population of all, and New Orleans also had a sizable free black community. While African Americans constituted a minority of urban residents, whites noted the increased numbers, often with negative feelings. As one African-American woman confessed, white prejudice based on "dislike to the color of the skin" had "often embittered" her feelings.

Events in Philadelphia showed how hazardous life for free blacks could be. Although a small elite group of blacks emerged in Philadelphia and in other cities as well, most African Americans did not enjoy the rewards of economic expansion and industrial progress. Black men, often with little or no education, held transient and frequently dangerous jobs. Black women, many of whom headed their households because the men were away working or had died, held jobs before and after marriage. In Philadelphia in 1849, almost half of the black women washed clothes for a living. Others took boarders into their homes thus adding to their domestic chores.

Northern whites, like southerners, believed in black inferiority and depravity and feared black competition. Although northern states had passed gradual abolition acts between 1780 and 1803 and the national government had banned slaves from entering new states to be formed out of the Northwest Territory, nowhere did any government extend equal rights and citizenship or economic opportunities to free blacks in their midst.

For a time in the early nineteenth century, some blacks living in the North were permitted to vote, but they soon lost that right. Beginning in the 1830s, in part because of the influx of fugitive slaves and manumitted blacks without property or jobs, Pennsylvania, Connecticut, and New Jersey disenfranchised blacks. New York allowed only those with three years' residence and property valued at $250 or more to vote. Only the New England states (with the exception of Connecticut), which had tiny black populations, preserved the right to vote regardless of color. By 1840, fully 93 percent of the northern free black population lived in states where law or custom prevented them from voting.

Other black civil rights were also restricted. In five northern states, blacks could not testify against whites or serve on juries. In most states, the two races were thoroughly segregated. Blacks increasingly endured separate and inferior facilities in railway cars, steamboats, hospitals, prisons, and other asylums. In some states, they could enter public buildings only as personal servants of white men. They sat in "Negro pews" in churches and took communion only after whites had left the church. Although most Protestant religious denominations in the antebellum period split into northern and southern branches over the issue of slavery, most northern churches were not disposed to welcome blacks as full members.

As the Philadelphia riot revealed, whites were driving blacks from their jobs. In 1839, *The Colored American* blamed the Irish. "These impoverished and destitute beings . . . are crowding themselves into every place of business . . . and driving the poor colored American citizen out." Increasingly after 1837, these "white niggers" became coachmen, stevedores, barbers, cooks, and house servants—all occupations blacks had once held.

Educational opportunities for blacks were also severely limited. Only a few school systems admitted blacks, in separate facilities. The case of Prudence Crandall illustrates the lengths to which northern whites would go to maintain racial segregation. In 1833, Crandall, a Quaker schoolmistress in Canterbury, Connecticut, announced that she would admit "young colored ladies and Misses" to her school. The outraged townspeople, fearful that New England would become the "Liberia of America," tried all sorts of persuasion and intimidation to stop Crandall.

Nonetheless, Crandall opened the school. Hostile citizens harassed and insulted students and teachers, refused to sell them provisions, and denied them medical care and admission to churches. Ministers preached against Crandall's efforts, and local residents poured manure in the school's well, set the school on fire, and knocked in walls with a battering ram. Crandall was arrested, and after two trials—in which free blacks were declared to have no citizenship rights—she finally gave up and moved to Illinois.

Crandall likely did not find the Old Northwest much more hospitable. The fast-growing western states were intensely committed to white supremacy and black exclusion. In Ohio, the response to talk of freeing the slaves was to pass "Black laws" excluding them from the state. Said one Ohioan, "The banks of the Ohio would be lined with men with muskets to keep off the emancipated slaves." In 1829 in Cincinnati, where evidence of freedom papers and $500 bond were demanded of blacks who wished to live in the city, white rioters ran nearly 2,000 blacks out of town.

As an Indiana newspaper editor observed in 1854, informal customs made life dangerous for blacks. They were "constantly subject to insults and annoyance in traveling and the daily avocations of life; [and] are practically excluded from all social privileges, and even from the Christian communion." An Indiana senator proclaimed in 1850 that a black could "never live together equally" with whites because "the same power that has given him a black skin, with less weight or volume of brain, has given us a white skin with greater volume of brain and intellect." A neighboring politician, Abraham Lincoln of Illinois, would not have disagreed with this assessment.

RURAL COMMUNITIES

Although the percentage of American workers involved in farming fell from 71 to 53 percent between 1830 and 1860, agriculture persisted as the country's most significant economic activity. The small family farm still characterized eastern and western agriculture, and farm products still made up most of the nation's exports.

Even though farming remained the dominant way of life, agriculture changed in the antebellum period. Vast new tracts of land came under cultivation in the West. Railroads, canals, and better roads pulled rural Americans into the orbit of the wider world. Some crops were shipped to regional markets; others, like grain, hides, and pork, stimulated industrial processing. Manufactured goods, ranging from cloth to better tools, flowed in return to farm families. Like city dwellers, farmers and their families read books, magazines, and papers that exposed them to new ideas. Commercial farming encouraged different ways of thinking and acting and lessened the isolation so typical before 1820.

Farming in the East

During the antebellum period, economic changes created new rural patterns in the Northeast. Marginal lands in New England, New York, and Pennsylvania, cultivated as more fertile lands ran out, yielded discouraging returns. Gradually, after 1830, farmers abandoned these farms, forest reclaimed farmland, and the New England hill country began a slow decline. A popular song of the 1840s captured the pattern of flight: "Come, all ye Yankee farmers who wish to change your lot, / Who've spunk enough to travel beyond your native spot. / And leave behind the village where Pa and Ma do stay, / Come follow me, and settle in Michigan, yea, yea."

By the 1830s, farmers remaining in the East realized that they could not compete with western grain and sought new agricultural opportunities created by better transportation and growing urban markets. One urban need was for fresh milk. Because some eastern cities had grown so large, milk was turning sour before it reached central marketplaces. Several cities, including New York, started urban dairies, where cows often fed on garbage and slop from distilleries and breweries. When railroad lines extended into rural areas, however, farmers living as far away as Vermont and upper New York State discovered that they could ship cooled milk to urban centers. In 1842 and 1843, the Erie Railroad carried 750,000 gallons of milk to New York City. New dairy farmers eventually drove the unsavory city dairies out of business. City residents had fresher, cheaper milk and drank more of it as a result.

Urban appetites encouraged other farmers to cultivate fruit and vegetables. Every city was surrounded by farmers growing produce for urban consumption. Railroads also prompted farmers miles away to turn to specialized farming. Upper New York State farmers began to raise and ship apples, while New Jersey and Delaware farmers became famous for their peaches. Thus, in July 1837, a Boston housewife could buy at the central market a wide variety of fresh vegetables and fruits, ranging from peas, summer squash, and cauliflower to grapes, cherries, and raspberries. Cookbooks began to include recipes calling for fresh ingredients.

As northern farmers adopted new crops, they began to consider farming as a scientific endeavor (see Chapter 9). By 1860, American farmers had developed thousands of special varieties of plants for local conditions. Many improvements resulted from experimentation, but farmers also enjoyed more and better information. New journals like the *New England Farmer*, the *Farmers' Register*, and the *Cultivator* informed readers of modern farming practices, fertilizers, scientific breeding, and methods for treating fruits and vegetables. Following New York's lead in 1819, many states established agricultural agencies to propagate new ideas. Although wasteful farming practices did not disappear, they became less characteristic of the Northeast. Improved farming methods contributed to increased agricultural output and helped reverse a two-hundred-year decline in farm productivity in some of the oldest areas of settlement. A "scientific" farmer in 1850 could often produce two to four times as much per acre as in 1820.

Farmers in the fertile area around Northampton, Massachusetts, illustrate the American farmer's adjustment to new economic conditions. As early as 1800, better roads, a turnpike, and stage routes reduced rural isolation. Canal improvements and then railroads strengthened new contacts. With markets ever more accessible, farmers began to change agricultural patterns. Rather than raising crops and animals for home use or for local barter, farmers started to cultivate crops "scientifically" to increase profits. Farming was becoming a business. At home, women found themselves freed from many of their traditional tasks. Peddlers brought goods to the door. The onerous duty of making cloth and clothing disappeared with the coming of inexpensive ready-made cloth and even ready-made clothes in the 1820s. Daughters liberated from the chores of home manufacturing went off to the mills or earned money by taking in piecework from local merchants.

As the rhythms of rural life in the Connecticut River valley quickened, attitudes also changed. Cash transactions replaced barter. Country stores became more reluctant to accept wood, rye, corn, oats, and butter as payment for goods instead of cash. Some farmers adopted the ethic of getting ahead, although

insurance companies. Others rented land from farmers who had bought more acres than they could manage. Tenants who furnished their own seeds and animals could expect to keep about one-third of the yield. Within a few years, some saved enough to buy their own farms. Even those without any capital could work as hired hands. Labor was scarce, so they earned good wages. In Indiana, German settler Jacob Schramm hired men "to help with heavy labors of lumbering and field work, ditch-digging, and so on." Five to ten years of frugal living and steady work for men like those hired by Schramm would bring the sum needed to get started.

Probably about one-quarter of the western farm population consisted of young men laboring as tenants or hired hands. Although they stood on the bottom rung of the agricultural ladder, their chances of moving up and joining the rural middle class were favorable. Widespread ownership of land characterized western rural communities. Lucinda Easteen knew as much when she told her younger sister to come to Illinois, where "you can have a home of your own, but never give your hand or heart to a lazy man."

Rural communities, unlike the cities, had no growing class of propertyless wage earners, but inequalities nevertheless existed in the Old Northwest. In Butler County, Ohio, for example, 16 percent of people leaving wills in the 1830s held half the wealth. By 1860, the wealthiest 8 percent held half the wealth. In a Wisconsin frontier county in 1860, the richest ten percent owned 40 percent of all property. Although rural wealth was not as concentrated as urban, a few residents benefited more from rapid economic development than others.

Nevertheless, the Northwest offered many American families the chance to become independent producers and to enjoy a "pleasing competence." The rigors of frontier life faded with time. As Catharine Skinner wrote to her sister from her new Illinois home in 1850, "We here have meetings instead of hearing the hunters gun and the woo[d]man's ax on the sabbath."

Commercial farming brought new patterns of family life. As one Illinois farmer told his wife and daughter, "Store away your looms, wheels, [and] warping bars . . . all of your utensils for weaving cloth up in the loft. The boys and I can make enough by increasing our herds." Many farm families had money to spend on new goods. As early as 1836, the *Dubuque Visitor* was advertising the availability of ready-made clothing and "Calicoes, Ginghams, Muslins, Cambricks, Laces and Ribbands." The next

year the *Iowa News* told of the arrival of "Ready Made Clothing from New York."

Agriculture and the Environment

Shifting agricultural patterns in the East and expanding settlement into the Old Northwest contributed to the changing character of the American landscape. As naturalist John Audubon mused in 1826, "A century hence," the rivers, swamps, and mountains "will not be here as I see them. Nature will have been robbed of many brilliant charms, the rivers will be

Timeline	
1805	*Palmer v. Mulligan*
1816	Second Bank of the United States chartered
1817	New York Stock Exchange established
1819	*Dartmouth College v. Woodward*
1820	City of Lowell, Massachusetts, founded by Boston Associates Land Act of 1820 The expression "woman's sphere" becomes current
1824	*Sturges v. Crowninshield*
1824–1850	Construction of canals in the Northeast
1825–1856	Construction of canals linking the Ohio, the Mississippi, and the Great Lakes
1828	Baltimore & Ohio Railroad begins operation
1830	Preemption Act
1830s	Boom in the Old Northwest Increasing discrimination against free blacks Public education movement spreads
1833	Philadelphia establishes small police force
1834	Philadelphia race riots Lowell work stoppage Cyrus McCormick patents his reaper
1837	Horace Mann becomes secretary of Massachusetts Board of Education
1837–1844	Financial panic and depression
1840	Agitation for 10-hour day
1840s–1850s	Rising tide of immigration Expansion of railroad system
1841	Distributive Preemption Act
1844	Anti-Catholic riots in Philadelphia
1849	Cholera epidemic in New York, St. Louis, Cincinnati
1850s	Rise of urban police forces
1857	Financial Panic

tormented and turned astray from their primitive course, the hills will be levelled with the swamps, and perhaps the swamps will have become a mount surmounted by a fortress of a thousand guns." His sense of the consequences of the movement of peoples and the exploitation of land was shared by one French visitor who remarked that Americans would never be satisfied until they had subdued nature.

More than the subjugation of nature was involved, however. When eastern farmers changed their agricultural practices as they became involved in the market economy, their decisions left an imprint on the land. Selling wood and potash stimulated clearing of forests, as did the desire for new tools, plow castings, threshing machines, and wagon boxes, which were produced in furnaces fueled by charcoal. As forests disappeared, so, too, did their wildlife. Even using mineral manures like gypsum or lime or organic fertilizers like guano to revitalize worn-out soil and increase crop yields meant the depletion of land elsewhere.

When farmers moved into the Old Northwest, they used new steel plows, like the one developed in 1837 by Illinois blacksmith John Deere. Unlike older eastern plows, the new ones could cut through the dense, tough prairie cover. Deep plowing and the intensive cultivation of large cash crops had immediate benefits. But these practices could result in robbing the soil of necessary minerals like phosphorous, carbon, and nitrogen. When farmers built new timber houses as frontier conditions receded, they helped fuel the destruction of the country's forests.

✦ *Conclusion*

THE CHARACTER OF PROGRESS

Between 1820 and 1860, the United States experienced tremendous growth and economic development. Transportation improvements facilitated the movement of people, goods, and ideas. Larger markets stimulated both agricultural and industrial production. There were more goods and ample food for the American people. Cities and towns were established and thrived. Visitors constantly remarked on the amazing bustle and rapid pace of American life. The United States was, in the words of one Frenchman, "one gigantic workshop, over the entrance of which there is the blazing inscription 'NO ADMISSION HERE, EXCEPT ON BUSINESS.' "

Although the wonders of American development dazzled foreigners and Americans alike, economic growth had its costs, as Susan Warner's novel made clear. Expansion was cyclic, and financial panics and depression punctuated the era. Industrial profits were based partly on low wages to workers. Time-honored routes to economic independence disappeared, and a large class of unskilled, impoverished workers appeared in U.S. cities. Growing inequality characterized urban and rural life, prompting some labor activists to criticize new economic and social arrangements. But workers, still largely unorganized, did not speak with one voice. Ethnic, racial, and religious diversity divided Americans in new and troubling ways.

Yet a basic optimism and sense of pride also characterized the age. To observers, however, it frequently seemed as if the East and the Old Northwest were responsible for the country's achievements. During these decades, many noted that the paths between the East, Northwest, and South seemed to diverge. The rise of King Cotton in the South, where slave rather than free labor formed the foundation of the economy, created a new kind of tension in American life, as the next chapter will show.

✦ Recommended Reading

Economic Growth

Thomas C. Cochran, *Frontiers of Change: Early Industrialism in America* (1981); Robert F. Dalzell Jr., *Enterprising Elite: The Boston Associates and the World They Made* (1987); David Freeman Hawke, *Nuts and Bolts of the Past: A History of American Technology, 1776–1860* (1988); David A. Hounshell, *From the American System to Mass Production, 1800–1832: The Development of Manufacturing Technology in the United States* (1984); David J. Jeremy, *Transatlantic Industrial Revolution: The Diffusion of Textile Technology Between Britain and America, 1790–1830* (1981); Nathan Rosenberg, *Technology and American Economic Growth* (1972); Charles G. Sellers, *The Market Revolution: Jacksonian America, 1815–1848* (1991); Carol Sheriff, *The Artificial River: The Erie Canal and the Paradox of Progress, 1817–1862* (1996).

Early Manufacturing

Mary H. Blewett, *Men, Women, and Work: Class, Gender, and Protest in the New England Shoe Industry, 1780–1910* (1988); Alan Dawley, *Class and Community: The*

Industrial Revolution in Lynn (1976); Thomas Dublin, *Women at Work: The Transformation of Work and Community in Lowell, Massachusetts, 1826–1860* (1979), and ed., *Farm to Factory: Women's Letters, 1830–1860* (1981); Bruce Laurie, *Artisans into Workers: Labor in Nineteenth-Century America* (1989); Steven J. Ross, *Workers on the Edge: Work, Leisure, and Politics in Industrializing Cincinnati, 1788–1890* (1985); Richard B. Stott, *Workers in the Metropolis: Class, Ethnicity, and Youth in Antebellum New York City* (1990); Sean Wilentz, *Chants Democratic: New York City & The Rise of the American Working Class, 1788–1850* (1984).

Urban Life

Stuart M. Blumin, *The Emergence of the Middle Class: Social Experience in the American City, 1760–1900* (1989); Tamara K. Hareven, ed., *Family and Kin in Urban Communities, 1700–1930* (1977); John F. Kasson, *Rudeness and Civility: Manners in Nineteenth-Century America* (1990); Gary B. Nash, *Forging Freedom: The Formation of Philadelphia's Black Community, 1720–1840* (1988); Edward Pessen, *Riches, Class, and Power Before the Civil War* (1973); Christopher Phillips, *Freedom's Port: The African-American Community of Baltimore, 1780–1860* (1997); Mary P. Ryan, *Cradle of the Middle Class: The Family in Oneida County, New York, 1790–1865* (1981); Christine Stansell, *City of Women: Sex and Class in New York, 1789–1860* (1986).

Rural Communities

Jeremy Atack and Fred Bateman, *To Their Own Soil: Agriculture in the Antebellum North* (1987); Christopher Clark, *The Roots of Rural Capitalism: Western Massachusetts, 1780–1860* (1992); Don H. Doyle, *The Social Order of a Frontier Community: Jacksonville, Illinois, 1825–1870* (1978); John Mack Faragher, *Sugar Creek: Life on the Illinois Prairies* (1986); Susan E. Gray, *The Yankee West: Community Life on the Michigan Frontier* (1996); John Denis Haeger, *The Investment Frontier: New York Businessmen and the Economic Development of the Old Northwest* (1981); Joan M. Jensen, *Loosening the Bonds: Mid-Atlantic Farm Women, 1750–1850* (1986); Robert Leslie Jones, *History of Agriculture in Ohio to 1880* (1983); Donald H. Parkerson, *The Agricultural Transition in New York State: Markets and Migration in Mid-Nineteenth Century America* (1995).

Fiction and Film

Nathaniel Hawthorne's novel *The Scarlet Letter* (1850, but use any edition), although set in the Puritan period, reveals more about the attitudes and controversies of the antebellum period than it does about the seventeenth century. The novels of James Fenimore Cooper provide a picture of the impact of social and economic change on the frontier. Susan Warner's *The Wide, Wide World* (any edition) as well as her other popular novels provide an excellent picture of female interests and concerns in this period (although certainly not all her readers were women). The feature film *Little Women* (1994) presents a moving picture of the domestic and family life so idealized by the middle class. It also suggests the struggle of the middle class to maintain its status in difficult times. Some critics have pointed out that this adaptation of Louisa May Alcott's novel has strong overtones of contemporary feminism. *Out of Ireland: The Story of Irish Emigration to America* (1994) gives a vivid picture of Irish emigration between 1840 and 1920.

✦ Discovering U.S. History Online

Whole Cloth: Discovering Science and Technology Through American History

www.si.edu.lemelson/centerpieces/whole_cloth/

The Jerome and Dorothy Lemelson Center for the Study of Invention and Innovation/Society for the History of Technology put together this site, which includes excellent activities and sources concerning early American manufacturing and industry.

Road Through the Wilderness

www.connerprairie.org/ntlroad.html

The National Road was a hot political topic in the early republic and was part of the beginning of the development of America's infrastructure. This site tells the history of the building of the National Road.

19th Century Scientific American Online

www.history.rochester.edu/Scientific_American/

Magazines and journals are windows through which we can view society. This site provides online editions of one of the more interesting nineteenth-century journals.

Jacksonian Medicine

www.connerprairie.org/historyonline/jmed.html

Survival was far from certain in the Jacksonian era. This site discusses some of the reasons for this as well as some of the possible cures of the times.

Penn 1830: A Virtual Tour

www.archives.upenn.edu/histy/features/1830

This "virtual tour" shows what a fairly typical campus looked like and what student life was like at one of the larger universities in the antebellum era.

A Brief History of Central Banking in the United States

http://odur.let.rug.nl/~usa/E/usbank/bank.xx.htm

Of particular interest at this site is the section on the Second Bank of the United States (1816–1836).

The Erie Canal

www.syracuse.com/features/eriecanal/

This site features an overview of the history of the Erie Canal as well as the section "Life on the Erie Canal," built around the diary of a 14-year-old girl who traveled from

Amsterdam to Syracuse, New York, in the early nineteenth century. It explores the construction and importance of the Erie Canal.

Inland Navigation: Connecting the New Republic, 1790–1840

www.xroads.virginia.edu/~HYPER/DETOC/transport/front.html

This illustrated site gives the history of American canals, rivers, railroads, and roads: "early systems of transportation [that] wove the new country together. . . ."

Lowell National Historic Park

www.nps.gov/lowe/home.htm

This well-illustrated site offers a detailed history of the Lowell textile mills and gives an overview of early manufacturing.

19th Century Schoolbooks

www.digital.library.pitt.edu/nietz/

This site offers an insight into nineteenth-century education with full-text, digital reproductions of nineteenth-century textbooks as well as two texts on the history of textbooks.

The Gentleman's Page: A Practical Guide for the 19th Century American Man

www.lahacal.org/gentleman/

Drawing from contemporary photographs and nineteenth-century etiquette books, this site lends insight to the attire and behavior expected of urban "gentlemen."

Common School Period

www.nd.edu/~rbarger/www7/common.html

This site presents several topics relevant to the 1840–1880 period in American education including a brief illustrated biography of Horace Mann, information on the "Catholic Controversy," compulsory attendance, and African-American education.

Connor Prairie Living History Museum

www.connerprairie.org/historyonline/

The online counterpart to a nineteenth-century living history museum that offers illustrated essays such as "Clothing of the 1830s," "The American Woman of the Early Nineteenth Century" and "Jacksonian Medicine." The site also has a series of articles on "Life in the 1880s" and online versions of the museum's exhibits, including "Taming the Wilderness: Rivers, Roads, Canals, and Railroads."

A History of American Agriculture

www.usda.gov/history2/front.htm

This government Web site offers an interactive timeline of American agriculture that contains several topics, including "Economic Cycles," "Farm Machinery and Technology," "Life on the Farm," and "Government Programs and Policy."

11 Slavery and the Old South

Engraved by J. C. Buttre from a Daguerreotype

The young Frederick Douglass, shown here in a photograph from about 1855, understood as well as any American the profound human, social, and political complexities and consequences of slavery. *(Photographs and Print Division, Schomburg Center for Research in Black Culture, The New York Public Library, Astor Lenox and Tilden Foundations)*

✦ *American Stories*

A YOUNG SLAVE DISCOVERS THE PATH TO FREEDOM

As a young slave, Frederick Douglass was sent by his master to live in Baltimore. When he first met his mistress, Sophia Auld, he was "astonished at her goodness" as she began to teach him to read. Her husband, however, ordered her to stop. Maryland law forbade teaching slaves to read. A literate slave was "unmanageable," "utterly unfit . . . to be a slave," he said. From this episode Douglass learned that "what he most dreaded, that I most desired . . . and the argument which he so warmly urged, against my learning to read, only served to inspire me with a desire and determination to learn."

In the seven years he lived with the Aulds, young Frederick used "various stratagems" to teach himself to read and write. In the narrative of his early life, written after his dramatic escape to the North, Douglass acknowledged that his master's "bitter opposition" had helped him achieve his freedom as much as did Mrs. Auld's "kindly aid."

Most slaves did not, like Douglass, escape. But all were as tied to their masters as Douglass was to the Aulds. Nor could whites in antebellum America escape the influence of slavery. Otherwise decent people were often compelled by the "peculiar institution" to act inhumanely. After Sophia Auld's husband's interference, Douglass observed that she was transformed into a demon by the "fatal poison of irresponsible power." Her formerly tender heart turned to "stone" when she ceased teaching him. "Slavery proved as injurious to her," Douglass wrote, "as it did to me."

Mr. Covey, a slavebreaker, to whom Douglass was sent in 1833 for discipline, also paid the cost of slavery. Covey succeeded for a time, Douglass sadly reported, in breaking his "body, soul, and spirit" by brutal work and discipline. But one hot August day in 1833 he could stand it no longer; the two men fought a long, grueling battle. Douglass won. Victory, he said, "rekindled the few expiring embers of freedom, and revived within me a sense of my own manhood." Although it would be four more years before his escape north, the young man never again felt like a slave. The key to Douglass's resistance to Covey's power was not just his strong will, or even the magical root he carried in his pocket, but rather his knowledge of how to challenge and jeopardize Covey's reputation and livelihood as a slavebreaker. The oppressed survive by knowing their oppressors.

As Mrs. Auld and Covey discovered, as long as some people were not free, no one was free. Douglass observed, "You cannot outlaw one part of the people without endangering the rights and liberties of all people. You cannot put a chain on the ankle of the bondsman without finding the other end of it about your own necks." After quarreling with a house servant, one plantation mistress complained that she "exercises dominion over me—or tries to do it. One would have thought . . . that I was the Servant, she the mistress." Many whites lived in constant fear of a slave revolt. A Louisiana planter recalled that he had "known times here when there was not a single planter who had a calm night's rest; they then never lay down to sleep without a brace of loaded pistols at their sides." In slave folktales, the clever Brer Rabbit usually outwitted the more powerful Brer Fox or Brer Wolf, thus reversing the roles of oppressed and oppressor.

Slavery was both an intricate web of human relationships and a labor system. After tracing the economic development of the Old South, in which slavery and cotton played vital roles, this chapter will emphasize the daily lives and relationships of masters and slaves who, like Douglass and the Aulds, lived, loved, learned, worked, and struggled with one another in the years before the Civil War.

Perhaps no issue in American history has generated as many interpretations or as much emotional controversy as slavery. Three interpretive schools developed over the years, each adding to our knowledge of the peculiar institution. The first saw slavery as a relatively humane and reasonable institution in which plantation owners took care of helpless, childlike slaves. The second depicted slavery as a harsh and cruel system of exploitation. The third, and most recent, interpretation described slavery from the perspective of the slaves, who did indeed suffer brutal treatment yet nevertheless survived with integrity, self-esteem, and a sense of community and culture.

The first and second interpretive schools emphasized workaday interactions among masters and mostly passive, victimized slaves, while the third focused on the creative energies and agency of life in the slave quarters from sundown to sunup. In a unique structure, this chapter follows these masters and slaves through their day, from morning in the Big House through hot afternoon in the fields to the slave cabins at night. Slavery was the crucial institution in defining the Old South. Although dominated by rich planters, many other southern social groups as well as international economic patterns contributed to the tremendous economic growth of the South from 1820 to 1860. We will look first at these diverse aspects of antebellum southern life and then follow whites and blacks through a southern day from morning to noon to night.

BUILDING A DIVERSE COTTON KINGDOM

Many myths obscure our understanding of the antebellum South. It was not a monolithic society filled only with large cotton plantations worked by hundreds of slaves. The realities were much more complex. Large-plantation agriculture was dominant in the antebellum South, but most southern whites (75 percent) were not even slaveholders, much less large planters. Although rich slaveholding planters dominated the political and social life of the South, middling, yeoman "self-working farmers" with few or no slaves played a significant role. Most southern farmers lived not in imposing mansions but in modestly small or dark, cramped, two-room cabins. Cotton was a key cash crop in the South, but more acreage was actually planted in corn. Some masters were kindly, but many were not; some slaves were contented, but most were not.

There were many Souths, encompassing several geographic regions, each with different economic bases and social structures, each reflecting its own cultural values. The older Upper South of Virginia, Maryland, North Carolina, and Kentucky grew different staple crops from those grown in the newer Lower or "Black Belt" South, from South Carolina to eastern Texas. Within each state, moreover, the economies of flat coastal areas differed from inland upcountry forests and pine barrens. A still further diversity existed between these areas and the Appalachian highlands, running from northern Alabama to western Virginia. Southern cities, few in number—New Orleans, Savannah, Charleston, and Richmond—differed dramatically from rural areas.

Although the South was diverse, agriculture dominated industry and commerce. In 1859, a Virginia planter complained about a neighbor who was considering abandoning his farm to become a merchant. "To me it seems to be a wild idea," the planter wrote in his diary. Southerners placed a high value on agriculture. Slavery was primarily a labor system intended to produce wealth for landowners. Although slavery in older areas was paternalistic, with masters and slaves owing mutual obligations, increasingly it became a capitalistic enterprise intended to maximize profits. As such, it was tied into a growing international web of economic relations.

The Expansion of Slavery in a Global Economy

In the 20 years preceding the Civil War, the South's agricultural economy grew slightly faster than the North's. Personal income in 1860 was 15 percent higher in the South than in the prosperous states of the Old Northwest. If the South had become an independent nation in 1860, it would have ranked as one of the wealthiest countries in the world in per capita income, a wealth based mainly on cotton.

The world was deeply involved in the tremendous economic growth of the South in the early nineteenth century. The expansion of cotton depended on five factors: technological developments, land, labor, demand, and a global system of trade. The technological breakthrough was the cotton gin, invented by Eli Whitney in 1793, which, as we saw in Chapter 9, allowed farmers to separate the cotton fibers from the sticky seeds in the hardier "short staple" cotton plant, which could grow anywhere in the South. This tied the southern economy to cotton production for a century, increased the need for more land and labor, and stimulated slavery's expansion southwestward into Alabama, Mississippi, western Tennessee and, with the Louisiana Purchase, into Louisiana, Arkansas, and

The Varied Economic Life in the South

Note the short-fiber, cotton-growing "Black Belt" running from southern Virginia to eastern Texas. Despite the economically varied South, cotton was "king."

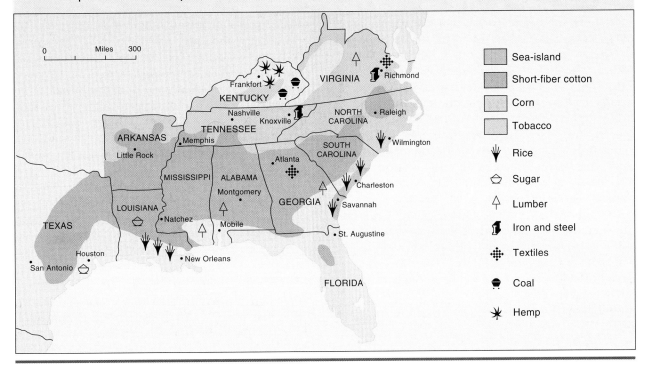

eastern Texas. The Haitian slave rebellion of Toussaint L'Ouverture in the 1790s had convinced Napoleon that he could not maintain a French presence in the Americas; therefore, he sold Louisiana to the United States. This opened up vast territories to cotton expansion that, ironically, given its birth in slave revolt, also meant the expansion and further entrenchment of slave labor in the United States.

Other crucial technological developments and demand for cotton came from Europe, especially England, tying the United States into a widening global economy. For several centuries, British, Dutch, French, and Spanish merchants had been developing a worldwide system of trade, exchanging European manufactured goods for gold and silver from Latin America; silk, spices, cotton, and tea from China and India; and tobacco, coffee, sugar, and lumber from the Caribbean and North America. Although many of these raw materials were taken by exploitative colonial powers, European mercantilists succeeded in establishing an international web of trade—that in turn motivated further technological developments that speeded the coming of the Industrial Revolution.

Starting in England in the late eighteenth century, industrialism began when the system of making clothes involving "putting out" various tasks to a cottage industry of rural people was replaced by the factory system. This was made possible by an agricultural revolution, which provided surplus food and labor for cities, and by inventions of the spinning jenny, the flying shuttle, and the steam engine, which mechanized textile manufacturing under one roof. Stimulating these developments was the demand by the British and other European nations' working classes to replace heavy linen and woollen clothes with lightweight, inexpensive cotton clothes. As British textile manufacturers sought to supply this demand, they eagerly bought all the cotton they could get from the American South. The British imported only 22 million pounds of cotton from the United States in the pre–cotton gin year of 1787, but by 1840, they imported 366 million pounds, making it the most important product in value in Great Britain.

To meet the huge demand for cotton, middling (yeoman) farmers as well as large planters rushed westward to fresh, fertile lands of the Gulf States to plant cotton as well as corn and other crops. However, only elite large-plantation owners could afford to buy gins and purchase vast lands, thereby spreading the plantation system and the emphasis on cotton. Large-scale farming increased, demanding ever more slave labor as a valuable investment.

Despite the abolition of slavery in the North and occasional talk of emancipation in the South, slavery became more deeply entrenched in southern life. Any thought of ending it could be dispelled by one word: cotton.

Although more acreage was planted in corn, cotton was the largest cash crop and for that reason was called "king." In 1820, the South became the world's largest producer of cotton, and after 1840, cotton represented more than half of all American exports. Cotton spurred economic growth not only in England but also throughout the United States. New England textile mills bought it, northern merchants profitably shipped, insured, and marketed it, northern bankers added capital from cotton sales, and western grain farmers found the South a major market for their foodstuffs.

The supply of cotton to Sheffield and Leeds in England, Brussels, and other European cities, as well as to Lowell and Lawrence, Massachusetts, grew at an astonishing rate. Cotton production soared from 461,000 bales in 1817 to 2.85 million in 1849, and peaked at 4.8 million bales in 1860, a more than tenfold jump.

Slavery in Latin America

Europeans depended on the slave-based economy in Latin America as well as the American South. As we saw in Chapter 3, Africans were enslaved not only in Virginia and the Carolinas but also in Jamaica, Barbados, Cuba, Martinique, and other British, Spanish, French, Dutch, and Danish islands in the West Indies, in Spanish Mexico and Central America, and in Peru, Venezuela, Guyana, and throughout South America, including Portuguese Brazil, which at 1 million in 1800 had the largest slave population in all the Americas. But in the next 60 years, while Brazil's slave population only climbed to 1,510,000, the United States' numbers reached over 4 million.

Historians used to think that because of restraints of Catholicism, Roman legal codes, and the greater frequency of racial intermarriage, slavery was more benign and less barbaric in Spanish Latin America than in the United States, and that slaves enjoyed more dignity as persons. Though it is true that Latin American slaves had more religious holidays and days of rest than in the North, and that caste distinctions based on gradations of color were more prevalent, it is now thought that slavery was just as harsh, if not more so, and that various differences within Latin America and between Latin and North American slavery were more economic, demographic, and regional than religious and cultural.

Slavery emerged in Latin America out of economic necessity to provide labor where the indigenous population of Indians, decimated by both disease and intermarriage, could not be replaced. Sugar was to Latin America as cotton was to the southern United States, doubling in output at the beginning of the nineteenth century to meet growing European demands. In Caribbean islands like Cuba, Jamaica, and Barbados, and in the Bahia region of Brazil, slaves were indispensable to the sugarcane industry, cutting, carting, milling, boiling, and refining sugar for a huge and growing global market that included rum and other liquor distilleries. By 1840, Cuba was the world's largest producer of cane sugar.

Enslaved Africans also worked in Peruvian and Chilean vineyards and in cacao, coca, cotton, and tobacco fields throughout Central and South America. They toiled in Mexican, Colombian, Peruvian, Venezuelan, and Brazilian gold, silver, and copper mines; as construction menials, cowboys, tradesmen, dockworkers, teamsters, and muleteers for overland and maritime transportation; and as servants to royal and religious officials. Few distinctions were made for women, who generally were expected to perform the same physical labor as men.

The conditions of work in Bolivian mines or Brazilian sugar fields were as harsh as in southern Black Belt cotton fields, and perhaps even worse. Slaves labored in gangs yet were held accountable as individuals. As market demands for sugar increased in the nineteenth century, sugar growers pressured slaves to increase their productivity, which rose from 1,500 to 2,500 pounds per year. Since slaves could produce enough sugar within two years to equal the value of their purchase, they were literally worked to debilitation and death, the average working life in the fields falling from 15 to 7 years and the death rate increasing from 6 to 10 percent. Whippings and stocks were used to enforce obedience, and strict supervision and control were maintained to prevent Africans from mixing with Indians and Europeans and fleeing to communities of escaped slaves, called maroons, in nearby jungles.

Perhaps the most distinctive aspect of Latin American slavery, especially in the seventeenth and eighteenth centuries, was the heavy preponderance of enslaved African men and the absence of women and families compared to the United States. By the nineteenth century, the gender ratio was 3 men to every 2 women, with a 2:1 ratio on the sugar estates of Brazil and Cuba; as late as 1875, only one in six Brazilian slaves was recorded as married. The birthrate was lower in Latin America, 40 births per 1,000 compared to 50 per 1,000 in the United States, and the death rate was appalling, the result of hard work, tropical epidemic diseases, malnutrition, and an extremely high infant-mortality rate. With low birthrates and lower life expectancy (age 23 in Brazil, 35 in the United States), the slave population in Latin America actually dropped in the nineteenth century.

Unlike in the United States, where natural births increased the slave population, Latin Americans used the African slave trade to replenish the lost labor. Between 1810 and 1870, after the 1807 abolition of the slave trade by Great Britain and the United States, nearly 2 million Africans were taken to the Americas, 60 percent to Brazil and 32 percent to Cuba and Puerto Rico, as compared to 2.7 percent smuggled illegally to the American South. The last American countries to abolish slavery were Puerto Rico (1873), Cuba (1880), and Brazil (1888).

Although slow to abolish slavery officially, intermarriages among Europeans, Indians, and Africans in Latin America led to an increase in the population of free people of color, who by mid-century outnumbered slaves (80 percent in Brazil), a balance strikingly different from the United States, where free African Americans were only 12 percent.

Latin American slaves obtained their freedom by various means: racial intermarriage, as payment for special favors and other contracts, in wills upon a master's death, and by purchasing their own freedom by extra work and hiring out. Relative autonomy and incentives such as presents, privileges, extra rations, holidays, and their own gardens to supplement diet deficiencies were given to many Latin American slaves. One slaveholder manual said: "the slave who owns neither flees nor causes disorder." Thus, although conditions in Latin America were as harsh as in the American South, the rights of slaves were more fluid, shifting with changing economic and demographic conditions.

White and Black Migrations in the South

Conditions changed in the United States, too. Seeking profits from the British and from the worldwide demand for cotton, southerners migrated southwestward in huge numbers between 1830 and 1860. Southern farmers, like their northern counterparts, followed parallel migration paths westward. From the coastal states they trekked westward into the lower Midwest and down into the Lower South. By the 1830s, the center of cotton production had shifted from South Carolina and Georgia to Alabama and Mississippi. This process continued in the 1850s as southerners forged into Arkansas,

Louisiana, and eastern Texas. A father and his sons would go first, find land and clear it, plant some corn and later some cotton, and begin to raise a cabin. Leaving the sons to finish, the father would return east, where his wife and daughters had been managing the farm, pack up the household, and bring it to the new home.

These migrating southern families were not only pulled by the prospect of fresh land, cheap labor, and new riches, but they were also pushed westward by deteriorating economic conditions. Beginning in the 1820s, the states of the Upper South entered a long depression affecting tobacco and cotton prices. Years of constant use had exhausted their lands, and families with many children struggled to give each child an inheritance or financial help to start a family and career. In a society that valued land ownership, farm families had several choices. One was to move west; another was to stay and diversify. Therefore, the older states of the Upper South continued to shift to grains, mainly corn and wheat. Because these crops required less labor than tobacco, slave owners, especially those with pressing debts, began to sell slaves.

The internal slave trade from Virginia and the Upper South "down the river" to the Old Southwest thus became a multimillion-dollar "industry" by the 1830s. An estimated 1 million slaves were transported southwestward by this trade. The practice was harsh and cruel. One of the busiest routes was from Alexandria, Virginia, almost within view of the nation's capital, to a huge depot near Natchez, Mississippi, one of the richest large-plantation areas of the South, indeed a city with more millionaires than any other in the United States. Although southern states occasionally attempted to outlaw or control the traffic in slaves, these efforts were poorly enforced and usually short-lived. Besides, the reason for outlawing the slave trade was generally not humanitarian but rather reflected fear of a rapid increase in the slave population. Alabama, Mississippi, and Louisiana all banned the importation of slaves after the Nat Turner revolt in Virginia in 1831 (described later in this chapter). But all three permitted the slave trade again during the profitable 1850s.

Congress acted in 1807 to end external slave imports formally on January 1, 1808, the earliest date permitted by the Constitution and the same year that Great Britain ended its slave trade. Enforcement by the United States was weak, however, and many thousands of blacks continued to be smuggled into North America until the end of the Civil War. The increase in the slave population was not the result of this illegal trade, however, but of natural reproduction, often encouraged by slave owners eager for more laborers and salable human property for higher profits.

Southern Dependence on Slavery

The rapid increase in the number of slaves, from 1.5 million in 1820 to 4 million in 1860, paralleled the South's economic growth and its dependence on both cotton and slavery, which was similar to the Latin American dependence on sugar and slavery. Senator Hugh Lawson White of Tennessee said that slavery was "sacred," the basis of civilization, and an English traveler said it would be easier to attack popery in Rome or Islam in Constantinople than slavery in the American South.

Although most slaves worked on plantations and medium-sized farms, just as in Latin America, they were found in all segments of the southern economy. In 1850, some 75 percent of all slaves were engaged in agricultural labor: 55 percent growing cotton, 10 percent tobacco, and 10 percent rice, sugar, and hemp. Of the remaining one-fourth, about 15 percent were domestic servants, while others were involved in mining, lumbering, construction, dock and steamship labor, and iron and tobacco factories.

The 300,000 slaves in 1850 who were not domestic or agricultural laborers worked as lumberjacks and turpentine producers in Carolina and Georgia forests; coal and salt miners in Virginia and Kentucky; boiler stokers and deckhands on

This engraving of a group of slaves in chains depicts the stark inhumanity of the slave trade. Note the white man (in the right corner) raising the whip to hurry the slaves along. In front of him are a woman and child, and another woman stares at him in moral disbelief. *(Library of Congress)*

Mississippi River steamships; textile laborers in Alabama cotton mills; dockworkers in Savannah and Charleston; and tobacco and iron workers in Richmond factories. A visitor to Natchez in 1835 saw slaves working as "mechanics, draymen, hostelers, labourers, hucksters, and washwomen, and the heterogeneous multitude of every other occupation, who fill the streets of a busy city—for slaves are trained to every kind of manual labour." The Tredegar Iron Company of Richmond, the largest in the South, manufacturing boilers and steam engines, axes and saws, and cannon and shot, decided in 1847 to shift from white labor "almost exclusively" to slave laborers, who were cheaper, easier to control, and not likely to organize. Others, like cotton mills advocate William Gregg of South Carolina, argued that poor whites should be given preference for factory work.

In fact, both practices were pursued, though the Tredegar policy foreshadowed that of many future companies as a way of both exploiting black labor and putting an economic squeeze on organized white workers, encouraging them to regard black workers as a threat. White artisans in the South (mechanics, blacksmiths, cabinetmakers, butchers, tanners, etc.) were similarly threatened by free and slave black artisans, whose work was, of course, cheaper. Even though granted superior status by their race, white artisans had limited economic opportunities and protested black competition; some opposed slavery.

Whether in towns, factories, mines, or cotton fields, slavery was profitable as a source of labor and capital investment. In 1859, the average plantation slave produced $78 in cotton earnings for his master annually while costing only about $32 to be fed, clothed, and housed. The "crop value per slave" increased from about $15 in 1800 to $125 in 1860. In 1844, a "prime field hand" sold for $600. A cotton boom beginning in 1849 raised this price to $1,800 by 1860. A female slave purchased for $450 at age 18 would not only triple or more in value in 20 years, but she would also bear from two to six children, which compounded her value. Therefore, slaves were a good investment.

The economic growth of the slaveholding South was impressive, but the dependence on a cotton and slave economy was limiting. Generally, agricultural growth spurs the rise of cities and industry, but this was not the case in the Old South. In 1860, the South had 35 percent of the U.S. population but only 15 percent of its manufacturing. Just before the Civil War, one southerner in fourteen was a city dweller, compared with one of every three northerners. The South would continue its economic

ANALYZING HISTORY

SLAVERY EXPANDS WITH THE COTTON BOOM

Although the South had a diverse agricultural economy, growing tobacco, rice, and sugar, cotton was the primary cash crop. Note the spectacular and simultaneous growth of cotton production and slave population between 1790 and 1860.

Reflecting on the Past In what 20-year period did the greatest growth occur? By 1860, which states have the densest concentration of cotton production? Where are the most slaves? How do you explain any differences? Why, for example, were there so many slaves in Virginia and South Carolina? What were the implications of the increasing importance of cotton for U.S. exports for relations with other countries, especially England?

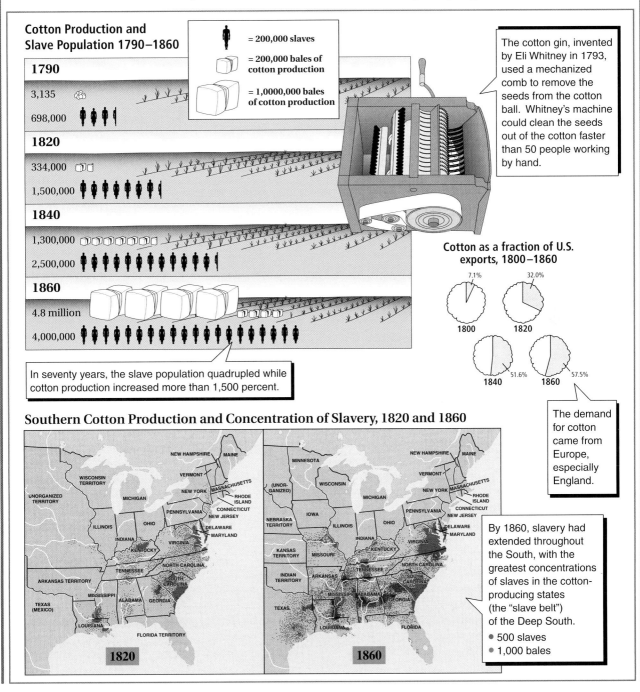

Cotton Production and Slave Population 1790–1860

= 200,000 slaves

= 200,000 bales of cotton production

= 1,0000,000 bales of cotton production

1790
3,135
698,000

1820
334,000
1,500,000

1840
1,300,000
2,500,000

1860
4.8 million
4,000,000

The cotton gin, invented by Eli Whitney in 1793, used a mechanized comb to remove the seeds from the cotton ball. Whitney's machine could clean the seeds out of the cotton faster than 50 people working by hand.

In seventy years, the slave population quadrupled while cotton production increased more than 1,500 percent.

Cotton as a fraction of U.S. exports, 1800–1860

7.1%   1800
32.0%   1820
51.6%   1840
57.5%   1860

The demand for cotton came from Europe, especially England.

Southern Cotton Production and Concentration of Slavery, 1820 and 1860

1820

1860

By 1860, slavery had extended throughout the South, with the greatest concentrations of slaves in the cotton-producing states (the "slave belt") of the Deep South.

● 500 slaves
● 1,000 bales

backwardness as long as whites with capital insisted on putting their business energies primarily toward cotton production.

Some southerners were aware of the dangers of following a single path to wealth. De Bow's *Review*, an important journal published in New Orleans, called for greater economic independence in the South through agricultural diversification, industrialization, and an improved transportation system. De Bow thought that slave labor could fuel an Industrial Revolution. But the planter class disagreed. As long as money could be made through a patriarchal, agricultural slave system that also valued honor and regulated race and gender relationships, plantation owners saw no reason to risk capital in new ventures.

Paternalism and Honor in the Planter Class

The aversion to industrialism in the South stemmed from the fact that most southerners, inheriting traditions of medieval chivalry, Protestantism, and their Celtic (Scottish, Scots-Irish, and Welsh) cultural heritage, espoused a definable life style and set of values. First among them was the importance of a refined paternalism based on a rigid sense of social-class hierarchy and obligations. Wealthy planters, emulating the English landowning aristocratic class, were aware of their privileged status as social "betters" and insisted on being treated with deference by those below them. This was especially important for those living in elegant mansions in isolated areas surrounded by black slaves and envious poor whites, circumstances that led to a violent undercurrent throughout the South.

The head of the plantation was aware of his obligations, one of which was to take good, paternal care of his inferiors, much like a kindly father. This meant providing the necessities of life to slaves (and white overseers), treating them humanely, and expecting faithful obedience, loyalty, and hard work in return. The plantation wife, or mistress, was an essential part of this culture. She was placed on a pedestal and expected to uphold genteel values of sexual purity, spiritual piety, and submissive patience as she managed the household and extended gracious hospitality to social equals. That she also had to put up with a double sexual standard and the hyper-masculinity of plantation life made it all the more important that she reflect lady-like virtues and be fiercely protected.

This intensely masculine code, which valued manly activities such as politics, war, hunting, and gambling, carried with it a rigid code of honor. Southern men enjoyed political and military ceremonies and reviews, as well as leisure activities of the hunt, cards, cockfighting, and horse racing. They were sensitive to lapses of appropriate, chivalrous behavior, to challenges to their honor, and to the slightest insults. Such slights led to duels, regulated by strict gentlemanly rules. One southern visitor said that the "smallest breach of courtesy, no matter how unintentional; the slightest suggestion of unfairness in a business deal; even a moment's awkwardness—were sufficient grounds for a challenge." Another described the life of the plantation elite in Natchez in 1847: "Many of the chivalric gentry whom I have been permitted to see dashing about here on highbred horses, seem to find their greatest enjoyment in recounting their bear hunts, 'great fights,' and occasional exploits with revolvers and Bowie knives." Although duels were outlawed in most states, such laws were routinely ignored. Ironically, the sometimes lawless and violent paternalistic code of honor in the Old South was intended to uphold law, order, and the plantation system.

Slavery, Class, and Yeoman Farmers

Slavery clearly served social purposes as well as economic ones. Although the proportion of southern white families that owned slaves slowly declined from 40 to 25 percent as some families sold slaves to cotton planters, the ideal of slave ownership still permeated all classes and determined southern society's patriarchal and hierarchical character. At the top stood the paternalistic planter aristocracy, much of it new wealth, elbowing its way among old established families like the Byrds and Carters of Virginia. Some 10,000 rich families owned 50 or more slaves in 1860; about 3,000 of these owned over 100. A slightly larger group of small planters held between 10 to 50 slaves. But the largest group, 70 percent of all slaveholders in 1860, comprised 270,000 middle-level, yeoman farm families with fewer than 10 slaves. The typical slaveholder worked a small family farm of about 100 acres with 8 or 9 slaves, who were perhaps members of the same family. The typical slave, however, was more likely to be in a group of 20 or more other slaves on a large farm or small plantation.

William Airs, a South Carolina Low Country farmer, owned nine slaves and worked 130 acres of mostly cotton in 1850. A decade later, with the addition of one more slave, he was able to buy more land and produced 54 bushels of rice in addition to cotton. In 1841, a young white North Carolinian, John Flintoff, went to Mississippi dreaming of wealth and prestige. Beginning as an overseer managing an uncle's farm, he bought a "negro boy 7 years old" even before he owned any land. After several years of unrewarding struggle, Flintoff married and returned to

Population Patterns in the South: Whites, Slaves, and Free Blacks, by State, 1860

Where were most free blacks, and how would you explain their location? How do you explain the tiny percentage of free blacks in South Carolina, Florida, and Louisiana, and where do you think they were? Which two states had the largest percentage of slaves, and how do you think that affected the regulation of race relations? Given the data on this map, where would you predict the strongest sentiments among whites for states' rights and even, perhaps, secession from the Union? Why?

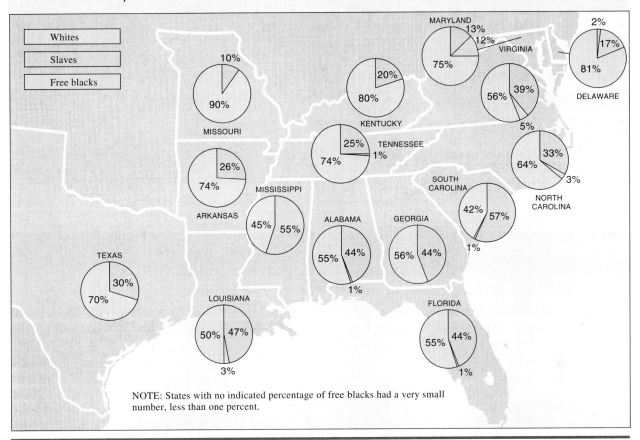

NOTE: States with no indicated percentage of free blacks had a very small number, less than one percent.

North Carolina. There he finally bought 124 acres and a few more cheap, young blacks, and by 1860, he had a modest farm with several slaves growing corn, wheat, and tobacco. Although he never realized his grand dreams, his son went to college, and his wife, he reported proudly, "has lived a Lady."

Slavery was a powerful force in the lives of middle-level farmers like Flintoff and Airs, who had only a few slaves, and even for those who owned none. Economic, social, and political standing depended on owning slaves. Flintoff hoped to purchase one slave, preferably a female who would bear children, and then climb the socioeconomic ladder. Most white southerners thus supported slavery whether they owned slaves or not. They also defended the institution because it gave them feelings of superiority

over blacks and of kinship, if not quite equality, with other whites. Although there was always a small element of southern society that believed in emancipation, most southerners did not. An Alabama farmer with a small farm told a northern visitor in the 1850s that if the slaves got their freedom, "they'd all think themselves just as good as we. . . . How would you like to hev a nigger feelin' just as good as a white man?"

As much as they defended slavery, the yeoman farmers, many of them of Scots-Irish descent, defended the independence of their household and property even more. Small as it was, their land and family household was indispensably important to their livelihood, self-esteem, and political rights in a region dominated by a privileged elite. Fiercely

White Class Structure in the South, 1860

In a pyramidal class structure, the richest southerners were those few with the largest number of slaves. As the chart shows, three-fourths of antebellum southerners held no slaves at all.

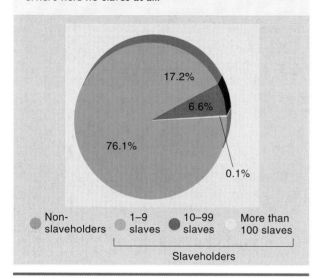

17.2%

6.6%

76.1%

0.1%

Non-slaveholders   1–9 slaves   10–99 slaves   More than 100 slaves

Slaveholders

proud of their independence and jealously protective of their modest properties, the yeoman farmers struggled for a share of political power against the planters. Other than defending states rights and their property against the national government (and sometimes against their powerful planter neighbors), yeoman political behavior focused on such local issues as militia organization and the election of sheriffs and tax collectors.

The yeoman households were also "households of faith," adamantly believing in an evangelical Christianity that endorsed both the sanctity of the family and of slavery. Although acknowledging spiritual equality (slaves, one woman said, may have "souls as well as white people"), they did not practice it. The contradictions did not end there. Calling themselves "self-working farmers," the yeoman household economic system included wives, the older children, and perhaps a handful of slaves or one slave hired on weekends. A neighbor said of Ezekiel Stokes of South Carolina that his slaves "were but three or four for help, and he and his family worked with [them] in the fields."

The Nonslaveholding South

Below Airs, Flintoff, and other middling farmers lived the majority of white southerners who owned no slaves. Some 30 to 50 percent were landless. This nonslaveholding class, 75 percent of all southerners, was scattered throughout the South. Newton Knight, for example, worked a harsh piece of land cut out of the pines of southern Mississippi. He and his wife lived in a crude log cabin, scratching out their livelihood by growing corn and sweet potatoes and raising chickens and hogs. A staunch Baptist given to fits of violence, Knight had once killed a black.

Abner Ginn lived in the South Carolina low country, and although he had 560 acres in 1850, most of it was woodland and swamp, and only 60 acres were cleared. On this land, worth only $1,000, he and his wife and nine children (six were under the age of 10) grew subsistence foodstuffs such as corn and sweet potatoes and managed a small herd of beef cattle and some dairy cows and pigs. He also managed to grow two bales of cotton for market. He had no slaves, though occasionally he would hire one on his off-time to help him split rails, dig fence posts, and cut shingles. During the 1850s, as Ginn's children grew older and were able to help more, he brought more land under cultivation and added wheat, rye, rice, and some horses. More successful than most nonslaveholding whites, the "hard-working" Abner Ginn was called "a well-off poor man." Success mainly meant retaining his independence and land and increasing its value.

Living throughout the South—low country, foothills, and upcountry—whites like Ginn and Knight generally worked poorer land than yeoman and planters. Far from commercial centers, they were largely self-sufficient, raising almost all their food and trading hogs, eggs, small game, or homemade items for cash and necessary manufactured items like kettles and rifles. With the indispensable help of their wives and children, they maintained a subsistence household economy, making soap, shoes, candles, whiskey, coarse textiles, and ax handles. They lived in two-room log houses separated by a "dog run." Their drab, isolated life was brightened when neighbors and families gathered at corn huskings and quilting parties, logrolling and wrestling matches, and political stump and revivalist camp meetings. They were Methodists and Baptists, believing both in a righteous God and slavery.

The nonslaveholding farmers were certainly in the majority. In 1860 in North Carolina, 70 percent of the farmers held fewer than 100 acres, whereas in Mississippi and Louisiana, reputedly large plantation states, more than 60 percent of the farms were smaller than 100 acres. Despite their numerical majorities, they were politically marginalized. Although many may have resented the tradition of political deference to "betters," they were not ready to challenge planters for political power. Most fought with the Confederacy during the Civil War; a few, such as those in southern Mississippi who organized a guerrilla band of Unionists, silently retained their Unionist views.

Another group of whites were herdsmen raising hogs and other livestock. They supplied bacon and pork to local slaveholders (who often thought hog raising beneath their dignity) and drove herds to stockyards in Nashville, Louisville, and Savannah. The South raised two-thirds of the nation's hogs. In 1860, the value of southern livestock was $500 million, twice that of cotton. Although much of the corn crop fed the hogs, many herdsmen preferred to let their stock roam loose in the woods. However valuable the total size of the hog business, hog herdsmen were low on the southern social ladder.

Below them were the poorest whites of the South, who comprised about 10 percent of the population. Often sneeringly called "dirt eaters" and "crackers,"

Southern yeoman farm families lived self-sufficient lives in cabins such as this one on the edge of a clearing. The isolation of the woman drawing water from a well was partly relieved by gatherings such as quilting parties, which created not only social contact but also a uniquely female American work of useful art. Note that men were also at the party, talking (politics, perhaps) by the stove, bouncing a baby, carrying food, and courting a young woman by the quilt. *(above, Abby Aldrich Rockefeller Folk Art Center; right, North Wind Picture Archives)*

they eked out a living in isolated, inhospitable areas growing vegetables, hunting small game, and raising a few pigs. Some made corn whiskey, and many hired out as farmhands for an average wage of $14 per month. Because of poor diet and bad living conditions, these poor whites often suffered from hookworm and malaria. This, and the natural debilitation of heat and poverty, gave them a reputation as lazy, shiftless, and illiterate. An English visitor described them as "the most degraded race of human beings claiming an Anglo-Saxon origin that can be found on the face of the earth."

Poor whites stayed poor partly because the slaveholding elite acquired a disproportionate amount of land and political power. High slave prices made entry into the planter class increasingly difficult, increasing class tensions except for the common white belief that all classes of whites were better than blacks. Because large planters dominated southern life and owned the most slaves, slavery and relations between slaves and masters is best understood by looking at plantation life during a typical day from morning to night.

MORNING: MASTER AND MISTRESS IN THE BIG HOUSE

It is early morning in the South. Imagine four scenes. In the first, William Waller of Virginia and a neighbor are preparing to leave with 20 choice slaves on a long trip to the slave market in Natchez, Mississippi. Waller is making this "intolerable" journey to sell some of his slaves in order to ease his heavy debts. Although he "loaths the vocation of slave trading," he must recover some money to see his family "freed from my bondage" of indebtedness. To ease his conscience, he intends to supervise the sale personally, thus securing the best possible deal not only for himself but also for his departing slaves.

On another plantation, owned by James Hammond of South Carolina, the horn blows an hour before daylight to awaken slaves for work in the fields. Hammond rises soon after, ever aware that "to continue" as a wealthy master he must "draw the rein tighter and tighter" to hold his slaves "in complete check." In general, he says, "15 to 20 lashes will be sufficient flogging" for most offenses, but "in extreme cases" the punishment "must not exceed 100 lashes in one day."

On an Alabama plantation, Hugh Lawson is up early, writing a sorrowful letter telling of the death of Jim, a "devotedly attached and faithful" slave. "I feel

desolate," Hugh writes, "my most devoted friend is gone and his place can never be supplied by another." As Lawson pens his letter, a female slave has already awakened and "walked across a frosty field in the early morning and gone to the big house to build a fire" for her mistress. As the mistress wakes up, she says to the slave, a grown woman responsible for the welfare of two families, "Well, how's my little nigger today?"

In a fourth household, a middling farm in upcountry Georgia not far from Hammond's plantation, Charles Brock wakes up at dawn and joins his two sons and four slaves to work his modest acreage of grains and sweet potatoes, while Brock's wife and a female slave tend the cows. On small or medium-sized family farms with five or fewer slaves, blacks and whites commonly worked together, as one observer noted, with the "axe of master and man [slave] falling with alternate strokes . . . [and] ploughing side by side."

As these diverse scenes suggest, slavery thoroughly permeated the lives of southern slaveholders. For the enslaved, morning was a time for getting up and going to work. But for white slaveholders, morning involved contact with slaves in many ways: as burdens of figuring profit and loss, as objects to be kept obedient and orderly, as intimates and fellow workers, and as ever-present reminders of fear, hate, and uncertainty.

The Burdens of Slaveholding

Robert Francis Withers Allston (1801–1864) was a major rice planter in a low, swampy, mosquito-infested tidal area of South Carolina where four rivers empty into Winyah Bay. It was a perfect spot for growing rice, but so unhealthy that few whites wanted to live there. The death rate among slaves was appallingly high. In 1840, a total of 18,274 slaves toiled there, but only 2,193 whites, many for only part of the year.

Robert was the fifth generation of Allstons to live in this inhospitable land. By 1860, he owned seven plantations along the Peedee River, totaling some 4,000 acres, in addition to another 9,500 acres of pasture and timberland. He held nearly 600 slaves, 236 of whom worked at the home plantation, Chicora Wood. The total value of his land and slaves in the 1850s was approximately $300,000. Rich in land and labor, he nevertheless had large mortgages and outstanding debts.

Allston was an enlightened, talented, public-spirited man. Educated at West Point and trained for the law, he did far more than practice agriculture. He served in the South Carolina state senate for 24 years and as governor from 1856 to 1858. As he wrote in 1838, his political creed of "virtue and purity" was based on "the principles of Thomas Jefferson." The core of his conviction was a "plain, honest, commonsense reading of the Constitution," which for Allston meant the constitutionality of slavery and nullification and the illegitimacy of abolitionism and the United States Bank.

Allston also reflected Jefferson's humane side. Active in the Episcopal church, he was an ardent reformer, advocating liberalization of South Carolina's poor laws; an improved system of public education open to rich and poor; humanitarian care of disabled people; and the improvement of conditions on the reservations of the Catawba Indians. In 1832, Allston married the equally enlightened Adele Petigru. She participated fully in the management of the plantation and ran it while Robert was away on political business. In a letter to her husband in 1850, Adele demonstrated her diverse interests by reporting on family affairs and the children's learning, sickness among the slaves, the status of spring plowing, the building of a canal and causeway, the bottling of some wine, and current politics. After Robert's death during the Civil War, she would assume control of the Allston plantations, abandoned when Union troops arrived (see Chapter 16).

State politics lured Allston from his land for part of each year, but he was by no means an absentee owner. Except during the worst periods of mosquitoes and heat, the Allstons were fully engaged in the operation of their plantations. Managing thousands of acres of rice required not only an enormous investment in labor and equipment but also careful supervision of both the slaves and an elaborate irrigation system. Although Allston's acreage and slave population were larger than those of most big planters and he grew rice rather than cotton, his concerns were typical.

Allston's letters frequently expressed the serious burdens of owning slaves. Although he was careful to distribute enough cloth, blankets, and shoes to his slaves and to give them sufficient rest, the sickness and death of slaves, especially young fieldworkers, headed his list of concerns. "I lost in one year 28 negroes," he complained, "22 of whom were task hands." He tried to keep slave families together, but sold slaves when necessary. In a letter to his son Benjamin, he expressed concern over the bad example set by a slave driver who was "abandon'd by his hands" because he had not worked with them the previous Sunday. In the same letter, Allston urged

Benjamin to keep up the "patrol duty," less to guard against runaway slaves, he said, than to restrain "vagabond whites." Clearly, the paternal planter class felt a duty to control lower-class whites as well as black slaves.

Other planters likewise saw slavery as both a duty and a burden. Many planters insisted that they worked harder than their slaves to feed and clothe them. R. L. Dabney of Virginia complained, "there could be no greater curse inflicted on us than to be compelled to manage a parcel of Negroes." Curse or not, Dabney and other planters profited from their burdens, a point they seldom admitted.

The Plantation Mistress

Adele Allston and other plantation wives experienced other kinds of burdens. "The mistress of a plantation," wrote Susan Dabney Smedes, "was the most complete slave on it." Southern women were expected to adhere to the cult of domesticity both by improving their husbands' morals, which often meant restraining them from excessive cruelty, and by beautifying their parlors for proper hospitality. Moreover, plantation mistresses suffered under a double standard of morality resulting from the plantation code of honor. They were expected to act as chaste ladies, while their husbands had virtually unrestricted sexual access to slave women. "God forgive us, but ours is a monstrous system," Mary Boykin Chesnut wrote in her diary, adding:

> Like the Patriarchs of old, our men live all in one house with their wives and their concubines; and the mulattoes one sees in every family partly resemble the white children. Any lady is ready to tell you who is the father of all the mulatto children in everybody's household but her own. Those, she seems to think, drop from the clouds.

But the plantation mistress had her own double standard: a former slave woman said of her mistress, Miss Betsy, that "though a warm-hearted woman, [she] was a violent advocate of slavery. I have since been puzzled how to reconcile this with her otherwise Christian character."

Chesnut called the sexual dynamics of slavery "the sorest spot." But there were others. Together with enslaved black females, plantation mistresses had to tend to the food, clothing, health, and welfare of not just their husbands and children, but the slaves, too. One woman complained to a northern visitor: "It is the slaves who own me. Morning, noon, and night, I'm obliged to look after them, to doctor them, and attend to them in every way." Adele

Adele and Robert F. W. Allston shared the work and burdens of managing their rice plantations, while their slaves, many of them women, as seen in these drawings, planted rice seeds by covering them with their feet (as was done in Africa), and later carried the harvested rice to flatboats, where it was taken to the threshing yard. *(Portraits, South Carolina Library, Columbia; Drawings, From Down by the Riverside, Charles Joyner, 1984, sketch by Alice R. Huger Smith, c. 1914; photograph from Photographs and Prints Division, Schomburg Center for Research in Black Culture, The New York Public Library, Astor, Lenox and Tilden Foundations)*

Allston added the management of crops to these duties, reporting to her husband away on business that she was "eager to get the field harvested, but Marcus (a slave) said it was not quite ripe enough . . . so I was forced to wait." A Tennessee planter's son remembered his mother and grandmother as "the busiest women I ever saw."

The plantation mistress, then, served many roles: as a potential humanizing influence on men; as a tough, resourceful, responsible manager of numerous plantation affairs; as a coercer of slaves and perpetuator of the system; and sometimes as a victim herself.

Justifying Slavery

The behavior of Douglass's mistress discussed at the beginning of this chapter suggests that as an institution slavery pressured well-intentioned people to act inhumanely. Increasingly attacked as immoral, slaveholders felt compelled to justify the institution, not only to opponents of the system, but perhaps also to themselves. Until the 1830s, they explained away slavery as a "necessary evil." But unlike in England, where opposition to slavery in the British West Indies succeeded in getting it abolished in 1834, in the United States, as abolitionists stepped up their attack in the 1830s, southerners defended slavery, in John C. Calhoun's words, as "a positive good." They used various arguments.

A biblical justification was based in part on the curse that had fallen upon the son of Ham, one of Noah's children, and in part on Old and New Testament admonitions to servants to obey their masters. As a historical justification, southerners claimed slavery had always existed and that great ancient civilizations—Egypt, Greece, Rome—as well as Spanish and Portuguese colonies in Latin America, had built their grandeur on slave labor. A leading southern economic magazine, De Bow's *Review*, said in 1851 that the South's peculiar institution "gradually enveloped the commercial world and bound the fortunes of American slaves so firmly to human progress, that civilization itself may almost be said to depend upon the continued servitude of blacks in America."

The legal justification rested on the U.S. Constitution's refusal to forbid slavery and on three passages clearly implying its legality: the "three-fifths" clause, the protection of the overseas slave trade for 20 years, and the mandate for returning fugitive slaves across state lines.

A fourth justification for slavery was scientific. Until the 1830s, most white southerners believed that blacks were degraded not by nature but by African climate and their slave condition. Claiming scientific authority, books were written to show black deficiency because of cranial shape and size. With the rise of the "positive good" defense in the 1830s, southerners began to argue that blacks had been created separately as an inherently inferior race, and therefore the destiny of the inferior Africans was to serve the superior Caucasians in work. At best, the slave system would domesticate uncivilized blacks. As Allston put it, "The educated master is the negro's best friend upon earth."

A sociological defense of slavery was implicit in Allston's paternalistic statement. As George Fitzhugh, a leading advocate of this view, argued, "the Negro is but a grown child and must be governed as a child," and so needed the paternal guidance, restraint, and protection of a white master. Many southerners believed that chaos and race mixing would ensue if blacks were freed. Allston wrote that emancipation was unthinkable because it would lead to "giving up our beautiful country to the ravages of the black race and amalgamation with savages." Fitzhugh compared the treatment of southern slaves favorably with that of free blacks and free laborers working in northern factories. These "wage slaves," he argued, worked as hard as slaves, yet with their paltry wages, they had to feed, clothe, and shelter themselves. Southern masters took care of all these ne-cessities. Emancipation, therefore, would be heartless, a burden to both blacks and whites.

Southern apologists for slavery faced the difficult intellectual task of justifying a system that ran counter to the main ideological directions of nineteenth-century American society: the expansion of individual liberty, mobility, economic opportunity, and democratic political participation. Moreover, the southern defense of slavery had to take into account the 75 percent of white families who owned no slaves but envied those who did. To deflect potential for class antagonisms among whites, wealthy planters developed a justification of slavery that pictured all whites as superior to all blacks but equal to one another, as contrasted with Latin America, where gradations of color (favoring the lighter-skinned) mattered. But in the American South, democratic equality among whites was made consistent with racism and slaveholding.

The underlying but rarely admitted motive behind all these justifications was that slavery was profitable, as it was in Latin America. As the southern defense of slavery intensified in the 1840s and 1850s, it aroused greater opposition from northerners and from slaves themselves. Perhaps slavery's worst cruelty was not physical but psychological: to be enslaved and barred from participation in a nation that put a high value on freedom and equality of opportunity.

NOON: SLAVES IN HOUSE AND FIELDS

It is 2 o'clock on a hot July afternoon on the plantation. The midday lunch break is over, and the slaves are returning to field work. Lunch was the usual cornmeal and pork. The slaves now work listlessly, their low stamina resulting from a deficient diet and suffocating heat and humidity. Douglass remembered that "we worked all weathers. . . . It was never too hot, or too cold." Mary Reynolds, a Louisiana slave, recalled that she hated most having to pick cotton "when the frost was on the bolls," which made her hands "git sore and crack open and bleed."

Daily Toil

The daily work schedule for most slaves, whether in the fields or the Big House, was long and demanding. Awakened before daybreak, they worked on an average day 14 hours in the summer and 10 hours in the winter; during harvest, an 18-hour workday was not uncommon. Depending on the size of the workforce and the crop, the slaves were organized either in gangs or according to tasks. Gangs, usually comprised of 20 to 25 slaves, worked the cotton rows under the watchful eye and quick whip of a driver. Ben Simpson, a Georgia slave, remembered vividly his master's "great, long whip platted out of rawhide" that struck any slave who would "fall behind or give out."

Under the task system, which slaves preferred and negotiated for cleverly, each slave had a specific task to complete daily. It gave slaves incentive to work hard enough to finish early, but their work was scrutinized constantly. An overseer's weekly report to Robert Allston in 1860 noted that he had "flogged for hoeing corn bad Fanny 12 lashes, Sylvia 12, Monday 12, Phoebee 12, Susanna 12, Salina 12, Celia 12, Iris 12." Black slave drivers were no less demanding. One reported to his master that because the slaves only got 1½ acres plowed instead of 7, "I gave them ten licks a peace [sic] upon their skins [and] I gave Julyann eight or ten licks for misplacing her hoe."

An average slave was expected to pick 130 to 150 pounds of cotton per day; work on sugar and rice plantations was even harder. Sugar demanded constant cultivation, digging ditches in snake-infested fields. At harvest time, cutting, stripping, and carrying the cane to the sugar house for boiling was exhausting, as was cutting and hauling huge quantities of firewood. Working in the low-country rice

Slaves survived nobly despite hard work, ill-health, a deficient diet, and poor living conditions. Enslaved families had a double burden of work and caring for their families, as seen in the photographs (top) of women working in the fields, one picking cotton with a child and the other helping till rice, and in the drawing (bottom left) of the woman cooking in her cabin while her children look out from the doorway. But female slaves also managed to develop networks of support while working, as seen in the drawing (bottom right) of the three women winnowing rice. *(Bottom right,* From Down by the Riverside, *Charles Joyner, 1984, sketch by Alice R. Huger Smith, c. 1914, top, photographs from Photographs and Prints Division, Schomburg Center for Research in Black Culture, The New York Public Library, Astor, Lenox and Tilden Foundations; bottom left, Private Collection)*

fields was worse: slaves spent long hours standing in water up to their knees.

House slaves, mostly women, had relatively easier assignments, though they were usually called on to help with the harvest. They worked in or near the Big House as maids, cooks, seamstresses, laundresses, coachmen, drivers, gardeners, and "mammies." Enslaved males did most of the skilled artisan work on the plantation; many became skilled carpenters, stonemasons, blacksmiths, weavers, mechanics, and millers. More intimacy between whites and blacks occurred near the house. House slaves ate and dressed better than those in the fields. But there were disadvantages: close supervision, duty day and night, and conflicts with whites that could range from being given unpleasant jobs to insults, spontaneous angry whippings, and sexual assault. The most feared punishment, however, other than sale to the Deep South, was to be sent to the fields.

Slave Health and Punishments

Although slave owners had an interest in keeping their workforce healthy, slaves led sickly lives. Home was a crude, one-room log cabin with a dirt floor and a fireplace. Cracks and holes allowed mosquitoes easy entry, disturbing sleep. Typical furnishings included a table, some stools or boxes to sit on, an iron pot and wooden dishes, and perhaps a bed. Cabins were crowded, usually housing more than one family. Clothing, issued once or twice a year, was shabby and uncomfortable, with shoes, men's cotton shirts and pants and, to the women, cotton and woollen cloth to make their own and their children's clothes.

Studies on the adequacy of the typical slave diet disagree, though most show that the food they ate was deficient in calories and vitamins. Diet was comparable to that of Latin American slaves, which was the worst on sugar and coffee plantations. North American slaves got an average ration of a peck of cornmeal per week, three to four pounds of salt pork or bacon, some molasses, and perhaps some sweet potatoes. The mainstay was corn. While some slaves (fewer than those in Latin America) were able to grow vegetables and to fish or hunt, they rarely enjoyed fresh meat, dairy products, fruits, or vegetables. The limitations of their diet led to the theft of food and the practice of eating dirt, which caused worms. Slave diet also resulted in skin disorders, cracked lips, sore eyes, vitamin deficiency diseases, and even mental illness.

Women slaves especially suffered weaknesses caused by vitamin deficiency, hard work, and disease, as well as those associated with menstruation and childbirth. Women were expected to do the same tasks in the fields as the men, in addition to cooking, sewing, child care, and traditional female jobs in the quarters when the fieldwork was finished. "Pregnant women," the usual rule stated, "should not plough or lift" and had a three-week recovery period following birth. But these guidelines were often violated. Mortality of slave children under five years of age was twice as high as for white children.

Life expectancy for American slaves was longer than for those in Latin America and the Caribbean, where the labor-intensive sugar industry used them up within a few years. Moreover, because of poor diet and the climate, slaves were highly susceptible to epidemics. Despite some resistance as a result of the sickle-cell trait, many slaves died from malaria, yellow fever, cholera, and other diseases spread by mosquitoes or bad water. Slaves everywhere suffered and died from intestinal ailments in the summer and respiratory diseases in the winter. An average of 20 percent (and sometimes 50 to 60 percent) of the slaves on a given plantation would be sick at one time, and no overseer's report was complete without recording sicknesses and days of lost labor.

The relatively frequent incidence of whippings and other physical punishments aggravated the poor physical condition of the slaves. Many slaveholders offered rewards—a garden plot, an extra holiday, hiring out, and passes—as inducements for faithful labor, and they withheld these privileges as punishment. But southern court records, newspapers, plantation diaries, and slave memoirs reveal that sadistic punishments were frequent and harsh.

The slave William Wells Brown reported that on his plantation, the whip was used "very frequently and freely" for inadequate or uncompleted work, stealing, running away, and insolence and lying. Whippings ranged from 10 to 100 strokes of the lash. Former slaves described a good owner as one who did not "whip too much" and a bad owner as one who "whipped till he'd bloodied you and blistered you." Slaveholders had many theories on the appropriate kind of lash to inflict sufficient pain and punishment without damaging a valuable laborer. Other punishments included confinement in stocks and jails during leisure hours, chains, muzzling, salting lash wounds, branding, mauling by dogs, and having to do "women's work."

Nothing testifies better to the physical brutality of slavery than the advertisements for runaways that slaveholders printed in antebellum newspapers. In searching for the best way to describe the physical characteristics of a missing slave, slave owners unwittingly condemned their own behavior. A Mississippi runaway was described as having "large raised scars . . . in the small of his back and

---

An Overseer's Report

W. Sweet to Adele Petigru Allston N[ightin]gale hall, 14th September, 1864

Dear madam I comence my harvest on last saterday on Boath Plantations the weather is very fin for harvest so far I will Bring some Rice in to the Barn yard at N[ightin]gale hall to Day and at ganderloss to morrow. I think that I will make about 2 Barrels of Syrrup on Each Place I finish grinding at ganderloss to Day I will not finish at Nightingale hall until the last of next weeak. litle Dianah was confined with a boy child on the 9 I am very sorry to say to you that one of Prisilia children a boy name July Dide on 12th with fits a[nd] fever I have had a grea[t] deal of fever among the children But not much among the grone negroes. old Rose is Stil quite sick mr Belflowers sent toney to mee on friday last I have concluded to let toney wife stay whare she is for a while as I understand that she is Pregnant and will not Be much survice in the harvest if I am Rong for soe Doing Pleas let mee know. the negroes all sends thare love to you an family my self and family is very un well.

N[ightin]gale hall

8th September	all hands hoing Bancks and grinding shugar cain no sick
9th September	all hands hoing Bancks grind shugar cain no sick
10th September	all hands cu[tt]ing Rice grinding shugar cain no sick
12th September	all hands harvesting grinding shugar cain 3 women with sick children
13th September	all hands harvesting grinding shugar cain 3 women with sick children
14th September	all hands harvesting grinding shugar cain 1 woman with sick child

Source: *The South Carolina Rice Plantation as Revealed in the Papers of Robert F. W. Allston*, ed., J. H. Easterby (1945).

---

on his abdomen nearly as large as a person's finger." A Georgia female was "considerably marked by the whip." Branding left even more vivid marks. One fugitive, Betty, was described as recently "burnt . . . with a hot iron on the left side of her face." "I tried to make the letter M," her master admitted in his diary.

Slave Law and the Family

Complicating master–slave relationships was the status of slaves as both human beings and property, a legal and psychological ambiguity the South never resolved. On the one hand, the slaves had names, personalities, families, and wills of their own, making them fellow humans. On the other hand, they were items of property, purchased to perform specific profit-making tasks. As a Kentucky court put the problem in 1836, "Although the law of this state considers slaves as property, . . . it recognizes their personal existence."

This ambiguity led to confusion in the laws governing treatment of slaves. Until the early 1830s, some southern abolitionist activity persisted, primarily in the Upper South, and slaves had slight hopes of being freed. But they also suffered careless, often brutal treatment. This confusion changed with the convergence in 1831 of Nat Turner's revolt and William Lloyd Garrison's attack on slavery in the *Liberator* (see Chapter 12). The South tightened up the slave system in the 1830s. Laws prohibited manumission, and slaves' hopes of freedom other than by revolt or escape vanished. At the same time, laws

protecting them from overly severe treatment were strengthened, and material conditions generally improved.

But laws were rarely enforced, and treatment varied with individual slaveholders and depended on their mood and other circumstances. Most planters, like Robert Allston, encouraged their slaves to marry and tried to keep families intact, believing that families made black males more docile and less inclined to run away. But some masters failed to respect slave marriages or broke them up because of financial problems, which southern law permitted them to do. As a North Carolina Supreme Court justice said in 1853, "Our law required no solemnity or form in regard to the marriage of slaves."

Adding to the pain of forced breakup of the slave family was the sexual abuse of black women. Although the frequency of such abuse is unknown, the presence of thousands of mulattoes in the antebellum era points to the practice. White men in the South took advantage of black enslaved women by offering gifts for sexual "favors," by threatening those who refused sex with physical punishment or the sale of a child or loved one, by purchasing concubines, and by outright rape. As Frederick Douglass put it, "The slave woman is at the mercy of the fathers, sons or brothers of her master."

To obtain cheap additional slaves for the workforce, slaveholders encouraged young slave women, whether married or not, to bear children. If verbal prodding and inducements such as less work and more rations did not work, masters would force mates on slave women. "Massa" Hawkins, for exam-

The breakup of families and friendships was an ever-present fear for slaves, who might be sold for purely economic reasons as well as in retribution for uncooperative behavior. In this painting of a slave market by an unidentified artist in the 1850s, note the varied colors of the African Americans (a sad, light-skinned young woman in the center, a mulatto male in the left foreground staring longingly at her, and dark-skinned women clutching their children to the right) and the diverse social class of the whites (the suave merchant leaning back in a chair on the porch, nattily attired slave auctioneers and buyers, and a gaudily dressed lower-class overseer cracking the whip over the separation of child from mother). All southern social classes perpetuated slavery, and African Americans of all hues were victimized by it. *(Anonymous American,* Slave Market, *c. 1860/The Carnegie Museum of Art, Gift of Mrs. W. Fitch Ingersoll)*

ple, chose Rufus to live with an unwilling 16-year-old Rose Williams. Years later, she recalled how she first repulsed him: "I puts de feet 'gainst him and give him a shove and out he go on de floor." When Rufus persisted, Rose took a poker and "lets him have it over de head." Hawkins threatened Rose with a "whippin' at de stake" or sale away "from my folks." This was too much for her. "What am I's to do? So I 'cides to do as de massa wish and so I yields."

Slaves, however, usually chose their own mates on the basis of mutual attraction during a courtship complicated by the threat of white interference. As among poor whites, premarital intercourse was frequent, but promiscuous behavior was rare. Most couples maintained affectionate, lasting relationships. This, too, led to numerous sorrows. Members of slave families, powerless to intervene, had to witness the flogging or physical abuse of loved ones. William Wells Brown remembered that "cold chills ran over me and I wept aloud" when he saw his mother whipped. To avoid these scenes, some slaves preferred to marry a spouse from another plantation.

Although motherhood was the key event in an enslaved woman's life, bearing children and the double burden of work and family responsibilities challenged her resourcefulness. Some masters provided time off for nursing mothers, but the more common practice was for them to work in the fields with their newborn infants lying nearby, wrapped in cloth for protection from the sun. Women developed support networks, looking after one another's children; meeting to sew, quilt, cook, or do laundry; and attending births, caring for the sick and dying, and praying together.

The worst trauma for slaves was the separation of families, a haunting fear rarely absent from slave consciousness. Although many slaveholders had both moral and economic reasons to maintain families, inevitably they found themselves destroying them. One study of 30 years of data from the Deep South shows that masters dissolved one-third of all slave marriages. Even then, the slaves tried to maintain contact with loved ones sold elsewhere. "My Dear Wife for you and my Children my pen cannot Express the Griffe I feel to be parted from you all," wrote Abream Scriven.

There was a sound basis, in fact, for the abolitionists' contention that slavery was a harsh, brutal system. However, two points need to be emphasized. First, although slavery led otherwise decent human beings to commit inhumane acts, many slaveholders throughout the South were neither sadistic nor cruel; they did what they could for their slaves, out of both economic self-interest and Christian morality. Second, whether under kind or cruel masters, the slaves endured with dignity, communal sensitivity, and even some joy. If daytime in the fields describes slavery at its worst, nighttime in the quarters, as examined from the

Administrator's Sale, by Order of the Ordinary.

A PRIME AND ORDERLY GANG OF

68 Long Cotton Field Negroes,

Belonging to the Estate of the late Christopher J. Whaley.

WILBUR & SON

Will sell at PUBLIC AUCTION in Charleston,

At the Mart in Chalmers Street,

On Thursday, Feb. 2d, 1860,

COMMENCING AT ELEVEN O'CLOCK,

THE FOLLOWING GANG OF LONG COTTON NEGROES,

Who are said to be remarkably prime, and will be sold as per Catalogue.

NAMES.		AGES.	NAMES.		AGES.
Jimmy,	driver,	30	Carter,		36
Flora,	seamstress,	24	Taffy,		13
James,		5	Rachel,	($ 720,)	8
Charles,	($ 125,)	1	Jannett,		18
August,		52	Phebe,	($ 860,)	40
Mathias,	($ 1,220,)	18	Judy,		8
Sandy,		16	Major,		40
John,		13	Lavinia,		30
Tom,		70	Billy,	($ 550,)	10
Jack,		38	Tamor,		6
James,		6	Jimmy,		52
Leah,		5	Kate,		46
Flora,		2	Susan,		25
Andrew,		42	Thomas,	($ 380,)	6
Binah,		40	Kate,		1
Phillis,		20	Edward,	coachman,	49
Mary,		15	Amey,		22
Lymus,		10	Teneh,	washer,	30
Abram,	($ 275,)	2	Josephine,		9
Binah,	2 mos.		Sam,		11
Andrew,		29	Isaac,		5
Hagar,		25	William,		1
Dayman,		4	Amey,		27
Cuffy,		21	Louisa,	($ 750,)	8
Hagar,	($ 1,320,)	20	Joe,		3
Margaret,		85	Sam,	ruptured,	65
Lucy,	cripple,	60	Andrew,	dropsical,	61
John,		22	Daniel,		70
Ellick,	($ 1,160,)	18	Lymus,		30
Libby,		19	Lucy,	nurse,	58

TERMS.

One-third Cash; balance in one and two years, secured by bond, and mortgage of the negroes, with approved personal security. Purchasers to pay us for papers.

29

Announcement of a slave sale in Charleston, 1860. What do you learn about the economics and morality of slavery from this poster?

black perspective, reveals the slaves' survival powers and their capacity to mold an African-American culture even under slavery.

NIGHT: SLAVES IN THEIR QUARTERS

It is near sundown, and the workday is almost over. Some slaves begin singing the gentle spiritual "Steal Away to Jesus," and others join in. To the unwary overseer or master, the song suggests happy slaves, content with their earthly lot and looking forward to heaven "in the sweet bosom of Jesus." To the slaves, however, the song is a signal that, as ex-slave Wash Wilson put it, they are to "steal away to Jesus" because "dere gwine be a 'ligious meetin' dat night."

In the slave quarters, away from whites and daily work, Wilson said, "sometimes us sing and pray all night." In the quarters, slaves preserved much of their African heritage and created an elaborate black community that helped them make sense out of their lives. In family life, religion, song, dance, the playing of musical instruments, and the telling of

stories, the slaves described their experiences and sought release from suffering.

Black Christianity

As suggested by the scene Wash Wilson described, Christian worship was indispensable to life in the slave quarters, mixed with elements of Islamic and African religious practices. The revivals of the early nineteenth century led to an enormous growth of Christianity among black Americans. Independent black Baptist and Methodist churches, especially in border areas, served both slaves and free blacks and occasionally even whites. These separate churches steered a careful path to maintain their freedom and avoid white interference.

But the vast majority of southern blacks were slaves, attending plantation churches set up by their masters. These churches were rigidly segregated, either by a roped off rear section for the blacks or, as one slave said, "us niggers sat on one side and de white folks sat on the other." Robert Allston built a prayer house for his slaves, reporting with pride that they were "attentive . . . and greatly improved in intelligence and morals." Black religious gatherings were usually forbidden unless white observers were present or white preachers led them. Although tolerating the presence of illiterate but eloquent slave preachers who occasionally administered baptisms, weddings, and funerals, masters sought to direct religion to their own ends.

For the slaveholders, religion was a form of social control. In the master's church, sermons emphasized the importance of work, obedience, honesty, and respect for the master's property. "All that preacher talked about," one slave remembered, "was for us slaves to obey our master and not to lie and steal." To enforce obedience, slaves were required to say catechisms that emphasized the masters' view of black inferiority and sinfulness: "Q. Who was the first Negro? A. Cain. Q. How did he become so? A. The Lord set a black mark upon him. Q. Did the Southern slave come from him? A. Yes." In another, contrasting their difficult toiling in the fields with Adam and Eve's easy work in the garden of Eden, slaves repeated the following:

Q. What makes the crops so hard to grow now?
A. Sin makes it.
Q. What makes you lazy?
A. My own wicked heart.
Q. How do you know your heart is wicked?
A. I feel it every day.

There were limits, however, to white control. Although some slaves accommodated to the master's brand of Christianity and patiently waited for heavenly deliverance, others rebelled and sought earthly liberty. Not far from Allston's plantation, several slaves were discovered (and imprisoned) for singing "We'll soon be free / We'll fight for liberty / When de Lord will call us home." Douglass organized an illegal Sabbath school, "the sweetest engagement with which I was ever blessed," where he and others risked whippings while learning about Christianity and how to read. In religious schools and meetings like these, the slaves created an "invisible" church. On Sunday morning, they dutifully sat through the "white fo'ks service in de mornin'," Sarah, an Alabama slave recalled, waiting for the "real meetin'" and "real preachin'" later that night.

Long into the night, they would sing, dance, shout, and pray in the call and response pattern characteristic of black religion to this day. "Ya' see," Sarah explained, "niggers lack ta shout a whole lot an' wid de white fo'ks al'round 'em, dey couldn't shout jes' lack dey want to." But at night they could, taking care to deaden the sound to keep the whites away by hanging curtains from the trees or, in an old African custom, to turn over a pot to "catch the sound." Another African practice, the ring shout, forbidden by Methodists, was transformed into the "ecstatic shout," praising the Lord. The religious ceremony in "the hush arbor" relieved the day's burdens and expressed communal religious values. "At night," another slave recalled with pride, "was when the darkies really did have they freedom of spirit."

Although many of the practices were African, the messages reiterated over again in the invisible slave church were the Judeo-Christian themes of suffering, thanksgiving, and deliverance from bondage. "We prayed a lot to be free," Anderson Edwards said. "The folks would sing and pray and testify and clap their hands," recalled Simon Brown, "just as if God was right there in the midst of them." The freedom the slaves sought was a complex blend of a peaceful soul and an earthly escape from slavery. Nothing better illustrated these mixed Christian themes of suffering and redemption than spirituals.

The Power of Song

A group of slaves gathers at night in the woods behind their quarters to sing and shout together. Two moods are expressed. First, they mourn with "trebbled spirit" being stolen from Africa, their families "sold apart." But second ("O brothers, don't get weary"), they sing: "There's a better day a-coming. / Will you go along with me? / There's a better day a-coming. / Go sound the jubilee."

Music was a crucial form of expression in the slave quarters on both secular and religious occa-

sions. The slaves were adept at creating a song, as one woman recalled, "on de spurn of de moment." Jeanette Robinson Murphy described a process of spontaneous creation that, whether in rural gospels or urban jazz, describes black music to this day. "We'd all be at the 'prayer house' de Lord's day," she said, when all of a sudden in the midst of a white preacher's sermon, "de Lord would come a-shinin' thoo dem pages and revive dis ole nigger's heart." She continued, "I'd jump up dar and den and holler and shout and sing and pat, and dey would all cotch de words and I'd sing it to some ole shout song I'd heard 'em sing from Africa, and dey'd all take it up and keep at it, and keep a-addin' to it, and den it would be a spiritual."

Spirituals reiterated the basic Judeo-Christian theme: A chosen people, the children of God, were held in bondage but would be delivered: "To the Promised Land I'm Bound to Go," "God Down Moses," and "Who Will Deliver Po' Me?" What they meant by deliverance often had a double meaning: freedom in heaven and freedom in the North. Where, exactly, was the desired destination of "Oh Canaan, sweet Canaan / I am bound for the land of Canaan"? Was it heaven? Freedom "anyplace else but here?" Or a literal reference to the terminus of the Underground Railroad in Canada? For different slaves, and at different times for the same person, it meant all of these.

Slave songs did not always contain double or hidden meanings. Sometimes slaves gathered simply for music, to play fiddles, drums, and other instruments fashioned in imitation of West African models. Some musicians were invited to perform at white ceremonies and parties, but most played for the slave community. Weddings, funerals, holiday celebrations, family reunions, and a successful harvest were all occasions for a communal gathering, usually with music.

So, too, was news of external events that affected their lives—a crisis in the master's situation, a change in the slave code, a Civil War battle, or emancipation. "The songs of the slave," Douglass wrote, "represent the sorrows of his heart." Indeed, they often expressed the sadness of broken families and the burdens of work; they were filled with images of trouble, toil, and homelessness. But they also expressed joy, triumph, and deliverance. Each expression of sorrow usually ended in an outburst of eventual liberation and justice. "O nobody knows a who I am" resolved itself into "bells a-ringing in my soul." And the deep sorrow of "Sometimes I feel like a motherless chile" was transformed later in the song into "Sometimes I feel like / A eagle in de air. . . . / Gonna spread my wings an' / Fly, fly, fly."

After sundown, when the work was done, slaves often gathered in "hush arbors" deep in the woods, away from the overseer's and master's interference. There they danced the "ring shout" and "praised de Lord" in ways that combined African and Christian forms of spiritual expression. This painting by John Antrobus shows a "Negro Burial." *(The Historic New Orleans Collection)*

The Enduring Family

The role of music in all milestones of family life suggests that the family was central to life in the slave quarters. Although sexual abuse and family separation were all too real, so was the hope for family continuity. Naming practices, for example, show that children were connected to large extended families.

The benefits of family cohesion were those of any group: love, protection, education, moral guidance, cultural transmission, status, role models, and support. All these existed in the slave quarters. As the slaves gathered in the quarters at the end of the day, parents passed onto their children the family story, language patterns and words, recipes, folktales, musical traditions, and models of strength and beauty. Thus, they preserved cultural traditions, which enhanced the identity and self-esteem of parents and children alike. Parents taught their children how to survive in the world and how to cope with slavery. As the young ones neared the age for full-time field work, their parents instructed them in the best ways to pick cotton or corn, how to avoid the overseer's

In the quarters at night, slave men, women, and children created a vibrant black community, socializing outdoors amid the physical objects typical of their daily life. *(© Collection of the New-York Historical Society)*

whip, whom to trust and learn from, and ways of fooling the master.

Opportunities existed on many plantations for parents to perform extra work for money to buy sugar or clothing; to hunt and fish, thereby adding protein to their family's diet; or to tend a small garden to grow vegetables. In such small ways, they improved the welfare of their families. J. W. C. Pennington proudly recalled helping his "father at night in making straw hats and willow-baskets, by which means we supplied our family with little articles of food, clothing and luxury."

Nor were slaves always totally at the mercy of abusive masters and overseers. Mary Prince used sass to tell her Antigua mistress that "she ought not to use me so," and her Bermuda master, who struck her for dropping some plates, that "he was a very indecent man—very spiteful" and that "I would not live longer with him." Occasionally, one family member could intervene to prevent the abuse of another. Harriet Jacobs fended off her master's advances partly by her cleverness and sass ("I openly . . . expressed my contempt for him"), and partly by threats to use her free grandmother's considerable influence in the community against him. That enraged but stopped him.

When family intervention, appeals for mercy, or conjurers' magic did not work, some slaves resorted to force. In 1800, a slave named Ben shot dead a white man for living with Ben's wife, and another slave killed an overseer in 1859 for raping his wife. Female slaves, too, risked serious consequences to protect themselves or family members. When Cherry Loguen was attacked by a knife-wielding rapist, she knocked him out with a large branch. When an Arkansas overseer abused a slave woman named Lucy, her son reported that she "jumped on him and like to tore him up."

The love and affection that slaves had for each other was sometimes a liability. Many slaves, women especially, were reluctant to run away because they did not want to leave their families. Those who fled were easily caught because, as an overseer near Natchez, Mississippi, told a northern visitor, they "almost always kept in the neighborhood, because they did not like to go where they could not sometimes get back and see their families." Others were reluctant to give up private means of supplementing their diet and resources by hiring out or growing food for trade.

As these episodes suggest, despite violence, sexual abuse, and separation, slave parents continued to serve as protectors, providers, comforters, transmitters of culture, and role models for their children.

Despite separation, sale, and sexual abuse by white masters, many slave families endured and provided love, support, and self-esteem to their members. This 1862 photograph shows five generations of a slave family, all born on the plantation of J. J. Smith of Beaufort, South Carolina. *(Library of Congress)*

Folktales

A frequent activity of family life in the slave quarters was telling stories. The folktale was an especially useful and indirect way in which older slaves could express hostility toward their masters, impart wisdom to the young, and teach them how to survive and gain a measure of freedom, while at the same time entertaining themselves. Folktales, cleverly indirect, reveal to historians a great deal about the enslaved Africans' view of their experience and aspirations.

Although the tales took many forms, perhaps the best known are the "Brer Rabbit" animal stories. The trickster rabbit, who existed originally in West African folklore (and in Brazilian fables as a tortoise), was weak and careless, often looked down on by the other animals. Like the slaves, he was a victim. But he was also boastful, outwardly happy, and full of mischief. More importantly, he knew how to use cleverness and cunning to outwit stronger foes (like Brer Wolf), usually by knowing them better than they knew him, a psychological necessity for all who are oppressed.

In one story, the powerful Brer Tiger took all the water and food for himself during a time of famine, leaving the weaker animals miserable. Brer Rabbit, however, turned things around. He played on Brer Tiger's fears that he would be blown away by a "big wind," which was secretly manufactured by the rabbit with the help of other creatures. The tiger was so afraid of the wind (perhaps the winds of revolt?) that he begged Brer Rabbit to tie him "tightly" to a tree to keep from being blown away. Brer Rabbit, although initially resistant in order to make Brer Tiger beg harder, was finally happy to oblige, after which all the creatures of the forest were able to share the cool water and juicy pears that the tiger had denied them.

In another folktale, Brer Rabbit fell into a well but then got out by tricking Brer Wolf into thinking it was better to be in the cool bottom of the well than outside where it was hot. As the wolf lowered himself down in one bucket, Brer Rabbit rose up in the other, laughingly saying as he passed Brer Wolf, "Dis am life; some go up and some go down." In these stories, the slaves vicariously outwitted their more powerful masters and usually reversed roles.

The accompanying story excerpt is from perhaps the most famous animal tale, "The Tar Baby Tricks Brer Rabbit." This version is by William J. Faulkner, who, after he retired as minister and dean of men at Fisk University, gathered and recorded the folktales he had heard in his youth in South Carolina from a former slave. Rev. Faulkner did not like to tell stories in dialect because he believed readers formed stereotyped judgments from the dialect and missed the significance of the tale itself. We enter the story as an angry Brer Wolf has decided on a plan to catch the lazy Brer Rabbit, who refused to help the wolf build a well and has been fooling him by drinking from the well while Brer Wolf was asleep.

When you have finished reading the story, ask yourself what you learned about slavery from this story. Did violence work for Brer Rabbit or did it only make things worse? What finally worked? How do you interpret the ending? Brer Rabbit returned to the briar patch, "the place where I was born." But is the briar patch, with all its thorns, scratches, and roots, more like Africa or slavery? Or what?

Reflecting on the Past   Think about the stories you heard as a child or now find yourself telling others. How do they express the realities, flaws, values, and dreams of the American people? The same question applies to the songs we sing, the art we make, the rhythms we move to, and the jokes we tell: What do they tell us about ourselves and our values? In answering these questions, we deepen our knowledge of history.

Tar Baby

Brer Wolf studied and studied to find a way to catch Brer Rabbit. He scratched his head, and he pulled his chin whiskers until by and by he said, "I know what I'll do. I'll make me a tar baby, and I'll catch that good-for-nothing rabbit."*

And so Brer Wolf worked and worked until he had made a pretty little girl out of tar. He dressed the tar baby in a calico apron and carried her up to the well, where he stood her up and fastened her to a post in the ground so that nobody could move her. Then Brer Wolf hid in the bushes and waited for Brer Rabbit to come for some water. But three days passed before Brer Rabbit visited the well again. On the fourth day, he came with a bucket in his hand. When he saw the little girl, he stopped and looked at her. Then he said, "Hello. What's your name? What are you doing here, little girl?"

The little girl said nothing.

This made Brer Rabbit angry, and he shouted at her, "You no-mannered little snip, you! How come you don't speak to your elders?"

The little girl still said nothing.

"I know what to do with little children like you. I'll slap your face and teach you some manners if you don't speak to me," said Brer Rabbit.

Still the little girl said nothing.

And then Brer Rabbit lost his head and said, "Speak to me, I say. I'm going to slap you." With that, Brer Rabbit slapped the tar baby in the face, and his right hand stuck.

"A-ha, you hold my hand, do you? Turn me loose, I say. Turn me loose. If you don't, I'm going to slap you with my left hand. And if I hit you with my left hand, I'll knock the day-lights out of you."

But the little girl said nothing. So Brer Rabbit drew back his left hand and slapped the little girl in her face, bim, and his left hand stuck.

"Oh, I see. You're going to hold both my hands, are you? You better turn me loose. If you don't, I'm going to kick you. And if I kick you, it's going to be like thunder and lightning!" With that, Brer Rabbit drew back his right foot and kicked the little girl in the shins with all his might, blap! Then his right foot stuck.

"Well, sir, isn't this something? You better turn my foot loose. If you don't, I've got another foot left, and I'm going to kick you with it, and you'll think a cyclone hit you." Then Brer Rabbit gave that little girl a powerful kick in the shins with his left foot, blip! With that, his left foot stuck, and there he hung off the ground, between the heavens and the earth. He was in an awful fix. But he still thought he could get loose.

So he said to the little girl, "You've got my feet and my hands all stuck up, but I've got one more weapon, and that's my head. If you don't turn me loose, I'm going to butt you! And if I butt you, I'll knock your brains out." Finally then, Brer Rabbit struck the little girl a powerful knock on the forehead with his head, and it stuck, and there he hung. Smart old Brer Rabbit, he couldn't move. He was held fast by the little tar baby.

Now, Brer Wolf was hiding under the bushes, watching all that was going on. And as soon as he was certain that Brer Rabbit was caught good by his little tar baby, he walked over to Brer Rabbit and said, "A-ha, you're the one who wouldn't dig a well. And you're the one who's going to catch his drinking water from the dew off the grass. A-ha, I caught the fellow who's been stealing my water. And he isn't anybody but you, Brer Rabbit. I'm going to fix you good."

"No, sir, Brer Wolf, I haven't been bothering your water. I was just going over to Brer Bear's house, and I stopped by here long enough to speak to this little no-manners girl," said Brer Rabbit.

"Yes, you're the one," said Brer Wolf. "You're the very one who's been stealing my drinking water all this time. And I'm going to kill you."

"Please, sir, Brer Wolf, don't kill me," begged Brer Rabbit. "I haven't done anything wrong."

"Yes, I'm going to kill you, but I don't know how I'm going to do it yet," growled Brer Wolf. "Oh, I know what I'll do. I'll throw you in the fire and burn you up."

"All right, Brer Wolf," said Brer Rabbit. "Throw me in the fire. That's a good way to die. That's the way my grandmother died, and she said it's a quick way to go. You can do anything with me, anything you want, but please, sir, don't throw me in the briar patch."

"No, I'm not going to throw you in the fire, and I'm not going to throw you in the briar patch. I'm going to throw you down the well and drown you," said Brer Wolf.

"All right, Brer Wolf, throw me down the well," said Brer Rabbit. "That's an easy way to die, but I'm surely going to smell up your drinking water, sir."

"No, I'm not going to drown you," said Brer Wolf. "Drowning is too good for you." Then Brer Wolf thought and thought and scratched his head and pulled his chin whiskers. Finally he said, "I know what I'm going to do with you. I'll throw you in the briar patch."

"Oh, no, Brer Wolf," cried Brer Rabbit. "Please, sir, don't throw me in the briar patch. Those briars will tear up my hide, pull out my hair, and scratch out my eyes. That'll be an awful way to die, Brer Wolf. Please, sir, don't do that to me."

"That's exactly what I'll do with you," said Brer Wolf all happy-like. Then he caught Brer Rabbit by his hind legs, whirled him around and around over his head, and threw him way over into the middle of the briar patch.

After a minute or two, Brer Rabbit stood up on his hind legs and laughed at Brer Wolf and said to him, "Thank you, Brer Wolf, thank you. This is the place where I was born. My grandmother and grandfather and all my family were born right here in the briar patch."

And that's the end of the story.

*Note: Masters often spread tar on fences to catch slaves who, when hungry, would sneak into fields and orchards to steal food. Tar stuck on the hands would betray the "guilty" slave.

Source: William J. Faulkner, *The Days When the Animals Talked.* Copyright © 1993. Used by permission of Africa World Press.

RESISTANCE AND FREEDOM

Songs, folktales (as seen in this chapter's "Recovering the Past" feature), and other forms of cultural expression enabled slaves to articulate their resistance to slavery. For example, in the song "Ole Jim," Jim was going on a "journey" to the "kingdom," and, as he invited others to "go 'long" with him, he taunted his owner: "O blow, blow, Ole Massa, blow de cotton horn / Ole Jim'll neber wuck no mo' in de cotton an' de corn." From refusal to work, it was a short step to outright revolt. In the song "Samson," the slaves clearly stated their determination to abolish the house of bondage: "An' if I had-'n my way / I'd tear the buildin' down! / . . . And now I got my way / And I'll tear this buildin' down." Every hostile song, story, or event, like Douglass's fight with Covey, was an act of resistance by which slaves asserted their dignity and gained a measure of freedom.

Forms of Black Protest

Slaves protested the burdensome demands of continuous forced labor in various "day-to-day" acts of resistance. These ranged from breaking tools to burning houses, from stealing food to defending fellow slaves from punishment, from self-mutilation to work slowdowns, and from poisoning masters to feigning illness.

Slave women, aware of their childbearing value, were adept at missing work on account of "disorders and irregularities," as a frustrated Virginia planter put it, "which cannot be detected by exterior symptoms," complaining that "you dare not set her to work . . . till she feels like taking the air again." Slave women established networks of support while winnowing and pounding rice or shucking corn, sharing miseries but also encouraging each other in private acts of sass and subtle defiance such as ruining the master's meals and faking sickness or painful menstrual cramps.

Overseers also suffered from these acts of disobedience, for their job depended on productivity, which in turn depended on the goodwill of the slave workers. Slaves adeptly played on the frequent struggles between overseer and master.

Many slaveholders resorted to using black drivers rather than overseers, but this created other problems. Slave drivers were "men between," charged with the tricky job of getting the master's work done without alienating fellow slaves or compromising their own loyalties. Although some drivers were as brutal as white overseers, many became leaders and role models for other slaves. A common practice of the drivers was to appear to punish without really

doing so. Solomon Northrup reported that he "learned to handle the whip with marvelous dexterity and precision, throwing the lash within a hair's breadth of the back, the ear, the nose, without, however, touching either of them."

Another form of resistance was to run away. The typical runaway was a young male who ran off alone and hid out in a nearby wood or swamp. He left to avoid a whipping or because he had just been whipped, to protest excessive work demands, or, as one master put it, for "no cause" at all. But there was a cause—the need to experience a period of freedom away from the restraints and discipline of the plantation. Many runaways would sneak back to the quarters for food, and after a few days, if not tracked down by hounds, they would return, perhaps to be whipped, but also perhaps with some concessions for better treatment. Some slaves left again and again. Remus and his wife Patty ran away from their master in Alabama three times; after each jailing, they escaped again.

Some runaways hid out for months and years in communities of escaped slaves known as *maroons*, especially in Florida, where Seminole and other Indians befriended them. In these areas, blacks and Indians, sharing a common hostility to whites, frequently intermarried, and established maroon communities deep in the Everglades. The Seminole resistance against the United States after the acquisition of Florida in 1819 was in fact a Black–Seminole alliance, which succeeded for several years in evading American troops. Although Creek and other Indians were hired to track down runaways and the Black Seminoles, re-enslaving and removing them to the Indian territory in Oklahoma, some succeeded in escaping permanently to the Texas-Mexico borderlands. Large maroon communities, also known as *cimarrons, quilombos,* and *palenques,* were in the mountains of Mexico, Colombia, Peru, and Brazil, as well as on West Indian islands.

Slaves were ingenious in their means of escape: forging passes, posing as master and servant, disguising one's gender, sneaking aboard ships, and pretending loyalty until taken by the master on a trip to the North. One slave even had himself mailed to the North in a large box. The Underground Railroad, organized by abolitionists, was a series of safe houses and stations where runaway slaves could rest, eat, and spend the night before continuing. Harriet Tubman, who led some 300 slaves out of the South on 19 separate trips, was the railroad's most famous "conductor." It is difficult to know exactly how many slaves actually escaped to the North and Canada, but the numbers were not large. One estimate suggests that in 1850, about 1,000 slaves (out of over 3 million) attempted to run away, and most of them were returned. Nightly patrols by white militiamen reduced the chances for any slave to escape and probably deterred many slaves from even trying.

Other ways in which slaves sought their freedom included petitioning Congress and state legislatures, bringing suit against their masters that they were being held in bondage illegally, and persuading masters to provide for emancipation in their wills. Many toiled to purchase their own freedom by hiring out to do extra work at night and on holidays.

Slave Revolts

The ultimate act of resistance was rebellion. Countless slaves committed individual acts of revolt. In addition, there were hundreds of conspiracies whereby slaves met to plan a group escape and often the massacre of whites. Most of these conspiracies never led to action, either because circumstances changed or the slaves lost the will to follow through or, more often, because some fellow slave—perhaps planted by the master—betrayed the plot. Such spies thwarted the elaborate conspiracies of Gabriel in Virginia in 1800 and Denmark Vesey in South Carolina in 1822. Both men were skilled, knowledgeable leaders who planned their revolts in hopes that larger events would support them—a possible war with France in 1800 and the Missouri debates in 1820. Both conspiracies were thwarted before revolts could begin, and both resulted in severe reprisals by whites, including mass executions of leaders and the random killing of innocent blacks. The severity of these responses indicated southern whites' enormous fear of slave revolt.

Only a few organized revolts ever actually took place, especially compared to Latin America where slaves revolted far more frequently: St. Domingue in 1791, Barbados in 1816, British Guiana (Demerara) in 1823, Jamaica in 1831–1832, Cuba in 1843–1844, and Brazil in 1810, 1814, 1835, 1843, and the 1880s. In Brazil, weaker military control, easier escape to rugged interior areas, the larger number of blacks to whites, the gender ratio of males to females (nearly 80 percent of Africans imported to Brazil in the 1830s were male), and the continued dependence on the African slave trade to replenish workers (rather than natural increase) explained these frequent revolts. Compared with the near 1:1 gender ratio of slaves in the United States, Latin American slaves had no family or female restraint on violent revolts.

The most famous slave revolt in North America, led by Nat Turner, occurred in Southampton County, Virginia, in 1831. Turner was an intelligent, skilled, unmarried, religious slave who had experienced many visions of "white spirits and black spirits engaged in battle." He believed himself "ordained for some great purpose in the hands of the Almighty." As Turner explained, he and his followers intended "to carry terror and devastation" throughout the country. On a hot, August night, Turner and his followers launched their revolt. They crept into the home of Turner's master—a "kind master" with "the greatest confidence in me"—and killed the entire family. Before the insurrection was finally put down, 55 white men, women, and children had been murdered and twice as many blacks killed in the aftermath. Turner hid for two weeks before he was apprehended and executed, but not before dictating a chilling confession to a white lawyer.

The Nat Turner revolt was a crucial moment for southern whites. A Virginia legislator suspected that there was "a Nat Turner . . . in every family," and slaveholders throughout the South slept less securely. The fact that Turner was an intelligent and trusted slave and yet led such a terrible revolt suggests again how difficult it is to generalize about slavery and slave behavior. Slaves, like masters, had diverse personalities and changeable moods, and their behavior could not be predicted easily. Sometimes humble and deferential, at other times obstinate and rebellious, the slaves made the best of a bad situation and did what they needed to do to survive with a measure of self-worth.

Free Blacks: Becoming One's Own Master

Frederick Douglass said of the slave, "Give him a bad master, and he aspires to a good master; give him a good master, and he wishes to become his own master." In 1838, Douglass forged a free black's papers as a seaman and sailed from Baltimore to become his own master in the North, where he found "great insecurity and loneliness." Apart from the immediate difficulties of finding food, shelter, and work, he realized that he was a fugitive in a land "whose inhabitants are legalized kidnappers" who could at any moment seize and return him to the South. Douglass thus joined the 12 percent of the African-American population who were not slaves.

Between 1820 and 1860, the number of free blacks in the United States doubled, from 233,500 to 488,000. This rise resulted from natural increase, successful escapes, "passing" as whites, purchasing of freedom, and manumission. Although a few free blacks left for Canada or the West Indies, most lived in the Upper South. The free African-American population actually decreased from 13.2 to 11 percent

Slave Revolts, Maroons, and the Abolition of Slavery in the Americas, 1790–1888

Throughout the Americas, enslaved Africans found many ways to protest their enslavement, including revolt, escape, and petitioning the abolition of slavery altogether. Maroons were communities of successful runaway slaves who fled to dense forested and largely inaccessible areas where they often intermarried with Indian groups. Some carried on a kind of guerilla warfare with Europeans who tried to track them down. **Reflecting on the Past** Do you see any patterns in the outbreaks of this partial mapping of slave revolts, either by place or time? What relationships do you see, if any, between slave revolts and abolition? Between national independence movements and abolition? What other observations would you make about the data on this map?

between 1820 and 1860, suggesting that the percentage of blacks in slavery grew faster than those who were free.

The presence of free blacks was a threat to whites, who saw them as an inducement to slave unrest. Many were scattered on impoverished, rural farmlands, and one-third of the southern free black population lived in cities. Over 80 percent were in the Upper South. Rural free blacks were poor farmhands, day laborers, or woodcutters. In the cities, they worked in factories and lived in appalling poverty. A few skilled jobs, such as barbering, shoemaking, and plastering, were reserved for black men; they were barred from more than 50 other trades. Women worked as cooks, laundresses, and domestics.

The 15 percent of free African Americans who lived in the Lower South were divided into two distinct castes. Most were poor. But in New Orleans, Charleston, and other southern cities, a small, mixed-blood free black elite emerged, closely connected to white society and distant from poor blacks. A "respectable" very few even owned land and slaves. In part because it took a long time to buy freedom, they tended to be older, more literate, and lighter-skinned than other African Americans. In 1860, over 40 percent of free blacks were mulattoes (compared with 10 percent of the slaves). With strong leadership, Baltimore, Richmond, Charleston, New Orleans, and other southern cities developed vibrant African-American communities, as free blacks formed churches, schools, and benevolent societies in the midst of white hostility.

Urban whites sought to restrain free blacks from mixing with whites in working-class grogshops, gambling halls, and brothels, as well as to confine them to certain sections of the city or (increasingly by the 1850s) to compel them to leave altogether. Those who stayed had trouble finding work, were required to carry papers, and had to have their actions supervised by a white guardian. Southern whites especially feared contact between free blacks and slaves, which did occur despite all attempts to limit it.

Most free blacks had little status or privileges. A Baltimore black paper said in 1826 that "though we are not slaves, we are not free." In most states, they could not vote, bear arms, buy liquor, assemble, speak in public, form societies, or testify against whites in court. Nevertheless, the African-American persistence to support each other in prayer meetings, burial societies, and back alleys was stronger than white efforts to impede it.

The key institution in these developments was the African-American church, "the Alpha and

Growth of Black Population: Slave and Free, 1820–1860

Although the number of free African Americans doubled in size between 1820 and 1860, their proportion relative to the total black population actually decreased. This indicates that the institution of slavery seemed unlikely to be ended voluntarily by southerners.

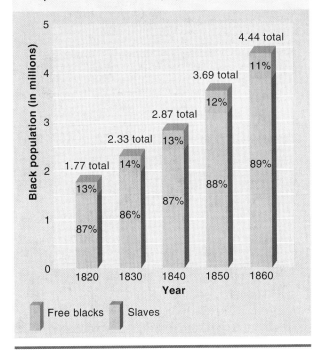

Omega of all things," Martin Delaney wrote to Douglass in 1849. Welcoming the freedom from white control, independent urban black churches grew enormously in the two decades before the Civil War. The African Methodist Episcopal (AME) Church in Baltimore doubled its membership between 1836 and 1856. By 1860, Baltimore had 15 African-American churches representing five different denominations. Fourteen new black Baptist churches in Virginia and four First African churches in Richmond were founded between 1841 and 1860. These institutions gave spiritual solace, set community standards, and offered a host of educational, insurance, self-help, and recreational opportunities.

Nor were African-American Catholics left out. Baltimore and New Orleans had strong black Catholic communities made up of Creoles, converts, former slaves, and refugees from Haiti. The first ordained black priests were three Georgia sons, born of a mulatto slave mother and an Irish immigrant father and educated at Holy Cross in the 1850s, though it would be three decades before the next one. In the absence of African-American

Churches for free blacks, rare before 1800, became a major source of social as well as religious activity by the 1840s. *(Library of Congress)*

priests, black sisterhoods took on special importance. The Sisters of the Holy Family and other communities of Catholic black women, begun in eastern cities, started schools and ministered to the aged and infirm as they spread with black Catholic communities westward to Louisville and St. Louis.

The African-American churches not only were centers of vital urban black community activities, but they also were springboards for activist black preachers seeking larger changes in American society. The Reverend J. C. Pennington, an escaped slave, attended lectures at Yale Divinity School (though he was denied the right to enroll or borrow books). Licensed to preach in 1838, he headed prominent black churches in New Haven, Hartford, and finally New York City. Pennington started several schools, was an abolitionist leader of the National Negro Convention movement, and founded the Union Missionary Society in 1841, a black organization that focused on African missions. Charles B. Ray was educated at Wesleyan University in Connecticut and, as minister of Bethesda Church in New York City for 20 years, was involved with the Underground Railroad and editor of *The Colored American*. Black religious leaders prepared the way not only for Civil War, but also for an unprecedented postwar growth of African-American churches.

A young minister, Henry M. Turner, later an AME bishop, proudly proclaimed in the 1850s, "We, as a race, have a chance to be Somebody, and if we are ever going to be a people, now is the time." Turner's exhortations were heralded 20 years earlier by Maria Stewart, the first African-American woman to give published public speeches. Stewart's religious conversion gave her the confidence to brave censure and ridicule in speaking out on behalf of

Timeline	
1787	Constitution adopted with proslavery provisions
1793	Eli Whitney invents cotton gin
1800	Gabriel conspiracy in Virginia
1808	External slave trade prohibited by Congress
1820	South becomes world's largest cotton producer
1822	Denmark Vesey's conspiracy in Charleston
1830s	Southern justification of slavery changes from a necessary evil to a positive good
1831	Nat Turner's slave revolt in Virginia
1845	*Narrative of the Life of Frederick Douglass* published
1850s	Cotton boom
1851	Indiana state constitution excludes free blacks
1852	Harriet Beecher Stowe publishes best-selling *Uncle Tom's Cabin*
1860	Cotton production and prices peak

abolitionism and equal rights for free blacks and women against those who cited St. Paul's opposition. "Did Saint Paul know of our wrongs and deprivations," Stewart said, "I presume he would make no objections to our pleading in public for our rights."

In part because free blacks were becoming more of a "people," they faced a crisis in the 1850s. Growing prosperity and the worsening conflict between the North and South over slavery in the territories caused many white southerners to be even more concerned than usual with the presence of free blacks. Pressures increased in the late 1850s either to deport or enslave them. Not surprisingly, some black leaders began to look more favorably on migration to Africa. That quest was interrupted, however, by the outbreak of the Civil War, rekindling in Douglass the "expiring embers of freedom."

✦ *Conclusion*

DOUGLASS'S DREAM OF FREEDOM

Frederick Douglass eventually won his freedom by forging a free black sailor's pass and escaping through Chesapeake Bay to New York. In a real sense, he wrote himself into freedom. The *Narrative of the Life of Frederick Douglass,* "written by himself" in 1845, was a way for Douglass both to expose the many evils of slavery and to create his own identity, even to the point of choosing his own name. Ironically, Douglass had learned to value reading and writing from his Baltimore masters, the Aulds. This reminds us again of the intricate and subtle ways in which the lives of slaves and masters were tied together in the antebellum South. Our understanding of the complexities of this relationship is enhanced as we consider the variations of life in the Big House in the morning, in the fields during the afternoons, in the slave quarters at night, and in the degrees of freedom blacks achieved through resistance, revolt, and free status.

In a poignant moment in his *Narrative,* Douglass described his boyhood dreams of freedom as he looked out at the boats on the waters of Chesapeake Bay. Contrasting his own enslavement with the boats he saw as "freedom's swift-winged angels," Douglass vowed to escape: "This very bay shall yet bear me into freedom.... There is a better day coming." As we will see later, southern white planters also bemoaned their lack of freedom relative to the North and made their own plans to achieve independent status through secession. Meanwhile, as that struggle brewed beneath the surface of antebellum life, many other Americans were dismayed by various evil aspects in their society, slavery among them, and sought ways of shaping a better America. We turn to these other dreams in the next chapter.

✦ Recommended Reading

Building a Diverse Cotton Kingdom
Eugene Genovese, *Roll, Jordan, Roll: The World the Slaves Made* (1974); Michele Gillespie, *Free Labor in an Unfree World: White Artisans in Slaveholding Georgia, 1789–1860* (2000); Stephanie McCurry, *Masters of Small Worlds: Yeoman Households, Gender Relations, & the Political Culture of the Antebellum South Carolina Lowcountry* (1995); Frank Owsley, *Plain Folk in the Old South* (1949); Mark Smith, *Debating Slavery: Economy and Society in the Antebellum American South* (1998).

Morning: Master and Mistress in the Big House
Victoria E. Bynum, *Unruly Women: The Politics of Social and Sexual Control in the Old South* (1990); Catherine Clinton, *The Plantation Mistress: Woman's World in the Old South* (1982); J. H. Easterby, ed., *The South Carolina Rice Plantation as Revealed in the Papers of Robert F. W. Allston* (1945); Elizabeth Fox-Genovese, *Within the Plantation Household: Black and White Women of the Old South* (1988); Jane H. Pease and William H. Pease, *A Family of Women: The Carolina Petigrus [Adele Allston] in Peace and War* (1999); Steven Stowe, *Intimacy and Power in the Old South: Rituals in the Lives of the Planters* (1987).

Noon: Slaves in House and Fields
Edward Ball, *Slaves in the Family* (1998); Ira Berlin, *Many Thousands Gone: The First Two Centuries of Slavery in North America* (1998); John Blassingame, ed., *Slave Testimony* (1977); Barbara Jeanne Fields, *Slavery and Freedom on the Middle Ground: Maryland during the Nineteenth Century* (1985); Larry E. Hudson, Jr., *To Have and to Hold: Slave Work and Family Life in Antebellum South Carolina* (1997); Jacqueline Jones, *American Work: Four Centuries of Black and White Labor* (1998); Peter Kolchin, *American Slavery, 1619–1877* (1993); Kenneth Stampp, *The Peculiar Institution: Slavery in the Antebellum South* (1956).

Night: Slaves in Their Quarters
William L. Andrews, *To Tell a Free Story: The First Century of Afro-American Autobiography, 1760–1865* (1986); John Blassingame, *The Slave Community*, rev. ed.

(1979); Jennifer Fleischner, *Mastering Slavery: Memory, Family, and Identity in Women's Slave Narratives* (1996); Herbert Gutman, *The Black Family in Slavery and Freedom, 1750–1925* (1976); Dwight Hopkins, *Down, Up, and Over: Slave Religion and Black Theology* (2000); James Oliver Horton, *Free People of Color: Inside the African-American Community* (1993); Charles Joyner, *Down by the Riverside: A South Carolina Slave Community* (1984); Lawrence Levine, *Black Culture and Black Consciousness: Afro-American Folk Thought from Slavery to Freedom* (1977); George Rawick, *From Sundown to Sunup: The Making of a Black Community* (1972); Albert Raboteau, *Slave Religion* (1978); Sterling Stuckey, *Slave Culture: Nationalist Theory and the Foundation of Black America* (1987); Deborah Gray White, *Arn't I a Woman?: Female Slaves in the Plantation South*, rev. ed. (1999).

Resistance and Freedom

William L. Andrews, ed., *The Oxford Frederick Douglass Reader* (1996); Herbert Aptheker, *Nat Turner's Slave Rebellion* (1966); Ira Berlin, *Slaves Without Masters: The Free Negro in the Antebellum South* (1976); Douglas R. Egerton, *He Shall Go Out Free: The Lives of Denmark Vesey* (1999); John Hope Franklin and Loren Schweninger, *Runaway Slaves: Rebels on the Plantation* (1999); Michael P. Johnson and James L. Roark, *No Chariot Down: Charleston's Free People of Color on the Eve of the Civil War* (1984); Gregory P. Lampe, *Frederick Douglass: Freedom's Voice, 1818–1845* (1998); Robert S. Levine, *Martin Delany, Frederick Douglass, and the Politics of Representative Identity* (1997); William S. McFeely, *Frederick Douglass* (1991); Melton McLaurin, *Celia, A Slave* (1991).

Fiction and Film

The Bondswoman's Narrative (2002) by Hannah Crafts, recently discovered and edited by Henry Louis Gates, Jr., is perhaps the earliest known novel by an African-American woman. Written in the 1850s, hers is a captivating story of a light-skinned North Carolina slave, part fiction and part autobiography, whose escape to New Jersey involved a series of horrifying experiences. Harriet Beecher Stowe's *Uncle Tom's Cabin* (1852) follows various black and white lives in antebellum Kentucky and the Deep South. Charles Johnson's *Middle Passage* (1990) is a novel about antebellum life in New Orleans and on slave trade ships between West Africa and the Caribbean. Toni Morrison's novel *Beloved* (1988) is a powerful and moving account of African-American life both during and after slavery. Margaret Walker's *Jubilee* (1966) is a black, female novelist's epic version of the African-American experience from slavery through Civil War and Reconstruction, and Alice Randall's *The Wind Done Gone* (2001) is a parody of Margaret Mitchell's *Gone With the Wind* (1936). *Kindred* (1979), by Octavia Butler, a contemporary African-American science fiction writer, is about a Los Angeles black woman who is transported back to 1815 where she endures the brutality of slavery even as she seeks to save the life of the son of her slave-owning white ancestors. *Amistad* is a 1997 Hollywood film based on a successful mutiny on a slave ship in 1839 near Cuba and the subsequent capture and trial of the mutineers in Connecticut, where they were defended by ex-President John Quincy Adams. The film, featuring the rebel leader Cinque, contains vivid scenes aboard slave ships. *Beloved* is a 1998 film version of Morrison's novel.

◆ Discovering U.S. History Online

Slave Culture

www.kingtisdell.org/exhibit.htm

An illustrated explanation of slavery culture in Savannah from antebellum Savannah to the end of the Reconstruction era.

Letters from the Slave States

www.fordham.edu/halsall/mod/1857stirling.html

A reprint of an article with interviews of plantation owners and former slaves.

African American Heritage

www.cr.nps.gov/aahistory

An examination of the places, objects, photos, and writings significant to African-American history.

Africans in America, 1791–1831

www.pbs.org/wgbh/aia/part3/index.html

PBS images and documents (both primary source and modern commentaries) on the growth and entrenchment of slavery, the rise of abolitionism (especially in Philadelphia), and the black church.

AFRO-American Almanac

www.toptags.com/aama

This multi-level site has gathered a large collection of material related to African-American history: biographies, historical documents, event descriptions, folk tales, and more.

Depictions of Slavery in Confederate Currency

www.lib.lsu.edu/cwc/BeyondFaceValue/beyondfacevalue.htm

With over 100 images, this site illustrates the relationship between art and politics in the Civil War era.

The Underground Railroad

www.nationalgeographic.com/features/99/railroad/

A richly illustrated online virtual "ride" along the Underground Railroad. The exhibit changes depending on the choices the viewer makes along the way.

Songs of the Underground Railroad

www.appleseedrec.com/underground/sounds.html

Samples of popular slavery songs and interpretations of the meaning of the lyrics.

Virginia Runaways

www.wise.virginia.edu/history/runaways

This Web site presents a "digital database" of the detailed "runaway and captured slave and servant advertisements from 18th-century Virginia newspapers."

Amistad

www.amistadamerica.org/new/main/html/history.html

Part of the Web site for the educational organization *Amistad AMERICA, Inc.*, this essay presents details of the Amistad incident and trial as well as an analysis of the present-day film.

12 Shaping America in the Antebellum Age

Marius and Emily Robinson, like other Americans, sought to find goodness and order in a society that seemed "everywhere unhinged." *(Anonymous,* Moving Day in the City, *c. 1829, Photo by Eric Schaal/LIFE Magazine © Time Inc.)*

✦ *American Stories*

EXPERIENCING THE COSTS OF COMMITMENTS

On November 19, 1836, as the second term of President Andrew Jackson neared its end, 30-year-old Marius Robinson and Emily Rakestraw were married near Cincinnati, Ohio. Two months after their wedding, he went on the road to speak against slavery and to organize abolitionist societies throughout Ohio. Emily stayed in Cincinnati to teach in a school for free blacks. During their 10-month separation, they exchanged affectionate letters that reflected their love and work.

Writing after midnight from Concord, Ohio, Marius complained of the "desolation of loneliness" he felt without her. Emily responded that she felt "about our separation just as you do" and confessed that her "womanish nature" did not much enjoy self-denial. In their letters, each imagined the "form and features" of the other and chided the other for not writing more often. Each voiced concern for the responsibilities and burdens of the other's work. Each expressed comfort and support, doubted his or her own abilities ("a miserable comforter I am"), and agreed that in their separation, as Marius put it, "we must look alone to God."

With such love for each other, what prompted this painful separation so early in their marriage? Emily wrote of their duty "to labor long in this cause so near and dear to us both," together if they could, but apart if so decreed by God. Marius, who had experienced a series of conversions inspired by the revivalist Charles G. Finney and his abolitionist disciple Theodore Dwight Weld, described the reason for their separation: "God and humanity bleeding and suffering demand our services apart." Thus motivated by a strong religious commitment to serve others, these two young reformers dedicated themselves to several social causes: the abolition of slavery, equal rights and education for free blacks, temperance, and women's rights.

Their commitments cost more than separation. When Emily went to Cincinnati to work with other young reformers, her parents disapproved. When she married Marius, who already had a reputation as a "rebel," her parents disowned her altogether. Emily wrote with sadness that her sisters and friends also "love me less . . . than they did in by-gone days." Marius responded that he wished he could dry her tears and sought to heal the rift. Although Emily's family eventually accepted their marriage, there were other griefs. Teaching at the school in Cincinnati was demanding, and Emily could not get rid of a persistent cough. Furthermore, the white citizens of the city resented the school and the young abolitionists in their midst, treating them with contempt. Earlier in the year, Marius had escaped an angry mob by disguising himself and mingling with the crowd that came to sack the offices of a reformist journal edited by James G. Birney. Emily, meanwhile, tirelessly persisted in the work of "our school" while worrying about the health and safety of her husband on the road.

She had good reason for concern, for Marius's letters were full of reports of mob attacks, disrupted meetings, stonings, and narrow escapes. At two lectures near Granville, Ohio, he was "mobbed thrice, once most rousingly," as he faced crowds of "the veriest savages I ever saw," armed with clubs, cudgels, and intense hatred for those speaking against slavery. In June, he was dragged from the home of his Quaker host and beaten, tarred, and feathered. Never quite recovering his health, Marius spent half a year in bed, weak and dispirited. For nearly 10 years after that, the Robinsons lived quietly on an Ohio farm, only slightly involved in the abolitionist movement. Despite the joyous birth of two daughters, they felt lonely, restless, and guilt-ridden, "tired of days blank of benevolent effort and almost of benevolent desires."

The work of Emily and Marius Robinson represents one response by the American people to the rapid social and economic changes of the antebellum era described in Chapters 10 and 11. In September 1835, a year before the Robinsons' marriage, the *Niles Register* commented on some 500 recent incidents of mob violence and social upheaval. "Society seems everywhere unhinged, and the demon of 'blood and slaughter' has been let loose upon us. . . . [The] character of our countrymen seems suddenly changed." How did Americans adapt to these changes? In a world that seemed everywhere "unhinged" and out of control, in which old rules and patterns no longer provided guidance, how did people maintain some sense of control over their lives? How did they seek to shape their altered world? How could they both adopt the benefits of change and reduce the accompanying disruptions?

One way was to embrace the changes fully. Thus, some Americans became entrepreneurs in new industries; invested in banks, canals, and railroads; bought more land and slaves; and invented new machines. Others went west or to the new textile mills, enrolled in common schools, joined trade unions, specialized their labor in both the workplace and the home, and celebrated the practical benefits that resulted from modernization. Marius Robinson eventually went into life insurance, though he and Emily never fully abandoned their reformist efforts and idealism.

But many Americans were uncomfortable with the character of the new era. Some worried about the unrestrained power and selfish materialism symbolized by the slave master's control over his slaves. Others feared that institutions like the U.S. Bank represented a "monied aristocracy" capable of undermining the country's honest producers. Seeking positions of leadership and authority, these critics of the new order tried to shape a nation that retained the benefits of economic change without sacrificing humane principles of liberty, equality of opportunity, and community virtue. This chapter examines four ways the American people, both men and women, responded to change by attempting to influence their country's development: religious revivalism, party politics, utopian communitarianism, and social reform.

RELIGIOUS REVIVAL AND REFORM PHILOSOPHY

When the Frenchman Alexis de Tocqueville visited the United States in 1831 and 1832, he observed that he could find "no country in the whole world in which the Christian religion retains a greater influence over the souls of men than in America." What de Tocqueville was describing was a new and powerful religious enthusiasm among American Protestants. Fired by the power of religious rebirth, some discovered that religion provided them with moorings in a fast-changing world. Others were inspired by revivalism to refashion American society, working through new political parties to shape an agenda for the nation or through reform associations organized to eliminate a particular social evil. Although not all evangelicals agreed about politics or even about what aspects of American society needed to be reformed, religion was the lens through which they viewed contemporary events and through which they sought to effect change.

Finney and the Second Great Awakening

From the late 1790s until the late 1830s, a wave of religious revivals that matched the intensity of the Great Awakening in the 1730s and 1740s swept through the United States. While there were many links between Protestant denominations in the United States and in Great Britain, the popular character of American revivalism gave it a distinctive stamp. British religion was becoming more conservative, while American Protestantism was becoming more democratic.

The camp meeting revivals of the frontier at the turn of the century and the New England revivals sparked by Lyman Beecher took on a new emphasis and location after 1830. Led by the spellbinding Charles G. Finney, under whose influence Marius Robinson had been converted, revivalism shifted to upstate New York and the Old Northwest. The Finney revivals followed the Erie Canal across upstate New York and eventually swept into Ohio. These areas had experienced profound economic and social changes, as the example of Rochester, New York, suggests.

By the 1830s, Rochester, like Lowell and Cincinnati, was a rapidly growing American city. Located on the recently completed Erie Canal, it was a flour-milling center for the rich wheat lands of western New York. The canal changed Rochester from a sleepy little village of 300 in 1815 to a bustling commercial and milling city of nearly 20,000 inhabitants by 1830. As in other cities, economic growth affected relationships between masters and workers, distancing them both physically and psychologically. As the gulf widened, the masters' control over their laborers weakened. Saloons and unions sprang up in workingmen's neighborhoods, and workers became more transient, following the canal and other opportunities westward.

In 1830, prompted partly by their concerns about poverty and absenteeism, both caused presumably by alcohol, prominent Rochester citizens invited Charles Finney to the city. He led what became one of the most successful revivals of the Second Great Awakening. Finney preached nearly every night and three times on Sundays, first converting the city's

Denominational Growth, 1780–1860

As this bar graph makes clear, the early nineteenth century was a time of explosive religious growth. What were the decades that saw the greatest growth? Which denominations expanded most quickly and which most slowly?

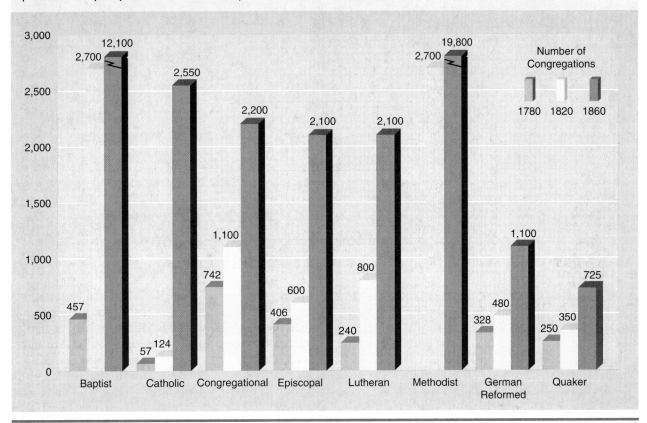

business elite, often through their wives with the help of his wife Lydia, and then converting many workers, redeeming them from sin and saving their wives from the abuses of drink. For six months, Rochester experienced a citywide prayer meeting in which one conversion led to another.

The Rochester revival was part of a wave of religious enthusiasm in America that contributed to the tremendous growth of Methodists, Baptists, and other evangelical denominations in the first half of the nineteenth century. By 1844, Methodism became the country's largest denomination with over a million members. To bring large numbers to accept Christ as their savior, revivalist preachers emphasized emotion over doctrine and softened Calvinist tenets like predestination that suggested that individual salvation resulted from God's decision rather than human effort and faith.

Finney rejected the formal approach to the ministry that had characterized mainline Protestant denominations. A lawyer when he experienced con-

version, he did not bother with ministerial training nor did he model himself on those who had attended seminary. Learned preachers reading their sermons from notes, he warned, were "calculated to make a sinner feel that religion is some mysterious thing that he cannot understand." "We must have exciting, powerful preaching, or the devil will have the people." But he also believed that a person's relationship with God was even more important than preaching, which empowered women.

Unlike Jonathan Edwards, who believed that revivals were God's miracles, Finney understood that the human "agency" of individuals and ministers were crucial in causing a revival. He even published a do-it-yourself manual for other revivalists. Few, however, could match Finney's powerful preaching style. The hypnotic effect of his eyes and voice carried such power that he could dissolve an audience into tears. When he threw an imaginary brick at the Devil, people ducked. When his finger pointed the descent of a sinner into hell, people in the back row

This 1839 painting of a camp meeting captures the religious fervor that many Americans turned to in the face of social and economic upheavals. These mass conversions led some believers to individual salvation and others to social reform. *(Old Dartmouth Historical Society-New Bedford Whaling Museum)*

stood up to see the final disappearance. Perhaps because he was a former lawyer, Finney used logic as well as emotion to bring about conversions, the purpose of which was to play a role in the perfectionist reform of society.

American Catholics also caught the revival fervor in the 1830s. Scattered in small but growing numbers in the East and the Ohio River valley, urban Catholic leaders recognized that survival as a small, often despised religion depended on constant reinvigoration and evangelism. Focusing on the parish mission, energetic retreats and revivals gathered Catholics from miles around to preserve a religious heritage seriously threatened by life in Protestant America.

Unlike Catholic and southern revivalism, which focused primarily on salvation, Finney revivals insisted that conversion and salvation were not the end of religious experience but the beginning. Finney believed that humans were not passive objects of God's predestined plan, but moral free agents who could choose good over evil and thereby eradicate sin. Finney's idea of the "utility of benevolence" called for a commitment on the part of converted Christians to do their sacred duty in reforming society, as we will see later in the chapter.

The Transcendentalists

No one knew this better than Ralph Waldo Emerson, a Concord, Massachusetts, essayist who was the era's foremost intellectual figure. Emerson's essays of the 1830s—"Nature," "American Scholar," and "Divinity School Address," among others—influenced the generation of reformist American intellectuals coming of age in mid-century and helped inspire artists and writers. The small but influential group of New England intellectuals who lived near Emerson were called Transcendentalists because of their belief that truth was found in intuition beyond sense experience. Casting off the European intellectual tradition and influenced to some extent by Eastern thought, Emerson urged Americans to look inward and to nature for self-knowledge, self-reliance, and the spark of divinity burning within all people. "To acquaint a man with himself," he wrote, would inspire a "reverence" for self and others, which would then lead outward to social reform. "What is man born for," Emerson wrote, "but to be a Reformer?"

Inspired by self-reflection, the Transcendentalists asked troublesome questions about the quality of American life. They questioned slavery, an obvious evil, but also the obsessive, competitive pace of economic life, the overriding concern for materialism, the restrictive conformity of social life and, with Margaret Fuller, the absence of women's voices.

A friend of Emerson, Margaret Fuller was called "a strange, wild woman" for her intellectual brilliance, for organizing "Conversations" among Boston area Transcendentalists, and for her unorthodox life style. She helped initiate and edit *The*

Dial, an influential Transcendentalist journal, and as a writer for Horace Greeley's *New York Tribune*, she broke ground by writing not just about women and women's rights but also about literature, prison reform, and other topics. When Greeley sent her to report from Europe, another first, she became a revolutionary, took an Italian lover and, returning to the States in 1850 with a baby, died in a shipwreck within sight of the American shore. Greeley called Fuller "the most remarkable woman in America."

Although not considered Transcendentalists, Nathaniel Hawthorne and Herman Melville, two giants of mid-century American literature, reflected Transcendentalist concerns in their fiction. Like Emerson and Fuller, they were romantic in spirit, celebrating emotion over reason, nature over civilization, and virtue over self-interest. Hawthorne's great subject was the "truth of the human heart," which he portrayed as more authentic than the calculating minds of scientists and their schemes. In his greatest novel, *The Scarlet Letter* (1850), Hawthorne sympathetically told the story of a courageous Puritan woman's adultery and her eventual loving triumph over the narrowness of both cold intellect and intolerant social conformity.

Herman Melville dedicated his epic novel *Moby Dick* (1851) to Hawthorne. At one level a rousing story of whaling on the high seas in pursuit of the great white whale, *Moby Dick* was actually an immense allegory of good and evil, bravery and weakness, innocence and experience. In Melville's other novels, he continued this sea voyage setting to make a powerful statement on behalf of the lowly seaman's claims for freedom and just social relations against the tyranny of the ship captain. Like Emerson and Fuller, Hawthorne and Melville mirrored the tensions of the age as they explored issues of freedom and control, and pushed the limits of self-reliance.

When Emerson wrote, "Whoso would be a man, must be a nonconformist," he described his friend Henry David Thoreau. No one thought more deeply about the virtuous natural life than Thoreau. On July 4, 1845, he went to live in a small hut by Walden Pond, near Concord. There he planned to confront the "essential facts of life"—to discover who he was and how to live well. When Thoreau left Walden two years later, he protested against slavery and the Mexican War by refusing to pay his taxes. He went to jail briefly and wrote an essay, "On Civil Disobedience" (1849), and a book, *Walden* (1854), which are still considered classic statements of what one person can do to protest unjust laws and wars and live a life of principle.

THE POLITICAL RESPONSE TO CHANGE

Transcendentalism touched only a few elite New Englanders, but perhaps as many as 40 percent of the American people were affected by the winds of evangelical Protestantism. Although economic, ethnic, and even regional factors played a part in shaping political loyalties, evangelical values and religious loyalties affected many people's understanding of the appropriate role of government and influenced their involvement in political activities. As politics became more of a popular than an elite interest, it was not surprising that religious commitments spilled over into the political sphere.

At the heart of American politics was the concern for the continued health of the republican experiment. As American society changed, so, too, did the understanding of what was needed to maintain that health. In the late 1850s, a Maine newspaper warned that the preservation of the nation's freedom depended on the willingness of its citizens to go to the polls. It was, in fact, the "positive duty of every citizen of a Republic to vote." This insistence on voting as crucial to the well-being of the country was a new emphasis in the United States and unique in the world at that time.

Before the 1820s, politics in both the United States and Europe was primarily an activity for the social and economic elite. In Europe, conservatives feared the political involvement of the lower classes and resisted pressures for change. In Great Britain, the country where the Industrial Revolution had begun, the Reform Bill of 1832 extended the parliamentary vote to middle-class men, still a minority. During the 1830s and 1840s, popular efforts to secure universal male suffrage and the secret ballot failed. Even when the House of Commons received a petition containing more than a million signatures, members still turned their backs on the request. In France, the government responded to efforts for political reform with repression and violence.

In the United States, however, the power of the Revolution's ideas and the relative weakness of the country's upper classes led to a gradual extension of the franchise to all white men. During the early nineteenth century, many states were voluntarily removing voting restrictions even though the majority of white men did not trouble themselves with political matters. But the Panic of 1819 and the spirited presidential campaigns for Andrew Jackson helped create widespread interest in politics and a distinctive American style of politics. For many Americans, political participation became an important way of asserting and supporting important values and promoting their vision of the republic.

Changing Political Culture

Jackson's presidency was crucial in bringing politics to the center of many Americans' lives. Styling himself as the people's candidate in 1828, Andrew Jackson derided the Adams administration as corrupt and aristocratic and promised a more democratic political system. He told voters that he intended to "purify" and "reform the Government," purging all "who have been appointed from political considerations or against the will of the people." Unlike in our own age, most Americans then believed the campaign rhetoric. Four times more men turned out to vote in the election of 1828 than had four years earlier. They gave Jackson a resounding 56 percent of their ballots. No other president in the century would equal that percentage of popular support.

Despite campaign rhetoric and his image as a democratic hero, Jackson was not personally very democratic, nor did the era he symbolized involve any significant redistribution of wealth. Jackson himself owned slaves, defended slavery, and condoned mob attacks on abolitionists like Marius Robinson. He disliked Indians and ordered the forcible removal of the southeastern Indian nations to west of the Mississippi River in blatant disregard of the treaty rights and a Supreme Court decision. Belying promises of widening opportunity, the rich got richer during the Jacksonian era, and most farming and urban laboring families did not prosper.

But the nation's political life changed in important ways. The old system of politics, based on elite coalitions bound together by ties of family and friendship and dependent on the deference of voters to their "betters," largely disappeared. In its place emerged a competitive party system, begun early in the republic but now oriented toward widespread voter participation. The major parties grew adept at raising money, selecting and promoting candidates, and bringing voters to the polls. A new "democratic" style of political life emerged as parties sponsored conventions, rallies (much like evangelical revivals in their flavor and fervor), and parades to encourage political participation and identification. Party politics became a central preoccupation for many adult white males. In the North, even women turned out for political hoopla, riding on floats at party parades.

Parties appealed to popular emotions, religious views, and ethnic prejudices. Party-subsidized newspapers regularly indulged in scurrilous attacks and the language of politics became contentious and militaristic. Jackson's rhetoric exemplified the new trends. He described an opponent as an "enemy" who waged "war against the cause of the people." Politicians talked of elections as battles and party members as their disciplined "rank and file." Strong party identification was part of the new national political culture. James Buchanan complained in 1839 about a colleague who urged politicians "to rise above mere party, and to go for our country." Instead, Buchanan said, "in supporting my party, I honestly believe I am . . . promoting the interest of my country."

Jackson's Path to the White House

The early career of Andrew Jackson gave few hints of his future political importance. Orphaned at 14, young Jackson grew up in poverty and was often in trouble. As a law student, he was "a most roaring, rollicking, game-cocking, horse-racing, card-playing, mischievous fellow." Despite these preoccupations, Jackson passed the bar and set out at the age of 21 to

More Americans Vote for President, 1824–1840

The single-party system (Jeffersonian Democratic Republican) that existed in 1824 collapsed with the intense personal rivalries and ideological differences of the 1820s and 1830s. The emergence of a two-party system in the Jacksonian era dramatically increased (white male) voter participation to percentages far exceeding those of modern U.S. presidential elections.

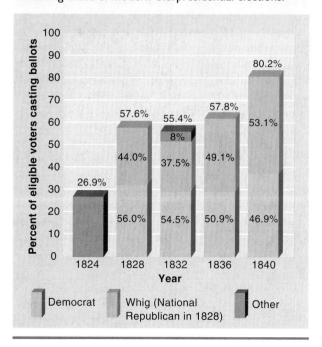

seek his fortune in the West. Settling in frontier Nashville, the tall, red-headed young man built up a successful law practice in Tennessee and went on to become state attorney general, a substantial land-owner, and a prominent citizen of Nashville.

Jackson's national reputation stemmed mainly from his military exploits, primarily against American Indians. As major general of the Tennessee militia, he proved able and popular. Jackson's troops admired his toughness and nicknamed him "Old Hickory." His victory over the Creek nation in the South in 1813 and 1814 brought notoriety and an appointment as major general in the U.S. Army. His victory at New Orleans in 1815 made him a na-tional hero, and by 1817, resolutions supporting a Jackson bid for the presidency began to appear in several states.

Although Jackson's aggressive military forays into Spanish Florida in 1818 bothered rival politicians and added to his reputation for scandal, they in-creased his popularity and his interest in the presi-dency. Jackson recognized that his greatest appeal lay with ordinary people. But he also secured effec-tive political backing. Careful political maneuvering in Tennessee in the early 1820s brought him elec-tion as a U.S. senator and a nomination for the pres-idency in 1824.

In the 1824 election, Jackson won both the popu-lar and the electoral votes but lost in the House of Representatives to John Quincy Adams. When Henry Clay threw his support to Adams and was named secretary of state, Jackson condemned this deal as a "corrupt bargain." By 1828, Jackson's loss had convinced him of the importance of having an effective political organization. He felt confident of his strength in the West, and support by Adams's vice president, John C. Calhoun, helped him in the South. Jackson organized his campaign by setting up loyal committees and newspapers in many states and by encouraging efforts to undermine Adams and Clay.

A loose coalition promoting Jackson's candidacy began to call itself the Democratic party. Politicians of diverse views from all sections of the country were drawn to it, including Martin Van Buren of New York. Jackson masterfully waffled on controver-sial issues. He concealed his dislike of banks and pa-per money and vaguely advocated a "middle and just course" on the tariff. He promised to cleanse government of corruption and privileged interests.

The Jackson–Adams campaign in 1828 degen-erated into a nasty but entertaining contest. The Democrats whipped up enthusiasm with barbe-cues, mass rallies, and parades and gave out buttons and hats with hickory leaves attached. Few people

Unlike rivals J. Q. Adams and Henry Clay, who deprived Jackson of the presidency in 1824, Jackson (nicknamed "Old Hickory" after America's toughest hardwood) claimed to honor the constitutional electoral system and the will of the people. *(© Collection of the New-York Historical Society)*

discussed issues, and both sides made slanderous personal attacks. Supporters of Adams and Clay, calling themselves National Republicans, branded Jackson "an adulterer, a gambler, a cockfighter, a brawler, a drunkard, and a murderer." His wife, Rachel, was maligned as common and immoral.

The Jacksonians, in turn, charged Adams with bribing Clay for his support in 1824. They described him as a "stingy, undemocratic" aristocrat deter-mined to destroy the people's liberties. Worse yet, Adams was an intellectual. Campaign slogans em-phasized the differences between the hero of New Orleans, "a man who can fight," and the wimpy Adams, "a man who can write." "Who do you want," one slogan asked, "John Quincy Adams, who quotes law, or Andy Jackson, who makes law?" The ques-tion left little doubt as to how proud Americans would vote.

Jackson's supporters in Washington worked to ensure his election by devising a tariff bill to win necessary support in key states. Under the leader-ship of Van Buren, who hoped to replace Calhoun as Jackson's heir apparent, Democrats in Congress put together enough votes to pass what opponents called the "Tariff of Abominations." It arbitrarily raised rates to protect New England textiles,

Pennsylvania iron, and some agricultural goods, winning voters in those states where the Democrats needed more support. John Randolph of Virginia sneered that the tariff "referred to manufactures of no . . . kind but the manufacture of a President of the United States."

The efforts of Jackson and his party paid off as he won an astonishing 647,286 ballots, about 56 percent of the total. Organization, money, effective publicity, and a popular style of campaigning had brought the 60-year-old Jackson to the presidency. His inauguration, however, horrified many. Washington was packed for the ceremonies. Daniel Webster noted that "persons have come five hundred miles to see General Jackson, and they really seem to think that the country is to be rescued from some dreadful danger." When Jackson stood to take the oath of office, wild cheering broke out. Few in the crowd heard him, but many hoped to shake the new president's hand, and Jackson was all but mobbed as he tried to make his way to his horse.

The White House reception soon got completely out of hand. A throng of people, "from the highest and most polished, down to the most vulgar and gross," Justice Joseph Story observed, poured into the White House with muddy boots to overturn furniture in a rush for food and punch. Jackson was forced to leave by a side door. When wine and ice cream were carried out to the lawn, many guests followed by diving through the windows. The inauguration, Story concluded, meant the "reign of King Mob." Another observer called it a "proud day for the people." These contrasting views on the events of the inauguration captured the essence of the Jackson era: for some, an era of the excesses of democracy; for others, democratic fulfillment.

Old Hickory's Vigorous Presidency

Although Jackson had taken vague positions on important issues during the campaign, as president he needed to confront many of them. His decisions, often controversial, helped sharpen what it meant to be a Democrat and what it meant to be "Democracy's opponent."

A few key convictions—the principle of majority rule, the limited power of the national government, the obligation of the national government to defend the interests of the nation's average people against the "monied aristocracy"—guided Jackson's actions as president. Seeing himself as the people's most authentic representative (only the president was elected by all the people), Jackson intended to be a vigorous executive. More than any previous president, Jackson used presidential power in the name

of the people and justified his actions by appeals to the people.

Jackson asserted his power most dramatically through the veto. His six predecessors had cast only nine vetoes, mostly against measures that they had believed unconstitutional. Jackson, however, argued that he had "undoubted right . . . to withhold . . . assent from bills on other grounds than their constitutionality." Jackson vetoed 12 bills during his two terms, often because they conflicted with his political agenda.

One of the abuses Jackson had promised to correct was what he described as an undemocratic and corrupt system of government officeholding. Too often, "unfaithful or incompetent" men clung to government jobs for years. Jackson proposed to throw these scoundrels out and establish a system of rotation of office. The duties of public office were so "plain and simple," he said, that ordinary men could fulfill them.

Jackson's rhetoric was more extreme than his actions. He did not replace officeholders wholesale. In the first year and a half of his presidency, he removed 919 officeholders of a total of 10,093, fewer than one in ten. Most of these were for good reason—corruption or incompetence. Nor were the new Democratic appointees especially plain, untutored, or honest; they were in fact much like their predecessors. Still, Jackson's rhetoric helped create a new kind of democratic political culture that would prevail for most of the nineteenth century.

His policy on internal improvements—roads, canals, and other forms of transportation—was less far-seeing. Like most Americans, Jackson recognized their economic importance and as president wished "to see them extended to every part of the country." But Jackson was against infringement on states' rights. When proposals for federal support for internal improvements seemed to rob local and state authorities of their proper function, he opposed them. In 1830, he vetoed the Maysville Road bill, which proposed federal funding for a road in Henry Clay's Kentucky. But projects of national significance, like river improvements or lighthouses, were different. During his presidency, Jackson supported an annual average of $1.3 million in internal improvements.

In a period of rapid economic change, tariffs stirred heated debate. New England and the Middle Atlantic states, centers of manufacturing, favored protective tariffs. The South had long opposed them because they made it more expensive to buy manufactured goods from the North or abroad and threatened to provoke foreign retaliation against southern cotton and tobacco exports. Feelings against the "Tariff of Abominations" ran particularly high in South Carolina. Some of that state's leaders mistakenly believed the tariff was the prime reason for the economic depression that hung over their state. In addition, some worried that the federal government might eventually interfere with slavery, a frightening prospect in a state where slaves outnumbered whites.

Vice President Calhoun, a brilliant political thinker and an opponent of the tariff, provided the appropriate theory to check federal power and to protect minority rights. "We are not a nation," he once remarked, "but a Union, a confederacy of equal and sovereign states." In 1828, the same year as the hateful tariff, Calhoun anonymously published *Exposition and Protest*, presenting the doctrine of nullification as a means by which southern states could protect themselves from harmful national action. When federal laws overstepped the limits of constitutional authority, he argued, a state had the right to declare that legislation null and void and to refuse to enforce it.

Two years later, Calhoun's doctrine was aired in a Senate debate over public land policy. South Carolina's Robert Hayne defined nullification and, in the name of liberty, urged western states to adopt the doctrine. Daniel Webster responded. The federal government, he said, was no mere agent of the state legislatures. It was "made for the people, made by the people, and answerable to the people." No state legislature, therefore, could ever be sovereign over the people. Aware that nullification raised the specter of a "once glorious Union . . . drenched . . . in fraternal blood," Webster cried out in his powerful closing words that the appropriate motto for the nation was not "Liberty first and Union afterwards, but Liberty and Union, now and forever, one and inseparable!"

The drama was repeated a month later at a dinner, when President Jackson declared himself on the issue. Despite his support of states' rights, Jackson did not believe that any state had the right to reject the will of the majority or to destroy the Union. Knowing that the supporters of nullification hoped to use the gathering to win adherents, Jackson rose for a toast, held high his glass, and said, "Our Union—it must be preserved." Thus challenged, Calhoun followed: "The Union—next to our liberty most dear." The split between them widened over personal as well as ideological issues, and in 1832, Calhoun resigned as vice president. Final rupture came in a collision over the tariff and nullification.

In 1832, hewing to Jackson's "middle course," Congress modified the tariff of 1828 by retaining high duties on goods such as wool, woollens, iron, and hemp but lowering other rates to an earlier

With references to the still-hated British royalty, this cartoon, which was widely distributed by Whigs (a name chosen with antimonarchical British politics in mind), shows President Jackson with a vetoed bill in one hand and kingly scepter in the other, trampling on the Constitution, the U.S. Bank, and internal improvements. *(Collection of The New-York Historical Society)*

level. Many southerners felt injured. A South Carolina convention later that year adopted an Ordinance of Nullification, voiding the tariffs of 1828 and 1832 in that state. The South Carolina legislature funded a volunteer army and threatened secession if the federal government tried to force the state to comply.

South Carolina had attacked the principles of federal union and majority rule. Jackson responded forcefully. To the "ambitious malcontents" in South Carolina, he proclaimed emphatically that "the laws of the United States must be executed. . . . Disunion by armed force is treason. . . . The Union will be preserved and treason and rebellion promptly put down."

Jackson's proclamation stimulated an outburst of patriotism all over the country, isolating South Carolina. Jackson asked Congress for legislation to enforce tariff duties (the Force Bill of 1833), and new tariff revisions, engineered by Henry Clay and supported by Calhoun, called for reductions over a 10-year period. South Carolina quickly repealed its nullification of the tariff laws but saved face by nullifying the Force Bill, which Jackson ignored. The crisis was over, but left unresolved were the constitutional issues it raised. Was the Union permanent? Was secession a valid way to protect minority rights? Such questions would trouble Americans for three decades.

Jackson's Indian Policy

Although Jackson only threatened force on South Carolina, he used it on the southeastern Indians. His policy of forcible removal and relocation west-ward and on reservations defined white American practice toward Native American Indians for the rest of the century. In the opening decades of the nineteenth century, the vast landholdings of the five "civilized nations" of the Southeast (the Cherokee, Choctaw, Chickasaw, Seminole, and Creek) had been seriously eroded by the pressures of land-hungry whites supported by successful military campaigns led by professional Indian fighters like Jackson. The Creek lost 22 million acres in southern Georgia and central Alabama after Jackson defeated them at Horseshoe Bend in 1814. Land cessions to the government and private sales accounted for even bigger losses: Cherokee holdings of more than 50 million acres in 1802 had dwindled to only 9 million acres 20 years later.

A Supreme Court decision in 1823 declaring that Indians could occupy but not hold title to land in the United States bolstered the trend. Seeing that their survival was threatened, Indian nations acted to end the pattern. By 1825, the Creek, Cherokee, and Chickasaw had each resolved to restrict land sales to government agents. The Cherokee, having

---

Key Court Cases on Indian Rights

These Supreme Court cases decided in the nineteenth century have provided the legal basis for Native American activism in the twentieth century. Although Indian victories in court during the Jacksonian period did not halt the ability of whites to take over tribal lands, in the twentieth century, these court decisions allowed Indian tribes to win numerous court victories.

1823 *Johnson & Graham's Lessee v. William Mcintosh*

This case focused on the status of a land grant from an Indian tribe to an individual person. The decision recognized the tribal sovereignty and its rights to land. The court stated that only the federal government was competent to negotiate with tribes for their lands.

"It has been contested that the Indian claims amounted to nothing. Their rights of possession has never been questioned . . . the Court is decidedly of the opinion, that the plaintiffs do not exhibit a title which can be sustained in the Courts of the United States."

1831 *Cherokee Nation v. Georgia*

This case involved the status of state law within the Cherokee nation. The court classified the Indian tribes as domestic dependent nations whose relationship was like that of a ward to a guardian.

"Though the Indians are acknowledged to have an unquestionable, and, heretofore, unquestioned right to the lands they occupy until that right shall be extinguished by a voluntary cession to our government, yet it may well be doubted whether those tribes . . . can, with strict accuracy, be denominated as foreign nations. They may more correctly, perhaps, be denominated as domestic dependent nations."

1832 *Worcester v. Georgia*

This case was prompted by the state of Georgia's attempt to extend state law over the Cherokee nation. The decision reaffirmed Indian political rights, stating that Georgia laws had no force in Native American territories and that only the federal government had jurisdiction in Indian territories.

"The Indian nations had always been considered as distinct, independent, political communities . . . the settled doctrine of the law of nations is, that a weaker power does not surrender its independence—its rights to self-government—by associating with a stronger."

1835 *Mitchell v. The United States*

This decision affirmed the rights Native Americans have as occupants (not owners) of the land.

"It is enough to consider as a settled principle, that the right of occupancy is considered as sacred as the fee simple of the white."

Indian Removals: Southeast and Midwest

This map shows the westward routes of Indians removed from the Southeast to the new Indian territory in Oklahoma and from the Midwest (Old Northwest Territory) to present-day Kansas.

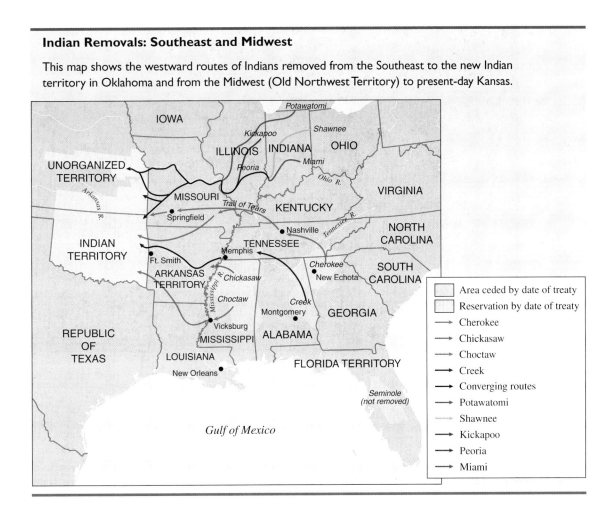

already assimilated such elements of white culture as dress, agricultural practices, and slaveholding (see Chapter 9), established a police force to prevent local leaders from selling off tribal lands. Indian determination to resist pressure confronted white resolve to gain southern lands for cotton planting and mining. Jackson's election in 1828 boosted efforts to relocate the Indians west of the Mississippi.

In Jackson's first annual message in 1829, he recommended removal of the southeastern tribes. Appealing at first to sympathy, Jackson argued that because the Indians were "surrounded by the whites with their arts of civilization," it was inevitable that the "resources of the savage" would be destroyed, dooming the Indians to "weakness and decay." Removal was justified, Jackson claimed, by both "humanity and national honor." He also insisted that state laws should prevail over the claims of either Indians or the federal government (thus contradicting his tariff policy).

The crisis came to a head in Georgia that same year, when the Georgia legislature declared the Cherokee tribal council illegal and claimed jurisdiction over both the tribe and its lands. In 1830,

the Cherokee were forbidden to defend their interests by bringing suits against whites into the Georgia courts or even by testifying in such cases. Without legal recourse on the state level, the Cherokee carried their protests to the Supreme Court. In 1832, Chief Justice Marshall supported their position in *Worcester* v. *Georgia,* holding that the Georgia law was "repugnant to the Constitution," adding that state laws could "have no force" over the Cherokee.

Legal victory could not, however, suppress white land hunger. With Jackson's blessing, Georgians defied the Court ruling. By 1835, harassment, intimidation, and bribery had persuaded a minority of chiefs to sign a removal treaty. That year, Jackson informed the Cherokee, "You cannot remain where you are. Circumstances . . . render it impossible that you can flourish in the midst of a civilized community." But when many Cherokee refused to leave, the nation split into two factions. Chief John Ross protested to Congress that the treaty was illegitimate. "We are stripped of every attribute of freedom. . . . Our property may be plundered . . . our lives may be taken away." His words did no good. In 1837 and 1838, the U.S. Army searched out and

Their attempts at assimilating into white society having failed, the Cherokee finally succumbed to white pressures and their own internal divisions and were forced to travel along the "Trail of Tears" to Oklahoma in 1838. About 4,000 died along the way. The Cherokee removal was actually the last major Indian group east of the Mississippi forced west. Upper-midwestern Indian nations such as the Shawnee, Potawatomi, Miami, Kickapoo, and Peoria had been removed to Missouri, Kansas, and Oklahoma in the 1810s and 1820s; the migration of southeastern nations began with the Choctaw in 1830. *(Woolaroc Museum, Bartlesville, Oklahoma)*

seized those opposed to migration westward and gathered them in stockades before herding them west to the "Indian Territory" in Oklahoma. An eyewitness described how the Cherokee trek began:

> Families at dinner were startled by the sudden gleam of bayonets in the doorway and rose to be driven with blows and oaths along the weary miles of trail that led to the stockade. Men were seized in their fields, or going along the road, women were taken from their [spinning] wheels and children from their play. In many cases, on turning for one last look as they crossed the ridge they saw their homes in flames, fired by the lawless rabble that followed on the heels of the soldiers to loot and pillage.

The removal, whose $6 million cost was deducted from the $9 million awarded the Cherokee for its eastern lands, killed perhaps a quarter of the 15,000 who set out. The Cherokee "Trail of Tears" followed those of other southeastern Indian nations. Tribal communities in the Old Northwest between 1821 and 1840 were also forced westward to Kansas and Oklahoma. The Chickasaw suffered as high a death rate as the Cherokee during their removal, while the Seminole and the Sac and Fox fought back. Although Jackson and the Removal Act of 1830 had promised to protect and forever guarantee the Indian lands in the West, within a generation those promises, like others before and since, would be broken. Indian removal left the eastern United States open for the enormous economic expansion described in Chapter 10.

Jackson's Bank War and "Van Ruin's" Depression

As the (white) people's advocate, Jackson could not ignore the Second Bank of the United States, which in 1816 had received a charter for 20 years. The bank generated intense feelings. Jackson called it a "monster" that threatened the people's liberties. But it was not as irresponsible as Jacksonians imagined.

Guided since 1823 by the aristocratic Nicholas Biddle, the Philadelphia bank and its 29 branches generally played a responsible economic role in an expansionary period. As the nation's largest commercial bank, the "B.U.S." could shift funds around the country as needed and could influence state banking activity. It restrained state banks from making unwise loans by insisting that they back their notes with specie (gold or silver coin) and by calling in its own loans to them. The bank accepted federal deposits, made commercial loans, and bought and sold government bonds. Businessmen, state bankers needing credit, and nationalist politicians such as Webster and Clay, who were on the bank's payroll, all favored it.

However, other Americans, led by the president, distrusted the bank. Businessmen and speculators in western lands resented its control over state banking and wanted cheap, inflated money to finance new projects and expansion. Some state bankers resented its power. Southern and western farmers regarded it as immoral because it dealt with paper, not landed property. Others simply thought it was unconstitutional and should be abolished.

Jackson had long opposed the B. U. S. He hated banks in general because of a near financial disaster in his own past and also because he and his advisers considered the B.U.S. the chief example of a special privilege monopoly that hurt the common man—farmers, craftsmen, and debtors. Jackson called the bank an "irresponsible power," a threat to the Republic. Its power and financial resources, he thought, made it a "vast electioneering engine" with "power to control the Government and change its character."

Aware of Jackson's hostility, Clay and Webster persuaded Biddle to ask Congress for a new charter in 1832, four years ahead of schedule. They reasoned that in an election year, Jackson would not risk a veto. The bill to recharter the bank swept through Congress and landed on the president's desk one hot, muggy day in July. Jackson took up the challenge. "The bank . . . is trying to kill me," he told Van Buren, "but I will kill it."

Jackson determined not only to veto the bill but also to carry his case to the public. His veto message, condemning the bank as undemocratic, un-American, and unconstitutional, was meant to stir up voters. He presented the bank as a dangerous monopoly that gave the rich special privileges and harmed "the humble members of society." He also pointed to the high percentage of foreign investors in the bank. Jackson's veto message turned the rechartering issue into a struggle between the people and the aristocracy. His oversimplified analysis made the bank into a symbol of everything that worried Americans in a time of change.

The bank furor helped to clarify party differences. In the election of 1832, the National Republicans, now calling themselves Whigs, nominated Henry Clay. Biddle and the Whigs spent thousands of dollars trying to defeat "King Andrew." Democratic campaign rhetoric pitted Jackson, the people, and democracy against Clay, the bank, and aristocracy. The Anti-Masons, the first third party in American political life and the first to hold a nominating convention, expressed popular resentments against the elitist Masonic order (Jackson was a member) and other secret societies.

Jackson won handsomely, with 124,000 more popular votes than the combined total for Clay and the Anti-Mason candidate, William Wirt. "He may be President for life if he chooses," said Wirt of Jackson.

Jackson, seeing the election as a victory for his bank policy, closed in on Biddle, even though the bank's charter had four years to run. He decided to weaken the B.U.S. by transferring $10 million in government funds to state banks. Although two secretaries of the treasury balked at the removal request as financially unsound, Jackson persisted until he found one, Roger Taney, willing to do it. His reward was being appointed the Chief Justice of the Supreme Court when John Marshall died in 1835.

Jackson's war with Biddle and the bank had serious economic consequences. A wave of speculation in western lands and ambitious new state internal improvement schemes in the mid-1830s produced inflated land prices and a flood of paper money. Even Jackson was concerned, and he tried to curtail irresponsible economic activity. In July 1836, he issued the Specie Circular, announcing that the government would accept only gold and silver in payment for public lands. Panicky investors rushed to change paper notes into specie, while banks started calling in loans. The result was the Panic of 1837. Jackson was blamed for this rapid monetary expansion followed by sudden deflation, but international trade problems with Britain and China probably contributed more to the panic and to the ensuing seven years of depression.

Whatever the primary cause, Jackson left his successor, Martin Van Buren (who was elected in 1836 over a trio of Whig opponents), with an economic crisis. Van Buren had barely taken the oath of office in 1837 when banks and businesses began to collapse. "Martin Van Ruin's" presidency was dominated by a severe depression. As New York banks suspended credit and began calling in loans, some $6 million was lost on defaulted debts. By the fall of 1837, one-third of America's workers were unemployed, and thousands of others had only part-time work. Those who kept their jobs saw wages fall by 30 to 50 percent within two years. The price of necessities like flour, pork, and coal nearly doubled. As winter neared in late 1837, a journalist estimated that 200,000 New Yorkers were "in utter hopeless distress with no means of surviving the winter but those provided by charity." They took to the streets demanding, "Bread! Meat! Rent! Fuel!" But as one worker said, most laborers called "not for the bread and fuel of charity, but for Work!"

The pride of workers was dampened as soup kitchens and bread lines grew faster than jobs. Laboring families found themselves defenseless, for the depression destroyed the trade union movement begun a decade earlier—a demise hastened by employers who imposed longer hours, cut wages and piece rates, and divided workers. One New England hat manufacturer offered to hire only those untouched by the "moral gangrene of Trades' Union principles." As the hardships of the depression grew worse, violence increased. In 1842, when

Philadelphia textile employers lowered wages below subsistence levels, angry hand-loom weavers, pursuing practices of the Luddites in England, broke machinery, destroyed cloth, and wrecked the homes of Irish strikebreakers.

Job competition, poverty, and ethnic animosities led to violent clashes in other eastern cities as well. "How is it," a Philadelphia mechanic asked in 1837, that in a country as rich as the United States so many people were "pinched for the common necessaries of life . . . [and] bowed down with gloom and despair?" President Van Buren's responses to the social misery behind this question were sympathetic but limited. An executive order in 1840 declaring a 10-hour day for federal employees affected few workers. Despite inadequate measures, political participation, as well as church membership, reached new heights during the depression, as Americans sought to alleviate their "gloom and despair."

The Second American Party System

By the mid-1830s, a new two-party system and a lively participatory national political culture had emerged in the United States. The parties had taken shape amid the conflicts of Jackson's presidency and the religious fervor of the Second Great Awakening. Although both parties included wealthy and influential leaders and mirrored the nation's growing diversity, Democrats had the better claim to be "the party of the common man" with nationwide strength.

Whigs represented greater wealth than Democrats and were strongest in New England and in areas settled by New Englanders across the Upper Midwest. In an appeal to businessmen and manufacturers, Whigs generally endorsed Clay's American System, which meant that they favored a national bank, federally supported internal improvements, and tariff protection for industry. Many large southern cotton planters joined the Whig party because of its position on bank credit and internal improvements. Whigs ran almost evenly with Democrats in the South for a decade, and artisans and laborers belonged equally to each party. The difficulty in drawing clear regional or class distinctions between Whigs and Democrats suggests that ethnic, religious, and cultural background also influenced party choice.

In the Jeffersonian tradition, the Democrats espoused liberty and local rule. They wanted freedom from legislators of morality, from religious tyranny, from special privilege, and from too much government. For them, the best society was one in which all Americans were free to follow their own individual interests. The Democrats appealed to members of denominations that had suffered discrimination in states where there had been an established church. Scots-Irish, French, German, and Irish Catholic immigrants, as well as free thinkers and labor organizers, tended to be Jacksonians. Democrats were less moralistic than Whigs on matters like drinking and slavery. Their religious background generally taught the inevitability of sin and evil, and

The Second American Party System

	Democrats	Whigs
Leaders	Andrew Jackson	Henry Clay
	John C. Calhoun	Daniel Webster
	Martin Van Buren	John Quincy Adams
	Thomas Hart Benton	William Henry Harrison
Political tradition	Republican party (Jefferson, Madison)	Federalist party (Hamilton, John Adams)
Major Political Beliefs		
	State and local autonomy	National power
	Opposition to monopoly and privilege	Support for U.S. Bank, high tariff
	Low land prices and tariffs	Internal improvements
	Freedom from government interference	Broad government role in reforming America
Primary Sources of Support		
Region	South and West	New England, Middle Atlantic, Upper Midwest
Class	Middle-class and small farmers, northeastern urban laborers and artisans	Big southern planters and wealthy businessmen, pockets of middling farmers in Midwest and South, artisans
Ethnicity	Scots-Irish, Irish, French, German, and Canadian immigrants	English, New England old stock
Religion	Catholics, frontier Baptists and Methodists, free thinkers	Presbyterians, Congregationalists, Quakers, moralists, reformers

FEDERAL BANK WHIG MOTTO.

"WE STOOP TO CONQUER."

FEDERAL-ABOLITION-WHIG TRAP,
TO CATCH VOTERS IN.

(Left) In the election of 1840, the Whigs "out-Jacksoned the Jacksonians" by playing to the popular political style of slogans, songs, and cider. They touted their candidate as a back-woodsy Indian fighter, the hero of the battle of Tippecanoe who lived in a log cabin and drank hard cider. *(Cincinnati Historical Society)* (Above) Louisiana Democrats responded to the Whig use of the log cabin and cider campaign with this cartoon, titled the "Federal-Abolition-Whig Trap to Catch Voters In," which shows an unwary voter, a member of the "industrious laboring classes," being lured under the log cabin by the promise of hard cider. "Just let him get a taste, " the text said, "and they come down at once upon him, hard and heavy, swig after swig, until they get him in a ranting way, shouting and bawling for Tip. and Ty." *(Library of Congress)*

Democrats sought to keep politics separate from moral issues.

By contrast, for many Whigs, religious and moral commitments shaped political goals and the way they understood issues. Calling themselves "the party of law and order," most Whigs did not think Americans needed more freedom, but rather they needed to learn to use the freedom they already had. If all men were to vote, they should learn how to use their political privileges. Old-stock New England Yankee Congregationalists and Presbyterians were usually Whigs. So were Quakers and evangelical Protestants, who believed that positive government action could change moral behavior and eradicate sin. Whigs supported a wide variety of reforms, such as temperance, antislavery, public education, and strict observance of the Sabbath, as well as government action to promote economic development.

Party identification played an increasingly large part in the lives of American men. Gaudy new electioneering styles were designed to recruit new voters into the political process and ensure party loyalty. Politics offered excitement, entertainment, camaraderie, and means to shape the changing world.

The election of 1840 illustrated the new political culture. Passing over Henry Clay, the Whigs nominated William Henry Harrison of Indiana, the aging hero of the Battle of Tippecanoe of 1811. Virginian John Tyler was nominated as vice president to underscore the regional diversity of the party. The Democrats had no choice but to renominate Van Buren, who conducted a quiet campaign. The Whig campaign, however, featured every form of popularized appeals for votes—songs, cartoons, barbecues, and torchlight parades. Whigs posed Harrison (who lived in a mansion) in front of a rural log cabin with a barrel of hard cider and dispensed jugs of cider to grateful voters.

The Whigs reversed conventional images by labeling Van Buren an aristocratic dandy and contrasting him with their simple candidate sitting in front of his cabin. Harrison reminded voters of General Jackson, and they swept him into office, with 234 electoral votes to Van Buren's 60. In one of the largest turnouts in American history, over 80 percent of eligible voters marched to the polls. A Democratic party journal acknowledged that "we taught them how to conquer us."

Concern over the new politics outlasted Harrison, who died only a month after taking office. One man complained during the campaign that he was tired of all the hoopla over "the Old Hero. Nothing but politics . . . mass-meetings are held in every groggery." The implied criticism of the role that alcohol played in party politics highlights the moral and religious perspective many Americans, especially Whigs, brought to politics. Others, however, rejected the political route and sought other means to impose order and morality on American society.

PERFECTIONIST REFORM AND UTOPIANISM

"Be ye therefore perfect even as your Father in heaven is perfect," commanded the Bible. Mid-nineteenth-century reformers, inspired by the Finney revivals, took the challenge seriously. Eventually, many believed, a perfected millennial era of 1,000 years of peace, harmony, and Christian brotherhood on earth would bring the Second Coming of Christ.

The perfectionist thrust in religion fit America's sense of itself as a redeemer nation chosen by God to reform the entire world. Religious commitment fused with patriotic duty. The motivating impulse to reform in the 1830s, then, had many deep-rooted causes. These included the Puritan idea of American mission; the secular examples of founding fathers like Benjamin Franklin to do good, reinforced by Republican ideology and romantic beliefs in the natural goodness of human nature; the social activist tendencies in Whig political ideology; anxiety over shifting class relationships and socioeconomic change; family influence and the desire of young

people to choose careers of principled service; and the direct influence of revivalism.

The International Character of Reform

Yet not all the forces leading to reformism came from within. During the early decades of the nineteenth century, the Atlantic Ocean was a highway for reform ideas and reformers. Many of the conditions that troubled Americans, often spawned by industrialization, also troubled Europeans. Women organized in Britain and the United States to reform prostitutes. Societies to encourage temperance flourished in Germany, Ireland, and England as well as the United States. French and British liberals agitated to end the slave trade as did their American counterparts.

A steady stream of men and women traveled from one side of the Atlantic to the other, raising money, publicizing their ideas, studying what had been done outside of their own country, and setting up social experiments. Abolitionists Frederick Douglass and William Lloyd Garrison visited England to gain support for their struggle against slavery, while English abolitionist George Thompson toured in the northern states to assist abolitionists there. Scottish cotton mill owner Robert Owen came to the United States in the 1820s to set up a socialist community after having created a model factory town in Scotland.

There was cross-fertilization across national boundaries of ideas and reform strategies. Owen's book, *The Book of the Moral World* (1820), inspired cooperative efforts of many kinds while the work of female antislavery societies in Britain and Scotland served as models for American women. Letters between reformers in different countries also helped to firm the reform commitment and inspire action. Hearing of a success elsewhere gave faith that change might come at home, while hearing about failures prompted discussions of appropriate strategies.

Motivations and Causes of Reform in America, 1830–1850

- Changing relationships between men and women, masters and workers as a result of the market economy, growth of cities, and increasing immigration
- Finney and other religious revivals in the Second Great Awakening
- Social activist and ethical impulses of the Whig party
- Psychological anxieties over shifting class and ethnic relationships
- Family traditions and youthful idealism
- Puritan and Revolutionary traditions of the American mission to remake the world
- Republican ideology and Enlightenment emphasis on virtue and good citizenship
- Romantic literary influences such as Transcendentalism

The Dilemmas of Reform

Throughout the Atlantic world, reformers faced difficult dilemmas about how best to effect change. Does one, for example, try to change attitudes first and then behavior, or the reverse? Which is more effective, to appeal to people's minds and hearts to change bad institutions, or to change institutions first, assuming that altered behavior will then change attitudes? Taking the first path, the reformer relies on education and on the moral suasion of sermons, tracts, literature, argument, and personal testimony. Following the second, the reformer acts politically and institutionally, seeking to pass laws, win elections, form unions, boycott goods, and create or abolish institutions.

Reformers, moreover, must decide whether to attempt to bring about limited, piecemeal practical change on a single issue or to go for perfection. Should they improve on a partly defective system or tear it down to build a utopian new one? Furthermore, should they use or recommend force or enter into coalitions with less principled potential allies? And as Thoreau asked, are their own attitudes and actions thoroughly consistent with the behavior they would urge on others?

As Marius and Emily Robinson understood, promoting change has its costs. Advocates of change experience enormous pressures, recriminations, and economic or physical persecution. Moreover, reformers invariably disagree on appropriate ideology and tactics, and so they end up quarreling with one another. Although reformers suffer pressure to conform and to cease questioning things, their duty to themselves, their society, and their God sustains their commitment. And so it was in the 1830s and 1840s.

Utopian Communities: Oneida and the Shakers

Thoreau tried to lead an ideal solitary life. Other reformers sought to create perfect communities. Emerson noted in 1840 that he hardly met a thinking man who did not have "a draft of a new community in his waistcoat pocket." One way to redeem a flawed society, one that seemed to be losing the cohesion and traditional values of small community life, was to create miniature utopian societies.

In 1831, as President Jackson and the South Carolina nullifiers squared off, as Nat Turner planned his revolt, and as the citizens of Rochester sought ways of controlling their workers' drinking habits, a young man in Putney, Vermont, heard Charles Finney preach on one of his whirlwind tours of New England. John Humphrey Noyes was an instant, if unorthodox, convert.

Noyes believed that the act of final conversion led to absolute perfection and complete release from sin. But his earthly happiness was soon sorely tested. In 1837, a woman he loved rejected both his doctrines and his marriage offer. Despondent, Noyes wrote to a friend, "when the will of God is done on earth as it is in heaven there will be no marriage." Among those who were perfect, he argued, all men and women belonged equally to each other, analogous to shared wealth in socioeconomic relationships. Others called his heretical doctrines "free love" and socialism. Noyes recovered from his unhappy love affair and married a loyal follower. When she bore four stillborn babies within six years, Noyes again revised his unconventional ideas about sex.

In 1848, Noyes and 51 devoted followers founded a "perfectionist" community at Oneida, New York. Under his strong leadership, it prospered, although many Americans found the community's rejection

In this sacred Shaker dance, sin is being shaken out of the body through the fingertips. Note the separation of women and men. *(Shaker Village of Pleasant Hill, Harrodsburg, Kentucky)*

of middle-class marriage norms immoral. Sexual life at the commune was subject to many regulations, including male continence except under carefully prescribed conditions. Only certain spiritually advanced males (usually Noyes) were allowed to father children. Other controversial practices included communal child rearing, sexual equality in work, the removal of the competitive spirit from both work and play, and an elaborate program of "mutual criticism" at community meetings presided over by "Father" Noyes.

Though creating considerable tension, these unorthodox sexual and social rules gave Oneidans a sense of uniqueness. Wise economic decisions bound community members in mutual prosperity. Forsaking the nostalgic agricultural emphasis that typified most other communes, Noyes opted for modern manufacturing. Oneida specialized at first in the fabrication of steel animal traps and later diversified into making silverware. Eventually abandoning religion to become a joint-stock company in which individual members held shares, Oneida thrived for many years and continues today as a silverware company.

Noyes greatly admired another group of communitarians, the Shakers, who also believed in perfectionism, communal property, and bringing on the millennial kingdom of heaven. Unlike the Oneidans, Shakers condemned sexuality and demanded absolute celibacy, so that only conversions could bring in new members. Founded by an Englishwoman, Mother Ann Lee, Shaker conversions grew in the Second Great Awakening and peaked around 6,000 souls by the 1850s, with communities from Maine to New York to Kentucky. Shakers believed that God had a dual personality, male and female, and that Ann Lee was the female counterpart to the masculine Christ. Shaker worship featured frenetic dancing intended to release (or "shake") sin out through the fingertips. Shaker communities, some of which survived long into the twentieth century, were known for their communal ownership of property, equality of women and men, simplicity, and beautifully crafted furniture.

Other Utopias

Over 100 utopian communities like Oneida and the Shaker colonies were founded. Some were religiously motivated; others were secular. Most were small and lasted only a few months or years. All eventually collapsed, though they gave birth to significant social ideas.

Pietist German-speaking immigrants founded the earliest utopian communities in America to preserve their language, spirituality, and ascetic lifestyle. The

most notable of these were the Ephrata colonists in Pennsylvania, the Harmonists in Indiana, the Zoar community in Ohio, and the Amana Society in Iowa. Some antebellum utopian communities focused less on otherworldly contemplation than on the regeneration of this world. In 1840, Adin Ballou founded Hopedale in Massachusetts as a "miniature Christian republic" based on the ethical teachings of Jesus. Hopedale's *The Practical Christian* advocated temperance, pacifism, women's rights, and other reforms.

Other antebellum communities, founded on the secular principles of reason inherited from the Enlightenment, responded more directly to the social misery and wretched working conditions accompanying the Industrial Revolution. These communities differed from religious ones in assuming that evil came from bad environments rather than individual acts of sin. They consequently believed that altered environments could eliminate or reduce poverty, ignorance, intemperance, and other ugly by-products of industrialism.

Robert Owen was the best known of the secular communalists. A Scottish industrialist who saw the miserable lives of cotton mill workers, he envisioned a society of small towns—"Agricultural and Manufacturing Villages of Unity and Mutual Cooperation"—with good schools and healthy work. Unemployment, poverty, and vice would be unknown in Owen's model communities. In 1824, he established his first town in America at New Harmony, Indiana, site of a Pietist community. But little harmony prevailed, and it failed within three years.

Brook Farm, founded by two Concord friends of Emerson, sought to integrate "intellectual and manual labor." Residents would hoe in the fields and shovel manure for a few hours each day and then study literature and recite poetry. Although the colony lasted less than three years, it produced some notable literature in Margaret Fuller's *The Dial*. (Although Fuller enjoyed the conversations, she thought the experiment was impractical and refused to live there.) Nathaniel Hawthorne briefly lived at Brook Farm and wrote a novel, *The Blithedale Romance* (1852), criticizing the utopians' naive optimism.

The utopian communities all failed for similar reasons. Americans seemed ill-suited to communal living and were unwilling to share either their property or their spouses. Nor did celibacy arouse much enthusiasm. Other recurring problems included unstable leadership, financial bickering, local hostility toward sexual experimentation and other unorthodox practices, the indiscriminate admission of members, and waning enthusiasm. Emerson

Utopian Communities before 1860

The Mormons retreated to the trans-Mississippi West to realize their vision of a better society, but most communitarians did not go so far away from "civilization" to establish their experiments. Why did they not flee more settled and ordinary communities? Why did they avoid the South?

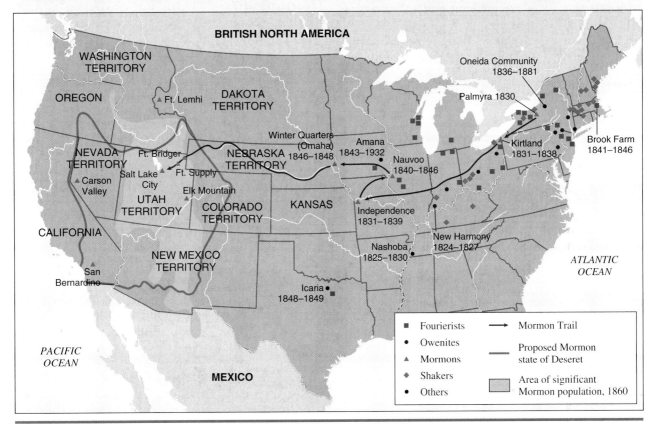

pinned the failure of the communities on their inability to confront human individualism. As he said of Brook Farm, an epitaph suitable for all utopian communities: "It met every test but life itself."

Millerites and Mormons

If utopian communities failed to bring about the millennium, an alternative hope was to leap directly past the thousand years of peace and harmony to the Second Coming of Christ. William Miller, a shy farmer from upstate New York, became so absorbed with the idea of the imminent coming of Christ that he figured out mathematically the exact time: 1843, probably in March. A sect gathered around him to prepare for Christ's return and the Day of Judgment.

A mixture of excitement and fear grew as the day of the predicted return came closer. Some people gave away all their worldly belongings, neglected business, put on robes, and flocked to high hills and rooftops to be nearer to the blessed event. When

1843 passed without the expected end, Miller recalculated and set new dates. Each new disappointment diminished his followers, and he died in 1848 a discredited man. But a small Millerite sect, the Seventh-Day Adventists, abandoned predicting the date of the Second Coming, instead choosing to live with the expectation that it will be "right soon." It continues to this day.

Other groups that emerged from the same religiously active area of upstate New York were more successful. As Palmyra, New York, was being swept by Finney revivalism, young Joseph Smith, who had been examining Methodism and other beliefs, claimed to be visited by the angel Moroni. According to Smith, Moroni led him to golden tablets buried in the ground near his home. On these were inscribed what later became *The Book of Mormon,* which described the one true church and a "lost tribe of Israel" missing for centuries. The book also predicted the appearance of an American prophet who would establish a new and pure kingdom of Christ in America. Smith published his book in 1830 and soon founded the Church of Jesus Christ of Latter-Day Saints (the Mormons). His visionary leadership attracted thousands of ordinary people trying to escape what they viewed as social disorder, religious impurity, and commercial degradation in the 1830s.

Smith and a steadily growing band of converts migrated first to Ohio, next to Missouri, and then back to Illinois. The frequent migrations were partly a consequence of the ridicule, persecution, and violence that they encountered. Hostility stemmed from their missionary work, their support for local Indian tribes, and from rumors of unorthodox sexual practices.

Despite external persecution and internal dissension caused by Smith's strong leadership style, the Mormons prospered. The policy of sending missionaries abroad resulted in substantial numbers of converts from England and northern Europe who traveled to join the Mormon community in the United States. By the mid-1840s, Nauvoo, Illinois, with a thriving population of nearly 15,000, was the showplace of Mormonism. Smith petitioned Congress for separate territorial status and ran for the presidency in 1844. This was too much for the citizens of nearby towns. Violence escalated and culminated in Smith's trial for treason and his murder by a mob. Under the brilliant leadership of Smith's successor, Brigham Young, the Mormons headed westward in 1846 in their continuing search for the "land of promise."

REFORMING SOCIETY

The Mormons and the utopian communitarians had as their common goal, in Brigham Young's words, "the spread of righteousness upon the earth." Most people, however, preferred to spread righteousness by focusing on a specific social evil rather than embracing whole new religions or joining utopian colonies.

"We are all a little wild here," Emerson wrote in 1840, "with numberless projects of social reform." Mobilized in part by their increased participation in the political parties of Jacksonian America, the reformers created and joined all kinds of societies for social betterment. The reform ranks were swelled by thousands of women, stirred to action by the religious revivals and freed from domestic burdens by delayed marriage and smaller families. Organized in hundreds of voluntary societies, women such as Emily Rakestraw joined men such as Marius Robinson in directing their energies to numerous social issues. Like men and women in many European countries, they tackled such issues as

alcohol; diet and health; sexuality; institutional treatment of the mentally ill, the disabled, paupers, and criminals; education; the rights of labor; slavery; and women's rights. It was a considerable agenda, much of it inspired by religious revivalism.

Temperance

On New Year's Eve in 1831, a Finney disciple, Theodore Dwight Weld, delivered a four-hour temperance lecture in Rochester. In graphic detail, he described the awful fate of those who refused to stop drinking and urged his audience not only to cease their tippling but also to stop others. Several were converted to abstinence on the spot. The next day, Elijah and Albert Smith, the largest providers of whiskey in Rochester, rolled their barrels out onto the sidewalk and smashed them. Cheering Christians applauded as the whiskey ran out onto Exchange Street.

Nineteenth century Americans drank heavily. It was said that "a house could not be raised, a field of wheat cut down, nor could there be a log rolling, a husking, a quilting, a wedding, or a funeral without the aid of alcohol." The corrosive effects of drinking were obvious: poverty, crime, illness, insanity, battered and broken families, and corrupt politics.

Early efforts at curbing alcohol consumption emphasized moderation. Local temperance societies agreed to limit how much they drank or to imbibe only beer and wine. Some met in local taverns to toast their commitment to moderation. But under the influence of the Beecher and Finney revivals, the movement achieved better organization and clearer goals. The American Temperance Society, founded in 1826, was dedicated not just to moderation but rather to total abstinence. Within a few years, thousands of local and state societies had formed with the goal of the "teetotal" pledge, foreswearing even the drinking of hard cider and communion wine.

Temperance advocates copied successful revival techniques. Fiery lecturers expounded on the evil consequences of drink and urged group pressure on the weak-willed. A deluge of graphic and sometimes gory and exaggerated temperance tracts poured out. "Some are killed instantly," one claimed, "some die a lingering, gradual death; some commit suicide in fits of intoxication; and some are actually burnt up." In another, an "intemperate man" died when his "breath caught fire by coming in contact with a lighted candle."

By 1840, disagreements over goals and methods split the temperance movement into many separate organizations. In depression times, when jobs and stable families were harder to find than whiskey and beer, laboring men and women moved more by

Here is an example of temperance propaganda. The journal, entitled *Cold Water Magazine*, gives a drastic picture of the effects of drinking. Here the drunkard is a father who abuses his wife and children. He has also reduced them to poverty as the bare house makes clear. *(The Library Company of Philadelphia [Pert 8, 51767.0, v. 1])*

practical concerns than religious fervor joined the crusade. The Washington Temperance Society, founded in a Baltimore tavern in 1840, was enormously popular with unemployed young workers and grew to an estimated 600,000 members in three years. The Washingtonians, arguing that alcoholism was a disease rather than moral failure, changed the shape of the temperance movement. They replaced revivalist techniques with those of the new party politics by organizing parades, picnics, melodramas, and festivals to encourage people to take the pledge.

Tactics in the 1840s also shifted away from moral suasion to political action. Temperance societies lobbied for local option laws, allowing communities to prohibit the sale, manufacture, and consumption of alcohol. The first such law in the nation was passed in Maine in 1851. Fifteen other states followed with similar laws before the Civil War. Despite weak enforcement, the per capita drinking fell dramatically in the 1850s. Interrupted by the Civil War, the movement reached its ultimate objective with passage of the Eighteenth Amendment in 1919.

The temperance crusade reveals the many practical motivations for Americans to join reform societies. For some, as in Rochester, temperance provided an opportunity for the Protestant middle classes to exert some control over laborers, migrants, and Catholics. Perfectionists saw abstinence as a way of practicing self-control. For many women, the temperance effort represented a way to control drunken abusers. For many young men, especially after the onset of the depression of 1837, a temper-

ance society provided entertainment, fellowship, and contacts to help their careers. In temperance societies as in political parties, Americans found jobs, purpose, support, spouses, and relief from the loneliness and uncertainty of a changing world.

Health and Sexuality

It was a short step from the physical and psychological ravages of drink to other potentially harmful effects on the body. Reformers were quick to attack too much eating, too many stimulants, and, above all, too much sex. Many endorsed a variety of special diets and exercise programs for maintaining good health. Some promoted panaceas. One of these was hydropathy, whereby clients sojourned at one of 70 special resorts for bathing and water purges of the body. Many of these resorts especially attracted women who not only found an escape from daily drudgery in the home but also found cures for chronic and untreated urogenital infections. Other panaceas, including hypnotism, phrenology (the study of bumps on the head), and various "spiritualist" seances, sought to cure problems of the mind.

Sylvester Graham, inventor of the Graham cracker, combined many of these enthusiasms into a focus on sexual purity. In 1834, he delivered a series of lectures on chastity, later published as an advice book. To those "troubled" by sexual desire, he recommended "cold baths" and "more active exercise in the open air." Graham advised women, apparently not as "passionless" as the Victorian stereotype suggested, to "have intercourse only for procreation." Although females learned to control sexuality for their own purposes, as we shall see, male "sexual purity" advocates urged sexual restraint to protect various male interests. One doctor argued that women ought not to be educated because blood needed for the womb would be diverted to the head, thus breeding "puny men." Men were warned not to "spend their seed" in unnatural acts.

The authors of antebellum "health" manuals advocated abstinence from sexual activity as vehemently as from alcohol. The body, they argued, was a closed energy system in which each organ had particular and limited functions to perform. Semen must be saved for reproductive purposes and should not be wasted in masturbation or intercourse only for pleasure. Such waste would cause enervation, disease, insanity, and death. Some argued further that the "expenditure" of sperm meant a loss of needed energy from the economy.

Humanizing the Asylum

Struggling to restore order to American society, some reformers preferred to work not to influence individuals but to change institutions such as asylums, almshouses, prisons, schools, and factories. Horace Mann, who led the struggle for common schools in Massachusetts (see Chapter 10), was a typical antebellum reformer. He blended dedicated idealism with a canny, practical sense of how to institutionalize educational improvements in one state: teacher training schools, higher teachers' salaries, and compulsory attendance laws.

Other reformers were less successful in achieving their goals. This was especially true in the treatment of society's outcasts. Colonial families or communities cared for orphans, paupers, the insane, and even criminals. Beginning early in the nineteenth century, states built asylums, houses of refuge, reform schools, jails, and other institutions to uplift and house social victims. In some, like prisons and almshouses, the sane and insane, children and hardened adult criminals were thrown together in terrible conditions. In 1843, Dorothea Dix, a frail New Englander, reported to a horrified Massachusetts legislature that the state's imprisoned insane people lived in the "extremest state of degradation and misery," confined in "cages, closets, stalls, pens! Chained, naked, beaten with rods, and lashed into obedience!" Dix recommended special asylums where the insane could be "humanly and properly controlled" by trained attendants.

Many perfectionist reformers like Dix believed that asylums could reform society's outcasts. Convinced that bad institutions corrupted basically good human beings, they reasoned that reformed

institutions could rehabilitate them. In 1853, Charles Loring Brace started a Children's Aid Society in New York City that was a model of change through effective education and self-help. Reformers like Dix and Brace, as well as Samuel Gridley Howe and Thomas Gallaudet, who founded institutions for the care and education of the blind and deaf, achieved remarkable results.

But all too often, results were disappointing. Prison reformers believed that a proper penitentiary could bring a hardened criminal "back to virtue." They argued intensely over the most appropriate structural design for rehabilitating criminals. Some preferred the rectangular prison at Auburn, New York, with its tiny cells and common workrooms, whereas others pointed to the Pennsylvania star-shaped system, where each inmate was in solitary confinement, though in a fairly modern cell. All prison reformers assumed that "penitents" in isolated cells, studying the Bible and reflecting on their wrongdoing, would eventually decide to become good citizens. In practice, many criminals went mad or committed suicide. Institutions built by well-intentioned reformers became dumping places for society's outcasts. By mid-century, American prisons and mental asylums had become sadly impersonal, understaffed, overcrowded institutions.

Working-Class Reform

Efforts to improve the institutional conditions of American life were not all top-down movements initiated and led by middle-class reformers. For working-class Americans, as in England, the social institution most in need of transformation was the factory. Workers, many of whom were involved in other issues such as temperance, peace, and abolitionism, tried to improve their own lives. As labor leader Seth Luther told a meeting of New England mechanics and laborers, "We must take our business into our own hands. Let us awake." And awake they did, forming both trade unions and workingmen's parties as Andrew Jackson neared the presidency.

Between 1828 and 1832, dozens of workingmen's parties arose. They advocated free, tax-supported schools, free public lands in the West, equal rights for the poor, and elimination of monopolistic privilege. Trade union activity began in Philadelphia in 1827 as skilled workers organized journeymen carpenters, plasterers, printers, weavers, tailors, and other tradesmen. That same year, 15 unions combined into a citywide federation, a process followed in other cities. The National Trades Union, founded in 1834, was the first attempt at a national labor organization.

Trade unions fared better than labor parties, as Jacksonian Democrats siphoned off workers' votes.

A popular workingmen's form of entertainment was the minstrel show, where whites would blacken their faces with burnt cork and perform songs and skits that negatively stereotyped blacks. Two oft-depicted types were thick-lipped, dim-witted slavish clowns and faithful "old Darkies," both incapable of coping with plantation life. Another was the northern pseudo-suave dandy like "Zip Coon," shown here who, despite his airs, was always humiliated so as to reassure white workers that free blacks posed no threat to take either their women or their jobs. *(The Harvard Theatre Collection, The Houghton Library)*

Union programs set more practical goals, including shorter hours, wages that would keep pace with rising prices, and ways (such as the closed shop) of warding off the competitive threat of cheap labor. In addition, both workers and their middle-class supporters called for the abolition of imprisonment for debt and of compulsory militia duty (both of which often cost workers their jobs), free public education, improved living conditions for workers, and the right to organize. Discouraged by anti-union decisions of New York State courts in 1835 and again in 1836, workers argued that unions were necessary to "resist the oppressions of avarice" and compared themselves with the Americans who dumped British tea in Boston's harbor in 1773.

Fired by revolutionary tradition, by increasing political influence, and by a union membership of near 300,000, workers struck some 168 times between 1834 and 1836. Over two-thirds of the strikes were over wages (see Chapter 10); the other strikes were for shorter hours. Identifying with the "blood of our fathers" shed on the battlefields of the American Revolution, Boston tradesmen struck in 1835 for a 10-hour day. They failed, but their attempt heralded the subsequent resurgence of a successful 10-hour-day movement in the 1850s. The Panic of 1837 ushered in a depression that dashed the hopes and efforts of American workers. But the organizational work of the 1830s promised that the labor movement would reemerge, strengthened, later in the century.

ABOLITIONISM AND THE WOMEN'S RIGHTS MOVEMENT

As American workers struggled in Lowell and other eastern cities for better wages and hours in 1834, Emily and Marius Robinson arrived in Cincinnati to fight for their causes. Along with many other young idealists, they were attracted by the newly founded Lane Seminary, a school to train abolitionist leaders. Financed by two wealthy New York brothers, Arthur and Lewis Tappan, Lane soon became a center of reformist activity. When nervous local residents persuaded President Lyman Beecher to crack down on the students, 40 "Lane rebels," led by Theodore Weld, fled to Oberlin in northern Ohio. The rebels turned Oberlin College into the first institution in the United States open both to women and men, blacks and whites. Thus, the movements to abolish slavery and for equal rights for women and free blacks were joined.

The goals of the struggle against slavery and subtle forms of racism and sexism often seemed as distant and unrealizable as the millennium itself. Yet antislavery and feminist advocates persisted in their efforts to abolish what they believed were concrete, visible, ingrained social wrongs. Whether seeking to eliminate coercion in the cotton fields or in the kitchen, they faced the dual challenge of pursuing elusive goals while achieving practical changes in everyday life.

Tensions within the Antislavery Movement

Although the antislavery movement was smaller than temperance advocacy, it revealed more clearly the difficulties of pursuing significant social change in America. As a young man of 22, William Lloyd Garrison passionately desired to improve, if not to perfect, the flawed world in which he lived. He was also ambitious and said that his name would "one day be known to the world." He was right. On January 1, 1831, eight months before Nat Turner's revolt,

This image of an imploring slave was one of the favorite abolitionist devices. Sometimes the caption asked, "Am I not a Man and a Brother?" In this case, the caption has been changed to encourage antislavery supporters to make weekly donations to the Massachusetts Anti-Slavery Society. The text suggested that abolitionism was a religious duty and drew upon the idea that slavery was a sin. *(Boston Public Library/Rare Books Department. Courtesy of the Trustees)*

Garrison published the first issue of *The Liberator*, soon to become the leading antislavery journal in the United States. "I am in earnest," he wrote. "I will not equivocate—AND I WILL BE HEARD." After organizing the New England Anti-Slavery Society with a group of blacks and whites in a church basement in Boston, in 1833 Garrison and 62 others established the American Anti-Slavery Society, which called for an immediate end to slavery.

Until then, most antislavery whites had advocated gradual emancipation by individual slave owners. Many joined the American Colonization Society, founded in 1816, which sent a few ex-slaves to Liberia. But these efforts proved inadequate and racist, the main goal being to rid the country of free blacks. Rejected by African Americans and violently attacked by Garrisonians, colonization lost much of it support.

Garrison and others in the American Anti-Slavery Society viewed slavery as a sin that had to be eliminated. They opposed gradualism and colonization and called for immediate emancipation in uncompromising language. As Garrison declared, "I do not

wish to think, or speak, or write, with moderation." There could be "no Union with slaveholders," he argued, condemning the Constitution that perpetuated slavery as "an agreement with Hell." Inspired by *The Liberator* and antislavery lecturers like Garrison, Marius Robinson, and the African-American writer and activist Maria Stewart, dozens of local male and female abolitionist societies dedicated to the immediate emancipation of the slaves arose, mostly in the Northeast and Northwest. A society founded by free black women in Boston in 1831, the African-American Female Intelligence Society, was the first antislavery organization dedicated to immediate emancipation.

The determination to eliminate slavery was reinforced by victories in the antislavery movement elsewhere in the world. Agitation against the international slave trade in several European countries and the abolition of slavery in the 1820s and 1830s in newly independent Latin American nations showed that change was possible. But it was the antislavery movement in Great Britain that most influenced American antislavery activists. British activists waged a decades-long campaign to persuade Parliament to emancipate slaves in Britain's Caribbean colonies. Antislavery societies of men and women provided an organizational basis for agitation, including massive petition campaigns. After achieving victory in 1833, these groups supported American efforts by providing advice, money, speakers, and an audience for traveling American abolitionists like Frederick Douglass.

Yet American antislavery reformers did not agree on how to achieve their goal. Some found the Garrisonian abolitionists far too radical for their tastes. Others differed over tactics. Their primary method was to convince slaveholders that slavery was a sin. Abolitionists tried to overwhelm slaveholders with moral guilt so that, repentant, they would free their slaves. Black abolitionist David Walker accused southern whites of Christian hypocrisy, citing cases of beating slaves as they were engaged in Christian worship. "Have not the Americans the Bible in their hands? Do they believe it? Surely they do not. See how they treat us in open violation of the Bible!!" But as Marius wrote to Emily Robinson, "The spirit of slavery is not confined to the South." His Ohio trip suggests that northerners were equally guilty in providing the support necessary to maintain the slave system.

The abolitionists had flooded the nation with over a million pieces of antislavery literature by 1837. Their writing described slave owners as "mansteaders" who gave up all claim to humanity. A slaveholder, Garrison wrote, led a life "of unbridled lust, . . . of haughty domination, of cowardly ruffian-ism, of boundless dissipation, of matchless inso-lence, of infinite self-conceit, of unequalled oppres-sion, of more than savage cruelty." In 1839, Weld published *American Slavery as It Is*, which described in the goriest possible detail the inhumane treat-ment of slaves.

Other abolitionists preferred more direct meth-ods. The main alternative lay in political action, such as bringing antislavery petitions before Congress and forming third parties. Boycotting goods made by slave labor was a third tactic.

A fourth approach was to call for slave rebellion, as did two northern blacks, David Walker in an 1829 pamphlet and Henry Highland Garnet in a speech at a convention of black Americans in 1843. As a free black living in Boston, Walker's powerful essay, "David Walker's Appeal," called upon other free blacks to "enlighten your brethren" to their ignorant "wretched condition" and upon slaves themselves to cease their submissiveness and rise up and throw off the yoke of slavery. "Now I ask you," Walker wrote, "had you not rather be killed than to be a slave to a tyrant, who takes the life of your mother, wife, and dear little children? Look upon your mother, wife and children, and answer God almighty; and believe this, that it is no more harm for you to kill a man, who is trying to kill you, than it is for you to take a drink of water when thirsty." It was Walker, however, who was mysteriously found dead on a Boston street a year after the publication of his "Appeal." Garnet's call for rebellion was clear:

"Brethren arise, arise! Strike for your lives and liber-ties. Now is the day and the hour. . . . You cannot be more oppressed than you have been—you cannot suffer greater cruelties than you have already. RATHER DIE FREEMEN, THAN LIVE TO BE SLAVES. Remember that you are THREE MILLIONS!"

Abolitionists' tactical disagreements helped splinter the movement. Garrison's unyielding per-sonal style and his commitment to even less popu-lar causes such as women's rights offended many abolitionists. In 1840, at its annual meeting in New York, which was intended as a unity convention to heal growing divisions, the American Anti-Slavery Society split. Several delegates walked out when a woman, Abby Kelley, was elected to a previously all-male committee. One group, which supported mul-tiple issues and moral suasion, stayed with Garrison; the other followed James Birney and the Tappans into the Liberty party and political action.

Class differences and race further divided aboli-tionists. Northern workers, though fearful of the po-tential job competition implicit in emancipation, nevertheless saw their "wage slavery" as similar to chattel slavery. Both violated fundamental republi-can values of freedom and equality. Strains between northern labor leaders and middle-class abolition-ists, who minimized the seriousness of working-men's concerns, were similar to those between white and black antislavery forces. Whites like Wendell Phillips decried slavery as a moral blot on American society, and blacks like Douglass were more con-cerned with the effects of slavery and discrimination

It was dangerous to be a public abolitionist in this period. In this Winslow Homer engrav-ing for *Harper's Weekly* titled "Expulsion of Negroes and Abolitionists from Tremont Temple, Boston, Massachusetts, on December 3, 1860," Homer shows Frederick Douglass being forced from the stage by pro-southern demonstrators, who interrupted the meeting called to debate "How can American slavery be Abolished?" The policeman removing Douglass for his safety was reported to have told him that he "must instantly leave," thus ending the de-bate and meeting before it had hardly begun. *(The Museum of Fine Arts, Houston; The Mavis P. Wilson Kelsey Collection of Winslow Homer Graphics)*

Slave Narratives

In the 1840s and 1850s, male and female abolitionists eagerly sought out and published book-length accounts of slavery written by runaway slaves themselves. These chilling stories of captivity and successful escapes, in the voices of former slaves, had enormous emotional power and were instrumental in the effort of abolitionists to influence public opinion and end slavery. According to one estimate, nearly 100 book-length "slave narratives" have been published, selections from two of which are included here.

The slave narratives were derived from three American autobiographical traditions: spiritual confessionals characteristic of Puritans like Jonathan Edwards; the rags-to-riches individualistic success story of Benjamin Franklin; and Indian captivity narratives. The last tradition, popular reading in the early nineteenth century, described the adventures of white captives who were dragged away from their villages by Indians; suffered the trials, tortures, and coping adaptations of living in an Indian village; and finally were freed and returned ("redeemed") home to white civilization.

The African-American slave narratives followed a similar three-stage pattern, beginning either with an idyllic childhood in a West African village or the relative innocence of childhood on a southern plantation. Aimed at northern white readers, the bulk of the story described, in vivid detail, the brutal oppressions of captivity and slavery, dwelling on the horrors of the slave ships, slave sales and the breakup of families, and the daily beatings, punishments, and harsh rigors of life on the plantation. But the narratives also described a creative and heroic will to survive: cunning strategies for avoiding work, sassing one's owner, connecting with loved ones, and learning how to read and write. The narratives concluded with the story of escape and the taking on of a new identity in freedom.

In fact, for many former slaves, the actual process of writing the narrative marked the attainment of their identity and freedom, often involving a ritual of self-naming. As William L. Andrews put it in *To Tell a Free Story,* for blacks to write their story was "in some ways uniquely self-liberating, the final, climactic act in the drama of their lifelong quests for freedom." Other themes included poignant appeals to white readers to agitate for the abolition of slavery; contrasts between the slaveholder's use of reli-

gion to justify slavery and the simple, spiritually based Christianity of the slaves themselves; and the supportive strength of the slave community and the white and black underground network in facilitating a successful runaway.

Although not the first, the prototypical slave narrative was that of Frederick Douglass, whose story is told in Chapter 11. You have seen how he grew up witnessing the horrors of slavery on a Maryland plantation and as an urban slave in Baltimore, learned to read and write, successfully defied the cruel Mr. Covey's efforts to break his will as a slave, and finally escaped to fight for abolitionism. Similar stories were told by Henry Bibb, William Wells Brown, Olaudah Equiano, Harriet Jacobs, Mattie Jackson, Solomon Northup, Sojourner Truth, and many, many others, all of which provided gory details of whippings and the wrenching loss of loved ones.

The two short selections here—from James W. C. Pennington's *Fugitive Blacksmith* (1849) and Harriet Jacobs's *Incidents in the Life of a Slave Girl* (1861)—focus not on white oppression but on the initial process of planning an escape. Note that Jacobs wrote under the pseudonym Linda Brent; as background to this passage, she discovers that her two children are to be brought to her master's plantation to be "broke in." As you read, look for restraints on running away, anticipated difficulties, sources of support, and the intelligent cleverness of the runaways.

Reflecting on the Past What role does religion play in their efforts? What about issues of family, trust, safety, and self-reliance? What do you learn about slavery in these brief descriptions of the first moments of self-emancipation? Can you imagine the impact they had on northern readers, and why abolitionists avidly used the narratives as part of their attack on slavery?

The Flight

It was the Sabbath: the holy day which God in his infinite wisdom gave for the rest of both man and beast. In the state of Maryland, the slaves generally have the Sabbath, except in those districts where the evil weed, tobacco, is cultivated; and then, when it is the season for setting the plant, they are liable to be robbed of this only rest.

It was in the month of November, somewhat past the middle of the month. It was a bright day, and all was quiet. Most of the slaves were resting about their quarters; others had leave to visit their friends on other plantations, and were absent. The evening previous I had arranged my little bundle of clothing, and had secreted it at some distance from the house. I had spent most of the forenoon in my workshop, engaged in deep and solemn thought.

It is impossible for me now to recollect all the perplexing thoughts that passed through my mind during that forenoon; it was a day of heartaching to me. But I distinctly remember the two great difficulties that stood in the way of my flight: I had a father and mother whom I dearly loved,——I had also six sisters and four brothers on the plantation. The question was, shall I hide my purpose from them? moreover, how will my flight affect them when I am gone? Will they not be suspected? Will not the whole family be sold off as a disaffected family, as is generally the case when one of its members flies? But a still more trying question was, how can I expect to succeed, I have no knowledge of distance or direction. I know that Pennsylvania is a free state, but I know not where its soil begins, or where that of Maryland ends? Indeed, at this time there was no safety in Pennsylvania, New Jersey, or New York, for a fugitive, except in lurking-places, or under the care of judicious friends, who could be entrusted not only with liberty, but also with life itself.

With such difficulties before my mind, the day had rapidly worn away; and it was just past noon. One of my perplexing questions I had settled——I had resolved to let no one into my secret; but the other difficulty was now to be met. It was to be met without the least knowledge of its magnitude, except by imagination. Yet of one thing there could be no mistake, that the consequences of a failure would be most serious. Within my recollection no one had attempted to escape from my master; but I had many cases in my mind's eye, of slaves of other planters who had failed, and who had been made examples of the most cruel treatment, by flogging and selling to the far South, where they were never to see their friends more. I was not without serious apprehension that such would be my fate. The bare possibility was impressively solemn; but the hour was now come, and the man must act and be free, or remain a slave for ever. How the impression came to be upon my mind I cannot tell; but there was a strange and horrifying belief, that if I did not meet the crisis that day, I should be self-doomed——that my ear would be nailed to the door-post for ever. The emotions of that moment I cannot fully depict. Hope, fear, dread, terror, love, sorrow, and deep melancholy were mingled in my mind together; my mental state was one of most painful distraction. When I looked at my numerous family—a beloved father and mother, eleven brothers and sisters, &c.; but when I looked at slavery as such; when I looked at it in its mildest form, with all its annoyances; and above all, when I remembered that one of the chief annoyances of slavery, in the most mild form, is the liability of being at any moment sold into the worst form; it seemed that no consideration, not even that of life itself, could tempt me to give up the thought of flight. And then when I considered the difficulties of the way—the reward that would be offered—the human blood-hounds that would be set upon my track—the weariness—the hunger—the gloomy thought, of not only losing all one's friends in one day, but of having to seek and to make new friends in a strange world. But, as I have said, the hour was come, and the man must act, or for ever be a slave.

Harriet Jacobs—from Incidents in the Life of a Slave Girl

Again and again I had traversed those dreary twelve miles, to and from the town; and all the way, I was meditating upon some means of escape for myself and my children. My friends had made every effort that ingenuity could devise to effect our purchase, but all their plans had proved abortive. Dr. Flint was suspicious, and determined not to loosen his grasp upon us. I could have made my escape alone; but it was more for my helpless children than for myself that I longed for freedom. Though the boon would have been precious to me, above all price, I would not have taken it at the expense of leaving them in slavery. Every trial I endured, every sacrifice I made for their sakes, drew them closer to my heart, and gave me fresh courage to beat back the dark waves that rolled and rolled over me in a seemingly endless night of storms. . . .

My plan was to conceal myself at the house of a friend, and remain there a few weeks till the search was over. My hope was that the doctor would get discouraged, and, for fear of losing my value, and also of subsequently finding my children among the missing, he would consent to sell us; and I knew somebody would buy us. I had done all in my power to make my children comfortable during the time I expected to be separated from them. . . .

Mr. Flint was hard pushed for house servants, and rather than lose me he had restrained his malice. I did my work faithfully, though not, of course, with a willing mind. They were evidently afraid I should leave them. Mr. Flint wished that I should sleep in the great house instead of the servants' quarters. His wife agreed to the proposition, but said I mustn't bring my bed into the house, because it would scatter feathers on her carpet. I knew when I went there that they would never think of such a thing as furnishing a bed of any kind for me and my little one. I therefore carried my own bed, and now I was forbidden to use it. I did as I was ordered. But now that I was certain my children were to be put in their power, in order to give them a stronger hold on me, I resolved to leave them that night. I remembered the grief this step would bring upon my dear old grandmother; and nothing less than the freedom of my children would have induced me to disregard her advice. I went about my evening work with trembling steps. Mr. Flint twice called from his chamber door to inquire why the house was not locked up. I replied that I had not done my work. "You have had time enough to do it," said he. "Take care how you answer me!"

I shut all the windows, locked all the doors, and went up to the third story, to wait till midnight. How long those hours seemed, and how fervently I prayed that God would not forsake me in this hour of utmost need! I was about to risk every thing on the throw of a die; and if I failed, O what would become of me and my poor children? They would be made to suffer for my fault.

At half past twelve I stole softly down stairs. I stopped on the second floor, thinking I heard a noise. I felt my way down into the parlor, and looked out of the window. The night was so intensely dark that I could see nothing. I raised the window very softly and jumped out. Large drops of rain were falling, and the darkness bewildered me. I dropped on my knees, and breathed a short prayer to God for guidance and protection. I groped my way to the road, and rushed towards the town with almost lightning speed. I arrived at my grandmother's house, but dared not see her. She would say, "Linda, you are killing me;" and I knew that would unnerve me. I tapped softly at the window of a room, occupied by a woman, who had lived in the house several years. I knew she was a faithful friend, and could be trusted with my secret. I tapped several times before she heard me. . . . I told her I had a hiding-place, and that was all it was best for her to know.

. . . The tidings made the old doctor rave and storm at a furious rate. It was a busy day for them. My grandmother's house was searched from top to bottom. As my trunk was empty, they concluded I had taken my clothes with me. Before ten o'clock every vessel northward bound was thoroughly examined, and the law against harboring fugitives was read to all on board. At night a watch was set over the town. Knowing how distressed my grandmother would be, I wanted to send her a message; but it could not be done. Every one who went in or out of her house was closely watched. The doctor said he would take my children, unless she became responsible for them; which of course she willingly did. The next day was spent in searching. Before night, the following advertisement was posted at every corner, and in every public place for miles round:—

$300 Reward! Ran away from the subscriber, an intelligent, bright, mulatto girl, named Linda, 21 years of age. Five feet four inches high. Dark eyes, and black hair inclined to curl; but it can be made straight. Has a decayed spot on a front tooth. She can read and write, and in all probability will try to get to the Free States. All persons are forbidden, under penalty of law, to harbor or employ said slave. $150 will be given to whoever takes her in the state, and $300 if taken out of the state and delivered to me, or lodged in jail.

Dr. Flint

Note: James Pennington successfully escaped to New York, where he became a Presbyterian minister and later performed Frederick Douglass's marriage rites. Harriet Jacobs hid for seven years in a cramped, tiny garret in her grandmother's house before finally escaping in disguise by ship; she eventually was reunited with her children. To mislead Dr. Flint as to her location, she wrote letters to him secreted to and postmarked from the North begging him to free her children.

431

on African Americans. Moreover, white abolitionists tended to see slavery and freedom as absolute moral opposites: a person was either a slave or free. African Americans, however, knew that there were degrees of freedom and that discriminatory restrictions on freedom existed for blacks in the North just as did relative degrees of servitude in the South.

Furthermore, black abolitionists themselves experienced prejudice, not just from ordinary northern citizens but also from their white abolitionist colleagues. Many antislavery businessmen refused to hire blacks. The antislavery societies usually provided less than full membership rights for blacks, permitted them to do only menial tasks rather than form policy, and, sometimes unknowingly, perpetuated racial stereotypes in their literature. One free black, in fact, described a white abolitionist as one who hated slavery, "especially that slavery which is 1,000 to 1,500 miles away," but who hated even more "a man who wears a black skin."

Conflict between Garrison and Douglass reflected these tensions. The famous runaway was one of the most effective orators in the movement. But after a while, rather than simply describing his life as a slave, Douglass began skillfully to analyze abolitionist policies. Garrison warned him that audiences would not believe he had ever been a slave, and other whites told him to stick to the facts and let them take care of the philosophy.

Douglass gradually moved away from Garrison's views, endorsing political action and sometimes even slave rebellion. Garrison's response, particularly when Douglass came out for the Liberty party, was to denounce his independence as "ungrateful . . . and malevolent in spirit." In 1847, Douglass started his own journal, the *North Star* (which later was called *Frederick Douglass's Paper*). In it, he expressed his appreciation for the help of that "noble band of white laborers" but declared that it was time for those who "suffered the wrong" to lead the way in advocating liberty.

Moving beyond Garrison, a few black nationalists, like the fiery Martin Delany, totally rejected white American society and advocated emigration and a new destiny in Africa. Most African Americans, however, agreed with Douglass to work to end slavery and discrimination in the United States. They believed that for better or worse, their home was America and not some distant land they had not known for generations.

These black leaders were practical. David Ruggles in New York and William Still in Philadelphia led black vigilance groups that helped fugitive slaves escape to Canada or to safe northern black settlements.

Ministers, writers, and orators such as Douglass, Garnet, Maria Stewart, William Wells Brown, Samuel Cornish, Lewis Hayden, and Sojourner Truth lectured and wrote journals and slave narratives on the evils of slavery. They also organized a National Negro Convention movement, which began holding annual meetings in 1830. These blacks met not only to condemn slavery but also to discuss issues of discrimination facing free blacks in the North.

Flood Tide of Abolitionism

Black and white abolitionists, however, agreed more than they disagreed and usually worked together well. They supported each other's publications. The first subscribers to Garrison's *Liberator* were nearly all African American, and an estimated 80 percent of the readers of Douglass's paper were white. Weld and Garrison often stayed in the homes of black abolitionists when they traveled. In addition, black and white "stations" cooperated on the Underground Railroad, passing fugitives from one hiding place to the next (for example, from a black church to a white farmer's barn to a Quaker meetinghouse to a black carpenter's shop).

The two races worked together fighting discrimination as well as slavery. When David Ruggles was dragged from the "white car" of a New Bedford, Massachusetts, railway in 1841, Garrison, Douglass, and 40 other protesters organized what may have been the first successful integrated "sit-in" act of civil disobedience in American history. Blacks and whites also worked harmoniously in protesting segregated schools; after several years of boycotts and legal challenges, they forced Massachusetts in 1855 to become the first to outlaw segregated public education. But not until 100 years later would the U.S. Supreme Court begin desegregating schools throughout the country.

White and black abolitionists were united perhaps most closely by defending themselves against the attacks of people who regarded them as dangerous fanatics bent on disrupting an orderly society. As abolitionists organized to rid the nation of slavery, they aroused many people—northerners as well as southerners—who were eager to rid the nation of abolitionists. Mob attacks like the one on Marius Robinson in Ohio in 1836 occurred frequently in the mid-1830s. Abolitionists were stoned, dragged through the streets, ousted from their jobs and homes, and reviled by northern mobs, often led by leading citizens. Theodore Weld, known as "the most mobbed man in the United States," could hardly finish a speech without disruption. Douglass endured similar attacks, and Garrison was saved from a Boston mob only by being put in jail. In 1837, Elijah Lovejoy, an antislavery editor from Illinois, was murdered.

Anti-abolitionists were as fervid as the abolitionists. "I warn the abolitionists, ignorant and infatuated barbarians as they are," growled one South Carolinian, "that if chance shall throw any of them into our hands, they may expect a felon's death." One widely circulated book in 1836 described opponents of slavery, led by the "gloomy, wild, and malignant" Garrison, as "crack-brained enthusiasts" and "female fanatics" with "disturbed minds." President Jackson joined in, denouncing the abolitionists in his annual message in 1835 as "incendiaries" who deserved to have their "unconstitutional and wicked" activities broken up by mobs, and he urged Congress to ban antislavery literature from the U.S. mails. A year later, southern Democratic congressmen, with the crucial support of Van Buren, succeeded in passing a "gag rule" to stop the flood of abolitionist petitions in Congress.

By the 1840s, despite factionalism and opposition, the antislavery movement had gained significant strength in American life. Many northerners, including workers otherwise unsympathetic to the goal of ending slavery, decried the mob violence, supported the right of free speech, and denounced the South as undemocratic. The gag rule, interference with the mails, and the killing of Lovejoy seemed proof of the growing pernicious influence of slave power. Former president John Quincy Adams, now a congressman, worked for several years for the repeal of the gag rule, which he finally achieved in 1844, keeping the matter alive until the question of slavery in the territories became the dominant national political issue of the 1850s (see Chapter 14). Meanwhile, black and white abolitionists continued their struggle to end slavery, using many different tactics without yet knowing that the only one that would eventually work would be violent civil war.

Women Reformers and Women's Rights

In an address in Boston in 1832, Maria Stewart said, "Methinks I heard a spiritual interrogation—'Who shall go forward, and take off the reproach that is cast upon the people of color? Shall it be a woman?' And my heart made this reply—'If it is thy will, be it even so, Lord Jesus!'" As a young Quaker teacher in Massachusetts four years later, Abby Kelley circulated petitions for the local antislavery society. Like Stewart and other antebellum reformers, she too

came to reform through religious conviction, writing in 1837, "'Tis a great joy to see the world grow better. . . . Indeed I think endeavors to improve mankind is the only object worth living for." Religiously motivated, women like Margaret Fuller, Ann Lee, Dix, Stewart, Kelley, and many others were active, as we have seen, in the movements for abolitionism, utopianism, care of society's outcasts, black rights, and other moral and political reforms. They were also engaged in a struggle for their own rights as women, beginning with the right to speak in public.

In 1838, Kelley braved the threats of an angry crowd in Philadelphia by delivering an abolitionist speech to a convention of antislavery women. Her speech was so eloquent that Weld told her that if she did not join the movement full-time, "God will smite you." Before the convention was over, a mob, incensed by both abolitionists and women speaking in public, attacked with stones and torches and burned the hall to the ground. Kelley left teaching to devote all her efforts to the antislavery movement and to women's rights. When she married Stephen Foster, she retained her own name and went on lecture tours of the West, while her husband stayed home to care for their daughter.

Other young women were also defining unconventional new relationships while illustrating the profound difficulty of both fulfilling traditional roles and speaking out for change. Angelina and Sarah Grimké, two demure but outspoken Quaker sisters from Philadelphia who had grown up in slaveholding South Carolina, went to New England in 1837 to lecture on abolitionism. Criticized for speaking to audiences containing both men and women, Angelina defended women's rights to speak in public. After the tour, Angelina married Theodore Weld and interrupted her public speaking to show that she could also be a good wife and mother. At the same time, she and Sarah, who moved in with her, undertook most of the research and writing for Weld's book attacking American slavery.

Young white couples like Kelley and Foster, Grimké and Weld, and Marius and Emily Robinson, while pursuing reform, also experimented with equal relationships in an age that assigned distinctly unequal roles to husbands and wives. The cult of domesticity told women that their sphere was the home, upholding piety and virtue, and influencing their husbands and children to lead morally upright lives in a harsh, changing economic world. As one clergyman said, although women were not expected to "step beyond the threshold" of the home, their ethical influence would be "felt around the globe."

This marriage certificate from 1848, detailing the respective marital requirements of husband and wife, makes clear male dominance and female subservience ("the wife hath not power of her own body"). In that same year, however, women's rights activists began their long struggle for equality at Seneca Falls, New York. *(Library of Congress)*

Given moral responsibilities like this, it is not surprising that many women joined the perfectionist movement to cleanse America of its sins.

Like their sisters in England, American women pursued several paths to achieve greater personal autonomy in the antebellum era. The choice depended on class, cultural background, and situation. Thus, in 1834, the Lowell textile workers went on strike to protest wage reductions while looking to marriage as an escape from millwork. Catharine Beecher argued that it was by accepting marriage and the home as a woman's sphere and by mastering domestic duties there that women could best achieve power and autonomy. In another form of "domestic feminism," American wives exerted considerable control over their own bodies by convincing their husbands to practice abstinence, coitus interruptus, and other forms of birth control.

Other women found an outlet for their role as moral guardians by attacking the sexual double standard. In 1834, a group of Presbyterian women formed the New York Female Moral Reform Society. Inspired by revivalism, they visited brothels and opened up a house of refuge in an effort to convert prostitutes to evangelical Protestantism; they even publicly identified brothel patrons. Within five years, 445 auxiliaries of the Female Moral Reform Society had blossomed.

Lowell mill workers and New York moral reformers generally accepted the duties—and attractions—of female domesticity. Other women, usually from upper-middle-class families, did not. They sought control over their lives by working directly for more legally protected equal rights with men, and even were engaged in the politics of the era. Campaigns to secure married women's control of their property and custody of their children involved many of them. Others gained from abolitionism a growing awareness of the similarities between the oppression of slaves and of women. Collecting antislavery signatures and speaking out publicly, they continued to face denials of their right to speak or act politically. American women "have good cause to be grateful to the slave," Kelley wrote, for in "striving to strike his iron off, we found most surely, that we were manacled *ourselves.*"

The more active women became in antislavery activities, the more hostility they encountered, especially from clergymen quoting the Bible to justify female inferiority and servility. Sarah Grimké was criticized once too often for her outspoken views. She struck back in 1837 with *Letters on the Condition of Women and the Equality of the Sexes,* concluding that "men and women were created equal" and that "whatever is right for man to do, is right for woman." Arguing that men ought to be sat-

Timeline

1824	New Harmony established
1825	John Quincy Adams chosen president by the House of Representatives
1826	American Temperance Society founded
1828	Calhoun publishes "Exposition and Protest" Jackson defeats Adams for the presidency Tariff of Abominations
1828–1832	Rise of workingmen's parties
1830	Webster–Hayne debate and Jackson–Calhoun toast Joseph Smith, *The Book of Mormon* Indian Removal Act
1830–1831	Charles Finney's religious revivals
1831	Garrison begins publishing *The Liberator*
1832	Jackson vetoes U.S. Bank charter Jackson reelected *Worcester v. Georgia*
1832–1833	Nullification crisis
1832–1836	Removal of funds from U.S. Bank to state banks
1833	Force Bill Compromise tariff Calhoun resigns as vice president American Anti-Slavery Society founded
1834	New York Female Moral Reform Society founded National Trades Union founded Whig party established
1835–1836	Countless incidents of mob violence

1836	"Gag rule" Specie Circular Van Buren elected president
1837	Financial panic and depression Sarah Grimké, *Letters on the Equality of the Sexes* Emerson's "American Scholar" address
1837–1838	Cherokee "Trail of Tears"
1840	William Henry Harrison elected president American Anti-Slavery Society splits World Anti-Slavery Convention Ten-hour day for federal employees
1840–1841	Transcendentalists found Hopedale and Brook Farm
1843	Dorothea Dix's report on treatment of the insane
1844	Joseph Smith murdered in Nauvoo, Illinois
1846–1848	Mormon migration to the Great Basin
1847	First issue of Frederick Douglass's *North Star*
1848	Oneida community founded First women's rights convention at Seneca Falls, New York
1850	Nathaniel Hawthorne's *Scarlet Letter* is published
1851	Maine prohibition law Herman Melville's *Moby Dick* is published
1853	Children's Aid Society established in New York City
1854	Thoreau's *Walden* is published
1855	Massachusetts bans segregated public schools

isfied with 6,000 years of dominion based on a false interpretation of the creation story, Grimké concluded that she sought "no favors for my sex. I surrender not our claim to equality. All I ask of our brethren is, that they will take their feet from off our necks and permit us to stand upright on that ground which God designed us to occupy."

Grimké's strong message soon was translated into an active movement for women's rights, and illustrative of its international character, the American movement was born in London. At the World Anti-Slavery Convention in 1840, attended by many American abolitionists, the delegates were divided about women's role and refused to let them participate. Two upstate New Yorkers who met each other in London, Elizabeth Cady Stanton and Lucretia Mott, a Quaker minister, had to sit behind curtains and were forbidden to speak. "Mrs. Mott was to me an entirely new revelation of womanhood," Stanton wrote later, "I sought every opportu-

nity to be at her side." They talked with each other about theology and women's conditions. Returning to the United States, they resolved to "form a society to advocate the rights of women." In 1848, in Seneca Falls, New York, their intentions (though delayed) were fulfilled in one of the most significant protest gatherings of the antebellum era.

In preparing for the meeting, Mott and Stanton drew up a list of women's grievances. Chief among them were the right to vote and the right for married women to control their own property and earnings. Modeling their "Declaration of Sentiments" on the Declaration of Independence, the women at Seneca Falls proclaimed it a self-evident truth that "all men and women are created equal" and that men had usurped women's freedom and dignity. The Declaration of Sentiments charged that a man "endeavored in every way he could, to destroy [woman's] confidence in her own powers, to lessen her self-respect, and to make her willing to lead a dependent and abject life." The remedy was expressed in 11 resolutions calling for equal opportunities in education and work, equality before the law, and the right to appear on public platforms. The most controversial resolution called for women's "sacred right to the elective franchise." The convention approved Mott and Stanton's list of resolutions.

Throughout the 1850s, led by Stanton and Susan B. Anthony, women continued to meet in annual conventions and worked by resolution, persuasion, and petition campaign to achieve equal political, legal, and property rights with men. The right to vote, however, was considered the cornerstone of the movement. It remained so for 72 years of struggle until 1920, when passage of the Nineteenth Amendment made woman suffrage part of the Constitution. The Seneca Falls convention was crucial in beginning the campaign for equal public rights. The seeds of psychological autonomy and self-respect, however, were sown in the struggles of countless women like Abby Kelley, Sarah Grimké, Maria Stewart, and Emily Robinson. The struggle for that kind of liberation continues today.

✦ *Conclusion*

PERFECTING AMERICA

Inspired by religious revivalism, advocates for women's rights and temperance, abolitionists, and other reformers carried on very different crusades from those waged by Andrew Jackson against Indians, nullifiers, and the U.S. Bank. In fact, Jacksonian politics and antebellum reform were often at odds. Most abolitionists and temperance reformers were anti-Jackson Whigs. Jackson and most Democrats repudiated the passionate moralism of reformers.

Yet both sides shared more than either side would admit. Reformers and political parties were both organized rationally. Both mirrored new tensions in a changing, growing society. Both had an abiding faith in change and the idea of progress yet feared that sinister forces jeopardized that progress. Whether ridding the nation of alcohol or the national bank, slavery or nullification, mob violence or political opponents, both forces saw these responsibilities in terms of patriotic duty. Whether inspired by religious revivalism or political party loyalty, both believed that by stamping out evil forces, they could shape a better America. In this effort, they turned to politics, religion, reform, and new lifestyles. Whether politicians like Jackson and Clay, religious community leaders like Noyes and Ann Lee, or reformers like Garrison, the Grimkés, and Emily and Marius Robinson, these antebellum Americans sought to remake their country politically and morally as it underwent social and economic change.

As the United States neared mid-century, slavery emerged as the most divisive issue. Against much opposition, the reformers had made slavery a matter of national political debate by the 1840s. Although both major political parties tried to evade the question, westward expansion and the addition of new territories to the nation would soon make avoidance impossible. Would new states be slave or free? The question increasingly aroused the deepest passions of the American people. For the pioneer family, who formed the driving force behind the westward movement, however, questions involving their fears and dreams seemed more immediate. We turn to this family and that movement in the next chapter.

✦ Recommended Reading

Religious Revival and Reform Philosophy
Robert Abzug, *Cosmos Crumbling: American Reform and the Religious Imagination* (1994); Richard J. Carwardine, *Evangelicals and Politics in Antebellum America* (1993); Charles E. Hambrick-Stowe, *Charles G. Finney and the Spirit of American Evangelicalism* (1996); Steven Mintz, *Moralists and Modernization: American Pre-Civil War Reformers* (1995); Richard Rabinowitz, *The Spiritual Self in Everyday Life: The Transformation of Personal Religious Experience in 19th Century New England* (1989); Mary Ryan, *Cradle of the Middle Class: The Family in Oneida County, New York, 1790–1865* (1981); Leonard I. Sweet, ed., *Communication and Change in American Religious History* (1993); Ronald Walters, *American Reformers, 1815–1860* (1978).

The Political Response to Change
Glenn C. Altschuler and Stuart Blumin, *Rude Republic: Americans and Their Politics in the Nineteenth Century* (2000); Jean Baker, *Affairs of Party* (1983); Donald B. Cole, *The Presidency of Andrew Jackson* (1993); Richard Ellis, *The Union at Risk: Jacksonian Democracy, States*

Rights, and the Nullification Crisis (1987); Daniel Feller, *The Jacksonian Promise, America, 1815–1840* (1995); Ronald Formisano, *The Transformation of Political Culture* (1983); Lawrence F. Kohl, *The Politics of Individualism: Parties and the American Character in the Jackson Era* (1989); Charles Sellers, *The Market Revolution: Jacksonian America, 1815–1846* (1992); Harry L. Watson, *Liberty and Power: The Politics of Jacksonian America* (1990).

Perfectionist Reform and Utopianism

Priscilla Brewett, *Shaker Communities, Shaker Lives* (1986); Robert Fogarty, ed., *American Utopianism* (1972); Lawrence Foster, *Women, Family, and Utopia: Communal Experiments of the Shakers, the Oneida Community, and the Mormons* (1991); William Kephart and William Zellner, *Extraordinary Groups: An Examination of Unconventional Life Styles*, 4th ed. (1991); Carol A. Kolmerten, *Women in Utopia: The Ideology of Gender in the American Owenite Communities* (1990); Grant Underwood, *The Millenarian World of Early Mormonism* (1993); Kenneth H. Winn, *Exiles in a Land of Liberty* (1989).

Reforming Society

Susan Cayleff, *Wash and Be Healed: The Water-Cure Movement and Women's Health* (1987); Lori D. Ginsberg, *Women and the Work of Benevolence: Morality, Politics and Class in Nineteenth-Century United States* (1990); Stephen Nissenbaum, *Sex, Diet, and Debility in Jacksonian America: Sylvester Graham and Health Reform* (1980); W. J. Rorabaugh, *The Alcoholic Republic: An American Tradition* (1979); David Rothman, *The Discovery of the Asylum: Social Order and Disorder in the New Republic* (1971); Ian Tyrrell, *Sobering Up: From Temperance to Prohibition in Antebellum America, 1800–1860* (1979); Sean Wilentz, *Chants Democratic: New York City and the Rise of the American Working Class, 1788–1850* (1983).

Abolitionism and the Women's Rights Movement

Ellen DuBois, *Feminism and Suffrage: The Emergence of an Independent Women's Movement in America,* *1848–1869* (1978); Paul Goodman, *Of One Blood: Abolitionism and the Origins of Racial Equality* (1998); Elisabeth Griffith, *In Her Own Right: The Life of Elizabeth Cady Stanton* (1984); Nancy Isenberg, *Sex & Citizenship in Antebellum America* (1998); Gerda Lerner, *The Grimké Sisters from South Carolina: Pioneers for Women's Rights and Abolition* (1967); Henry Mayer, *All on Fire: William Lloyd Garrison and the Abolition of Slavery* (1999); Julie Roy Jeffrey, *The Great Silent Army of Abolitionism: Ordinary Women in the Antislavery Movement* (1998); Jane A. Pease and William H. Pease, *They Who Would Be Free: Blacks' Search for Freedom, 1830–1861* (1974); Kathryn Kish Sklar, *Women's Rights Emerges Within the Antislavery Movement, 1830–1870: A Brief History with Documents* (2000); Dorothy Sterling, *Ahead of Her Time: Abby Kelley and the Politics of Antislavery* (1991).

Fiction and Film

Nathaniel Hawthorne's *Blithdale Romance* (1852), a novel set in a utopian community much like Brook Farm, reveals the challenges of perfecting America through socialistic communal experiments and other reforms such as woman suffrage, spiritualism, and prison reform. Hawthorne's *The Scarlet Letter* (1850) and *Celestial Railroad and Other Stories* (1963 edition, reprinting stories written in the 1830s and 1840s)—in particular, "The Birthmark," "Rappaccini's Daughter," and the title story—show the author's struggles to balance the head and the heart, scientific and romantic perfectionism. *Not for Ourselves Alone: The Story of Elizabeth Cady Stanton and Susan B. Anthony* is a superb documentary produced by Ken Burns for PBS in 1999. Other film possibilities include *Frederick Douglass: When the Lion Wrote History* (1994) and a dramatization of *Uncle Tom's Cabin* (1987). *The Journey of August King*, a 1996 film based on a 1971 novel, deals with the decision of a North Carolina frontiersman to help a female fugitive slave.

✦ Discovering U.S. History Online

Women in America

www.xroads.virginia.edu/~HYPER/DETOC/FEM/home.htm

This University of Virginia site takes a look at women in antebellum America, 1820–1842.

The Amistad Affair

www.amistad.mysticseaport.org/main/welcome.html

This site reveals issues of slavery, race, and abolitionism.

Godey's Lady's Book Online Home Page

www.history.rochester.edu/godeys/

Here is online text of this interesting nineteenth-century journal.

Influence of Prominent Abolitionists

www.loc.gov/exhibits/african/influ.html

This Library of Congress exhibit site, with pictures and text, discusses some key African-American abolitionists and their efforts to end slavery.

In Search of Tocqueville's Democracy in America

www.tocqueville.org/

Text, images, and teaching suggestions are part of this companion site to C-SPAN's recent programming on de Tocqueville.

Thomas Cole
www.yale.edu/amstud/cole/
This site features paintings by Thomas Cole. They include landscapes of wilderness and domesticated scenes.

Transcendentalists
www.transcendentalists.com/
This site has background information on Transcendentalists, interactive information on Thoreau and Emerson, as well as information on other Transcendentalists.

Religion and the National Culture in the Nineteenth Century
www.nhc.rtp.nc.us:8080/tserve/nineteen.htm
Using essays and contemporary photos and primary sources, this site was "designed to help teachers of American history bring their students to a greater understanding of the role religion has played in the development of the United States."

Andrew Jackson
www.ipl.org/ref/POTUS/ajackson.html
This site contains basic factual data about Jackson's election, presidency, and speeches, as well as online biographies.

The Trail of Tears
www.ourgeorgiahistory.com/indians/cherokee/trail_of_tears.html
A thorough interactive essay explains the history of the Trail of Tears. The site also presents information on Cherokee forts and a map of the various routes traveled during this period of Indian removal.

America's First Look into the Camera: Daguerreotype Portraits and Views, 1839–1864
www.memory.loc.gov/ammem/daghtml/dagpres.html
This exhibit presents samples of the major subjects of this searchable database of more than 650 daguerreotypes. Portraits, architectural views, and some street scenes make up most of the collection.

Social History of the Antebellum Period
www.moa.cit.cornell.edu/moa/index.html
This site contains primary sources in American social history from the antebellum period through Reconstruction.

Reform Movements
www.womhist.binghamton.edu/datelist.htm
This site includes many essays and primary sources relevant to the antebellum reform movements including "The Appeal of Female Moral Reform," "The Nineteenth-Century Dress Reform Movement, 1838–1881," and "Lucretia Mott's Reform Networks, 1840–1860."

Charles Loring Brace
www.childrensaidsociety.org/about/history/
A brief biography of reformer Charles Loring Brace as well as a description of the orphan train movement.

Woman Suffrage in Words and Pictures
www.lcweb2.loc.gov/ammem/naw/nawshome.html
www.memory.loc.gov/ammem/vfwhtml/vfwhome.html
These Library of Congress sites consist of searchable databases. The first contains 167 books, pamphlets, and other artifacts documenting the suffrage campaign, while the second consists of 38 photographs as "a pictorial partner for the text documents."

13 Moving West

This painting by Albert Bierstadt captures the majesty of the western landscape, which dwarfs the Native Americans depicted in the foreground. *(The Rocky Mountains, Lander's Peak, 1863, The Metropolitan Museum of Art, Rogers Fund, 1907 [07.123] Photograph by Geoffrey Clements)*

✦ *American Stories*

THE SURPRISES OF A MISSIONARY LIFE

It was July 4, 1836, but nothing in her 28 years had prepared Narcissa Whitman for the sights and sounds that marked this particular holiday. Earlier in the day, Narcissa and the party with which she was traveling had crossed over the South Pass of the Rocky Mountains, a memorable milestone for the nation's birthday. Now, evening had come, and the caravan had set up camp for the night. Suddenly, wild cries and the sound of gunshots and galloping horses broke the silence. Fourteen or fifteen men, most dressed as Indians, advanced toward the camp. Frightened by the threatening appearance of the horsemen, the noise, and the bullets whizzing over her head, Narcissa may well have wondered if her journey and even her life were to end. But as the horsemen approached, the anxious travelers could make out a white flag tied to one of the rider's rifles. These were not foes but friends who had ridden out from the annual fur traders' rendezvous to greet the caravan.

440

Two days later, Narcissa reached the rendezvous site where hundreds of Indians as well as 200 whites, mostly traders and trappers, were gathered to exchange furs, tell stories, drink, and enjoy themselves. Some of the mounted Indians, "carrying their war weapons, wearing their war emblems and implements of music," put on a special display. The exhibition was a novelty for Narcissa as was her presence for the Indians. Narcissa found herself the center of attention "in the midst of [a] gazing throng" of curious Indians. The experience was not unpleasant, and Narcissa's impression of the Indians was favorable. "They all like us and that we have come to live with them."

Narcissa Whitman was one of the first white women to cross the Rocky Mountains and live in Oregon territory in the 1830s. While many more Americans would follow her, only a few would share her reasons for coming west. They would come to farm, dig for gold, speculate in land, open a store, or practice law. However, Narcissa and her husband, Dr. Marcus Whitman, did not go west to better their lives but to carry God's word to the Native Americans. Inspired by the revivals of the Second Great Awakening and convinced that all non-Christians were headed toward eternal damnation, Narcissa and her husband came to settle among the Indians in Oregon territory and to convert them to Christianity and the American way of life.

This dream of becoming a missionary was one Narcissa had nourished since her early teens. But once the Whitmans had established their mission station in the Walla Walla valley, Narcissa slowly discovered that missionary work was nothing like her youthful fantasies. Although the Cayuse Indians listened to the missionaries and even adopted some Christian practices, they never lived up to the Whitmans' high standards. None of them had conversion experiences that the Whitmans judged necessary for admittance to the Presbyterian church nor were they quick to abandon Indian customs. They continued to consult their medicine men and refused to settle permanently next to the mission station. Cayuse women seemed little interested in the middle-class domestic skills Narcissa wished to teach them. Narcissa's positive impression of Native Americans disappeared. The Cayuse, she wrote, were "insolent, proud, domineering, arrogant, and ferocious."

There were other disappointments and personal tragedies as well. Marcus was often away from the mission on medical business, and Narcissa was lonely and sometimes frightened when he was absent. Her beloved daughter fell into the river and drowned. Often sick and unhappy, Narcissa did not conceive again.

As time passed, however, Narcissa's dismay and depression over her lack of success faded as hopeful signs of new possibilities other than Indian missionary work appeared. As she wrote to her mother in 1840, "a tide of immigration appears to be moving this way rapidly." In the following years, more and more American families made their way past the mission station, headed for the Willamette valley. In one wagon train, there was a family of children who had been orphaned during their journey. The Whitmans took them in and adopted all seven children. Narcissa threw herself into caring for them and found herself too busy to work actively with the Cayuse.

The Indians were dismayed at the numbers of whites coming into the territory, but the Whitmans, convinced that the future of the West lay with the emigrants, welcomed them. The day of the Indians had passed. As a "hunted, despised and unprotected" people, the Whitmans believed that the Native Americans were headed toward "entire extinction." But in an unexpected turn of events, some of the Cayuse protested against this vision, turned against the Whitmans, and killed them both. Such violent actions did nothing to hold back the swarm of Americans heading west.

Narcissa Whitman and her husband, Marcus, were among thousands of Americans who played a part in the nation's expansion into the trans-Mississippi West. While the religious faith that drove them west differentiated them from many crossing the western plains and prairies, the Whitmans' cultural beliefs about the inferiority of the Native Americans and the necessity of American settlement were widely shared. Shared too was the conviction that American values and way of life were superior to those of the Native Americans and Mexicans who occupied the land.

This chapter concerns movement into the trans-Mississippi West between 1830 and 1865. First we will con-

sider how and when Americans moved west, by what means the United States acquired the vast territories that in 1840 belonged to other nations, and the meaning of "Manifest Destiny," the slogan used to defend the conquest of the continent west of the Mississippi River. Then we explore the nature of life on the western farms, in western mining communities where Latin American, Chinese, and European adventurers mingled with American fortune seekers, and in western cities. Finally, the chapter examines responses of Native Americans and Mexican Americans to expansion and illuminates the ways different cultural traditions intersected in the West.

PROBING THE TRANS-MISSISSIPPI WEST

Until the 1840s, most Americans lived east of the Mississippi in a nation with fluid and changing boundaries. By 1860, however, some 4.3 million Americans had moved beyond the great river into the trans-Mississippi West, and the United States had acquired fixed boundaries with Canada and Mexico and reached the western edge of the continent.

The International Context for American Expansionism

When the Whitmans arrived in Oregon territory in 1836, they stayed at Fort Vancouver, a bustling British fur trading post. The large fort with its "neat" village, gardens, orchards, and fields was home to hundreds of workers, French Canadians, English men and women, Scots, and many from mixed European–Indian backgrounds. The establishment symbolized the international setting within which American expansionism occurred. The shifting interests and fortunes of several European nations helped to shape the character and timing of westward emigration even though individual settlers might not recognize the large forces affecting their experiences.

In 1815, except for Louisiana territory, Spain held title to most of the trans-Mississippi West. For hundreds of years, explorers, soldiers, settlers, and missionaries had marched north from Mexico to explore and settle the lands lying beyond the Rio Grande and to spread Spanish culture to native peoples. Eventually, Spanish holdings included present-day Texas, Arizona, New Mexico, Nevada, Utah, western Colorado, California, and small parts of Wyoming, Kansas, and Oklahoma. Spanish rulers

tried to keep foreigners out of its northern frontier areas but increasingly found this policy difficult to enforce. Not only was the area vast, but Spain itself was experiencing internal difficulties that weakened its hold on its New World colonies. In 1820, the conservative Spanish monarch faced liberal revolt at home. These same ideas inspired liberation movements in the New World. In 1821, Mexico took advantage of Spain's difficulties and declared its independence from Spain.

The new country inherited Spain's territories in the trans-Mississippi West and its population that included 75,000 Spanish-speaking inhabitants and numerous Native Americans tribes. While maintaining control of this distant region and its peoples would have been difficult under any circumstances, Mexico was not successful in forming a strong or a stable government until the 1860s. Wracked by financial, political, and military problems, Mexico was in a weak position to resist the avid American appetite for expansion.

North of California lay Oregon country, a vaguely defined area extending to Alaska. Russia, Spain, Great Britain, and Spain all had claims to Oregon, but negotiations with Russia and Spain in 1819 and 1824 left just the United States and Britain in contention for the territory. Joint British–American occupation, agreed upon in 1818 and 1827, delayed settling the boundary question. In fact, as the Whitmans knew, the British presence was a formidable one while only a handful of Americans were actually living in the territory during the 1830s. The future of Oregon would depend partly on how Britain, the world's richest and most powerful country, defined its interests there as Americans began to stream into Oregon in the 1840s.

North and South America, 1800–1836

Events in Europe had a dramatic impact on the Americas. Napoleon's defeat of the Spanish king in 1808 and the popularization of the ideas of the French revolution contributed to ending Spanish rule in the New World. Note how rapidly countries claimed their independence in the southern hemisphere and Latin America. **Reflecting on the Past** How did the changing political landscape of the Americas affect the power and influence of the United States in the region?

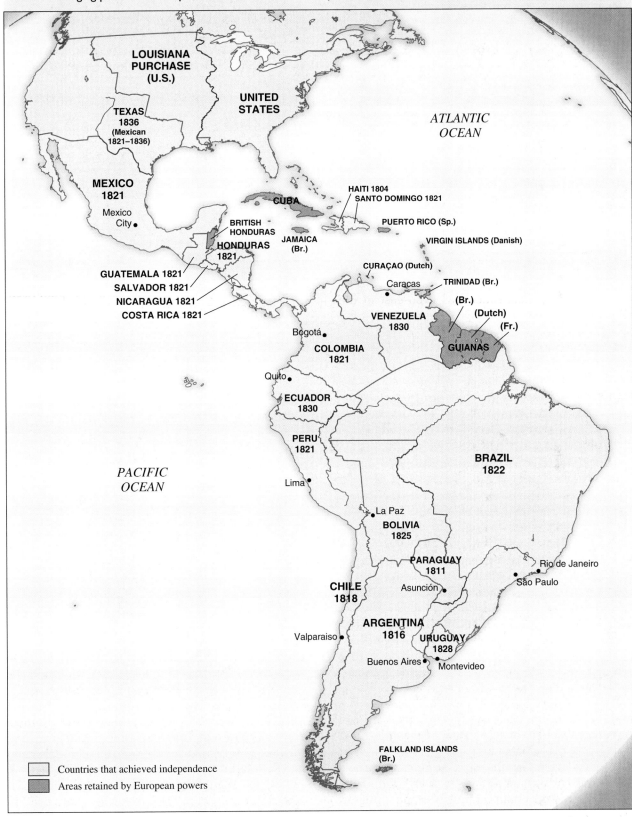

LOUISIANA PURCHASE (U.S.)

UNITED STATES

TEXAS 1836 (Mexican 1821–1836)

ATLANTIC OCEAN

MEXICO 1821

Mexico City

HAITI 1804
SANTO DOMINGO 1821
CUBA
PUERTO RICO (Sp.)
VIRGIN ISLANDS (Danish)

BRITISH HONDURAS
HONDURAS 1821
JAMAICA (Br.)

GUATEMALA 1821
SALVADOR 1821
NICARAGUA 1821
COSTA RICA 1821

CURAÇAO (Dutch)
Caracas
TRINIDAD (Br.)
(Br.)
(Dutch)
(Fr.)
GUIANAS

VENEZUELA 1830

Bogotá

COLOMBIA 1821

Quito

ECUADOR 1830

PERU 1821

Lima

BRAZIL 1822

PACIFIC OCEAN

La Paz
BOLIVIA 1825

PARAGUAY 1811

Rio de Janeiro
São Paulo

CHILE 1818

Asunción

ARGENTINA 1816

Valparaiso

URUGUAY 1828

Buenos Aires
Montevideo

FALKLAND ISLANDS (Br.)

Countries that achieved independence

Areas retained by European powers

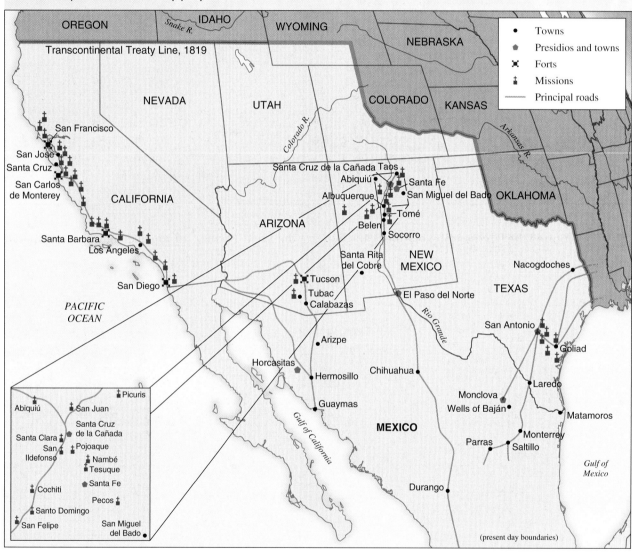

 Mexico in 1821

Mexico won its independence from Spain in 1821 and inherited vast Spanish territories north of the Rio Grande River. This map suggests the modest development of these northern holdings and their distance from the center of Mexico. **Reflecting on the Past** How might the geographical realities represented in this map have affected the attitudes of American and Mexican diplomats and ordinary people?

Early Interest in the West

Americans had penetrated the trans-Mississippi West long before the great migrations of the 1840s and 1850s. Commercial goals fueled early interest as traders first sought beaver skins in Oregon territory as early as 1811 and then bison robes prepared by the Plains tribes in the area around the upper Missouri River and its tributaries. Many of the men in the fur business married Indian women, thereby making valuable connections with Indian tribes in-

volved in trapping. Along with their wives, they occupied a cultural middle ground, adopting elements from both American and native ways of life. When the beaver was all but exterminated in the mid-1830s, some of the early traders and trappers acted as guides for Americans who would have little tolerance for the hybrid ways of the mountain men and their families.

Like the Whitmans, Methodist missionaries established outposts in Oregon territory and tried to teach native tribes Christian and American practices. Roman Catholic priests, sent from Europe, also worked among the native peoples. More tolerant of Indian culture than their Protestant counterparts, the Catholics had greater initial success in converting native peoples to Christianity.

In the Southwest, the collapse of the Spanish Empire gave American traders an opportunity they had long sought. Each year, caravans from "the States," loaded with weapons, tools, and brightly colored calicoes, followed the Santa Fe Trail over the plains and mountains. New Mexico's 40,000 inhabitants proved eager buyers, exchanging precious metals and furs for manufactured goods. Eventually, some "Anglos" settled there. Their economic activities prepared the way for military conquest.

To the south, in Texas, land for cotton rather than trade or missionary fervor attracted settlers and squatters in the 1820s at the very time that the Tejano population of 2,000 was adjusting to Mexican independence. The lure of cheap land drew more Americans to that area than to any other. By 1835, almost 30,000 Americans were living in Texas. They constituted the largest group of Americans living outside the nation's boundaries at that time.

On the Pacific, a few New England traders carrying sea otter skins to China anchored in the harbors of Spanish California in the early nineteenth century. By the 1830s, as the near extermination of the animals ruined this trade, a commerce based on California cowhides and tallow developed. New England ships brought clothes, boots, hardware, and furniture manufactured in the East to exchange for hides collected from local ranches.

Among the earliest easterners to settle in the trans-Mississippi West were tribes from the South and the Old Northwest whom the American government forcibly relocated in present-day Oklahoma and Kansas. Ironically, some of these eastern tribes acted as agents of white civilization by introducing cotton, the plantation system, black slavery, and schools. Other tribes triggered conflicts that weakened the western tribes with whom they came into contact. The Cherokee, Shawnee, and Delaware forced the Osage out of their Missouri and Arkansas hunting grounds, and tribes from the Old Northwest successfully claimed hunting areas long used by Kansas plains tribes. These disruptions foreshadowed white incursions later in the century.

The fact that most of the trans-Mississippi West lay outside U.S. boundaries and that the government had guaranteed Indian tribes permanent possession of some western territories did not curtail American activities. By the 1840s, a growing volume of published information fostered dreams of possession. Government reports by explorers like Zebulon Pike and John C. Frémont provided detailed information about the interior, and guidebooks and news articles described the routes that fur trappers such as Jim Bridger, Kit Carson, and Jedediah Smith had mapped out. Going west was clearly possible. Lansford Hastings's *Emigrants' Guide to Oregon and California* (1845) provided not only the practical information that emigrants would need but also the encouragement that heading for the frontier was the right thing to do.

In his widely read guide, Hastings minimized the importance of Mexican and British sovereignty. California, as a Mexican possession, presented a problem, he conceded, but Oregon did not. "So far from having any valid claim to any portion of it," Hastings argued, Great Britain "had no right even to occupy it." Furthermore, American settlers were already trickling into the Pacific Northwest, bringing progress with them. Surely the day could not be far distant, he wrote approvingly, "when genuine Republicanism and unsophisticated Democracy shall be reared up . . . upon the now wild shores, of the great Pacific," to replace "ignorance, superstition, and despotism."

Hastings's belief that Americans would obtain rights to foreign holdings in the West came true within a decade. In the course of the 1840s, the United States, through war and diplomacy, acquired Mexico's territories in the Southwest and on the Pacific (1,193,061 square miles, including Texas) as well as title to the Oregon country up to the 49th parallel (another 285,580 square miles). Later, with the Gadsden Purchase in 1853, the country incorporated another 29,640 square miles of Mexican territory.

Manifest Destiny

Bursts of florid rhetoric accompanied territorial growth, and Americans used the slogan "Manifest Destiny" to justify and account for it. The phrase, coined in 1845 by John L. O'Sullivan, editor of the *Democratic Review*, expressed the conviction that the country's superior institutions and culture gave Americans a God-given right, even an obligation, to spread their civilization across the entire continent. This sense of uniqueness and mission was a legacy of early Puritan utopianism and Revolutionary republicanism. By the 1840s, the successful absorption of the Louisiana Territory, rapid population growth, and advances in transportation, communication, and industry bolstered the idea of national superiority. Publicists of Manifest Destiny proclaimed that the nation not only could but must absorb new territories.

WINNING THE TRANS-MISSISSIPPI WEST

Manifest Destiny justified expansion, but events in Texas triggered the government's determination to acquire territories west of the Mississippi River. The Texas question originated in the years when Spain held most of the Southwest. Although some settlements such as Santa Fe, founded in 1609, were almost as old as Jamestown, the sparsely populated and underdeveloped Southwest acted primarily as a buffer zone for Mexico. The main centers of Spanish settlement were geographically distant from one another and thousands of miles from Mexico City. This weak defensive perimeter was increasingly vulnerable as Spain weakened, but its legal status was recognized internationally in the Transcontinental Treaty. Moreover, in its treaty negotiations with Spain in 1819, the United States, in return for Florida, accepted a southern border excluding Texas, to which the Americans had vague claims stemming from the Louisiana Purchase.

Annexing Texas, 1845

By the time the treaty was ratified in 1821, Mexico had won its independence from Spain but scarcely had an opportunity to cope with the borderlands, their people, and their problems or to achieve national stability. Mexicans soon had reason to won-

der whether the American disavowal of any claim to Texas in the Transcontinental Treaty would last, for political leaders like Henry Clay began to cry out for "reannexation." Fear about American expansionism, fueled by several attempts to buy Texas and by continuing aggressive American statements, permeated Mexican politics.

In 1823, the Mexican government resolved to strengthen border areas by increasing population. To attract settlers, it offered land in return for token payments and pledges to become Roman Catholics and Mexican citizens. Stephen F. Austin, whose father had gained rights from Spain to bring 200 families into Texas two years earlier, was among the first of the American impresarios, or contractors, to take advantage of this opportunity. His call for settlers brought an enthusiastic response, as Mary Austin Holley recalled. "I was a young thing then, but 5 months married, my husband . . . failed in Tennessee, proposed to commence business in New Orleans. I ready to go anywhere . . . freely consented. Just then Stephen Austin and Joe Hawkins were crying up Texas—beautiful country, land for nothing, etc.—Texas fever rose then . . . there we must go. There without much reflection, we did go." Like the Holleys, most of the American settlers came from the South, and some brought slaves. By the end of the decade, some 15,000 white Americans and 1,000 slaves lived in Texas, far outnumbering the 5,000 Tejano inhabitants.

This 1872 painting by John Gast—with its large, goddess-like figure trailing telegraph lines, its parade of settlers, and its depiction of technological progress—captures the confidence of white Americans that the acquisition of the West was a positive and inevitable event. It also presents the conventional picture of the settlement of the frontier as a process generated by the movement of people from east to west. In fact, the West was also settled by emigrants moving from Mexico northward and by Indian tribes moving south. (*The Museum of the City of New York*)

United States Territorial Expansion by 1860

This map reveals that it took over 100 years for the United States to expand from the original 13 colonies to Mississippi. You can see the substantial gains Americans won as a result of the Revolution. Then, as the map shows, within the span of a lifetime, the United States acquired the vast territories across the Mississippi River.

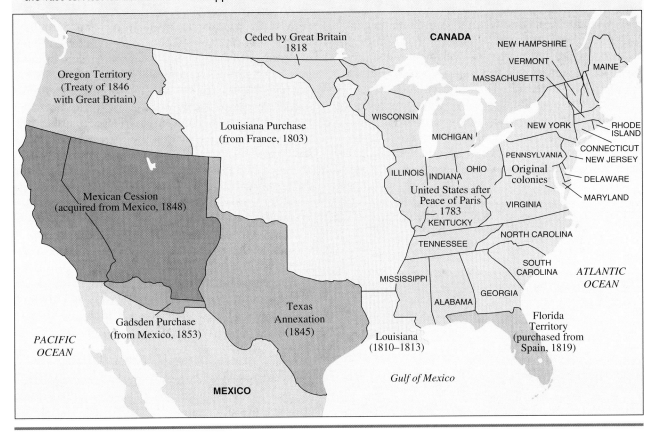

Mexican officials soon had second thoughts. Although Stephen Austin converted to Roman Catholicism, few settlers gave signs of honoring their bargain with the Mexican government. Most remained far more American than Mexican. Some were malcontents who disliked Mexican laws and customs and the limitations on their economic and commercial opportunities. In late 1826, a small group of them rebelled and declared the Republic of Fredonia. Although Stephen Austin and others assisted in putting down the brief uprising, American newspapers hailed the rebels as "apostles of democracy" and called Mexico an "alien civilization."

Mexican anxiety grew apace. Secretary of Foreign Relations Lucas Aláman accused American settlers of being advance agents of the United States. "They commence by introducing themselves into the territory which they covet," he told the Mexican Congress, "grow, multiply, become the predominant party in the population. . . . These pioneers excite . . . movements which disturb the political state of the country . . . and then follow discontents and dissatisfaction."

In 1829, the Mexican government altered its Texas policy. Determined to curb American influence, the government abolished slavery in Texas in 1830 and forbade further emigration from the United States. Officials began to collect customs duties on goods crossing the Louisiana border. But little changed in Texas. American slave owners freed their slaves and then forced them to sign life indenture contracts. Emigrants still crossed the border and outnumbered Mexicans.

Tensions escalated, and in October 1835, a skirmish between the colonial militia and Mexican forces opened hostilities. Sam Houston, onetime governor of Tennessee and army officer, became commander in chief of the Texas forces. Although Texans called the war with Mexico a revolution, a Vermont soldier perhaps more accurately observed, "It is in fact a rebellion."

The new Mexican dictator and general Antonio López de Santa Anna hurried north to crush the rebellion with an army of 6,000 conscripts. Although he had a numerical advantage, many of his soldiers were Mayan Indians who had been drafted unwillingly, spoke no Spanish, and were exhausted by the long march. Supply lines were spread thin. Nevertheless, Santa Anna and his men won the initial engagements of the war: the Alamo at San Antonio fell to him, as did the fortress of Goliad, to the southeast. All the Americans were killed, even though the Americans holding Goliad had surrendered.

As he pursued Houston and the Texans toward the San Jacinto River, carelessness proved Santa Anna's undoing. Although fully anticipating an American attack, the Mexican general and his men settled down to their usual siesta on April 21, 1836,

The Texas Revolution, 1836

This map shows the significance of the American settlement in Texas and the major military engagements of the war. The map also suggests how far the Mexican army had traveled before meeting the Texans on the battlefield.

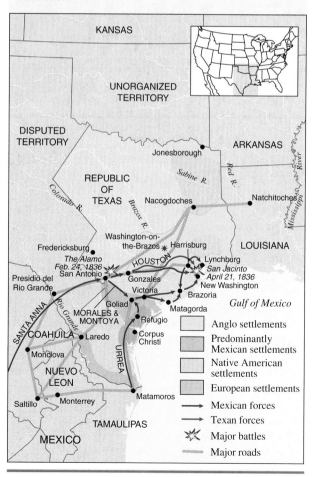

without posting an adequate guard. As the Mexicans dozed, the Americans attacked. With cries of "Remember the Alamo! Remember Goliad!" the Texans overcame the army, captured its commander in his slippers, and won the war within 20 minutes. Their casualties were minimal: 8 or 9 dead, 17 wounded. But 630 Mexicans lay dead.

With the victory at San Jacinto, Texas gained its independence. Threatened with lynching, Santa Anna saw little choice but to sign the treaty of independence setting the republic's boundary at the Rio Grande. When news of the disastrous events reached Mexico City, however, the Mexican Congress repudiated an "agreement carried out under the threat of death." Mexico maintained that Texas was still part of Mexico.

The new republic started off shakily, financially unstable, unrecognized by its enemy, rejected by its friends. Although Texans immediately sought admission to the Union, their bid failed. Jackson, whose agent in Texas reported that the republic's "future security must depend more upon the weakness and imbecility of her enemy than upon her own strength," was reluctant to run the risk of war with Mexico. With the union precariously balanced with 13 free and 13 slave states, many northerners violently opposed annexation of another slave state. Petitions poured into Congress in 1837 opposing annexation, and John Quincy Adams repeatedly denounced the idea. Annexation was too explosive a political issue to pursue; debate finally died down and then disappeared.

For the next few years, the Lone Star Republic led a precarious existence. Mexico refused to recognize its independence but could send only an occasional raiding party across the border. Texans skirmished with Mexican bands, did their share of border raiding, and suffered an ignominious defeat in an ill-conceived attempt to capture Santa Fe in 1841. Diplomatic maneuvering in European capitals for financial aid and recognition was only moderately successful. Financial ties with the United States increased, however, as trade grew and many Americans invested in Texas bonds and lands.

Texas became headline news again in 1844. "It is the greatest question of the age," an Alabama expansionist declared, "and I predict will agitate the country more than all the other public questions ever have." He was right. Although President John Tyler (who assumed office after Harrison's sudden death) reopened the question of annexation hoping to ensure his reelection, the issue exploded. It brought to life powerful sectional, national, and political tensions and demonstrated the divisiveness of the questions connected to the western expansion of slavery. Southern Democrats insisted that the South's future hinged on the annexation of Texas. "Now is the time to vindicate and save our institutions," John C. Calhoun insisted.

Other wings of the Democratic party capitalized more successfully on the issue, however. Senators like Lewis Cass of Michigan, Stephen Douglas of Illinois, and Robert Walker of Mississippi vigorously supported annexation, not because it would expand slavery, a topic they carefully avoided, but because it would spread the benefits of American civilization. Their arguments, classic examples of the basic tenets of Manifest Destiny, put the question into a national context of expanding American freedom. So powerfully did they link Texas to Manifest Destiny and avoid sectional issues that their candidate, James Polk of Tennessee, secured the Democratic nomination in 1844. Polk called for "the reannexation of Texas at the earliest practicable period" and the occupation of the Oregon Territory. Manifest Destiny had come of age.

Whigs tended to oppose annexation, fearing slavery's expansion and the growth of southern power. They accused the Democrats of exploiting Manifest Destiny, more as a means of securing office than of bringing freedom to Texas.

The Whigs were right that the annexation issue would bring victory to the Democrats. Polk won a close election in 1844. But by the time he took the oath of office in March 1845, Tyler had resolved the question of annexation by pushing through Congress a joint resolution admitting Texas to the Union. Unlike a treaty, which required the approval of two-thirds of the Senate and which Tyler had already failed to win, a joint resolution needed only majority support. Nine years after its revolution, Texas finally joined the Union with the unusual right to divide into five states if it chose to do so.

War with Mexico, 1846–1848

When Mexico learned of Texas's annexation, it promptly severed diplomatic ties with the United States. It was easy for Mexicans to interpret the events from the 1820s on as part of an American plot to steal Texas. During the war for Texas independence, American newspapers, especially those in the South, had enthusiastically hailed the efforts of the rebels, while southern money and volunteers had aided the Texans in their struggle. Now that the Americans had gained Texas, would they want still more?

In his inaugural address in 1845, President Polk pointed out "that our system may easily be extended to the utmost bounds of our territorial limits, and that as it shall be extended the bonds of our Union, so far from being weakened will become stronger." What were those territorial limits? Did they extend into the territory the Mexican government considered its own?

Polk, like many other Americans, failed to appreciate how the annexation of Texas humiliated Mexico and increased pressures on its government to respond belligerently. Knowing that Mexico was weak, the president anticipated that it would grant his grandiose demands: a Texas boundary at the Rio Grande rather than the Nueces River 150 miles to the north, as well as California and New Mexico.

Even before the Texans could accept the invitation to join the Union, rumors of a Mexican invasion were afloat. As a precautionary move, Polk ordered General Zachary Taylor to move "on or near the Rio Grande." By October 1845, Taylor and 3,500 American troops had reached the Nueces River. The presence of the army did not mean that Polk actually expected war. Rather, he hoped that military might, coupled with secret diplomacy, would bring the desired concessions. In November, the president sent his agent, John L. Slidell, to Mexico City. When the Mexican government refused to receive Slidell, Polk angrily decided to force Mexico into accepting American terms. He ordered Taylor south to the Rio Grande. To the Mexicans, who insisted that the Nueces River was the legitimate boundary, their presence constituted an act of war. Democratic newspapers and expansionists enthusiastically hailed Polk's provocative decision; the Whigs opposed it.

It was only a matter of time before an incident occurred to justify American hostilities. In late April, the Mexican government declared a state of defensive war. Two days later, a skirmish between Mexican and American troops resulted in 16 American casualties. When Polk received Taylor's report, he quickly drafted a war message for Congress. The president claimed that Mexico had "passed the boundary of the United States . . . invaded our territory and shed American blood upon American soil." "War exists," he claimed, adding untruthfully, "notwithstanding all our efforts to avoid it, exists by act of Mexico."

Although Congress declared war, the conflict bitterly divided Americans. Many Whigs, including Abraham Lincoln, questioned the accuracy of Polk's initial account of the events, and their opposition grew more vocal as time passed. Lincoln called the war one "of conquest brought into existence to catch votes." The American Peace Society revealed sordid examples of army misbehavior in Mexico, and Frederick Douglass accused the country of "cupidity and love of dominion." Many workers also criticized the war.

The Mexican-American War

This map shows not only the movements of American troops during the Mexican-American War but also the large area that was in dispute. Note how far into Mexico American troops penetrated during the conflict.

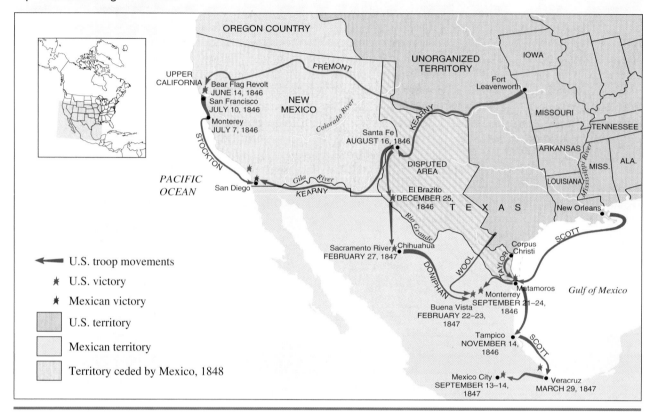

Debate continued as American troops swept into Mexico and advanced toward the capital. Although the Mexicans were also fighting Indian tribes on their northern border, the government refused to admit defeat and end the hostilities. The war dragged on. The *American Review*, a Whig paper, proclaimed that the conflict was a "crime over which angels may weep." In 1847, a month after General Winfield Scott took Mexico City, Philadelphian Joseph Sills wrote in his diary, "There is a widely spread conviction . . . that it is a wicked & disgraceful war."

Yet Polk enjoyed the enthusiastic support of expansionists. Most soldiers were eager volunteers. Some expansionists even urged permanent occupation of Mexico. Illinois Democratic Senator Sidney Breese told the Senate, "The avowed objects of the war . . . [were] to obtain redress of wrongs, a permanent and honorable peace, and indemnity for the past and security for the future." To secure these goals, Breese could even contemplate permanent occupation with "great ultimate good" to the United States, to Mexico, "and to humanity."

Inflated rhetoric did not win the war, however. In the end, chance helped draw hostilities to a close. Mexican moderates approached Polk's diplomatic representative, Nicholas Trist, who accompanied the American army in Mexico. In Trist's baggage were detailed though out-of-date instructions outlining Polk's requirements: the Rio Grande boundary, Upper California, and New Mexico. Although the president had lost confidence in Trist and had ordered him home, Trist stayed in Mexico to negotiate an end to the war. Having obtained most of Polk's objectives, he returned to Washington to an ungrateful president who fired him from his job at the State Department and denounced him as an "unqualified scoundrel."

California and New Mexico

Although Texas and Mexico dominated the headlines, Polk made it clear that California and New Mexico were part of any resolution of the Mexico crisis. Serious American interest in California dated only from the late 1830s. Those few Americans who

In February 1847, American forces, depleted by the departure of 9,000 troops for the Veracruz campaign, met Santa Anna's much larger army several miles north of the hacienda of Buena Vista. The Americans, largely inexperienced volunteers, dug themselves into the valley's gullies and ravines. After bitter conflict, the Americans won the day with far fewer casualties than their Mexican opponents. This victory secured northeastern Mexico for the Americans and helped make General Zachary Taylor into a popular hero and potential political candidate. (*Frances Flora Bond Palmer after Joseph H. Eaton,* Battle of Buena Vista. View of the Battle-Ground of "The Angostura" fought near Buena Vista, Mexico February 23rd. 1847. [Looking S. West] *Amon Carter Museum, Fort Worth, Texas 1971.48)*

were living in California before then constituted only a small part of the Spanish-speaking Californio population. Many had married into Californio families and taken Mexican citizenship. But gradual recognition of California's fine harbors, its favorable position for the China trade, and the suspicion that other countries, especially Great Britain, had designs on the region nourished the conviction that it must become part of the United States.

In 1842, a comic dress rehearsal for rebellion occurred when U.S. naval commodore Thomas Catsby Jones, believing that war had broken out with Mexico, sailed into Monterey, forced the Mexican commander to surrender, and proclaimed California's annexation. Learning of his error, Jones apologized and watched the Mexican flag hoisted once more. Yet the arrival of 1,500 American overland emigrants in a three-year period intensified the friction. These newcomers wanted an American California. As one resident realized, "The American population will soon be sufficiently numerous to play the Texas game."

In 1845, Polk appointed Thomas Larkin, a successful American merchant in Monterey, as his confidential agent. Larkin had clear instructions should Californians decide to break with Mexico. "While the President will make no effort and use no influence to induce California to become one of the free and independent states of the Union," wrote Polk's secretary of state, James Buchanan, to Larkin, "yet if the people should desire to unite their destiny with ours, they would be received as brethren." Polk's efforts to purchase California suggested that he was sensitive to the fragility of American claims to the region. But Santa Anna, who bore the burden of having lost Texas, was in no position to sell. Thus, in 1846, a few armed American settlers rose up against Mexican "tyranny" and established the "Bear Flag Republic."

New Mexico was also on Polk's list. Ties with the United States dated to the beginning of American trade with Santa Fe in the 1820s. Economic profits stimulated American territorial appetites. As the oldest and largest Mexican group in North America (60,000 out of 75,000), however, New Mexicans had little desire for annexation. The unsuccessful attempt by the Texans to capture Santa Fe in 1841 and border clashes in the two following years did not enhance the attractiveness of their Anglo neighbors.

But, standing awkwardly in the path of westward expansion and further isolated from Mexico by the annexation of Texas in 1846, New Mexico had a shaky future as a Mexican province.

In June 1846, shortly after the declaration of war with Mexico, the Army of the West, led by Colonel Stephen W. Kearney, left Fort Leavenworth, Kansas, for New Mexico. Kearney had orders to occupy Mexico's northern provinces and to protect the lucrative Santa Fe trade. Two months later, the army took Santa Fe without a shot, although one eyewitness noticed the "surly countenances" and the "wail of grief . . . above the din of our horses' tread." New Mexico's upper class, who had already begun to intermarry with American merchants and send some sons to colleges in the United States, readily accepted the new rulers. However, ordinary Mexicans and Pueblo Indians did not take conquest so lightly. After Kearney departed for California, resistance erupted in New Mexico. Californios also fought the American occupation force. Kearney was wounded, and the first appointed American governor of New Mexico was killed. In the end, however, superior American military strength won the day. By January 1847, both California and New Mexico were firmly in American hands.

The Treaty of Guadalupe Hidalgo, 1848

Negotiated by Trist and signed on February 2, 1848, the Treaty of Guadalupe Hidalgo resolved the original issues by setting the Rio Grande as the boundary between Mexico and the United States and by transferring the Southwest and California into American hands. The United States abandoned the grandiose idea of annexing Mexico but took in the 75,000 Spanish-speaking inhabitants and its 150,000 Native Americans living in the Southwest and California. American territory increased by 529,017 square miles, almost one-third of Mexico's extent. Mexico received $15 million and in 1853 would receive another $10 million for large tracts of land in southern Arizona and New Mexico (the Gadsden Purchase). In the treaty, the United States guaranteed the civil and political rights of former Mexican citizens and their rights to land and also agreed to satisfy all American claims against Mexico.

If the territorial gains were immense, some costs were equally huge: 13,000 American lives were lost, mostly to diseases such as measles and dysentery, and $97 million was expended for military operations. Although sporadic violence would continue for years in the Southwest as Mexicans protested the new status quo, the war was over, and the Americans had won.

The Oregon Question, 1844–1846

Belligerence and war secured vast areas of the Southwest and California for the United States. In the Pacific Northwest, the presence of mighty Great Britain rather than the weak, crisis-ridden Mexican government suggested reliance on diplomacy rather than war. Glossing over the disputed nature of American claims, Polk set out the American position that settlement carried the presumption of possession. He assured the inauguration day crowd huddled under umbrellas that "our title to the country of Oregon is 'clear and unquestionable,' . . . already our people are preparing to perfect that title by occupying it with their wives and children." But the British did not agree. As the *London Times* warned, "Ill regulated, overbearing, and aggressive . . . [Polk's] pretensions amount, if acted upon, to the clearest *causa belli* which has yet arisen between Great Britain and the American Union."

Though the British considered the president's speech belligerent, Polk recognized the reality that Americans had not hesitated to settle the disputed territories. Between 1842 and 1845, the number of Americans in Oregon grew from 400 to over 5,000.

The Oregon Country

This map highlights the extravagant claims to Oregon voiced during the election of 1844 and the eventual boundaries established with Great Britain. The major trails that brought American settlers to the West suggest the population movements that lay behind the Oregon controversy.

Most located south of the Columbia River in the Willamette valley. By 1843, these settlers had written a constitution and soon after elected a legislature.

At the same time, changing conditions set the stage for an eventual compromise. British interests in the area were declining as the near destruction of the beaver caused the fur trade to dwindle. The riches produced in Britain by the Industrial Revolution made colonies appear less important than they had had been in the eighteenth century, and Britain had already granted Canada self rule. Attractive commercial opportunities were opening up in other parts of the world like India and China, while New Zealand, annexed in 1840, and Australia became magnets for British emigration.

Polk was not willing to go to war with Great Britain for Oregon, but his flamboyant posture and expansive American claims complicated the conflict's resolution. The Democratic platform and the slogan that helped elect Polk set the boundary at 54°40′. Privately, he considered reasonable a boundary at the 49th parallel, which would extend the existing Canadian–American border to the Pacific and secure the harbors of Puget Sound for the United States. But Polk could hardly admit this to his Democratic supporters, who had so recently and enthusiastically shouted "Fifty-four forty or fight."

Soon after his inaugural, Polk offered his compromise to Great Britain—but in a tone that antagonized the British. Polk compounded his error by gracelessly withdrawing his suggestion. In his year-end address to Congress in 1845, the president created more diplomatic difficulties. Urging the protection of American settlers in Oregon, he again publicly claimed that Oregon belonged to the United States. In addition, he asked Congress to give Britain the one-year notice required by previous agreements to terminate joint occupation there.

Discussions about Oregon occupied Congress for months in early 1846. Debate, however, gradually revealed deep divisions about Oregon and the possibility of war with Great Britain. Despite slogans, most Americans did not want to fight for Oregon and preferred to resolve the crisis diplomatically. As war with Mexico loomed, this task became more urgent.

The British, too, were eager to settle. In June 1846, the British agreed to accept the 49th-parallel boundary if Vancouver Island remained British. Polk took the unorthodox step of forwarding this proposal to the Senate for a preliminary response. Within days, the Senate overwhelmingly approved the compromise. Escaping some of the responsibility for retreating from slogans by sharing it with the Senate, Polk ended the crisis just a few weeks before the declaration of war with Mexico.

Manifest Destiny was an idea that supported and justified expansionist policies. At the most basic level, it corresponded to what Americans believed— that expansion was both necessary and right. As early as 1816, American geography books pictured the nation's western boundary at the Pacific and included Texas. Poems, essays, and stories about winning the West, enlivened with illustrations of covered wagons and Indian fighters, were standard reading fare. Popular literature typically described Indians as a dying race that had failed in the basic tasks of cultivating the soil and conquering the wilderness. Mexicans were dismissed as "unjust and injurious neighbor[s]." Only whites could make the wilderness flower. Thus, as lands east of the Mississippi filled up, Americans automatically called on familiar ideas to justify expansion.

GOING WEST AND EAST

Americans lost little time in moving into the new territories. During the 1840s, 1850s, and 1860s, thousands of Americans left their homes for the West. By 1860, California alone had 380,000 settlers. At the same time, thousands of Chinese headed south and east to destinations like Australia, Hawaii, and North and South America to escape the unrest caused by the opium wars in the 1840s with Great Britain, internal unrest, and poor economic conditions. Sixty-three thousand had come to the United States by 1870. Most were in California, the land of the "Gold Mountain."

One Chinese folk song depicted the "perilous journey" to the United States "sailing [in] a boat with bamboo poles across the sea." The Chinese, of course, had little choice on their travel route to the American West, but American migrants did. Some chose the sea route; although the trip was expensive, one could sail from Atlantic or Gulf Coast ports around South America to the West Coast or embark for Panama, cross the isthmus by land, and then continue by sea. Most emigrants from the states, however, chose land routes. In 1843, the first large party succeeded in crossing the plains and mountains to Oregon. More followed. Between 1841 and 1867, some 350,000 traveled the overland trails to California or Oregon, while others trekked part of the way to intermediate points like Colorado and Utah.

The Emigrants

Most of the emigrants who headed for the Far West, where slavery was prohibited, were white and American-born. They came from the Midwest and the Upper South. A few free blacks made the trip as well. Pioneer Margaret Frink remembered seeing a "Negro woman . . . tramping along through the heat and dust, carrying a cast iron black stove on her head, with her provisions and a blanket piled on top . . . bravely pushing on for California." Emigrants from the Deep South usually selected Arkansas or Texas as their destination, and many took their slaves with them. By 1840, over 11,000 slaves toiled in Texas and 20,000 in Arkansas.

The many pioneers who kept journals during the five- to six-month overland trip captured the human dimension of emigrating. Their journals, usually their only contribution to the historical record, focused on day-to-day events and expressed some of the thoughts and emotions experienced on the long journey west. One migrant, Lodisa Frizzell, described her feelings at parting in 1852:

> Who is there that does not recollect their first night when started on a long journey, the well known voices of our friends still ring in our ears, the parting kiss feels still warm upon our lips, and that last separating word farewell! sinks deeply into the heart! It may be the last we ever hear from some or all of them, and to those who start . . . there can be no more solemn scene of parting only at death.

Most emigrants traveled with family and relatives. Only during the gold rush years did large numbers, usually young men, travel independently. Migration was a family experience, mostly involving men and women in their late twenties to early forties. A sizable number of them had recently married. And for most, migration was a familiar experience. Like other geographically mobile Americans, emigrants to the Far West had earlier moved to other frontiers, often as children or as newlyweds. The difference was the vast distance to this frontier and the seemingly final separation from home.

Migrants' Motives

What led so many Americans to sell most of their possessions and embark on an unknown future thousands of miles away? Many believed that frontier life would offer rich opportunities. A popular folk song expressed this widespread conviction:

> *Since times has been hard, I'll tell you sweetheart,*
> *I've a notion to leave off my plow and my cart,*
> *Away to Californy a journey pursue,*
> *To double my fortunes as other men do.*

The kinds of opportunities emigrants expected varied widely. Thousands sought riches in the form of gold. Others anticipated making their fortune as merchants, shopkeepers, and peddlers. Some intended to speculate in land, acquiring large blocks of public lands and then selling them later to settlers at a handsome profit. The possibility of professional rewards gained from practicing law or medicine attracted still others.

Most migrants dreamed of bettering their life by cultivating the land. As one settler explained, "The motive that induced us to part with pleasant associates and dear friends of our childhood days, was to obtain from the government of the United States a grant of land that 'Uncle Sam' had promised." Federal and state land policies made the acquisition of land increasingly alluring. Preemption acts during the 1830s and 1840s gave "squatters" the right to settle public lands before the government offered them for sale and then allowed them to purchase these lands at the minimum price once they came on the market. At the same time, the amount of land a family had to buy shrank to only 40 acres. In 1862, the Homestead Act went further by offering 160 acres of government land free to citizens or future citizens over 21 who lived on the property, improved it, and paid a small registration fee. Oregon's land policy, which predated the Homestead Act, was even more generous. It awarded a single man 320 acres of free land and a married man 640 acres, provided he occupied his claim for four years and made improvements.

Some emigrants hoped the West would restore them to health. Settlers from the Mississippi valley wished to escape the region's debilitating malarial fevers. Doctors advised those suffering the dreaded tuberculosis that the long out-of-doors trip and the western climate might cure them. Even invalids grasped at the advice offered by one doctor in 1850, who urged them to "attach themselves to the companies of emigrants bound for Oregon or Upper California."

Others pursued religious or cultural missions in the West. Missionary couples like David and Catherine Blaine, who settled in Seattle when it was a frontier outpost, were determined to bring Protestantism and education west. Stirred by tales of the "deplorable morals" on the frontier, they willingly left the comforts of home to evangelize and educate westerners. Still others, like the Mormons, made the long trek to Utah to establish a society in conformity with their religious beliefs.

Not everyone who dreamed of setting off for the frontier could do so, however. Unlike the moves to earlier frontiers, the trip to the Far West involved considerable expense. The sea route, while probably the most comfortable, was the most costly, an estimated $600 per person for the trip around Cape Horn. For the same sum, four people could travel overland. And if the emigrants sold their wagons and oxen at the journey's end, the final expenses might amount to only $220. Clearly, however, the initial financial outlay was considerable enough to rule out the trip for the very poor. Despite increasingly liberal land policies, American migration to the Far West (with the exception of group migration to Utah) was a movement of the middle class.

Like Americans, Chinese migrants were also inspired by the dream of bettering their condition. Most were married men who faced limited opportunities in their villages. Labor circulars proclaimed that Americans "want the Chinaman to come and make him very welcome.... Money is in great plenty and to spare in America." The message was reinforced when emigrants to Hawaii and the United States returned with money in their pockets. In the 1860s, Chinese laborers could earn $30 a month working for the railroad, far more than the $3 to $5 they could expect if they stayed home.

The Overland Trails

The trip started for most American emigrants in the late spring when they left their homes for starting points in Iowa and Missouri: Council Bluffs, Independence, Westport, St. Joseph. There, companies of wagons gathered, and when grass was up for the stock, usually by the middle of May, they set out. Emigrant trains first followed the valley of the Platte River. Making only 15 miles a day, they slowly wound their way through the South Pass of the Rockies, heading for destinations in California or Oregon.

Emigrants found the first part of the trip novel and even enjoyable. The Indians, one woman noted, "proved better than represented"; some even helped emigrants cross rivers swollen by spring rains. The scenery, with its spring and early summer flowers, was new. Familiar chores were a challenge out in the open. The traditional division of labor persisted. Generally, men did the "outdoor" work. They drove and repaired the wagons, ferried cattle and wagons across rivers, hunted, and stood guard at night. Women labored at domestic chores, caring for children, cooking meals, and washing clothes. As they had at home, women procured small treats, trading with each other and with Indians for buffalo meat, fish, or moccasins. During travel, young children stayed out of the way in the wagons, while older brothers and sisters walked alongside and lent a hand to their elders. Many of the children remembered the trip as an exciting adventure. Sometimes a

This illustration of a young woman being carried away by a Comanche chief came from a book entitled *Thrilling Adventures Among the Indians*, published in 1850. An increasingly racist view of Native Americans, nourished by popular accounts of Indians as "savage brute[s]," colored emigrants' views of the Indians they encountered in the trans-Mississippi West and seemed to justify disregarding native rights. *(The Newberry Library)*

day off from traveling provided a chance for fun. Wagon trains might stop to observe the Sabbath, allowing men and animals time to rest and women an opportunity to catch up on the laundry.

As the trip lengthened, difficulties multiplied. Cholera often took a heavy toll. Conflict with Indians became a problem only in the 1850s and made emigrants jumpy during the second half of the trip. (Between 1840 and 1860, Indians killed about 400 emigrants, most during the second half of the trip; the emigrants themselves killed at least that many Indians.) Traveling grew more arduous as deserts and mountains replaced rolling prairies.

Emigrants had to cross the final mountain ranges of the Sierras and the Cascades before the first snowfall, so there was a pressing need to push ever onward. Animals weakened by travel, poor feed, and bad water sickened, collapsed, and often died. As families faced the harsh realities, they had to lighten their wagons by throwing out beloved possessions from home. Food grew scarce.

Personal Diaries

Nineteenth-century journals kept by hundreds of ordinary men and women traveling west on the overland trails constitute a rich source for exploring the nature of the westward experience. They are also an example of how private sources can be used to deepen our understanding of the past. Diaries, journals, and letters all provide us with a personal perspective on major happenings. These sources tend to focus on the concrete, so they convey the texture of daily life in the nineteenth century, daily routines and amusements, clothing, habits, and interactions with family and friends. They also provide evidence of the varied concerns, attitudes, and prejudices of the writers, thus providing a test of commonly accepted generalizations about individual and group behavior.

Like any historical source, personal documents must be used carefully. It is important to note the writer's age, gender, class, and regional identification. Although this information may not be available, some of the writer's background can be deduced from what he or she has written. It is also important to consider for what purpose and for whom the document was composed. This information will help explain the tone or character of the source and what has been included or left out. It is, of course, important to avoid generalizing too much from one or even several similar sources. Only after reading many diaries, letters, and journals is it possible to make valid generalizations about life in the past.

Here we present excerpts from two travel journals of the 1850s. Few of the writers considered their journals to be strictly private. Often, they were intended as a family record or as information for friends back home. Therefore, material of a personal nature has often been excluded. Nineteenth-century Americans referred to certain topics, such as pregnancy, only indirectly or not at all.

One excerpt comes from Mary Bailey's 1852 journal. Mary was 22 years old when she crossed the plains to California with her 32-year-old doctor husband. Originally a New Englander, Mary had lived in Ohio for six years before moving west. The Baileys were reasonably prosperous and were able to restock necessary supplies on the road west. The other writer, Robert Robe, was 30 years old when he crossed along the same route a year earlier than the Baileys, headed for Oregon. Robert was a native of Ohio and a Presbyterian minister.

As you read these excerpts, notice what each journal reveals about the trip west. What kinds of challenges did the emigrants face on their journey? Do these correspond to the picture you may have formed from novels, television, and movies? What kinds of work needed to be done, and who did it? Can you see any indication of a division of work based on gender? What kinds of interactions appear to have occurred between men and women on the trip? What does the pattern tell us about nineteenth-century society? How does the painting of the "emigrant train" reinforce the journal accounts of men's and women's roles?

Reflecting on the Past Even these short excerpts suggest that men and women, as they traveled west, may have had different concerns and different perspectives on the journey. In what ways do the two accounts differ, and in what ways are they similar?

(Benjamin Reinhardt, The Emigrant Train Bedding Down for the Night, 1867, 40 × 70 in. oil on canvas. In the Collection of the Corcoran Gallery of Art, Washington, D.C., Gift of Mr. and Mrs. Landsell K. Christie, 59.21)

Journal of Mary Stuart Bailey

Wednesday, April 13, 1852 Left our hitherto happy home in Sylvania amid the tears of parting kisses of dear friends, many of whom were endeared to me by their kindness shown to me when I was a stranger in a strange land, when sickness and death visited our small family & removed our darling, our only child in a moment, as it were. Such kindness I can never forget. . . .

Friday, 21st [May] Rained last night. Slept in the tent for the first time. I was Yankee enough to protect myself by pinning up blankets over my head. I am quite at home in my tent.

12:00 Have traveled in the rain all day & we are stuck in the mud. I sit in the wagon writing while the men are at work doubling the teams to draw us out. . . .

Sunday, 23rd. Walked to the top of the hill where I could be quiet & commune with nature and nature's God. This afternoon I was annoyed by something very unpleasant & shed many tears and felt very unhappy. . . .

Thursday, 4th [June] Very cold this morning after the shower. . . . We stopped on the banks of the Platte to take dinner. I am sitting on the banks of the Platte with my feet almost in the water. Have been writing to my Mother. How I wish I had some of my own relations with me. . . .

Sunday, 4th [July] Started at 3 o'clock to find feed or know where it was. Had to go 4 or 5 miles off the road.

Found water & good grass. Camped on the sand with sage roots for fuel. It is wintery, cold & somewhat inclined to rain, not pleasant. Rather a dreary Independence Day. We speak of our friends at home. We think they are thinking of us. . . .

Monday, 12th. Stayed in camp another day to get our horse better. He is much improved. It is cold enough. Washed in the morning & had the sick headache in the afternoon. . . .

Thursday, 12th [August] Very warm. Slept until we stopped to take breakfast. Mr. Patterson starts as soon as light & stops in the heat of the day to rest the animals. We do not have much time to do anything except 4 or 5 hours in the middle of the day. . . .

Friday, 17th [September] Have been confined ever since Monday with ague in my face which is very much swollen. Have suffered very much. We are now in Carson Valley. Plenty of trees but the country is very barren.

Saturday, 18th. Very pleasant, delightful weather. Feel much better today. We are not stirring this afternoon. We have heard to a great deal of suffering, people being thrown out on the desert to die & being picked up & brought to the hospital. . . .

Source: Sandra L. Myers, ed., *Ho for California! Women's Overland Diaries from the Huntington Library* (San Marino, CA: Henry F. Huntington Library, 1980).

Journal of Robert Robe

[May] 19, [1851] A fine day. The first spent in travelling on the plains of the Platte river.

20. Continue our journey up the Platte valley which I would judge to be here some 12 miles wide on this side of the river. The only game seen here are the antelope and wolf beside some wild fowl.

21. A rainy morning started early passed an old Pawnee village in ruins. The houses are constructed by placing timbers in forks and upon these without placing upright poles then rushes bound with [illegible] and finally earth. Chimney in center. Day became more & more rainy and wound up with a storm which beggared description.

22. Bluff approach the river—travelling less monotonous river finely skirted with timber.

23. Roads very muddy in afternoon. Today our wagon severed itself from our former companions & joined a company of Californians.

24. Before starting a trader direct from Ft. Kearney arrived at our camp. He informs us it is yet 25 miles thither. Travelling is by no means dangerous a waggon of provisions passing with only three guards. In the afternoon passed the entrance of the Independence Weston & St. Jo. roads. Emigrants became more numerous.

25. Passed Fort Kearney this morning and after a short drive encamped. Having conversed with some of the soldiers I find they consider life very monotonous.

26. Roads heavy—short drive—a storm.

27. High Bluffs on the opposite side of river approach and present a beautiful appearance. At night a fearful storm.

28. Roads heavy nothing singular.

29. Have arrived in the region abounding in Buffalo. At noon a considerable herd came in sight. The first any of us had ever seen. Thus now for the chase—the horsemen proved too swift in pursuit and frightened them into the Bluffs without capturing any—the footmen pursued however and killed three pretty good success for the first.

30. Nothing remarkable today.

31. Game being abundant we resolved to rest our stock and hunt today—Started in the morning on foot. Saw probably 1,000 Buffalo. Shot at several and killed one. Where ever we found them wolves were prowling around as if to guard them. Their real object is however no doubt to seize the calves as their prey. Saw a town of Prairie dogs, they are nearly as large as a gray squirrel. They bark fiercely when at a little distance but on near approach flee to their holes. Wherever they are we see numerous owls. After a very extensive ramble and having seen a variety of game we returned at sunset with most voracious appetites.

June 1. The Bluffs became beautifully undulating losing their precipitous aspect and the country further back is beautifully rolling prairie.

2. In the evening camped beside our old friends Miller and Dovey. They had met with a great loss this morning their 3 horses having taken fright at a drove of buffalo and ran entirely away. Some of our company killed more buffalo this evening & a company went in the night with teams to bring them in.

Source: *Pacific Northwest Quarterly* 19 (January 1928): 52–63.

Overland Trails to the West

The various trails over which thousands of Americans traveled during the 1840s, 1850s, and 1860s are depicted on this map. The geographic features begin to suggest the increasing number of natural obstacles that travelers faced during the last months of their trip.

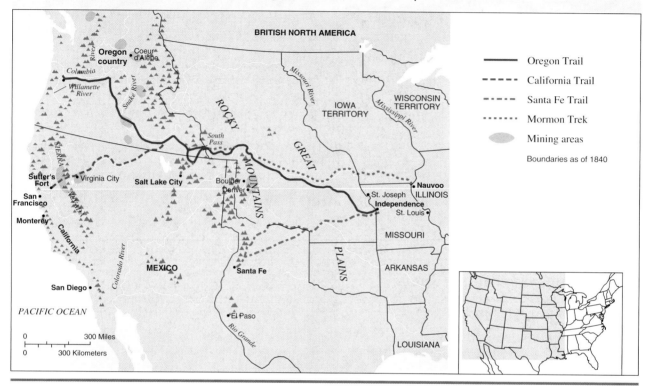

The familiar division of responsibilities often broke down. Women found themselves driving wagons, loading them, even helping to drag them over rocky mountain trails. Their husbands worked frantically with the animals and the wagons as the time of the first snowfall approached. Tempers frayed among tired, overworked, and anxious families. Finally, five or six months after setting out, emigrants arrived, exhausted and often penniless, in Oregon or California. As one wrote on a September day in 1854, her journey had ended, "which for care, fatigue, tediousness, perplexities and dangers of various kinds, can not be excelled."

The trip's strains led some groups to draw up rules and elect officers. This did not prevent dissension, however. Many companies split because of arguments over the pace of travel or the number of rest stops or because some changed their minds about their eventual destination. Family harmony often collapsed under the strain of increased workloads, the irritations of travel, and crises of sickness and even death. Mary Power, who with her husband and three children crossed in 1853, revealed exasperation and depression in her journal: "I felt my courage must fail me, for there we were in a strange land, almost without anything to eat, [with] a team that was not able to pull an empty wagon." In a letter she was even more candid: "I felt as though myself and the little ones were at the mercy of a madman." Men, too, lost nerve as they confronted the hazards of travel. Oregon-bound John Minto described coming upon a father of four, "lying on his back upon a rock, taking the rain in his face, seemingly given up all thought of manly struggle," while the cry of Indians sent some men in another train into their wagons to hide.

LIVING IN THE WEST

When emigrants finally reached their destinations, their feelings ranged from acute disappointment to buoyant enthusiasm. But whether elated or depressed, they had no choice but to start anew. As they turned toward building a new life, they naturally drew on their experiences back East. "Pioneers though we are, and proud of it, we are not content with the wilds . . . with the idleness of the land, the rudely construct[ed] log cabin," one Oregon settler explained. "Pioneers are not that kind of folks."

This view of a Mormon wagon train in the 1850s gives some idea of the rough terrain that emigrant families encountered as they went west. The Mormon migrations were the most organized of the migrations into the trans-Mississippi West, although not all Mormons were lucky enough to travel by wagon. Some emigrants to Utah pushed handcarts across the plains to their destination. *(Used by permission, Utah State Historical Society, all rights reserved. Photo no. 10077)*

Farming in the West

Pioneer farmers faced the urgent task of establishing their homesteads. First, the family had to locate a suitable claim. Clearing the land and constructing a crude shelter followed. Only then could crops be planted.

As farmers labored "to get the land subdued and the wilde nature out of it," they repeated a process that had occurred on earlier frontiers. Felling timber, pulling out native plants that seemed to have no value, and planting familiar crops began a transformation of the landscape. The results were often unanticipated. When they planted their crops, for example, farmers unknowingly introduced weeds whose seeds were mixed in with plant seeds from home. Some of the weeds, like the Canadian thistle, might do even better than the intended crops. Over time, the weeds could become much more than a nuisance to be pulled out of the ground. The Canadian thistle, for example, moved from field to pasture, where it gradually displaced grass and rendered the land useless for livestock grazing.

As they began their agricultural operations, emigrants did not recognize the ecological patterns that seem clear to us today. The goal of taming nature was so central and the task so challenging that there was little time or inclination to question long-range consequences.

Because emigrants brought so few of their possessions west, the work of getting started was even more difficult than it would have been in the East. A young Oregon bride who set up housekeeping in the 1840s with only a stew kettle and three knives was not unusual. A letter from Sarah Everett to her sister-in-law in the East told the tale of hardship. Pleased with a gift of pretty trimmings, Sarah confessed, "I am a very old woman. My face is thin sunken and wrinkled, my hands bony and withered and hard—I shall look strangely I fear with your nice undersleeves and coquettish cherry bows." Sarah was 29 years old.

After months of intense closeness with other travelers, families found themselves alone on their claims. The typical frontier household consisted of parents with one to four children. Although frontier families might interact with nearby Indians, cultural biases made close friendships difficult. No wonder the pioneers often felt lonely and thought longingly of old friends. No wonder either that women helped men with their work and men assisted their wives in domestic chores such as washing.

At first, such isolation was the rule. One pioneer remembered, "We were . . . 'all told,' eleven families within a radius of six or eight miles, widely separated by our holdings and three hundred and twenty acres to each family. In those days anyone residing within twenty miles was considered a neighbor."

But the isolation usually ended within a few years as most areas attracted new emigrants and old settlers seeking better claims.

As rural communities grew, settlers worked to establish schools, churches, and clubs. These organizations drew together people from different places and backgrounds and helped mold them into a new community. They also served to redefine acceptable forms of behavior and remind members of conventional standards and beliefs.

The determination to reestablish familiar institutions was most apparent in politics and law. In Oregon, for example, the pioneers set up a political system based on eastern models before the status of the territory was resolved. Before permanent schools or churches existed, men resumed the familiar political rituals of voting, electioneering, and talking politics. They were also going to court to resolve controversies and to ensure law and order. Although modern popular culture suggests that violence was a part of everyday life on the frontier, this was not true on the farming frontier. Courts, rather than rough-and-ready vigilante groups, usually handled the occasional violence.

Setting up a common school system was more difficult and less urgent in the eyes of many frontier communities than beginning political life. Few settlers initially thought education important enough to tax themselves for permanent public schools. There were schools, of course. But most operated sporadically and only for students who could pay at least part of the fees.

Various obstacles hindered organized religion. Although settlers often attended early church services no matter what the denomination, community growth proved a mixed blessing. When confirmed believers gathered in their own churches, they often discovered to their dismay that the congregation was too small to sustain the new church financially. Nor were converts plentiful, for many settlers had grown out of the habit of regular churchgoing. In early Seattle, Catherine and David Blaine were shocked. "Observation and experience have taught us since we left home," David remarked, "the unwelcome lesson that separation from gospel influences has rendered them quite indifferent to gospel truth." This pattern of low church attendance (the lowest in the nation) characterized the West during both the nineteenth and twentieth centuries.

The chronic shortage of cash on the frontier retarded the growth of both schools and churches. Until farmers could send their goods to market, they had little cash to spare. Geographic mobility also contributed to institutional instability. Up to three-quarters of the population of a frontier county might vanish within a 10-year period as emigrants left to seek better land. Some farmed in as many as four locations until they found a satisfactory claim. Institutions that relied on continuing personal and financial support suffered accordingly.

Yet even if their efforts to re-create familiar institutional life often faltered, settlers did not lose sight of their goals. Newspapers, journals, and books, which circulated early on the frontier, reinforced familiar values and norms and kept determination strong. As more settlers arrived, the numbers willing to support educational, religious, and cultural institutions grew. In the end, as one pioneer pointed out, "We have a telegraph line from the East, a daily rail road train, daily mail and I am beginning to feel quite civilized. And here ended my pioneer experience." Only 16 years had passed since she had crossed the Plains.

Although the belief in the frontier's special economic and social opportunities encouraged emigration, the dream was often illusory. Western society rapidly acquired a social and economic structure similar to that of the East. Frontier newspapers referred to leading settlers as the "better" sort, giving voice to an emerging world of social and economic distinctions. The appearance of workers for hire and tenant farmers also pointed to real economic differences and hinted at the difficulties those on the bottom would face as they tried to improve their situation.

Their widespread geographic mobility also indicates that many found it difficult to capitalize on the benefits of homesteading. Census data show that those who moved were generally less successful than the core of stable residents, who became the community's economic and social leaders. Of course, those on the move may have believed that fortune would finally smile on them at their next stop. But one wife was not so hopeful. When her husband announced that they were to move once again, she commented, "Perhaps I was not quite so enthusiastic as he. I seemed to have heard all this before."

Mining Western Resources

The mineral riches of the trans-Mississippi West prompted people to leave their ordinary lives behind and set out to make their fortunes. News of the discovery of gold in 1848 in California swept the country like "wildfire," according to one Missouri emigrant. Thousands raced to cash in on the bonanza. Within a year, California's population ballooned from 14,000 to almost 100,000. By 1852, that figure had more than doubled.

Like migrants who planned to establish farms in the West, the "forty-niners" were mostly young (in 1850, over half the people in California were in their twenties). Unlike pioneers headed for rural homesteads, however, the gold seekers were unmarried, predominantly male, and heterogeneous. Of those pouring into California in 1849, about 80 percent came from the United States, 8 percent from Mexico, and 5 percent from South America. The rest came from Europe and Asia. California was thus one of the most diverse places in the country. Few of its residents, however, were as interested in settling the West as they were in extracting its precious metals and returning home rich.

California was the first and most dramatic of the western mining discoveries. But others followed. Rumors of gold propelled between 25,000 and 30,000 emigrants, many from California, to British Columbia in Canada in 1858. A year later, news of gold strikes in Colorado set off another rush for fortune. Precious metals unearthed in the Pacific Northwest early in the decade and in Montana and Idaho a few years later kept dreams alive and prospectors moving. In the mid-1870s, more gold, this time in the Black Hills of North Dakota, attracted hordes of fortune seekers.

In contrast to the agricultural settlements, where early residents were isolated and the community expanded gradually, the discovery of gold or silver spurred rapid, if usually short-lived, growth. Mining camps, ramshackle and often hastily constructed, soon housed hundreds or even thousands of miners and people serving them. Merchants, saloonkeepers, cooks, druggists, gamblers, and prostitutes hurried into boom areas as fast as prospectors. Usually, about half the residents of any mining camp were there to prospect the miners rather than the mines.

Given the motivation, character, and ethnic diversity of those flocking to boomtowns and the feeble attempts to set up local government in what were perceived as temporary communities, it was hardly surprising that mining life was often disorderly. Racial antagonism between American miners and foreigners, whom they labeled "greasers" (Mexicans), "chinks" (Chinese), "keskedees" (Frenchmen), and lesser "breeds," led to ugly riots and lynchings. Miners had few qualms about eliminating those who interfered with the race for riches. Fistfights, drunkenness, and murder occurred often enough to become part of the lore of the gold rush. Wrote one woman, "In the short space of twenty four days, we have had murders, fearful accidents, bloody deaths, a mob, whippings, a hanging, an attempt at suicide, and a fatal duel."

If mining life was usually not this violent, it tolerated behavior unacceptable farther east. Miners were not trying to re-create eastern communities but to get rich. Married men, convinced of the raucous character of mining communities, hesitated to bring wives and families west. As one declared, "I would much prefer that a wife of mine should board

This 1852 photograph of miners and the constructions they built on the American River hints at some of the environmental consequences of mining activity. The formal clothing of the woman contrasts sharply with that worn by the men and suggests that she has not forgotten the standards of civilized life. (Courtesy of the California History Room, California State Library, Sacramento, California)

in a respectable bawd house in the city of New York than live anywhere in the city of San Francisco."

Although the lucky few struck it rich or at least made enough money to return home with their pride intact, miners' journals and letters reveal that many made only enough to keep going. Wrote one, "Everybody in the States who has friends here is always writing for them to come home. Now they all long to go home. . . . But it is hard for a man to leave . . . with nothing. . . . I have no pile yet, but you can bet your life I will never come home until I have something more than when I started." The problem was that easily mined silver and gold deposits soon ran out. Chinese miners proved adept at finding what early miners overlooked. Working individually or in small companies, they became a familiar sight in their distinctive clothes, big hats, and pigtails. But even their patient efforts brought decreasing rewards. The remaining rich deposits lay deeply embedded in rock or gravel. Extraction required cooperative efforts, capital, technological experience, and expensive machinery. Eventually, mining became a corporate industrial concern, with miners as wage earners. As early as 1852, the changing nature of mining in California had transformed most of the shaggy miners into wage workers.

Probably 5 percent of early gold rush emigrants to California were women and children. Many of the women also anticipated getting "rich in a hurry." Because there were so few of them, the cooking, nursing, laundry, and hotel services women provided had a high value. When Luzena Wilson arrived in Sacramento, a miner offered to pay her $10 for a biscuit. That night, Luzena dreamt she saw "crowds of bearded miners striking gold from the earth with every blow of the pick, each one seeming to leave a share for me." Yet it was wearying work. As Mary Ballou thought it over, she decided, "I would not advise any Lady to come out here and suffer to toil and fatigue I have suffered for the sake of a little gold." As men's profits shrank, so, too, did those of the women who served them.

Some of the first women to arrive were prostitutes. They rejected the hard labor of cooking and washing that "respectable" women performed, hoping that the gender ratio would make their profession especially profitable. Prostitutes may have constituted as much as 20 percent of California's female population in 1850, and they probably vastly outnumbered other women in early mining camps. During boom days, they made good money and sometimes won a recognized place in society. But prostitutes always ran risks in a disorderly environment and often were the victims of murder and violence.

The Mexicans, South Americans, Chinese, and small numbers of blacks seeking their fortunes in California soon discovered that although they contributed substantially to California's growth, racial discrimination flourished. At first, American miners hoped to force foreigners of color out of the gold fields altogether. But an attempt to declare mining illegal for foreigners failed. A high tax on foreign miners proved more successful. Thousands of Mexicans left the mines, while the Chinese found other jobs in San Francisco and Sacramento. As business stagnated in mining towns, however, white

This magazine illustration shows Chinese miners searching for gold deposits in areas probably abandoned by other miners. The illustration highlights the foreign character of these miners, emphasizing the men's queues—the braid of hair hanging in the back—and Chinese clothes. But the tone of the illustration is descriptive and does not appear to carry a negative message.

This picture of the near–ghost town of Ophir City, Nevada, taken in the 1870s, points to the way the mining frontier left its mark on the landscape and suggests the unstable nature of such a frontier. *(Denver Public Library, Western History Department)*

miners had second thoughts about the levy and reduced it. By 1870, when the tax was declared unconstitutional, the Chinese, who had paid 85 percent of it, had "contributed" $5 million to California for the right to prospect. The hostility that led to this legislation also fed widespread violence against the Chinese and Mexicans.

Black Americans found that their skin color placed them in a situation akin to that of foreigners. Deprived of the vote, forbidden to testify in civil or criminal cases involving whites, excluded from the bounties of the homestead law, blacks led a precarious existence. When news arrived of the discovery of gold in British Columbia in the late 1850s, hundreds of blacks as well as thousands of Chinese left the state, hoping that Canada would be more hospitable than California.

For the Native American tribes of the interior, the mining rushes were disasters. Accustomed to foraging for food, they found fish and game increasingly scarce as miners diverted streams, hunted game, or drove it from mining areas altogether. When Indians responded by raiding mining camps, miners erupted with fury. They stalked and killed native men and women, sometimes collecting bounties offered by some mining communities for their scalps. Indian women were raped; children were kidnapped and offered as apprentices. As one miner pointed out, "Indians seven or eight years old are worth $100 . . . [and] it is a damn poor Indian that's not worth $50."

Without legal recourse because of their skin color, Native Americans could not withstand the onslaught of white society. Subjected not only to violence but to white disease, Indians died by the thousands. In 1849, there had been about 150,000 Indians in California. In just over 20 years, numbers had tumbled to fewer than 30,000.

Although the mining experience was never as brutal for whites as for people of color, white men and women's fantasies of dazzling riches rarely came true. The ghost towns of the West testify to the typical pattern: boom, bust, decay, death. The empty streets and rotting buildings stood as symbols of dashed hopes and disappointed dreams. Also left behind were other physical signs recalling the presence and passing of mining operations. Forests had been decimated to provide timber for the flumes to divert rivers from their channels in the hopes of exposing rich gold deposits in the dry river beds. Slurries and ditches created mounds of debris that during floods or heavy rains oozed over fields and choked rivers and streams. Consumed by visions of glittering metal, miners had been blind to the realities of eroding soil, deforested mountains, diverted waterways, and silt.

It was difficult, however, to recognize some of the negative consequences of the discovery of gold, for it had many positive effects on the West as a whole. Between 1848 and 1883, California mines supplied two-thirds of the country's gold. Gold transformed

San Francisco from a sleepy town into a bustling metropolis. It fueled the agricultural and commercial development of California and Oregon, as miners provided a market for goods and services. Gold built harbors, railroads, and irrigation systems not just in California and Oregon but all over the West. Though few people made large fortunes, both the region and the nation profited from gold.

Establishing God's Kingdom

In the decades before 1860, many emigrants heading for the Far West stopped to rest and buy supplies in Salt Lake City, the heart of the Mormon state of Deseret. There they encountered a society that seemed familiar, yet foreign and shocking. Visitors admired the attractively laid out town with its irrigation ditches, gardens, and tidy houses. But as they noted the decorous nature of everyday life, they gossiped about polygamy and searched for signs of rebellion in the faces of Mormon women. Emigrants who opposed slavery were fond of comparing the Mormon wife to the black slave. They were amazed that so few Mormon women seemed interested in escaping from the bonds of plural marriage.

Violent events brought the Mormons to the arid Great Basin area. Two years after Joseph Smith's murder in 1844, angry mobs chased the last of the "Saints" out of Nauvoo, Illinois. As they struggled to join their advance groups at temporary camps in Iowa, Smith's successor, Brigham Young, realized that the Saints' best hope for survival lay in situating the kingdom of God somewhere in the West, far removed from the United States.

The Mexican-American War unexpectedly furthered Mormon plans. At first, most Mormons probably agreed with Hosea Stout, who hoped that the war "might never end until the States were entirely destroyed." But Brigham Young realized that war might provide desperately needed capital. By recruiting 500 young Mormons for Kearney's Army of the West, Young acquired vital resources. The battalion's advance pay bought wagonloads of supplies for starving and sick Mormons strung out along the trail between Missouri and Iowa and helped finance the impending great migration.

Young selected the Great Basin area, technically part of Mexico, as the best site for his future kingdom. It was arid and remote, 1,000 miles from its nearest "civilized" neighbors. But Mormon leaders concluded that if irrigated, the area might prove as fertile as the fields and vineyards of ancient Israel.

In April 1847, Young led an exploratory expedition of 143 men, 3 women, and 2 children to this promised land. In late July, after reaching Salt Lake,

Young exclaimed, "This is the place." Before returning to Iowa to prepare Mormons for the trip to Utah, he announced his land policy. Settlers would receive virtually free land on the basis of a family's size and its ability to cultivate it. After Young left, the expeditionary group followed his directions to construct irrigation ditches and begin planting.

The following months and years tested Young's organizational talents and his followers' cooperative abilities. By September 1847, fully 566 wagons and 1,500 of the Saints had made the arduous trek to Salt Lake City. Still more Mormons came the next year, inspired by visions of a new Zion in the West. Their trip was also a collective venture, planned and directed by Church leaders. By 1850, the Mormon settlement had attracted over 11,000 settlers. Missionary efforts in the United States and abroad, especially in Great Britain and Scandinavia, drew thousands of converts to the Great Basin. The Church emigration society and a loan fund facilitated the journey for many who could never have otherwise undertaken the trip. By the end of the decade, over 30,000 Saints lived in Utah, not only in Salt Lake City but also in more than 90 village colonies Young had planned. Though hardship marked these early years, the Mormons thrived. As

This photograph shows the Mormon settlement in Nauvoo, Illinois. In the background, you can see the Mormon temple, a dignified and substantial building that could almost be an academy or New England church. The town's development points to the organization and leadership of the new religion. When mobs chased the Mormons out of Nauvoo in the mid-1840s and killed Joseph Smith, the Mormons moved west and built up a new community in Utah. *(Archives of the Church of Jesus Christ of Latter-Day Saints)*

one early settler remarked, "We have everything around us we could ask."

Non-Mormon, or "Gentile," emigrants passing through Utah found much that was recognizable. The government had familiar characteristics. Most Mormons were farmers; many of them came originally from New England and the Midwest and shared mainstream customs and attitudes. But outsiders also perceived profound differences, for the heart of Mormon society was not the individual farmer on his own homestead but the cooperative village.

Years of persecution had nourished a strong sense of group identity and acceptance of Church leadership. Organized by the Church leaders, who made the essential decisions, farming became a collective enterprise. All farmers were allotted land. All had irrigation rights, for water belonged to the community. During Sunday services, the local bishop might give farming instructions to his congregation along with his sermon. As Young explained, "I have looked upon the community of Latter-day Saints in a vision and beheld them organized as the great family of heaven, each person performing his several duties in his line of industry, working for the good of the whole more than for individual aggrandizement." In this vast communal effort, every Mormon was expected to work for success, men and women alike. "We do not believe in having any drones in the hive," one woman said tartly.

The Church was omnipresent in Utah; in fact, nothing separated Church and state. Despite familiar government forms, Church leaders occupied all important political posts. Brigham Young's Governing Quorum contained the high priests of the Church, who made both religious and political decisions.

When it became clear that Utah would become a territory, Mormon leaders drew up a constitution dividing religious and political power. But once in place, powers overlapped. As one Gentile pointed out, "This intimate connection of church and state seems to pervade everything that is done. The supreme power in both being lodged in the hands of the same individuals, it is difficult to separate their two official characters, and to determine whether in any one instance they act as spiritual or merely temporal officers."

Although the Treaty of Guadalupe Hidalgo officially incorporated Utah into the United States, it had little effect on political and religious arrangements. Brigham Young became territorial governor. Local bishops continued as spiritual leaders and civil magistrates. Mormons had come to Utah to establish a kingdom rather than a republic. Their motives dictated the unique politico-religious nature of the Utah experience.

Other aspects of the Mormon frontier were distinctive. Mormon policy toward the Indian tribes was remarkably enlightened. As one prominent Mormon explained, "It has been our habit to shoot Indians with tobacco and bread biscuits rather than with powder and lead, and we are most successful with them." After two expeditions against the Timpanago and Shoshone in 1850, Mormons concentrated on converting rather than killing Native Americans. Mormon missionaries learned Bannock, Ute, Navajo, and Hopi languages to bring the faith to these tribes. They also encouraged Native Americans to ranch and farm.

Although most Gentiles could tolerate some of the differences they encountered in Utah, few could accept polygamy and the seemingly immoral extended family structure that plural marriage entailed. Although Joseph Smith and other Church leaders had secretly practiced polygamy in the early 1840s, Brigham Young publicly revealed the doctrine only in 1852, when the Saints were safely in Utah. Smith believed that the highest or "celestial" form of marriage brought special rewards in the afterlife. Because wives and children contributed to these rewards, polygamy was a means of sanctification. From a practical standpoint, polygamy served to incorporate into Mormon society single female converts who had left their families to come to Utah.

Although most Mormons accepted the doctrine and its religious justification, some found it hard to follow. One woman called it a "great trial of feelings." Actually, relatively few families were polygamous. During the 40-year period in which Mormons practiced plural marriage, only 10 to 20 percent of Mormon families were polygamous. Few men had more than two wives. Because of the expense of maintaining several families and the personal strains involved, usually only the most successful and visible Mormon leaders practiced polygamy.

Polygamous family life was a far cry from the lascivious arrangement outsiders fantasized. Jealousy among wives could destroy the institution of plural marriage, so Mormon leaders minimized the role of romantic love and sexual attraction in courtship and marriage. Instead, they encouraged marriages founded on mutual attachment, with sex for procreation rather than pleasure.

To the shock of outsiders, Mormon women did not consider themselves slaves but highly regarded members of the community. Whether plural wives or not, they saw polygamy as the cutting edge of their society and defended it to the outside world. Polygamy was preferable to monogamy, which left the single woman without the economic and social protection of family life and forced some of them into prostitution; as Brenda Pratt explained, "Polygamy...tends directly to the chastity of women, and the sound health and morals...of their children."

Although they faced obvious difficulties, many plural wives found rewards in polygamy. Without the constant presence of husbands, they had an unusual opportunity for independence. Many treated husbands when they visited as revered friends; their children, not their spouses, provided them with day-to-day emotional satisfaction. Occasionally, plural wives lived together and shared domestic work, becoming close friends. As one such wife put it, "We three...loved each other more than sisters" and would "go hand in hand together down till eternity."

Although the Mormon settlement seemed alien to outsiders, it succeeded in terms of its numbers, its growing economic prosperity, and its group unity. Long-term threats loomed, however, once the region became part of the United States. Attacks on Young's power as well as heated verbal denunciations of polygamy proliferated. Efforts began in Congress to outlaw polygamy. In the years before the Civil War, Mormons withstood these assaults on their way of life. But as Utah became more connected to the rest of the country, the tide would turn against them.

Cities in the West

Many emigrants went west not to claim farmland or to pan for gold but rather to settle in cities like San Francisco, Denver, and Portland. There they hoped to find business and professional opportunities or, perhaps, the chance to make a fortune by speculating in town lots. Others first tried occupations like mining or worked on railroad construction and then headed for the city. In San Francisco, a Chinese community took shape as men left both activities for jobs in the city. In 1860, almost 3,000 Chinese lived in Chinatown; 10 years later, 12,022 did.

Cities were an integral part of western life and, in some cases, preceded agricultural settlement. Some communities turned into bustling cities as they catered to the emigrant trade. St. Joseph, Missouri, outfitted families setting out on the overland journey. Salt Lake City offered weary pioneers headed for California an opportunity to rest and restock. Portland was the destination of many emigrants and became a market and supply center for homesteaders.

Some cities grew so rapidly that they have been called "instant cities." San Francisco and Denver turned into cities almost overnight; in a mere 12 years, San Francisco's population zoomed from 812 to 56,802. The discovery of precious metals sent thousands of miners to and through these places. And once the strike ran out, many miners returned to make a new start. Still other places supplied farmers and served as their markets. They only gradually acquired urban characteristics.

Commercial life bustled in western cities, offering residents a wide range of occupations and services. As a Portland emigrant remarked in 1852, only a few years after that community's beginning, "In many ways life here...was more primitive than it was in the early times in Illinois and Missouri. But in others it was far more advanced.... We could get the world's commodities here which could not be had then, or scarcely at all, in the interior of Illinois or Missouri."

Young, single men seeking their fortunes made up a disproportionate share of the urban population. Early Portland had more than three men for every woman. Predictably, city life was often noisy, rowdy, and occasionally violent. The presence of so many young men could not help but affect urban families. Mothers worried that their children would fall into bad company. Some attempted to reform the atmosphere by pressing for Sunday store closings or prohibition. Other women, of course, en-

This 1853 view of San Francisco reveals the rapid transformation of the city. Brick buildings (several stories high, with elaborate cornices), board sidewalks, kerosene street lamps, and the inevitable grid street pattern give San Francisco the appearance of an eastern city rather than a raw western community, though it was only four years after the gold rush. (*The Bancroft Library, University of California, Berkeley*)

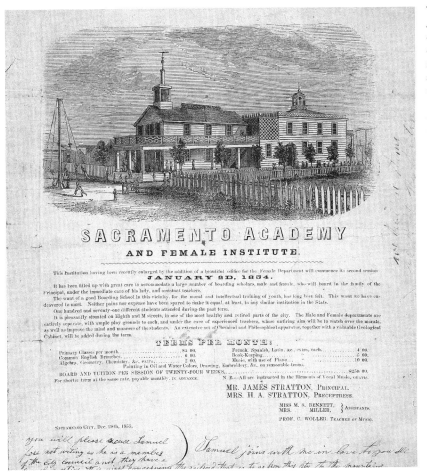

This circular advertising the Sacramento Academy and Female Institute shows settlers' desire to re-create familiar patterns of life. The circular informs interested parents that the school's teachers would watch over "the morals, as well as improve the minds and manners of our students." It was possible to study French, Latin, and Spanish and to study piano for an extra fee. *(Courtesy of the California History Room, California State Library, Sacramento, California)*

joyed all the attention that came with the presence of so many young men. Eventually, the gender ratio became balanced, but as late as 1880, fully 18 of the 24 largest western cities had more men than women.

Although western cities began with distinctive characters, they soon resembled eastern cities. As a western publication boasted, "Transport a resident of an Eastern city and put him down in the streets of Portland, and he would observe little difference between his new surroundings and those he beheld but a moment before in his native city."

The history of Portland suggests the common pattern of development. In 1845, Portland was only a clearing in the forest, large enough for four streets and 16 blocks. Speculation in town lots was lively. By the early 1850s, Portland had grown into a small trading center with a few rough log structures and muddy tracks for streets. As farmers poured into Oregon, the city became a regional commercial center. More permanent structures were built, giving the city an "eastern" appearance.

The belief that urban life in the West abounded with special opportunities initially drew many young men to Portland and other western cities.

Many of them did not find financial success there. Opportunities were greatest for newcomers who brought assets with them. These residents became the elite of the community. By the 1860s, when the city's population had reached 2,874, Portland's Social Club symbolized the emergence of that city's elite. Portland's businessmen, lawyers, and editors controlled an increasing share of the community's wealth and set its social standards. Their elaborate parties, summer trips, and exclusive clubs showed how far Portland had come from its raw frontier beginnings.

CULTURES IN CONFLICT

Looking at westward expansion through the eyes of white emigrants provides only one view of the migration experience. In such a diverse region, many other views existed.

Some of those heading to the American West came from south China. Mostly men, they planned to work for a few years and then return home to their families. Initially, California welcomed the Chinese. One San Francisco merchant reported in

1855 that the Chinese were "received like guests" and treated "with politeness. From far and near we came and were pleased." However, such tolerance soon disappeared as more Chinese arrived on the West Coast. Chinese workers met hostility, violence, and ridicule as they labored in mining camps, on the railroads, and in other jobs. A telegram from Chinese miners in the California mountains betrayed the anxieties many must have felt: "Am afraid there will be big fight." Increasingly perceived by whites as racial threats, called "nagurs" with an appearance supposedly "but a slight removal from the African race," Chinese workers faced many forms of harassment. In 1880, California legislators expressed white hostility by passing a law that made illegal any marriage between a white person and a "negro, mulatto, or Mongolian."

Confronting the Plains Tribes

Some whites likened the Chinese to the Native Americans, another group that would see the western experience differently from white emigrants. An entry from an Oregon Trail journal hints at what one

This dark image, made in about 1851, provides a rare glimpse of one of California's Native American children. The boy's cloth shirt hints at the disappearance of Indian culture as people rushed into California to mine its treasures. The gold rush was a disaster for Native American tribes in California, where violence against Native Americans was all too common. *(M. Lee Fatherree/Oakland Museum of California)*

such perspective might be. On May 7, 1864, Mary Warner, a bride of only a few months, described a frightening event. That day, a "fine-looking" Indian had visited the wagon train and tried to buy her. Mary's husband, probably uncertain how to handle the situation, played along, agreeing to trade his wife for two ponies. The Indian generously offered three. "Then," wrote Mary, "he took hold of my shawl to make me understand to get out [of the wagon]. About this time I got frightened and really was so hysterical [that] I began to cry." Everyone laughed at her, she reported, though surely the Indian found the whole incident no more amusing than she had.

This ordinary encounter on the overland trail only begins to point to the social and cultural differences separating white Americans moving west and the native peoples with whom they came in contact. Confident of their values and rights, emigrants had little regard for those who had lived in the West for centuries and no compunction in seizing their lands. Like the Whitmans, many predicted that the Indian race would die out, a just reward for tribal "degeneracy."

During the 1840s, white Americans, for the first time, came into extensive contact with the powerful Plains tribes, whose culture differed from that of the more familiar eastern Woodlands tribes. Probably a quarter million Native Americans occupied the area from the Rocky Mountains to the Missouri River and from the Platte River to New Mexico. Nearest the Missouri and Iowa frontier lived the "border" tribes—the Pawnee, Omaha, Oto, Ponca, and Kansa. These Indians, unlike other Plains tribes, lived in villages and raised crops, though they supplemented their diet with buffalo meat during the summer months. On the Central Plains lived the Brulé and Oglala Sioux, the Cheyenne, Shoshone, and Arapaho, aggressive tribes who followed the buffalo and often raided the border tribes. In the Southwest were the Comanche, Ute, Navajo, and some Apache bands; the Kiowa, Wichita, Apache, and southern Comanche claimed northern and western Texas as their hunting grounds. Many of the southwestern tribes had adopted aspects of Spanish culture and European domestic animals like cattle, sheep, and horses.

Although differences existed, the Plains tribes shared important similarities. Most had adopted a nomadic way of life after the introduction of Spanish horses in the sixteenth century increased their seasonal mobility from 50 to 500 miles. Horses allowed Indian braves to hunt the buffalo with such success that tribes (with the exclusion of the border groups) came to depend on the beasts for food, clothing, fuel, teepee dwellings, and trading purposes. Because women were responsible for processing buffalo products, some men had more than one wife to tan skins for trading.

Mobility also increased tribal contact and conflict. War played a central part in the lives of the Plains tribes. No male became a fully accepted member of his tribe until he had proved himself in battle. But tribal warfare was not like the warfare of white men. Indians sought not to exterminate their enemies or to claim territory but rather to steal horses and to prove individual prowess. They considered it braver to touch an enemy than to kill or scalp him. Moreover, because individual tribes were loosely organized, chiefs had only limited authority. As Chief Low Horn, a Blackfoot, explained, chiefs "could not restrain their young men . . . their young men were wild, and ambitious, in their turn to be braves and chiefs. They wanted by some brave act to win the favor of their young women, and bring scalps and horses to show their prowess."

This pattern of conflict on the Plains discouraged political unity. But even so, armed with guns, mounted on fast ponies, and skilled in warfare and raiding, the Plains tribes posed a fearsome obstacle to white expansion. They had signed no treaties with the United States and had few friendly feelings toward whites. Their contact with white society had brought gains through trade in skins, but the trade had also introduced alcohol and destructive epidemics of smallpox and scarlet fever.

In the early 1840s, relations between Indians and whites were peaceable. But the intrusion of whites set in motion an environmental cycle that eventually caused conflict. Indian tribes depended on the buffalo but respected this source of life. The Teton Sioux performed rituals to ensure a continuing supply of the animals, while hunters often ritualistically apologized to the Great Unseen Buffalo for slaughtering what the tribe needed. The grasses that nourished the buffalo also sustained the Indians' own ponies and the animals that supported horse traders like the Cheyenne.

Whites, however, put their stock to graze on the grass that both the Indians' ponies and the buffalo needed. And they adopted the "most exciting sport," the buffalo hunt. As the great herds began to shrink, Native American tribes began to battle one another for hunting grounds and food. The powerful Sioux swooped down into the hunting grounds of their enemies and mounted destructive raids against the Pawnee and other smaller tribes. In an 1846 petition to President Polk, the Sioux explained that "for several years past the Emigrants going over the Mountains from the United States, have been the

cause that Buffalo have in great measure left our hunting grounds, thereby causing us to go into the Country of Our Enemies to hunt, exposing our lives daily for the necessary subsistence of our wives and Children and getting killed on several occasions." Despite their plight, the Sioux had "all along treated the Emigrants in the most friendly manner, giving them free passage through our hunting grounds."

The Sioux requested compensation for white damages. When the president denied their request, they tried to extract taxes from those passing over their lands. Emigrants were outraged. Frontier newspapers printed letters denouncing the Sioux, demanding adequate protection for travelers and some chastening of the "savages." However, little was done to relieve the suffering of the tribes bearing the brunt of Sioux aggression, the dismay of the Sioux at the white invasion, or the fears of the emigrants themselves.

This drawing, done by an unknown Indian artist sometime in the 1840s, contrasts the traditionally clad Indians and the wild animals they hunted with the formally dressed white men and their stock animals. Has the artist depicted whites in a sympathetic manner? *(Archives de Jesuites, St. Jerome Quebec)*

Indian Land Cessions in 1840

This map of Indian tribes and groupings reveals locations in 1840, but it presents too static a picture of tribal territories. Some of the Indian groups in the West had been forced across the Mississippi by events in the Midwest. What the map does make obvious, however, is the rapid pace of Indian land cessions in the nineteenth century, especially in the trans-Mississippi West.

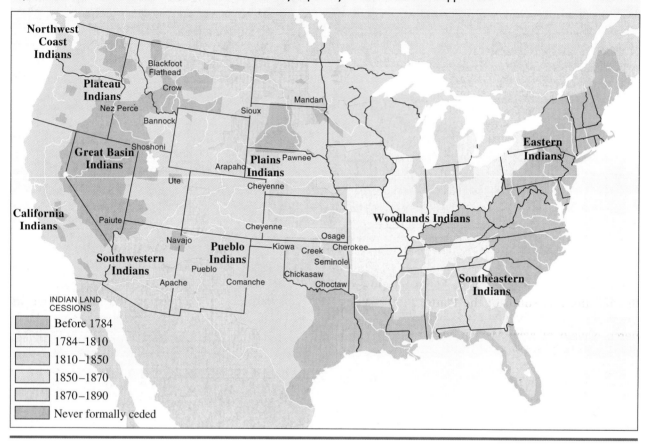

The discovery of gold in California, which lured over 20,000 across the Plains in 1849 alone, became the catalyst for federal action. The vast numbers of gold seekers and their animals wrought such devastation in the Platte valley that it rapidly became a wasteland for the Indians. The dreaded cholera that whites carried with them spread to the Indians, killing thousands.

To meet the crisis, government officials devised a two-pronged plan. The government would construct a chain of forts to protect emigrants and, simultaneously, call the tribes to a general conference. Officials expected that in return for generous presents, Indians would end tribal warfare and limit their movements to prescribed areas. They instructed tribes to select chiefs to speak for them at the conference.

The Fort Laramie Council, 1851

In 1851, the tribal council convened at Fort Laramie. As many as 10,000 Indians, hopeful of ending the destruction of their way of life and eager for the promised presents, gathered at the fort. Tribal animosities simmered, however. Skirmishes occurred on the way to the fort, and the border tribes, fearful of the Sioux, declined to participate. The Comanche, Kiowa, and Apache also refused to come, because their enemies, the Sioux and the Crow, were to be there.

At the conference, whites told the gathered tribes that times had changed. In the past, "you had plenty of buffalo and game . . . and your Great Father well knows that war has always been your favorite amusement and pursuit. He then left the question of peace and war to yourselves. Now, since the settling of the districts West . . . by the white men, your condition has changed." There would be compensation for the destruction of their grass, timber, and buffalo and annual payments of goods and services. But in return, the tribes had to give up their rights of free movement. The government drew tribal boundaries, and chiefs promised to stay within them. In most cases, some tribal lands were sold.

The Fort Laramie Treaty was the first agreement between the Plains tribes and the U.S. government. It expressed the conviction of whites that Indians must stay in clearly defined areas apart from white civilization.

But this system of isolation and its purported benefits were still in the future. During the conference, ominous signs appeared that more trouble would precede any "resolution" of Indian–white affairs. Sioux Chief Black Hawk told whites, "You have split the country and I do not like it." His powerful tribe refused to be restricted to lands north of the Platte, for south of the river lay their recently conquered lands. "These lands once belonged to the Kiowas and the Crows," one Sioux explained, "but we whipped those nations out of them and in this we did what the white men do when they want the lands of the Indians." The words suggested that Indians, despite agreements, would not willingly abandon their traditional way of life for confinement. In the following years, it would become evident that Americans and Sioux had conflicting interests south of the Platte. Elsewhere in the trans-Mississippi West, other tribes, like the fierce Navajo of New Mexico, also resisted white attempts to confine them.

Overwhelming the Mexican Settlers

In the Southwest, in Texas, and in California, Americans encountered a Spanish-speaking population and Hispanic culture. Expansionist senator Lewis Cass expressed Americans' scorn for both. Speaking in a congressional debate on the annexation of New Mexico, Cass stated, "We do not want the people of Mexico, either as citizens or as subjects. All we want is a portion of territory . . . with a population, which would soon recede, or identify itself with ours." Americans regarded Mexicans as lazy, ignorant, and cunning, the "dregs of society." Although Mexicans easily recognized such cultural arrogance, they lacked the numbers to fend off American aggression.

Although Anglo–Mexican interaction differed, few Anglos heeded the Treaty of Guadalupe Hidalgo's assurances that Mexicans would have citizens' rights and the "free enjoyment of their liberty and property." The greatest numbers of Spanish-speaking people lived in New Mexico, and, of all former Mexican citizens, they probably fared the best. Most were of mixed blood, living marginally as ranch hands for rich landowners or as farmers and herdsmen in small villages dominated by a *patron*, or headman. As the century wore on, Americans pro-

duced legal titles and took over lands long occupied by peasant farmers and stock raisers. But despite economic reversals, New Mexicans survived, carrying their rural culture well into the twentieth century.

Light-skinned, upper-class landowners fared better. Even before the conquest, rich New Mexicans had protected their future by establishing contacts with American businessmen and by sending their sons east to American schools. When the United States annexed New Mexico, this substantial and powerful class contracted strategic marriage and business alliances with the Anglo men slowly trickling into the territory. Only rarely did they worry about their poorer countrymen. Class interests outweighed ethnic or cultural considerations.

In Texas, the Spanish-speaking residents, only 10 percent of the population in 1840, shrank to a mere 6 percent by 1860. Although the upper class also intermarried with Americans, they lost most of their power, as Germans, Irish, French, and Americans poured into the state. Poor, dark-skinned Hispanics clustered in low-paying and largely unskilled jobs.

In California, the discovery of gold radically changed the situation for the Californios. In 1848, there were 7,000 Californios and about twice as many Anglos. By 1860, the Anglo population had ballooned to 360,000. Hispanic-Americans were hard-pressed to cope with the rapid influx of outsiders. At first, Californios and several thousand Mexicans from Sonora joined Anglos and others in the gold fields. But competition there fed antagonism and finally open conflict. Posters warned foreigners out of the gold fields. In Anglo eyes, one Hispanic was much like another, even if one claimed to be a Californio with political rights and another a Sonoran. Taxes and terrorism ultimately succeeded in forcing most Spanish speakers out of the mines and established the racial contours of the new California.

Other changes were more disastrous. In 1851, Congress passed the Gwinn Land Law, supposedly a measure for validating Spanish and Mexican land titles. The law violated the pledge contained in a Statement of Protocol accompanying the Treaty of Guadalupe Hidalgo that stated the government "did not in any way" intend to annul the grants of lands made by Mexico, for it forced California landowners to defend their property and encouraged squatters to settle on land in the hopes that the Californios' titles would prove false. The process was slow—it took an average of 17 years to establish clear title to land—and unfamiliar. As one woman explained, her mother had been "totally unprepared for the problems that came with American rule. Not only was the language foreign to her, but also the concept of

This watercolor of the Rancho San Miguelito was not created as a decoration but rather as evidence of land ownership. After the United States defeated Mexico, land owners in California were forced to prove that they had valid legal titles to the lands they claimed. This process was expensive and difficult, and Californios often ended up losing their land holdings. If you had to make a judgment of ownership based on this watercolor, what would you decide? *(National Archives)*

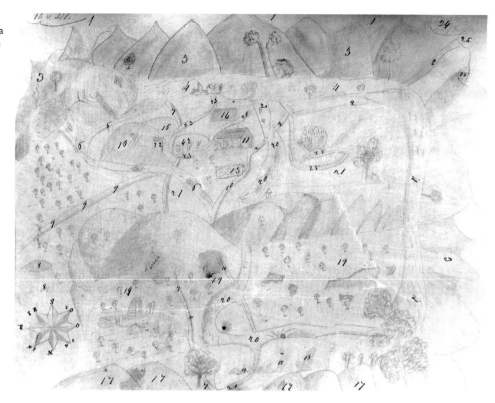

property taxes, mortgages and land title regulations." Landowners found themselves paying American lawyers large fees, often in land, and borrowing at high interest rates to pay for court proceedings. A victory at court often proved hollow when legal expenses forced owners to sell their lands to pay debts. In the South, where Anglos judged land less valuable than in the mining North, the process of dispossession was slower. But by the early 1860s, the ranching class there had also lost most of its extensive holdings and slid into relative poverty.

For working-class Hispanic Americans, who became laborers for Anglo farmers or mining or railroad companies, the arrival of Anglos was the start of a steadily deteriorating situation. Whatever their

Timeline

1803–1806	Lewis and Clark expedition
1818	Treaty on joint U.S.–British occupation of Oregon
1819	Spain cedes Spanish territory in United States and sets transcontinental boundary of Louisiana Purchase, excluding Texas
1821	Mexican independence Opening of Santa Fe Trail Stephen Austin leads American settlement of Texas
1821–1840	Indian removals
1830	Mexico abolishes slavery in Texas
1836	Texas declares independence Battles of the Alamo and San Jacinto
1840s	Emigrant crossings of Overland Trail
1844	James Polk elected president
1845	"Manifest Destiny" coined United States annexes Texas and sends troops to the Rio Grande Americans attempt to buy Upper California and New Mexico
1846	Mexico declares defensive war United States declares war and takes Santa Fe Resolution of Oregon question
1847	Attacks on Veracruz and Mexico City Mormon migration to Utah begins
1848	Treaty of Guadalupe Hidalgo
1849	California gold rush begins
1850	California admitted to the Union
1851	Fort Laramie Treaty
1853	Gadsden Purchase
1862	Homestead Act

employment, Hispanic Americans earned less and did more unpleasant jobs than Anglo workers. By 1870, the average Hispanic-American worker's property was worth only about one-third of what its value had been 20 years earlier.

Some resisted American expansion into the Southwest. Tiburcio Vásquez, a notorious *bandido* in southern California, told his story:

> As I grew to manhood I was in the habit of attending balls and parties given by the native Californians, into which the Americans, then beginning to become numerous, would force themselves and shove the native born men aside. . . . This was about 1852. A spirit of ha-

tred and revenge took possession of me. . . . I believed we were unjustly and wrongfully deprived of the social rights that belonged to us.

Other Hispanics adopted different tactics. In New Mexico, members of Las Gorras Blancas ripped up railroad ties and cut the barbed-wire fences of Anglo ranchers and farmers. The religiously oriented Penitentes tried to work through the ballot box. Ordinary men, women, and children resisted efforts to convert them to Protestantism and clung to familiar customs and beliefs even as they learned some of the skills needed to survive in a changing culture.

✦ *Conclusion*

FRUITS OF MANIFEST DESTINY

Like Narcissa Whitman and her husband, many nineteenth-century Americans decided that they had a unique right to settle the West and make it flower. They were not much concerned with the fate of those who had lived for centuries on the land. The process of acquiring the western half of the continent was so swift that there seemed little point in worrying about the losers. The tale of western expansion loomed large in the imagination of the American people for many years. Some western

settlers became folk heroes. The Whitmans were remembered by the founding of Whitman College in Walla Walla, Washington. All white Americans could be thankful for the special opportunities and the new chance that the West seemed to hold out. Certainly, the nation did gain vast natural wealth in the trans-Mississippi West. But only a small fraction of the hopeful emigrants heading for the frontier realized their dreams of success. And the move west and east had a dark side, as the acquisition of new territories fueled the controversy over the future of slavery.

✦ Recommended Reading

Probing the Trans-Mississippi West
William Cronon, George Miles, and Jay Gitlin, eds., *Under An Open Sky: Rethinking America's Western Past* (1992); David Hamer, *New Towns in the New World: Images and Perceptions of the Nineteenth-Century Frontier* (1990); Theodore J. Karamanski, *Fur Trade and Exploration: Opening the Far Northwest, 1821–1852* (1983); Patricia Nelson Limerick, *The Legacy of Conquest: The Unbroken Past of the American West* (1987); William H. Troettner, *The West as America: Reinterpreting Images of the Frontier, 1820–1920* (1991).

Winning the Trans-Mississippi West
David Pletcher, *The Diplomacy of Annexation: Texas, Oregon, and the Mexican War* (1973); Cecil Robinson, ed., *The View From Chapultepec: Mexican Writers on the Mexican-American War* (1989); Anders Stephanson, *Manifest Destiny: American Expansionism and the Empire of Right* (1995); David J. Weber, *The Mexican Frontier, 1821–1846* (1982).

Going West and East
John Mack Faragher, *Women and Men on the Overland Trail* (1978); Sandra Myres, ed., *Ho for California!*

Women's Overland Diaries from the Huntington Library (1980); John D. Unruh, Jr., *The Plains Across: The Overland Emigrants and the Trans-Mississippi West, 1840–1860* (1979).

Living in the West
Peter G. Boag, *Environment and Experience: Settlement Culture in Nineteenth-Century Oregon* (1992); Richard L. Bushman, *Joseph Smith and the Beginnings of Mormonism* (1984); Arrell Morgan Gibson, *Yankees in Paradise: The Pacific Basin Frontier* (1993); Julie Roy Jeffrey, *Frontier Women "Civilizing" the West? 1840–1880*, 2nd ed. (1998); Laurie F. Maffly-Kipp, *Religion and Society in Frontier California* (1994); Dean L. May, *Three Frontiers: Family, Land, and Society in the American West, 1850–1900* (1994).

Cultures in Conflict
Julie Roy Jeffrey, *Converting the West: A Biography of Narcissa Whitman* (1991); Timothy M. Marovina, *Tejano Religion and Ethnicity: San Antonio, 1821–1860* (1995); Jacqueline Peters, *Sacred Encounters: Father DeSmet and the Indians of the Rocky Mountain West* (1993); Robert J. Rosenbaum, *Mexicano Resistance in the Southwest: "The*

Sacred Right of Self-Preservation" (1981); Theodore Stern, *Chiefs & Chief Traders: Indian Relations at Fort Nez Perces, 1818–1855* (1993); Ronald Takaki, *A Different Mirror: A History of Multicultural America* (19930; Sylvia Van Kirk, *Many Tender Ties: Women in the Fur Trade Society, 1670–1870* (1983); Elliott West, *The Contested Plains: Indians, Goldseekers, and the Rush to Colorado* (1998); David J. Wishart, *An Unspeakable Sadness: The Dispossession of the Nebraska Indians* (1994).

Fiction and Film

Mark Twain's *Roughing It* (1872) is often humorous, but through the humor you can see Twain's insightful comments about westerners' values and standards. James C.

Work's *Gunfight!* (1996) contains a selection of gunfight stories originally printed in popular magazines. For an example of an early "dime novel," see Ann Sophia Winterbotham Stephens's *Malaeska: Indian Wife of the White Hunter* (1861, but use any edition). *The West* (1996) is a nine-part series by Ken Burns that was first shown on television. The films provide a sympathetic and critical account of the settlement and its impact on Native Americans. *The Donner Party* (1992) is a PBS video of the disastrous experience of a party of emigrants caught in the Sierra Nevadas during the winter of 1846–1847. One critic notes a dark tone to the film, which is characteristic of the New Western History.

✦ Discovering U.S. History Online

Fort Scott National Historic Site

www.nps.gov/fosc/mandest.htm

This illustrated site recounts the role of dragoon soldiers from Fort Scott as armed escorts for settlers traveling over the Santa Fe and Oregon Trails.

The Mexican-American War

www.sunsite.unam.mx/revistas/1847/

This well-illustrated site offers several sections (each available in English or Spanish) that explain the causes, courses, and outcomes of the Mexican-American War.

Alamo History

www.drtl.org/History/

An illustrated timeline of the Alamo mission, including its role in the famous battle.

The Treaty of Guadalupe Hidalgo

www.loc.gov/exhibits/ghtreaty

This site gives background on the treaty and has an exhibit of digitized images of each page of the treaty, including the seals. A map of the area of negotiation is also presented.

The Oregon Trail

www.ukans.edu/carrie/kancoll/index.html
www.isu.edu/~trinmich/Oregontrail.html

The Kansas Collection site holds several good primary sources with images concerning the Oregon Trail and America's early movement westward. The second site is a companion to the PBS film *The Oregon Trail* The authors present audio clips from historians, illustrated essays, maps, and images about this famous trail.

The Donner Party

www.members.aol.com/danmrosen/donner/index.htm

This site includes logs recreated from primary sources from the infamous party that resorted to extreme measures to survive. It also has images of the region.

James Knox Polk

www.ipl.org/ref/POTUS/jkpolk.html

This site contains basic factual data about Polk, including his presidency, speeches, cabinet members, and election information.

American Mountain Men

www.xmission.com/~drudy/amm.html

Private letters can speak volumes about the concerns and environment of the writers and recipients. Letters from early settlers west of the Mississippi River are offered on this site, which is an online research center devoted to the trappers, explorers, and traders known as the Mountain Men.

California in the Gold Rush Decade

www.huntington.org/Education/GoldRush
www.museumca.org/goldrush

The first site is a presentation of the "Huntington Library's remarkable collection of Gold Rush manuscripts, drawings, and rare printed materials." The second is a well-illustrated interactive site on the Gold Rush exhibit formerly on display at the Oakland Museum of California.

The National Museum of the American Indian, Smithsonian Institution and The George Gustav Heye Center

www.conexus.si.edu/main.htm

A cooperative effort of these two institutions, this site hosts several virtual exhibits about Native American culture and history.

Native American Women

www.gowest.coalliance.org/exhib/gallery4/leadin.htm

This site is an annotated photographic gallery of Native American women.

14 The Union in Peril

George Caleb Bingham's *Stump Speaking* (1856) captures the democratic energy of politics at mid-century. Note the Lincolnlike figure sitting to the right. *(From the Art Collection of Bank of America)*

✦ *American Stories*

FOUR MEN RESPOND TO THE UNION IN PERIL

The autumn of 1860 was a time of ominous rumors and expectations. The election was held on November 6 in an atmosphere of crisis. In Springfield, Illinois, Abraham Lincoln, taking coffee and sandwiches prepared by the "ladies of Springfield," waited as the telegraph brought in the returns. By 1 A.M., victory was certain. He reported later, "I went home, but not to get much sleep, for I then felt, as I never had before, the responsibility that was upon me." Indeed, he and the American people faced the most serious crisis since the founding of the Republic.

Lincoln won an unusual four-party election with only 39 percent of the popular vote. He had appealed almost exclusively to northern voters in a blatantly sectional campaign, defeating his three opponents by carrying every free state except New Jersey. Of the candidates, only Illinois Senator Stephen Douglas campaigned actively in every section of the country. For his efforts, he received the second-highest number of votes. Douglas's appeal, especially in the closing days of the campaign, was "on behalf of the Union," which he feared—correctly—was in imminent danger of splitting apart.

Other Americans sensed the mood of crisis that fall and faced their own fears and responsibilities. A month before the election, plantation owner Robert Allston wrote his oldest son, Benjamin, that "disastrous consequences" would follow from a Lincoln victory. Although his letter mentioned the possibility of secession, he dealt mostly with plantation concerns: a new horse, the mood of the slaves, ordering supplies from the city, instructions for making trousers on a sewing machine. After Lincoln's election, Allston corresponded with a southern colleague about the need for an "effective military organization" to resist "Northern and Federal aggression." In his shift from sewing machines to military ones, Robert Allston prepared for what he called the "impending crisis."

Frederick Douglass greeted the election of 1860 with characteristic optimism. Not only was this an opportunity to "educate . . . the people in their moral and political duties," he said, but "slaveholders know that the day of their power is over when a Republican President is elected." But no sooner had Lincoln's victory been determined than Douglass's hopes turned sour. He noted that Republican leaders, in their desire to keep the border states from seceding, sounded more antiabolitionist than antislavery. They vowed not to touch slavery in areas where it already existed, which included the District of Columbia, and they promised to enforce the hated Fugitive Slave Act and to put down slave rebellions. In fact, Douglass bitterly contested, slavery would "be as safe, and safer" with Lincoln than with a Democrat.

Michael Luark, an Iowa farmer, was not so sure. Born in Virginia, Luark was a typically mobile nineteenth-century American. Growing up in Indiana, he followed the mining booms of the 1850s to Colorado and California, then returned to the Midwest to farm. Luark sought a good living and resented the furor over slavery. He could not, however, avoid the issue. Writing in his diary on the last day of 1860, Luark looked ahead to 1861 with a deep sense of fear. "Startling" political changes would occur, he predicted, perhaps even the "Dissolution of the Union and Civil War with all its train of horrors." He blamed abolitionist agitators, perhaps reflecting his Virginia origins. On New Year's Day, he expressed his fears that Lincoln would let the "most ultra sectional and Abolition" men disturb the "vexed Slavery question" even further, as Frederick Douglass wanted. But if this happened, Luark warned, "then farewell to our beloved Union of States."

Within four months of this diary entry, the guns of the Confederate States of America fired on a federal fort in South Carolina. The Civil War had begun. Luark's fears, Douglass's hopes, and Lincoln's and Allston's preparations for responsibility all became realities. The explanation of the peril and dissolution of the Union forms the theme of this chapter.

Such a calamitous event as Civil War had numerous causes, large and small. The reactions of Allston, Douglass, and Luark to Lincoln's election suggest some of them: moral duties, sectional politics, growing apprehensions over emotional agitators, and a concern for freedom and independence on the part of blacks, white southerners, and western farmers. But as Douglass understood, by 1860, it was clear that "slavery is the real issue, the single bone of contention between all parties and sections. It is the one disturbing force, and explains the confused and irregular motion of our political machine."

This chapter analyzes how the momentous issue of slavery disrupted the political system and eventually the Union itself. We will look at how four major developments between 1848 and 1861 contributed to the Civil War: first, a sectional dispute over the extension of slavery into the western territories; second, the breakdown of the political party system; third, growing cultural differences in the views and lifestyles of southerners and northerners; and fourth, intensifying emotional and ideological polarization between the two regions over losing their way of life and sacred republican rights at the hands of the other. A preview of civil war, bringing all four causes together, occurred in 1855–1856 in Kansas. Eventually, emotional events, mistrust, and irreconcilable differences made conflict inevitable. The election of Lincoln was the spark that touched off the conflagration of civil war, with all its "train of horrors."

SLAVERY IN THE TERRITORIES

Narcissa Whitman's experiences suggested the various possibilities and pitfalls of the westward movement (see Chapter 13). Their own lives endangered, white migrants threatened the safety, freedom, and cultural integrity of Native Americans and Mexicans whose land stood in the way. But the westward movement also jeopardized freedom by causing a collision between Yankees and slaveholders.

The North and the South had contained their differences over slavery, with only occasional difficulties, during the 60 years after the Constitutional Convention. Compromise in 1787 had resolved questions of the slave trade and the matter of counting slaves for congressional representation. Although slavery threatened ("like a fireball in the night," Jefferson had said) the uneasy sectional harmony in 1820, the Missouri Compromise had established a workable balance of free and slave states and had defined a geographic line (36°30′) to determine future decisions. In 1833, compromise had defused South Carolina's attempt at nullification, and the gag rule in 1836 had kept abolitionist petitions off the floor of Congress.

Each apparent resolution, however, raised the level of emotional conflict between North and South and postponed ultimate settlement of the slavery question. One reason why these compromises temporarily worked was the two-party system, with Whigs and Democrats in both North and South. Party loyalties served as an "antidote," as Van Buren put it, to sectional allegiance. The parties differed over cultural and economic issues, but the volatile issue of slavery was largely kept out of political campaigns and congressional debates. This changed in the late 1840s, which would prove catastrophic to the Union.

Free Soil or Constitutional Protection?

When the war with Mexico broke out in 1846, it seemed likely that the United States would acquire new territories in the Southwest. Would they be slave or free? Philadelphia Congressman David Wilmot added an amendment to a war appropriations bill declaring that "neither slavery nor involuntary servitude shall ever exist" in any territories acquired from Mexico. The debates in Congress over the Wilmot Proviso were significant because legislators voted not as Whigs and Democrats but as northerners and southerners.

A Boston newspaper prophetically observed that Wilmot's resolution "brought to a head the great question which is about to divide the American people." When the Mexican-American War ended, several solutions were presented to deal with this question of slavery in the territories. The first was the "free soil" idea of preventing any extensions of slavery. But did Congress have the power or right to do so? Two precedents suggested that it did. One was the Northwest Ordinance, which had prohibited the entry of slaves into states created in the Upper Midwest; the other was the Missouri Compromise.

Supporters of free soil had mixed motives. For some, slavery was a moral evil to be attacked and destroyed because it trampled on principles of liberty and equality. But for many northern white farmers looking to move westward, the threat of economic competition with an expanding system of large-scale slave labor was even more serious. Nor did they wish to compete for land with free blacks. As Wilmot put it, his proviso was intended to preserve the area for the "sons of toil, of my own race and own color." Other northerners supported the Proviso as a means of restraining what seemed to them the growing political power and "insufferable arrogance" of the "spirit and demands of the Slave Power."

Opposed to the free-soil position were the arguments of Senator John C. Calhoun of South Carolina, expressed in several resolutions introduced in the Senate in 1847. Not only did Congress lack the constitutional right to exclude slavery from the territories, Calhoun argued, but it had a positive duty to protect it. The Wilmot Proviso, therefore, was unconstitutional, as was the Missouri Compromise and any other federal act that prevented slaveholders from taking their slave property into the territories of the United States.

Economic, political, and moral considerations stood behind the Calhoun position. Many southerners hungered for new cotton lands in the West and Southwest, even in Central America and the Caribbean. Politically, southerners feared that northerners wanted to trample on their liberties—namely, the right to protect their institutions against abolitionism. Southern leaders saw the Wilmot Proviso as a moral issue that raised questions about basic republican principles. One congressman called it "treason to the Constitution," and Senator Robert Toombs of Georgia warned that if Congress passed the proviso, he would favor disunion rather than "degradation."

Popular Sovereignty and the Election of 1848

With such divisive potential, it was natural that many Americans sought a compromise solution to keep slavery out of politics. Polk's secretary of state, James Buchanan of Pennsylvania, proposed that the Missouri Compromise line be extended through the lands acquired from Mexico to the Pacific Ocean. This would avoid thorny questions about the morality of slavery and the constitutionality of congressional authority. So would "popular sovereignty," Michigan Senator Lewis Cass's proposal to leave decisions about permitting slavery to the local territorial legislature. The idea appealed to the American democratic belief in local self-government but left many details unanswered. At what point in the progress toward statehood could a territorial legislature decide about slavery? Cass preferred to leave such questions ambiguous, reasoning that both northern and southern politicians would conclude that popular sovereignty favored their interests.

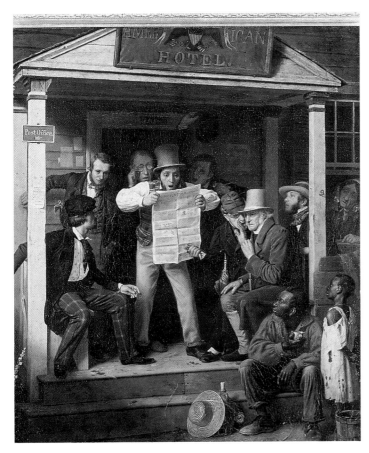

This 1848 painting by Richard Caton Woodville, titled *War News from Mexico,* captures the mood of the period from the Mexican-American War through the Civil War; in towns across the country, outside of countless "American Hotels," the American people listened eagerly to the latest news in an era of steadily worsening political, socioeconomic, and constitutional crises. Separate from the men on the porch, but clearly a part of the picture, are a black father and daughter in rags; they await the war news with special interest, for black Americans would have most to lose by an outcome of the war that led to the expansion of slavery into the territories. *(National Academy of Design, New York)*

Senate Speeches

The history of ordinary Americans is recovered in letters, diaries, folktales, and other nontraditional sources. But in times of political conflict, as in the years before the Civil War, historians turn to more conventional sources such as congressional speeches. Recorded in the *Congressional Globe*, these speeches are a revealing means of recovering the substance, tone, and drama of political debate.

The mid-nineteenth century was an era of giants in the U.S. Senate: Daniel Webster, Henry Clay, Thomas Hart Benton, John C. Calhoun, William Seward, and Stephen Douglas. When Congress debated a major issue, such as the tariff, nullification, or the extension of slavery, large crowds packed the Senate galleries. The speeches would be quickly printed and widely distributed. These spectacular oratorical encounters provided mass entertainment and political instruction. Such was the case with the Senate speeches over the Compromise of 1850. The three principal figures early in the debates were Clay (Kentucky), Calhoun (South Carolina), and Webster (Massachusetts), each of whom delivered memorable speeches to crown brilliant careers.

Born within five years of each other as the American Revolution was ending (1777–1782), each man began his political career in the House of Representatives in the War of 1812 era. Each served a term as secretary of state; in addition, Clay was speaker of the House and Calhoun secretary of war and vice president. Each served for over a decade in the Senate (Clay, 13 years; Calhoun, 15 years; Webster, 19 years). Clay and Webster were leaders of the Whig party, and Calhoun was a leader of the Democrats. During their 40 years of public service, they represented strong nationalistic positions as well as their various states and sections. All three were failing candidates for president between 1824 and 1844. All three spent most of their careers in the political shadow of Andrew Jackson, and all three clashed with him.

Forty years of political and ideological conflict with each other not only sharpened their oratorical skills but also led to mutual respect. Webster said of Calhoun that he was "the ablest man in the Senate. He could have demolished Newton, Calvin, or even John Locke as a logician." Calhoun said of Clay, "He is a bad man, but by god, I love him." And "Old Man Eloquent" himself, John Quincy Adams, said of Webster that he was "the most consummate orator of modern times."

It was therefore a momentous event when they each prepared speeches and met for one last encounter early in 1850. Clay was over 70 years old and in failing health, but he sought to keep the Union together by defending his compromise proposals in a four-hour speech spread over two days in February. The Senate galleries were so packed that listeners were pushed into hallways and even into the rotunda of the Capitol. Copies of his speech were in such demand that over 100,000 were printed.

A month later, on March 7, Webster rose to join Clay in defending the compromise, three days after a seriously ill Calhoun had "tottered into the Senate" on the arm of a friend to hear James Mason of Virginia read his rejection of the compromise. Within a month, Calhoun was dead. Clay and Webster followed him to the grave two years later, and Senate leadership passed on to Seward, Douglas, and others.

Reflecting on the Past   As you read these brief excerpts from each speech, try to imagine yourself sitting in the gallery overlooking the Senate floor absorbing the drama. What oratorical devices does each speaker use? How do they differ? To what extent does each man reflect his section, or not, especially on the fugitive slave issue? To what extent do they appeal to an indivisible Union? On whom do you put the burden of resolving the conflicts? Which passages convey the most emotional power? Which speaker is most persuasive to you? Why?

Henry Clay

February 5–6, 1850

I have seen many periods of great anxiety, of peril, and of danger in this country, and I have never before risen to address any assemblage so oppressed, so appalled, and so anxious; and sir, I hope it will not be out of place to do here, what again and again I have done in my private chamber, to implore of Him who holds the destinies of nations and individuals in His hands, to bestow upon our country His blessing, to calm the violence and rage of party, to still passion, to allow reason once more to resume its empire. . . .

Mr. President, it is passion, passion-party, party, and intemperance—that is all I dread in the adjustment of the great questions which unhappily at this time divide our distracted country. Sir, at this moment we have in the legislative bodies of this Capitol and in the States, twenty old furnaces in full blast, emitting heat, and passion, and intemperance, and diffusing them throughout the whole extent of this broad land. Two months ago all was calm in comparison to the present moment. All now is uproar, confusion, and menace to the existence of the Union, and to the happiness and safety of this people. . . .

Sir, when I came to consider this subject, there were two or three general purposes which it seemed to me to be most desirable, if possible, to accomplish. The one was, to settle all the contro-verted questions arising out of the subject of slavery. . . . I therefore turned my attention to every subject connected with this institution of slavery, and out of which controverted questions had sprung, to see if it were possible or practicable to accommodate and adjust the whole of them. . . .

We are told now, and it is rung throughout this entire country, that the Union is threatened with subversion and destruction. Well, the first question which naturally rises is, supposing the Union to be dissolved,—having all the causes of grievance which are complained of,—How far will a dissolution furnish a remedy for those grievances? If the Union is to be dissolved for any existing causes, it will be dissolved because slavery is interdicted or not allowed to be introduced into the ceded territories; because slavery is threatened to be abolished in the District of Columbia, and because fugitive slaves are not returned, as in my opinion they ought to be, and restored to their masters. These, I believe, will be the causes; if there be any causes, which can lead to the direful event to which I have referred. . . .

Mr. President, I am directly opposed to any purpose of secession, of separation. I am for staying within the Union, and defying any portion of this Union to expel or drive me out of the Union.

John C. Calhoun

March 4, 1850

Having now, Senators, explained what it is that endangers the Union, and traced it to its cause, and explained its nature and character, the question again recurs—How can the Union be saved? To this I answer, there is but one way by which it can be—and that is—by adopting such measures as will satisfy the States belonging to the Southern section, that they can remain in the Union consistently with their honor and their safety. . . .

But will the North agree to this? It is for her to answer the question. But, I will say, she cannot refuse, if she has half the love of the Union which she professes to have, or without justly exposing herself to the charge that her love of power and aggrandizement is far greater than her love of the Union. At all events, the responsibility of saving the Union rests on the North, and not on the South. . . .

Daniel Webster

March 7, 1850

Mr. President: I wish to speak to-day, not as a Massachusetts man, nor as a Northern man, but as an American, and a member of the Senate of the United States. . . .

I speak to-day for the preservation of the Union. "Hear me for my cause." I speak to-day, out of a solicitous and anxious heart, for the restoration to the country of that quiet and that harmony which make the blessing of this Union so rich, and so dear to us all. . . . I shall bestow a little attention, Sir, upon these various grievances existing on the one side and on the other. I begin with complaints of the South . . . and especially to one which has in my opinion just foundation; and that is, that there has been found at the North, among individuals and among legislators, a disinclination to perform fully their constitutional duties in regard to the return of persons bound to service who have escaped into the free States. In that respect, the South, in my judgment, is right, and the North is wrong. Every member of every Northern legislature is bound by oath, like every other officer in the country, to support the Constitution of the United States; and the article of the Constitution which says to these States they shall deliver up fugitives from service is as binding in honor and conscience as any other article. . . .

Where is the line to be drawn? What States are to secede? What is to remain American? What am I to be? An American no longer? Am I to become a sectional man, a local man, a separatist, with no country in common with the gentlemen who sit around me here, or who fill the other house of Congress? Heaven forbid! Where is the flag of the republic to remain? Where is the eagle still to tower? or is he to cower, and shrink, and fall to the ground?

Democrats, liking popular sovereignty because it could mean all things to all people, nominated Cass for president in 1848. Cass denounced abolitionists and the Wilmot Proviso but otherwise avoided the issue of slavery. The Democrats, however, cleverly printed two campaign biographies of Cass, one for the South and one for the North.

The Whigs found an even better way to hold the party together by evading the slavery issue. Rejecting Henry Clay, they nominated the Mexican-American War hero General Zachary Taylor, a Louisiana slaveholder. Taylor compared himself with Washington as a "no party" man above politics. This was about all he stood for. Southern Whigs supported Taylor because they thought he might understand the burdens of slaveholding, and northern Whigs were pleased that he took no stand on the Wilmot Proviso.

The evasions of the two major parties disappointed Calhoun, who tried to create a new, unified southern party. His "Address to the People of the Southern States" threatened secession and called for a united stand against further attempts to interfere with the southern right to extend slavery. Although only 48 of 121 southern representatives signed the address, Calhoun's argument raised the specter of secession and disunion.

Warnings also came from the North. A New York Democratic faction bolted to support Van Buren for president. At first, the split had more to do with internal state politics than moral principles, but it soon involved the question of slavery in the territories. Disaffected "conscience" Whigs from Massachusetts, unhappy with a slaveholder as their party standard-bearer, also explored a third-party alternative. These groups met in Buffalo, New York, to form the Free-Soil party and nominate Van Buren for president. The platform of the new party, an uneasy mixture of ardent abolitionists and opponents of free blacks moving into western lands, pledged to fight for "free soil, free speech, free labor and free men."

General Taylor won easily, largely because defections from Cass to the Free-Soilers cost the Democrats New York and Pennsylvania. Although weakened, the two-party system survived. Purely sectional parties had failed. The Free-Soilers took only about 10 percent of the popular vote, and no electoral votes.

The Compromise of 1850

Taylor won the election by avoiding slavery questions. But as president, he had to deal with them. When he was inaugurated in 1849, four compelling issues faced the nation. First, the rush of some 80,000 gold miners to California qualified it for statehood. But California's entry as a free state would upset the balance between slave and free states in the Senate that had prevailed since 1820.

Henry Clay argues for the compromise package of 1850 in this painting by R. Whitechurch, entitled *The United States Senate, 1850.* Clay warned that failure to adopt his bill would lead to "furious" and "bloody" civil war. *(Library of Congress)*

The Compromise of 1850

"I have seen many periods of great anxiety, of peril, and of danger in this country," Henry Clay told the Congress in February 1850, "and I have never before risen to address any assemblage so oppressed, so appalled, and so anxious." What followed were the debates that led eventually to the passage of the Compromise of 1850. Can you find three of the four major parts of the bill on the map? What was the fourth?

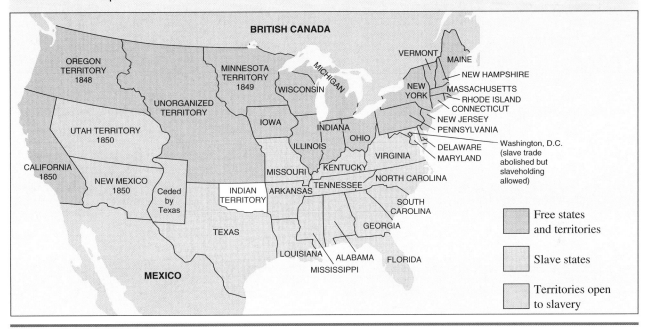

The unresolved status of the Mexican cession in the Southwest posed a second problem. The longer the area remained unorganized, the louder local inhabitants called for an application of either the Wilmot Proviso or the Calhoun doctrine. The Texas–New Mexico boundary was also disputed, with Texas claiming everything east of Santa Fe. Northerners feared that Texas might split into five or six slave states.

A third problem, especially for abolitionists, was the existence of slavery and one of the largest slave markets in North America in the nation's capital. Fourth, southerners resented the lax federal enforcement of the Fugitive Slave Act of 1793. They called for a stronger act that would end protection for runaways fleeing to Canada.

Although Taylor was a newcomer to politics (he had never even voted in a presidential election before 1848), he tackled these problems in a statesmanlike, if evasive, manner. Sidestepping the issue of slavery in the territories, he invited California and New Mexico to apply immediately for statehood, presumably as free states. But soon he alienated both southern supporters such as Calhoun and mainstream Whig leaders such as Clay and Webster.

Early in 1850, the old compromiser Henry Clay sought to regain control of the Whig party by proposing solutions to the divisive issues before the nation. With Webster's support, Clay introduced a series of resolutions in an omnibus package intended to settle these issues once and for all. The stormy debates, great speeches, and political maneuvering that followed provided a crucial and dramatic moment in American history. Despite some 70 speeches on behalf of the compromise, the Senate defeated Clay's Omnibus Bill. The tired and disheartened 73-year-old Clay left Washington, hoping to regain his strength. He never did, and soon died. Into the gap stepped Senator Stephen Douglas of Illinois, who saw that Clay's resolutions had a better chance of passing if voted on individually. Under Douglas's leadership, and with the support of Millard Fillmore, who succeeded to the presidency upon Taylor's sudden death, a series of bills was finally passed.

The Compromise of 1850 put Clay's resolutions, slightly altered, into law. First, California entered the Union as a free state, ending the balance of free and slave states, 16 to 15. Second, territorial governments were organized in New Mexico and Utah, letting local people decide whether to permit slavery. The Texas–New Mexico border was settled, denying

Texas the disputed area. In return, the federal government gave Texas $10 million to pay debts owed to Mexico. Third, the slave trade, but not slavery, was abolished in the District of Columbia.

The fourth and most controversial part of the compromise was the Fugitive Slave Act, containing many provisions that offended northerners. One denied alleged fugitives a jury trial, leaving special cases for decision by commissioners (who were paid $5 for setting a fugitive free but $10 for returning a fugitive). An especially repugnant provision compelled northern citizens to help catch runaways.

Consequences of Compromise

The Compromise of 1850 was the last attempt to keep slavery out of politics. Voting behavior on the different bills varied, with legislators following sectional lines on some issues and party lines on others. Douglas felt pleased with his "final settlement" of the slavery question.

But the compromise only delayed more serious sectional conflict, and it added two new ingredients to American politics. First, political realignment along sectional lines moved closer. Second, although repudiated by most ordinary citizens, ideas like secessionism, disunion, and a "higher law" than the Constitution entered political discussions.

People wondered whether the question of slavery in the territories could be compromised away the next time it arose.

Others were immediately upset. The new fugitive slave law angered many northerners because it brought the evils of slavery right into their midst. The owners of runaway slaves hired agents, labeled "kidnappers" in the North, to hunt down fugitives. In a few dramatic episodes, most notably in Boston, literary and religious intellectuals led mass protests to resist slave hunters. When Senator Webster supported the law, New England abolitionists denounced him as "indescribably base and wicked." Theodore Parker called the new law a "hateful statute of kidnappers," and Ralph Waldo Emerson said he would not obey the "filthy law."

Frederick Douglass would not obey it either. As a runaway slave himself, he was threatened with arrest and return to the South until friends overcame his objections and purchased his freedom. Douglass still risked harm by his strong defiance of the Fugitive Slave Act. Arguing the "rightfulness of forcible resistance," he urged free blacks to arm themselves and even wondered whether it was justifiable to kill kidnappers. "The only way to make the Fugitive Slave Law a dead letter," he said in Pittsburgh in 1853, "is to make a half dozen or more dead kidnappers." Douglass raised money for black

As a group of runaways makes its way north in this painting by Theodor Kaufmann entitled *On to Liberty* (1867), the peril of the journey, even if successful, is reflected in this broadside published by Boston abolitionist Theodore Parker, which alerted the city's black community in 1851 to the dangers posed by the Fugitive Slave Act. *(left: The Metropolitan Museum of Art, gift of Erving and Joyce Wolf, 1982 [1982.443.3]; right: Chicago Public Library)*

fugitives, hid runaways in his home, helped hundreds escape to Canada, and supported black organizations such as the League of Freedom in Boston.

Other northerners, white and black, stepped up their work for the Underground Railroad and helped runaway slaves evade capture. Several states passed "personal liberty laws" that prohibited the use of state officials and institutions in the recovery of fugitive slaves. But most northerners complied. Of some 200 blacks arrested in the first six years of the law, only 15 were rescued, and only 3 of these by force. Failed rescues, in fact, had more emotional impact than successful ones. In two cases in the early 1850s (Thomas Sims in 1851 and Anthony Burns in 1854), angry mobs of abolitionists in Boston, reminiscent of the pre-revolutionary days of the Tea Party, failed to prevent the forcible return of blacks to the South. These celebrated cases aroused antislavery emotions in more northerners than the abolitionists had been able to do in all their tracts and speeches. Amos Lawrence, a textile tycoon in Massachusetts, wrote of the trial of Anthony Burns that sent him back to the South: "We went to bed one night old fashioned, conservative Compromise Union Whigs and waked up stark mad abolitionists."

Longtime abolitionists escalated their rhetoric, fueling emotions over slavery in the aftermath of the Fugitive Slave Act. In an Independence Day speech in 1852, Frederick Douglass wondered, "What, to the American slave, is your 4th of July?" It was, he said, the day that revealed to the slave the "gross injustice and cruelty to which he is the constant victim." To a slave, the American claims of national greatness were vain and empty; the "shouts of liberty and equality" were "hollow mockery, . . . mere bombast, fraud, deception, impiety, and hypocrisy." Douglass's speeches, like those of the former slave Sojourner Truth, took on an increasingly strident tone in the early 1850s.

At a women's rights convention in Akron, Ohio, in 1851, Truth made one of the decade's boldest statements for minority rights. The convention was attended by clergymen who heckled female speakers. Up stood Sojourner Truth to speak in words still debated by historians. She pointed to her many years of childbearing and hard, backbreaking work as a slave, crying out in a repetitive refrain, "And ar'n't I a woman?" Referring to Jesus, she asked where he came from: "From God and a woman: Man had nothing to do with Him." Referring to Eve, she concluded, "If the first woman God ever made was strong enough to turn the world upside down all alone, these women together ought to be able to turn it back, and get it right side up again! And now

they is asking to do it, the men better let them." Her speech silenced the hecklers.

As Truth spoke, another American woman, Harriet Beecher Stowe, was finishing *Uncle Tom's Cabin,* a novel that would go far toward turning the world upside down and trying to right it again. As politicians were hoping the American people would forget slavery, Stowe's novel brought it to the attention of thousands. She gave readers an absorbing indictment of the horrors of slavery and its impact on both northerners and southerners. Published initially in serial form, each month's chapter ended at a nail-biting dramatic moment. Readers throughout the North cheered Eliza's daring escape across the ice floes on the Ohio River, cried over Uncle Tom's humanity and Little Eva's death, suffered under the lash of Simon Legree, and rejoiced in the reuniting of black family members.

Although it outraged the South when published in full in 1852, *Uncle Tom's Cabin* became one of the all-time best-sellers in American history. In the first year, over 300,000 copies were printed, and Stowe's novel was eventually published in 20 languages. When President Lincoln met Stowe in 1863, he is reported to have said to her: "So you're the little woman who wrote the book that made this great war!"

POLITICAL DISINTEGRATION

The response to *Uncle Tom's Cabin* and the Fugitive Slave Act indicated that politicians had congratulated themselves too soon for saving the Republic in 1850. Political developments, not all dealing with slavery, were already weakening the ability of political parties—and ultimately the nation—to withstand the passions slavery aroused.

Weakened Party Politics in the Early 1850s

As we see today, political parties seek to convince voters that their party stands for moral values and economic policies crucially different from those of the opposition. In the period between 1850 and 1854 (as perhaps now), these differences were blurred, thereby undermining party loyalty.

Both parties scrambled to convince voters that they had favored the Compromise of 1850. In addition, several states rewrote their constitutions and remodeled their laws in the early 1850s, standardizing many political and economic procedures. One effect of these changes was to reduce the number of patronage jobs that were available for party victors to dispense. Another effect was to regularize the process, begun in the 1830s, for securing banking,

Changing Political Party Systems and Leaders

It is characteristic of American politics that when the two major parties fail to respond to the pressing issues of the day, third parties are born and major party realignment occurs. This happened in the 1850s over the issue of slavery and its extension into the territories, which resulted in the collapse of the Whigs and the emergence of the Republican party. Note that the "Republican" party begins in one tradition and ends up in the other. Is political realignment happening again in American politics?

First Party System: 1790s–1820s

Republican	Federalist
Jefferson	Hamilton
Madison	John Adams
Monroe	

Transition: 1824 and 1828

Democrat-Republican	National Republican
Jackson	J. Q. Adams

Second Party System: 1830s–1850s

Democrat	Whig
Jackson	Clay
Van Buren	Webster
Calhoun	W. H. Harrison
Polk	

Third Party System: 1856–1890s

Democrat	Republican
Douglas	Lincoln
Pierce	Seward
Buchanan	Grant

railroad, and other corporate charters, removing the role formerly played by legislatures. Both of these weakened the importance of the party in citizens' lives.

Another development that weakened parties was economic. For almost a quarter of a century, Whigs and Democrats had disagreed over such issues as the tariff, money and banking systems, and government support for internal improvements. But economic conditions improved markedly in the early 1850s. In a time of prosperity, party distinctions over economic policies seemed less important. An ample money supply made the revenues of a high tariff less necessary. Moreover, in the rush for railroad charters during the boom of the early 1850s, local connections were more important than national party politics.

Economic issues persisted, but the battles were fought at the local rather than national level. Thus Georgia voters in 1851 disagreed over commercial banking laws, taxes for internal improvements, and, as an Augusta newspaper put it, "the jealousies of the poor who owned no slaves, against the rich

slaveholder." In Indiana, where Congressman George Julian observed that people "hate the Negro with a perfect if not a supreme hatred," legislators rewrote the state constitution in 1851, depriving blacks of the rights to vote, attend white schools, and make contracts. Those who could not post a $500 bond were expelled from the state, and an 1852 law made it a crime for blacks to settle in Indiana. In Massachusetts, temperance reform and a law limiting the working day to 10 hours were hot issues. Fleeting political alliances developed around particular issues and local personalities. As a Baltimore businessman said, "The two old parties are fast melting away."

The election of 1852 illustrated the lessening significance of political parties. The Whigs nominated General Winfield Scott, another Mexican-American War hero, who they hoped would repeat Taylor's success four years earlier. With Clay and Webster both dead, party leadership passed to Senator William Seward of New York, who wanted a president he could influence more successfully than the pro-southern Fillmore. Still, it took 52 ballots to nominate Scott over Fillmore, alienating southern Whigs. Democrats had their own problems choosing a candidate. After 49 ballots, the party turned to a lackluster compromise candidate, Franklin Pierce of New Hampshire.

The two parties offered little choice. Both played down issues so as not to widen intraparty divisions. Voter interest diminished. "Genl. Apathy is the strongest candidate out here," was the report from Ohio, while the Baltimore *Sun* remarked that "there is no issue that much interests the people." Democratic prospects were aided by thousands of new Catholic immigrants from Ireland and Germany, who could be naturalized and were eligible to vote after only three years. Democrats resorted to bribes and drinks to buy their support. Internal conflicts and defections seriously weakened the Whigs, and Pierce won easily, 254 to 42 electoral votes.

The Kansas-Nebraska Act

The Whig party's final disintegration came on a February day in 1854 when southern Whigs stood to support Stephen Douglas's Nebraska bill, thus choosing to be more southern than Whig. The Illinois senator had many reasons for introducing a bill organizing the Nebraska Territory (which included Kansas). As an ardent nationalist and chairman of the Committee on Territories, he was concerned for the continuing development of the West. As a solid citizen of Illinois in a period of explosive railroad building, he wanted the eastern terminus

In George Caleb Bingham's *Verdict of the People* (after 1855), the American flag flies proudly over a happy throng celebrating the outcome of the political process. However, the process of deciding the Kansas-Nebraska Act marked the collapse of the second party system and moved the Union a step closer to disruption and civil war. In an earlier version of the painting, the women on a hotel balcony in the upper right display a banner announcing (ironically?) "Freedom for Virtue." *(Courtesy of the R.W. Norton Art Gallery, Shreveport, Louisiana)*

for a transcontinental railroad in Chicago rather than in rival St. Louis. This meant organizing the lands west of Iowa and Missouri.

Politics also played a role. Douglas hoped to recapture the party leadership he had held in passing the Compromise of 1850. He also harbored presidential ambitions. Although he had replaced Cass as the great advocate of popular sovereignty, which won him favor among northern Democrats, he needed southern Democratic support. Many southerners, especially neighboring Missouri slaveholders, opposed organizing the Nebraska Territory unless it were open to slavery. The problem, as Douglas knew well, was that the entire Nebraska Territory lay north of the line where the Missouri Compromise had prohibited slavery.

Douglas's bill, introduced early in 1854, recommended using popular sovereignty in organizing the Kansas and Nebraska territories. This meant that inhabitants could vote slavery in, thereby violating the Missouri Compromise. Douglas reasoned, however, that the climate and soil of the prairies in Kansas and Nebraska would never support slavery-based agriculture, and the people would decide to be a free state. Therefore, he could win the votes he needed for the railroad without also getting slavery. By stating that the states created out of the Nebraska Territory would enter the Union "with or without slavery, as their constitution may prescribe at the time of their admission," his bill ignored the Missouri Compromise.

Douglas miscalculated. Northerners from his own party immediately attacked him and his bill as a "criminal betrayal of precious rights" and as part of a plot promoting his own presidential ambitions by turning free Nebraska over to "slavery despotism." The outrage among Whigs and abolitionists was even greater. Frederick Douglass branded the act a "hateful" attempt to extend slavery, the result of the "audacious villainy of the slave power."

But Stephen Douglas was a fighter. The more he was attacked, the harder he fought. Eventually his bill passed, but not without seriously damaging the political party system. What began as a railroad measure ended in reopening the question of slavery in the territories that Douglas and others had thought was finally settled in 1850. What began as a way of avoiding conflict ended up in violence over whether Kansas would enter the Union slave or free. What began as a way of strengthening party lines over issues ended up destroying one party (Whigs), planting deep, irreconcilable divisions in another (Democrats), and creating two new ones (Know-Nothings and Republicans).

Expansionist "Young America" in the Larger World

The Democratic party was weakened in the early 1850s not only by the Kansas-Nebraska Act but also by an ebullient, expansive energy that led Americans to adventures far beyond Kansas. As republican revolutions erupted in 1848 in Europe (Austria-Hungary,

Expansionist "Young America" in the 1850s: Attempted Raids into Latin America

Note the flurry of expansionist American raids and forays southward into Mexico and the Caribbean between the mid-1840s and mid-1850s. **Reflecting on the Past** What major events and motives caused the expansionist interest? Why was Cuba a key target?

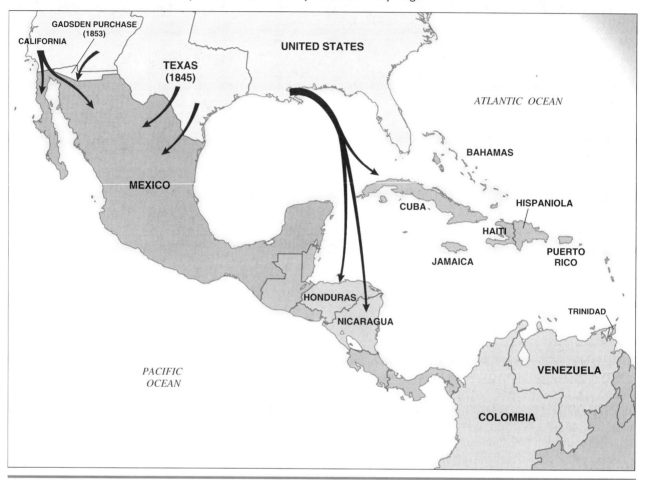

France, Germany) and had initial successes, Americans greeted them as evidence that the American model of free republican institutions was the wave of the future; they were disheartened when counterrevolutionary monarchial forces resumed control. Americans dedicated to the idea of a national mission, which ironically included the spread of slavery, were called "Young America." An early expression of the spirit of Young America was the enthusiastic reception given the exiled Hungarian revolutionary Louis Kossuth, who was fighting for an independent Hungary, while on a tour of the United States in 1851.

Pierce's platform in 1852 reflected American expansionist nationalism, declaring that the war with Mexico had been "just and necessary." Many Democrats took the overwhelming victory as a man-

date to continue adding territory to the Republic. A Philadelphia newspaper in 1853 described the United States as a nation bound on the "East by sunrise, West by sunset, North by the Arctic Expedition, and South as far as we darn please." Southward expansion into Latin America looked very attractive as those newly independent countries were wracked by internal and external disputes, struggling for power with the Catholic church, one of the largest landowners in the region, and with peasants over distribution of land.

Many of Pierce's diplomatic appointees were southerners interested in adding new cotton-growing lands to the national domain. Pierce's ambassador to Mexico, for example, South Carolinian James Gadsden, had instructions to negotiate with Mexican President Santa Anna for the acquisition of large parts of northern Mexico. Gadsden did not get all he wanted, but he did manage to purchase a strip of southwestern desert for a transcontinental railroad linking the Deep South with the Pacific Coast.

Failure to acquire more territory from Mexico legally did not discourage expansionist Americans from pursuing illegal means. During the 1850s, Texans and Californians staged dozens of raids (called "filibusters") into Mexico. The most daring adventurer of the era was William Walker, a 100-pound Tennessean with a zest for danger and power. After migrating to southern California, Walker made plans to add slave lands to the country. In 1853, he invaded Lower California (the Baja Peninsula) with fewer than 300 men and declared himself president of the independent Republic of Sonora. Although eventually arrested and tried in the United States, he was acquitted after eight minutes of deliberation.

Back Walker went, invading Nicaragua two years later. He overthrew the government, proclaimed himself an elected dictator, and issued a decree legalizing slavery. The Nicaraguans regained control with British help who, as the dominant influence in the Caribbean, sought to thwart Walker's efforts to further U. S. expansion. But the U.S. Navy rescued Walker. After a triumphant tour in the South, he tried twice more to conquer Nicaragua. Walker came to a fitting end in 1860 when, invading Honduras this time, he was captured and shot by a firing squad.

Undaunted by failures in the Southwest, the Pierce administration looked to the acquisition of Cuba. Many Americans thought this Spanish colony was destined for U.S. annexation and would be an ideal place for expanding the slave-based economy. Some argued that Cuba belonged to the United States because it was physically connected by alluvial deposits from the Mississippi River. "What God has joined together let no man put asunder," one said.

In the 1840s, the Polk administration had offered $10 million for Cuba, but Spain had refused the offer. Unsuccessful efforts were then made to foment a revolution among Cuban sugar planters, who were expected to request annexation by the United States. One Latin adventurer organized an invasion of Cuba, launched from New Orleans in 1850. When his attempt failed, he was executed, and hundreds of captured comrades were sent to Spain. The citizens of New Orleans rioted in protest, storming the Spanish consulate, which forced an embarrassed Congress to pay an indemnity. A few years later, a former governor of Mississippi, with the support of his friend, Secretary of War Jefferson Davis, planned

to raise $1 million and 50,000 troops to invade the island. The proposed expedition, intended to carve Cuba into several new slave states, was aborted.

Although President Pierce did not support these illegal efforts, his administration did want Cuba. Secretary of State William Marcy instructed the emissary to Spain, Pierre Soulé, to offer $130 million for Cuba, upping the price. If that failed, Marcy suggested stronger measures. In 1854, the secretary arranged for Soulé and the American ministers to France and England to meet in Belgium, where they issued the Ostend Manifesto to pressure Spain to sell Cuba to the United States.

The manifesto argued that Cuba "belongs naturally" to the United States. Both geographically and economically, the fortunes and interests of Cubans and southerners were so "blended" that they were "one people with one destiny." Trade and commerce in the hemisphere would "never be secure" until Cuba was part of the United States. Moreover, southern slaveholders feared that a slave rebellion would "Africanize" Cuba, like Haiti, suggesting all kinds of "horrors to the white race" in the nearby southern United States. The American acquisition of Cuba was necessary, therefore, to "preserve our rectitude and self-respect." If Spain refused to sell, the ministers at Ostend threatened a Cuban revolution with American support. If that failed, "we should be justified in wresting it from Spain."

Even Secretary Marcy was shocked when he received the document from Belgium, and he quickly rejected it. Like the Kansas-Nebraska Act, Democrats supported the Ostend Manifesto in order to further the expansion of slavery. The outraged reaction of northerners in both cases divided and further weakened the Democratic Party.

Nativism, Know-Nothings, and Republicans

Foreign immigration damaged an already enfeebled Whig party and created concern among many native-born Americans. To the average hardworking Protestant American, the foreigners pouring into the cities and following the railroads westward spoke unfamiliar languages, wore funny clothes, drank alcohol freely, and bred crime and pauperism. Moreover, they seemed content with a lower standard of living by working for lower wages and thus threatened to take jobs away from American workers.

Worst of all from the Protestant perspective, Irish and German immigrants spearheaded an unprecedented growth of American Catholicism. By the

The American (Know-Nothing) party campaign against the immigrants is shown dramatically in this cartoon of a whiskey-drinking Irishman and beer-barreled German stealing the ballot box while native-born Americans fight at the election poll in the background. The Know-Nothing flag (right) makes starkly clear the origin of the danger. One can only imagine what American Indians thought of this banner. *(cartoon: New York Public Library, Astor, Lenox & Tilden Foundations; photo: Courtesy of the Milwaukee County Historical Society)*

1850s, there were nearly 3 million Catholics in the United States, not only in eastern cities but expanding westward into the Ohio valley (Germans in Wheeling, Cincinnati, and St. Louis) and along old French-Canadian trade routes through Detroit, Green Bay, and Vincennes. A surprising and, to many, disturbing development was Catholic success in converting Protestants. As one Catholic explained, it was "a time when great throngs of Americans began to flock to the Roman Catholic Church despite bitterly intense propaganda and overt opposition."

Two notable conversions in 1844 compelled Protestant Americans to take the threat seriously. Orestes Brownson, a lifelong Jacksonian Democrat and spiritual seeker, moved successively through Congregationalism, Presbyterianism, Unitarianism, and Transcendentalism until finally converting to a Catholicism he argued was fully compatible with democracy. His disciple, the Methodist German immigrant Isaac Hecker, converted to Catholicism two months earlier in 1844. Joining the Redemptorist order, Hecker served poor German immigrants and, with papal permission, shifted in the 1850s to the active recruiting of Protestants.

Led by the Redemptorists and Jesuits, over 400 parish mission revivals and retreats were held in the 1850s in an aggressive effort to convert urban American Protestants to Roman Catholicism. "All America can be reformed," one religious superior told a group of seminarians in 1856, calling them "instruments in the hands of God which He will use to effect a wonderful change—a spiritual revolution in this country." Sending their children to Catholic schools offended Protestants. Perhaps worst of all, many charged that Catholic immigrants corrupted American politics.

Most Catholics preferred the Democratic party out of traditional loyalties and because Democrats were less inclined than Whigs to interfere with religion, schooling, drinking, and other aspects of personal behavior. It was mostly former Whigs, therefore, who in 1854 founded the American party to oppose the new immigrants. Members wanted a longer period of naturalization to guarantee the "vital principles of Republican Government" and pledged never to vote for Irish Catholics, whose highest loyalty was supposedly to the pope. They also agreed to keep information about their order secret. If asked, they would say, "I know nothing." Hence, they were dubbed the Know-Nothing party.

The Know-Nothings appealed to the middle and lower classes—workers worried about their jobs and to farmers and small-town Americans nervous about disruptive new forces in their lives. A New Yorker said in 1854, "Roman Catholicism is feared more than American slavery." It was widely believed

The Emerging Third-Party System: Presidential Elections, 1852–1860

Year	Candidates	Party	Popular Vote	Electoral Vote
1852	FRANKLIN PIERCE	Democrat	1,601,474 (51%)	254
	Winfield Scott	Whig	1,386,578 (44%)	42
	John P. Hale	Free-Soil	156,149 (5%)	0
1856	JAMES BUCHANAN	Democrat	1,838,169 (45%)	174
	John C. Frémont	Republican	1,335,264 (33%)	114
	Millard Fillmore	American	874,534 (22%)	8
1860	ABRAHAM LINCOLN	Republican	1,866,352 (40%)	180
	Steven A. Douglas	Democrat	1,375,157 (29%)	12
	John C. Breckinridge	Democrat	847,953 (18%)	72
	John Bell	Constitutional Union	589,581 (13%)	39

Note: Winners' names appear in capital letters.

that Catholics slavishly obeyed the orders of their priests, who represented a Church associated with European despotism. The opposition of the Catholic church to the revolutionary movements of 1848 in Europe intensified the fears of many Protestant Americans that Catholic voters and the Catholic revivals deeply threatened their democratic order. The call to parish missions by Hecker to "make Yankeedom the Rome of the modern world" confirmed their fears. In the 1854 and 1855 elections, the Know-Nothings gave anti-Catholicism a national, political focus for the first time.

To other northerners, however, the "slave power" seemed a more serious threat. No sooner had the debates over Nebraska ended than a group of former Whigs and Free-Soilers met and formed the nucleus of another new party, called the Republican party. Concerned about southern expansionism, as reflected in the Kansas-Nebraska Act, the Ostend Manifesto, and plans to build a transcontinental railroad from the South to California on land acquired in the Gadsden Purchase, the party sought to respond to popular sentiments by mobilizing sectional fears and ethnic and religious concerns.

Composed almost entirely of northerners, former "conscience" Whigs, and disaffected Democrats, the Republican party combined four main elements. The first group—led by William Seward and Charles Sumner of Massachusetts and Salmon P. Chase and Joshua Giddings of Ohio—was fired by a moral fervor to prohibit slavery in the territories. They also sought to divorce the federal government from the support of slavery by freeing slaves in the District of Columbia, repealing the Fugitive Slave Act, and eliminating the internal slave trade. There were, however, limits to the idealism of most Republicans. A more moderate and larger group, typified by

Abraham Lincoln of Illinois, opposed slavery in the western territories only but would not interfere with it where it already existed. This group also opposed equal rights for northern free blacks.

Many Republicans were anti-Catholic as well as antislavery. A third element of the party, true to traditional Whig reformist and revivalist impulses, wanted to cleanse America of its sins of intemperance, impiety, parochial schooling, and other forms of immorality. Another evil included voting for Democrats, who catered to the "grog shops, foreign vote, and Catholic brethren" and combined the "forces of Jesuitism and Slavery."

The fourth element of the Republican party, a Whig legacy from Henry Clay's American System, included those who wanted the federal government to promote commercial and industrial development. This fourth group not only supported economic growth but also idealized free labor, believing that both led to progress. At the heart of both the new party and the future of America, Republicans proclaimed, were hardworking, middle-class, mobile, free white laborers—farmers, small businessmen, and independent craftsmen. Lincoln's home town paper, the Springfield *Republican,* said in 1856 that the Republican party's strength came from "those who work with their hands, who live and act independently, who hold the stakes of home and family, of farm and workshop, of education and freedom."

The strengths of the Republican and Know-Nothing (American) parties were tested in 1856. Which party could best oppose the Democrats? The American party nominated Fillmore, who had strong support in the Upper South and border states. The Republicans chose John C. Frémont, an ardent Free-Soiler from Missouri with virtually no political experience but with a military record against Mexicans in California. The Democrats nominated James Buchanan of Pennsylvania, a "northern man with southern principles." Frémont carried several free states, while Fillmore took only Maryland. Buchanan, benefiting from a divided opposition, won with only 45 percent of the popular vote.

After 1856, the Know-Nothings died out, largely because Republican leaders cleverly redirected nativist fears—and voters—to their broader program. Moreover, Know-Nothing secrecy, hatreds, and occasional violent attacks on Catholic voters damaged their image. Still, the Know-Nothings represented a powerful current in American politics that would return each time social and economic changes seemed to threaten the nation. It became convenient to label certain people "un-American" and try to root them out. The Know-Nothing party disappeared after 1856, but nativism did not.

KANSAS AND THE TWO CULTURES

The slavery issue also would not go away. As Democrats sought to expand slavery and other American institutions westward across the Plains and south into Cuba, Republicans wanted to halt the advance of slavery to prove to the world, as Seward said, that the American "experiment in self-government" still worked. In 1854, Lincoln worried that it was slavery that "deprives our republican example of its just influence in the world." The specific cause of his concern was the likelihood that slavery might be extended into Kansas as a result of the passage that year of Stephen Douglas's Kansas-Nebraska Act.

Competing for Kansas

During the congressional debates over the Nebraska bill, Seward accepted the challenge of slave-state senators to "engage in competition for the virgin soil of Kansas." Passage of the Kansas-Nebraska Act in 1854 opened the way for proslavery and antislavery forces to clash over Kansas. No sooner had the bill passed Congress than the Massachusetts Emigrant Aid Society was founded to recruit free-soil settlers for Kansas. Frederick Douglass called for "companies of emigrants from the free states . . . to possess the goodly land." By the summer of 1855, about 1,200 New England colonists had migrated to Kansas.

One migrant was Julia Louisa Lovejoy, a Vermont minister's wife. As a riverboat carried her into a slave state for the first time, she described the dilapidated plantation homes on the monotonous Missouri shore as the "blighting mildew of slavery." By the time she and her husband arrived in the Kansas Territory, Julia had concluded that the "morals" of the slaveholding Missourians moving into Kansas were of an "*undescribably repulsive* and undesirable character." To her, northerners came to bring the "energetic Yankee" virtues of morality and economic enterprise to drunken, unclean slaveholders.

Perhaps she had in mind David Atchison, Democratic senator from Missouri. Atchison believed that Congress must protect slavery in the territories, allowing Missouri slaveholders into Kansas. In 1853, he pledged "to extend the institutions of Missouri over the Territory at whatever sacrifice of blood or treasure." He described New England migrants as "negro thieves" and "abolition tyrants." He recommended to fellow Missourians that they defend their property and interests "with the *bayonet* and with *blood*" and, if need be, "to kill every God-damned abolitionist in the district."

Under Atchison's inflammatory leadership, secret societies sprang up in the Missouri counties adjacent to Kansas dedicated to combatting the Free-Soilers. One editor exclaimed that northerners came to Kansas "for the express purpose of stealing, running off and hiding runaway negroes from Missouri [and] taking to their own bed . . . a stinking negro wench." Not slaveholders, he said, but New Englanders, were immoral, uncivilized, and hypocritical. Rumors of 20,000 such Massachusetts migrants spurred Missourians to action. Thousands poured across the border late in 1854 to vote on permitting slavery in the territory. Twice as many ballots were cast as the number of registered voters; in one polling place only 20 of over 600 voters were legal residents.

The proslavery forces overreacted to their fear of the New Englanders. The permanent population of Kansas consisted primarily of migrants from Missouri and other border states—people more concerned with land titles than slavery. They opposed any blacks—slave or free—moving into their state. As one clergyman put it, "I kem to Kansas to live in a free state and I don't want niggers a-trampin' over my grave."

In March 1855, a second election was held to select a territorial legislature. The pattern of border crossings, intimidation, and illegal voting was repeated. Atchison himself, drinking "considerable whiskey," led an armed band across the state line to vote and frighten away would-be free-soil voters. Not surprisingly, swollen numbers of illegal voters elected a proslavery tritorial legislature. Free-

Soilers, meanwhile, held their own convention in Lawrence and created a free-soil government at Topeka. It banned blacks from the state. The proslavery legislature settled in Lecompton, giving Kansas two governments.

The struggle shifted to Washington. President Pierce could have nullified the illegal election, but he did nothing. Congress debated the wrongs in Kansas and sent an investigating committee, further inflaming passions. Throughout 1855, the call to arms grew more strident. One proslavery newspaper invited southerners to bring their weapons and "send the scoundrels" from the North "back to whence they came, or . . . to hell, it matters not which." In South Carolina, Robert Allston wrote his son Benjamin that he was "raising men and money . . . to counteract the effect of the Northern hordes. . . . We are disposed to fight the battle of our rights . . . on the field of Kansas."

Both sides saw Kansas as a holy battleground. An Alabama Colonel sold his slaves to raise money to hire an army of 300 men to fight for slavery in Kansas, promising free land to his recruits. A Baptist minister blessed their departure from Montgomery, promised them God's favor, and gave each man a Bible. Northern Christians responded in kind. At Yale University, the noted minister Henry Ward Beecher presented 25 Bibles and 25 Sharps rifles to young men who would go fight for the Lord in Kansas. "There are times," he said, "when self-defense is a religious duty. If that duty was ever imperative it is now, and in Kansas." Beecher suggested that rifles would be of greater use than Bibles. Missourians dubbed them "Beecher's Bibles" and vowed, as one newspaper put it, "Blood for Blood!"

"Bleeding Kansas"

As civil war threatened in Kansas, a Brooklyn poet, Walt Whitman, heralded American democracy in his epic poem *Leaves of Grass* (1855). Whitman identified himself as the embodiment of average Americans "of every hue and caste, . . . of every rank and religion." Ebulliently, Whitman embraced urban mechanics, southern woodcutters, planters' sons, runaway slaves, mining camp prostitutes, and a long list of others in his poetic celebration of "the word Democratic, the word En-Masse." But Whitman's faith in the American masses faltered in the mid-1850s. He worried that a knife plunged into the "breast" of the Union would bring on the "red blood of civil war."

Blood indeed flowed in Kansas. In May 1856, supported by a pro-southern federal marshal, a mob entered Lawrence, smashed the offices and presses of a free-soil newspaper, fired several cannonballs into the Free State Hotel, and destroyed homes and

Led by Senator David Atchison, thousands of gun-toting Missourians crossed into Kansas in 1854 and 1855 to vote illegally for a proslavery territorial government. The ensuing bloodshed made Kansas a preview of the Civil War. *(The Newberry Library, Chicago)*

"Bleeding Kansas"

Sites of violence in the divided territory.

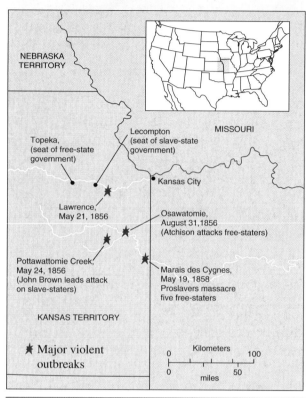

Major violent outbreaks

shops. Three nights later, believing he was doing God's will, John Brown led a small New England band, including four of his sons, to a proslavery settlement near Pottawatomie Creek. There they dragged five men out of their cabins and, despite the terrified entreaties of their wives, hacked them to death with swords.

Violence also entered the halls of Congress. That same week, abolitionist Senator Charles Sumner delivered a tirade known as "The Crime Against Kansas." He lashed out at the "murderous robbers" and "incredible atrocities of the Assassins and . . . Thugs" from the South. He accused proslavery Senate leaders, especially Atchison and Andrew Butler of South Carolina, of cavorting with the "harlot, Slavery." Two days later, Butler's nephew, Congressman Preston Brooks, avenged the honor of his colleague by beating Sumner senseless with his cane as he sat at his Senate desk.

The sack of Lawrence, the massacre at Pottawatomie Creek, and the caning of Sumner set off a minor civil war that historians have called "Bleeding Kansas." It lasted throughout the summer. Crops were burned, homes were destroyed, fights broke out in saloons and streets, and night raiders

tortured and murdered their enemies. For residents like Charles Lines, who just wanted to farm his land in peace, it was impossible to remain neutral. Lines hoped his neighbors near Lawrence would avoid "involving themselves in trouble." But when proslavery forces tortured to death a mild-mannered neighbor, Lines joined the battle. "Blood," he wrote, "must end in the triumph of the right."

Even before the bleeding of Kansas began, the New York *Tribune* warned, "We are two peoples. We are a people for Freedom and a people for Slavery. Between the two, conflict is inevitable." As the rhetoric and violence in Kansas demonstrated, competing visions of two separate cultures for the future destiny of the United States were at stake. Despite many similarities between the North and the South, the gap between the two sides widened with the hostilities of the 1850s.

Northern Views and Visions

As Julia Lovejoy suggested, the North saw itself as a prosperous land of bustling commerce and expanding, independent agriculture. Northern farmers and workers were self-made free men and women who believed in individualism and democracy. The "free labor system" of the North, as both Seward and Lincoln often said, offered equality of opportunity and upward mobility. Both generated more wealth. Although the North contained many growing cities, northerners revered the values of the small towns that spread from New England across the Upper Midwest. These values included a respect for the rights of the people, tempered by the rule of law; individual enterprise, balanced by a concern for one's neighbors; and a fierce morality rooted in Calvinist Protestantism. Northerners would regulate morality—by persuasion if possible but by legislation if necessary—to purge irreligion, illiteracy, and intemperance from American society. It was no accident that the ideas of universal public education and laws against the sale and consumption of alcohol both began in New England.

Northerners valued the kind of republican government that guaranteed the rights of free men, enabling them to achieve economic progress. This belief supported government action to promote free labor, industrial growth, some immigration, foreign trade (protected by tariffs), and the extension of railroads and free farm homesteads westward across the continent. Energetic mobility, both westward and upward, would dissolve state, regional, and class loyalties and increase the sense of nationhood. A strong Union could achieve national and even international greatness. These were the conditions befitting a chosen people that would, as Seward put it, spread American institutions around the world and "renovate the condition of mankind." These were the principles of the Republican party.

Only free men could achieve economic progress and moral society. In northerner's eyes, therefore, the worst sin was the loss of one's freedom. Slavery was the root of all evil. It was, Seward said, "incompatible with all . . . the elements of the security, welfare, and greatness of nations." The South was the antithesis of everything that northerners saw as good. Southerners were backward, economically stagnant, uneducated, lawless, immoral, and in conflict with the values and ideals of the nineteenth century. Julia Lovejoy's denunciation of slaveholding Missourians was mild. Other migrants to Kansas saw southerners as subhuman, unclean, and uncivilized. They were, as one put it, "drunken ourangoutans," "wild beasts" who drank whiskey, ate dirt, uttered oaths, raped slave women, and fought or dueled at the slightest excuse. In the slang of the day, they were "Pukes."

The Southern Perspective

Southerners were a diverse people who, like northerners, shared certain broad values, generally those of the planter class. If in the North the values of economic enterprise were most important, southerners revered social values most. They admired the English gentry and saw themselves as courteous, refined, hospitable, honorable, and chivalrous. By contrast, they saw northern "Yankees" as coarse, ill-mannered, aggressive, and materialistic. In a society where one person in three was a black slave, racial distinctions and paternalistic relationships were crucial in maintaining order and white supremacy. Fear of slave revolt was ever-present. The South had five times more military schools than the North. Northerners educated the many for economic utility; southerners educated the few for grace and character. In short, the white South saw itself as an ordered society guided by the planters' genteel code.

Southerners agreed with northerners that sovereignty in a republic rested in the people, who created a government of laws to protect life, liberty, and property. But unlike people in the North, southerners believed that the democratic principle of self-government was best preserved in local political units such as the states. Southerners were ready to fight to defend their sacred rights against any tyrannical encroachment on their liberty, as they had in 1776. They saw themselves as true revolutionary patriots. Like northerners, southerners

cherished the Union. But they preferred the loose confederacy of the Jeffersonian past to the centralized nationalism Seward kept invoking.

To southerners, Yankees were in too much of a hurry—to make money, to reform the behavior of others, to put dreamy theories (like racial equality) into practice. Two images dominated the South's view of northerners: either they were stingy, hypocritical, moralizing Puritans, or they were grubby, slum-dwelling, Catholic immigrants. A Georgia paper combined both images in an 1856 editorial: "Free society! we sicken at the name. What is it but a conglomeration of greasy mechanics, filthy operatives, small-fisted farmers, and moon-struck theorists?" These northerners, the paper said, "are devoid of society fitted for well-bred gentlemen."

Each side, then, saw the other threatening its freedom and degrading proper republican society. Each saw the other imposing barriers to its vision for America's future, which included the economic systems described in Chapters 10 and 11. As hostilities rose, the views each section had of the other grew steadily more rigid and conspiratorial. Northerners saw the South as a "slave power," determined to foist the slave system on free labor throughout the land. Southerners saw the North as full of "black Republicanism," determined to destroy their way of life.

POLARIZATION AND THE ROAD TO WAR

The struggle over Kansas solidified the image of the Republicans as a northern party and seriously weakened the Democrats. Further events, still involving the question of slavery in the territories, split the Democratic party irrevocably into sectional halves: the Dred Scott decision of the Supreme Court (1857), the constitutional crisis in Kansas (1857), the Lincoln–Douglas debates in Illinois (1858), John Brown's raid in Virginia (1859), and Lincoln's election (1860). These incidents further polarized the negative images each culture held of the other and accelerated the nation down the final road to civil war.

The Dred Scott Case

The events of 1857 reinforced the arguments of those who believed in a slave power conspiracy. Two days after James Buchanan's inauguration, the Supreme Court finally ruled in *Dred Scott* v. *Sanford*. The case had been pending before the Court for nearly three years, longer for the Scott slave family. Back in 1846, Dred and Harriet Scott had filed suit in

These scenes illustrate the contrasting socioeconomic cultures of the antebellum North and South. Chicago (top) was a rapidly growing, bustling northern city in the 1850s; situated on the Great Lakes and a developing railroad hub, Chicago became the distribution center for industrial and agricultural goods throughout the Midwest. The vital unit of southern commerce was, by contrast, the individual plantation (bottom), with steamboats and flatboats carrying cotton and sugar to port cities for trade with Europe. *(top: Corbis; bottom: Library of Congress)*

Missouri for their freedom. They argued that their master had taken them into Minnesota, Wisconsin, and other territories where the Missouri Compromise prohibited slavery, and therefore they should be freed. By the time the case reached the Supreme Court, the issue of slavery in the territories was a hot political issue.

When the Court, with its southern majority, issued a 7-2 decision, it made three rulings. First, because blacks were, as Chief Justice Roger Taney put it, "beings of an inferior order [who] had no rights which white men were bound to respect," Dred

Scott was not a citizen and had no right to sue in federal courts. Justice Peter Daniel of Virginia was even more indelicate in his consenting opinion, saying that the "African Negro race" did not belong "to the family of nations" but rather was a subject for "commerce or traffic." The second ruling stated that the Missouri Compromise was unconstitutional because Congress had no power to ban slavery in a territory. Third, the court decided that taking the Scotts in and out of free states did not affect their status. Despite two eloquent dissenting opinions, Dred and Harriet Scott remained slaves.

The implications of these decisions went far beyond the Scotts' personal freedom. The arguments about black citizenship infuriated many black and white northerners. Frederick Douglass called the ruling "a most scandalous and devilish perversion of the Constitution, and a brazen misstatement of the facts of history." Many citizens worried about the few rights free blacks still held. Even more troubling, the decision hinted that slavery might be legal in the free states of the North. People who suspected a conspiracy were not calmed when Buchanan endorsed the Dred Scott decision as a final settlement of the right of citizens to take their "property of any kind, including slaves, into the common Territories . . . and to have it protected there under the Federal Constitution." Rather than settling the political issue of slavery in the territories, as Buchanan had hoped, the Dred Scott decision threw it back into American politics, opened new questions, and further intensified sectional hostilities.

Constitutional Crisis in Kansas

The *Dred Scott* decision and Buchanan's endorsement fed northern suspicions of a slave power conspiracy to impose slavery everywhere. Events in Kansas, which still had two governments, heightened these fears. In the summer of 1857, Kansas had yet another election, with so many irregularities that only 2,000 out of a possible 24,000 voters participated. A proslavery slate of delegates was elected to a constitutional convention meeting at Lecompton as a preparation for statehood. The convention barred free blacks from the state, guaranteed the property rights of the few slaveholders in Kansas, and asked voters to decide in a referendum whether to permit more slaves.

The proslavery Lecompton constitution, clearly unrepresentative of the wishes of the majority of the people of Kansas, was sent to Congress for approval. Eager to retain southern Democratic support, Buchanan endorsed it. Stephen Douglas challenged the president's power and jeopardized his standing with southern Democrats by opposing it. Facing reelection to the Senate from Illinois in 1858, Douglas needed to hold the support of the northern wing of his party. Congress sent the Lecompton constitution back to the people of Kansas for another referendum. This time they defeated it, which meant that Kansas remained a territory rather than becoming a slave state. While Kansas was left in an uncertain status, the larger political effect of the struggle was to split the Democratic party almost beyond repair.

No sooner had Douglas settled the Lecompton question than he faced reelection in Illinois. Douglas's opposition to the Lecompton constitution had restored his prestige in the North as an opponent of the slave power. This cut some ground out from under the Republican party claim that only it could stop the spread of southern power. Republican party leaders from the West, however, had a candidate who understood the importance of distinguishing Republican moral and political views from those of the Democrats.

Lincoln and the Illinois Debates

Although relatively unknown nationally and out of elective office for several years, by 1858, Abraham Lincoln emerged in Illinois to challenge William Seward for leadership of the Republican party. Lincoln's character was shaped on the midwestern frontier, where he had educated himself, developed mild abolitionist views, and dreamed of America's greatness.

Douglas was clearly the leading Democrat, so the 1858 election in Illinois gave a preview of the presidential election of 1860. The other Douglass, Frederick, observed that "the slave power idea was the ideological glue of the Republican party." Lincoln's handling of this idea would be crucial in distinguishing him from Stephen Douglas. The Illinois campaign featured a series of seven debates between Lincoln and Douglas, which took place in different cities. Addressing a national as well as a local audience, the debaters confronted the heated racial issues before the nation.

Lincoln set a solemn tone when he accepted the Republican senatorial nomination in Chicago. The American nation, he said, was in a "crisis" and building toward a worse one. "A House divided against itself cannot stand. I believe this government cannot endure, permanently half *slave* and half *free*." Lincoln said he did not expect the Union "to be dissolved" or "the house to fall," but rather that "it will become *all* one thing, or *all* the other." Then he rehearsed the history of the South's growing influence over national policy since the Kansas-Nebraska Act, which he blamed on Douglas. Lincoln stated his firm opposition to the *Dred Scott* decision, which he believed part of a conspiracy involving Pierce, Buchanan, Taney, and Douglas. Lincoln explained that he and others who opposed this conspiracy wished to place slavery on a "course of ultimate extinction."

In the ensuing debates with Douglas, Lincoln reiterated these controversial themes. He also expressed his views on race and slavery, formed from a blend of experience, principle, and politics. Although far from being a radical abolitionist, in

The overwhelming stress of leading the nation through the Civil War is evident in these two images of Abraham Lincoln. To the left is a portrait from 1860 *(Chicago Historical Society)* and on the right is an April 1865 photograph taken just before his assassination. *(Library of Congress)*

these debates Lincoln skillfully staked out a moral position not only in advance of Douglas but well ahead of his time.

Lincoln was also very much a part of his time. He believed in white superiority, opposed granting specific equal civil rights to free blacks, and said that physical and moral differences between whites and blacks would "forever forbid the two races from living together on terms of social and political equality." He recommended "separation" and colonization in Liberia or Central America as the best solution to racial differences.

Lincoln, however, differed from most contemporaries in his deep commitment to the equality and dignity of all human beings. Countering Douglas's racial slurs, Lincoln said that he believed not only that blacks were "entitled to all the natural rights . . . in the Declaration of Independence" but also that they had many specific economic rights as well, like "the right to put into his mouth the bread that his own hands have earned." In these rights, blacks were, Lincoln said, "my equal and the equal of Judge Douglas, and the equal of every living man."

Unlike Douglas, Lincoln hated slavery. At Galesburg, he said, "I contemplate slavery as a moral, social, and political evil." In Quincy, he said

that the difference between a Republican and a Democrat was quite simply whether one thought slavery wrong or right. Douglas was more equivocal and dodged the issue in Freeport by pointing out that slavery would not exist if favorable local legislation did not support it. Douglas's moral indifference to slavery was clear in his admission that he did not care if a territorial legislature voted it "up or down." Republicans did care, Lincoln answered, warning that by stopping the expansion of slavery, the course toward "ultimate extinction" had begun. Although barred by the Constitution from interfering with slavery where it already existed, Lincoln said that because Republicans believed slavery was wrong, "we propose a course of policy that shall deal with it as a wrong."

What Lincoln meant by "policy" was not yet clear, even to himself. However, he did succeed in affirming that the Republican party was the only moral and political force capable of stopping the slave power. It seems ironic now, though not at the time, that Douglas won the election. When he and Lincoln met again two years later, this time for the presidency, the order of their finish would be reversed. Elsewhere, in 1858, Democrats did poorly, losing 18 congressional seats.

This modern mural captures both the madness and passionate larger-than-life commitment of John Brown against a backdrop of flag-covered wagon trains across the Great Plains, a raging tornado and angry sky (God's wrath?), struggling slaves (by his left knee), and a violent confrontation between those for and against slavery. *(Kansas State Historical Society)*

John Brown's Raid

Unlike Lincoln, John Brown was prepared to act decisively against slavery. On October 16, 1859, he and a band of 22 men attacked a federal arsenal at Harpers Ferry, Virginia (now West Virginia). He hoped to provoke a general uprising of slaves throughout the Upper South or at least provide the arms for slaves to make their way to freedom. Although he seized the arsenal for a time, federal troops soon overcame him. Nearly half his men were killed, including two sons. Brown himself was captured, tried, and hanged for treason. So ended a lifetime of failures.

In death, however, Brown was not a failure. His daring if foolhardy raid and his dignified behavior during his trial and speedy execution unleashed powerful passions. The North–South gap widened. Although widely condemned, many northerners responded to Brown's death with an outpouring of sympathy; memorial rallies, parades, and prayer meetings were held. Admirers wrote poems, songs, and speeches in Brown's honor. Thoreau compared him to Christ, calling Brown an "angel of light." Abolitionist William Lloyd Garrison, a pacifist, wished "success to every slave insurrection" in the South. Ministers called slave revolt a "divine weapon" and glorified Brown's treason as "holy."

Brown's raid, Frederick Douglass pointed out, showed that slavery was a "system of brute force" that would only be ended when "met with its own weapons." Southerners were filled with "dread and terror" over the possibility of a wave of slave revolts led by hundreds of imaginary John Browns and Nat Turners, and they concluded that northerners would stop at nothing to free the slaves. This atmosphere of suspicion eroded freedom of thought and expression. A North Carolinian described a "spirit of terror, mobs, arrests, and violence" in his state. Twelve families in Berea, Kentucky, were evicted from the state for their mild abolitionist sentiments. A Texas minister who criticized the treatment of slaves in a sermon was given 70 lashes.

In response to the Brown raid, southerners also became more convinced, as the governor of South Carolina put it, that a "black Republican" plot in the North was "arrayed against the slaveholders." In this atmosphere of mistrust, southern Unionists lost their influence, and power became concentrated in the hands of those favoring secession. Only one step remained to complete the southern sense of having become a permanent minority within the United States: withdrawal to form a new nation. Senator Robert Toombs of Georgia, insistent that northern "enemies" were plotting the South's

In the aftermath of John Brown's raid, passions fed by fear were unleashed throughout the South against northern sympathizers, and vice versa. A year later, the editor of a Massachusetts newspaper who expressed Democratic, southern sympathies found himself the victim of the time-honored mob punishment of tarring and feathering. *(The New York Public Library, Astor, Lenox & Tilden Foundations)*

ruin, warned fellow southerners late in 1859, "Never permit this Federal government to pass into the traitorous hands of the black Republican party."

The Election of 1860

When the Democratic convention met in Charleston, South Carolina, a secessionist hotbed, it sat for a record 10 days and went through 59 ballots without being able to name a candidate. Southern delegates withdrew twice, forcing adjournments. Reconvening in Baltimore, the Democrats acknowledged their irreparable division by choosing two candidates at two separate conventions: Douglas for northern Democrats and John C. Breckinridge, Buchanan's vice president, for the proslavery South. The Constitutional Union party, made up of former southern Whigs and border-state nativists, claimed the middle ground and nominated John Bell, a slaveholder from Tennessee who favored compromise.

With Democrats split and a new party in contention, the Republican strategy aimed at keeping the states carried by Frémont in 1856 and adding Pennsylvania, Illinois, and Indiana. Seward, the

leading candidate for the nomination, had been tempering his antislavery views to appear more electable. So had Abraham Lincoln, who seemed more likely than Seward to carry those key states. After shrewd maneuvers emphasizing his "availability" as a moderate, Lincoln was nominated.

The Republican platform also exuded moderation, opposing only slavery's extension. Mostly it spoke of tariff protection, subsidized internal improvements, free labor, and a homestead bill. Above all, the Republicans, like southern Democrats, defended their view of what republican values meant for America's future. It did not include the equal rights envisioned by Frederick Douglass. An English traveler in 1860 observed that in America "we see, in effect, two nations—one white and another black—growing up together within the same political circle, but never mingling on a principle of equality."

The Republican moderate strategy worked as planned. Lincoln was elected by sweeping the entire Northeast and Midwest. Although he got less than 40 percent of the popular vote nationwide, his triumph in the North was decisive. Even a united Democratic party could not have defeated him.

Two Maps of the Presidential Election of 1860

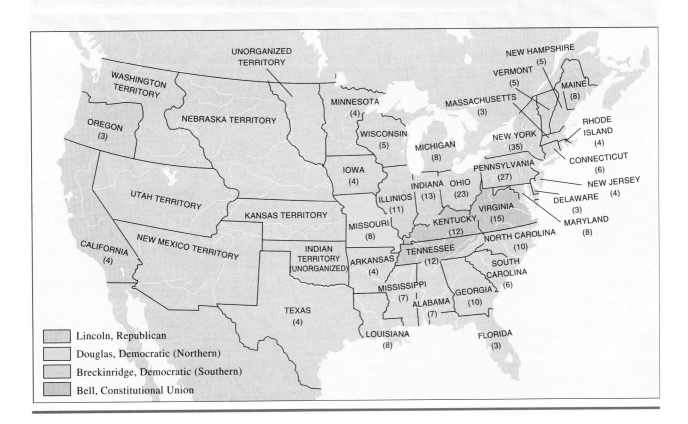

This 1860 pre-election cartoon shows Lincoln and Douglas fighting for the midwestern states (and California and Oregon), while Breckinridge tears off the South, and the compromise candidate Bell, standing on the chair, tries to hold the nation together with a little glue. Lincoln won with only 40 percent of the popular vote. Note on the map the states Lincoln and Breckinridge won: what does that suggest? Although he was second in many states, Douglas took only one, Missouri, perhaps for both real and symbolic reasons. Why do you think so? How do you explain the three states Bell won? *(Cartoon: Library of Congress)*

Lincoln, Republican
Douglas, Democratic (Northern)
Breckinridge, Democratic (Southern)
Bell, Constitutional Union

With victory assured, Lincoln finished his sandwich and coffee on election night in Springfield and prepared for his awesome new responsibilities. They came even before his inauguration.

THE DIVIDED HOUSE FALLS

The Republicans overestimated Unionist sentiment in the South. They could not believe that the secessionists would prevail after Lincoln's victory. A year earlier, some southern congressmen had walked out in protest when the House chose an antislavery speaker. A Republican leader, Carl Schurz, recalling

this act, said that the southerners had taken a drink and then come back. Now, Schurz predicted, they would walk out, take two drinks, and come back again. He was wrong.

Secession and Uncertainty

On December 20, 1860, South Carolina seceded from the Union, declaring the "experiment" of putting people with "different pursuits and institutions" under one government a failure. By February 1, the other six Deep South states (Mississippi, Florida, Alabama, Georgia, Louisiana, and Texas) had also seceded. A week later, delegates met in

The Causes of the Civil War

Using this chart as a summary, how would you explain the primary cause of the Civil War? Which four or five of the "issues and events" would you use to support your argument?

Date	Issues and Events	Deeper, Underlying Causes of Civil War
1600s–1860s	Slavery in the South	Major underlying pervasive cause
1700s–1860s	Development of two distinct socioeconomic systems and cultures	Further reinforced slavery as fundamental socioeconomic, cultural, moral issue
1787–1860s	States' rights, nullification doctrine	Ongoing political issue, less fundamental as cause
1820	Missouri Compromise (36°30′)	Background for conflict over slavery in territories
1828–1833	South Carolina tariff nullification crisis	Background for secession leadership in South Carolina
1831–1860s	Antislavery movements, southern justification	Thirty years of emotional preparation for conflict
1846–1848	War with Mexico (Wilmot Proviso, Calhoun, popular sovereignty)	Options for issue of slavery in territories

Date	Issues and Events	Specific Impact on the Road to War
1850	Compromise of 1850	Temporary and unsatisfactory "settlement" of divisive issue
1851–1854	Fugitive slaves returned and rescued in North; personal liberty laws passed in North; Harriet Beecher Stowe's *Uncle Tom's Cabin*	Heightened northern emotional reactions against the South and slavery
1852–1856	Breakdown of Whig party and national Democratic party; creation of a new party system with sectional basis	Made national politics an arena where sectional and cultural differences over slavery were fought
1854	Ostend Manifesto and other expansionist efforts in Central America	Reinforced image of Democratic party as favoring slavery
	Formation of Republican party	Major party identified as opposing the extension of slavery
	Kansas-Nebraska Act	Reopened "settled" issue of slavery in the territories
1856	"Bleeding Kansas"; Senator Sumner physically attacked in Senate	Foretaste of Civil War (200 killed, $2 million in property lost) inflamed emotions and polarized North and South
1857	Dred Scott decision; proslavery Lecompton constitution in Kansas	Made North fear a "slave power conspiracy," supported by President Buchanan and the Supreme Court
1858	Lincoln–Douglas debates in Illinois; Democrats lose 18 seats in Congress	Set stage for election of 1860
1859	John Brown's raid and reactions in North and South	Made South fear a "black Republican" plot against slavery; further polarization and irrationality
1860	Democratic party splits in half; Lincoln elected president; South Carolina secedes from Union	Final breakdown of national parties and election of "northern" president; no more compromises
1861	Six more southern states secede by February 1; Confederate Constitution adopted February 4; Lincoln inaugurated March 4; Fort Sumter attacked April 12	Civil War begins

Montgomery, Alabama, created the Confederate States of America, adopted a constitution, and elected Jefferson Davis, a Mississippi senator and cotton planter, its provisional president. The divided house had fallen, as Lincoln had predicted. But it was not yet certain whether the house could be put back together or whether disunion necessarily meant civil war.

The government in Washington had three options. First was compromise, but the emotions of the time ruled out that possibility. Most proposed compromises were really concessions to the secessionist states. Second, as suggested by Horace Greeley, editor of the New York *Tribune,* was to let the seven states "go in peace," taking care not to lose the border states. This was opposed by northern businessmen, who would lose profitable economic ties with the South, and by those who believed in an indissoluble Union. The third option was to compel secessionist states to return, which probably meant war.

Republican hopes that southern Unionism would assert itself and make none of these options necessary seemed possible in February 1861. The momentum toward disunion slowed, and no other southern states seceded. The nation waited and watched, wondering what Virginia and the border states would do, what outgoing President Buchanan would do, and what Congress would do. Pro-southern and determined not to start a civil war in the last weeks of his already dismal administration, Buchanan did nothing. Congress made some feeble efforts to pass compromise legislation, waiting in vain for the support of the president-elect. And as Union supporters struggled with secessionists, Virginia and the border states, like the entire nation, waited for Lincoln.

Frederick Douglass waited, too, without much hope. He wanted nothing less than the "complete and universal *abolition* of the whole slave system," as well as equal suffrage and other rights for free blacks. His momentary expectation during the presidential campaign, that Lincoln and the Republicans had the will to do this, had been thoroughly dashed. In November, the voters of New York State had defeated a referendum for black suffrage by more votes than a similar measure 14 years earlier. Moreover, Douglass saw northern politicians and businessmen "granting the most demoralizing concessions to the Slave Power."

In his despair, Douglass began to explore possibilities for emigration and colonization in Haiti, an idea he had long opposed. To achieve full freedom and citizenship in the United States for all blacks, he said in January 1861, he would "welcome the hardships consequent upon a dissolution of the Union."

In February, Douglass said, "Let the conflict come." He opposed all compromises, hoping that with Lincoln's inauguration in March it would "be decided, and decided forever, which of the two, Freedom or Slavery, shall give law to this Republic."

Lincoln and Fort Sumter

As Douglass penned these thoughts, Lincoln began a long, slow train ride from Springfield, Illinois, to Washington, writing and rewriting his inaugural address. Lincoln's quietness in the period between his election and his inauguration led many to judge him weak and indecisive. He was not. Lincoln firmly opposed secession and any compromises with the principle of stopping the extension of slavery. He would neither conciliate secessionist southern states nor force their return.

Lincoln believed in his constitutional responsibility to uphold the laws of the land, and on this significant point he would not yield. The focus of his attention was a federal fort in the harbor of Charleston, South Carolina. Major Robert Anderson, the commander of Fort Sumter, was running out of provisions and had requested new supplies from Washington. Lincoln would enforce the laws and protect federal property at Fort Sumter.

As the new president delivered his inaugural address on March 4, he faced a tense and divided nation. Federal troops, fearing a Confederate attack on the nation's capital, were everywhere. Lincoln asserted his unequivocal intention to enforce the laws of the land, arguing that the Union was constitutionally "perpetual" and indissoluble. He reminded the nation that the "only substantial dispute" was that "one section of our country believes slavery is *right,* and ought to be extended, while the other believes it is *wrong,* and ought not to be extended." Still hoping to appeal to Unionist strength among southern moderates, Lincoln said he would make no attempts to interfere with existing slavery and would respect the law to return fugitive slaves. Nearing the end of his address, Lincoln urged against rash actions and put the burden of initiating a civil war on the "dissatisfied fellow-countrymen" who had seceded. As if foreseeing the horrible events that might follow, he closed his speech eloquently:

> I am loath to close. We are not enemies, but friends. We must not be enemies. Though passion may have strained, it must not break our bonds of affection. The mystic chords of memory, stretching from every battlefield, and patriot grave, to every living heart and hearthstone, all over this broad land, will yet swell the chorus of the Union, when again touched, as surely they will be, by the better angels of our nature.

Frederick Douglass was not impressed with Lincoln's "honied phrases" and accused him of "weakness, timidity and conciliation." Also unmoved, Robert Allston wrote his son from Charleston, where he was watching the developing crisis over Fort Sumter, that the Confederacy's "advantage" was in having a "much better president than they have."

On April 6, Lincoln notified the governor of South Carolina that he was sending "provisions only" to Fort Sumter. No effort would be made "to throw in men, arms, or ammunition" unless the fort were attacked. On April 10, Jefferson Davis directed General P. G. T. Beauregard to demand the surrender of Fort Sumter. Davis told Beauregard to reduce the fort if Major Anderson refused.

On April 12, as Lincoln's relief expedition neared Charleston, Beauregard's batteries began shelling Fort Sumter, and the Civil War began. Frederick Douglass was about to leave for Haiti when he heard the news. He immediately changed his plans: "This is no time . . . to leave the country." He announced his readiness to help end the war by aiding the Union to organize freed slaves "into a liberating army" to "make war upon . . . the savage barbarism of slavery." The Allstons had changed places, and it was Benjamin who described the events in Charleston harbor to his father. On April 14, Benjamin reported exuberantly the "glorious, and astonishing news that Sumter has fallen." With it fell America's divided house.

✦ *Conclusion*

THE "IRREPRESSIBLE CONFLICT"

Lincoln had been right. The nation could no longer endure half-slave and half-free. The collision between North and South, William Seward said, was not an "accidental, unnecessary" event but an "irrepressible conflict between opposing and enduring forces." Those forces had been at work for many decades, but they developed with increasing intensity after 1848 in the conflict over the extension of slavery into the territories. Although economic, cultural, political, constitutional, and emotional forces all contributed to the developing opposition between North and South, slavery was the fundamental, enduring force that underlay all others, causing what Walt Whitman called the "red blood of civil war." Abraham Lincoln, Frederick Douglass, the Allston family, Michael Luark, and the American people all faced a radically altered national scene. Together they wondered if the American democratic system would be able to withstand this challenge.

✦ Recommended Reading

Overviews of the Imperiled Union and Crises of the 1850s
Eric Foner, ed., *Politics and Ideology in the Age of the Civil War* (1980); Bruce Levine, *Half Slave and Half Free: The Roots of the Civil War* (1992); James M. McPherson, *Battle Cry of Freedom: The Civil War Era* (1988); David Potter, *The Impending Crisis, 1848–1861* (1976); Brian Holden Reid, *The Origins of the American Civil War* (1996); Richard Sewall, *A House Divided: Sectionalism and Civil War, 1848–1865* (1988).

Slavery in the Territories
Frederick Moore Binder, *James Buchanan and the American Empire* (1994); William W. Freehling, *The Road to Disunion: I. Secessionists at Bay, 1776–1854* (1990); Robert W. Johanssen, *The Frontier, the Union, and Stephen A. Douglas* (1989) and *Stephen Douglas* (1973); Michael A. Morrison, *Slavery and the American West: The Eclipse of Manifest Destiny and the Coming of the Civil War* (1997); Mark J. Stegmaier, *Texas, New Mexico, and the Compromise of 1850: Boundary Dispute & Sectional Crisis* (1996).

Political Disintegration
Tyler Anbinder, *Nativism and Slavery: The Northern Know-Nothings and the Politics of the 1850s* (1992); Irving H. Bartlett, *John C. Calhoun: A Biography* (1993); Eric Foner, *Free Soil, Free Labor, Free Men: The Ideology of the Republican Party Before the Civil War* (1970); William E. Gienapp, *The Origins of the Republican Party, 1852–1856* (1987); Anthony Gronowicz, *Race and Class Politics in New York City before the Civil War* (1997); Michael Holt, *The Political Crisis of the 1850s* (1978) and *The Rise and Fall of the American Whig Party: Jacksonian Politics and the Onset of the Civil War* (1999); Merrill Peterson, *The Great Triumvirate: Webster, Clay, and Calhoun* (1987); Robert V. Remini, *Daniel Webster: The Man and His Time* (1997).

Kansas and the Two Cultures
William J. Cooper, *The South and the Politics of Slavery* (1978); Donald Fehrenbacher, *Slavery, Law, and Politics: The Dred Scott Case in Historical Perspective* (1981); Thomas F. Gossett, *Uncle Tom's Cabin and American Culture* (1985); David Grimsted, *American Mobbing, 1828–1861: Toward Civil War* (1998); David S. Heidler, *Pulling the Temple Down: The Fire-Eaters and the Destruction of the Union* (1994); Jerome Loving, *Walt Whitman: The Song of Himself* (1999); Nell Irvin Painter, *Sojourner Truth: A Life, A Symbol* (1996); Albert J. von Frank, *The Trials of Anthony Burns: Freedom and Slavery in Emerson's Boston* (1998); Steven Weisenburger, *Modern Media: A Family Story of Slavery and Child-Murder from the Old South* (1998).

The Divided House Falls
Steven Channing, *Crisis of Fear: Secession in South Carolina* (1970); David H. Donald, *Lincoln* (1995); Don Fehrenbacher, ed., *Abraham Lincoln: A Documentary Portrait Through His Speeches and Writings* (1977); Maury Klein, *Days of Defiance: Sumter, Secession, and the Coming of the Civil War* (1997); Mark E. Neely, *The Last Best Hope of Earth: Abraham Lincoln and the Promise of America* (1993); Kenneth Stampp, *And the War Came: The North and the Secession Crisis, 1860–61* (1950) and *America in 1857: A Nation on the Brink* (1990); David Zarefsky, *Lincoln, Douglas and Slavery in the Crucible of Public Debate* (1990).

Fiction and Film
The most important novel about slavery during the antebellum era was Harriet Beecher Stowe's *Uncle Tom's Cabin* (1852). Written in serial form, each episode stopped at a nail-biting moment and aroused the conscience of the North. Walt Whitman's collection of poems, *Leaves of Grass* (1855), celebrates not only the poet's own ego but also the common people and democratic American values in a decade that sorely tested those values. Russell Banks's *Cloudsplitter* (1998) is a long but riveting novel about John Brown and his activities during the 1850s, told through the eyes of one of his sons. *The Bondswoman's Daughter* by Hannah Crafts (2002), recently discovered by Henry Louis Gates, Jr., is a captivating story of a runaway slave woman in the 1850s. Toni Morrison's award-winning novel *Beloved* (1988), later made into a feature film, tells the story, based on a true event in 1856, of an escaped slave mother who killed her child as bounty hunters were about to seize her family and return them to slavery. Part I of Ken Burns's PBS film series *The Civil War* (1989) sets the slavery and 1850s background for his haunting documentary portrayal of the Civil War. Another fine video is *John Brown's Holy War* (1999) from the PBS series *The American Experience*.

✦ Discovering U.S. History Online

Zachary Taylor
www.ipl.org/div/potus/ztaylor.html
This site contains basic factual data about Taylor, including his presidency, speeches, cabinet members, and election information.

Compromise of 1850
www.loc.gov/exhibits/treasures/trm043.html
This exhibit shows digitized images of compromise documents by John C. Calhoun and Daniel Webster's notes for introductory remarks.

Uncle Tom's Cabin and American Culture

www.iath.virginia.edu/utc/sitemap.html

Along with searchable access to the text of *Uncle Tom's Cabin*, this site contains an archive of primary material (texts, images, songs, 3-D objects, film clips, etc.), an interactive timeline, and virtual exhibits designed for exploring and understanding the primary material.

Franklin Pierce

www.ipl.org/div/potus/fpierce.html

This site contains basic factual data about Pierce, including his presidency, speeches, cabinet members, and election information.

The Rise and Fall of the Know-Nothings

www.smithsonianmag.si.edu/smithsonian/issues96/nov96/knownothings.html

This site contains an abstract about the Know-Nothing party as well as links to articles on contemporary objects illustrating the politics of the era.

Bleeding Kansas

www.kancoll.org/galbks.htm

A collection of contemporary and later accounts of America's rehearsal for the Civil War make up this University of Kansas site.

Africans in America 1831–1865

www.pbs.org/wgbh/aia/part4/index.html

A large collection of people and events, historical documents, and modern voices on antebellum slavery, abolitionism, slavery in the territories, John Brown's raid, and the Civil War.

The Dred Scott Case

www.library.wustl.edu/vlib/dredscott/

This site presents digital images and transcriptions of 85 original documents (HTML or Word format), as well as a timeline of events surrounding the case.

John Brown's Holy War

www.pbs.org/wgbh/amex/brown

This companion Web site to the film contains primary source material (excerpts from letters, speeches, and an editorial), biographical information, a timeline, profiles of related people and events, information on the song "John Brown's Body," and a bibliography.

Lincoln's Election

www.iath.virginia.edu/vshadow2/outlines/election.html

A thorough collection of sources on the 1860 election, including a breakdown of the votes and various contemporary newspaper articles.

Crisis at Fort Sumter

www.tulane.edu/~latner/CrisisMain.html

This site presents "an interactive historical simulation and decision making program. . . . Using text, images, and sound, it reconstructs the dilemmas of policy formation and decision making in the period between Abraham Lincoln's election in November 1860 and the battle of Fort Sumter in April 1861."

15 The Union Severed

Artist Winslow Homer captured a Union sharpshooter in one of his early paintings. *(Portland Museum of Art, Maine. Gift of Barbro and Bernard Osher, 3.1993.3)*

✦ *American Stories*

A WAR THAT TOUCHED LIVES

In his remarks to Congress in 1862, Abraham Lincoln reminded congressmen that "We cannot escape history. We of this Congress and this administration will be remembered in spite of ourselves. No personal significance, or insignificance, can spare . . . us. The fiery trial through which we pass, will light us down, in honor or dishonor, to the latest generation." Lincoln's conviction that Americans would long remember him and other major actors of the Civil War was correct. Jefferson Davis, Robert E. Lee, Ulysses S. Grant—these are the men whose characters, actions, and decisions have been the subject of continuing discussion and analysis, whose statues and memorials dot the American countryside and grace urban squares. Whether seen as heroes or villains, great men have dominated the story of the Civil War.

Yet from the earliest days, the war touched the lives of even the most uncelebrated Americans. From Indianapolis, 20-year-old Arthur Carpenter wrote to his parents in Massachusetts begging for permission to enlist in the volunteer army: "I have always longed for the time to come when I could enter the army and be a military man, and when this war broke out, I thought the time had come, but you would not permit me to enter the service . . . now I make one more appeal to you." The pleas worked, and Carpenter enlisted, spending most of the war fighting in Kentucky and Tennessee.

In that same year, in Tennessee, George and Ethie Eagleton faced anguishing decisions. Though not an abolitionist, George, a 30-year-old Presbyterian preacher, was unsympathetic to slavery and opposed to secession. But when his native state left the Union, George felt compelled to follow and enlisted in the 44th Tennessee Infantry. Ethie, his 26-year-old wife, despaired over the war, George's decision, and her own forlorn situation.

> Mr. Eagleton's school dismissed—and what for? O my God, must I write it? He has enlisted in the service of his country—to war—the most unrighteous war that ever was brought on any nation that ever lived. Pres. Lincoln has done what no other Pres. ever dared to do—he has divided these once peaceful and happy United States. And Oh! the dreadful dark cloud that is now hanging over our country—'tis enough to sicken the heart of any one. . . . Mr. E. is gone. . . . What will become of me, left here without a home and relatives, a babe just nine months old and no George.

Both Carpenter and the Eagletons survived the war, but the conflict transformed each of their lives. Carpenter had difficulty settling down. Filled with bitter memories of the war years in Tennessee, the Eagletons moved to Arkansas. Ordinary people such as Carpenter and the Eagletons are historically anonymous. Yet their actions on the battlefield and behind the lines helped to shape the course of events, as their leaders realized, even if today we tend to remember only the famous and influential.

For thousands of Americans, from Lincoln and Davis to Carpenter and the Eagletons, war was both a profoundly personal and a major national event. Its impact reached far beyond the four years of hostilities. The war that was fought to conserve two political, social, and economic visions ended by changing familiar ways of life in both North and South. War was a transforming force, both destructive and creative in its effect on the structure and social dynamics of society and on the lives of ordinary people. This theme underlies this chapter's analysis of the war's three stages: the initial months of preparation, the years of military stalemate between 1861 and 1865, and, finally, resolution.

ORGANIZING FOR WAR

The Confederate bombardment of Fort Sumter on April 12, 1861, and the surrender of Union troops the next day ended the uncertainty of the secession winter. The North's response to Fort Sumter was a virtual declaration of war as President Lincoln called for state militia volunteers to crush southern "insurrection." His action pushed several slave states (Virginia, North Carolina, Tennessee, and Arkansas) off the fence and into the southern camp. Other states (Maryland, Kentucky, and Missouri) agonizingly debated which way to go. The "War Between the States" was now a reality.

Many Americans were unenthusiastic about the course of events. Southerners like George Eagleton reluctantly followed Tennessee out of the Union. When he enlisted, he complained of the "disgraceful cowardice of many who were last winter for secession and war ... but are now refusing self and means for the prosecution of war." Robert E. Lee of Virginia also hesitated but finally decided that he could not "raise [a] hand against ... relatives ... children ... home." Whites living in the southern uplands (where blacks were few and slaveholders were heartily disliked), yeomen farmers in the Deep South (who owned no slaves), and many border state residents were dismayed at secession and war. Many would eventually join the Union forces.

In the North, large numbers had supported neither the Republican party nor Lincoln. Irish immigrants fearing the competition of free black labor and southerners now living in Illinois, Indiana, and Ohio harbored misgivings. Indeed, northern Democrats at first blamed Lincoln and the Republicans almost as much as southern secessionists for the nation's crisis.

Nevertheless, the days following Fort Sumter and Lincoln's call for troops saw an outpouring of support on both sides, fueled in part by relief at decisive action, in part by patriotism and love of adventure, and in part by unemployment. Northern blacks and even some southern freedpeople proclaimed themselves "ready to go forth and do battle," while whites like Carpenter enthusiastically flocked to enlist. In some places, workers were so eager to join up that trade unions collapsed. Sisters, wives, and mothers set to work making uniforms. A New Yorker, Jane Woolsey, described the drama of those early days "of terrible excitement."

> Outside the parlor windows the city is gay and brilliant with excited crowds, the incessant movement and music of marching regiments and all the thousands of flags, big and little, which suddenly came fluttering out of every window and door. . . . In our little circle of friends, one mother has just sent away an idolized son; another, two; another, four. . . . One sweet young wife is

In May 1861, the first Michigan Regiment mustered in Detroit before boarding the train to Washington. The people crowded in the square, on the porches of the Rail-Road Hotel, and on rooftops suggest the patriotic enthusiasm of the send-off. Many women shared the fervor for the coming conflict. Thousands of them would be involved in war work at home or in army hospitals or camps. As one explained, "As the soldiers went from among us, there came the yearning wish to lessen somewhat the hardships of their lonely camp life, especially when sick in hospital or wounded." *(Courtesy of the Burton Historical Collection, Detroit Public Library)*

packing a regulation valise for her husband today, and doesn't let him see her cry.

The war fever produced so many volunteers that neither northern nor southern officials could handle the throng. Northern authorities turned aside offers from blacks to serve. Both sides sent thousands of white would-be soldiers home. The conviction that the conflict would rapidly come to a glorious conclusion fueled the eagerness to enlist. "We really did not think that there was going to be an actual war," remembered Mary Ward, a young Georgia woman. "We had an idea that when our soldiers got upon the ground and showed, unmistakably that they were really ready and willing to fight . . . the whole trouble would be declared at an end." Lincoln's call for 75,000 state militiamen for only 90 days of service, and a similar enlistment term for Confederate soldiers, supported the notion that the war would be short.

The Balance of Resources

The Civil War was one of several military conflicts during the nineteenth century that sought national independence. In Europe, Italian and German patriots struggled to create new nations out of individual states. Unlike their European counterparts, however, southern nationalists proclaimed their independence by withdrawing from an already unified state. Likening their struggle to that of the Revolutionary generation that had broken away from Great Britain's tyranny, southerners argued that they were "now enlisted in The Holy Cause of Liberty and Independence." While they legitimized secession by appealing to freedom, however, southerners were also preserving freedom's antithesis, slavery.

The outcome of the southern bid for autonomy was far from clear. Statistics of population and industrial development suggested that the Union would prevail. Yet Great Britain had enjoyed enormous statistical advantages in 1775 and still had lost the War of American Independence. Many northern assets would only become effective over time. The federal army was small (16,000 men), supplemented by state militia volunteers called up in April 1861. Probably a quarter of the regular army officers, like Robert E. Lee, had resigned. Thus the Confederate army, authorized in March 1861, could count on the service of able military men like Lee, Joseph E. Johnston, and Albert Sidney Johnston. Its president, Jefferson Davis, was an 1828 graduate of West Point.

The North's white population greatly exceeded that of the South, suggesting a powerful military advantage. Yet in the early days of war, the armies were not unevenly matched. Almost 187,000 Union

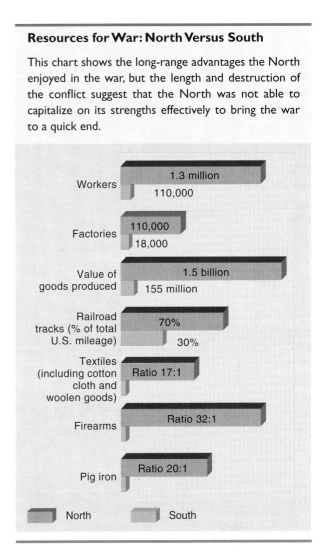

Resources for War: North Versus South

This chart shows the long-range advantages the North enjoyed in the war, but the length and destruction of the conflict suggest that the North was not able to capitalize on its strengths effectively to bring the war to a quick end.

	North	South
Workers	1.3 million	110,000
Factories	110,000	18,000
Value of goods produced	1.5 billion	155 million
Railroad tracks (% of total U.S. mileage)	70%	30%
Textiles (including cotton cloth and woolen goods)	Ratio 17:1	
Firearms	Ratio 32:1	
Pig iron	Ratio 20:1	

troops bore arms in July 1861, while just over 112,000 men marched under Confederate colors. Even if numerically inferior, southerners believed that their population would prove the superior fighting force because it was more accustomed to outdoor life and the use of firearms. Furthermore, slaves could carry on vital work behind the lines, freeing most adult white males for service.

The Union also enjoyed impressive economic advantages. In the North, 1.3 million workers in 110,000 manufacturing concerns produced goods valued at $1.5 billion annually, while 110,000 southern workers in 18,000 manufacturing concerns produced goods valued at only $155 million a year. The North had one factory for every southern industrial worker, and 70 percent of the nation's railroad tracks were in the North. Producing 17 times as much cotton cloth and woollen goods, 32 times as many firearms, and 20 times as much pig iron as the South, the North could clothe and arm troops and move them and their supplies on a scale that the

Railroads in 1860

This map shows the railroads at the beginning of the Civil War. What does it reveal about the differences in the transportation systems in the North and the South? In what ways was the war effort of each side helped or hindered by the rail system? In what ways did the configuration of southern transportation benefit the South?

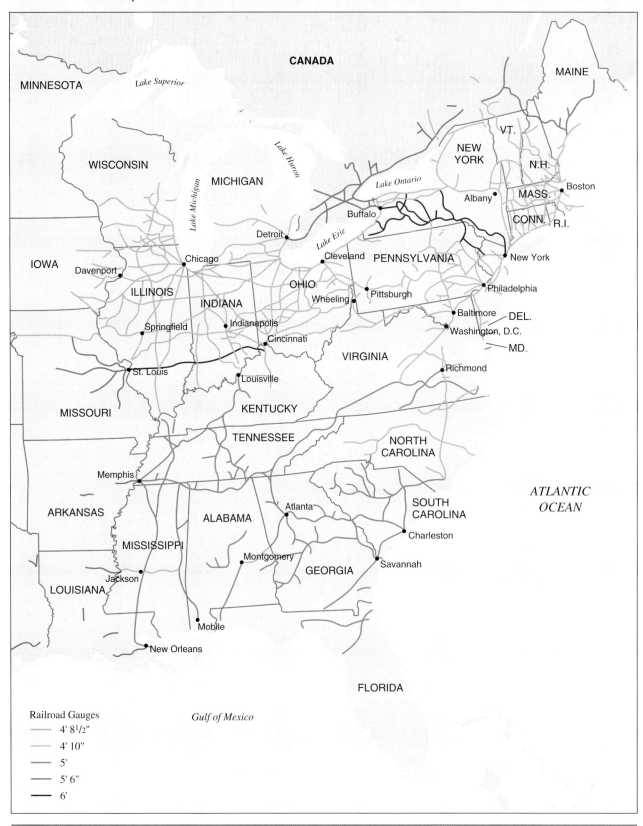

South could not match. But to be effective, northern industrial resources had to be mobilized for war. That would take time, especially because the government did not intend to direct production. Furthermore, the depleted northern treasury made the government's first task the raising of funds to pay for military necessities.

The South traditionally depended on imported manufactured goods from the North and from Europe. If Lincoln cut off that trade, the South would face the daunting task of creating its industry almost from scratch. Moreover, its railroad system was organized to move cotton, not armies and supplies. Yet the agricultural South had important resources of food, draft animals, and, of course, cotton, which hopefully would secure British and French support. Finally, in choosing to wage a defensive war, the South could tap regional loyalty and would enjoy protected lines of supply and support.

Union forces, however, were embarked on an expensive and difficult war of conquest. Because many parts of the South raised cotton and tobacco rather than food crops, Union armies could not forage for necessary food and fodder. Supplying northern forces in the South presented significant logistic problems and dangers. Extended supply lines were always vulnerable to attack, rendering northern armies less mobile and secure than southern troops. The Union had to win a war of conquest and occupation. The South merely had to survive until its enemy tired and gave up.

The Border States

Uncertainty over the war's outcome and divided loyalties produced indecision in the border states. When the seven states of the Deep South seceded during the winter of 1860–1861, the border states adopted a wait-and-see attitude. Their decisions were critically important to both North and South.

The states of the Upper South offered natural borders for the Confederacy along the Ohio River, access to its river traffic, and vital resources, wealth, and population. The major railroad link to the West ran through Maryland and western Virginia. Virginia boasted the South's largest ironworks, and Tennessee as the region's principal source of grain. Missouri provided the road to Kansas and the West and was strategically placed to control Mississippi River traffic. It was difficult to imagine the long- or short-term success of the Confederacy without the border states.

For the North, every border state that remained loyal represented a psychological triumph for the idea of Union. Nor was the North indifferent to the economic and strategic advantages of keeping the border states with the Union. Lincoln's call for troops precipitated decisions in several states, however. Between April 17 and May 20, 1861, Virginia, Arkansas, Tennessee, and North Carolina joined the Confederacy.

The significance of border-state loyalty was soon dramatized in Maryland. Slave-owning tobacco and wheat planters from the state's southern counties and eastern shore favored secession. Confederate enthusiasts abounded in Baltimore. But in the western and northern parts of the state, small farmers, often of German background, opposed slavery and supported the Union cause.

On the morning of April 19, the 6th Massachusetts Regiment arrived in Baltimore headed for Washington. Because the regiment had to change railroad lines, the soldiers set out across the city on foot and in horsecars. As they marched through the streets, a mob of some 10,000 southern sympathizers, flying Confederate flags, attacked them with paving stones, then bayonets and bullets. "A scene of bloody confusion followed." In the commotion, would-be secessionists burned the railroad bridges connecting Baltimore to the North and to the South. Washington, cut off from the rest of the Union, became an island in the middle of hostile territory.

Lincoln took stern measures to secure Maryland. The president agreed temporarily to route troops around Baltimore. In return, the governor called the state legislature into session at Frederick, a center of Union sentiment in western Maryland. This action and Lincoln's swift violation of civil rights damped secessionist enthusiasm. Hundreds of southern sympathizers, including 19 state legislators and Baltimore's mayor, were arrested and languished in prison without trial. Although the chief justice of the United States, Roger B. Taney, challenged the legality of the president's action and issued a writ of habeas corpus for the release of John Merryman, a southern supporter, Lincoln ignored him. A month later, Taney ruled in *Ex parte Merryman* that if the public's safety was endangered, only Congress had the right to suspend a writ of habeas corpus. By then, Lincoln had secured Maryland for the Union.

Though Lincoln's quick response ensured Maryland's loyalty, he was more cautious elsewhere. Above all, he had to deal with slavery prudently, for hasty action would push border states into the waiting arms of the Confederacy. Thus, when General John C. Frémont enthusiastically issued an unauthorized declaration of emancipation in Missouri in August 1861, Lincoln revoked the order. As the president explained, if certain key states left the Union, others would follow. "I think to lose Kentucky is nearly the same as to lose the whole game. Kentucky gone, we cannot hold Missouri, nor, as I think,

Secession of the Southern States

This map provides a chronology of secession and shows the geographic importance of the border states. The map also highlights the vulnerable position of Washington and explains many of Lincoln's actions in the early days of the war.

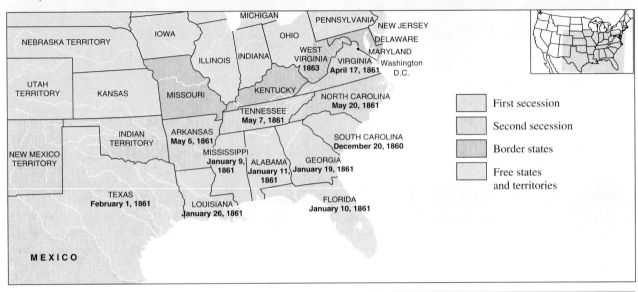

Maryland. These all against us, and the job on our hands is too large for us." In the end, after some fighting and much maneuvering, Kentucky and Missouri, like Maryland, stayed in the Union.

Challenges of War

The tense weeks after Fort Sumter spilled over with unexpected challenges. Neither side could handle the floods of volunteers. Both faced enormous organizational problems as they readied for war. In the South, a nation-state had to be created and its apparatus set in motion. Everything from a constitution and government departments to a flag and postage stamps had to be devised. As one onlooker observed, "The whole country was new. Everything was to be done—and to be made."

In February 1861, the original seceding states sent delegates to Montgomery, Alabama, to work on a provisional framework and to select a provisional president and vice president. The delegates swiftly wrote a constitution resembling the federal constitution of 1787 except in its emphasis on the "sovereign and independent character" of the states and its explicit recognition of slavery. The provisional president, Jefferson Davis of Mississippi, tried to assemble a geographically and politically balanced cabinet of moderates. His cabinet was balanced but contained few of his friends and, more serious, few men of political stature. As time passed, it turned out to be unstable as well.

Davis's cabinet appointees faced the formidable challenge of creating government departments from scratch. They had to hire employees and initiate administrative procedures with woefully inadequate resources. The president's office was in a hotel parlor. The Confederate Treasury Department was merely a room in an Alabama bank "without furniture of any kind; empty . . . of desks, tables, chairs or other appliances for the conduct of business." Treasury Secretary Christopher G. Memminger bought furniture with his own money; operations lurched forward in fits and starts. In those early days, when an army captain came to the treasury with a warrant from Davis for blankets, he found only one clerk. After reading the warrant, the clerk offered the captain a few dollars of his own, explaining, "This, Captain, is all the money that I will certify as being in the Confederate Treasury at this moment." Other departments faced similar difficulties.

Despite such challenges, the new Confederate government could count on widespread civilian enthusiasm and a growing sense of nationalism. Ordinary people spoke proudly of the South as "our nation" and referred to themselves as the "southern people." Georgia's governor insisted that "poor and rich, have a common interest, a common destiny." Southern Protestant ministers encouraged a sense of collective identity and reminded southerners that they were God's chosen people. The conflict was a sacred one.

Unlike Davis, Lincoln did not have to establish a postal system or decide the status of laws passed before 1861. But he too faced organizational problems. Military officers and government clerks daily left the capital for the South. The treasury was empty. The Republicans had won their first presidential election, and floods of office seekers thronged the White House looking for rewards.

Nor was it easy for Lincoln, who knew few of the "prominent men of the day," to select a cabinet. Finally, he appointed important Republicans from different factions of the party to cabinet posts whether they agreed with him or not. Most were almost strangers. Several scorned him as a bumbling backwoods politician. Treasury Secretary Salmon P. Chase actually hoped to replace Lincoln as president in four years' time. Soon after the inauguration, Secretary of State William Seward sent Lincoln a memo condescendingly offering to oversee the formulation of presidential policy.

Lincoln and Davis

A number of Lincoln's early actions illustrated his leadership skills. As his Illinois law partner, William Herndon, pointed out, Lincoln's "mind was tough—solid—knotty—gnarly, more or less like his body." In his reply to Seward's memo, the president firmly indicated that he intended to run his own administration. After Sumter, he swiftly called up the state militias, expanded the navy, and suspended habeas corpus. He ordered a naval blockade of the South and approved the expenditure of funds for military purposes, all without congressional sanction, because Congress was not in session. As Lincoln told legislators later, "The dogmas of the quiet past are inadequate to the stormy present. . . . As our case is new, so must we think anew, and act anew . . . and then we shall save our country." This willingness to "think anew" was a valuable personal asset, even though some regarded the expansion of presidential power as despotic.

By coincidence, Lincoln and his rival, Jefferson Davis, were born only 100 miles apart in Kentucky. However, the course of their lives diverged radically. Lincoln's father had migrated north and eked out a simple existence as a farmer in Indiana and Illinois. Lincoln's formal education was rudimentary; he was largely self-taught. Davis's family had moved south to Mississippi and become cotton planters. Davis grew up in comfortable circumstances, went to Transylvania University and West Point, and fought in the Mexican-American War before his election to the U.S. Senate. His social, political, and economic prominence led to his appointment as secretary of war under Franklin Pierce (1853–1857). Tall,

distinguished-looking, and very rich, he appeared every inch the aristocratic southerner.

Although Davis was not eager to accept the presidency, he loyally responded to the call of the provisional congress in 1861 and worked tirelessly until the war's end. His wife, Varina, observed that "the President hardly takes time to eat his meals and works late at night." Some contemporaries suggested that Davis's inability to let subordinates handle details explained this schedule. Others observed that he was sickly, reserved, humorless, too sensitive to criticism, and hard to get along with. But, like Lincoln, Davis found it necessary to "think anew." He reassured southerners in his inaugural address that his aims were conservative, "to preserve the Government of our fathers in spirit." Yet under the pressure of events, he moved toward creating a new kind of South.

CLASHING ON THE BATTLEFIELD, 1861–1862

The Civil War was the most brutal and destructive conflict in American history. Much of the bloodshed resulted from changing military technology coupled with inadequate communications. By 1861, the range of rifles had increased from 100 to 500 yards, in part owing to the new French minié bullet, which traveled with tremendous velocity and accuracy. The greater reach of the new rifles meant that it was no longer possible to position the artillery close enough to enemy lines to support an infantry charge. Therefore, during the Civil War, attacking infantry soldiers faced a final, often fatal, dash of 500 yards in the face of deadly enemy fire.

As it became clear that infantry charges resulted in horrible carnage, military leaders increasingly valued the importance of the strong defensive position. Although Confederate soldiers criticized General Lee as "King of Spades" when he first ordered them to construct earthworks, the epithet evolved into one of affection as it became obvious that earthworks saved lives. Union commanders followed suit. By the end of 1862, both armies dug defensive earthworks and trenches whenever they interrupted their march.

War in the East

The war's brutal character only gradually revealed itself. The Union commanding general, 70-year-old Winfield Scott, at first pressed for a cautious, long-term strategy, known as the Anaconda Plan. Scott proposed weakening the South gradually through blockades on land and at sea until the northern army was strong enough for the kill or southerners abandoned the conflict. The excited public, however, hungered for action and quick victory. So did Lincoln, who knew that the longer the war lasted, the more embittered both sides would both become, making reunion more difficult. Under the cry of "Forward to Richmond!" 35,000 partially trained men led by General Irwin McDowell headed out from Washington in sweltering July weather.

On July 21, 1861, only 25 miles from the capital at Manassas Creek, or Bull Run, as it is also called, inexperienced northern troops confronted 25,000 raw Confederate soldiers commanded by Brigadier General P. G. T. Beauregard, a West Point classmate of McDowell's. Although sightseers, journalists, and politicians accompanied the Union troops, expecting only a Sunday outing, the encounter at Bull Run was no picnic. The course of battle swayed back and forth before the arrival of 2,300 fresh Confederate troops, brought by trains, decided the day. Union soldiers and sightseers fled toward Washington in terror and confusion. An English journalist described the troops flooding into Washington on July 22:

> I saw a steady stream of men covered with mud, soaked through with rain . . . pouring irregularly, without any semblance of order, up Pennsylvania Avenue toward the Capitol. . . . Hastily [I] . . . ran downstairs and asked an officer . . . where the men were coming from. . . . "Well, sir, I guess we're all coming out of Virginny as far as we can, and pretty well whipped too. . . . I'm going home. I've had enough of fighting to last my lifetime."

"Whipped" the Union forces certainly were. Yet inexperienced Confederate troops failed to turn the rout into a decisive victory. As General Joseph E. Johnston recognized, his men were disorganized, confused by victory, and insufficiently supplied with food to chase the Union army back toward Washington.

In many ways, the Battle of Bull Run was prophetic. Victory would come neither quickly nor

Eastern Theater of the Civil War, 1861–1862

This map reveals the military actions in the East during the early years of the war. Initially, military planners hoped to end the war quickly by capturing Richmond. They soon discovered that the Confederate army was too powerful to allow them an easy victory. Eventually, Lincoln decided to combine military pressure on Virginia with an effort in the West aimed at cutting the Confederacy in two.

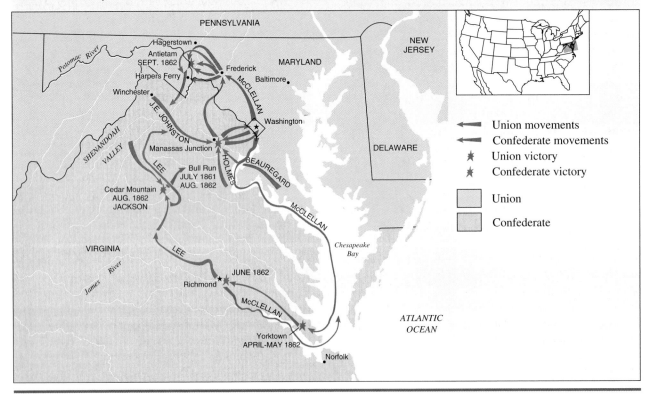

easily. The disorganization and confusion on both sides demonstrated that both armies lacked professionalism and highlighted serious logistical problems. The Civil War put more men in the field than any previous American engagement. Supplying and moving so many men and ensuring adequate communication, especially during battle, were tasks of an unprecedented kind. It was hardly surprising that the armies floundered trying to meet these challenges.

The prominent South Carolina rice planter Robert Allston, viewing the battlefield at Bull Run, declared it had been a "glorious tho bloody" day. For the Union, however, the loss at Bull Run was sobering. Replacing McDowell with 34-year-old General George McClellan, Lincoln began his search for a northern commander capable of winning the war. McClellan, formerly an army engineer, undertook the task of transforming the Army of the Potomac into a fighting force. Short-term militias went home. When Scott retired in the fall of 1861, McClellan became general in chief of the Union armies.

McClellan had considerable organizational ability but no desire to be a daring battlefield commander. Convinced that the North must combine military victory with efforts to persuade the South to return to the Union, he sought to avoid unnecessary and embittering loss of life and property. He intended to win the war "by maneuvering rather than fighting."

In March 1862, pushed by an impatient Lincoln, McClellan finally led his invasion force of 130,000 toward Richmond, now the Confederate capital. By late June, his army was close enough to hear Richmond's church bells pealing. But just as it seemed that victory was within grasp, Lee counterattacked and slowly drove the Union forces away from the city. Finally, orders came from Washington: abandon the Peninsula campaign.

Other Union defeats followed in 1862 as commanders came and went. In September, the South took the offensive with a bold invasion of Maryland. Lee well understood the need for aggressive actions that would weaken northern will and encourage southerners to believe in the eventual success of their cause. Antietam was a costly engagement in which more than 5,000 soldiers were slaughtered and another 17,000 wounded. Lee retreated to Virginia. While he did not gain the victory for which he had hoped, the defeat at Antietam was not conclusive. In the following 10 months, Lee won significant engagements at Fredericksburg and Chancellorsville. His success made him the focus of Confederate loyalty and the symbol of southern hopes. But final victory eluded both sides. The war in the East was stalemated.

This dying horse, stripped of saddle and bridle, was the mount of a Confederate officer killed during the battle of Antietam. The stark character of the picture reveals the devastating nature of the Civil War battlefield. *(Library of Congress [LC-B8184-558])*

War in the West

The early struggle in the East focused on Richmond, the Confederacy's capital and one of its most important railroad, industrial, and munitions centers. But the East was only one of three theaters of action. Between the Appalachian Mountains and the Mississippi lay the western theater, the states of Kentucky, Tennessee, Mississippi, and Alabama. At its edge lay the Mississippi, with its vital river trade and its great port, New Orleans. Here both George Eagleton and Arthur Carpenter served. Beyond lay the trans-Mississippi West—Louisiana, Arkansas, Missouri, Texas, and the Great Plains—where Native American tribes joined the conflict on both sides.

In the western theater, the Union had two strategic objectives: the domination of Kentucky and eastern Tennessee, which were the avenues to the South and West, and the control of the Mississippi River to split the South in two. Major campaigns sought strategic points along rivers and railroads.

It was in the western theater that Ulysses S. Grant rose to prominence. His modest military credentials included a West Point education, service in the Mexican-American war, and an undistinguished stint in the peacetime army. After his resignation, he went bankrupt. At the war's opening, he was working in his family's leather store in Illinois. Soon after Fort Sumter, Grant enlisted as a colonel in an Illinois militia regiment. Within two months, he was a brigadier general.

Trans-Mississippi Campaign of the Civil War

The military movements in the trans-Mississippi West appear here. Union forces operating in the Mississippi valley were attempting to separate Texas, Arkansas, and Louisiana from other southern states as part of an attempt to squeeze the Confederacy.

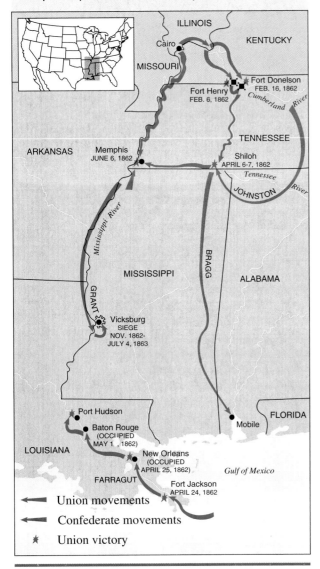

cesses there raised fears among Confederate leaders that southern mountaineers, loyal to the Union, would rush to Grant's support.

Despite Grant's grasp of strategy, his army was nearly destroyed by a surprise Confederate attack at Shiloh Church in Tennessee. The North won this battle, but victory proved enormously costly. In that two-day engagement, the Union suffered over 13,000 casualties, while 10,000 Confederates lay dead or wounded. More men fell in this single battle than in the American Revolution, the War of 1812, and the Mexican-American War combined. Because neither army offered sufficient care on the battlefield, untreated wounds caused many of the deaths. A full day after the battle had ended, 90 percent of the wounded still lay in the rain. Many died of exposure; others drowned in the downpour. Those who survived had infected wounds by the time they received medical attention. Though more successful than efforts in the East, such devastating Union campaigns failed to bring decisive results. Western plans were never coordinated with eastern military activities. Victories there did not force the South to its knees.

The war in the trans-Mississippi West was a sporadic, far-flung struggle to control the region's manpower and natural resources. California was a prize, luring both armies into the Southwest. Confederate troops from Texas took Albuquerque and Santa Fe briefly in 1862. Volunteer soldiers from the Colorado mining fields, joined by Mexican Americans and other soldiers, drove the Texas Confederates from New Mexico. A Union force from California, arriving after the Confederates were gone, spent the remainder of the war battling the Apache and the Navajo nations.

Farther east lay another prize, the Missouri River, which flowed into the Mississippi River, bordered Illinois, and affected military campaigns in Kentucky and Tennessee. Initially, Confederate troops succeeded here, as they had in New Mexico. But in March 1862, at Pea Ridge in northern Arkansas, the balance tilted in favor of the Union. There the Union forces defeated a Confederate army of 16,000 that included a brigade of Native Americans from the Five Civilized Nations. Missouri entered the Union camp for the first time in the war, but fierce guerrilla warfare continued in the region.

Naval Warfare

At the beginning of the war, Lincoln decided to strangle the South with a naval blockade. But an effective blockade proved elusive. With no more than 33 ships, the Union navy tried to close up 189 ports along a 3,500-mile coastline. In 1861, the navy intercepted only about one blockade runner in ten and

Grant's military genius consisted of an ability to see beyond individual battles to larger goals. In 1862, he realized that the Tennessee and Cumberland rivers offered paths for a successful invasion of Tennessee. A premature Confederate invasion of Kentucky allowed Grant to bring his forces into that state without arousing sharp local opposition. Assisted by gunboats, Grant was largely responsible for the capture of Fort Henry and Fort Donelson, key points on the rivers, in February 1862. His sucin 1862 one in eight. In the short run, the blockade did little damage to the South.

More successful were operations to gain footholds along the southern coast. In November 1861, a Union expedition took Port Royal Sound, where it freed the first slaves, and the nearby South Carolina Sea Islands. A few months later, the navy defeated a Confederate force on Roanoke Island, North Carolina. By gaining fueling stations and other important coastal points, the navy increased the possibility of making the blockade effective. The Union's greatest naval triumph in the early war years was the capture of New Orleans in 1862. The loss of the South's greatest port seriously weakened the Confederacy. The success of this amphibious effort stimulated other joint attempts to cut the South in two.

The Confederate leadership, recognizing that the South could not match the Union fleet, concentrated on developing new weapons like torpedoes and formidable ironclad vessels, a concept the French navy had successfully tested. Because the Union fleet consisted primarily of wooden ships, iron ships might literally crash through the Union blockade.

The *Merrimac* was one key to southern naval strategy. Originally a U.S. warship sunk as the federal navy hurriedly abandoned the Norfolk Navy Yard early in the war, the Confederates raised the vessel and covered it with heavy iron armor. Rechristened the *Virginia,* the ship steamed out of Norfolk in March 1862, heading directly for the Union ships blocking the harbor. Using its 1,500-pound ram and guns, the *Virginia* drove a third of the ships aground and destroyed the squadron's largest ships. But victory was short-lived. The next day, the *Virginia* confronted the *Monitor,* a newly completed and better designed Union iron vessel. While the *Virginia* survived the crash, it withdrew and was burned during the evacuation of Norfolk that May. Southern attempts to buy and produce ironclad ships failed, and southern hopes of evading the northern noose faded.

Though technological innovation failed to break the blockade, the Confederate navy's policy of harming northern commerce brought some success. Confederate raiders, many built in England, wreaked havoc on northern shipping. In its two-year career, the raider *Alabama* destroyed 69 Union merchant vessels valued at more than $6 million. But while such blows were costly to the North, they did not seriously damage its overall war effort.

Throughout the first two years of conflict, both sides achieved victories, but the war remained deadlocked. Although the South was far from being defeated, the North was as far from giving up or accepting southern independence. The costs of war, in manpower and supplies, far exceeded what either side had anticipated. The need to replace lost men and supplies thus loomed ever more serious at the end of 1862.

Cotton Diplomacy

Both sides in the Civil War realized the critical importance of European attitudes to the outcome of the struggle. Diplomatic recognition of the Confederacy would legitimize the new nation in the eyes of the world. Furthermore, just as French and Dutch aid had helped the American colonies win their independence, European loans and assistance might bring the South victory. But if the European nations refused to recognize the South, the fiction of the Union was kept alive, undermining Confederate chances for long-term survival. The European powers, of course, consulted their own national interests. Neither England nor France, the two most important nations, wished to back the losing side. Nor did they wish to upset Europe's delicate balance of power by hasty intervention in American affairs.

Men Present for Duty in the Civil War

This chart demonstrates the growing superiority of the North in terms of manpower and the impact of draft laws. After 1863, blacks, like native-born Americans and Irish and German immigrants, served in the armed forces.

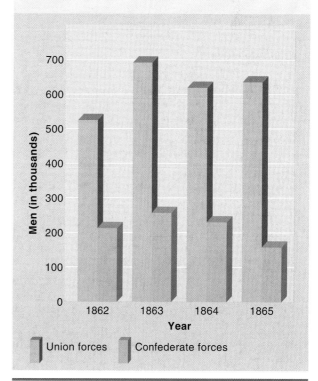

One by one, therefore, the European states declared a policy of neutrality.

Southerners were sure that cotton would be their trump card. English and French textile mills needed cotton, and southerners believed that their owners would eventually force government recognition of the Confederacy and an end to the North's blockade. But a glut of cotton in 1860 and 1861 left foreign mill owners oversupplied. As stockpiles dwindled, European industrialists found cotton in India and Egypt. The conviction that cotton was "the king who can shake the jewels in the crown of Queen Victoria" proved false.

Union Secretary of State Seward sought above all else to prevent diplomatic recognition of the Confederacy. The North had its own economic ties with Europe, so the Union was not as disadvantaged as southerners thought. Seward daringly threatened Great Britain with war if it interfered in what he insisted was an internal matter. Some called his boldness reckless, even mad. Nevertheless, his policy succeeded. Even though England allowed the construction of Confederate raiders in its ports, it did not intervene in American affairs in 1861 or 1862. Nor did the other European powers. Unless the military situation changed dramatically, the Europeans were willing to sit on the sidelines.

Common Problems, Novel Solutions

As the conflict dragged on into 1863, unanticipated problems appeared in both the Union and the Confederacy, and leaders devised novel approaches to solve them. War acted as a catalyst for changes that no one could have imagined in the heady spring days of 1861.

The problem of fighting a long war was partly monetary. Both treasuries had been empty initially, and the war proved extraordinarily expensive. Neither side considered trying to finance the war by imposing direct taxes. Such an approach violated custom and risked alienating support. Nevertheless, each side was so starved for funds that it initiated taxation on a small scale. Ultimately, taxes financed 21 percent of the North's war expenses (but only 1 percent of southern expenses). Both treasuries also tried borrowing. Northerners bought over $2 billion worth of bonds, but southerners proved reluctant to buy their government's bonds.

As in the American Revolution, the unwelcome solution was to print paper money. In August 1861, the Confederacy put into circulation $100 million in crudely engraved bills. Millions more followed the next year. Five months later, the Union issued $150 million in paper money, soon nicknamed "greenbacks" because of their color. Although financing

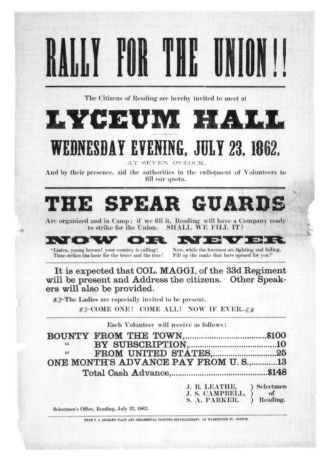

This 1862 poster invites "one" and "all" to come to the rally in Reading, Massachusetts. While there would be speeches and perhaps even patriotic music, the point of the meeting was to fill the town's military quota with "volunteers." Note how the poster appeals to young men with its appeal to "young heroes," whose enlistment would certainly be approved by the "Ladies" invited to be present. In addition to the use of patriotic language, the poster offered very clear financial rewards to those who signed up. In 2001 dollars, $148 would be worth over $2,800. *[Library of Congress (rbpe 06901800 urn [port. 69, fol. 18])]*

the war with paper money was unexpected, the resulting inflation was not. Inflation was particularly troublesome in the Confederacy, but a "modest" 80 percent increase in food prices brought southern city families near starvation and contributed to urban unhappiness during the war.

Both sides confronted similar manpower problems as initial enthusiasm for the war evaporated. Soldiering, it turned out, was nothing like the militia parades and outings familiar to most American males. Young men were shocked at the deadly diseases that accompanied the army and were unprepared for the boredom of camp life. As one North Carolina soldier explained, "If anyone wishes to become used to the crosses and trials of this life, let him enter camp life." None were prepared for the vast and impersonal destruction of the battlefield, which mocked values like courage and honor. It was with anguish that Robert Carter of Massachusetts saw bodies tossed into trenches "with not a prayer, eulogy or tear to distinguish them from so many animals." Many in the service longed to go home. The swarm of volunteers disappeared. Rather than fill their military quotas from within, rich northern communities began offering bounties of $800 to $1,000 to outsiders who would join up.

Arthur Carpenter's letters give a good picture of life in the ranks and his growing disillusionment with the war. As Carpenter's regiment moved into Kentucky and Tennessee in the winter of 1862, his enthusiasm for army life evaporated. "Soldiering in Kentucky and Tennessee," he complained, "is not so pretty as it was in Indianapolis. . . . We have been half starved, half frozen, and half drowned. The mud in Kentucky is awful." Soldiering often meant marching over rutted roads carrying 50 or 60 pounds of equipment with insufficient food, water, or supplies. One blanket was not enough in the winter. In the summer, stifling woollen uniforms attracted lice and other vermin. Poor food, bugs, inadequate sanitation, and exposure invited disease. Carpenter marched through Tennessee suffering from diarrhea and then fever. His regiment left him behind in a convalescent barracks in Louisville. Fearing the hospital at least as much as the sickness, he fled as soon as he could.

Confederate soldiers, even less well supplied than their northern counterparts, complained similarly. In 1862, a Virginia captain described what General Lee called the best army "the world ever saw":

> During our forced marches and hard fights, the soldiers have been compelled to throw away their knapsacks and there is scarcely a private in the army who has a change of clothing of any kind. Hundreds of men are perfectly barefooted and there is no telling when they can be supplied with shoes.

Such circumstances prompted some to desert. An estimated one of every seven Union soldiers and one of every nine men enlisting in the Confederate armies deserted. The majority, however, stayed with their units. As one southern soldier explained, "I am determined to anything and do everything I can for my country."

Manpower needs led both governments to resort to the draft. Despite the sacrosanct notion of states' rights, the Confederate Congress passed the first conscription act in American history in March 1862. Four months later, the Union Congress approved a draft measure. Rather than forcing men to serve, both laws sought to encourage men already in the army to reenlist and to attract volunteers. Ultimately, over 30 percent of the Confederate army were drafted. But because the northern draft law allowed payment to secure volunteers, only 6 percent of the Union forces were draftees.

The Confederacy relied more heavily on the draft than the Union did because the North's initial manpower pool was larger and growing. During the war, 180,000 foreigners of military age poured into the northern states. Some came specifically to claim bounties and fight. Immigrants constituted at least 20 percent of the Union army.

Necessary though they were, draft laws were very unpopular. The first Confederate conscription declared all able-bodied men between 18 and 35 eligible for military service but allowed numerous exemptions and the purchase of substitutes. Critics complained that the provision entitling every planter with more than 20 slaves to one exemption from military service favored rich slave owners. Certainly, the legislation fed class tension in the South and undermined the loyalty of the poorer classes, particularly southern mountaineers. The advice one woman shouted after her husband as he was dragged off to the army was hardly unique. "You desert again, quick as you kin. . . . Desert, Jake!" The law, as one southerner pointed out, "aroused a spirit of rebellion." But as long as the South won battlefield victories, the discontent did not reach dangerous proportions.

Northern legislation was neither more popular nor fair. The 1863 draft allowed the hiring of substitutes, and $300 bought an exemption from military service. Already suffering from inflation, workers resented the ease with which moneyed citizens could avoid army duty. In July 1863, the resentment boiled over in New York City in the largest civil disturbance of the nineteenth century. The violence demonstrated that northern morale and support for the war also wavered as the conflict persisted.

The three-day riot was sparked by the process of selecting several thousand conscripts on an early July weekend. By Monday, workers opposed to the draft were parading through the streets. Several Irish members of the Black Joker Volunteer Fire Company, whose names had been listed, were determined to destroy draft records and the hated Enrollment Office. Events spun out of control as a mob torched the armory, plundered the houses of the rich, and looted jewelry stores. African Americans, whom the Irish hated as economic competitors and the cause of the war, became special targets. Crowds shouting "Vengeance on every nigger in New York" beat and lynched African Americans and even burned the Colored Orphan Asylum. More than 100 people died in the violence.

There was much truth in the accusation that the war on both sides was a rich man's war but a poor man's fight.

Political Dissension, 1862

As the war continued, rumbles of dissension grew louder. On February 24, 1862, the *Richmond Examiner* summarized many southerners' frustration. "The Confederacy has had everything that was required for success but one, and that one thing it was and is supposed to possess more than anything else, namely Talent." As victory proved elusive, necessitating unpopular measures like the draft, criticism of Confederate leaders mounted. Jefferson Davis's vice president, Alexander Stephens of Georgia, became one of the administration's bitterest accusers. Public criticism reflected private disapproval. Wrote one southerner to a friend, "Impeach Jeff Davis for incompetency & call a convention of the States. . . . West Point is death to us & sick Presidents & Generals are equally fatal."

Because the South had no party system, dissatisfaction with Davis and his handling of the war tended to be factional, petty, and personal. No party mechanism channeled or curbed irresponsible criticism. Detractors rarely felt it necessary to offer programs in place of Davis's policies. Davis suffered personally from the carping comments of his detractors. More important, the Confederacy suffered. Without a party leader's traditional weapons and rewards, Davis had no mechanism to generate enthusiasm for his war policies.

Although Lincoln has since become a folk hero, at the time, many northerners derided his performance and eagerly looked forward to a new president in 1864. Peace Democrats, called Copperheads, claimed that Lincoln betrayed the Constitution and that working-class Americans bore the brunt of his conscription policy. New York Democrats warned the city's Irish residents that freed blacks would "steal the work and bread of honest Irish." Immigrant workers in eastern cities and those who lived in the southern parts of the Midwest had little sympathy for abolitionism or blacks, and they supported the antiwar stance of the Copperheads. Even Democrats favoring the war effort found Lincoln arbitrary and tyrannical. They also worried that extreme Republicans would push Lincoln into making the war a crusade for the abolition of slavery.

Republicans were themselves divided. Moderates favored a cautious approach toward winning the war, fearing the possible consequences of emancipating the slaves, confiscating Confederate property, or arming blacks. The radicals, however, urged Lincoln to make emancipation a wartime objective.

They hoped for a victory that would revolutionize southern social and racial arrangements.

Before the war, Lincoln had advocated ending slavery's expansion in the West but not its abolition in the South. In the early stages of the conflict, he retained his moderate stance. He hoped that pro-Union sentiment would emerge in the South and compel its leaders to abandon their rebellion. He began changing his mind in early 1862. The reduction of the congressional Republican majority in the fall elections of 1862 made it imperative that Lincoln listen not only to both factions of his party but also to the Democratic opposition.

THE TIDE TURNS, 1863–1865

Hard political realities as well as Lincoln's sense of the public's mood help explain why he delayed an emancipation proclamation until 1863. Like congressional Democrats, many northerners supported a war for the Union but not one for emancipation. Not only did many, if not most, whites see blacks as inferior, but they also suspected that emancipation would trigger a massive influx of former slaves who would steal white men's jobs and political rights. Race riots in New York, Brooklyn, Philadelphia, and Buffalo dramatized white attitudes. In Cincinnati, Irish dockworkers attacked blacks who were offering to work for less pay with the cry, "Let's clear out the niggers." Arthur Carpenter's evaluation of blacks was typical of many northern soldiers confronting blacks for the first time. In December 1861, he wrote to his parents:

> No one who has ever seen the nigger in all its glory on the southern plantations . . . will ever vote for emancipation. . . . If emancipation is to be the policy of the war (and I think it will not) I do not care how quick the country goes to pot. The negro never was intended to be equal with the white man.

The Emancipation Proclamation, 1863

If the president moved too fast on emancipation, he risked losing the allegiance of people like Carpenter, offending the border states, and increasing the Democrats' chances for political victory. But if Lincoln did not move at all, he would alienate abolitionists and lose the support of radical Republicans, which he could ill afford.

For these reasons, Lincoln proceeded cautiously. At first, he hoped the border states would take the initiative. In the early spring of 1862, he urged Congress to pass a joint resolution offering federal compensation to states beginning a "gradual abolishment of slavery." Border-state opposition killed

This depiction of African Americans celebrating the Emancipation Proclamation appeared in the French publication *Le Monde Illustre.* The artist has provided a triumphant and sympathetic picture of rejoicing freed-people. The appearance of such a picture in France points to the importance of the Emancipation Proclamation in legitimizing the Union cause in Europe.

the idea, for people there refused to believe, as Lincoln did, that the "friction and abrasion" of war would finally end slavery. Abolitionists and northern blacks, however, greeted Lincoln's proposal with a "thrill of joy."

That summer, Lincoln told his cabinet he intended to emancipate the slaves. Secretary of State Seward urged the president to delay any general proclamation until the North won a decisive military victory. Otherwise, he warned, Lincoln would appear to be urging racial insurrection behind the Confederate lines to compensate for northern military bungling.

Lincoln followed Seward's advice, using that summer and fall to prepare the North for the shift in the war's purpose. To counteract white racial fears of free blacks, he promoted various schemes for establishing free black communities in Haiti and Panama. Seizing unexpected opportunities, he lay the groundwork for the proclamation itself. In August, Horace Greeley, the influential abolitionist editor of the New York *Tribune*, printed an open letter to Lincoln attacking him for failing to act on slavery. In his reply, Lincoln linked the idea of emancipation to military necessity. His primary goal, he wrote, was to save the Union:

> If I could save the Union without freeing any slave, I would do it; and if I could save it by freeing all the slaves, I would do it; and if I could do it by freeing some and leaving others alone, I would also do that. What I

do about Slavery and the colored race, I do because I believe it helps to save this Union.

If Lincoln attacked slavery, then, it would be because emancipation would save white lives, preserve the democratic process, and bring victory.

In September 1862, the Union success at Antietam gave Lincoln the opportunity to issue a preliminary emancipation proclamation. It stated that unless rebellious states (or parts of states in rebellion) returned to the Union by January 1, 1863, the president would declare their slaves "forever free." Although supposedly aimed at bringing the southern states back into the Union, Lincoln no longer expected the South to lay down arms. Rather, he was preparing northerners to accept the eventuality of emancipation on the grounds of necessity. Frederick Douglass greeted the president's action with jubilation. "We shout for joy," he wrote, "that we live to record this righteous decree."

Not all northerners shared Douglass's joy. In fact, the September proclamation probably harmed Lincoln's party in the fall elections. As one Democratic ditty put it:

> *"De Union!" used to be de cry—*
> *For dat we want it strong;*
> *But now de motto seems to be,*
> *"De nigger, right or wrong."*

Although the elections of 1862 weakened the Republicans' grasp on the national government,

This photograph was taken in the summer of 1862 in Cumberland Landing, Virginia. Sitting in front of the cabin are about 20 men and women who had fled to Union lines and freedom. The flight of slaves, called contrabands, had the potential of seriously undermining the southern war effort and southern morale, but their presence also posed difficulties for Union commanders and northern leaders who were often not sure what to do with them. *(Library of Congress [LC-B811-0383])*

they did not destroy it. Still, cautious cabinet members begged Lincoln to forget about emancipation. His refusal demonstrated his vision and humanity, as did his efforts to reduce racial fears. "Is it dreaded that the freed people will swarm forth and cover the whole land?" he asked. "Are they not already in the land? Will liberation make them any more numerous? Equally distributed among the whites of the whole country, and there would be but one colored to seven whites. Could the one, in any way, greatly disturb the other?"

Finally, on New Year's Day, 1863, Lincoln issued the promised Emancipation Proclamation. It was an "act of justice, warranted by the Constitution upon military necessity." Thus, what had started as a war to save the Union now also became a struggle that, if victorious, would free the slaves. Yet the proclamation had no immediate impact on slavery. It affected only slaves living in the unconquered portions of the Confederacy. It was silent about slaves in the border states and in parts of the South already in northern hands. These limitations led Elizabeth Cady Stanton and Susan B. Anthony to establish the women's Loyal National League to lobby Congress to emancipate all southern slaves.

Though the Emancipation Proclamation did not immediately liberate southern slaves from their masters, it had a tremendous symbolic importance and changed the nature of the war. On New Year's Day, blacks gathered outside the White House to cheer the president and tell him that if he would "come out of that palace, they would hug him to death." For the first time, the government had committed itself to freeing slaves. Jubilant blacks could only believe that the president's action heralded a new era for their race. More immediately, the proclamation sanctioned the policy of accepting blacks as soldiers. Blacks also hoped that the news would reach southern slaves, encouraging them either to flee to Union lines or to subvert the southern war effort by refusing to work for their masters.

Diplomatic concerns also lay behind the Emancipation Proclamation. Lincoln and his advisers anticipated that the commitment to abolish slavery would favorably impress foreign powers. European statesmen, however, remained cautious. The English prime minister called the proclamation "trash." But important segments of the English public who opposed slavery now regarded any attempt to help the South as immoral. Foreigners could better understand and sympathize with a war to free the slaves than they could with a war to save the Union. In diplomacy, where image is so important, Lincoln had created a more attractive picture of the North. The Emancipation Proclamation became the North's symbolic call for human freedom.

Unanticipated Consequences of War

The Emancipation Proclamation was but another example of the war's surprising consequences. Innovation was necessary for victory. In the final two years of the war, both North and South experimented on the battlefields and behind the lines in desperate efforts to conclude the conflict successfully.

One of the Union's experiments involved using black troops for combat duty. Blacks had offered themselves as soldiers in 1861 but had been rejected. They were serving as cooks, laborers, teamsters, and carpenters in the army, however, and composed as much as a quarter of the navy. But as white casualties mounted, so did the interest in black service on the battlefield. The Union government allowed states to escape draft quotas if they enlisted enough volunteers, and they allowed them to count southern black enlistees on their state rosters. Northern governors grew increasingly interested in black military service. One piece of doggerel reflected changing attitudes:

> *Some tell us 'tis a burnin' shame*
> *To make the naygers fight;*
> *And that the thrade of bein' kilt*
> *Belongs but to the white:*
> *But as for me, upon my soul!*
> *So liberal are we here.*
> *I'll let Sambo be murthered instead of myself*
> *On every day in the year.*

Beyond white self-interest lay the promises of the Emancipation Proclamation and the desire to prove blacks' value to the Union. Black leaders like Frederick Douglass pressed for military service.

Newspaper engravings provided civilians with images of the conflict. This colored lithograph by Currier & Ives was produced a generation after the war, but it is very much like the journalistic images of the time. The picture shows a famous black regiment, the 54th Massachusetts, valiantly storming Fort Wagner, South Carolina. James Gooding, a member of the volunteer regiment and a free black from New Bedford, Massachusetts, described the assault. "We went at it, over the ditch and on to the parapet through a deadly fire; but we could not get into the fort. We met the foe on the parapet of Wagner with the bayonet—we were exposed to a murderous fire. . . . Mortal men could not stand such a fire, and the assault on Wagner was a failure." The experiences of the 54th form the basis for the Hollywood movie *Glory*. *(Library of Congress)*

"Once let the black man get upon his person the brass letter, U.S., let him get an eagle on his button, and a musket on his shoulder and bullets in his pocket," Douglass believed that "there is no power on earth that can deny that he has earned the right to citizenship." By the war's end, 186,000 blacks (10 percent of the army) had served the Union cause, 134,111 of them escapees from slave states.

Enrolling blacks in the Union army was an important step toward citizenship and acceptance of blacks by white society. But the black experience in the army highlighted some of the obstacles to racial acceptance. Black soldiers, usually led by white officers, were second-class soldiers for most of the war, receiving lower pay ($10 a month as compared with $13), poorer food, often more menial work, and fewer benefits than whites. Even whites working to equalize black and white pay often considered blacks inferior. Many white soldiers, including an entire regiment from Illinois, quit the service rather than fight alongside blacks.

The army's racial experiment had mixed results. But the faithful and courageous service of black troops helped modify some of the most demeaning white racial stereotypes of blacks. The black soldiers, many former slaves, who conquered the South felt a sense of pride and dignity as they performed their duties. Wrote one, "We march through these fine thoroughfares where once the slave was forbid being out after nine P.M. . . . Negro soldiers!— with banners floating."

As the conflict continued, basic assumptions weakened about how it should be waged. One wartime casualty was the courtly idea that war involved only armies. Early in the war, many officers tried to protect civilians and their property. In the Richmond campaign, General McClellan actually posted guards to prevent stealing. Such concern for rebel property soon vanished, and along with it went chickens, corn, livestock, and, as George Eagleton noted with disgust, even the furnishings of churches, down to the binding of the Bible in the pulpit. Southern troops, on the few occasions when they came North, also lived off the land. War touched all of society, not just the battlefield participants.

Changing Military Strategies, 1863–1865

In the early war years, the South's military strategy combined defense with selective maneuvers. Until the summer of 1863, the strategy seemed to be succeeding, at least in the eastern theater. But an occasional victory over the invading northern army, such as at Fredericksburg in December 1862, did not change the course of the war. Realizing this, Lee reviewed his strategy and concluded, "There is nothing to be gained by this army remaining quietly on the defensive." Unless the South won victories in the North, he believed, civilian confidence would disintegrate, and the North would continue its efforts to crush the southern bid for independence. He was willing to take risks to gain peace and national recognition.

In the summer of 1863, Lee led the Confederate army of northern Virginia across the Potomac into Maryland and southern Pennsylvania. Hoping for a victory that would threaten both Philadelphia and Washington, he even dreamed of capturing a northern city. Such spectacular feats would surely bring diplomatic recognition and might even force the North to sue for peace. On a practical level, Lee sought provisions for his men and their animals.

At Gettysburg on a hot and humid July 1, Lee came abruptly face-to-face with a Union army led by General George Meade. During three days of fighting, Lee ordered costly infantry assaults that probably lost him the battle. On July 3, Lee sent three divisions, about 15,000 men in all, against the Union center. The assault, known as Pickett's Charge, was as futile as it was gallant. At 700 yards, the Union artillery opened fire. One southern officer described the scene: "Pickett's division just seemed to melt away in the blue musketry smoke which now covered the hill. Nothing but stragglers came back."

Despite his losses, Lee did procure the food and fodder he needed and captured thousands of prisoners. Gettysburg was a defeat, but neither Lee, nor his men, nor southern civilians regarded it as conclusive. Fighting would continue for another year and a half. In 1864, one high army officer revealed his continuing belief in the struggle's outcome. "Our hearts are full of hope," he wrote. "Oh! I do pray that we may be established as an independent people, . . . [and] recognized as God's Peculiar People!" While many remained hopeful, Lee's Gettysburg losses were so heavy that he could never mount another southern offensive.

Despite the Gettysburg victory, Lincoln was dissatisfied with General Meade, who had failed to finish off Lee's retreating army. His disappointment faded with news of a great victory on July 4 at Vicksburg in the western theater. The capture of the city completed the Union campaign to gain control of the Mississippi River and to divide the South. Ulysses S. Grant, who was responsible for the victory, demonstrated the boldness and flexibility that Lincoln had been looking for in a commander.

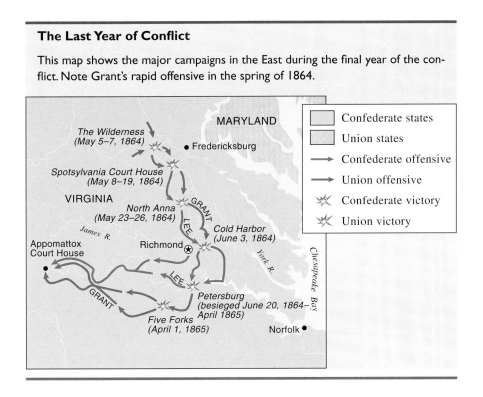

The Last Year of Conflict

This map shows the major campaigns in the East during the final year of the conflict. Note Grant's rapid offensive in the spring of 1864.

By the summer of 1863, the Union controlled much of Arkansas, Louisiana, Mississippi, Missouri, Kentucky, and Tennessee. The following spring, Lincoln appointed Grant general in chief of the Union armies. Grant planned for victory within a year. "The art of war is simple enough," he reasoned. "Find out where your enemy is. Get at him as soon as you can. Strike at him as hard as you can, and keep moving on."

As an outsider to the prewar military establishment, Grant easily rejected conventional military wisdom. "If men make war in slavish observance of rules, they will fail," he asserted. He anticipated no one decisive engagement but rather a grim campaign of annihilation, using the North's superior resources of men and supplies to wear down and defeat the South. Although Grant's plan entailed large casualties on both sides, he justified the strategy by arguing that "now the carnage was to be limited to a single year."

A campaign of annihilation involved the destruction not only of enemy armies but also of the resources that fueled the southern war effort. Although the idea of cutting the enemy off from needed supplies was implicit in the naval blockade, economic or "total" warfare was a relatively new and shocking idea. Grant, however, "regarded it as humane to both sides to protect the persons of those found at their homes, but to consume everything that could be used to support or supply armies."

Following this policy, he set out after Lee's army in Virginia. General William Tecumseh Sherman, who pursued General Joseph Johnston from Tennessee toward Atlanta, further refined this plan.

The war, Sherman believed, must also be waged in the minds of civilians, and he intended to make southerners "fear and dread" their foes. His campaign to seize Atlanta and his march to Savannah spread destruction and terror. Ordered to forage "liberally" on the land, his army left desolation in its wake. "Reduction to poverty," Sherman asserted, "brings prayers for peace." A Georgia woman described in her diary the impact of Sherman's march:

> There was hardly a fence left standing all the way from Sparta to Gordon. The fields were trampled down and the road was lined with carcasses of horses, hogs and cattle that the invaders, unable either to consume or to carry away with them, had wantonly shot down, to starve out the people. . . . The dwellings that were standing all showed signs of pillage, and on every plantation we saw . . . charred remains.

This destruction, with its goal of total victory, demonstrated once more how conflict produced the unexpected. The war that both North and South had hoped would be quick and relatively painless was ending after four long years with great cost to both sides. But the bitter nature of warfare during that final year threatened Lincoln's hopes for reconciliation.

The Progress of War, 1861–1865

In this map you can see the very slow progression of the North's effort to conquer the South. For much of the war, the South controlled large areas of contiguous territory. This control of the southern homeland helped southerners to feel that it was possible for them to win the war. At what point in time might the realities depicted in this map have made southerners decide their cause was lost?

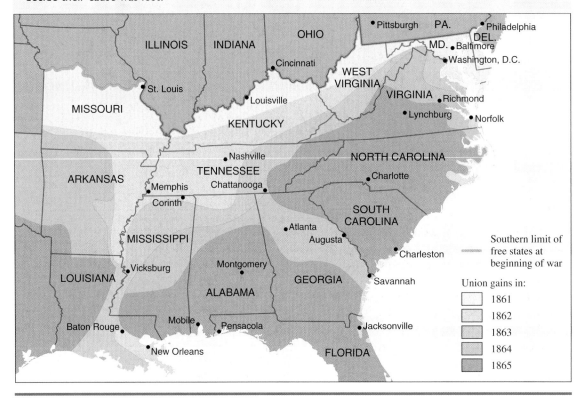

This albumen print by Timothy H. O'Sullivan is entitled *A Harvest of Death, Gettysburg, Pennsylvania, July, 1863*. It captures the quiet and misery of the battlefield and suggests the important role photography was starting to play in recording the sweep of American life. *(Rare Books Division, The New York Public Library, Astor, Lenox and Tilden Foundations)*

CHANGES WROUGHT BY WAR

As bold new tactics emerged both on and off the battlefield, both governments took steps that changed their societies in surprising ways. Of the two, the South, which had left the Union to conserve a traditional way of life, experienced the more radical transformation.

A New South

The expansion of the central government's power in the South, starting with the passage of the 1862 Conscription Act, continued in the last years of the war. Secession grew out of the concept of states' rights, but, ironically, winning the war depended on central direction and control. Many southerners denounced Davis because he recognized the need for the central government to take the lead. Despite the accusations, the Confederate Congress cooperated with him and established important precedents. In 1863, it enacted a comprehensive tax law and an impressment act that allowed government agents to requisition food, horses, wagons, and other necessary war materials, often for only about half their market price. These were prime examples of the central government's power to interfere with private property. Government impressment of slaves for war work in 1863 affected the very form of private property that had originally driven the South from the Union.

The Conscription Act of 1862 did not solve the Confederate army's manpower problems. By 1864, the southern armies were only one-third the size of the Union forces. Hence, in February 1864, an expanded conscription measure made all white males between the ages of 17 and 50 subject to the draft. By 1865, the necessities of war had led to the unthinkable: arming slaves as soldiers. Black companies were recruited in Richmond and other southern towns. However, because the war soon ended, no blacks actually fought for the Confederacy.

In a message sent to Congress in November 1864, Davis speculated on some of the issues involved in arming slaves. "Should a slave who had served his country" be retained in servitude, he wondered, "or should his emancipation be held out to him as a reward for faithful service, or should it be granted at once on the promise of such service . . . ?" The war fought by the South to preserve slavery ended in the contemplation of emancipation.

Southern agriculture also changed under the pressure of war. Earlier, the South had imported food from the North, concentrating on the production of staples such as cotton and tobacco for market. Now, more and more land was turned over to food crops. Some farmers voluntarily shifted crops, but others responded only to state laws reducing the acreage permitted for cotton and tobacco cultivation. These measures never succeeded in raising enough food to feed southerners adequately. But they contributed to a dramatic decline in the production of cotton, from 4.5 million bales in 1861 to 300,000 bales in 1864.

The South had always relied on imported manufactured goods. Even though some blockade runners were able to evade the Union ships, the noose tightened after 1862. The Confederacy could not, in any case, rely on blockade runners to arm and equip the army. Thus, war triggered the expansion of military-related industries in the South. Here, too, the government played a crucial role. The war and navy offices directed industrial development, awarding contracts to private manufacturing firms like Richmond's Tredegar Iron Works and operating other factories themselves. The number of southern industrial workers rose dramatically. In 1861, the Tredegar Iron Works employed 700 workers; two years later, it employed 2,500, more than half of them black. The head of the Army Ordinance Bureau reflected on the amazing transformation: "Where three years ago we were not making a gun, pistol nor a sabre, no shot nor shell . . . we now make all these in quantities to meet the demands of our large armies." At the end of the war, the soldiers were better supplied with arms and munitions than with food.

Although the war did not transform the southern class structure, relations between the classes began to change. The pressures of the struggle undermined the solidarity of whites, which was based on racism and supposed political unanimity. Draft resistance and desertion reflected the alienation of some southerners from a war perceived as serving only the interests of upper-class plantation owners. More and more yeoman families suffered grinding poverty as the men went off to war and government officials and armies requisitioned needed resources. Harlan Fuller, a poor farmer from Georgia, explained his family's situation in the spring of 1864. Even though Fuller was 50, he was now eligible for the draft. "I am liable at any time to be taken away from my little crops leaving my family almost without provisions & no hope of making any crop atal. I have sent six sons to the war & now the seventh enrolled he being the last I have no help left atal." This new poverty was an ominous hint of the decline of the yeoman farming class in postwar years.

The North

Although changes in the South were more noticeable, the Union's government and economy also responded to the demands of war. Like Davis, Lincoln was accused of being a dictator. Although he rarely tried to control Congress, veto its legislation, or direct government departments, Lincoln did use executive power freely. He violated the writ of habeas corpus by suspending the civil rights of over 13,000 northerners, who languished in prison without trials; curbed the freedom of the press because of supposedly disloyal and inflammatory articles; established conscription; issued the Emancipation Proclamation; and removed army generals. Lincoln argued that this vast extension of presidential power was temporarily justified because, as president, he was responsible for defending and preserving the Constitution.

Many of the wartime changes in government proved more permanent than Lincoln imagined. The financial necessities of war helped revolutionize the country's banking system. Ever since Andrew Jackson's destruction of the Bank of the United States, state banks had served American financial needs. Treasury Secretary Chase found this banking system inadequate and proposed to replace it. In 1863 and 1864, Congress passed banking acts that established a national currency issued by federally chartered banks and backed by government bonds. The country had a federal banking system once again.

The northern economy also changed under wartime demands. The need to feed soldiers and civilians stimulated the expansion of agriculture and new investment in farm machinery. With so many men off soldiering, farmers were at first short of labor. McCormick reapers performed the work of four to six men, and farmers began to buy them. During the war, McCormick sold 165,000 of his machines. Northern farming, especially in the Midwest, was well on the way to becoming mechanized. Farmers not only succeeded in growing enough grain to feed civilians and soldiers but also gathered a surplus to export as well.

The war also selectively stimulated manufacturing. Although it is easy to imagine that northern industry as a whole expanded during the Civil War, in fact, the war retarded overall economic growth. War consumed rather than generated wealth. Between 1860 and 1870, the annual rate of increase in real manufacturing value added was only 2.3 percent, in contrast with 7.8 percent for the years between 1840 and 1860 and 6 percent for the period 1870 to 1900. Some important prewar industries, like cotton textiles, languished without a supply of southern cotton.

However, industries that produced for the war machine, especially those with advantages of scale, expanded and made large profits. Each year, the Union army required 1.5 million uniforms and 3 million pairs of shoes; the woollen and leather industries grew accordingly. Meatpackers and producers of iron, steel, and pocket watches all profited from wartime opportunities. Cincinnati was one city that flourished from supplying soldiers with everything from pork to soap and candles.

On the Home Front, 1861–1865

Events on the battlefield were intimately connected to life behind the lines. As both northern and southern leaders realized, civilian morale was crucial to the war's outcome. If civilians lost faith, they would lack the will to continue the conflict.

The war stimulated religious efforts to generate enthusiasm and loyalty on the homefront. On both sides, Protestant clergymen threw themselves behind the war effort. As northern preacher Henry Ward Beecher proclaimed, "God hates lukewarm patriotism as much as lukewarm religion, and we hate it too." Southern ministers gave similar messages and urged southerners to reform their lives, for victory could not come without moral change. In North and South, every defeat was a cause for soul searching. Fast days and revivals provided a spiritual dimension to the conflict and helped people deal with discouragement and death.

In numerous ways, the war transformed northern and southern society. The very fact of conflict established a new perspective for most civilians. War news vied with local events for their attention. They read newspapers and national weekly magazines with a new eagerness. The use of the mails increased dramatically as they corresponded with faraway relatives and friends. Wrote one North Carolina woman, "I never liked to write letters before, but it is a pleasure as well as a relief now." Distant events became almost as real and vivid as those at home. The war helped make Americans less parochial, integrating them into the larger world.

For some Americans, like John D. Rockefeller and Andrew Carnegie, war brought army contracts and unanticipated riches. The New York *Herald* reported that New York City had never been "so gay, . . . so crowded, so prosperous," as it was in March 1864. Residents of Cincinnati noted people who "became suddenly immensely wealthy, and in their fine equipages, with liveried servants, rolled in magnificence along the city streets." In the South, blockade runners made fortunes slipping luxury goods past Union ships.

For the majority of Americans, however, war meant deprivation. The war effort gobbled up a large

My only support—both boys gone to the war. I wonder if they would take me?

Appearing on a printed envelope, this image reveals several aspects of female experience during wartime. This woman's life has been adversely affected by the conflict. Before the war, her sons supported her, but now she struggles to earn money by washing clothes. Instead of being resentful because her sons are in the army, however, the widow exhibits her patriotism when she wonders whether she can perform her humble duties in the military. In fact, washerwomen accompanied the armies wherever they went. (Collection of the New-York Historical Society [PR-022-3-88-5])

part of each side's resources, and ultimately ordinary people suffered. To be sure, the demand for workers ended unemployment and changed employment patterns. Large numbers of women and blacks entered the workforce, a phenomenon that would be repeated in all future American wars. But whereas work was easy to get and wages appeared to increase, real income actually declined. Inflation, especially destructive in the South, was largely to blame. By 1864, eggs sold in Richmond for $6 a dozen; butter brought $25 a pound. Strikes and union organizing pointed to working-class discontent.

Low wages compounded the problem of declining income and particularly harmed women workers. Often forced into the labor market because husbands could save little from small army stipends, army wives and other women took what pay they could get. As more women entered the workforce, employers cut costs by slashing wages. In 1861, the Union government paid Philadelphia

seamstresses 17 cents per shirt. At the height of inflation, three years later, the government reduced the piecework rate to 15 cents. Private employers paid even less, about 8 cents a shirt. Working women in the South fared no better. War may have brought prosperity to a few Americans in the North and South, but for most it meant trying to survive on an inadequate income.

Economic dislocation caused by the war reduced the standard of living for civilians. Shortages and hardships were severe in the South, which bore the brunt of the fighting. Most white southerners did without food, manufactured goods, and medicine during the war. Farming families without slaves to help with field work fared poorly. As one Georgia woman explained, "I can't manage a farm well enough [alone] to make a suporte." Conditions were most dismal in cities, where carts brought in vital supplies, because trains were reserved for military use. Hunger was rampant. Food riots erupted in Richmond and other cities; crowds of hungry whites broke into stores to steal food. The very cleanliness of southern cities pointed to urban hunger. As one Richmond resident noted, everything was so "cleanly consumed that no garbage or filth can accumulate."

Thousands of southerners who fled as Union armies advanced suddenly found themselves homeless. "The country for miles around is filled with refugees," noted an army officer in 1862. "Every house is crowded and hundreds are living in churches, in barns and tents." Caught up in the effort of mere survival, refugees worried about what had happened to homes and possessions left behind and whether anything would remain when they returned. Life was probably just as agonizing for those who chose to stay put when Union troops arrived. Virginia Gray, an Arkansas woman, wrote in her diary of her fear of the "Feds" and the turmoil they caused when they suddenly appeared and then disappeared.

White flight also disrupted slave life. Even the arrival of Union forces could prove a mixed blessing. One slave described the upsetting behavior of the Yankees at his plantation in Arkansas: "Them folks stood round there all day. Killed hogs . . . killed cows. . . . Took all kinds of sugar and preserves. . . . Tore all the feathers out of the mattresses looking for money. Then they put Old Miss and her daughter in the kitchen to cooking." So frightened was this slave's mother that she hid in her bed, only to be roused by the lieutenant, who told her, "We ain't a-going to do you no hurt. . . . We are freeing you." But the next day, the Yanks were

The dislocations caused by the war were many. These southerners, forced to leave their home by invading troops, have packed what few belongings they could transport and stand ready to evacuate their homestead. *(Library of Congress)*

gone and the Confederates back. During Sherman's march through Georgia in 1864, his troops stole not only from whites but from slaves as well. Indeed some soldiers flogged blacks who tried to stop the looting.

Wartime Race Relations

The journal kept by Emily Harris in South Carolina conveys some of the character of life behind the lines. She revealed not only the predictable story of shortages, hardships, and the psychological burdens of those at home but also the subtle social changes the war stimulated. Emily and her husband David lived on a 500-acre farm with their seven young children and ten slaves. When David went to war, Emily had to manage the farm, even though David worried that she would be "much at a loss with the . . . farm and the negroes."

Emily's early entries establish two themes that persist for the years she kept her diary. She worried about how David would survive the "privation and hardships" of army life and was also anxious about her own "load of responsibilities." Her December 1862 entry provides a poignant picture of a wife's thoughts. "All going well as far as I can judge but tonight it is raining and cold and a soldier's wife cannot be happy in bad weather and during a battle." The dozens of tasks she had to do depressed her. "I shall never get used to being left as the head of affairs," she wrote in January 1863. "I am not an independent woman nor ever shall be." As time passed and the war went badly, the dismal news and mounting list of casualties heightened her concern about David's safety.

Her relations with her slaves compounded Emily's problems. As so many southerners discovered, war transformed the master–slave relationship. Because Emily was not the master David had been, her slaves gradually claimed unaccustomed liberties. At Christmas in 1864, several left the farm without her permission; others stayed away longer than she allowed. "Old Will" boldly requested his freedom. Worse yet, she discovered that her slaves had helped three Yankees who had escaped from prison camp.

The master–slave relationship was crumbling, and Emily reported in her journal the consequences for whites. "It seems people are getting afraid of negroes." Although not admitting to fear, she revealed that she could no longer control the blacks, who were increasingly unwilling to play a subservient role.

Understanding what was at stake, slaves, in their own way, often worked for their freedom. Said one later, "Us slaves worked den when we felt like it, which wasn't often." Emily's journal entry for February 22 confessed a "painful necessity." "I am reduced," she said, "to the use of a stick but the negroes are becoming so impudent and disrespectful that I cannot bear it." A mere two weeks later she added, "The Negroes are all expecting to be set free very soon and it causes them to be very troublesom."

Similar scenes occurred throughout the South. Insubordination, refusal to work, and refusal to accept punishment marked the behavior of black slaves, especially those who worked as fieldhands. Thousands of blacks (probably 20 percent of all slaves), many of them women who had been exploited as workers and as sexual objects, fled toward Union lines after the early months of the war. Their flight pointed to the changing nature of race relations and the harm slaves could do to the southern cause. Reflected one slaveowner, "The 'faithful slave' is about played out."

Women and the War

If Emily Harris's journal reveals that she was sometimes overwhelmed by her responsibilities and shocked by the changes in dealings with her slaves, it also illustrates how the war affected women's lives. Nineteenth-century ideology promoted women's domestic role and minimized their economic importance. But the war made it impossible for many women to live according to conventional norms. So many men on both sides had gone off to fight that, just like many of their grandmothers during the American Revolution, women had to find jobs and carry on farming operations. During the war years, southern women who had no slaves to help with the farmwork and northern farm wives who labored without the assistance of husbands or sons carried new physical and emotional burdens. For southern women, who faced shortages and even displacement, sanity sometimes seemed at stake. Emily Harris felt she was going crazy. Others found their patriotism waning and urged their men to come home.

Women supported the war effort by participating in numerous war-related activities. In both North and South, they entered government service in large numbers. In the North, hundreds of women became military nurses. Under the supervision of Drs. Emily and Elizabeth Blackwell; Dorothea Dix, superintendent of army nurses; and Clara Barton, northern women nursed the wounded and dying for low pay or even for none at all. They also attempted to improve hospital conditions by attacking red tape and bureaucracy. The diary of a volunteer, Harriet Whetten, revealed the activist attitude of many others:

> I have never seen such a dirty disorganized place as the Hospital. The neglect of cleanliness is inexcusable. All sorts of filth, standing water, and the embalming house near the Hospital. . . . No time had to be lost. Miss Gill and I set the contrabands at work making beds & cleaning.

Although men largely staffed southern military hospitals, Confederate women also cared for the sick and wounded in their homes and in makeshift hospitals behind the battle lines. Grim though the work was, many women felt that they were participating in the real world for the first time in their lives.

Women moved outside the domestic sphere in other forms of volunteer war work. Some women gained administrative experience in soldiers' aid societies and in the U.S. Sanitary Commission that raised $50 million by the war's end for medical supplies, nurses' salaries and other wartime necessities. Others made bandages and clothes, put together packages for soldiers at the front, and helped army wives and disabled soldiers find jobs.

Many of the changes women experienced during war years ended when peace returned. Jobs in industry and government disappeared when the men came to reclaim them. Women turned over the operation of farms to returning husbands. But for women whose men came home maimed or not at all, the work had not ended. Nor had the discrimination. Trying to pick up the threads of their former lives, they found it impossible to forget what they had done to help the war effort. At least some of them were sure they had equaled their men in courage and commitment.

The Election of 1864

In the North, the election of 1864 brought some of the transformations of wartime into the political arena. The Democrats, seeking to regain power by capitalizing on war weariness, nominated General George McClellan for president. The party proclaimed the war a failure and demanded an armistice with the South. During the campaign, Democrats accused Lincoln of arbitrarily expanding executive power and denounced sweeping economic measures such as the banking bills. Arguing that the president had transformed the war from one for Union into one for emancipation, they tried to inflame racial passions by insinuating that if the Republicans won, a fusion of blacks and whites would result.

Although Lincoln gained the Republican renomination because of his tight control over party machinery and patronage, his party did not unite behind him. Lincoln seemed to please no one. His veto of the radical reconstruction plan for the South, the Wade-Davis bill, led to cries of "usurpation." The Emancipation Proclamation did not sit well with conservatives. Union defeats during the summer encouraged those who wanted to make peace with the South. In August 1864, a gloomy Lincoln told his cabinet that he expected to lose the election. As late as September, some Republicans actually hoped to reconvene the convention and select another candidate.

Sherman's capture of Atlanta in September 1864 and the march through Georgia to Savannah helped swing voters to Lincoln. In the end, Republicans had no desire to see the Democrats oust their party. Lincoln won 55 percent of the popular vote and swept the electoral college.

Photography

The invention of photography in 1839 expanded the visual and imaginative world of nineteenth-century Americans. For the first time, Americans could visually record events in their own lives and see the images of people and incidents from far away. Photographs, of course, also expand the boundaries of the historian's world. As photographic techniques became simpler, more and more visual information about the nineteenth century was captured. Historians can use photographs to discover what nineteenth-century Americans wore, how they celebrated weddings and funerals, and what their families, houses, and cities looked like. Pictures of election campaigns, parades, strikes, and wars show the texture of public life. But historians can also study photographs, as they do paintings, to glean information about attitudes and norms. The choice of subjects, the way people and objects are arranged and grouped, and the relationships between people in photographs are all clues to the social and cultural values of nineteenth-century Americans.

Some knowledge of the early history of photography helps place the visual evidence in the proper perspective. The earliest type of photograph, the daguerreotype, was not a print but the negative itself on a sheet of silver-plated copper. The first daguerreotype required between 15 and 30 minutes for the proper exposure. This accounts for the stiff and formal quality of many of these photographs. Glass ambrotypes (negatives on glass) and tintypes (negatives on gray iron bases), developed after the daguerreotype, were easier and cheaper to produce. But both techniques produced only one picture and required what to us would seem an interminable time for exposure.

A major breakthrough came in the 1850s with the development of the wet-plate process. In this process, the photographer coated a glass negative with a sensitive solution, exposed the negative (i.e., took the picture), and then quickly developed it. The new procedure required a relatively short exposure time of perhaps five seconds out-of-doors and one minute inside. Action shots, however, were still not feasible. The entire process tied the photographer to the darkroom. Traveling photographers carried their darkrooms with them. The advantage of the

Mathew Brady, *Confederate Captives, Gettysburg.* (National Archives)

Mathew Brady, *Burial Party at Cold Harbor.* (Chicago Historical Society)

wet-plate process was that it was possible to make many paper prints from one negative, opening new commercial vistas for professional photographers.

Mathew Brady, a fashionable Washington photographer, realized that the camera was the "eye of history" and asked Lincoln for permission to record the war with his camera. He and his team of photographers left about 8,000 glass negatives, currently stored in the Library of Congress and the National Archives, as their record of the Civil War. Shown here are two photographs, one of three Confederate soldiers captured at Gettysburg, the other of the battlefield of Cold Harbor in Virginia.

In the first photograph, study and describe the three soldiers. How are they posed? What kind of clothes are they wearing? What about their equipment? What seems to be their physical condition?

The second picture was taken in April 1865, about a year after the battle at Cold Harbor. In the background, you can see two Union soldiers digging graves. In the foreground are the grisly remains of the battle. What do you think is the intent of the photograph? The choice of subject matter shows clearly that photography reveals attitudes as well as facts. What attitude toward war and death is con-

veyed in this picture? Why is the burial taking place a full year after the battle? What does this tell us about the nature of civil warfare? Notice that the soldiers ordered to undertake this ghastly chore are black, as was customary. What might this scene suggest about the experience of black soldiers in the Union army?

Reflecting on the Past Using the photograph of Confederate captives as evidence, what might you conclude about the southern soldier—his equipment, uniforms, shoes? How well-fed do the men in the picture appear? What attitudes are conveyed through their facial expressions and poses? What kind of mood was the northern photographer trying to create? What might a northern viewer conclude about the South's war effort after looking at this picture?

These photographs just begin to suggest what can be discovered from old photographs. Your local historical society and library probably have photograph collections available to you. In addition, at home or in a relative's attic, you may find visual records of your family and its history.

Why the North Won

In the months after Lincoln's reelection, the war drew to an agonizing conclusion. Sherman moved north from Atlanta to North Carolina, while Grant pummeled Lee's forces in Virginia. The losses Grant sustained in Virginia were staggering: 18,000 in the Battle of the Wilderness, over 8,000 at Spotsylvania, and another 12,000 at Cold Harbor. New recruits stepped forward to replace the dead. On April 9, 1865, Grant accepted Lee's surrender at Appomattox. Southern soldiers and officers were allowed to return home with their personal equipment after promising to remain there peaceably. The war was finally over.

Technically, the war was won on the battlefield and at sea. But Grant's military strategy succeeded because the Union's manpower and economic resources could survive staggering losses of men and equipment while the Confederacy's could not. As Union armies pushed back the borders of the Confederacy, the South lost control of territories essential for their war effort. Finally, naval strategy eventually paid off because the North could build enough ships to make its blockade work. In 1861, fully 90 percent of the blockade runners were slipping through the naval cordon. By the war's end, only half made it.

The South had taken tremendous steps toward meeting war needs. But despite the impressive growth of manufacturing and the increasing acreage devoted to foodstuffs, the southern army and the southern people were poorly fed and poorly clothed. As one civilian realized, "The question of bread and meat . . . is beginning to be regarded as a more serious one even than that of War." Women working alone or with disgruntled slaves on farms could not produce enough food. Worn-out farm equipment was not replaced. The government's impressment of slaves and animals cut production. The half million blacks who fled to Union lines also played their part in pulling the South down in defeat.

New industries could not meet the extraordinary demands of wartime, and advancing Union forces destroyed many of them. A Confederate officer in northern Virginia observed, "Many of our soldiers are thinly clothed and without shoes and in addition to this, very few of the infantry have tents. With this freezing weather, their sufferings are indescribable." Skimpy rations, only one-third of a pound of meat for each soldier a day by 1864, weakened the Confederate force, whose trail was "traceable by the deposit of dysenteric stool" it left behind. By that time, the Union armies were so well supplied that soldiers often threw away heavy blankets and coats as they advanced.

The South's woefully inadequate transportation system also contributed to defeat. Primitive roads deteriorated and became all but impassable without repairs. The railroad system, geared to the needs of cotton, not war, was inefficient. When tracks wore out or were destroyed, they were not replaced. Rails were too heavy for blockade runners to bother with, and as the Confederate railroad coordinator observed in 1865, "Not a single bar of railroad iron has been rolled in the Confederacy since the war, nor can we hope to do better." Thus, food

This photograph of the South Side Railroad at Appomattox Station, Virginia, shows the condition of a southern railroad at the end of the war. You can see the poor condition of the tracks and the destroyed train lying beside the tracks. The breakdown of the Confederate transportation system through battle, sabotage, and simple wear and tear contributed to the defeat of the Confederacy. (*Library of Congress*)

intended for the army rotted awaiting shipment. Supplies were tied up in bottlenecks and soldiers went hungry. Food riots in southern cities pointed to the hunger, anger, and growing demoralization of civilians.

Ironically, measures the Confederacy took to strengthen its ability to win the war, as one Texan later observed, "weakened and paralyzed it." Conscription, impressment, and taxes all contributed to resentment and sometimes open resistance. They fueled class tensions already strained by the poverty war brought to many yeoman farmers and led some of them to assist the invaders or to join the Union army. The proposal to use slaves as soldiers called into question the war's purpose. The many southern governors who refused to contribute men, money, and supplies on the scale Davis requested implicitly condoned disloyalty to the cause.

It is natural to compare Lincoln and Davis as war leaders. There is no doubt that Lincoln's humanity, his awareness of the terrible costs of war, his determination to save the Union, and his eloquence set him apart as one of this country's most extraordinary presidents. Yet the men's personal characteristics were probably less important than the differences between the political and social systems of the two regions. Without the support of a party behind him, Davis failed to engender enthusiasm or loyalty. Even though the Republicans rarely united behind Lincoln, they uniformly wanted to keep the Democrats from office. Despite all the squabbles, Republicans tended to support Lincoln's policies in Congress and back in their home districts. Commanding considerable resources of patronage, Lincoln was able to line up federal, state, and local officials behind his party and administration.

Just as the northern political system provided Lincoln with more flexibility and support, its social system also proved more able to meet the war's extraordinary demands. Although both societies adopted innovations in an effort to secure victory, northerners were more cooperative, disciplined, and aggressive in meeting the organizational and production challenges of wartime. In the southern states, old attitudes, habits, and values impeded the war effort. Southern governors, wedded to states' rights, refused to cooperate with the Confederate government. North Carolina, the center of the southern textile industry, actually kept back most uniforms for its own regiments. At the war's end, 92,000 uniforms and thousands of blankets, shoes, and tents still lay in its warehouses. When Sherman approached Atlanta, Georgia's governor would not turn over the 10,000 men in the state army to Confederate commanders. Even slaveholders,

whose property had been the cause for secession, resisted the impressment of their slaves for war work.

In the end, the Confederacy collapsed, exhausted and bleeding. Hungry soldiers received letters from their families revealing desperate situations at home. They worried and then slipped away. By December 1864, the Confederate desertion rate had passed 50 percent. Replacements could not be found. Farmers hid livestock and produce from tax collectors. Many southerners felt their cause was lost and resigned themselves to defeat. But some fought on till the end. One northerner described them as they surrendered at Appomattox:

> Before us in proud humiliation stood the embodiment of manhood: men whom neither toils and sufferings, nor the fact of death, nor disaster, nor hopelessness could bend from their resolve; standing before us now, thin, worn, and famished, but erect, and with eyes looking level into ours, waking memories that bound us together as no other bond.

The Costs of War

The long war was over, but the memories of that event would fester for years to come. About 3 million American men, one-third of all free males between the ages of 15 and 59, had served in the army. Each would remember his own personal history of the war. For George Eagleton, who had worked in army field hospitals, the history was one of "Death and destruction! Blood! Blood! Agony! Death! Gaping flesh wounds, broken bones, amputations, bullet and bomb fragment extractions." Of all wars Americans have fought, none has been more deadly. The death rate during this war was over five times as great as the death rate during World War II. About 360,000 Union soldiers and another 258,000 Confederate soldiers died, about one-third of them because their wounds were either improperly treated or not treated at all. Disease claimed more lives than combat. Despite the efforts of men like Eagleton and the women army nurses, hospitals could not handle the scores of wounded and dying. "Glory is not for the private soldier, such as die in the hospitals," reflected one Tennessee soldier, "being eat up with the deadly gangrene, and being imperfectly waited on."

Thousands upon thousands of men would be reminded of the human costs of war by the injuries they carried with them to the grave, by the missing limbs that marked them as Civil War veterans. About 275,000 on each side were maimed. Another 410,000 (195,000 northerners and 215,000 southerners) would remember wretchedly overcrowded and unsanitary prison camps. The lucky ones would recall only the dullness and boredom. The worst memory was of those who rotted in prison camps, such as Andersonville in Georgia, where 31,000 Union soldiers were confined. At the war's end, over 12,000 graves were counted there.

Some Americans found it hard to throw off wartime experiences and adjust to peace. As Arthur Carpenter's letters suggest, he gradually grew accustomed to army life. War provided him with a sense of purpose. When it was over, he felt aimless. A full year after the war's end, he wrote, "Camp life agrees with me better than any other." Many others had difficulty returning to civilian routines and finding a new focus for life. Even those who adjusted successfully discovered that they looked at life from a different perspective. The experience of fighting, of mixing with all sorts of people from many places, and of traveling far from home had lifted former soldiers out of their familiar local world and widened their vision. Fighting the war made the concept of national union real.

Unanswered Questions

What, then, had the war accomplished? On the one hand, death and destruction. Physically, the war devastated the South. Historians have estimated a 43 percent decline in southern wealth during the war years, exclusive of the value of slaves. Great cities like Atlanta, Columbia, and Richmond lay in ruins. Fields lay weed-choked and uncultivated. Tools were worn out. One-third or more of the South's stock of mules, horses, and swine had disappeared. Two-thirds of the railroads had been destroyed. Thousands were hungry, homeless, and bitter about their four years of what now appeared a useless sacrifice. Over 4 million slaves, a vast financial investment, were free.

On the other hand, the war had resolved the question of union and ended the debate over the relationship of the states to the federal government. During the war, Republicans seized the opportunity to pass legislation that would foster national union and economic growth: the Pacific Railroad Act of 1862, which set aside huge tracts of public land to finance the transcontinental railroad; the Homestead Act of 1862, which was to provide yeoman farmers cheaper and easier access to the public domain; the Morrill Act of 1862, which established support for agricultural (land-grant) colleges; and the banking acts of 1863 and 1864.

The war had also resolved the issue of slavery, the thorny problem that had so long plagued American life. Yet uncertainties outnumbered certainties. What would happen to the former slaves? When blacks had fled to Union lines during the war, commanders had not known what to do with them. Now the problem became even more pressing. Were blacks to have the same civil and political rights as whites? In the Union army, they had been second-class soldiers. The behavior of Union forces toward liberated blacks in the South showed how deep the stain of racism went. One white soldier, caught stealing a quilt by a former slave, shouted, "I'm fighting for $14 a month and the Union"—not to end slavery. Would blacks be given land, the means for economic independence? What would be their relations with their former owners?

What, indeed, would be the status of the conquered South in the nation? Should it be punished for the rebellion? Some people thought so. Should southerners keep their property? Some people thought not. There were clues to Lincoln's intentions. As early as December 1863, the president had announced a generous plan of reconciliation. He was willing to recognize the government of former Confederate states established by a group of citizens equal to 10 percent of those voting in 1860, as long as the group swore to support the Constitution and to accept the abolition of slavery. He began to restore state governments in three former Confederate

Timeline	
1861	Lincoln calls up state militia and suspends habeas corpus
	First Battle of Bull Run
	Union blockades the South
1862	Battles at Shiloh, Bull Run, and Antietam
	Monitor and *Virginia* battle
	First black regiment authorized by Union
	Union issues greenbacks
	South institutes military draft
	Pacific Railroad Act
	Homestead Act
	Morrill Land–Grant College Act
1863	Lincoln issues Emancipation Proclamation
	Congress adopts military draft
	Battles of Gettysburg and Vicksburg
	Union Banking Act
	Southern tax laws and impressment act
	New York draft riots
	Southern food riots
1864	Sherman's march through Georgia
	Lincoln reelected
	Union Banking Act
1865	Lee surrenders at Appomattox
	Lincoln assassinated; Andrew Johnson becomes president
	Congress passes Thirteenth Amendment, abolishing slavery

states on that basis. But not all northerners agreed with his leniency, and the debate continued.

In his 1865 inaugural address, Lincoln urged Americans to harbor "malice towards none . . . and charity for all." "Let us strive," he urged, "to finish the work we are in; to bind up the nation's wounds . . . to do all which may achieve a just and lasting peace." Privately, the president said the same thing. Generosity and goodwill would pave the way for reconciliation. On April 14, he pressed the point home to his cabinet. His wish was to avoid persecution and bloodshed. That same evening, only five days after the surrender at Appomattox, the presi-

dent attended a play at Ford's Theatre. There, as one horrified eyewitness reported,

> a pistol was heard and a man . . . dressed in a black suit of clothes leaped onto the stage apparently from the President's box. He held in his right hand a dagger whose blade appeared about 10 inches long. . . . Every one leaped to his feet, and the cry of "the President is assassinated" was heard—Getting where I could see into the President's box, I saw Mrs. Lincoln . . . in apparent anguish.

John Wilkes Booth, a southern sympathizer, had killed the president.

✦ *Conclusion*

AN UNCERTAIN FUTURE

As the war ended, many Americans grieved for the man whose decisions had so marked their lives for five years. "Strong men have wept tonight & the nation will mourn tomorrow," wrote one eyewitness to the assassination. Many more wept for friends and relations who had not survived the war, but whose actions had in one way or another contributed to its outcome. The lucky ones, like Arthur Carpenter and

George and Ethie Eagleton, now faced the necessity of putting their lives back together and moving forward into an uncertain future. Perhaps not all Americans realized how drastically the war had altered their lives, their prospects, their nation. It was only as time passed that the war's impact became clear to them. And it was only with time that they recognized how many problems the war had left unsolved. It is to these years of Reconstruction that we turn next.

✦ Recommended Reading

Organizing for War
Joseph T. Glatthatt, *Partners in Command: The Relationship between Leaders in the Civil War* (1994); James McPherson, *Battle Cry of Freedom: The Civil War Era* (1988) and *Drawn to the Sword: Reflections on the American Civil War* (1996); Phillip S. Paludan, *"A People's Contest": The Union and the Civil War, 1861–1865* (1989); Peter J. Parrish, *The American Civil War* (1985).

Clashing on the Battlefield, 1861–1862
Thomas B. Buell, *The Warrior Generals: Combat Leadership in the Civil War* (1997); Benjamin Franklin Colling, *Fort Donelson's Legacy: War and Society in Kentucky and Tennessee, 1862–1863* (1997); Gary W. Gallagher, *The Confederate War* (1997); Perry D. Jamieson, *Attack and Die: Civil War Tactics and the Southern Heritage* (1982); Russell F. Weigley, *The American Way of War: A History of U.S. Military Strategy and Policy* (1973).

The Tide Turns, 1863–1865
Richard E. Beringer, Herman Hattaway, Archer Jones, and William N. Still, Jr., *Why the South Lost the Civil War* (1986) and *The Elements of Confederate Defeat: Nationalism, War Aims, and Religion* (1988); William W. Freehling, *The South vs. the South: How Anti-Confederate Southerners Shaped the Course of the Civil War* (2001); Gary Gallagher, *Lee and His Army in Confederate History* (2001); Laurence M. Hauptman, *The*

Iroquois in the Civil War: From Battlefield to Reservation (1993); Randall C. Jimerson, *The Private Civil War* (1988); Gerald F. Linderman, *Embattled Courage: The Experience of Combat in the American Civil War* (1987); Malcolm C. McMillan, *The Disintegration of a Confederate State* (1986); James M. McPherson, *For Cause and Comrades: Why Men Fought in the Civil War* (1997); Reid Mitchell, *The Vacant Chair: The Northern Soldier Leaves Home* (1993).

Changes Wrought by War
Ira Berlin, ed., *Freedom: A Documentary History of Emancipation, 1861–1867*, Series I and II (1979, 1982); David W. Blight and Brooks D. Simpson, eds., *Union & Emancipation: Essays on Politics and Race in the Civil War Era* (1997); Michael Burlingame, *The Inner World of Abraham Lincoln* (1994); Catherine Clinton, *Tara Revisited: Women, War, and the Plantation Legend* (1995); Mary A. Decredico, *Patriotism for Profit: Georgia's Urban Entrepreneurs and the Confederate War Effort* (1990); David Donald, *Lincoln* (1995); Wayne K. Durrell, *War of Another Kind: A Southern Community in the Great Rebellion* (1990); Laura F. Edwards, *Scarlett Doesn't Live Here Anymore: Southern Women in the Civil War Era* (2000); Drew Gilpin Faust, *Mothers of Invention: Women of the Slaveholding South in the American Civil War* (1996); Eric Foner, *Politics and Ideology in the Age of Civil*

War (1980); Gary W. Gallagher, *The Confederate War* (1997); J. Matthew Gallman, *Mastering Wartime: A Social History of Philadelphia During the Civil War* (1990); Theodore J. Karamanski, *Rally 'Round the Flag: Chicago and the Civil War* (1993); Elizabeth D. Leonard, *Yankee Women: Gender Battles in the Civil War* (1994); Glenn M. Lindend and Thomas J. Pressly, eds., *Voices From the House Divided* (1995); David E. Long, *The Jewel of Liberty: Abraham Lincoln's Re-Election and the End of Slavery* (1994); Clarence L. Mohr, *On the Threshold of Freedom* (1986); Wendy Hamand Venet, *Neither Ballots Nor Bullets: Women Abolitionists and the Civil War* (1991).

Fiction and Film

Stephen Crane's *The Red Badge of Courage* (1895) examines the soldier's experience during the war, while MacKinlay Kantor's novel *Andersonville* (1955) provides an insight into the Civil War's worst prison camp. *Enemy Women* (2002) by Paulette Jiles follows the journey of a young Missouri woman who tries to rescue her father who has been carried off by the Union militia to St. Louis. The feature film *Glory* (1989) focuses on a black regiment, the 54th Massachusetts, that demonstrated its heroism in the midst of battle. You will get a better sense of the character of warfare and race relations if you see this film. The classic *Gone with the Wind* (1939) offers a romanticized but powerful picture of southern life before, during, and after the Civil War. Ken Burns's famous documentary series *The Civil War* (1990) is a powerful evocation of that period with ample use of period photographs and documents.

✦ Discovering U.S. History Online

Index of Civil War Information on the Internet

www.cwc.lsu.edu/

A good starting place for research, this index has as its mission to "locate, index, and make available all appropriate private and public data on the Internet regarding the Civil War" and to promote the study of the Civil War from the perspectives of all professions, occupations, and academic disciplines. It includes a guide on evaluating sources of information on the Internet.

Causes of the Civil War

www.members.aol.com/jfepperson/causes.html

The site offers a collection of "primary documents from the period of the secession crisis ... with the goal of shedding light on the causes of secession, hence of the war." Document sections include "Party Platforms and Secession Documents," "Compromise Proposals," and "Abraham Lincoln's Speeches and Letters," as well as documents from individual states, other quotes, and political speeches and commentaries.

Crisis at Fort Sumter

www.tulane.edu/~latner/CrisisMain.html

This well-crafted use of hypermedia with assignments and problems explains and explores the events and causes leading to the Civil War.

Charleston

www.awod.com/gallery/probono/cwchas/cwlayout.html

William Hamilton, the author, attorney and Civil War reenactor, presents the history of the Civil War in and around Charleston, South Carolina, via timelines, biographies, primary sources, battleground information, and illustrations.

Abraham Lincoln

www.ipl.org/ref/POTUS/alincoln.html

This site contains basic factual data about Lincoln, including his presidency, speeches, cabinet members, and election information.

Black American Contributions to Union Intelligence During the Civil War

www.odci.gov/cia/publications/dispatches/

This illustrated article, reprinted from the CIA journal *Studies in Intelligence* (Winter 1998–1999) offers information about this little-known contribution to the Union war effort.

16 The Union Reconstructed

In this Winslow Homer painting entitled *A Visit from the Old Mistress,* imagine Adele Allston returning to her plantation to reunite with former slaves. What kind of new relationships would they form in the transformed world after a wrenching Civil War? *(National Museum of American Art, Smithsonian Institution)*

◆ *American Stories*

BLACKS AND WHITES REDEFINE THEIR DREAMS AND RELATIONSHIPS

In April 1864, a year before Lincoln's assassination, Robert Allston died, leaving his wife Adele and his daughter Elizabeth to manage their many rice plantations. Elizabeth was left with a "sense of terrible desolation and sorrow" as the Civil War raged around her. With Union troops moving through coastal South Carolina in the late winter of 1864–1865, Elizabeth's sorrow turned to "terror" as Union soldiers arrived and searched for liquor, firearms, and valuables. The Allston women endured an insulting search and then fled.

Later, Yankee troops encouraged the Allston slaves to take furniture, food, and other goods from the Big House. "My house at Chicora Wood plantation has been robbed of every article of furniture and much defaced," Adele complained to the local Union commander, adding, "all my provisions of meat, lard, coffee and tea [were] taken [and] distributed among the Negroes." Moreover, before they left, the liberating Union soldiers gave the keys to the crop barns to the semi-free slaves.

After the war, Adele Allston swore allegiance to the United States and secured a written order requiring the newly freed blacks to relinquish the keys. She and Elizabeth returned in the summer of 1865 to reclaim the plantations and reassert white authority. She was assured that although the blacks had guns and were determined to have the means to a livelihood, "no outrage has been committed against the whites except in the matter of property." But property was the issue. Possession of the keys to the barns, Elizabeth wrote, would be the "test case" of whether former masters or former slaves would control land, labor, and its fruits, as well as the subtle aspects of interpersonal relations.

Nervously, Adele and Elizabeth Allston rode up in a carriage to confront their ex-slaves at Chicora Wood. To their surprise, a pleasant reunion took place as the Allston women greeted the blacks by name, inquired after their children, and caught up on their lives. A trusted black foreman handed over the keys to the barns. This harmonious scene was repeated elsewhere.

But at one plantation, owned by a son who was absent during most of the war because he was fighting with the Confederate army, the Allston women met defiant and armed African Americans, who lined both sides of the road as the carriage arrived. Tension grew when the carriage stopped. An old black driver, Uncle Jacob, was unsure whether to yield the keys to the barns full of rice and corn, put there by black labor. Mrs. Allston insisted. As Uncle Jacob hesitated, an angry young man shouted out: "If you give up de key, blood'll flow." Uncle Jacob slowly slipped the keys back into his pocket.

The blacks sang freedom songs and brandished hoes, pitchforks, and guns to discourage anyone from going to town for help. Two blacks, however, slipped away to find some Union officers. The Allston women spent the night safely, if restlessly, in their house. Early the next morning, they were awakened by a knock at the unlocked front door. Adele slowly opened the door, and there stood Uncle Jacob. Without a word, he gave back the keys.

The story of the keys reveals most of the essential human ingredients of the Reconstruction era. Defeated southern whites were determined to resume control of both land and labor. Rebellion aside, the law and federal enforcement generally supported the original owners of the land. The Allston women were friendly to the blacks in a genuine but maternal way and insisted on restoring the deferential relationships that existed before the war. Adele and Elizabeth, in short, both feared and cared about their former slaves.

The African-American freedpeople likewise revealed mixed feelings toward their former owners: anger, loyalty, love, resentment, and pride. They paid respect to the person of the Allstons but not to their property and crops. They wanted not revenge but economic independence and freedom.

In this encounter between former slaves and their mistresses, the role of the northern federal officials is also revealing. Union soldiers, literally and symbolically, gave the keys of freedom to the freedmen and women but did not stay around long enough to guarantee that freedom. Although encouraging blacks to plunder the master's house and seize the crops, in the crucial encounter, Union officials had disappeared. Understanding the limits of northern help, Uncle Jacob handed the keys to land and liberty back to his former owner. The blacks realized that if they wanted to ensure their freedom, they would have to do it themselves.

This chapter describes what happened to the conflicting goals and dreams of three groups as they sought to redefine new social, economic, and political relationships during the postwar Reconstruction era. Amid devastation and divisions of class and race, Civil War survivors sought to put their lives back together. Victorious but variously motivated northern officials, defeated but defiant southern planters, and impoverished but hopeful African Americans could not all fulfill their conflicting goals, yet each had to try. This guaranteed that Reconstruction would be divisive, leaving a mixed legacy of human gains and losses.

THE BITTERSWEET AFTERMATH OF WAR

"There are sad changes in store for both races," the daughter of a Georgia planter wrote in her diary early in the summer of 1865, adding, "I wonder the Yankees do not shudder to behold their work." To understand the bittersweet nature of Reconstruction, we must look at the state of the nation after the assassination of President Lincoln.

The United States in 1865

The "Union" faced constitutional crisis in April 1865. What was the status of the 11 former Confederate states? The North had denied the South's constitutional right to secede but needed four years of civil war and over 600,000 deaths to win the point. Were the 11 southern states part of the Union or not? Lincoln's official position had been that they had never left the Union, which was "constitutionally indestructible," and were only "out of their proper relation" with the United States. The president, therefore, as commander in chief, had the authority to decide how to set relations right again.

Lincoln's congressional opponents argued that by declaring war on the Union, the Confederate states had broken their constitutional ties and reverted to a kind of pre-statehood status, like territories or "conquered provinces." Congress, therefore, should resolve the constitutional issues and assert its authority over the Reconstruction process.

Politically, differences between Congress and the White House mirrored a wider struggle between two branches of the national government. During war, as has usually been the case, the executive branch assumed broad powers necessary for rapid mobilization of resources and domestic security. Many believed, however, that Lincoln had far exceeded his constitutional authority and that his successor, Andrew Johnson, was even worse. Would Congress reassert its authority?

In April 1865, the Republican party ruled virtually unchecked. Republicans had made immense achievements in the eyes of the northern public: winning the war, preserving the Union, and freeing the slaves. They had enacted sweeping economic programs on behalf of free labor and free enterprise. These included a high protective tariff, a national banking system, broad use of the power to tax and to borrow and print money, generous federal appropriations for internal improvements, the Homestead Act, and an act to establish land-grant colleges to teach agricultural and mechanical skills. Alexander Hamilton, John Quincy Adams, and Henry Clay might all have applauded. But the party remained an uneasy grouping of former Whigs, Know-Nothings, Unionist Democrats, and antislavery idealists.

The Democrats, by contrast, were in shambles. Republicans depicted southern Democrats as rebels, murderers, and traitors, and they blasted northern Democrats as weak-willed, disloyal, and opposed to economic growth and progress. Nevertheless, in the election of 1864, needing to show that the war was a bipartisan effort, the Republicans nominated a Unionist Tennessee Democrat, Andrew Johnson, as Lincoln's vice president. Now the tactless Johnson headed the government.

Economically, the United States in the spring of 1865 presented stark contrasts. Northern cities hummed with productive activity; southern cities and railroads lay in ruin. Northern banks flourished; southern financial institutions were bankrupt. Mechanized northern farms were more productive than ever, as free farmers took pride that they had

Conflicting Goals During Reconstruction

Examine these conflicting goals which, at a human level, were the challenge of Reconstruction. How could each group possibly fulfill its goals when so many of them are in conflict with other groups? You may find yourself referring back to this chart throughout the chapter. How can each group fulfill its goals?

Victorious Northern ("Radical") Republicans

- Justify the war by remaking southern society in the image of the North
- Inflict political but not physical or economic punishment on Confederate leaders
- Continue programs of economic progress begun during the war: high tariffs, railroad subsidies, national banking
- Maintain the Republican party in power
- Help the freedpeople make the transition to full freedom by providing them with the tools of citizenship (suffrage) and equal economic opportunity

Northern Moderates (Republicans and Democrats)

- Quickly establish peace and order, reconciliation between North and South
- Bestow on the southern states leniency, amnesty, and merciful readmission to the Union
- Perpetuate land ownership, free labor, market competition, and other capitalist ventures
- Promote local self-determination of economic and social issues; limit interference by the national government
- Provide limited support for black suffrage

Old Southern Planter Aristocracy (Former Confederates)

- Ensure protection from black uprising and prevent excessive freedom for former slaves
- Secure amnesty, pardon, and restoration of confiscated lands
- Restore traditional plantation-based, market-crop economy with blacks as cheap labor force
- Restore traditional political leaders in the states
- Restore traditional paternalistic race relations as basis of social order

New "Other South": Yeoman Farmers and Former Whigs (Unionists)

- Quickly establish peace and order, reconciliation between North and South
- Achieve recognition of loyalty and economic value of yeoman farmers
- Create greater diversity in southern economy: capital investments in railroads, factories, and the diversification of agriculture
- Displace the planter aristocracy with new leaders drawn from new economic interests
- Limit the rights and powers of freedpeople; extend suffrage only to the educated few

Black Freedpeople

- Secure physical protection from abuse and terror by local whites
- Achieve economic independence through land ownership (40 acres and a mule) and equal access to trades
- Receive educational opportunity and foster the development of family and cultural bonds
- Obtain equal civil rights and protection under the law
- Commence political participation through the right to vote

---

amply fed the Union army and cities throughout the war. By contrast, southern farms and plantations, especially those along Sherman's march, resembled a "howling waste." Said one resident, "The Yankees came through . . . and just tore up everything."

Socially, the South was largely devastated as soldiers, many missing limbs and suffering from hunger, demobilized and returned home in April 1865. One-half million southern whites faced starvation. Yet, as a later southern writer, Wilbur Cash, explained, "If this war had smashed the Southern world, it had left the essential Southern mind and will . . . entirely unshaken." Many white southerners braced to resist Reconstruction and restore their former life while the minority who had remained quietly loyal to the Union dreamed of reconciliation.

Whatever the extremes of southern white attitudes, the dominant social reality in the spring of 1865 was that nearly 4 million freedpeople faced the challenges of freedom. After initial joy and celebration in jubilee songs, the freedmen and women quickly realized their continuing dependence on former owners. A Mississippi woman said:

> I used to think if I could be free I should be the happiest of anybody in the world. But when my master come to me, and says—Lizzie, you is free! it seems like I was in a kind of daze. And when I would wake up in the morning I would think to myself, Is I free? Hasn't I got to get up before day light and go into the field of work?

For Lizzie and 4 million other blacks, everything—and nothing—had changed.

The United States in 1865: Crises at the End of the Civil War

Given these enormous casualties, costs, and crises of the immediate aftermath of the Civil War, what attitudes, behaviors, and goals would you predict for the major combatants in the war?

Military Casualties

360,000 Union soldiers dead
260,000 Confederate soldiers dead
620,000 Total dead
375,000 Seriously wounded and maimed
995,000 Casualties nationwide in a total male population of 15 million (nearly 1 in 15)

Physical and Economic Crises

The South devastated; its railroads, industry, and some major cities in ruins; its fields and livestock wasted

Constitutional Crisis

Eleven former Confederate states not a part of the Union, their status unclear and future status uncertain

Political Crisis

Republican party (entirely of the North) dominant in Congress; a former Democratic slaveholder from Tennessee, Andrew Johnson, in the presidency

Social Crisis

Nearly 4 million black freedpeople throughout the South facing challenges of survival and freedom, along with thousands of hungry, demobilized Confederate soldiers and displaced white families

Psychological Crisis

Incalculable stores of resentment, bitterness, anger, and despair, North and South, white and black

Hopes Among the Freedpeople

Throughout the South in the summer of 1865, optimism surged through the old slave quarters. As Union soldiers marched through Richmond, prisoners in slave-trade jails chanted: "Slavery chain done broke at last! Gonna praise God till I die!" The slavery chain, however, broke slowly, link by link. After Union troops swept through an area, as one man said, "they would tell us we was free and we'd begin celebratin'." But Confederate soldiers would follow, or master and overseer would return, and "tell us to go back to work, and we would go." Another slave recalled celebrating emancipation "about twelve times" in one North Carolina county. The freedmen and women learned, therefore, not to rejoice too quickly or openly.

Gradually, though, blacks began to test the reality of freedom. Typically, their first step was to leave the plantation, if only for a few hours or days. "If I stay here I'll never know I am free," said a South Carolina woman, who went to work as a cook in a nearby town. Some freedpeople cut their ties entirely, returning to an earlier master, or, more often, going into towns and cities to find jobs, family members, churches, and schools.

The freedpeople made education a priority. A Mississippi farmer vowed, "If I nebber does do nothing more, I shall give my children a chance to go to school, for I consider education next best ting to liberty." An official in Virginia echoed the observation of many when he said that the freedmen were "down right crazy to learn." As the war ended, impatient for teachers, they set up schools "taught by colored people who have got a little learning." One traveler throughout the South counted "at least five hundred" such schools, observing that blacks were "determined to be self-taught."

Many freedpeople left the plantation in search of a spouse, parent, or child who had been sold away years before. Advertisements detailing these sorrowful searches filled African-American newspapers. For those who found a spouse and those who had been living together in slave marriages, freedom meant getting married legally, sometimes in mass ceremonies, which were common in the first months of emancipation. Legal marriage was important morally, but it also established the legitimacy of children and meant access to land titles and other economic opportunities. Marriage meant special burdens for black women who assumed the now familiar double role of housekeeper and breadwinner. Their determination to create a family life and to educate their children resulted in the withdrawal of many women from plantation field labor.

Freedpeople also demonstrated their new status by choosing surnames. Names connoting independence, such as Washington, were common. Revealing their mixed feelings toward their former masters, some would adopt their master's name, while others would pick "any big name 'ceptin' their master's." Emancipation changed black manners around whites as well. Masks fell, and expressions of humility—tipping a hat, stepping aside, feigning happiness, addressing whites with titles of deference—diminished. For the blacks, these changes were necessary expressions of selfhood, proving that social relationships were different. Whites, however, saw these new behaviors as acts of "insolence" and "insubordination."

Other than the passion for education, the primary goal for most African Americans was securing jobs and land. "All I want is to git to own fo' or five acres ob land, dat I can build me a little house on and call my home," a Mississippi black said. Only through eco-

Both white southerners and their former slaves suffered in the immediate aftermath of the Civil War, as illustrated by this engraving from *Frank Leslie's Illustrated Newspaper*, February 23, 1867. *(The Granger Collection, New York)*

nomic independence, the American means of controlling one's own labor and land, could freedpeople like Lizzie be certain that emancipation was real.

During the war, some Union generals had put liberated slaves in charge of confiscated and abandoned lands. In the Sea Islands of South Carolina and Georgia, African Americans had been working 40-acre plots of land and harvesting their own crops for several years. Farther inland, freedpeople who received land were the former slaves of Cherokees and Creeks. Some blacks held title to these lands. Northern philanthropists had organized others to grow cotton for the Treasury Department to prove the superiority of free labor over slavery. In Mississippi, thousands of blacks worked 40-acre tracts on leased lands formerly owned by Jefferson Davis. In this highly successful experiment, they made profits sufficient to repay the government for initial costs, and then lost the land to Davis's brother.

Many freedpeople expected a new economic order as fair payment for their years of involuntary work. "It's de white man's turn ter labor now," a black preacher in Florida told a group of fieldhands, adding that "de Guverment is gwine ter gie ter ev'ry Nigger forty acres of lan' an' a mule." Others were willing to settle for less: a freedman in Virginia offered to take only one acre of land—"Ef you make it de acre dat Marsa's house sets on." Another was more guarded, aware of how easy the power could shift back to white planters: "Gib us our own land and we take care ourselves; but widout land, de ole massas can hire us or starve us, as dey please."

Such cautions aside, freedpeople hoped that the promised "40 acres and a mule" was forthcoming. Once they obtained land, family unity, and education, many looked forward to civil rights and the vote—along with protection from vengeful defeated confederates.

Everything—and nothing—had changed: In the early months of freedom, the daily life of former slaves was both the same and different. Here (top) we see a photograph of freedpeople, led by a crew leader much like during slavery days, leaving the cotton fields after a full day of gang labor carrying cotton on their heads, and a sketch (above) of a Freedmen's Bureau school in 1866, which many men, women, and children attended at night. *(Top, © Collection of The New-York Historical Society; Above, The Newberry Library)*

The Promise of Land: 40 Acres

Note the progression in various documents in this chapter from promised lands (this page), to lands restored to whites (page 551), to work contracts (page 557), to semi-autonomous tenant farms (page 559). Freedom came by degrees to freedpeople.

To All Whom It May Concern
Edisto Island, August 15th, 1865

George Owens, having selected for settlement forty acres of Land, on Theodore Belab's Place, pursuant to Special Field Orders, No. 15, Headquarters Military Division of the Mississippi, Savannah, Ga., Jan. 16, 1865; he has permission to hold and occupy the said Tract, subject to such regulations as may be established by proper authority; and all persons are prohibited from interfering with him in his possession of the same.

By command of   R. SAXTON
                             Brev't Maj. Gen.,
                             Ass't Comm.
                             S.C., Ga., and Fla.

The White South's Fearful Response

White southerners had equally mixed goals and expectations. Middle-class (yeoman) farmers and poor whites stood beside rich planters in bread lines, all hoping to regain land and livelihood. Suffering from "extreme want and destitution," as a Cherokee County, Georgia, resident put it, southern whites responded to the immediate postwar crises with feelings of outrage, loss, and injustice. "I tell you it is mighty hard," said one man, "for my pa paid his own money for our niggers; and that's not all they've robbed us of. They have taken our horses and cattle and sheep and everything." Others felt the loss more personally, as former faithful slaves for whom they felt great affection suddenly left. "Something dreadful has happened," a Florida woman wrote in 1865. "My dear black mammy has left us. . . . I feel lost, I feel as if someone is dead in the house. Whatever will I do without my Mammy?"

A more dominant emotion than sorrow, however, was fear. The entire structure of southern society was shaken, and the semblance of racial peace and order that slavery had provided was shattered. Many white southerners could hardly imagine a society without blacks in bondage. Having lost control of all that was familiar and revered, whites feared everything—from losing their cheap labor supply to having blacks sit next to them on trains. Many feared the inconvenience of doing chores like housework that they had rarely done before. A

Georgia woman, Eliza Andrews, complained that it seemed to her a "waste of time for people who are capable of doing something better to spend their time sweeping and dusting while scores of lazy negroes that are fit for nothing else are lying around idle." Worse yet was the "impudent and presumin'" new manners of former slaves, a North Carolinian put it, worrying, with others, that blacks wanted social equality.

Ironically, given the rape of black women during slavery, southern whites' worst fears were of rape and revenge. African-American "impudence," some thought, would lead to legal intermarriage and "Africanization," the destruction of the purity of the white race. The presence of black soldiers was especially ominous. These fears were groundless, as demobilization of black militia units came quickly, and rape and violence by blacks against whites was extremely rare.

Believing their world turned upside down, the former planter aristocracy tried to set it right again. To reestablish white dominance, southern legislatures passed "Black codes" in the first year after the war. Many of the codes granted freedpeople the right to marry, sue and be sued, testify in court, and hold property. But these rights were qualified. Complicated passages explained under exactly what circumstances blacks could testify against whites or own property (mostly they could not) or exercise other rights of free people. Rights expressly denied were bearing arms, racial intermarriage, possessing alcoholic beverages, sitting on trains (except in baggage compartments), being on city streets at night, and congregating in large groups.

Many of the qualified rights guaranteed by the Black codes—testimony in court, for example—were passed only to induce the federal government to withdraw its remaining troops from the South. This was a crucial issue, for in many places marauding groups of whites were terrorizing virtually defenseless blacks. In one small district in Kentucky, for example, a government agent reported the following in 1865:

> Twenty-three cases of severe and inhuman beating and whipping of men; four of beating and shooting; two of robbing and shooting; three of robbing; five men shot and killed; two shot and wounded; four beaten to death; one beaten and roasted; three women assaulted and ravished; four women beaten; two women tied up and whipped until insensible; two men and their families beaten and driven from their homes, and their property destroyed; two instances of burning of dwellings, and one of the inmates shot.

The Black codes, widespread violence against freedpeople, and President Johnson's veto of the Civil Rights Bill gave rise to the sardonic question "Slavery Is Dead?" Note the irony of blind justice presiding over two violations of the freedpeople's rights (described in the newspaper headings at the bottom on either side of a death's head encircled by "state rights"). *(The Newberry Library, Chicago)*

Freedpeople clearly needed protection and the right to testify in court against whites.

For white planters, the violence was another sign of social disorder that could be eased only by restoring a plantation-based society. Besides, they needed African-American labor. Key provisions of the Black codes regulated freedpeople's economic status. "Vagrancy" laws provided that any blacks not "lawfully employed" (by a white employer) could be arrested, jailed, fined, or hired out to a man who would assume responsibility for their debts and behavior. The codes regulated black laborers' work contracts with white landowners, including severe penalties for leaving before the yearly contract was fulfilled and rules for proper behavior, attitude, and manners. Thus, southern leaders sought to reestablish their dominance, agreeing with the Texan who advocated adopting "a coercive system of labor." A Kentucky newspaper was more direct: "The tune . . . will not be 'forty acres and a mule,' but . . . 'work nigger or starve.'"

NATIONAL RECONSTRUCTION POLITICS

The Black codes directly challenged the national government in 1865. Would it use its power to uphold the codes or to defend freedpeople? Would the federal government support the property rights and self-interest of the few or the rights and liberties of the many? The Reconstruction drama took place both in the South and in Washington. Although the primary story pitted white landowners against black freedmen over land and labor on southern plantations, in the background of these local struggles lurked the debate over Reconstruction policy among politicians in the nation's capital. This dual drama would extend well into the twentieth century.

Presidential Reconstruction by Proclamation

After initially demanding that the defeated Confederates be punished for "treason," President

Johnson soon adopted a more lenient policy. On May 29, 1865, he issued two proclamations setting forth his Reconstruction program. Like Lincoln's, it rested on the claim that the southern states had never left the Union.

Johnson's first proclamation continued Lincoln's policies by offering "amnesty and pardon, with restoration of all rights of property" to most former Confederates who would swear allegiance to the Constitution and the Union. Johnson revealed his Jacksonian hostility to "aristocratic" planters by exempting former Confederate government leaders and rich rebels with taxable property valued over $20,000. They could, however, apply for individual pardons, which Johnson granted to nearly all applicants.

In his second proclamation, Johnson accepted the reconstructed government of North Carolina and prescribed the steps by which other southern states could reestablish state governments. First, the president would appoint a provisional governor, who would call a state convention representing those "who are loyal to the United States," including

Promised Land Restored to Whites

Richard H. Jenkins, an applicant for the restoration of his plantation on Wadmalaw Island, S. C., called "Rackett Hall," the same having been unoccupied during the past year and up to the 1st of Jan. 1866, except by one freedman who planted no crop, and being held by the Bureau of Refugees, Freedmen and Abandoned Lands, having conformed to the requirements of Circular No. 15 of said Bureau, dated Washington, D. C., Sept. 12, 1865, the aforesaid property is hereby restored to his possession.

. . . The Undersigned, Richard H. Jenkins, does hereby solemnly promise and engage, that he will secure to the Refugees and Freedmen now resident on his Wadmalaw Island Estate, the crops of the past year, harvested or unharvested; also, that the said Refugees and Freedmen shall be allowed to remain at their present houses or other homes on the island, so long as the responsible Refugees and Freedmen (embracing parents, guardians, and other natural protectors) shall enter into contracts, by leases or for wages, in terms satisfactory to the Supervising Board.

Also, that the undersigned will take the proper steps to enter into contracts with the above described responsible Refugees and Freedmen, the latter being required on their part to enter into said contracts on or before the 15th day of February, 1866, or surrender their right to remain on the said estate, it being understood that if they are unwilling to contract after the expiration of said period, the Supervising Board is to aid in getting them homes and employment elsewhere.

persons who took the oath of allegiance or were otherwise pardoned. The convention must ratify the Thirteenth Amendment, which abolished slavery; void secession; repudiate Confederate debts; and elect new state officials and members of Congress.

Under this lenient plan, all southern states completed Reconstruction and sent representatives to the Congress that convened in December 1865. Defiant southern voters elected dozens of former officers and legislators of the Confederacy, including a few not yet pardoned. Some state conventions hedged on ratifying the Thirteenth Amendment, and some asserted former owners' right to compensation for lost slave property. No state convention provided for black suffrage, and most did nothing to guarantee civil rights, schooling, or economic protection for the freedpeople. Eight months after Appomattox, the southern states were back in the Union, freedpeople were working for former masters under annual contracts, and the new president seemed firmly in charge. Reconstruction seemed to be over. A young French reporter, Georges Clemenceau, wondered if the North, having made so many "painful sacrifices," would "let itself be tricked out of what it had spent so much trouble and perseverance to win."

Congressional Reconstruction by Amendment

Late in 1865, northern leaders painfully saw that almost none of their postwar goals were being fulfilled. The South seemed far from reconstructed. The freedpeople had received neither equal citizenship nor economic independence. And the Republicans were not likely to maintain their political power. Would Democrats and the South gain by postwar elections what they had been unable to achieve by civil war?

A song popular in the North in 1866 posed the question: "Who shall rule this American Nation?"— those who would betray their country and "murder the innocent freedmen" or those "loyal millions" who had shed their "blood in battle"? The answer was obvious. Congressional Republicans, led by Congressman Thaddeus Stevens of Pennsylvania and Senator Charles Sumner of Massachusetts, decided to set their own policies for Reconstruction. Although labeled "radicals," the vast majority of Republicans were moderates on the economic and political rights of African Americans.

Rejecting Johnson's position that the South had already been reconstructed, Congress exercised its constitutional authority to decide on its own membership. It refused to seat the new senators and representatives from the former Confederate states. It also established the Joint Committee on Reconstruction to investigate conditions in the South. Its report documented white resistance, disorder, and the appalling treatment and conditions of freedpeople.

Even before the report came out in 1866, Congress passed a civil rights bill to protect the fragile rights of African Americans and extended for two more years the Freedmen's Bureau, an agency providing emergency assistance at the end of the war. Johnson vetoed both bills and called his congressional opponents "traitors." His actions drove moderates into the radical camp, and Congress passed both bills over his veto—both, however, watered down by weakening the power of enforcement. Southern courts, therefore, regularly disallowed black testimony against whites, acquitted whites of violence, and sentenced blacks to compulsory labor.

In such a climate, southern racial violence erupted. In May 1866, white mobs in Memphis, encouraged by local Irish police violence against black Union soldiers stationed nearby, went on the rampage. For over 40 hours of terror, they killed, beat, robbed, and raped virtually helpless black residents and burned houses, schools, and churches. A Memphis newspaper suggested that "the negro can do the country more good in the cotton field than in the camp," and prominent local officials urged the mob to "go ahead and kill the last damned one of the nigger race." Forty-eight people died, all but two of them black. The local Union army commander took his time restoring order, arguing that his troops "hated Negroes too." A congressional inquiry found that Memphis blacks had "no protection from the law whatever."

A month later, Congress sent to the states for ratification the Fourteenth Amendment, the most significant act of the Reconstruction era. The first section of the amendment promised permanent constitutional protection of the civil rights of blacks by defining them as citizens. States were prohibited from depriving "any person of life, liberty, or property, without due process of law," and all people were guaranteed the "equal protection of the laws." Section 2 granted black male suffrage in the South, putting the word "male" into the Constitution for the first time, and stating that those states denying the black vote would have their "basis of representation" reduced proportionally. Other sections of the amendment barred leaders of the Confederacy from national or state offices (except by act of Congress), and repudiated the Confederate debt and claims of compensation to former slave owners. Johnson urged the southern states to reject the Fourteenth Amendment, and 10 immediately did so.

The Fourteenth Amendment was the central issue of the 1866 midterm election. Johnson barnstormed the country asking voters to throw out the radical Republicans and trading insults with hecklers. Democrats north and south appealed openly to racial prejudice in attacking the Fourteenth Amendment. The nation would be "Africanized," they charged, with black equality threatening both

Reconstruction Amendments

Constitutional Seeds of Dreams Deferred for 100 Years (or More)

Substance	Outcome of Ratification Process	Final Implementation and Enforcement
Thirteenth Amendment—Passed by Congress January 1865		
Prohibited slavery in the United States	Ratified by 27 states, including 8 southern states, by December 1865	Immediate, although economic freedom came by degrees
Fourteenth Amendment—Passed by Congress June 1866		
(1) Defined equal national citizenship; (2) reduced state representation in Congress proportional to number of disenfranchised voters; (3) denied former Confederates the right to hold office; (4) Confederate debts and lost property claims voided and illegal	Rejected by 12 southern and border states by February 1867; Congress made readmission depend on ratification; ratified in July 1868	Civil Rights Act of 1964
Fifteenth Amendment—Passed by Congress February 1869		
Prohibited denial of vote because of race, color, or previous servitude (but not sex)	Ratification by Virginia, Texas, Mississippi, and Georgia required for readmission; ratified in March 1870	Voting Rights Act of 1965

Note: See exact wording in U.S. Constitution in the Appendix.

A white mob burned this freedpeople's school during the Memphis riot of May 1866. *(Library Company of Philadelphia)*

the marketplace and the bedroom. Republicans responded by calling Johnson a drunkard and a traitor and by "waving the bloody shirt," reminding voters of Democrats' treason and draft dodging during the civil war. Governor Oliver P. Morton of Indiana described the Democratic party as a "common sewer and loathsome receptacle [for] inhumanity and barbarism." But self-interest and local issues moved voters more than speeches, and the result was an overwhelming Republican victory. The mandate seemed clear: presidential Reconstruction had not worked, and Congress could present its own.

Early in 1867, Congress passed three Reconstruction acts. The southern states were divided into five military districts, whose military commanders had broad powers to maintain order and protect civil and property rights. Congress also defined a new process for readmitting a state. Qualified voters—including blacks but excluding unreconstructed rebels—would elect delegates to state constitutional conventions that would write new constitutions guaranteeing black suffrage. After the new voters of the states had ratified these constitutions, elections would be held to choose governors and state legislatures. When a state ratified the Fourteenth Amendment, its representatives to

Congress would be accepted, completing readmission to the Union.

The President Impeached

Congress also restricted presidential powers and launched an era of legislative dominance over the executive branch. The Tenure of Office Act, designed to prevent Johnson from firing the outspoken Secretary of War Edwin Stanton, limited the president's appointment powers. Other measures trimmed his power as commander in chief.

Johnson responded exactly as congressional Republicans had anticipated. He vetoed the Reconstruction acts, removed cabinet officers and other officials sympathetic to Congress, hindered the work of Freedmen's Bureau agents, and limited the activities of military commanders in the South. The House Judiciary Committee investigated, charging the president with "usurpations of power" and of acting in the "interests of the great criminals" who had led the southern rebellion. But moderate House Republicans defeated the impeachment resolutions.

In August 1867, Johnson dismissed Stanton and asked for Senate consent. When the Senate refused, the president ordered Stanton to surrender his office, which he refused, barricading himself inside.

The House quickly approved impeachment resolutions, charging the president with "high crimes and misdemeanors." The three-month trial in the Senate early in 1868 featured impassioned oratory, similar to the trial of President Bill Clinton 131 years later. Evidence was skimpy, however, that Johnson, like Clinton, had committed any constitutional crime justifying his removal. With seven moderate Republicans joining Democrats against conviction, the effort to find the president guilty fell one vote short of the required two-thirds majority. Not until the late twentieth century (Nixon and Clinton) would an American president face removal from office through impeachment.

Moderate Republicans, satisfied with the changes wrought by the Civil War, may have feared the consequences of removing Johnson, for the next man in line for the presidency, Senator Benjamin Wade of Ohio, was a leading radical Republican. Wade had endorsed woman suffrage, rights for labor unions, and civil rights for blacks in both southern and northern states. As moderate Republicans gained strength in 1868 through their support of the presidential election winner, Ulysses S. Grant, radicalism lost much of its power within Republican ranks.

What Congressional Moderation Meant for Rebels, Blacks, and Women

The impeachment crisis revealed that most Republicans were more interested in protecting themselves than the freedpeople and in punishing Johnson rather than the South. Congress's political battle against the president was not matched by a commitment to African Americans. State and local elections of 1867 showed that voters preferred moderate Reconstruction policies. In the enduring national effort to embody principles of justice, freedom, and rights, it is important to look not only at what Congress did during Reconstruction but also at what it did not do.

With the exception of Jefferson Davis, Congress did not imprison rebel Confederate leaders, and only one person, the commander of the infamous Andersonville prison camp, was executed. Congress did not insist on a lengthy probation before southern states could be readmitted to the Union. It did not reorganize southern local governments. It did not mandate a national program of education for freedpeople. It did not confiscate and redistribute land to the freedpeople, nor did it prevent Johnson from taking land away from those who had gained titles during the war. It did not, except indirectly, provide economic help to black citizens.

What Congress did do was to grant citizenship and suffrage to freedpeople, although only to southern black men. Northerners were no more prepared than southerners to make all blacks fully equal citizens. Between 1865 and 1869, several states held referendums proposing black (male) suffrage. Voters in Kansas, Ohio, Michigan, Missouri, Wisconsin, Connecticut, New York, and the District of Columbia all turned down the proposals. Only in Iowa and Minnesota (on the third try, and then only by devious wording) did northern whites grant the vote to blacks.

Proposals to give black men the vote gained support in the North only after the election of 1868, when General Grant, the supposedly invincible military hero, barely won the popular vote in several states. To ensure grateful black votes, Congressional Republicans, who had twice rejected a suffrage amendment, took another look at the idea. After a bitter fight, in 1870 the Fifteenth Amendment, forbidding all states to deny the vote "on account of race, color, or previous condition of servitude," became part of the Constitution. A black preacher from Pittsburgh observed that "the Republican party had done the Negro good, but they were doing themselves good at the same time."

One casualty of the Fourteenth and Fifteenth Amendments was the goodwill of white women. They had been fighting for rights, including the right to vote, since the Seneca Falls convention in 1848, and hoped that grateful male legislators would recognize their willing suspension of their campaign in order to support the Union during the war. The Woman's Loyal League, headed by Elizabeth Cady Stanton and Susan B. Anthony, had gathered nearly 400,000 signatures petitioning Congress to pass the Thirteenth Amendment. They were therefore shocked when the Fourteenth (and later the Fifteenth) Amendments applied only to "male" voters.

Some suffragists such as Lucy Stone were willing to accept delay, recognizing the plea of Frederick Douglass, a longtime proponent of woman suffrage, that this was "the Negro's hour." But Stanton and Anthony, veteran suffragists, campaigned against an amendment that left them out, refusing to ask women to continue to rely on fathers and husbands to protect their rights. Anthony vowed to "cut off this right arm of mine before I will ever work for or demand the ballot for the Negro and not the woman."

Disappointment over the suffrage issue helped split the women's movement in 1869. Anthony and Stanton continued their fight for a national amendment for woman suffrage and a long list of property, educational, and sexual rights, while other women focused on securing the vote state by state.

Abandoned by radical and moderate men alike, women had few champions in Congress and their efforts were put off for half a century.

The moderate Congress compromised the rights of African Americans as well as women. It gave blacks the vote but not the land, the opposite of what they wanted. Almost alone, Thaddeus Stevens argued that "forty acres . . . and a hut would be more valuable . . . than the . . . right to vote." But Congress never seriously considered his plan to confiscate the land of the "chief rebels" and give a small portion of it, divided into 40-acre plots, to the freedpeople, for this would have violated deeply held American beliefs in the sacredness of private property. Moreover, northern business interests looking to develop southern industry and invest in southern land liked the prospect of a large pool of property-less black workers.

Congress did, however, pass the Southern Homestead Act of 1866 making public lands available to blacks and loyal whites in five southern states. But the land was poor and inaccessible; no transportation, tools, or seed was provided; and most blacks were bound by contracts that prevented them from making claims before the deadline. Only about 4,000 black families even applied for the Homestead Act lands, and fewer than 20 percent of them saw their claims completed. White claimants did little better. Congressional moderation, therefore, ironically strengthened southern white landowners while leaving freedmen and women economically weak and with only paper rights as they faced the challenges of freedom.

THE LIVES OF FREEDPEOPLE

Union army major George Reynolds boasted to a friend late in 1865 that in the area of Mississippi under his command, he had "kept the negroes at work, and in a good state of discipline." Clinton Fisk, a well-meaning white who helped found a black college in Tennessee, told freedmen in 1866 that they could be "as free and as happy" working again for their "old master . . . as any where else in the world." Such pronouncements reminded blacks of white preachers' exhortations during slavery to work hard and obey their masters. Ironically, Fisk and Reynolds were agents of the Freedmen's Bureau, the agency intended to aid the black transition from slavery to freedom.

The Freedmen's Bureau

Never before in American history had one small agency—underfinanced, understaffed, and under-supported—been given a harder task than the Bureau of Freedmen, Refugees and Abandoned Lands. But with amnesty restoring lands to former owners, the Bureau controlled less than 1 percent of southern lands. Its name is telling; its fate epitomizes Reconstruction.

The Freedmen's Bureau performed many essential services. It issued emergency food rations, clothed and sheltered homeless victims of the war, and established medical and hospital facilities. It provided funds to relocate thousands of freedpeople. It helped blacks search for relatives and get legally married. It represented African Americans in local civil courts to see that they got fair trials. In conjunction with northern missionary aid societies and southern black churches, the Bureau was responsible for an extensive education program, authorizing a half million dollars for freedpeople's schooling.

Many of the earliest teachers were Quaker and Yankee "schoolmarms" who volunteered through the American Missionary Association to teach in the South. In October, 1865, Esther Douglass found "120 dirty, half naked, perfectly wild black children" in her schoolroom near Savannah, Georgia. Eight months later, she reported, "their progress was wonderful"; they could read, sing hymns, and repeat Bible verses. Bureau Commissioner General O. O. Howard estimated that by 1868, one-third of southern black children had been educated by Bureau schools. By 1870, there were almost 250,000 pupils in 4,329 agency schools when Bureau funds for education were terminated.

The Bureau's largest task was to provide African-American economic survival, serving as an employment agency. This included settling blacks on abandoned lands and getting them started with tools, seed, and draft animals, as well as arranging work contracts with white landowners. But in this area, the Freedmen's Bureau, although not intending to instill a new dependency, often supported the needs of whites to find cheap labor rather than helping blacks to become independent farmers.

Although some agents were eager to help freedpeople adjust to freedom, others were Union army officers more concerned with social order than social transformation. Working in a postwar climate of resentment and violence, Freedmen's Bureau agents were overworked, underpaid, spread too thin (at its peak only 900 agents were scattered across 11 states), and constantly harassed by local whites. Even the best-intentioned agents would have agreed with General Howard's belief in the nineteenth-century American values of self-help, minimal government interference in the marketplace, the sanctity

The Freedmen's Bureau had fewer resources in relation to its purpose than any agency in the nation's history. *Harper's Weekly* published this engraving of freedpeople lining up for aid in Memphis in 1866. *(Library of Congress)*

of private property, contractual obligations, and white superiority. The Bureau's work served to uphold these values as it sought to aid the freedpeople.

On a typical day, these overburdened agents would visit local courts and schools, file reports, supervise the signing of work contracts, and handle numerous complaints, most involving contract violations between whites and blacks or property and domestic disputes among blacks. A Georgia agent wrote that he was "*tired out* and *broke down*. . . . Every day for 6 months, day after day, I have had from 5 to 20 complaints, *generally trivial* and of no moment, yet requiring consideration & attention coming from both Black & White." Another, reflecting his growing frustrations, complained that the freedpeople were "disrespectful and greatly in need of instruction." In finding work for freedmen and imploring freedwomen to hold their husbands accountable as providers, agents often sided with white landowners by telling blacks to obey orders, trust employers, and accept disadvantageous contracts. One agent sent a man who had complained of a severe beating back to work with the advice, "Don't be sassy [and] don't be lazy when you've got work to do."

Despite numerous constraints and even threats on their lives, the agents accomplished much. In little more than two years, the Freedmen's Bureau issued 20 million rations (nearly one-third to poor whites); reunited families and resettled some 30,000 displaced war refugees; treated some 450,000 people for illness and injury; built 40 hospitals and hundreds of schools; provided books, tools, and furnishings to the freedmen; and occasionally protected their civil rights. W.E.B. Du Bois, arguably the greatest African-American scholar of the twentieth century, wrote, "In a time of perfect calm, amid willing neighbors and streaming wealth," it "would have been a herculean task" for the Bureau to fulfill its many purposes. But in the midst of hunger, hate, sorrow, suspicion, and cruelty, "the work of . . . social regeneration was in large part foredoomed to failure." The Bureau's greatest success was education; providing land was its greatest failure. By 1868, all agents were gone as Congress stopped funding.

Economic Freedom by Degrees

Despite the best efforts of the Freedmen's Bureau, the failure of Congress to provide the promised 40 acres and a mule forced freedmen and women into a new economic dependency on former masters. Blacks made some progress, however, in degrees of economic autonomy and were partly responsible, along with international economic developments, in forcing the white planter class into making major changes in southern agriculture.

First, a land-intensive system replaced the labor intensity of slavery. Land ownership was concentrated into fewer and even larger holdings than before the war. From South Carolina to Louisiana, the wealthiest tenth of the population owned about 60 percent of the real estate in the 1870s. Second, these large planters increasingly concentrated on one crop, usually cotton, and were tied into the international market. This resulted in a steady drop in food production (both grains and livestock). Third, one-crop farming created a new credit system whereby

most farmers—black and white—were forced into dependence on local merchants for renting seed, farm implements and animals, provisions, housing, and land. These changes affected race relations and class tensions among whites.

This new system, however, took a few years to develop after emancipation. At first, most African Americans signed contracts with white landowners and worked fields in gangs very much as during slavery. Supervised by superintendents who still used the lash, they toiled from sunrise to sunset for a meager wage and a monthly allotment of bacon and meal. All members of the family had to work to receive their rations.

Freedpeople resented this new semi-servitude, refused to sign the contracts, and sought a measure of independence working their own lands. A South

---

A Freedman's Work Contract

As you read this rather typical work contract defining the first economic relationship between whites and blacks in the early months of the postwar period, note the regulation of social behavior and deportment, as well as work and "pay" arrangements. How different is this from slavery? As a freedman or freedwoman, would you have signed such an agreement? Why or why not? What options did you have?

State of South Carolina
Darlington District
Articles of Agreement

This Agreement entered into between Mrs. Adele Allston Exect of the one part, and the Freedmen and Women of The Upper Quarters plantation of the other part Witnesseth:

That the latter agree, for the remainder of the present year, to reside upon and devote their labor to the cultivation of the Plantation of the former. And they further agree, that they will in all respects, conform to such reasonable and necessary plantation rules and regulations as Mrs. Allston's Agent may prescribe; that they will not keep any gun, pistol, or other offensive weapon, or leave the plantation without permission from their employer; that in all things connected with their duties as laborers on said plantation, they will yield prompt obedience to all orders from Mrs. Allston or his [sic] agent; that they will be orderly and quiet in their conduct, avoiding drunkenness and other gross vices; that they will not misuse any of the Plantation Tools, or Agricultural Implements, or any Animals entrusted to their care, or any Boats, Flats, Carts or Wagons; that they will give up at the expiration of this Contract, all Tools & c., belonging to the Plantation, and in case any property, of any description belonging to the Plantation shall be willfully or through negligence destroyed or injured, the value of the Articles so destroyed, shall be deducted from the portion of the Crops which the person or persons, so offending, shall be entitled to receive under this Contract.

Any deviations from the condition of the foregoing Contract may, upon sufficient proof, be punished with dismissal from the Plantation, or in such other manner as may be determined by the Provost Court; and the person or persons so dismissed, shall forfeit the whole, or a part of his, her or their portion of the crop, as the Court may decide.

In consideration of the foregoing Services duly performed, Mrs. Allston agrees, after deducting Seventy five bushels of Corn for each work Animal, exclusively used in cultivating the Crops for the present year; to turn over to the said Freedmen and Women, one half of the remaining Corn, Peas, Potatoes, made this season. He [sic] further agrees to furnish the usual rations until the Contract is performed.

All Cotton Seed Produced on the Plantation is to be reserved for the use of the Plantation. The Freedmen, Women and Children are to be treated in a manner consistent with their freedom. Necessary medical attention will be furnished as heretofore.

Any deviation from the conditions of this Contract upon the part of the said Mrs. Allston or her Agent or Agents shall be punished in such manner as may be determined by a Provost Court, or a Military Commission. This agreement to continue till the first day of January 1866.

Witness our hand at The Upper Quarters this 28th day of July 1865.

Carolina freedman said, "If I can't own de land, I'll hire or lease land, but I won't contract." Freedwomen especially wanted to send their children to school rather than to the fields and, except for small vegetable gardens, insisted on "no more outdoor work."

A Georgia planter observed that freedpeople wanted "to get away from all overseers, to hire or purchase land, and work for themselves." Many broke contracts, haggled over wages, engaged in work slowdowns or strikes, burned barns, and otherwise expressed their displeasure with the contract labor system. In the Sea Islands and rice-growing regions of coastal South Carolina and Georgia, resistance was especially strong. On the Heyward plantations, near the Allstons, blacks "refuse work at any price," a Bureau agent reported, and the women "wish to stay in the house or the garden all the time." Even when offered livestock and other incentives, the Allstons' blacks refused to sign their contracts, and in 1869 Adele Allston was forced to sell much of her vast landholdings.

Blacks' insistence on autonomy and land of their own was the major impetus for the change from the contract system to tenancy and sharecropping. Families would hitch mules to their old slave cabin and drag it to their plot as far from the Big House as possible. Sharecroppers received seed, fertilizer, implements, food, and clothing. In return, the landlord (or a local merchant) told them what and how much to grow, and he took a share—usually half—of the harvest. The croppers' half usually went to pay for goods bought on credit (at high interest rates) from the landlord. Sharecroppers remained only semi-autonomous, tied to the landlord for economic survival.

Tenant farmers had only slightly more independence. Before a harvest, they promised to sell their crop to a local merchant in return for renting land, tools, and other necessities. From the merchant's store they also had to buy goods on credit (at a higher price than whites paid) against the harvest. At "settling up" time, income from sale of the crop was compared with accumulated debts. It was possible, especially after an unusually bountiful season, to come out ahead and eventually to own one's own land. But tenants rarely did; in debt at the end of each year, they had to pledge the next year's crop. World cotton prices remained low, and whereas big landowners still generated profits through their large scale of operation, sharecroppers rarely made much money. When they were able to pay their debts, landowners frequently altered loan agreements. Thus, debt peonage replaced slavery, ensuring a continuing cheap labor supply to grow cotton and other staples in the South.

Despite this bleak picture, painstaking, industrious work by African Americans helped many gradually accumulate a measure of income, personal property, and autonomy, especially in the household economy of producing eggs, butter, meat, food

Sharecroppers and tenant farmers, though more autonomous than contract laborers, remained dependent on the landlord for their survival. *(Brown Brothers)*

The Rise of Tenancy in the South, 1880

Although no longer slaves and after resisting labor contracts and the gang system of field labor, the freedpeople (as well as many poor whites) became tenant farmers, working on shares in the New South. The former slaves on the Barrow Plantation in Georgia, for example, moved their households to individual 25 to 30 acre tenant farms, which they rented from the Barrow family in annual contracts requiring payment in cotton and other cash crops. Where was the highest percentage of tenant farms, and how do you explain it? How would you explain the low percentage areas? What do you notice about how circumstances have changed—and not changed—on the Barrow plantation?

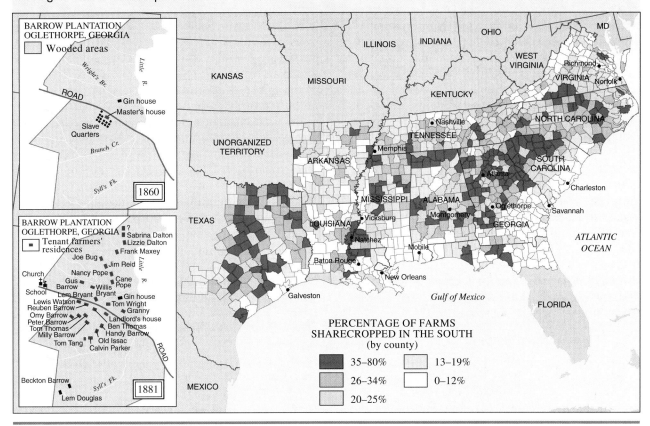

crops, and other staples. Debt did not necessarily mean a lack of subsistence. In Virginia the declining tobacco crop forced white planters to sell off small parcels of land to blacks. Throughout the South, a few African Americans became independent landowners—about 3–4 percent by 1880, but closer to 25 percent by 1900.

White Farmers During Reconstruction

Changes in southern agriculture affected yeoman and poor white farmers as well, and planters worried about a coalition between poor black and pro-Unionist white farmers. As a white Georgia farmer said in 1865, "We should tuk the land, as we did the niggers, and split it, and giv part to the niggers and part to me and t'other Union fellers." But confiscation and redistribution of land was no more likely for white farmers than for the freedpeople. Whites, too, had to concentrate on growing staples, pledging their crops against high-interest credit, and facing perpetual indebtedness. In the upcountry piedmont area of Georgia, for example, the number of whites working their own land dropped from nine in ten before the Civil War to seven in ten by 1880, while cotton production doubled.

Reliance on cotton meant fewer food crops and therefore greater dependence on merchants for provisions. In 1884, Jephta Dickson of Jackson County, Georgia, purchased over $50 worth of flour, meal, meat, syrup, peas, and corn from a local store;

25 years earlier he had been almost completely self-sufficient. Fencing laws seriously curtailed the livelihood of poor whites raising pigs and hogs, and restrictions on hunting and fishing reduced the ability of poor whites and blacks alike to supplement incomes and diets.

In the worn-out flatlands and barren mountainous regions of the South, poor whites' antebellum poverty, health, and isolation worsened after the war. A Freedmen's Bureau agent in South Carolina described the poor whites in his area as "gaunt and ragged, ungainly, stooping and clumsy in build." They lived a marginal existence, hunting, fishing, and growing corn and potato crops that, as a North Carolinian put it, "come up puny, grow puny, and mature puny." Many poor white farmers, in fact, were even less productive than black sharecroppers. Some became farmhands at $6 a month and board. Others fled to low-paying jobs in cotton mills, where they would not have to compete against blacks.

The cultural life of poor southern whites reflected both their lowly position and their pride. Their religion centered on the emotional camp meeting revivals. In backwoods clearings, men and women told tall tales of superhuman feats and exchanged folk remedies for poor health. Their ballads and folklore told of debt, chain gangs, and deeds of drinking prowess. Their quilt making and house construction reflected a marginal culture in which everything was saved and reused.

In part because their lives were so hard, poor whites clung to their belief in white superiority. A federal officer reported in 1866, "The poorer classes of white people . . . have a most intense hatred of the Negro, and swear he shall never be reckoned as part of the population." Many joined the Ku Klux Klan and other southern white terror groups that emerged in 1866 to resist Reconstruction. The Klan was founded initially in Tennessee by six Confederate veterans and populated by a cross section of southern white society. With a fierce belief in white superiority, the Klan terrorized freedpeople and their white Republican allies. The Klan expressed its hatred in midnight raids on teachers in black schools, laborers who disputed their landlords' discipline, Republican voters, and any black whose "impudence" caused him not to "bow and scrape to a white man, as was done formerly."

Black Self-Help Institutions

Enforced by the Klan, African Americans were beaten, killed, sentenced to chain gangs for the slightest crimes, and bound to a life of debt, degradation, and dependency. Their hopes and dreams

after emancipation had soured. Texan Felix Haywood recalled:

> We thought we was goin' to be richer than white folks, 'cause we was stronger and knowed how to work, and the whites . . . didn't have us to work for them anymore. But it didn't turn out that way. We soon found out that freedom could make folks proud but it didn't make 'em rich.

Haywood understood the limitations of programs and efforts on behalf of the freedpeople. It was clear to many black leaders, therefore, that because white people and institutions could not fulfill the promises of emancipation, blacks would have to do it themselves.

They began, significantly, with churches. The tradition of black community self-help survived in the organized churches and schools of the antebellum free Negro communities and in the "invisible" religious and cultural institutions of the slave quarters. As Union troops liberated areas of the Confederacy, blacks fled white churches for their own, causing an explosion in the growth of membership in African-American churches. The Negro Baptist Church grew from 150,000 members in 1850 to 500,000 in 1870, while the membership of the African Methodist Episcopal Church increased in the postwar decade from 50,000 to 200,000, and by 1896 to over 400,000 members. Other denominations such as the Colored (later Christian) Methodist Episcopal (CME) Church, the Reformed Zion Union Apostolic Church, and the Colored Presbyterian Church all broke with their white counterparts to establish indigenous black churches in the first decade after emancipation.

African-American ministers continued to exert community leadership. Many led efforts to oppose discrimination, some by entering politics: over one-fifth of the black officeholders in South Carolina were ministers. Most preachers, however, focused on sin, conversion, salvation, and revivalist enthusiasm. An English visitor to the South in 1867 and 1868, after observing a revivalist preacher in Savannah arouse nearly 1,000 people to "sway, and cry, and groan," noted the intensity of black "devoutness." Despite some efforts by urban blacks to restrain the emotionalism characteristic of black worship, most congregations preferred traditional forms of religious expression. One woman, when urged to pray more quietly, complained: "We make noise 'bout ebery ting else . . . I want ter go ter Heaben in de good ole way."

The freedpeople's desire for education was as strong as for religion. Even before the Freedmen's Bureau ceased operating schools, African Americans assumed more responsibility for their costs and operation. Black South Carolinians contributed

$17,000, 16 percent of the cash cost of education, and more in labor and supplies. Louisiana and Kentucky blacks contributed more to education than the Bureau itself. Georgia African Americans increased the number of "freedom schools" from 79 to 232 in 1866–1867, despite attacks by local whites who stoned them on their way home and threatened to "kill every d——d nigger white man" who worked in the schools.

Black teachers increasingly replaced whites. By 1868, 43 percent of the Bureau's teachers were African American, working for four or five dollars a month and boarding with families. Although white teachers played a remarkable role in the education of freedpeople during Reconstruction, black teachers were more persistent and positive. Charlotte Forten, for example, who taught in a school in the Sea Islands, noted that even after a half day's "hard toil" in the fields, her older pupils were "as bright and as anxious to learn as ever." Despite the taunting degradation of "the haughty Anglo-Saxon race," she said, blacks showed "a desire for knowledge, and a capability for attaining it."

Indeed, by 1870 there was a 20 percent gain in freed black adult literacy, a figure that, against difficult odds, would continue to grow for all ages to the end of the century, when there were more than 1.5 million black children in school with 28,560 black teachers. This achievement was remarkable in the face of crowded facilities, limited resources, local opposition, and absenteeism caused by the demands of fieldwork. In Georgia, for example, only 5 percent of black children went to school for part of any one year between 1865 and 1870, as opposed to 20 percent of white children. To train teachers like Forten, northern philanthropists founded Fisk, Howard, Atlanta, and other black universities in the South between 1865 and 1867.

Black schools, like churches, became community centers. They published newspapers, provided training in trades and farming, and promoted political participation and land ownership. A black farmer in Mississippi founded both a school and a society to facilitate land acquisition and better agricultural methods. These efforts made black schools objects of local white hostility. A Virginia freedman told a congressional committee that in his county, anyone starting a school would be killed and blacks were "afraid to be caught with a book." In Alabama, the Klan hanged an Irish-born teacher and four black men. In 1869, in Tennessee alone, 37 black schools were burned to the ground.

Along with equal civil rights and land of their own, what the freedpeople wanted most was education. Despite white opposition and limited facilities for black schools, one of the most positive outcomes of the Reconstruction era was education in freedpeople's schools. *(Valentine Museum, Richmond, Virginia)*

White opposition to black education and land ownership stimulated African-American nationalism and separatism. In the late 1860s, Benjamin "Pap" Singleton, a Tennessee slave who had escaped to Canada, observed that "whites had the lands and . . . blacks had nothing but their freedom." Singleton urged them to abandon politics and migrate westward. He organized a land company in 1869, purchased public property in Kansas, and in the early 1870s took several groups from Tennessee and Kentucky to establish separate black towns in the prairie state. In following years, thousands of "exodusters" from the Lower South bought some 10,000 infertile acres in Kansas. But natural and human obstacles to self-sufficiency often proved insurmountable. By the 1880s, despairing of ever finding economic independence in the United States, Singleton and other nationalists urged emigration to Canada and Liberia. Frederick Douglass and other African-American leaders continued to press for full citizenship rights within the United States.

RECONSTRUCTION IN THE SOUTHERN STATES

Douglass's confidence in the power of the ballot seemed warranted in the enthusiastic early months under the Reconstruction Acts of 1867. With President Johnson neutralized, national Republican leaders finally could prevail. Local Republicans, taking advantage of the inability or refusal of many southern whites to vote, overwhelmingly elected their delegates to state constitutional conventions in the fall of 1867. Guardedly optimistic and sensing the "sacred importance" of their work, black and white Republicans began creating new state governments.

Republican Rule

Contrary to early pro-southern historians, the southern state governments under Republican rule were not dominated by illiterate black majorities intent on "Africanizing" the South by passing compulsory racial intermarriage laws, as many whites feared. Nor were these governments unusually corrupt or extravagant, nor did they use massive numbers of federal troops to enforce their will. By 1869, only 1,100 federal soldiers remained in Virginia, and most federal troops in Texas were guarding the frontier against Mexico (temporarily under French-imposed monarchial rule) and hostile Indians. Lacking strong military backing, the new state governments tried to do their work in a climate of economic distress and increasingly violent harassment.

Diverse coalitions made up the new governments elected under congressional Reconstruction. These "black and tan" governments (as opponents called them) were actually predominantly white, except for the lower house of the South Carolina legislature. Some new leaders came from the old Whig elite of bankers, industrialists, and others interested far more in economic growth and sectional reconciliation than in radical social reforms. A second group consisted of northern Republican capitalists who headed south to invest in land, railroads, and new industries. Others included Union veterans and missionaries and teachers inspired to work in Freedmen's Bureau schools. Such people were unfairly labeled "carpetbaggers."

Moderate African Americans made up a third group in the Republican state governments. A large percentage of black officeholders were mulattos, many of them well-educated preachers, teachers, and soldiers from the North. Others were self-educated tradesmen or representatives of the small landed class of southern blacks. In South Carolina, for example, of some 255 black state and federal officials elected between 1868 and 1876, two-thirds were literate and one-third owned real estate; only 15 percent owned no property at all. This class composition meant that African-American leaders often supported land policies that largely ignored the land redistribution needs of the black masses. Their goals fit squarely into the American republican tradition. Black leaders reminded whites that they, too, were southerners: "the dust of our fathers mingles with yours in the same grave yards," an 1865 petition put it, seeking only that "the same laws which govern white men shall govern black men."

The primary accomplishment of Republican rule in the South was to eliminate undemocratic features from prewar state constitutions. All states provided universal male suffrage and loosened requirements for holding office. Underrepresented counties got more legislative seats. Automatic imprisonment for debt was ended, and laws were enacted to relieve poverty and care for the handicapped. Many southern states passed their first divorce laws and provisions granting property rights to married women. Lists of crimes punishable by death were shortened, in one state from 26 to 5.

Republican governments reconstructed the South financially and physically by overhauling tax systems and approving generous railroad and other capital investment bonds. Harbors, roads, and bridges were rebuilt; hospitals and asylums were established. Most important, the Republican governments created the South's first public school systems. As in the North, these schools were largely

The Establishment of Historically Black Colleges in the South During Reconstruction

Note the scattered location of Freedmen's Bureau agencies in eight of the eleven former Confederate states. How well do you imagine agents were able to serve the 4 million freedpeople in their areas? The establishment of black colleges during Reconstruction by mostly white philanthropic monies suggests that self-help through the preparation of black preachers, teachers, and other educated leaders had more long-term potential for achieving the freedpeople's goals. What else do you see here?

Legend:
- ○ Locations of Freedmen's Bureaus
- Black colleges established during the Reconstruction Era
- Black colleges established before the Civil War
- Former Confederate states with Freedmen's Bureaus
- Former Confederate states without Freedmen's Bureaus
- Border states during Civil War

segregated, but for the first time, rich and poor, black and white alike had access to education. By the 1880s, African-American school attendance increased from 5 to over 40 percent, and white attendance increased from 20 to over 60 percent. All this cost money, and so the Republicans also increased tax rates and state debts.

These considerable achievements came in the face of opposition like that expressed at a convention of Louisiana planters, which labeled the Republican leaders the "lowest and most corrupt body of men ever assembled in the South." There was some corruption, mostly in land sales, railway bonds, and construction contracts. Such graft had become a way of life in postwar American politics, South and North.

But given their lack of experience with politics, the black role was remarkable. As Du Bois put it, "There was one thing that the White South feared more than negro dishonesty, ignorance, and incompetence, and that was negro honesty, knowledge, and efficiency."

Despite its effectiveness in modernizing southern state governments, the Republican coalition did not survive. The map on page 564 shows that Republican rule lasted for different periods in different states. A Georgia newspaper in 1868 charged that Republican rulers would "see this fair land drenched in blood from the Potomac to the Rio Grande rather than lose their power." True to their word, in Georgia and Virginia, Republicans ruled hardly at all. Situated in the shadow of Washington,

The Return of Conservative Democratic Control in Southern States During Reconstruction

Note that the length of time Republican governments were in power to implement even moderate Reconstruction programs varied from state to state. In North Carolina and Georgia, for example, Republican rule was very brief, while in Virginia it never took place at all. "Redemption," the return of conservative control, took longest in the three Deep South states where electoral votes were hotly contested in the election of 1876.

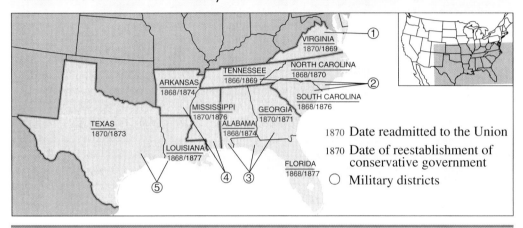

conservatives in Virginia professed agreement with Congress's Reconstruction guidelines while doing as they pleased. In South Carolina, white violence and African-American leaders' unwillingness to use their power to help black laborers contributed to a loss of political control to the Democrats in 1876.

Republican rule lasted longest in the Black Belt Gulf states. In Louisiana, Reconstruction began with General Ben Butler's occupation of New Orleans in 1862. Although he granted civil rights to blacks, he was quickly replaced by a succession of Republican governors in the late 1860s more interested in graft, election laws, and staying in office than in the rights and welfare of freedpeople. Class tensions and divisions among blacks in Louisiana also helped to weaken the Republican regime there. Alabama received a flood of northern capital to develop railroads and the rich coal, iron ore, and timber resources of the northern third of the state. Republican rule in Alabama typified the greater role for merchants and the emergence of a new class structure to replace the old planter aristocracy. Mississippi was another story, as we see in the next section.

Violence and "Redemption"

Democrats used violence, intimidation, and coercion to regain power. As one southern editor put it, "We must render this either a white man's government, or convert the land into a Negro man's cemetery." The Ku Klux Klan was only one of several secret organizations that used violent force to drive black and white Republicans from power. Although violence was terrible throughout the South, Mississippi and North Carolina typify the pattern.

After losing a close election in North Carolina in 1868, conservatives waged a concentrated terror campaign in several piedmont counties, areas of strong Unionist support. If the Democrats could win these counties in 1870, they would most likely win statewide. In the year before the election, several prominent Republicans were killed, including a white state senator, whose throat was cut, and a leading black Union League organizer, who was hanged in the courthouse square with a sign pinned to his breast: "Bewar, ye guilty, both white and black." Scores of citizens were flogged, tortured, fired from their jobs, or driven in the middle of the night from burning homes and barns. The courts consistently refused to prosecute anyone for these crimes, which local papers blamed on "disgusting negroes and white Radicals." The conservative campaign worked. In the election of 1870, some 12,000 fewer Republicans voted in the two crucial counties than had voted two years earlier, and the Democrats swept back into power.

In Mississippi's state election 1875, Democrats used similar tactics, openly announcing that "the thieves . . . robbers, and scoundrels" in power "deserve death and ought to be killed." In what became known as the Mississippi Plan, local Democratic clubs formed armed militias, marching defiantly through black areas, breaking up Republican meetings, and provoking riots to justify killing hundreds. Armed men were posted during voter registration to intimidate Republicans. At the election itself, voters were either "helped" by gun-toting whites to cast a Democratic ballot, or they were chased away by clubs. Counties that had given Republican majorities in the thousands managed a total of less than a dozen votes in 1875.

Democrats called their victory "redemption." As conservative Democrats resumed control of each state government, Reconstruction ended. Redemption succeeded with a combination of persistent white southern resistance, including violence and coercion, and a failure of northern will. Albion Tourgée summed up the Reconstruction era in his novel *A Fool's Errand* (1879): "The spirit of the dead Confederacy was stronger than the mandate of the nation to which it had succumbed in battle."

Congress did not totally ignore southern violence. Three force acts, passed in 1870 and 1871, gave the president strong powers to use federal supervisors to ensure that citizens were not prevented from voting by force or fraud. The third act, known as the Ku Klux Klan Act, declared illegal secret organizations that used disguise and coercion to deprive others of equal protection of the laws. Congress created a joint committee to investigate Klan violence,

and in 1872 its report filled 13 huge volumes with horrifying testimony.

President Grant, who supported these measures, sent messages to Congress proclaiming the importance of the right to vote, issued proclamations condemning lawlessness, and even dispatched troops to Hamburg, South Carolina, to restore order when several blacks were killed in court by a white mob dispensing its own form of "justice" to black militiamen arrested for parading on Independence Day. Republicans, however, lost interest in defending African Americans, whose votes they took for granted or no longer thought they needed. Besides, they were much more concerned with northern issues. In 1875, Grant's advisers told him that Republicans might lose important Ohio elections if he continued protecting blacks, so he rejected appeals by Mississippi blacks for troops to guarantee free elections. He and the nation "had tired of these annual autumnal outbreaks," the president said.

The success of the Mississippi Plan in 1875, repeated a year later in South Carolina and Louisiana, indicated that congressional reports, presidential proclamations, and the Force Acts did little to stop the reign of terror against black and white Republicans throughout the South. Despite hundreds of arrests, all-white juries refused to find whites guilty of crimes against blacks. The U.S. Supreme Court backed them, in two 1874 decisions

"The negroes of the South are free—ree as air," says the parliamentary Waterson. This is what the *State*, a well-known Democratic organ of Tennessee, says, in huge capitals, on the subject: 'Let it be known before the election that the farmers have agreed to spot every leading Radical negro in the county, and treat him as an enemy for all time to come. The rotten ring must and shall be broken at any and all costs. The Democrats have determined to withdraw all employment from their enemies. Let this fact be known.'

Although the Fourteenth and Fifteenth Amendments gave African-American males the right to vote in the late 1860s, by the 1870s white southerners opposed to black suffrage found many illegal ways of influencing and eventually depriving that vote, thus returning white Democrats to office. In this cartoon, titled "Of course he wants to vote the Democratic Ticket," one of the two pistol-wielding men is saying: "You're as free as air, ain't you? Say you are, or I'll blow your black head off!" Note that another freedman is being led down the street to the polling place, no doubt to vote Democratic also. (*Corbis*)

These two scenes vividly contrast family life during Reconstruction in the North and South. For most white northerners, as shown in this 1868 Currier & Ives print (top), the end of the Civil War meant renewing the good life of genteel middle-class values. *(Museum of the City of New York, The Harry T. Peters Collection)* For many freedpeople, however, family life was constantly threatened by the intrusion of Klan violence. *(The Granger Collection, New York)*

throwing out cases against whites convicted of preventing blacks from voting and declared key parts of the Force Acts unconstitutional. Although the Klan's power ended officially, the attitudes (and tactics) of Klansmen would continue long into the next century.

Shifting National Priorities

The American people in the North, like their leaders, were tired of battles over freedpeople. Frustrated with the difficulties of trying to transform an unwilling South, the easiest course was to give citizenship and the vote to African Americans, and leave them to fend for themselves. Americans of increasing ethnic diversity were primarily interested in starting families, finding work, and making money. Slovakian immigrants fired furnaces in steel plants in Pittsburgh; Chinese men pounded in railroad ties for the Central Pacific over the Sierra Nevada mountains and across the Nevada desert; Yankee women taught in one-room schoolhouses in Vermont for $23 a month; Mexican vaqueros drove Texas cattle herds to Kansas; and Scandinavian families battled heat, locusts, and high railroad rates on farmsteads in the Dakotas.

American priorities had shifted, at both the individual and national levels. Failing to effect a smooth transition from slavery to freedom for freedpeople, northern leaders focused their efforts on accelerating and solidifying their program of economic growth and industrial and territorial expansion.

As North Carolina Klansmen convened in dark forests in North Carolina in 1869, the Central Pacific and Union Pacific railroads met in Utah, linking the Atlantic and Pacific. As southern cotton production revived, northern iron and steel manufacturing and western settlement of the mining, cattle, and agricultural frontiers also surged. As black farmers haggled over work contracts with landowners in Georgia, white workers were organizing the National Labor Union in Baltimore. As Elizabeth and Adele Allston demanded the keys to their crop barns in the summer of 1865, the Boston Labor Reform Association was demanding that "our . . . education, morals, dwellings, and the whole Social System" needed to be "reconstructed." If the South would not be reconstructed, labor relations might be.

The years between 1865 and 1875 featured not only the rise (and fall) of Republican governments in the South but also a spectacular rise of working-class organizations. Stimulated by the Civil War to improve working conditions in northern factories, trade unions, labor reform associations, and labor parties flourished, culminating in the founding of the National Labor Union in 1866. Before the depression of 1873, an estimated 300,000 to 500,000 American workers enrolled in some 1,500 trade unions, the largest such increase in the nineteenth century. This growth inevitably stirred class tensions. In 1876, hundreds of freedmen in the rice region along the Combahee River in South Carolina went on strike to protest a 40-cent-per-day wage cut, clashing with local sheriffs and white Democratic rifle clubs. A year later, also fighting wage cuts, thousands of northern railroad workers went out in a nationwide wave of strikes, clashing with police and the National Guard.

As economic relations changed, so did the Republican party. Heralded by the moderate tone of state elections of 1867 and Grant's election in 1868, the Republicans changed from a party of moral reform to one of material interest. In the continuing struggle in American politics between "virtue and commerce," self-interest was again winning. Abandoning the Freedmen's Bureau as an inappropriate federal intervention, Republican politicians had no difficulty handing out huge grants of money and land to the railroads. As freedpeople were told to help themselves, the Union Pacific was getting subsidies of between $16,000 and $48,000 for each mile of track laid across western plains and mountains. As Susan B. Anthony and others tramped through the snows of upstate New York with petitions for the rights of suffrage and citizenship, Boss Tweed and other machine politicians defrauded New York taxpayers of millions of dollars. As Native Americans in the Great Plains struggled to preserve their sacred Black Hills from greedy gold prospectors protected by U.S. soldiers, corrupt government officials in the East "mined" public treasuries.

By 1869, the year financier Jay Gould almost cornered the gold market, the nation was increasingly defined by its sordid, materialistic "go-getters." Henry Adams, a descendant of two presidents, was living in Washington, D.C., during this era. As he wrote in his 1907 autobiography *The Education of Henry Adams*, he had had high expectations in 1869 that Grant, like George Washington, would restore moral order and peace. But when Grant announced his cabinet, a group of army cronies and rich friends to whom he owed favors, Adams felt betrayed, charging that Grant's administration "outraged every rule of decency."

Honest himself, Grant showed poor judgment of others. The scandals of his administration touched his relatives, his cabinet, and two vice presidents. Outright graft, loose prosecution, and generally negligent administration flourished in a half dozen

RECOVERING THE PAST

Novels

We usually read novels, short stories, and other forms of fiction for pleasure, that is, for the enjoyment of plot, style, symbolism, and character development. In addition to being well-written, "classic" novels such as *Moby Dick, Huckleberry Finn, The Great Gatsby, The Invisible Man,* and *Beloved,* explore timeless questions of good and evil, of innocence and knowledge, of noble dreams fulfilled and shattered. We enjoy novels because we often find ourselves identifying with one of the major characters. Through that person's problems, joys, relationships, and search for identity, we gain insights about our own.

Even though novels may be historically untrue, we can also read them as historical sources, for they reveal much about the attitudes, dreams, fears, and ordinary, everyday experiences of human beings in a particular period. They also show how people responded to the major events of that era. The novelist, like the historian, is a product of time and place and has an interpretive point of view. Consider the two novels about Reconstruction that are quoted here. Neither is reputed for great literary merit, yet both reveal much about the various interpretations and impassioned attitudes of the post–Civil War era. *A Fool's Errand* was written by Albion Tourgée, a northerner, while *The Clansman* was written by Thomas Dixon, Jr., a southerner.

Tourgée was a young northern teacher and lawyer who fought with the Union army and moved to North Carolina after the war, partly for health reasons and partly to begin a legal career. He became a judge and was an active Republican, supporting black suffrage and helping to shape the new state constitution and the codification of North Carolina laws. But because he boldly criticized the Ku Klux Klan for its campaign of terror against blacks, his life was threatened many times. When he left North Carolina in 1879, he published an autobiographical novel about his experiences as a judge challenging the Klan's violence against the freedpeople.

The "fool's errand" in the novel is that of the northern veteran Comfort Servosse, who, like Tourgée, seeks to fulfill humane goals on behalf of both blacks and whites in post–Civil War North Carolina. His efforts are thwarted, however, by

threats, intimidation, a campaign of violent "outrages" against Republican leaders in the county, and a lack of support from Congress. Historians have verified the accuracy of many of the events in Tourgée's novel. While exposing the brutality of the Klan, Tourgée features loyal southern Unionists, respectable planters ashamed of Klan violence, and even guiltridden, poor white Klansmen who try to protect or warn intended victims.

In 1905, the year of Tourgée's death, another North Carolinian published a novel with a very different analysis of Reconstruction and its fate. Thomas Dixon was a lawyer, North Carolina state legislator, Baptist minister, pro-Klan lecturer, and novelist. *The Clansman,* subtitled *A Historical Romance of the Ku Klux Klan,* reflects turn-of-the-century attitudes most white southerners still had about Republican rule during Reconstruction. According to Dixon, once the "Great Heart" Lincoln was gone, a power-crazed, vindictive, radical Congress, led by scheming Austin Stoneman (Thaddeus Stevens), sought to impose corrupt carpetbagger and brutal black rule by bayonet on a helpless South. Only through the inspired leadership and redemptive role of the Ku Klux Klan was the South saved from the horrors of rape and revenge.

Dixon dedicated *The Clansman* to his uncle, who was a Grand Titan of the Klan in North Carolina during the time when two crucial counties were being transformed from Republican to Democratic through intimidation and terror. No such violence shows up in Dixon's novel. When the novel was made the basis of D. W. Griffith's film classic *Birth of a Nation* in 1915, the novel's attitudes were firmly imprinted on the twentieth-century American mind.

Both novels convey Reconstruction attitudes toward the freedpeople. Both create clearly defined heroes and villains. Both include exciting chase scenes, narrow escapes, daring rescues, and tragic deaths. Both include romantic subplots in which a southern man falls in love with a northern woman (both white). Yet the two novels are strikingly different.

Reflecting on the Past Even in these brief excerpts, what differences of style and attitude do you see in the descriptions of Uncle Jerry and Old Aleck? What emotional responses do you have to these passages? How do you think turn-of-the-twentieth-century Americans might have responded?

When the second Christmas came, Metta wrote again to her sister:

"The feeling is terribly bitter against Comfort on account of his course towards the colored people. There is quite a village of them on the lower end of the plantation. They have a church, a sabbath school, and are to have next year a school. You can not imagine how kind they have been to us, and how much they are attached to Comfort. . . . I got Comfort to go with me to one of their prayer-meetings a few nights ago. I had heard a great deal about them, but had never attended one before. It was strangely weird. There were, perhaps, fifty present, mostly middle-aged men and women. They were singing in a soft, low mono-tone, interspersed with prolonged exclamatory notes, a sort of rude hymn, which I was surprised to know was one of their old songs in slave times. How the chorus came to be endured in those days I can not imagine. It was

'Free! free! free, my Lord, free!
An' we walks de hebben-ly way!'

"A few looked around as we came in and seated our-selves; and Uncle Jerry, the saint of the settlement, came forward on his staves, and said, in his soft voice,

"'Ev'nin', Kunnel! Sarvant, Missus! Will you walk up, an' hev seats in front?'

"We told him we had just looked in, and might go in a short time; so we would stay in the back part of the audience.

"Uncle Jerry can not read nor write; but he is a man of strange intelligence and power. Unable to do work of any account, he is the faithful friend, monitor, and director of others. He has a house and piece of land, all paid for, a good horse and cow, and, with the aid of his wife and two boys, made a fine crop this season. He is one of the most promising colored men in the settle-ment: so Comfort says, at least. Everybody seems to have great respect for his character. I don't know how many people I have heard speak of his religion. Mr. Savage used to say he had rather hear him pray than any other man on earth. He was much prized by his master, even after he was disabled, on account of his faithfulness and character."

At noon Ben and Phil strolled to the polling-place to watch the progress of the first election under Negro rule. The Square was jammed with shouting, jostling, perspiring negroes, men, women, and children. The day was warm, and the African odour was supreme even in the open air. . . .

The negroes, under the drill of the League and the Freedman's Bureau, protected by the bayonet, were voting to enfranchise themselves, disfranchise their former masters, ratify a new constitution, and elect a legislature to do their will. Old Aleck was a candidate for the House, chief poll-holder, and seemed to be in charge of the movements of the voters outside the booth as well as inside. He appeared to be omnipresent, and his self-importance was a sight Phil had never dreamed. He could not keep his eyes off him. . . .

[Aleck] was a born African orator, undoubtedly descended from a long line of savage spell-binders, whose eloquence in the palaver houses of the jungle had made them native leaders. His thin spindle-shanks supported an oblong, protruding stomach, resembling an elderly monkey's, which seemed so heavy it swayed his back to carry it.

The animal vivacity of his small eyes and the flexibil-ity of his eyebrows, which he worked up and down rapidly with every change of countenance, expressed his eager desires.

He had laid aside his new shoes, which hurt him, and went barefooted to facilitate his movements on the great occasion. His heels projected and his foot was so flat that what should have been the hollow of it made a hole in the dirt where he left his track.

He was already mellow with liquor, and was dressed in an old army uniform and cap, with two horse-pistols buckled around his waist. On a strap hanging from his shoulder were strung a half-dozen tin canteens filled with whiskey.

departments. Most scandals involved large sums of public money. The Whiskey Ring affair, for example, cost the public millions of dollars in lost tax revenues siphoned off to government officials. Gould's gold scam received the unwitting aid of Grant's Treasury Department and the knowing help of the president's brother-in-law.

Nor was Congress pure. Crédit Mobilier, a dummy corporation supposedly building the transcontinental railroad, received generous bonds and contracts in exchange for giving congressmen gifts of money, stocks, and railroad lands. An Ohio congressman described the House of Representatives in 1873 as an "auction room where more valuable considerations were disposed of under the speaker's hammer than any place on earth." In Henry Adams's 1880 novel *Democracy*, written about Washington life during this period, the main character, Mrs. Madeleine Lee, sought to uncover "the heart of the great American mystery of democracy and government." What she found were corrupt legislators and lobbyists in an unprincipled pursuit of power and wealth. "Surely something can be done to check corruption?" Mrs. Lee asked her friend one evening, adding, "Is a respectable government impossible in a democracy?" His answer was that "no responsible government can long be much better or much worse than the society it represents."

The election of 1872 showed the public uninterested in moral issues. "Liberal" Republicans, disgusted with Grant, formed a third party calling for lower tariffs and fewer grants to railroads, civil service reform, and the removal of federal troops from the South. Their candidate, Horace Greeley, editor of the New York *Tribune,* was also nominated by the Democrats, whom he had spent much of his earlier career assailing. Despite his wretched record, Grant easily won a second term. Greeley was beaten so badly, he said, "I hardly knew whether I was running for the Presidency or the Penitentiary."

The End of Reconstruction

Soon after Grant's second inauguration, a financial panic, caused by commercial overexpansion into railroads, railroad mismanagement, and the collapse of some eastern banks, started a terrible depression that lasted throughout the mid-1870s. In these hard times, economic issues dominated politics, further diverting attention from the freedpeople. As Democrats took control of the House of Representatives in 1874 and looked toward winning the White House in 1876, politicians talked about new Grant scandals, unemployment and public works projects, the currency, and tariffs. No one said much about civil rights. In 1875, a guilt-ridden Congress did pass Senator Charles Sumner's civil rights bill to put teeth into the Fourteenth Amendment. But the act was not enforced, and after eight years, the Supreme Court declared it unconstitutional. Congressional Reconstruction, long dormant, was over. The election of 1876, which was the closest in American history until 2000, sealed the end.

As their presidential candidate in 1876, the Republicans chose a former governor of Ohio, Rutherford B. Hayes, partly because of his reputation for honesty, partly because he had been a Union officer (a necessity for post–Civil War candidates), and partly because, as Henry Adams put it, he was "obnoxious to no one." The Democrats nominated Governor Samuel J. Tilden of New York, a well-known civil service reformer who had broken the corrupt Tweed ring.

Like Al Gore in 2000, Tilden won a popular-vote majority and appeared to have enough electoral votes (184 to 165) for victory—except for 20 disputed votes, all but one in the Deep South states of Florida, Louisiana, and South Carolina, where some federal troops remained and where Republicans still controlled the voting apparatus despite Democratic intimidation. To settle the dispute, Congress created a special electoral commission of eight Republicans and seven Democrats, who voted along party lines to give Hayes all 20 votes and a narrow electoral-college victory, 185 to 184.

As in the election of 2000, outraged Democrats protested the outcome and threatened to stop the Senate from officially counting the electoral votes, preventing Hayes's inauguration. There was talk of a new civil war but a North–South compromise emerged. Northern investors wanted the government to subsidize a New Orleans-to-California railroad. Southerners wanted northern dollars but not northern political influence—no social agencies, no federal enforcement of the Fourteenth and Fifteenth Amendments, and no military occupation, not even the symbolic presence left in 1876.

As the March 4 inauguration date approached, and as newspapers echoed outgoing President Grant's call for "peace at any price," the forces of mutual self-interest concluded the "compromise of 1877." Democrats agreed to suspend their resistance to the counting of the electoral votes, and on March 2, Hayes was declared president. After his inauguration, he ordered the last federal troops out of the South, sending them west to fight Indians,

Under a caption quoting a Democratic party newspaper, "This is a white man's government," this Thomas Nast cartoon from 1868 shows three white groups (stereotyped as apelike northern Irish workers, unrepentant former Confederates, and rich northern capitalists) joining hands to bring Republican Reconstruction to an end almost before it began. The immigrant's vote, the Kluxer's knife, and the capitalist's dollars would restore a "white man's government" on the back of the freedman, still clutching the Union flag and reaching in vain for the ballot box. What else do you see here? No single image better captures the story of the end of Reconstruction. *(Harper's Weekly, September 5, 1868/The Granger Collection, New York)*

appointed a former Confederate general to his cabinet, supported federal aid for economic and railroad development in the South, and promised to let southerners handle race relations themselves. On a goodwill trip to the South, he told blacks that "your rights and interests would be safer if this great mass of intelligent white men were let alone by the general government." The message was clear: Hayes would not enforce the Fourteenth and Fifteenth Amendments, initiating a pattern of governmental inaction and white northern abandonment of African Americans that lasted to the 1960s. But the immediate crisis was averted, officially ending Reconstruction.

✦ *Conclusion*

A MIXED LEGACY

In the 12 years between Appomattox and Hayes's inauguration, victorious northern Republicans, defeated white southerners, and hopeful black freedpeople each wanted more than the others would give. Each saw some fulfillment of their dreams. The compromise of 1877 cemented the reunion of South and North, providing new opportunities for economic development in both regions. The Republican party achieved its economic goals and generally held the White House, though not always Congress, until 1932. The former Confederate states came back into the Union, and southerners retained their grip on southern lands and black labor, though not without struggle and some changes. Elizabeth Allston resumed authority over the family plantations for a time but eventually faced black resistance to work contracts and had to sell much of her land—to whites.

What of the freedpeople? In 1880, Frederick Douglass wrote: "Our Reconstruction measures were radically defective. . . . To the freedmen was given the machinery of liberty, but there was denied to them the steam to put it in motion. They were given the uniform of soldiers, but no arms; they were called citizens, but left subjects; they were called free, but left almost slaves. The old master class . . . retained the power to starve them to death, and wherever this power is held there is the power of slavery." The wonder, Douglass said, was "not that freedmen have made so little progress, but, rather, that they have made so much; not that they have been standing still, but that they have been able to stand at all." Freedpeople had made strong gains in education and economic and family survival. Despite sharecropping and tenancy, black laborers organized themselves to achieve a measure of autonomy and opportunity in their lives. The three great Reconstruction amendments, despite flagrant violation over the next 100 years, held out the promise that the dreams of equal citizenship and political participation would yet be realized.

But there was still an underlying tragedy to Reconstruction, as a short story by W. E. B. Du Bois, written in 1903, makes sadly clear. Two boyhood playmates, both named John, one black and one white, are sent from the fictional town of Altamaha, Georgia, north to school to prepare for leadership of their respective communities, the black John as a teacher and the white John as a judge and possibly governor. While they were away, the black and white people of Altamaha, each race thinking of its own John and not of the other, waited for "the coming of two young men, and dreamed . . . of new things that would be done and new thoughts that all would think." After several years, both Johns returned to Altamaha, but a series of tragic events shattered their hopes. Neither John understood the people of the town, and each was in turn misunderstood. Black John's school was closed because he taught ideals of liberty. Heartbroken and discouraged as he walked through the forest near town, he surprised white John in an attempted rape of his sister. Without a word, black John picked up a fallen limb, and with "all the pent-up hatred of his great black arm," killed his boyhood friend. Within hours he was lynched.

Du Bois's story captures the human cost of the Reconstruction era. The black scholar's hope for reconciliation by a "union of intelligence and sympathy across the color-line" was smashed in the tragic encounter between the two Johns. Both young men, each once filled with glorious dreams, lay dead under the pines of the Georgia forest. Dying with them were hopes that interracial harmony, intersectional trust, and equal opportunities and rights for freedpeople might be the legacies of Reconstruction. Conspicuously absent in the forest scene was the presence of northerners. They had turned their attention to other, less noble, causes.

✦ Recommended Reading

The Bittersweet Aftermath of War
W. E. B. Du Bois, *Black Reconstruction* (1935); Laura Edwards, *Gendered Strife & Confusion: The Political Culture of Reconstruction* (1997); Eric Foner, *Reconstruction: America's Unfinished Revolution, 1863–1877* (1988); John Hope Franklin, *Reconstruction After the Civil War* (1961); Leon Litwack, *Been in the Storm So Long: The Aftermath of Slavery* (1980); James M. McPherson, *Ordeal by Fire: Civil War and Reconstruction*, 3rd ed. (2000).

National Reconstruction Politics
Richard H. Abbott, *The Republican Party and the South, 1855–1877* (1986); Michael Les Benedict, *A Compromise of Principle: Congressional Republicans and Reconstruction,*

1863–1869 (1974); David Donald, *The Politics of Reconstruction* (1965); William Gillette, *Retreat from Reconstruction, 1869–1879* (1979); Ward M. McAfee, *Religion, Race, and Reconstruction: The Public Schools in the Politics of the 1870s* (1998); William McFeeley, *Grant: A Biography* (1981); Heather Cox Richardson, *The Death of Reconstruction: Race, Labor, and Politics in the post–Civil War North, 1865–1901* (2001); Brooks D. Simpson, *The Reconstruction Presidents* (1998); Hans L. Trefousse, *Thaddeus Stevens: Nineteenth-Century Egalitarian* (1997); Allen Trelease, *Andrew Johnson: A Biography* (1989).

The Lives of Freedpeople

Paul Cimbala and Randall M. Miller, eds., *The Freedmen's Bureau and Reconstruction: Reconsiderations* (1999); Paul Cimbala, *Under the Guardianship of the Nation: The Freedmen's Bureau and the Reconstruction of Georgia, 1865–1870* (1997); Eric Foner, *Nothing but Freedom: Emancipation and Its Legacy* (1983); Noralee Frankel, *Freedom's Women: Black Women and Families in Civil War Era Mississippi* (1999); Sharon Ann Holt, *Making Freedom Pay: North Carolina Freedpeople Working for Themselves, 1865–1900* (2000); Tera Hunter, *To 'Joy My Freedom: Southern Black Women's Lives and Labors after the Civil War* (1997); Jacqueline Jones, *Soldiers of Light and Love: Northern Teachers and Georgia Blacks, 1865–1873* (1980); Robert Kenzer, *Enterprising Southerners: Black Economic Success in North Carolina, 1865–1915* (1997); Leon Litwack, *Been in the Storm So Long: The Aftermath of Slavery* (1980); Roger Ransom and Richard Sutch, *One Kind of Freedom: The Economic Consequences of Emancipation* (1977); Elizabeth Regosin, *Freedom's Promise: Ex-Slaves and Citizenship in the Age of Emancipation* (2002); Edward Royce, *The Origins of Southern Sharecropping* (2002); Julie Saville, *The Work of Reconstruction: From Slave to Wage Laborer in South Carolina, 1860–1870* (1994).

Reconstruction in the Southern States

W. Fitzhugh Brundage, *Lynching in the New South: Georgia and Virginia, 1880–1930* (1993); Dan T. Carter, *When the War Was Over: The Failure of Self-Reconstruction in the South* (1985); Thomas Holt, *Black over White: Negro Political Leadership in South Carolina During Reconstruction* (1977); Edward A. Miller, *Gullah Statesman: Robert Smalls from Slavery to Congress, 1839–1915* (1995); George C. Rable, *But There Was No Peace: The Role of Violence in the Politics of Reconstruction* (1984); Scott Reynolds, *Iron Confederacies: Southern Railways, Klan Violence, and Reconstruction* (1999); Joel Williamson, *The Crucible of Race* (1984) and *A Rage for Order: Black/White Relations in the American South Since Emancipation* (1986).

Fiction and Film

W. E. B. Du Bois's *The Quest of the Silver Fleece* (1911) is a little-known novel by the sociologist-historian about the lives of sharecroppers during Reconstruction. Howard Fast's *Freedom Road* (1944) is a novel about the heroic but ultimately failed efforts of poor whites and blacks to unite for mutual benefit during the era. Ernest Gaines's *The Autobiography of Miss Jane Pittman* (1971), framed as an autobiography, is a gripping fictional account of a proud centenarian black woman who lived from the time of the Civil War to the era of civil rights. In *A Fool's Errand* (1879), as described in the "Recovering the Past" section, Albion Tourgee takes the viewpoint of a sympathetic white judge who helps the freedpeople in North Carolina during Reconstruction. Margaret Walker's *Jubilee* (1966) is a black woman novelist's epic version of the African-American experience in the Civil War era, and Alice Randall's *The Wind Done Gone* (2001) is a parody of Margaret Mitchell's *Gone With the Wind* (1936); both follow black and white families from slavery to Reconstruction. Toni Morrison's *Beloved* (1988), an extraordinary novel set near Cincinnati in 1873 that includes flashbacks, is about the lasting traumas of slavery as black women especially seek to put their lives together and pursue their dreams of freedom. The film of the same name (1998), though slow moving, follows the time disconnections of the novel well with many moving scenes. *Birth of a Nation*, the classic 1913 film by D. W. Griffith that portrays the rise of the Ku Klux Klan as the defender of white supremacy and womanhood, is based on Thomas Dixon's *The Clansman* (1905) (which is described in the "Recovering the Past" section of the chapter).

✦ Discovering U.S. History Online

A Documentary History of Emancipation, 1861–1867

www.inform.umd.edu/ARHU/Depts/History/Freedman/home.html

A rich collection of primary sources from the Freedom and Southern Society Project of the University of Maryland, containing superb links to four completed of nine projected volumes of collected documents.

Civil War, Reconstruction and Recovery in Brazoria County, Texas

www.bchm.org/wrr/

This illustrated exhibit focuses on Reconstruction and recovery in Texas as an example of these issues in the South.

Nineteenth Century African-American Legislators and Constitutional Convention Delegates of Texas

www.tsl.state.tx.us/exhibits/forever/index.html

This exhibit documents the political struggles in the post–Reconstruction South via the stories of the "52 African-American men who served Texas as either state legislative members or Constitutional Convention delegates."

The Impeachment of Andrew Johnson

www.andrewjohnson.com

Over 200 excerpts from contemporary issues of *Harper's Weekly* (1865–1869) provide in-depth information about Andrew Johnson and the impeachment process.

Images of African-Americans from the Nineteenth Century

www.digital.nypl.org/schomburg/images_aa19/

A vast collection of visual images by artists, engravers, and photographers capturing elements of African-American life in the nineteenth century.

Reports on Black America, 1857–1874

www.blackhistory.harpweek.com

Fascinating text and imagery found in the pages of *Harper's Weekly* magazine.

African-American Perspectives, 1818–1907

www.memory.loc.gov/ammem/aap/aaphome.html

This searchable collection is filled with links to Reconstruction topics and political speeches and manuscripts from the Federal Writers' Project interviews with ex-slaves in the 1930s.

Diary and Letters of Rutherford B. Hayes

www.ohiohistory.org/onlinedoc/hayes/index.cfm

The center offers a searchable database of 3,000 pages digitized from the five volume set of Hayes's presidential diaries and letters.

Central Pacific Railroad

www.cprr.org

This searchable site traces the history of the completion of the first transcontinental railroad. The Web site includes photographs, 3-D stereographs, engravings, documents, railroad and survey maps, and other related materials.

Freedmen's Bureau in Augusta County, Virginia

www.vcdh.virginia.edu/afam/reconst.html

"This student-made project traces the attempts by Augusta County African Americans and the U.S. Freedmen's Bureau to reunite families, establish fair labor practices, and build community institutions."

THE DECLARATION OF INDEPENDENCE IN CONGRESS, JULY 4, 1776

The Unanimous Declaration of the Thirteen United States of America

When, in the course of human events, it becomes necessary for one people to dissolve the political bonds which have connected them with another, and to assume, among the powers of the earth, the separate and equal station to which the laws of nature and of nature's God entitle them, a decent respect to the opinions of mankind requires that they should declare the causes which impel them to the separation.

We hold these truths to be self-evident: That all men are created equal; that they are endowed by their Creator with certain unalienable rights; that among these are life, liberty, and the pursuit of happiness; that, to secure these rights, governments are instituted among men, deriving their just powers from the consent of the governed; that whenever any form of government becomes destructive of these ends, it is the right of the people to alter or to abolish it, and to institute new government, laying its foundation on such principles, and organizing its powers in such form, as to them shall seem most likely to effect their safety and happiness. Prudence, indeed, will dictate that governments long established should not be changed for light and transient causes; and accordingly all experience hath shown that mankind are more disposed to suffer, while evils are sufferable, than to right themselves by abolishing the forms to which they are accustomed. But when a long train of abuses and usurpations, pursuing invariably the same object, evinces a design to reduce them under absolute despotism, it is their right, it is their duty, to throw off such government, and to provide new guards for their future security. Such has been the patient sufferance of these colonies; and such is now the necessity which constrains them to alter their former systems of government. The history of the present King of Great Britain is a history of repeated injuries and usurpations, all having in direct object the establishment of an absolute tyranny over these states. To prove this, let facts be submitted to a candid world.

He has refused his assent to laws, the most wholesome and necessary for the public good.

He has forbidden his governors to pass laws of immediate and pressing importance, unless suspended in their operation till his assent should be obtained; and, when so suspended, he has utterly neglected to attend to them.

He has refused to pass other laws for the accommodation of large districts of people, unless those people would relinquish the right of representation in the legislature, a right inestimable to them, and formidable to tyrants only.

He has called together legislative bodies at places unusual, uncomfortable, and distant from the depository of their public records, for the sole purpose of fatiguing them into compliance with his measures.

He has dissolved representative houses repeatedly, for opposing, with manly firmness, his invasions on the rights of the people.

He has refused for a long time, after such dissolutions, to cause others to be elected; whereby the legislative powers, incapable of annihilation, have returned to the people at large for their exercise; the state remaining, in the mean time, exposed to all the dangers of invasions from without and convulsions within.

He has endeavored to prevent the population of these states; for that purpose obstructing the laws for naturalization of foreigners; refusing to pass others to encourage their migration hither, and raising the conditions of new appropriations of lands.

He has obstructed the administration of justice, by refusing his assent to laws for establishing judiciary powers.

He has made judges dependent on his will alone, for the tenure of their offices, and the amount and payment of their salaries.

He has erected a multitude of new offices, and sent hither swarms of officers to harass our people and eat out their substance.

He has kept among us, in times of peace, standing armies, without the consent of our legislatures.

He has affected to render the military independent of, and superior to, the civil power.

He has combined with others to subject us to a jurisdiction foreign to our constitution, and unacknowledged by our laws, giving his assent to their acts of pretended legislation:

For quartering large bodies of armed troops among us;

For protecting them, by a mock trial, from punishment for any murder which they should commit on the inhabitants of these states;

For cutting off our trade with all parts of the world;

For imposing taxes on us without our consent;

For depriving us, in many cases, of the benefits of trial by jury;

For transporting us beyond seas, to be tried for pretended offenses;

For abolishing the free system of English laws in a neighboring province, establishing therein an arbitrary government, and enlarging its boundaries, so as to render it at once an example and fit instrument for introducing the same absolute rule into these colonies;

For taking away our charters abolishing our most valuable laws, and altering fundamentally the forms of our governments;

For suspending our own legislatures, and declaring themselves invested with power to legislate for us in all cases whatsoever.

He has abdicated government here, by declaring us out of his protection and waging war against us.

He has plundered our seas, ravaged our coasts, burned our towns, and destroyed the lives of our people.

He is at this time transporting large armies of foreign mercenaries to complete the works of death, desolation, and tyranny already begun with circumstances of cruelty and perfidy scarcely paralleled in the most barbarous ages, and totally unworthy the head of a civilized nation.

He has constrained our fellow-citizens, taken captive on the high seas, to bear arms against their country, to become the executioners of their friends and brethren, or to fall themselves by their hands.

He has excited domestic insurrection among us, and has endeavored to bring on the inhabitants of our frontiers the merciless Indian savages, whose known rule of warfare is an undistinguished destruction of all ages, sexes, and conditions.

In every stage of these oppressions we have petitioned for redress in the most humble terms; our repeated petitions have been answered only by repeated injury. A prince, whose character is thus marked by every act which may define a tyrant, is unfit to be the ruler of a free people.

Nor have we been wanting in our attentions to our British brethren. We have warned them, from time to time, of attempts by their legislature to extend an unwarrantable jurisdiction over us. We have reminded them of the circumstances of our emigration and settlement here. We have appealed to their native justice and magnanimity; and we have conjured them, by the ties of our common kindred, to disavow these usurpations, which would inevitably interrupt our connections and correspondence. They, too, have been deaf to the voice of justice and of consanguinity. We must, therefore, acquiesce in the necessity which denounces our separation, and hold them, as we hold the rest of mankind, enemies in war, in peace friends.

We, therefore, the representatives of the United States of America, in General Congress assembled, appealing to the Supreme Judge of the world for the rectitude of our intentions, do, in the name and by the authority of the good people of these colonies, solemnly publish and declare, that these United Colonies are, and of right, ought to be, FREE AND INDEPENDENT STATES; that they are absolved from all allegiance to the British crown, and that all political connection between them and the state of Great Britain is, and ought to be, totally dissolved; and that, as free and independent states, they have full power to levy war, conclude peace, contract alliances, establish commerce, and do all other acts and things which independent states may of right do. And for the support of this declaration, with a firm reliance on the protection of Devine Providence, we mutually pledge to each other our lives, our fortunes, and our sacred honor.

JOHN HANCOCK

BUTTON GWENNETT	FRANCIS LIGHTFOOT LEE	JNO. WITHERSPOON
LYMAN HALL	CARTER BRAXTON	FRAS. HOPKINSON
GEO. WALTON	ROBT. MORRIS	JOHN HART
WM. HOOPER	BENJAMIN RUSH	ABRA. CLARK
JOSEPH HEWES	BENJA. FRANKLIN	JOSIAH BARTLETT
JOHN PENN	JOHN MORTON	WM. WHIPPLE
EDWARD RUTLEDGE	GEO. CLYMER	SAML. ADAMS
THOS. HEYWARD, JUNR.	JAS. SMITH	JOHN ADAMS
THOMAS LYNCH, JUNR.	GEO. TAYLOR	ROBT. TREAT PAINE
ARTHUR MIDDLETON	JAMES WILSON	ELBRIDGE GERRY
SAMUEL CHASE	GEO. ROSS	STEP. HOPKINS
WM. PACA	CAESAR RODNEY	WILLIAM ELLERY
THOS. STONE	GEO. READ	ROGER SHERMAN
CHARLES CARROLL OF CARROLLTON	THO. MÍKEAN	SAMÍEL. HUNTINGTON
GEORGE WYTHE	WM. FLOYD	WM. WILLIAMS
RICHARD HENRY LEE	PHIL. LIVINGSTON	OLIVER WOLCOTT
TH. JEFFERSON	FRANS. LEWIS	MATHEW THORNTON
BENJA. HARRISON	LEWIS MORRIS	
THS. NELSON, JR.	RICHD. STOCKTON	

THE CONSTITUTION OF THE UNITED STATES OF AMERICA*

PREAMBLE

We the People of the United States, in Order to form a more perfect Union, establish Justice, insure domestic Tranquility, provide for the common defence, promote the general Welfare, and secure the Blessings of Liberty to ourselves and our Posterity, do ordain and establish this Constitution for the United States of America.

ARTICLE I.

Section 1   All legislative Powers herein granted shall be vested in a Congress of the United States, which shall consist of a Senate and House of Representatives.

Section 2   The House of Representatives shall be composed of Members chosen every second Year by the People of the several States, and the Electors in each State shall have the Qualifications requisite for Electors of the most numerous Branch of the State Legislature.

No Person shall be a Representative who shall not have attained to the Age of twenty five Years, and been seven Years a Citizen of the United States, and who shall not, when elected, be an Inhabitant of that State in which he shall be chosen.

Representatives and direct Taxes shall be apportioned among the several States which may be included within this Union, according to their respective Numbers, *which shall be determined by adding to the whole Number of free Persons, including those bound to Service for a Term of Years, and excluding Indians not taxed, three fifths of all other Persons.* The actual Enumeration shall be made within three Years after the first Meeting of the Congress of the United States, and within every subsequent Term of ten Years, in such Manner as they shall by Law direct. The Number of Representatives shall not exceed one for every thirty Thousand, but each State shall have at Least one Representative; *and until such enumeration shall be made, the State of New Hampshire shall be entitled to chuse three, Massachusetts eight, Rhode-Island and Providence Plantations one, Connecticut five, New-York six, New Jersey four, Pennsylvania eight, Delaware one, Maryland six, Virginia ten, North Carolina five, South Carolina five, and Georgia three.*

When vacancies happen in the Representation from any State, the Executive Authority thereof shall issue Writs of Election to fill such Vacancies.

The House of Representatives shall chuse their Speaker and other Officers; and shall have the sole Power of Impeachment.

Section 3   The Senate of the United States shall be composed of two Senators from each State, chosen by the Legislature thereof, for six Years; and each Senator shall have one Vote.

Immediately after they shall be assembled in Consequence of the first Election, they shall be divided as equally as may be into three Classes. The Seats of the Senators of the first Class shall be vacated at the Expiration of the second Year, of the second Class at the Expiration of the fourth Year, and of the third Class at the Expiration of the sixth Year, so that one third may be chosen every second Year; and if Vacancies happen by Resignation, or otherwise, during the Recess of the Legislature of any State, the Executive thereof may make temporary Appointments until the next Meeting of the Legislature, which shall then fill such Vacancies.

No Person shall be a Senator who shall not have attained to the Age of thirty Years, and been nine Years a Citizen of the United States, and who shall not, when elected, be an Inhabitant of that State for which he shall be chosen.

The Vice President of the United States shall be President of the Senate, but shall have no Vote, unless they be equally divided.

The Senate shall choose their other Officers, and also a President *pro tempore,* in the Absence of the Vice President, or when he shall exercise the Office of President of the United States.

The Senate shall have the sole Power to try all Impeachments. When sitting for that Purpose, they shall be on Oath or Affirmation. When the President of the United States is tried the Chief Justice shall preside: And no Person shall be convicted without the Concurrence of two thirds of the Members present.

Judgment in Cases of Impeachment shall not extend further than to removal from Office, and disqualification to hold and enjoy any Office of honor, Trust or Profit under the United States: but the Party convicted shall nevertheless be liable and subject to Indictment, Trial, Judgment and Punishment, according to Law.

Section 4   The Times, Places and Manner of holding Elections for Senators and Representatives, shall be prescribed in each State by the Legislature thereof; but the Congress may at any time by Law make or alter such Regulations, except as to the Places of chusing Senators.

The Congress shall assemble at least once in every Year, and such Meeting *shall be on the first Monday in December, unless they shall by Law appoint a different Day.*

Section 5   Each House shall be the Judge of the Elections, Returns and Qualifications of its own Members, and a Majority of each shall constitute a Quorum to do Business; but a smaller Number may adjourn from day to day, and may be authorized to compel the Attendance of absent Members, in such

---

* The Constitution became effective March 4, 1789. Any portion of the text that has been amended is printed in italics.

Manner, and under such Penalties as each House may provide.

Each House may determine the Rules of its Proceedings, punish its Members for disorderly Behaviour, and, with the Concurrence of two thirds, expel a Member.

Each House shall keep a Journal of its Proceedings, and from time to time publish the same, excepting such Parts as may in their Judgment require Secrecy; and the Yeas and Nays of the Members of either House on any question shall, at the Desire of one fifth of those Present, be entered on the Journal.

Neither House, during the Session of Congress, shall, without the Consent of the other, adjourn for more than three days, nor to any other Place than that in which the two Houses shall be sitting.

Section 6   The Senators and Representatives shall receive a Compensation for their Services, to be ascertained by Law, and paid out of the Treasury of the United States. They shall in all Cases, except Treason, Felony and Breach of the Peace, be privileged from Arrest during their Attendance at the Session of their respective Houses, and in going to and returning from the same; and for any Speech or Debate in either House, they shall not be questioned in any other Place.

No Senator or Representative shall, during the Time for which he was elected, be appointed to any civil Office under the Authority of the United States, which shall have been created, or the Emoluments whereof shall have been encreased during such time; and no Person holding any Office under the United States, shall be a Member of either House during his Continuance in Office.

Section 7   All Bills for raising Revenue shall originate in the House of Representatives; but the Senate may propose or concur with Amendments as on other Bills.

Every Bill which shall have passed the House of Representatives and the Senate, shall, before it become a Law, be presented to the President of the United States; If he approve he shall sign it, but if not he shall return it, with his Objections to that House in which it shall have originated, who shall enter the Objections at large on their Journal, and proceed to reconsider it. If after such Reconsideration two thirds of that House shall agree to pass the Bill, it shall be sent, together with the Objections, to the other House, by which it shall likewise be reconsidered, and if approved by two thirds of that House, it shall become a Law. But in all such Cases the Votes of both Houses shall be determined by yeas and Nays, and the Names of the Persons voting for and against the Bill shall be entered on the Journal of each House respectively. If any Bill shall not be returned by the President within ten Days (Sundays excepted) after it shall have been presented to him, the Same shall be a Law, in like Manner as if he had signed it, unless the Congress by their Adjournment prevent its Return, in which Case it shall not be a Law.

Every Order, Resolution, or Vote to which the Concurrence of the Senate and House of Representatives may be necessary (except on a question of Adjournment) shall be presented to the President of the United States; and before the Same shall take Effect, shall be approved by him, or being disapproved by him, shall be repassed by two thirds of the Senate and House of Representatives, according to the Rules and Limitations prescribed in the Case of a Bill.

Section 8   The Congress shall have Power:

To lay and collect Taxes, Duties, Imposts and Excises, to pay the Debts and provide for the common Defence and general Welfare of the United States; but all Duties, Imposts and Excises shall be uniform throughout the United States;

To borrow Money on the credit of the United States;

To regulate Commerce with foreign Nations, and among the several States, and with the Indian Tribes;

To establish an uniform Rule of Naturalization, and uniform Laws on the subject of Bankruptcies throughout the United States;

To coin Money, regulate the Value thereof, and of foreign Coin, and fix the Standard of Weights and Measures;

To provide for the Punishment of counterfeiting the Securities and current Coin of the United States;

To establish Post Offices and post Roads;

To promote the Progress of Science and useful Arts, by securing for limited Times to Authors and Inventors the exclusive Right to their respective Writings and Discoveries;

To constitute Tribunals inferior to the supreme Court;

To define and punish Piracies and Felonies committed on the high Seas, and Offences against the Law of Nations;

To declare War, grant Letters of Marque and Reprisal, and make Rules concerning Captures on Land and Water;

To raise and support Armies, but no Appropriation of Money to that Use shall be for a longer Term than two Years;

To provide and maintain a Navy;

To make Rules for the Government and Regulation of the land and naval Forces;

To provide for calling forth the Militia to execute the Laws of the Union, suppress Insurrections and repel Invasions;

To provide for organizing, arming, and disciplining, the Militia, and for governing such Part of them as may be employed in the Service of the United

States, reserving to the States respectively, the Appointment of the Officers, and the Authority of training the Militia according to the discipline prescribed by Congress;

To exercise exclusive Legislation in all Cases whatsoever, over such District (not exceeding ten Miles square) as may, by Cession of particular States, and the Acceptance of Congress, become the Seat of the Government of the United States, and to exercise like Authority over all Places purchased by the Consent of the Legislature of the State in which the Same shall be, for the Erection of Forts, Magazines, Arsenals, dock-Yards, and other needful Buildings;

To make all Laws which shall be necessary and proper for carrying into Execution the foregoing Powers, and all other Powers vested by this Constitution in the Government of the United States, or in any Department or Officer thereof.

Section 9   *The Migration or Importation of such Persons as any of the States now existing shall think proper to admit, shall not be prohibited by the Congress prior to the Year one thousand eight hundred and eight, but a Tax or duty may be imposed on such Importation, not exceeding ten dollars for each Person.*

The Privilege of the Writ of Habeas Corpus shall not be suspended, unless when in Cases of Rebellion or Invasion the public Safety may require it.

No Bill of Attainder or ex post facto Law shall be passed.

No Capitation, or other direct, Tax shall be laid, unless in Proportion to the Census or Enumeration herein before directed to be taken.

No Tax or Duty shall be laid on Articles exported from any State.

No Preference shall be given by any Regulation of Commerce or Revenue to the Ports of one State over those of another: nor shall Vessels bound to, or from, one State, be obliged to enter, clear, or pay Duties in another.

No Money shall be drawn from the Treasury, but in Consequence of Appropriations made by Law; and a regular Statement and Account of the Receipts and Expenditures of all public Money shall be published from time to time.

No Title of Nobility shall be granted by the United States: And no Person holding any Office of Profit or Trust under them, shall, without the Consent of the Congress, accept of any present, Emolument, Office, or Title, of any kind whatever, from any King, Prince, or foreign State.

Section 10   No State shall enter into any Treaty, Alliance, or Confederation; grant Letters of Marque and Reprisal; coin Money; emit Bills of Credit; make any Thing but gold and silver Coin a Tender in Payment of Debts; pass any Bill of Attainder, ex post facto Law, or Law impairing the Obligation of Contracts, or grant any Title of Nobility.

No State shall, without the Consent of the Congress, lay any Imposts or Duties on Imports or Exports, except what may be absolutely necessary for executing it's inspection Laws: and the net Produce of all Duties and Imposts, laid by any State on Imports or Exports, shall be for the Use of the Treasury of the United States; and all such Laws shall be subject to the Revision and Controul of the Congress.

No State shall, without the Consent of Congress, lay any Duty of Tonnage, keep Troops, or Ships of War in time of Peace, enter into any Agreement or Compact with another State, or with a foreign Power, or engage in War, unless actually invaded, or in such imminent Danger as will not admit of delay.

ARTICLE II.

Section 1   The executive Power shall be vested in a President of the United States of America. He shall hold his Office during the Term of four Years, and, together with the Vice President, chosen for the same Term, be elected, as follows

Each State shall appoint, in such Manner as the Legislature thereof may direct, a Number of Electors, equal to the whole Number of Senators and Representatives to which the State may be entitled in the Congress: but no Senator or Representative, or Person holding an Office of Trust or Profit under the United States, shall be appointed an Elector.

The Electors shall meet in their respective States, and vote by Ballot for two Persons, of whom one at least shall not be an Inhabitant of the same State with themselves. And they shall make a List of all the Persons voted for, and of the Number of Votes for each; which List they shall sign and certify, and transmit sealed to the Seat of Government of the United States, directed to the President of the Senate. The President of the Senate shall, in the Presence of the Senate and House of Representatives, open all the Certificates, and the Votes shall then be counted. The Person having the greatest Number of Votes shall be the President, if such Number be a Majority of the whole Number of Electors appointed; and if there be more than one who have such Majority, and have an equal Number of Votes, then the House of Representatives shall immediately chuse by Ballot one of them for President; and if no Person have a Majority, then from the five highest on the List the said House shall in like Manner chuse the President. But in chusing the President, the Votes shall be taken by States, the Representation from each State having one Vote; A quorum for this Purpose shall consist of a Member or Members from two thirds of the States, and a Majority of all the States shall be necessary to a Choice. In every Case, after the Choice of the President, the Person having the greatest Number of

Votes of the Electors shall be the Vice President. But if there should remain two or more who have equal Votes, the Senate shall chuse from them by Ballot the Vice President. The Congress may determine the Time of chusing the Electors, and the Day on which they shall give their Votes; which Day shall be the same throughout the United States.

No Person except a natural born Citizen, *or a Citizen of the United States, at the time of the Adoption of this Constitution,* shall be eligible to the Office of President; neither shall any Person be eligible to that Office who shall not have attained to the Age of thirty five Years, and been fourteen Years a Resident within the United States.

In Case of the Removal of the President from Office, or of his Death, Resignation, or Inability to discharge the Powers and Duties of the said Office, the Same shall devolve on the Vice President, and the Congress may by Law provide for the Case of Removal, Death, Resignation or Inability, both of the President and Vice President declaring what Officer shall then act as President, and such Officer shall act accordingly, until the Disability be removed, or a President shall be elected.

The President shall, at stated Times, receive for his Services, a Compensation, which shall neither be increased nor diminished during the Period for which he shall have been elected, and he shall not receive within that Period any other Emolument from the United States, or any of them.

Before he enter on the Execution of his Office, he shall take the following Oath or Affirmation: "I do solemnly swear (or affirm) that I will faithfully execute the Office of President of the United States, and will to the best of my Ability, preserve, protect and defend the Constitution of the United States."

Section 2　The President shall be Commander in Chief of the Army and Navy of the United States, and of the Militia of the several States, when called into the actual Service of the United States; he may require the Opinion, in writing, of the principal Officer in each of the executive Departments, upon any Subject relating to the Duties of their respective Offices, and he shall have Power to grant Reprieves and Pardons for Offences against the United States, except in Cases of Impeachment.

He shall have Power, by and with the Advice and Consent of the Senate, to make Treaties, provided two thirds of the Senators present concur; and he shall nominate, and by and with the Advice and Consent of the Senate, shall appoint Ambassadors, other public Ministers and Consuls, Judges of the supreme Court, and all other Officers of the United States, whose Appointments are not herein otherwise provided for, and which shall be established by Law: but the Congress may by Law vest the Appointment of such inferior Officers, as they think proper, in the President alone, in the Courts of Law, or in the Heads of Departments.

The President shall have Power to fill up all Vacancies that may happen during the Recess of the Senate, by granting Commissions which shall expire at the End of their next Session.

Section 3　He shall from time to time give to the Congress Information of the State of the Union, and recommend to their Consideration such Measures as he shall judge necessary and expedient; he may, on extraordinary Occasions, convene both Houses, or either of them, and in Case of Disagreement between them, with Respect to the Time of Adjournment, he may adjourn them to such Time as he shall think proper; he shall receive Ambassadors and other public Ministers; he shall take Care that the Laws be faithfully executed, and shall Commission all the Officers of the United States.

Section 4　The President, Vice President and all civil Officers of the United States, shall be removed from Office on Impeachment for, and Conviction of, Treason, Bribery, or other high Crimes and Misdemeanors.

ARTICLE III.

Section 1　The judicial Power of the United States, shall be vested in one supreme Court, and in such inferior Courts as the Congress may from time to time ordain and establish. The Judges, both of the supreme and inferior Courts, shall hold their Offices during good Behaviour, and shall, at stated Times, receive for their Services, a Compensation which shall not be diminished during their Continuance in Office.

Section 2　The judicial Power shall extend to all Cases, in Law and Equity, arising under this Constitution, the Laws of the United States, and Treaties made, or which shall be made, under their Authority;—to all Cases affecting Ambassadors, other public Ministers and Consuls;—to all Cases of admiralty and maritime Jurisdiction;—to Controversies to which the United States shall be a Party;—to Controversies between two or more States;—*between a State and Citizens of another State;*—between Citizens of different States;—between Citizens of the same State claiming Lands under Grants of different States, and between a State, or the Citizens thereof, and foreign States, Citizens or Subjects.

In all Cases affecting Ambassadors, other public Ministers and Consuls, and those in which a State shall be Party, the supreme Court shall have original Jurisdiction. In all the other Cases before mentioned, the supreme Court shall have appellate Jurisdiction, both as to Law and Fact, with such Exceptions, and under such Regulations as the Congress shall make.

The Trial of all Crimes, except in Cases of Impeachment, shall be by Jury; and such Trial shall be held in the State where the said Crimes shall have been committed; but when not committed within any State, the Trial shall be at such Place or Places as the Congress may by Law have directed.

Section 3   Treason against the United States, shall consist only in levying War against them, or in adhering to their Enemies, giving them Aid and Comfort. No Person shall be convicted of Treason unless on the Testimony of two Witnesses to the same overt Act, or on Confession in open Court.

The Congress shall have Power to declare the Punishment of Treason, but no Attainder of Treason shall work Corruption of Blood, or Forfeiture except during the Life of the Person attainted.

ARTICLE IV.

Section 1   Full Faith and Credit shall be given in each State to the public Acts, Records, and judicial Proceedings of every other State. And the Congress may by general Laws prescribe the Manner in which such Acts, Records and Proceedings shall be proved, and the Effect thereof.

Section 2   The Citizens of each State shall be entitled to all Privileges and Immunities of Citizens in the several States.

A Person charged in any State with Treason, Felony, or other Crime, who shall flee from Justice, and be found in another State, shall on Demand of the executive Authority of the State from which he fled, be delivered up, to be removed to the State having Jurisdiction of the Crime.

No Person held to Service or Labour in one State, under the Laws thereof, escaping into another, shall, in Consequence of any Law or Regulation therein, be discharged from such Service or Labour, but shall be delivered up on Claim of the Party to whom such Service or Labour may be due.

Section 3   New States may be admitted by the Congress into this Union; but no new State shall be formed or erected within the Jurisdiction of any other State; nor any State be formed by the Junction of two or more States, or Parts of States, without the Consent of the Legislatures of the States concerned as well as of the Congress.

The Congress shall have Power to dispose of and make all needful Rules and Regulations respecting the Territory or other Property belonging to the United States; and nothing in this Constitution shall be so construed as to Prejudice any Claims of the United States, or of any particular State.

Section 4   The United States shall guarantee to every State in this Union a Republican Form of Government, and shall protect each of them against Invasion; and on Application of the Legislature, or of the Executive (when the Legislature cannot be convened) against domestic Violence.

ARTICLE V.

The Congress, whenever two thirds of both Houses shall deem it necessary, shall propose Amendments to this Constitution, or, on the Application of the Legislatures of two thirds of the several States, shall call a Convention for proposing Amendments, which, in either Case, shall be valid to all Intents and Purposes, as Part of this Constitution, when ratified by the Legislatures of three fourths of the several States, or by Conventions in three fourths thereof, as the one or the other Mode of Ratification may be proposed by the Congress; Provided that *no Amendment which may be made prior to the Year One thousand eight hundred and eight shall in any Manner affect the first and fourth Clauses in the Ninth Section of the first Article; and* that no State, without its Consent, shall be deprived of its equal Suffrage in the Senate.

ARTICLE VI.

All Debts contracted and Engagements entered into, before the Adoption of this Constitution, shall be as valid against the United States under this Constitution, as under the Confederation.

This Constitution, and the Laws of the United States which shall be made in Pursuance thereof; and all Treaties made or which shall be made, under the Authority of the United States, shall be the supreme Law of the Land; and the Judges in every State shall be bound thereby, any Thing in the Constitution or Laws of any State to the Contrary notwithstanding.

The Senators and Representatives before mentioned, and the Members of the several State Legislatures, and all executive and judicial Officers, both of the United States and of the several States, shall be bound by Oath or Affirmation, to support this Constitution; but no religious Test shall ever be required as a Qualification to any Office or public Trust under the United States.

ARTICLE VII.

The Ratification of the Conventions of nine States, shall be sufficient for the Establishment of this Constitution between the States so ratifying the Same.

Done in Convention by the Unanimous Consent of the States present the Seventeenth Day of September in the Year of our Lord one thousand seven hundred and Eighty seven and of the Independence of the United States of America the Twelfth IN WITNESS whereof We have hereunto subscribed our Names,

GEORGE WASHINGTON,
President and Deputy from Virginia

North Carolina	*South Carolina*	*Massachusetts*
WILLIAM BLOUNT	J. RUTLEDGE	NATHANIEL GORHAM
RICHARD DOBBS SPRAIGHT	CHARLES C. PINCKNEY	RUFUS KING
HU WILLIAMSON	PIERCE BUTLER	
		Connecticut
Pennsylvania	*Virginia*	WILLIAM S. JOHNSON
BENJAMIN FRANKLIN	JOHN BLAIR	ROGER SHERMAN
THOMAS MIFFLIN	JAMES MADISON, JR.	
ROBERT MORRIS		*New York*
GEORGE CLYMER	*New Jersey*	ALEXANDER HAMILTON
THOMAS FITZSIMONS	WILLIAM LIVINGSTON	
JARED INGERSOLL	DAVID BREARLEY	
JAMES WILSON	WILLIAM PATERSON	*New Hampshire*
GOUVERNEUR MORRIS	JONATHAN DAYTON	JOHN LANGDON
		NICHOLAS GILMAN
Delaware	*Maryland*	
GEORGE READ	JAMES MCHENRY	*Georgia*
GUNNING BEDFORD, JR.	DANIEL OF ST. THOMAS JENIFER	WILLIAM FEW
JOHN DICKINSON	DANIEL CARROLL	ABRAHAM BALDWIN
RICHARD BASSETT		
JACOB BROOM		

AMENDMENTS TO THE CONSTITUTION*

Amendment I
Congress shall make no law respecting an establishment of religion, or prohibiting the free exercise thereof; or abridging the freedom of speech, or of the press; or the right of the people peaceably to assemble, and to petition the Government for a redress of grievances.

Amendment II
A well regulated Militia, being necessary to the security of a free State, the right of the people to keep and bear Arms, shall not be infringed.

Amendment III
No Soldier shall, in time of peace be quartered in any house, without the consent of the Owner, nor in time of war, but in a manner to be prescribed by law.

Amendment IV
The right of the people to be secure in their persons, houses, papers, and effects, against unreasonable searches and seizures, shall not be violated, and no Warrants shall issue, but upon probable cause, supported by Oath or affirmation, and particularly describing the place to be searched, and the persons or things to be seized.

Amendment V
No person shall be held to answer for a capital, or otherwise infamous crime, unless on a presentment or indictment of a Grand Jury, except in cases arising in the land or naval forces, or in the Militia, when in actual service in time of War or public danger; nor shall any person be subject for the same offence to be twice put in jeopardy of life or limb; nor shall be compelled in any criminal case to be a witness against himself, nor be deprived of life, liberty, or property, without due process of law; nor shall private property be taken for public use, without just compensation.

Amendment VI
In all criminal prosecutions, the accused shall enjoy the right to a speedy and public trial, by an impartial jury of the State and district wherein the crime shall have been committed, which district shall have been previously ascertained by law, and to be informed of the nature and cause of the accusation; to be confronted with the witnesses against him; to have compulsory process for obtaining witnesses in his favor, and to have the Assistance of Counsel for his defence.

Amendment VII
In Suits at common law, where the value in controversy shall exceed twenty dollars, the right of trial by jury shall be preserved, and no fact tried by a jury, shall be otherwise re-examined in any Court of the United States, than according to the rules of the common law.

Amendment VIII
Excessive bail shall not be required, nor excessive fines imposed, nor cruel and unusual punishments inflicted.

Amendment IX
The enumeration in the Constitution, of certain rights, shall not be construed to deny or disparage others retained by the people.

* The first ten amendments (the Bill of Rights) were adopted in 1791.

Amendment X

The powers not delegated to the United States by the Constitution, nor prohibited by it to the States, are reserved to the States respectively, or to the people.

Amendment XI [Adopted 1798]

The Judicial power of the United States shall not be construed to extend to any suit in law or equity, commenced or prosecuted against one of the United States by Citizens of another State, or by Citizens or Subjects of any Foreign State.

Amendment XII [Adopted 1804]

The Electors shall meet in their respective states, and vote by ballot for President and Vice-President, one of whom, at least, shall not be an inhabitant of the same state with themselves; they shall name in their ballots the person voted for as President, and in distinct ballots the person voted for as Vice-President, and they shall make distinct lists of all persons voted for as President, and of all persons voted for as Vice-President, and of the number of votes for each, which list they shall sign and certify, and transmit sealed to the seat of the government of the United States, directed to the President of the Senate;—The President of the Senate shall, in the presence of the Senate and House of Representatives, open all the certificates and the votes shall then be counted;—The person having the greatest number of votes for President, shall be the President, if such number be a majority of the whole number of Electors appointed; and if no person have such majority, then from the persons having the highest numbers not exceeding three on the list of those voted for as President, the House of Representatives shall choose immediately, by ballot, the President. But in choosing the President, the votes shall be taken by states, the representation from each state having one vote; a quorum for this purpose shall consist of a member or members from two thirds of the states, and a majority of all the states shall be necessary to a choice. And if the House of Representatives shall not choose a President whenever the right of choice shall devolve upon them, before the *fourth day of March* next following, then the Vice-President shall act as President, as in the case of the death or other constitutional disability of the President.

The person having the greatest number of votes as Vice-President, shall be the Vice-President, if such number be a majority of the whole number of Electors appointed, and if no person have a majority, then from the two highest numbers on the list, the Senate shall choose the Vice-President; a quorum for the purpose shall consist of two thirds of the whole number of Senators, and a majority of the whole number shall be necessary to a choice. But no person constitutionally ineligible to the office of President shall be eligible to that of Vice-President of the United States.

Amendment XIII [Adopted 1865]

Section 1   Neither slavery nor involuntary servitude, except as a punishment for crime whereof the party shall have been duly convicted, shall exist within the United States, or any place subject to their jurisdiction.

Section 2   Congress shall have power to enforce this article by appropriate legislation.

Amendment XIV [Adopted 1868]

Section 1   All persons born or naturalized in the United States, and subject to the jurisdiction thereof, are citizens of the United States and of the State wherein they reside. No State shall make or enforce any law which shall abridge the privileges or immunities of citizens of the United States; nor shall any State deprive any person of life, liberty, or property, without due process of law; nor deny to any person within its jurisdiction the equal protection of the laws.

Section 2   Representatives shall be apportioned among the several States according to their respective numbers, counting the whole number of persons in each State, excluding Indians not taxed. But when the right to vote at any election for the choice of electors for President and Vice-President of the United States, Representatives in Congress, the Executive and Judicial officers of a State, or the members of the Legislature thereof, is denied to any of the male inhabitants of such State, being twenty-one years of age, and citizens of the United States, or in any way abridged, except for participation in rebellion, or other crime, the basis of representation therein shall be reduced in the proportion which the number of such male citizens shall bear to the whole number of male citizens twenty-one years of age in such State.

Section 3   No person shall be a Senator or Representative in Congress, or elector of President and Vice-President, or hold any office, civil or military, under the United States, or under any State, who, having previously taken an oath, as a member of Congress, or as an officer of the United States, or as a member of any State legislature, or as an executive or judicial officer of any State, to support the Constitution of the United States, shall have engaged in insurrection or rebellion against the same, or given aid or comfort to the enemies thereof. But Congress may by a vote of two thirds of each House, remove such disability.

Section 4   The validity of the public debt of the United States, authorized by law, including debts incurred for payment of pensions and bounties for services in suppressing insurrection or rebellion, shall not be questioned. But neither the United States nor any State shall assume or pay any debt or obligation incurred in aid of insurrection or rebellion against the United States, or any claim for the loss or emancipation of any slave; but all such debts, obligations and claims shall be held illegal and void.

Section 5 The Congress shall have power to enforce, by appropriate legislation, the provisions of this article.

Amendment XV [Adopted 1870]

Section 1 The right of citizens of the United States to vote shall not be denied or abridged by the United States or by any State on account of race, color, or previous condition of servitude.

Section 2 The Congress shall have power to enforce this article by appropriate legislation.

Amendment XVI [Adopted 1913]

The Congress shall have power to lay and collect taxes on incomes, from whatever source derived, without apportionment among the several States, and without regard to any census or enumeration.

Amendment XVII [Adopted 1913]

The Senate of the United States shall be composed of two Senators from each State, elected by the people thereof, for six years; and each Senator shall have one vote. The electors in each State shall have the qualifications requisite for electors of the most numerous branch of the State legislatures.

When vacancies happen in the representation of any State in the Senate, the executive authority of such State shall issue writs of election to fill such vacancies: *Provided,* That the legislature of any State may empower the executive thereof to make temporary appointments until the people fill the vacancies by election as the legislature may direct.

This amendment shall not be so construed as to affect the election or term of any Senator chosen before it becomes valid as part of the Constitution.

Amendment XVIII [Adopted 1919; Repealed 1933]

Section 1 After one year from the ratification of this article the manufacture, sale, or transportation of intoxicating liquors within, the importation thereof into, or the exportation thereof from the United States and all territory subject to the jurisdiction thereof for beverage purposes is hereby prohibited.

Section 2 The Congress and the several States shall have concurrent power to enforce this article by appropriate legislation.

Section 3 This article shall be inoperative unless it shall have been ratified as an amendment to the Constitution by the legislatures of the several States, as provided in the Constitution, within seven years from the date of the submission hereof to the States by the Congress.

Amendment XIX [Adopted 1920]

Section 1 The right of citizens of the United States to vote shall not be denied or abridged by the United States or by any State on account of sex.

Section 2 Congress shall have power to enforce this article by appropriate legislation.

Amendment XX [Adopted 1933]

Section 1 The terms of the President and Vice-President shall end at noon on the 20th day of January, and the terms of Senators and Representatives at noon on the third day of January, of the years in which such terms would have ended if this article had not been ratified; and the terms of their successors shall then begin.

Section 2 The Congress shall assemble at least once in every year, and such meeting shall begin at noon on the third day of January, unless they shall by law appoint a different day.

Section 3 If, at the time fixed for the beginning of the term of the President, the President elect shall have died, the Vice-President elect shall become President. If a President shall not have been chosen before the time fixed for the beginning of his term, or if the President elect shall have failed to qualify, then the Vice-President elect shall act as President until a President shall have qualified; and the Congress may by law provide for the case wherein neither a President elect nor a Vice-President elect shall have qualified, declaring who shall then act as President, or the manner in which one who is to act shall be selected, and such person shall act accordingly until a President or Vice-President shall have qualified.

Section 4 The Congress may by law provide for the case of the death of any of the persons from whom the House of Representatives may choose a President whenever the right of choice shall have devolved upon them, and for the case of the death of any of the persons from whom the Senate may choose a Vice-President whenever the right of choice shall have devolved upon them.

Section 5 Sections 1 and 2 shall take effect on the 15th day of October following the ratification of this article.

Section 6 This article shall be inoperative unless it shall have been ratified as an amendment to the Constitution by the legislatures of three fourths of the several States within seven years from the date of its submission.

Amendment XXI [Adopted 1933]

Section 1 The eighteenth article of amendment to the Constitution of the United States is hereby repealed.

Section 2 The transportation or importation into any State, Territory, or possession of the United States for delivery or use therein of intoxicating liquors, in violation of the laws thereof, is hereby prohibited.

Section 3 This article shall be inoperative unless it shall have been ratified as an amendment to the Constitution by conventions in the several States, as provided in the Constitution, within seven years from the date of the submission hereof to the States by the Congress.

Amendment XXII [Adopted 1951]

Section 1   No person shall be elected to the office of the President more than twice, and no person who has held the office of President, or acted as President, for more than two years of a term to which some other person was elected President shall be elected to the office of the President more than once. But this Article shall not apply to any person holding the office of President when this Article was proposed by the Congress, and shall not prevent any person who may be holding the office of President, or acting as President, during the term within which this Article becomes operative from holding the office of President or acting as President during the remainder of such term.

Section 2   This article shall be inoperative unless it shall have been ratified as an amendment to the Constitution by the legislatures of three fourths of the several States within seven years from the date of its submission to the States by the Congress.

Amendment XXIII [Adopted 1961]

Section 1   The District constituting the seat of Government of the United States shall appoint in such manner as the Congress may direct:

A number of electors of President and Vice-President equal to the whole number of Senators and Representatives in Congress to which the District would be entitled if it were a State, but in no event more than the least populous State; they shall be in addition to those appointed by the States, but they shall be considered, for the purposes of the election of President and Vice-President, to be electors appointed by a State; and they shall meet in the District and perform such duties as provided by the twelfth article of amendment.

Section 2   The Congress shall have power to enforce this article by appropriate legislation.

Amendment XXIV [Adopted 1964]

Section 1   The right of citizens of the United States to vote in any primary or other election for President or Vice-President, for electors for President or Vice-President, or for Senator or Representative in Congress, shall not be denied or abridged by the United States or any State by reason of failure to pay any poll tax or other tax.

Section 2   The Congress shall have power to enforce this article by appropriate legislation.

Amendment XXV [Adopted 1967]

Section 1   In case of the removal of the President from office or his death or resignation, the Vice-President shall become President.

Section 2   Whenever there is a vacancy in the office of the Vice-President, the President shall nominate a Vice-President who shall take the office upon confirmation by a majority vote of both houses of Congress.

Section 3   Whenever the President transmits to the President pro tempore of the Senate and the Speaker of the House of Representatives his written declaration that he is unable to discharge the powers and duties of his office, and until he transmits to them a written declaration to the contrary, such powers and duties shall be discharged by the Vice-President as Acting President.

Section 4   Whenever the Vice-President and a majority of either the principal officers of the executive departments, or of such other body as Congress may by law provide, transmit to the President pro tempore of the Senate and the Speaker of the House of Representatives their written declaration that the President is unable to discharge the powers and duties of his office, the Vice-President shall immediately assume the powers and duties of the office as Acting President.

Thereafter, when the President transmits to the President pro tempore of the Senate and the Speaker of the House of Representatives his written declaration that no inability exists, he shall resume the powers and duties of his office unless the Vice-President and a majority of either the principal officers of the executive department, or of such other body as Congress may by law provide, transmit within four days to the President pro tempore of the Senate and the Speaker of the House of Representatives their written declaration that the President is unable to discharge the powers and duties of his office. Thereupon Congress shall decide the issue, assembling within 48 hours for that purpose if not in session. If the Congress, within 21 days after receipt of the latter written declaration, or, if Congress is not in session, within 21 days after Congress is required to assemble, determines by two-thirds vote of both houses that the President is unable to discharge the powers and duties of his office, the Vice-President shall continue to discharge the same as Acting President; otherwise, the President shall resume the powers and duties of his office.

Amendment XXVI [Adopted 1971]

Section 1   The right of citizens of the United States, who are eighteen years of age or older, to vote shall not be denied or abridged by the United States or any state on account of age.

Section 2   The Congress shall have power to enforce this article by appropriate legislation.

Amendment XXVII [Adopted 1992]

No law, varying the compensation for the services of Senators and Representatives, shall take effect until an election of Representatives have intervened.

PRESIDENTIAL ELECTIONS

Year	Candidates	Parties	Popular Vote	Electoral Vote	Voter Participation
1789	GEORGE WASHINGTON		*	69	
	John Adams			34	
	Others			35	
1792	GEORGE WASHINGTON		*	132	
	John Adams			77	
	George Clinton			50	
	Others			5	
1796	JOHN ADAMS	Federalist	*	71	
	Thomas Jefferson	Democratic-Republican		68	
	Thomas Pinckney	Federalist		59	
	Aaron Burr	Dem.-Rep.		30	
	Others			48	
1800	THOMAS JEFFERSON	Dem.-Rep.	*	73	
	Aaron Burr	Dem.-Rep.		73	
	C. C. Pinckney	Federalist		64	
	John Jay	Federalist		1	
1804	THOMAS JEFFERSON	Dem.-Rep.	*	122	
	C. C. Pinckney	Federalist		14	
1808	JAMES MADISON	Dem.-Rep.	*	122	
	C. C. Pinckney	Federalist		47	
	George Clinton	Dem.-Rep.		6	
1812	JAMES MADISON	Dem.-Rep.	*	128	
	De Witt Clinton	Federalist		89	
1816	JAMES MONROE	Dem.-Rep.	*	183	
	Rufus King	Federalist		34	
1820	JAMES MONROE	Dem.-Rep.	*	231	
	John Quincy Adams	Dem.-Rep.		1	
1824	JOHN Q. ADAMS	Dem.-Rep.	108,740 (10.5%)	84	26.9%
	Andrew Jackson	Dem.-Rep.	153,544 (43.1%)	99	
	William H. Crawford	Dem.-Rep.	46,618 (13.1%)	41	
	Henry Clay	Dem.-Rep.	47,136 (13.2%)	37	
1828	ANDREW JACKSON	Democratic	647,286 (56.0%)	178	57.6%
	John Quincy Adams	National Republican	508,064 (44.0%)	83	
1832	ANDREW JACKSON	Democratic	687,502 (55.0%)	219	55.4%
	Henry Clay	National Republican	530,189 (42.4%)	49	
	John Floyd	Independent		11	
	William Wirt	Anti-Mason	33,108 (2.6%)	7	
1836	MARTIN VAN BUREN	Democratic	765,483 (50.9%)	170	57.8%
	W. H. Harrison	Whig		73	
	Hugh L. White	Whig	739,795 (49.1%)	26	
	Daniel Webster	Whig		14	
	W. P. Magnum	Independent		11	
1840	WILLIAM H. HARRISON	Whig	1,274,624 (53.1%)	234	80.2%
	Martin Van Buren	Democratic	1,127,781 (46.9%)	60	
	J. G. Birney	Liberty	7,069	—	
1844	JAMES K. POLK	Democratic	1,338,464 (49.6%)	170	78.9%
	Henry Clay	Whig	1,300,097 (48.1%)	105	
	J. G. Birney	Liberty	62,300 (2.3%)	—	
1848	ZACHARY TAYLOR	Whig	1,360,967 (47.4%)	163	72.7%
	Lewis Cass	Democratic	1,222,342 (42.5%)	127	
	Martin Van Buren	Free-Soil	291,263 (10.1%)	—	
1852	FRANKLIN PIERCE	Democratic	1,601,117 (50.9%)	254	69.6%
	Winfield Scott	Whig	1,385,453 (44.1%)	42	
	John P. Hale	Free-Soil	155,825 (5.0%)	—	

Year	Candidates	Parties	Popular Vote	Electoral Vote	Voter Participation
1856	JAMES BUCHANAN	Democratic	1,832,955 (45.3%)	174	78.9%
	John C. Fremont	Republican	1,339,932 (33.1%)	114	
	Millard Fillmore	American	871,731 (21.6%)	8	
1860	ABRAHAM LINCOLN	Republican	1,865,593 (39.8%)	180	81.2%
	Stephen A. Douglas	Democratic	1,382,713 (29.5%)	12	
	John C. Breckinridge	Democratic	848,356 (18.1%)	72	
	John Bell	Union	592,906 (12.6%)	39	
1864	ABRAHAM LINCOLN	Republican	2,213,655 (55.0%)	212	73.8%
	George B. McClellan	Democratic	1,805,237 (45.0%)	21	
1868	ULYSSES S. GRANT	Republican	3,012,833 (52.7%)	214	78.1%
	Horatio Seymour	Democratic	2,703,249 (47.3%)	80	
1872	ULYSSES S. GRANT	Republican	3,597,132 (55.6%)	286	71.3%
	Horace Greeley	Democratic; Liberal Republican	2,834,125 (43.9%)	66	
1876	RUTHERFORD B. HAYES	Republican	4,036,298 (48.0%)	185	81.8%
	Samuel J. Tilden	Democratic	4,300,590 (51.0%)	184	
1880	JAMES A. GARFIELD	Republican	4,454,416 (48.5%)	214	79.4%
	Winfield S. Hancock	Democratic	4,444,952 (48.1%)	155	
1884	GROVER CLEVELAND	Democratic	4,874,986 (48.5%)	219	77.5%
	James G. Blaine	Republican	4,851,981 (48.2%)	182	
1888	BENJAMIN HARRISON	Republican	5,439,853 (47.9%)	233	79.3%
	Grover Cleveland	Democratic	5,540,309 (48.6%)	168	
1892	GROVER CLEVELAND	Democratic	5,556,918 (46.1%)	277	74.7%
	Benjamin Harrison	Republican	5,176,108 (43.0%)	145	
	James B. Weaver	People's	1,041,028 (8.5%)	22	
1896	WILLIAM McKINLEY	Republican	7,104,779 (51.1%)	271	79.3%
	William J. Bryan	Democratic People's	6,502,925 (47.7%)	176	
1900	WILLIAM McKINLEY	Republican	7,207,923 (51.7%)	292	73.2%
	William J. Bryan	Dem.-Populist	6,358,133 (45.5%)	155	
1904	THEODORE ROOSEVELT	Republican	7,623,486 (57.9%)	336	65.2%
	Alton B. Parker	Democratic	5,077,911 (37.6%)	140	
	Eugene V. Debs	Socialist	402,283 (3.0%)	—	
1908	WILLIAM H. TAFT	Republican	7,678,908 (51.6%)	321	65.4%
	William J. Bryan	Democratic	6,409,104 (43.1%)	162	
	Eugene V. Debs	Socialist	420,793 (2.8%)	—	
1912	WOODROW WILSON	Democratic	6,293,454 (41.9%)	435	58.8%
	Theodore Roosevelt	Progressive	4,119,538 (27.4%)	88	
	William H. Taft	Republican	3,484,980 (23.2%)	8	
	Eugene V. Debs	Socialist	900,672 (6.0%)	—	
1916	WOODROW WILSON	Democratic	9,129,606 (49.4%)	277	61.6%
	Charles E. Hughes	Republican	8,538,221 (46.2%)	254	
	A. L. Benson	Socialist	585,113 (3.2%)	—	
1920	WARREN G. HARDING	Republican	16,152,200 (60.4%)	404	49.2%
	James M. Cox	Democratic	9,147,353 (34.2%)	127	
	Eugene V. Debs	Socialist	919,799 (3.4%)	—	
1924	CALVIN COOLIDGE	Republican	15,725,016 (54.0%)	382	48.9%
	John W. Davis	Democratic	8,386,503 (28.8%)	136	
	Robert M. La Follette	Progressive	4,822,856 (16.6%)	13	
1928	HERBERT HOOVER	Republican	21,391,381 (58.2%)	444	56.9%
	Alfred E. Smith	Democratic	15,016,443 (40.9%)	87	
	Norman Thomas	Socialist	267,835 (0.7%)	—	
1932	FRANKLIN D. ROOSEVELT	Democratic	22,821,857 (57.4%)	472	56.9%
	Herbert Hoover	Republican	15,761,841 (39.7%)	59	
	Norman Thomas	Socialist	881,951 (2.2%)	—	

Year	Candidates	Parties	Popular Vote	Electoral Vote	Voter Participation
1936	FRANKLIN D. ROOSEVELT	Democratic	27,751,597 (60.8%)	523	61.0%
	Alfred M. Landon	Republican	16,679,583 (36.5%)	8	
	William Lemke	Union	882,479 (1.9%)	—	
1940	FRANKLIN D. ROOSEVELT	Democratic	27,244,160 (54.8%)	449	62.5%
	Wendell L. Willkie	Republican	22,305,198 (44.8%)	82	
1944	FRANKLIN D. ROOSEVELT	Democrat	25,602,504 (53.5%)	432	55.9%
	Thomas E. Dewey	Republican	22,006,285 (46.0%)	99	
1948	HARRY S TRUMAN	Democratic	24,105,695 (49.5%)	304	53.0%
	Thomas E. Dewey	Republican	21,969,170 (45.1%)	189	
	J. Strom Thurmond	State-Rights Democratic	1,169,021 (2.4%)	38	
	Henry A. Wallace	Progressive	1,156,103 (2.4%)	—	
1952	DWIGHT D. EISENHOWER	Republican	33,936,252 (55.1%)	442	63.3%
	Adlai E. Stevenson	Democratic	27,314,992 (44.4%)	89	
1956	DWIGHT D. EISENHOWER	Republican	35,575,420 (57.6%)	457	60.5%
	Adlai E. Stevenson	Democratic	26,033,066 (42.1%)	73	
	Other	—	—	1	
1960	JOHN F. KENNEDY	Democratic	34,227,096 (49.9%)	303	62.8%
	Richard M. Nixon	Republican	34,108,546 (49.6%)	219	
	Other	—	—	15	
1964	LYNDON B. JOHNSON	Democratic	43,126,506 (61.1%)	486	61.7%
	Barry M. Goldwater	Republican	27,176,799 (38.5%)	52	
1968	RICHARD M. NIXON	Republican	31,770,237 (43.4.%)	301	60.6%
	Hubert H. Humphrey	Democratic	31,270,633 (42.7%)	191	
	George Wallace	American Indep.	9,906,141 (13.5%)	46	
1972	RICHARD M. NIXON	Republican	47,169,911 (60.7%)	520	55.2%
	George S. McGovern	Democratic	29,170,383 (37.5%)	17	
	Other	—	—	1	
1976	JIMMY CARTER	Democratic	40,828,587 (50.0%)	297	53.5%
	Gerald R. Ford	Republican	39,147,613 (47.9%)	241	
	Other	—	1,575,459 (2.1%)	—	
1980	RONALD REAGAN	Republican	43,901,812 (50.7%)	489	52.6%
	Jimmy Carter	Democratic	35,483,820 (41.0%)	49	
	John B. Anderson	Independent	5,719,722 (6.6%)	—	
	Ed Clark	Libertarian	921,188 (1.1%)	—	
1984	RONALD REAGAN	Republican	54,455,075 (59.0%)	525	53.3%
	Walter Mondale	Democratic	37,577,185 (41.0%)	13	
1988	GEORGE H.W. BUSH	Republican	48,886,000 (45.6%)	426	57.4%
	Michael S. Dukakis	Democratic	41,809,000 (45.6%)	111	
1992	WILLIAM J. CLINTON	Democratic	43,728,375 (43%)	370	55.0%
	George H.W. Bush	Republican	38,167,416 (38%)	168	
	Ross Perot	—	19,237,247 (19%)	—	
1996	WILLIAM J. CLINTON	Democratic	45,590,703 (50%)	379	48.8%
	Robert Dole	Republican	37,816,307 (41%)	159	
	Ross Perot	Independent	7,866,284 (9%)		
2000	GEORGE W. BUSH	Republican	50,456,062 (47%)	271	51.0%
	Albert Gore	Democratic	50,996,582 (49%)	267	
	Ralph Nader	Independent	2,858,843 (3%)	—	

STATES OF THE UNITED STATES

State	Date of Admission	State	Date of Admission
Delaware	December 7, 1787	Michigan	January 16, 1837
Pennsylvania	December 12, 1787	Florida	March 3, 1845
New Jersey	December 18, 1787	Texas	December 29, 1845
Georgia	January 2, 1788	Iowa	December 28, 1846
Connecticut	January 9, 1788	Wisconsin	May 29, 1848
Massachusetts	February 6, 1788	California	September 9, 1850
Maryland	April 28, 1788	Minnesota	May 11, 1858
South Carolina	May 23, 1788	Oregon	February 14, 1859
New Hampshire	June 21, 1788	Kansas	January 29, 1861
Virginia	June 25, 1788	West Virginia	June 19, 1863
New York	July 26, 1788	Nevada	October 31, 1864
North Carolina	November 21, 1789	Nebraska	March 1, 1867
Rhode Island	May 29, 1790	Colorado	August 1, 1876
Vermont	March 4, 1791	North Dakota	November 2, 1889
Kentucky	June 1, 1792	South Dakota	November 2, 1889
Tennessee	June 1, 1796	Montana	November 8, 1889
Ohio	March 1, 1803	Washington	November 11, 1889
Louisiana	April 30, 1812	Idaho	July 3, 1890
Indiana	December 11, 1816	Wyoming	July 10, 1890
Mississippi	December 10, 1817	Utah	January 4, 1896
Illinois	December 3, 1818	Oklahoma	November 16, 1907
Alabama	December 14, 1819	New Mexico	January 6, 1912
Maine	March 15, 1820	Arizona	February 14, 1912
Missouri	August 10, 1821	Alaska	January 3, 1959
Arkansas	June 15, 1836	Hawaii	August 21, 1959

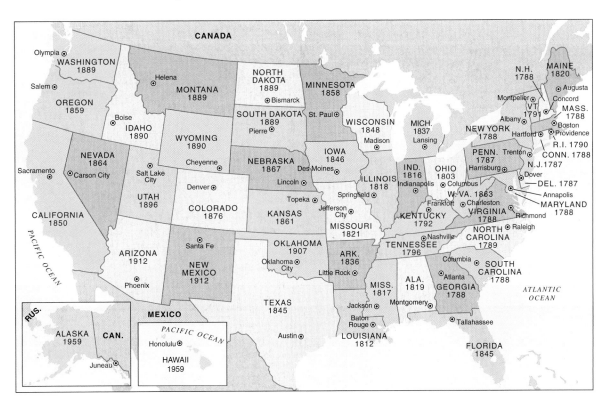

POPULATION OF THE UNITED STATES

Year	Number of States	Population	Percent Increase	Population per Square Mile
1790	13	3,929,214		4.5
1800	16	5,308,483	35.1	6.1
1810	17	7,239,881	36.4	4.3
1820	23	9,638,453	33.1	5.5
1830	24	12,866,020	33.5	7.4
1840	26	17,069,453	32.7	9.8
1850	31	23,191,876	35.9	7.9
1860	33	31,443,321	35.6	10.6
1870	37	39,818,449	26.6	13.4
1880	38	50,155,783	26.0	16.9
1890	44	62,947,714	25.5	21.2
1900	45	75,994,575	20.7	25.6
1910	46	91,972,266	21.0	31.0
1920	48	105,710,620	14.9	35.6
1930	48	122,775,046	16.1	41.2
1940	48	131,669,275	7.2	44.2
1950	48	150,697,361	14.5	50.7
1960	50	179,323,175	19.0	50.6
1970	50	203,235,298	13.3	57.5
1980	50	226,545,805	11.5	64.1
1990	50	248,709,873	9.8	70.3
2000	50	281,421,906	13.0	77.0

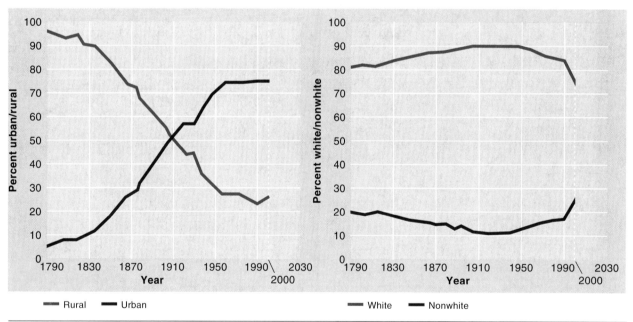

Source: U.S. Bureau of the Census estimates.

The World

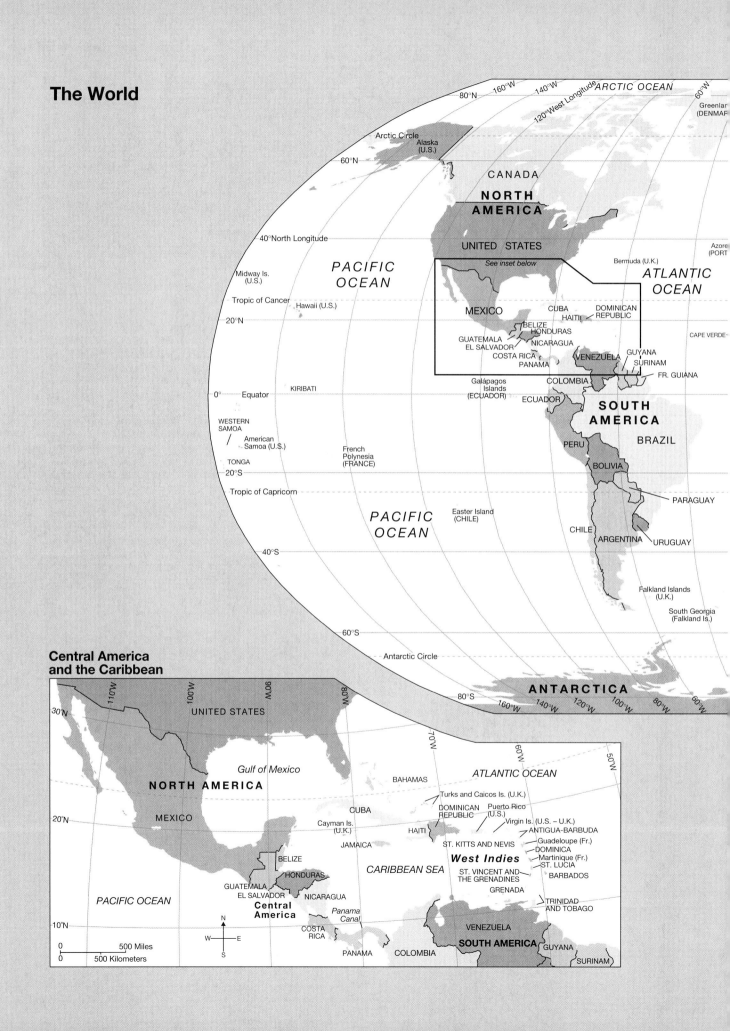

ARCTIC OCEAN
80°N
160°W
140°W
120°West Longitude
60°W

Greenlar (DENMAR

Arctic Circle
Alaska
(U.S.)
60°N

CANADA

NORTH AMERICA

UNITED STATES

40°North Longitude

See inset below

Bermuda (U.K.)

Azore (PORT

ATLANTIC OCEAN

PACIFIC OCEAN

Midway Is.
(U.S.)

Tropic of Cancer
20°N

Hawaii (U.S.)

MEXICO

CUBA
HAITI
DOMINICAN REPUBLIC

CAPE VERDE

BELIZE
HONDURAS
GUATEMALA
EL SALVADOR
NICARAGUA

GUYANA
SURINAM

VENEZUELA

FR. GUIANA

COSTA RICA
PANAMA

KIRIBATI

Galápagos
Islands
(ECUADOR)

COLOMBIA

0° Equator

ECUADOR

SOUTH AMERICA

WESTERN
SAMOA

American
Samoa (U.S.)

BRAZIL

French
Polynesia
(FRANCE)

PERU

TONGA
20°S

BOLIVIA

Tropic of Capricorn

Easter Island
(CHILE)

PARAGUAY

PACIFIC OCEAN

CHILE

ARGENTINA

URUGUAY

40°S

Falkland Islands
(U.K.)

South Georgia
(Falkland Is.)

60°S

Antarctic Circle

**Central America
and the Caribbean**

80°S

ANTARCTICA

160°W
140°W
120°W
100°W
80°W
60°W

110°W
100°W
90°W
80°W

30°N

UNITED STATES

Gulf of Mexico

BAHAMAS

70°W

60°W

50°W

ATLANTIC OCEAN

NORTH AMERICA

CUBA

Turks and Caicos Is. (U.K.)

DOMINICAN
REPUBLIC

Puerto Rico
(U.S.)

20°N

MEXICO

Cayman Is.
(U.K.)

Virgin Is. (U.S. – U.K.)

ANTIGUA-BARBUDA

HAITI

Guadeloupe (Fr.)

JAMAICA

ST. KITTS AND NEVIS

DOMINICA

BELIZE

West Indies

Martinique (Fr.)

ST. LUCIA

PACIFIC OCEAN

HONDURAS

CARIBBEAN SEA

ST. VINCENT AND
THE GRENADINES

BARBADOS

GUATEMALA
EL SALVADOR

**Central
America**

NICARAGUA

GRENADA

Panama
Canal

TRINIDAD
AND TOBAGO

10°N

COSTA
RICA

VENEZUELA

0   500 Miles

SOUTH AMERICA

GUYANA

0   500 Kilometers

N
W   E
S

PANAMA

COLOMBIA

SURINAM

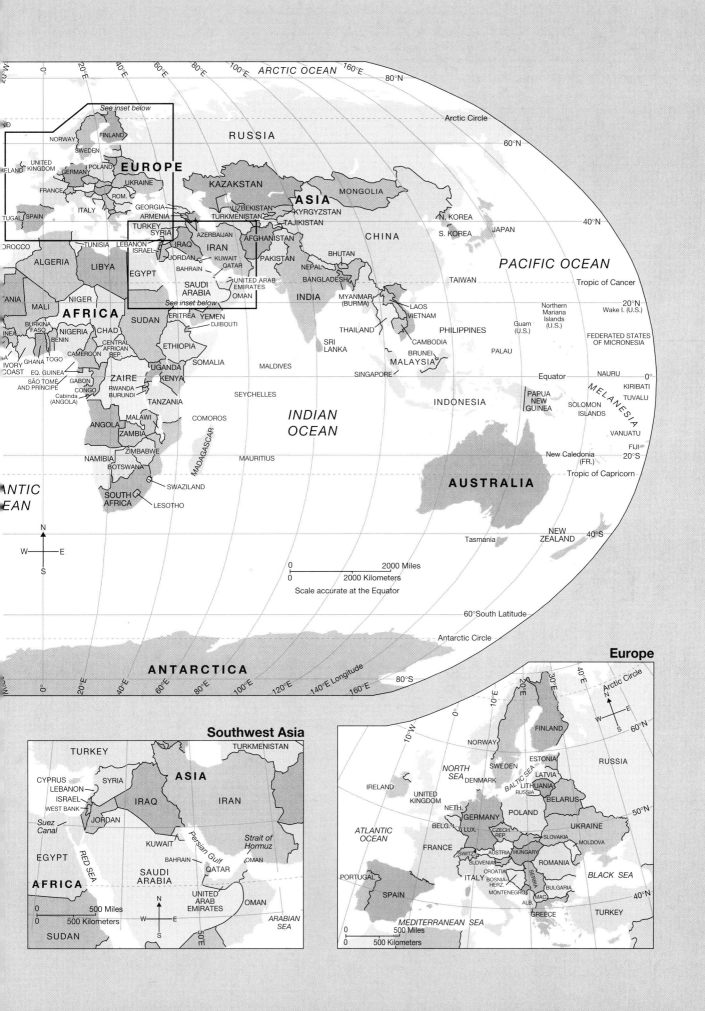

STUDY QUESTIONS

CHAPTER 1

MULTIPLE CHOICE. Choose the one alternative that best completes the statement or answers the question.

1. Paleo-anthropologists generally agree that the first inhabitants traveled to North America 14,000–25,000 years ago utilizing which of the following?
   A. sailing ships
   B. ice bridges
   C. canoes
   D. land bridges

2. The Europeans and Native Americans differed primarily in their
   A. attitudes toward land and social organization.
   B. economic practices such as farming and hunting.
   C. lifestyles such as sedentary versus nomadic.
   D. dedication to religious values.

3. When European settlers crossed the Appalachian Mountains and found hundreds of ceremonial mounds and other earthworks, they reasoned the Mound Builders were possibly all of the following EXCEPT
   A. Phoenicians
   B. Atlantis survivors
   C. Lost Tribes of Israel
   D. Native Americans

4. The developments that made the European age of exploration possible included all of the following EXCEPT the
   A. replacement of the feudal system with monarchies.
   B. development of merchant-dominated city-states.
   C. Black Death's effect on feudal power.
   D. spread of Christianity across North Africa.

5. The Renaissance involved all of the following EXCEPT
   A. a greater appreciation of the classics of Greece and Rome.
   B. a new confidence in the ability of humans.
   C. a new emphasis on religion and the life hereafter.
   D. more freedom of thought.

6. Iroquois women controlled the timing of male military forays through all of the following methods EXCEPT
   A. withholding food supplies for the foray.
   B. withholding moccasins for the foray.
   C. withholding sexual relations from their husbands.
   D. demanding enemy captives for fallen clan members.

7. All of the following were brought to America by Europeans EXCEPT
   A. pigs
   B. horses
   C. oxen
   D. potatoes

8. The last great West African trading empire before the area devolved into smaller states more susceptible to the Atlantic slave trade was
   A. Songhai
   B. Kongo
   C. Mali
   D. Ghana

9. According to pre-Colombian Native Americans,
   A. the natural world was a resource for human use.
   B. every part of the natural environment was sacred.
   C. the belief that spirits resided in nature was superstition.
   D. land ownership was the basis of individual status and identity.

10. From the fifth to the fourteenth centuries, West Africa was
    A. a savage land of nomadic hunters.
    B. colonized and exploited by a succession of various European nations.
    C. engaged in perpetual warfare with Muslims from the Middle East.
    D. organized into a series of kingdoms with relatively advanced cultures and complex political structures.

11. Which of the following was NOT a feature of slavery in West Africa?
    A. Slaves were entitled to protection under the law.
    B. Slavery was not inherited by children of slaves.
    C. Slaves were allowed the privileges of marriage and parenthood.
    D. Slavery was a permanent status.

12. All of the following were effects of the Black Death EXCEPT
    A. It promoted the creation of early modern states.
    B. Feudal lords treated peasants better because of a shortage of labor.
    C. Because of the misery there were peasant revolts and worker strikes.
    D. The economy greatly improved for the survivors.

13. Prince Henry the Navigator led which country into the unknown Atlantic in the early 1400s?
    A. Spain
    B. England
    C. Portugal
    D. France

SHORT ANSWER. Complete each statement or answer the question with a word or phrase.

14. In the fifteenth century, Europe was invigorated by a renewed interest in ideas, the arts, the past, and human capability. This period was called the _____.

15. Native Americans, unlike _____, believed that nature was sacred; that exploiting it was wrong; and that land should be held as communal property.

16. The revival of Europe is associated with the decline of the _____, the political and economic system that dominated Europe between the ninth and fifteenth centuries.

17. The great Native American winter gatherings in the Northwest where chiefs gave away possessions and maintained their power were called _____ .

18. The Iroquois had _____ families where family ownership was determined through the female line and women shared political power.

19. Mansa Musa created an Islamic _____ in Timbuktu, the center of the Mali Empire.

20. One of the first large empires in West Africa, noted for its sculpture and metalwork, was the kingdom of _____.

21. _____ led Italy's commercial cities to greatness as city states.

22. During Europe's Middle Ages the Ghana Empire supplied two-thirds of the _____ in the Christian Mediterranean region.

TRUE/FALSE. Determine if each statement is true or false.

23. Communal ownership of property promoted equality within pre-Colombian Native American societies.

24. The production of domesticated plant food encouraged early Americans to settle into villages.

25. The feudal system in Europe ensured the growth of independent and powerful monarchies.

26. In 1519 Cortes's army was amazed by the grandeur and technology of the Aztec people in Techochtitlan.

27. The Mound Builders were geographically insulated by mountain ranges and rivers so they probably had little contact with people outside of the Midwest region.

28. Native Americans generally believed land should be held in communal ownership.

29. The aristocracy in Late Middle Age Continental Europe thought the maximization of profit was not proper behavior for a gentleman.

30. The rights of slaves in West Africa were much the same as the rights of slaves in America.

VOCABULARY. Define each term or phrase.

African Empires
Black Death
enclosure movement
feudal system
Magna Carta
Marco Polo
matrilineal
Mound Builders
Mansa Musa
merchants
Muslim
polytheism
potlatch
pre-Colombian
Prince Henry
Renaissance
Tenochtitlan

CHAPTER 2

MULTIPLE CHOICE. Choose the one alternative that best completes the statement or answers the question.

1. Europeans saw the Native Americans as all of the following EXCEPT
   A. flesh-eating savages who slaughtered all in their path.
   B. gentle, naive people who welcomed newcomers with open arms.
   C. crafty, sly businessmen out to make a profit.
   D. noble savages who were culturally inferior to Europeans.

2. Between 1518 and 1548, Spanish conquistadores conquered most of the New World, motivated by the
   A. belief that an all-water western route to the Orient existed.
   B. urge to claim more territory for Spain.
   C. desire to advance national glory, serve God, and seek personal wealth.
   D. drive to settle colonies in the New World.

3. The Protestant Reformation was important because it
   A. reduced the intensity of religious devotion and activity in Europe.
   B. promoted national rivalries and wars.
   C. abandoned the idea of returning to a purer, "primitive" Christianity.
   D. discouraged and created apathy among Roman Catholics.

4. According to the text, the history of the New World in the 1500s and 1600s is primarily the story of the
   A. intermingling and exchange among different cultures.
   B. conquest and settlement by the Europeans.
   C. struggle for control of North America among Spain, England, and France.
   D. effect of European arrival on the natives.

5. The arrival of the Europeans had a major impact on the Native Americans because it
   A. destroyed their religious beliefs.
   B. freed them from a limited, structured existence.
   C. provided new crops and more nutrition.
   D. brought deaths from disease.

6. According to Martin Luther,
   A. only a chosen few deserved salvation.
   B. only Protestants could ever be saved.
   C. salvation came through faith in God's grace.
   D. salvation was earned through good works.

7. Which of the following best describes England's motivations for moving westward to North America?
   A. the quest for new fisheries
   B. the quest for gold and silver
   C. religious and trading rivalry with Spain
   D. the desire to Christianize heathen Indians

8. Which of the following pairs is NOT correctly matched?
   A. Pizarro/Incas
   B. Cortes/Aztecs
   C. Coronado/Pueblos
   D. De Soto/Shawnee

9. The Spanish armada was defeated in 1588 by a force led by the English sea dog
   A. Richard Hakluyt
   B. Thomas Harriot
   C. Francis Drake
   D. John Winthrop

10. Olaudah Equiano provided a graphic description of the middle passage of the slave trade. Equiano witnessed this misery as a
    A. slave trader
    B. sailor
    C. minister
    D. slave

11. Which product did the most to transform the early African slave trade?
    A. tobacco
    B. indigo
    C. sugar
    D. cotton

12. The English arguments created to justify dispossessing Native Americans of their land included
    A. denying the humanity of Native Americans.
    B. claiming the legal right to take Native American land.
    C. the perspective of Native Americans as partners in commercial exchange.
    D. the perspective of Native Americans as converted Christians.

SHORT ANSWER. Complete each statement or answer the question with a word or phrase.

13. The movement begun by Martin Luther to purify the Christian church was known as the _____.

14. The introduction of European diseases for which Native Americans had no immunity, plus their enslavement and being forced into hard labor, had a major impact on the native population and resulted in the tragedy known as the _____.

15. The Spanish extraction of immense amounts of _____ from the New World vastly inflated prices throughout Europe in the sixteenth century.

16. England's colonization of _____ in the 1560s and 1570s shaped their thinking on how to deal with "savage" peoples when they later colonized North America.

17. The _____ made the original decision that divided the Spanish and Portuguese spheres of exploration.

18. Native Americans were more susceptible to smallpox and measles because of their _____.

19. England's first interest in North America centered on _____.

20. _____ was the first English settlement in North America, which probably succumbed to Indian attacks and disappeared.

21. The disease _____ was apparently an export from America to Europe in the 1500s.

TRUE/FALSE. Determine if each statement is true or false.

22. The two Richard Hakluyts were important as merchant adventurers who promoted English colonies in the New World.

23. The Spanish Armada was a weapon used to advance the Protestant Reformation.

24. Christopher Columbus never realized that he had "discovered" the New World.

25. John Calvin argued that, by performing good "works" in life, any devout Christian was assured of salvation.

26. Calvinism appealed primarily to upper-class and middle-class Europeans.

27. Most early English colonies in North America were financed by private capital raised by profit-seeking merchants.

28. Old World swine thrived and were destructive in many areas of the New World.

29. The Spanish were the first European slave traders.

30. Europeans encouraged slave trade wars in Africa by providing tens of thousands of weapons to African nations.

VOCABULARY. Define each term or phrase.

Calvinism
conquistadores
John Cabot
Christopher Columbus
Columbian Exchange
Hernan de Soto
Olaudah Equiano
Leif Eriksson
Martin Luther
price revolution
Protestant Reformation
Richard Hakluyt
Roanoke Island
Spanish Armada
Treaty of Tordesillas

CHAPTER 3

MULTIPLE CHOICE. Choose the one alternative that best completes the statement or answers the question.

1. English Pilgrims who came to Plymouth Plantation were
   A. Separatists.
   B. Puritans.
   C. Quakers.
   D. Antinomians.

2. Roger Williams was banished from Massachusetts Bay for all of the following reasons EXCEPT
   A. he argued the Puritans had no right to take Indian land.
   B. he called for a complete separation from the Church of England.
   C. he opposed compulsory church attendance.
   D. he tried to replace John Winthrop as governor.

3. In accordance with their plans to bring political stability to their new colony, the proprietors of South Carolina called for a society
   A. of small farms.
   B. with democratic government.
   C. with social equality.
   D. with a hereditary aristocracy.

4. Bacon's Rebellion reflected the
   A. desire of Virginia's ambitious young frontier settlers to have more opportunity.
   B. governor of Virginia's policy of aggression toward the Indians.
   C. Powhatan Indians' desire for revenge against White encroachers on their land.
   D. unpopularity of the king's rule in Virginia.

5. The conditions of daily life in the early years of the Chesapeake Bay area are revealed by all of the following EXCEPT the
   A. genteel way of life of the large plantation owners.
   B. crude, earthfast cabins of the farmers.

C. breakdown in families from death and remarriage.

D. coming and going of strangers in the household.

6. In 1624, as a result of the massacre of 1622 and the difficulty making a profit, Jamestown lost its original charter and
   A. became a royal colony under the king's control.
   B. obtained a commercial charter to promote growth.
   C. re-established itself as a proprietary colony.
   D. signed a treaty of cooperation with the Indians.

7. The founders of Pennsylvania and Massachusetts differed in their
   A. Indian policy.
   B. immigration policy.
   C. tolerance toward religious dissenters.
   D. all of the above

8. The fur trade, as a profitable economic activity, did all of the following EXCEPT
   A. promote immigration into New France.
   B. create wars between Indian tribes.
   C. create rivalry between European powers.
   D. strengthen the colonies of the Dutch and French.

9. King Philip's War was named after
   A. Philip IV of France.
   B. Philip II of Spain.
   C. Metacomet of the Wampanoags.
   D. John Sassamon of the Powhatans.

10. Mercantilists claimed that colonies were valuable as all the following EXCEPT
    A. markets for English goods.
    B. manufacturers of finished goods.
    C. sources of raw materials.
    D. sources of tax income for the crown.

11. The witchcraft trials in Salem, Massachusetts Bay, were a result of all of the following EXCEPT the
    A. political instability following the overthrow of the Dominion of New England.
    B. determination of the new governor to root out and solve the problems in New England society.
    C. distress among Puritans about the loss of their colony's charter.
    D. anxiety among Puritans over having failed in their mission to establish a Godly society.

12. The most harmonious relations between English colonists and Native American Indians were found in
    A. Pennsylvania.
    B. Carolina.
    C. Massachusetts Bay.
    D. Virginia.

13. Which one of the following was NOT among the tenets of the Puritans?
    A. inward light
    B. work ethic
    C. sense of mission
    D. covenant of grace

14. New England enjoyed a steadier population growth than the Chesapeake colonies because it had all the following EXCEPT a
    A. healthier climate.
    B. higher birth rate.
    C. better diet.
    D. lower infant mortality rate.

SHORT ANSWER. Complete each statement or answer the question with a word or phrase.

15. The colonial laws to restrict the rights and activities of slaves were known as _____.

16. Both King Philip's War and Bacon's Rebellion were the upshot of frontier colonists' desire for _____.

17. The _____ rejected the ideas of original sin and eternal predestination, but embraced both the spiritual equality of the sexes and pacifism.

18. The population of the United States, like that of early Pennsylvania, is composed of peoples of many different religious and ethnic backgrounds, a characteristic called cultural _____.

19. The early period of Jamestown's history, when disease was rampant and food was scarce, was known as the _____ time.

20. Along with the trade in deerskins, the most important commercial activity for South Carolina during its early years was the capture and sale of _____.

21. To hold their dispersing settlements together and provide greater defense against the French, Dutch, and Indians, Puritan leaders established the _____, the first American attempt at federalism.

TRUE/FALSE. Determine if each statement is true or false.

22. Leisler's Rebellion showed that the colonial elite thought rule by the people meant rule by the mob.

23. Powhatan was the chief of the Pequot Indians who led bloody raids on southern New England settlements during the Pequot War in 1637.

24. When Jamestown became a royal colony, it lost its primary institution of self-government, the House of Burgesses.

25. The town meeting showed that the Puritans believed in the local exercise of authority.

26. The Salem witchcraft trials reflected social tensions and anxiety over change in that Massachusetts Bay community.

27. The Puritans were a homogeneous religious group who insisted on conformity to their ideas and beliefs.

28. The Puritans' initial errand into the wilderness was to establish the perfect, Godly society and separate themselves from the corruption of the Old World.

29. The theory of mercantilism was responsible for England's policy of regulating the trade to and from the colonies.

30. William Penn provided vigilant and effective leadership for Pennsylvania for years.

VOCABULARY. Define each term or phrase.

Anne Hutchinson
Bacon's Rebellion
black codes
Confederation of New England
covenant of grace
covenant of works
cultural pluralism
errand into the wilderness
Fundamental Constitutions
indentured servants
Jamestown
John Winthrop
joint-stock company
King Philip
Lord Baltimore
mercantilism
New Netherland
perpetual enmity
Pilgrims
Puritans
Quakers
reciprocal responsibility
religious commonwealth
Roger Williams
royal colony
Salem witchcraft
starving time
town meeting
William Penn
work ethic

CHAPTER 4

MULTIPLE CHOICE. Choose the one alternative that best completes the statement or answers the question.

1. The results of the Great Awakening included all of the following EXCEPT
   A. a new legitimacy for Protestant dissenters.
   B. the weakening of the idea of one official church.
   C. the founding of church colleges that admitted all faiths.
   D. a new acceptance of authority and correct thought.

2. The power of the purse, held by the assemblies in the English colonies, was important because it
   A. provided a means for women to redress their grievances in a male-dominated society.
   B. provided a means for assemblies to gain power at the expense of royal officials.
   C. was used to exploit the backcountry residents of the colonies by the tidewater elite.
   D. was used by the lower classes in the colonies to redistribute wealth.

3. The Peace of Utrecht of 1713
   A. reflected the military advantage France had gained over England in Queen Anne's War.
   B. cost Spain most of her vast New World empire.
   C. transferred French Louisiana to England.
   D. awarded England the privilege of supplying slaves to the Spanish empire in America.

4. Contact with the Europeans and involvement with the fur trade changed Native American culture by
   A. making them more religious and less savage.
   B. threatening their ethos of oneness with nature.
   C. stimulating them to adopt European legal practices.
   D. making them reject commercial hunting as exploitative.

5. New Light preachers did all of the following EXCEPT
   A. break down the connection between church and state.
   B. attack the upper classes and the accumulation of wealth.
   C. promote personal, emotional religion.
   D. bring the people together and unite the churches.

6. Louis Jolliet and Father Jacques Marquette were famous for
   A. converting Indians to Catholicism.
   B. convincing Indians to be French mercenaries.
   C. claiming the Mississippi valley for France.
   D. building forts and missions in the Mississippi valley.

7. Between 1699 and 1754 the French increased their activity in North America and
   A. built a series of outposts from the Great Lakes to the Gulf of Mexico.
   B. fortified Florida against British expansion.
   C. reconciled themselves to British colonial expansion.
   D. substantially increased the number of settlements with families.

8. English colonists shifted from the use of White indentured servitude to African slave labor because
   A. the typical price of a slave became equivalent to two years' worth of a free White laborer's wages.
   B. the supply of indentured servants declined.
   C. planters came to perceive indentured servants as a threat.
   D. all of the above

9. In the northern colonies, colonists made money on slavery by
   A. owning slaves.
   B. building and outfitting slave ships.
   C. participating in the slave trade.
   D. all of the above

10. In contrast to other slaves in the New World, North American slaves
    A. lived in a decidedly unhealthy natural environment.
    B. were never able to establish a balanced sex ratio in their population.
    C. increased their numbers more by natural reproduction than by immigration.
    D. more frequently and successfully organized rebellions against the planters' authority.

11. Jonathan Edwards was important for the Great Awakening because he
    A. led the movement to reject all intellectual content in theology.
    B. led the "New Light" Presbyterians across the South.
    C. wrote the first description of a local revival.
    D. aroused a popular attack on governmental authorities.

12. After 1730, the interior, or backcountry, of the English colonies developed its own culture characterized by
    A. a hard-driving, progressive, ambitious mentality.
    B. unchanging folkways as a result of isolation.
    C. a class system with the gentry on top.
    D. a well-to-do, socially conservative society.

13. In the late colonial period, colonial elites tried to do all the following EXCEPT
    A. fundamentally alter the social arrangements of the Old World.
    B. foster social and political stability.
    C. maintain a system of social gradations and subordination.
    D. maintain a stratified society.

SHORT ANSWER. Complete each statement or answer the question with a word or phrase.

14. In the seventeenth century, the large-scale cultivation of _____ in the New World transformed the Atlantic slave trade into a massive forced migration of African peoples.

15. Most of the products for everyday life in the colonies were made by the _____ who lived in colonial cities and villages and worked at handicraft industries.

16. *Poor Richard's Almanack* by _____ was filled with adages about how to live the moral, religious life.

17. _____ believed that concentrated power was the enemy of liberty.

18. The French Jesuit priest who explored the Mississippi River valley with Louis Jolliet was Father _____.

19. One of the major slave rebellions in the English colonies was the _____ Rebellion in South Carolina in 1739.

20. Made from West Indian sugar, _____ became one of the principal commodities traded for slaves on the African coast.

21. In _____, slaves working on rice plantations outnumbered Whites and were thus able to retain much of their African culture.

22. In their struggle to find meaning and worth in their existence, the slaves' religion and their _____ played a central role.

23. The kind of government that pitted the interests of monarchy, aristocracy, and democracy against one another was called a _____ government.

TRUE/FALSE. Determine if each statement is true or false.

24. Between 1699 and 1754, the French moved to establish an empire along the Ohio and Mississippi rivers and block British expansion westward.

25. Enlightenment thinkers wanted to acquire knowledge in order to perfect society.

26. Women living on plantations in the South were sheltered from the world and had no important roles or responsibilities.

27. The Peace of Utrecht signaled an increase in international power for England.

28. Extralegal crowd action, such as Boston's impressment riot, rarely had any success in protecting colonists' rights.

29. New Light preachers inspired the common people to question authority.

30. In both King William's and Queen Anne's wars, French Louisiana was the geographical area of greatest importance to the two belligerents.

VOCABULARY. Define each term or phrase.

American dilemma
Dominion of New England
Jonathan Edwards
enumerated articles
Ben Franklin
Father Jacques Marquette
Great Awakening
Gullah
King William's War
New Light preachers
Peace of Utrecht
Protestant Association
racial caste
Rene de Robert La Salle
Stono Rebellion
stratified society
Whigs

CHAPTER 5

MULTIPLE CHOICE. Choose the one alternative that best completes the statement or answers the question.

1. The main tactic of the successful colonial protest against the Townsend Acts was
   A. widespread rioting.
   B. economic boycott.
   C. declaration of independence.
   D. French negotiation.

2. The Albany Congress of 1754
   A. indicated that the colonists thought of themselves as Americans.
   B. showed that the Iroquois were under British control.
   C. demonstrated the inability of colonists to unite in pursuit of common purposes.
   D. proved that the colonists believed in a federalist system of government.

3. The neutrality of the Iroquois in the early years of the Seven Years' War showed that the
   A. position of the Indians made little difference in the war.
   B. Iroquois were too weak to become involved safely.
   C. British ignored them as unimportant and irrelevant.
   D. Indians set their policy according to their own self-interest.

4. The Seven Years' War was important for all of the following reasons EXCEPT it
   A. cost the colonies a great deal compared to the British.
   B. offered the colonists new opportunities.
   C. increased the costs of maintaining the empire.
   D. reduced the colonists' need for the empire.

5. During 1772 and 1773, the colonial radicals, to keep their faltering effort alive,
   A. relied on economic sanctions and nonimportation agreements.
   B. kept the common people stirred up with mob action.
   C. developed committees of correspondence to tie the colonists together.
   D. tried to influence the British to pass more taxes.

6. The British issued the Proclamation of 1763 for all the following reasons EXCEPT to
   A. fulfill their wartime agreements with the Indians.
   B. promote the interests of colonial land speculators.
   C. stabilize the frontier.
   D. limit the expense of defending an expanded empire.

7. After the Glorious Revolution in 1688, England began constructing a more coherent imperial administration by doing all the following EXCEPT
   A. strengthening the customs service.
   B. giving royal governors more freedom in deciding how to enforce the navigation acts.
   C. creating a professional Board of Trade to administer colonial affairs.
   D. establishing vice-admiralty courts in North America.

8. When Parliament began playing a more active role in colonial administration, it was primarily concerned with maintaining
   A. economic regulation.
   B. military occupation.
   C. religious orthodoxy.
   D. social harmony.

9. Which of the following territorial transfers was NOT in the Treaty of Paris of 1763?
   A. French Canada to Britain
   B. New Orleans to France
   C. France's Trans-Mississippi empire to Spain
   D. Florida to Britain

10. The 1764 Sugar Act did NOT
    A. add more colonial products to the list of enumerated articles.
    B. require colonial merchants to guarantee their observance of trade regulations.
    C. affect the operation of vice-admiralty courts.
    D. raise the tax on the molasses that the colonists imported from the French West Indies.

11. The political ideas colonists used to justify their revolt against British authority had roots in all the following EXCEPT
    A. mercantilist doctrine.
    B. English political thought.
    C. Enlightenment theories.
    D. their own experience as colonists.

12. Colonists came to see revolt against British authority as important to their
    A. constitutional rights.
    B. economic interests.
    C. moral character.
    D. all of the above

SHORT ANSWER. Complete each statement or answer the question with a word or phrase.

13. The ideology motivating and justifying the colonists' rejection of parliamentary authority was known as revolutionary _____.

14. The _____ were the small farmers who rebelled against the existing political and social power structure in North Carolina in the 1760s and 1770s.

15. The _____ placed a user's tax on items such as newspapers and legal documents in the American colonies.

16. The initial clashes between British and French colonists that led to the Seven Years' War occurred in the _____ River valley.

17. The turning point of the Seven Years' War came after _____ became prime minister in 1757.

18. The revenue program proposed by British prime minister _____ in 1763 initiated a rift between England and the colonies that twelve years later culminated in revolution.

19. Known as the _____ in America, the Coercive Acts were passed to punish Boston for the Tea Party.

20. In 1776, Thomas Paine's revolutionary pamphlet, _____, speeded the colonists toward an open declaration of independence.

21. The woman who warned that American women would "foment a rebellion" against male authority if men did not heed women's rightful claims to political power was _____.

TRUE/FALSE. Determine if each statement is true or false.

22. The Proclamation of 1763 was in part an effort to establish an interracial policy of peace between interior tribes and American colonists.

23. Revolutionary republicanism reflected the fact that the colonists initially were fighting for their rights as Englishmen, not for political independence from the British empire.

24. The policy of the Iroquois Confederacy during the Seven Years' War was a crucial factor in determining whether the French or British won in North America.

25. The Townshend duties, unlike the Sugar Act and Stamp Act, provoked more protest in the South than in Massachusetts and New England.

26. The British Tea Act in 1733 would have actually provided colonists with cheaper tea than the Dutch tea they had been smuggling.

27. The colonists considered the Sugar Act worse than the Molasses Act because it raised the duty on imported French molasses to a level too high for colonial merchants to continue to make a profit.

28. The Committees of Correspondence were first organized in Boston and then were adopted by other colonial legislatures.

29. The Tea Act levied taxes on paper, lead, painter's colors, and tea imported by colonists.

30. The most politically active people in America during the crisis with England in the 1760s and early 1770s lived in the cities.

VOCABULARY. Define each term or phrase.

Albany Congress
Board of Trade
Boston Massacre
Boston Tea Party
Coercive Acts
Committees of Correspondence
Common Sense
Currency Act
Declaratory Act
First Continental Congress
Iroquois Confederacy
mob rule
Molasses Act
nonimportation agreements
Regulators
revolutionary republicanism
Seven Years' War
Sons of Liberty
Stamp Act
Sugar Act
Townshend duties
William Pitt

CHAPTER 6

MULTIPLE CHOICE. Choose the one alternative that best completes the statement or answers the question.

1. The ideology of revolutionary republicanism to which the colonists turned to justify the overthrow of British authority
   A. was a single set of ideas that united the colonists in their common effort.
   B. argued that liberty could be defended only with the adequate use of political power.
   C. assumed that colonists' liberties were threatened by corruption and conspiracy in England.
   D. asserted that economic self-interest, not political principles, justified revolution.

2. The death rate was high for soldiers during the American Revolution because of all of the following reasons EXCEPT
   A. Americans were fighting a civil war.
   B. weapons and tactics dictated fighting at close range.
   C. unlike European warfare, the fighting continued year round.
   D. disease was rampant in military camps.

3. The Articles of Confederation
   A. established a strong central government.
   B. adopted the idea of separation of powers among several branches of government.
   C. provided for an association of essentially sovereign states.
   D. gave the country an effective, flexible government.

4. In the era of the Revolution, a state's constitution, drawn up by a constitutional convention rather than by the legislature, was considered
   A. better, because the constitution was supposed to be above the government.
   B. wasteful, because the legislature was already available to govern.
   C. worse, because the legislature reflected the people's will.
   D. equivalent, because both the legislature and convention were elected by the people.

5. The passage of the Olive Branch Petition in 1775 indicates that
   A. there was hope of colonial reconciliation with Parliament before the battle of Concord.
   B. many colonists wanted reconciliation with Parliament even after fighting began.
   C. Lord North's government tried to make peace with the colonists.
   D. George III could not overcome the hotheads in Parliament.

6. Loyalists supported Britain and rejected independence because they
   A. sought positions dependent on British power.
   B. feared that revolution threatened law and order.
   C. resented the rule of the colonial elite.
   D. all the above

7. The use of "out of doors" or mob action during the Revolution brought all of the following EXCEPT
   A. praise from radicals as a form of direct democracy.
   B. abandonment of the doctrine of balanced government in the thirteen new states.
   C. demands for more popular participation in politics.
   D. concern from conservatives worried about political chaos.

8. The Treaty of Paris of 1783, which ended the Revolutionary War,
   A. was accomplished only with the aid of Foreign Minister Vergennes and the French government.
   B. was negotiated by Thomas Jefferson.

C. gave the United States territory as far west as the Mississippi River.

D. required no concessions from the victorious Americans.

9. To make the common man believe in and sacrifice for the Revolution, ministers used various arguments including all of the following EXCEPT
   A. America's independence was a sign of the Second Coming.
   B. America had a special covenant with God to preserve liberty.
   C. God's law justified and sanctioned revolution against tyranny.
   D. the Revolution would finally result in the separation of church and state.

10. The primary strategy of the American continental army during the Revolutionary War was
    A. defensive, surviving by avoiding major battles.
    B. aggressive, seeking to dislodge the British from wherever they were encamped.
    C. to hide from British forces while waiting for French aid.
    D. to let the British have the coastal cities while protecting the frontier against Indians.

11. The American Patriots won the Revolutionary War for all the following reasons EXCEPT
    A. the administrative talents and determination of General Washington.
    B. British indecisiveness and failure of will.
    C. the enormous drain on England's financial resources.
    D. the readiness of the state militias when the war began.

SHORT ANSWER. Complete each statement or answer the question with a word or phrase.

12. The battle in 1777 that encouraged the British to move their campaign to the southern colonies was the battle of _____.

13. The first constitution of the United States, ratified in 1781, was the _____.

14. In most of the new states, the right to vote was restricted to those who owned _____.

15. The Indian league, which played a major role in the frontier fighting in the Mid-Atlantic states, was composed of the _____.

16. The British offer of freedom for all Virginia slaves in exchange for their fighting against the colonial rebellion was made by that colony's royal governor, _____.

17. The ratification of the Articles of Confederation was delayed by a dispute over ownership of _____.

18. When they left the states, most Loyalists settled in _____.

19. The constitution of _____, which provided for a single-house legislature, represented the most radical thrust of revolutionary republicanism.

20. The new state constitution of _____ was the only one to allow women to vote.

TRUE/FALSE. Determine if each statement is true or false.

21. Governments of men differ from governments of law in that in the former the leaders are above the law.

22. Unlike Britain, the new states in the United States did not use property qualifications to restrict voting.

23. The Iroquois Six Nations tried initially to remain neutral during the Revolutionary War.

24. "Out of doors" politics meant that prior to and during the Revolution, people affected political decisions by acting outside formal governmental bodies, thereby weakening or discrediting them.

25. The state constitutional conventions were devised as a way to have the people rather than the government approve the new state constitutions.

26. American commissioners who violated their instructions from Congress negotiated the Treaty of Paris of 1783.

27. The divisive, destructive effect of factions on republics made the American revolutionary leaders believe that only small, homogeneous societies could last as republics.

28. The Revolutionary generation was persuaded that tyranny was more often the result of too much government power, rather than too little.

29. John Adams was the main architect of Massachusetts's first state constitution.

30. George III's rejection of the Olive Branch Petition made the colonists traitors and revolutionaries even before they declared themselves independent.

VOCABULARY. Define each term or phrase.

American constitutionalism
Articles of Confederation
Battle of Saratoga
faction
guerrilla warfare
Iroquois Six Nations
Lord Dunmore's proclamation
Loyalists
Olive Branch Petition
out of doors
public virtue
tyranny of the people
Yorktown

CHAPTER 7

MULTIPLE CHOICE. Choose the one alternative that best completes the statement or answers the question.

1. The Land Ordinance of 1785
   A. is an example of the failures of the Articles of Confederation government.
   B. provided for the political organization of the territory lying north of the Ohio River.
   C. established the procedure for surveying and selling land lying west of the Appalachians.
   D. prevented White settlers from entering Native American territories.

2. During the Revolutionary War, all the following went up EXCEPT
   A prices and wages.
   B. taxes.
   C. purchasing power.
   D. private and public debt.

3. People in several states demanded a bill of rights be added to the Constitution in return for their vote to ratify the Constitution because they wanted
   A. limitations placed on the power of the national government.
   B. limitations placed on the power of the state governments.
   C. the readoption of a system of balanced government.
   D. to assure the supremacy of the national legislature over executive powers.

4. Federalists believed that a stronger central government was necessary for all of the following reasons EXCEPT
   A. the attribute of public virtue was weaker than they had anticipated.
   B. property rights seemed increasingly threatened under the Articles of Confederation.
   C. the national security seemed in jeopardy.
   D. the country was expanding too rapidly and chaotically.

5. The introduction of the Virginia Plan was a crucial development at the Constitutional Convention of 1787 because
   A. without it no compromise would have occurred.
   B. it was a call for a whole new Constitution.
   C. it combined the Articles of Confederation with new ideas.
   D. it represented the ideas of the Anti-Federalists.

6. Shays's Rebellion could best be described as representing how
   A. irresponsible the farmers and shopkeepers were.
   B. greedy and unprincipled the commercial banks in Massachusetts were.
   C. debtors thought a republican government should respond to their needs.
   D. radicals wanted to overthrow the government.

7. British occupation of military and fur-trading posts in the Old Northwest Territory in the 1780s was important primarily because it
   A. interfered with U.S. fur-trading operations.
   B. showed how inadequate the Treaty of Paris of 1783 was.
   C. indicated how weak and vulnerable the United States was under the Articles of Confederation.
   D. revealed continued rivalry for empire in North America between Britain and France.

8. The Confederation Congress had grave financial difficulties during and after the Revolutionary War for all of the following reasons EXCEPT
   A. states failed to honor Congress's requests for contributions.
   B. its expenditures were much too great.
   C. it could not tax or impose trade duties.
   D. it was deeply in debt to foreign creditors.

9. The Anti-Federalists opposed the Constitution of 1787 because they believed all of the following EXCEPT
   A. a geographically large republic could not survive the factions it would contain.
   B. a strong, centralized government would become tyrannical.
   C. emphasis on separation of executive, legislative, and judicial branches would make government too complex.
   D. reliance on local authority would interfere with equal rights for all.

10. The 1787 land ordinance governing the Old Northwest Territory provided for all the following EXCEPT
   A. political organization of that territory.
   B. the systematic survey and sale of land in that territory.
   C. no further introduction of slaves into that territory.
   D. a procedure for the admission of new states from that territory.

11. In the 1780s, White Americans looked upon Native Americans of the interior as
   A. a conquered people.
   B. potential political and military allies.
   C. a domestic independent nation.
   D. all of the above

12. Federalists were troubled by the Confederation Congress's inability to deal successfully with all of the following EXCEPT
   A. establishment of public credit.
   B. restoration of overseas trade.
   C. funding the national debt.
   D. disposing of western lands.

13. Delegates at the Constitutional Convention had to reconcile the conflicting interests of all of the following EXCEPT
   A. large and small states.
   B. national and state governments.
   C. nationalists and Federalists.
   D. slave and free states.

14. The Great Compromise at the Constitutional Convention resolved the key controversy involving
    A. representation in Congress.
    B. Congress's taxing power.
    C. the Supreme Court's authority to review the constitutionality of congressional legislation.
    D. the procedure for electing the president.

15. Delegates at the Constitutional Convention sanctioned the
    A. gradual abolition of slavery.
    B. use of the words "slave" and "slavery" in the Constitution.
    C. capture and return of runaway slaves.
    D. immediate abolition of the foreign slave trade.

16. The argument James Madison made in Federalist No. 10 was that
    A. a strong central government was inherently corrupted and a threat to liberty.
    B. the function of government was to peacefully compromise the difference between conflicting groups in society.
    C. factions in society were inherently self-interested and a threat to the common good.
    D. that government is best which governs least.

17. The legal disestablishment of the churches by most of the states in the 1770s and the 1780s meant all of the following EXCEPT
    A. the end of religious discrimination.
    B. the separation of church and state.
    C. greater opportunity for freedom of conscience.
    D. the loss of tax monies to support churches.

SHORT ANSWER. Complete each statement or answer the question with a word or phrase.

18. The social unrest in Massachusetts in 1786 threatening the social order and motivating some to call for a Constitutional Convention was _____ Rebellion.

19. The army officers camped at _____, New York, demanded compensation and implicitly threatened to take action against the Confederation government if their grievances were not satisfied.

20. Madison's proposal for a strong central government, introduced at the Constitutional Convention by Edmund Randolph, was known as the _____ Plan.

21. The _____ Plan at the Constitutional Convention proposed that states have equal rather than proportional representation in Congress.

22. Delegates to the Constitutional Convention decided that the president would not be chosen by popular vote, but by the vote of an _____.

23. In what were later called _____ clauses, delegates at the Constitutional Convention laid the groundwork for a vast expansion of the powers of the national government.

TRUE/FALSE. Determine if each statement is true or false.

24. The Bill of Rights was adopted to fulfill a promise the Federalists had made to those who were reluctant to ratify the Constitution.

25. Shays's Rebellion was in part the result of the accumulation of a massive private debt and the failure of state government to help those debtors on the bottom of society.

26. The outcome of the Confederation Congress's effort to remove British troops from the Northwest posts in the 1780s is a good example of the new republic's success at defending its interests in a world of strong monarchies.

27. The Federalists were Patriots during the Revolution who became convinced the United States could not succeed, perhaps not even continue to exist, without more respect for order, property, and talent.

28. The Pennsylvania constitution of 1790 indicated that the United States was emphasizing order rather than freedom by the late 1780s.

29. States passed "stay laws" to try to control the movement of Indian tribes in the interior.

30. Delegates at the Constitutional Convention recommended that their new Constitution be submitted to each state legislature for ratification.

VOCABULARY. Define each term or phrase.

Anti-Federalists
conquest theory
disestablishment
just price
elastic clauses
electoral college
Federalist Papers
Federalists
fugitive slave clause
Great Compromise
Jay-Gardoqui Treaty
Newburgh incident
New Jersey Plan
Northwest Ordinance
Pennsylvania constitution
Robert Morris
Shays's Rebellion
stay laws
Treaty of Fort Stanwyix
Virginia Plan
Western Confederation

CHAPTER 8

MULTIPLE CHOICE. Choose the one alternative that best completes the statement or answers the question.

1. The Whiskey Rebellion was
   A. an expression of public outrage at the high level of alcohol consumption in the West.
   B. an expression of popular resentment toward the arrogance of government officials.
   C. a serious threat to the safety of the new federal government.
   D. an example of the anarchy resulting from the government's failure to enforce the law.

2. The Bill of Rights
   A. was an integral part of the Constitution written in 1787.
   B. protected individual liberties from the power of the national government.
   C. was added to the Constitution to fulfill a promise made to the Jeffersonian Republican party.
   D. is composed of the first twelve amendments to the Constitution.

3. Citizen Genet, the minister from the French republic to the United States, became an embarrassment for the pro-French Jeffersonians for all of the following reasons EXCEPT he
   A. was more popular than Jefferson.
   B. threatened the U.S. government's sovereignty.
   C. endangered U.S. neutrality abroad.
   D. appealed to Congress to reverse Washington's neutral policy.

4. The election of 1800 was referred to as the "Revolution of 1800" for all of the following reasons EXCEPT
   A. it resulted in the first transfer of power from one party to another.
   B. Republicans had won control of both the presidency and Congress.

C. Jeffersonians thought liberty and the people had triumphed over special interests.

D. Jefferson's wide margin of victory in the electoral college gave him a strong mandate to change federal policy.

5. The French Revolution divided Americans in the 1790s because it represented something different to various groups EXCEPT for which of the following?

A. Jeffersonians, an extension of the American struggle for liberty and equality.

B. Federalists, an anarchic attack on all order and civilization.

C. Hamiltonians, a threat to Britain and American commercial interests.

D. Republicans, a chance to free the United States from organized Christianity.

6. The public furor following the XYZ Affair stimulated the national government to

A. negotiate a peace accord with Great Britain resulting in Jay's Treaty.

B. suppress opposition to administration policies through the Alien and Sedition Acts.

C. take military action against the Whiskey Rebellion.

D. remove Jefferson as vice-president.

7. The effect of Thomas Malthus's arguments was to convince Americans of the need

A. for a pro-British foreign policy.

B. to isolate the United States from European affairs.

C. for the United States to expand territorially in North America.

D. for a larger government offering more social services.

8. In his single term as president, John Adams was a strong advocate of

A. a powerful and active national government.

B. rapidly expanding political democracy.

C. a massive build-up of the nation's army.

D. war with France.

9. By 1800, Jeffersonian Republicans received strong electoral support from all the following EXCEPT

A. New England merchants.

B. southern planters.

C. northern and southern small farmers.

D. urban workers.

10. In Hamilton's view, "implied powers" could be derived from the _____ in the Constitution.

A. "necessary and proper" clause

B. "due process" amendment

C. Bill of Rights

D. Three-fifths Compromise

11. In the 1790s, Democratic-Republican societies campaigned for all of the following EXCEPT

A. British removal from western frontier posts.

B. greater representation of frontier communities in state legislatures.

C. restoration of republican principles of government.

D. U.S. neutrality toward the war between Britain and revolutionary France.

12. The Lewis and Clark expedition

A. led the first party of American settlers to the Pacific Northwest.

B. explored the West, following the Mississippi River.

C. was a military expedition to lay claim to and conquer the Far West.

D. was a scientific and commercial expedition to collect information and open the fur trade.

SHORT ANSWER. Complete each statement or answer the question with a word or phrase.

13. Congressional opposition to Hamilton's proposal to create a national bank was sectional; most of the opposition came from representatives from _____ states.

14. The act of 1798 allowing the president to expel radical immigrants was the _____ Act.

15. Congress rejected the proposals Hamilton requested in his 1791 "Report on _____."

16. The incident in which three French commissioners demanded a gratuity in exchange for negotiating an accord with the United States became known as the _____ Affair.

17. The uprising of Pennsylvania farmers against Hamilton's excise taxes was known as the _____ Rebellion.

18. In the Treaty of _____, Spain granted the United States free navigation of the Mississippi River and allowed U.S. merchants to transship their goods from New Orleans.

19. The state declarations in response to the Alien and Sedition Acts that the states could declare federal laws unconstitutional and nullify them were the _____ Resolutions.

20. The legislation that expanded the federal judiciary at the end of John Adams's administration was the _____ of 1801.

21. The United States's first secretary of the treasury was _____.

TRUE/FALSE. Determine if each statement is true or false.

22. The "Revolution of 1800" involved the political defeat of John Adams, the Federalists, and the policy of suppression of dissent.

23. The French Revolution overturned more of the social order in France than the American Revolution did in the United States.

24. President Jefferson organized the Lewis and Clark expedition to lay claim to Louisiana and force the French to sell it to the United States.

25. Citizen Genet failed to increase diplomatic support for France during his mission to the United States but succeeded in increasing popular support for France.

26. Alexander Hamilton was the single most important influence on policy during Washington's administration.

27. The Whiskey Rebellion involved the problem of how to balance the interests of individual citizens with the need of the government to maintain its authority and public order.

28. The outbreak of war between Britain and France in 1793 quickly destroyed U.S. commerce and plunged New England into economic depression.

29. The XYZ Affair demonstrated how sensitive most Americans were about the sovereignty and honor of the United States in the 1790s.

30. Alexander Hamilton believed the proper role of the new federal government was to sharply curtail the government's activity in promoting economic enterprise.

VOCABULARY. Define each term or phrase.

agrarian republic
Alexander Hamilton
Alien Act
assumption plan
Bank of the United States
Bill of Rights
Citizen Genet
commercial republic
Democratic-Republican societies
excise taxes
Federalist party
French Revolution
funding the debt
implied powers
impressment
Jay's Treaty
Jeffersonian Republicans
Lewis and Clark
Louisiana Purchase
Thomas Malthus
National Gazette
neutral rights
Report on Manufactures
Sedition Act
The Gazette of the United States
Treaty of San Lorenzo
Twelfth Amendment
Virginia and Kentucky Resolutions
Washington's Farewell Address
Whiskey Rebellion
XYZ Affair

MULTIPLE CHOICE. Choose the one alternative that best completes the statement or answers the question.

1. The establishment of the Second Bank of the United States in 1816 revealed all of the following EXCEPT the
    A. Jeffersonians' acceptance of Hamiltonian ideas.
    B. unsatisfactory operation of the First Bank of the United States.
    C. need for more controls on currency and finance.
    D. nation's desire to expand commercially.

2. Most northern states had laws, such as Ohio's "Black laws," which
    A. provided protection for Blacks' rights.
    B. divided churches into those for and against slavery.
    C. restricted and segregated Blacks.
    D. protected runaways from fugitive slave laws.

3. The cotton gin made it possible to use which form of cotton that grew across large areas of the South?
    A. long-staple
    B. organic
    C. short-staple
    D. native

4. The Missouri Compromise of 1820
    A. maintained sectional equality in the Senate.
    B. resulted in the adoption of the American System.
    C. kept slavery out of the Northwest Territory.
    D. banned slavery from all states and territories north of 36 degrees 30 minutes latitude.

5. Dysentery and typhoid were spread in early 1800s cities by
    A. inadequate hygiene.
    B. fleas from rats.

C. contaminated water.

D. unknown sources.

6. By 1800, the rural Northeast was characterized by all the following EXCEPT

   A. small family farms.

   B. increasing economic opportunity.

   C. the sale of agricultural surpluses in local markets.

   D. general use of the system of letting land lie in fallow for a season.

7. The Cherokee, under such leaders as John Ross, did all of the following EXCEPT

   A. adopt a "blood law" to prevent the loss of Cherokee lands.

   B. incur more White hostility by successfully adopting White ways.

   C. abandon their claim to be an independent, sovereign nation.

   D. become more "civilized" by expanding the practice of slavery.

8. The Monroe Doctrine, when issued in December 1823, was all of the following EXCEPT

   A. a call for U.S. domination of Latin America.

   B. representative of the rising American nationalism after the War of 1812.

   C. an effort to stop further European colonization in the Americas.

   D. an indication of the rising strength and power of the United States.

9. The Battle of Fallen Timbers in 1794

   A. proved the new federal government could not clear the way for western settlement.

   B. indicated the Shawnee would fight to the last to defend Ohio.

   C. led to the Shawnee ceding the southern two-thirds of Ohio.

   D. ended the Shawnee threat in the Old Northwest.

10. The Second Great Awakening did NOT

    A. focus on the salvation of individual souls.

    B. emphasize the equality of all believers.

    C. call on believers to demonstrate their faith by doing good works in society.

    D. fail to reach America's upper class.

11. The U.S. government attempted assimilation of Native Americans into White society by

    A. isolating them on reservations.

    B. providing them abundant supplies of rum.

    C. encouraging missionaries to convert Native Americans to Christianity.

    D. encouraging Native Americans to keep their traditional culture.

12. Which of the following was aimed at using commerce as a tool of diplomacy with England or France?

    A. Adams-Onis Treaty

    B. Embargo Act

    C. Hartford Convention

    D. Monroe Doctrine

13. Early nineteenth-century objectives of U.S. Indian policy did NOT include

    A. negotiating treaties with Indian tribes.

    B. regulating the fur trade.

    C. civilizing and Christianizing Indians.

    D. conquering Indian land.

SHORT ANSWER Complete each statement or answer the question with a word or phrase.

14. The U.S. policy statement of 1823 stipulating the Americas were no longer open to European colonization was the _____.

15. Shawnee chief _____ attempted to unite Native Americans from the north and south against Whites to regain their land.

16. Members of the _____ Society, believing that Blacks and Whites could not coexist as free persons, called for the abolition of slavery and the settling of freed Blacks in colonies in Africa.

17. The Second _____ was a surge of Protestant religious enthusiasm that began in the 1790s and brought the promise of individual salvation to people in all classes in all sections of the United States.

18. The _____ attempted to prevent their removal from Georgia by creating a common government and a written constitution similar to that of the United States.

19. The _____ was designed to encourage U.S. economic expansion and self-sufficiency through tariffs and internal improvements.

20. Southern cotton production soared and the institution of Black slavery was given new life after _____ invented the cotton gin in 1793.

21. The Battle of _____ led by Andrew Jackson's Tennessee volunteers defeated British troops launching an invasion of the mouth of the Mississippi River.

22. The Battle of _____ broke the back of Creek Indian resistance to White expansion into the Old Southwest.

TRUE/FALSE. Determine if each statement is true or false.

23. As the nineteenth century began, antislavery sentiment in the United States was declining and fear of slave revolts was increasing.

24. Delegates to the Hartford Convention in 1814 signed a resolution calling for New England's secession from the Union unless President Madison immediately ended the war with England.

25. The 1807 Embargo Act actually did more damage to New England's economy than to Britain's, against which it was directed.

26. In the treaty ending the War of 1812, Britain made important territorial concessions to the United States and agreed to honor America's claims to neutral rights in the future.

27. In the South the spread of cotton cultivation greatly increased the value of slave labor.

28. Although the Cherokee adopted the accommodationist policy of John Ross, they resisted the authority of the states and the loss of their land.

29. The center of early 1800s urban Black life was found in Black schools.

30. The Monroe Doctrine had an immediate impact on international affairs and saved Latin America from the re-establishment of a Spanish colonial empire.

VOCABULARY. Define each term or phrase.

Adams-Onis Treaty
American Colonization Society
American System
Battle of Fallen Timbers
Battle of Horseshoe Bend
Battle of New Orleans
Black laws
Chesapeake Incident
Hartford Convention
John Marshall
John Ross
Marbury v. Madison
McCulloch v. Maryland
Missouri Compromise
Monroe Doctrine
Non-Importation Act
Second Great Awakening
Tecumseh
Treaty of Ghent
War Hawks

CHAPTER 10

MULTIPLE CHOICE. Choose the one alternative that best completes the statement or answers the question.

1. The American economy between 1820 and 1860 became increasingly industrialized because of the
   A. expansion of the "putting out" system.
   B. reorganization of production processes.
   C. nation's commitment to a free trade commercial policy.
   D. increased demand for luxury items.

2. The development of factories with machines created a new class of laborers in industry—
   A. craftsmen.
   B. unskilled workers.
   C. journeymen.
   D. apprentices.

3. Immigration from Europe increased after 1840 for all of the following reasons EXCEPT
   A. an increase in population.
   B. natural disasters threatening starvation.
   C. the failure of technology to keep up with growth.
   D. political oppression.

4. Between 1820 and 1860 the American economy was characterized by all of the following EXCEPT
   A. periods of prosperity and depression.
   B. a doubling of per capita income.
   C. a greater interdependence among regions.
   D. greater job security for workers.

5. Urban violence increased in early-nineteenth-century cities for all of the following reasons EXCEPT
   A. the existence of racism.
   B. disagreement over constitutional issues.
   C. overcrowding and poor living conditions.
   D. competition for jobs.

6. All of the following developments changed the nature of work and the work force in the early nineteenth century EXCEPT the
   A. replacement of women workers with male immigrant workers.
   B. development of the progression from journeyman to master.
   C. reliance on the clock to set schedules.
   D. worker's sale of his labor rather than a product made by his labor.

7. In 1840 the types of cities included all of the following EXCEPT
   A. commercial centers on the coasts.
   B. railroad centers on the rails.
   C. mill towns on rivers.
   D. transportation centers on lakes and rivers.

8. Cities, which grew rapidly between 1820 and 1860, were characterized by all of the following EXCEPT
   A. an increasing proportion of poor immigrants among their inhabitants.
   B. equitable provision of public services to all residents.
   C. an increasingly heterogeneous population.
   D. increases in upward and downward social mobility.

9. Which one of the following is NOT true of both railroads and canals in the early nineteenth century?
   A. They strengthened links between the Old Northwest and the East.
   B. They supplied reliable access to distant markets.
   C. They could be built almost anywhere.
   D. They encouraged western settlement.

10. Young women came to work in the Lowell mills because
   A. of the promise of high job mobility.
   B. they otherwise faced desperate poverty.
   C. their productive role at home was declining.
   D. the work was easy.

11. At the core of worker discontent in the early nineteenth century was the fear that the industrial system
    A. was unconstitutional.
    B. condemned them to economic dependency.
    C. made them compete for jobs with their social inferiors.
    D. compelled them to change their work habits.

SHORT ANSWER. Complete each statement or answer the question with a word or phrase.

12. The first cotton-spinning machine in America was produced by a former English textile worker, _____.

13. The National Road and the Erie Canal were both examples of government-funded _____.

14. Early-nineteenth-century industrial workers used the phrase "_____" to describe the growing fear of their permanent dependence on earning wages by working for others.

15. The Massachusetts educational reformer who valued schools as purveyors of intellect and training grounds for productive work habits was _____.

16. The early-nineteenth-century concept of _____ confined women to their homes as housekeepers and emphasized the private nature of family life.

17. The new notions of family life and definition of childhood in early-nineteenth-century middle-class homes supported the use of _____ for the first time in American history.

18. Early-nineteenth-century urban violence was often the consequence of resentment between _____ _____ and Irish immigrants with whom they competed for jobs.

19. In early-nineteenth-century America, _____ remained the dominant way of life, the most significant economic activity, and the source of most of the nation's export goods.

20. The most ecologically damaging impact of economic growth in early-nineteenth-century America derived from the seemingly insatiable demand for _____.

TRUE/FALSE. Determine if each statement is true or false.

21. American society placed increased emphasis on middle-class values after 1820 because the traditional controls of the corporate society were weakening in a society of greater individualism.

22. Such popular middle-class publications as *Godey's Lady's Book* suggested that women had a special role to save the republic through moral leadership at home.

23. Early-nineteenth-century farmers increasingly produced for market as commercial farmers and less for their families as subsistence farmers.

24. The period between 1820 and 1860 had the fastest rate of urbanization in American history.

25. Most early-nineteenth-century cities suffered from violence in part because they did not have a police force.

26. While railroads encouraged western settlement in the early nineteenth century, they had little influence on where in the West people actually settled.

27. The introduction of new technology in the New England textile industry caused early-nineteenth-century clothing prices to increase dramatically.

28. Working conditions for female "outworkers" in the clothing industry in the 1850s improved considerably with the introduction of the sewing machine.

29. In most cases, skilled workers headed early-nineteenth-century labor protests and union activity.

30. The widening gap between rich and poor in early-nineteenth-century America was most extreme in the cities.

VOCABULARY Define each term or phrase.

boom and bust
commercial farming
concentration of wealth
Dartmouth College v. Woodward
entrepreneurial spirit
Erie Canal
Godey's Lady's Book
Horace Mann
international improvements
Lowell mill
McGuffey readers
middle-class values
outworkers
Palmer v. Mulligan
potato famine
Samuel Slater
Sturges v. Crowninshield
textile manufacturing
urbanization
wage slavery

CHAPTER 11

MULTIPLE CHOICE. Choose the one alternative that best completes the statement or answers the question.

1. The cotton kingdom of the antebellum South was
   A. a monolithic society of big plantations and slaveowners.
   B. socially diverse, but economically dependent on one cash crop.
   C. tending toward economic diversity and social equality by 1860.
   D. sharply divided over the morality of slavery after 1830.

2. Nat Turner's revolt
   A. resulted in new laws requiring harsher punishment for slaves.
   B. provoked an increase in demands for manumission.
   C. was motivated by religious zeal, not harsh punishment.
   D. was betrayed by spies before it achieved its goals.

3. The use of slave labor by the Tredegar Iron Company of Richmond is indicative of the
   A. unreasonable demands by White labor unions.
   B. wide range of skills that slaves gained.
   C. desire of southerners to avoid "wage slavery."
   D. anticapitalist attitude of southerners.

4. After 1831, most Whites in the South increasingly
   A. argued that slavery was a "necessary evil."
   B. advocated manumission.
   C. claimed slavery was a "positive good."
   D. called for colonization of Blacks in Africa.

5. The masculine code in the plantation south featured all of the following EXCEPT
   A. a rigid code of honor.
   B. dueling.

C. hunting and cockfighting.

D. abolitionist activities.

6. The yeoman farmers of the South, whom Jefferson had viewed as the backbone of the republic,
   A. were generally opposed to slavery.
   B. were southern Unionists during the Civil War.
   C. were dependent on the planter class for their livelihoods.
   D. owned few, if any, slaves.

7. The difference between the gang system and the task system for organizing the slaves' work was the
   A. gang system potentially allowed more leisure time.
   B. task system involved fewer whippings.
   C. gang system reduced the work load for the individual.
   D. task system involved more scrutiny.

8. All of the following are true of the antebellum South EXCEPT
   A. the economy grew faster than the North's.
   B. personal income was higher than in the Old Northwest.
   C. the price of slaves increased.
   D. the proportion of families who owned slaves increased.

9. Most antebellum slaves did NOT
   A. lack dignity and self-esteem.
   B. live in the Lower South.
   C. work on plantations.
   D. lead sickly lives.

10. Nonslaveholding southerners
    A. were outnumbered by slaveowners.
    B. defended slavery.
    C. did not aspire to own slaves.
    D. were economically dependent on planters.

11. Southern defenders of slavery pointed out that the Constitution implied the legitimacy of slavery in all the following places EXCEPT the
    A. Three-fifths Clause.
    B. necessary and proper clause.
    C. fugitive slave clause.
    D. slave trade moratorium clause.

12. The most traumatic problem for slaves was
    A. getting enough to eat.
    B. being forced to attend White religious services.
    C. being separated from their families.
    D. finding ways to resist their enslavement.

13. Most antebellum free Blacks were NOT
    A. living in the South.
    B. more literate and skilled than slaves.
    C. mulattoes.
    D. poor.

SHORT ANSWER. Complete each statement or answer the question with a word or phrase.

14. The northerner whose invention of the cotton gin reinvigorated slavery and allowed cotton production to dominate the southern economy and society was _____.

15. The antebellum South, largely dependent on one cash crop, was known as the _____ kingdom.

16. The single worst slave uprising in North America, _____ revolt, occurred in Virginia in 1831.

17. The idea that, according to the biblical account, the descendants of Ham were condemned to eternal servitude is known as the curse of _____.

18. The slaves who enforced the planters' orders were called _____.

19. Whites who were hired to enforce the planter's orders and see that slaves were productive laborers were called _____.

20. The two primary ways of organizing slave labor were the gang system and the _____ system.

21. Some runaway slaves, called _____, lived in communities of runaways, especially in the Florida swamps, where Seminole Indians befriended them.

22. Slaves and free Blacks who were the offspring of unions between White men and slave women were called _____.

TRUE/FALSE. Determine if each statement is true or false.

23. The South was referred to as the cotton kingdom because most Whites were planters with king-like powers.

24. The yeoman farmers of the South comprised about 75 percent of the antebellum southern population.

25. Slave drivers were slaves in positions of authority and sometimes used physical punishment to enforce rules.

26. Free Blacks tended to congregate in their own communities in part because of White restrictions.

27. Life expectancy for American slaves was longer than that for those in Latin America and the Caribbean.

28. The Tredegar Iron Company's policies showed how Blacks and Whites who shared a lower economic status could be divided and turned against one another.

29. According to the proslavery polygenesis theory, Blacks had been created separately from Whites and were an inherently inferior people.

30. Advertisements for runaways and southern court records, diaries, and newspapers reveal that sadistic slave punishments were rare.

VOCABULARY. Define each term or phrase.

antebellum South
Black Belt
cotton kingdom
curse of Canaan
De Bow's Review
Eli Whitney
Frederick Douglass
free Blacks
fugitive slave clause
George Fitzhugh
Harriet Tubman
Maroons
Nat Turner revolt
polygenesis
poor Whites
slave artisans
slave drivers
task system
Tredegar Iron Company
underground railroad
Upper South

CHAPTER 12

MULTIPLE CHOICE. Choose the one alternative that best completes the statement or answers the question.

1. Charles G. Finney was all of the following EXCEPT
   A. a leading evangelist.
   B. a proponent of a complex theology.
   C. an advocate of social reform.
   D. a skillful organizer.

2. The Jacksonian Democrats formed a party in the 1820s based on all of the following EXCEPT
   A. the republican principles of Thomas Jefferson.
   B. the military reputation of Andrew Jackson.
   C. the representation of the common man's interest.
   D. limiting the power of the president as the national leader.

3. The American Temperance Society, one of several approaches to combating the widespread consumption of alcohol in the early nineteenth century,
   A. advocated the perfectionist ideal of total abstinence.
   B. set personal moderation as its goal.
   C. called for local option laws so each community could decide.
   D. argued alcoholism was a disease, not a moral failure.

4. The development of utopian communities such as John Humphrey Noyes's Oneida and Mother Ann Lee's Shakertown was based on all of the following EXCEPT the
   A. felt need to restore small, homogeneous communities.
   B. anxiety created by the need for controls on individualism.
   C. possibility of reaching perfection through religious enthusiasm.
   D. opposition to experiments in new, unusual relationships among people.

5. The National Trades Union was representative of the
   A. strong political power of workingmen's parties during the 1830s.
   B. right to organize granted to labor by the New York state courts.
   C. workingmen's identification of themselves with the resistance to tyranny.
   D. growth of trade unionism after the Panic of 1837.

6. Jackson's adoption of a rotation-in-office system for governmental officeholders indicated that
   A. the Democrats believed the Republicans had been in power too long.
   B. Jackson's followers thought the government was corrupt.
   C. Jackson believed that administrative experts were needed for good government.
   D. Jackson thought rewarding political supporters with government offices would cause corruption.

7. William Lloyd Garrison and his newspaper, *The Liberator*,
   A. continued the work of the American Colonization Society.
   B. were dedicated to ending slavery to the exclusion of other social reforms.
   C. attacked the Constitution as a proslavery document.
   D. advocated ending slavery immediately through slave rebellion.

8. The development of the second party system in the 1830s meant that
   A. for a time, the United States had four major parties.
   B. Whigs took over Jeffersonian policies.
   C. a more democratic political system had emerged.
   D. the ideas of the Jeffersonians and Federalists were abandoned.

9. In his "Expostion and Protest," John C. Calhoun formulated
   A. a defense of protective tariff legislation.
   B. an attack on the Second Bank of the United States.
   C. a doctrine of nullification.
   D. a justification for Indian removal.

10. A social reformer from New England would most likely have voted for _____ candidates; an Irish Catholic immigrant mechanic would most likely have voted for the _____.
    A. Whig; Democrats
    B. Whig; Whigs
    C. Democratic; Whigs
    D. Democratic; Democrats

11. Andrew Jackson was a champion of all the following EXCEPT
    A. majority rule.
    B. limited government.
    C. social reform.
    D. the common man.

12. Most Second Great Awakening evangelical revivalists emphasized
    A. individual salvation.
    B. predestination.
    C. original sin.
    D. social reform.

13. To Transcendentalists, truth was found in
    A. rational thought.
    B. the Bible.
    C. human intuition.
    D. technological progress.

14. Which of the following was founded by secular communalists?
    A. New Harmony
    B. Oneida
    C. Shakertown
    D. Ephrata

15. In 1851 Maine passed a law that became a model for which of the following reform movements?
    A. abolitionism
    B. temperance
    C. Sabbath-keeping
    D. common schools

SHORT ANSWER. Complete each statement or answer the question with a word or phrase.

16. The leader of the effort to improve conditions in asylums and prisons as a way to promote the rehabilitation of their inmates was _____.

17. The first third party in American history and the first to hold a national nominating convention was the _____ party.

18. The convention of 1848 that called for the equal treatment of women and their right to vote was the _____ Convention.

19. The organization established to reduce the consumption of alcohol through abstinence was the _____.

20. The derisive title of the 1828 legislation that became a target of South Carolina nullifiers in 1832 was the _____.

21. Many social reformers tried to rally support for their cause by using _____, that is, attempting to educate others as to the sinful unacceptability of a particular social evil.

22. When the state of Georgia tried to deny them title to their land, the _____ Indians took their case to the Supreme Court—and won.

TRUE/FALSE. Determine if each statement is true or false.

23. In the second party system, Whigs usually represented the wealthier people; Democrats the poorer.

24. The Transcendentalists reflected the romanticism of the early nineteenth century and its emphasis on emotion rather than intellect.

25. Robert Owen, as a promoter of utopian communitarianism, believed in perfectionism through religion.

26. The rotation-in-office system would, according to Jackson, make the government more representative of the people's will.

27. The Jacksonian Democrats redefined politics by appealing to ordinary people and drawing them into campaigns and elections.

28. One of the most extreme forms of the millennialist belief was that of William Miller, who prophesied that 1843 would see the end of the world.

29. William Lloyd Garrison exemplified the passionate, almost fanatical desire of some to perfect society and to do so immediately.

30. The most controversial issue at the Seneca Falls Convention was women's right to vote.

VOCABULARY. Define each term or phrase.

abolitionists
American Temperance Society
Anti-Masons
Bank War
Charles G. Finney
communitarianism
Dorothea Dix
Exposition and Protest
Henry David Thoreau
Jacksonian Democrats
log cabin campaign
Maysville Road bill
millennialism
National Trades Union
Ordinance of Nullification
perfectionism
Robert Owen
rotation system
second party system
Seneca Falls Convention
Specie Circular
Tariff of Abominations
Trail of Tears
Transcendentalists
Webster-Hayne debate
Whigs
William Lloyd Garrison
Worcester v. Georgia

CHAPTER 13

MULTIPLE CHOICE. Choose the one alternative that best completes the statement or answers the question.

1. The Treaty of Guadalupe-Hidalgo of 1848
   A. fell far short of obtaining President Polk's objectives.
   B. required Mexico to pay millions of dollars in debt claims to the United States.
   C. transferred about a third of Mexico's territory to the United States.
   D. forced Mexico to pay a $15 million war indemnity to the United States.

2. Stephen F. Austin
   A. commanded the Texan army at the Battle of San Jacinto.
   B. took advantage of Mexican land offers to settle Americans in Texas.
   C. ordered the abolition of slavery in the Anglo settlements of Texas.
   D. was the first president of the Republic of Texas.

3. The Fort Laramie Council of 1851
   A. moved the Plains Indians onto reservations in Kansas and Oklahoma.
   B. paid the Indians to reduce the range of their movement.
   C. was the final resolution of White-Plains Indian conflict.
   D. was attended by all the major Plains tribes.

4. The campaign slogan of 1844, "fifty-four forty or fight," was indicative of all of the following EXCEPT
   A. the willingness of many Americans to expand the nation's boundaries by force.
   B. the ability of the Democrats to use expansionist rhetoric to gain popular support.
   C. Polk's willingness to go to war with Great Britain for all of Oregon.
   D. the conviction that the United States should claim the west coast north to Alaska.

5. The Mormons, under the direction of Brigham Young, were able to migrate to Utah as a result of all the following EXCEPT their
   A. exceptional dedication to rugged individualism.
   B. willingness to serve as paid soldiers in the Mexican War.
   C. ability to provide for the needs of emigrants moving west.
   D. desire to create a kingdom rather than a republic.

6. The mining frontier was characterized by all of the following EXCEPT
   A. boomtowns that could rapidly appear and disappear.
   B. little attention to the impact of mining operations on the natural environment.
   C. settlers interested in economic growth and political stability.
   D. a mixed population manifesting violence and racism.

7. The idea of Manifest Destiny was all of the following EXCEPT
   A. the result of previous successful expansion westward.
   B. an expression of the Puritan belief in a God-given mission.
   C. the cause of U.S. acquisition of the Louisiana Territory.
   D. in accord with the Founders' vision of the United States.

8. The experience of emigrants on the overland trails in the 1840s included all of the following EXCEPT
   A. better relations with the Indians than expected.
   B. a frantic rush to beat the snow to the Sierra Nevada Mountains.
   C. a rapid and complete breakdown in the traditional social roles.
   D. a group effort punctuated by tension and disputes.

9. It seems clear that the Mexican War of 1846–1848 was caused by
   A. Polk's determination to have a war.
   B. Mexico's refusal to receive Ambassador Slidell.
   C. American military occupation of disputed territory.
   D. Mexican demands to have Texas returned.

10. The Mexican government wanted settlers in Texas because
   A. the area was underpopulated and a weak defensive perimeter.
   B. it needed converts to the Roman Catholic church.
   C. it hoped to see American law introduced into the area.
   D. it wanted to attract slave labor to the area to speed economic development.

11. Most overland emigrants traveled
   A. alone.
   B. with relatives and friends.
   C. with people of their own religion.
   D. without their families.

12. The Mormon settlement in Utah was characterized by all the following EXCEPT
   A. communal agriculture.
   B. polygamy.
   C. authoritarian government.
   D. economic failure.

SHORT ANSWER. Complete each statement or answer the question with a word or phrase.

13. The federal legislation requiring the validation of Spanish and Mexican land titles was the _____ Land Law.

14. The overland trail of the early and mid-1840s leading west along the Platte River, through South Pass, and down the Snake and Columbia rivers led to settlements in _____.

15. The agreement ending the Mexican War was the Treaty of _____.

16. One of the first and most famous impresarios or contractors in Texas was _____.

17. The government established by American settlers who rebelled against Mexican authority in California was the _____ Republic.

18. The meeting of 1851 between the U.S. government and the tribes of the northern plains was the _____ Council.

19. The idea that spread in the 1840s that U.S. expansion was God's intention and therefore undeniable was _____.

20. In 1846 the British and American governments agreed on the _____ as the northern boundary of the Oregon Territory.

21. The leader of the Mormons who led them to Utah after Joseph Smith's death was _____.

22. Texas was annexed to the United States by a _____ of Congress because, unlike a treaty, it required only a simple majority vote to pass.

TRUE/FALSE. Determine if each statement is true or false.

23. Texas did not join the United States in 1836 because most Texans wanted to have their own independent republic.

24. American impresarios brought settlers into Mexico who were rarely prepared to meet the conditions imposed by Mexican authorities.

25. The Mexican War had almost unanimous support in the U.S. Congress and public.

26. Manifest Destiny was a self-righteous justification for territorial expansion.

27. Life on the Oregon Trail invariably drew families together and forged the rugged individualism that won the West.

28. The mining frontier was dominated by the desire for quick profit, not permanent settlement.

29. In Utah, Brigham Young established a society based on communal and cooperative values.

30. The Fort Laramie Council was another attempt to move the Indians out of the path of the Whites.

VOCABULARY. Define each term or phrase.

bandidos
Battle of San Jacinto
Bear Flag Republic
Brigham Young
corporate mining
Emigrants' Guide to Oregon and California
Fifty-four forty or fight
Fort Laramie Council
Gwinn Land Law
John Slidell
Lone Star Republic
Manifest Destiny
Mexican War
Mormons
Oregon Trail
polygamy
Preemption Acts
Santa Fe Trail
Stephen F. Austin
The Alamo
Treaty of Guadalupe-Hidalgo

CHAPTER 14

MULTIPLE CHOICE. Choose the one alternative that best completes the statement or answers the question.

1. The rise of nativism in the United States during the 1850s revealed all of the following EXCEPT
   A. rising tensions and anxieties in the United States as the result of change and conflict.
   B. the Irish and German immigrants were considered both different and inferior.
   C. the Protestant tradition identified Catholics as oppressors and undemocratic.
   D. the desire to fully and finally drive the Native Americans out of the way of White settlement.

2. Several states passed personal liberty laws in the 1850s
   A. because the federal government was attempting to enforce a national moral standard.
   B. to protect free Blacks from southern slave catchers.
   C. to protect those who were enforcing the Fugitive Slave Act.
   D. as a way to defend the South and slavery from abolitionist literature.

3. The Massachusetts Emigrant Aid Society was established to
   A. help the newly arrived German and Irish immigrants.
   B. promote the nativist cause in New England.
   C. prevent proslavery forces from controlling the Kansas Territory.
   D. spread the Christian doctrine to the tribes transplanted to Kansas and Oklahoma.

4. The Wilmot Proviso was important because
   A. the debate over it limited congressional appropriations for the Mexican War.
   B. it raised the question of whether the United States should gain new territories.

C. it revealed that sectional loyalties could be stronger than party loyalties.

D. it questioned the constitutionality of the Missouri Compromise.

5. The phrase "Bleeding Kansas" refers to all of the following EXCEPT

A. the fact that the Kansas struggle was a fore-runner of the Civil War.

B. individual acts of violence in the name of righteousness over slavery.

C. Kansas's admission to the Union under the Lecompton Constitution.

D. the increasing distrust between the North and South provoked by slavery.

6. The Compromise of 1850 was necessitated by all of the following EXCEPT the

A. California gold rush.

B. Kansas-Nebraska Act.

C. boundary dispute between Texas and New Mexico.

D. existence of slavery in Washington, D.C.

7. The Dred Scott case, decided in 1857,

A. suggested the whole Union might fall to slavery.

B. upheld the Missouri Compromise of 1820.

C. allowed Dred and Harriet Scott their free-dom.

D. distressed the South by even considering the constitutionality of slavery.

8. The term "Young America" in the 1850s referred to the

A. effect of the frontier experience on succes-sive generations of Americans.

B. declining average age resulting from mas-sive immigration.

C. belief that republics such as the United States were the wave of the future.

D. growing influence of youth on American culture.

9. John Brown's raid on Harpers Ferry did all of the following EXCEPT

A. make Brown into a martyr for liberty and equality.

B. make the South believe the North would support slave uprisings.

C. cause the South to feel like an estranged minority.

D. encourage Republican leaders to place an abolitionist plank in their 1860 platform.

10. The Compromise of 1850 included all of the following provisions EXCEPT

A. increased federal responsibility to capture and return runaway slaves.

B. alteration of the free state—slave state bal-ance in favor of the free states.

C. abolition of slavery in federal territories.

D. application of the popular sovereignty concept.

11. The Know-Nothing party advocated

A. government funding of Catholic parochial schools.

B. extending the time required for naturaliza-tion to citizenship.

C. giving new immigrants the right to vote.

D. granting free homesteads to new immigrants.

12. The Republican party in 1860

A. was uncompromising in its defense of allowing territorial residents to decide the fate of slavery in their territory.

B. took a moderate position opposing the extension of slavery in the territories.

C. was controlled by its abolitionist wing.

D. advocated equal rights for northern free Blacks.

13. Of the options facing him as he awaited his inauguration, Lincoln favored

A. conciliating the secessionists.

B. recognizing the Confederate government.

C. a preemptive surprise attack against the Confederacy.

D. enforcing the law of the land.

SHORT ANSWER. Complete each statement or answer the question with a word or phrase.

14. Harriet Beecher Stowe's novel, _____, an absorbing indictment of the horrors of slavery, captivated the attention and evoked the sympathy of thousands of northerners.

15. The attack by private citizens on the federal arsenal at Harpers Ferry, Virginia, on October 16, 1859, was known as _____ raid.

16. The _____ threatened U.S. seizure of Cuba if the Spanish refused to sell the island.

17. The doctrine that proposed that each territory determine whether it should be free or slave was _____.

18. The South Carolina senator who proposed that the federal government was constitutionally obligated to protect slavery in the territories was _____.

19. The laws passed by several northern states in reaction to the Fugitive Slave Act were known as _____ laws.

20. The unreasoning fear and hatred of foreigners and recent immigrants in the 1850s gave birth to a new political party popularly known as the _____ party.

21. The congressional agreement that was fashioned by Henry Clay and was intended as a "final settlement" of the slavery question was the _____.

22. The Supreme Court decision that declared slaves were not citizens and the Missouri Compromise was unconstitutional was the _____ decision.

TRUE/FALSE. Determine if each statement is true or false.

23. After Kansas adopted the Lecompton constitution, it entered the Union as a slave state.

24. Popular sovereignty was appealing because it allowed the politicians to take no position on the issue of extending slavery into the territories.

25. The most controversial part of the Compromise of 1850 was the decision to ban the slave trade from Washington, D.C.

26. Stephen Douglas sponsored the Kansas-Nebraska Act as a means of appealing to northern and southern supporters simultaneously.

27. The personal liberty laws were intended to prevent the federal government from forcing state officials to recover runaway slaves.

28. The Dred Scott decision supported the North's position on slavery in the territories.

29. The Wilmot Proviso was significant because the subsequent congressional debate split congressmen along party lines.

30. The Lincoln-Douglas debates were important because they revealed Lincoln's belief in ending slavery immediately and providing political and social equality for all men.

VOCABULARY. Define each term or phrase.

Beecher's Bibles
Bleeding Kansas
Dred Scott case
free labor ideology
free soil
Free-Soil party
Fugitive Slave Act
Gadsden Purchase
John Brown's raid
Kansas-Nebraska Act
Know-Nothings
Lecompton constitution
Lincoln-Douglas debates
Massachusetts Emigrant Aid Society
nativism
Ostend Manifesto
personal liberty laws
popular sovereignty
Republican party
slave power
The Crime Against Kansas
Uncle Tom's Cabin
William Walker
Wilmot Proviso
Yankees
Young America

CHAPTER 15

MULTIPLE CHOICE. Choose the one alternative that best completes the statement or answers the question.

1. The Civil War did NOT
   A. completely transform the southern class structure.
   B. initiate the decline of the southern yeoman farming class in the postwar years.
   C. undermine the solidarity of southern Whites.
   D. stimulate manufacturing or alter the pattern of prewar agriculture in the South.

2. All of the following border states eventually joined the Union EXCEPT
   A. Tennessee.
   B. Kentucky.
   C. Maryland.
   D. Missouri.

3. On the day it was issued, the Emancipation Proclamation declared the freedom of
   A. slaves in the border states.
   B. slaves in areas already conquered by Union armies.
   C. slaves in still unconquered parts of the Confederacy.
   D. all slaves.

4. The North's advantages in the Civil War included all of the following EXCEPT the
   A. South was under attack, fighting a defensive war.
   B. South had fewer factories.
   C. North had a large influx of immigrants during the war.
   D. North could produce a surplus of foodstuffs.

5. Radical Republicans favored all the following EXCEPT
   A. confiscating Confederate property.
   B. arming ex-slaves and enlisting northern free Blacks.

C. emancipating southern slaves.

D. negotiating a peace with the Confederates.

6. The Impressment Act adopted by the Confederacy in 1863
   A. revealed how the Confederate war effort required centralized government.
   B. showed how much the Confederate navy needed more sailors.
   C. enrolled Native Americans and Blacks in the Confederate army.
   D. made each Confederate state responsible for raising its own regiments.

7. The importance of the border states for both the North and the South can be seen in all of the following EXCEPT
   A. Lincoln's revocation of General Fremont's emancipation order in Missouri.
   B. the temporary isolation of Washington, D.C., by Maryland secessionists.
   C. the river traffic provided to the Confederacy by Kentucky's secession.
   D. Missouri's geographic position, which would affect navigation on the Mississippi and Ohio rivers.

8. The western theater of war during the Civil War was important for all of the following reasons EXCEPT
   A. Union control of the Mississippi River would cut the South in two.
   B. control of the Missouri River would determine the outcome of the war.
   C. the Tennessee River was an invasion route into the South.
   D. it offered the prize of California.

9. The strategy of Winfield Scott, the Union commanding general when the Civil War began, was to
   A. strike quickly before the Confederates could organize.
   B. seize the southern capital, disregarding the southern army.

C. strangle the Confederacy by surrounding and isolating it.

D. allow the Confederacy to discover it could not exist independently.

10. The factors contributing to the Confederacy's defeat included all of the following EXCEPT the
    A. loss of morale in the Confederate army and its unwillingness to fight.
    B. South's belief in states' rights and the sanctity of private property.
    C. South's inadequate transportation system.
    D. South's prewar emphasis on growing cash crops rather than foodstuffs.

11. The activities of Clara Barton and others indicated that during the war women
    A. stayed within the cult of domesticity and the role of custodian of morals.
    B. gained new social status and replaced men permanently in many positions.
    C. worked in the war effort often without compensation.
    D. shunned all activities except the women's rights movement.

12. Cotton diplomacy did not work because
    A. the Union blockade effectively closed all ship traffic into and out of southern ports.
    B. the Union opened cotton trade with Egypt.
    C. when the war began, the South was short of cotton.
    D. Britain and France found alternative sources of cotton.

13. Gettysburg was an important battle because
    A. it provided Lincoln with a victory that enabled him to announce the Emancipation Proclamation.
    B. it gained the Union control of the Ohio-Mississippi river traffic.
    C. Lee was never thereafter able to launch another southern offensive.
    D. Lincoln had at last found his aggressive general.

SHORT ANSWER. Complete each statement or answer the question with a word or phrase.

14. The Union's capture of _____ in July 1863 effectively completed the Union's campaign to gain control of the Mississippi River and to divide the South.

15. The announcement by Lincoln on January 1, 1863 concerning slavery was the _____.

16. The battle of 1863 that offered Lincoln the opportunity to issue the preliminary Emancipation Proclamation occurred at _____.

17. The paper money printed by the Union during the Civil War became known as _____ because of their appearance.

18. Winfield Scott's strategy for winning the war was called the _____ plan.

19. Those northern Democrats who wanted to end the war immediately were called _____ by northerners.

20. The legislation of 1863 that allowed the Confederate government to seize or requisition whatever property was needed for the war effort was the _____ Act.

21. General Sherman's army's capture of _____ helped swing voters and assure Lincoln's reelection in 1864.

TRUE/FALSE. Determine if each statement is true or false.

22. The fact that the North was fighting a war of conquest meant it had a more difficult and expensive task than the South.

23. The concept of states' rights tended to weaken the Confederacy because the southern states often refused to provide the Confederate central government material that was necessary for the war effort.

24. During the Civil War, women took many jobs outside the domestic sphere that led to new long-range careers in the postwar period.

25. The preliminary Emancipation Proclamation was immediately and immensely popular in the North and brought Republicans victories in the fall elections in 1862.

26. The mixed feelings about secession in the border states made Lincoln cautious in all of his policies concerning those states.

27. The printing of paper money to finance the Civil War led to only modest inflation in both the North and the South.

28. The Impressment Act of 1863 indicated that the war was requiring the Confederacy to jeopardize the principles for which it was fighting.

29. Both Union and Confederate draft laws were so unpopular because neither allowed for many exceptions to serving in the military.

30. The Emancipation Proclamation proved that Lincoln thought all men should be political and social equals.

VOCABULARY. Define each term or phrase.

Anaconda plan
Antietam
border states
Bull Run
Clara Barton
Confederate Conscription Act
Copperheads
cotton diplomacy
Emancipation Proclamation
ex parte Merryman
Fort Sumter
George McClellan
Gettysburg
greenbacks
Impressment Act
Merrimac
Morrill Act
Pacific Railroad Act
radical Republicans
states' rights
total war
Vicksburg

CHAPTER 16

MULTIPLE CHOICE. Choose the one alternative that best completes the statement or answers the question.

1. After the Civil War, the liberated slaves did NOT
   A. leave the plantations.
   B. seek legal confirmation of their marriages.
   C. choose their own surnames.
   D. seek revenge on Whites.

2. When they were liberated, ex-slaves most wanted
   A. their own land.
   B. the right to vote.
   C. social equality with Whites.
   D. to work for wages.

3. Radical Republicans in Congress were upset with Johnson's presidential plans for Reconstruction because under that plan southerners did all the following EXCEPT
   A. elect former Confederate officials to Congress.
   B. balk at ratifying the Thirteenth Amendment.
   C. fail to provide for Black suffrage.
   D. repudiate the Confederate debt.

4. By their actions, Freedmen's Bureau agents revealed they valued all the following EXCEPT
   A. government control of the marketplace.
   B. self-help.
   C. the sanctity of private property.
   D. White supremacy.

5. Radical Republican governments in the South during Reconstruction
   A. were dominated by illiterate Black legislators.
   B. were usually corrupt or financially extravagant.
   C. relied on massive numbers of federal troops to enforce their will.
   D. democratized southern state governments.

6. The Compromise of 1877
   A. was the beginning of the end for Republican rule in the post-Civil War South.
   B. revealed the power of Black self-interest in the Reconstruction era.
   C. showed the strong northern commitment to civil rights.
   D. was a victory for northern and southern Whites at the expense of the freedmen.

7. The Freedmen's Bureau did all of the following EXCEPT
   A. provide economic independence for Blacks.
   B. act as an unemployment agency for Blacks.
   C. establish schools to educate Blacks.
   D. provide food and shelter to refugees of the Civil War.

8. Presidential reconstruction under Andrew Johnson
   A. had the primary objective of punishing the South.
   B. was a major departure from Lincoln's plan for Reconstruction.
   C. stipulated federal protection for freedmen's rights.
   D. provided for quick and easy re-entry into the Union.

9. The first effort to establish a dependable, stable labor system in the South after the Civil War was
   A. sharecropping.
   B. tenant farming.
   C. contract labor.
   D. "forty acres and a mule."

10. The vagrancy laws passed by the southern state governments were supposed to do all of the following EXCEPT
   A. establish a stable labor force.
   B. pressure the federal government to give Blacks land.
   C. regulate Black economic status and behavior.
   D. restore and maintain White supremacy.

11. "Carpetbaggers" was a name southerners derisively applied to all of the following EXCEPT
   A. northern idealists who went South to help people.
   B. former Union soldiers who sought a new life in the South.
   C. northern Democrats who believed in White supremacy.
   D. northern emigrants who were looking for economic opportunity.

12. During the Civil War, congressional legislation was marked by the
   A. adoption of free trade policies.
   B. ideas of Jacksonian democracy.
   C. desire to promote business.
   D. belief in a strong, dominant president.

SHORT ANSWER. Complete each statement or answer the question with a word or phrase.

13. Southern state legislatures guided by the planter aristocracy adopted _____—special laws limiting freedmen's rights—to reestablish White domination after the Civil War.

14. The federal agency responsible for providing basic rights and needs of Blacks during and after the Civil War was the _____.

15. The constitutional amendment that stipulated race, color, or previous condition of servitude could not be used to deny suffrage was the _____ Amendment.

16. The act passed by Congress to limit the appointment power of President Johnson and give dominance to Congress was the _____ Act.

17. After the Civil War, the liberated slaves were commonly called _____.

18. The amendment to the Constitution that defined citizenship and provided equal protection of the law to any person was the _____ Amendment.

19. A campaign tactic used by Republicans in the post-Civil War years to discredit Democrats politically was to "wave the _____."

20. The political agreement that marked the end of Reconstruction was the _____.

21. Black "_____," disappointed with their economic future in the South, sought to establish self-sufficient Black towns on the Great Plains.

TRUE/FALSE. Determine if each statement is true or false.

22. Redemption meant the return of control of the South to advocates of White supremacy.

23. The Freedmen's Bureau had an unblemished record of advancing the rights and interests of freedmen.

24. The Fifteenth Amendment satisfied women's suffrage advocates who had been disappointed by the Fourteenth Amendment's voting provisions.

25. The Federalist-Whig economic program ended with the Civil War and the arrival in power of the Republican party.

26. Under contract labor, freedmen worked under conditions similar to slavery.

27. Presidential Reconstruction under presidents Lincoln and Johnson was an unnecessarily harsh and unjust policy toward the South.

28. The greatest fear of White southerners after the Civil War was that their former slaves would not work.

29. The Civil War destroyed the plantation system in the South where land ownership was concentrated in the hands of relatively few people.

30. President Lincoln viewed the former Confederate states as "conquered provinces" need-

ing congressional approval for their readmission to statehood in the Union.

VOCABULARY. Define each term or phrase.

amnesty
Black codes
carpetbaggers
contract labor
Credit Mobilier
debt peonage
exodusters
Federalist-Whig economic program
Fifteenth Amendment
Force Acts
forty acres and a mule
Fourteenth Amendment
Freedmen's Bureau
impeachment
Ku Klux Klan
liberal Republicans
Presidential Reconstruction
radical Republicans
Reconstruction Acts
redemption sharecropping
Tenure of Office Act
Thirteenth Amendment
vagrancy laws
waving the bloody shirt

ANSWER KEY

CHAPTER 1

MULTIPLE CHOICE

1. D
2. A
3. D
4. D
5. C
6. C
7. D
8. A
9. B
10. D
11. D
12. D
13. C

SHORT ANSWER

14. Renaissance
15. Europeans
16. feudal system
17. potlatch
18. matrilineal
19. university
20. Ghana
21. Merchants
22. gold

TRUE/FALSE

23. T
24. T
25. F
26. T
27. F
28. T
29. T
30. F

CHAPTER 2

MULTIPLE CHOICE

1. C
2. C
3. B
4. A
5. D
6. C
7. C
8. D
9. C
10. D
11. C
12. A

SHORT ANSWER

13. Protestant Reformation
14. Great Dying
15. silver
16. Ireland
17. pope
18. geographic isolation
19. fishing
20. Roanoke Island
21. syphilis

TRUE/FALSE

22. T
23. F
24. T
25. F
26. T
27. T
28. T
29. F
30. T

CHAPTER 3

MULTIPLE CHOICE

1. A
2. D
3. D
4. A
5. A
6. A
7. D
8. A
9. C
10. B
11. B
12. A
13. A
14. B

SHORT ANSWER

15. black codes
16. land
17. Quakers
18. pluralism
19. starving
20. Indians
21. Confederation of New England

TRUE/FALSE

22. T
23. F
24. F
25. T
26. T
27. T
28. T
29. T
30. F

CHAPTER 4

MULTIPLE CHOICE

1. D
2. B
3. D
4. B
5. D
6. C
7. A
8. A
9. D
10. C
11. C
12. B
13. A

SHORT ANSWER

14. sugar
15. artisans
16. Benjamin Franklin
17. Whigs
18. Jacques Marquette
19. Stono
20. rum
21. South Carolina
22. churches
23. balanced

TRUE/FALSE

24. T
25. T
26. F
27. T
28. F
29. T
30. F

CHAPTER 5

MULTIPLE CHOICE

1. B
2. C
3. D
4. A
5. C
6. B
7. B
8. A
9. B
10. D
11. A
12. D

SHORT ANSWER

13. republicanism
14. Regulators
15. stamp
16. Ohio
17. William Pitt
18. George Grenville
19. Intolerable Act
20. *Common Sense*
21. Abigail Adams

TRUE/FALSE

22. T
23. T
24. T
25. F
26. T
27. F
28. T
29. F
30. T

CHAPTER 6

MULTIPLE CHOICE

1. C
2. C
3. C
4. A
5. D
6. D
7. B
8. C
9. D
10. A
11. D

SHORT ANSWER

12. Saratoga
13. Articles of Confederation
14. property
15. Iroquois
16. Lord Dunmore
17. Western lands
18. Canada
19. Pennsylvania
20. New Jersey

TRUE/FALSE

21. T
22. F
23. T
24. T
25. T
26. T
27. T
28. T
29. T
30. T

CHAPTER 7

MULTIPLE CHOICE

1. C
2. C
3. A
4. D
5. B
6. C
7. C
8. B
9. D
10. B
11. A
12. D
13. C
14. A
15. C
16. B
17. A

SHORT ANSWER

18. Shays's
19. Newburgh
20. Virginia
21. New Jersey
22. electoral college
23. elastic

TRUE/FALSE

24. T
25. T
26. F
27. T
28. T
29. F
30. F

CHAPTER 8

MULTIPLE CHOICE

1. B
2. B
3. A
4. D
5. D
6. B
7. C
8. A
9. A
10. A
11. D
12. C

SHORT ANSWER

13. southern
14. Alien
15. Manufactures
16. XYZ
17. Whiskey
18. San Lorenzo
19. Virginia and Kentucky
20. Judiciary Act
21. Alexander Hamilton

TRUE/FALSE

22. T
23. T
24. F
25. T
26. T
27. T
28. F
29. T
30. F

CHAPTER 9

MULTIPLE CHOICE

1. B
2. C
3. C
4. A
5. C
6. B
7. C
8. D
9. C
10. D
11. C
12. B
13. D

SHORT ANSWER

14. Monroe Doctrine
15. Tecumseh
16. American Colonization
17. Great Awakening
18. Cherokee
19. American system
20. Eli Whitney
21. New Orleans
22. Horseshoe Bend

TRUE/FALSE

23. T
24. F
25. T

26. F
27. T
28. T
29. F
30. F

CHAPTER 10

MULTIPLE CHOICE

1. B
2. B
3. C
4. D
5. B
6. B
7. B
8. B
9. C
10. C
11. B

SHORT ANSWER

12. Samuel Slater
13. internal improvements
14. wage slavery
15. Horace Mann
16. domesticity
17. contraceptives
18. free Blacks
19. farming
20. wood

TRUE/FALSE

21. T
22. T
23. T
24. T
25. T
26. F
27. F
28. F
29. T
30. T

CHAPTER 11

MULTIPLE CHOICE

1. B
2. C
3. B
4. C
5. D
6. D
7. D
8. D
9. A
10. B
11. B
12. C
13. C

SHORT ANSWER

14. Eli Whitney
15. cotton
16. Nat Turner's
17. Canaan
18. slave drivers
19. overseers
20. task
21. Maroons
22. mulattoes

TRUE/FALSE

23. F
24. T
25. T
26. T
27. T
28. T
29. T
30. F

CHAPTER 12

MULTIPLE CHOICE

1. B
2. D
3. A
4. D
5. C
6. B
7. C
8. C
9. C
10. A
11. C
12. A
13. C
14. A
15. B

SHORT ANSWER

16. Dorothea Dix
17. Anti-Masonic
18. Seneca Falls
19. American Temperance Society
20. Tariff of Abominations
21. moral suasion
22. Cherokee

TRUE/FALSE

23. T
24. T
25. F
26. T
27. T
28. T
29. T
30. T

CHAPTER 13

MULTIPLE CHOICE

1. C
2. B
3. B
4. C
5. A
6. C
7. C
8. C
9. C
10. A
11. B
12. D

SHORT ANSWER

13. Gwinn
14. Oregon
15. Guadalupe-Hidalgo
16. Stephen Austin
17. Bear Flag
18. Fort Laramie
19. Manifest Destiny
20. 98th parallel
21. Brigham Young
22. joint resolution

TRUE/FALSE

23. F
24. T
25. F
26. T
27. F
28. T
29. T
30. T

CHAPTER 14

MULTIPLE CHOICE

1. D
2. B
3. C
4. C
5. C
6. B
7. A
8. C
9. D
10. C
11. B
12. B
13. D

SHORT ANSWER
14. *Uncle Tom's Cabin*
15. John Brown's
16. Ostend Manifesto
17. Popular Sovereignty
18. John C. Calhoun
19. personal liberty
20. Know-Nothing
21. Compromise of 1850
22. Dred Scott

TRUE/FALSE
23. F
24. T
25. F
26. T
27. T
28. F
29. F
30. F

CHAPTER 15

MULTIPLE CHOICE
1. A
2. A
3. C
4. A
5. D
6. A
7. C
8. B
9. C
10. A
11. C
12. D
13. C

SHORT ANSWER
14. Vicksburg
15. Emancipation Proclamation
16. Antietam

17. greenbacks
18. Anaconda
19. Copperheads
20. Impressment
21. Atlanta

TRUE/FALSE
22. T
23. T
24. F
25. F
26. F
27. F
28. T
29. F
30. F

CHAPTER 16

MULTIPLE CHOICE
1. D
2. A
3. D
4. A
5. D
6. D
7. A
8. D
9. C
10. B
11. C
12. C

SHORT ANSWER
13. Black codes
14. Freedmen's Bureau
15. Fifteenth
16. Tenure of Office
17. freedman
18. Fourteenth
19. bloody shirt
20. Compromise of 1877
21. exodusters

TRUE/FALSE
22. T
23. F
24. F
25. F
26. T
27. F
28. F
29. F
30. F